Teacher Wraparound Edition

Glencoe Spanish 2

# ¡Buen viaje!

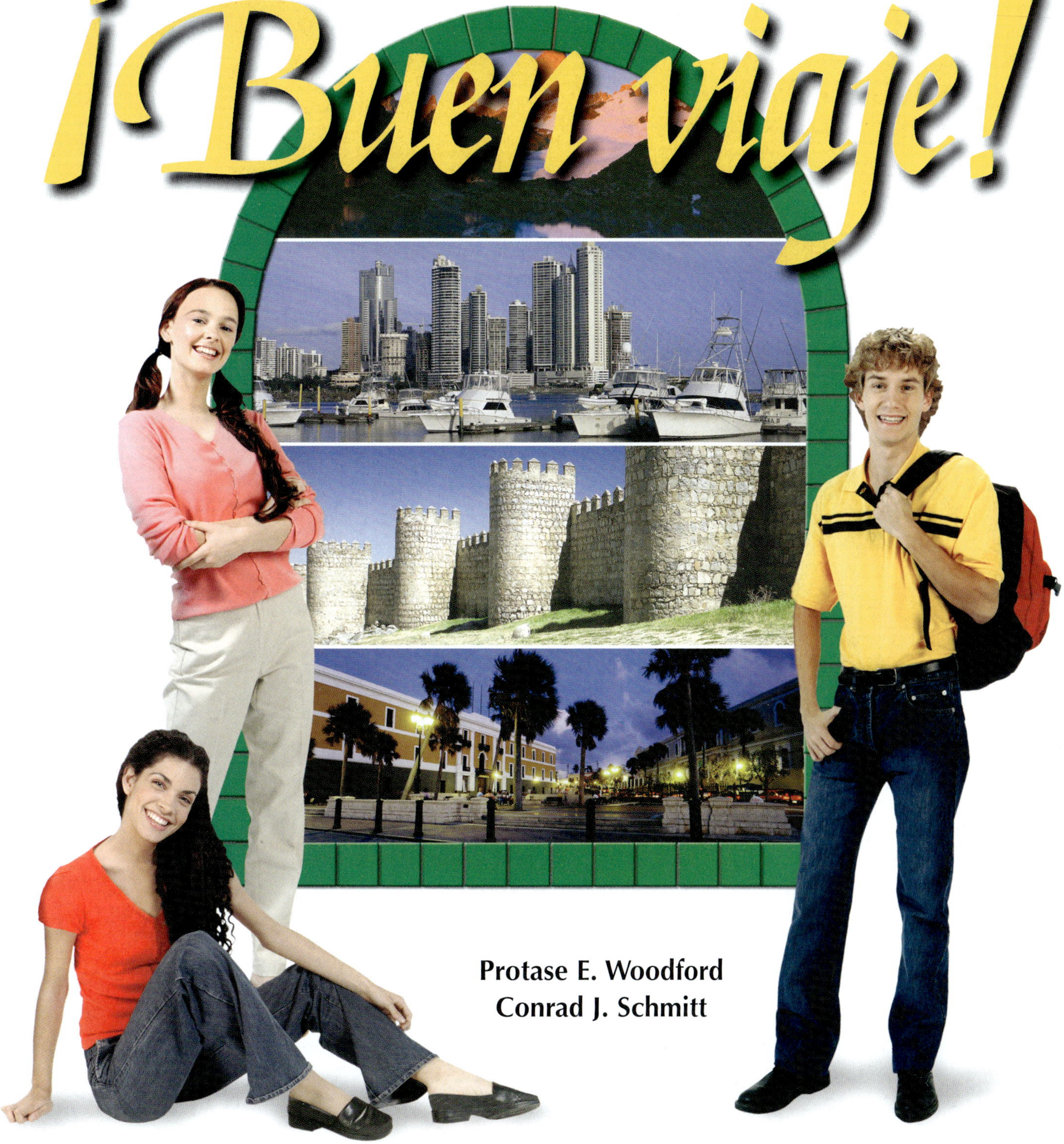

Protase E. Woodford
Conrad J. Schmitt

New York, New York Columbus, Ohio Chicago, Illinois Peoria, Illinois Woodland Hills, California

The McGraw-Hill Companies



Send all inquiries to:
Glencoe/McGraw-Hill
8787 Orion Place
Columbus, Ohio 43240-4027

ISBN 0-07-861970-X *(Student Edition)*
ISBN 0-07-861971-8 *(Teacher Wraparound Edition)*

Printed in the United States of America

2 3 4 5 6 7 8 9 10 055/071 10 09 08 07 06 05 04

# From the Authors

**Itinerary for Success**

- ✓ Exposure to Hispanic culture
- ✓ Clear expectations and goals
- ✓ Thematic, contextualized vocabulary
- ✓ Useful and thematically linked structure
- ✓ Progressive practice
- ✓ Real-life conversation
- ✓ Cultural readings in the target language
- ✓ Connections to other disciplines . . . in Spanish!
- ✓ Recycling and review
- ✓ High-interest articles from **People en español**

Dear Spanish Teacher,

Welcome to Glencoe's **¡Buen viaje!** Spanish program. We hope you will find that the way in which we have organized the presentation of the Spanish language and Hispanic cultures will make the Spanish language more teachable for you and more learnable for your students.

Upon completion of each chapter of **¡Buen viaje!** your students will be able to communicate in Spanish in a real-life situation. The high-frequency, productive vocabulary presented at the beginning of the chapter focuses on a specific communicative topic and covers key situations where students would have to use Spanish to survive. The structure point that follows the vocabulary presentation will enable students to put their new words together to communicate coherently.

After students acquire the essential vocabulary and structure needed to function in a given situation, we present a realistic conversation that uses natural, colloquial Spanish and, most importantly, Spanish that students can readily understand. To introduce students to the culture of the Hispanic world, the chapter topic is subsequently presented in a cultural milieu in narrative form. The **Lecturas culturales** recombine known language and enable students to read and learn—in Spanish—about the fascinating cultures of the people who speak Spanish.

Any one of us who has taught Spanish realizes the importance of giving students the opportunity to practice, a factor so often overlooked in many textbooks today. Throughout **¡Buen viaje!** we provide students with many opportunities to use their Spanish in activities with interesting and varied, but realistic, formats. The activities within each chapter progress from simple, guided practice to more open-ended activities that may use all forms of the particular structure in question. Finally, activities that encourage completely free communication enable students to recall and reincorporate all the Spanish they have learned up to that point.

We are aware that your students have varied learning styles and abilities. For this reason we have provided a great deal of optional material in **¡Buen viaje!** to permit you to pick and choose material appropriate for the needs of your classes. In this Teacher Wraparound Edition we have clearly outlined the material that is required, recommended, or optional in each chapter.

Many resources accompany **¡Buen viaje!** to help you vary and enliven your instruction. We hope you will find these materials not only useful but an integral part of the program. However, we trust you will agree that the Student Text is the lifeline of any program; the supporting materials can be used to reinforce and expand upon the themes of the main text.

Again, we hope that your yearlong journey with each of your classes will indeed be a **¡Buen viaje!**

Atentamente,

*Conrad J. Schmitt* • *Protase E. Woodford*

# Teacher Edition

# Student Edition

Glencoe's **¡Buen viaje!** is a carefully articulated program written by experienced authors. The Scope and Sequence of **¡Buen viaje!** ensures that students are presented with material in a way that enables them to build the skills they need to become proficient in Spanish. To allow you flexibility in moving through the program there is a review section at the beginning of **¡Buen viaje!** Level 2. In addition Chapters 13 and 14 of Level 1 are repeated as Chapters 1 and 2 of Level 2. The subjunctive is presented in Chapter 12 of **¡Buen viaje!** Level 2 but is presented as brand new material in **¡Buen viaje!** Level 3

## LEVEL 1

### Preliminary Lessons

#### Topics
- Greeting people
- Saying good-bye
- Being courteous
- Ordering food
- Days of the week
- Asking the day
- Months of the year
- Asking the date
- Numbers 0–30
- Seasons

#### Culture
- Calendario maya
- Puerto Vallarta, México
- El besito, dar la mano, el abrazo
- Formality
- Salamanca, España
- Guanajuato, México
- Buenos Aires, Argentina
- El Cinco de Mayo

#### Functions
- How to greet people
- How to say good-bye to people
- How to express simple courtesies
- How to find out and tell the days of the week
- How to find out and tell the months of the year
- How to count from 0–30
- How to find out and tell the seasons of the year

### Capítulo 1

#### Topics
- Describing people
- Describing places
- Numbers 0–30

#### Culture
- Francisco de Goya, *Muchachos trepando a un árbol*
- *El Quijote,* the novel
- Miguel de Cervantes Saavedra
- Map of Spain (featuring La Mancha)
- Pablo Picasso, *Don Quijote*
- Alicia Bustelo, student from Venezuela
- Map of Venezuela
- Two Latin American heroes: Simón Bolívar and José de San Martín
- Connections—Geographical terms in Spanish

#### Functions
- How to ask or tell who someone is
- How to ask or tell what something is
- How to describe yourself or someone else
- How to ask or tell where someone is from
- How to ask or tell what someone is like

#### Structure
- Singular forms of definite and indefinite articles—**el, la, un, una**
- Singular forms of adjectives
- Present singular forms of the verb **ser**

### Capítulo 2

#### Topics
- School
- Class subjects
- Numbers 31–99
- Telling time
- Nationalities

#### Culture
- Juan Carlos Liberti, *Concierto barroco*
- Alejandro Chávez and Guadalupe Garza, two Mexican Americans
- Raúl Ugarte and Marta Dávila, two Cuban Americans
- San Antonio, a bilingual city
- The Alamo, San Antonio, Texas
- Coyoacán, México
- The Frida Kahlo museum
- Connections—Latin American ethnicities
- Diego Rivera, *La almendra del cacao*

#### Functions
- How to describe people and things
- How to talk about more than one person or thing
- How to discuss classes in school
- How to express opinions about classes
- How to tell time
- How to tell at what time an event takes place

#### Structure
- Plural forms of nouns, articles, and adjectives
- Present plural forms of **ser**
- Telling time

## LEVEL 1

## Capítulo 3

### Topics
- School supplies
- Shopping
- Clothing, sizes
- Color
- Numbers 100–1999

### Culture
- Joaquín Torres-García, *Art in Five Tones and Complimentaries*
- Julio Torres, a student from Madrid
- Discussing differences between school in the United States and in Spanish-speaking countries
- El Retiro, Madrid, España
- Indigenous clothing in Central and South America
- A famous clothing designer: Oscar de la Renta
- Connections—Computers and technology

### Functions
- How to identify and describe school supplies
- How to describe articles of clothing
- How to ask questions while shopping
- How to state color and size preference
- How to speak to people formally and informally

### Structure
- Singular forms of **-ar** verbs (present tense)
- **Tú** versus **usted**

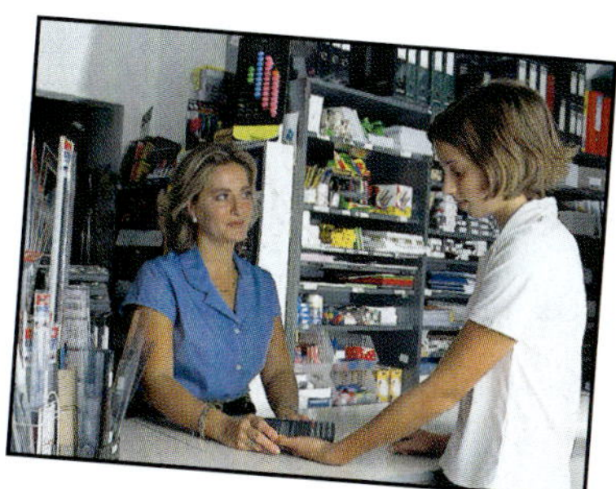

## Capítulo 4

### Topics
- Going to school
- The school day
- Activities at school
- Numbers 1,000–999,999,999

### Culture
- Diego Rivera, *Alfabetización*
- Paula and Armando, two students from Miraflores, Perú
- Differences between schools in the United States and in Spanish-speaking countries
- Miraflores, Perú
- La Universidad de Santo Domingo
- Chilean poet, Gabriela Mistral
- Connections—Biology terms in Spanish

### Functions
- How to discuss going to school
- How to talk about school activities
- How to greet people and ask how they feel
- How to tell how you feel
- How to describe where you and others go
- How to describe where you and others are

### Structure
- Plural forms of **-ar** verbs (present tense)
- Present of **ir**, **dar**, and **estar**
- Contractions **al** and **del**

## Capítulo 5

### Topics
- Eating at a café
- Foods and beverages
- Shopping for food

### Culture
- Bernardita Zegers, *Don Diego y doña Patricia*
- A café in Madrid, España
- Meal times in Spanish-speaking countries
- Buenos Aires, Argentina
- Open-air markets and supermarkets in Spanish-speaking countries
- Connections—Math terms in Spanish

### Functions
- How to order food or a beverage at a café
- How to identify some food
- How to shop for food
- How to talk about activities

### Structure
- Forms of **-er** and **-ir** verbs (present tense)

LEVEL 1

## Capítulo 6

### Topics
- Family relationships
- Houses and apartments
- Rooms in houses and apartments
- Telling your age, birthdays

### Culture
- María Izquierdo, *Mis sobrinos*
- The Hispanic family
- La Sagrada Familia, Barcelona, España
- La quinceañera
- Diego Velázquez, *Las Meninas*
- Connections—Great artists from Spain and Latin America
- Frida Kahlo, *Autorretrato*
- Francisco de Goya, *El tres de mayo*
- José Clemente Orozco, *Zapatistas*
- El Greco, *El entierro del Conde de Orgaz*

### Functions
- How to talk about your family
- How to describe your home
- How to tell your age and find out someone else's age
- How to tell what you have to do
- How to tell what you are going to do
- How to tell what belongs to you and to others

### Structure
- Present of **tener**
- **Tener que, ir a**
- Possessive adjectives

## Capítulo 7

### Topics
- El fútbol
- Parts of the body
- Baseball
- Basketball

### Culture
- Ángel Zarraga, *Futbolistas en el llano*
- El fútbol in Spain
- The World Cup
- Baseball
- Jai alai
- Connections—Archeological terms in Spanish
- Copán, Honduras
- Chichén Itzá, México
- Ponce, Puerto Rico

### Functions
- How to talk about team sports and other physical activities
- How to tell what you want to, begin to, and prefer to do
- How to talk about people's activities
- How to express what interests, bores, or pleases you

### Structure
- Stem-changing verbs in the present e → ie
- Stem-changing verbs in the present o → ue
- **Interesar, aburrir,** and **gustar**

## Capítulo 8

### Topics
- Minor illness
- Emotions
- The doctor's office
- More parts of the body
- The pharmacy

### Culture
- Pablo Picasso, *Head of a Medical Student*
- Visiting the doctor's office
- Differences between pharmacies in the United States and in Spanish-speaking countries
- Cuban American doctor Antonio Gassett
- Connections—Information about nutrition in Spanish

### Functions
- How to explain a minor illness to a doctor
- How to describe some feelings
- How to have a prescription filled at a pharmacy
- How to describe characteristics and conditions
- How to tell where things are and where they're from
- How to tell where someone or something is now
- How to tell what happens to you or someone else

### Structure
- **Ser** and **estar**
- **Me, te, nos**

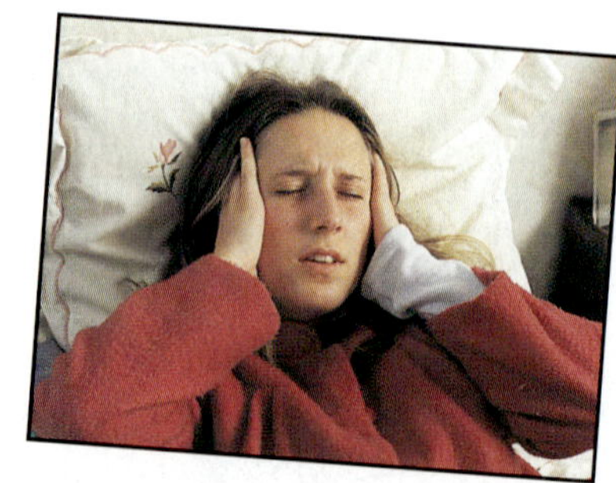

## LEVEL 1

## Capítulo 9

### Topics
- Summer weather and activities
- Winter weather and activities

### Culture
- Daniel Hernández, *A Breath of Fresh Air*
- World-class beaches and resorts in Spanish-speaking countries
- Marbella, España
- Cancún, México
- La playa de Varadero, Cuba
- Playa de Guajataca, Puerto Rico
- Pocitos, Uruguay
- Opposite seasons in the northern and southern hemispheres
- Snowboarding in Chile and Argentina
- Connections—Weather and climate in Spanish-speaking countries

### Functions
- How to describe summer and winter weather
- How to talk about summer activities and sports
- How to talk about winter sports
- How to discuss past actions and events
- How to refer to people and things already mentioned

### Structure
- Preterite tense of **-ar** verbs
- Pronouns—**lo, la, los, las**
- **Ir** and **ser** in the preterite

## Capítulo 10

### Topics
- Attending cultural events
- Taking the bus, subway

### Culture
- Rufino Tamayo, *Músicos*
- Dating in Spanish-speaking countries
- Teatro Colón, Lima, Perú
- La Zarzuela
- El Ballet Folklórico de México
- Connections—Fine Arts in the Spanish-speaking world

### Functions
- How to discuss movies, museums, and theater
- How to discuss cultural events
- How to relate more past actions or events
- How to tell for whom something is done

### Structure
- Preterite of **-er** and **-ir** verbs
- Indirect object pronouns—**le, les**

## Capítulo 11

### Topics
- Air travel

### Culture
- Alexander Aramburo Maldonado, *San Francisco to New York in One Hour*
- The importance of air travel in South America
- The Andes mountains
- The Amazon river
- Comparing the flight time from New York to Madrid and the flight time from Caracas to Buenos Aires
- The Nazca lines in Perú
- Connections—Everyday finances in the Spanish-speaking world

### Functions
- How to check in for a flight
- How to talk about some services on board the plane
- How to get through the airport after deplaning
- How to tell what you or others are currently doing
- How to tell what you know and whom you know

### Structure
- Present tense of **hacer, poner, traer**, and **salir**
- Present progressive
- Present tense of **saber** and **conocer**

## LEVEL 1

## Capítulo 12

### Topics
- Daily routines
- Grooming habits
- Having breakfast
- Camping

### Culture
- Susana González-Pagliere, *Southern Lake*
- Iván Orama describes a backpacking trip in northern Spain
- El lago Enol en el Parque Nacional de Covadonga, España
- San Sebastián, España
- El Camino de Santiago
- The cathedral in Santiago de Compostela, España
- Galicia, España
- Hostal de los Reyes Católicos, Santiago de Compostela
- Connections—Ecology in the Spanish-speaking world

### Functions
- How to describe your personal grooming habits
- How to talk about your daily routine
- How to tell some things you do for yourself

### Structure
- Reflexive verbs
- Stem-changing reflexive verbs

## Capítulo 13

### Topics
- The train station
- Traveling by train

### Culture
- Casimiro Castro, *Álbum del ferrocarril mexicano*
- Taking the AVE from Madrid to Sevilla
- Plaza de España, Sevilla
- Torre del Oro, Sevilla
- Taking a train from Cuzco to Machu Picchu
- La Plaza de Armas, Cuzco
- El valle del Urubamba, Perú
- Machu Picchu
- Connections—The 24-hour clock and the metric system

### Functions
- How to use expressions related to train travel
- How to purchase a train ticket and request information about arrival, departure, etc.
- How to talk about more past events or activities
- How to tell what people say

### Structure
- Preterite of **hacer**, **querer**, and **venir**
- Irregular verbs in the preterite
- Present and preterite of **decir**

## Capítulo 14

### Topics
- Restaurants
- Eating utensils
- Types of food

### Culture
- Hernán Miranda, *Interiores con mesa*
- Typical Mexican cuisine
- Diego Rivera, *El cultivo del maíz*
- Typical Spanish cuisine
- Typical Caribbean cuisine
- Connections—Regional variations of pronunciation and vocabulary in the Spanish-speaking world

### Functions
- How to order food or a beverage at a restaurant
- How to identify eating utensils and dishes
- How to identify more foods
- How to make a reservation at a restaurant
- How to talk about present and past events

### Structure
- Stem-changing verbs in the present e → i
- Stem-changing verbs in the preterite e → i, o → u

## LEVEL 2

## Repaso

The **Repaso** section reviews the material taught in **¡Buen viaje!** Level 1. In addition Chapters 13 and 14 in **¡Buen viaje!** Level 1 are the same as Chapters 1 and 2 in **¡Buen viaje!** Level 2. The **Repaso** section provides the opportunity to review the following functions and structures.

### Functions

- How to describe the school day
- How to purchase school supplies
- How to describe clothing while shopping
- How to describe another person
- How to talk about family
- How to describe the inside of a house or apartment
- How to shop for food at the market
- How to talk about sports
- How to talk about air travel
- How to talk about daily routines
- How to talk about minor illness
- How to talk about the doctor's office
- How to talk about winter and summer activities

### Structure

- Present tense **-ar** verbs
- **ir, dar, estar**
- Present tense of **ser**
- Agreement of nouns, articles, and adjectives
- Present tense of **-er** and **-ir** verbs
- **Tener**
- Possessive adjectives
- Stem-changing verbs
- Verbs like **aburrir, interesar,** and **gustar**
- Present of irregular verbs
- **Ser** and **estar**
- Reflexive verbs
- The preterite
- Direct object pronouns

## Capítulo 1

### Topics

- The train station
- Traveling by train

### Culture

- Casimiro Castro, *Álbum del ferrocarril mexicano*
- Taking the AVE from Madrid to Sevilla
- Plaza de España, Sevilla
- Torre del Oro, Sevilla
- Taking a train from Cuzco to Machu Picchu
- La Plaza de Armas, Cuzco
- El valle del Urubamba, Perú
- Machu Picchu
- Connections—The 24-hour clock and the metric system

### Functions

- How to use expressions related to train travel
- How to purchase a train ticket and request information about arrival, departure, etc.
- How to talk about more past events or activities
- How to tell what people say

### Structure

- Preterite of **hacer, querer,** and **venir**
- Irregular verbs in the preterite
- Present and preterite of **decir**

## Capítulo 2

### Topics

- Restaurants
- Eating utensils
- Types of food

### Culture

- Hernán Miranda, *Interiores con mesa*
- Typical Mexican cuisine
- Diego Rivera, *El cultivo del maíz*
- Typical Spanish cuisine
- Typical Caribbean cuisine
- Connections—Regional variations of pronunciation and vocabulary in the Spanish-speaking world

### Functions

- How to order food or a beverage at a restaurant
- How to identify eating utensils and dishes
- How to identify more foods
- How to make a reservation at a restaurant
- How to talk about present and past events

### Structure

- Stem-changing verbs in the present e → i
- Stem-changing verbs in the preterite e → i, o → u

## LEVEL 2

## Capítulo 3

### Topics
- Describing the parts of a computer
- Telling how to use a computer
- Telling how to use a fax
- Telephones
- Answering the telephone

### Culture
- Ernesto Bertani, *Nueva visión*
- Carmen Tordesillas, engineering student in Madrid
- Madrid, España
- Phone cards in Spain and in the United States
- The use of cell phones in Spanish-speaking countries and in the United States
- Connections—Computers and technology

### Functions
- How to talk about computers, e-mail, the Internet, faxes, and telephones
- How to talk about past habitual and routine actions
- How to describe people and events in the past
- How to make and receive telephone calls in Spanish

### Structure
- Imperfect of **-ar** verbs
- Imperfect of **-er** and **-ir** verbs
- Imperfect of **ser** and **ir**
- Uses of the imperfect

## Capítulo 4

### Topics
- Men's clothing
- Women's clothing
- Shoes
- Jewelry
- Shopping for food

### Culture
- Pedro de Vega Muñoz, *Market Day, Seville*
- Open-air markets and supermarkets in the Spanish-speaking world
- The market in Chichicastenango, Guatemala
- Indigenous clothing in Guatemala
- Connections—Commerce and marketing

### Functions
- How to shop for apparel and food in Spanish-speaking countries
- How to ask for the quantities and sizes you want
- How to find out prices
- How to talk about different types of past actions
- How to talk in general terms about what is done

### Structure
- The preterite and the imperfect
- Narrating sequence of events
- Expressing feelings in the past
- Passive voice with **se**

## Capítulo 5

### Topics
- Pastimes and hobbies
- The park
- Amusement parks

### Culture
- Gonzalo Cienfuegos, *The Enchanted Crystal*
- Sunday in the park
- Parque de Chapultepec, Ciudad de México
- Palermo, Buenos Aires, Argentina
- Sevilla, España
- Video arcades in Spanish-speaking countries
- Dominoes
- Connections—Literature

### Functions
- How to talk about popular hobbies and games
- How to talk about activities in the park
- How to give details about location
- How to talk about what will happen in the future
- How to compare objects and people
- How to describe your favorite pastime

### Structure
- Future tense of regular verbs
- Comparatives and superlatives

## LEVEL 2

### Capítulo 6

#### Topics
- Staying in a hotel
- Hotel rooms

#### Culture
- José Agustín Arrieta, *View of the Patio*
- Los paradores
- Youth hostels in Spanish-speaking countries
- Hotels
- Connections—Exercise

#### Functions
- How to check into and out of a hotel
- How to ask for things you may need while at a hotel
- How to talk about future events
- How to refer to previously mentioned people

#### Structure
- Future tense of irregular verbs
- Using direct and indirect objects in a sentence

### Capítulo 7

#### Topics
- Inside an airplane
- At the airport
- Geographic terminology

#### Culture
- Susana González-Pagliere, *Village with Volcano*
- The airport in La Paz, Bolivia
- Areas surrounding La Paz
- Latin American aviation hero, Emilio Carranza
- Connections—Geography of Spain

#### Functions
- How to talk about air travel
- How to discuss the influence of geography on travel in Latin America
- How to talk about things that would happen under certain conditions

#### Structure
- The conditional of regular verbs
- The conditional of irregular verbs
- Changing **le, les** to **se** before direct object pronouns

### Capítulo 8

#### Topics
- Parts of the body
- Minor medical problems
- The emergency room
- In the hospital

#### Culture
- Manuel Jiménez Prieto, *Hospital Visit*
- Practicantes in rural, Spanish-speaking countries
- The Buena Vista hospital
- Medical problems
- Connections—Medical terminology

#### Functions
- How to talk about accidents and medical problems
- How to talk about hospital stays
- How to discuss things that you and others have done recently
- How to compare things with like characteristics

#### Structure
- Present perfect
- Irregular past participles
- Comparison of like things

## LEVEL 2

### Capítulo 9

#### Topics
- The city
- Transportation in the city
- The country
- Farm animals

#### Culture
- María Eugenia Terrazas, *Inmensidad cordillerana*
- Buenos Aires, Argentina
- Raising cattle in Argentina
- Lima, Perú
- Santa Fe, New Mexico, United States
- Connections—Demography of Latin America

#### Functions
- How to talk about life in the city
- How to talk about life in the country
- How to describe things that were happening
- How to refer to things already mentioned
- How to indicate where things are located

#### Structure
- Imperfect progressive
- Placement of direct and indirect object pronouns
- Adjectives and demonstrative pronouns

### Capítulo 10

#### Topics
- The kitchen
- Cooking
- Types of food
- Using a recipe

#### Culture
- Manuel Serrano, *A Mexican Kitchen in 1885*
- Recipe for paella
- Valencia, España
- History of the tomato in Spanish-speaking countries and in the United States
- History of corn and potatoes, foods indigenous to Latin America
- Connections—Nutrition and diet

#### Functions
- How to talk about foods and food preparation
- How to give commands
- How to refer to people and things previously mentioned
- How to prepare some regional specialties

#### Structure
- Commands (regular forms)
- Commands (irregular forms)
- Placement of direct object pronouns with a command

### Capítulo 11

#### Topics
- Cars
- Gas stations
- Driving on the highway
- Driving in the city

#### Culture
- Norberto Russo, *De mi Buenos Aires*
- The Pan American highway
- Parking in Spanish-speaking countries
- International traffic signs
- Connections—Ecology and pollution

#### Functions
- How to check in for a flight
- How to talk about some services on board the plane
- How to get through the airport after deplaning
- How to tell what you or others are currently doing
- How to tell what you know and whom you know

#### Structure
- **Tú** commands (regular forms)
- **Tú** commands (irregular forms)
- Negative **tú** commands

## LEVEL 2

### Capítulo 12

**Topics**
- The hair salon
- Washing clothes
- Mailing letters and packages
- The bank

**Culture**
- Hernán Miranda, *Metro*
- Students from Madrid visit Andalucía
- Palacio de la Moneda, Santiago de Chile
- Hairstyles in the Spanish-speaking world
- Connections—Finance

**Functions**
- How to talk about going to the hair salon
- How to talk about having your clothes cleaned
- How to talk about using the services of the post office and bank
- How to talk about things that may or may not happen

**Structure**
- The subjunctive
- Expressing wishes and orders with the subjunctive
- Expressing opinions with the subjunctive

### Capítulo 13

**Topics**
- Birthdays
- Weddings
- Christmas
- The New Year
- Three Kings Day
- Hanukkah

**Culture**
- Alfredo Ramos Martínez, *Casamiento indio*
- New Year's Eve in Madrid
- Engagement and marriage in Spanish-speaking countries
- A wedding announcement
- Connections—Spanish painting

**Functions**
- How to describe and talk about parties and weddings
- How to talk about some holidays
- How to give advice and make recommendations
- How to express doubt, uncertainty, or disbelief
- How to express emotional reactions to what others do

**Structure**
- Subjunctive of stem-changing verbs
- Subjunctive of verbs like **pedir** and **aconsejar**
- Expressing doubt with the subjunctive
- Expressing emotion with the subjunctive

### Capítulo 14

**Topics**
- Professions
- Trades
- Looking for a job
- Job applications and interviews

**Culture**
- Antonio Gattorno, *Agricultores*
- Story of an ambassador to Latin America
- The importance of learning foreign languages
- Advertisements for jobs
- Connections—Economics

**Functions**
- How to talk about professions and occupations
- How to interview for a job
- How to state work qualifications
- How to talk about future events
- How to talk about probable events

**Structure**
- Infinitive versus subjunctive
- Subjunctive with **ojalá** and **quizá(s)**
- Subjunctive in relative clauses

## LEVEL 3

### Capítulo 1

#### Topics
- The geography of Spain
- The history of Spain
- Spanish culture

#### Culture
- Trains of the future
- Immigrants in Tarifa

#### Functions
- How to express past actions
- How to refer to specific things
- How to express ownership

#### Structure
- The preterite of regular verbs
- The preterite of stem-changing verbs
- The preterite of irregular verbs
- Nouns that begin with **a-** and **ha-**
- Irregular nouns that end in **-a**
- Demonstrative pronouns
- Possessive pronouns

### Capítulo 2

#### Topics
- The geography of Ecuador, Peru, and Bolivia
- The history of Ecuador, Peru and Bolivia
- The culture of Ecuador, Peru, and Bolivia

#### Culture
- Tungurahua volcano
- Peruvian woman who celebrates her 110th birthday

#### Functions
- How to describe habitual past actions
- How to talk about past events
- How to express what may or may not take place
- How to express necessity and possibility
- How to express wishes, preferences, and demands

#### Structure
- The imperfect
- The imperfect versus the preterite
- Expressing two past actions in the same sentence
- The subjunctive
- Expressing necessity and possibility with the subjunctive
- Expressing wishes, preferences, and demands with the subjunctive

### Capítulo 3

#### Topics
- The geography of Chile, Argentina, Paraguay, and Uruguay
- The history of Chile, Argentina, Paraguay, and Uruguay
- The culture of Chile, Argentina, Paraguay, and Uruguay

#### Culture
- Summer fashion
- Leaving home to go to college

#### Functions
- How to state location and origin
- How to state characteristics and conditions
- How to express surprise, interest, and annoyance
- How to express likes, dislikes, and needs
- How to express affirmative and negative ideas
- How to express emotions, doubt, or uncertainty

#### Structure
- **Ser** versus **estar** with location and origin
- **Ser** versus **estar** with characteristics and conditions
- Special uses of **ser** and **estar**
- Using verbs with indirect objects to express surprise, interest, and annoyance
- Expressing likes and needs with **gustar** and **faltar**
- Affirmative and negative words
- Using the subjunctive to express emotion
- Using the subjunctive to express doubt or uncertainty
- Using the subjunctive in adverbial clauses

## LEVEL 3

### Capítulo 4

#### Topics
- The geography of Central American countries
- The history of Central American countries
- The culture of Central American countries

#### Culture
- Public announcements in the newspaper
- Microchip implants in pets for identification

#### Functions
- How to express future events
- How to refer to people and things already mentioned
- How to express emotions and possibilities about past events
- How to use time expressions such as **en cuanto** and **hasta que**

#### Structure
- The future tense
- The conditional tense
- Direct and indirect object pronouns
- The imperfect subjunctive
- The subjunctive with conjunctions of time

### Capítulo 5

#### Topics
- The geography of Mexico
- The history of Mexico
- The culture of Mexico

#### Culture
- Windsurfing
- Mexican families

#### Functions
- How to express what you have done recently
- How to give commands
- How to describe actions in progress
- How to refer to people and things already mentioned
- How to describe actions completed prior to other actions
- How to express what you would have done and will have done
- How to express indefinite ideas and the known and unknown

#### Structure
- The present perfect
- Commands
- The progressive tenses
- Placement of direct and indirect object pronouns
- Direct and indirect object pronouns with commands
- The pluperfect
- The conditional perfect
- The future perfect
- Using the subjunctive with indefinite ideas
- Using the subjunctive in relative clauses

### Capítulo 6

#### Topics
- The geography of Cuba, Puerto Rico, and the Dominican Republic
- The history of Cuba, Puerto Rico, and the Dominican Republic
- The culture of Cuba, Puerto Rico, and the Dominican Republic

#### Culture
- Synchronized swimming
- Educational programs in prisons in the Dominican Republic

#### Functions
- How to express what people do for themselves
- How to express reciprocal actions
- How to make comparisons
- How to express *although* and *perhaps*
- How to express opinions and feelings about what has or had happened
- How to discuss contrary-to-fact situations

#### Structure
- Reflexive verbs
- Reciprocal verbs
- Regular forms of comparatives and superlatives
- Irregular forms of comparatives and superlatives
- Stating like qualities
- The subjunctive with **aunque**
- The subjunctive with **quizás** and **tal vez**
- The present perfect subjunctive
- **Si** clauses

## LEVEL 3

### Capítulo 7

#### Topics
- The geography of Venezuela and Colombia
- The history of Venezuela and Colombia
- The culture of Venezuela and Colombia

#### Culture
- Different kinds of teachers
- Gasoline in Colombia

#### Functions
- How to use shortened forms of adjectives
- How to use articles
- How to use prepositional pronouns
- How to use **por** and **para**
- How to express duration of time using **hace** and **hacía**

#### Structure
- Shortened forms of adjectives
- Special uses of definite and indefinite articles
- Addressing and referring to people with the definite article
- The definite article with days of the week
- The definite article with clothing and parts of the body
- The indefinite article when telling one's profession
- Pronouns after prepositions
- **Por** versus **para**
- **Por** and **para** with expressions of time
- **Por** and **para** with the infinitive
- Other uses of **por** and **para**
- Expressing duration of time with **hace** and **hacía**

### Capítulo 8

#### Topics
- The geography of the United States
- The history of the United States
- The culture of the United States

#### Culture
- Growth of the Hispanic population in the United States
- A storm and mudslides in California

#### Functions
- How to tell how actions are carried out
- How to express more activities in the present and past
- How to tell what was done or what is done in general

#### Structure
- Adverbs ending in **-mente**
- **-uir** verbs in the past and present
- Passive voice
- Passive voice with **se**

# Pacing and Leveling

Each chapter of **¡Buen viaje!** contains required, recommended, and optional material. **Vocabulario, Estructura,** and **Conversación** sections are always required. The recommended sections include the first cultural reading in **Lecturas culturales, ¡Te toca a ti!,** and **Assessment. Lectura opcional, Conexiones,** and **Tecnotur** are optional. The following chart provides you with a guide to the number of required, recommended, and optional pages in each of the fourteen chapters.

## Chapter Planning in the Student Edition

| | required number of pages | recommended number of pages | optional number of pages |
|---|---|---|---|
| Chapter 1 | 15 | 7 | 8 |
| Chapter 2 | 13 | 7 | 8 |
| Chapter 3 | 13 | 7 | 8 |
| Chapter 4 | 17 | 7 | 8 |
| Chapter 5 | 15 | 7 | 8 |
| Chapter 6 | 15 | 7 | 8 |
| Chapter 7 | 17 | 7 | 8 |
| Chapter 8 | 15 | 7 | 8 |
| Chapter 9 | 15 | 7 | 8 |
| Chapter 10 | 15 | 7 | 8 |
| Chapter 11 | 13 | 7 | 8 |
| Chapter 12 | 17 | 7 | 8 |
| Chapter 13 | 17 | 7 | 8 |
| Chapter 14 | 13 | 7 | 8 |
| Total: | 210 required | 98 recommended | 112 optional |

**Note:** Chapters 13 and 14 of **¡Buen viaje! Level 1** are repeated as Chapters 1 and 2 of **¡Buen viaje! Level 2** for additional flexibility.

Watch for the "little green man." This icon indicates that you have finished the new material in the chapter.

**LEVELING**

The activities, conversations, and reading within each chapter are marked according to level of difficulty. E indicates easy. A indicates average. C indicates challenging. Some activities cover a range of difficulty. In some activities, for example, advanced students will be able to produce more extensive responses while students who learn at a different rate may give less detailed responses. The leveling indicators will help you individualize instruction to best meet your students' needs.

# Analytic Scoring Guide for Rating Speaking Products

| VOCABULARY | GRAMMAR | PRONUNCIATION | MESSAGE CONTENT |
|---|---|---|---|
| **4.** Vocabulary is generally accurate and appropriate to the task; minor errors, hesitations, and circumlocutions may occur. | **4.** Grammar may contain some inaccuracies, but these do not negatively affect comprehensibility. | **4.** Completely or almost completely comprehensible; pronunciation errors, rhythm and/or intonation problems do not create misunderstandings. | **4.** Relevant, informative response to the task. Adequate level of detail and creativity. |
| **3.** Vocabulary is usually accurate; errors, hesitations, and circumlocutions may be frequent. | **3.** Some grammatical inaccuracies may affect comprehensibility; some control of major patterns. | **3.** Generally comprehensible, but pronunciation errors, rhythm and/or intonation problems may create misunderstandings. | **3.** Response to the task is generally informative; may lack some detail and/or creativity. |
| **2.** Vocabulary is not extensive enough for the task; inaccuracies or repetition may be frequent; may use English words. | **2.** Many grammatical inaccuracies may affect comprehensibility; little control of major patterns. | **2.** Difficult to comprehend because of numerous pronunciation errors, rhythm, and intonation problems. | **2.** Response incomplete; lacks some important information. |
| **1.** Vocabulary inadequate for most basic aspects of the task. | **1.** Almost all grammatical patterns inaccurate, except for a few memorized patterns | **1.** Practically incomprehensible. | **1.** Response not informative; provides little or no information. |
| **0.** No response. | **0.** No response. | **0.** No response. | **0.** No response. |

Luis Delgado

Owen Franken/CORBIS

# Analytic Scoring Guide for Rating Writing Products

## VOCABULARY

**4.** Vocabulary is generally accurate and appropriate to the task; minor errors may occur.

**3.** Vocabulary is usually accurate; occasional inaccuracies may occur.

**2.** Vocabulary is not extensive enough for the task; inaccuracies may be frequent; may use English words.

**1.** Vocabulary inadequate for most basic aspects of the task.

**0.** No response.

## GRAMMAR

**4.** Grammar may contain some inaccuracies, but these do not negatively affect comprehensibility.

**3.** Some grammatical inaccuracies may affect comprehensibility; some control of major patterns.

**2.** Many grammatical inaccuracies may affect comprehensibility; little control of major patterns.

**1.** Almost all grammatical patterns inaccurate, except for a few memorized patterns.

**0.** No response.

## SPELLING

**4.** Good control of the mechanics of Spanish; may contain occasional errors in spelling, diacritics, or punctuation, but these do not affect comprehensibility.

**3.** Some control of the mechanics of Spanish; contains errors in spelling, diacritics, or punctuation that sometimes affect comprehensibility.

**2.** Weak control of the mechanics of Spanish; contains numerous errors in spelling, diacritics, or punctuation that seriously affect comprehensibility.

**1.** Almost no control of the mechanics of Spanish.

**0.** No response.

## MESSAGE CONTENT

**4.** Relevant, informative response to the task. Adequate level of detail and creativity.

**3.** Response to the task is generally informative; may lack some detail and/or creativity.

**2.** Response incomplete; lacks some important information.

**1.** Response not informative; provides little or no information.

**0.** No response.

wen Franken/CORBIS

# How Can I Use the Internet to Teach Foreign Language?

From the Internet to round-the-clock live newscasts, teachers and students have never before had so much information at their fingertips. Yet never before has it been so confusing to determine where to turn for reliable content and what to do with it once you have found it. In today's world, foreign language teachers must not only use the Internet as a source of up-to-the-minute information for students; they must teach students how to find and evaluate sources on their own.

## What's available On the Internet?

✔ **Teacher-Focused Web Sites**
These Web sites provide teaching tips, detailed lesson plans, and links to other sites of interest to teachers and students.

✔ **Cultural Information**
Sites on the Web provide information to help students explore both "Big C" and "Little C" culture. Information about museums, stores, restaurants, schools, holiday celebrations, and customs can be found on Web sites that allow the student to virtually immerse into the culture.

✔ **Geographical Information**
The Web holds a variety of geographical resources, from historical, physical, and political maps; to interactive mapping programs; to information about people and places around the world.

✔ **Statistics**
Government Web sites are rich depositories for statistics of all kinds, including census data and information about climate, education, the economy, and political processes and patterns.

✔ **Reference Sources**
Students can access full-text versions of encyclopedias, dictionaries, atlases, and other reference books. Students have easy access to newspapers written in the target language.

✔ **News**
Traditional media sources, including television, radio, newspapers, and news magazines, sponsor Web sites that provide updates, as well as in-depth news coverage and analysis.

✔ **Topical Information**
Among the most numerous Web sites are those organized around a particular topic or issue. These Internet pages may contain essays, analyses, and other commentaries, as well as primary source documents, maps, photographs, video and audio clips, bibliographies, and links to related online resources.

✔ **Organizations**
Many organizations such as museums post Web pages that provide online exhibits, archives, and other information.

## Glencoe Online

Glencoe provides engaging **Student Web Activities** plus **Self-Check Quizzes** for each chapter that let you and your students assess their knowledge. There are games in each chapter to afford students extra practice. You can also access additional resources,

including enrichment links.

**Finding Things on the Internet**

*The greatest asset of the Internet—its vast array of materials—is also its greatest deterrent. Many excellent foreign language-specific sites provide links to relevant content. Using Internet search engines can also help you find what you need.*

- ✔ A search engine is an Internet search tool. You type in a keyword, name, or phrase, and the search engine lists the URLs for Web sites that match your search. However, a search engine may find things that are not at all related or may miss sites that you would consider of interest. The key is to find ways to define your search.
- ✔ Not all search engines are the same. Each seeks out information a little bit differently. Different search engines use different criteria to determine what constitutes a "match" for your search topic. The Internet holds numerous articles that compare search engines and offer guidelines for choosing those that best meet your needs.
- ✔ An advanced search allows you to refine the search by using a phrase or a combination of words. The way to conduct an advanced search varies from search engine to search engine; check the search engine's *Help* feature for information. Encourage students to review this information regularly for each of the search engines they use.

## How do I teach students to evaluate Web sites?

*Anyone can put up a Web site. Web content is easy to change, too, so Webmasters constantly update their Web sites by adding, modifying, and removing content. These characteristics make evaluating Web sites both more challenging and more important than traditional print resources. Teach students to critically evaluate Web resources, using the questions and criteria below.*

1. ***Purpose:*** *What is the purpose of the Web site or Web page? Is it an informational Web page, a news site, a business site, an advocacy site, or a personal Web page? Many sites serve more than one purpose. For instance, a news site may provide current events accompanied by banner ads that market the products advertisers think readers might want.*

2. ***URL:*** *What is the URL, or Web address? Where does the site originate? That can sometimes tell you about the group or business behind the Web page. For example, URLs with .edu and .gov domain names indicate that the site is connected to an educational institution or a government agency, respectively. A .com suffix usually means that a commercial or business interest hosts the Web site, but may also indicate a personal Web page. A nonprofit organization's Web address may end with .org.*

3. ***Authority:*** *Who wrote the material or created the Web site? What qualifications does this person or group have? Who has ultimate responsibility for the site? If the site is sponsored by an organization, are the organization's goals clearly stated?*

4. ***Accuracy:*** *How reliable is the information? Are sources listed so that they can be verified? Is the Web page free from surface errors in spelling and grammar? How does it compare with other sources you've found on the Web and in print?*

5. ***Objectivity:*** *If the site presents itself as an informational site, is the material free from bias? If there is advertising, is it easy to tell the difference between the ads and other features? If the site mixes factual information with opinion, can you spot the difference between the ads and other features? If the site advocates an opinion or viewpoint, is the opinion clearly stated and logically defended?*

6. ***Currency:*** *When was the information first placed on the Web? Is the site updated on a regular basis? When was the last revision? If the information is time-sensitive, are the updates frequent enough?*

7. ***Coverage:*** *What topics are covered on the Web site? What is the depth of coverage? Are all sides of an issue presented? How does the coverage compare with other Web and print sources?*

# Addressing the Needs of Special Students

## How can I help ALL my students learn foreign language?

Today's classroom contains students from a variety of backgrounds and with a variety of learning styles, strengths, and challenges. With careful planning, you can address the needs of all students in the foreign language classroom. The following tips for instruction can assist your efforts to help all students reach their maximum potential.

- ✔ Survey students to discover their individual differences. Use interest inventories of their unique talents so you can encourage contributions in the classroom.
- ✔ Model respect of others. Adolescents crave social acceptance. The student with learning differences is especially sensitive to correction and criticism—particularly when it comes from a teacher. Your behavior will set the tone for how students treat one another.
- ✔ Expand opportunities for success. Provide a variety of instructional activities that reinforce skills and concepts.
- ✔ Establish measurable objectives and decide how you can best help students meet them.
- ✔ Celebrate successes and praise "work in progress".
- ✔ Keep it simple. Point out problem areas—if doing so can help a student affect change. Avoid overwhelming students with too many goals at one time.
- ✔ Assign cooperative group projects that challenge all students to contribute to solving a problem or creating a product.

### How do I reach students with learning disabilities?

- ✔ Provide support and structure. Clearly specify rules, assignments, and responsibilities.
- ✔ Practice skills frequently. Use games and drills to help maintain student interest.
- ✔ Incorporate many modalities into the learning process. Provide opportunities to say, hear, write, read, and act out important concepts and information.
- ✔ Link new skills and concepts to those already mastered.
- ✔ Allow students to record answers on audiotape.
- ✔ Allow extra time to complete tests and assignments.
- ✔ Let students demonstrate proficiency with alternative presentations, including oral reports, role plays, art projects, and with music.
- ✔ Provide outlines, notes, or recordings of readings.
- ✔ Pair students with peer helpers, and provide class time for pair interaction.

### How do I reach students with behavioral disorders?

- ✔ Provide a structured environment with clear-cut schedules, rules, seat assignments, and safety procedures.
- ✔ Reinforce appropriate behavior and model it for students.
- ✔ Cue distracted students back to the task through verbal signals and teacher proximity.
- ✔ Set very small goals that can be achieved in the short term. Work for long-term improvement in the big areas.

### How do I reach students with physical challenges?

- ✔ Openly discuss with the student any uncertainties you have about when to offer aid.
- ✔ Ask parents or therapists and students what special devices or procedures are needed, and whether any special safety precautions need to be taken.
- ✔ Welcome students with physical challenges into all activities, including field trips, special events, and projects.
- ✔ Provide information to help able-bodied students and adults understand other students' physical challenges.

### How do I reach students with visual impairments?

- ✔ Facilitate independence. Modify assignments as needed.
- ✔ Teach classmates how and when to serve as guides.
- ✔ Limit unnecessary noise in the classroom if it distracts the student with visual impairments.
- ✔ Provide tactile models whenever possible.
- ✔ Foster a spirit of inclusion.

Describe people and events as they occur in the classroom. Remind classmates that the student with visual impairments cannot interpret gestures and other forms of nonverbal communication.

- ✔ Provide taped lectures and reading assignments.
- ✔ Team the student with a sighted peer for written work.

## How do I reach students with hearing impairments?

- ✔ Seat students where they can see your lip movements easily and where they can avoid visual distractions.
- ✔ Avoid standing with your back to the window or light source.
- ✔ Use an overhead projector to maintain eye contact while writing.
- ✔ Seat students where they can see speakers.
- ✔ Write out all assignments on the board, or hand out written instructions.
- ✔ If the student has a manual interpreter, allow both student and interpreter to select the most favorable seating arrangements.
- ✔ Teach students to look directly at each other when they speak.

## How do I reach English language learners?

- ✔ Remember, students' ability to speak English does not reflect their academic abilities.
- ✔ Try to incorporate the students' cultural experience into your instruction. The help of a bilingual aide may be effective.
- ✔ Avoid cultural stereotypes.
- ✔ Pre-teach important vocabulary and concepts.
- ✔ Be cognizant of difficulties that may arise from learning a new written notation.
- ✔ Encourage students to make comparisons between their heritage culture and language and the target culture and language.
- ✔ Encourage students to preview text before they begin reading, noting headings, graphic organizers, photographs, and maps.

## How do I reach gifted students?

- ✔ Make arrangements for students to take selected subjects early and to work on independent projects.
- ✔ Ask "what if" questions to develop high-level thinking skills. Establish an environment safe for risk taking.
- ✔ Call on gifted students to provide more open-ended responses. Use the material as optional for enrichment.
- ✔ Emphasize concepts, theories, ideas, relationships, and generalizations.
- ✔ Promote interest in the past by inviting students to make connections to the present.
- ✔ Let students express themselves in alternate ways, such as creative writing, acting, debate, simulations, drawing, or music.
- ✔ Provide students with a catalog of helpful resources, listing such things as agencies that provide free and inexpensive materials, appropriate community services and programs.
- ✔ Assign extension projects that allow students to solve real-life problems related to their communities.

## Hints for Inclusion Classes

**Advice from Diane Russell**
**Delaware City Schools**
**Delaware, Ohio**

In an inclusion setting, all students can respond to and get immediate feedback when using a set of dry-erase boards (cut at the local hardware store from a 4′ by 8′ laminated panel). For vocabulary review, students can write dictated words or sketch their meanings on the boards. Students can also be asked to draw what they hear from a story read aloud by the teacher to check listening comprehension. When students take turns illustrating different pages of a story, the pictures can be displayed on the chalk ledge as cues for retelling or writing a summary.

# The What, Why, and How of Reading

Reading is a learned process. You have been reading in your first language for a long time and noe your challenge is to transfer what you know to enable you to read fluently in Spanish. Reading will help you improve your vocabulary, cultural knowledge, and productive skills in Spanish. The strategies in the chart are reading strategies you are probably familiar with. Review them and apply them as you continue to improve your spanish reading skills.

## Skill/Strategy

| What is it? | Why It's Important | How To Do It |
|---|---|---|
| **Preview**<br>Previewing is looking over a selection before you read. | Previewing lets you begin to see what you already know and what you'll need to know. It helps you set a purpose for reading. | Look at the title, illustrations, headings, captions, and graphics. Look at how ideas are organized. Ask questions about the text. |
| **Skim**<br>Skimming is looking over an entire selection quickly to get a general idea of what the piece is about. | Skimming will tell you what a selection is about. If the selection you skim isn't what you're looking for, you won't need to read the entire piece. | Read the title of the selection and quickly look over the entire piece. Read headings and captions and maybe part of the first paragraph to get a general idea of the selection's content. |
| **Scan**<br>Scanning is glancing quickly over a selection in order to find specific information. | Scanning helps you pinpoint information quickly. It saves you time when you have a number of selections to look at. | As you move your eyes quickly over the lines of text, look for key words or phrases that will help you locate the information you're looking for. |
| **Predict**<br>Predicting is taking an educated guess about what will happen in a selection. | Predicting gives you a reason to read. You want to find out if your prediction and the selection events match, don't you? As you read, adjust or change your prediction if it doesn't fit what you learn. | Combine what you already know about an author or subject with what you learned in your preview to guess at what will be included in the text. |
| **Summarize**<br>Summarizing is stating the main ideas of a selection in your own words and in a logical sequence. | Summarizing shows whether you've understood something. It teaches you to rethink what you've read and to separate main ideas from supporting information. | Ask yourself: What is this selection about? Answer who, what, where, when, why, and how? Put that information in a logical order. |

| What is it? | Why It's Important | How To Do It |
|---|---|---|
| **Clarify**<br>Clarifying is looking at difficult sections of text in order to clear up what is confusing. | Authors will often build ideas one on another. If you don't clear up a confusing passage, you may not understand main ideas or information that comes later. | Go back and reread a confusing section more slowly. Look up words you don't know. Ask questions about what you don't understand. Sometimes you may want to read on to see if further information helps you. |
| **Question**<br>Questioning is asking yourself whether information in a selection is important. Questioning is also regularly asking yourself whether you've understood what you've read. | When you ask questions as you read, you're reading strategically. As you answer your questions, you're making sure that you'll get the gist of a text. | Have a running conversation with yourself as you read. Keep asking yourself, Is this idea important? Why? Do I understand what this is about? Might this information be on a test later? |
| **Visualize**<br>Visualizing is picturing a writer's ideas or descriptions in your mind's eye. | Visualizing is one of the best ways to understand and remember information in fiction, nonfiction, and informational text. | Carefully read how a writer describes a person, place, or thing. Then ask yourself, What would this look like? Can I see how the steps in this process would work? |
| **Monitor Comprehension**<br>Monitoring your comprehension means thinking about whether you're understanding what you're reading. | The whole point of reading is to understand a piece of text. When you don't understand a selection, you're not really reading it. | Keep asking yourself questions about main ideas, characters, and events. When you can't answer a question, review, read more slowly, or ask someone to help you. |

| What is it? | Why It's Important | How To Do It |
|---|---|---|
| **Identify Sequence**<br>Identifying sequence is finding the logical order of ideas or events. | In a work of fiction, events usually happen in chronological order. With nonfiction, understanding the logical sequence of ideas in a piece helps you follow a writer's train of thought. You'll remember ideas better when you know the logical order a writer uses. | Think about what the author is trying to do. Tell a story? Explain how something works? Present how something works? Present information? Look for clues or signal words that might point to time order, steps in a process, or order of importance. |
| **Determine the Main Idea**<br>Determining an author's main idea is finding the most important thought in a paragraph or selection. | Finding main ideas gets you ready to summarize. You also discover an author's purpose for writing when you find the main ideas in a selection. | Think about what you know about the author and the topic. Look for how the author organizes ideas. Then look for the one idea that all of the sentences in a paragraph or all the paragraphs in a selection are about. |
| **Respond**<br>Responding is telling what you like, dislike, find surprising or interesting in a selection. | When you react in a personal way to what you read, you'll enjoy a selection more and remember it better. | As you read, think about how you feel about story elements or ideas in a selection. What's your reaction to the characters in a story? What grabs your attention as you read? |
| **Connect**<br>Connecting means linking what you read to events in your own life or to other selections you've read. | You'll "get into" your reading and recall information and ideas better by connecting events, emotions, and characters to your own life. | Ask yourself: Do I know someone like this? Have I ever felt this way? What else have I read that is like this selection? |
| **Review**<br>Reviewing is going back over what you've read to remember what's important and to organize ideas so you'll recall them later. | Reviewing is especially important when you have new ideas and a lot of information to remember. | Filling in a graphic organizer, such as a chart or diagram, as you read helps you organize information. These study aids will help you review later. |
| **Interpret**<br>Interpreting is using your own understanding of the world to decide what the events or ideas in a selection mean. | Every reader constructs meaning on the basis of what he or she understands about the world. Finding meaning as you read is all about interacting with the text. | Think about what you already know about yourself and the world. Ask yourself: What is the author really trying to say here? What larger idea might these events be about? |

| What is it? | Why It's Important | How To Do It |
|---|---|---|
| **Infer**<br>Inferring is using your reason and experience to guess at what an author does not come right out and say. | Making inferences is a large part of finding meaning in a selection. Inferring helps you look more deeply at characters and points you toward the theme or message in a selection. | Look for clues the author provides. Notice descriptions, dialogue, events, and relationships that might tell you something the author wants you to know. |
| **Draw Conclusions**<br>Drawing conclusions is using a number of pieces of information to make a general statement about people, places, events, and ideas. | Drawing conclusions helps you find connections between ideas and events. It's another tool to help you see the larger picture. | Notice details about characters, ideas, and events. Then make a general statement on the basis of these details. For example, a character's actions might lead you to conclude that he is kind. |
| **Analyze**<br>Analyzing is looking at separate parts of a selection in order to understand the entire selection. | Analyzing helps you look critically at a piece of writing. When you analyze a selection, you'll discover its theme or message, and you'll learn the author's purpose for writing. | To analyze a story, think about what the author is saying through the characters, setting, and plot. To analyze nonfiction, look at the organization and main ideas. What do they suggest? |
| **Synthesize**<br>Synthesizing is combining ideas to create something new. You may synthesize to reach a new understanding or you may actually create a new ending to a story. | Synthesizing helps you move to a higher level of thinking. Creating something new of your own goes beyond remembering what you learned from someone else. | Think about the ideas or information you've learned in a selection. Ask yourself: Do I understand something more than the main ideas here? Can I create something else from what I now know? |
| **Evaluate**<br>Evaluating is making a judgment or forming an opinion about something you read. You can evaluate a character, an author's craft, or the value of the information in a text. | Evaluating helps you become a wise reader. For example, when you judge whether an author is qualified to speak about a topic or whether the author's points make sense, you can avoid being misled by what you read. | As you read, ask yourself questions such as: Is this character realistic and believable? Is this author qualified to write on this subject? Is this author biased? Does this author present opinions as facts? |

# Expand your students' view of the Spanish-speaking world

## El mundo hispanohablante

Spanish is the language of more than 350 million people around the world. Spanish had its origin in Spain. It is sometimes fondly called the "language of Cervantes," the author of the world's most famous novel and character, *Don Quijote*. The Spanish **conquistadores** and **exploradores** brought their language to the Americas in the fifteenth and sixteenth centuries. Spanish is the official language of almost all the countries of Central and South America. It is the official language of Mexico and several of the larger islands in the Caribbean. Spanish is also the heritage language of forty million people in the United States.

España

México

Perú

## El mundo hispanohablante

**Costa Rica**

CAPITAL
San José

POPULATION
3,896,000

FUN FACT
Many consider Costa Rica a very special place. Its residents, Ticos, are polite, peaceful, and extremely friendly. Costa Rica has no army and prides itself on having more teachers than police officers. Costa Rica is a country of sun-drenched beaches on the Pacific, tropical jungles along the Caribbean coast, cosmopolitan cities such as San José, and high mountains in the central valley. Costa Rica is a tourist's paradise as well as home to many expatriates.

**Panamá**

CAPITAL
Panamá

POPULATION
2,961,000

FUN FACT
Panama is a country of variety—a variety of races, customs, natural wonders, and attractions. It is a country of tropical forests, mountains, beautiful beaches, excellent fishing, picturesque lakes, rivers, two oceans, and—the most incredible engineering feat—the Panama Canal. Panama is also the largest financial center of Latin America. All this in a mere 77,432 square kilometers!

**Cuba**

CAPITAL
La Habana

POPULATION
11,263,000

FUN FACT
Havana, the capital of Cuba, is known for its gorgeous colonial architecture. This lush island, not far from Florida, is one of the world's greatest producers of sugar cane. Cuba has been ruled by Fidel Castro since 1959 when he overthrew the dictator Fulgencio Batista.

**La República Dominicana**

CAPITAL
Santo Domingo

POPULATION
8,716,000

FUN FACT
The Dominican Republic shares with Haiti the island of Hispaniola in the greater Antilles. The oldest university in our hemisphere, la Universidad de Santo Domingo, was founded in Santo Domingo. The Dominicans are ardent fans or aficionados of baseball, and this rather small island nation has produced some of the finest major league players.

**Puerto Rico**

CAPITAL
San Juan

POPULATION
3,886,000

FUN FACT
Puerto Ricans have an endearing term for their beloved island—la isla del encanto—island of enchantment. A commonwealth of the United States, Puerto Rico is a lush, tropical island with beaches along its Atlantic and Caribbean shores and gorgeous mountains with Alpine-like views in its interior. Puerto Rico is the home of the beloved coquí—a little frog that lives only in Puerto Rico and who lets no one see him.



Glencoe's **El mundo hispanohablante** will take your students to the many places where they will be able to use their Spanish.

Maps, facts, and figures will serve as a valuable resource for you and your students throughout your journey.

# Awaken your students' interest with an introduction to the chapter theme in a cultural context

**Itinerary for Success**

- ✓ Exposure to Hispanic culture
- ✓ Clear expectations and goals
- ✓ Thematic, contextualized vocabulary
- ✓ Useful and thematically linked structure
- ✓ Progressive practice
- ✓ Real-life conversation
- ✓ Cultural readings in the target language
- ✓ Connections to other disciplines . . . in Spanish!
- ✓ Recycling and review
- ✓ High-interest articles from **People en español**

Objectives let students know what they will be able to do at the end of the chapter.

Capítulo 4

De tiendas

**Objetivos**

In this chapter you will learn to:

- shop for apparel and food in Spanish-speaking countries
- ask for the quantities and sizes you want
- find out prices
- talk about different types of past actions
- talk in general terms about what is done
- talk about shopping practices in Spanish-speaking countries

Pedro de Vega Muñoz *Market Day, Seville*

90 noventa

FOX DELICIAS MALL

Opening photo provides a cultural backdrop for the chapter.

Fine Art related to the chapter enriches students' cultural knowledge. The Fine Art pieces are also available on transparencies.

# Give students something to talk about with thematic, contextualized vocabulary

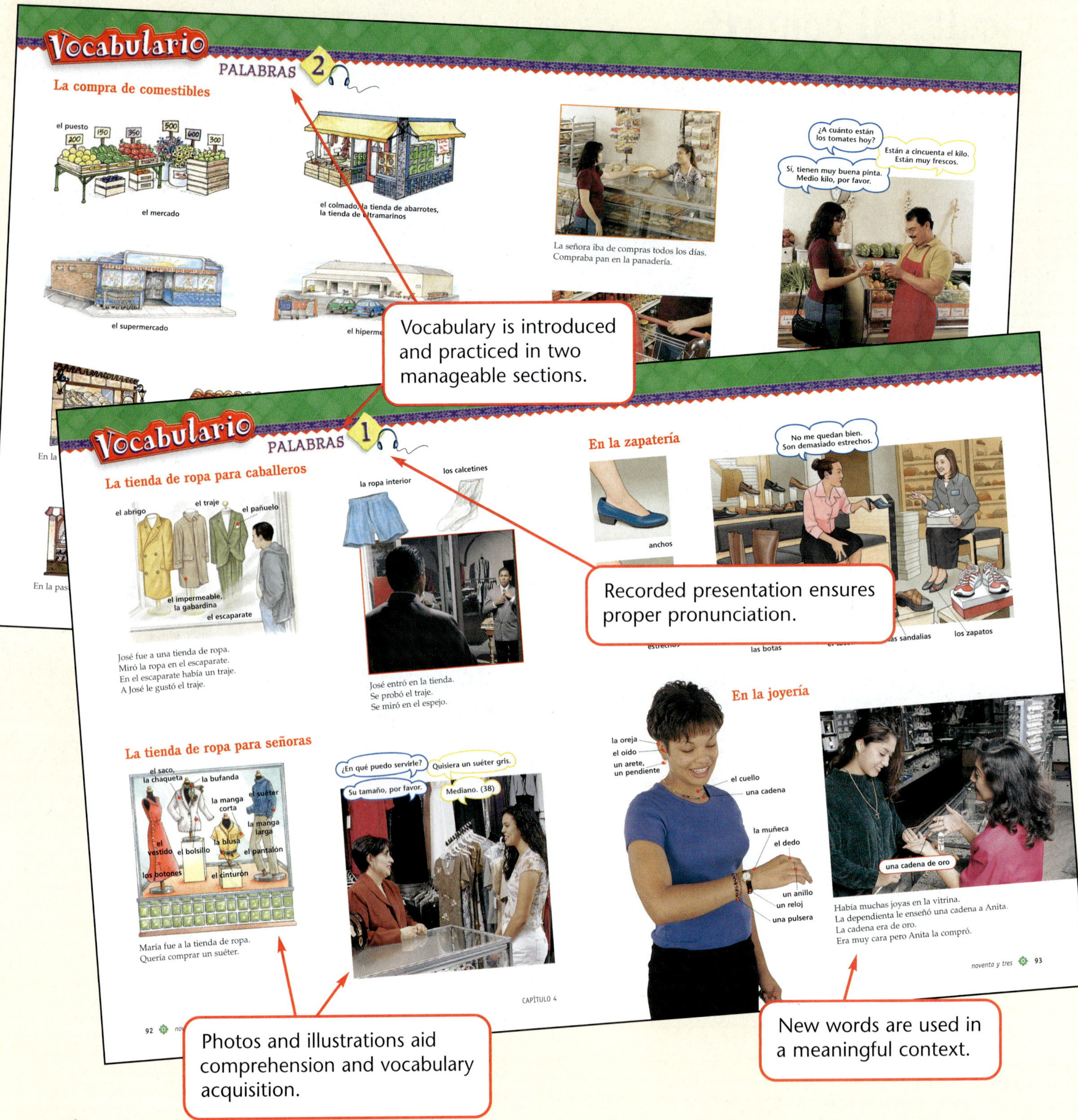

# Provide practice for the mastery of new vocabulary

**Itinerary for Success**

- ✓ Exposure to Hispanic culture
- ✓ Clear expectations and goals
- ✓ Thematic, contextualized vocabulary
- ✓ Useful and thematically linked structure
- ✓ Progressive practice
- ✓ Real-life conversation
- ✓ Cultural readings in the target language
- ✓ Connections to other disciplines . . . in Spanish!
- ✓ Recycling and review
- ✓ High-interest articles from **People en español**

**Historieta** enables students to tell and retell a story, using their new words.

Vocabulario

¿Qué palabra necesito?

7 **De compras** Contesten.
1. Alicia necesitaba pan. ¿Adónde fue ella?
2. Ella quería comprar un biftec. ¿Adónde fue?
3. Quería ostras frescas y un filete de pescado. ¿Adónde fue?
4. Necesitaba una docena de naranjas. ¿Adónde fue?
5. Quería comprar un pastel delicioso. ¿Adónde fue?

8 **Historieta Al supermercado** Contesten.
1. ¿Fue al mercado o al supermercado la señora Galdós?
2. ¿Empujó un carrito por los pasillos?
3. ¿Fue de un departamento a otro?
4. ¿Qué compró en la carnicería?
5. ¿Qué compró en el departamento de productos congelados?
6. Quería hacer un bocadillo de jamón y queso. ¿Cuántas rebanadas de jamón compró?
7. ¿Compró un frasco de mayonesa?
8. ¿Dónde pagó?
9. ¿En qué puso la señora sus compras?



Una panadería, México

Un supermercado, San José, Costa Rica

9 **Preguntas personales** Contesten.
1. ¿Quién en tu familia compra la comida?
2. ¿Hace las compras en un mercado o en un supermercado?
3. ¿Qué productos congelados compra con frecuencia?
4. ¿Compra la carne en una carnicería o en el supermercado?
5. En el supermercado donde ustedes compran, ¿usan bolsas de plástico o de papel?

98 noventa y ocho

CAPÍTULO 4



Vocabulario

10 **¿A cuánto está?** Contesten según el anuncio.
1. la bolsa de patatas fritas
2. la lata de tomate
3. el jamón serrano
4. la caja de queso castellano
5. el frasco de mermelada

11 **¿Cuánto?** Tú eres el/la dependiente(a) en el mercado. El/La cliente (tu compañero[a]) pide uno de los siguientes productos y tú le preguntas la cantidad que quiere, en kilos, latas, paquetes, bolsas, botellas, etc. Luego cambien de rol.

ternera · cola · zanahorias congeladas · atún · mayonesa

12 **Los favoritos** Prepara dos listas: una lista de los comestibles que te gustan y otra de los comestibles que no te gustan. Luego trabaja con un(a) compañero(a). Comparen sus listas y determinen los gustos que tienen en común.

13 **¡Qué invitación!** Estás viviendo con los Menéndez, una familia mexicana. ¡Qué coincidencia! Los «Dallas Cowboys» están en México y los señores Menéndez invitan a los «Cowboys» a cenar. Con el señor o la señora Menéndez (tu compañero[a]), planeen el menú para la comida que van a servir. Discutan las cantidades que van a necesitar. A propósito, *a ton* en español es «una tonelada».

Un poco más: For more practice using words from **Palabras 2**, do Activity 4 on page H5 at the end of this book.

Plaza San Jacinto, Ciudad de México

DE TIENDAS

Paired and small-group activities allow students to communicate about the chapter topic.

# Build communicative competence with thematically linked structure

New structures are presented in simple terms with familiar vocabulary.

Immediate reinforcement shows students how structure works to build meaning.

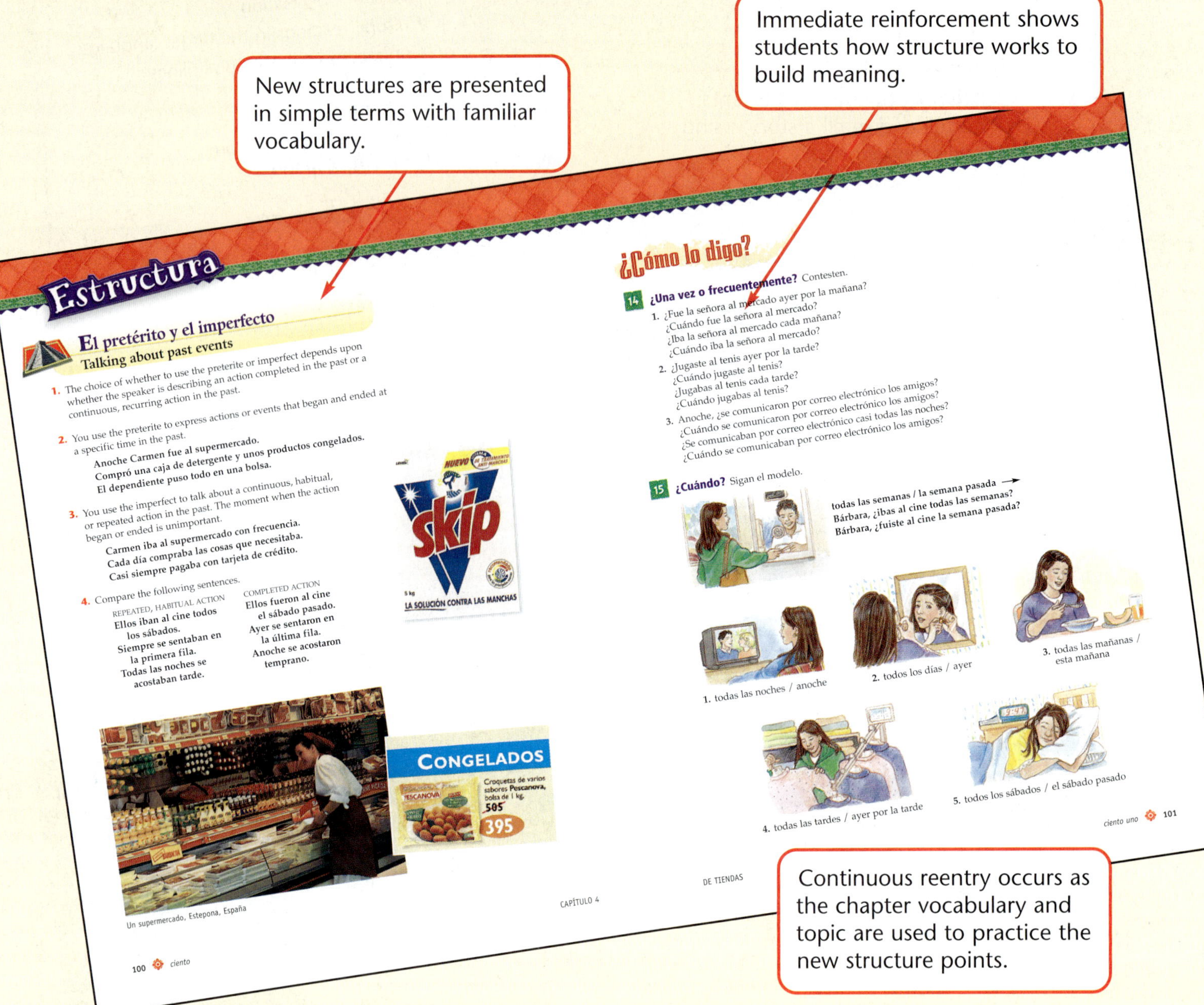

## Estructura

### El pretérito y el imperfecto
#### Talking about past events

1. The choice of whether to use the preterite or imperfect depends upon whether the speaker is describing an action completed in the past or a continuous, recurring action in the past.

2. You use the preterite to express actions or events that began and ended at a specific time in the past.
   **Anoche Carmen fue al supermercado.**
   **Compró una caja de detergente y unos productos congelados.**
   **El dependiente puso todo en una bolsa.**

3. You use the imperfect to talk about a continuous, habitual, or repeated action in the past. The moment when the action began or ended is unimportant.
   **Carmen iba al supermercado con frecuencia.**
   **Cada día compraba las cosas que necesitaba.**
   **Casi siempre pagaba con tarjeta de crédito.**

4. Compare the following sentences.

| REPEATED, HABITUAL ACTION | COMPLETED ACTION |
|---|---|
| **Ellos iban al cine todos los sábados.** | **Ellos fueron al cine el sábado pasado.** |
| **Siempre se sentaban en la primera fila.** | **Ayer se sentaron en la última fila.** |
| **Todas las noches se acostaban tarde.** | **Anoche se acostaron temprano.** |



Un supermercado, Estepona, España

## ¿Cómo lo digo?

**14 ¿Una vez o frecuentemente?** Contesten.

1. ¿Fue la señora al mercado ayer por la mañana?
   ¿Cuándo fue la señora al mercado?
   ¿Iba la señora al mercado cada mañana?
   ¿Cuándo iba la señora al mercado?
2. ¿Jugaste al tenis ayer por la tarde?
   ¿Cuándo jugaste al tenis?
   ¿Jugabas al tenis cada tarde?
   ¿Cuándo jugabas al tenis?
3. Anoche, ¿se comunicaron por correo electrónico los amigos?
   ¿Cuándo se comunicaron por correo electrónico los amigos?
   ¿Se comunicaban por correo electrónico casi todas las noches?
   ¿Cuándo se comunicaban por correo electrónico los amigos?

**15 ¿Cuándo?** Sigan el modelo.

**todas las semanas / la semana pasada →**
**Bárbara, ¿ibas al cine todas las semanas?**
**Bárbara, ¿fuiste al cine la semana pasada?**

1. todas las noches / anoche
2. todos los días / ayer
3. todas las mañanas / esta mañana
4. todas las tardes / ayer por la tarde
5. todos los sábados / el sábado pasado

100 ciento   CAPÍTULO 4   DE TIENDAS   ciento uno 101

Continuous reentry occurs as the chapter vocabulary and topic are used to practice the new structure points.

# Strengthen proficiency with continuous reinforcement and reentry

**Itinerary for Success**

- ✓ Exposure to Hispanic culture
- ✓ Clear expectations and goals
- ✓ Thematic, contextualized vocabulary
- ✓ Useful and thematically linked structure
- ✓ Progressive practice
- ✓ Real-life conversation
- ✓ Cultural readings in the target language
- ✓ Connections to other disciplines . . . in Spanish!
- ✓ Recycling and review
- ✓ High-interest articles from **People en español**

Students build confidence as they complete activities that progress from easy to more challenging.

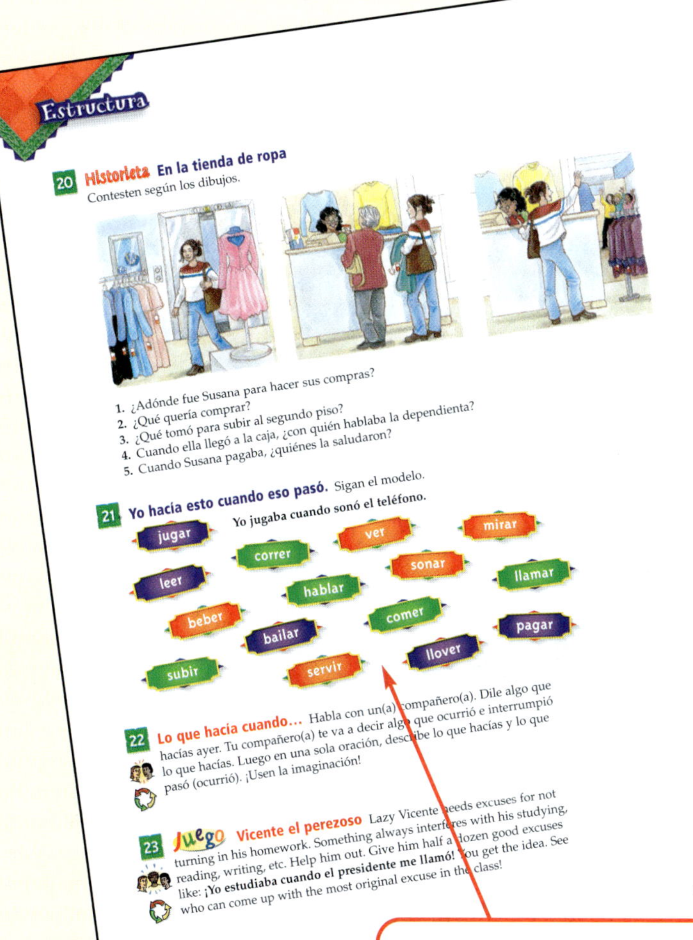

Estructura

**20 Historieta En la tienda de ropa**
Contesten según los dibujos.

1. ¿Adónde fue Susana para hacer sus compras?
2. ¿Qué quería comprar?
3. ¿Qué tomó para subir al segundo piso?
4. Cuando ella llegó a la caja, ¿con quién hablaba la dependienta?
5. Cuando Susana pagaba, ¿quiénes la saludaron?

**21 Yo hacía esto cuando eso pasó.** Sigan el modelo.
**Yo jugaba cuando sonó el teléfono.**

jugar, correr, ver, mirar, leer, sonar, llamar, hablar, beber, comer, bailar, pagar, llover, subir, servir

**22 Lo que hacía cuando...** Habla con un(a) compañero(a). Dile algo que hacías ayer. Tu compañero(a) te va a decir algo que ocurrió e interrumpió lo que hacías. Luego en una sola oración, describe lo que hacías y lo que pasó (ocurrió). ¡Usen la imaginación!

**23 Juego Vicente el perezoso** Lazy Vicente needs excuses for not turning in his homework. Something always interferes with his studying, reading, writing, etc. Help him out. Give him half a dozen good excuses like: **¡Yo estudiaba cuando el presidente me llamó!** You get the idea. See who can come up with the most original excuse in the class!

104 ciento cuatro

CAPÍTULO 4

## Dos acciones en una oración
### Narrating a sequence of events

1. Often a sentence may have two or more verbs in the past. The verbs may be in the same tense or in different tenses. In the sentence below, both verbs are in the preterite. Both describe simple actions that began and ended at a specific time in the past.
   **Laura llegó ayer y Pepe la vio.**
2. In the sentence below, the two verbs are in the imperfect because they both describe habitual or continuous actions. The moment when the actions began or ended is unimportant.
   **Durante los inviernos, Adela iba a las montañas a esquiar, pero yo trabajaba.**
3. In the sentence below, the verb **estudiaba** is in the imperfect; it describes the background—what was going on. The verb in the preterite, **entró**, expresses the action or event that interrupted the ongoing action.
   **Yo estudiaba cuando Julia entró.**

## ¿Cómo lo digo?

**19 Historieta ¿Qué hacías cuando... ?**
Contesten.

1. ¿Estabas en casa cuando sonó el teléfono?
2. ¿Mirabas un video cuando sonó?
3. ¿Contestaste el teléfono cuando sonó?
4. ¿Hablabas por teléfono cuando tu padre volvió a casa?
5. ¿Preguntó tu padre con quién hablabas?
6. ¿Con quién hablabas cuando tu padre entró?

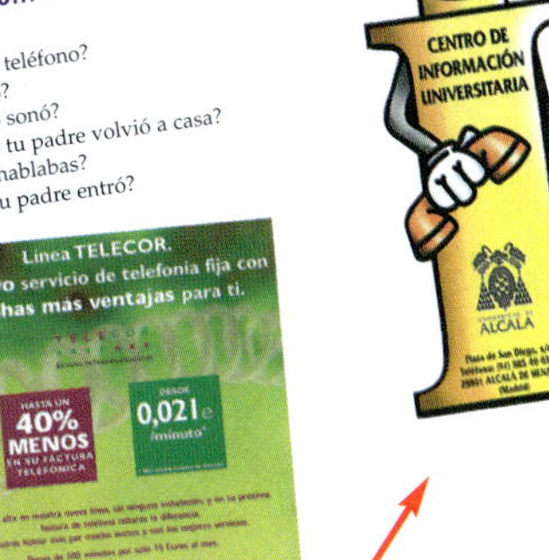


DE TIENDAS

ciento tres 103

Graphic organizers and clear examples aid comprehension.

Realia adds interest to the lesson. Students see language they are learning in real-life contexts.

# Engage students in real conversation

Students can watch and participate in the interactive conversation on CD-ROM.

Students apply newly learned vocabulary and structures to real-life situations.

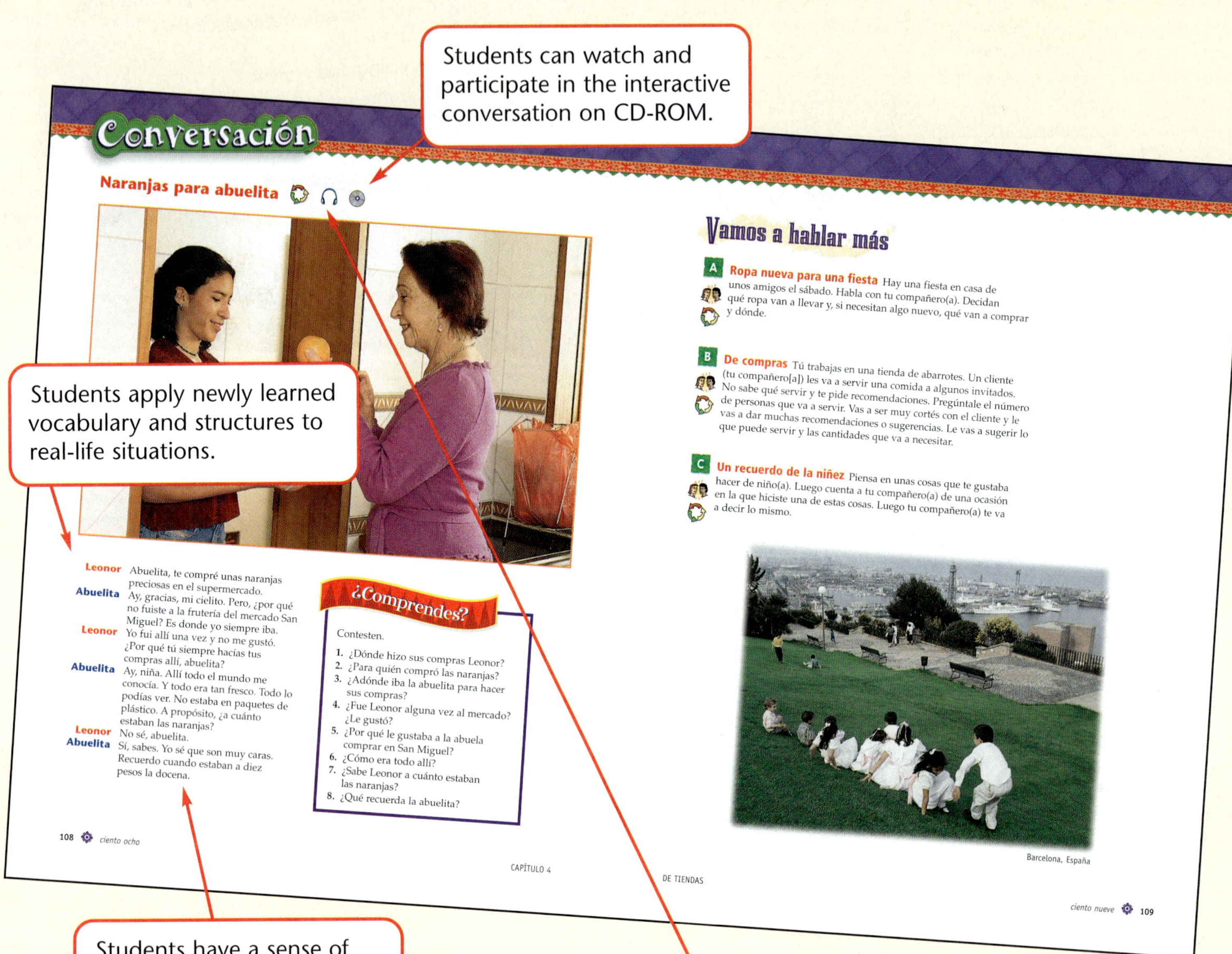

Conversación

Naranjas para abuelita

**Leonor** Abuelita, te compré unas naranjas preciosas en el supermercado.
**Abuelita** Ay, gracias, mi cielito. Pero, ¿por qué no fuiste a la frutería del mercado San Miguel? Es donde yo siempre iba.
**Leonor** Yo fui allí una vez y no me gustó. ¿Por qué tú siempre hacías tus compras allí, abuelita?
**Abuelita** Ay, niña. Allí todo el mundo me conocía. Y todo era tan fresco. Todo lo podías ver. No estaba en paquetes de plástico. A propósito, ¿a cuánto estaban las naranjas?
**Leonor** No sé, abuelita.
**Abuelita** Sí, sabes. Yo sé que son muy caras. Recuerdo cuando estaban a diez pesos la docena.

¿Comprendes?

Contesten.

1. ¿Dónde hizo sus compras Leonor?
2. ¿Para quién compró las naranjas?
3. ¿Adónde iba la abuelita para hacer sus compras?
4. ¿Fue Leonor alguna vez al mercado? ¿Le gustó?
5. ¿Por qué le gustaba a la abuela comprar en San Miguel?
6. ¿Cómo era todo allí?
7. ¿Sabe Leonor a cuánto estaban las naranjas?
8. ¿Qué recuerda la abuelita?

108 ciento ocho — CAPÍTULO 4

Vamos a hablar más

A **Ropa nueva para una fiesta** Hay una fiesta en casa de unos amigos el sábado. Habla con tu compañero(a). Decidan qué ropa van a llevar y, si necesitan algo nuevo, qué van a comprar y dónde.

B **De compras** Tú trabajas en una tienda de abarrotes. Un cliente (tu compañero[a]) les va a servir una comida a algunos invitados. No sabe qué servir y te pide recomendaciones. Pregúntale el número de personas que va a servir. Vas a ser muy cortés con el cliente y le vas a dar muchas recomendaciones o sugerencias. Le vas a sugerir lo que puede servir y las cantidades que va a necesitar.

C **Un recuerdo de la niñez** Piensa en unas cosas que te gustaba hacer de niño(a). Luego cuenta a tu compañero(a) de una ocasión en la que hiciste una de estas cosas. Luego tu compañero(a) te va a decir lo mismo.

Barcelona, España

DE TIENDAS — ciento nueve 109

Students have a sense of accomplishment when they are able to comprehend the conversation.

Students listen to speakers from diverse areas of the Spanish-speaking world to improve pronunciation.

# Heighten students' cultural awareness

**Itinerary for Success**

- ✓ Exposure to Hispanic culture
- ✓ Clear expectations and goals
- ✓ Thematic, contextualized vocabulary
- ✓ Useful and thematically linked structure
- ✓ Progressive practice
- ✓ Real-life conversation
- ✓ Cultural readings in the target language
- ✓ Connections to other disciplines . . . in Spanish!
- ✓ Recycling and review
- ✓ High-interest articles from **People en español**

Recorded reading on CD provides options for addressing various skills and learning styles.

Reading Strategies help students develop reading skills.

## Lecturas culturales

**Reading Strategy**

**Skimming** Skimming is the quickest way to find out what a reading selection is about. When you skim, look at the titles, subtitles, and any words in bold print. Also look at the photographs. All of these will indicate to you the topic of the reading and will help you understand it better.

### De compras

**Mercados**

En los países hispanos la gente tradicionalmente compraba la comida en el mercado. Los mercados municipales tenían puestos para los diferentes productos. Había pescaderías, carnicerías, fruterías, verdulerías, etc. La señora hacía sus compras todos los días—generalmente temprano por la mañana. En el mercado iba de un puesto a otro. Conocía a todos los vendedores y conversaba (charlaba) con ellos. Llevaba una bolsa o un capacho[1] para sus compras. Los vendedores no las ponían en bolsas de plástico.

Sant Feliu de Guixols, España

**Supermercados**

En todas las ciudades hispanas hay supermercados también. Son modernos, limpios[2] y sobre todo convenientes. En el supermercado uno toma un carrito. Lo empuja por los pasillos y en un solo establecimiento puede comprar todo lo que necesita.

[1]capacho *a cloth shopping bag*
[2]limpios *clean*

Caracas, Venezuela

Estepona, España

**Hipermercados**

Recientemente llegó otra posibilidad para hacer las compras—el hipermercado. El hipermercado es un enorme establecimiento comercial, normalmente en las afueras[3] de la ciudad. El hipermercado tiene lugar para miles de automóviles.

En el hipermercado se puede comprar comida, obviamente. Pero también se puede comprar de todo: ropa, aparatos electrónicos, libros, casi cualquier[4] tipo de producto. El hipermercado tiene docenas de pasillos y cajas registradoras. Si uno quiere, puede pagar sus compras con tarjeta de crédito.

Hoy en día nadie tiene bastante tiempo. Todos estamos muy ocupados. El hipermercado ayuda a conservar tiempo. Podemos comprar todo lo que necesitamos sin tener que ir a más de una tienda.

Pero todavía hay muchos que prefieren el mercado donde todo es muy fresco y todo el mundo se conoce. Los mercados municipales todavía existen y muchas personas siguen haciendo sus compras allí.

[3]afueras *outskirts* [4]cualquier *any*

**¿Comprendes?**

**A De compras** Contesten.

1. ¿Dónde compraba la gente la comida?
2. ¿Cuáles son tres puestos que se encuentran en el mercado?
3. ¿Cuándo hacía sus compras la señora?
4. ¿Con quiénes conversaba en el mercado?
5. ¿Para qué llevaba ella un capacho?
6. ¿Dónde hay supermercados?
7. ¿Por qué prefieren algunas personas el supermercado?
8. ¿Qué es un hipermercado?
9. ¿Dónde están los hipermercados normalmente?
10. ¿Por qué prefieren algunas personas el hipermercado?

**B El hipermercado y el mercado tradicional** Comparen el mercado tradicional y el hipermercado.

DE TIENDAS

ciento once  111

Cultural reading uses learned language to reinforce chapter theme.

Many visuals help students comprehend what they read.

Activities reinforce vocabulary skills and comprehension.

# Enrich students' cultural knowledge

Optional cultural readings reinforce the chapter theme.

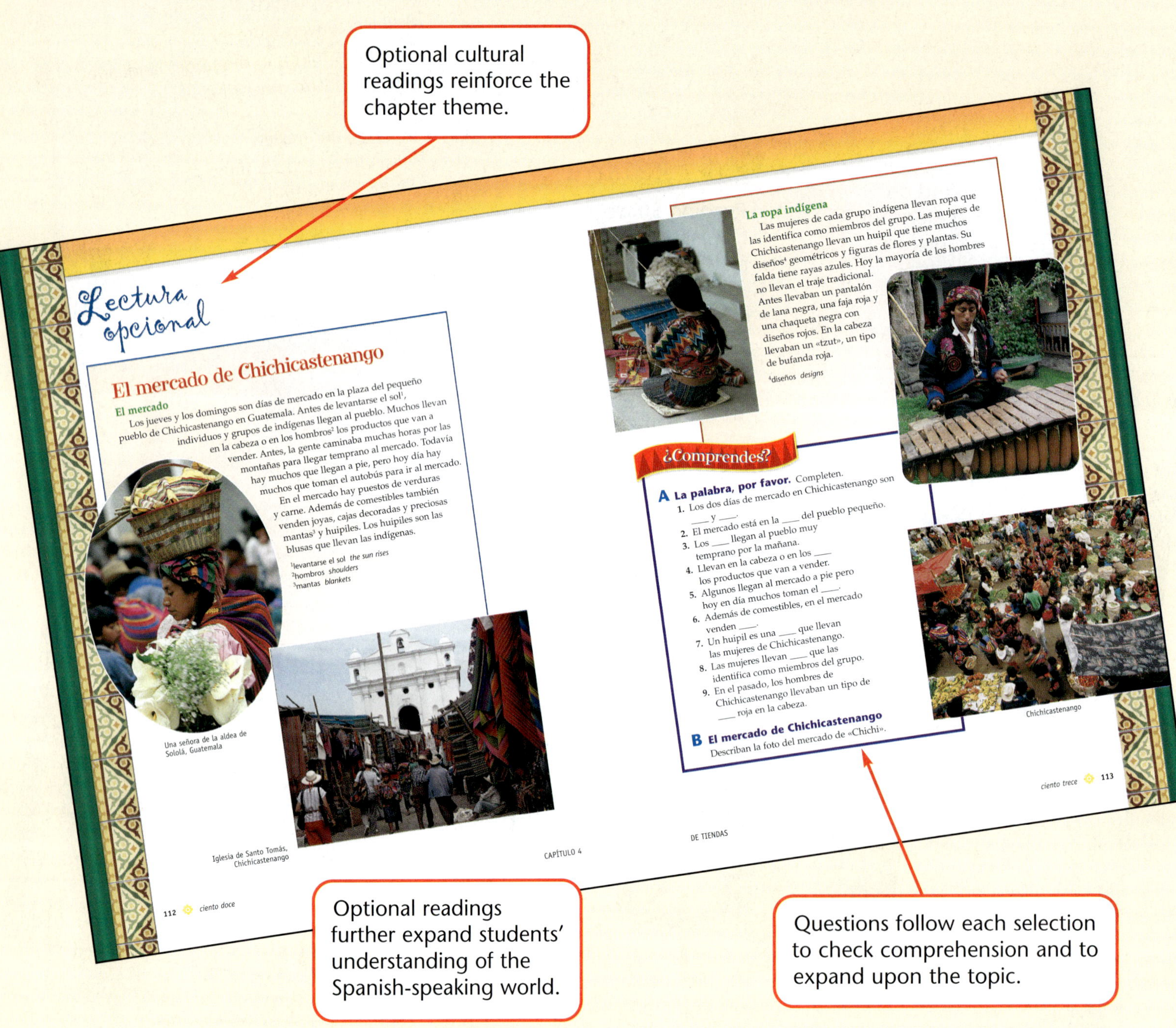

Lectura opcional

## El mercado de Chichicastenango

**El mercado**

Los jueves y los domingos son días de mercado en la plaza del pequeño pueblo de Chichicastenango en Guatemala. Antes de levantarse el sol[1], individuos y grupos de indígenas llegan al pueblo. Muchos llevan en la cabeza o en los hombros[2] los productos que van a vender. Antes, la gente caminaba muchas horas por las montañas para llegar temprano al mercado. Todavía hay muchos que llegan a pie, pero hoy día hay muchos que toman el autobús para ir al mercado.

En el mercado hay puestos de verduras y carne. Además de comestibles también venden joyas, cajas decoradas y preciosas mantas[3] y huipiles. Los huipiles son las blusas que llevan las indígenas.

[1]levantarse el sol *the sun rises*
[2]hombros *shoulders*
[3]mantas *blankets*

Una señora de la aldea de Sololá, Guatemala

Iglesia de Santo Tomás, Chichicastenango

**La ropa indígena**

Las mujeres de cada grupo indígena llevan ropa que las identifica como miembros del grupo. Las mujeres de Chichicastenango llevan un huipil que tiene muchos diseños[4] geométricos y figuras de flores y plantas. Su falda tiene rayas azules. Hoy la mayoría de los hombres no llevan el traje tradicional. Antes llevaban un pantalón de lana negra, una faja roja y una chaqueta negra con diseños rojos. En la cabeza llevaban un «tzut», un tipo de bufanda roja.

[4]diseños *designs*

**¿Comprendes?**

**A La palabra, por favor.** Completen.

1. Los dos días de mercado en Chichicastenango son ___ y ___.
2. El mercado está en la ___ del pueblo pequeño.
3. Los ___ llegan al pueblo muy temprano por la mañana.
4. Llevan en la cabeza o en los ___ los productos que van a vender.
5. Algunos llegan al mercado a pie pero hoy en día muchos toman el ___.
6. Además de comestibles, en el mercado venden ___.
7. Un huipil es una ___ que llevan las mujeres de Chichicastenango.
8. Las mujeres llevan ___ que las identifica como miembros del grupo.
9. En el pasado, los hombres de Chichicastenango llevaban un tipo de ___ roja en la cabeza.

**B El mercado de Chichicastenango** Describan la foto del mercado de «Chichi».

Chichicastenango

112 ciento doce — CAPÍTULO 4 — DE TIENDAS — ciento trece 113

Optional readings further expand students' understanding of the Spanish-speaking world.

Questions follow each selection to check comprehension and to expand upon the topic.

# Connect with other disciplines

**Itinerary for Success**

- ✓ Exposure to Hispanic culture
- ✓ Clear expectations and goals
- ✓ Thematic, contextualized vocabulary
- ✓ Useful and thematically linked structure
- ✓ Progressive practice
- ✓ Real-life conversation
- ✓ Cultural readings in the target language
- ✓ Connections to other disciplines . . . in Spanish!
- ✓ Recycling and review
- ✓ High-interest articles from **People en español**

Introduction to the **Conexiones** provides the background for students to understand the reading.

# Conexiones

## *El comercio*

### El mercadeo

One of the most important subjects for business students is marketing. **Mercadeo** is the Spanish word for *marketing*, but the English word is more often used all over the Spanish-speaking world—**el marketing.** A major focus of marketing is the promotion and advertising of a product or service.



### El mercado

Antes de definir el término «marketing», es necesario dar una definición de la palabra «mercado». El mercado es el conjunto de todos los posibles compradores (los consumidores) de un producto o de un servicio. Ejemplos de un producto son un coche o un pantalón. Ejemplos de un servicio son un banco o una agencia de viajes.

**El marketing**

En términos generales, el marketing es la creación de un mercado para un producto o servicio antes de comenzar a producir el producto o servicio. Es la responsabilidad del departamento de marketing de informar a los posibles compradores sobre la existencia del producto y las características del producto.



114 ciento catorce

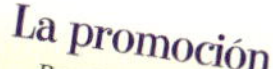

### La promoción

Para informar al público de la existencia y de las características de un producto, un aspecto muy importante del marketing es la promoción. Y la propaganda[1] juega un rol primordial, muy importante, en la promoción. Para lanzar[2] un buen programa de promoción, el personal de marketing tiene que emplear muchos medios de comunicación como la radio, la televisión, los anuncios en los periódicos y en las revistas.

**Diferentes productos y mercados**

Hay algunos productos y servicios que la gente necesita. Hay otros que la gente no necesita pero quiere. No es necesario convencer a la gente de comprar comida o gasolina. ¡Pero otra cosa es el perfume!

La industria de la ropa es un caso muy interesante. La gente necesita ropa porque todos tenemos que vestirnos. Pero hay también ropa que la gente no necesita pero que quiere. Uno puede comprar un pantalón que cuesta treinta dólares. O puede comprar un pantalón que cuesta trescientos dólares. Los dos satisfacen la necesidad de vestirse. Pero la persona que paga trescientos dólares no compra solamente algo que necesita—un artículo de ropa. Compra algo que quiere—prestigio. Y la propaganda tiene que convencer a los clientes que la belleza, la calidad y el prestigio valen el precio que les ponen.

[1]propaganda *advertising* [2]lanzar *to launch*

Carolina Herrera

### ¿Comprendes?

**A El mercadeo** Digan que sí o que no.

1. El coche es un producto.
2. El banco es otro producto.
3. Los consumidores compran sólo productos que necesitan.
4. Los consumidores no tienen que conocer las características de un producto.
5. El perfume se considera una necesidad.
6. El prestigio es una necesidad.

**B Definiciones** Den una definición de las siguientes palabras.

1. el consumidor
2. el comprador
3. el mercado
4. el producto
5. el servicio
6. la necesidad

**C Un anuncio** Preparen un anuncio para un artículo de ropa.

CAPÍTULO 4

ciento quince 115

Students further their knowledge of other disciplines—in Spanish!

# Encourage students to apply what they have learned

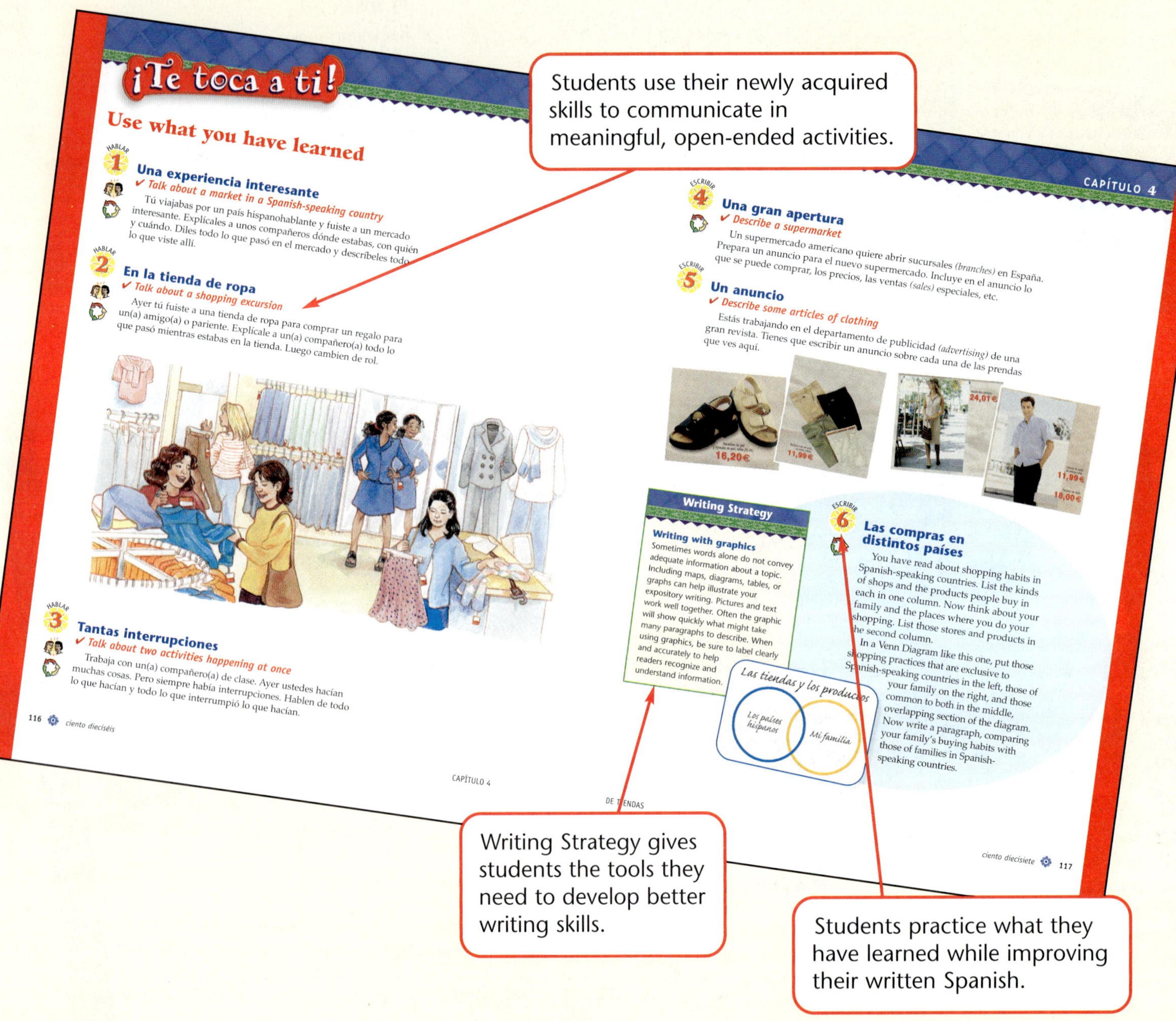

¡Te toca a ti!

## Use what you have learned

HABLAR 1

### Una experiencia interesante

✓ *Talk about a market in a Spanish-speaking country*

Tú viajabas por un país hispanohablante y fuiste a un mercado interesante. Explícales a unos compañeros dónde estabas, con quién y cuándo. Diles todo lo que pasó en el mercado y descríbeles todo lo que viste allí.

HABLAR 2

### En la tienda de ropa

✓ *Talk about a shopping excursion*

Ayer tú fuiste a una tienda de ropa para comprar un regalo para un(a) amigo(a) o pariente. Explícale a un(a) compañero(a) todo lo que pasó mientras estabas en la tienda. Luego cambien de rol.

HABLAR 3

### Tantas interrupciones

✓ *Talk about two activities happening at once*

Trabaja con un(a) compañero(a) de clase. Ayer ustedes hacían muchas cosas. Pero siempre había interrupciones. Hablen de todo lo que hacían y todo lo que interrumpió lo que hacían.

116 ciento dieciséis

CAPÍTULO 4

ESCRIBIR 4

### Una gran apertura

✓ *Describe a supermarket*

Un supermercado americano quiere abrir sucursales (*branches*) en España. Prepara un anuncio para el nuevo supermercado. Incluye en el anuncio lo que se puede comprar, los precios, las ventas (*sales*) especiales, etc.

ESCRIBIR 5

### Un anuncio

✓ *Describe some articles of clothing*

Estás trabajando en el departamento de publicidad (*advertising*) de una gran revista. Tienes que escribir un anuncio sobre cada una de las prendas que ves aquí.

16,20€ 11,99€ 24,01€ 11,99€ 18,00€

**Writing Strategy**

**Writing with graphics** Sometimes words alone do not convey adequate information about a topic. Including maps, diagrams, tables, or graphs can help illustrate your expository writing. Pictures and text work well together. Often the graphic will show quickly what might take many paragraphs to describe. When using graphics, be sure to label clearly and accurately to help readers recognize and understand information.

ESCRIBIR 6

### Las compras en distintos países

You have read about shopping habits in Spanish-speaking countries. List the kinds of shops and the products people buy in each in one column. Now think about your family and the places where you do your shopping. List those stores and products in the second column.

In a Venn Diagram like this one, put those shopping practices that are exclusive to Spanish-speaking countries in the left, those of your family on the right, and those common to both in the middle, overlapping section of the diagram. Now write a paragraph, comparing your family's buying habits with those of families in Spanish-speaking countries.



DE TIENDAS

ciento diecisiete 117

Students use their newly acquired skills to communicate in meaningful, open-ended activities.

Writing Strategy gives students the tools they need to develop better writing skills.

Students practice what they have learned while improving their written Spanish.

# Check students' progress

**Itinerary for Success**

- ✓ Exposure to Hispanic culture
- ✓ Clear expectations and goals
- ✓ Thematic, contextualized vocabulary
- ✓ Useful and thematically linked structure
- ✓ Progressive practice
- ✓ Real-life conversation
- ✓ Cultural readings in the target language
- ✓ Connections to other disciplines . . . in Spanish!
- ✓ Recycling and review
- ✓ High-interest articles from **People en español**

Assessment activities give students a chance to evaluate what they have really learned.

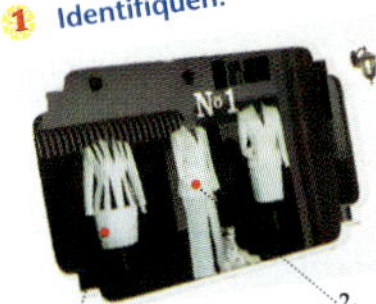

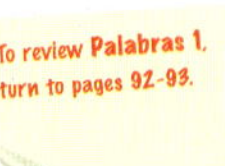

"Sticky" notes direct students to the correct pages for review.

# Take students beyond the text to learn more about culture and language Give students opportunities to review and use their vocabulary in creative ways

The illustration provided at the end of each chapter recombines material students have learned to remind them of what they know how to say in Spanish. Use this illustration as a prompt to allow your students to demonstrate all they know how to say or write.

Students can use the list as a self-check at the end of the chapter.

## ¡Hablo como un pro!

Tell all you can about this illustration.

ZARA

## Vocabulario

**Identifying more stores**
la zapatería
la joyería

**Shopping for clothes and jewelry**
mirar en el escaparate (la vitrina)
probarse la ropa
¿En qué puedo servirle?
Quisiera...
No me (le) queda(n) bien.

**Identifying more clothing**
el bolsillo
el saco, la chaqueta
el abrigo
el impermeable, la gabardina
el suéter
la camisa de mangas cortas (largas)
el vestido
el cinturón
el pañuelo
la ropa interior
la bufanda
los botones
las sandalias
las botas
el tacón

**Identifying jewelry**
las joyas
una pulsera
una cadena
un anillo
un arete, un pendiente
un reloj

**Identifying more parts of the body**
la muñeca
el cuello
el dedo
la oreja, el oído

**Describing clothing and jewelry**
mediano(a)
ancho(a)
estrecho(a)
de oro

**Identifying more food stores**
el colmado, la tienda de abarrotes, la tienda de ultramarinos
el puesto
el supermercado
el hipermercado
la panadería
la carnicería
la pescadería
la pastelería
la verdulería
la frutería

**Foods**
el pan
la carne
el pescado
los mariscos
los pasteles
las legumbres, los vegetales

**Shopping for food**
hacer las compras, ir de compras
¿A cuánto están... ?
tener buena pinta
empujar el carrito
fresco(a)
la bolsa de plástico
una tajada, una rebanada
un frasco
una caja
una docena

**VIDEOTUR**
**Episodio 4**
In this video episode, you will join Francisco and Julián on a trip to the supermarket. See page 483 for more information.

**How well do you know your vocabulary?**
- Choose any type of store you like to shop in.
- Tell what you like to buy there.

DE TIENDAS

ciento veintiuno 121

Vocabulary is categorized to help recall.

# People en español motivates students to read and learn about the diverse cultures of the Spanish-speaking world

**Itinerary for Success**

- ✓ Exposure to Hispanic culture
- ✓ Clear expectations and goals
- ✓ Thematic, contextualized vocabulary
- ✓ Useful and thematically linked structure
- ✓ Progressive practice
- ✓ Real-life conversation
- ✓ Cultural readings in the target language
- ✓ Connections to other disciplines . . . in Spanish!
- ✓ Recycling and review
- ✓ High-interest articles from **People en español**

**People en español** articles throughout **¡Buen viaje!** take students to different regions in the world where Spanish is spoken.

People en español

## Entérate Estados Unidos

### Datos interesantes sobre los latinos en Estados Unidos

■ En 1970 el gobierno de Estados Unidos inventó el término "hispanos" para dar un solo nombre a esta diversa población. Muchos "hispanos" prefieren el término "latinos" porque indica el origen de Latinoamérica.
■ Estados Unidos es el 5º país de habla hispana en el mundo, y los latinos son la minoría más numerosa de este país.
■ De mayor a menor, estos son los grupos que viven en Estados Unidos: mexicanos, puertorriqueños, cubanos, dominicanos, salvadoreños, colombianos; el resto son hispanos de orígenes diversos.
■ Muchos mexicanos del suroeste tienen un origen diferente al resto de los hispanos, porque ellos ya vivían ahí cuando Estados Unidos conquistó[1] estos territorios.
■ Los valores[2] culturales más importantes para los hispanos son preservar la lengua española y la unión de la familia.

[1]conquistó: conquered
[2]valores: values

### California, su pasado español

Los colonizadores[1] españoles dejaron su marca más obvia en los numerosos nombres españoles de los diferentes lugares. En la arquitectura también es notable su presencia. Las misiones californianas son un ejemplo del estilo español. Los indígenas construyeron estos bellos edificios de adobe. Hay 21 misiones en todo el estado y hoy día son una gran atracción turística.

Santa Bárbara, fundada en 1786

[1]colonizadores: settlers

### Las tiendas latinas

Hay "bodegas" en todos los barrios latinos; son tiendas de comestibles donde la atención personal es muy importante. Como para los latinos es extremadamente importante "verse bien"[1], es una buena idea tener un salón de belleza en sus barrios. Las tiendas donde venden hierbas[2], medicamentos naturales, incienso y velas[3] especiales se llaman botánicas.

[1]"verse bien": "looking good" [2]hierbas: herbs [3]velas: candles

126

## SUCESOS

César Chávez

**César Chávez** es un líder muy respetado entre los chicanos y los trabajadores extranjeros. Latinos en su mayoría, los que recogen[1] las frutas en Estados Unidos hoy reciben un mejor salario gracias al trabajo de Chávez. Un momento importante en su carrera fue en 1970, cuando los rancheros aceptaron pagar más y mejorar las condiciones de trabajo para estas personas. César Chávez murió en 1993.
**Sábados Gigantes** es uno de los programas más famosos y populares de la televisión hispana. Desde hace 40 años, el chileno "Don Francisco" conduce el programa, un récord que pasó al Libro Guinness de los Récords.

[1]recogen: pick

Chef Douglas Rodríguez

### El "Mango Gang"

Más y más estadounidenses conocen la diferencia entre una "tortilla" en un restaurante mexicano y en un restaurante español. Pero... ¿quién conoce al "Mango Gang"? Ellos hicieron popular la "Nuevo Latino Cuisine". En Miami, el chef cubanoamericano, Douglas Rodríguez, y sus colegas Norman Van Aken, Robin Haas, Allen Susser y Mark Militello re-inventaron la cocina tradicional latina. Ellos usan frijoles negros y arroz, mangos, aguacates[1], pescado caribeño y los preparan de una manera diferente.

[1]aguacates: avocados

La parada puertorriqueña

### Calendario de fiestas

**5 de mayo** En el suroeste, y poco a poco[1] en otras partes de Estados Unidos, se celebra el patrimonio cultural mexicano. En México, la fiesta conmemora la victoria de los mexicanos sobre los invasores franceses.
**12 de octubre** En 1492 llegaron los españoles a América y hoy se celebra el "Día de la Raza[2]" en esta fecha. Esta fiesta conmemora el patrimonio cultural de todos los latinos en Estados Unidos. Además, el mes de octubre es el "Mes de la Hispanidad".
**1º de noviembre** "El Día de los Muertos[3]" era una fiesta exclusivamente de los mexicanos al sur de la frontera. Hoy día, más y más mexicanamericanos celebran esta fiesta en Estados Unidos porque les gusta recordar[4] a sus familiares en forma festiva.
**6 de junio** El segundo domingo del mes de junio se celebra "El día nacional de los puertorriqueños" en la Ciudad de Nueva York. Las estrellas del cine, del deporte y también el alcalde[5] y otras autoridades van a la parada en la Quinta Avenida, donde hay carrozas[6] y mucha música y baile.

[1]poco a poco: little by little
[2]raza: race
[3]muertos: dead
[4]recordar: to remember
[5]alcalde: mayor
[6]carrozas: floats

## micocina

**Primero, las tortillas y ahora ¡las pupusas!**
Esta comida típica salvadoreña se come con la mano y es muy popular entre los latinos de todas partes. Es como una tortilla gorda rellena[1] con carne, queso, frijoles o una combinación de todos estos ingredientes. *(Atención: No es bueno llamar "tortillas" a las pupusas frente a un salvadoreño.)*

**Pupusas de frijol con queso**
**Ingredientes**
*(Para la masa[2])*
2 tazas de harina de maíz
1 taza de agua tibia[3]
1 poco de sal
*(Para el relleno)*
1 lata de frijoles molidos[4]
250g de queso rallado[5]

**Preparación**
Mezclar la harina, el agua y la sal para hacer la masa. Formar 12 bolitas medianas. Ahuecar[6] el centro y rellenar con los frijoles y el queso. Luego, aplastar[7] y formar una tortilla gruesa (1/4 pulgada). Freír en aceite caliente y servir con salsa de tomates frescos.

[1]rellena: filled
[2]masa: dough
[3]tibia: lukewarm
[4]molidos: ground
[5]rallado: grated
[6]ahuecar: hollow
[7]aplastar: flatten

Pupusas de frijol con queso

127

Students learn about topics that interest them—holidays, foods, entertainment, and famous people—in Spanish they can read!

# Enhance appreciation of literature and culture

Literary Companion affords students yet another opportunity to apply their reading skills in Spanish.

Literary selections present another view of Hispanic culture.

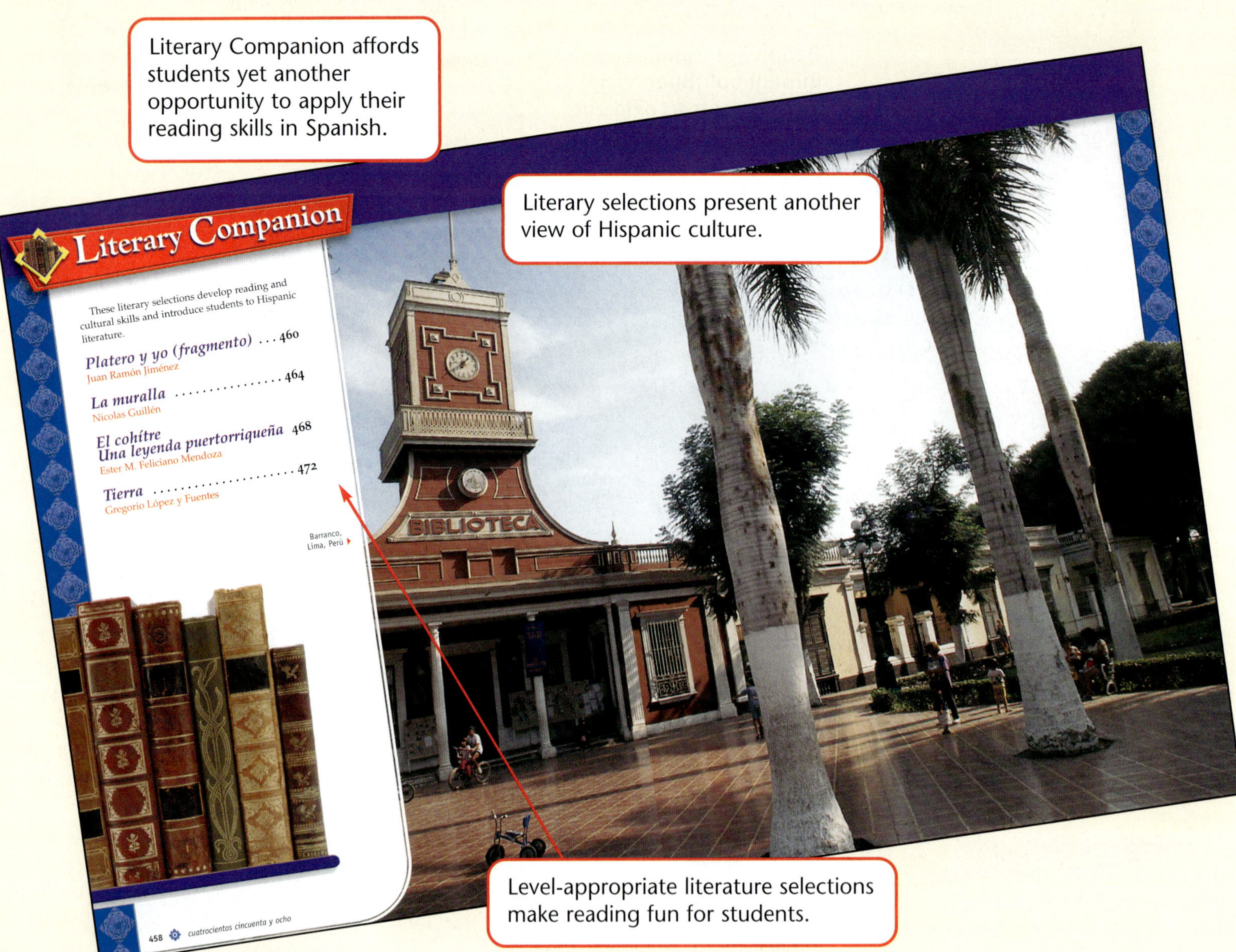


Level-appropriate literature selections make reading fun for students.

# Take your students on a tour of the Spanish-speaking world with ¡Viva el mundo hispano!

**Itinerary for Success**

- ✓ Exposure to Hispanic culture
- ✓ Clear expectations and goals
- ✓ Thematic, contextualized vocabulary
- ✓ Useful and thematically linked structure
- ✓ Progressive practice
- ✓ Real-life conversation
- ✓ Cultural readings in the target language
- ✓ Connections to other disciplines . . . in Spanish!
- ✓ Recycling and review
- ✓ High-interest articles from **People en español**

**¡Viva el mundo hispano!**, filmed in eight Spanish-speaking countries, lets your students experience the diversity of the Spanish-speaking world while reinforcing the language they have learned and improving their listening and viewing skills.

## Video Companion

### Using video in the classroom

The use of video in the classroom can be a wonderful asset to the World Languages teacher and a most beneficial learning tool for the language student. Video enables students to experience whatever it is they are learning in their textbook in a real-life setting. With each lesson, they are able to take a vicarious field trip. They see people interacting at home, at school, at the market, etc., in an authentic milieu. Students sitting in a classroom can see real people going about their real life in real places. They may experience the target culture in many countries. The cultural benefits are limitless.

**Developing listening and viewing skills**

In addition to its tremendous cultural value, video, when properly used, gives students much needed practice in developing good listening and viewing skills. Video allows students to look for numerous clues that are evident in a tone of voice, facial expressions, and gestures. Through video students can see and hear the diversity of the target culture and, as discerning viewers and listeners, compare and contrast the Spanish-speaking cultures to each other and to their own culture. Video introduces a dimension into classroom instruction that no other medium—teachers, overhead, text, audio CDs—can provide.

**Reinforcing learned language**

Video that is properly developed for classroom use has speakers reincorporate the language students have learned in a given lesson. In keeping with reality, however, speakers introduce some new words, expressions, and structures because students functioning in a real-life situation would not know every word native speakers use with them in a live conversation. The lively and interactive nature of video allows students to use their listening and viewing skills to comprehend new language in addition to seeing and hearing the language they have learned come to life.

**Getting the most out of video**

The intrinsic benefit of video is often lost when students are allowed to read the scripted material before viewing. In many cases, students will have come to understand language used by the speakers in the video by means of reading comprehension, thus negating the inherent benefits of video as a tool to develop listening and viewing skills. Because today's students are so accustomed to the medium of video as a tool for entertainment and learning, a well-written and well-produced video program will help them develop real-life language skills and confidence in those skills in an enjoyable way.



478 cuatrocientos setenta y ocho

### On Location

Your students will love seeing the adventures and mishaps of the teen characters in **¡Viva el mundo hispano!**

Francisco.
Madrid, España.

Students will visit places where they will hear different accents, dialects, and languages spoken. **¡Viva el mundo hispano!** will take you and your students on an exciting tour of Spanish-speaking world.

# Preview and objectives let you know what to plan for

**Spotlight on Culture** gives you facts and information about the art and photographs on the page. Your students will think you know everything.

References to the National Standards are made for you.

Capítulo 10

**Preview**

In this chapter, students will learn to talk about food and its preparation. Students will also increase their communication skills by learning the formal imperative forms as well as the placement of object pronouns with them. The cultural focus of this chapter is on the variety of foods and recipes available in the Spanish-speaking world and the important role that cuisine plays in it.

**National Standards**

**Communication**
In Chapter 10 students will learn to communicate in spoken and written Spanish on the following topics:
- foods
- food preparation
- the origins of specific foods

Students will obtain and provide information about these topics and engage in conversations that would typically take place in a kitchen as they fulfill the chapter objectives listed on this page.

Capítulo 10

**La cocina hispana**

**Objetivos**

In this chapter you will learn to:
- talk about foods and food preparation
- give commands
- refer to people and things previously mentioned
- prepare some regional specialties
- talk about the origin of several foods

Manuel Serrano *A Mexican Kitchen in 1885*

290 doscientos noventa



Capítulo 10

**Spotlight on Culture**

**Fotografía** The photo shows traditional Spanish foods. Pictured are varieties of **embutidos** (the generic word for *sausages*): **chorizos, salchichones,** and others. There is also a whole **jamón serrano**. On the wall is a **ristra** (*string of hot peppers*) called **chiles picantes** in Mexico or **guindillas** in Spain.

The poster is of Trujillo in the province of Cáceres, in the region of Extremadura. Trujillo was the home of three of the most famous **conquistadores,** Francisco Pizarro and his brothers Gonzalo and Hernando.

**LEVELING**

The activities, conversations, and readings within each chapter are marked according to level of difficulty. E indicates easy. A indicates average. C indicates challenging. Some activities cover a range of difficulty. In some activities, for example, advanced students will be able to produce more extensive responses while students who learn at a different rate may give less detailed responses. The leveling indicators will help you individualize instruction to best meet your students' needs.

**¡Buen viaje!** is written to address learners with different ability levels. The activities, conversations, and readings throughout the text are marked to indicate their level of difficulty to help you individualize instruction.

# Step-by-step hints help you through the chapter

**Resource Manager** lets you know which resources you will need for each part of the chapter.

**Bellringer Reviews** (also available in the Transparency Binder) provide quick checks of previously taught material.

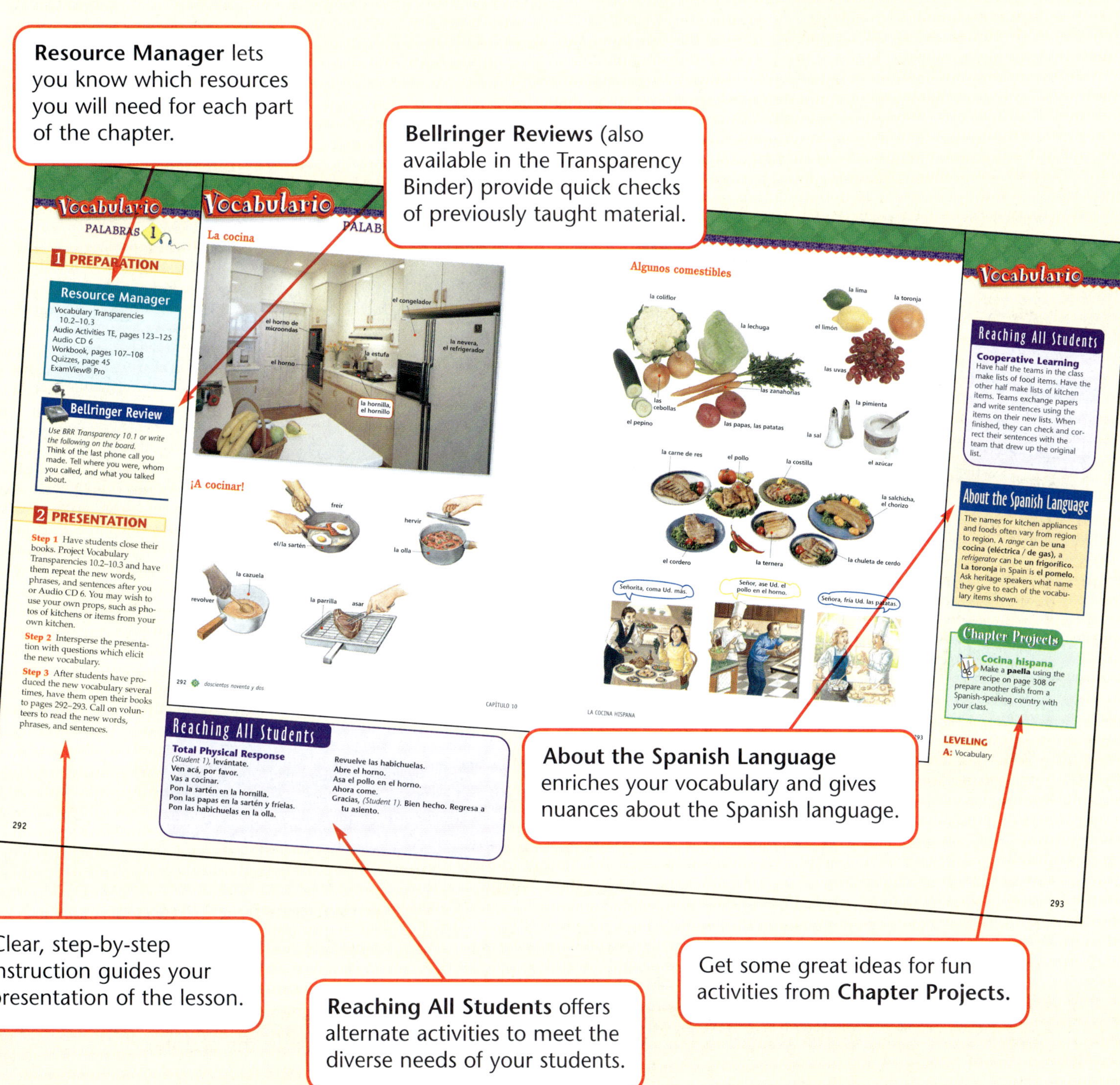

Vocabulario

PALABRAS 1

1 PREPARATION

Resource Manager

Vocabulary Transparencies 10.2–10.3
Audio Activities TE, pages 123–125
Audio CD 6
Workbook, pages 107–108
Quizzes, page 45
ExamView® Pro

Bellringer Review

*Use BRR Transparency 10.1 or write the following on the board.*
Think of the last phone call you made. Tell where you were, whom you called, and what you talked about.

2 PRESENTATION

**Step 1** Have students close their books. Project Vocabulary Transparencies 10.2–10.3 and have them repeat the new words, phrases, and sentences after you or Audio CD 6. You may wish to use your own props, such as photos of kitchens or items from your own kitchen.

**Step 2** Intersperse the presentation with questions which elicit the new vocabulary.

**Step 3** After students have produced the new vocabulary several times, have them open their books to pages 292–293. Call on volunteers to read the new words, phrases, and sentences.

Reaching All Students

**Total Physical Response**
*(Student 1)*, levántate.
Ven acá, por favor.
Vas a cocinar.
Pon la sartén en la hornilla.
Pon las papas en la sartén y fríelas.
Pon las habichuelas en la olla.
Revuelve las habichuelas.
Abre el horno.
Asa el pollo en el horno.
Ahora come.
Gracias, *(Student 1)*. Bien hecho. Regresa a tu asiento.

292

Vocabulario

La cocina



¡A cocinar!



292 descientos noventa y dos

CAPÍTULO 10

Algunos comestibles



LA COCINA HISPANA

Vocabulario

Reaching All Students

**Cooperative Learning** Have half the teams in the class make lists of food items. Have the other half make lists of kitchen items. Teams exchange papers and write sentences using the items on their new lists. When finished, they can check and correct their sentences with the team that drew up the original list.

About the Spanish Language

The names for kitchen appliances and foods often vary from region to region. A *range* can be **una cocina (eléctrica / de gas)**, a *refrigerator* can be **un frigorífico. La toronja** in Spain is **el pomelo.** Ask heritage speakers what name they give to each of the vocabulary items shown.

Chapter Projects

**Cocina hispana**
Make a **paella** using the recipe on page 308 or prepare another dish from a Spanish-speaking country with your class.

**LEVELING**
**A:** Vocabulary

293

**About the Spanish Language** enriches your vocabulary and gives nuances about the Spanish language.

Clear, step-by-step instruction guides your presentation of the lesson.

**Reaching All Students** offers alternate activities to meet the diverse needs of your students.

Get some great ideas for fun activities from **Chapter Projects.**

# Painless presentation of structure makes it easier for you to reach your students

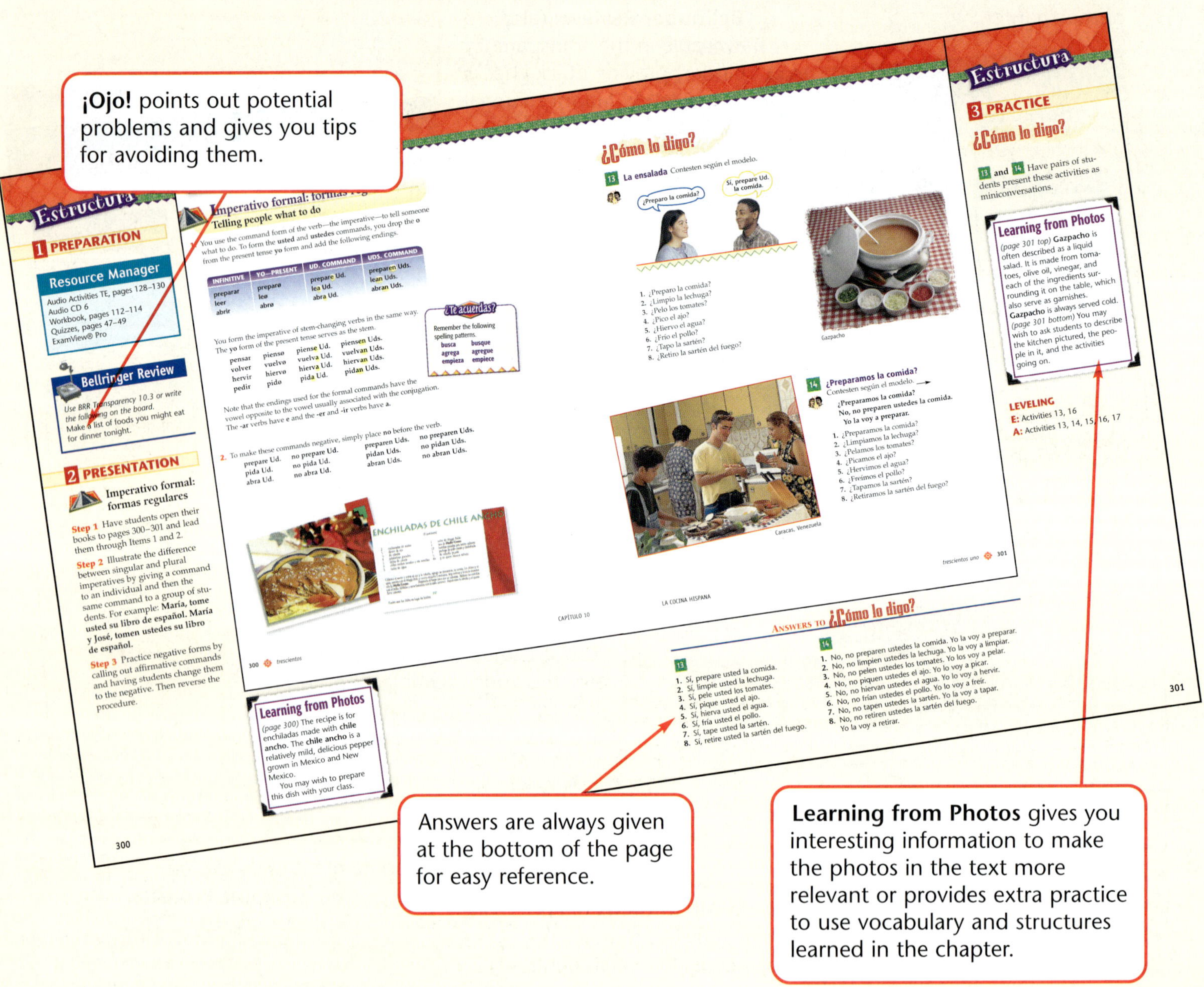

**¡Ojo!** points out potential problems and gives you tips for avoiding them.

Answers are always given at the bottom of the page for easy reference.

**Learning from Photos** gives you interesting information to make the photos in the text more relevant or provides extra practice to use vocabulary and structures learned in the chapter.

# Help your students feel confident about their speaking skills

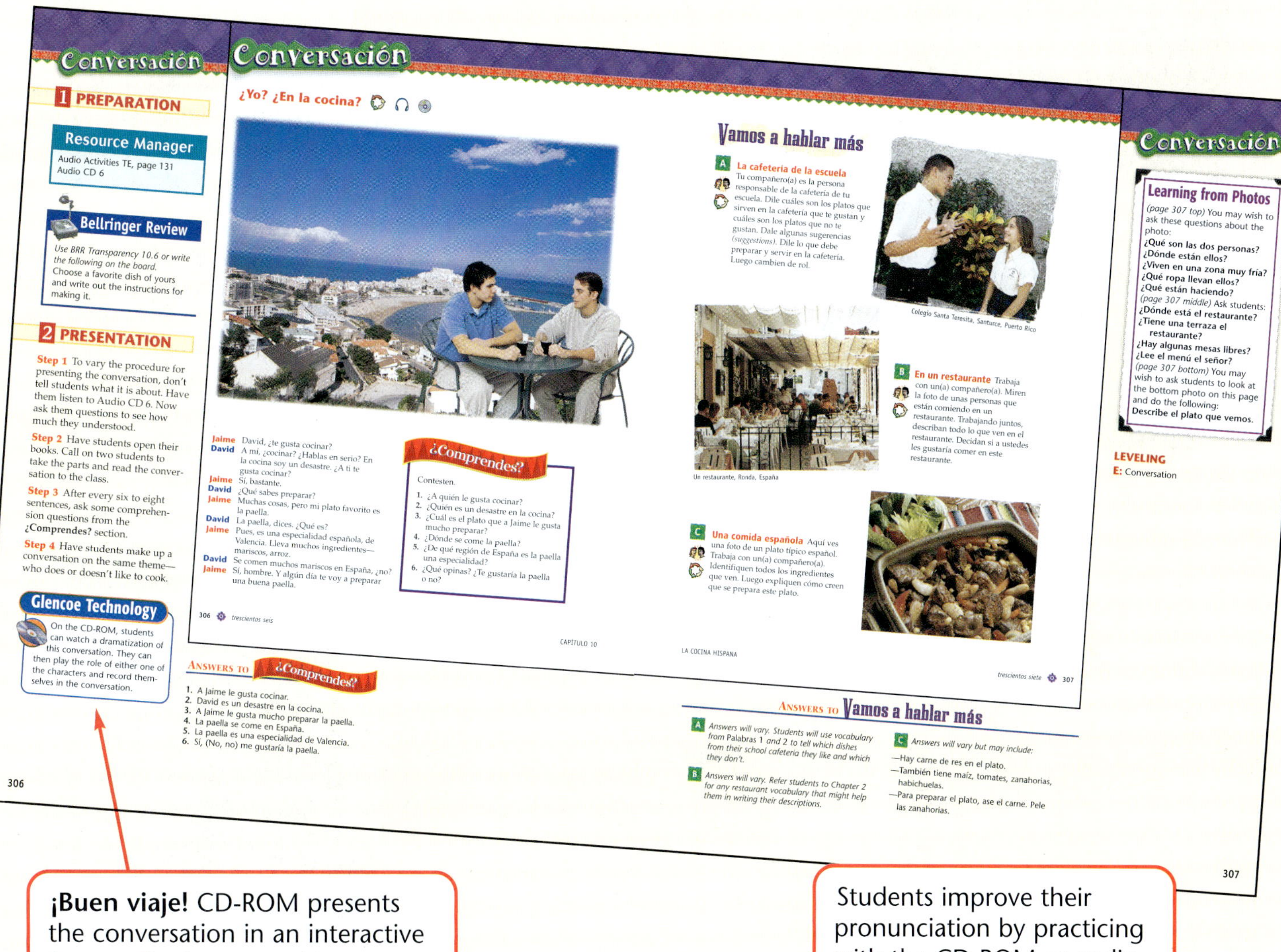

Conversación

**1 PREPARATION**

**Resource Manager**

Audio Activities TE, page 131
Audio CD 6

**Bellringer Review**

*Use BRR Transparency 10.6 or write the following on the board.*
Choose a favorite dish of yours and write out the instructions for making it.

**2 PRESENTATION**

**Step 1** To vary the procedure for presenting the conversation, don't tell students what it is about. Have them listen to Audio CD 6. Now ask them questions to see how much they understood.

**Step 2** Have students open their books. Call on two students to take the parts and read the conversation to the class.

**Step 3** After every six to eight sentences, ask some comprehension questions from the **¿Comprendes?** section.

**Step 4** Have students make up a conversation on the same theme—who does or doesn't like to cook.

**Glencoe Technology**

On the CD-ROM, students can watch a dramatization of this conversation. They can then play the role of either one of the characters and record themselves in the conversation.

Conversación

**¿Yo? ¿En la cocina?**

**Jaime** David, ¿te gusta cocinar?
**David** A mí, ¿cocinar? ¿Hablas en serio? En la cocina soy un desastre. ¿A ti te gusta cocinar?
**Jaime** Sí, bastante.
**David** ¿Qué sabes preparar?
**Jaime** Muchas cosas, pero mi plato favorito es la paella.
**David** La paella, dices. ¿Qué es?
**Jaime** Pues, es una especialidad española, de Valencia. Lleva muchos ingredientes—mariscos, arroz.
**David** Se comen muchos mariscos en España, ¿no?
**Jaime** Sí, hombre. Y algún día te voy a preparar una buena paella.

**¿Comprendes?**

Contesten.

1. ¿A quién le gusta cocinar?
2. ¿Quién es un desastre en la cocina?
3. ¿Cuál es el plato que a Jaime le gusta mucho preparar?
4. ¿Dónde se come la paella?
5. ¿De qué región de España es la paella una especialidad?
6. ¿Qué opinas? ¿Te gustaría la paella o no?

306 trescientos seis    CAPÍTULO 10

**Vamos a hablar más**

**A La cafetería de la escuela** Tu compañero(a) es la persona responsable de la cafetería de tu escuela. Dile cuáles son los platos que sirven en la cafetería que te gustan y cuáles son los platos que no te gustan. Dale algunas sugerencias (*suggestions*). Dile lo que debe preparar y servir en la cafetería. Luego cambien de rol.

Colegio Santa Teresita, Santurce, Puerto Rico

**B En un restaurante** Trabaja con un(a) compañero(a). Miren la foto de unas personas que están comiendo en un restaurante. Trabajando juntos, describan todo lo que ven en el restaurante. Decidan si a ustedes les gustaría comer en este restaurante.

Un restaurante, Ronda, España

**C Una comida española** Aquí ves una foto de un plato típico español. Trabaja con un(a) compañero(a). Identifiquen todos los ingredientes que ven. Luego expliquen cómo creen que se prepara este plato.

LA COCINA HISPANA    trescientos siete 307

Conversación

**Learning from Photos**

*(page 307 top)* You may wish to ask these questions about the photo:
**¿Qué son las dos personas?**
**¿Dónde están ellos?**
**¿Viven en una zona muy fría?**
**¿Qué ropa llevan ellos?**
**¿Qué están haciendo?**
*(page 307 middle)* Ask students:
**¿Dónde está el restaurante?**
**¿Tiene una terraza el restaurante?**
**¿Hay algunas mesas libres?**
**¿Lee el menú el señor?**
*(page 307 bottom)* You may wish to ask students to look at the bottom photo on this page and do the following:
**Describe el plato que vemos.**

**LEVELING**
**E:** Conversation

**ANSWERS TO ¿Comprendes?**

1. A Jaime le gusta cocinar.
2. David es un desastre en la cocina.
3. A Jaime le gusta mucho preparar la paella.
4. La paella se come en España.
5. La paella es una especialidad de Valencia.
6. Sí, (No, no) me gustaría la paella.

**ANSWERS TO Vamos a hablar más**

**A** *Answers will vary. Students will use vocabulary from* Palabras 1 *and* 2 *to tell which dishes from their school cafeteria they like and which they don't.*

**B** *Answers will vary. Refer students to Chapter 2 for any restaurant vocabulary that might help them in writing their descriptions.*

**C** *Answers will vary but may include:*
—Hay carne de res en el plato.
—También tiene maíz, tomates, zanahorias, habichuelas.
—Para preparar el plato, ase el carne. Pele las zanahorias.

306    307

**¡Buen viaje!** CD-ROM presents the conversation in an interactive format. Students are able to converse with native speakers with this interactive technology.

Students improve their pronunciation by practicing with the CD-ROM or audio program.

## Build proficiency in all language skills

### Provide Meaningful and Varied Practice for Your Students!

The **¡Buen viaje! Workbook** includes numerous activities to reinforce every concept presented in the Student Edition. Varied activities provide several ways for students to practice and apply the material you have presented in class. **Un poco más** provides additional opportunity to have students practice with realia. **Mi autobiografía** provides a tool for portfolio assessment.

### Improve Listening and Speaking Skills!

The **Audio CDs** provide recordings of the vocabulary words and some of the activities from the Student Edition as well as new activities to reinforce and expand upon what students have learned. The cultural readings are also recorded. Students may use the Audio Activities sheets to guide them through the **Audio Activities.**

### StudentWorks Plus™ Helps Lighten the Load!

**StudentWorks Plus™** includes the **Student Edition** and **Workbook and Audio Activities.** This alternative to the textbook is available on CD or online at spanish.glencoe.com.

**Glencoe Spanish Online** gives students many opportunities to review, practice, and explore. There are chapter-related activities, online quizzes, and many links to Web sites throughout the vast Hispanic world. Go to spanish.glencoe.com.

# Have students learn by interacting in Spanish!

**¡Viva el mundo hispano!** takes students on many adventures through the Spanish-speaking world. Students become involved with the escapades of six teens and travel to eight different countries. Each episode is related to a chapter of the textbook by its theme. The language provides comprehensible input and gives the students opportunities to hear many regionalisms and dialects. **¡Viva el mundo hispano!** is available on VHS and DVD.

With the **Interactive Conversations CD-ROM** students have an opportunity to interact with a native speaker by participating in the chapter conversation. Students first watch a video of the conversation. They then choose to play the role of one of the characters in the conversation, record their own voice into the conversation and compare their pronunciation and fluency to that of the native speaker.

The **MindJogger** is a video review game that saves teachers precious time and that students love to play. Each chapter of the text (Levels 1 and 2) has an accompanying MindJogger segment in which students are quizzed about the vocabulary, structure, and culture of the chapter. You may form teams and play MindJogger as a class activity or students may play the MindJogger DVD individually on a computer. MindJogger is available on VHS and DVD.

# ¡Buen viaje! Resources

## Save planning time with ancillaries organized and filed by chapter!

We make your life easier by organizing your written resources by chapter in convenient **FastFile Booklets**. The FastFile booklets include several essential resources

- **Letter to Parents** Explains goals and suggests activities to do at home.
- **Workbook Teacher Edition** In your version of the student workbook answers are provided for all activities.
- **Audio Program Teacher Edition** The Audio Program TE includes the scripts to the audio activities and the answers to the students' activities. The audio activities found on these pages are recorded on the ¡Buen viaje! Audio Program CDs.
- **TPR Storytelling** We have written a story for each chapter and provided the illustrations to allow you to implement TPR Storytelling in your classroom. The stories are written using the vocabulary and structure for each chapter.
- **Situation Cards** Provide your students with topics they can talk about with the Situation Cards. Several scenarios are provided for each chapter. There are blank cards provided as well should you or your students want to make up new situations.
- **Quizzes** Quizzes are provided to cover every concept taught in each chapter. These quizzes give you immediate feedback about your students' progress.
- **Tests** There are four kinds of tests with each chapter: Reading and Writing, Listening, Speaking, and Proficiency. The Listening Tests are available on CD. You can be sure that you are assessing your students' proficiency in each of the skill areas. In addition, the Reading and Writing Tests are leveled, meaning that there is a separate test for average students and another more challenging test for more able students.
- **Performance Assessment** The Performance Assessment Tasks allow your students to show you what they can do with their language skills at the end of each chapter. Rubrics are provided to help you evaluate your students' performances.

# Multimedia resources help you diversify your instruction!

## Enhance Your Lessons Visually!

The **Transparency Binder** gives you all the visual support you need to enhance your presentation.

- **Vocabulary** transparencies include the photos and art you see on the Student Edition pages, overlays with the Spanish words, and Spanish/English vocabulary lists for chapter vocabulary.
- **Maps** help you present the Hispanic world.
- **Bellringer Review** transparencies provide a quick review activity to begin each class.
- **Pronunciation** transparencies provide a visual for pronunciation practice.
- **Communication** transparencies illustrate the chapter theme. These can be used for communicative practice or for assessment.
- **Assessment** transparencies replicate the Assessment pages of the student text. Assessment Answer transparencies allow you to easily review the answers with your students in class.

**Fine Art** transparencies are full-color reproductions of the fine art from the text. These transparencies can be used to reinforce the cultural topics introduced in the text and improve your students' awareness of Hispanic Fine Art.

The **Vocabulary PuzzleMaker** allows you to create four kinds of puzzles at the touch of a key. The Vocabulary PuzzleMaker includes all the vocabulary introduced in your **¡Buen viaje!** It is also easy to add your own words to the vocabulary banks.

The **Audio CDs** provide additional practice to reinforce the material presented in **¡Buen viaje!** Students benefit from hearing a variety of voices from around the entire Spanish-speaking world.

The **Test Program CD** includes the recorded portion for the Listening Tests.

**Interactive Chalkboard** provides ready-made, customizable PowerPoint presentations with sound, interactive graphics and video. This presentation tool will help you vary your lessons and reach all students in your classroom.

**ExamView®Pro** helps you make a test in a matter of minutes by choosing from existing banks of questions, editing them, or creating your own test questions. You can also print several versions of the same test. The clip art bank allows you to create a test using visuals from the text.

**TeacherWorks** is your all-in-one planner and resource center. This convenient tool will help you reduce the time you spend planning for classes. Simply populate your school year calendar with customizable lesson plans. TeacherWorks will also allow you to easily view your resources without carrying around a heavy bag of books. TeacherWorks provides correlations to standards.

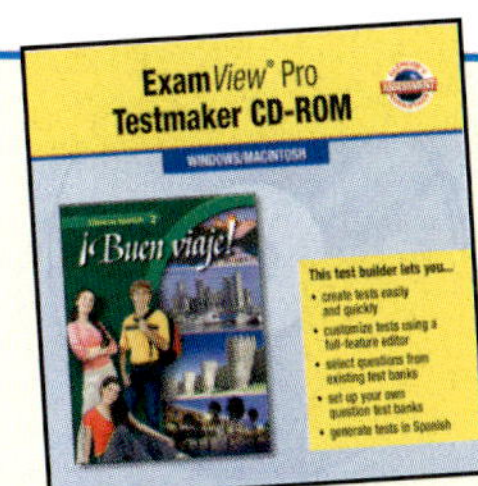

# Spanish Names

**The following are some Spanish boys' and girls' names that you may wish to give to your students.**

## Chicos

Adán
Alberto
Alejandro
Alfonso
Álvaro
Andrés
Antonio
Arnulfo
Arturo
Benjamín
Benito
Camilo
Carlos
César
Cristóbal
Daniel
David
Diego
Eduardo
Efraím
Emilio
Enrique
Ernesto
Esteban
Federico
Felipe
Fernando
Francisco
Gabriel
Gerardo
Gilberto
Guillermo
Gustavo
Héctor
Ignacio
Jaime
Javier
Jorge
José
Juan
Julio
Justo
Leonardo
Luis
Manuel
Marcos
Mateo
Miguel
Nicolás
Octavio
Omar
Óscar
Pablo
Paco
Patricio
Pedro
Rafael
Ramón
Raúl
Ricardo
Rigoberto
Roberto
Rubén
Santiago
Teodoro
Timoteo
Tomás
Víctor
Wilfredo

## Chicas

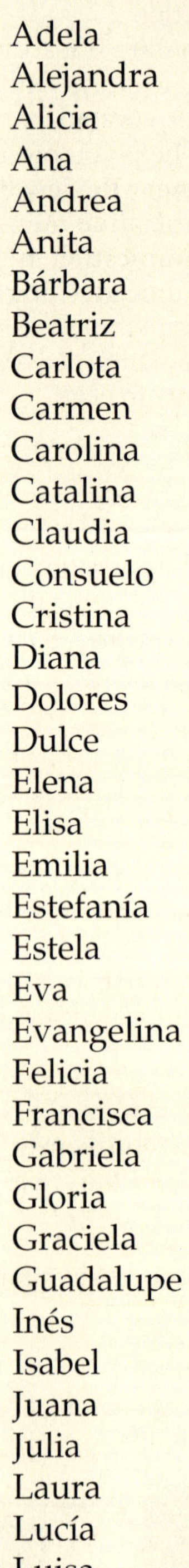

Adela
Alejandra
Alicia
Ana
Andrea
Anita
Bárbara
Beatriz
Carlota
Carmen
Carolina
Catalina
Claudia
Consuelo
Cristina
Diana
Dolores
Dulce
Elena
Elisa
Emilia
Estefanía
Estela
Eva
Evangelina
Felicia
Francisca
Gabriela
Gloria
Graciela
Guadalupe
Inés
Isabel
Juana
Julia
Laura
Lucía
Luisa
Lupe
Luz

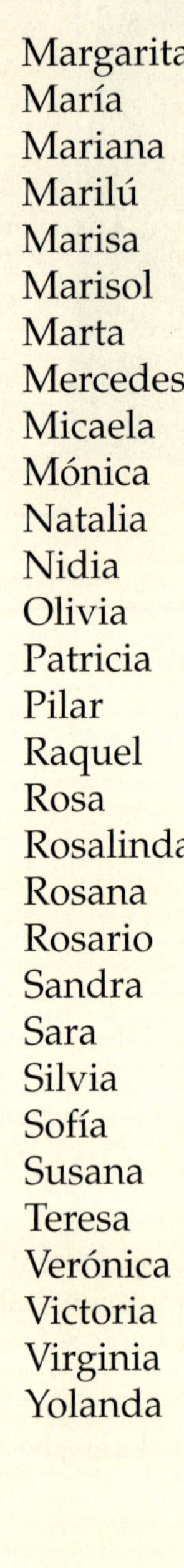

Margarita
María
Mariana
Marilú
Marisa
Marisol
Marta
Mercedes
Micaela
Mónica
Natalia
Nidia
Olivia
Patricia
Pilar
Raquel
Rosa
Rosalinda
Rosana
Rosario
Sandra
Sara
Silvia
Sofía
Susana
Teresa
Verónica
Victoria
Virginia
Yolanda

# Classroom Expressions

**Below is a list of words and expressions frequently used when conducting a Spanish class.**

| | |
|---|---|
| **el papel** | paper |
| **la hoja de papel** | sheet of paper |
| **el cuaderno** | notebook, workbook |
| **el libro** | book |
| **el diccionario** | dictionary |
| **la regla** | ruler |
| **la cinta** | tape |
| **el bolígrafo, la pluma** | ballpoint pen |
| **el lápiz** | pencil |
| **el sacapuntas** | pencil sharpener |
| **la goma** | eraser |
| **la tiza** | chalk |
| **la pizarra, el pizarrón** | chalkboard |
| **el borrador** | chalkboard eraser |
| **el escritorio** | desk |
| **la silla** | chair |
| **la fila** | row |
| **el CD** | CD |
| **la computadora, el ordenador** | computer |
| **el DVD** | DVD |
| **la pantalla** | the screen |
| **el video** | video |

| | | |
|---|---|---|
| **Ven.** | **Vengan.** | Come. |
| **Ve.** | **Vayan.** | Go. |
| **Entra.** | **Entren.** | Enter. |
| **Sal.** | **Salgan.** | Leave. |
| **Espera.** | **Esperen.** | Wait. |
| **Pon.** | **Pongan.** | Put. |
| **Dame.** | **Denme.** | Give me. |
| **Dime.** | **Díganme.** | Tell me. |
| **Repite.** | **Repitan.** | Repeat. |
| **Practica.** | **Practiquen.** | Practice. |
| **Estudia.** | **Estudien.** | Study. |
| **Contesta.** | **Contesten.** | Answer. |
| **Aprende.** | **Aprendan.** | Learn. |
| **Escoge.** | **Escojan.** | Choose. |
| **Prepara.** | **Preparen.** | Prepare. |
| **Mira.** | **Miren.** | Look at. |
| **Describe.** | **Describan.** | Describe. |
| **Empieza.** | **Empiecen.** | Begin. |
| **Pronuncia.** | **Pronuncien.** | Pronounce. |
| **Escucha.** | **Escuchen.** | Listen. |
| **Habla.** | **Hablen.** | Speak. |
| **Lee.** | **Lean.** | Read. |
| **Escribe.** | **Escriban.** | Write. |
| **Pregunta.** | **Pregunten.** | Ask. |
| **Sigue el modelo.** | **Sigan el modelo.** | Follow the model. |
| **Abre.** | **Abran.** | Open. |
| **Cierra.** | **Cierren.** | Close. |
| **Continúa.** | **Continúen.** | Continue. |
| **Siéntate.** | **Siéntense.** | Sit down. |
| **Levántate.** | **Levántense.** | Get up. |
| **Cállate.** | **Cállense.** | Be quiet. |
| **Presta atención.** | **Presten atención.** | Pay attention. |

| | |
|---|---|
| **Atención, por favor.** | Your attention, please. |
| **Silencio.** | Quiet. |
| **Otra vez.** | Again. |
| **Todos juntos.** | All together. |
| **En voz alta.** | Out loud. |
| **Más alto, por favor.** | Louder, please. |
| **En español, por favor.** | In Spanish, please. |
| **En inglés, por favor.** | In English, please. |

# Standards for Foreign Language Learning

**¡Buen viaje!** has been written to help you meet the Standards for Foreign Language Learning as set forth by ACTFL. The focus of the text is to provide students with the skills they need to create language for communication. Culture is integrated throughout the text, from the basic introduction of vocabulary to the photographic contributions of the National Geographic Society. Special attention has been given to meeting the standard of Connections with a reading in Spanish in each chapter about another discipline. Linguistic and cultural comparisons are made throughout the text. Suggestions are made for activities that encourage students to use their language skills in their immediate community and more distant ones. Students who complete the **¡Buen viaje!** series are prepared to participate in the Spanish-speaking world.

Specific correlations to each chapter are provided on the teacher pages preceeding each chapter.

## Communication

| | | |
|---|---|---|
| Communicate in Languages Other than English | **Standard 1.1** | Students engage in conversations, provide and obtain information, express feelings and emotions, and exchange opinions. |
| | **Standard 1.2** | Students understand and interpret written and spoken language on a variety of topics. |
| | **Standard 1.3** | Students present information, concepts, and ideas to an audience of listeners or readers on a variety of topics. |

## Cultures

| | | |
|---|---|---|
| Gain Knowledge and Understanding of Other Cultures | **Standard 2.1** | Students demonstrate an understanding of the relationship between the practices and perspectives of the culture studied. |
| | **Standard 2.2** | Students demonstrate an understanding of the relationship between the products and perspectives of the culture studied. |

## Connections

| | | |
|---|---|---|
| Connect with Other Disciplines and Acquire Information | **Standard 3.1** | Students reinforce and further their knowledge of other disciplines through the foreign language. |
| | **Standard 3.2** | Students acquire information and recognize the distinctive viewpoints that are only available through the foreign language and its cultures. |

## Comparisons

| | | |
|---|---|---|
| Develop Insight into the Nature of Language and Culture | **Standard 4.1** | Students demonstrate understanding of the nature of language through comparisons of language studied and their own. |
| | **Standard 4.2** | Students demonstrate understanding of the concept of culture through comparisons of the cultures studied and their own. |

## Communities

| | | |
|---|---|---|
| Participate in Multilingual Communities at Home and Around the World | **Standard 5.1** | Students use the language both within and beyond the school setting. |
| | **Standard 5.2** | Students show evidence of becoming life-long learners by using the language for personal enjoyment and enrichment. |

Glencoe Spanish 2

# ¡Buen viaje!

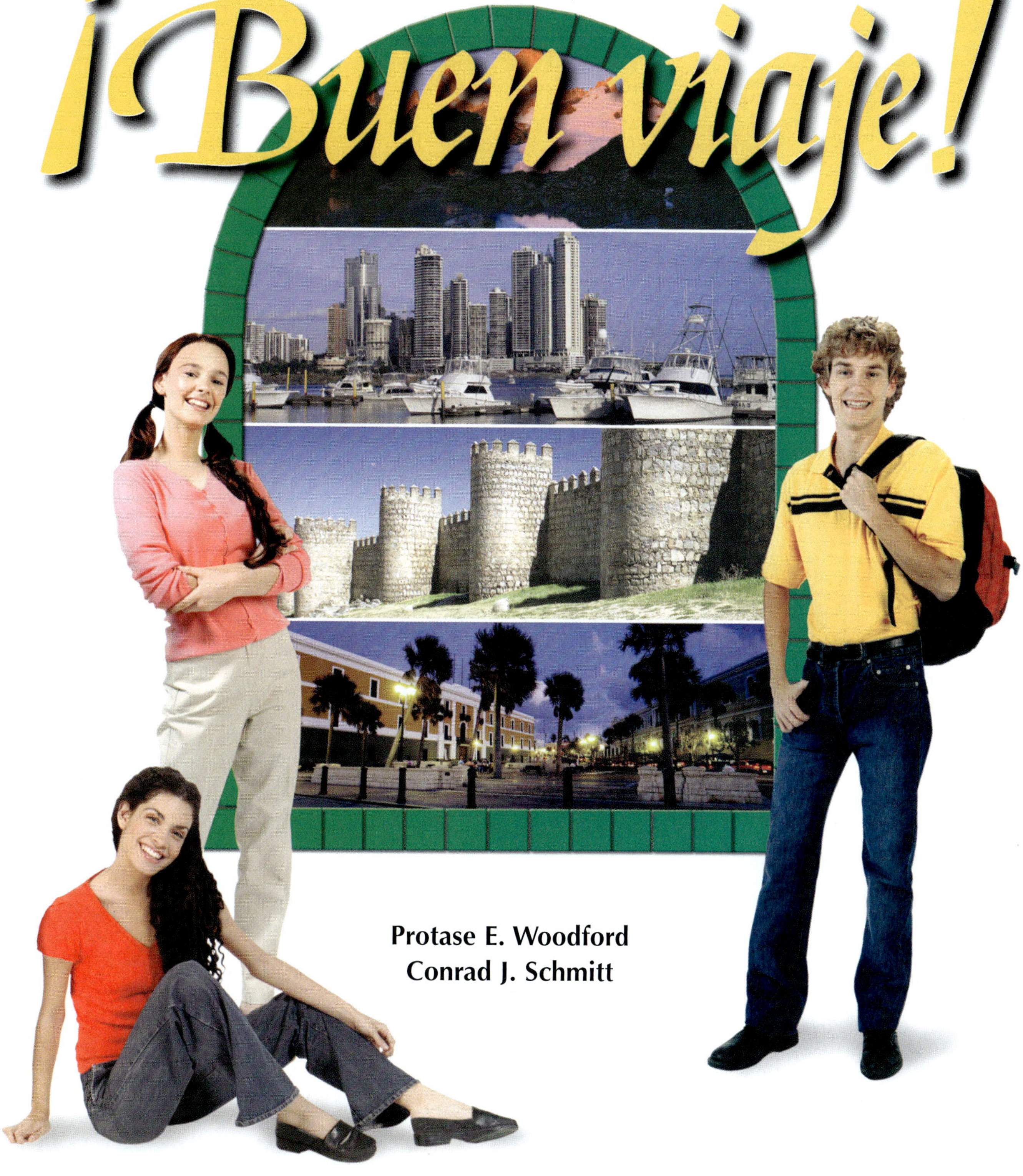

Protase E. Woodford
Conrad J. Schmitt

New York, New York Columbus, Ohio Chicago, Illinois Peoria, Illinois Woodland Hills, California

The McGraw-Hill Companies



Send all inquiries to:
Glencoe/McGraw-Hill
8787 Orion Place
Columbus, OH 43240-4027

ISBN: 0-07-861970-X *(Student Edition)*
ISBN: 0-07-861971-8 *(Teacher Wraparound Edition)*

Printed in the United States of America.

2 3 4 5 6 7 8 9 10 055/071 10 09 08 07 06 05 04

# About the Authors

## Conrad J. Schmitt

Conrad J. Schmitt received his B.A. degree magna cum laude from Montclair State College, Upper Montclair, NJ. He received his M.A. from Middlebury College, Middlebury, VT. He did additional graduate work at Seton Hall University and New York University. Mr. Schmitt has taught Spanish and French at the elementary, junior, and senior high school levels, as well as at the undergraduate and graduate levels. In addition, he has traveled extensively throughout Spain, Central and South America, and the Caribbean.

## Protase E. Woodford

Protase "Woody" Woodford has taught Spanish at all levels from elementary through graduate school. At Educational Testing Service in Princeton, NJ, he was Director of Test Development, Director of Language Programs, Director of International Testing Programs and Director of the Puerto Rico Office. He has served as a consultant to the United Nations Secretariat, UNESCO, the Organization of American States, the U.S. Office of Education, and many ministries of education in Asia, Latin America, and the Middle East.

# For the Parent or Guardian

We are excited that your child has decided to study Spanish. Foreign language study provides many benefits for students in addition to the ability to communicate in another language. Students who study another language improve their first language skills. They become more aware of the world around them and they learn to appreciate diversity.

You can help your child be successful in his or her study of Spanish even if you are not familiar with that language. Encourage your child to talk to you about the places where Spanish is spoken. Engage in conversations about current events in those places. The section of their Glencoe Spanish book called **El mundo hispanohablante** on pages xxi–xxxiii may serve as a reference for you and your child. In addition, you will find information about the geography of the Spanish-speaking world and links to foreign newspapers at **spanish.glencoe.com**.

The methodology employed in the Glencoe Spanish books is logical and leads students step by step through their study of the language. Consistent instruction and practice are essential for learning a foreign language. You can help by encouraging your child to review vocabulary each day. As he or she progresses through the text, you will want to use the study tips on pages H16–H31 to help your child learn Spanish. If you have Internet access, encourage your child to practice using the activities, games, and practice quizzes at **spanish.glencoe.com**.

*¡Buen viaje!*



iii

# Contenido

## Repaso

# Capítulo 1 

## Objetivos

In this chapter you will learn to:

- use expressions related to train travel
- purchase a train ticket and request information about arrival, departure, etc.
- talk about more past events or activities
- tell what people say
- discuss an interesting train trip in Spain and in Peru

# Un viaje en tren



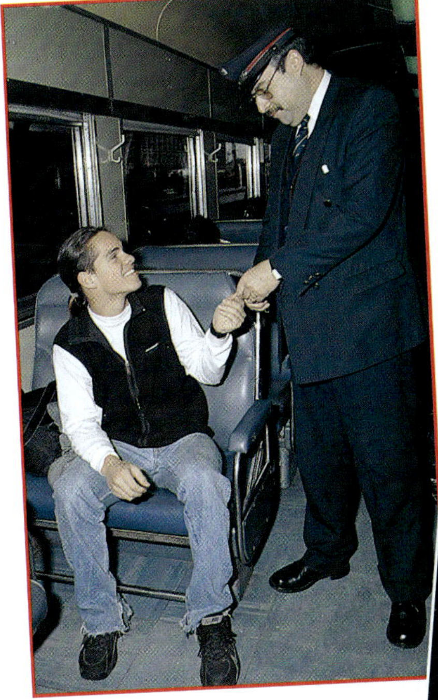

# Capítulo 2

## Objetivos

In this chapter you will learn to:

- order food or a beverage at a restaurant
- identify eating utensils and dishes
- identify more foods
- make a reservation at a restaurant
- talk about present and past events
- describe some cuisines of the Hispanic world

## En el restaurante

# Capítulo 3 Telecomunicaciones

## Objetivos

In this chapter you will learn to:

- talk about computers, e-mail, the Internet, faxes, and telephones
- talk about past habitual and routine actions
- describe people and events in the past
- make and receive telephone calls in Spanish

# Contenido

# Capítulo 4 De tiendas

## Objetivos

In this chapter you will learn to:

- shop for apparel and food in Spanish-speaking countries
- ask for the quantities and sizes you want
- find out prices
- talk about different types of past actions
- talk in general terms about what is done
- talk about shopping practices in Spanish-speaking countries

# Capítulo 5

## Los pasatiempos

### Objetivos

**In this chapter you will learn to:**

- talk about popular hobbies and games
- talk about activities in the park
- give details about location
- talk about what will happen in the future
- compare objects and people
- describe your favorite pastime
- talk about pastimes in Spanish-speaking countries

# Capítulo 6 En el hotel

## Objetivos

**In this chapter you will learn to:**

- **check into and out of a hotel**
- **ask for things that you may need while at a hotel**
- **talk about future events**
- **refer to previously mentioned people or things**
- **talk about lodging in the Hispanic world**

# Capítulo 7 El vuelo

## Objetivos

**In this chapter you will learn to:**

- **talk about air travel**
- **discuss the influence of geography on travel in Latin America**
- **talk about things that would happen under certain conditions**
- **talk about air travel in Hispanic countries**

# Contenido

## Capítulo 8

### Objetivos

In this chapter you will learn to:

- talk about accidents and medical problems
- talk about hospital stays
- discuss things that you and others have done recently
- compare things with like characteristics
- talk about health care in various areas of the Spanish-speaking world

## Emergencias médicas



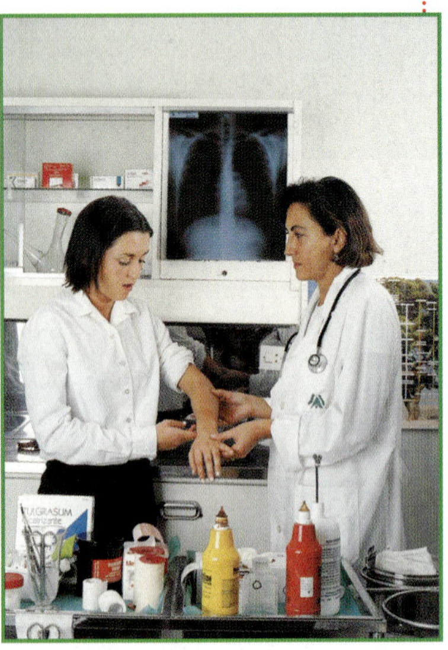

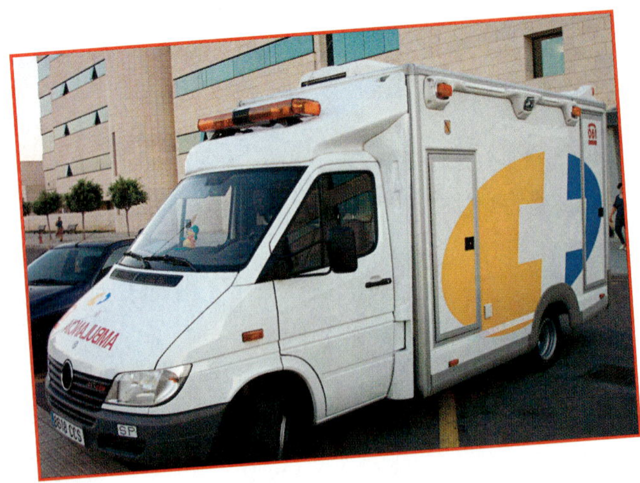

# Capítulo 9

## Objetivos

In this chapter you will learn to:

- talk about life in the city
- talk about life in the country
- describe things that were happening
- refer to things that were already mentioned
- indicate where things are located
- talk about some cities in the Spanish-speaking world

## Ciudad y campo

Contenido

# Capítulo 10 La cocina hispana

**Objetivos**

**In this chapter you will learn to:**

- **talk about foods and food preparation**
- **give commands**
- **refer to people and things previously mentioned**
- **prepare some regional specialities**
- **talk about the origin of several foods**

# Capítulo 11 El coche y la carretera

**Objetivos**

In this chapter you will learn to:

- talk about cars and driving
- give directions on the road
- tell family and friends what to do and what not to do
- talk about highways in the Hispanic world

# Capítulo 12 Los servicios al público

## Objetivos

In this chapter you will learn to:

- talk about going to the hairdresser/barber shop
- talk about having your clothes cleaned
- talk about using the services of the post office and bank
- talk about things that may or may not happen
- express what you would like, wish, or hope others would do

# Capítulo 13 ¡Fiestas!

## Objetivos

In this chapter you will learn to:

- describe and talk about parties and weddings
- talk about some holidays
- give advice and make recommendations
- express doubt, uncertainty, or disbelief
- express emotional reactions to what others do
- talk about New Year's Eve in the Hispanic world

Contenido

# Capítulo 14 Profesiones y oficios

## Objetivos

In this chapter you will learn to:

- talk about professions and occupations
- interview for a job
- state work qualifications
- talk about future events
- talk about probable events

# Literary Companion



# Video Companion

# Handbook



## Guide to Symbols

Throughout **¡Buen viaje!** you will see these symbols, or icons. They will tell you how to best use the particular part of the chapter or activity they accompany. Following is a key to help you understand these symbols.

**Audio link** This icon indicates material in the chapter that is recorded on compact disk.

**Recycling** This icon indicates sections that review previously introduced material.

**Paired Activity** This icon indicates sections that you can practice orally with a partner.

**Group Activity** This icon indicates sections that you can practice together in groups.

**Un poco más** This icon indicates additional practice activities that review knowledge from each chapter.

**¡Adelante!** This icon indicates the end of new material in each chapter. All remaining material is recombination and review.

**Literary Companion** This icon appears in the review lessons to let you know that you are prepared to read the literature selection indicated if you wish.

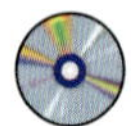

**Interactive CD-ROM** This icon indicates that the material is also on the Interactive CD-ROM.

# El mundo hispanohablante

Spanish is the language of more than 350 million people around the world. Spanish had its origin in Spain. It is sometimes fondly called the "language of Cervantes," the author of the world's most famous novel and character, *Don Quijote*. The Spanish **conquistadores** and **exploradores** brought their language to the Americas in the fifteenth and sixteenth centuries. Spanish is the official language of almost all the countries of Central and South America. It is the official language of Mexico and several of the larger islands in the Caribbean. Spanish is also the heritage language of forty million people in the United States.

▼ España

▲ México

◀ Perú

▲ Chile

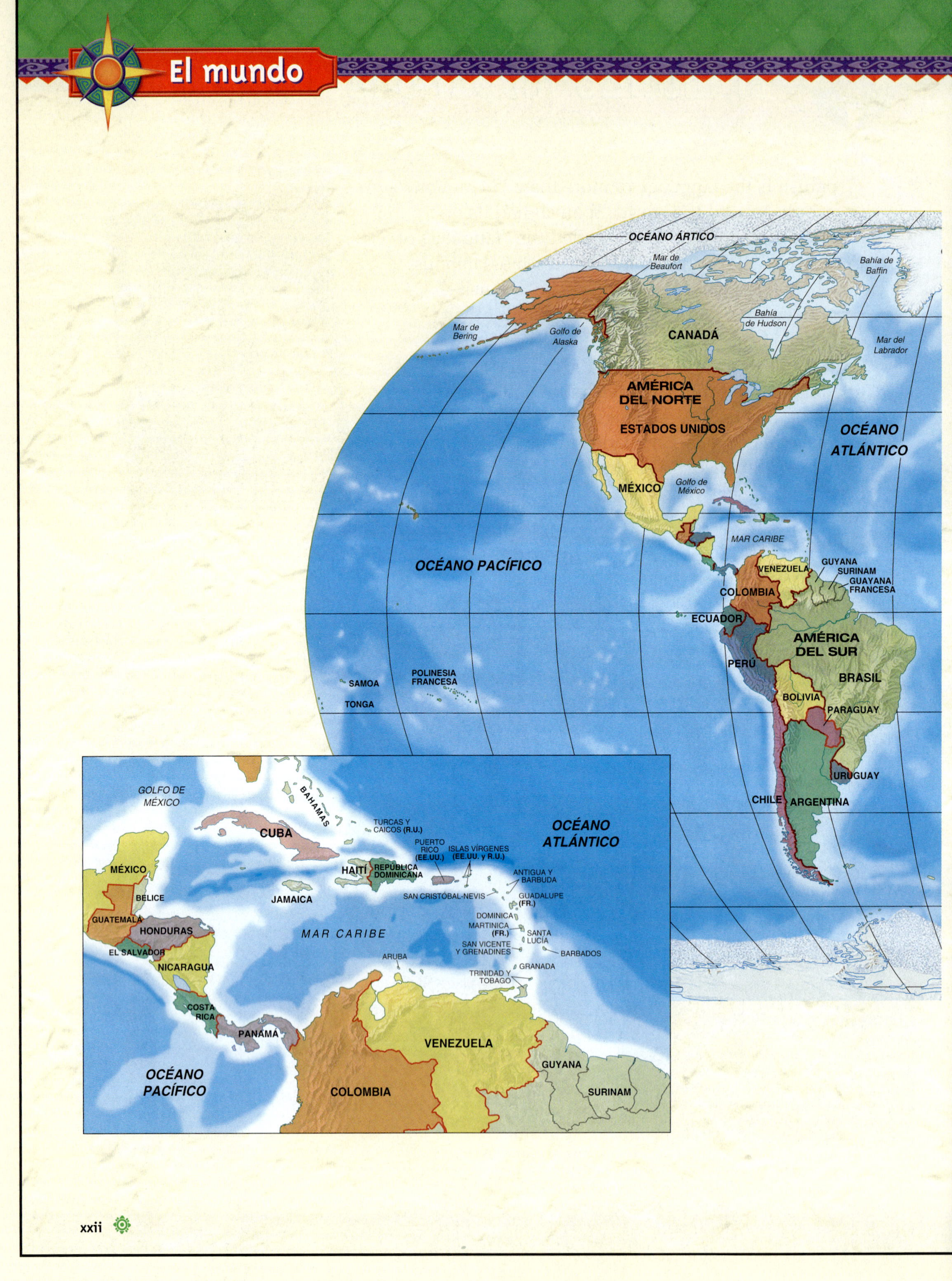
OCÉANO ÁRTICO
Mar de Beaufort
Bahía de Baffin
Mar de Bering
Golfo de Alaska
CANADÁ
Bahía de Hudson
Mar del Labrador
AMÉRICA DEL NORTE
ESTADOS UNIDOS
OCÉANO ATLÁNTICO
MÉXICO
Golfo de México
MAR CARIBE
OCÉANO PACÍFICO
VENEZUELA
GUYANA
SURINAM
GUAYANA FRANCESA
COLOMBIA
ECUADOR
AMÉRICA DEL SUR
PERÚ
BRASIL
BOLIVIA
PARAGUAY
SAMOA
POLINESIA FRANCESA
TONGA
URUGUAY
CHILE
ARGENTINA
GOLFO DE MÉXICO
BAHAMAS
TURCAS Y CAICOS (R.U.)
OCÉANO ATLÁNTICO
CUBA
PUERTO RICO (EE.UU.)
ISLAS VÍRGENES (EE.UU. y R.U.)
MÉXICO
HAITÍ
REPÚBLICA DOMINICANA
ANTIGUA Y BARBUDA
BELICE
JAMAICA
SAN CRISTÓBAL-NEVIS
GUADALUPE (FR.)
DOMINICA
GUATEMALA
HONDURAS
MARTINICA (FR.)
SANTA LUCÍA
MAR CARIBE
EL SALVADOR
SAN VICENTE Y GRENADINES
BARBADOS
ARUBA
NICARAGUA
GRANADA
TRINIDAD Y TOBAGO
COSTA RICA
PANAMÁ
VENEZUELA
GUYANA
OCÉANO PACÍFICO
COLOMBIA
SURINAM

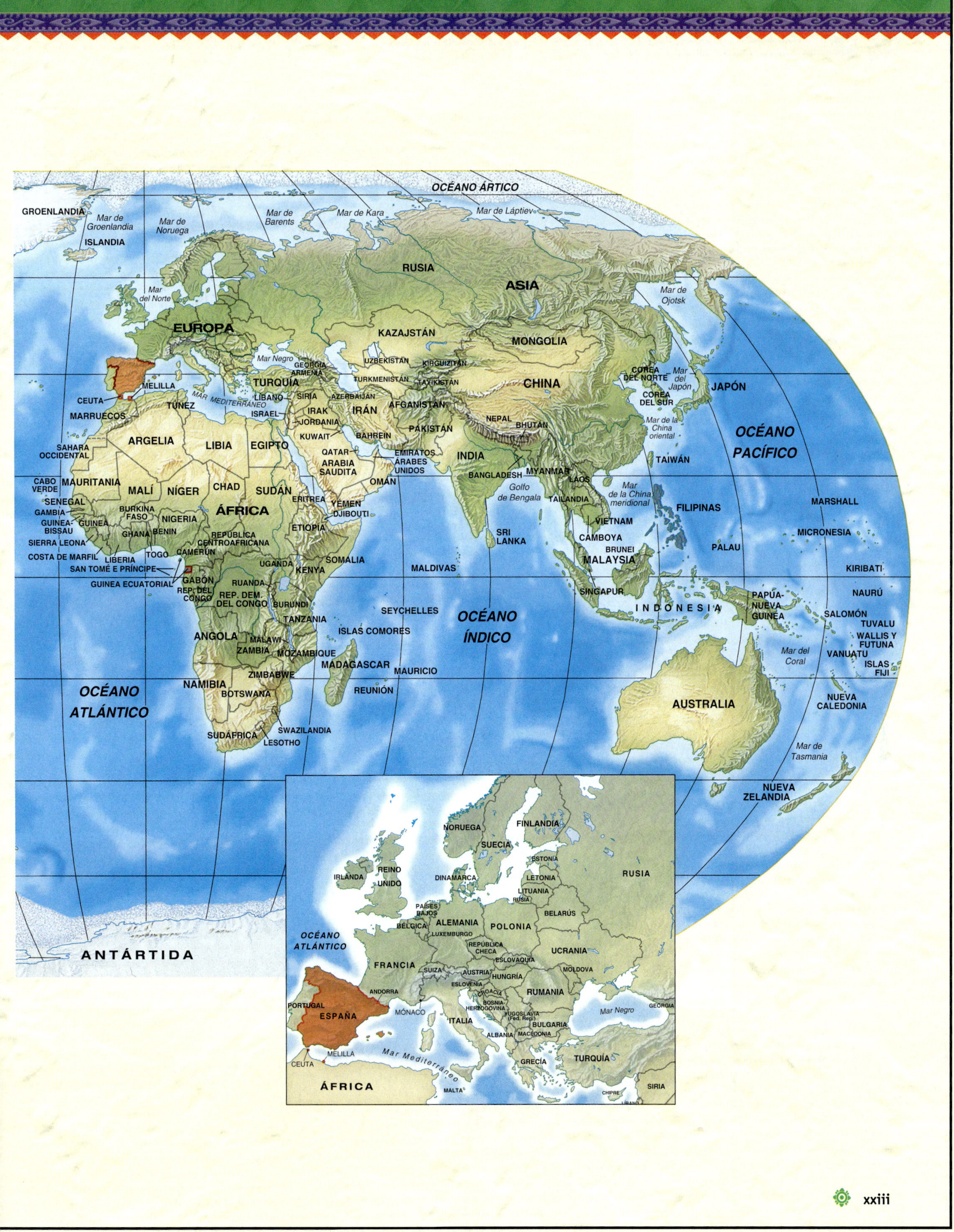
OCÉANO ÁRTICO
GROENLANDIA
Mar de Groenlandia
ISLANDIA
Mar de Noruega
Mar de Barents
Mar de Kara
Mar de Láptiev
RUSIA
ASIA
Mar de Ojotsk
Mar del Norte
EUROPA
KAZAJSTÁN
MONGOLIA
Mar Negro
GEORGIA
ARMENIA
UZBEKISTÁN
KIRGUIZISTÁN
TURKMENISTÁN
TAYIKISTÁN
TURQUÍA
CHINA
COREA DEL NORTE
Mar del Japón
JAPÓN
COREA DEL SUR
MELILLA
CEUTA
MAR MEDITERRÁNEO
LÍBANO
SIRIA
AZERBAIJÁN
TÚNEZ
ISRAEL
IRAK
IRÁN
AFGANISTÁN
MARRUECOS
JORDANIA
NEPAL
BHUTÁN
Mar de la China oriental
KUWAIT
BAHREIN
PAKISTÁN
ARGELIA
LIBIA
EGIPTO
OCÉANO PACÍFICO
SAHARA OCCIDENTAL
QATAR
EMIRATOS ÁRABES UNIDOS
INDIA
TAIWÁN
ARABIA SAUDITA
BANGLADESH
MYANMAR
CABO VERDE
MAURITANIA
OMÁN
LAOS
MALÍ
NÍGER
CHAD
SUDÁN
Golfo de Bengala
Mar de la China meridional
SENEGAL
ERITREA
YEMEN
TAILANDIA
FILIPINAS
MARSHALL
GAMBIA
BURKINA FASO
ÁFRICA
DJIBOUTI
GUINEA-BISSAU
GUINEA
NIGERIA
VIETNAM
ETIOPÍA
GHANA
BENIN
SRI LANKA
MICRONESIA
SIERRA LEONA
REPÚBLICA CENTROAFRICANA
CAMBOYA
CAMERÚN
BRUNEI
PALAU
COSTA DE MARFIL
LIBERIA
TOGO
SOMALIA
MALAYSIA
SAN TOMÉ E PRÍNCIPE
UGANDA
KENYA
MALDIVAS
KIRIBATI
GUINEA ECUATORIAL
GABÓN
RUANDA
REP. DEL CONGO
REP. DEM. DEL CONGO
BURUNDI
SINGAPUR
NAURÚ
SEYCHELLES
INDONESIA
PAPÚA-NUEVA GUINEA
TANZANIA
OCÉANO ÍNDICO
SALOMÓN
TUVALU
ISLAS COMORES
ANGOLA
MALAWI
WALLIS Y FUTUNA
ZAMBIA
MOZAMBIQUE
Mar del Coral
VANUATU
MADAGASCAR
ISLAS FIJI
MAURICIO
NAMIBIA
ZIMBABWE
OCÉANO ATLÁNTICO
BOTSWANA
REUNIÓN
AUSTRALIA
NUEVA CALEDONIA
SWAZILANDIA
SUDÁFRICA
LESOTHO
Mar de Tasmania
NUEVA ZELANDIA
ANTÁRTIDA
NORUEGA
FINLANDIA
SUECIA
ESTONIA
RUSIA
IRLANDA
REINO UNIDO
DINAMARCA
LETONIA
LITUANIA
RUSIA
PAÍSES BAJOS
BELARÚS
BÉLGICA
ALEMANIA
POLONIA
OCÉANO ATLÁNTICO
LUXEMBURGO
REPÚBLICA CHECA
UCRANIA
ESLOVAQUIA
FRANCIA
SUIZA
AUSTRIA
MOLDOVA
HUNGRÍA
ESLOVENIA
CROACIA
ANDORRA
RUMANIA
BOSNIA-HERZEGOVINA
PORTUGAL
ESPAÑA
MÓNACO
YUGOSLAVIA (Fed. Rep.)
Mar Negro
GEORGIA
ITALIA
BULGARIA
ALBANIA
MACEDONIA
MELILLA
Mar Mediterráneo
CEUTA
GRECIA
TURQUÍA
ÁFRICA
MALTA
CHIPRE
SIRIA

# El mundo hispanohablante

## España

**CAPITAL**
*Madrid*

**POPULATION**
*40,217,000*

**FUN FACT**
*The verdant hills of Galicia, the golden fields of Castilla, and the white villages of Andalucía as well as the industrial areas of Cataluña and the Basque Country are all a part of beautiful Spain. Once home to Iberians, Carthaginians, Romans, Celts, and Moors, Spain is the birthplace of Spanish—the language of many nations scattered on five continents of the globe. Madrid, in the exact center of the country, is considered a major cultural center of Europe.*

## México

**CAPITAL**
*Ciudad de México*

**POPULATION**
*104,908,000*

**FUN FACT**
*Beautiful Mexico shares a border with the United States. This magnificent nation of Aztec, Mayan, and Spanish heritage is a country of contrasts: cosmopolitan cities such as Mexico City; industrial centers such as Monterrey; quaint towns such as Taxco and San Miguel de Allende; world-famous beaches like Acapulco and Cancún; as well as magnificent vestiges of pre-Columbian civilization in Chichén Itzá and Tulum.*

## Estados Unidos

**CAPITAL**
*Washington, D.C.*

**POPULATION**
*290,343,000*

**FUN FACT**
*The influence of Spanish and Mexican heritage has been evident in Texas and in the Southwest of the United States for generations. More recent is the proliferation of Hispanic or Latin cultures in all areas of the United States. New arrivals from the Caribbean, Central America, and South America bring their language, customs, music, and foods, adding to the rich cultural diversity of this "melting pot" country. Today Spanish is heard in New York, Chicago, Minneapolis, Denver, and Miami as well as El Paso, Phoenix, and Los Angeles.*

xxiv

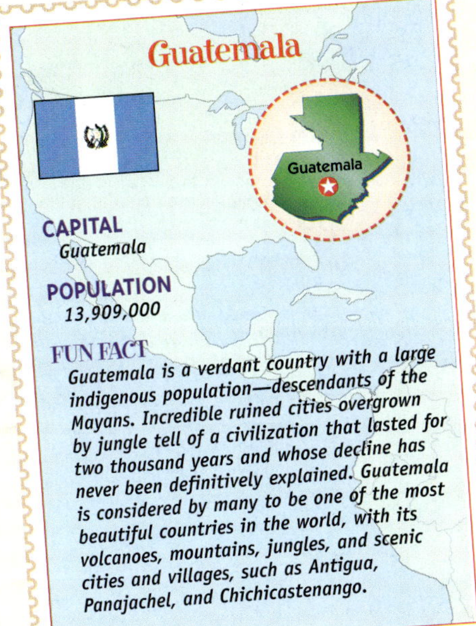
Guatemala
Guatemala
CAPITAL
Guatemala
POPULATION
13,909,000
FUN FACT
Guatemala is a verdant country with a large indigenous population—descendants of the Mayans. Incredible ruined cities overgrown by jungle tell of a civilization that lasted for two thousand years and whose decline has never been definitively explained. Guatemala is considered by many to be one of the most beautiful countries in the world, with its volcanoes, mountains, jungles, and scenic cities and villages, such as Antigua, Panajachel, and Chichicastenango.

El Salvador
San Salvador
CAPITAL
San Salvador
POPULATION
6,470,000
FUN FACT
El Salvador is the smallest and most densely populated of the Central American republics. It is also the only one that has no Atlantic seaboard. The country is traversed by two mountain ranges with many impressive volcanic peaks.

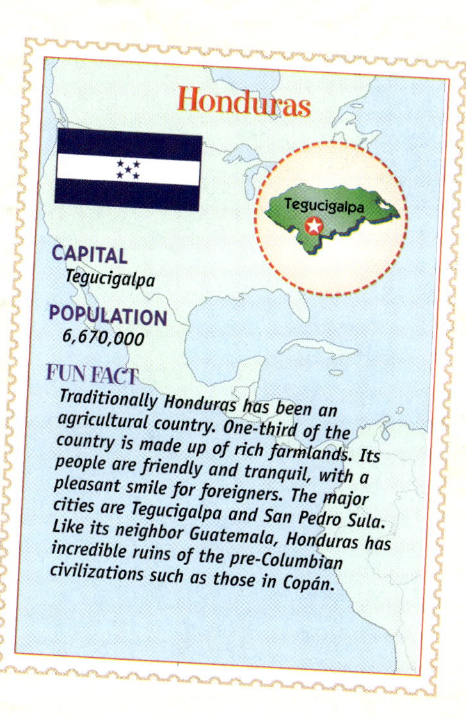
Honduras
Tegucigalpa
CAPITAL
Tegucigalpa
POPULATION
6,670,000
FUN FACT
Traditionally Honduras has been an agricultural country. One-third of the country is made up of rich farmlands. Its people are friendly and tranquil, with a pleasant smile for foreigners. The major cities are Tegucigalpa and San Pedro Sula. Like its neighbor Guatemala, Honduras has incredible ruins of the pre-Columbian civilizations such as those in Copán.

Nicaragua
Managua
CAPITAL
Managua
POPULATION
5,129,000
FUN FACT
Nicaragua is a country that has more than 40 volcanoes, many of which have erupted in recent years. The capital, Managua, is on the shores of Lake Managua, the only inland lake inhabited by sharks. Northwest of Managua is the lovely university city of León with its colonial churches and eighteenth-century cathedral.



XXV

# El mundo hispanohablante

## Costa Rica

**CAPITAL**
*San José*

**POPULATION**
*3,896,000*

**FUN FACT**
*Many consider Costa Rica a very special place. Its residents, Ticos, are polite, peaceful, and extremely friendly. Costa Rica has no army and prides itself on having more teachers than police officers. Costa Rica is a country of sun-drenched beaches on the Pacific, tropical jungles along the Caribbean coast, cosmopolitan cities such as San José, and high mountains in the central valley. Costa Rica is a tourist's paradise as well as home to many expatriates.*

## Panamá

**CAPITAL**
*Panamá*

**POPULATION**
*2,961,000*

**FUN FACT**
*Panama is a country of variety—a variety of races, customs, natural wonders, and attractions. It is a country of tropical forests, mountains, beautiful beaches, excellent fishing, picturesque lakes, rivers, two oceans, and—the most incredible engineering feat—the Panama Canal. Panama is also the largest financial center of Latin America. All this in a mere 77,432 square kilometers!*

## Cuba

**CAPITAL**
*La Habana*

**POPULATION**
*11,263,000*

**FUN FACT**
*Havana, the capital of Cuba, is known for its gorgeous colonial architecture. This lush island, not far from Florida, is one of the world's greatest producers of sugar cane. Cuba has been ruled by Fidel Castro since 1959 when he overthrew the dictator Fulgencio Batista.*

## La República Dominicana

**CAPITAL**
*Santo Domingo*

**POPULATION**
*8,716,000*

**FUN FACT**
*The Dominican Republic shares with Haiti the island of Hispaniola in the greater Antilles. The oldest university in our hemisphere, la Universidad de Santo Domingo, was founded in Santo Domingo. The Dominicans are ardent fans or aficionados of baseball, and this rather small island nation has produced some of the finest major league players.*

## Puerto Rico

**CAPITAL**
*San Juan*

**POPULATION**
*3,886,000*

**FUN FACT**
*Puerto Ricans have an endearing term for their beloved island—la isla del encanto—island of enchantment. A commonwealth of the United States, Puerto Rico is a lush, tropical island with beaches along its Atlantic and Caribbean shores and gorgeous mountains with Alpine-like views in its interior. Puerto Rico is the home of the beloved coquí—a little frog that lives only in Puerto Rico and who lets no one see him.*

xxvi

## Venezuela

**CAPITAL**
*Caracas*

**POPULATION**
*24,655,000*

**FUN FACT**
*Venezuela was the name given to this country by Spanish explorers in 1499, when they came across indigenous villages where people lived on the water and where all commerce was conducted by dugout canoes. The waterways reminded them of Venice, Italy. Caracas is a teeming cosmopolitan city of high-rises surrounded by mountains and tucked in a narrow nine-mile valley. Angel Falls in southern Venezuela is the highest waterfall in the world, reaching a height of 3,212 feet with an unbroken fall of 2,648 feet.*

## Colombia

**CAPITAL**
*Bogotá*

**POPULATION**
*41,662,000*

**FUN FACT**
*Colombia covers over 440,000 square miles of tropical and mountainous terrain. Bogotá is situated in the center of the country in an Andean valley 8,640 feet above sea level. The Caribbean coast in the North boasts many beautiful beaches; the South is covered by jungle, and the southern port of Leticia is on the Amazon River.*

## Ecuador

**CAPITAL**
*Quito*

**POPULATION**
*13,710,000*

**FUN FACT**
*Ecuador takes its name from the equator, which cuts right across the country. Ecuador is the meeting place of the high Andean sierra in the center, the tropical coastal plain to the west, and the Amazon Basin jungle to the east. Snowcapped volcanoes stretch some 400 miles from north to south. The beautiful colonial section of the capital, Quito, is sometimes called "the Florence of the Americas."*

## Perú

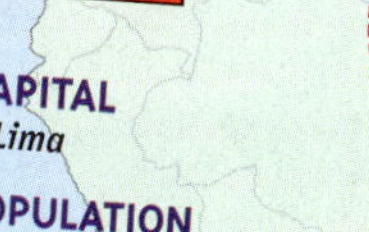


**CAPITAL**
*Lima*

**POPULATION**
*28,410,000*

**FUN FACT**
*Peru, like Ecuador, is divided into three geographical areas—a narrow coastal strip of desert along the Pacific, the Andean highlands where nearly half the population lives, and the Amazon jungle to the east. Lima is on the coast, and for almost nine months out of the year it is enshrouded in a fog called* la garúa. *Peru is famous for its Incan heritage. Nothing can prepare visitors for the awe-inspiring view of the Incan city of Machu Picchu, an imposing architectural complex high in the Andes.*

## Bolivia

**CAPITAL**
*La Paz*

**POPULATION**
*8,568,000*

**FUN FACT**
*Bolivia is one of two landlocked countries in South America. Mountains dominate the Bolivian landscape. La Paz is the highest city in the world at an altitude of 12,500 feet. Bolivia also has the world's highest navigable lake, Lake Titicaca, which is surrounded by the picturesque villages of the Aymara Indians.*



xxvii

# El mundo hispanohablante

## Chile

**CAPITAL**
*Santiago*

**POPULATION**
*15,665,000*

**FUN FACT**
*Chile, a "string bean" country never more than 111 miles wide, stretches 2,666 miles from north to south along the Pacific Coast. The imposing Andes isolate it from Bolivia and Argentina. The northern part of the country is characterized by the super-arid Atacama desert, the South by the spectacular wind-swept glaciers and fjords of Patagonia. Over one-third of the country's population lives in the Santiago area.*

## Argentina

**CAPITAL**
*Buenos Aires*

**POPULATION**
*38,741,000*

**FUN FACT**
*Argentina is often considered the most European country of South America. Buenos Aires is a beautiful city of parks, boutiques, restaurants, and wide boulevards. Argentina is famous for its beef from the cattle that graze on the huge estancias of the grassy Pampas. Farther south on the Chilean border is the gorgeous lake area with Swiss-like villages around Bariloche. To the south is Patagonia with its rocky countryside where the Welsh still graze sheep.*

## Paraguay

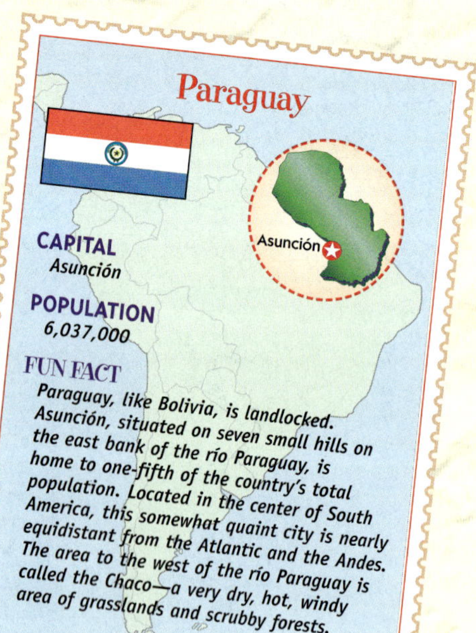


**CAPITAL**
*Asunción*

**POPULATION**
*6,037,000*

**FUN FACT**
*Paraguay, like Bolivia, is landlocked. Asunción, situated on seven small hills on the east bank of the río Paraguay, is home to one-fifth of the country's total population. Located in the center of South America, this somewhat quaint city is nearly equidistant from the Atlantic and the Andes. The area to the west of the río Paraguay is called the Chaco—a very dry, hot, windy area of grasslands and scrubby forests.*

## Uruguay

**CAPITAL**
*Montevideo*

**POPULATION**
*3,413,000*

**FUN FACT**
*Uruguay is the smallest country in South America. Most of the country's terrain is grazing land for sheep and cattle. Montevideo, situated where the río de la Plata empties into the Atlantic, is a rather peaceful city whose suburbs look more like beautiful resorts. The beaches of Uruguay's Atlantic coastline, particularly Punta del Este, attract many people from Brazil and Argentina.*



xxviii

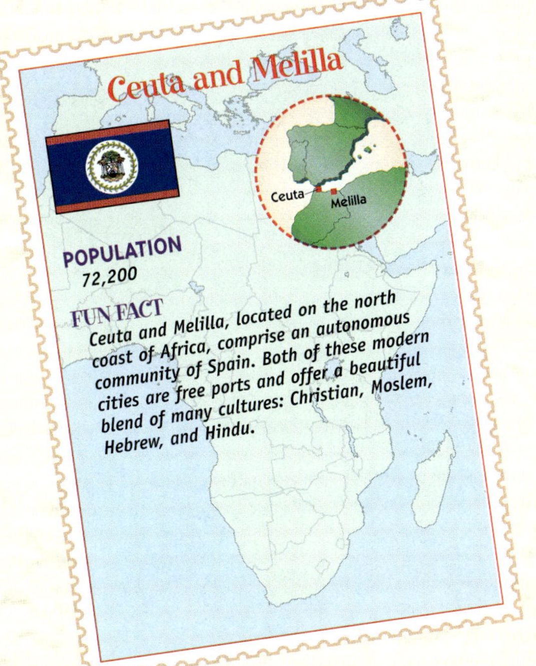
Ceuta and Melilla
Ceuta
Melilla
POPULATION
72,200
FUN FACT
Ceuta and Melilla, located on the north coast of Africa, comprise an autonomous community of Spain. Both of these modern cities are free ports and offer a beautiful blend of many cultures: Christian, Moslem, Hebrew, and Hindu.

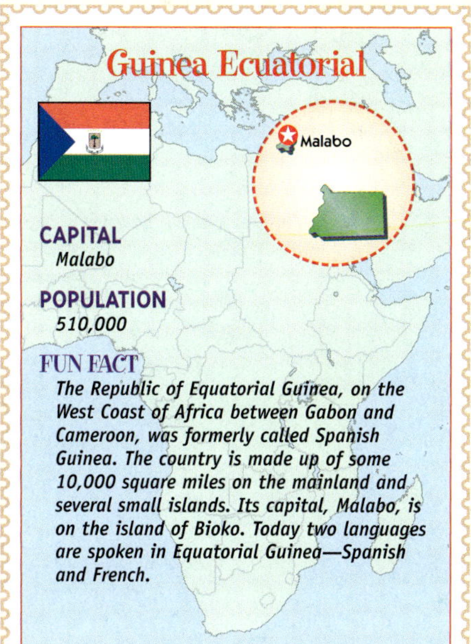
Guinea Ecuatorial
Malabo
CAPITAL
Malabo
POPULATION
510,000
FUN FACT
The Republic of Equatorial Guinea, on the West Coast of Africa between Gabon and Cameroon, was formerly called Spanish Guinea. The country is made up of some 10,000 square miles on the mainland and several small islands. Its capital, Malabo, is on the island of Bioko. Today two languages are spoken in Equatorial Guinea—Spanish and French.

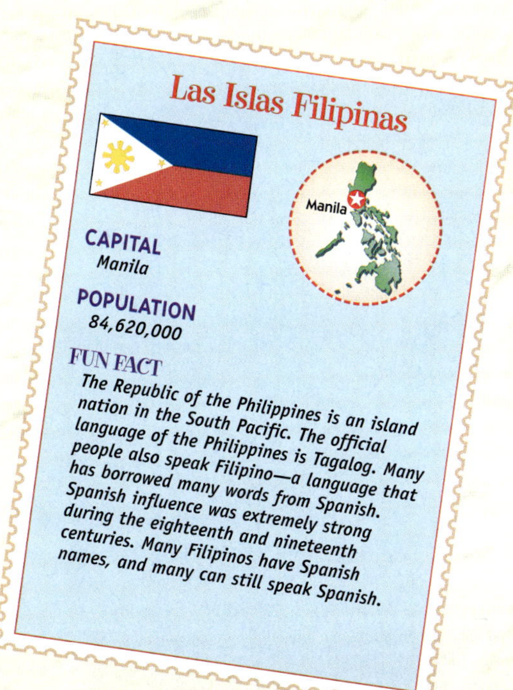
Las Islas Filipinas
Manila
CAPITAL
Manila
POPULATION
84,620,000
FUN FACT
The Republic of the Philippines is an island nation in the South Pacific. The official language of the Philippines is Tagalog. Many people also speak Filipino—a language that has borrowed many words from Spanish. Spanish influence was extremely strong during the eighteenth and nineteenth centuries. Many Filipinos have Spanish names, and many can still speak Spanish.



xxix

España
OCÉANO ATLÁNTICO
MAR CANTÁBRICO
Golfo de Vizcaya
FRANCIA
ANDORRA
La Coruña
Santiago de Compostela
Galicia
Oviedo
Asturias
Santander
Cantabria
San Sebastián
Bilbao
País Vasco
Roncesvalles
Pamplona
Navarra
LOS PIRINEOS
CORDILLERA CANTÁBRICA
León
Burgos
Rioja
Castilla y León
Río Ebro
Cataluña
Barcelona
Valladolid
Río Duero
Zaragoza
Aragón
Salamanca
Segovia
Ávila
SIERRA DE GUADARRAMA
Madrid
Madrid
Río Tajo
PORTUGAL
ESPAÑA
Comunidad Valenciana
Valencia
Castilla-la Mancha
Menorca
Islas baleares
Palma
Mallorca
Ibiza
Formentera
Lisboa
Río Guadiana
Extremadura
Alicante
Murcia
Murcia
Cartagena
MAR MEDITERRÁNEO
Río Guadalquivir
Córdoba
Sevilla
Granada
Andalucía
SIERRA NEVADA
Jerez de la Frontera
Málaga
COSTA DEL SOL
Cádiz
Marbella
Estepona
Gibraltar (R.U.)
Estrecho de Gibraltar
Ceuta (Esp.)
Tánger
Melilla (Esp.)
OCÉANO ATLÁNTICO
ARGELIA
MARRUECOS
Islas Canarias
La Palma
Santa Cruz de Tenerife
Lanzarote
Fuerteventura
Gomera
Tenerife
Las Palmas
Hierro
Gran Canaria
MARRUECOS
ÁFRICA
OCÉANO ATLÁNTICO
SAHARA OCCIDENTAL

La América del Sur
MAR CARIBE
OCÉANO ATLÁNTICO
Barranquilla
Cartagena
Maracaibo
Caracas
Lago de Maracaibo
Río Orinoco
VENEZUELA
Medellín
Río Magdalena
Santafé de Bogotá
GUYANA
SURINAM
GUAYANA FRANCESA
Cali
COLOMBIA
Ecuador
Otavalo
Quito
ECUADOR
Islas Galápagos (Ecuador)
Guayaquil
Cuenca
Río Amazonas
PERÚ
BRASIL
El Callao
Lima
CORDILLERA DE LOS ANDES
Cuzco
Lago Titicaca
BOLIVIA
La Paz
Cochabamba
Santa Cruz
Sucre
Brasília
PARAGUAY
Trópico de Capricornio
Asunción
CHILE
Vicuña
Río Paraná
Córdoba
OCÉANO PACÍFICO
Valparaíso
Santiago
Rosario
URUGUAY
Buenos Aires
Montevideo
ARGENTINA
La Plata
Río de la Plata
Mar del Plata
Puerto Montt
PATAGONIA
OCÉANO ATLÁNTICO
Estrecho de Magallanes
Islas Malvinas (R.U.)
Tierra del Fuego
Punta Arenas
Cabo de Hornos
xxxi

# México, la América Central y el Caribe

# Estados Unidos

## The Spanish-Speaking World

**Culture** Knowing Spanish will open doors to you around the world. As you study the language, you will come to understand and appreciate the way of life, customs, values, and cultures of people from many different areas of the world. Look at the map on pages xxii–xxiii to see where Spanish is spoken, either as a first or second language.

Learning Spanish can be fun and will bring you a sense of accomplishment. You'll be really pleased when you are able to carry on a conversation in Spanish. You will be able to read the literature of Spain and Latin America, keep up with current events in magazines and newspapers from Spain and Latin America, and understand Spanish language films without relying on subtitles.

The Spanish language will be a source of enrichment for the rest of your life—and you don't have to leave home to enjoy it. In all areas of the United States there are Hispanic radio and television stations, Latin musicians, Spanish-language magazines and newspapers, and a great diversity of restaurants serving foods from all areas of the Spanish-speaking world. The Latin or Hispanic population of the United States today totals forty million people and is the fastest growing segment of the population.

# Career Opportunities

**Business** Your knowledge of Spanish will also be an asset to you in a wide variety of careers. Many companies from Spain and Latin America are multinational and have branches around the world, including the United States. Many U.S. corporations have great exposure in the Spanish-speaking countries. With the growth of the Hispanic population in the U.S., bilingualism is becoming an important asset in many fields including retail, fashion, cosmetics, pharmaceutical, agriculture, automotive, tourism, airlines, technology, finance, and accounting.

You can use your Spanish in all these fields, not only abroad but also in the United States. On the national scene there are innumerable possibilities in medical and hospital services, banking and finance, law, social work, and law enforcement. The opportunities are limitless.

# Language Link

Another benefit to learning Spanish is that it will improve your English. Once you know another language, you can make comparisons between the two and gain a greater understanding of how languages function. You'll also come across a number of Spanish words that are used in English. Just a few examples are: **adobe, corral, meseta, rodeo, poncho, canyon, llama, alpaca.** Spanish will also be helpful if you decide to learn yet another language. Once you learn a second language, the learning process for acquiring other languages becomes much easier.

Spanish is a beautiful, rich language spoken on many continents. Whatever your motivation is for choosing to study it, Spanish will expand your horizons and increase your job opportunities. **¡Viva el español! Y ¡buen viaje!**

## Preview

There are seven **Repasos (A–G)** at the beginning of **¡Buen viaje! Level 2.** In **Repaso A,** students review vocabulary relating to school, getting to school, and buying school supplies and clothing. In the **Estructura** section, students review the present tense of **-ar** verbs and the verbs **ir, dar,** and **estar.**

Students practice this vocabulary and these structures as they talk about school, after-school activities, and shopping for clothes.

### National Standards

**Communication**

In Review Chapter A, students will communicate in spoken and written Spanish on the following topics:

- School activities
- Buying clothing and supplies for school

Students will also learn to narrate present events. They will obtain and provide information about school and shopping.

# Repaso A

# Las compras para la escuela

Diego Rivera *Fin del corrido*

## Learning from Photos

*(page R1)* You may wish to ask the following questions about the photo of **Calle Serrano,** a shopping and residential street in the upscale area of Salamanca in Madrid:

**¿Es de noche o es de día?**
**¿Es una calle bonita?**
**¿Hay muchas tiendas en la calle?**
**¿Hay mucho tráfico?**

Repaso A

## Vocabulario

### Resource Manager

Workbook, pages R1–R6
Tests, pages R1–R2, R19, R31

### Bellringer Review

*Use BRR Transparency R.1 or write the following on the board.*
Write as many words as you can think of associated with school.

### PRESENTATION

¡OJO! Before you begin your presentation, you may wish to ask students to say anything they can about the illustrations. If you find that they have a good command of the vocabulary, you can skip this review material and do the activities immediately.

**Step 1** Have students open their books. Point to individual items in the illustrations and have the class repeat **el bus escolar,** for example. Then build to the complete sentences.

**Step 2** As you present the sentences, ask comprehension questions such as: **¿Llegan los alumnos a la escuela? ¿Quiénes llegan? ¿Adónde llegan? ¿Llegan a eso de las ocho menos cuarto? ¿A qué hora llegan?**

**Step 3** After reviewing the vocabulary orally, have students read the material for additional reinforcement.





## Vocabulario

Los alumnos llegan a la escuela a las ocho menos cuarto.
Algunos toman el bus escolar.
Otros van a la escuela a pie.

Los alumnos estudian mucho.
Toman apuntes.
Escuchan a la profesora cuando habla.
La profesora enseña.

José está en la papelería.
Necesita materiales escolares.
Compra un cuaderno, un lápiz y un bolígrafo.

Teresa está en la tienda de ropa.
Compra una blusa para llevar a la escuela.
Mira la blusa.
Paga en la caja.



### Learning from Photos

*(page R3)* Remind students that **Calle Florida** is a lovely shopping street in the heart of Buenos Aires.

You may wish to ask the following questions about the photo:
**¿Dónde está el muchacho?**
**¿Qué mira?**
**¿Qué opinas? ¿Es cara o barata la camisa? ¿Cuesta mucho o poco?**

## 1 Historieta En la escuela Contesten.

1. ¿Cómo llegan los alumnos a la escuela? ¿Toman el bus, van en carro o van a pie?
2. ¿A qué hora llegan a la escuela?
3. ¿Con quién hablan los alumnos cuando entran en la sala de clase?
4. ¿Quiénes toman exámenes y quién da los exámenes?
5. ¿Sacan los alumnos notas altas?
6. ¿Prestan ellos atención cuando la profesora habla?

## 2 Historieta A la papelería Escojan.

1. Alicia necesita materiales escolares. ¿Adónde va ella?
   **a.** a la cafetería **b.** a la tienda de ropa **c.** a la papelería
2. ¿Con quién habla Alicia en la papelería?
   **a.** con el empleado **b.** con el profesor **c.** con el mesero
3. ¿Qué compra Alicia en la papelería?
   **a.** un refresco **b.** un pantalón corto **c.** un cuaderno
4. ¿Dónde paga Alicia?
   **a.** cien pesos **b.** en la caja **c.** en el parque
5. ¿En qué lleva ella los materiales escolares?
   **a.** en una mochila **b.** en un cuaderno **c.** en una asignatura

## 3 Historieta En la tienda de ropa

Contesten según se indica.

1. ¿Adónde va Roberto? (a la tienda de ropa)
2. ¿Qué necesita? (una camisa de mangas cortas)
3. ¿Busca una camisa verde? (no, roja y azul)
4. ¿Qué talla usa? (38)
5. ¿Compra Roberto una camisa? (sí)
6. ¿Cuánto cuesta? (125 pesos)
7. ¿Dónde paga Roberto? (en la caja)

Calle Florida, Buenos Aires, Argentina



# Repaso A

## Vocabulario

### PRACTICE

**¡OJO!** When students are doing the activities, accept any answer that makes sense. The purpose of these activities is to have students use the new vocabulary. They are not factual recall activities. Thus, it is not necessary for students to remember specific factual information from the vocabulary presentation when answering. If you wish, have students use the photo on this page as a stimulus, when possible.

**Historieta** Each time **Historieta** appears, it means that the answers to the activity form a short story. Encourage students to look at the title of the **Historieta,** since it can help them do the activity.

**1** This activity can be done orally with books closed.
**Expansion:** After going over Activity 1, call on a student to retell the story in his or her own words.

**2** Have students read Activity 2 aloud.

**3** Activity 3 can be done orally with books closed.

## Answers to  Repaso

**1**

1. Los alumnos toman el bus (van en carro, van a pie) a la escuela.
2. Llegan a la escuela a las ___.
3. Los alumnos hablan con ___ cuando entran en la sala de clase.
4. Los alumnos toman exámenes y el / la profesor(a) da los exámenes.
5. Sí (No), los alumnos (no) sacan notas altas.
6. Sí (No), ellos (no) prestan atención cuando la profesora habla.

**2**

1. c
2. a
3. c
4. b
5. a

**3**

1. Roberto va a la tienda de ropa.
2. Necesita una camisa de mangas cortas.
3. No, busca una camisa roja y azul.
4. Usa la talla 38.
5. Sí, Roberto compra una camisa.
6. Cuesta 125 pesos.
7. Roberto paga en la caja.

## Conversación

### PRESENTATION

**Step 1** Call on two students to read the **Conversación** aloud using as much expression as possible.

**Step 2** After the conversation has been read, go over the **¿Comprendes?** activity.

### Learning from Realia

*(page R4)* You may wish to ask the following questions about **Papelería Monog:**

**¿Es Monog el nombre de una papelería o de una tienda de ropa?**
**¿Qué venden en la tienda Monog?**
**¿Dónde está?**
**¿Quién es la propietaria?**

# Conversación

## La apertura de clases

**Paco** Elena, ¿cómo estás?
**Elena** Muy bien, Paco. ¿Y tú?
**Paco** Bien. ¿Adónde vas?
**Elena** Voy a la papelería. Necesito comprar algunas cosas para la apertura de clases.
**Paco** Verdad. Septiembre una vez más. ¡Es increíble!

PAPELERIA MONOG
TODO PARA EL ESTUDIANTE
TODO PARA LA OFICINA
Y MIL COSAS MAS.
Rosa María de Valdéz
PROPIETARIA
Av. Obregon 721
Tel. y Fax 2-54-55
Nogales, Sonora, Mex.

### ¿Comprendes?

Contesten.

1. ¿Con quién habla Elena?
2. ¿Cómo está Paco?
3. ¿Son amigos Elena y Paco?
4. ¿Adónde va Elena?
5. ¿Qué necesita ella?
6. ¿De qué hablan los dos amigos?



### Answers to ¿Comprendes?

1. Elena habla con Paco.
2. Paco está bien.
3. Sí, Elena y Paco son amigos.
4. Elena va a la papelería.
5. Ella necesita comprar algunas cosas para la apertura de clases.
6. Los dos amigos hablan de la apertura de clases.

# Estructura

## Presente de los verbos en -ar

1. Review the forms of the present tense of regular **-ar** verbs.

| | | | | | | |
|---|---|---|---|---|---|---|
| MIRAR | **miro** | **miras** | **mira** | **miramos** | ***miráis*** | **miran** |
| TOMAR | **tomo** | **tomas** | **toma** | **tomamos** | ***tomáis*** | **toman** |

2. Remember, to make a sentence negative you put **no** before the verb.

   **No hablamos francés. Hablamos español.**

3. Remember to use **tú** when talking to a friend, family member, or person your own age. Use **usted** when speaking to an adult, a person you do not know well, or someone to whom you wish to show respect.

   **¿Tú estudias español, Roberto?**
   **¿Y usted, señora? ¿Usted también estudia español?**

**4 Entrevista** Contesten personalmente.

1. ¿En qué escuela estudias?
2. ¿Cómo llegas a la escuela por la mañana?
3. ¿Cuántos cursos tomas?
4. ¿En qué llevas los materiales escolares?
5. ¿Estudian mucho los alumnos de tu escuela?
6. ¿Sacan ustedes buenas notas?
7. ¿Toman ustedes muchos exámenes?
8. ¿Escuchan ustedes cuando la profesora habla?

Universidad Nacional, San Andrés, Colombia

## Answers to Repaso

**4**

1. Estudio en la Escuela ___.
2. Llego a pie (en carro, en bus).
3. Tomo ___ cursos.
4. Llevo los materiales escolares en una mochila.
5. Sí (No), los alumnos de mi escuela (no) estudian mucho.
6. Sí, (No, no) sacamos buenas notas.
7. Sí, (No, no) tomamos muchos exámenes.
8. Sí, (No, no) escuchamos cuando la profesora habla.

Repaso A

## Estructura

### Bellringer Review

*Use BRR Transparency R.2 or write the following on the board.*
Use the following expressions in a sentence.
**estudiar mucho**
**tomar apuntes**
**prestar atención**
**sacar notas**

### PRESENTATION

#### Presente de los verbos en -ar

**Step 1** Have students read the forms of the **-ar** verbs aloud.

**Step 2** Write the two verbs on the board and underline the endings.

**Step 3** Read the information in Item 3 to the class. Review this point as quickly as possible.

### PRACTICE

**4** Activity 4 can be done as an interview. Have one student ask the questions and another respond.

# Estructura

## PRACTICE *(continued)*

**5** Have students do Activity 5 with books open.

### Learning from Photos

*(page R6)* Ask the following questions about the photo:

**¿Están en una fiesta los jóvenes?**
**¿Cuántos muchachos hay? ¿Y cuántas muchachas hay?**
**¿Qué llevan?**
**¿Qué toman?**
**¿Dónde está la casa?**
**¿Dónde está Guatemala?**

## PRESENTATION

### Los verbos ir, dar, estar

**Step 1** Have students look at the verbs on page R6. Point out to them that the endings are the same as regular **-ar** verbs except for the **yo** form.

**Step 2** Have students repeat **estoy, doy, voy.** Then have them repeat all the forms.

**Step 3** Read the explanation about **al** in Item 2 aloud.



**5** **Historieta En la fiesta** Completen.

1. Durante la fiesta todos nosotros ____. (bailar)
2. Felipe ____ el piano. (tocar)
3. Mientras él ____ el piano, Elena y Carlos ____. (tocar, cantar)
4. ¿____ ustedes refrescos durante la fiesta? (preparar)
5. ¿____ ustedes fotos durante la fiesta? (tomar)
6. Sí, y todos nosotros ____ las fotografías. (mirar)

Una fiesta en la Ciudad de Guatemala

### Los verbos ir, dar, estar

1. Note that the verbs **ir, dar,** and **estar** are the same as regular **-ar** verbs in all forms except **yo.**

| | | | | | | |
|---|---|---|---|---|---|---|
| ESTAR | **estoy** | **estás** | **está** | **estamos** | ***estáis*** | **están** |
| DAR | **doy** | **das** | **da** | **damos** | ***dais*** | **dan** |
| IR | **voy** | **vas** | **va** | **vamos** | ***vais*** | **van** |

2. The preposition **a** often follows the verb **ir.** Remember that **a** contracts with **el** to form one word—**al.**

   **Voy al café. No voy a la tienda.**



## Answers to Repaso

**5**

1. bailamos
2. toca
3. toca, cantan
4. Preparan
5. Toman
6. miramos

**6** **Historieta Voy a la escuela.** Contesten.

1. ¿Vas a la escuela?
2. ¿A qué hora vas a la escuela?
3. ¿Con quién vas a la escuela?
4. ¿Están ustedes en la escuela ahora?
5. ¿Cómo van ustedes a la escuela?

**7** **Historieta A la tienda de ropa**
Completen.

Estepona, España

Yo __1__ (ir) a la tienda de ropa. Emilio __2__ (ir) también. Él y yo __3__ (estar) en la tienda. Yo __4__ (comprar) una camiseta y él __5__ (comprar) un blue jean. Nosotros no __6__ (necesitar) mucha ropa porque __7__ (llevar) uniforme a la escuela.

Elena y Tomás __8__ (llevar) uniforme a la escuela también. Ellos __9__ (ir) a una escuela en las afueras de Lima, en Miraflores.

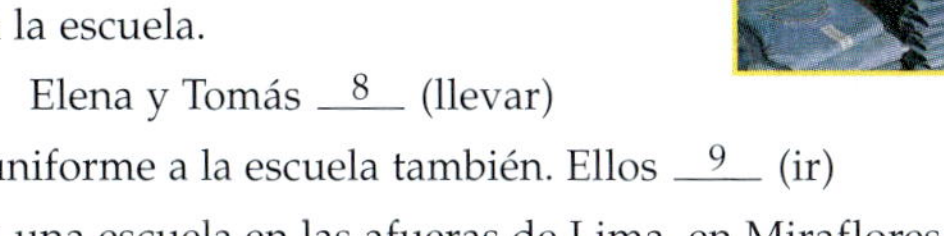

**8** **¿Cuándo? ¿En clase, después de las clases o en la fiesta?** Work with a classmate. He or she will suggest an activity. You will tell where you and your friends typically take part in the activity.

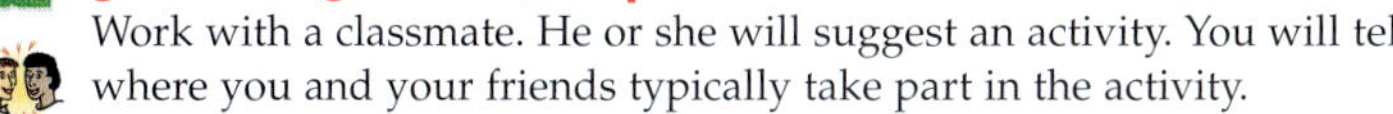

**9** **En la tienda de ropa** You are at a clothing store. You need to buy some things. Your partner will be the sales clerk. Have a conversation with each other and then reverse roles.

**10** **Juego ¿Quién es?** Work in small groups. One person tells what someone in the class is wearing. The others have to guess who it is. If several people are wearing the same thing, the person giving the clues will have to give more details.

# Repaso A

## Estructura

### PRACTICE

**6** Activity 6 can be done orally with books closed.

**7** Go over Activity 7 with books open.

### Writing Development

Have students rewrite the information from Activity 7 in paragraph form.

### Learning from Photos

*(page R7)* You may wish to ask the following questions about the photo:
**¿Dónde está el muchacho?**
**¿Qué hay en la tienda?**
**¿Qué mira el muchacho?**
**¿De qué color es?**

**¡OJO!** Note that the activities are color-coded. All the activities in the text are communicative. However, the ones with blue titles are guided communication. The red titles indicate that the answers to the activity are more open-ended and can vary more. You may wish to correct students' mistakes more so in the guided activities than in the activities with a red title, which lend themselves to a freer response.

## Answers to Repaso

**6**

1. Sí, voy a la escuela.
2. Voy a la escuela a las ___.
3. Voy a la escuela con ___.
4. Sí, (No, no) estamos en la escuela ahora.
5. Vamos a la escuela a pie (en carro, en bus).

**7**

1. voy
2. va
3. estamos
4. compro
5. compra
6. necesitamos
7. llevamos
8. llevan
9. van

**8** *Answers will vary. Students will use* -ar *verbs, the verbs* ir, dar, *and* estar, *and vocabulary related to school and leisure-time activities.*

**9** *Answers will vary. Students will use* -ar *verbs, the verbs* ir, dar, *and* estar, *and vocabulary related to shopping for clothes.*

**10** *Answers will vary. Students will use vocabulary related to clothing.*

# Preview

In **Repaso B,** students review the vocabulary they need to describe people and things and to identify nationalities. In the **Estructura** section, they review the verb **ser** and agreement of nouns and adjectives.

Students practice this vocabulary and these structures as they talk about their friends, classes, and teachers.

## National Standards

### Communication

In Review Chapter B, students will communicate in spoken and written Spanish on the following topics:

- Describing people
- Talking about their courses

Students will also learn to narrate present events. They will obtain and provide information and engage in conversations about friends and school.

Repaso B

# Amigos y alumnos

Carolina Larrea *Arvores*

R8

## Learning from Photos

*(pages R8–R9)* You may wish to ask the following questions about the photo of the students seated at **Café México Mágico, Calle Presidente, la Ciudad de México:**
**¿Están los jóvenes en un café?**
**¿Qué toman los jóvenes?**
**¿Qué hay en la mesa?**
**¿Qué llevan los jóvenes?**

## Vocabulario

### Resource Manager

Workbook, pages R7–R10
Tests, pages R3–R4, R20, R32

### Bellringer Review

*Use BRR Transparency R.3 or write the following on the board.*
Write any words you can use to describe a person.

### PRESENTATION

**Step 1** Students should be quite familiar with this vocabulary. It should be possible to review it very quickly.

**Step 2** Call on a student to read the sentences below each photo.

**Step 3** Ask questions about the sentences. Then have students say anything they can about the photos.

### PRACTICE

**¡OJO!** When students are doing the activities, accept any answer that makes sense. The purpose of these activities is to have students use the new vocabulary. They are not factual recall activities. Thus, it is not necessary for students to remember specific factual information from the vocabulary presentation when answering. If you wish, have students use the photos on this page as a stimulus, when possible.

**Historieta** Each time **Historieta** appears, it means that the answers to the activity form a short story. Encourage students to look at the title of the **Historieta,** since it can help them do the activity.

**1** and **2** These activities can be done orally with books closed.





## Vocabulario

Es María Gorostiza.
Ella es mexicana.
Es rubia y bastante alta.
María es de Guadalajara.
Ella es alumna en el Colegio Hidalgo.

Felipe y Teresa son amigos.
Ellos son alumnos en la misma escuela.
Son alumnos buenos. Son inteligentes.
Y ellos son bastante cómicos.

**1** **Historieta María Gorostiza**

Contesten.

1. ¿De qué nacionalidad es María Gorostiza?
2. ¿De dónde es?
3. ¿Cómo es ella?
4. ¿Es ella alumna?
5. ¿Dónde es alumna María?

**2** **Historieta Felipe y Teresa**

Corrijan las oraciones falsas.

1. Felipe y Teresa son hermanos.
2. Ellos son alumnos en escuelas diferentes.
3. Ellos son alumnos muy malos.
4. No son inteligentes.
5. Son muy serios y tímidos.



### Answers to Repaso

**1**

1. María Gorostiza es mexicana.
2. Es de Guadalajara.
3. Es rubia y bastante alta.
4. Sí, ella es alumna.
5. Es alumna en el Colegio Hidalgo.

**2**

1. Felipe y Teresa son amigos.
2. Ellos son alumnos en la misma escuela.
3. Ellos son alumnos buenos.
4. Son inteligentes.
5. Son bastante cómicos.

# Conversación

## ¿De dónde son?

**Julio** ¡Hola!
**Rosa** ¡Hola! ¿Qué tal?
**Julio** Bien, ¿y tú?
**Rosa** Bien. Oye, ¿eres un amigo de Teresa Irizarry, ¿no?
**Julio** Sí, soy Julio Arenal.
**Rosa** ¿De dónde eres, Julio?
**Julio** ¿Yo? Soy de San Juan. Y tú eres de Ponce como Teresa, ¿no?
**Rosa** Sí, soy ponceña.

### ¿Comprendes?

Contesten.

1. ¿Son puertorriqueños los dos muchachos?
2. ¿De dónde es Julio?
3. ¿Es Julio un amigo de Teresa Irizarry?
4. ¿De dónde son Teresa y Rosa?

Ponce, Puerto Rico



Repaso B

## Conversación

### PRESENTATION

**Step 1** Call on two students to come to the front of the class. Have them read the **Conversación** with as much expression as possible.

**Step 2** Have students make up their own conversations with similar information. Ask for volunteers to present their conversations to the class.

**Step 3** Now quickly do the **¿Comprendes?** activity.

### Learning from Photos

*(page R11)* Ponce is the second largest city in Puerto Rico. It is on the Caribbean coast in the southern part of the island.

### Answers to ¿Comprendes?

1. Sí, los dos muchachos son puertorriqueños.
2. Julio es de San Juan.
3. Sí, Julio es un amigo de Teresa Irizarry.
4. Teresa y Rosa son de Ponce.

## Estructura

### Bellringer Review

*Use BRR Transparency R.4 or write the following on the board.*
Answer.
1. **¿Quién eres?**
2. **¿De dónde eres?**
3. **¿De qué nacionalidad eres?**

### PRESENTATION

**Presente del verbo ser**

**Step 1** Quickly go over the forms of **ser** and have students do the activities.

### PRACTICE

**3** Have students work in pairs and ask each other the questions in Activity 3.

### Writing Development

After going over Activity 4 have students rewrite the story in their own words.

### Learning from Photos

*(page R12)* Santo Domingo is the capital of the Dominican Republic. The Dominican Republic and Haiti form the island of Hispaniola. Columbus first sailed to Hispaniola in 1492.





# Estructura

## Presente del verbo ser

Review the forms of the irregular verb **ser**.

| SER | soy | eres | es | somos | *sois* | son |
|---|---|---|---|---|---|---|

*Acrílico sobre tela de Tony Capellán. Arma de doble filo*

**3 Entrevista** Contesten personalmente.

1. ¿Quién eres?
2. ¿De qué nacionalidad eres?
3. ¿Dónde eres alumno o alumna?
4. ¿Cómo es tu escuela?

**4 Historieta El amigo de Andrés**
Completen con **ser**.

Yo __1__ un amigo de Andrés. Andrés __2__ muy simpático. Y él __3__ gracioso. Andrés y yo __4__ dominicanos. __5__ de la República Dominicana.

La capital de la República Dominicana __6__ Santo Domingo. Nosotros __7__ alumnos en un colegio en Santo Domingo. Nosotros __8__ alumnos de inglés. La profesora de inglés __9__ la señorita White. Ella __10__ americana.

Fortaleza de Orzama, Santo Domingo



## Answers to Repaso

**3**

1. Soy ___.
2. Soy americano(a), (cubano[a], mexicano[a], etc.).
3. Soy alumno(a) en la Escuela ___.
4. Mi escuela es ___.

**4**

1. soy
2. es
3. es
4. somos
5. Somos
6. es
7. somos
8. somos
9. es
10. es

## Sustantivos, artículos y adjetivos

1. Spanish nouns are either masculine or feminine. Most nouns ending in **o** are masculine and most nouns ending in **a** are feminine. The definite articles **el** and **los** accompany masculine nouns; **la** and **las** accompany feminine nouns.

| | | | |
|---|---|---|---|
| **el alumno** | **los alumnos** | **la amiga** | **las amigas** |
| **el curso** | **los cursos** | **la escuela** | **las escuelas** |

2. An adjective must agree with the noun it describes or modifies. Adjectives that end in **o** have four forms.

| | |
|---|---|
| **el amigo sincero** | **los amigos sinceros** |
| **la amiga sincera** | **las amigas sinceras** |

3. Adjectives that end in **e** or a consonant have only two forms.

| | |
|---|---|
| **el curso interesante** | **los cursos interesantes** |
| **la asignatura interesante** | **las asignaturas interesantes** |
| **el curso difícil** | **los cursos difíciles** |
| **la asignatura difícil** | **las asignaturas difíciles** |

Unas amigas chilenas, Elqui, Chile



# Repaso B

## Estructura

### Bellringer Review

*Use BRR Transparency R.5 or write the following on the board.*

Write the following in the plural.

1. **Él es americano.**
2. **La muchacha es bonita.**
3. **El colegio es moderno.**
4. **El curso es fácil.**

## PRESENTATION

### Sustantivos, artículos y adjetivos

**Step 1** As you go over the explanation, have students repeat the words and phrases in Items 1–3 after you. Point to a specific person or object as you use the definite article.

### Learning from Photos

*(page R13)* You may wish to ask the following questions about the photo of the girls in Elqui, Chile:

**¿Cuántas muchachas hay en la fotografía?**
**¿De dónde son ellas?**
**¿Cómo viajan?**
**¿Tienen un carro?**

# Repaso B

## Estructura

### PRACTICE

**5** Have students say as much as they can about the girl.

### Writing Development

After going over Activity 6 orally in class, have students write about what they see in the photo.

### Recycling

You may also review time expressions by asking students questions about the school schedule in Activity 7.

### Learning from Photos

*(page R14 middle)* San Ángel is a lovely, rather quiet colonial section in the southern part of Mexico City. Every Saturday there is a popular market in San Ángel, called **el bazar sábado.**

**5 Julia** Describan a la muchacha.

Una muchacha de San Juan, Puerto Rico

**6 Los amigos** Describan al grupo de amigos.

En la colonia de San Ángel, Ciudad de México

**7 Mi clase favorita** Describan su clase favorita.

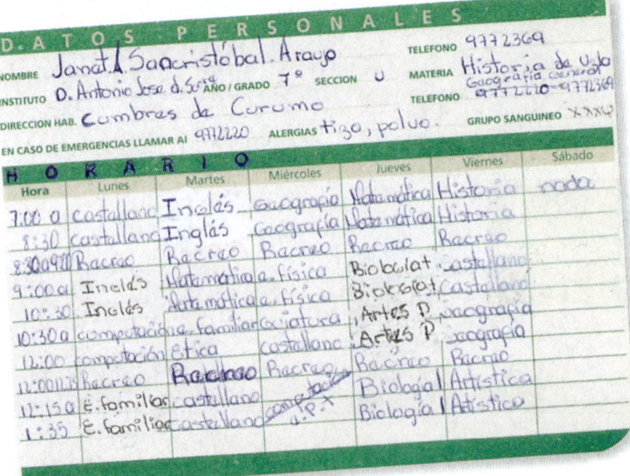

DATOS PERSONALES

NOMBRE Janet A. Sancristóbal Araujo TELEFONO 9772369
INSTITUTO D. Antonio José d. Sucre AÑO / GRADO 7° SECCION U MATERIA Historia de Vzla, Geografía general
DIRECCION HAB. Cumbres de Curumo TELEFONO 9772220-9772369
EN CASO DE EMERGENCIAS LLAMAR AI 9772220 ALERGIAS tizo, polvo. GRUPO SANGUINEO XXXX

HORARIO

| Hora | Lunes | Martes | Miércoles | Jueves | Viernes | Sábado |
|---|---|---|---|---|---|---|
| 7:00 a | castellano | Inglés | Geografía | Matemática | Historia | nada |
| 8:30 | castellano | Inglés | Geografía | Matemática | Historia | |
| 8:30 a 9:00 | Recreo | Recreo | Recreo | Recreo | Recreo | |
| 9:00 a | Inglés | Matemática | Ed. física | Biología | castellano | |
| 10:30 | Inglés | Matemática | Ed. física | Biología | castellano | |
| 10:30 a | computación | Ed. familiar | Agricultura | Artes P. | Geografía | |
| 12:00 | computación | Ética | castellano | Artes P. | Geografía | |
| 12:00 a 12:15 | Recreo | Recreo | Recreo | Recreo | Recreo | |
| 12:15 a | E. familiar | castellano | computación | Biología | Artística | |
| 1:35 | E. familiar | castellano | [illegible] | Biología | Artística | |



### Answers to Repaso

**5**, **6**, and **7** *Answers will vary. Students will use vocabulary and structure previously learned in* **¡Buen viaje! Level 1.**

8 **¡Qué clase tan difícil!** Work in groups of three or four. In each group, rate your courses as **fácil, difícil, regular, aburrido, fantástico.** Tally the results and report the information to the class.

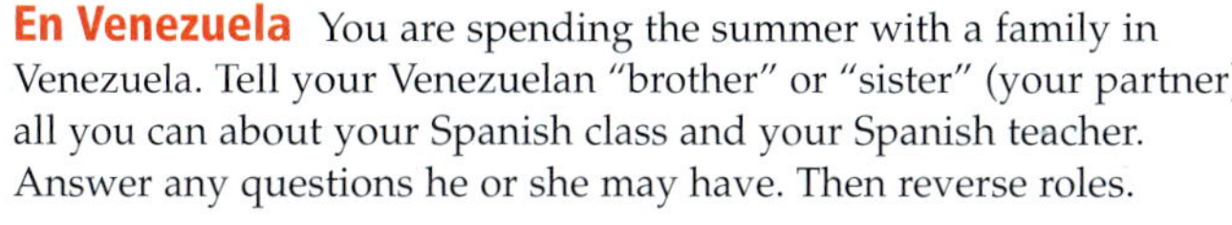

9 **En Venezuela** You are spending the summer with a family in Venezuela. Tell your Venezuelan "brother" or "sister" (your partner) all you can about your Spanish class and your Spanish teacher. Answer any questions he or she may have. Then reverse roles.

Salto Ángel, Venezuela

10 **Cursos** You are speaking with an exchange student from Peru (your partner). He or she wants to know about your school, your schedule, and your classes. Tell as much as you can about your school and then ask him or her about school life in Peru.

Una alumna, Lima, Perú



## Repaso B

## Estructura

8, 9, and 10 These activities allow students to use the vocabulary and structures of the chapter in open-ended, real-life situations. They also give students another opportunity to use words and structures from previous chapters. Have students work on as many activities as you wish. You may also allow them to select those activities they want to do. Different groups can work on different activities.

### Learning from Photos

*(page R15 top)* Angel Falls gets its name from the American bush pilot Jimmy Angel, who first saw it in 1935 when he was trying to explore the table mountain, **Auyantepuy.** He was looking for a mountain of gold. Two years later, he and his wife and a small group of colleagues returned and attempted a landing on the summit of the mountain. They crashed, and for many years his plane standing on its nose was a tourist attraction. His party emerged from the forest eleven days after the crash. They had discovered the fifteen or twenty tallest falls in the world. Angel Falls has a total height of 3,212 feet, with an unbroken fall of 2,648 feet—fifteen times taller than Niagara Falls.
*(page R15 bottom)* Have students look at the photo of the student from Lima, Peru, and say as much as they can about it.

### Answers to Repaso

8, 9, and 10 *Answers will vary. Students will use vocabulary and structure previously learned in* **¡Buen viaje! Level 1.**

Repaso C

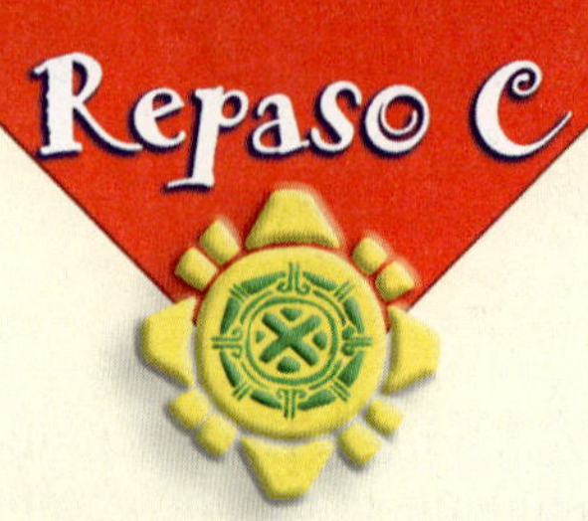

## Preview

In **Repaso C,** students review vocabulary relating to family and home; they also discuss some of their daily activities. In the **Estructura** section, they review the present of **-er** and **-ir** verbs, the verb **tener,** and possessive adjectives.

Students practice this vocabulary and these structures as they talk about their families, homes, and neighbors.

### National Standards

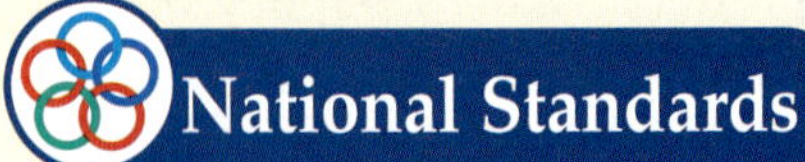

**Communication**

In Review Chapter C, students will communicate in spoken and written Spanish on the following topics:

- Describing their family
- Describing their home

Students will also learn to narrate present events. They will obtain and provide information and engage in conversations about home and family.

Repaso C

# La familia

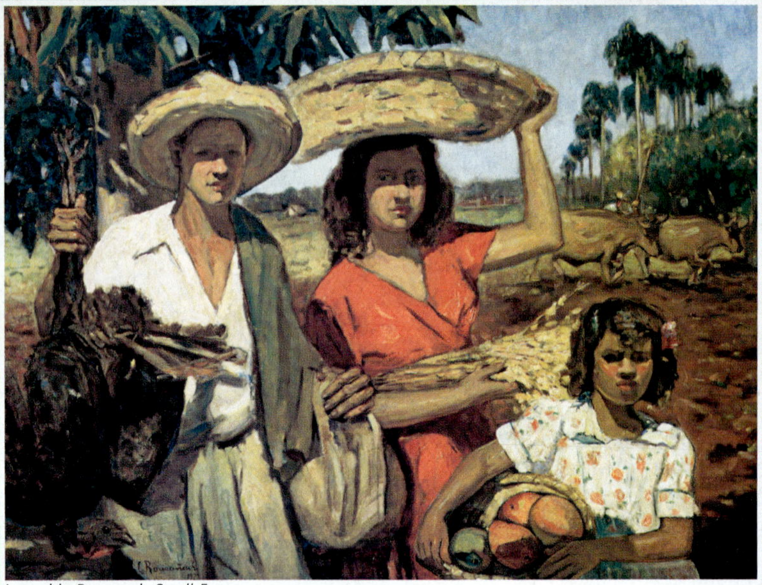

Leopoldo Romanach *Small Farmers*

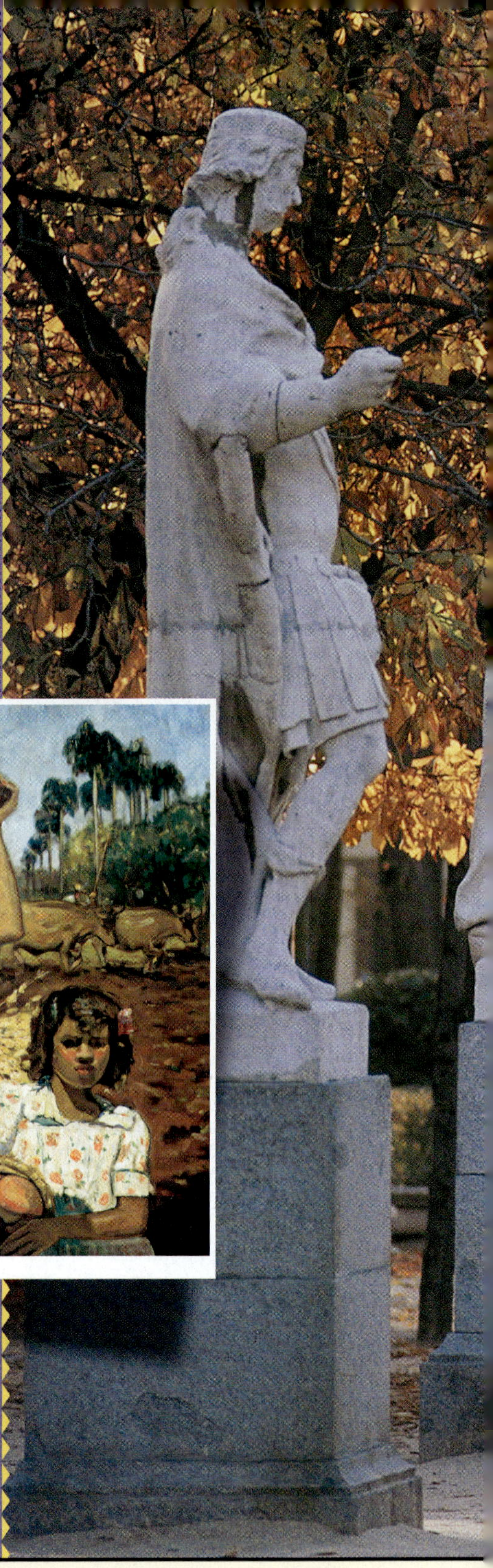

## Learning from Photos

*(pages R16–R17)* Ask the following questions about the photo of the **Parque del Retiro** after presenting the vocabulary on page R18.

**¿Está la familia en el parque?**
**El parque está en Madrid.**
**¿Es la primavera o el otoño en Madrid?**
**¿Lleva la familia ropa de invierno o ropa de verano?**
**¿Anda la familia por el parque?**
**¿Da la familia un paseo?**

## Vocabulario

### Resource Manager

Workbook, pages R11–R18
Tests, pages R5–R6, R19, R31

### Bellringer Review

*Use BRR Transparency R.6 or write the following on the board.*
Complete.

1. **El hermano de mi padre es mi ___.**
2. **La hija de mis tíos es mi ___.**
3. **Yo soy ___ de los padres de mis padres.**
4. **Los padres de mis padres son mis ___.**

### PRESENTATION

**Step 1** Have students open their books to page R18. As you review the vocabulary, have students repeat the words and sentences after you.

**Step 2** Ask questions such as: **¿Es la familia Ramos? ¿Cuántas personas hay en la familia Ramos? ¿Dónde tienen ellos una casa? ¿En qué país viven ellos? ¿Son hondureños?**

**Step 3** Once you have asked your questions about all the illustrations and photos, have students say everything they can about them.



## Vocabulario

Es la familia Ramos.
En la familia Ramos hay cinco personas.
Ellos tienen una casa en San Pedro Sula.
Ellos viven en Honduras.

Su casa tiene siete cuartos.

La familia está en la sala.
La señora Ramos lee un libro.
Su esposo lee el periódico.
José ve la televisión.
Una hermana de José escribe una carta.

En el mercado venden frutas y vegetales.
Venden carne también.
La señora compra un kilo de tomates.
Los tomates están a 50 pesos el kilo.

## 1 Historieta La familia Ramos Contesten.

1. ¿Cuántas personas hay en la familia Ramos?
2. ¿Tienen ellos una casa o un apartamento?
3. ¿Dónde viven ellos?
4. ¿Cuántos cuartos tiene su casa?
5. ¿Cuáles son los cuartos de la casa?

San Miguel de Allende, México

## 2 Expresiones Pareen.

| | |
|---|---|
| 1. leer | a. mucho en la escuela |
| 2. escribir | b. al quinto piso |
| 3. vivir | c. una novela |
| 4. aprender | d. un alumno bueno y serio |
| 5. vender | e. una carta con bolígrafo |
| 6. comer | f. una limonada |
| 7. ver | g. en una casa particular |
| 8. ser | h. una emisión deportiva |
| 9. subir | i. CDs en una tienda |
| 10. beber | j. carne, ensalada y papas |

## 3  ¿Cuáles son? Contesten.

1. ¿Cuáles son algunas cosas que comemos?
2. ¿Cuáles son algunas cosas que bebemos?
3. ¿Cuáles son algunas cosas que leemos?
4. ¿Cuáles son algunas cosas que escribimos?



## Answers to Repaso

**1**

1. Hay cinco personas en la familia Ramos.
2. Tienen una casa.
3. Ellos viven en Honduras.
4. Su casa tiene siete cuartos.
5. Son la sala, el comedor, la cocina, el cuarto de baño y tres cuartos (recámaras).

**2** *(Please note that numbers 5 and 7 have more than one possible answer. However, for the activity to work as a whole, only one answer is possible for each question.)*

| | |
|---|---|
| 1. c | 6. j |
| 2. e | 7. h |
| 3. g | 8. d |
| 4. a | 9. b |
| 5. i | 10. f |

**3** *Answers will vary. Students should attempt to recall vocabulary they have previously learned.*

# Repaso C

## Vocabulario

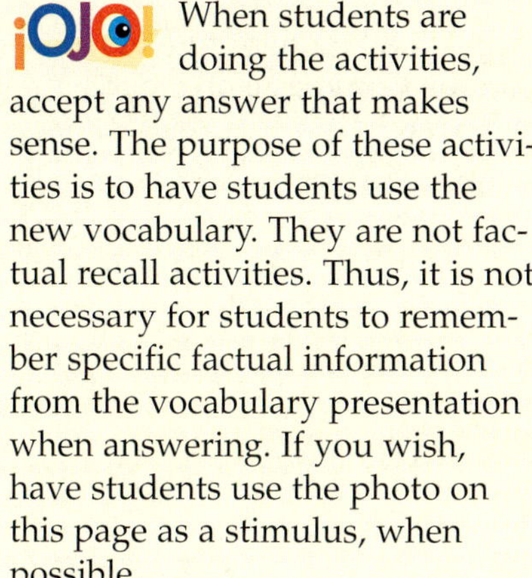

### PRACTICE

**¡OJO!** When students are doing the activities, accept any answer that makes sense. The purpose of these activities is to have students use the new vocabulary. They are not factual recall activities. Thus, it is not necessary for students to remember specific factual information from the vocabulary presentation when answering. If you wish, have students use the photo on this page as a stimulus, when possible.

**Historieta** Each time **Historieta** appears, it means that the answers to the activity form a short story. Encourage students to look at the title of the **Historieta,** since it can help them do the activity.

**¡OJO!** Go over the activities as quickly as possible. If students appear to have a good command of the vocabulary, it is not necessary that they write the activities.

However, if you feel students need additional reinforcement of the vocabulary, have them write the activities after you go over them orally in class.

**3 Juego** You may wish to have students work in small groups to play this game. See which group can come up with the longest list for each category.

### Learning from Photos

*(page R19)* Students learned something about San Miguel de Allende in **¡Buen viaje! Level 1.** Ask them if they remember anything about San Miguel.

You may also wish to have them say as much as they can about the house in the photo.

Repaso C

## Conversación

### PRESENTATION

**Step 1** Call on two students to read the **Conversación** aloud.

**Step 2** Then go over the **¿Comprendes?** activity.

# Conversación

## ¿Dónde viven?

**Tomás** Elena, ¿tienes una familia grande?
**Elena** Sí, bastante grande. Somos seis.
**Tomás** ¿Viven ustedes aquí en la capital?
**Elena** Sí, vivimos en la calle Mayor. Nuestro apartamento está en el edificio Bolívar.

### ¿Comprendes?

Contesten.

1. ¿Con quién habla Tomás?
2. ¿Tiene Elena una familia bastante grande?
3. ¿Cuántas personas hay en su familia?
4. ¿Viven ellos en la capital?
5. ¿En qué calle viven?
6. ¿Dónde tienen un apartamento?

Málaga, España



### Answers to ¿Comprendes?

1. Tomás habla con Elena.
2. Sí, Elena tiene una familia bastante grande.
3. Hay seis personas en su familia.
4. Sí, ellos viven en la capital.
5. Viven en la calle Mayor.
6. Tienen un apartamento en el edificio Bolívar.

# Estructura

## Presente de los verbos en -er e -ir

1. Review the following forms of regular **-er** and **-ir** verbs.

| | | | | | | |
|---|---|---|---|---|---|---|
| COMER | como | comes | come | comemos | *coméis* | comen |
| BEBER | bebo | bebes | bebe | bebemos | *bebéis* | beben |
| VIVIR | vivo | vives | vive | vivimos | *vivís* | viven |
| SUBIR | subo | subes | sube | subimos | *subís* | suben |

2. Note that the **-er** and **-ir** verbs have the same endings in all forms except **nosotros** (and **vosotros**).

| | |
|---|---|
| comemos | vivimos |
| *coméis* | *vivís* |

Lima, Perú



# Estructura

### Bellringer Review

*Use BRR Transparency R.7 or write the following on the board.*
Do the following.
1. Write five things you can eat.
2. Write three things you can drink.
3. Write the names of the three meals.

## PRESENTATION

### Presente de los verbos en -er e -ir

**Step 1** Have students repeat all the verb forms after you.

**Step 2** Write two of the verbs (one **-er** and one **-ir** verb) on the board and have students repeat all forms after you.

**Step 3** Read Item 2 aloud and underline the endings to emphasize that **-er** and **-ir** verbs have the same endings in all forms except **nosotros** (and **vosotros**).

### Learning from Photos

*(page 21)* With a metropolitan population of over seven million, Lima is the capital and largest city of Peru. The city has an abundance of residential neighborhoods, with a mixture of colonial and high-rise architecture.

# Repaso C

## Estructura

### Bellringer Review

*Use BRR Transparency R.8 or write the following on the board.*
Write an original sentence using each of the following verbs.

1. **vivir**
2. **leer**
3. **escribir**
4. **aprender**

**¡OJO!** Go over the activities orally in class. If you feel students need additional review, have them write the activities for homework.

**4 Tú y tus amigos** Contesten.

1. ¿Qué comes cuando vas a un café?
2. ¿Qué bebes cuando estás en un café?
3. ¿Qué aprenden tú y tus amigos en la escuela?
4. ¿Qué leen ustedes en la clase de inglés?
5. ¿Qué escriben ustedes?
6. ¿Comprenden los alumnos cuando la profesora de español habla?
7. ¿Reciben ustedes notas buenas en todas sus asignaturas?

**5 Historieta En un café** Completen.

En el café los clientes __1__ (ver) al mesero. Ellos __2__ (hablar) con el mesero. Los clientes __3__ (leer) el menú y __4__ (decidir) lo que van a tomar. Los meseros __5__ (tomar) la orden y __6__ (escribir) la orden en un cuaderno pequeño o un bloc. Los meseros no __7__ (leer) el menú. Y los clientes no __8__ (escribir) la orden.

RINCÓN EXTREMEÑO, S. L.
HOTEL ★ · CAFETERIA · RESTAURANTE !!
C/. Vidrieras, 6
Teléfs.: (927) 41 11 50 - 41 11 54 - 41 11 58
Fax (927) 42 06 27
10600 PLASENCIA (Cáceres)
C. I. F.: B-10034379

CLIENTE MESA Nº 1
D.N.I. :
FECHA FACT. 28/09
FRA. NUMERO 0004240
N.º HABITACION

| N.º ALBARAN | FECHA | CONCEPTO | UNIDADES | PRECIO DTO. | IMPORTE |
|---|---|---|---|---|---|
| 0000001 | 28/09 | CRIADILLAS DE TIERRA AL AJO | 1.00 | 9,00 | 9,00 |
| 0000001 | 28/09 | REVUELTO DE PIG. Y TRIG. | 1.00 | 6,60 | 6,60 |
| 0000001 | 28/09 | PIQUILLO RELLENO | 1.00 | 6,00 | 6,00 |
| 0000001 | 28/09 | CABRITO AJILLO | 1.00 | 9,50 | 9,50 |
| 0000001 | 28/09 | FRASCA DE LA CASA 3/4 | 1.00 | 3,30 | 3,30 |
| 0000001 | 28/09 | AGUA 1/2 L. O GASEOSA | 1.00 | 1,50 | 1,50 |
| 0000001 | 28/09 | PAN | 2.00 | ,50 | ,50 |
| 0000001 | 28/09 | POSTRES | 1.00 | 1,30 | 1,30 |

SUMA 37,70
7.00 % I. V. A. 2,64
TOTAL 40,34

Manta, Ecuador



### Answers to Repaso

**4**

1. Como ___ cuando voy a un café.
2. Bebo ___ cuando voy a un café.
3. Mis amigos y yo aprendemos ___en la escuela.
4. Nosotros leemos ___ en la clase de inglés.
5. Nosotros escribimos ___.
6. Sí (No), los alumnos (no) comprenden cuando la profesora de español habla.
7. Sí (No), nosotros (no) recibimos notas buenas en todas nuestras asignaturas.

**5**

1. ven
2. hablan
3. leen
4. deciden
5. toman
6. escriben
7. leen
8. escriben

## El verbo **tener**

1. Review the forms of the irregular verb **tener.**

   TENER **tengo** **tienes** **tiene** **tenemos** ***tenéis*** **tienen**

2. Note that the expression **tener que** followed by an infinitive means *to have to.*

   **Tenemos que estudiar y aprender mucho.**

Barcelona, España

**6 Historieta Mi familia** Contesten.

1. ¿Tienes una familia grande o pequeña?
2. ¿Cuántos hermanos tienes?
3. ¿Cuántos años tienen ellos?
4. ¿Y cuántos años tienes tú?
5. ¿Tienen ustedes un perro o un gato?
6. ¿Tiene tu padre o tu madre un carro?
7. En la escuela, ¿tienes que estudiar mucho?
8. ¿Y tienen que trabajar mucho tus padres?

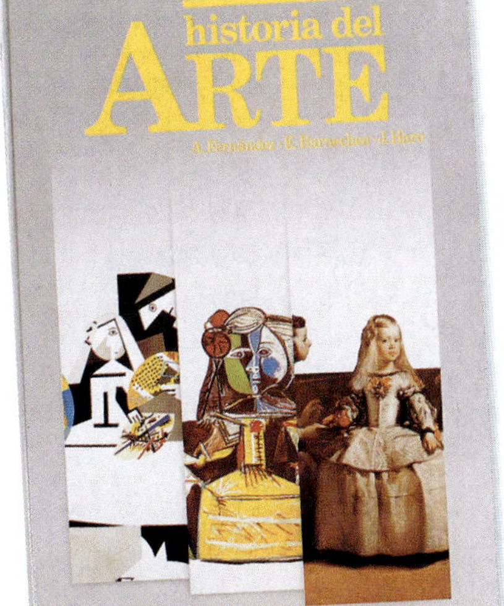


**7 Historieta La familia Bravo**
Completen con **tener.**

La familia Bravo __1__ un piso o apartamento en Madrid. Su piso __2__ seis cuartos. Está en Salamanca, una zona muy bonita de la ciudad. Muchas calles en la zona Salamanca __3__ los nombres de artistas famosos—la calle Goya, la calle Velázquez.

Hay cuatro personas en la familia Bravo. Teresa __4__ diecisiete años y su hermano __5__ quince años. Ellos __6__ un perro adorable.



## Repaso C

### Estructura

#### PRESENTATION

**El verbo tener**

**Step 1** Have students repeat the forms of the verb **tener.**

**Step 2** Read the information in Item 2 about **tener que** to the class.

**Step 3** Have students make up additional sentences using **tener que.**

#### PRACTICE

**Paired Activity**
Activity 6 can be done in pairs as an interview.

**Writing Development**
After going over Activity 6 orally, have students rewrite the information in their own words in paragraph form.

### Answers to Repaso

**6**

1. Tengo una familia grande (pequeña).
2. Tengo ___ hermano(a)(s). (No tengo hermanos[as]).
3. Ellos tienen ___ años.
4. Yo tengo ___ años.
5. Sí, nosotros tenemos un perro (un gato). (No, no tenemos un perro [un gato]).
6. Sí, mi padre (mi madre) tiene un carro.
7. Sí, (No, no) tengo que estudiar mucho en la escuela.
8. Sí (No), mis padres (no) tienen que trabajar mucho.

**7**

1. tiene
2. tiene
3. tienen
4. tiene
5. tiene
6. tienen

# Repaso C

## Estructura

### Bellringer Review

*Use BRR Transparency R.9 or write the following on the board.*
Answer.

1. **¿Dónde vives?**
2. **¿Tienes una familia grande o pequeña?**
3. **¿Cuántos años tienes?**
4. **Y tu hermano(a), ¿cuántos años tiene?**
5. **¿Tienen ustedes un perro o gato?**

## PRESENTATION

### Adjetivos posesivos

**Step 1** Have students open their books to page R24. Go over Items 1 and 2 with them. Have them read the model sentences aloud.

**Step 2** After you have gone over the explanation with them, ask students to make up some original sentences using the possessive adjectives.

**Step 3** Go over the activities orally in class. Assign them for written homework if you feel additional review and reinforcement are necessary.

### Learning from Realia

*(page R24)* You may wish to ask the following question about the realia:
**¿Es *Hogares* una revista o un periódico?**

## Adjetivos posesivos

1. Review the forms of the possessive adjectives **mi, tu,** and **su.** These adjectives have only two forms.

   **¿Dan una fiesta tu hermana y tus primos?**
   **Sí, mi hermana y mis primos dan una fiesta.**
   **Todos sus amigos van a recibir una invitación a su fiesta.**

2. The possessive adjective **nuestro** has four forms.

   **Nuestro primo, nuestra tía, nuestras sobrinas y nuestros abuelos viven todos en Madrid.**

### ¿Te acuerdas?

In Spain, **vuestro** is the adjective that corresponds to **vosotros:**
**vuestro piso**
**vuestra prima**

### 8 Historieta Mi familia y mi casa Contesten.

1. ¿Dónde está tu casa o tu apartamento?
2. ¿Cuántos cuartos tiene tu casa o tu apartamento?
3. ¿Cuántas personas hay en tu familia?
4. ¿Dónde viven tus abuelos?
5. Y tus primos, ¿dónde viven?

### 9 Historieta Nuestra casa Completen.

Nosotros vivimos en ___ *(name of city or town)*. _1_ casa está en la calle ___ *(name of street)*. _2_ padres tienen un carro. _3_ carro es bastante nuevo. Yo tengo una bicicleta. _4_ bicicleta está en el garaje con el carro de _5_ padres. Nosotros tenemos un perro. _6_ perro es adorable. _7_ perro está en el jardín. Mi hermano y _8_ amigos siempre juegan en el jardín alrededor de _9_ casa.

## Answers to Repaso

**8**

1. Mi casa (apartamento) está en ___.
2. Mi casa (apartamento) tiene ___ cuartos.
3. Hay ___ personas en mi familia.
4. Mis abuelos viven en ___.
5. Mis primos viven en ___.

**9**

1. Nuestra
2. Nuestros
3. Nuestro
4. Mi
5. mis
6. Nuestro
7. Nuestro
8. sus
9. nuestra

**10** **Apartamentos** With a classmate, look at this plan of the fourth floor of an apartment building. A different family lives in each of the two apartments. Give each family a name. Then say as much as you can about each family and their activities. Don't forget to describe their apartment. Be as original as possible.

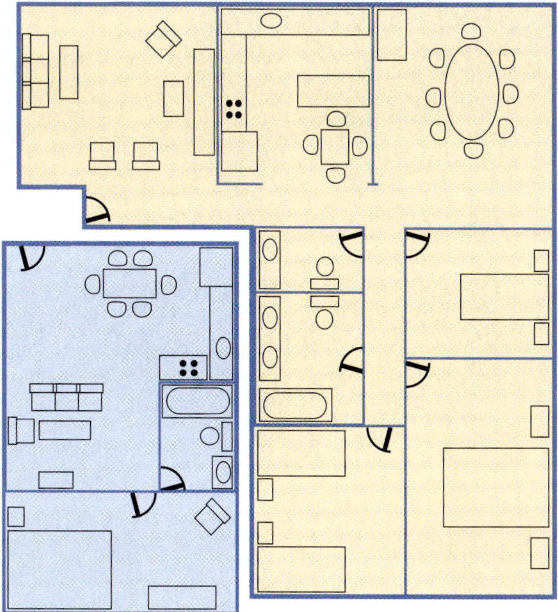

**11** **En el café** Work in groups of three or four. You're all friends from Uruguay. After school you go to a café where you talk about lots of things—school, teachers, friends, home, family, etc. One of you will be the waiter or waitress. You have to interrupt the conversation once in a while to take the orders and serve. Take turns.

Montevideo, Uruguay

## Estructura

### PRACTICE

**¡OJO!** Note that the activities are color-coded. All the activities in the text are communicative. However, the ones with blue titles are guided communication. The red titles indicate that the answers to the activity are more open-ended and can vary more. You may wish to correct students' mistakes more so in the guided activities than in the activities with a red title, which lend themselves to a freer response.

**10** Encourage students to be as creative as possible when doing this activity. They can make up a lot of funny things.

**11** Have students present their conversations to the entire class.

### Answers to Repaso

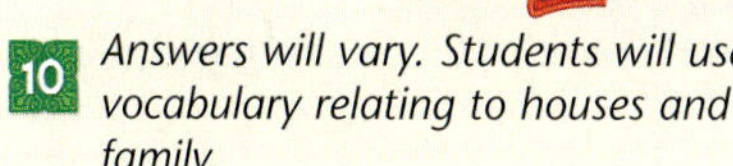

**10** *Answers will vary. Students will use vocabulary relating to houses and family.*

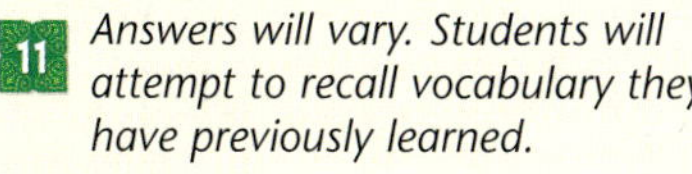

**11** *Answers will vary. Students will attempt to recall vocabulary they have previously learned.*

# Repaso D

## Preview

In **Repaso D,** students review vocabulary associated with team sports. In the **Estructura** section they review the present tense of stem-changing verbs and expressions with **aburrir, interesar,** and **gustar.**

Students practice this vocabulary and these structures as they talk about the sports and teams that they like.

### National Standards

**Communication**

In Review Chapter D, students will communicate in spoken and written Spanish on the following topic:

- Individual and team sports

Students will also learn to narrate present events. They will obtain and provide information and engage in conversations about sports.

Repaso D

# Los deportes

Pablo Picasso *Footballeurs*

### Learning from Photos

*(pages R26–R27)* You may wish to ask the following questions about the photo of **el Estadio Azteca** in Mexico City:

**¿Hay muchos espectadores en el estadio?**

**En tu opinión, ¿cuántos espectadores hay?**

**¿Dónde están los jugadores?**

**¿Se divierten los espectadores?**

## Vocabulario

### Resource Manager

Workbook, pages R19–R24
Tests, pages R7–R8, R22, R34

### Bellringer Review

*Use BRR Transparency R.10 or write the following on the board.*
Do the following.
1. Write six words associated with soccer.
2. Write five words associated with baseball.
3. Write four words associated with tennis.

### PRESENTATION

**Step 1** Have students open their books to page R28. Ask them questions such as: **¿Cuántos equipos hay? ¿Qué juegan? ¿Qué empieza? ¿Adónde vuelven los jugadores? ¿Qué quieren hacer los dos equipos?**

**Step 2** Have students repeat the miniconversation with as much expression as possible.

**Step 3** After going over the specific vocabulary on this page, have students say all the words they remember that are associated with team sports.

## Vocabulario

Los dos equipos juegan (al) fútbol.
Empieza el segundo tiempo.
Los jugadores vuelven al campo de fútbol.
Los dos equipos quieren ganar.

Es un partido de béisbol.
El jugador batea la pelota.
Luego corre de una base a otra.

## 1 Historieta El juego de fútbol

Contesten según se indica.

1. ¿Cuántos tiempos hay en un juego de fútbol? (dos)
2. ¿Cuántos jugadores hay en un equipo de fútbol? (once)
3. ¿Dónde juegan fútbol? (en el campo de fútbol)
4. ¿Quién guarda la portería? (el portero)
5. ¿Qué bloquea? (el balón)
6. ¿Quieren perder los dos equipos? (no, ganar)
7. ¿Pierde un equipo si el tanto queda empatado? (no)

## 2 ¿Qué deporte es? Escojan.

1. El jugador lanza el balón con el pie.
2. Hay cinco jugadores en el equipo.
3. Hay nueve entradas en el partido.
4. El jugador corre de una base a otra.
5. El portero para o bloquea el balón.
6. El jugador tira el balón y encesta.

## 3 Gustos Contesten.

1. ¿Cuáles son los deportes que a ti te gustan?
2. ¿Cuáles son los comestibles que te gustan?
3. ¿Cuáles son los cursos que te interesan?
4. ¿Cuáles son algunas cosas que no te gustan, que te aburren?



# Repaso D

## Vocabulario

### PRACTICE

**¡OJO!** When students are doing the activities, accept any answer that makes sense. The purpose of these activities is to have students use the new vocabulary. They are not factual recall activities. Thus, it is not necessary for students to remember specific factual information from the vocabulary presentation when answering. If you wish, have students use the photos on this page as a stimulus, when possible.

**Historieta** Each time **Historieta** appears, it means that the answers to the activity form a short story. Encourage students to look at the title of the **Historieta,** since it can help them do the activity.

**1** Go over the activity orally with books closed.

**Expansion:** After going over Activity 1, have one or more students describe a soccer game in their own words. They can use this activity as a guide.

**2** Activity 2 can be done as a game.

**3** Activity 3 gives students the opportunity to recycle a great deal of general vocabulary from **¡Buen viaje! Level 1.**

### ANSWERS TO Repaso

**1**

1. Hay dos tiempos en un juego de fútbol.
2. Hay once jugadores en un equipo de fútbol.
3. Juegan fútbol en el campo de fútbol.
4. El portero guarda la portería.
5. Bloquea el balón.
6. No, los dos equipos quieren ganar.
7. No, un equipo no pierde si el tanto queda empatado.

**2**

1. el fútbol
2. el baloncesto
3. el béisbol
4. el béisbol
5. el fútbol
6. el baloncesto

**3** *Answers will vary. Students will attempt to recall vocabulary previously learned.*

Repaso D

## Conversación

### PRESENTATION

**Step 1** Call on two students to read the **Conversación** aloud with as much expression as possible.

**Step 2** After students have read the conversation, do the **¿Comprendes?** activity.

### About the Spanish Language

When referring to a sports team, one says **el Real** or **el Valencia,** for example, because the word **equipo** is understood.

Repaso D

# Conversación

## Un partido importante

**Tadeo** Isabel, ¿quieres ir al café Solís con nosotros?
**Isabel** Gracias, Tadeo, pero no puedo. Quiero ver el partido.
**Tadeo** ¿De qué partido hablas?
**Isabel** El Real juega contra el Valencia.
**Tadeo** ¿Cuál es tu equipo favorito? ¿Cuál te gusta más?
**Isabel** El Real.

ATLETICO de MADRID
¡AUPA ATLETI!

### ¿Comprendes?

Contesten.

1. ¿Adónde van los amigos de Tadeo?
2. ¿Quiere ir con ellos Isabel?
3. ¿Por qué no puede ir?
4. ¿Qué quiere ver?
5. ¿Qué equipos juegan?
6. ¿Cuál es el equipo favorito de Isabel?

Manuel Martínez
PRESENTADOR DEPORTIVO
CANAL CUATRO
TELEFONOS: 24-1015 - 24-4555
FAX (503) 24-5708
APARTADO POSTAL 444
SAN SALVADOR,
EL SALVADOR, C. A.

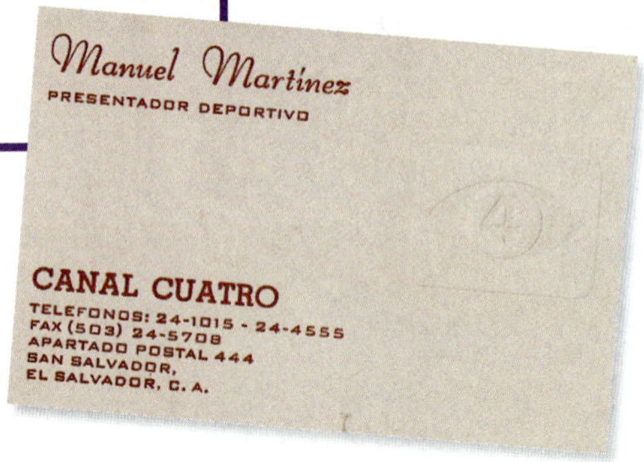

### Answers to ¿Comprendes?

1. Los amigos de Tadeo van al café Solís.
2. No, Isabel no quiere ir con ellos.
3. No puede ir porque quiere ver el partido.
4. Quiere ver el partido.
5. El Real juega contra el Valencia.
6. El Real es el equipo favorito de Isabel.

# Estructura

## Verbos de cambio radical

1. Review the following forms of stem-changing verbs. Remember that the **e** changes to **ie** in all forms except **nosotros** (and **vosotros**).

| | | | | | | |
|---|---|---|---|---|---|---|
| EMPEZAR | **empiezo** | **empiezas** | **empieza** | **empezamos** | *empezáis* | **empiezan** |
| PERDER | **pierdo** | **pierdes** | **pierde** | **perdemos** | *perdéis* | **pierden** |

2. The following verbs change the **o** to **ue** in all forms except **nosotros** (and **vosotros**).

| | | | | | | |
|---|---|---|---|---|---|---|
| VOLVER | **vuelvo** | **vuelves** | **vuelve** | **volvemos** | *volvéis* | **vuelven** |
| PODER | **puedo** | **puedes** | **puede** | **podemos** | *podéis* | **pueden** |

3. The verb **jugar** also has a stem change.

| | | | | | | |
|---|---|---|---|---|---|---|
| JUGAR | **juego** | **juegas** | **juega** | **jugamos** | *jugáis* | **juegan** |

**4** **Historieta Un juego de béisbol** Completen.

El juego de béisbol __1__ (empezar) a las tres y media. Habla Teresa:
—Hoy yo __2__ (querer) ser la pícher.

La verdad es que Teresa __3__ (ser) una pícher muy buena. Ella __4__ (jugar) muy bien. Nosotros __5__ (tener) un equipo bueno. Todos nosotros __6__ (jugar) bien. Nuestro equipo no __7__ (perder) mucho.

Caracas, Venezuela

# Estructura

## Bellringer Review

*Use BRR Transparency R.11 or write the following on the board.*
Complete.
1. Nosotros ___ en ___. (vivir)
2. Mi primo ___ francés y yo ___ español. (estudiar)
3. Nosotros no ___ en la misma clase. (estar)
4. Yo ___ alumno(a) en la Escuela ___. (ser)

## PRESENTATION

### Verbos de cambio radical

**Step 1** Have students repeat all the verb forms after you.

**Step 2** Then have students repeat all the **nosotros** forms.

**Step 3** Now have them repeat all the **yo** forms to contrast the stem change.

## PRACTICE

### Writing Development

After going over Activity 4 orally, have students rewrite the information in their own words in paragraph form.

### Learning from Photos

*(page R31)* Have students say everything they can about the photo of the baseball game in Caracas, Venezuela.

Answers to Repaso

**4**

1. empieza
2. quiero
3. es
4. juega
5. tenemos
6. jugamos
7. pierde

## Estructura

### PRACTICE *(continued)*

**5** Students can ask each other these questions.

**6** **Juego** Encourage students to give as many answers as they can. Elicit multiple responses so students can review the use of the infinitive after an auxiliary verb.

#### Bellringer Review

*Use BRR Transparency R.12 or write the following on the board.*
Write the names of six school subjects.

### PRESENTATION

**Verbos como aburrir, interesar y gustar**

As you go over the explanation and the activities, have students point to themselves as they say **me** and have them look at a friend as they say **te.**

**5** **Historieta Una fiesta** Contesten.

1. ¿Quieres ir a la fiesta?
2. ¿Quieren ustedes bailar durante la fiesta?
3. ¿A qué hora empieza la fiesta?
4. ¿Puedes llegar a tiempo?
5. ¿Pueden ustedes tomar el bus a la fiesta?
6. ¿A qué hora vuelven ustedes a casa?

**6** **Juego Puedo, quiero, prefiero**

1. **Puedo…** Tell all that you can do.
2. **Quiero…** Tell all that you want to do.
3. **Quiero pero no puedo…** Tell all that you want to do but for some reason you cannot do.
4. **No quiero porque prefiero…** Tell something you don't want to do because you prefer to do something else.

## Verbos como **aburrir, interesar** y **gustar**

1. The verbs **interesar** and **aburrir** function the same in Spanish and English.

   **¿Te aburre el arte?**
   *Does art bore you?*
   **¿Te aburren los deportes?**
   *Do sports bore you?*
   **No, los deportes me interesan.**
   *No, sports interest me.*

2. The verb **gustar** functions the same as **interesar** and **aburrir. Gustar** conveys the meaning "to like," but it actually means "to be pleasing to."

   **¿Te gusta el béisbol?**
   **Sí, me gusta mucho.**
   **¿Te gustan los deportes?**
   **Sí, me gustan.**

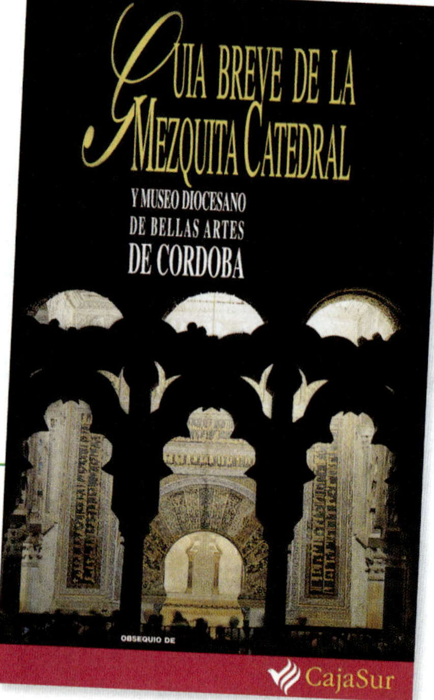

### Answers to Repaso

**5**

1. Sí, (No, no) quiero ir a la fiesta.
2. Sí, (No, no) queremos bailar durante la fiesta.
3. La fiesta empieza a las ___.
4. Sí, (No, no) puedo llegar a tiempo.
5. Sí (No), nosotros (no) podemos tomar el bus a la fiesta.
6. Nosotros volvemos a casa a las ___.

**6** *Answers will vary. Students will practice using the infinitive form after these verbs; they will also recall vocabulary they have previously learned.*

7 **Gustos** Sigan el modelo.

**¿A mí? ¿Los tomates? ⟶**
**Me gustan mucho los tomates.**

1. ¿A mí? ¿El pescado?
2. ¿A mí? ¿Los vegetales?
3. ¿A mí? ¿La carne?
4. ¿A mí? ¿El jamón?
5. ¿A mí? ¿Los mariscos?

8 **¿Sí o no?** Contesten.

1. ¿Te interesan o te aburren las matemáticas? ¿Te gustan o no?
2. ¿Te interesa o te aburre la historia? ¿Te gusta o no?
3. ¿Te interesan o te aburren las ciencias? ¿Te gustan o no?
4. ¿Te interesa o te aburre la literatura? ¿Te gusta o no?
5. ¿Te interesa o te aburre la geografía? ¿Te gusta o no?

9 **¿Qué te gusta hacer?** Contesten según los dibujos.

1. 
2. 
3. 
4. 

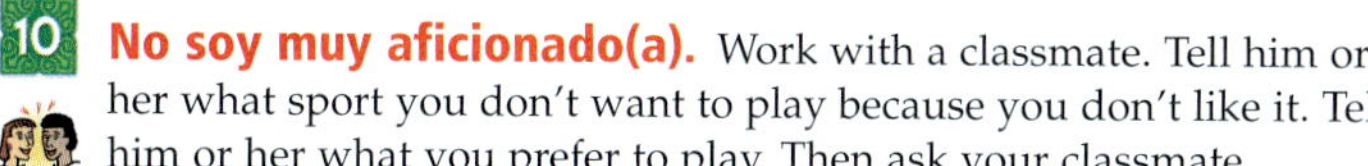

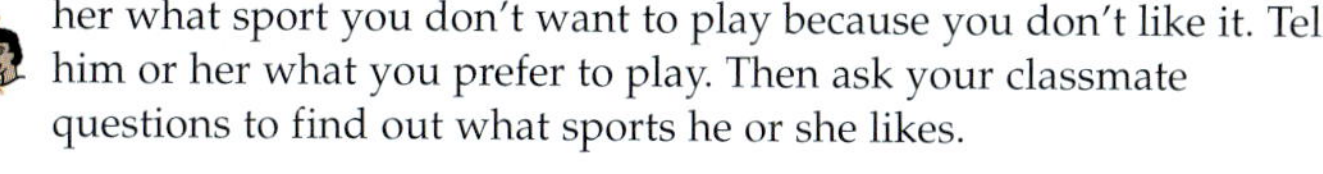

10 **No soy muy aficionado(a).** Work with a classmate. Tell him or her what sport you don't want to play because you don't like it. Tell him or her what you prefer to play. Then ask your classmate questions to find out what sports he or she likes.

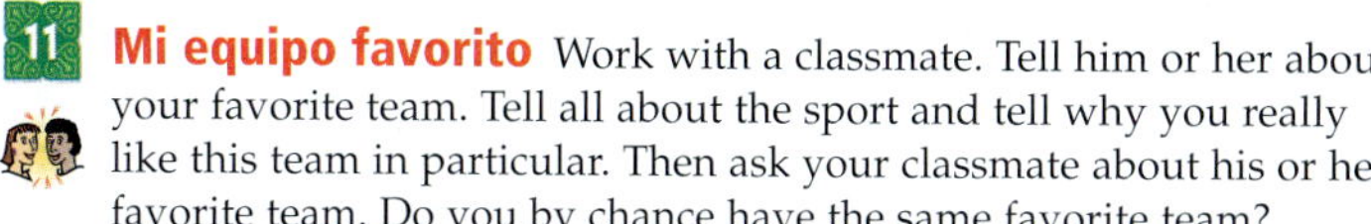

11 **Mi equipo favorito** Work with a classmate. Tell him or her about your favorite team. Tell all about the sport and tell why you really like this team in particular. Then ask your classmate about his or her favorite team. Do you by chance have the same favorite team?

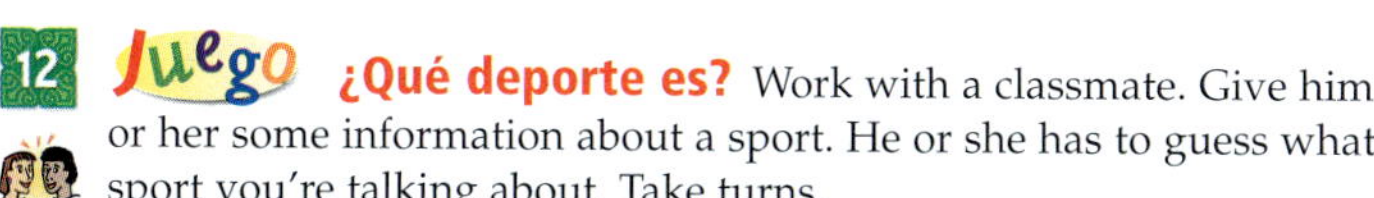

12 **Juego** **¿Qué deporte es?** Work with a classmate. Give him or her some information about a sport. He or she has to guess what sport you're talking about. Take turns.



# Repaso D

## Estructura

### PRACTICE

**¡OJO!** Note that the activities are color-coded. All the activities in the text are communicative. However, the ones with blue titles are guided communication. The red titles indicate that the answers to the activity are more open-ended and can vary more. You may wish to correct students' mistakes more so in the guided activities than in the activities with a red title, which lend themselves to a freer response.

**7 and 8** Have students do these activities orally using as much expression as possible.

**9** Have students refer to the illustrations as they do Activity 9.

**10, 11, and 12 Juego** Let students choose the activity or activities they wish to do.

## ANSWERS TO Repaso

**7**

1. Me gusta mucho el pescado.
2. Me gustan mucho los vegetales.
3. Me gusta mucho la carne.
4. Me gusta mucho el jamón.
5. Me gustan mucho los mariscos.

**8**

1. Me interesan (Me aburren) las matemáticas. Sí, (No, no) me gustan.
2. Me interesa (Me aburre) la historia. Sí, (No, no) me gusta.
3. Me interesan (Me aburren) las ciencias. Sí, (No, no) me gustan.
4. Me interesa (Me aburre) la literatura. Sí, (No, no) me gusta.
5. Me interesa (Me aburre) la geografía. Sí, (No, no) me gusta.

**9**

1. Me gusta cantar.
2. Me gusta comer.
3. Me gusta leer.
4. Me gusta escuchar música.

**10 and 11** *Answers will vary. Students will use vocabulary related to sports, stem-changing verbs, and verbs like* aburrir, interesar, *and* gustar.

**12** *Answers will vary but may include the following:*
—El jugador batea.
—Hay dos tiempos de 45 minutos.
—Los jugadores corren de una base a otra.

## Preview

In **Repaso E,** students review vocabulary dealing with airline travel and airports. In the **Estructura** section, students review the present tense of verbs with an irregular **yo** form, the difference between **saber** and **conocer,** and the present progressive.

Students practice this vocabulary and these structures as they plan a trip to a Spanish-speaking country and role-play making airline reservations.

### National Standards

**Communication**

In Review Chapter E, students will communicate in spoken and written Spanish on the following topic:

- Traveling by plane

Students will also learn to narrate in the present about whom and what they know. They will obtain and provide information and engage in conversations about traveling by plane.

# Un viaje en avión

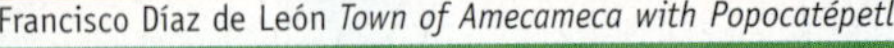

Francisco Díaz de León *Town of Amecameca with Popocatépetl*

**Learning from Photos**

*(pages R34–R35)* The relatively new international airport of Guanajuato is called **Aeropuerto el Bajío.** The **el Bajío** area was always known for its rich farmland but today is becoming more and more industrialized. Traffic at the **el Bajío** Airport has been increasing about twenty percent annually.

## Vocabulario

### Resource Manager

Workbook, pages R25–R30
Tests, pages R9–R10, R23, R35

### Bellringer Review

*Use BRR Transparency R.13 or write the following on the board.*
Write original sentences using the following verbs.
1. **mirar**
2. **tomar**
3. **leer**
4. **escribir**
5. **vivir**

### PRESENTATION

**¡OJO!** Before you begin your presentation, you may wish to ask students to say anything they can about the illustrations. If you find that they have a good command of the vocabulary, you can skip this review material and do the activities immediately.

**Step 1** Have students open their books to page R36. As you present the sentences, ask comprehension questions such as: **¿La agente revisa los boletos o revisa las maletas? ¿La agente tiene que revisar los pasaportes también? ¿El vuelo 102 sale con destino a México o con destino a Chile? ¿Sale a tiempo o sale con una demora?**

**Step 2** After reviewing the vocabulary orally, have students read the material for additional reinforcement.





## Vocabulario

Los pasajeros están en el aeropuerto.
La agente de la línea aérea revisa los boletos (billetes).
Tiene que mirar los pasaportes también.

Los pasajeros hacen un viaje en avión.
El vuelo 102 con destino a México sale de la puerta número diez.
El vuelo está saliendo a tiempo.
No sale con una demora.

Los pasajeros traen bastante equipaje de mano.
Ponen su equipaje de mano debajo del asiento.



### Learning from Photos

*(page R37 top)* You may wish to ask the following questions about the photo:
**¿Están haciendo cola los pasajeros delante del mostrador de la línea aérea?**
**¿Es larga la cola?**
**¿Cuántas personas hay en la cola?**
**¿Tienen mucho equipaje los pasajeros?**
**¿Tienen que facturar su equipaje?**

## 1 Historieta En el aeropuerto

Contesten. Inventen una historia.

1. ¿Están en el aeropuerto los pasajeros?
2. ¿Hacen un viaje en avión?
3. ¿Hablan con la agente de la línea aérea?
4. ¿Qué tiene que revisar la agente?
5. ¿Para dónde sale el vuelo?
6. ¿Está saliendo a tiempo o con una demora?
7. ¿Qué traen los pasajeros?
8. ¿Dónde ponen su equipaje de mano?

## 2 ¿Sí o no? Digan que sí o que no.

1. El avión aterriza cuando sale.
2. El avión despega cuando llega a su destino.
3. Un vuelo internacional es un vuelo que va a un país extranjero.
4. Los agentes de la línea aérea que trabajan en el mostrador en el aeropuerto son los asistentes de vuelo.
5. La tripulación consiste en los empleados que trabajan a bordo del avión.

Aerolínea argentina



## Answers to Repaso

**1**

1. Sí, los pasajeros están en el aeropuerto.
2. Sí, hacen un viaje en avión.
3. Sí, hablan con la agente de la línea aérea.
4. La agente tiene que revisar los boletos.
5. El vuelo sale para ___.
6. Está saliendo a tiempo (con una demora).
7. Los pasajeros traen equipaje de mano.
8. Ponen su equipaje de mano debajo del asiento.

**2**

1. No
2. No
3. Sí
4. No
5. Sí

# Repaso E

## Vocabulario

### PRACTICE

**¡OJO!** When students are doing the activities, accept any answer that makes sense. The purpose of these activities is to have students use the new vocabulary. They are not factual recall activities. Thus, it is not necessary for students to remember specific factual information from the vocabulary presentation when answering. If you wish, have students use the photos on this page as a stimulus, when possible.

**Historieta** Each time **Historieta** appears, it means that the answers to the activity form a short story. Encourage students to look at the title of the **Historieta,** since it can help them do the activity.

**1** This activity can be done orally with books closed.
**Expansion:** After going over Activity 1, call on a student to retell the story in his or her own words.

**2** Have students correct the false statements in Activity 2.

**¡OJO!** After going over the activities in class, you may have students write them for homework for additional reinforcement. Since this is review work, however, you may find that it is not necessary to have students do this. Try to get through these review lessons as quickly as possible.

## Conversación

### Bellringer Review

*Use BRR Transparency R.14 or write the following on the board.*
Write five words associated with an airport.

### PRESENTATION

**Step 1** Have the entire class repeat the **Conversación** once after you.

**Step 2** Call on two students to read the conversation using as much expression as possible.

**Step 3** Go over the **¿Comprendes?** activity.

**Expansion:** Have one or more students retell the information from the conversation in narrative form.

### Learning from Realia

*(page R38)* Have students answer the following questions:
**¿De qué país es el pasaporte?**
**¿Dónde está Nicaragua?**

# Conversación

## En el aeropuerto

**Felipe** Están anunciando la salida de nuestro vuelo, ¿no?
**Alejandra** Sí, sí. Es nuestro vuelo.
**Felipe** ¿De qué puerta sale?
**Alejandra** Sale de la puerta número once.
**Felipe** ¿Tenemos que pasar por el control de seguridad?
**Alejandra** Sí, tienen que tomar unos rayos equis de nuestro equipaje de mano.

### ¿Comprendes?

Corrijan las oraciones.

1. Están anunciando la llegada del vuelo de Felipe y Alejandra.
2. Su vuelo va a salir de la puerta número dos.
3. Ellos tienen que pasar por migración.
4. Tienen que tomar unos rayos equis de sus boletos y pasaportes.

### Answers to ¿Comprendes?

1. Están anunciando la salida del vuelo de Felipe y Alejandra.
2. Su vuelo sale de la puerta once.
3. Ellos tienen que pasar por el control de seguridad.
4. Tienen que tomar unos rayos equis de su equipaje de mano.

# Estructura

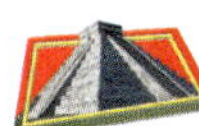

## Presente de algunos verbos irregulares

1. Many verbs that are irregular in the present tense are irregular only in the **yo** form. All other forms are regular. Study the following verbs that have a **g** in the **yo** form.

   | | |
   |---|---|
   | HACER | **hago** |
   | PONER | **pongo** |
   | TRAER | **traigo** |
   | SALIR | **salgo** |

2. The verbs **saber** and **conocer** also have an irregular **yo** form.

   | | |
   |---|---|
   | SABER | **sé** |
   | CONOCER | **conozco** |

   **Saber** is used to express knowledge of simple facts. **Conocer** means "to know" in the sense of to be acquainted with someone or something.

   **Yo sé que Madrid está en España.**
   **Yo conozco Madrid.**
   **Yo conozco a Eduardo también.**
   **Yo sé que él es de Madrid.**

Madrid, España

### 3 Historieta Un viaje imaginario

Contesten.

1. ¿Haces un viaje a España?
2. ¿Haces el viaje en avión?
3. Antes, ¿haces las maletas?
4. ¿Qué pones en las maletas?
5. ¿Cuándo sales?
6. ¿Sales para el aeropuerto en taxi?
7. ¿A qué hora sale tu vuelo?
8. A bordo del avión, ¿dónde ponen los pasajeros su equipaje de mano?
9. ¿Conoces la ciudad de Madrid?
10. ¿Sabes hablar español?

IBERIA TARJETA DE EMBARQUE

INFORMACION AL PASAJERO

| Vuelo | Destin | Hora Límite | Puerta | Clase | Su asiento |
|---|---|---|---|---|---|
| IB3127 | MAD | 12.45 | 15 | C | 8C |

LUNA/GABRIEL

LIS/22APR C 048

Conserve esta tarjeta hasta su destino



## Answers to Repaso

**3**

1. Sí, (No, no) hago un viaje a España.
2. Sí, (No, no) hago el viaje en avión.
3. Sí (No), antes, (no) hago las maletas.
4. Pongo ___ en las maletas.
5. Salgo a las ___.
6. Sí, (No, no) salgo para el aeropuerto en taxi.
7. Mi vuelo sale a las ___.
8. A bordo del avión, los pasajeros ponen su equipaje de mano debajo del asiento.
9. Sí, (No, no) conozco la ciudad de Madrid.
10. Sí, (No, no) sé hablar español.

## Repaso E

## Estructura

### Bellringer Review

*Use BRR Transparency R.15 or write the following on the board.*
Complete the following.

1. **Yo ___ un viaje en avión. (hacer)**
2. **Yo ___ para el aeropuerto en taxi. (salir)**
3. **Yo ___ la maleta en la maletera del taxi. (poner)**
4. **Yo___ adonde yo ___. (saber, ir)**

### PRESENTATION

#### Presente de algunos verbos irregulares

**Step 1** Have students repeat the **yo** form of these verbs several times.

**Step 2** Write all the forms of two or three of the verbs on the board to show students that all forms other than **yo** conform to the regular pattern. Have students repeat all forms.

**Step 3** Read the explanation in Item 2 about the use of **saber** and **conocer** to the class. Have students repeat the model sentences aloud.

### PRACTICE

**3** Go over this activity orally with books closed.

**Expansion:** Have a student retell all the information in Activity 3 in his or her own words.

#### Learning from Realia

*(page R39)* Have students find the following information: **el nombre del pasajero, el número del vuelo, el destino, la fecha del vuelo, la puerta, el número del asiento.** Explain: **El pasajero viaja en Clase C. C es el código para** *Business Class.*

# Estructura

## PRACTICE *(continued)*

**4** Have students prepare Activity 4 before you go over it in class.

## PRESENTATION

### El presente progresivo

**Step 1** Read Steps 1 and 2 aloud to the class.

**Step 2** Have students repeat the model sentences.

**4** **La maleta** Completen con **hacer, poner** o **salir.**

1. Juan ___ su maleta. Él ___ una camisa en la maleta. Él ___ para Málaga.
2. Nosotros ___ nuestra maleta. Nosotros ___ blue jeans en la maleta porque ___ para Cancún en México.
3. ¿Tú ___ tu maleta? ¿Qué ___ en la maleta? ¿Para dónde ___?
4. Mis padres ___ su maleta. Ellos ___ muchas cosas en la maleta. Ellos ___ su maleta porque ___ para Miami.

Málaga, España

## El presente progresivo

1. The present progressive tense is used to express an action or activity that is presently going on.

2. To form the present progressive, you use the present tense of the verb **estar** and the present participle. Review the forms of the present participle.

| | |
|---|---|
| HABLAR | **hablando** |
| COMER | **comiendo** |
| SALIR | **saliendo** |

**¿Qué está haciendo Teresa?**
**Teresa está esperando el avión porque está saliendo para México.**



## Answers to Repaso

**4**

1. hace, pone, sale
2. hacemos, ponemos, salimos
3. haces, pones, sales
4. hacen, ponen, hacen, salen

## 5 Historieta En el aeropuerto

Contesten según se indica.

1. ¿Adónde están llegando los pasajeros? (al aeropuerto)
2. ¿Cómo están llegando? (en taxi)
3. ¿Adónde están viajando? (a Colombia)
4. ¿Cómo están haciendo el viaje? (en avión)
5. ¿Dónde están facturando su equipaje? (en el mostrador de la línea aérea)
6. ¿Qué está mirando la agente? (los boletos y los pasaportes)

San Andrés, Colombia

## 6 Un boleto para Mérida

Work with a classmate. You want to fly from your hometown to Mérida, México. Call the airline to get a reservation. Your partner will be the reservations agent. Before you call, think about all the information you will need to give or get from the agent: date of departure, time, arrival time in Mérida, flight number, price, etc. Take turns.

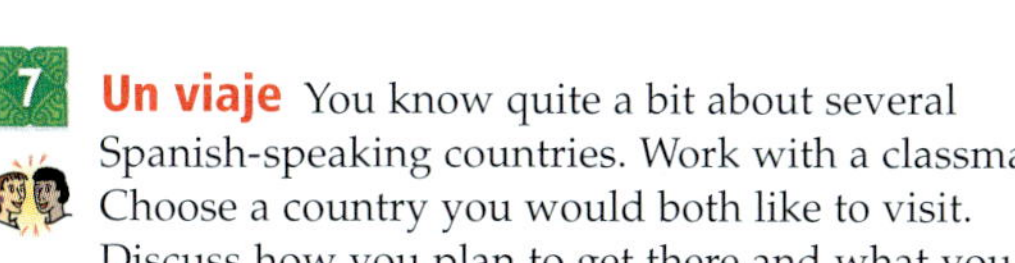

## 7 Un viaje

You know quite a bit about several Spanish-speaking countries. Work with a classmate. Choose a country you would both like to visit. Discuss how you plan to get there and what you are going to do and see there.

Mérida, México

## 8 El aeropuerto

Work with a classmate. Look at the illustration of the many activities taking place at an airport. Tell all about the illustration in your own words.

# Repaso E

## Estructura

### PRACTICE

¡OJO! Note that the activities are color-coded. All the activities in the text are communicative. However, the ones with blue titles are guided communication. The red titles indicate that the answers to the activity are more open-ended and can vary more. You may wish to correct students' mistakes more so in the guided activities than in the activities with a red title, which lend themselves to a freer response.

**5** Go over Activity 5 orally with books open.

**6**, **7**, and **8** These activities give students another opportunity to use words and structures learned previously. Have students work on as many activities as you wish. You may also allow them to select those activities they want to do. Different groups can work on different activities.

### Learning from Photos

*(page R41 top)* San Andrés, a small Columbian island located in the western Caribbean Sea, is one of several islands that make up the San Andrés Archipelago. San Andrés and the other islands in the archipelago are surrounded by an extensive coral reef and are considered luxury tourist destinations.
*(page R41 bottom)* Mérida is the capital of the Mexican state of Yucatán. It is home to the oldest cathedral on the American continent. At one time, Mérida was considered among the great Spanish colonial cities.

## Answers to Repaso

**5**

1. Los pasajeros están llegando al aeropuerto.
2. Están llegando en taxi.
3. Están viajando a Colombia.
4. Están haciendo el viaje en avión.
5. Están facturando su equipaje en el mostrador de la línea aérea.
6. La agente está mirando los boletos y los pasaportes.

**6**, **7**, and **8** *Answers will vary. Students will use the vocabulary relating to travel and airplanes, as well as the present tense of* hacer, poner, traer, *and* salir.

# Preview

In **Repaso F,** students review the vocabulary they need to discuss their daily routines and some good health and hygiene practices. In the **Estructura** section, they review the uses of **ser** and **estar** and reflexive verbs.

Students practice this vocabulary and these structures as they talk about a typical day and a visit to the doctor.

## National Standards

**Communication**

In Review Chapter F, students will communicate in spoken and written Spanish on the following topics:

- Daily routine
- Home activities

Students will also learn to narrate present events. They will obtain and provide information and engage in conversations about daily routines.

Repaso F

# La rutina y la salud

Gustavo Montoya *La merced*

R42

## Learning from Photos

*(pages R42–R43)* Lake Titicaca in Bolivia is the world's highest navigable lake (12,500 ft.). The lake has several islands, and its shoreline of bays and inlets is covered with farms going up terraced hills. Two indigenous groups, the Quechua and the Aymara, inhabit the area.

## Vocabulario

### Resource Manager

Workbook, pages R31–R36
Tests, pages R11–R12, R24, R36

### Bellringer Review

*Use BRR Transparency R.16 or write the following on the board.*

Match the following words.

| | |
|---|---|
| **1. cepillar** | **a. la cena** |
| **2. peinar** | **b. el almuerzo** |
| **3. desayunar** | **c. el desayuno** |
| **4. almorzar** | **d. el cepillo** |
| **5. cenar** | **e. el peine** |

### PRESENTATION

**Step 1** Have students open their books to page R44 and look at the photos.

**Step 2** Have them repeat the sentences two or three times after you.



# Vocabulario

Estefanía está bien.
Ella se levanta cada mañana a las seis y media.

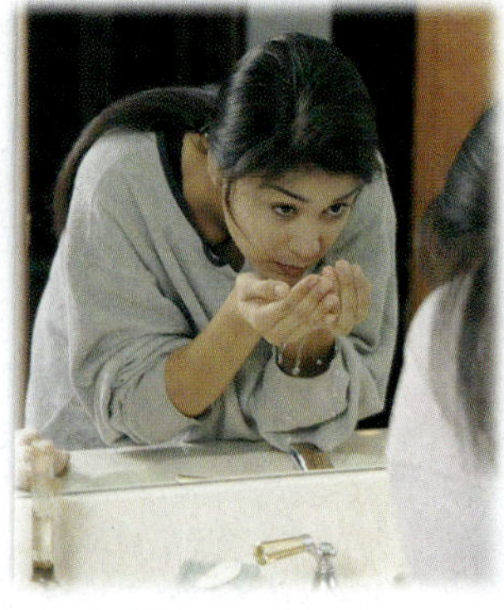

Ella se lava la cara.

Se peina.
Estefanía se mira en el espejo cuando se peina.

Juan no está bien hoy.
Está enfermo.
Tiene fiebre.
Tiene (una) tos.
Está en cama.

Juan va al consultorio de la médica.
Está en el consultorio.
La médica examina a Juan.

**1** **Historieta** **La rutina diaria** Contesten.

1. ¿A qué hora se levanta Claudia cada mañana?
2. ¿Ella se desayuna en casa?
3. Después de desayunarse, ¿se cepilla los dientes?
4. ¿Se lava la cara?
5. ¿A qué hora se acuesta ella cada noche?

**2** **La salud** Digan que sí o que no.

1. Cuando estamos cansados, queremos dormir.
2. Cuando estamos enfermos, vamos a ver al médico.
3. Tenemos que ir al hospital cuando tenemos un catarro.
4. Tenemos fiebre cuando tenemos la gripe.
5. Estamos contentos y nos sentimos bien cuando tenemos la temperatura elevada.
6. Tenemos que guardar cama cuando tenemos dolor de cabeza.

**3** **Juego** **El cuerpo** ¿Cuáles son los nombres de todas las partes del cuerpo que sabes en español?

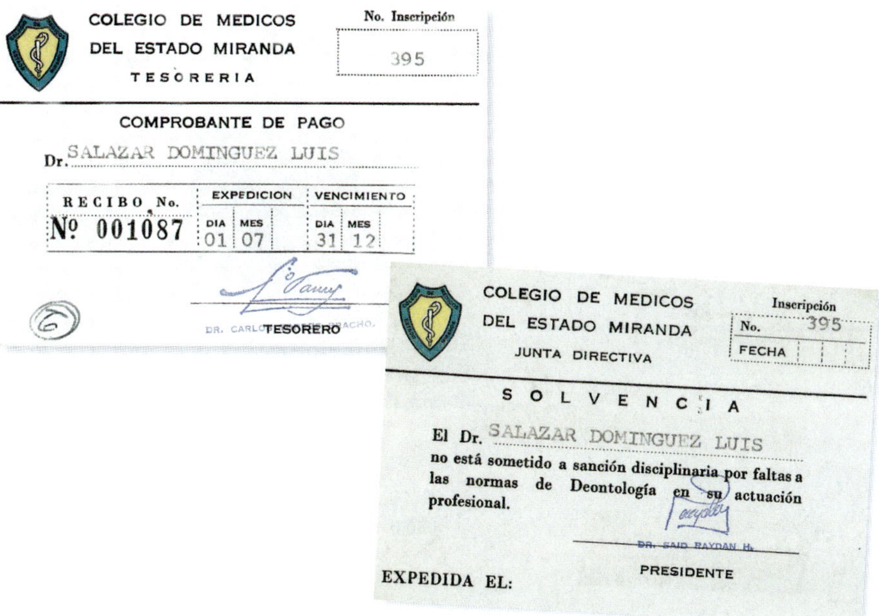

COLEGIO DE MEDICOS DEL ESTADO MIRANDA
TESORERIA
No. Inscripción 395

COMPROBANTE DE PAGO

Dr. SALAZAR DOMINGUEZ LUIS

| RECIBO No. | EXPEDICION DIA | EXPEDICION MES | VENCIMIENTO DIA | VENCIMIENTO MES |
|---|---|---|---|---|
| Nº 001087 | 01 | 07 | 31 | 12 |

TESORERO

COLEGIO DE MEDICOS DEL ESTADO MIRANDA
JUNTA DIRECTIVA
Inscripción No. 395
FECHA

SOLVENCIA

El Dr. SALAZAR DOMINGUEZ LUIS no está sometido a sanción disciplinaria por faltas a las normas de Deontología en su actuación profesional.

DR. SAID RAYDAN H.
PRESIDENTE

EXPEDIDA EL:



## Answers to Repaso

**1**

1. Claudia se levanta cada mañana a las ___.
2. Sí (No), ella (no) se desayuna en casa.
3. Sí (No), después de desayunarse, (no) se cepilla los dientes.
4. Sí, (No, no) se lava la cara.
5. Ella se acuesta a las ___ cada noche.

**2**

1. Sí
2. Sí
3. No
4. Sí
5. No
6. No

**3** *Answers will vary. Students will use the vocabulary relating to parts of the body learned in* **¡Buen viaje! Level 1.**

# Repaso F

## Vocabulario

### PRACTICE

**¡OJO!** When students are doing the activities, accept any answer that makes sense. The purpose of these activities is to have students use the new vocabulary. They are not factual recall activities. Thus, it is not necessary for students to remember specific factual information from the vocabulary presentation when answering. If you wish, have students use the photos on this page as a stimulus, when possible.

**Historieta** Each time **Historieta** appears, it means that the answers to the activity form a short story. Encourage students to look at the title of the **Historieta,** since it can help them do the activity.

**1** Go over this activity orally with books closed.

**2** Have students correct the false statements in this activity.

**3** **Juego**  You may wish to have each student do this individually and see who can prepare the longest list.

# Repaso F

## Conversación

### PRESENTATION

**Step 1** Call on two students to read this short conversation to the class.

**Step 2** Go over the **¿Comprendes?** activity.

### Learning from Realia

*(page R46)* Have students read the ad. You may wish to explain to them that **¿Es muy perro?** means *Is it awful, really bad?* Have them tell you in their own words what the advertisement means.

## Conversación

### ¿Cómo estás?

**Sandra** ¿Cómo estás, Pepe?
**Pepe** La verdad es que no me siento muy bien.
**Sandra** ¿Estás enfermo? ¿Qué tienes?
**Pepe** Tengo dolor de garganta y estoy cansado.
**Sandra** Pues, sabes donde está la consulta del médico, ¿no?

### ¿Comprendes?

Contesten.

1. ¿Cómo está Pepe?
2. ¿Cómo se siente él?
3. ¿Qué tiene?
4. ¿Tiene mucha energía?
5. ¿Está cansado?
6. ¿Adónde debe ir?

### Answers to ¿Comprendes?

1. Pepe no está bien.
2. Él no se siente muy bien.
3. Tiene dolor de garganta.
4. No, no tiene mucha energía.
5. Sí, está cansado.
6. Debe ir a la consulta del médico.

# Estructura

## Ser y estar

1. The verbs **ser** and **estar** both mean "to be." **Ser** is used to tell where someone or something is from. It is also used to describe an inherent trait or characteristic.

 **Roberto es de Miami.**
 **Él es inteligente y guapo.**

2. **Estar** is used to tell where someone or something is located. It is also used to describe a temporary state or condition.

 **Roberto es de Miami pero ahora está en Madrid.**
 **Madrid está en España.**
 **Roberto está muy contento en Madrid.**

### 4 Historieta ¿En qué clase estás?

Contesten.

1. ¿Estás en la escuela ahora?
2. ¿Dónde está la escuela?
3. ¿En qué clase estás?
4. ¿Está la profesora en la clase también?
5. ¿Cómo es la profesora?
6. Y, ¿cómo es la clase de español?
7. ¿De dónde es la profesora?
8. Y tú, ¿de dónde eres?
9. ¿Cómo estás hoy?
10. Y la profesora, ¿cómo está?

Alumnos ecuatorianos, Manta, Ecuador

## Repaso F

## Estructura

### Bellringer Review

*Use BRR Transparency R.17 or write the following on the board.*
List all of your family members and tell where each of them is right now.

### PRESENTATION

#### Ser y estar

**Step 1** Have students open their books to page R47. Now read the explanation to the class.

**Step 2** Have students give additional examples for each use of **ser** and **estar.**

**Step 3** Write some of their examples on the board and have the class read them aloud.

### PRACTICE

**4** This activity can be done orally with books closed.

### Answers to Repaso

**4**

1. Sí, estoy en la escuela ahora.
2. La escuela está en ___.
3. Estoy en la clase de español.
4. Sí, la profesora está en la clase también.
5. La profesora es ___.
6. La clase de español es ___.
7. La profesora es de ___.
8. Yo soy de ___.
9. Hoy (no) estoy bien.
10. La profesora (no) está bien.

# Repaso F

## Estructura

### PRACTICE *(continued)*

**Writing Development**
After going over Activity 5, have students write about Ángel in their own words.

**Bellringer Review**
*Use BRR Transparency R.18 or write the following on the board.*
Make a list of all of your usual morning activities.

### PRESENTATION

**Verbos reflexivos**

**Step 1** Write one of the verb paradigms from page R48 on the board or on a transparency.

**Step 2** Circle the reflexive pronoun in each sentence, underline the subject pronoun and draw a line from the reflexive pronoun to the subject pronoun to stress that they refer to the same person.

**Step 3** Explain to students that in a negative sentence **no** comes right before the reflexive pronoun.

**Learning from Photos**
*(page R48)* You may wish to ask the following questions about the photo:
¿Hay muchos edificios altos en Caracas?
¿Son modernos y bonitos?
¿Hay montañas alrededor de Caracas?
¿Son altas las montañas?
¿Está en un valle la ciudad de Caracas?





**5** **Historieta Ángel** Completen con **ser** o **estar.**

Ángel __1__ de Caracas. Él __2__ muy simpático. __3__ gracioso también. Ahora Ángel __4__ en Nueva York. __5__ estudiante en la universidad. Ángel __6__ muy contento en Nueva York.

Nueva York __7__ en el nordeste de Estados Unidos. La Ciudad de Nueva York __8__ muy grande y __9__ muy interesante. A Ángel le gusta mucho Nueva York.

Caracas, Venezuela

## Verbos reflexivos

The subject of a reflexive verb both performs and receives the action of the verb. Each subject has its corresponding reflexive pronoun. Review the following forms.

| INFINITIVE | levantarse | acostarse |
|---|---|---|
| yo | me levanto | me acuesto |
| tú | te levantas | te acuestas |
| él, ella, Ud. | se levanta | se acuesta |
| nosotros(as) | nos levantamos | nos acostamos |
| *vosotros(as)* | *os levantáis* | *os acostáis* |
| ellos, ellas, Uds. | se levantan | se acuestan |



**Answers to Repaso**

**5**

1. es
2. es
3. Es
4. está
5. Es
6. está
7. está
8. es
9. es

**6** **¿Y tú?** Contesten personalmente.

1. ¿A qué hora te acuestas?
2. ¿Te duermes enseguida?
3. Y, ¿a qué hora te despiertas?
4. Cuando te despiertas, ¿te levantas enseguida?
5. ¿Te lavas en el cuarto de baño?
6. ¿Te desayunas en casa?
7. Después, ¿te cepillas los dientes?

**7** **Su rutina** Describan cada foto.

1. Ellos
   Nosotros
   Ustedes

2. Yo
   Ella
   Tú

**8** **Un día típico** Work with a classmate. Compare a typical day in your life with a typical day in your partner's life. Then tell what activities you have in common.

**9** **En la consulta del médico** This is a really busy doctor's office. There is a lot going on at the same time. With a classmate, describe all that you see in the illustration.

Repaso F

## Estructura

### PRACTICE

¡OJO! Note that the activities are color-coded. All the activities in the text are communicative. However, the ones with blue titles are guided communication. The red titles indicate that the answers to the activity are more open-ended and can vary more. You may wish to correct students' mistakes more so in the guided activities than in the activities with a red title, which lend themselves to a freer response.

### Paired Activity

Activity 6 can be done orally as an interview. It can also be done as a paired activity.

**7** Have students refer to the photos when doing Activity 7.

**8** and **9** Allow students to choose the activities they wish to do or choose those you consider most appropriate.

## Answers to Repaso

**6** *Answers will vary but may include:*

1. Me acuesto a (eso de) las ___.
2. Sí, (No, no) me duermo enseguida.
3. Me despierto a (eso de ) las ___.
4. Sí (No), cuando me despierto, (no) me levanto enseguida.
5. Sí, (No, no) me lavo en el cuarto de baño.
6. Sí, (No, no) me desayuno en casa.
7. Sí (No), después, (no) me cepillo los dientes.

**7**

1. Ellos se peinan.
   Nosotros nos peinamos.
   Uds. se peinan.
2. Yo me lavo la cara.
   Ella se lava la cara.
   Tú te lavas la cara.

**8** *Answers will vary. Students will recall vocabulary relating to daily routine that they learned in* **¡Buen viaje! Level 1** *as they practice reflexive verbs.*

**9** *Answers will vary but may include:*

Hay muchas personas en la consulta del médico. Un señor tiene un brazo roto. Otro señor tiene dolor de cabeza. Una señora estornuda. La médica examina al paciente. Él abre la boca y ella examina la garganta.

## Preview

In **Repaso G,** students review the vocabulary they need to talk about activities people do on summer and winter vacations. In the **Estructura** section, they review the preterite of regular verbs and object pronouns.

Students practice this vocabulary and these structures as they talk about what season they prefer and where they would like to vacation.

### National Standards

**Communication**

In Review Chapter G, students will communicate in spoken and written Spanish on the following topics:

- Seasons
- Summer and winter activities

Students will also learn to narrate past events. They will obtain and provide information and engage in conversations about summer and winter activities.

Repaso G

# El verano y el invierno

Arturo Gordon Vargas *Caserío costero*

## Learning from Photos

*(pages R50–R51)* After reviewing the vocabulary, have students look at this photo of the **Fiesta Americana Hotel** in Quintana Roo and say everything they can about it.

## Vocabulario

### Resource Manager

Workbook, pages R37–R42
Tests, pages R13–R14, R25, R37

### Bellringer Review

*Use BRR Transparency R.19 or write the following on the board.*
Write at least five things you do when you are on vacation.

### PRESENTATION

**Step 1** Have students open their books to page R52. Review the vocabulary using suggestions given for previous review lessons.

**Step 2** After reviewing the specific vocabulary on this page, have students give additional vocabulary they remember that deals with summer and winter activities.

Repaso G

## Vocabulario

Raúl pasó el verano en la playa.
Nadó en el mar.

Tomó el sol.
Volvió a casa muy bronceado.

Susana pasó una semana en una estación de esquí.
Tomó el telesilla para subir la montaña.
Subió en el telesilla.

Ella bajó la pista para expertos.
No bajó la pista para principiantes.

## 1 Historieta En la playa

Contesten.

1. ¿Fue José a la playa?
2. ¿Nadó en el mar?
3. ¿Esquió en el agua?
4. ¿Se sentó en la arena?
5. ¿Tomó el sol?
6. ¿Volvió a casa muy bronceado?

Acapulco, México

Los Andes, Chile

## 2 Historieta En la estación de esquí

Contesten.

1. ¿Fueron a una estación de esquí los amigos?
2. ¿Salieron ellos muy temprano por la mañana?
3. ¿Pasaron el día entero en las pistas?
4. ¿Subieron la montaña en el telesilla?
5. ¿Bajaron la pista para expertos o para principiantes?
6. ¿Volvieron a casa el mismo día?



# Repaso G

## Vocabulario

### PRACTICE

**¡OJO!** When students are doing the activities, accept any answer that makes sense. The purpose of these activities is to have students use the new vocabulary. They are not factual recall activities. Thus, it is not necessary for students to remember specific factual information from the vocabulary presentation when answering. If you wish, have students use the photos on this page as a stimulus, when possible.

**Historieta** Each time **Historieta** appears, it means that the answers to the activity form a short story. Encourage students to look at the title of the **Historieta,** since it can help them do the activity.

**1 and 2** These activities can be done orally with books closed.
**Expansion:** After going over Activities 1 and 2, call on one or more students to retell all the information from the activities in their own words.

### Learning from Photos

*(page R53)* Have students describe the weather in each of the photos. Then ask them to name articles of clothing they would need in each place.

## Answers to Repaso

**1**

1. Sí (No), José (no) fue a la playa.
2. Sí, (No, no) nadó en el mar.
3. Sí, (No, no) esquió en el agua.
4. Sí, (No, no) se sentó en la arena.
5. Sí, (No, no) tomó el sol.
6. Sí, (No, no) volvió a casa muy bronceado.

**2**

1. Sí (No), los amigos (no) fueron a una estación de esquí.
2. Sí (No), ellos (no) salieron muy temprano por la mañana.
3. Sí, (No, no) pasaron el día entero en las pistas.
4. Sí, (No, no) subieron la montaña en el telesilla.
5. Sí, (No, no) bajaron la pista para principiantes (expertos).
6. Sí, (No, no) volvieron a casa el mismo día.

# Repaso G

## Conversación

### PRESENTATION

**Step 1** Have two students read the **Conversación** to the class, using as much expression as possible.

**Step 2** Go over the **¿Comprendes?** activity.

### Recycling

Have students identify all the items pictured on this page. Now ask them to make up original sentences using these words.

## Conversación

### ¿Qué hicieron los amigos?

**José** ¿Adónde fuiste ayer, Adriana?
**Adriana** Fui a casa de Elena.
**José** ¿Y... ?
**Adriana** Jugamos tenis.
**José** ¿Tiene Elena una cancha de tenis?
**Adriana** No, hay canchas en un parque cerca de su casa. Pero Elena tiene una piscina.
**José** ¿Sí? ¿Nadaron ustedes?
**Adriana** Sí, nadamos después de jugar tenis.

Fuerte, España

### ¿Comprendes?

Digan que sí o que no.

1. José fue con Adriana a casa de Elena.
2. La casa de Elena tiene una cancha de tenis.
3. Adriana y Elena jugaron tenis.
4. Jugaron en una cancha en un parque.
5. Nadaron también.
6. Nadaron en una piscina en el parque.

### Answers to ¿Comprendes?

1. No
2. No
3. Sí
4. Sí
5. Sí
6. No

# Estructura

## El pretérito

1. Review the forms of the preterite of regular verbs.

| INFINITIVE | nadar | comer | subir |
|---|---|---|---|
| yo | nadé | comí | subí |
| tú | nadaste | comiste | subiste |
| él, ella, Ud. | nadó | comió | subió |
| nosotros(as) | nadamos | comimos | subimos |
| *vosotros(as)* | *nadasteis* | *comisteis* | *subisteis* |
| ellos, ellas, Uds. | nadaron | comieron | subieron |

2. The forms of the verbs **ir** and **ser** are the same in the preterite. The meaning is made clear by the context of the sentence.

   **fui fuiste fue fuimos *fuisteis* fueron**

3. The preterite is used to express an event or action that began and ended at a definite time in the past.

   **Ellos pasaron el año pasado en México.**
   **Fueron a Acapulco.**

**3** **Historieta En la escuela** Contesten.

1. ¿Fuiste a la escuela ayer?
2. ¿A qué hora llegaste a la escuela?
3. ¿Hablaste con el/la profesor(a) de español?
4. ¿Tomaste un examen?
5. ¿En qué curso tomaste el examen?
6. ¿Saliste bien en el examen?
7. ¿Comiste en la cafetería de la escuela?
8. ¿A qué hora volviste a casa?

# Repaso G

## Estructura

### Bellringer Review

*Use BRR Transparency R.20 or write the following on the board.*
Write down six things you did this past weekend.

### PRESENTATION

**El pretérito**

**Step 1** Have students repeat the verbs in Items 1 and 2 after you.

**Step 2** Write one form of a verb on the board and challenge volunteers to fill in the rest of the paradigm.

**Step 3** Read Items 2 and 3 to the class aloud.

**Step 4** Have students make up additional sentences, using the past tense.

### PRACTICE

**3** Activity 3 can be done orally with books closed.

## ANSWERS TO Repaso

**3**

1. Sí, (No, no) fui a la escuela ayer.
2. Llegué a la escuela a (eso de) las ___.
3. Sí, (No, no) hablé con el / la profesor(a) de español.
4. Sí, (No, no) tomé un examen.
5. Tomé el examen en (mi curso de) ___. (No tomé un examen.)
6. Sí, (No, no) salí bien en el examen.
7. Sí, (No, no) comí en la cafetería de la escuela.
8. Volví a casa a (eso de) las ___.

## Estructura

### PRACTICE *(continued)*

**4** Activity 4 can be done orally with books closed. Have students write it as a homework assignment.

### PRESENTATION

**Los pronombres de complemento**

**Step 1** Have students open their books to page R56. Now read the explanation to the class.

**Step 2** Write some examples from Item 2 on the board. As you write them, draw a line from **el boleto** to **lo,** etc., so students can visualize which word the pronoun replaces.

**Note:** This point is rather difficult for students and it will be reviewed again.

**4** **Muchas actividades** Contesten.

1. ¿Fuiste al cine ayer?
   ¿Viste una película?
   ¿Tomaste un refresco en el cine?
2. ¿Salieron ustedes anoche?
   ¿Fueron a una fiesta?
   ¿Bailaron y cantaron durante la fiesta?
3. ¿Esquió Sandra?
   ¿Subió la montaña en el telesilla?
   ¿Bajó la pista para expertos?
4. ¿Pasaron los amigos el fin de semana en la playa?
   ¿Te escribieron una tarjeta postal?
   ¿Nadaron y esquiaron en el agua?

**CANAL SUR**

| | |
|---|---|
| 8.00 | TELETRASTO (Infantil) «LA FAMILIA BIONICA», «EL INSPECTOR GADGET», «TRASTO» |
| 9.00 | HOSPITAL |
| 10.00 | ANDALUCIA NUESTRA |
| 10.30 | VECINOS |
| 11.00 | LAS MAÑANAS DE CANAL SUR |
| 12.00 | CINE MATINAL «LAS PROTEGIDAS» |
| 13.30 | SIEMPRE HAY UNA SUEGRA |
| 14.30 | EL DIARIO 1 |
| 15.00 | EL TIEMPO |
| 15.05 | PIGMALION |
| 15.30 | IMAGINA |

## Los pronombres de complemento

1. The object pronouns **me, te,** and **nos** can be either a direct or an indirect object. Note that the object pronoun precedes the conjugated verb.

| | |
|---|---|
| **Él me miró.** | **Él me habló por teléfono.** |
| **¿Te invitó Carlos?** | **¿Te dio una invitación?** |

2. **Lo, los, la,** and **las** function as direct objects only. They can replace either persons or things.

| | |
|---|---|
| **Pablo compró el boleto.** | **Pablo lo compró.** |
| **Pablo compró los boletos.** | **Pablo los compró.** |
| **Teresa compró la raqueta.** | **Teresa la compró.** |
| **Teresa compró las raquetas.** | **Teresa las compró.** |
| **Yo vi a los muchachos.** | **Yo los vi.** |

3. **Le** and **les** function as indirect objects only.

**Yo le escribí una carta (a él, a ella, a usted).**
**Yo les escribí una carta (a ellos, a ellas, a ustedes).**

### ANSWERS TO Repaso

**4**

1. Sí, (No, no) fui al cine ayer.
   Sí, (No, no) ví una película.
   Sí, (No, no) tomé un refresco en el cine.
2. Sí, (No, no) salimos anoche.
   Sí, (No, no) fuimos a una fiesta.
   Sí, (No, no) bailamos y (no) cantamos durante la fiesta.
3. Sí (No), Sandra (no) esquió.
   Sí, (No, no) subió la montaña en el telesilla.
   Sí, (No, no) bajó la pista para expertos.
4. Sí (No), los amigos (no) pasaron el fin de semana en la playa.
   Sí, (No, no) me escribieron una tarjeta postal.
   Sí, (No, no) nadaron y (no) esquiaron en el agua.

### 5 Historieta A la consulta del médico Contesten.

1. ¿Fuiste a la consulta del médico?
2. ¿Te habló el médico?
3. ¿Te examinó?
4. ¿Te dio una diagnosis?
5. ¿Te recetó unos antibióticos?

### 6 Aquí lo tienes. Sigan el modelo.

**la toalla →**
**Aquí la tienes.**

1. la toalla playera
2. la crema bronceadora
3. el bañador
4. el traje de baño
5. los anteojos de sol
6. los boletos para el telesilla
7. los esquís
8. las raquetas

### 7 Historieta En el aeropuerto Completen con **le** o **les.**

La señora Iturria fue al mostrador de la línea aérea. Ella __1__ habló al agente. __2__ habló en español; no __3__ habló en inglés. Ella __4__ dio su boleto y él lo miró. Ella __5__ dio su pasaporte también.

A bordo del avión los asistentes de vuelo __6__ hablaron a los pasajeros. __7__ dieron la bienvenida a bordo y __8__ explicaron las reglas de seguridad.

### 8 Las estaciones

Work with a classmate. Tell whether you prefer summer or winter. Explain why you prefer one over the other. Tell what you do during that season. Take turns.

### 9 ¡A viajar!

Look at these postcards. Work with a classmate. Tell where you prefer to go and why. Take turns.

## Repaso G

## Estructura

### PRACTICE

¡OJO! Note that the activities are color-coded. All the activities in the text are communicative. However, the ones with blue titles are guided communication. The red titles indicate that the answers to the activity are more open-ended and can vary more. You may wish to correct students' mistakes more so in the guided activities than in the activities with a red title, which lend themselves to a freer response.

**8 and 9** Have students choose the activities they wish to do.

## Answers to Repaso

**5**

1. Sí, (No, no) fui a la consulta del médico.
2. Sí (No), el médico (no) me habló.
3. Sí, (No, no) me examinó.
4. Sí, (No, no) me dio una diagnosis.
5. Sí, (No, no) me recetó unos antibióticos.

**6**

1. Aquí la tienes.
2. Aquí la tienes.
3. Aquí lo tienes.
4. Aquí lo tienes.
5. Aquí los tienes.
6. Aquí los tienes.
7. Aquí los tienes.
8. Aquí las tienes.

**7**

1. le
2. Le
3. le
4. le
5. le
6. les
7. Les
8. les

**8 and 9** *Answers will vary. Students will use vocabulary relating to summer and winter.*

# Planning for Chapter 1

## SCOPE AND SEQUENCE, PAGES 1–29

### Topics

- ❖ Train travel
- ❖ Travel-related activities

### Culture

- ❖ José Luis and Maripaz take the AVE train to Seville
- ❖ Taking the train from Cuzco to Machu Picchu
- ❖ La Plaza de Armas, Cuzco
- ❖ Machu Picchu
- ❖ The 24-hour clock and the metric system

### Functions

- ❖ How to use words and expressions related to train travel
- ❖ How to describe various types of trains and train services
- ❖ How to talk about events or activities that took place at a definite time in the past
- ❖ How to tell what people say

### Structure

- ❖ **Hacer, querer,** and **venir** in the preterite
- ❖ Irregular verbs in the preterite
- ❖ **Decir** in the present and in the preterite

### National Standards

- ❖ Communication Standard 1.1 pages 4, 5, 8, 10, 11, 13, 14, 15, 24
- ❖ Communication Standard 1.2 pages 5, 9, 11, 16, 17, 18–19, 20–21, 23, 24, 25
- ❖ Communication Standard 1.3 pages 9, 25
- ❖ Cultures Standard 2.1 pages 16, 17
- ❖ Cultures Standard 2.2 pages 5, 18–19, 20–21
- ❖ Connections Standard 3.1 pages 22–23
- ❖ Comparisons Standard 4.2 pages 22–23
- ❖ Communities Standard 5.1 pages 5, 29

## PACING AND PRIORITIES

**The chapter content is color coded below to assist you in planning.**

**■ required ■ recommended ■ optional**

**Vocabulario** *(required)* *Days 1–4*

- ■ Palabras 1
  En la estación de ferrocarril
- ■ Palabras 2
  En el tren

**Estructura** *(required)* *Days 5–7*

- ■ **Hacer, querer** y **venir** en el pretérito
- ■ Verbos irregulares en el pretérito
- ■ **Decir** en el presente y en el pretérito

**Conversación** *(required)*

- ■ En la ventanilla

**Pronunciación** *(recommended)*

- ■ Las consonantes **ñ, ch**

**Lecturas culturales**

- ■ En el AVE *(recommended)*
- ■ De Cuzco a Machu Picchu *(optional)*

**Conexiones**

- ■ Conversiones aritméticas *(optional)*

■ **¡Te toca a ti!** *(recommended)*

■ **Assessment** *(recommended)*

■ **¡Hablo como un pro!** *(optional)*

## RESOURCE GUIDE

| Section | Pages | Section Resources |
|---|---|---|
| **Vocabulario PALABRAS 1** | | |
| En la estación de ferrocarril | 2–5 | Vocabulary Transparencies 1.2–1.3<br>Audio CD 2<br>Audio Activities TE, pages 1–4<br>Workbook, pages 1–2<br>Quiz 1, page 1<br>ExamView® Pro |
| **Vocabulario PALABRAS 2** | | |
| En el tren | 6–9 | Vocabulary Transparencies 1.4–1.5<br>Audio CD 2<br>Audio Activities TE, pages 5–6<br>Workbook, pages 3–4<br>Quiz 2, page 2<br>ExamView® Pro |
| **Estructura** | | |
| **Hacer, querer** y **venir** en el pretérito<br>Verbos irregulares en el pretérito<br>**Decir** en el presente y en el pretérito | 10–11<br>12–14<br>14–15 | Audio CD 2<br>Audio Activities TE, pages 7–9<br>Workbook, pages 5–8<br>Quizzes 3–5, pages 3–5<br>ExamView® Pro |
| **Conversación** | | |
| En la ventanilla | 16 | Audio CD 2<br>Audio Activities TE, pages 9–10<br>Interactive CD-ROM |
| **Pronunciación** | | |
| Las consonantes **ñ, ch** | 17 | Audio CD 2<br>Audio Activities TE, page 10 |
| **Lecturas culturales** | | |
| En el AVE<br>De Cuzco a Machu Picchu | 18–19<br>20–21 | Audio CD 2<br>Audio Activities TE, page 11<br>Tests, pages 3, 5–6 |
| **Conexiones** | | |
| Conversiones aritméticas | 22–23 | Tests, page 7 |
| **¡Te toca a ti!** | | |
| | 24–25 | **¡Viva el mundo hispano!** Video, Episode 1<br>Video Activities, pages 61–65<br>Spanish Online Activities spanish.glencoe.com |
| **Assessment** | | |
| | 26–27 | Communication Transparency C 1<br>Quizzes 1–5, pages 1–5<br>Performance Assessment, Task 1<br>Tests, pages 1–14<br>Situation Cards, Chapter 1<br>ExamView® Pro<br>**Maratón mental** Videoquiz |

# Using Your Resources for Chapter 1

## Transparencies

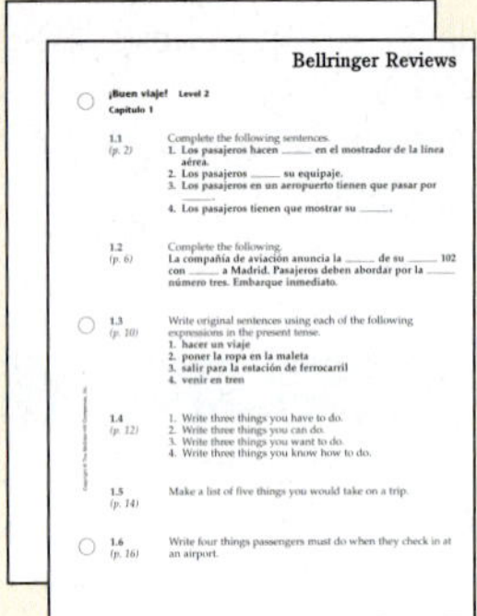

Bellringer 1.1–1.6

Vocabulary 1.1–1.5

Communication C 1

## Workbook

Vocabulary, pages 1–4

Structure, pages 5–8

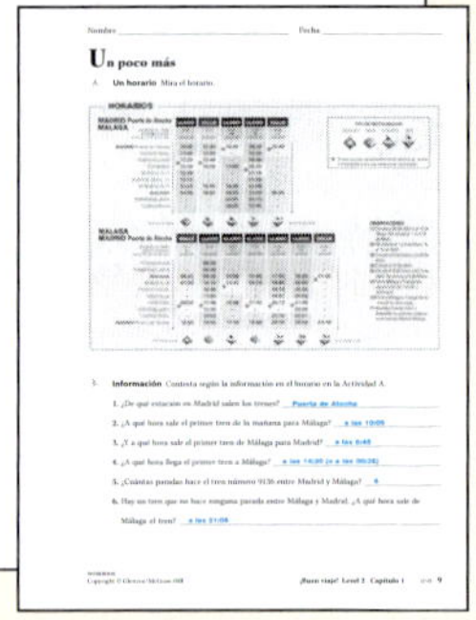

Enrichment, pages 9–12

## Audio Activities

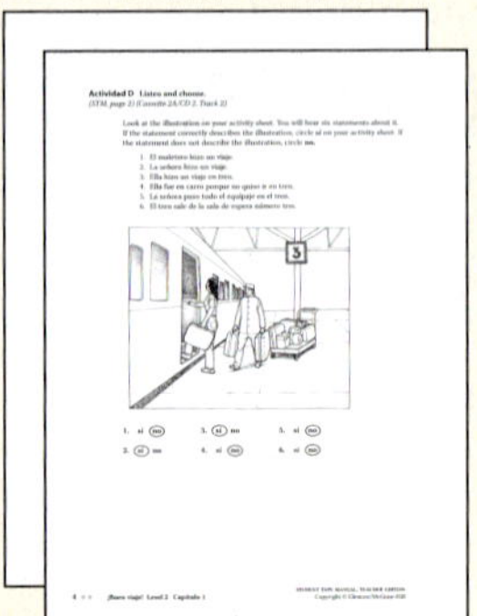

Vocabulary, pages 1–6

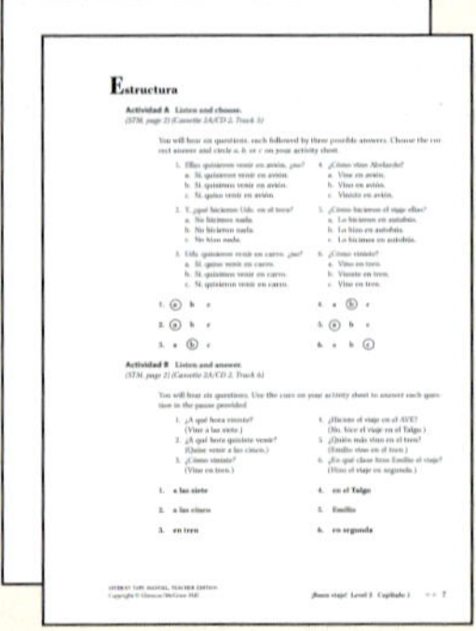

Structure, pages 7–9

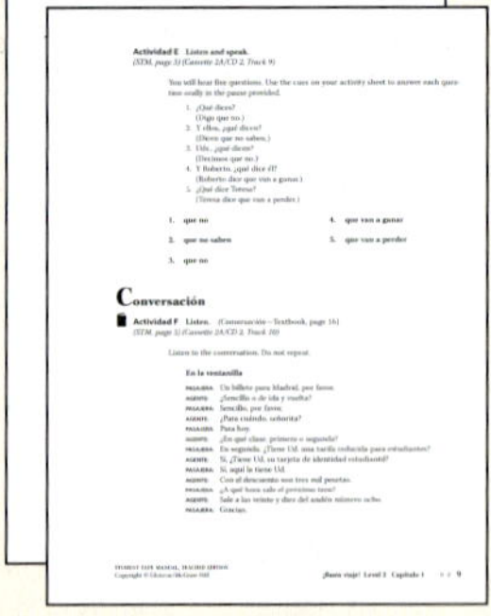

Conversation, pages 9–10
Pronunciation, page 10

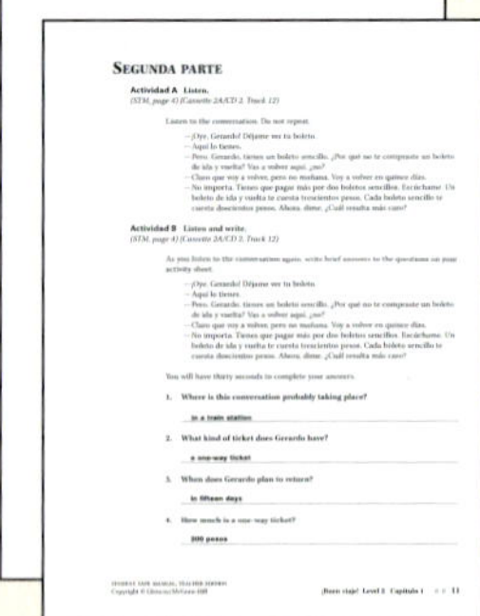

Additional Practice, pages 11–12

# Assessment

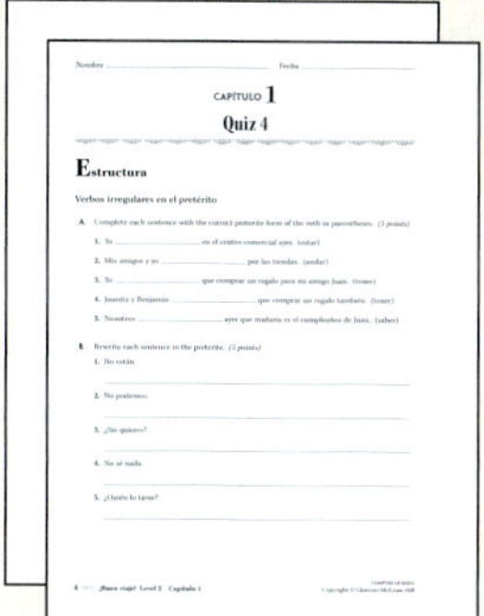

Vocabulary and Structure Quizzes, pages 1–5

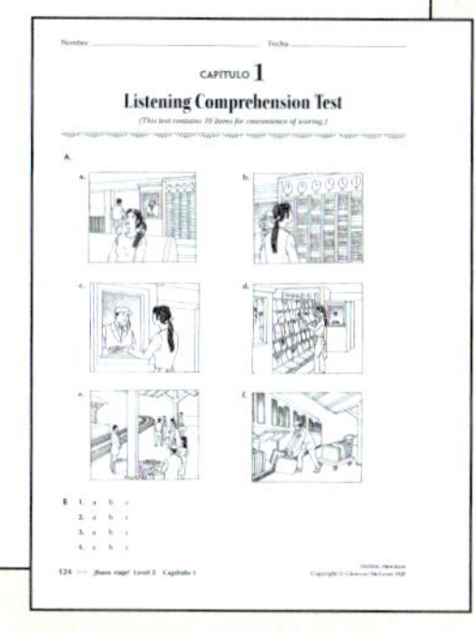

Chapter Tests, pages 1–14

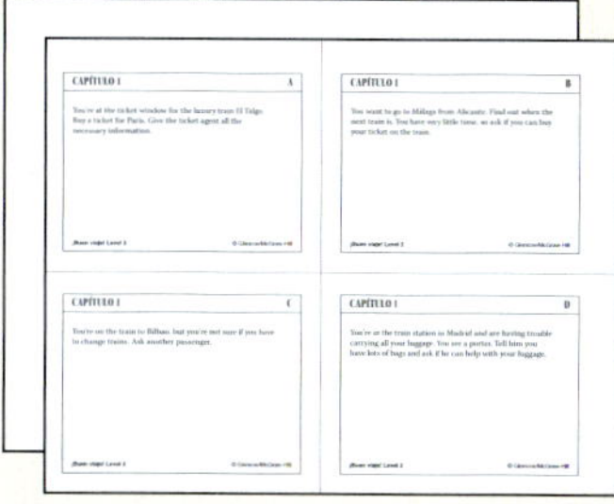

Situation Cards, Chapter 1

MindJogger Videoquiz, ExamView® Pro, Chapter 1

## Timesaving Teacher Tools

### TeacherWorks™

TeacherWorks™ is your all-in-one teacher resource center. Personalize lesson plans, access resources from the Teacher Wraparound Edition, connect to the Internet, or make a to-do list. These are only a few of the many features that can assist you in the planning and organizing of your lessons.

Includes:

- A calendar feature
- Access to all program blackline masters
- Standards correlations and more

### ExamView® Pro

Test Bank software for Macintosh and Windows makes creating, editing, customizing, and printing tests quick and easy.

## Technology Resources

In the Chapter 1 Internet Activity, you will have a chance to learn more about the Spanish-speaking world. Visit spanish.glencoe.com

On the interactive CD–ROM, students can listen to and take part in a recorded version of the conversation in Chapter 1.

**¡Viva el mundo hispano!** Video and Video Activities, Chapter 1. Available on VHS and DVD.

Help your students prepare for the chapter test by playing the **Maratón mental** Videoquiz game show. Teams will compete against each other to review chapter vocabulary and structure and sharpen listening comprehension skills. Available on VHS and DVD.

**¡Buen viaje!** is also available on CD or Online.

## Preview

In this chapter, students will learn to talk about a train trip. In order to do this they will learn vocabulary related to the train station and train travel. They will also continue to learn how to talk about past events by learning the preterite forms of some irregular verbs. The cultural focus of the chapter is on train travel in Spain and Latin America.

### National Standards

**Communication**

In Chapter 1 students will communicate in spoken and written Spanish on the following topics:

- purchasing a train ticket and consulting a timetable
- getting through a train station
- traveling on board a train

Students will obtain and provide information about these topics and learn to engage in conversations with a ticket agent, train conductor, and fellow passengers as they fulfill the chapter objectives listed on this page.

### LEVELING

The activities, conversations, and readings within each chapter are marked according to level of difficulty. **E** indicates easy. **A** indicates average. **C** indicates challenging. Some activities cover a range of difficulty. In some activities, for example, advanced students will be able to produce more extensive responses while students who learn at a different rate may give less detailed responses. The leveling indicators will help you individualize instruction to best meet your students' needs.

Capítulo 1

# Un viaje en tren

### Objetivos

**In this chapter you will learn to:**

- use expressions related to train travel
- purchase a train ticket and request information about arrival, departure, etc.
- talk about more past events or activities
- tell what people say
- discuss an interesting train trip in Spain and in Peru

Casimiro Castro *Álbum del ferrocarril mexicano*

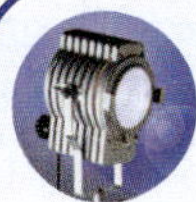

## Spotlight on Culture

**Arte** Casimiro Castro (1826–1889) is considered a master 19th century Mexican illustrator, lithographer, and water color painter. He is known for nationalistic themes—with a particular interest in Mexico City—portrayed in many of his works.

**Fotografía** This photo was taken at the Estació de Sants in Barcelona. Note that the name of the station is in **catalán.** There are two other train stations in Barcelona.

## Learning from Photos

*(page 1)* You may wish to ask the following questions about the photo after presenting the new vocabulary on pages 2–3:

**¿Dónde están los jóvenes?**
**¿Qué está mirando la muchacha?**
**¿El muchacho tiene un plano de qué ciudad?**
**¿Cómo se llama el periódico que tiene el muchacho?**
**¿Cuántos trenes ves en la foto?**

# Vocabulario

PALABRAS 1

## 1 PREPARATION

### Resource Manager

Vocabulary Transparencies 1.2–1.3
Audio Activities TE, pages 1–4
Audio CD 2
Workbook, pages 1–2
Quizzes, page 1
ExamView® Pro

### Bellringer Review

*Use BRR Transparency 1.1 or write the following on the board.*
Complete the following sentences.

1. **Los pasajeros hacen ___ en el mostrador de la línea aérea.**
2. **Los pasajeros ___ su equipaje.**
3. **Los pasajeros en un aeropuerto tienen que pasar por ___.**
4. **Los pasajeros tienen que mostrar su ___.**

## 2 PRESENTATION

**Step 1** Have students close their books. Present the vocabulary using Vocabulary Transparencies 1.2–1.3.

**Step 2** Now have students open their books and repeat the new words and sentences after you or Audio CD 2.

**Step 3** Have students act out the short dialogue on page 2.

**Step 4** As you present the new vocabulary, intersperse it with questions such as the following:

**¿La muchacha compra un billete de primera o segunda clase?**
**¿Compra un billete sencillo o de ida y vuelta?**

**LEVELING**

**A:** Vocabulary

# Vocabulario

PALABRAS 1

## En la estación de ferrocarril

### Reaching All Students

**Total Physical Response** A piece of paper with the word **maleta** written on it can represent a suitcase.

*(Student 1),* **levántate y ven acá, por favor.**
**Vas a hacer algunos gestos. Aquí tienes una maleta.**
**Toma la maleta. Mira la maleta.**
**Abre la maleta. Pon la ropa en la maleta.**
**Cierra la maleta.**
**Ve al teléfono. Llama un taxi.**
**Toma la maleta y ve a la calle.**
**Espera el taxi.**
**El taxi llega. Pon la maleta en la maletera del taxi. Abre la puerta del taxi.**
**Sube al taxi. Siéntate.**
**Gracias,** *(Student 1).* **Y ahora puedes volver a tu asiento.**

La señora hizo un viaje.
Hizo el viaje en tren.
Tomó el tren porque no quiso ir en carro.
Subió al tren.

El mozo vino con el equipaje.
El mozo puso el equipaje en el tren.
Los mozos ayudaron a los pasajeros con su equipaje.

El tren salió del andén número dos.
Algunos amigos estuvieron en el andén.



## Vocabulario

**¿Tiene el mozo bolsas y maletas?**
**¿Qué tiene el mozo?**
**¿Dónde puso el equipaje?**

Have students answer with complete sentences or sometimes just have them use the specific word or phrase that responds to the question word.

### About the Spanish Language

- The word **el billete** is used in Spain. **El boleto** is used in Latin America. The expression *to buy a ticket* is **sacar un billete** in Spain and **comprar un boleto** in Latin America.
- **El tablero** is the word used for an arrival or departure board. In some stations there is a modern type of TV screen that is called either **la pantalla** or **el monitor.**

### Assessment

As an informal assessment, you may wish to show Vocabulary Transparencies 1.2–1.3 again and let students identify items at random. Then have students make up questions about what they see on the transparencies. You may answer the questions yourself or have them call on other students to answer.

## Reaching All Students

**Total Physical Response** Have your desk be **la ventanilla.** One student can be **el agente** and another student can be **el pasajero.** Numbers on the board can represent **los andenes.** A piece of paper with the word **boleto** or **billete** can be the ticket.

*(Student 1),* **levántate y ven acá.**
**Estamos en la sala de espera. Dame la maleta.**
**Compra un boleto.**
**Págale al agente.**
**Toma tu boleto. Mira el boleto.**
**Pon el boleto en tu bolsillo.**
**Ven acá. Toma la maleta.**
**Busca el andén número dos.**
**Aquí viene el tren. Sube al tren.**
**Gracias,** *(Student 1).* **Regresa a tu asiento.**

Vocabulario

## 3 PRACTICE

## ¿Qué palabra necesito?

¡OJO! When students are doing the **¿Qué palabra necesito?** activities, accept any answer that makes sense. The purpose of these activities is to have students use the new vocabulary. They are not factual recall activities. Thus, it is not necessary for students to remember specific factual information from the vocabulary presentation when answering. If you wish, have students use the photos on this page as a stimulus, when possible.

**Historieta** Each time **Historieta** appears, it means that the answers to the activity form a short story. Encourage students to look at the title of the **Historieta,** since it can help them do the activity.

**1** Have students retell the story from Activity 1 in their own words.

**2** After completing Activity 2, have students ask questions using the other answer choices from this activity.

### Learning from Photos

*(page 4)* Until recently, **Atocha** was falling into disuse and serving very few destinations. There was even talk of closing the station. Instead, the station was completely renovated for the inauguration of the high speed AVE train in 1992. Today it serves points south and east of Madrid. The **Chamartín** station serves trains heading to the north and to Barcelona. The **Norte** station is primarily for local trains serving the western suburbs.

Vocabulario

## ¿Qué palabra necesito?

### 1 Historieta En la estación de ferrocarril

Contesten según se indica.

1. ¿Cómo vino la señora a la estación? (en taxi)
2. ¿Dónde puso sus maletas? (en la maletera del taxi)
3. En la estación, ¿adónde fue? (a la ventanilla)
4. ¿Qué compró? (un billete)
5. ¿Qué tipo de billete compró? (de ida y vuelta)
6. ¿En qué clase? (segunda)
7. ¿Dónde puso su billete? (en su bolsa)
8. ¿Qué consultó? (el horario)
9. ¿Adónde fue? (al andén)
10. ¿De qué andén salió el tren? (del número dos)
11. ¿Por qué hizo la señora el viaje en tren? (no quiso ir en coche)

Atocha, una estación de ferrocarril en Madrid

la estación de Atocha

### 2 Historieta Antes de abordar el tren

Escojan.

1. ¿Dónde espera la gente el tren?
   **a.** en la ventanilla **b.** en la sala de espera **c.** en el quiosco
2. ¿Dónde venden o despachan los billetes?
   **a.** en la ventanilla **b.** en el equipaje **c.** en el quiosco
3. ¿Qué venden en el quiosco?
   **a.** boletos **b.** maletas **c.** periódicos y revistas
4. ¿Qué consulta el pasajero para verificar la hora de salida del tren?
   **a.** la llegada **b.** la vía **c.** el horario
5. ¿Quién ayuda a los pasajeros con el equipaje?
   **a.** el mozo **b.** el tablero **c.** el andén
6. ¿De dónde sale el tren?
   **a.** de la ventanilla **b.** del andén **c.** del tablero



### Answers to ¿Qué palabra necesito?

**1**

1. La señora vino a la estación en taxi.
2. Puso sus maletas en la maletera del taxi.
3. En la estación fue a la ventanilla.
4. Compró un billete.
5. Compró un billete de ida y vuelta.
6. Compró un billete en segunda (clase).
7. Puso su billete en su bolsa.
8. Consultó el horario.
9. Fue al andén.
10. El tren salió del andén número dos.
11. La señora hizo el viaje en tren porque no quiso ir en coche.

**2**

1. b
2. a
3. c
4. c
5. a
6. b

**3 Historieta El billete del tren** Contesten.

1. ¿De qué estación sale el tren?
2. ¿Adónde va el tren?
3. ¿Cuál es la fecha del billete?
4. ¿A qué hora sale el tren?
5. ¿Está el asiento en la sección de fumar o de no fumar?
6. ¿Qué clase de billete es?
7. ¿Con qué pagó el/la pasajero(a)?

**4 RENFE (Red Nacional de Ferrocarriles Españoles)**

You're in Spain and you want to visit one of the cities on the map. A classmate will be the ticket agent. Get yourself a ticket and ask the agent any questions you have about your train trip.

## Learning from Realia

*(page 5)* Have students look at the train ticket. Ask them to guess what the word **metálico** under **Forma de pago** means. What do we say in English instead of **metálico?** *(cash)*

**¡OJO!** Note that the activities are color-coded. All the activities in the text are communicative. However, the ones with blue titles are guided communication. The red titles indicate that the answers to the activity are more open-ended and can vary more. You may wish to correct students' mistakes more so in the guided activities than in the activities with a red title, which lend themselves to a freer response.

**4** You may wish to have some students present their skits to the class.

**LEVELING**

**E:** Activities 1, 2, 3

**A:** Activities 2, 3, 4

## Answers to ¿Qué palabra necesito?

**3**

1. El tren sale de la estación de Atocha.
2. El tren va a Ciudad Real.
3. La fecha del billete es 06/07.
4. El tren sale a las 15:30.
5. El asiento está en la sección de no fumar.
6. Es un billete de primera clase.
7. El / La pasajero(a) pagó en metálico.

**4** *Answers will vary. Students may use the conversation on page 2 as a model.*

# Vocabulario

PALABRAS 2

## 1 PREPARATION

### Resource Manager

Vocabulary Transparencies 1.4–1.5
Audio Activities TE, pages 5–6
Audio CD 2
Workbook, pages 3–4
Quizzes, page 2
ExamView® Pro

### Bellringer Review

*Use BRR Transparency 1.2 or write the following on the board.*
Complete the following.
**La compañía de aviación anuncia la ___ de su ___ 102 con ___ a Madrid. Pasajeros deben abordar por la ___ número tres. Embarque inmediato.**

## 2 PRESENTATION

**Step 1** Have students close their books. Present the vocabulary, using Vocabulary Transparencies 1.4–1.5. Have students repeat each word or expression two or three times after you or Audio CD 2.

**Step 2** Ask the following questions as you present the vocabulary: **¿Los jóvenes están en el tren o están en la ventanilla? ¿Qué tiene que ver el revisor? ¿Hay muchos o pocos asientos libres en el coche? ¿Los pasajeros toman asiento o se sientan en el pasillo? ¿Qué hacen los pasajeros en el coche-cama? ¿En el coche-comedor? ¿El tren sale a tiempo o sale tarde? ¿Sale con retraso? ¿Dónde bajan los pasajeros?**

# Vocabulario

PALABRAS 2

## En el tren

## Reaching All Students

**Total Physical Response** Set up an area in the front of the classroom as **el tren** and place three chairs together. Tell students that those chairs are seats in the train. Then call on one student to act as **el / la pasajero(a).**

*(Student 1),* **levántate y ven acá, por favor.**
**Sube al tren. Busca tu asiento.**
**Pon tu maleta en el asiento. Abre la maleta.**
**Saca un libro de la maleta.**
**Cierra la maleta.**
**Pon la maleta en el compartimiento.**
**Siéntate. Toma tu asiento.**
**Abre tu libro. Lee el libro.**
**Gracias,** *(Student 1).* **Y ahora puedes volver a tu asiento.**

# Vocabulario

| MADRID Puerta de Atocha CADIZ | LLANO | |
|---|---|---|
| NUMERO DE TREN | 9220 | 41 (1) |
| DIAS DE CIRCULACION | LMXJVSD | LMXJVSD |
| **MADRID** Puerta de Atocha | 10:05 | 16:05 |
| CIUDAD REAL | 11:06 | 17:06 |
| PUERTOLLANO | 11:23 | 17:23 |
| CORDOBA | 12:12 | 18:11 |
| SEVILLA Santa Justa | 13:19 | 19:26 |
| JEREZ DE LA FRONTERA | 14:16 | 20:23 |
| EL PUERTO DE STA. MARIA | 14:27 | 20:36 |
| SAN FERNANDO DE CADIZ | 14:41 | 20:50 |
| **CADIZ** | 14:55 | 21:05 |

El tren salió a tiempo.
No salió tarde.
No salió con retraso (con una demora).

Los pasajeros van a bajar en la próxima parada (estación).
Van a transbordar en la próxima parada.

**bajar(se) del tren**

**transbordar**



## About the Spanish Language

Note that we have used the expression **bajar del tren,** which is grammatically correct. In many areas of Latin America one will hear **bajarse del tren.** In contemporary novels, **bajar** and **bajarse** are sometimes used in the same work.

## Chapter Projects

**Un viaje en tren** Have groups plan a rail trip through Spain using a guide such as the one from Eurail (available at many travel agencies). Give them a time limit and have them include at least one overnight stay. They should plan arrival and departure times and the length of each stop on the itinerary. Groups can describe their trips to the class.

**Una ciudad** Have the groups select one city from the itinerary they wrote in the **Un viaje en tren** project, and have them find out some information about it. They can do a brief report for a presentation to the class.

## SPANISH Online

The Glencoe Spanish Web site **(spanish.glencoe.com)** offers options that enable you and your students to experience the Spanish-speaking world via the Internet. For each **Capítulo,** there are activities, games, and quizzes. in addition, an *Enrichment* section offers students an opportunity to visit Web sites related to the theme of the chapter.

## Vocabulario

# 3 PRACTICE

## ¿Qué palabra necesito?

**5, 6, and 7** After going over these activities, students can summarize all the information in their own words.

### FUN-FACTS

Students have already learned about the importance of air travel in South America in Chapter 11 of **¡Buen viaje! Level 1.** Train travel in South America can be very interesting, but in many areas it is not convenient (and in some cases it is nonexistent). In addition to long distances, there are often mechanical delays, flooding during the rainy season, and rugged terrain, all of which can make travel slow and tedious. The railway service is fairly good in Argentina and Chile. Most of Chile's 5,200 miles of track run north to south.

**LEVELING**

**E:** Activities 5, 6

**A:** Activities 7, 9

**C:** Activities 7, 8, 9



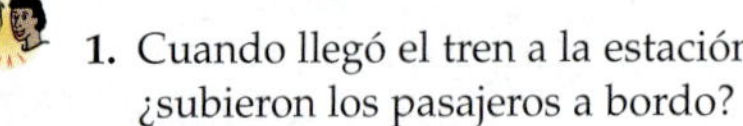

## ¿Qué palabra necesito?

**5 Historieta En el tren**

Contesten.

1. Cuando llegó el tren a la estación, ¿subieron los pasajeros a bordo?
2. ¿El tren salió tarde?
3. ¿Con cuántos minutos de demora salió?
4. ¿Vino el revisor?
5. ¿Revisó él los boletos?

Santiago, Chile

Madrid, España

**6** 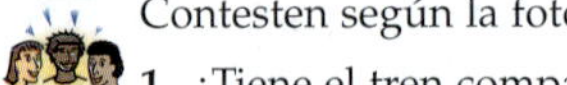 **Historieta El tren**

Contesten según la foto.

1. ¿Tiene el tren compartimientos?
2. ¿Tiene el coche o vagón un pasillo?
3. ¿Cuántos asientos hay a cada lado del pasillo?
4. ¿Hay asientos libres o están todos ocupados?
5. ¿Está completo el tren?
6. ¿Hay pasajeros de pie en el pasillo?

**7 Historieta Un viaje en tren** Completen.

1. Entre Granada y Málaga el tren local hace muchas ____.
2. No hay un tren directo a Benidorm. Es necesario cambiar de tren. Los pasajeros tienen que ____.
3. Los pasajeros que van a Benidorm tienen que ____ en la próxima ____ o ____.
4. ¿Cómo lo sabes? El ____ nos informó que nuestro tren no es directo.



### ANSWERS TO ¿Qué palabra necesito?

**5**

1. Sí, cuando el tren llegó a la estación, los pasajeros subieron a bordo.
2. Sí (No), el tren (no) salió tarde.
3. Salió con una demora de ___ minutos.
4. Sí, el revisor vino.
5. Sí, él revisó los boletos.

**6**

1. No, el tren no tiene compartimientos.
2. Sí, el coche (vagón) tiene un pasillo central.
3. Hay tres asientos a cada lado del pasillo.
4. Hay asientos libres.
5. No, el tren no está completo.
6. No, no hay pasajeros de pie en el pasillo.

**7**

1. paradas
2. transbordar
3. transbordar, parada, estación
4. revisor

**8** ## ¿Qué tienes que hacer?

Work with a classmate. You are spending a month in Madrid and your Spanish hosts are taking you to San Sebastián. You're trying to pack your bags and their child (your partner) has a lot of questions. Answer his or her questions and try to be patient. The child has never taken a train trip before.

Madrid

San Sebastián

**9** ## De Santiago a Puerto Montt

You're planning a trip from Santiago de Chile to Puerto Montt. A classmate will be your travel agent. Get as much information as you can about the trip from Santiago to Puerto Montt. It gets rather cold and windy there and it rains a lot. You may want to find out if there are frequent delays. The following are some words and expressions you may want to use with the travel agent: **la demora, la tarifa, reservar, el número de paradas, el horario, el boleto de ida y vuelta, primera (segunda) clase.**

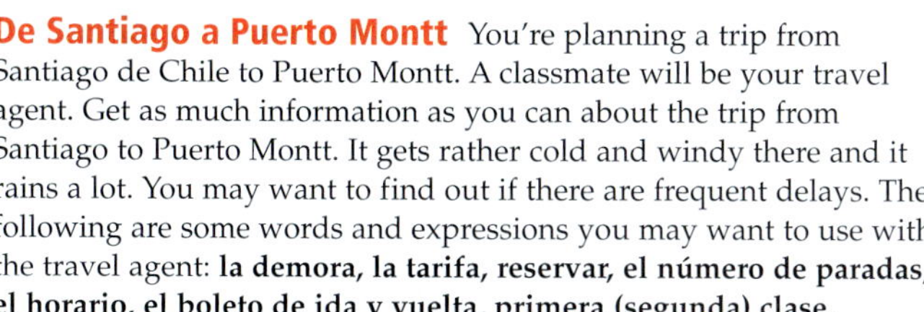

*For more practice using words from **Palabras 2**, do Activity 1 on page H2 at the end of this book.*

## Vocabulario

**8** and **9** These activities encourage students to use the chapter vocabulary and structures in open-ended situations. It is not necessary to have them do all the activities. Choose the ones you consider most appropriate.

**8** Before students begin this activity, have them make a list of questions they will ask. You may wish to have students present their conversations to the class.

**9** Have students working on Activity 9 locate Puerto Montt on the map of South America on page xxxi or on Map Transparency M 3.

### Geography Connection

You may either have students look up some information on Puerto Montt on the Internet or give them the following information.

Puerto Montt is a city of some 120,000 inhabitants, many of German descent. A large number of its small houses are unpainted, and one can see the Germanic influence in the architecture. In bakery shop windows there are still signs in Spanish and German—**Pasteles** and **Kuchen.**

Puerto Montt is the northernmost town in Chilean Patagonia. The weather can be very harsh with strong winds and a great deal of rain. The train trip to Puerto Montt from Santiago takes twenty hours.

### Answers to ¿Qué palabra necesito?

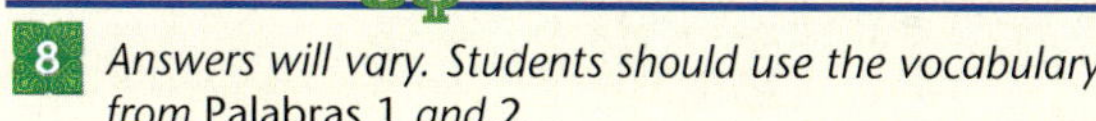

**8** *Answers will vary. Students should use the vocabulary from* Palabras 1 *and* 2*.*

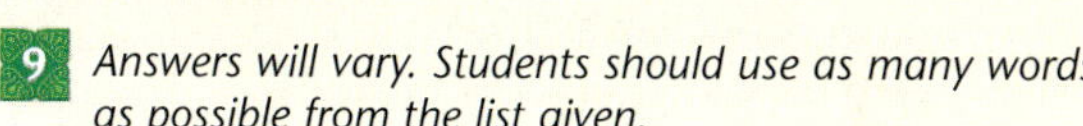

**9** *Answers will vary. Students should use as many words as possible from the list given.*

UN POCO MÁS This *InfoGap* Activity will allow students to practice in pairs. The activity should be very manageable for them, since all vocabulary and structures are familiar to them.

### Learning from Photos

*(page 9 left)* This is a view of the **Gran Vía** in Madrid. The **Gran Vía** has many hotels, clubs, stores, and **cafeterías**.
*(page 9 right)* For information on San Sebastián, see Learning from Photos, **¡Buen viaje! Level 1**, Chapter 12, page 390.

# Estructura

## 1 PREPARATION

### Resource Manager

Audio Activities TE, pages 7–9
Audio CD 2
Workbook, pages 5–8
Quizzes, pages 3–5
ExamView® Pro

### Bellringer Review

*Use BRR Transparency 1.3 or write the following on the board.*
Write original sentences using each of the following expressions in the present tense.

1. **hacer un viaje**
2. **poner la ropa en la maleta**
3. **salir para la estación de ferrocarril**
4. **venir en tren**

## 2 PRESENTATION

### Hacer, querer y venir en el pretérito

**Step 1** Have students open their books to page 10. Read Items 1 and 2 to the class.

**Step 2** Have the class repeat the verb forms aloud.

**Step 3** Call on an individual to read the model sentences.

**Step 4** Point out to students that all these irregular verbs have the ending **e** in the **yo** form.

**Note:** Many of the verbs students will be learning in this chapter are not used very frequently in the preterite. For this reason, it is recommended that you do not spend a great deal of time on this topic. The most important verbs are **venir, hacer,** and **poner.**

# Estructura

## Hacer, querer y venir en el pretérito

### Relating more past actions

1. The verbs **hacer, querer,** and **venir** are irregular in the preterite. Note that they all have an **i** in the stem and the endings for the **yo, él, ella,** and **usted** forms are different from the endings of regular verbs.

| INFINITIVE | hacer | querer | venir |
|---|---|---|---|
| yo | hice | quise | vine |
| tú | hiciste | quisiste | viniste |
| él, ella, Ud. | hizo | quiso | vino |
| nosotros(as) | hicimos | quisimos | vinimos |
| *vosotros(as)* | *hicisteis* | *quisisteis* | *vinisteis* |
| ellos, ellas, Uds. | hicieron | quisieron | vinieron |

2. The verb **querer** has several special meanings in the preterite.

**Quise ayudar.** *I tried to help.*
**No quise ir en carro.** *I refused to go by car.*

For more information about travel in Peru and other areas of the Spanish-speaking world, go to the Glencoe Spanish Web site: spanish.glencoe.com

## ¿Cómo lo digo?

### 10 Historieta ¿Cómo viniste?

Contesten.

1. ¿Viniste a la estación en taxi?
2. ¿Viniste en un taxi público o privado?
3. ¿Hiciste el viaje en tren?
4. ¿Hiciste el viaje en el tren local?
5. ¿Lo hiciste en tren porque no quisiste ir en carro?

Poconchile, Chile



## Answers to ¿Cómo lo digo?

**10**

1. Sí, vine a la estación en taxi.
2. Vine en un taxi público.
3. Sí, hice el viaje en tren.
4. Sí, (No, no) hice el viaje en el tren local.
5. Sí, lo hice en tren porque no quise ir en coche. (No, no lo hice en tren porque quise ir en coche.)

### LEVELING

**E:** Activities 10, 12, 13
**A:** Activities 12, 13
**C:** Activity 11

11 **No quisieron.** Completen.

1. —Ellos no __1__ (querer) hacer el viaje.
   —¿No lo __2__ (querer) hacer?
   —No, de ninguna manera.
   —Pues, ¿qué pasó entonces? ¿Lo __3__ (hacer) o no lo __4__ (hacer)?
   —No lo __5__ (hacer).
2. —¿Por qué no __6__ (venir) ustedes esta mañana?
   —Nosotros no __7__ (venir) porque no __8__ (hacer) las reservaciones.
3. —Carlos no __9__ (querer) hacer la cama.
   —Entonces, ¿quién la __10__ (hacer)?
   —Pues, la __11__ (hacer) yo.
   —¡Qué absurdo! ¿Tú la __12__ (hacer) porque él no la __13__ (querer) hacer?

12 **¡Rebelde!** A friend of yours (your classmate) is in trouble with his or her parents because he or she didn't help to get ready for their trip. Find out what your friend didn't do and why. Use the model as a guide.

hacer la maleta
reservar un taxi
comprar los billetes
llamar a los parientes
hacer las reservaciones

13 **¿Qué hiciste durante el fin de semana?** With a classmate, take turns asking each other what you and other friends did over the weekend.

**Estructura**

## 3 PRACTICE

### ¿Cómo lo digo?

10 Activity 10 on page 10 practices the **tú** and **yo** forms.

11 Have students present Activity 11 as a series of miniconversations.

12 Ask for volunteers to role-play the model dialogue. Have them do one or two examples from the handwritten list on the right before students work on their own in pairs.
**Expansion:** Encourage students to come up with their own list of things they were supposed to do.

13 This is a good warm-up activity to begin the class period. Students might begin by saying: **¿Qué hiciste durante el fin de semana?** or **¿Qué hicieron ustedes durante el fin de semana?**

### Answers to ¿Cómo lo digo?

11

1. quisieron
2. quisieron
3. hicieron
4. hicieron
5. hicieron
6. vinieron
7. vinimos
8. hicimos
9. quiso
10. hizo
11. hice
12. hiciste
13. quiso

12 *Answers will vary, but students should follow the model.*

13 *Answers will vary, but students should use the preterite tense.*

# Estructura

## 1 PREPARATION

### Bellringer Review

*Use BRR Transparency 1.4 or write the following on the board.*

1. Write three things you have to do.
2. Write three things you can do.
3. Write three things you want to do.
4. Write three things you know how to do.

## 2 PRESENTATION

### Verbos irregulares en el pretérito

**Step 1** Have students open their books to page 12. Read Items 1 and 2 to the class.

**Step 2** Have the class repeat the verb forms from the chart.

**Step 3** Call on an individual to read the model sentences in Item 2.

### Art Connection

Show the Fine Art Transparency from the Transparency Binder of ***Vista de Toledo*** by El Greco. You may wish to have students read the background information accompanying this transparency and do the related activities.

**Expansion:** Have students look at a photo of Toledo today. Ask them if they see a resemblance between today's photo and El Greco's painting done about four centuries ago.

# Estructura

## Verbos irregulares en el pretérito
### Describing more past actions

1. The verbs **estar, andar,** and **tener** are irregular in the preterite. They all have a **u** in the stem. Study the following forms.

| INFINITIVE | estar | andar | tener |
|---|---|---|---|
| yo | estuve | anduve | tuve |
| tú | estuviste | anduviste | tuviste |
| él, ella, Ud. | estuvo | anduvo | tuvo |
| nosotros(as) | estuvimos | anduvimos | tuvimos |
| *vosotros(as)* | *estuvisteis* | *anduvisteis* | *tuvisteis* |
| ellos, ellas, Uds. | estuvieron | anduvieron | tuvieron |

2. The verb **andar** means *to go,* but not to a specific place. The verb **ir** is used with a specific place.

    **Fueron a Toledo.**
    *They went to Toledo.*

    **Anduvieron por las plazas pintorescas de Toledo.**
    *They wandered through (walked around) the picturesque squares of Toledo.*

*Vista de Toledo* de El Greco



### About the Spanish Language

In Spain the verb **andar** means *to walk.* **Caminar** is used in Latin America. **Ir a pie** means *to go on foot,* and **dar un paseo** or **pasear(se)** means *to take a walk.*

3. The verbs **poder, poner,** and **saber** are also irregular in the preterite. Like the verbs **estar, andar,** and **tener,** they all have a **u** in the stem. Study the following forms.

| INFINITIVE | poder | poner | saber |
|---|---|---|---|
| yo | pude | puse | supe |
| tú | pudiste | pusiste | supiste |
| él, ella, Ud. | pudo | puso | supo |
| nosotros(as) | pudimos | pusimos | supimos |
| *vosotros(as)* | *pudisteis* | *pusisteis* | *supisteis* |
| ellos, ellas, Uds. | pudieron | pusieron | supieron |

4. Like **querer,** the verbs **poder** and **saber** have special meanings in the preterite.

**Pude parar.** *(After trying hard) I managed to stop.*
**No pude parar.** *(I tried but) I couldn't stop.*
**Yo lo supe ayer.** *I found it out (learned it) yesterday.*

## ¿Cómo lo digo?

**14 Historieta ¿Dónde está mi tarjeta de identidad estudiantil?**
Contesten según se indica.

1. ¿Estuviste ayer en la estación de ferrocarril? (sí)
2. ¿Tuviste que tomar el tren a Toledo? (sí)
3. ¿Pudiste comprar un billete de precio reducido? (no)
4. ¿Tuviste que presentar tu tarjeta de identidad estudiantil? (sí)
5. ¿Dónde la pusiste? (no sé)
6. ¿La perdiste? (sí, creo)
7. ¿Cuándo supiste que la perdiste? (cuando llegué a la estación)

Toledo, España



## Estructura

**Step 4** Have the class repeat the verb forms from the chart in Item 3.

**Step 5** Point out to students that all these irregular verbs have a **u** in the stem.

**Step 6** Call on an individual to read the model sentences from Item 4.

## 3 PRACTICE

### ¿Cómo lo digo?

**14** Allow students to refer to the verb charts on these two pages as they do the activity.

### Writing Development

Have students write a note telling someone what happened in Activity 14.

### History Connection

Toledo is one of the most magnificent cities in Spain. The rock on which it stands was inhabited in prehistoric times. The Romans came in 192 B.C. and built a large fort where the **Alcázar** now stands. Toledo was inhabited by the Iberians, Romans, Visigoths, and the Moors, who arrived early in the eighth century.

Alfonso VI, aided by El Cid, took Toledo from the Moors in 1085. During the Renaissance, Toledo was a center of humanism. However, it began to decline in the sixteenth century. The expulsion of the Jews in 1492 had severe economic consequences, and the decision in 1561 to move the court to Madrid led to Toledo's political decline. The years El Greco spent in Toledo (1572 until his death in 1614) were the years of Toledo's decline.

## Answers to ¿Cómo lo digo?

**14**

1. Sí, ayer estuve en la estación de ferrocarril.
2. Sí, tuve que tomar el tren a Toledo.
3. No, no pude comprar un billete de precio reducido.
4. Sí, tuve que presentar mi tarjeta de identidad estudiantil.
5. No sé dónde la puse.
6. Sí, creo que la perdí.
7. Supe que la perdí cuando llegué a la estación.

# Estructura

## 3 PRACTICE *(continued)*

15 For additional practice, have students retell the story in their own words.

## 1 PREPARATION

### Bellringer Review

*Use BRR Transparency 1.5 or write the following on the board.*
Make a list of five things you would take on a trip.

## 2 PRESENTATION

### Decir en el presente y en el pretérito

**Step 1** Have students open their books to page 14 and repeat the forms of the verb **decir** after you.

**Step 2** Write the forms of the verb on the board. Underline the stem for each form.

**Step 3** Now do the activities on page 15.

### Learning from Realia

*(page 14)* The **quetzal** is the monetary unit of Guatemala. The **quetzal** is a multicolored bird, and it is the national symbol of Guatemala.

Ask students: **¿Cuántos quetzales hay en la página 14?**

**15 Historieta En el mercado**

Completen.

El otro día yo __1__ (estar) en el mercado de Chichicastenango, en Guatemala. Ramón __2__ (estar) allí también. Nosotros __3__ (andar) por el mercado pero no __4__ (poder) comprar nada. No es que no __5__ (querer) comprar nada, es que no __6__ (poder) porque __7__ (ir) al mercado sin un quetzal.

Chichicastenango, Guatemala

## Decir en el presente y en el pretérito

### Telling what people say

1. The verb **decir** *(to say)* is irregular in the present and preterite tenses. Study the following forms.

| | Presente | Pretérito |
|---|---|---|
| yo | digo | dije |
| tú | dices | dijiste |
| él, ella, Ud. | dice | dijo |
| nosotros(as) | decimos | dijimos |
| *vosotros(as)* | *decís* | *dijisteis* |
| ellos, ellas, Uds. | dicen | dijeron |



### Answers to ¿Cómo lo digo?

15

1. estuve
2. estuvo
3. anduvimos
4. pudimos
5. quisimos
6. pudimos
7. fuimos

# ¿Cómo lo digo?

 **¿Qué dices?** Sigan el modelo.

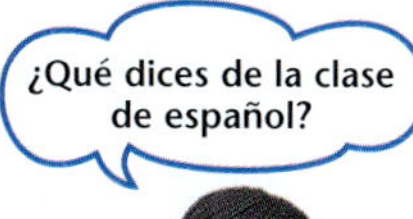

1. ¿Qué dices de la clase de matemáticas?
2. ¿Qué dices de la clase de inglés?
3. ¿Qué dices de la clase de biología?
4. ¿Qué dices de la clase de educación física?
5. ¿Qué dices de la clase de historia?

**17 ¿Qué dicen todos?** Completen con la forma apropiada del presente de **decir.**

Yo __1__ que quiero ir en tren pero Elena me __2__ que prefiere tomar el avión. Ella y Tomás también __3__ que no hay mucha diferencia entre la tarifa del avión y la tarifa del tren.

—¿Qué __4__ tú?

—Yo __5__ que es mejor ir en tren.

—Bien. Tú y yo __6__ la misma cosa. Estamos de acuerdo.

**18 ¿Qué dijeron todos?** Contesten.

1. ¿Dijiste tú que quieres ir?
2. ¿Dijeron ustedes que es mejor ir en tren?
3. ¿Dije yo que sí?
4. ¿Dijo Elena que ella tiene los boletos?
5. ¿Dijimos la misma cosa?

## Estructura

### 3 PRACTICE

### ¿Cómo lo digo?

**16** Have students do Activity 16 as a miniconversation, working in pairs.

**Expansion:** Have students think of additional topics to talk about, such as their school teams and clubs. For example:

**—¿Qué dices del equipo de fútbol?**

**—Pues, yo digo que es fantástico porque está ganando.**

**17** This activity uses all forms of **decir** in the present.

**18** This activity uses all forms of **decir** in the preterite.

**¡Adelante!** At this point in the chapter, students have learned all the vocabulary and structure necessary to complete the chapter. The conversation and cultural readings that follow recycle all the material learned up to this point.

**LEVELING**

**A:** Activities 16, 17

**C:** Activities 15, 18

### Answers to ¿Cómo lo digo?

 *Answers will follow the model.*

1. digo
2. dice
3. dicen
4. dices
5. digo
6. decimos

**18**

1. Sí, (No, no) dije que quiero ir.
2. Sí, (No, no) dijimos que es mejor ir en tren.
3. Sí, (No, no) dijiste que sí.
4. Sí (No), Elena (no) dijo que ella tiene los boletos.
5. Sí, (No, no) dijimos (dijeron) la misma cosa.

## 1 PREPARATION

### Resource Manager

Audio Activities TE, pages 9–10
Audio CD 2

### Bellringer Review

*Use BRR Transparency 1.6 or write the following on the board.*
Write four things passengers must do when they check in at an airport.

## 2 PRESENTATION

**Step 1** Have students close their books. Read the conversation to them or play Audio CD 2.

**Step 2** Have the class repeat each line after you once.

**Step 3** Call on two students to read the conversation with as much expression as possible.

**Step 4** After completing the conversation, have students summarize it in their own words.

**Step 5** After presenting the conversation, go over the **¿Comprendes?** activity. If students can answer the questions with relative ease, move on. Students should not be expected to memorize the conversation.

### Learning from Photos

*(page 16)* The photo on this page was taken at the Toledo train station, which has beautiful mosaics and tilework.

# Conversación

## En la ventanilla   

**Pasajera** Un billete para Madrid, por favor.
**Agente** ¿Sencillo o de ida y vuelta?
**Pasajera** Sencillo, por favor.
**Agente** ¿Para cuándo, señorita?
**Pasajera** Para hoy.
**Agente** ¿En qué clase, primera o segunda?
**Pasajera** En segunda. ¿Tiene usted una tarifa reducida para estudiantes?
**Agente** Sí. ¿Tiene usted su tarjeta de identidad estudiantil?
**Pasajera** Sí, aquí la tiene usted.
**Agente** Con el descuento son veintidós euros.
**Pasajera** ¿A qué hora sale el próximo tren?
**Agente** Sale a las veinte y diez del andén número ocho.
**Pasajera** Gracias.

### ¿Comprendes?

Contesten.

1. ¿Dónde está la señorita?
2. ¿Adónde va?
3. ¿Qué tipo de billete quiere?
4. ¿Para cuándo lo quiere?
5. ¿En qué clase quiere viajar?
6. ¿Es alumna la señorita?
7. ¿Hay una tarifa reducida para estudiantes?
8. ¿Qué tiene la señorita?
9. ¿Cuánto cuesta el billete con el descuento estudiantil?
10. ¿A qué hora sale el tren?
11. ¿De qué andén sale?



### Answers to ¿Comprendes?

1. La señorita está en la ventanilla.
2. Va a Madrid.
3. Quiere un billete sencillo.
4. Lo quiere para hoy.
5. Quiere viajar en segunda (clase).
6. Sí, la señorita es alumna.
7. Sí, hay una tarifa reducida para estudiantes.
8. La señorita tiene su tarjeta de identidad estudiantil.
9. Con el descuento estudiantil el billete cuesta tres mil pesetas.
10. El tren sale a las veinte y diez.
11. Sale del andén número ocho.

# Vamos a hablar más

**A** **El horario** Look at the train schedule. With a classmate, ask and answer as many questions as you can about it.

**B** **Vamos a Barcelona.** You and a classmate are spending a semester in Spain. You will be going to Barcelona for a couple of days. One of you is going to fly and the other is going to take the train. Compare your trips: time, cost, and what you have to do the day of departure.

## Pronunciación

### La consonante ñ y la combinación ch

The **ñ** is a separate letter of the Spanish alphabet. The mark over it is called a **tilde**. Note that it is pronounced similarly to the *ny* in the English word *canyon*. Repeat the following.

**señor** **otoño** **España**
**señora** **pequeño** **cumpleaños**
**año**

**Ch** is pronounced much like the *ch* in the English word *church*. Repeat the following.

**coche** **chaqueta**
**chocolate** **muchacho**

Repeat the following sentences.

**El señor español compra un coche cada año en el otoño.**
**El muchacho chileno duerme en una cama pequeña en el coche-cama.**
**El muchacho pequeño lleva una chaqueta color chocolate.**

## Conversación

### 3 PRACTICE

### Vamos a hablar más

**A** Give students a few minutes to study the train schedule before they begin the activity.

**B** Students should write down their answers and then compare notes with their partners.

### Glencoe Technology

On the CD-ROM, students can watch a dramatization of this conversation. They can then play the role of either one of the characters and record themselves in the conversation.

### Pronunciación

**Step 1** Most students have no particular problem with these sounds. Have them pronounce each word carefully after you or Audio CD 2.

**Step 2** Have students open their books to page 17. Call on individuals to read the words and sentences.

**Step 3** All model sentences on page 17 can be used for dictation.

### Answers to Vamos a hablar más

**A** *Answers will vary. Students may discuss departure times, departure and destination cities, the number of stops, and any other observations, such as the day of travel.*

**B** *Answers will vary, but students should include the time of departure, the cost of the trip, and a brief description of what they have to do the day they leave.*

### LEVELING

**E:** Conversation

# Lecturas culturales

## Resource Manager

Audio Activities TE, page 11
Audio CD 2

## National Standards

**Cultures**
The reading about the AVE train in Spain and the related activities on page 19 allow students to demonstrate an understanding of the importance of train travel in Spain.

## PRESENTATION

### Pre-reading

**Step 1** Have students open their books to page 18 and read the information in the Reading Strategy.

**Step 2** Tell them that the illustration at the bottom of the page is of **un ave.**

**Step 3** Then have them scan the **Lectura** and the photos to look for the connection between the bird and the train.

**Step 4** Have students locate Madrid and Sevilla on the map of Spain on page xxx or use Map Transparency M 2.

### Reading

**Step 1** Call on a student to read three or four sentences aloud.

**Step 2** Intersperse the oral reading with comprehension questions from **¿Comprendes?** Activity A, page 19.



# Lecturas culturales

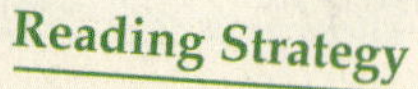

**Reading Strategy**

**Interpretation of images** Reading passages sometimes use images as a symbol to create an impression. Many times these images are animals. If you are able to identify an image, it is helpful to stop for a moment and think about the qualities and characteristics of the particular symbol the author is using in his or her imagery. Then when you have finished reading, go back and think about how the image and the topic of the reading are alike.

## En el AVE

José Luis y su hermana, Maripaz, pasan dos días en Sevilla. Vinieron a visitar a sus abuelos. El viaje que hicieron de Madrid, donde viven, fue fantástico. Tomaron el tren y llegaron a Sevilla en sólo dos horas y quince minutos. Salieron de Atocha en Madrid a las 17:00 y bajaron del tren en Sevilla a las 19:15. ¿Es posible recorrer el trayecto[1] Madrid–Sevilla en dos horas quince minutos? Es una distancia de 538 kilómetros. ¡Es increíble!

[1]recorrer el trayecto *cover the route*

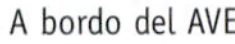

A bordo del AVE

Plaza de España, Sevilla

Sí, es increíble, pero es verdad. El tren español de alta velocidad es uno de los trenes más rápidos del mundo. Viaja a 250 kilómetros por hora. El tren se llama el AVE. ¿Por qué el AVE? Porque el tren vuela como un ave o pájaro.

José Luis y Maripaz tomaron el AVE. Según ellos, el viaje fue fantástico. ¿Por qué? Primero la velocidad. Pero el tren es también muy cómodo[2]. Lleva ocho coches en tres clases. Los pasajeros pueden escuchar música estereofónica o mirar tres canales de video. El tren también dispone de[3] teléfono por si acaso[4] un pasajero quiere o necesita hacer una llamada telefónica.

[2]cómodo *comfortable*
[3]dispone de *has available*
[4]por si acaso *in case*

Torre del Oro, Sevilla

## ¿Comprendes?

**A Una visita a los abuelos** Contesten.

1. ¿Quiénes hicieron un viaje de Madrid a Sevilla?
2. ¿Quiénes vinieron a Sevilla, José Luis y su hermana o sus abuelos?
3. ¿Cómo hicieron el viaje?
4. ¿Qué tal fue el viaje?
5. ¿Cuánto tiempo tardó el viaje?
6. ¿A qué hora salieron de Madrid?
7. ¿A qué hora llegaron a Sevilla?

**B Información** Busquen la información.

1. uno de los trenes más rápidos del mundo
2. el nombre del tren
3. el número de coches que lleva el tren
4. el número de clases que tiene
5. algunas comodidades que el tren ofrece a los pasajeros

Plaza de España, Sevilla



# Lecturas culturales

### Post-reading

**Step 1** Assign the reading and the **¿Comprendes?** activities on page 19 for homework.

**Step 2** Have a student summarize the reading selection in his or her own words.

### History Connection

The grandiose structure on the **Plaza de España** was designed by the architect Aníbal González. It was Spain's pavillion at the 1929 Hispanic-American Exhibition Fair. There are four bridges over the ornamental lake. One of the bridges is seen here. Each bridge represents one of the medieval kingdoms of the Iberian peninsula.

For information about the **Torre del Oro**, see Geography Connection, Chapter 5, page 149.

### ¿Comprendes?

**A** Allow students to refer to the reading to look up the answers, or you may use this activity as a testing device for factual recall.

**B** Have individual students read the appropriate phrase or sentence aloud. Make sure all students find the information in the **Lectura.**

**LEVELING**

**E:** Reading

### Answers to ¿Comprendes?

**A**

1. José Luis y su hermana, Maripaz, hicieron un viaje de Madrid a Sevilla.
2. José Luis y su hermana vinieron a Sevilla.
3. Hicieron el viaje en el tren.
4. El viaje fue fantástico.
5. El viaje tardó dos horas quince minutos.
6. Salieron de Madrid a las 17:00.
7. Llegaron a Sevilla a las 19:15.

**B**

1. el tren español de alta velocidad
2. el AVE
3. ocho
4. tres
5. música estereofónica, tres canales de video, teléfono

# Lectura opcional

## National Standards

**Cultures**

This reading about Machu Picchu in Peru and the related activities on page 21 allow students to develop an appreciation for one of the unique archeological sites in the Spanish-speaking world.

**¡OJO!** This reading is optional. You may skip it completely, have the entire class read it, have only several students read it and report to the class, or assign it for extra credit.

## PRESENTATION

**Step 1** Have students locate Cuzco on the map of South America on page xxxi or use Map Transparency M 3.

**Step 2** Have students read the passage quickly as they look at the photos that accompany it. The photos will increase their comprehension because students will be able to visualize what they are reading about.

**Step 3** Have students discuss the information that they find interesting.

# Lectura opcional

## De Cuzco a Machu Picchu

Un viaje muy interesante en tren es el viaje de Cuzco a Machu Picchu en el Perú. Cada día a las siete de la mañana, un tren de vía estrecha[1] sale de la estación de San Pedro en Cuzco y llega a Machu Picchu a las diez y media. Cuzco está a unos 3.500 metros sobre el nivel del mar. El tren tiene que bajar a 2.300 metros para llegar a Machu Picchu. Tiene que bajar 1.200 metros y en el viaje de regreso tiene que subir 1.200 metros.

Pero, ¿quiénes toman el tren para ir a Machu Picchu? Es un tren que lleva a muchos turistas que quieren ir a ver las famosas ruinas de los incas. Machu Picchu es una ciudad entera, totalmente aislada[2] en un pico andino al borde de[3] un cañón. Un dato histórico increíble es que los españoles no

[1]de vía estrecha *narrow gauge*
[2]aislada *isolated*
[3]al borde de *on the edge of*

La Plaza de Armas, Cuzco

El valle del Urubamba, Perú

Machu Picchu

descubrieron a Machu Picchu durante su conquista de Perú. Los historiadores creen que Machu Picchu fue el último refugio de los nobles incas al escaparse[4] de los españoles.

Machu Picchu fue descubierto por Hiram Bingham, el explorador y senador de Estados Unidos, en 1911. ¿Cómo llegó Bingham a Machu Picchu en 1911? ¡A pie! Y aún hoy hay sólo dos maneras de ir a Machu Picchu—a pie o en el tren que sale a las siete y media de Cuzco.

[4]al escaparse *upon escaping*

## ¿Comprendes?

**¿Sí o no?** Digan que sí o que no.

1. Machu Picchu está a una altura más elevada que Cuzco.
2. El tren que va de Machu Picchu a Cuzco tiene que subir 1.200 metros.
3. El viaje de Cuzco a Machu Picchu toma tres horas y media.
4. Hay muy pocos turistas en el tren a Machu Picchu.
5. En Machu Picchu hay ruinas famosas de los incas.
6. Machu Picchu fue una ciudad de los incas.
7. Los españoles descubrieron la ciudad de Machu Picchu durante su conquista de Perú.
8. Hiram Bingham fue un senador de Estados Unidos.
9. Él también fue a Machu Picchu en tren.



## Learning from Photos

*(page 20 top)* This photo, taken through a stone portal or doorway, gives us a beautiful view of one of the many terraces at Machu Picchu. Many of the original stone buildings have been reconstructed. However, since the original roofs were made of thatch, they have not been rebuilt.

*(page 20 middle)* This is the train that takes tourists from Cuzco to Machu Picchu.

*(page 20 bottom right)* This valley is referred to as the "Sacred Valley of the Incas." The name "Inca" originally applied to the royal family only. Today it is used to describe the people as a whole.

*(page 20 bottom left)* Cuzco is a city of 200,000 people. Its population is a blend of Indian, **mestizo**, and Spanish cultures. In the days of the Incas, the **Plaza de Armas** was called **Huacaypata.** This square was lined with the sumptuous palaces of dead and mummified Incas and with the imperial residences of the living Incas. Today, the palaces have been replaced by Spanish mansions. The first floors of these mansions are occupied by small stores and restaurants.

**LEVELING**

**A:** Reading

## Answers to ¿Comprendes?

1. No
2. Sí
3. Sí
4. No
5. Sí
6. Sí
7. No
8. Sí
9. No

## Assessment

As an informal assessment, you may wish to use the **¿Comprendes?** activity to see how well students understood the reading selection.

# Conexiones

## National Standards

**Connections**

This reading about the 24-hour clock and the metric system establishes a connection with another discipline, allowing students to reinforce and further their knowledge of mathematics through the study of Spanish.

**Comparisons**

This reading allows students to compare the English system of measurement with the metric system, which is used in most of the Spanish-speaking world.

**¡OJO!** The readings in the **Conexiones** section are optional. They focus on some of the major disciplines taught in schools and universities. The vocabulary is useful for discussing such topics as history, literature, art, economics, business, science, etc. You may choose any of the following ways to do the readings in the **Conexiones** sections.

**Independent reading** Have students read the selections and do the post-reading activities as homework, which you collect. This option is least intrusive on class time and requires a minimum of teacher involvement.

**Homework with in-class follow-up** Assign the readings and post-reading activities as homework. Review and discuss the material in class the next day.

**Intensive in-class activity** This option includes a pre-reading vocabulary presentation, in-class reading and discussion, assignment of the activities for homework, and a discussion of the assignment in class the following day.

# Conexiones

## *Las matemáticas*

### Conversiones aritméticas

When traveling through many of the Spanish-speaking countries, you will need to make some mathematical conversions. For example, train as well as plane schedules and hours for formal events, radio, and television are given using the twenty-four-hour clock. The metric system rather than the English system is used for weights and measures. Let's take a look at some of the conversions that must be made.

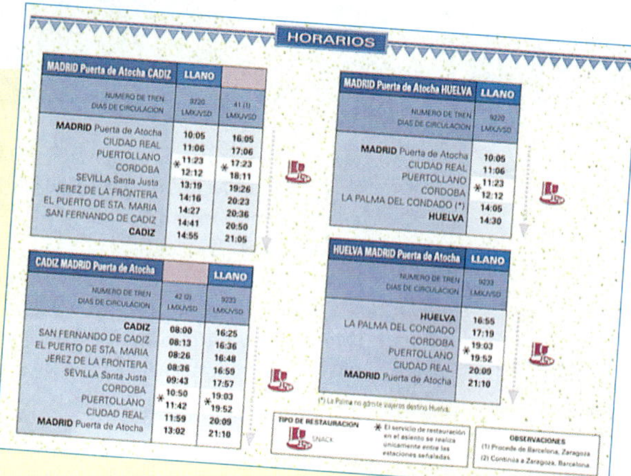

HORARIOS

| MADRID Puerta de Atocha CADIZ | LLANO | |
|---|---|---|
| NUMERO DE TREN / DIAS DE CIRCULACION | 9720 / LMXJVSD | 41 (1) / LMXJVSD |
| **MADRID** Puerta de Atocha | 10:05 | 16:05 |
| CIUDAD REAL | 11:06 | 17:06 |
| PUERTOLLANO | * 11:23 | * 17:23 |
| CORDOBA | 12:12 | 18:11 |
| SEVILLA Santa Justa | 13:19 | 19:26 |
| JEREZ DE LA FRONTERA | 14:16 | 20:23 |
| EL PUERTO DE STA. MARIA | 14:27 | 20:36 |
| SAN FERNANDO DE CADIZ | 14:41 | 20:50 |
| **CADIZ** | 14:55 | 21:05 |

| CADIZ MADRID Puerta de Atocha | | LLANO |
|---|---|---|
| NUMERO DE TREN / DIAS DE CIRCULACION | 42 (2) / LMXJVSD | 9723 / LMXJVSD |
| **CADIZ** | 08:00 | 16:25 |
| SAN FERNANDO DE CADIZ | 08:13 | 16:36 |
| EL PUERTO DE STA. MARIA | 08:26 | 16:48 |
| JEREZ DE LA FRONTERA | 08:36 | 16:59 |
| SEVILLA Santa Justa | 09:43 | 17:57 |
| CORDOBA | * 10:50 | * 19:03 |
| PUERTOLLANO | 11:42 | 19:52 |
| CIUDAD REAL | 11:59 | 20:09 |
| **MADRID** Puerta de Atocha | 13:02 | 21:10 |

| MADRID Puerta de Atocha HUELVA | LLANO |
|---|---|
| NUMERO DE TREN / DIAS DE CIRCULACION | 9220 / LMXJVSD |
| **MADRID** Puerta de Atocha | 10:05 |
| CIUDAD REAL | 11:06 |
| PUERTOLLANO | * 11:23 |
| CORDOBA | 12:12 |
| LA PALMA DEL CONDADO (*) | 14:05 |
| **HUELVA** | 14:30 |

| HUELVA MADRID Puerta de Atocha | LLANO |
|---|---|
| NUMERO DE TREN / DIAS DE CIRCULACION | 9233 / LMXJVSD |
| **HUELVA** | 16:55 |
| LA PALMA DEL CONDADO | 17:19 |
| CORDOBA | * 19:03 |
| PUERTOLLANO | 19:52 |
| CIUDAD REAL | 20:09 |
| **MADRID** Puerta de Atocha | 21:10 |

(*) La Palma no admite viajeros destino Huelva.

TIPO DE RESTAURACION
SNACK
* El servicio de restauración en el asiento se realiza únicamente entre las estaciones señaladas.

OBSERVACIONES
(1) Procede de Barcelona, Zaragoza
(2) Continúa a Zaragoza, Barcelona

### La hora

Cuando lees el horario para el tren o un anuncio para un programa cultural, dan la hora usando las 24 horas. La una (1:00) es la una de la mañana y las doce (12:00) es el mediodía. Las trece (13:00), una hora después del mediodía, es la una de la tarde y las veinticuatro horas (00:00) es la medianoche.

Nuestros amigos José Luis y Maripaz salieron de Madrid a las 17:00 y llegaron a Sevilla a las 19:15. Es decir que salieron de Madrid a las 5:00 de la tarde y llegaron a las 7:15 de la tarde.

### El sistema métrico—pesos y medidas[1]

**Pesos**

Las medidas tradicionales para peso en los Estados Unidos son la onza, la libra y la tonelada. En el sistema métrico decimal, las medidas para peso están basadas en el kilogramo, o kilo.

[1]pesos y medidas *weights and measures*



## About the Spanish Language

Terms from the English system—**el pie, la yarda, el galón**—are seldom heard in Spanish.

Hay mil gramos en un kilo. El kilo es igual a 2,2 libras. Una libra estadounidense es un poco menos de medio kilo.

**Líquidos**

Las medidas para líquidos en Estados Unidos son la pinta, el cuarto y el galón. En el sistema métrico es el litro. Un litro contiene un poco más que un cuarto.

**Distancia y altura**

Para medir la distancia y la altura en Estados Unidos usamos la pulgada, el pie, la yarda y la milla. El sistema métrico usa el metro. El metro es un poco más que una yarda. Un kilómetro (mil metros) es 0,621 millas—un poco más que media milla.

## ¿Comprendes?

**A La hora** Read the schedule on page 22 and give the arrival and departure times of the trains using our system of telling time.

**B El sistema métrico** Contesten según las fotografías.

1. ¿Cuánto cuesta un litro de gasolina?
2. ¿Cuál es el límite de velocidad?
3. ¿Cuánto cuesta un litro de leche?
4. ¿Cuánto cuesta un kilo de carne?

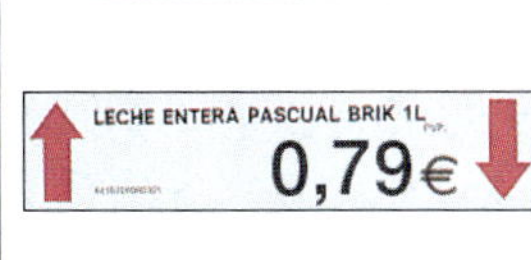

# Conexiones

## PRESENTATION

### *Las matemáticas*
### Conversiones aritméticas

**¡OJO!** The material in this section will probably be of more interest to students who like math and science. However, it is useful information for all students because when traveling through most areas of the Spanish-speaking world, one has to use the metric system.

**Step 1** Have students read the introduction in English on page 22.

**Step 2** Now have them read the selection quickly. Students should already be familiar with the metric terms used in the reading.

**Step 3** Explain to students some basic strategies to use when reading unfamiliar material. They should learn to: (1) recognize cognates and (2) derive meaning from context.

**Step 4** Now do the **¿Comprendes?** activities.

**LEVELING**

**A:** Reading

## ANSWERS TO ¿Comprendes?

**A** *Answers will vary. Students will have to convert from 24-hour clock times to our system of telling time.*

**B**

1. Un litro de gasolina super cuesta 0.869.
2. El límite de velocidad es de 60 kilómetros por hora.
3. Un litro de leche cuesta 0,79 euros.
4. Un kilo de carne cuesta 7,95 euros.

¡Te toca a ti!

## Use what you have learned

 **Recycling**

These activities allow students to use the vocabulary and structure from this chapter in completely open-ended, real-life situations.

### PRESENTATION

Encourage students to say as much as possible when they do these activities. Tell them not to be afraid to make mistakes, since the goal of the activities is real-life communication. If someone in the group makes an error, allow the others to politely correct him or her. Let students choose the activities they would like to do.

You may wish to divide students into pairs or groups. Encourage students to elaborate on the basic theme and to be creative. They may use props, pictures, or posters if they wish.

### PRACTICE

1 You may wish to assign one type of travel to each group.

### Writing Development

Have students keep a notebook or portfolio containing their best written work from each chapter. These selected writings can be based on assignments from the Student Textbook and the Workbook. Activities 4 and 5 on page 25 are examples of writing assignments that may be included in each student's portfolio. On page 12 in the Workbook, students will begin to develop an organized autobiography **(Mi autobiografía)**. These workbook pages may also become a part of their portfolio.

# ¡Te toca a ti!

## Use what you have learned

### 1 El tren, el bus o el avión

✔ *Discuss train, bus, and plane travel*

Work in groups of three or four. Discuss the advantages **(las ventajas)** and the disadvantages **(las desventajas)** of bus, train, and air travel. In your discussion, include such things as speed, price, location of stations, and anything else you consider important.

### 2 Y ahora, ¿qué hacemos?

✔ *Discuss what to do if you miss your train*

You and a classmate are on a bus on the way to the Atocha station in Madrid. There's an awful traffic jam **(un tapón, un atasco)**. You know you are going to miss your train. Discuss your predicament with one another and figure out what you can do.

La estación de ferrocarril, Málaga



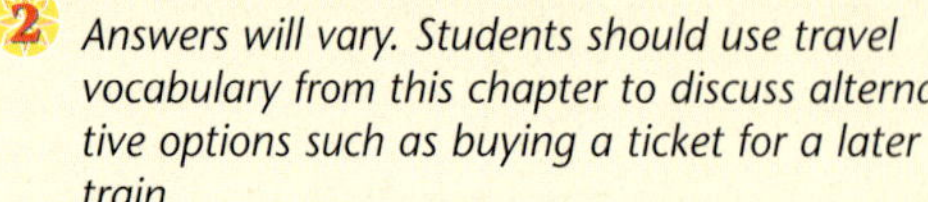

**Answers to ¡Te toca a ti!**

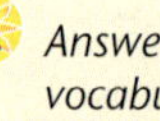

1 *Answers will vary. Students should use train vocabulary from this chapter and air travel vocabulary from* **¡Buen viaje! Level 1,** *Chapter 11.*

2 *Answers will vary. Students should use travel vocabulary from this chapter to discuss alternative options such as buying a ticket for a later train.*

## 3 En la estación de ferrocarril

✔ *Talk about activities at a train station*

With a classmate look at the photograph and talk about it.

## 4 ¡Una experiencia!

✔ *Write about an interesting train trip in Spain*

You took the AVE from Madrid to Sevilla. Write home and tell all about it.

## 5 Un viaje excelente

Write about a trip you took to a place you love. The place can be real or imaginary. Describe how and where you went and when. Then describe what the weather is like in that place and what clothing you need there. Continue writing about what you saw and how you got to each place you visited. In your description of the place, try to make your readers understand what it is about the place that you think is so great.

### Writing Strategy

**Writing a descriptive paragraph** Your overall goal in writing a descriptive paragraph is to enable the reader to visualize your scene. To achieve this you must select and organize details that create an impression. Using a greater number of specific nouns and vivid adjectives will make your writing livelier.



### Writing Strategy

**Writing a descriptive paragraph** Have students read the Writing Strategy on page 25. Your students may enjoy writing about a trip to Machu Picchu or one of the other beautiful tourist destinations in the Spanish-speaking world. To help stimulate your students' "creative juices," have them find a photo in the textbook of a place they'd like to visit. Ask them to look at the photo for inspiration as they do Activity 5 on page 25.

### LEVELING

These activities encompass all three levels. All students will be able to do them at a sophistication level commensurate with their ability in Spanish. Some students will be able to speak for several minutes, and others may be able to give just a few sentences. This is to be expected when students are functioning completely on their own generating their own language to the best of their ability.

### Answers to ¡Te toca a ti!

3. *Answers will vary. Students should discuss all activities associated with train travel.*

4. *Answers will vary. Students should use the preterite tense to describe their train trip.*

5. *Answers will vary. Students should use the preterite tense to describe their train trip.*

Assessment

## Resource Manager

Communication Transparency C 1
Quizzes, pages 1–5
Performance Assessment, Task 1
Tests, pages 1–14
Situation Cards, Chapter 1
ExamView® Pro, Chapter 1
**Maratón mental** Videoquiz, Chapter 1

## Assessment

This is a pre-test for students to take before you administer the chapter test. Note that each section is cross-referenced so students can easily find the material they have to review in case they made errors. You may use Assessment Answers Transparency A 1 to do the assessment in class, or you may assign this assessment for homework. You can correct the assessment yourself, or you may prefer to project the answers on the overhead in class.

## Glencoe Technology

**MINDJOGGER VHS/DVD**
You may wish to help your students prepare for the chapter test by playing the MindJogger game show. Teams will compete against each other to review chapter vocabulary and structure and sharpen listening comprehension skills.

Assessment

# Vocabulario

To review **Palabras 1**, turn to pages 2–3.

**1 Completen.**

1. Elena va de Madrid a Córdoba y va a volver a Madrid. Quiere un billete ____.
2. Los pasajeros esperan el tren en el andén o en la ____.
3. El ____ de llegadas indica a qué hora llegan los trenes a la estación.
4. Venden periódicos y revistas en el ____ en la estación de ferrocarril.
5. Un tren tiene varios vagones o ____.

To review **Palabras 2**, turn to pages 6–7.

**2 ¿Sí o no?**

6. El revisor trabaja en la estación de ferrocarril.
7. Una litera es un tipo de cama donde puede dormir un pasajero en un tren.
8. El tren que salió a tiempo salió con una demora.
9. Los pasajeros que van de Cuzco a Machu Picchu bajan del tren en Cuzco.

## Answers to Assessment

1. de ida y vuelta
2. sala de espera
3. tablero
4. quiosco
5. coches

6. No
7. Sí
8. No
9. No

# Estructura

**3** **Escriban en el pretérito.**

10. Los turistas andan por la plaza principal.
11. Él hace la cama por la mañana.
12. Lo pongo en la maleta.
13. ¿Quién lo sabe?
14. No estamos en la capital.

To review the preterite, turn to pages 10, 12, and 13.

**4** **Completen con decir.**

15–16. Yo lo ____ ahora y lo ____ ayer.
17–18. Ellos lo ____ ahora y lo ____ ayer.

To review decir, turn to page 14.

# Cultura

**5** **Contesten.**

19. ¿Qué es el AVE?
20. ¿A qué ciudad de Andalucía fueron José Luis y su hermana?

To review this cultural information, turn to page 18.

## Assessment

**FOLDABLES™ Study Organizer** **Dinah Zike's Study Guides**

Your students may wish to use Foldable 11 to organize, display, and arrange data as they learn to use the preterite tense in Spanish. You may wish to encourage them to add pairs of sentences as they continue to expand their understanding of how to use the past and present tenses.

*Large sentence strips* are also ideal for having students compare and contrast other grammatical structures that they will learn.

## Answers to Assessment

10. Los turistas anduvieron por la plaza principal.
11. Él hizo la cama en la mañana.
12. Lo puse en la maleta.
13. ¿Quién lo supo?
14. No estuvimos en la capital.

15. digo
16. dije
17. dicen
18. dijeron

19. El AVE es un tren español de alta velocidad.
20. José Luis y su hermana fueron a Sevilla.

# ¡Hablo como un pro!

This unique page gives students the opportunity to speak freely and say whatever they can, using the vocabulary and structures they have learned in the chapter. The illustration serves to remind students of precisely what they know how to say in Spanish. There are no activities that students do not have the ability to describe or talk about in Spanish. The art not only depicts the vocabulary and content of this chapter, but also reinforces what they learned in previous chapters.

You may wish to use this page in many ways. Some possibilities are to have students do the following:

1. Look at the illustration and identify items by giving the correct Spanish words.
2. Make up sentences about what they see in the illustration.
3. Make up questions about the illustration. They can call on another class member to respond if you do this as a class activity, or you may prefer to allow students to work in small groups. This activity is extremely beneficial because it enables students to actively use interrogative words.
4. Answer questions you ask them about the illustration.
5. Work in pairs and make up a conversation based on the illustration.
6. Look at the illustration and give a complete oral review of what they see.
7. Look at the illustration and write a paragraph (or essay) about it.

You can also use this page as an assessment or testing tool, taking into account individual differences by having students go from simple to quite complicated tasks.

# ¡Hablo como un pro!

Tell all you can about this illustration.

The assessment can be either oral or written. You may wish to use the rubrics provided on pages T20–T21 as you give students the following directions.

1. Identify the topic or situation of the illustration.
2. Give the Spanish words for as many items as you can.
3. Think of as many sentences as you can to describe the illustration.
4. Go over your sentences and put them in the best sequencing to give a coherent story based on the illustration.

### Getting around a train station

la estación de ferrocarril
la ventanilla
el billete, el boleto sencillo
de ida y vuelta
la sala de espera
el mozo, el maletero
el equipaje
la maleta
la bolsa
el tablero de llegadas, de salidas
el horario
el quiosco
el tren
el andén
la vía
en segunda (clase)
en primera (clase)

**How well do you know your vocabulary?**

- Choose five words from the vocabulary list.
- Use the words in original sentences to tell a story.

### Describing activities at a train station

bajar(se) del tren
subir al tren
transbordar
salir a tiempo
con retraso, con una demora

### On board the train

el coche, el vagón
el pasillo
el compartimiento
el asiento, la plaza
libre
ocupado(a)
reservado(a)
completo(a)
el coche-cama
el coche-comedor, el coche-cafetería
la litera
el revisor
la parada
en la próxima parada

**VIDEOTUR**

## Episodio 1

In this video episode, you will join Claudiá and Francisco in an unusual train experience. See page 480 for more information.



Vocabulario

## Vocabulary Review

The words and phrases in the **Vocabulario** have been taught for productive use in this chapter. They are summarized here as a resource for both student and teacher. This list also serves as a convenient resource for the **¡Te toca a ti!** activities on pages 24 and 25. There are approximately four cognates in this vocabulary list. Have students find them.

**¡OJO!** You will notice that the vocabulary list here is not translated. This has been done intentionally, since we feel that by the time students have finished the material in the chapter they should be familiar with the meanings of all the words. If there are several words they still do not know, we recommend that they refer to the **Palabras 1** and **2** sections in the chapter or go to the dictionaries at the end of this book to find the meanings. However, if you prefer that your students have the English translations, please refer to Vocabulary Transparency 1.1, where you will find all these words with their translations.

**VIDEO VHS/DVD**

The Video Program allows students to see how the chapter vocabulary and structures are used by native speakers within an engaging story line. For maximum reinforcement, show the video episode as a final activity for Chapter 1.

# Planning for Chapter 2

## SCOPE AND SEQUENCE, PAGES 30–57

### Topics

- ❖ Restaurants
- ❖ Foods and eating utensils

### Culture

- ❖ Typical cuisine from Mexico
- ❖ Typical cuisine from Spain
- ❖ Typical foods from the Caribbean
- ❖ Regional vocabulary in the Spanish-speaking world

### Functions

- ❖ How to order food or beverage at a restaurant
- ❖ How to identify eating utensils and dishes
- ❖ How to make a reservation at a restaurant
- ❖ How to explain how you like certain foods prepared
- ❖ How to talk about present and past events and activities

### Structure

- ❖ Stem-changing verbs in the present
- ❖ Stem-changing verbs in the preterite

### National Standards

- ❖ Communication Standard 1.1 pages 34, 35, 38, 39, 40, 41, 42, 52
- ❖ Communication Standard 1.2 pages 35, 39, 41, 43, 44, 45, 46–47, 48, 49, 50–51, 52, 53
- ❖ Communication Standard 1.3 pages 45, 53
- ❖ Cultures Standard 2.1 page 44
- ❖ Cultures Standard 2.2 pages 46–47, 48, 49, 50
- ❖ Connections Standard 3.1 pages 50–51
- ❖ Comparisons Standard 4.1 pages 50–51
- ❖ Communities Standard 5.1 page 57
- ❖ Communities Standard 5.2 page 38

## PACING AND PRIORITIES

**The chapter content is color coded below to assist you in planning.**

**■ required ■ recommended ■ optional**

**Vocabulario** *(required)* *Days 1–4*
- ■ Palabras 1
  En el restaurante
- ■ Palabras 2
  Más alimentos o comestibles

**Estructura** *(required)* *Days 5–7*
- ■ Verbos con el cambio **e → i** en el presente
- ■ Verbos con el cambio **e → i, o → u** en el pretérito

**Conversación** *(required)*
- ■ En el restaurante

**Pronunciación** *(recommended)*
- ■ La consonante **x**

**Lecturas culturales**
- ■ La comida mexicana *(recommended)*
- ■ La comida española *(optional)*
- ■ La comida del Caribe *(optional)*

**Conexiones**
- ■ El lenguaje *(optional)*

■ **¡Te toca a ti!** *(recommended)*

■ **Assessment** *(recommended)*

■ **¡Hablo como un pro!** *(optional)*

## RESOURCE GUIDE

| Section | Pages | Section Resources |
|---|---|---|
| **Vocabulario PALABRAS 1** | | |
| En el restaurante | 32–35 | Vocabulary Transparencies 2.2–2.3<br>Audio CD 2<br>Audio Activities TE, pages 14–16<br>Workbook, pages 13–14<br>Quiz 1, page 7<br>ExamView® Pro |
| **Vocabulario PALABRAS 2** | | |
| Más alimentos o comestibles | 36–39 | Vocabulary Transparencies 2.4–2.5<br>Audio CD 2<br>Audio Activities TE, pages 16–19<br>Workbook, pages 15–16<br>Quiz 2, pages 8–9<br>ExamView® Pro |
| **Estructura** | | |
| Verbos con el cambio **e → i** en el presente<br>Verbos con el cambio **e → i, o → u** en el pretérito | 40–41<br>42–43 | Audio CD 2<br>Audio Activities TE, pages 19–20<br>Workbook, pages 17–18<br>Quizzes 3–4, pages 10–11<br>ExamView® Pro |
| **Conversación** | | |
| En el restaurante | 44 | Audio CD 2<br>Audio Activities TE, page 21 |
| **Pronunciación** | | |
| La consonante **x** | 45 | Audio CD 2<br>Audio Activities TE, page 22<br>Interactive CD-ROM |
| **Lecturas culturales** | | |
| La comida mexicana<br>La comida española<br>La comida del Caribe | 46–47<br>48<br>49 | Audio CD 2<br>Audio Activities TE, page 22<br>Tests, pages 17, 21 |
| **Conexiones** | | |
| El lenguaje | 50–51 | Tests, page 22 |
| **¡Te toca a ti!** | | |
| | 52–53 | **¡Viva el mundo hispano!** Video, Episode 2<br>Video Activities, pages 66–68<br>Spanish Online Activities spanish.glencoe.com |
| **Assessment** | | |
| | 54–55 | Communication Transparency C 2<br>Quizzes 1–4, pages 7–11<br>Performance Assessment, Task 2<br>Tests, pages 15–28<br>Situation Cards, Chapter 2<br>ExamView® Pro<br>**Maratón mental** Videoquiz |

# Using Your Resources for Chapter 2

## Transparencies

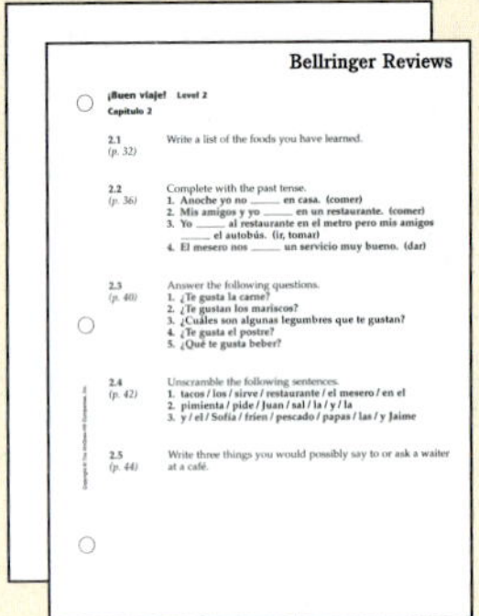
Bellringer 2.1–2.5

Vocabulary 2.1–2.5

Communication C 2

## Workbook

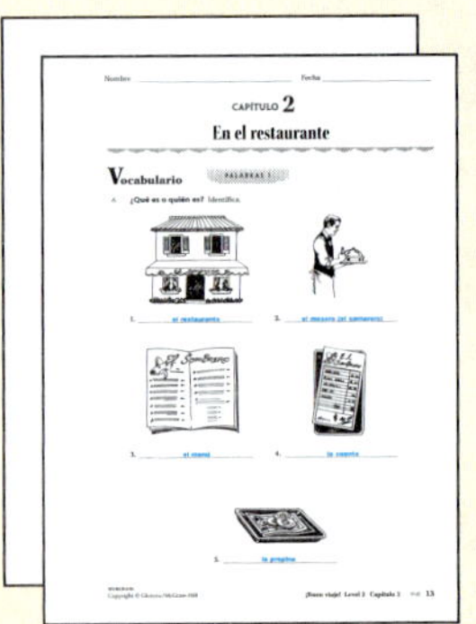
Vocabulary, pages 13–16

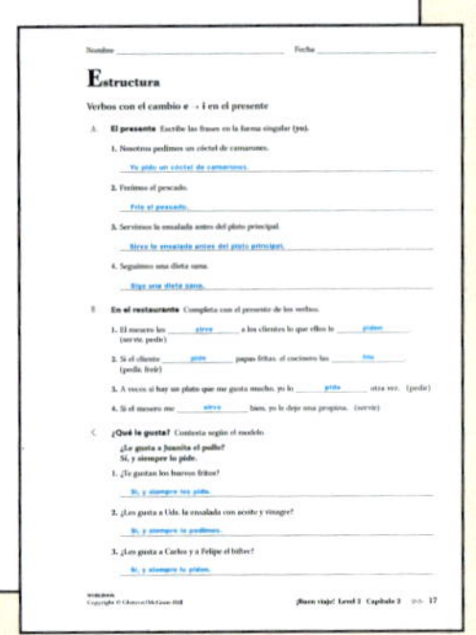
Structure, pages 17–18

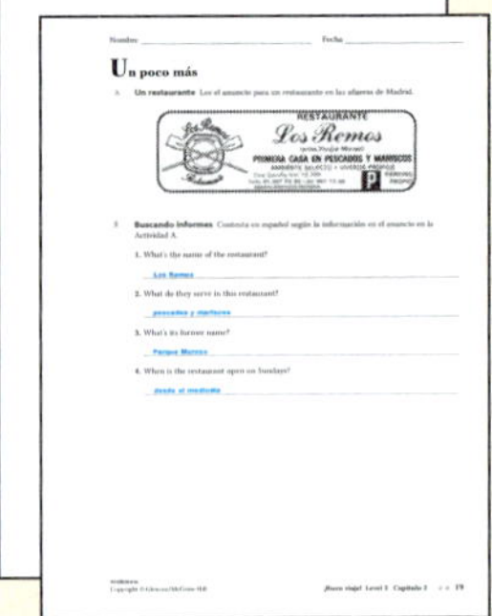
Enrichment, pages 19–22

## Audio Activities

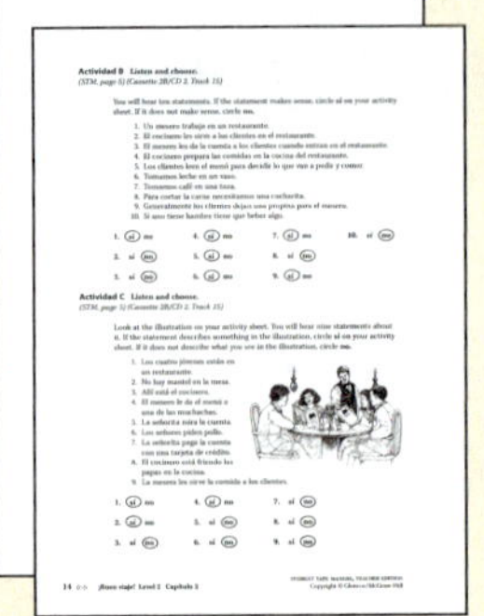
Vocabulary, pages 14–19

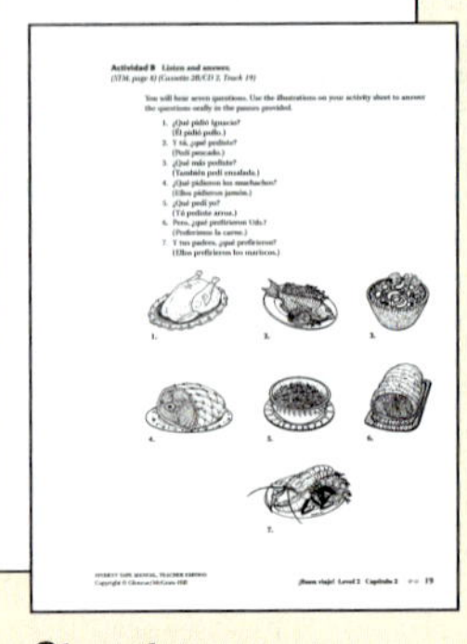
Structure, pages 19–20

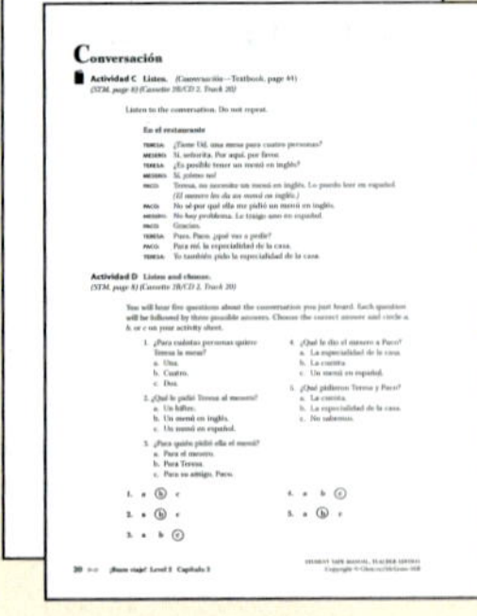
Conversation, page 21
Pronunciation, page 22

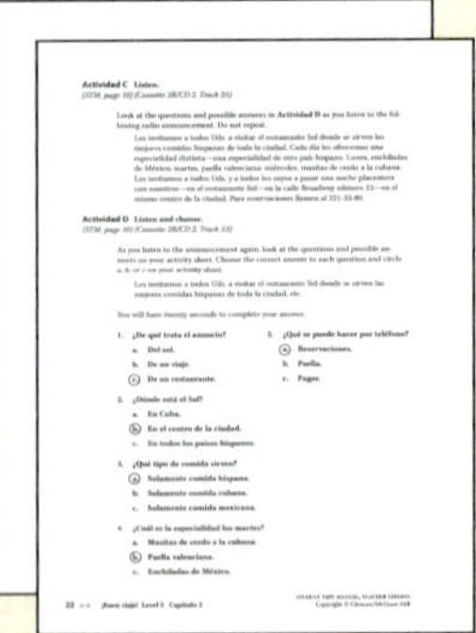
Additional Practice, pages 22–24

# Assessment

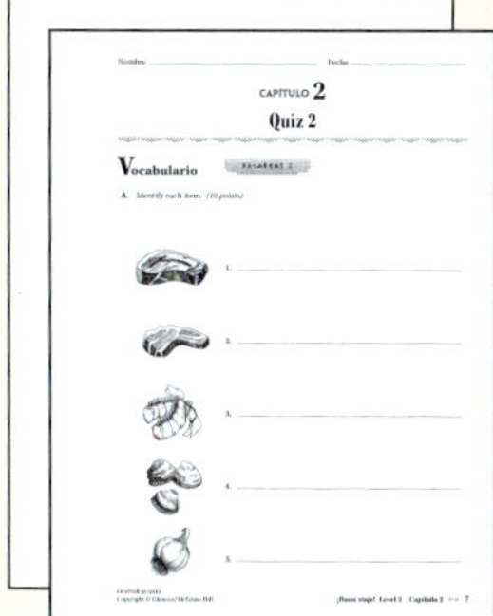

**Vocabulary and Structure Quizzes, pages 7–11**

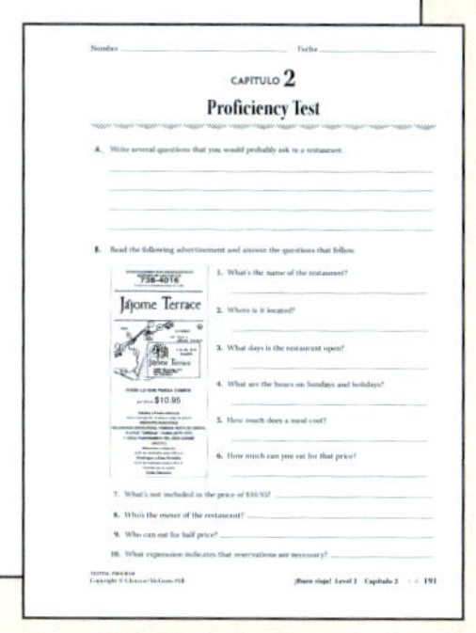

**Chapter Tests, pages 15–28**

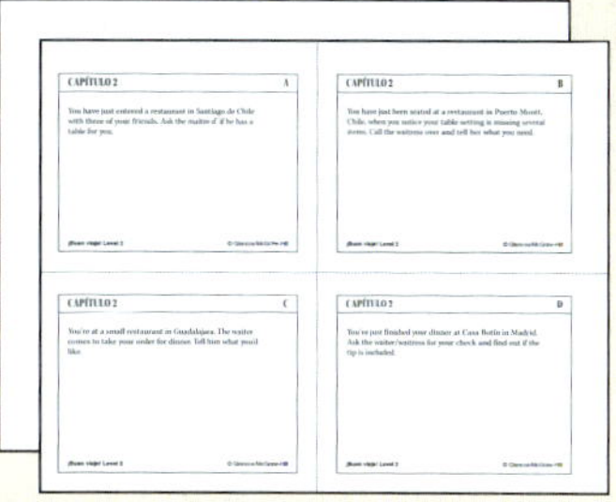

**Situation Cards, Chapter 2**

**MindJogger Videoquiz, ExamView® Pro, Chapter 2**

## Timesaving Teacher Tools

### TeacherWorks™

TeacherWorks™ is your all-in-one teacher resource center. Personalize lesson plans, access resources from the Teacher Wraparound Edition, connect to the Internet, or make a to-do list. These are only a few of the many features that can assist you in the planning and organizing of your lessons.

Includes:

- A calendar feature
- Access to all program blackline masters
- Standards correlations and more

### ExamView® Pro

Test Bank software for Macintosh and Windows makes creating, editing, customizing, and printing tests quick and easy.

## Technology Resources

In the Chapter 2 Internet Activity, you will have a chance to learn more about the Spanish-speaking world. Visit spanish.glencoe.com

On the interactive CD–ROM, students can listen to and take part in a recorded version of the conversation in Chapter 2.

**¡Viva el mundo hispano!** Video and Video Activities, Chapter 2. Available on VHS and DVD.

Help your students prepare for the chapter test by playing the **Maratón mental** Videoquiz game show. Teams will compete against each other to review chapter vocabulary and structure and sharpen listening comprehension skills. Available on VHS and DVD.

**¡Buen viaje!** is also available on CD or Online.

Capítulo 2

## Preview

In this chapter, students will learn how to order food in a restaurant. To do this, they will learn expressions needed to speak with a server, vocabulary associated with utensils, and additional items of food. They will continue to narrate in the present and past by learning the present and preterite of stem-changing verbs they can use at a restaurant—**pedir, servir, repetir.** The cultural focus of the chapter is on some typical cuisines of the Spanish-speaking world.

### National Standards

**Communication**

In Chapter 2 students will learn to communicate in spoken and written Spanish on the following topics:

- ordering a meal
- describing a restaurant experience
- discussing cuisines of the Spanish-speaking world

Students will obtain and provide information about these topics and engage in conversations that would typically take place at a restaurant as they fulfill the chapter objectives listed on this page.

### LEVELING

The activities, conversations, and readings within each chapter are marked according to level of difficulty. **E** indicates easy. **A** indicates average. **C** indicates challenging. Some activities cover a range of difficulty. In some activities, for example, advanced students will be able to produce more extensive responses while students who learn at a different rate may give less detailed responses. The leveling indicators will help you individualize instruction to best meet your students' needs.

Hernán Miranda *Interiores con mesa*

Capítulo 2

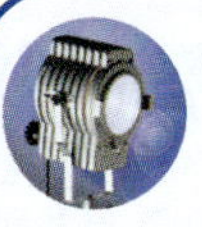

## Spotlight on Culture

**Arte** Hernán Miranda (1960) is a self-taught, contemporary Paraguayan artist. From 1993 until 1997, he was Professor of Art at the **Escuela Nacional de Bellas Artes** in Asunción. His recent works focus primarily on the objects of daily life such as utensils, fruit, and dishware.

**Fotografía** The restaurant shown on this page is in Lima.

## Learning from Photos

*(pages 30–31)* Ask the following questions about the photo after presenting the new vocabulary in this chapter:

**¿Es un restaurante económico o elegante?**

**¿Está poniendo la mesa el mesero?**

**Identifica todo lo que ves en la mesa.**

**¿Cuántas personas hay en la familia que está en el restaurante?**

**¿Cómo está vestido el papá? ¿Qué lleva?**

**¿Qué leen la mamá y el papá?**

PALABRAS 1

# 1 PREPARATION

## Resource Manager

Vocabulary Transparencies 2.2–2.3
Audio Activities TE, pages 14–16
Audio CD 2
Workbook, pages 13–14
Quizzes, page 7
ExamView® Pro

## Bellringer Review

*Use BRR Transparency 2.1 or write the following on the board.*
Write a list of the foods you have learned.

# 2 PRESENTATION

**Step 1** Have students close their books. Show Vocabulary Transparencies 2.2–2.3. Point to individual items and have students repeat each word or expression two or three times after you or Audio CD 2.

**Step 2** Intersperse the presentation with simple questions that enable students to use the new words. For example: **¿Tienes hambre? ¿Quieres comer? ¿Tienes sed? ¿Qué pone el mesero? ¿Usas la taza para beber o para cortar la carne?** Have students answer with complete sentences or sometimes have them answer with a word or an expression.

**Step 3** After presenting the vocabulary orally, have students open their books and read the new vocabulary aloud. You can have the class read in chorus or call on individuals to read. Intersperse with questions such as those outlined above.

# Vocabulario

PALABRAS 1

## En el restaurante

El mesero pone la mesa.

Tengo hambre y quiero comer.

Tengo sed y quiero beber algo.

32

## Reaching All Students

**Total Physical Response** Teach the following words by using the appropriate gestures as you say each expression: **cubre, dobla, a la derecha, a la izquierda, deja.**

*(Student 1),* **ven acá, por favor.**
**Vas a poner la mesa.**
**Cubre la mesa con un mantel.**
**Dobla las servilletas.**
**Pon un plato en la mesa.**
**Luego pon la cucharita y el cuchillo a la derecha.**
**Pon el tenedor a la izquierda. Gracias.**
*(Student 2),* **ven acá, por favor.**
**Vas a hacer unos gestos.**
**Toma el menú. Abre el menú.**
**Lee el menú. Cierra el menú.**
**Corta la carne con el cuchillo. Come.**
**Bebe. Deja una propina para el mesero.**
**Gracias,** *(Student 2).* **Regresa a tu asiento.**

# Vocabulario

La señorita pide el menú.

El cocinero fríe las papas.
Está friendo las papas.

El mesero le sirve la comida.



La señorita pide la cuenta.
El servicio no está incluido.
Ella deja una propina.

## Fun Facts

In Spain and in many countries of Latin America, a saltshaker is put on the table but not a pepper shaker or pepper mill. If you want pepper you have to ask for it. The only exceptions would be in some international restaurants and hotels.

## Reaching All Students

**Additional Practice** You may have students make up a brief conversation using the words **hambre** and **sed**. For example:
**¿Sabes? Tengo hambre.**
**¿Ah sí? ¿Qué quieres comer?**
**Pues, creo que voy a pedir ___.**

**For the Younger Students** You may wish to bring in silverware and have students set a table as they learn to identify each item.

**LEVELING**
**A:** Vocabulary

## About the Spanish Language

- The word **mesero** is used in Latin America. **Camarero** is used in Spain.
- The word **el menú** is universally understood. Other words frequently used for **menú** are **la minuta** and **la carta.**
- We have presented the words **sal** and **pimienta** but not **el salero** and **el pimentero,** since these words are hardly ever used. One would say: **Sal, por favor.**

Vocabulario

## 3 PRACTICE

## ¿Qué palabra necesito?

**¡OJO!** When students are doing the **¿Qué palabra necesito?** activities, accept any answer that makes sense. The purpose of these activities is to have students use the new vocabulary. They are not factual recall activities. Thus, it is not necessary for students to remember specific factual information from the vocabulary presentation when answering. If you wish, have students use the photos on this page as a stimulus, when possible.

**Historieta** Each time **Historieta** appears, it means that the answers to the activity form a short story. Encourage students to look at the title of the **Historieta,** since it can help them do the activity.

**1** Have students work with a partner.
**Expansion:** Ask students to volunteer additional items. For example: **Para tomar una limonada, una sopa,** etc.

**2** After going over Activity 2, have students retell the story in their own words.

Vocabulario

# ¿Qué palabra necesito?

**1** **¿Qué necesitas?** Contesten según el modelo.

**¿Para tomar leche? →**
**Para tomar leche necesito un vaso.**

1. ¿Para tomar agua?
2. ¿Para tomar café?
3. ¿Para comer la ensalada?
4. ¿Para comer el postre?
5. ¿Para cortar la carne?

**2** **Historieta** **En el restaurante**
Contesten.

1. ¿Cuántas personas hay en la mesa?
2. ¿Tiene hambre María?
3. ¿Pide María el menú?
4. ¿Le trae el menú el mesero?
5. ¿Qué pide María?
6. ¿El mesero le sirve?
7. ¿El mesero le sirve bien?
8. Después de la comida, ¿le pide la cuenta al mesero?
9. ¿Le trae la cuenta el mesero?
10. ¿Paga con su tarjeta de crédito María?
11. ¿María le da (deja) una propina al mesero?
12. Después de la comida, ¿tiene hambre María?



## ANSWERS TO ¿Qué palabra necesito?

**1**

1. Para tomar agua necesito un vaso.
2. Para tomar café necesito una taza.
3. Para comer la ensalada necesito un tenedor.
4. Para comer el postre necesito una cucharita (un tenedor).
5. Para cortar la carne necesito un cuchillo.

**2**

1. Hay una persona en la mesa.
2. Sí, María tiene hambre.
3. Sí, María pide el menú.
4. Sí, el mesero le trae el menú.
5. María pide ___.
6. Sí, el mesero le sirve.
7. Sí, el mesero le sirve bien.
8. Sí, le pide la cuenta al mesero después de la comida.
9. Sí, el mesero le trae la cuenta.
10. Sí (No), María (no) paga con su tarjeta de crédito.
11. Sí, María le da (deja) una propina al mesero.
12. No, María no tiene hambre después de la comida.

## 3 Palabras relacionadas Pareen las palabras relacionadas.

| | |
|---|---|
| 1. la mesa | a. el servicio |
| 2. la cocina | b. la bebida |
| 3. servir | c. el cocinero |
| 4. freír | d. la comida |
| 5. comer | e. el mesero |
| 6. beber | f. frito |

Alcalá de Henares, España

## 4 Historieta El mesero pone la mesa. Completen.

1. Para comer, los clientes necesitan ___, ___, ___ y ___.
2. Dos condimentos son la ___ y la ___.
3. El mesero cubre la mesa con ___.
4. En la mesa el mesero pone una ___ para cada cliente.
5. El niño pide un ___ de leche y sus padres piden una ___ de café.
6. Ellos tienen ___ y piden una botella de agua mineral.

## 5 En el restaurante

Look at the advertisement for a restaurant in Santiago de Chile. Tell as much as you can about the restaurant based on the information in the advertisement. A classmate will tell whether he or she wants to go to the restaurant and why.

## Vocabulario

**3** This activity helps students learn to identify word families.

**¡OJO!** Note that the activities are color-coded. All the activities in the text are communicative. However, the ones with blue titles are guided communication. The red titles indicate that the answers to the activity are more open-ended and can vary more. You may wish to correct students' mistakes more so in the guided activities than in the activities with a red title, which lend themselves to a freer response.

**5** Students should base their descriptions on both the descriptive paragraph and the two photos in this ad. Explain to the class that the phrase **e informal** is not a spelling error. After students have done **Palabras 2,** pages 36–37, see how many seafood items they can identify in this ad.

### Learning from Realia

*(page 34)* The name of the restaurant on the check is **Alkalde.** It is a Basque restaurant. The Basques are considered to be some of the best cooks in Spain.
*(page 35)* There is something in this ad that indicates that the restaurant must be in South America. What is it? **(del Pacífico Sur)**

### LEVELING

**E:** Activities 1, 2, 3
**A:** Activities 1, 2, 4, 5

## Answers to ¿Qué palabra necesito?

**3**

1. e
2. c
3. a
4. f
5. d
6. b

**4**

1. un plato, un tenedor, un cuchillo, una cucharita (una cuchara)
2. sal, pimienta
3. un mantel
4. servilleta
5. vaso, taza
6. sed

**5** *Answers will vary; however, students should mention the type of dishes served* (pescados y mariscos) *and whether the restaurant is formal or informal.*

# Vocabulario

PALABRAS 2

## 1 PREPARATION

### Resource Manager

Vocabulary Transparencies 2.4–2.5
Audio Activities TE, pages 16–19
Audio CD 2
Workbook, pages 15–16
Quizzes, pages 8–9
ExamView® Pro

### Bellringer Review

*Use BRR Transparency 2.2 or write the following on the board.*
Complete with the past tense.

1. Anoche yo no ___ en casa. (comer)
2. Mis amigos y yo ___ en un restaurante. (comer)
3. Yo ___ al restaurante en el metro pero mis amigos ___ el autobús. (ir, tomar)
4. El mesero nos ___ un servicio muy bueno. (dar)

# Vocabulario

PALABRAS 2

## Más alimentos o comestibles

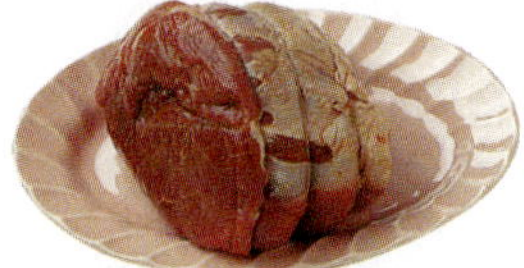

la carne

la carne de res, el biftec

la ternera

el cerdo

el cordero

el pescado

los mariscos

los camarones

las almejas

la langosta

## Reaching All Students

### Total Physical Response

*(Student 1),* levántate y ven acá, por favor.
Estamos en el restaurante Mendoza.
Lee el menú y llama al mesero.
*(Student 2),* ven acá. Tú vas a ser el mesero.
*(Student 1),* pídele al mesero lo que quieres comer.
*(Student 2),* escribe lo que pide.
Ve a la cocina y vuelve con la comida.
Pon los platos en la mesa.
*(Student 1),* come.

*(Student 2),* ve a la mesa.
*(Student 1),* dale el plato.
Pide la cuenta y mira la cuenta.
Saca el dinero de tu bolsillo.
Paga, levántate y sal del restaurante.
Gracias, *(Student 1).* Ahora puedes volver a tu asiento.
Y tú también, *(Student 2).* Gracias.

La joven pidió un biftec.
El mesero sirvió el biftec.
La comida está rica, deliciosa.

# Vocabulario

## 2 PRESENTATION

**Step 1** Have students close their books. Then model the new vocabulary on pages 36–37 using Vocabulary Transparencies 2.4–2.5. Have students repeat each word or expression two or three times after you or Audio CD 2.

**Step 2** Clarify any cuts of meat that are not evident. For example, students may not know **carne de res** *(beef)*, **ternera** *(veal)*, **cerdo** *(pork)*, **cordero** *(lamb)*.

**Step 3** Have students read the dialogue on page 37 aloud. You may want to have several students perform the telephone conversation for the class.

### Vocabulary Expansion

You may wish to introduce the following expressions:

| | |
|---|---|
| **bien hecho(a), cocido(a)** | *well-done* |
| **a término medio** | *medium* |
| **casi crudo, no muy cocido(a)** | *rare* |

A waiter will frequently ask:
**¿Qué les apetece?** *(What would you like to order?)*

## About the Spanish Language

- Explain the difference between **La comida está buena** and **La comida es buena. (La comida está buena significa que la comida está deliciosa, que tiene buen sabor. La comida es buena significa que es buena para la salud—contiene vitaminas, etc.)**
- In addition to el maíz, you will also hear **el elote** (Mexico) and **el choclo** (South America).
- In addition to **la alcachofa**, you will also hear **la cotufa.**
- There are several ways to say *shrimp.* The differences in names reflect type and size. In addition to **el camarón** you will hear **la gamba** (usually small shrimp in Spain), **el langostino** (large, but not a lobster), and **la quisquilla.**
- **Biftec** and **bistec** are commonly used for **steak**. You will also hear **filete** and **entrecot. Filete**, however, can be a filet of any type of meat or fish. **El entrecot** is meat only. The word **lomo** refers to any cut from the loin area. **Lomo de carne de res** is similar to a sirloin steak. **Solomillo** or **lomo fino** is similar to a tenderloin or filet mignon. In many areas of Latin America **el churrasco** is a grilled steak.

## 3 PRACTICE

## ¿Qué palabra necesito?

**¡OJO!** It is recommended that you go over all the activities in class before assigning them for homework.

**6** After doing Activity 6, go back to page 36 and ask students whether they like the other food items on that page.

**7** After doing Activity 7, have one or two students retell the story in their own words.

**Learning from Photos**

*(page 38)* Have students describe what they see in these photos in their own words.

Vocabulario

## ¿Qué palabra necesito?

**6** **¿Te gusta(n) o no te gusta(n)?** Contesten según los dibujos.

1.

2.

3.

4.

5.

6.

Barcelona, España

**7** **Historieta Cenó en el restaurante.**
Contesten.

1. ¿Fue Victoria al restaurante anoche?
2. ¿Quién le sirvió?
3. ¿Pidió Victoria un biftec?
4. ¿Pidió también una ensalada?
5. ¿Le sirvió el mesero una ensalada de lechuga y tomate?
6. ¿Le sirvió una comida deliciosa o una comida mala?

**SPANISH Online**
For more information about varieties of food in the Spanish-speaking world, go to the Glencoe Spanish Web site: spanish.glencoe.com



## ANSWERS TO ¿Qué palabra necesito?

1. (No) Me gusta el biftec.
2. (No) Me gusta el pescado.
3. (No) Me gustan los camarones (las gambas).
4. (No) Me gustan los guisantes.
5. (No) Me gusta el maíz.
6. (No) Me gustan las almejas.

1. Sí, Victoria fue al restaurante anoche.
2. El mesero le sirvió.
3. Sí (No), Victoria (no) pidió un biftec.
4. Sí, (No, no) pidió una ensalada.
5. Sí (No), el mesero (no) le sirvió una ensalada de lechuga y tomate.
6. Le sirvió una comida deliciosa (mala).

# Vocabulario

**8 ¿Qué te gusta?** Contesten personalmente.

1. ¿Te gusta la ensalada?
2. ¿Te gusta la ensalada con aceite y vinagre?
3. ¿Te gusta el biftec?
4. ¿Te gusta el sándwich de jamón y queso? ¿Te gusta más con pan tostado?
5. ¿Te gusta la tortilla de queso?
6. ¿Te gustan los huevos con jamón?

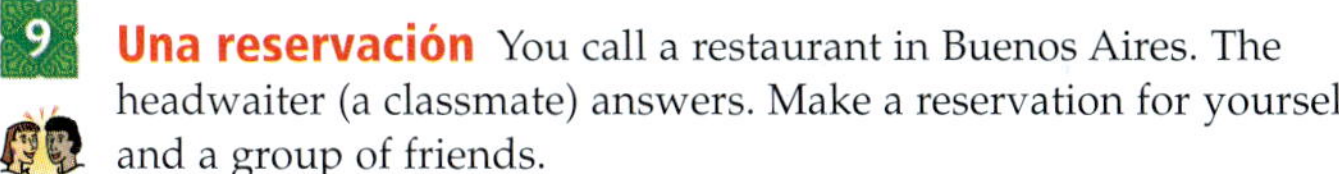

**9 Una reservación** You call a restaurant in Buenos Aires. The headwaiter (a classmate) answers. Make a reservation for yourself and a group of friends.

**10 ¿Qué recomienda usted?** Here's a menu from a very famous restaurant in Madrid. In fact, it's the oldest restaurant in the city, dating from 1725. There are many items on the menu that you will be able to recognize. A classmate will be the server. Ask what he or she recommends and then order.

CARTA
I.V.A. 7% INCLUIDO

RESTAURANT
3ª Categoría

ENTRADAS

Jugos de tomate, naranja ........ 2,60
Pimientos asados con bacalao ........ 6,40
Lomo ibérico de bellota ........ 15,00
Jamón ibérico de bellota ........ 16,50
Surtido ibérico de bellota ........ 14,10
Melón con jamón ........ 13,00
Queso (manchego) ........ 5,80
Ensalada riojana ........ 6,20
Ensalada de lechuga y tomate ........ 3,10
ENSALADA BOTIN (con pollo y jamón) ........ 7,90
Ensalada de rape y langostinos ........ 17,00
Ensalada de endivias con perdiz ........ 13,00
Morcilla de Burgos ........ 4,80
Croquetas de pollo y jamón ........ 5,80
Manitas de cochinillo rebozadas ........ 5,20
Salmón ahumado ........ 13,20

SOPAS

Sopa al cuarto de hora (de pescados) ........ 10,60
SOPA DE AJO CON HUEVO ........ 3,80
Caldo de ave ........ 3,20
Gazpacho ........ 5,30

HUEVOS

Revuelto de la casa (morcilla y patatas) ........ 5,50
Huevos revueltos con espárragos trigueros ........ 6,60
Huevos revueltos con salmón ahumado ........ 7,00
Tortilla de gambas ........ 7,00

VERDURAS

Espárragos con mahonesa ........ 8,90
Menestra de verduras salteadas con jamón ibérico ........ 7,80
Alcachofas salteadas con jamón ibérico ........ 5,90
Judías verdes con jamón ibérico ........ 5,90
Setas a la segoviana ........ 6,40
Patatas fritas ........ 2,40
Patatas asadas ........ 2,40

PESCADOS

Angulas ........ (según mercado)
ALMEJAS BOTIN ........ 15,70
Langostinos con mahonesa ........ 24,00
Gambas al ajillo ........ 17,00
Gambas a la plancha ........ 17,00
Cazuela de pescados ........ 18,00
Rape en salsa ........ 17,40
Merluza al horno o frita ........ 20,00
Lenguado frito, al horno o a la plancha (pieza) ........ 16,00
Calamares fritos ........ 10,00
CHIPIRONES EN SU TINTA (arroz blanco) ........ 10,10

ASADOS Y PARRILLAS

COCHINILLO ASADO ........ 15,40
CORDERO ASADO ........ 16,00
Pollo asado 1/2 ........ 6,30
Pollo en cacerola 1/2 ........ 8,40
Perdiz estofada (pieza) ........ 16,40
Filete de ternera a la plancha ........ 12,00
Escalope de ternera ........ 12,00
Ternera asada con guisantes ........ 12,00
Solomillo a la plancha ........ 17,00
SOLOMILLO BOTIN (al champiñón) ........ 17,00
"Entrecotte" de cebón a la plancha ........ 16,00

POSTRES

Cuajada ........ 4,30
Tarta helada ........ 4,40
Tarta de la casa (crema y bizcocho) ........ 4,50
Tarta de chocolate ........ 4,70
Tarta de frambuesa ........ 5,30
Pastel ruso (crema de praliné) ........ 5,20
Flan de la casa ........ 2,70
Flan de la casa con nata ........ 4,50
Helado de chocolate o caramelo ........ 3,40
Helado de vainilla con salsa de chocolate ........ 3,50
Surtido de buñuelos ........ 5,70
Hojaldre de crema ........ 4,80
Piña natural al dry-sack ........ 4,00
Fresón con nata ........ 5,10
Sorbete de limón ........ 3,80
Melón ........ 4,20
Bartolillos (sábados y domingos) ........ 4,70

MENU DE LA CASA
(Primavera - Verano)
Precio: 26,00 €
Gazpacho campero
Cochinillo asado
Helado



HORAS DE SERVICIO: ALMUERZO, de 1:00 A 4:00 - CENA, de 8:00 A 12:00
ABIERTO TODOS LOS DIAS
HAY HOJAS DE RECLAMACION



## Vocabulario

**8** Students can do this activity in pairs.

**Expansion:** You may wish to have students expand Activity 8 into a miniconversation:

**—¿Te gusta la ensalada?**
**—Sí, mucho. ¿Y a ti te gusta?**
**—Sí, me gusta. (No, no me gusta.)**

**9** Students should use the dialogue on page 37 as a model.

**10** The famous **Casa de Botín** restaurant specializes in **cordero asado** and **cochinillo asado. Cochinillo** is called **lechón** in Latin America. You may also wish to point out that the word **carta** is used here, rather than **menú.**

### Chapter Projects

**Visita a un restaurante hispano** Plan a class outing to an inexpensive restaurant that serves food from a Spanish-speaking country. If possible, distribute the restaurant's menu in advance so students can think about what they will order. You may also have them use the menus to practice ordering in Spanish.

### LEVELING

**E:** Activities 6, 7, 8
**A:** Activities 7, 8, 9, 10
**C:** Activity 10

## Answers to ¿Qué palabra necesito?

**8**

1. Sí, (No, no) me gusta la ensalada.
2. Sí, (No, no) me gusta la ensalada con aceite y vinagre.
3. Sí, (No, no) me gusta el biftec.
4. Sí, (No, no) me gusta el sándwich de jamón y queso. Sí, (No, no) me gusta más con pan tostado.
5. Sí, (No, no) me gusta la tortilla de queso.
6. Sí, (No, no) me gustan los huevos con jamón.

**9** *Answers will vary. Students should use the conversation on page 37 as a model.*

**10** *Answers will vary. Students should use* recomendar *and the foods listed on the menu.*

Estructura

## 1 PREPARATION

**Resource Manager**

Audio Activities TE, pages 19–20
Audio CD 2
Workbook, pages 17–18
Quizzes, pages 10–11
ExamView® Pro

**Bellringer Review**

*Use BRR Transparency 2.3 or write the following on the board.*
Answer the following questions.

1. **¿Te gusta la carne?**
2. **¿Te gustan los mariscos?**
3. **¿Cuáles son algunas legumbres que te gustan?**
4. **¿Te gusta el postre?**
5. **¿Qué te gusta beber?**

## 2 PRESENTATION

### Verbos con el cambio e → i en el presente

**Step 1** Have students open their books to page 40. Write the verb forms on the board. Underline the stem and have students repeat each form after you.

**Note:** Oral practice with these verbs is important, because if students pronounce them correctly, they will be inclined to spell them correctly.

**Step 2** When going over the verb **seguir**, review with students the following sound / spelling correspondence: **ga, gue, gui, go, gu.**

# Estructura

## Verbos con el cambio e → i en el presente
### Describing more present activities

1. The verbs **pedir, servir, repetir, freír, seguir** *(to follow)*, and **vestirse** *(to get dressed)* are stem-changing verbs. The **e** of the infinitive stem changes to **i** in all forms of the present tense except the **nosotros** and **vosotros** forms. Study the following forms. Note the spelling of **seguir.**

| INFINITIVE | pedir | servir | seguir | vestirse |
|---|---|---|---|---|
| yo | pido | sirvo | sigo | me visto |
| tú | pides | sirves | sigues | te vistes |
| él, ella, Ud. | pide | sirve | sigue | se viste |
| nosotros(as) | pedimos | servimos | seguimos | nos vestimos |
| *vosotros(as)* | *pedís* | *servís* | *seguís* | *os vestís* |
| ellos, ellas, Uds. | piden | sirven | siguen | se visten |

## ¿Cómo lo digo?

**11 Lo que yo pido** Digan si piden lo siguente o no.

1.

2.

3.

4.

5.

6.



### ANSWERS TO ¿Cómo lo digo?

**11**

1. Sí, (No, no) pido una langosta.
2. Sí, (No, no) pido queso.
3. Sí, (No, no) pido papas.
4. Sí, (No, no) pido un pollo.
5. Sí, (No, no) pido una botella de agua mineral.
6. Sí, (No, no) pido una ensalada.

**LEVELING**

**E:** Activities 11, 14
**A:** Activities 11, 12, 13, 15

## 12 Lo que pedimos en el restaurante

Sigan el modelo.

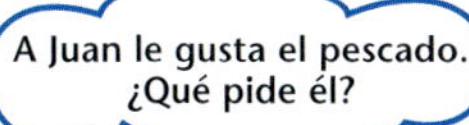


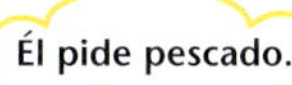

1. A Teresa le gustan los mariscos. ¿Qué pide ella?
2. A Carlos le gusta el biftec. ¿Qué pide él?
3. A mis amigos les gustan las legumbres. ¿Qué piden ellos?
4. A mis padres les gusta mucho la ensalada. ¿Qué piden ellos?
5. Nos gusta el postre. ¿Qué pedimos?
6. Nos gustan las tortillas. ¿Qué pedimos?
7. ¿Qué pides cuando tienes sed?
8. ¿Qué pides cuando tienes hambre?

## 13 Historieta Vamos al restaurante. Completen.

Cuando mi amiga y yo __1__ (ir) al restaurante, nosotros __2__ (pedir) casi siempre una hamburguesa. Yo la __3__ (pedir) con lechuga y tomate y ella la __4__ (pedir) con queso. A mi amiga le __5__ (gustar) mucho las papas fritas. Ella __6__ (decir) que le __7__ (gustar) más cuando el cocinero las __8__ (freír) en aceite de oliva.

Marbella, España

## 14 Entrevista Contesten personalmente.

1. Cuando vas a un restaurante, ¿qué pides?
2. ¿Pides papas? Si no pides papas, ¿pides arroz?
3. ¿Qué más pides con la carne y las papas o el arroz?
4. ¿Quién te sirve en el restaurante?
5. Si te sirve bien, ¿qué le dejas?

## 15 ¿Por qué no pides... ?

You're in a restaurant with a friend (a classmate). You are hungry and thirsty, but you don't know what to order. Your friend will suggest something. Then you decide.

*For more practice using words from **Palabras 2** and the verb **pedir**, do Activity 2 on page H3 at the end of this book.*



# Estructura

## 3 PRACTICE

## ¿Cómo lo digo?

**11** Students will answer using the **yo** form.

**12** Activity 12 reviews the use of **gustar** as it practices stem-changing verbs.

**13** After going over Activity 13, students can summarize the information in their own words.

**14** Activity 14 may be done in pairs.

**15** In this activity, the first student can begin by asking: **¿Te gusta(n)... ?** or **¿Por qué no pides... ?**

UN POCO MÁS This *InfoGap* Activity will allow students to practice in pairs. The activity should be very manageable for them, since all vocabulary and structures are familiar to them.

## Answers to ¿Cómo lo digo?

**12**

1. Ella pide mariscos.
2. Él pide biftec.
3. Ellos piden legumbres.
4. Ellos piden ensalada.
5. Pedimos postre.
6. Pedimos tortillas.
7. Cuando tengo sed pido ___.
8. Cuando tengo hambre pido ___.

**13**

1. vamos
2. pedimos
3. pido
4. pide
5. gustan
6. dice
7. gusta
8. fríe

**14**

1. Cuando voy a un restaurante, pido ___.
2. Sí, (No, no) pido papas. Sí, si no pido papas, pido arroz. (No, si no pido papas, no pido arroz.)
3. Pido ___.
4. El mesero me sirve en el restaurante.
5. Si me sirve bien le dejo una propina.

**15** *Answers will vary. Students should use the phrase* ¿Por qué no pides... ? *to make their suggestions.*

# Estructura

## 1 PREPARATION

### Bellringer Review

*Use BRR Transparency 2.4 or write the following on the board.*
Unscramble the following sentences.

1. **tacos / los / sirve / restaurante / el mesero / en el**
2. **pimienta / pide / Juan / sal / la / y / la**
3. **y / el / Sofía / fríen / pescado / papas / las / y Jaime**

## 2 PRESENTATION

### Verbos con el cambio e → i, o → u en el pretérito

**Step 1** Have students repeat the verb forms shown in the charts on page 42, paying particular attention to the stem changes and correct pronunciation.

## 3 PRACTICE

### ¿Cómo lo digo?

**16** The items in Activity 16 describe an unfortunate experience in a restaurant.

**Expansion:** After going over Activity 16, have students make up original stories about a horrible experience in a restaurant. This can be done as a narrative.

**Note:** This is a good preparatory activity for Activity 18, page 43. In that activity students converse with the restaurant manager about a problem with their meal and the service.

# Estructura

## Verbos con el cambio e → i, o → u en el pretérito

### Describing more activities in the past

**1.** The verbs **pedir, repetir, freír, servir,** and **vestirse** have a stem change in the preterite. The **e** of the infinitive stem changes to **i** in the **él** and **ellos** forms.

| INFINITIVE | pedir | repetir | vestirse |
|---|---|---|---|
| yo | pedí | repetí | me vestí |
| tú | pediste | repetiste | te vestiste |
| él, ella, Ud. | pidió | repitió | se vistió |
| nosotros(as) | pedimos | repetimos | nos vestimos |
| *vosotros(as)* | *pedisteis* | *repetisteis* | *os vestisteis* |
| ellos, ellas, Uds. | pidieron | repitieron | se vistieron |

**2.** The verbs **preferir, divertirse,** and **dormir** also have a stem change in the preterite. The **e** in **preferir** and **divertirse** changes to **i** and the **o** in **dormir** changes to **u** in the **él** and **ellos** forms.

| INFINITIVE | preferir | divertirse | dormir |
|---|---|---|---|
| yo | preferí | me divertí | dormí |
| tú | preferiste | te divertiste | dormiste |
| él, ella, Ud. | prefirió | se divirtió | durmió |
| nosotros(as) | preferimos | nos divertimos | dormimos |
| *vosotros(as)* | *preferisteis* | *os divertisteis* | *dormisteis* |
| ellos, ellas, Uds. | prefirieron | se divirtieron | durmieron |

## ¿Cómo lo digo?

**Historieta Servicio bueno o malo** Contesten según se indica.

1. ¿Qué pediste en el restaurante? (una ensalada)
2. ¿Cómo la pediste? (sin aceite y vinagre)
3. ¿Cuántas veces repetiste «sin aceite y vinagre»? (dos veces)
4. Y, ¿cómo sirvió el mesero la ensalada? (con aceite y vinagre)
5. ¿Qué hiciste? (pedí otra ensalada)
6. ¿Qué pidió tu amigo? (puré de papas)
7. ¿Y qué pasó? (el cocinero frió las papas)
8. ¿Qué sirvió el mesero? (papas fritas)
9. ¿Pidieron ustedes una bebida? (sí)
10. ¿Qué pidieron para beber? (una limonada)
11. ¿Qué sirvió el mesero? (un té)
12. ¿Le dieron ustedes una propina al mesero? (no)



## Answers to ¿Cómo lo digo?

**16**

1. Pedí una ensalada en el restaurante.
2. La pedí sin aceite y vinagre.
3. Repetí «sin aceite y vinagre» dos veces.
4. El mesero sirvió la ensalada con aceite y vinagre.
5. Pedí otra ensalada.
6. Mi amigo pidió puré de papas.
7. El cocinero frió las papas.
8. El mesero sirvió papas fritas.
9. Sí, pedimos una bebida.
10. Pedimos una limonada.
11. El mesero sirvió un té.
12. No, no le dimos una propina al mesero.

**17** **Historieta Preparando la comida**
Completen con el pretérito.

Anoche mi hermano y yo __1__ (preparar) la comida para la familia. Yo __2__ (freír) el pescado. Mi hermano __3__ (freír) las papas. Mamá __4__ (poner) la mesa. Y papá __5__ (servir) la comida. Todos nosotros __6__ (comer) muy bien. A todos nos __7__ (gustar) mucho el pescado. Mi hermano y mi papá __8__ (repetir) el pescado. Luego yo __9__ (servir) el postre, un sorbete. Después de la comida mi hermano tomó una siesta. Él __10__ (dormir) media hora. Yo no __11__ (dormir). No me gusta dormir inmediatamente después de comer.

Valparaíso, Chile

**18**   **Lo siento mucho.** You're in a restaurant and you're fed up with the waiter. He hasn't done a thing right. Call over the manager (a classmate) and tell him or her all that happened. He or she will apologize and say something to try to make you happy.

# Estructura

**17** After doing Activity 17, have several students retell the story in their own words.

**Learning from Photos**

*(page 43)* Have students describe the family members and their activities in this photo.

**18** Have students examine the illustration accompanying Activity 18 carefully. There are quite a few things that have gone wrong!

Before students begin to work on their conversations, you may wish to ask them to describe the people in the illustration and to have them say what's wrong. See who can come up with the longest list.

**¡Adelante!**
At this point in the chapter, students have learned all the vocabulary and structure necessary to complete the chapter. The conversation and cultural readings that follow recycle all the material learned up to this point.

**LEVELING**

**A:** Activities 16, 18
**C:** Activity 17

## Answers to ¿Cómo lo digo?

**17**

1. preparamos
2. freí
3. frió
4. puso
5. sirvió
6. comimos
7. gustó
8. repitieron
9. serví
10. durmió
11. dormí

**18** *Answers will vary. Students should use the illustration as a prompt for ideas. Students may also want to use the sentences from Activity 16 on page 42 as a model.*

# Conversación

## 1 PREPARATION

**Resource Manager**

Audio Activities TE, page 21
Audio CD 2

**Bellringer Review**

*Use BRR Transparency 2.5 or write the following on the board.*
Write three things you would possibly say to or ask a waiter at a café.

## 2 PRESENTATION

**Step 1** Have students close their books. Tell them that they will hear a conversation between Teresa, Paco, and a waiter. Then read the conversation to them or play Audio CD 2.

**Step 2** After introducing the conversation, you may wish to set up a café in the classroom and have groups of students perform the conversation for the class.

**Step 3** Have students summarize the conversation in their own words.

**Step 4** After presenting the conversation, go over the **¿Comprendes?** activity. If students can answer the questions with relative ease, move on. Students should not be expected to memorize the conversation.

# Conversación

## En el restaurante   

**Teresa** ¿Tiene usted una mesa para dos personas?
**Mesero** Sí, señorita. Por aquí, por favor.
**Teresa** ¿Es posible tener un menú en inglés?
**Mesero** Sí, ¡cómo no!
**Paco** Teresa, no necesito un menú en inglés. Lo puedo leer en español.
*(El mesero les da un menú en inglés.)*
**Paco** No sé por qué ella me pidió un menú en inglés.
**Mesero** No hay problema. Le traigo uno en español.
**Paco** Gracias.
**Teresa** Pues, Paco, ¿qué vas a pedir?
**Paco** Para mí, la especialidad de la casa.
**Teresa** Yo también pido la especialidad de la casa.

### ¿Comprendes?

Completen.

1. ¿Para cuántas personas quiere la mesa Teresa?
2. ¿Tiene el mesero una mesa libre?
3. ¿Qué tipo de menú pide Teresa?
4. ¿Necesita un menú en inglés Paco?
5. ¿Sabe él por qué ella le pidió un menú en inglés?
6. ¿Qué va a pedir Paco?
7. Y Teresa, ¿qué pide ella?



### Answers to ¿Comprendes?

1. Teresa quiere la mesa para dos personas.
2. Sí, el mesero tiene una mesa libre.
3. Teresa pide un menú en inglés.
4. No, Paco no necesita un menú en inglés.
5. No, no sabe por qué ella le pidió un menú en inglés.
6. Paco va a pedir la especialidad de la casa.
7. Ella también pide la especialidad de la casa.

# Vamos a hablar más

**A** **Fuimos al restaurante.** You and your parents went to a restaurant last night. A classmate will ask you questions about your experience. Answer him or her.

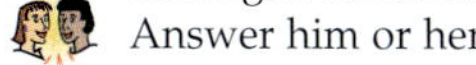

**B** **Preferencias** Work with a classmate and discuss whether you prefer to eat at home or in a restaurant. Give reasons for your preferences.

## Pronunciación

### La consonante x

An **x** between two vowels is pronounced much like the English *x* but a bit softer. It's like a **gs: examen → eg-samen.** Repeat the following.

**exacto** **examen**
**éxito** **próximo**

When **x** is followed by a consonant, it is often pronounced like an **s.** Repeat the following.

**extremo** **explicar** **exclamar**

Repeat the following sentence.

**El extranjero exclama que baja en la próxima parada.**

## Answers to Vamos a hablar más

**A** *Answers will vary, but students may use the conversation on page 44 as a model.*

**B** *Answers will vary; however, students will typically begin the conversation by asking:* ¿Prefieres comer en casa o en el restaurante?

### Learning from Realia

*(page 45)* Have students take a look at the ad to see how much of the vocabulary they already know.

## Conversación

### 3 PRACTICE

## Vamos a hablar más

**A** Students can base their answers on any outing to a restaurant with their parents. They may wish to use the conversation on page 44 as a model.

**B** Students should use the verb **preferir** for this exchange.

## Pronunciación

**¡OJO!** Whenever **x** is followed by a consonant in Spanish, it is pronounced as **s.** There are no exceptions to this rule.

However, there is a variation in the pronunciation of **x** between two vowels. In some geographic areas the **x** in the word **exacto,** for example, is pronounced like **s (esacto)** and in others it is **gs (eg-sacto).**

**Step 1** Have students repeat the words after you or Audio CD 2. Have them imitate very carefully.

**Step 2** Have students open their books to page 45. Call on individuals to read the words and sentences carefully.

**Step 3** The model sentence on page 45 can be used for dictation.

### Glencoe Technology

On the CD–ROM, students can watch a dramatization of this conversation. They can then play the role of either one of the characters and record themselves in the conversation.

**LEVELING**

**E:** Conversation

# Lecturas culturales

## Resource Manager

Audio Activities TE, page 22
Audio CD 2

## National Standards

**Cultures**

The reading about Mexican cuisine on page 46 and the related activity on page 47 familiarize students with typical Mexican food and dishes.

## PRESENTATION

### Pre-reading

**Step 1** Have students open their books and do the Reading Strategy activity on page 46. Then ask them what they think the reading is about.

**Step 2** Have students tell some things they already know about Mexican food.

### Reading

**Step 1** Now have students open their books. Call on individuals to read.

**Step 2** Intersperse oral reading with some comprehension questions. Then continue reading.

### Post-reading

**Step 1** Have students tell what they see on the plate at the bottom of the page.

**Step 2** Go over the **¿Comprendes?** activity on page 47 orally. Then assign it for homework. Go over the activity again the following day.

# Lecturas culturales

## La comida mexicana

Es muy difícil decir lo que es la comida hispana porque la comida varía mucho de una región hispana a otra.

Aquí en Estados Unidos la comida mexicana es muy popular. Hay muchos restaurantes mexicanos. Algunos sirven comida típicamente mexicana y otros sirven variaciones que vienen del suroeste de Estados Unidos donde vive mucha gente de ascendencia mexicana.

La base de muchos platos mexicanos es la tortilla. La tortilla es un tipo de panqueque. Puede ser de harina[1] de maíz o de trigo[2]. Con las tortillas, los mexicanos preparan tostadas, tacos, enchiladas, etc. Rellenan[3] las tortillas de pollo, carne de res o frijoles y queso.

[1]harina *flour*
[2]trigo *wheat*
[3]Rellenan *They fill*

**Reading Strategy**

**Thinking while reading** Good readers always think while reading. They think about what the passage might be about after reading the title and looking at the visuals. They predict, create visual images, compare, and check for understanding; they continually think while the author is explaining.

San Miguel de Allende, México

## Learning from Photos

*(page 46 right)* Ask the following questions about the photo:
**¿Dónde está la señora?**
**¿Qué está haciendo ella?**
**¿Tortillas o arroz?**

## Chapter Projects

**La cocina hispana**
Prepare a dish from a Spanish-speaking country or have students prepare some Hispanic foods. A number of typical dishes are described in this chapter. Students can go to the library to find recipes for these dishes.

*El cultivo del maíz*
de Diego Rivera

SECRETARIA DE EDUCACION, CULTURA
Y RECREACION
MUSEO CASA
"DIEGO RIVERA"
GUANAJUATO, GTO.
COOPERACION N$ 5.00

## ¿Comprendes?

**La comida mexicana** Contesten.

1. ¿Varía mucho la cocina hispana de una región a otra?
2. ¿Dónde es popular la comida mexicana?
3. ¿De dónde vienen muchas variaciones de la cocina mexicana?
4. ¿Qué sirve de base para muchos platos mexicanos?
5. ¿Qué es una tortilla? ¿De qué puede ser?
6. ¿De qué rellenan las tortillas?



# Lecturas culturales

## ¿Comprendes?

Allow students to refer to the story to look up the answers, or you may use this activity as a testing device for factual recall.

## Art Connection

Throughout his life, Diego Rivera was vitally interested in the suffering of Mexico's poor. Ask students if they can figure out why he would do a painting depicting someone cultivating corn. (Corn is extremely important to Mexico because it is the sustenance for Mexico's poor. Corn is for Mexico what potatoes, bread, or rice are to people in other parts of the world.)

**Expansion:** Show the Fine Art Transparency of ***El cultivo del maíz*** by Diego Rivera. You may wish to have students read the background information accompanying this transparency and do the related activities.

**LEVELING**

**E:** Reading

## Answers to ¿Comprendes?

1. Sí, la comida hispana varía mucho de una región a otra.
2. La comida mexicana es popular aquí en Estados Unidos.
3. Vienen del suroeste de Estados Unidos.
4. La tortilla sirve de base para muchos platos mexicanos.
5. Una tortilla es un tipo de panqueque. Puede ser de harina de maíz o de harina de trigo.
6. Rellenan las tortillas de pollo, carne de res o frijoles y queso.

Lectura opcional 1

**National Standards**

**Cultures**
This reading about Spanish cuisine and the related activity on this page familiarize students with some typical foods from Spain.

**¡OJO!** This reading is optional. You may skip it completely, have the entire class read it, have only several students read it and report to the class, or assign it for extra credit.

## PRESENTATION

**Step 1** Have students read the passage quickly as they look at the photos that accompany it. The photos will increase comprehension because students can visualize what they are reading about.

**Step 2** Have students discuss the information they find interesting.

### Learning from Photos

*(page 48)* Have students look at the three photos on this page to see how many items they can identify.

**LEVELING**

**E:** Readings 1, 2

# Lectura opcional 1

Málaga, España

## La comida española

En España, como en México, hay tortillas también. Pero hay una gran diferencia entre una tortilla mexicana y una tortilla española. La tortilla española no es de maíz. El cocinero español prepara la tortilla con huevos. La tortilla española, que es muy típica, lleva patatas (papas) y cebollas[1].

La cocina española es muy buena y muy variada. Como España es un país que tiene mucha costa, muchos platos españoles llevan marisco y pescado. Y los cocineros preparan muchos platos con aceite de oliva.

[1]cebollas *onions*

Málaga, España

### ¿Comprendes?

**La cocina española** Contesten.

1. ¿Cuál es la diferencia entre una tortilla española y una tortilla mexicana?
2. ¿Qué lleva la típica tortilla española?
3. ¿Por qué llevan marisco y pescado muchos platos españoles?
4. ¿Qué usan muchos cocineros españoles para preparar una comida?



### ANSWERS TO ¿Comprendes?

1. La tortilla española no es de maíz. El cocinero español la prepara con huevos.
2. Lleva patatas y cebollas.
3. Muchos platos españoles llevan marisco y pescado porque España es un país que tiene mucha costa.
4. Usan aceite de oliva para preparar una comida.

# Lectura opcional 2

## La comida del Caribe

En el Caribe, en Puerto Rico, Cuba y la República Dominicana, la gente come muchos mariscos y pescado. Es natural porque Puerto Rico, Cuba y la República Dominicana son islas. Pero la carne favorita de la región es el puerco o el lechón[1]. No hay nada más delicioso que un buen lechón asado[2]. Sirven el lechón con arroz, frijoles (habichuelas) y tostones. Para hacer tostones el cocinero corta en rebanadas[3] un plátano, una banana grande, verde y dura. Luego fríe las rebanadas en manteca[4].

Humacao, Puerto Rico

[1]lechón *suckling pig*
[2]asado *roast*
[3]rebanadas *slices*
[4]manteca *lard*

### ¿Comprendes?

**¿Lo sabes?** Busquen la información.

1. algunos países de la región del Caribe
2. por qué come la gente muchos mariscos y pescado en la región del Caribe
3. una carne favorita de los puertorriqueños, cubanos y dominicanos
4. lo que sirven con el lechón asado
5. lo que son tostones



# Lectura opcional 2

### National Standards

**Cultures**
This reading about Caribbean cuisine and the related activity familiarize students with some typical foods from the Spanish-speaking countries of the Caribbean.

**¡OJO!** This reading is optional. You may skip it completely, have the entire class read it, have only several students read it and report to the class, or assign it for extra credit.

### PRESENTATION

**Step 1** Have students read the selection to themselves.

**Step 2** Now have students do the **¿Comprendes?** activity on page 49.

### Learning from Photos

*(page 49 bottom)* Have students look at the meal in the photo. Point out to them that the dish in the foreground contains **arroz, tostones,** and **habichuelas rosadas.** Tell them that red beans are favored in Puerto Rico and black beans are favored in Cuba.

### Answers to ¿Comprendes?

1. Puerto Rico, Cuba y la República Dominicana
2. porque son islas
3. el puerco o el lechón
4. arroz, frijoles (habichuelas) y tostones
5. rebanadas de plátano fritas en manteca

### Geography Connection

Humacao is on the western coast of Puerto Rico. The well-known resort and condominium complex **Palmas del Mar** is in Humacao.

## National Standards

### Connections

This reading about linguistic differences in the Spanish-speaking world establishes a connection with another discipline, allowing students to reinforce and further their knowledge of the humanities through the study of Spanish.

### Comparisons

This reading on regional differences in pronunciation and vocabulary in Spanish and the related activities, which illustrate the same concepts in English, give students a better understanding of the nature of language.

**¡OJO!** The readings in the **Conexiones** section are optional. They focus on some of the major disciplines taught in schools and universities. The vocabulary is useful for discussing such topics as history, literature, art, economics, business, science, etc. You may choose any of the following ways to do the readings in the **Conexiones** sections.

**Independent reading** Have students read the selections and do the post-reading activities as homework, which you collect. This option is least intrusive on class time and requires a minimum of teacher involvement.

**Homework with in-class follow-up** Assign the readings and post-reading activities as homework. Review and discuss the material in class the next day.

**Intensive in-class activity** This option includes a pre-reading vocabulary presentation, in-class reading and discussion, assignment of the activities for homework, and a discussion of the assignment in class the following day.

# Conexiones

## *Las humanidades*

### El lenguaje

As we already know, Spanish is a language that is spoken in many areas of the world. In spite of the fact that the Spanish-speaking world covers a large area of the globe, it is possible to understand a speaker of Spanish regardless of where he or she is from. Although there are regional differences, these differences do not cause serious comprehension problems.

However, pronunciation does change from area to area. For example, people from San Juan, Puerto Rico; Buenos Aires, Argentina; and Madrid, Spain have pronunciations that are quite different from one another. However, the same is true of English. People from New York, Memphis, and London also have a distinct pronunciation, but they can all understand one another.

The use of certain words also changes from one area to another. This is particularly true in the case of words for foods. Let's look at some regional differences with regard to vocabulary.

### Regionalismos

**Comestibles**

En España son patatas y en todas partes de Latinoamérica son papas.

En casi todas partes es el maíz, pero en México es el maíz o el elote y en Chile es el choclo.

En España son cacahuetes; en muchas partes de Latinoamérica son cacahuates, pero en el Caribe son maní.

En muchas partes es jugo de naranja, pero en Puerto Rico es jugo de china y en España es zumo de naranja.

Las judías verdes tienen muchos nombres. Además de judías verdes son habichuelas tiernas, chauchas, vainitas, ejotes y porotos.

The Glencoe Spanish Web site **(spanish.glencoe.com)** offers options that enable you and your students to experience the Spanish-speaking world via the Internet. For each **Capítulo,** there are activities, games, and quizzes. In addition, an *Enrichment* section offers students an opportunity to visit Web sites related to the theme of the chapter.

**Cosas que no son comestibles**

Tomamos el autobús en España, el camión en México y la guagua en el Caribe y en las Islas Canarias.

En España todos duermen en el dormitorio o en la habitación. En México duermen en la recámara y en muchas partes en el cuarto o en el cuarto de dormir.

En España sacas un billete en la ventanilla y en Latinoamérica compras un boleto en la ventanilla o en la boletería.

## ¿Comprendes?

**A Hispanohablantes** If any of your classmates are heritage speakers of Spanish, ask them to compare the way they say things. Have them share this information with you.

**B El inglés** There are variations in the use of English words. Discuss the following terms and where they might be heard.

1. bag, sack
2. soda, pop
3. elevator, lift
4. line, queue
5. pram, baby carriage
6. truck, lorry
7. traffic circle, rotary, roundabout
8. subway, underground



# Conexiones

## PRESENTATION

### *Las humanidades*

### El lenguaje

**Step 1** Have students read the introduction in English on page 50.

**Step 2** You may wish to have students skim this section for general interest.

**Step 3** For a more in-depth treatment, have students identify each item of food pictured on page 50. Then have them give the additional regional names for each item. Now do the same with regard to the nonfood items in the photos on page 51.

### ¿Comprendes?

**B** Ask students whether they know of additional examples in English. They might mention: purse / pocketbook.

### Reaching All Students

**For the Heritage Speakers** Have heritage speakers make a list of at least twenty common items of food and clothing. Then have each student compare his or her list with those of the other heritage speakers in the class. Finally, have them make a list of the items that have different names.

## Answers to ¿Comprendes?

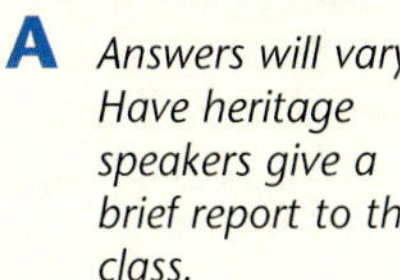

**A** *Answers will vary. Have heritage speakers give a brief report to the class.*

**B** *Answers will include the following:*

1. bag: U.S.
   sack: UK and parts of U.S.
2. soda: East and West Coasts, South
   pop: Midwest
3. elevator: U.S.
   lift: UK
4. line: U.S.
   queue: UK
5. pram: UK
   baby carriage: U.S.
6. truck: U.S.
   lorry: UK
7. traffic circle: U.S.
   rotary: New England states, Canada
   roundabout: UK
8. subway: U.S.
   underground: UK

# ¡Te toca a ti!

## Use what you have learned

### Recycling

These activities allow students to use the vocabulary and structure from this chapter in completely open-ended, real-life situations.

### PRESENTATION

Encourage students to say as much as possible when they do these activities. Tell them not to be afraid to make mistakes, since the goal of the activities is real-life communication. If someone in the group makes an error, allow the others to politely correct him or her. Let students choose the activities they would like to do.

You may wish to divide students into pairs or groups. Encourage students to elaborate on the basic theme and to be creative. They may use props, pictures, or posters if they wish.

### PRACTICE

**1** This activity is an excellent follow-up to the readings in Chapter 2, pages 46–49.

**2** This is a good activity to use when students need a "break" during the class period or as an opening or closing activity.

# ¡Te toca a ti!

## Use what you have learned

HABLAR

### 1 Vamos a un restaurante

✔ *Order food and beverages at a restaurant*

Pretend your Spanish class is at a restaurant. The restaurant serves food from Spain or Latin America. All the waiters and waitresses are Spanish speaking. Order your meal in Spanish and speak together in Spanish during your meal.

HABLAR

### 2 Una comida hispana

✔ *Describe a meal from some area of the Spanish-speaking world*

Work with a classmate. You have learned about some Hispanic cuisines. Talk about a meal or dish that you want to try **(probar).**

HABLAR

### 3 La comida

✔ *Talk about categories of food*

Mention a food category, such as meat, seafood, fruit, vegetable. Your partner will give the name of a food that belongs in that category. Take several turns each. Try to use as much as possible of the food vocabulary you've learned.

Café • Restaurante

EN EL CENTRO DE GRANADA

Restaurante CHIKITO

## ANSWERS TO ¡Te toca a ti!

**1** *Answers will vary. Students should order foods presented in this chapter. After ordering, students may discuss regional differences in foods, the restaurant, or any other topic.*

**2** *Answers will vary. Students might use the names of foods and dishes from the readings on pages 46–49.*

**3** *Answers will vary. Students should use the foods presented in this chapter and the foods presented in* **¡Buen viaje! Level 1,** *Chapter 5.*

**4** *Answers will vary. The selections for each meal should be logical.*

**5** *Answers will vary. The illustration on page 53 gives clues as to what students could say in their letter.*

# ¡Te toca a ti!

## El menú

✔ *Plan a menu*

Write out the menu for several meals in Spanish. You can plan meals for **el desayuno, el almuerzo,** and **la cena.**

35° Aniversario

**La Estancia**

**ASADOR CRIOLLO**

| | |
|---|---|
| Lechón al Asador | $ 14,00 |
| Chivito «La Estancia» | $ 16,00 |
| Asado al Asador | $ 11,00 |

**COCINA**

| | |
|---|---|
| Costilla de Cerdo con puré de manzana | $ 10,00 |
| Costilla de Cerdo a la Riojana | $ 12,00 |
| Lomo a la Pimienta con papas a la crema | $ 16,00 |
| Lomo al Champignon | $ 17,00 |
| Milanesa de Lomo | $ 6,50 |
| Milanesa de Lomo a la Napolitana | $ 9,50 |
| Milanesa de Pollo | $ 6,00 |
| Milanesa de Pollo a la Napolitana | $ 9,00 |
| Suprema de Pollo «La Estancia» | $ 10,50 |
| Suprema de Pollo a la Maryland | $ 10,00 |
| 1/2 Pollo deshuesado a la Parrilla | $ 10,00 |

**BIFES**

| | |
|---|---|
| Bife de costilla con Lomo con guarnición de papas fritas | $ 8,50 |
| Bife de Chorizo | $ 7,50 |
| Bife especial «La Estancia» | $ 14,50 |
| Bife de Lomo especial «La Estancia» | $ 15,00 |
| Costillas de Cerdo | $ 8,00 |
| Chorizos (c/u) | $ 2,50 |
| Salchicha Criolla (c/u) | $ 3,00 |
| Morcillas (c/u) | $ 2,50 |
| Matambrito Tiernizado | $ 10,00 |
| Bife Aniversario con Lomo | $ 17,00 |
| Mollejas porción | $ 11,00 |
| Longaniza (c/u) | $ 4,00 |
| Riñones porción | $ 5,00 |
| Chinchulines de Ternera porción | $ 5,00 |
| Chinchulines de Cordero porción | $ 9,00 |
| Ubre porción | $ 4,50 |

### Writing Strategy

**Writing a letter of complaint** When you write a letter of complaint, you must clearly identify the problem and suggest solutions; you should use a businesslike tone. You might be angry when you write a letter of complaint. But to be effective, you must control your emotions since your goal is to get the problem corrected. Your tone of voice is reflected in writing as much as it is in speech; your results will be better if you address the situation calmly and reasonably.In addition, it is important that the letter be addressed to the person who has the most authority.

ESCRIBIR 5

## ¡Qué desastre!

Pretend you went to a restaurant where you had a very bad experience. The waiter didn't serve you what you ordered nor the way you ordered it. Write a letter to the management complaining about the food and the service.

### Writing Development

Have students keep a notebook or portfolio containing their best written work from each chapter. These selected writings can be based on assignments from the Student Textbook and the Workbook. The activities on page 53 are examples of writing assignments that may be included in each student's portfolio. On page 22 in the Workbook, students will begin to develop an organized autobiography **(Mi autobiografía).** These workbook pages may also become a part of their portfolio.

4 Students can use the food items taught in **¡Buen viaje! Level 1,** Chapter 5, as well as those taught in this chapter. Encourage students to list only those foods that they know how to say in Spanish.

### Writing Strategy

**Writing a letter of complaint** Have students do the Writing Strategy activity on page 53. Based on the strategy, ask students which statement in the Critical Thinking Activity below would be most effective when writing a letter of complaint.

### LEVELING

These activities encompass all three levels. All students will be able to do them at a sophistication level commensurate with their ability in Spanish. Some students will be able to speak for several minutes, and others may be able to give just a few sentences. This is to be expected when students are functioning completely on their own generating their own language to the best of their ability.

### Critical Thinking Activity

**Drawing conclusions** Ask students which of the following statements would be most effective when writing a letter of complaint.

1. **Tuvimos que esperar cinco minutos para la mesa y no pudimos leer el menú en español.**
2. **Nos gustó la comida, pero hay un problema con el servicio.**
3. **¡Su restaurante es horrible!**

Assessment

## Resource Manager

Communication Transparency C 2
Quizzes, pages 7–11
Performance Assessment, Task 2
Tests, pages 15–28
Situation Cards, Chapter 2
ExamView® Pro, Chapter 2
**Maratón mental** Videoquiz, Chapter 2

## Assessment

This is a pre-test for students to take before you administer the chapter test. Note that each section is cross-referenced so students can easily find the material they have to review in case they made errors. You may use Assessment Answers Transparency A 2 to do the assessment in class, or you may assign this assessment for homework. You can correct the assessment yourself, or you may prefer to project the answers on the overhead in class.

## Glencoe Technology

### MINDJOGGER VHS/DVD

You may wish to help your students prepare for the chapter test by playing the MindJogger game show. Teams will compete against each other to review chapter vocabulary and structure and sharpen listening comprehension skills.

Assessment

# Vocabulario

To review **Palabras 1**, turn to pages 32–33.

**1** **Identifiquen.**

To review **Palabras 2**, turn to pages 36–37.

**2** **Identifiquen.**

6.

7.

8.

9.

10.

**3** **¿Sí o no?** Indiquen si la persona contesta bien.

11. —¿Para cuándo quiere usted la reservación?
—Para cuatro.
12. —¿A nombre de quién, por favor?
—Conforme, señor Pereda.



ANSWERS TO Assessment

**1**

1. el mantel
2. el plato
3. el cuchillo
4. la taza
5. la servilleta

**2**

6. el aceite
7. el arroz
8. la carne
9. el pescado
10. los camarones

**3**

11. No
12. No

# Estructura

## 4 Completen con el presente.

13. El mesero les ____ a los clientes en el restaurante. (servir)
14. Yo siempre ____ la misma cosa, un biftec. (pedir)
15. Ellas ____ elegantemente para ir al restaurante. (vestirse)
16. Nosotros no lo ____. (repetir)
17. El cocinero ____ las papas. (freír)

To review the present of stem-changing verbs, turn to page 40.

## 5 Sigan el modelo.

**Él lo pidió. →**
**Y yo lo pedí, también.**

18. Ellos se divirtieron.
    Y yo ____, también.
19. Yo dormí bien.
    Y él ____ bien, también.
20. Tú lo repetiste.
    Y nosotros lo ____, también.
21. Ellos lo prefirieron.
    Y su amigo lo ____, también.
22. Nos vestimos.
    Y ellos ____, también.

To review the preterite of stem-changing verbs, turn to page 42.

# Cultura

## 6 Contesten.

23. ¿Cuál es la base de muchas comidas mexicanas?
24. ¿Qué es una tortilla mexicana?
25. ¿De qué rellenan las tortillas para hacer tacos y enchiladas?

To review this cultural information, turn to page 46.



## Assessment

**FOLDABLES™ Study Organizer** **Dinah Zike's Study Guides**

Your students may wish to use Foldable 13 to organize, display, and arrange data as they review the vocabulary, verbs, and verb forms they know in Spanish. You may wish to encourage them to add information from each unit as they continue to expand their vocabulary.

A *sentence strip* holder foldable is also ideal as students continue their study of Spanish and learn more and more words.

## Answers to Assessment

13. sirve
14. pido
15. se visten
16. repetimos
17. fríe

18. me divertí
19. durmió
20. repetimos
21. prefirió
22. se vistieron

6

23. La base de muchas comidas mexicanas es la tortilla.
24. Una tortilla mexicana es un tipo de panqueque.
25. Rellenan las tortillas de pollo, carne de res o frijoles y queso.

# ¡Hablo como un pro!

This unique page gives students the opportunity to speak freely and say whatever they can, using the vocabulary and structures they have learned in the chapter. The illustration serves to remind students of precisely what they know how to say in Spanish. There are no activities that students do not have the ability to describe or talk about in Spanish. The art not only depicts the vocabulary and content of this chapter, but also reinforces what they learned in previous chapters.

You may wish to use this page in many ways. Some possibilities are to have students do the following:

1. Look at the illustration and identify items by giving the correct Spanish words.
2. Make up sentences about what they see in the illustration.
3. Make up questions about the illustration. They can call on another class member to respond if you do this as a class activity, or you may prefer to allow students to work in small groups. This activity is extremely beneficial because it enables students to actively use interrogative words.
4. Answer questions you ask them about the illustration.
5. Work in pairs and make up a conversation based on the illustration.
6. Look at the illustration and give a complete oral review of what they see.
7. Look at the illustration and write a paragraph (or essay) about it.

You can also use this page as an assessment or testing tool, taking into account individual differences by having students go from simple to quite complicated tasks. The assessment can be either oral or written. You may wish to use the rubrics provided on pages T20–T21 as you give students the following directions.

1. Identify the topic or situation of the illustration.
2. Give the Spanish words for as many items as you can.
3. Think of as many sentences as you can to describe the illustration.
4. Go over your sentences and put them in the best sequencing to give a coherent story based on the illustration.

# ¡Hablo como un pro!

Tell all you can about this illustration.

# Vocabulario

### Getting along at a restaurant

| | |
|---|---|
| el restaurante | el menú |
| la mesa | la cuenta |
| el/la mesero(a), el/la camarero(a) | la tarjeta de crédito |
| | la propina |
| el/la cocinero(a) | el dinero |

### Identifying a place setting

| | |
|---|---|
| el vaso | la cucharita |
| la taza | la cuchara |
| el platillo | el mantel |
| el plato | la servilleta |
| el tenedor | |
| el cuchillo | |

**How well do you know your vocabulary?**

- Choose a food category from the list, for example, **la carne.**
- Have classmates choose the names of foods that belong to that category.

### Describing some restaurant activities

| | |
|---|---|
| poner la mesa | repetir |
| pedir | reservar |
| servir | tener hambre |
| freír | tener sed |

### Identifying more foods

| | | | |
|---|---|---|---|
| la carne | el cordero | la langosta | el maíz |
| la carne de res, el biftec | el pescado | el ajo | la sal |
| | los mariscos | la berenjena | la pimienta |
| la ternera | los camarones | la alcachofa | el aceite |
| el cerdo | las almejas | el arroz | el vinagre |

### Describing food

rico(a), delicioso(a)

**VIDEOTUR**

## Episodio 2

In this video episode, you will join Vicky and Alberto as they help out at his father's restaurant. See page 481 for more information.

# Vocabulario

## Vocabulary Review

The words and phrases in the **Vocabulario** have been taught for productive use in this chapter. They are summarized here as a resource for both student and teacher. This list also serves as a convenient resource for the **¡Te toca a ti!** activities on pages 52 and 53. There are approximately eight cognates in this vocabulary list. Have students find them.

**¡OJO!** You will notice that the vocabulary list here is not translated. This has been done intentionally, since we feel that by the time students have finished the material in the chapter they should be familiar with the meanings of all the words. If there are several words they still do not know, we recommend that they refer to the **Palabras 1** and **2** sections in the chapter or go to the dictionaries at the end of this book to find the meanings. However, if you prefer that your students have the English translations, please refer to Vocabulary Transparency 2.1, where you will find all these words with their translations.

**VIDEO VHS/DVD**

The Video Program allows students to see how the chapter vocabulary and structures are used by native speakers within an engaging story line. For maximum reinforcement, show the video episode as a final activity for Chapter 2.

# Planning for Chapter 3

## SCOPE AND SEQUENCE, PAGES 58–89

### Topics

- Computer terminology
- Fax terminology
- Telephone terminology
- Telephone etiquette

### Culture

- Carmen Tordesillas, a future engineer
- The telephone card in Spain
- The cellular telephone in the Spanish-speaking world
- Advances in computer technology

### Functions

- How to use the computer
- How to send a fax
- How to make a telephone call
- How to use proper telephone etiquette
- How to talk about habitual past actions

### Structure

- Imperfect tense of **-ar** verbs
- Imperfect tense of **-er** and **-ir** verbs
- Imperfect tense of the verbs **ser** and **ir**
- Uses of the imperfect tense

### National Standards

- Communication Standard 1.1 pages 62, 63, 66, 67, 69, 70, 71, 72, 74, 75, 77, 84
- Communication Standard 1.2 pages 63, 67, 70, 72, 73, 75, 76, 77, 78, 79, 80, 81, 83, 84
- Communication Standard 1.3 page 85
- Cultures Standard 2.1 page 78
- Cultures Standard 2.2 pages 75, 76, 77, 78, 80
- Connections Standard 3.1 pages 82–83
- Connections Standard 3.2 pages 75, 80
- Comparisons Standard 4.2 pages 80, 81
- Communities Standard 5.1 page 89

## PACING AND PRIORITIES

**The chapter content is color coded below to assist you in planning.**

**required** **recommended** **optional**

**Vocabulario** *(required)* *Days 1–4*

- Palabras 1
  La computadora
  El fax, el facsímil
- Palabras 2
  El teléfono

**Estructura** *(required)* *Days 5–7*

- Imperfecto de los verbos en **-ar**
- Imperfecto de los verbos en **-er** e **-ir**
- Imperfecto de los verbos **ser** e **ir**
- Usos del imperfecto

**Conversación** *(required)*

- Una llamada internacional

**Lecturas culturales**

- Futura ingeniera *(recommended)*
- La tarjeta telefónica—una innovación popularísima *(optional)*
- La solución a un problema de comunicaciones *(optional)*

**Conexiones**

- La computadora *(optional)*

- **¡Te toca a ti!** *(recommended)*
- **Assessment** *(recommended)*
- **¡Hablo como un pro!** *(optional)*

## RESOURCE GUIDE

| SECTION | PAGES | SECTION RESOURCES |
|---|---|---|
| **Vocabulario PALABRAS 1** | | |
| La computadora<br>El fax, el facsímil | 60, 62–63<br>61, 62–63 | Vocabulary Transparencies 3.2–3.3<br>Audio CD 3<br>Audio Activities TE, pages 25–27<br>Workbook, page 23<br>Quiz 1, page 11<br>ExamView® Pro |
| **Vocabulario PALABRAS 2** | | |
| El teléfono | 64–67 | Vocabulary Transparencies 3.4–3.5<br>Audio CD 3<br>Audio Activities TE, pages 28–30<br>Workbook, pages 24–25<br>Quiz 2, page 12<br>ExamView® Pro |
| **Estructura** | | |
| Imperfecto de los verbos en **-ar**<br>Imperfecto de los verbos en **-er** e **-ir**<br>Imperfecto de los verbos **ser** e **ir**<br>Usos del imperfecto | 68–70<br>70–72<br>72–73<br>74–75 | Audio CD 3<br>Audio Activities TE, pages 31–32<br>Workbook, pages 26–28<br>Quizzes 3–5, pages 13–15<br>ExamView® Pro |
| **Conversación** | | |
| Una llamada internacional | 76–77 | Audio CD 3<br>Audio Activities TE, page 33<br>Interactive CD-ROM |
| **Lecturas culturales** | | |
| Futura ingeniera<br>La tarjeta telefónica—una innovación popularísima<br>La solución a un problema de comunicaciones | 78–79<br>80<br>81 | Audio CD 3<br>Audio Activities TE, page 34<br>Tests, pages 32, 36 |
| **Conexiones** | | |
| La computadora | 82–83 | Tests, pages 37–38 |
| **¡Te toca a ti!** | | |
| | 84–85 | **¡Viva el mundo hispano!** Video, Episode 3<br>Video Activities, pages 69–75<br>Spanish Online Activities spanish.glencoe.com |
| **Assessment** | | |
| | 86–87 | Communication Transparency C 3<br>Quizzes 1–5, pages 11–15<br>Performance Assessment, Task 3<br>Tests, pages 29–44<br>Situation Cards, Chapter 3<br>ExamView® Pro<br>**Maratón mental** Videoquiz |

# Using Your Resources for Chapter 3

## Transparencies

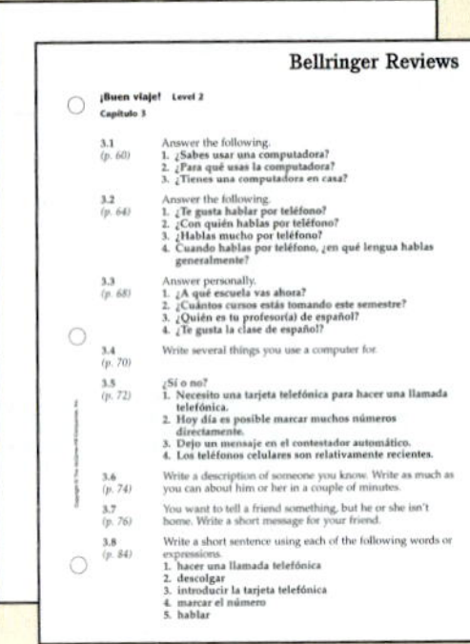
Bellringer 3.1–3.8

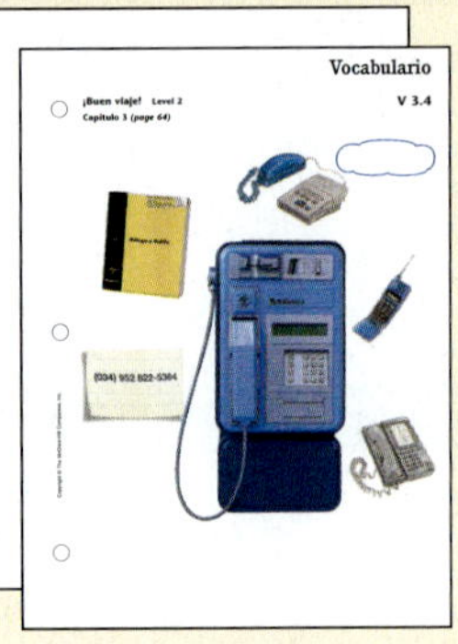
Vocabulary 3.1–3.5

Communication C 3

## Workbook

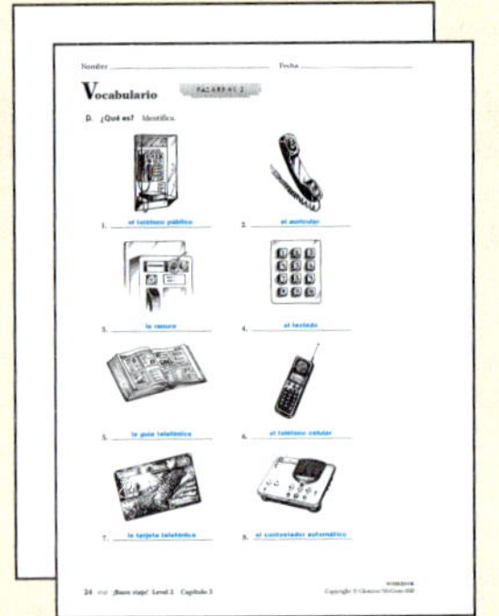
Vocabulary, pages 23–25

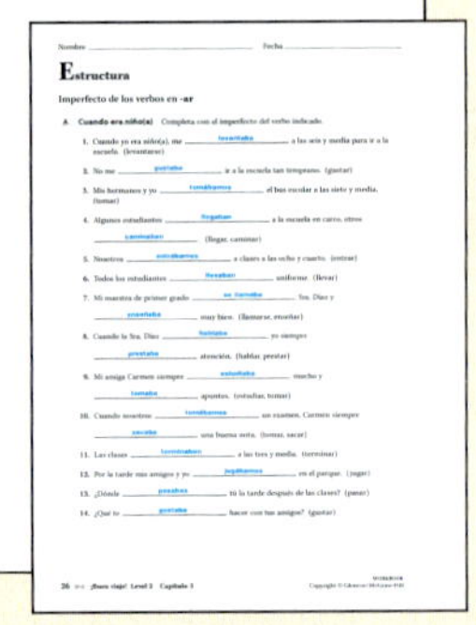
Structure, pages 26–28

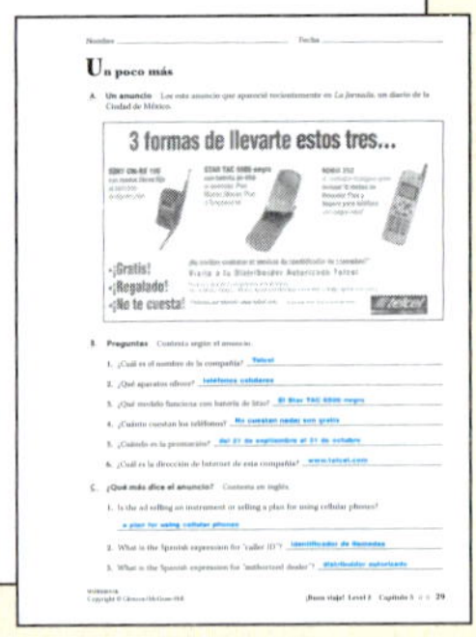
Enrichment, pages 29–32

## Audio Activities

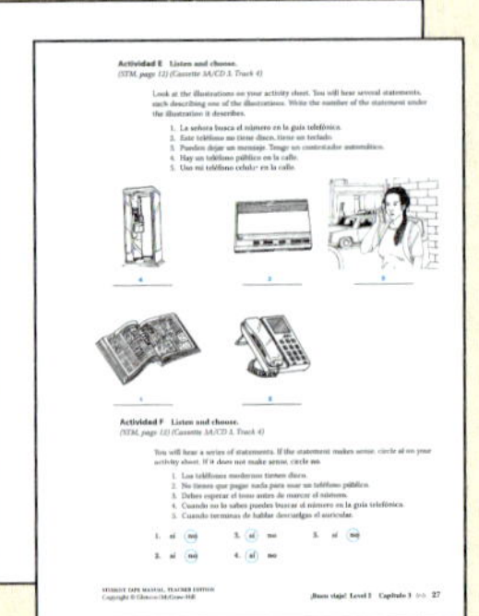
Vocabulary, pages 25–30

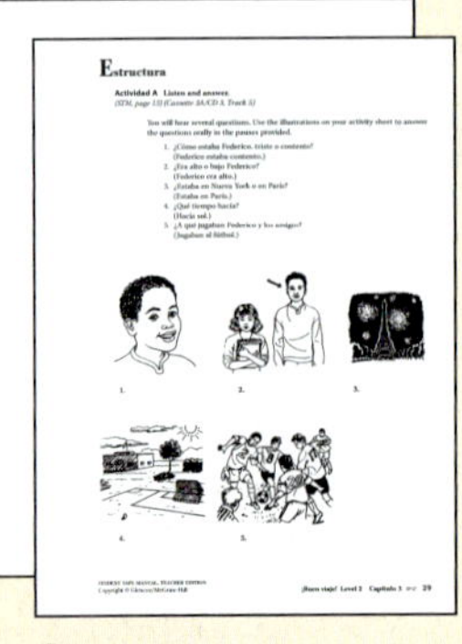
Structure, pages 31–32

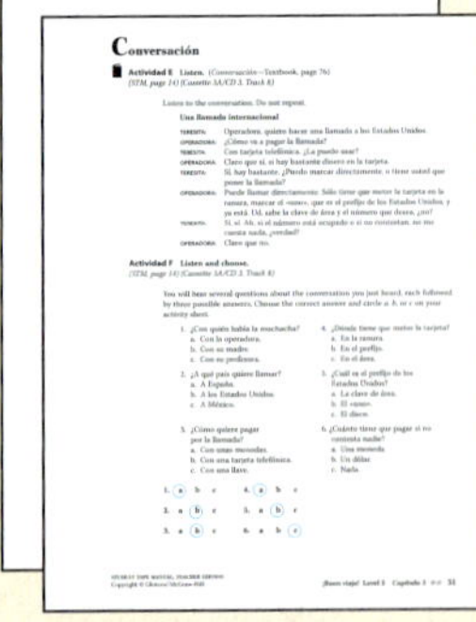
Conversation, page 33

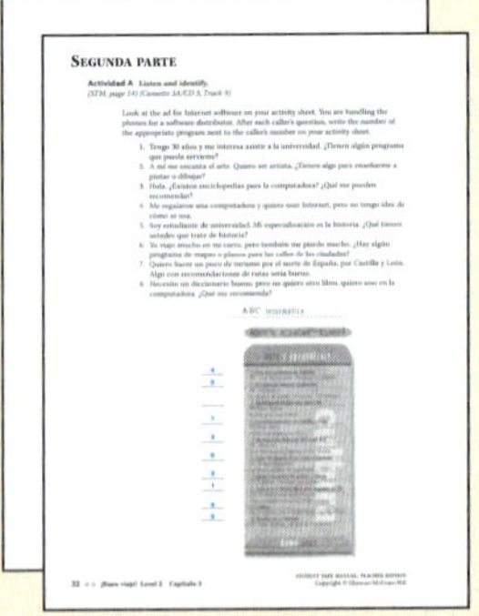
Additional Practice, pages 35–37

## Assessment

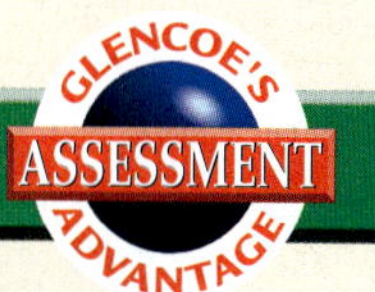


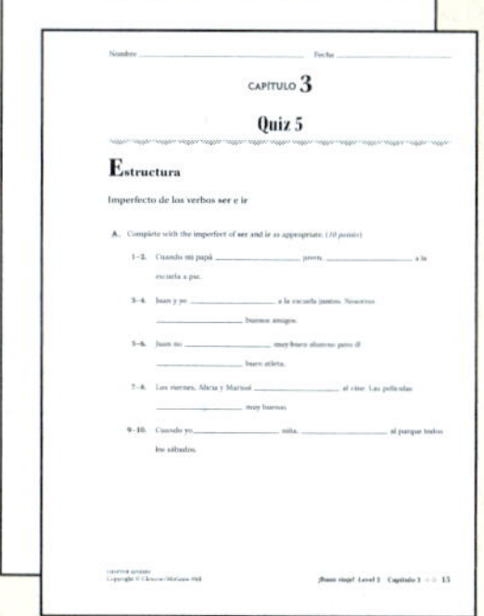

Vocabulary and Structure Quizzes, pages 11–15

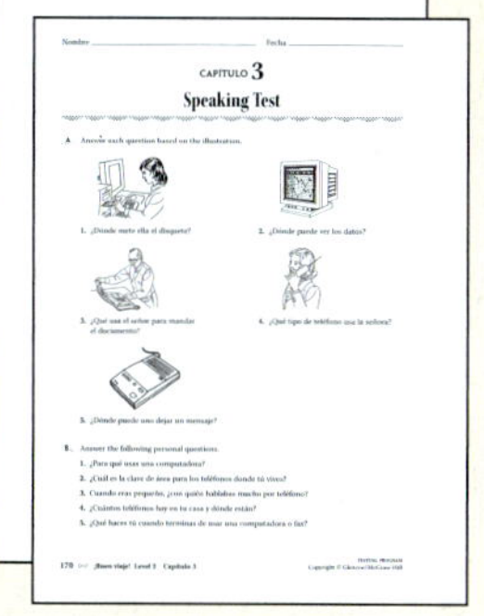

Chapter Tests, pages 29–44

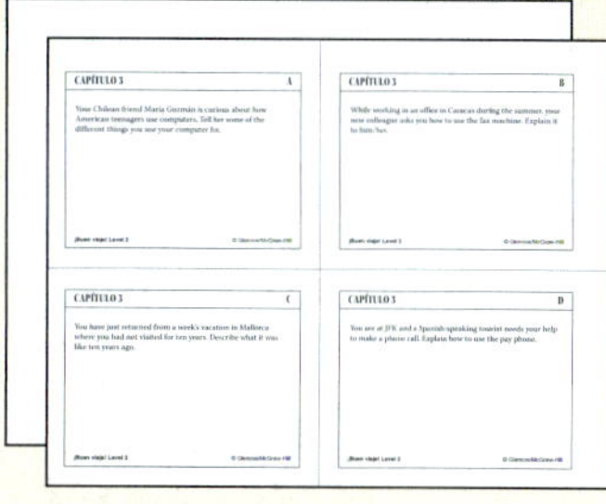

Situation Cards, Chapter 3

MindJogger Videoquiz, ExamView® Pro, Chapter 3

## Timesaving Teacher Tools

### TeacherWorks™

TeacherWorks™ is your all-in-one teacher resource center. Personalize lesson plans, access resources from the Teacher Wraparound Edition, connect to the Internet, or make a to-do list. These are only a few of the many features that can assist you in the planning and organizing of your lessons.

Includes:

- A calendar feature
- Access to all program blackline masters
- Standards correlations and more

### ExamView® Pro

Test Bank software for Macintosh and Windows makes creating, editing, customizing, and printing tests quick and easy.

## Technology Resources

In the Chapter 3 Internet Activity, you will have a chance to learn more about the Spanish-speaking world. Visit spanish.glencoe.com

On the interactive CD–ROM, students can listen to and take part in a recorded version of the conversation in Chapter 3.

**¡Viva el mundo hispano!** Video and Video Activities, Chapter 3. Available on VHS and DVD.

Help your students prepare for the chapter test by playing the **Maratón mental** Videoquiz game show. Teams will compete against each other to review chapter vocabulary and structure and sharpen listening comprehension skills. Available on VHS and DVD.

**¡Buen viaje!** is also available on CD or Online.

# Preview

In this chapter, students will learn to talk about computers, e-mail, and the Internet. They will also learn how to send a fax and make a telephone call in a Spanish-speaking country. Students will also learn the formation and uses of the imperfect tense. The cultural focus of the chapter is on a comparison of telephone service of yesterday and today in the Spanish-speaking world and on modern telecommunications technology.

## National Standards

### Communication

In Chapter 3, students will communicate in spoken and written Spanish on the following topics:

- computers, e-mail, and the Internet
- using the telephone and fax machine
- activities that they used to do

Students will provide and obtain information, express opinions, and participate in conversations dealing with computers and the telephone as they fulfill the chapter objectives listed on this page.

## LEVELING

The activities, conversations, and readings within each chapter are marked according to level of difficulty. **E** indicates easy. **A** indicates average. **C** indicates challenging. Some activities cover a range of difficulty. In some activities, for example, advanced students will be able to produce more extensive responses while students who learn at a different rate may give less detailed responses. The leveling indicators will help you individualize instruction to best meet your students' needs.

Capítulo 3

# Telecomunicaciones

### Objetivos

**In this chapter you will learn to:**

- talk about computers, e-mail, the Internet, faxes, and telephones
- talk about past habitual and routine actions
- describe people and events in the past
- make and receive telephone calls in Spanish

Ernesto Bertani *Nueva visión*

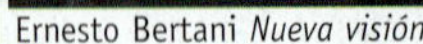

# Capítulo 3

## Spotlight on Culture

**Arte** Ernesto Bertani (1949) is an award-winning, contemporary Argentine painter. He is heavily influenced by the Belgian surrealist painter, Renee Magritte (1898–1967). Bertani's use of everyday objects painted in a hyperrealist style, questions general assumptions about who we are and the nature of the world in which we live.

**Fotografía** The photo shows the **Plaza de la Cibeles** with the **Fuente de la Cibeles** as its centerpiece. **La Cibeles** is to Madrid what the Eiffel Tower is to Paris. The plaza is situated at the intersection of two major arteries, the **Paseo del Prado** and the **Calle de Alcalá.**

**La Cibeles** is the Cybele of Greek and Roman mythology. Cybele was responsible for maintaining and reproducing the wild things of the earth. She was also the guardian of cities and nations and was entrusted with the general welfare of the people. She is usually represented, as she is here, in a chariot drawn by lions.

Behind **La Cibeles** is the main post office building, **El Palacio de Comunicaciones** (1918). The cathedral-like design of the building led **madrileños** to jokingly call it **Nuestra Señora de los Correos.**

# Vocabulario

## PALABRAS 1

## 1 PREPARATION

### Resource Manager

Vocabulary Transparencies 3.2–3.3
Audio Activities TE, pages 25–27
Audio CD 3
Workbook, page 23
Quizzes, page 11
ExamView® Pro

### Bellringer Review

*Use BRR Transparency 3.1 or write the following on the board.*
Answer the following.

1. **¿Sabes usar una computadora?**
2. **¿Para qué usas la computadora?**
3. **¿Tienes una computadora en casa?**

## 2 PRESENTATION

**Step 1** Have students close their books. Introduce the **Palabras 1** vocabulary using Vocabulary Transparencies 3.2–3.3. Have students repeat each word after you or the recording on Audio CD 3 two or three times as you point to the appropriate visual on the transparencies.

**Step 2** When presenting the sentences, intersperse questions to enable students to use the new words immediately. Build from simple to more complex questions. **¿Es un CD? ¿Es la ranura? ¿Mete la muchacha un CD en la ranura? ¿Qué mete en la ranura? ¿Dónde mete el CD?**

# Vocabulario

## PALABRAS 1

### La computadora

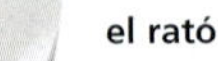

La muchacha prende la máquina.

Ella mete un CD en la ranura.

Ella usa la computadora para hacer las tareas. Ella entra los datos.

La muchacha no pierde los datos porque los guarda.

Después se comunica con los amigos. Usa el correo electrónico.

Cuando termina, ella apaga la máquina y saca el CD.



### Reaching All Students

**Total Physical Response** If you don't have a computer in your classroom, students can pantomime the actions. However, if you do have a computer, you may wish to have students actually perform the actions on the computer as you call them out.

*(Student 1),* **levántate.**
**Ve a la computadora.**
**Indica el monitor.**
**Indica el teclado.**
**Indica el ratón.**
**Prende la máquina.**
**Mete un disquete en la ranura.**
**Entra los datos.**
**Guarda los datos.**
**Apaga la máquina y saca el disquete.**
**Gracias,** *(Student 1).* **Puedes volver a tu asiento.**

# El fax, El facsímil

el facsímil

El señor manda el documento por fax.

Él mete el documento boca arriba.
No lo mete boca abajo.

Él pulsa el botón.

Él transmite el documento.



## Vocabulario

**Teacher Tips**

If you have a computer in class, you can use the actual computer to teach much of this vocabulary. When presenting the vocabulary relating to a fax on page 61, use a sheet of paper to actually show **boca arriba** vs. **boca abajo.**

## About the Spanish Language

In Spain the word for *computer* is **el ordenador;** in most of Latin America it is **la computadora.** The difference is probably due to the influence of other languages—French in Spain and English in Latin America. The French word for *computer* is **ordinateur.**

## Chapter Projects

**Postales electrónicas**

Your students may enjoy sending electronic postcards and greeting cards from the **Glencoe Spanish Web site** (spanish.glencoe.com).

**LEVELING**

**A:** Vocabulary

Vocabulario

# 3 PRACTICE

## ¿Qué palabra necesito?

¡OJO! When students are doing the **¿Qué palabra necesito?** activities, accept any answer that makes sense. The purpose of these activities is to have students use the new vocabulary. They are not factual recall activities. Thus, it is not necessary for students to remember specific factual information from the vocabulary presentation when answering. If you wish, have students use the photos on this page as a stimulus, when possible.

**Historieta** Each time **Historieta** appears, it means that the answers to the activity form a short story. Encourage students to look at the title of the **Historieta,** since it can help them do the activity.

**1** It is suggested that you go over Activity 1 orally in class with books closed. Then have students write the answers for homework and go over the activity once again the following day.

**2** Students can do Activity 2 on their own and then read their answers aloud to a partner or to the class.

Vocabulario

## ¿Qué palabra necesito?

**1 ¿Usas una computadora?**
Contesten personalmente.

1. ¿Sabes usar una computadora?
2. ¿Cuáles son tres partes de la computadora?
3. El monitor, ¿es de color o blanco y negro?
4. ¿Usas el correo electrónico?
5. ¿Con quién te comunicas por correo electrónico?
6. ¿Haces tus tareas en la computadora?
7. ¿Para qué clase o clases usas la computadora?
8. ¿Usas Internet?
9. ¿Tienes CD-ROM?
10. ¿Cuál es tu juego favorito en la computadora?

Caracas, Venezuela

**2 Los pasos a seguir** Pongan las oraciones en orden lógico.

1. Meto un CD en la ranura.
2. Entro los datos.
3. Prendo la computadora.
4. Saco el CD.
5. Apago la máquina.
6. Guardo los datos.

**3 Historieta En la oficina**
Contesten según la foto.

1. ¿Qué quiere hacer la señorita?
2. ¿Usa la señorita la máquina de fax o la computadora?
3. ¿Está prendida la máquina?
4. ¿Cómo mete el documento, boca arriba o boca abajo?
5. ¿Qué pulsa ella?



### Answers to ¿Qué palabra necesito?

**1** *Answers will vary but may include:*

1. Sí, (No, no) sé usar una computadora.
2. Tres partes de la computadora son el monitor o la pantalla, el teclado y el ratón.
3. El monitor es de color.
4. Sí, (No, no) uso el correo electrónico.
5. Me comunico con mis amigos por correo electrónico.
6. Sí, (No, no) hago mis tareas en la computadora.
7. Uso la computadora para la clase de ___.
8. Sí, (No, no) uso Internet.
9. Sí, (No, no) tengo CD-ROM.
10. Mi juego favorito en la computadora es ___. (No tengo un juego favorito.)

**2**

3, 1, 2, 6, 4 (5), 5 (4)

**3**

1. La señorita quiere enviar un fax.
2. Usa la máquina de fax.
3. Sí, la máquina está prendida.
4. Mete el documento boca abajo (arriba).
5. Pulsa el botón.

**4 ¿Cómo uso la computadora?** Un(a) alumno(a) de Latinoamérica quiere aprender a usar tu computadora. Explícale.

**5 ¿Cómo mando un fax?** Tú y tu compañero(a) están trabajando en una oficina. Tú sabes usar la máquina de fax, pero tu compañero(a), no. Explícale.

**6 Programas de software** Con un(a) compañero(a), hablen de cómo pasan el tiempo en la computadora. ¿Juegan mucho o hacen las tareas? Discutan los programas de software que ustedes usan. ¿Son los mismos o no? Luego miren la siguiente pantalla de la computadora. Discutan lo que ven en el monitor. Decidan si consideran útil tal programa.

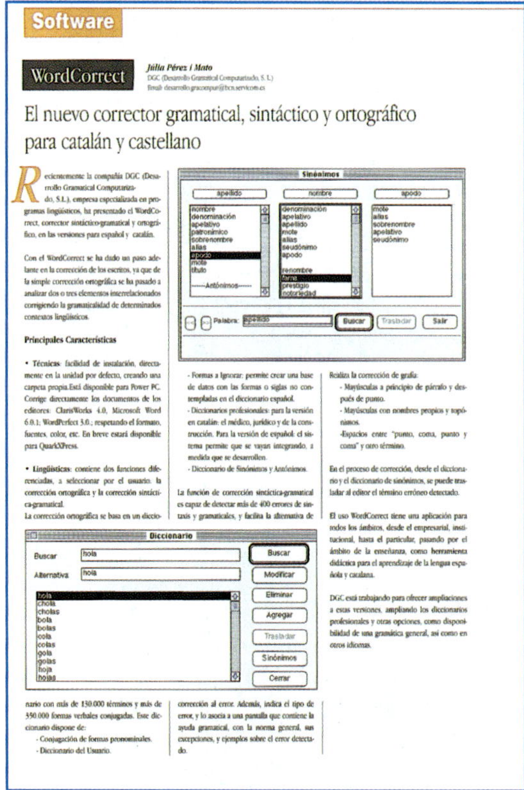

**Software**

**WordCorrect**

*Júlia Pérez i Mato*
DGC (Desarrollo Gramatical Computarizado, S. L.)
Email: desarrollo.gracompur@bcn.servicom.es

El nuevo corrector gramatical, sintáctico y ortográfico para catalán y castellano

Recientemente la compañía DGC (Desarrollo Gramatical Computarizado, S.L.), empresa especializada en programas lingüísticos, ha presentado el WordCorrect, corrector sintáctico-gramatical y ortográfico, en las versiones para español y catalán.

Con el WordCorrect se ha dado un paso adelante en la corrección de los escritos, ya que de la simple corrección ortográfica se ha pasado a analizar dos o tres elementos interrelacionados corrigiendo la gramaticalidad de determinados contextos lingüísticos.

**Principales Características**

• **Técnicas**: facilidad de instalación, directamente en la unidad por defecto, creando una carpeta propia. Está disponible para Power PC. Corrige directamente los documentos de los editores: ClarisWorks 4.0, Microsoft Word 6.0.1; WordPerfect 3.0.; respetando el formato, fuentes, color, etc. En breve estará disponible para QuarkXPress.

• **Lingüísticas**: contiene dos funciones diferenciadas, a seleccionar por el usuario: la corrección ortográfica y la corrección sintáctica-gramatical.

La corrección ortográfica se basa en un diccionario con más de 150.000 términos y más de 350.000 formas verbales conjugadas. Este diccionario dispone de:

- Conjugación de formas pronominales.
- Diccionario del Usuario.
- Formas a Ignorar: permite crear una base de datos con las formas o siglas no contempladas en el diccionario español.
- Diccionarios profesionales: para la versión en catalán: el médico, jurídico y de la construcción. Para la versión de español: el sistema permite que se vayan integrando, a medida que se desarrollen.
- Diccionario de Sinónimos y Antónimos.

La función de corrección sintáctica-gramatical es capaz de detectar más de 400 errores de sintaxis y gramaticales, y facilita la alternativa de corrección al error. Además, indica el tipo de error, y lo asocia a una pantalla que contiene la ayuda gramatical, con la norma general, sus excepciones, y ejemplos sobre el error detectado.

Realiza la corrección de grafía:

- Mayúsculas a principio de párrafo y después de punto.
- Mayúsculas con nombres propios y topónimos.
- Espacios entre "punto, coma, punto y coma" y otro término.

En el proceso de corrección, desde el diccionario y el diccionario de sinónimos, se puede trasladar al editor el término erróneo detectado.

El uso WordCorrect tiene una aplicación para todos los ámbitos, desde el empresarial, institucional, hasta el particular, pasando por el ámbito de la enseñanza, como herramienta didáctica para el aprendizaje de la lengua española y catalana.

DGC está trabajando para ofrecer ampliaciones a estas versiones, ampliando los diccionarios profesionales y otras opciones, como disponibilidad de una gramática general, así como en otros idiomas.



**SPANISH Online**

For more information about computers and search engines in the Spanish-speaking world, go to the Glencoe Spanish Web site: spanish.glencoe.com



## Answers to ¿Qué palabra necesito?

 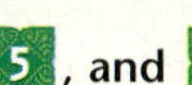 

**4, 5, and 6** *Answers will vary. Students will use the vocabulary from* Palabras 1 *to answer the questions.*

**Vocabulario**

## Writing Development

Have students write the answers to Activity 3 on page 62 in a paragraph to illustrate how all of the items tell a story.

**¡OJO!** Note that the activities are color-coded. All the activities in the text are communicative. However, the ones with blue titles are guided communication. The red titles indicate that the answers to the activity are more open-ended and can vary more. You may wish to correct students' mistakes more so in the guided activities than in the activities with a red title, which lend themselves to a freer response.

## About the Spanish Language

The generic word for *office* is **la oficina.** However, specific kinds of offices often have specific names. The office of a lawyer is **un bufete** and a doctor's office is **una consulta.** The actual office room, especially in a business, is usually called **un despacho.**

### LEVELING

**E:** Activities 1, 3
**A:** Activities 2, 4, 5
**C:** Activities 4, 5, 6

The Glencoe Spanish Web site **(spanish.glencoe.com)** offers options that enable you and your students to experience the Spanish-speaking world via the Internet. For each **Capítulo,** there are activities, games, and quizzes. In addition, an *Enrichment* section offers students an opportunity to visit Web sites related to the theme of the chapter.

Vocabulario

PALABRAS 2

## 1 PREPARATION

### Resource Manager

Vocabulary Transparencies 3.4–3.5
Audio Activities TE, pages 28–30
Audio CD 3
Workbook, pages 24–25
Quizzes, page 12
ExamView® Pro

### Bellringer Review

*Use BRR Transparency 3.2 or write the following on the board.*
Answer the following.

1. **¿Te gusta hablar por teléfono?**
2. **¿Con quién hablas por teléfono?**
3. **¿Hablas mucho por teléfono?**
4. **Cuando hablas por teléfono, ¿en qué lengua hablas generalmente?**

## 2 PRESENTATION

**Step 1** For the initial presentation of the new vocabulary, have students close their books and repeat the words orally as you point to the appropriate visual on Vocabulary Transparencies 3.4–3.5.

### Learning from Realia

*(page 64 top left)* The phone book is for Málaga and Melilla. Melilla is one of two Spanish enclaves in Morocco; the other is Ceuta. Melilla was conquered by Spanish forces under the Duque de Medina Sidonia in 1496.

PALABRAS 2

## El teléfono

la guía telefónica

el teléfono celular

la ranura
el auricular
el teclado
la tecla
el teléfono público

el prefijo de país
(34) 952 822-5364
la clave de área
el número de teléfono

*Nota* **Un aparato** is usually a device like a telephone or an appliance; **una máquina** is usually something more complex, like a computer.



### Reaching All Students

**Total Physical Response**
*(Student 1),* **levántate.**
**Ven acá, por favor.**
**Toma la guía telefónica.**
**Abre la guía telefónica.**
**Mira adentro.**
**Busca un número.**
**Ve al teléfono público.**
**Descuelga.**
**Introduce la tarjeta telefónica.**
**Espera el tono.**
**Marca el número.**
**Habla.**
**Cuelga.**
**Gracias,** *(Student 1).* **Puedes regresar a tu asiento ahora.**

Rafael va a hacer una llamada telefónica.

Él descuelga el auricular.

Él introduce la tarjeta telefónica. No introduce una moneda.

Él espera el tono.

Cuando oye el tono, él marca el número.

El teléfono suena.

La hermana de su amiga contesta.

Cuando yo estaba en Madrid, vivía en una residencia para estudiantes.

Yo llamaba a mis padres a menudo (con frecuencia).
Yo siempre quería hablar mucho. Pero las llamadas largas costaban mucho.
Eran muy caras.



# Vocabulario

**Step 2** After the oral presentation, have students open their books and read aloud for reinforcement.

**Step 3** Have students act out the short telephone conversation.

**Note:** Parts of this **Vocabulario** section introduce students to the forms of the imperfect. The imperfect tense will be taught in the **Estructura** section of this chapter.

## FUN-FACTS

Student **residencias,** unlike our college or university dorms, are not run directly by the universities. They are more like student hotels, although there is university oversight and students are under a certain degree of supervision. Another option for students in Spain is a **colegio mayor,** also a type of student residence. Some **colegios mayores** are actually run by the universities. Others are run privately, usually by religious orders.

Vocabulario

## 3 PRACTICE

## ¿Qué palabra necesito?

**7** Go over this activity orally with books closed. Ask each question and call on a student to respond.
**Expansion:** After going over Activity 7, have one student (or two) provide all the answers. The answers will give directions on how to make a telephone call.

**8** Go over Activity 8 with books open. You may wish to assign it first.

### Writing Development

Students can write the answers to Activity 7 in paragraph form. The answers will form a coherent story.

UN POCO MÁS This *InfoGap* Activity will allow students to practice in pairs. The activity should be very manageable for them, since all vocabulary and structures are familiar.

Vocabulario

# ¿Qué palabra necesito?

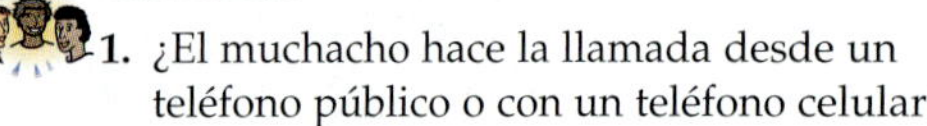

## 7 Historieta Una llamada telefónica

Contesten.

1. ¿El muchacho hace la llamada desde un teléfono público o con un teléfono celular?
2. ¿Es un teléfono de disco o de botones?
3. ¿Qué tiene que esperar antes de marcar el número?
4. Si no sabe el número, ¿dónde puede buscar el número?
5. Si no es un número local, ¿qué tiene que marcar primero?
6. Y si es una llamada a un país extranjero, ¿qué tiene que marcar?

Lima, Perú

## 8 Aparatos y máquinas Escojan.

1. Las computadoras y los teléfonos públicos tienen ____.
   **a.** ranuras **b.** teclas **c.** monitores
2. Si una persona no está en casa cuando llamas, puedes dejar un mensaje en el ____.
   **a.** teclado **b.** auricular **c.** contestador automático
3. Cuando estás en un coche o cuando no estás cerca de un teléfono público, puedes usar un teléfono ____.
   **a.** automático **b.** celular **c.** electrónico
4. Para usar cualquier máquina eléctrica, primero tienes que ____ la máquina.
   **a.** prender **b.** apagar **c.** marcar
5. Y cuando terminas, tienes que ____ la máquina.
   **a.** esperar **b.** meter **c.** apagar

UN POCO MÁS *For more practice using words from **Palabras 1** and **Palabras 2**, do Activity 3 on page H4 at the end of this book.*



## Answers to ¿Qué palabra necesito?

**7**

1. El muchacho hace la llamada desde un teléfono público.
2. Es un teléfono de botones.
3. Tiene que esperar el tono antes de marcar el número.
4. Si no sabe el número, puede buscar el número en la guía telefónica.
5. Si no es un número local, tiene que marcar la clave de área primero.
6. Si es una llamada a un país extranjero tiene que marcar el prefijo de país.

**8**

1. b
2. c
3. b
4. a
5. c

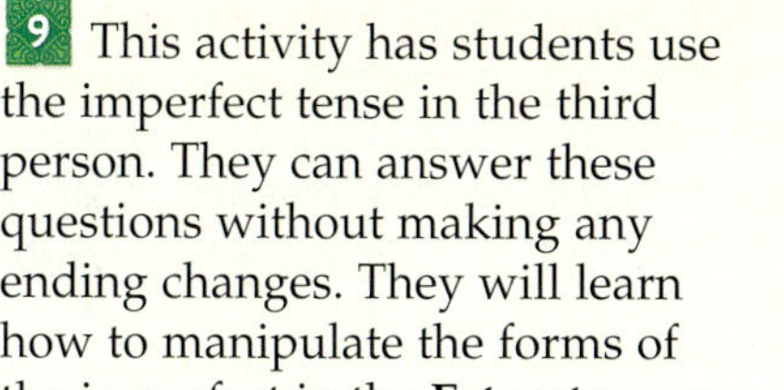

**9** **Historieta** **Linda, la americanita en Madrid**

Contesten.

1. ¿Dónde vivía Linda cuando era alumna en Madrid? (en una residencia para estudiantes)
2. ¿Cuándo llamaba a sus padres? (a menudo)
3. ¿Quién siempre contestaba el teléfono? (su madre)
4. ¿Quería hablar mucho Linda? (sí, siempre)
5. ¿Hablaban mucho Linda y su madre? (sí)
6. ¿Costaban mucho las llamadas cortas? (no, largas)
7. ¿Cómo eran las llamadas largas? (caras)

Madrid, España

Puerta del Sol, Madrid

**10** **Un número equivocado** Llamas a un(a) amigo(a) por teléfono, pero otra persona (tu compañero[a]) contesta y dice que tu amigo(a) no vive allí. Dile a la persona el número que marcaste. La persona va a decir que el número es correcto, pero la clave de área, no, y te va a dar la clave de área correcta.

1. (201) 899–6645 Felipe / (301)
2. (513) 371–8302 Andrea / (313)
3. (917) 356–3223 Tomás / (817)
4. (516) 384–1475 Inés / (517)

**11** **¿Cómo lo hago?** Estás en Madrid y quieres hacer una llamada telefónica. No sabes usar el teléfono público que está en la calle. Le pides ayuda a una persona en la calle (tu compañero[a]). Le preguntas a la persona cómo hacer la llamada. Él o ella te va a explicar lo que tienes que hacer.

**9** This activity has students use the imperfect tense in the third person. They can answer these questions without making any ending changes. They will learn how to manipulate the forms of the imperfect in the **Estructura** section of this chapter.

## Learning from Photos

*(page 67 left)* This telephone at **Puerta del Sol** has slots for coins, telephone cards, and credit cards.

*(page 67 right)* This typical **residencia para estudiantes** is located in the city close to, but not on, the campus of the university. A **residencia** will usually provide meals, laundry facilities, reading and TV rooms, and a number of other amenities in addition to a bedroom.

### LEVELING

**E:** Activities 7, 8, 9, 10

**A:** Activities 8, 9, 10, 11

**C:** Activity 11

## Answers to ¿Qué palabra necesito?

**9**

1. Linda vivía en una residencia para estudiantes cuando era alumna en Madrid.
2. Llamaba a sus padres a menudo.
3. Su madre siempre contestaba el teléfono.
4. Sí, siempre quería hablar mucho.
5. Sí, hablaban mucho.
6. No, las llamadas largas costaban mucho.
7. Las llamadas largas eran caras.

**10** and **11** *Answers will vary, but students will use the vocabulary presented in* Palabras 2.

# Estructura

## 1 PREPARATION

### Resource Manager

Audio Activities TE, pages 31–32
Audio CD 3
Workbook, pages 26–28
Quizzes, pages 13–15
ExamView® Pro

### Bellringer Review

*Use BRR Transparency 3.3 or write the following on the board.*
Answer personally.

1. **¿A qué escuela vas ahora?**
2. **¿Cuántos cursos estás tomando este semestre?**
3. **¿Quién es tu profesor(a) de español?**
4. **¿Te gusta la clase de español?**

## 2 PRESENTATION

### Imperfecto de los verbos en -ar

**Step 1** Have students open their books to page 68. Read Item 1 to them aloud.

**Step 2** Read to students the definition of the imperfect in Item 2.

**Step 3** Write the **-ar** verb forms on the board. Underline the endings and have students read all forms aloud.

**Step 4** Read the model sentences aloud. Tell students to concentrate on the fact that these are things Carlos always did. Read the sentences once and then have students repeat them.

# Estructura

## Imperfecto de los verbos en -ar
### Talking about habitual past actions

1. In Spanish there are two simple past tenses. The preterite tense, which you have already learned, is used to state an action that began and ended at a specific time in the past. The other simple past tense is the imperfect.

2. The imperfect tense is used to describe a habitual or repeated action in the past. The exact times when the action began and ended are not important. These are the forms of regular **-ar** verbs in the imperfect.

| INFINITIVE | tomar | llamar | ENDINGS |
|---|---|---|---|
| STEM | tom- | llam- | |
| yo | tomaba | llamaba | -aba |
| tú | tomabas | llamabas | -abas |
| él, ella, Ud. | tomaba | llamaba | -aba |
| nosotros(as) | tomábamos | llamábamos | -ábamos |
| *vosotros(as)* | *tomabais* | *llamabais* | *-abais* |
| ellos, ellas, Uds. | tomaban | llamaban | -aban |

**Carlos siempre se levantaba temprano.**
**Él tomaba el bus escolar a las siete.**
**El bus llegaba a la escuela a las siete y media.**
**Algunos muchachos caminaban a la escuela.**
**Todos los alumnos entraban a clase a las ocho.**

**¿Lo sabes?**

Verbs that have a stem change in the present do not have one in the imperfect.

**jugar: jugaba**
**acostarse: me acostaba**

San Juan, Puerto Rico



**LEVELING**

**E:** Activities 12, 13
**A:** Activity 14

# ¿Cómo lo digo?

**12 Historieta Carlota iba a la escuela.** Contesten.

1. ¿Carlota se levantaba tarde o temprano todos los días?
2. ¿Carlota caminaba a la escuela o tomaba el bus?
3. ¿A qué hora llegaba a la escuela?
4. ¿Todos los alumnos caminaban a la escuela?
5. ¿A qué hora entraban todos a clase?

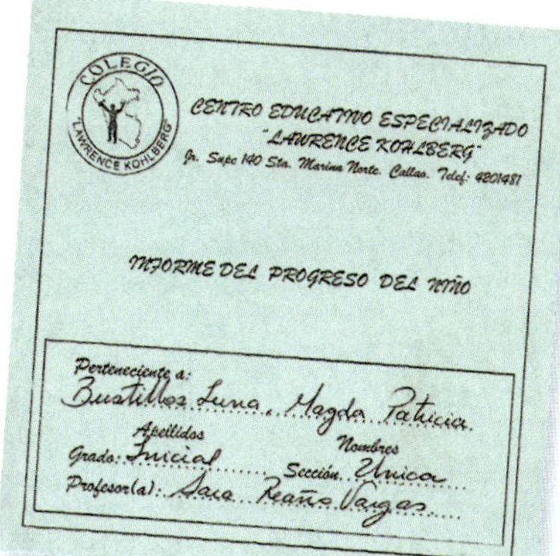

COLEGIO "LAWRENCE KOHLBERG"

CENTRO EDUCATIVO ESPECIALIZADO
"LAWRENCE KOHLBERG"
Jr. Supe 140 Sta. Marina Norte. Callao. Telef: 4201481

INFORME DEL PROGRESO DEL NIÑO

Perteneciente a: Bustillos Luna Magda Patricia
Apellidos Nombres
Grado: Inicial Sección: Unica
Profesor(a): Sara Reaño Vargas

**13 Historieta En el primer grado** Contesten.

1. En el primer grado, ¿tú caminabas a la escuela?
2. ¿Cómo se llamaba tu maestro(a) de primer grado?
3. ¿Qué estudiabas en el primer grado?
4. ¿Tomabas el almuerzo en casa o en la escuela?
5. ¿Dónde estaba tu escuela?
6. ¿A qué hora terminaban las clases?
7. ¿Qué te gustaba hacer por la tarde?
8. ¿Con quién jugabas?

**14 Historieta La oficina de Carmen** Completen con el imperfecto.

Todos los veranos Carmen __1__ (trabajar) en una oficina. La oficina __2__ (estar) en la ciudad. Más de treinta personas __3__ (trabajar) allí. Carmen __4__ (tomar) el tren para ir a la ciudad. El tren __5__ (llegar) a las ocho. Carmen __6__ (caminar) de la estación a la oficina. Carmen __7__ (usar) una computadora. Ella __8__ (entrar) datos y los __9__ (revisar). Ella también __10__ (mandar) copias de documentos por fax. A las doce, Carmen y sus amigas __11__ (tomar) el almuerzo. A las cinco, ellas __12__ (terminar) de trabajar. Entonces Carmen __13__ (apagar) las máquinas y __14__ (regresar) a su casa.

Paseo de la Reforma,
la Ciudad de México, México



## Estructura

**¡OJO!** It is strongly recommended that you do not give students the English equivalents for the imperfect tense. Students must grasp the concept that the imperfect is used to express an ongoing, continuing action. Its beginning and end points are unimportant. When students hear that *used to* is an English equivalent of the imperfect, it confuses them and interferes with the concept because *used to* implies *but no longer*, suggesting an end at a given point in time.

## 3 PRACTICE

### ¿Cómo lo digo?

**12 and 13** These activities can be done first orally with books closed.

**13** Once students have done this activity orally, they can open their books, read the questions, and then answer aloud for additional reinforcement.

**14** Have students prepare Activity 14 before going over it in class.

**Expansion:** After going over all the activities, students can retell the story of each one in their own words.

## Answers to ¿Cómo lo digo?

**12**

1. Carlota se levantaba temprano (tarde) todos los días.
2. Carlota caminaba (tomaba el bus) a la escuela.
3. Llegaba a la escuela a las ___.
4. Sí (No), todos los alumnos (no) caminaban a la escuela.
5. Todos entraban a clase a las ___.

**13** *Answers will vary but may include:*

1. Sí (No), en el primer grado (no) caminaba a la escuela.
2. Mi maestro(a) de primer grado se llamaba ___.
3. En el primer grado estudiaba ___.
4. Tomaba el almuerzo en casa (en la escuela).
5. Mi escuela estaba en la calle ___.
6. Las clases terminaban a las ___.
7. Me gustaba ___ por la tarde.
8. Jugaba con ___.

**14**

1. trabajaba
2. estaba
3. trabajaban
4. tomaba
5. llegaba
6. caminaba
7. usaba
8. entraba
9. revisaba
10. mandaba
11. tomaban
12. terminaban
13. apagaba
14. regresaba

Estructura

## 1 PREPARATION

### Bellringer Review

*Use BRR Transparency 3.4 or write the following on the board.*
Write several things you use a computer for.

## 2 PRESENTATION

### Imperfecto de los verbos en -er e -ir

**Step 1** Have students open their books to page 70. Read Item 1 to them.

**Step 2** Write the infinitives of the verbs **comer** and **vivir** on the board. Cross out the infinitive endings, leaving just the stems.

**Step 3** Write the forms of **comer** and **vivir** in the imperfect on the board. Underline the endings.

**Step 4** Have students read all the verb forms aloud.

**Step 5** Write all the imperfect forms of **querer** and **volver** on the board. Have students repeat them.

**Step 6** Now go over Item 2. Explain to students that the form **había** never changes.

**Note:** It is better not to mention the **n** to English-speaking students because it may confuse them. If you have native speakers in class, you may have to explain that **había** is also used when followed by a plural. **Habían** is wrong. This is a very common error made by native speakers.



**15 El verano pasado** Mira la lista de palabras. Escoge una y pregúntale a tu compañero(a) si hacía eso con frecuencia durante el verano. Luego cambien de rol. Sigan hasta terminar con la lista.

## Imperfecto de los verbos en -er e -ir

### Talking about habitual past actions

1. The imperfect tense forms of regular **-er** and **-ir** verbs are identical.

| INFINITIVE | leer | comer | escribir | vivir | ENDINGS |
|---|---|---|---|---|---|
| STEM | le- | com- | escrib- | viv- | |
| yo | leía | comía | escribía | vivía | -ía |
| tú | leías | comías | escribías | vivías | -ías |
| él, ella, Ud. | leía | comía | escribía | vivía | -ía |
| nosotros(as) | leíamos | comíamos | escribíamos | vivíamos | -íamos |
| *vosotros(as)* | *leíais* | *comíais* | *escribíais* | *vivíais* | *-íais* |
| ellos, ellas, Uds. | leían | comían | escribían | vivían | -ían |

2. The imperfect of **hay** is **había.**

   **No había papel en el fax.**
   **No había mensajes en el contestador automático.**

**¿Te acuerdas?**
Remember that verbs that have a stem change in the present do not have one in the imperfect.
**querer: quería**
**volver: volvía**

## ¿Cómo lo digo?

**16 Cuando yo tenía doce años...** Contesten.

1. Cuando tenías doce años, ¿dónde vivías?
2. ¿A qué escuela asistías?
3. ¿Tenías muchos amigos?
4. ¿Podías hablar español?
5. ¿Sabías usar una computadora?
6. ¿Leías muchos libros?
7. ¿Tenías que estudiar mucho?



### ANSWERS TO ¿Cómo lo digo?

**15** *Answers will vary but may include:*

—¿Nadabas con frecuencia durante el verano?
—Sí, (No, no) nadaba con frecuencia durante el verano.
—¿Estudiabas con frecuencia durante el verano?
—Sí, (No, no) estudiaba con frecuencia durante el verano.

**16** *Answers will vary but may include:*

1. Cuando tenía doce años vivía en ___.
2. Asistía a la Escuela ___.
3. Sí, (No, no) tenía muchos amigos.
4. Sí, (No, no) podía hablar español.
5. Sí, (No, no) sabía usar una computadora.
6. Sí, (No, no) leía muchos libros.
7. Sí, (No, no) tenía que estudiar mucho.

17 **¿Qué hacía la gente en la oficina?** Contesten según los dibujos.

1. ¿Qué hacía la señorita Flores?

2. ¿Qué hacían los señores?

3. ¿Qué hacía Eugenio?

4. ¿Qué hacía Teresita?

5. ¿Qué hacían ustedes?

6. ¿Qué hacías tú?

18 **Historieta Las amiguitas de Ramona** Completen.

Cuando Ramona __1__ (tener) cuatro años, ella __2__ (vivir) en el campo. Los padres de Ramona __3__ (tener) una hacienda con muchos animales. Ramona __4__ (divertirse) mucho en el campo. Ella __5__ (tener) muchas amiguitas imaginarias. Ella les __6__ (servir) café a sus amiguitas. Las amigas la __7__ (querer) mucho a Ramona. Los padres no __8__ (poder) ver a las amiguitas, pero ellos __9__ (saber) que, para Ramona, las amiguitas sí __10__ (existir). Y Ramona nunca __11__ (aburrirse).

En el campo, Casares, España



## Estructura

### 3 PRACTICE

### ¿Cómo lo digo?

16 After going over Activity 16 on page 70, let students say everything they can about things they often did **cuando tenían doce años.**

17 Point out to students that questions with **hacer** are often answered with another verb.

**Writing Development**
Have students write Activity 18 as a unified paragraph.

**Reaching All Students**

**Additional Practice** In Activity 18 the word **amiguitas** appears a number of times. Ask students why there is a **u** in **amiguitas.** Ask students what they think the diminutive of **amigo** would be.

**Geography Connection**

You may wish to let students know that Casares is located in Andalucia in southern Spain, and that it has Arab origins.

**LEVELING**

**E:** Activities 16, 17

**A:** Activities 15, 17, 18

### ANSWERS TO ¿Cómo lo digo?

1. La señorita Flores escribía.
2. Los señores leían.
3. Eugenio comía.
4. Teresita trabajaba (mandaba un fax).
5. Nosotros nos divertíamos.
6. Yo dormía.

18

1. tenía
2. vivía
3. tenían
4. se divertía
5. tenía
6. servía
7. querían
8. podían
9. sabían
10. existían
11. se aburría

## PRACTICE *(continued)*

**19** If there are any other Spanish-speaking teachers at your school, students may enjoy interviewing them and reporting back to the class.

## 1 PREPARATION

### Bellringer Review

*Use BRR Transparency 3.5 or write the following on the board.*

**¿Sí o no?**

1. **Necesito una tarjeta telefónica para hacer una llamada telefónica.**
2. **Hoy día es posible marcar muchos números directamente.**
3. **Dejo un mensaje en el contestador automático.**
4. **Los teléfonos celulares son relativamente recientes.**

## 2 PRESENTATION

### Imperfecto de los verbos ser e ir

**Step 1** Write the infinitives of the verbs **ser** and **ir** on the board.

**Step 2** Write all the forms on the board in paradigm order. Have students repeat all the forms after you.

**Step 3** When going over the verbs **ser** and **ir**, stress the importance of learning these verbs since they are used very often.

## 3 PRACTICE

### ¿Cómo lo digo?

**20** After going over Activity 20 call on an individual student to do the activity in its entirety, retelling the story in his or her own words.

**19 Entrevista** Prepara una entrevista con tu profesor o profesora de español (tu compañero[a]). Entre otras cosas, tú quieres saber algo de su vida cuando asistía a la escuela secundaria. ¡Usen la imaginación!

## Imperfecto de los verbos ser e ir
### Talking about habitual past actions

The verbs **ser** and **ir** are irregular in the imperfect tense.

| INFINITIVE | ser | ir |
|---|---|---|
| yo | era | iba |
| tú | eras | ibas |
| él, ella, Ud. | era | iba |
| nosotros(as) | éramos | íbamos |
| *vosotros(as)* | *erais* | *ibais* |
| ellos, ellas, Uds. | eran | iban |

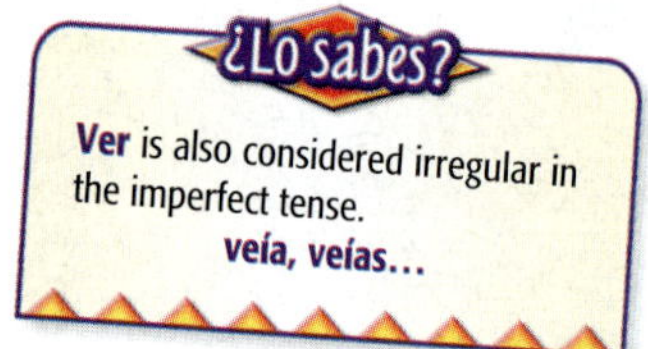

**¿Lo sabes?**

**Ver** is also considered irregular in the imperfect tense.
**veía, veías...**

## ¿Cómo lo digo?

**20 Historieta En la primaria**

Contesten.

1. ¿Quiénes eran tus amigos?
2. ¿Adónde iban tus amigos por la tarde?
3. ¿Adónde iban ustedes los sábados?
4. ¿Quién era tu profesor(a) de español?
5. ¿Cómo ibas a la escuela?
6. ¿Quiénes eran tus maestros favoritos?

Estepona, España



## Answers to ¿Cómo lo digo?

**19** *Answers will vary. Students should use the imperfect tense.*

**20** *Answers will vary but may include:*

1. Mis amigos eran ___.
2. Mis amigos iban ___ por la tarde.
3. Nosotros íbamos ___ los sábados.
4. Mi profesor(a) de español era ___. (No tenía profesor[a] de español en la primaria.)
5. Iba a la escuela a pie (en carro, en el bus escolar, etc.).
6. Mis maestros favoritos eran ___.

## 21 Historieta Buenos amigos

Completen con la forma correcta de **ser** o **ir.**

Cuando Maribel y Paco __1__ jóvenes, __2__ muy buenos amigos. Ellos __3__ a la escuela juntos. Ellos __4__ a comer juntos. Maribel no __5__ muy buena alumna, pero ella __6__ excelente atleta. Y Paco no __7__ buen atleta, pero __8__ excelente alumno. Maribel __9__ a casa de Paco para hacer la tarea con él. Los dos muchachos __10__ al gimnasio donde Maribel le enseñaba a Paco a hacer los ejercicios. Todo el mundo decía que los dos __11__ a ser buenos amigos para siempre.

Málaga, España

## 22 Los maestros de cuarto y quinto

Dile a tu compañero(a) cómo eran tus maestros(as) de cuarto y quinto grado. Tu compañero(a) va a hacer lo mismo. Después digan quiénes eran y cómo eran sus buenos(as) amigos(as) en esos grados.

Una clase de primaria





### Writing Development

Have students write Activity 21 as a unified paragraph.

**22** You may wish to have some groups present their conversations to the entire class.

### Learning from Photos

*(page 73 bottom)* Ask the students to read the poem in the photo. You may want to help them by providing the meaning of a few unfamiliar words such as **miel.** The art on the chart should help them figure out what the poem is about.

### Vocabulary Expansion

The soccer ball shown in the photo on page 72 is **un balón.** A basketball is also called **un balón,** but a smaller ball such as a baseball or a jai-alai ball is **una pelota.** Just to confuse things a bit, while a golf ball is referred to as **una pelota** in Spain, it's **una bola** in most of Latin America. A billiard ball is **una bola** and so is a bowling ball.

### LEVELING

**E:** Activity 20

**A:** Activities 21, 22

**C:** Activity 19

## Answers to ¿Cómo lo digo?

**21**

1. eran
2. eran
3. iban
4. iban
5. era
6. era
7. era
8. era
9. iba
10. iban
11. iban

**22** *Answers will vary. Students should answer using the imperfect tense to describe what their fourth and fifth grade teachers were like.*

## 1 PREPARATION

### Bellringer Review

*Use BRR Transparency 3.6 or write the following on the board.*
Write a description of someone you know. Write as much as you can about him or her in a couple of minutes.

## 2 PRESENTATION

### Usos del imperfecto

**Step 1** Emphasize the fact that the imperfect is used for description in the past.

**Step 2** Ask students to open their books to page 74. Read the sentences as if they were part of an ongoing story in the past.

## 3 PRACTICE

### ¿Cómo lo digo?

**23** Go over Activity 23 once in class. Call on a different student to respond to each question. Then give students a couple of minutes to think about the answers and make up their own story.

**24** After going over Activity 24, call on students to give a description of don Quijote and another one of Sancho Panza.

### Writing Development

Have students write a description of don Quijote and Sancho Panza based on their answers to Activity 24.



## Usos del imperfecto
### Describing things in the past

In addition to expressing repeated, habitual actions or events in the past, the imperfect is used to describe persons, places, objects, events, weather, and time in the past.

| | |
|---|---|
| APPEARANCE | Victoria era alta y fuerte. |
| AGE | Tenía dieciséis años. |
| PHYSICAL CONDITION | Estaba cansada. |
| EMOTIONAL STATE | Pero estaba muy contenta. |
| ATTITUDES AND DESIRES | Ella quería ganar el campeonato. |
| LOCATION | Todos los equipos estaban en la cancha. |
| DATE | Era el ocho de octubre. |
| TIME | Eran las cuatro de la tarde. |
| WEATHER | Hacía bastante frío. |

## ¿Cómo lo digo?

**23 Victoria la victoriosa** Contesten.

1. ¿Cómo era Victoria?
2. ¿Tenía veinte años?
3. ¿Estaba enferma o cansada?
4. ¿Estaba triste?
5. ¿Qué quería Victoria?
6. ¿Dónde estaban todos los atletas?
7. ¿Cuál era la fecha?
8. Y, ¿qué hora era?
9. ¿Qué tiempo hacía?

**24 Don Quijote y Sancho Panza** Contesten.

1. ¿Quién era alto? (Don Quijote)
2. ¿Quién era bajo? (Sancho Panza)
3. ¿Quién tenía un asno? (Sancho Panza)
4. ¿Quién tenía un caballo? (Don Quijote)
5. ¿Quién era idealista? (Don Quijote)
6. ¿Quién era realista? (Sancho Panza)
7. ¿Quién quería viajar? (Don Quijote)
8. ¿Quién quería volver a casa? (Sancho Panza)
9. ¿Quién quería conquistar los males del mundo? (Don Quijote)
10. ¿Quién estaba loco? (Don Quijote)



## Answers to ¿Cómo lo digo?

**23**

1. Era alta y fuerte.
2. No, tenía dieciséis años.
3. Estaba cansada.
4. No, estaba muy contenta.
5. Quería ganar el campeonato.
6. Estaban en la cancha.
7. Era el ocho de octubre.
8. Eran las cuatro de la tarde.
9. Hacía bastante frío.

**24**

1. Don Quijote era alto.
2. Sancho Panza era bajo.
3. Sancho Panza tenía un asno.
4. Don Quijote tenía un caballo.
5. Don Quijote era idealista.
6. Sancho Panza era realista.
7. Don Quijote quería viajar.
8. Sancho Panza quería volver a casa.
9. Don Quijote quería conquistar los males del mundo.
10. Don Quijote estaba loco.

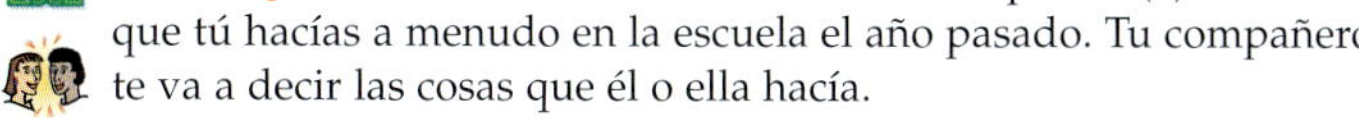

**25 El año pasado en la escuela** Dile a tu compañero(a) las cosas que tú hacías a menudo en la escuela el año pasado. Tu compañero(a) te va a decir las cosas que él o ella hacía.

**26 Eventos culturales** Tú asististe a uno de los siguientes eventos culturales. Descríbelo en detalle a un(a) compañero(a). Incluye el local, el día, la hora, etc. Di por qué querías asistir. Luego cambien de rol.

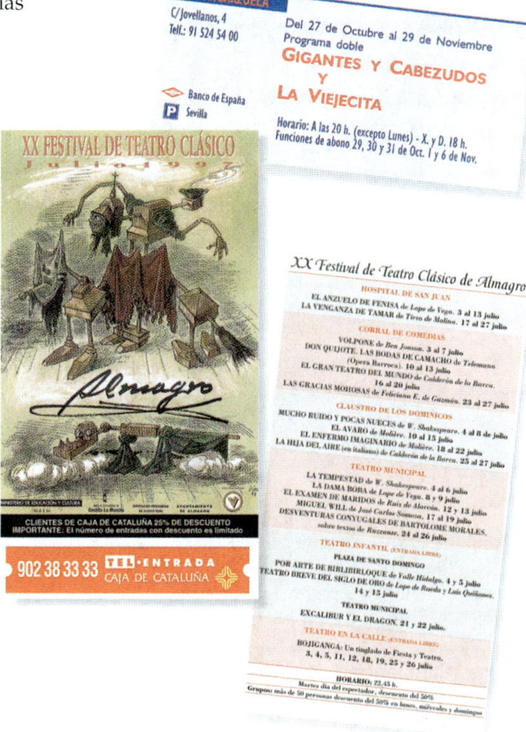

## Estructura

**25** Give students some other expressions that mean **a menudo: con frecuencia, frecuentemente, muchas veces.**

### Learning from Realia

*(page 74)* You may wish to ask students the following questions about the **software educativo:**

**¿Cómo se llama el programa?**

**¿Quién es el autor de *El Quijote?***

**¿Para quiénes fue adaptada la obra?**

**¿Qué contiene el programa?**

*(page 75 top right)* Have students look at the ticket to the **Teatro de la Zarzuela.** The **zarzuela** is a cross between an American musical and an opera. There is spoken dialogue, song, and dance. What is unique, however, is that the setting of every **zarzuela** is Spain, and most often Madrid. The **zarzuela** is a uniquely Spanish art form.

### ¡Adelante!

At this point in the chapter, students have learned all the vocabulary and structure necessary to complete the chapter. The conversation and cultural readings that follow recycle all the material learned up to this point.

### Answers to ¿Cómo lo digo?

**25 and 26** *Answers will vary, but students will use imperfect verb forms and vocabulary from previous chapters to describe what they did last year and what cultural events they attended.*

### Leveling

**E:** Activities 23, 24

**A:** Activities 24, 25

**C:** Activity 26

## Conversación

### 1 PREPARATION

**Resource Manager**

Audio Activities TE, page 33
Audio CD 3

**Bellringer Review**

*Use BRR Transparency 3.7 or write the following on the board.*
You want to tell a friend something, but he or she isn't home. Write a short message for your friend.

### 2 PRESENTATION

**Step 1** Have students listen to the conversation on Audio CD 3.

**Step 2** Now have them open their books. Call on one student to read the part of Teresita and another to read the part of **la operadora.**

**Step 3** As students are reading aloud, you may wish to intersperse questions from the **¿Comprendes?** section.

**Step 4** Have students retell the information from the **Conversación** in their own words.

## Conversación

### Una llamada internacional   

**Ricardo** Operadora, quiero hacer una llamada a Estados Unidos.
**Operadora** ¿Cómo va a pagar la llamada?
**Ricardo** Con tarjeta telefónica. ¿La puedo usar?
**Operadora** Claro que sí, si hay bastante dinero en la tarjeta.
**Ricardo** Sí, hay bastante. ¿Puedo marcar directamente, o tiene usted que poner la llamada?
**Operadora** Puede llamar directamente. Sólo tiene que meter la tarjeta en la ranura, marcar el «uno», que es el prefijo de Estados Unidos, y ya está. Usted sabe la clave de área y el número que desea, ¿no?
**Ricardo** Sí, sí. Ah, si el número está ocupado o si no contestan, no me cuesta nada, ¿verdad?
**Operadora** Claro que no.

**¿Comprendes?**

Contesten.

1. ¿A dónde quiere llamar Ricardo?
2. ¿Qué le pregunta la operadora?
3. ¿Qué tiene Ricardo?
4. ¿Hay bastante dinero en la tarjeta?
5. ¿La operadora tiene que poner la llamada?
6. ¿Dónde tiene que meter la tarjeta Ricardo ?
7. ¿Por qué tiene que marcar el «uno»?
8. Si nadie contesta, ¿le cuesta algo a Ricardo?



**ANSWERS TO ¿Comprendes?**

1. Ricardo quiere llamar a Estados Unidos.
2. La operadora le pregunta cómo va a pagar la llamada.
3. Tiene una tarjeta telefónica.
4. Sí, hay bastante dinero en la tarjeta.
5. No, la operadora no tiene que poner la llamada.
6. Ricardo tiene que meter la tarjeta en la ranura.
7. Tiene que marcar el «uno» porque es el prefijo de Estados Unidos.
8. No, no le cuesta nada.

# Vamos a hablar más

**A** **Los abuelos cuando eran jóvenes** Dile a tu compañero(a) todo lo que sabes de tus abuelos cuando ellos eran jóvenes: cómo eran, dónde vivían y trabajaban, qué hacían con tus padres, etc. Tu compañero(a) va a hacer lo mismo.

**B** **El/La operador(a) internacional** Tú eres el/la operador(a) internacional. Una persona (tu compañero[a]) llama para saber los prefijos de país y las claves de área para las ciudades a donde quiere llamar. Después cambien de rol.

| PAÍS | PREFIJO DE PAÍS | CIUDAD | CLAVE DE ÁREA |
|---|---|---|---|
| Chile | 56 | Valparaíso | 32 |
| Ecuador | 593 | Quito | 2 |
| España | 34 | Sevilla | 5 |
| México | 52 | Acapulco | 74 |
| Perú | 51 | Lima | 1 |
| Uruguay | 598 | Paysandú | 722 |

**C** **Las cosas que nos gustaban** Habla con tu compañero(a) de las cosas que les gustaba hacer cuando eran pequeños, pero que no les gusta hacer ahora.

**D** **Juego** **¿Para qué lo/la uso?** With a partner, look at the following photos. One of you will make up a sentence describing something you do with one of the items in the photos. The other will guess which item you need. Take turns. Use the model as a guide.

**—Quiero buscar el número de teléfono de mi tía.**
**—Ah, necesitas la guía telefónica.**

1. 2. 3. 4. 5.



## Answers to Vamos a hablar más

**A** *Students can say anything they wish about the childhood of their grandparents using vocabulary they know. The verbs will be in the imperfect.*

**B** *Answers will vary.*

**C** *Students will use the imperfect tense and vocabulary they have learned to talk about what they liked to do when they were younger.*

## Conversación

### 3 PRACTICE

### Vamos a hablar más

**A**, **B**, and **C** Allow students to choose the activities they would like to do.

**D** **Juego** This is a good end-of-class activity.

### Learning from Realia

*(page 77 top)* You may wish to ask students these questions about the area codes:

**¿Qué ciudad tiene una clave de área de tres dígitos?**
**¿Qué ciudades tienen claves de área de un solo dígito?**
**¿Qué países tienen prefijos de país de tres dígitos?**

### About the Spanish Language

The Mazatlán, México, telephone directory shown here is called a **Directorio telefónico.** Ask students if they remember what the Málaga and Melilla (page 64) phone book was called **(Guía telefónica).** This is a good opportunity to remind students that different terms are used in different Spanish-speaking countries. Ask them if they can think of any examples in English of different ways of saying things in different places.

### Glencoe Technology

On the CD-ROM, students can watch a dramatization of this conversation. They can then play the role of either one of the characters and record themselves in the conversation.

# Lecturas culturales

## Resource Manager

Audio Activities TE, page 34
Audio CD 3

## National Standards

**Cultures**
The reading about the telephone on page 78 and the related activity on page 79 familiarize students with the Spanish telephone system, both now and in the past.

## PRESENTATION

### Pre-reading

Give students a brief oral summary (in Spanish) of the reading.

### Reading

**Step 1** Call on an individual to read two or three sentences.

**Step 2** Ask questions about the sentences just read and call on volunteers to answer them.

**Step 3** Continue in this way until the entire selection has been read and discussed.

### Post-reading

Assign the **¿Comprendes?** activities for homework. Go over the activities the following day.

### Teaching Tip

Call on students other than the reader to answer your comprehension questions. Most students have difficulty comprehending what they are reading when reading aloud, since they tend to concentrate on their pronunciation.

# Lecturas culturales

## Futura ingeniera

Carmen Tordesillas es estudiante de ingeniería[1] en Madrid. El año que viene va a trabajar para la Compañía de Teléfonos, «la Telefónica». Ella nos habla.

—Cuando yo era niña siempre quería ser ingeniera. Los aparatos electrónicos me fascinaban, especialmente el teléfono. Mi papá me permitía hacer llamadas a casa desde los teléfonos públicos. Era una aventura. Él me levantaba. Me daba unas monedas. Yo las metía en la ranura. Cuando mami contestaba, las monedas caían[2] y empezábamos a hablar. Después de unos minutos sonaba un tono que decía que iba a terminar la conexión. Yo le pedía más monedas a papá. Cuando me daba las monedas, yo estaba contenta; si no, yo protestaba.

Hoy no necesitamos monedas, porque tenemos tarjetas telefónicas y teléfonos celulares que son muy convenientes.

Y van a ver lo que el futuro nos trae. Yo voy a trabajar en «la Telefónica». ¡Voy a crear una revolución en las telecomunicaciones!

[1]ingeniería *engineering*
[2]caían *dropped*

### Reading Strategy

**Asking questions** There are several types of questions you can ask about a reading selection. One type is an inference question. An inference question is one that can be answered by logical reasoning from the information given in the text. You can also ask questions involving an opinion or thought. Asking any number of these different types of questions will usually aid comprehension.

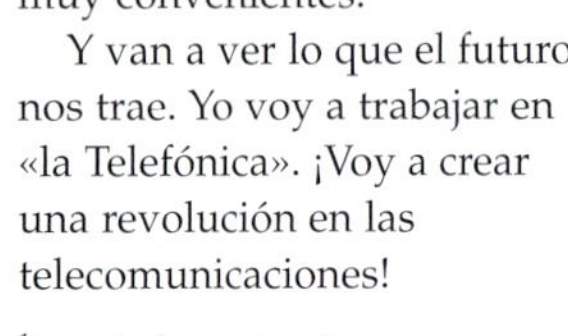

## ¿Comprendes?

**Carmen Tordesillas** Contesten.

1. Actualmente, ¿Carmen trabaja o estudia?
2. ¿Dónde quiere Carmen trabajar?
3. ¿Qué quería ser Carmen cuando era pequeña?
4. ¿Qué le interesaba mucho a la pequeña Carmen?
5. ¿Qué le permitía hacer su padre?
6. Cuando alguien contestaba, ¿qué pasaba con las monedas?
7. ¿Por qué le pedía más monedas a su padre?
8. ¿Su padre siempre le daba monedas a Carmen?
9. ¿Por qué no necesitamos monedas para llamar hoy?
10. ¿Qué va a hacer Carmen en el futuro?

Madrid, España

El Palacio Real, Madrid, España



# Lecturas culturales

### FUN FACTS

**Telefónica** was the Spanish national telephone service until 1998, when the government monopoly ended and the company was privatized. Today **Telefónica** is one of the most important international telecommunications companies. It owns or has a major interest in many telephone systems in Latin America.

### Learning from Photos

*(page 79 top)* This subway station is at the University of Madrid. The statue is by Ana Hyatt Huntington, a prominent American sculptor who created it in the 1930s.

*(page 79 bottom)* The **Palacio Real** is an enormous edifice built entirely of stone. Carlos III was the first king to move into the palace in 1764. The last king to live there was Alfonso XIII, who lived there until his abdication in 1931. There are a number of museums within the Palace, including the Royal Armory, which has a superb collection of weaponry. The Royal Library has over 300,000 volumes, thousands of maps, manuscripts, and music.

**LEVELING**

**A:** Reading

## Answers to ¿Comprendes?

1. Actualmente, Carmen estudia.
2. Carmen quiere trabajar para la Compañía de Teléfonos.
3. Quería ser ingeniera.
4. Le interesaban mucho los aparatos electrónicos.
5. Su padre le permitía hacer llamadas a casa desde los teléfonos públicos.
6. Cuando alguien contestaba las monedas caían.
7. Porque después de unos minutos sonaba un tono que decía que iba a terminar la conexión.
8. No, su padre no siempre le daba monedas a Carmen.
9. Hoy no necesitamos monedas porque tenemos tarjetas telefónicas y teléfonos celulares.
10. Carmen va a trabajar en «la Telefónica».

# Lectura opcional 1

## National Standards

**Cultures**
This reading and the related activity on this page familiarize students with the use of telephone cards in Spain.

**Comparisons**
In this selection students learn that phone cards were introduced in Spain earlier than in the United States.

**¡OJO!** This reading is optional. You may skip it completely, have the entire class read it, have only several students read it and report to the class, or assign it for extra credit.

## Assessment

You may want to quiz those students who read this selection.

1. **¿Dónde usaban primero la tarjeta telefónica?**
2. **¿Se puede usar la tarjeta telefónica con un teléfono público?**
3. **¿Qué tienen las tarjetas?**
4. **¿En dónde introduces la tarjeta cuando haces una llamada?**

**LEVELING**
**E:** Reading 1
**A:** Reading 2

# Lectura opcional 1

## La tarjeta telefónica—una innovación popularísima

La introducción de la tarjeta telefónica ocurrió en España antes que en Estados Unidos. Allí usan este conveniente método de hacer llamadas con teléfonos públicos. Las tarjetas tienen un microchip que registra la cantidad de dinero para llamadas. Introduces la tarjeta en la ranura del teléfono para hacer la conexión. Las tarjetas son muy convenientes. No tienes que llevar muchas monedas o ir a las tiendas para pedir cambio[1]. Y las compañías ahora tienen otro medio de propaganda. Muchas tarjetas llevan un anuncio[2] comercial. Y algunas compañías regalan tarjetas con sus anuncios a sus buenos clientes. La tarjeta telefónica es un invento muy popular.

[1]cambio *change* [2]anuncio *advertisement, announcement*

## ¿Comprendes?

**¿Sí o no?** Digan que sí o que no.

1. La introducción de la tarjeta telefónica ocurrió primero en Estados Unidos.
2. Usan las tarjetas en los teléfonos públicos.
3. Hay un microchip en las tarjetas telefónicas.
4. Para usar las tarjetas necesitas muchas monedas.
5. Las compañías venden las tarjetas a todos sus clientes.
6. Algunas tarjetas llevan anuncios.



## Answers to ¿Comprendes?

1. No
2. Sí
3. Sí
4. No
5. No
6. Sí

## Learning from Realia

*(page 80)* You may wish to ask students questions about the **tarjetas telefónicas:**

**¿De qué país es la tarjeta de arriba?**
**¿Qué valor (dinero) tenía la tarjeta española?**
**¿De qué país es la tarjeta de abajo?**
**¿Cuál es el valor de la tarjeta?**

# Lectura opcional 2

Quito, Ecuador

## La solución a un problema de comunicaciones

En Estados Unidos y en España y las grandes ciudades de Latinoamérica, los teléfonos celulares son muy populares. Los hombres y las mujeres mantienen contacto con la oficina o con los clientes mientras viajan de casa al trabajo y viceversa. Pero en muchos pueblos de Latinoamérica el teléfono celular tiene otro rol.

Hay algunos pueblos y ciudades donde el sistema telefónico está en muy malas condiciones. Las familias tienen que esperar años para la instalación de un teléfono. Donde hay una necesidad, siempre hay una solución. En muchos pueblos y en algunas ciudades, empresarios[1] obtienen[2] teléfonos celulares o aún teléfonos de disco[3] y una conexión con el sistema telefónico. En las calles y las plazas hay mesitas donde un empleado se sienta con un teléfono. Si una persona quiere hacer una llamada, puede usar el teléfono y pagar al empleado. Así el pequeño empresario gana dinero y el público tiene acceso al servicio telefónico.

[1]empresarios *entrepreneurs, businesspeople*
[2]obtienen *obtain*
[3]de disco *rotary*

Plaza de Armas, Trujillo, Peru

## ¿Comprendes?

**A El teléfono celular** Contesten.

1. ¿Quiénes usan mucho el teléfono celular?
2. ¿Para qué usan el teléfono celular?
3. ¿Cuál es el problema con el sistema telefónico en algunas partes de Latinoamérica?
4. ¿Qué problema tienen las familias?
5. ¿Dónde puedes ver los teléfonos en partes de Latinoamérica?
6. ¿Qué puede hacer una persona que quiere hacer una llamada?

**B La solución a un problema** Expliquen, en sus propias palabras, el uso de un teléfono celular o de disco que describen en la lectura.



## Answers to ¿Comprendes?

**A**

1. Los hombres y las mujeres que trabajan en oficinas usan mucho el teléfono celular.
2. Usan el teléfono celular para mantenerse en contacto con la oficina o con los clientes mientras viajan de casa al trabajo y viceversa.
3. El sistema telefónico está en muy malas condiciones.
4. Las familias tienen que esperar años para la instalación de un teléfono.
5. Puedes ver los teléfonos en mesitas en calles y plazas.
6. Una persona que quiere hacer una llamada puede usar el teléfono celular y pagar al empleado.

**B** *Answers will vary. Students should use vocabulary and information from* Lectura opcional 2.

# Lectura opcional 2

### National Standards

**Cultures**
This reading and the related activities on this page familiarize students with the use of cell phones in Latin America.

**Comparisons**
In this selection, students learn that because of the poor condition of the phone system in some areas of Latin America, people who are otherwise without a phone can pay to make calls from cell phones provided on the street by enterprising businesspeople.

**¡OJO!** This reading is optional. You may skip it completely, have the entire class read it, have only several students read it and report to the class, or assign it for extra credit.

### PRESENTATION

You may wish to explain to students that in some areas the phone is not necessarily a cell phone. They actually have a regular phone installed, and people line up to use it and pay for each call.

### Learning from Photos

*(page 81 top)* Located 9,350 feet above sea level, Quito, Ecuador is considered by many to be one of the most beautiful cities in South America. Quito is surrounded by volcanoes and is known for its wonderful climate and well-preserved colonial architecture.

*(page 81 bottom)* Known for its balmy weather, Trujillo is located in the northern Peruvian province of La Libertad. Trujillo was the first northern city to declare its independence from Spanish rule (1820) and it is now considered an important economic and cultural center.

# Conexiones

## National Standards

**Connections**

This reading about changes in computer technology and the prevalence of English in the field of computer science establishes a connection with another discipline, allowing students to reinforce and further their knowledge of technology through the study of Spanish.

**Comparisons**

This reading points out how much of the computer vocabulary in Spanish has been derived from English and gives students a better understanding of the interrelatedness of the two languages.

**¡OJO!** The readings in the **Conexiones** section are optional. They focus on some of the major disciplines taught in schools and universities. The vocabulary is useful for discussing such topics as history, literature, art, economics, business, science, etc. You may choose any of the following ways to do the readings in the **Conexiones** sections.

**Independent reading** Have students read the selection and do the post-reading activities as homework, which you collect. This option is least intrusive on class time and requires a minimum of teacher involvement.

**Homework with in-class follow-up** Assign the reading and post-reading activities as homework. Review and discuss the material in class the next day.

**Intensive in-class activity** This option includes a pre-reading vocabulary presentation, in-class reading and discussion, assignment of the activities for homework, and a discussion of the assignment in class the following day.

# Conexiones

## *La tecnología*

### La computadora

It's hard to imagine life before the computer and the fax machine. The computer has revolutionized travel, medicine, architecture, the military, banking, and commerce. Hardly a field has been unaffected by computers. Even agriculture and the arts make extensive use of the new technology. The changes have been tremendous. Because the United States has led the way in computer science, much of the vocabulary used worldwide is in English or derived from English. Let's read about some of these changes in technology and the prevalence of English in this field.

### Los avances en las telecomunicaciones

Las computadoras de hace treinta años eran enormes. Una computadora antigua, como la original ENIAC de 1946, procesaba menos datos que un PC moderno y llenaba toda una sala. Hoy hay computadoras portátiles que pesan menos de 2 kilos. Lo que ha facilitado el progreso en las computadoras es la «miniaturización». Un solo microchip puede almacenar[1] miles y miles de datos. Los primeros aparatos de transmisión de facsímil también eran muy grandes y las copias que salían en el destino muchas veces no se podían leer.

[1]almacenar *store*

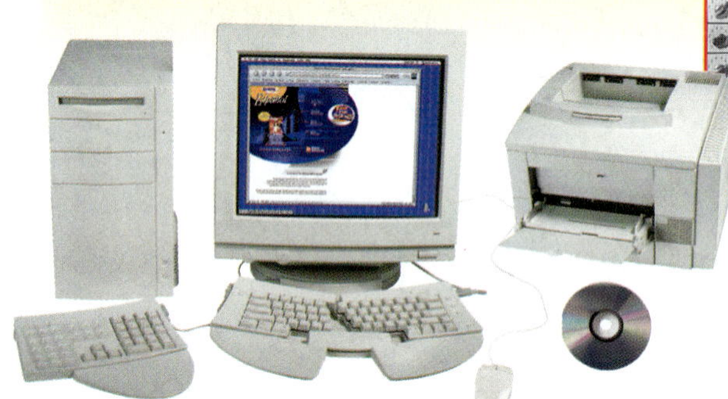

Computadora ENIAC



**Learning from Photos**

*(page 82 right)* ENIAC stood for *Electronic Numerical Integrator and Computer.* ENIAC, with its thousands of electron tubes, was the first electronic digital computer.

Laura Ballesteros trabaja en uno de los ministerios del gobierno chileno. Ella es recepcionista. El edificio es del siglo XIX, pero los aparatos que usa Laura son muy modernos. Ella tiene una computadora y un fax. En el colegio Laura estudiaba inglés. Buena idea, porque hay mucho inglés en el vocabulario de la informática[2]. Por ejemplo, tienes que hacer «clic» en un «icono» para tener acceso a un programa de «software». Y un «virus» puede infectar los programas.

Aquí hay otros ejemplos del predominio del inglés en el mundo de las computadoras: monitor, datos, disquete, memoria, documentación, drive, formateo, site de Internet. ¿Sabes lo que son en inglés?

[2]informática *computer science*

Edificio del siglo XIX

Interior del mismo edificio

## ¿Comprendes?

**A ¿Cómo se llama... ?** Den la palabra en español.

1. icon
2. access
3. memory
4. program
5. click
6. data

**B ¿Qué es?** Identifiquen.

1. el proceso de hacer muy pequeño un aparato u otra cosa
2. una copia exacta y precisa
3. la pantalla como la de un televisor en donde proyectan la información de la computadora
4. el disco pequeño para guardar datos que pueden sacar de la computadora
5. el disco grande con mucha memoria dentro de la computadora
6. una computadora muy pequeña que pueden llevar de viaje

# Conexiones

## PRESENTATION

### *La tecnología*
### La computadora

Since many students are interested in computers, you may wish to have all students scan or read this selection quickly just to get some general information and acquaint themselves with some vocabulary for receptive purposes.

## Reaching All Students

**Additional Practice** You may wish to ask students what the following computer terms mean in English:
**procesar**
**tarjeta de sonido**
**micrófono sobremesa**
**placa base**
**salidas**

**LEVELING**

**A:** Reading

## Answers to ¿Comprendes?

**A**

1. icono
2. acceso
3. memoria
4. programa
5. clic
6. datos

**B**

1. la «miniaturización»
2. un fax
3. el monitor
4. el disquete
5. el drive
6. una computadora portátil

# ¡Te toca a ti!

## Use what you have learned

### 1 PREPARATION

**Bellringer Review**

*Use BRR Transparency 3.8 or write the following on the board.*
Write a short sentence using each of the following words or expressions.
1. **hacer una llamada telefónica**
2. **descolgar**
3. **introducir la tarjeta telefónica**
4. **marcar el número**
5. **hablar**

 **Recycling**

These activities allow students to use the vocabulary and structure from this chapter in completely open-ended, real-life situations.

### 2 PRESENTATION

Encourage students to say as much as possible when they do these activities. Tell them not to be afraid to make mistakes, since the goal of the activities is real-life communication. If someone in the group makes an error, allow the others to politely correct him or her. Let students choose the activities they would like to do.

You may wish to divide students into pairs or groups. Encourage students to elaborate on the basic theme and to be creative. They may use props, pictures, or posters if they wish.

**Writing Strategy**

**Expository writing** Have students read the Writing strategy on page 85. Some topic suggestions:
- how to call from a public phone
- how to use a computer

Have students exchange their letter with a classmate. The classmate can then provide feedback.

# ¡Te toca a ti!

## Use what you have learned

HABLAR **1**

### ¿Qué pasa?

✔ *Talk about computers, e-mail, faxes, and cell phones*

Con un(a) compañero(a), miren las fotos. Cada uno(a) va a escoger una y explicar lo que pasa.

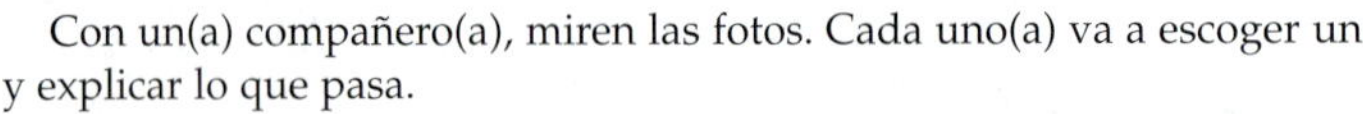

a.

b.

c.

HABLAR **2**

### Un mensaje telefónico

✔ *Leave a message on an answering machine*

Tú y tu compañero(a) tienen muchos amigos de habla española. Cada uno(a) de ustedes debe pensar en un mensaje en español para el contestador automático. Comparen sus mensajes y escojan uno para usar en el contestador automático.

HABLAR **3**

### Los veranos de mi niñez

✔ *Talk about past habitual actions*

Pregúntale a un(a) compañero(a) de clase lo que hacía en el verano cuando era pequeño(a). Pregúntale adónde iba, con quién, lo que hacía, etc. Luego cambien de papel.

HABLAR **4**

### Un juego telefónico

✔ *Describe routine actions*

Divide the class into teams by rows. Using the imperfect, the last person in each row will whisper to the person in front of him or her one sentence about what he or she always did in the past. Each person will whisper the same sentence to the next person until the message reaches the front of the row. The first person in each row will say the sentence to the class. The team whose final sentence most clearly resembles the original wins.



## Answers to ¡Te toca a ti!

 **1** *Answers will vary but may include:*

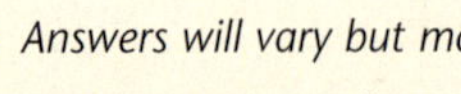
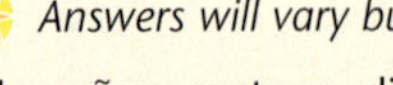

**a.** La señora mete un disco en la ranura.
**b.** El señor habla por teléfono. Usa su teléfono celular.
**c.** El señor manda un fax.

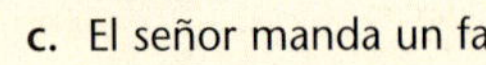

**2** *Answers will vary, but students should use vocabulary from the chapter.*

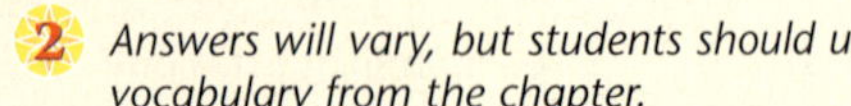

**3** *Answers will vary, but students should use the imperfect tense.*

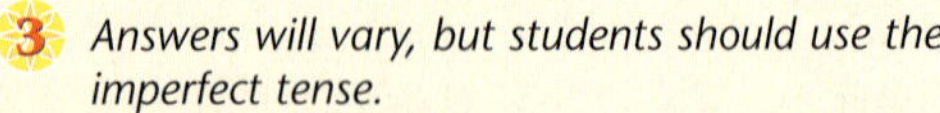

# ¡Te toca a ti!

## 5 Recuerdos de mi niñez

*✔ Write about people and events in the past*

Cuando eras niño(a), ¿ibas con frecuencia a visitar a unos primos o amigos? En un párrafo, describe a quién (quiénes) visitabas, cómo eran, qué tipo de casa tenían. Incluye en tu párrafo todo lo que hacían cuando estaban juntos.

Barcelona, España

## 6 Una historieta o un cuento

*✔ Narrate in the past*

Escribe un cuento utilizando las siguientes categorías como guía.

- Fecha
- Tiempo
- Personajes y lugar (quiénes y dónde)
- Descripción física y emocional de los personajes
- Actitudes
- Deseos
- Actividades usuales

### Writing Strategy

**Expository writing** Expository writing is writing that explains and informs. It helps one understand a topic. Two important expressions to think about while writing an expository piece are "how to" and "why." Use familiar terms in your definitions and descriptions. Be careful not to omit important facts and steps. Be certain not to present steps out of order. These measures will help you present a clear and concise explanation that readers will find interesting and informative.

## 7 Un trabajo interesante

You had a job this past summer with a service organization in the Hispanic community in your town. You got the job because you speak Spanish. Since you've never worked in an office before, you were excited about learning to use equipment that was all new to you. Write to Octavio, your Peruvian pen pal, and explain some of the things you did in the office and what equipment you used. Since you know that Octavio has never worked in an office and is not familiar with office machines, be as clear and logical as you can in your explanation.



### Writing Development

Have students keep a notebook or portfolio containing their best written work from each chapter. These selected writings can be based on assignments from the Student Textbook and the Workbook. The activities on page 85 are examples of writing assignments that may be included in each student's portfolio. On page 32 in the Workbook, students will begin to develop an organized autobiography **(Mi autobiografía)**. These workbook pages may also become a part of their portfolio.

## 3 PRACTICE

4 You may wish to do this game as a whole-class activity.

5 Have students edit each others' paragraphs.

### Answers to ¡Te toca a ti!

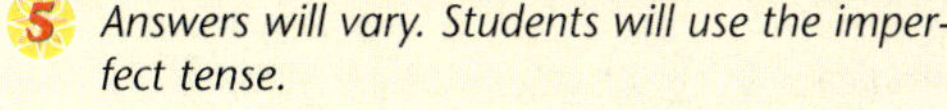

5 *Answers will vary. Students will use the imperfect tense.*

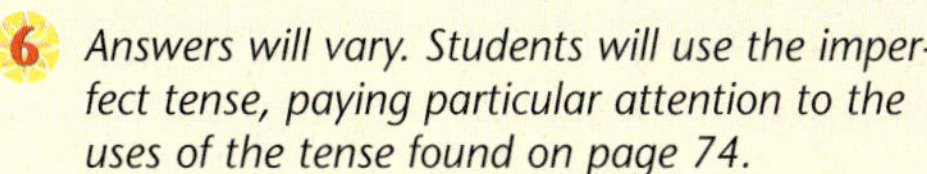

6 *Answers will vary. Students will use the imperfect tense, paying particular attention to the uses of the tense found on page 74.*

### LEVELING

These activities encompass all three levels. All students will be able to do them at a sophistication level commensurate with their ability in Spanish. Some students will be able to speak for several minutes, and others may be able to give just a few sentences. This is to be expected when students are functioning completely on their own generating their own language to the best of their ability.

# Assessment

## Resource Manager

Communication Transparency C 3
Quizzes, pages 11–15
Performance Assessment, Task 3
Tests, pages 29–44
ExamView® Pro, Chapter 3
Situation Cards, Chapter 3
**Maratón mental** Videoquiz, Chapter 3

## Assessment

This is a pre-test for students to take before you administer the chapter test. Note that each section is cross-referenced so students can easily find the material they have to review in case they made errors. You may use Assessment Answers Transparency A 3 to do the assessment in class, or you may assign this assessment for homework. You can correct the assessment yourself, or you may prefer to project the answers on the overhead in class.

## Glencoe Technology

**MINDJOGGER VHS/DVD**

You may wish to help your students prepare for the chapter test by playing the MindJogger game show. Teams will compete against each other to review chapter vocabulary and structure and sharpen listening comprehension skills.

# Assessment

## Vocabulario

To review **Palabras 1**, turn to pages 60–61.

**1 Escojan.**

1. Antes de empezar a trabajar, es necesario ____ la computadora.
   **a.** guardar **b.** meter **c.** prender
2. La joven mete su CD en ____.
   **a.** el teclado **b.** el dato **c.** la ranura
3. La joven no pierde los datos. Los ____.
   **a.** guarda **b.** entra **c.** saca
4. Ve lo que entra en la computadora en ____.
   **a.** el ratón **b.** el teclado **c.** la pantalla

**2 Den lo contrario.**

5. prender la máquina
6. meter el CD
7. boca arriba

To review **Palabras 2**, turn to pages 64–65.

**3 Identifiquen.**

8. 

9.  (34) 952 822-5364

10. 

ANSWERS TO 

1. c
2. c
3. a
4. c

5. apagar la máquina
6. sacar el disquete
7. boca abaja

8. la guía telefónica
9. el número de teléfono
10. el contestador automático

## 4 Completen.

11. Él ____ el auricular para hacer una llamada telefónica.
12. Él no introduce una moneda en la ranura. Introduce su ____.
13. Cuando oye el ____, marca el número.

# Estructura

## 5 Escriban en el imperfecto.

14. Él habla mucho.
15. Él hace muchas llamadas telefónicas.
16. Tomo fotos de la casa.
17. Yo vivo en la casa.
18. ¿Comes en la cafetería de la escuela?
19. ¿Tomas el desayuno en la escuela?
20. Escribimos muchas cartas a nuestros abuelos.

To review regular -ar, -er, and -ir verbs in the imperfect tense, turn to pages 68 and 71.

## 6 Completen.

21–22. Cuando yo ____ muy joven, ____ a la escuela a pie. (ser, ir)

To review ser and ir in the imperfect tense, turn to page 72.

## 7 Completen en el pasado.

23–25. Sancho Panza ____ (ser) el escudero de don Quijote. Don Quijote siempre ____ (querer) conquistar los males del mundo. Los dos ____ (viajar) por toda España.

To review the imperfect tense, turn to pages 68–75.



## Assessment

**FOLDABLES™ Study Organizer** **Dinah Zike's Study Guides**

Your students may wish to use Foldable 1 to organize, display, and arrange data as they learn more numbers in Spanish. You may wish to encourage them to add information from each unit as they continue to learn and use numbers in Spanish.

A *vocabulary book* foldable is an ideal reference, especially as students begin to make word associations and write simple passages in Spanish.

## Answers to Assessment

11. descuelga
12. tarjeta telefónica
13. tono

14. Él hablaba mucho.
15. Él hacía muchas llamadas telefónicas.
16. Tomaba fotos de la casa.
17. Yo vivía en la casa.
18. ¿Comías en la cafetería de la escuela?
19. ¿Tomabas el desayuno en la escuela?
20. Escribíamos muchas cartas a nuestros abuelos.

21. era
22. iba

23. era
24. quería
25. viajaban

# ¡Hablo como un pro!

This unique page gives students the opportunity to speak freely and say whatever they can, using the vocabulary and structures they have learned in the chapter. The illustration serves to remind students of precisely what they know how to say in Spanish. There are no activities that students do not have the ability to describe or talk about in Spanish. The art not only depicts the vocabulary and content of this chapter, but also reinforces what they learned in previous chapters.

You may wish to use this page in many ways. Some possibilities are to have students do the following:

1. Look at the illustration and identify items by giving the correct Spanish words.
2. Make up sentences about what they see in the illustration.
3. Make up questions about the illustration. They can call on another class member to respond if you do this as a class activity, or you may prefer to allow students to work in small groups. This activity is extremely beneficial because it enables students to actively use interrogative words.
4. Answer questions you ask them about the illustration.
5. Work in pairs and make up a conversation based on the illustration.
6. Look at the illustration and give a complete oral review of what they see.
7. Look at the illustration and write a paragraph (or essay) about it.

You can also use this page as an assessment or testing tool, taking into account individual differences by having students go from simple to quite complicated tasks. The assessment can be either oral or written. You may wish to use the rubrics provided on pages T20–T21 as you give students the following directions.

1. Identify the topic or situation of the illustration.
2. Give the Spanish words for as many items as you can.
3. Think of as many sentences as you can to describe the illustration.
4. Go over your sentences and put them in the best sequencing to give a coherent story based on the illustration.

# ¡Hablo como un pro!

Tell all you can about this illustration.

### Describing a computer

la computadora, el ordenador
el teclado
el monitor, la pantalla
el disquete
el disco compacto
el ratón
la impresora
la ranura
el correo electrónico
el CD-ROM
Internet

### Describing computer activities

prender la máquina
meter un disquete
entrar los datos
hacer las tareas
guardar
comunicarse
terminar
apagar
sacar

### Describing how to send a fax

el facsímil, el fax
el aparato
el documento
boca arriba
boca abajo
mandar, transmitir
meter
pulsar el botón

**VIDEOTUR**

## Episodio 3

In this video episode, you will see Julián try to help Alejandra with a dilemma. See page 482 for more information.

### Describing a telephone

el teléfono público
la ranura
el auricular
el disco
el teléfono de botones
la tecla
el teléfono celular
el contestador automático
dejar un mensaje

### Describing telephone numbers

la guía telefónica
el prefijo de país
la clave de área
el número de teléfono

### Making a telephone call

hacer una llamada telefónica, llamar
descolgar el auricular
introducir la tarjeta telefónica
oír el tono
marcar el número
sonar
contestar
¿Está... ?
¿De parte de quién?

**How well do you know your vocabulary?**

- Choose words to describe your favorite method of communication.
- Write a brief explanation of sending an e-mail or making a telephone call.

### Other useful expressions

a menudo
con frecuencia



Vocabulario

## Vocabulary Review

The words and phrases in the **Vocabulario** have been taught for productive use in this chapter. They are summarized here as a resource for both student and teacher. This list also serves as a convenient resource for the **¡Te toca a ti!** activities on pages 84 and 85. There are approximately fifteen cognates in this vocabulary list. Have students find them.

**¡OJO!** You will notice that the vocabulary list here is not translated. This has been done intentionally, since we feel that by the time students have finished the material in the chapter they should be familiar with the meanings of all the words. If there are several words they still do not know, we recommend that they refer to the **Palabras 1** and **2** sections in the chapter or go to the dictionaries at the end of this book to find the meanings. However, if you prefer that your students have the English translations, please refer to Vocabulary Transparency 3.1, where you will find all these words with their translations.

**VIDEO VHS/DVD**

The Video Program allows students to see how the chapter vocabulary and structures are used by native speakers within an engaging storyline. For maximum reinforcement, show the video episode as a final activity for Chapter 3.

# Planning for Chapter 4

## SCOPE AND SEQUENCE, PAGES 90–121

### Topics

- Men's clothing and apparel
- Women's clothing and apparel
- Food
- Quantities, prices, and sizes

### Culture

- Shopping in the Spanish-speaking world
- The traditional market at Chichicastenango
- The science of marketing
- **Vistas de Chile**

### Functions

- How to shop for clothing
- How to shop for food
- How to differentiate between continuous habitual past actions and those completed at a definite time
- How to express two past actions in the same sentence

### Structure

- Preterite versus imperfect
- Two actions in the same sentence
- Verbs such as **querer** and **creer** in the past
- The passive voice with **se**

### National Standards

- Communication Standard 1.1 pages 94, 95, 98, 99, 101, 102, 103, 104, 105, 106, 107, 109, 116
- Communication Standard 1.2 pages 95, 99, 102, 104, 105, 107, 108, 109, 110–111, 112–113, 114–115, 116
- Communication Standard 1.3 page 117
- Cultures Standard 2.1 pages 108, 110–111, 112–113
- Cultures Standard 2.2 page 97
- Connections Standard 3.1 pages 114–115
- Comparisons Standard 4.2 pages 110–111
- Communities Standard 5.1 page 121
- Communities Standard 5.2 page 102

## PACING AND PRIORITIES

**The chapter content is color coded below to assist you in planning.**

**■ required ■ recommended ■ optional**

**Vocabulario** *(required)* *Days 1–4*

- ■ Palabras 1
  - La tienda de ropa para caballeros
  - La tienda de ropa para señoras
  - En la zapatería
  - En la joyería
- ■ Palabras 2
  - La compra de comestibles

**Estructura** *(required)* *Days 5–7*

- ■ El pretérito y el imperfecto
- ■ Dos acciones en una oración
- ■ Verbos como **querer** y **creer** en el pasado
- ■ La voz pasiva con **se**

**Conversación** *(required)*

- ■ Naranjas para abuelita

**Lecturas culturales**

- ■ De compras *(recommended)*
- ■ El mercado de Chichicastenango *(optional)*

**Conexiones**

- ■ El mercadeo *(optional)*

■ **¡Te toca a ti!** *(recommended)*

■ **Assessment** *(recommended)*

■ **¡Hablo como un pro!** *(optional)*

## RESOURCE GUIDE

| SECTION | PAGES | SECTION RESOURCES |
| --- | --- | --- |
| **Vocabulario PALABRAS 1** | | |
| La tienda de ropa para caballeros<br>La tienda de ropa para señoras<br>En la zapatería<br>En la joyería | 92, 94–95<br>92, 94–95<br>93, 94–95<br>93, 94–95 | Vocabulary Transparencies 4.2–4.3<br>Audio CD 3<br>Audio Activities TE, pages 38–41<br>Workbook, pages 33–34<br>Quiz 1, page 16<br>ExamView® Pro |
| **Vocabulario PALABRAS 2** | | |
| La compra de comestibles | 96–99 | Vocabulary Transparencies 4.4–4.5<br>Audio CD 3<br>Audio Activities TE, pages 41–43<br>Workbook, pages 35–36<br>Quiz 2, page 17<br>ExamView® Pro |
| **Estructura** | | |
| El pretérito y el imperfecto<br>Dos acciones en una oración<br>Verbos como **querer** y **creer** en el pasado | 100–102<br>103–104<br>105 | Audio CD 3<br>Audio Activities TE, pages 44–45<br>Workbook, pages 37–41<br>Quizzes 3–6, pages 18–21<br>ExamView® Pro |
| **Conversación** | | |
| Naranjas para abuelita | 108–109 | Audio CD 3<br>Audio Activities TE, pages 45–46<br>Interactive CD-ROM |
| **Lecturas culturales** | | |
| De compras<br>El mercado de Chichicastenango | 110–111<br>112–113 | Audio CD 3<br>Audio Activities TE, page 47<br>Tests, pages 49, 53 |
| **Conexiones** | | |
| El mercadeo | 114–115 | Tests, pages 54–55 |
| **¡Te toca a ti!** | | |
| | 116–117 | **¡Viva el mundo hispano!** Video, Episode 4<br>Video Activities, pages 76–80<br>Spanish Online Activities spanish.glencoe.com |
| **Assessment** | | |
| | 118-119 | Communication Transparency C 4<br>Quizzes 1–6, pages 16–21<br>Performance Assessment, Task 4<br>Tests, pages 45–60<br>Situation Cards, Chapter 4<br>ExamView® Pro<br>**Maratón mental** Videoquiz |

# Using Your Resources for Chapter 4

## Transparencies

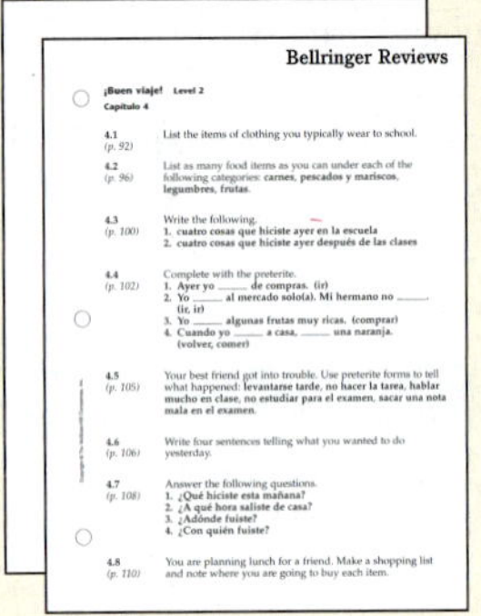


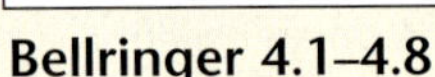

Bellringer 4.1–4.8

Vocabulary 4.1–4.5

Communication C 4

## Workbook

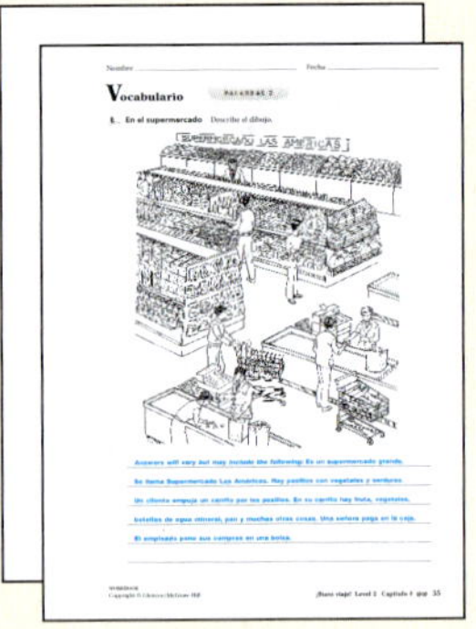

Vocabulary, pages 33–36

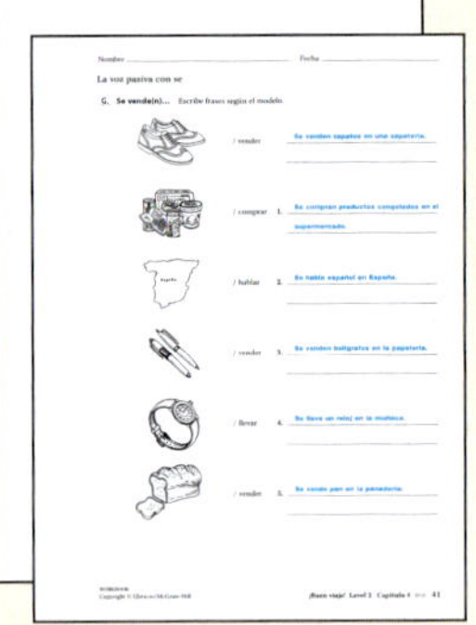

Structure, pages 37–41

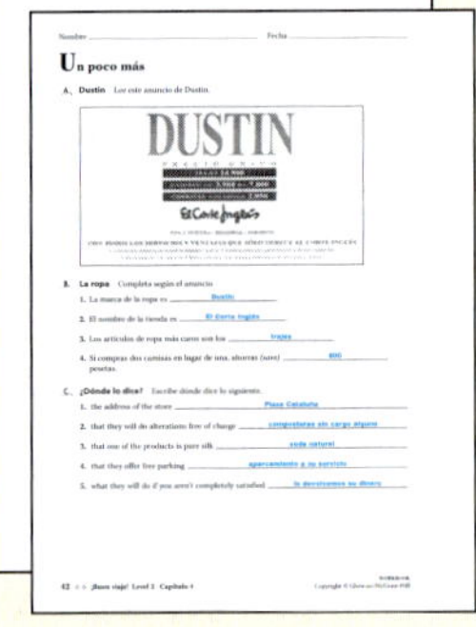


Enrichment, pages 42–44

## Audio Activities

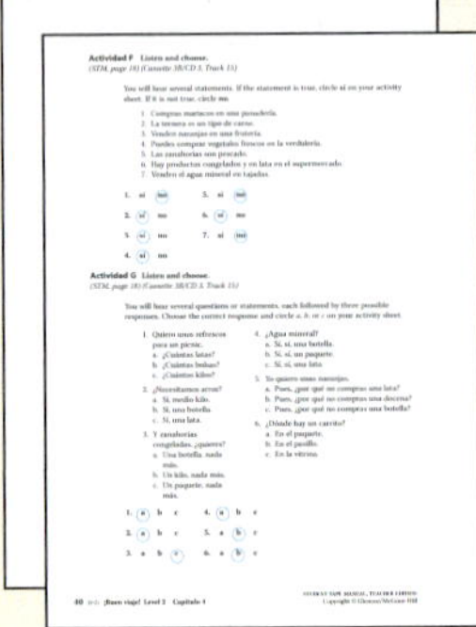

Vocabulary, pages 38–43

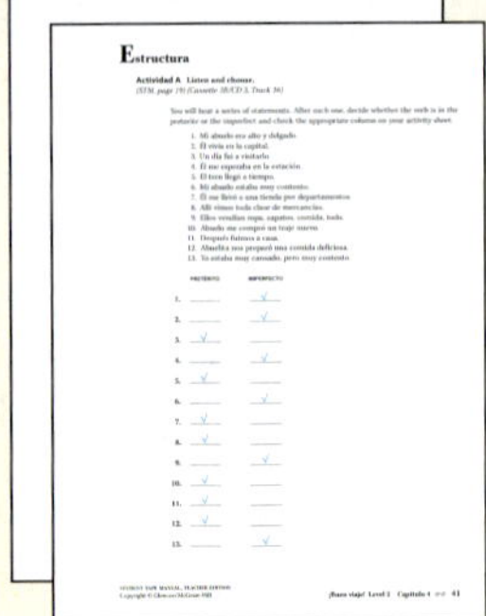


Structure, pages 44–45

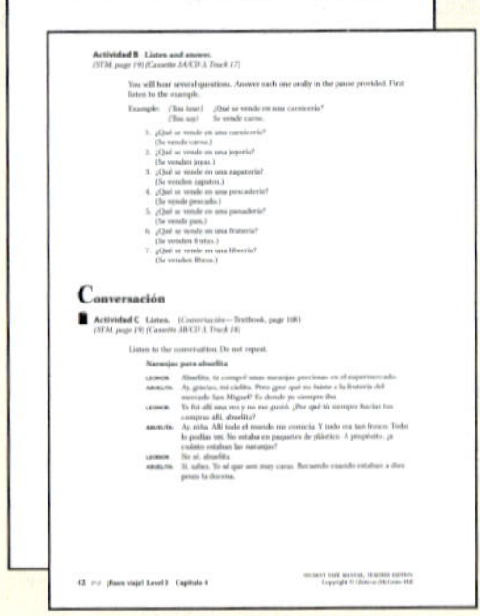


Conversation, pages 45–46

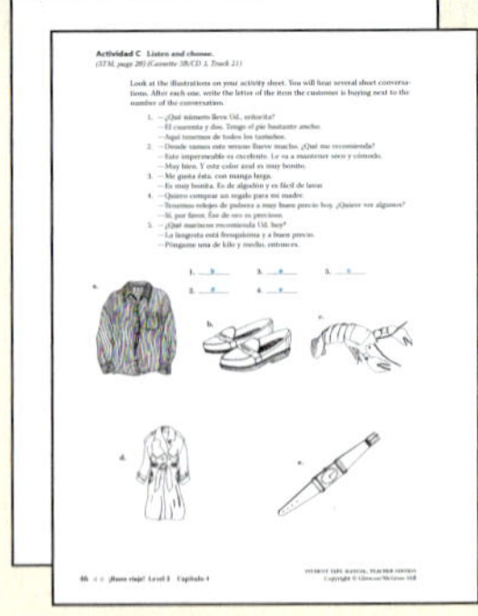

Additional Practice, pages 48–50

# Assessment

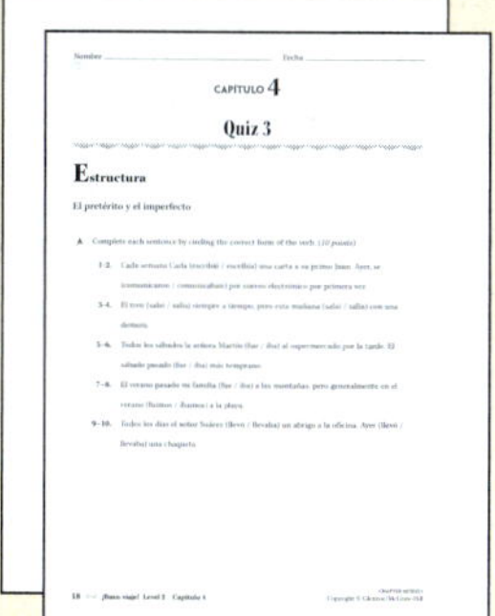
Vocabulary and Structure Quizzes, pages 16–21

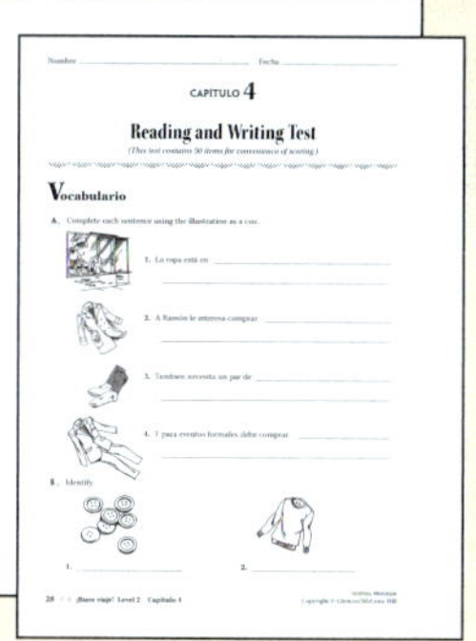
Chapter Tests, pages 45–60

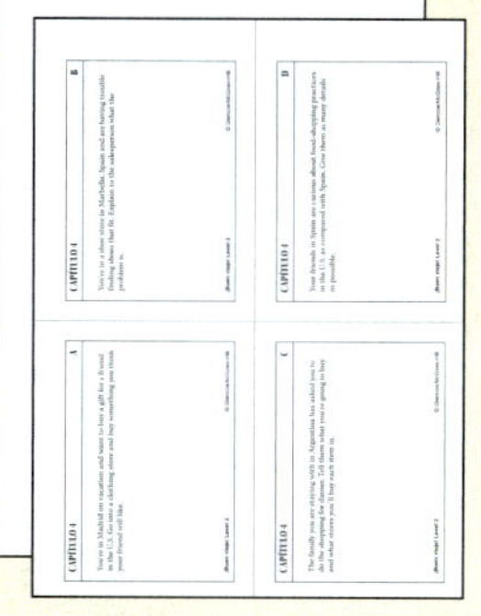
Situation Cards, Chapter 4

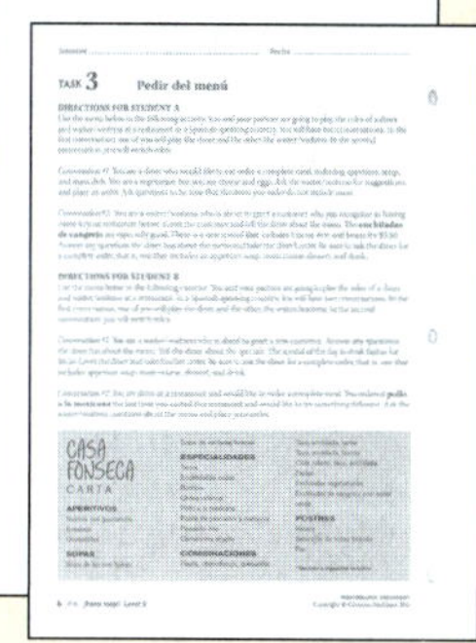
Performance Assessment, pages 1–8

MindJogger Videoquiz, ExamView® Pro, Chapter 4

## Timesaving Teacher Tools

### TeacherWorks™

TeacherWorks™ is your all-in-one teacher resource center. Personalize lesson plans, access resources from the Teacher Wraparound Edition, connect to the Internet, or make a to-do list. These are only a few of the many features that can assist you in the planning and organizing of your lessons.

Includes:

- A calendar feature
- Access to all program blackline masters
- Standards correlations and more

### ExamView® Pro

Test Bank software for Macintosh and Windows makes creating, editing, customizing, and printing tests quick and easy.

## Technology Resources

In the Chapter 4 Internet Activity, you will have a chance to learn more about the Spanish-speaking world. Visit spanish.glencoe.com

On the interactive CD–ROM, students can listen to and take part in a recorded version of the conversation in Chapter 4.

**¡Viva el mundo hispano!** Video and Video Activities, Chapter 4. Available on VHS and DVD.

Help your students prepare for the chapter test by playing the **Maratón mental** Videoquiz game show. Teams will compete against each other to review chapter vocabulary and structure and sharpen listening comprehension skills. Available on VHS and DVD.

**¡Buen viaje!** is also available on CD or Online.

## Preview

In this chapter, students will learn about shopping for clothing and jewelry, as well as about grocery shopping in different types of markets. Students will learn the difference between the preterite and the imperfect, how to express feelings in the past, and how to talk in general terms using the passive voice. The cultural focus of the chapter is on grocery shopping in the Spanish-speaking world.

### National Standards

**Communication**

In Chapter 4 students will learn to communicate in spoken and written Spanish on the following topics:

- buying clothing, jewelry, and food
- asking for sizes, amounts, and prices
- grocery shopping in Spanish-speaking countries

Students will obtain and provide information about these topics and engage in conversations that would typically take place in clothing stores and in grocery stores or traditional markets as they fulfill the chapter objectives listed on this page.

### LEVELING

The activities, conversations, and readings within each chapter are marked according to level of difficulty. **E** indicates easy. **A** indicates average. **C** indicates challenging. Some activities cover a range of difficulty. In some activities, for example, advanced students will be able to produce more extensive responses while students who learn at a different rate may give less detailed responses. The leveling indicators will help you individualize instruction to best meet your students' needs.

Capítulo 4

# De tiendas

### Objetivos

**In this chapter you will learn to:**

- shop for apparel and food in Spanish-speaking countries
- ask for the quantities and sizes you want
- find out prices
- talk about different types of past actions
- talk in general terms about what is done
- talk about shopping practices in Spanish-speaking countries

Pedro de Vega Muñoz *Market Day, Seville*

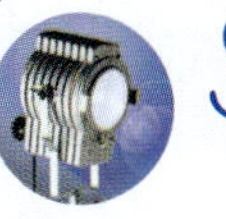

## Spotlight on Culture

**Fotografía** *(pages 90–91)* The modern shopping mall seen here is in the southern Puerto Rican city of Ponce, on the Caribbean coast. Many visitors to Ponce go to see the varied **ponceño** architectural styles of the restored buildings on **Calle Reina Isabel,** one of the city's major residential streets. The Fox Delicias Mall is at the intersection of **Calle Reina Isabel** and the **Plaza de las Delicias.**

## Chapter Projects

### Mi comida favorita

Tell students that, as they progress through the chapter, they are to keep track of the names of their favorite foods as they learn them. This vocabulary is important since these are the words students will probably use most when ordering in restaurants or shopping for food. At the end of the chapter, have students make up their own personal grocery lists and ideal restaurant menus.

# Vocabulario

PALABRAS 1

## 1 PREPARATION

### Resource Manager

Vocabulary Transparencies 4.2–4.3
Audio Activities TE, pages 38–41
Audio CD 3
Workbook, pages 33–34
Quizzes, page 16
ExamView® Pro

### Bellringer Review

*Use BRR Transparency 4.1 or write the following on the board.*
List the items of clothing you typically wear to school.

## 2 PRESENTATION

**Step 1** Have students close their books. Use Vocabulary Transparencies 4.2–4.3 for the initial presentation of vocabulary. Point to each item and have students repeat after you or the recording on Audio CD 3.

**Step 2** After presenting the vocabulary orally, have students open their books and read for additional reinforcement.

**Step 3** When going over the sentences, intersperse with questions such as: **¿Fue José a la tienda de ropa? ¿Adónde fue? ¿Qué miró en el escaparate? ¿Dónde miró la ropa? ¿Qué había en el escaparate? A José, ¿le gustó el traje?**

**Step 4** Have students act out the miniconversation on this page.



# Vocabulario

PALABRAS 1

## La tienda de ropa para caballeros

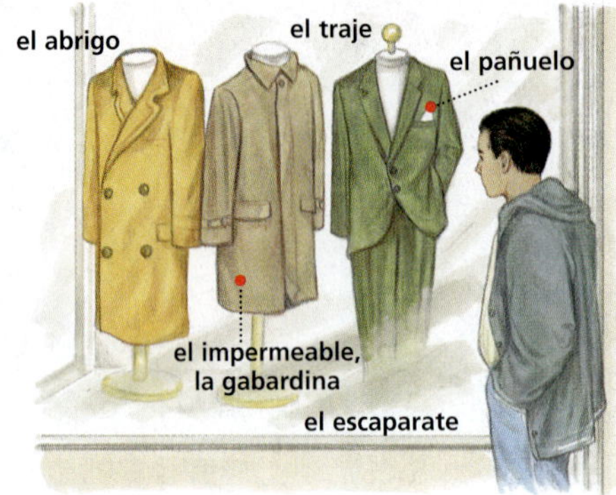


José fue a una tienda de ropa.
Miró la ropa en el escaparate.
En el escaparate había un traje.
A José le gustó el traje.

José entró en la tienda.
Se probó el traje.
Se miró en el espejo.

## La tienda de ropa para señoras

María fue a la tienda de ropa.
Quería comprar un suéter.

### Vocabulary Expansion

Students may wish to know the names of articles of **ropa interior:**

| HOMBRES | |
|---|---|
| **los calzoncillos** | *underpants* |
| **la camiseta** | *undershirt* |
| MUJERES | |
| **la lencería** | *lingerie* |
| **las bragas, los pantis, el calzón** | *panties* |
| **el sostén** | *bra* |

## En la zapatería

anchos

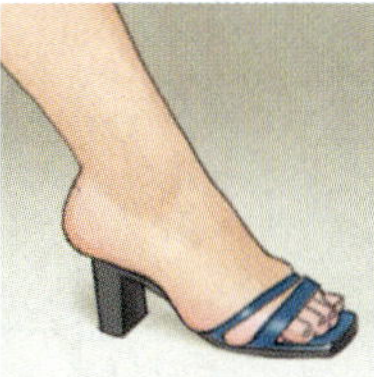
estrechos

## En la joyería

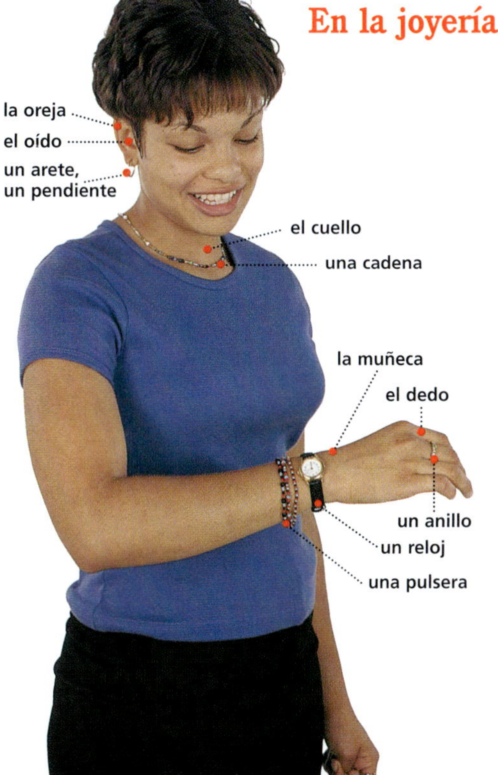

Había muchas joyas en la vitrina.
La dependienta le enseñó una cadena a Anita.
La cadena era de oro.
Era muy cara pero Anita la compró.



# Vocabulario

**Step 5** You can use gestures and facial expressions to help convey the meaning of **No me quedan bien. Son demasiado estrechos.**

**Step 6** You can also use a student or yourself to teach or reinforce: **la oreja (el oído), el cuello, la muñeca, el dedo.**

### About the Spanish Language

You may wish to remind students that **la oreja** is only the outer ear. The ear in the sense of the inner ear and / or the sense of hearing is **el oído**. An earache is **un dolor de oídos.**

**LEVELING**

**A:** Vocabulary

### About the Spanish Language

The names of articles of clothing vary from country to country. For example, *sport coat:* **la americana, el saco, la chaqueta;** *men's suit:* **el traje, el terno;** *sweater:* **el jersey, el suéter, la chompa, el pulóver.**

### Reaching All Students

**Total Physical Response**

Atención, todos.
Si ustedes llevan un artículo que yo digo, levanten la mano.
Veo un suéter.
Veo una blusa con mangas largas (cortas).
Veo un reloj.
Veo una pulsera.
Veo unas botas (sandalias).
Veo calcetines blancos (negros).
Veo un cinturón.
Veo aretes.
Veo una cadena.
Gracias. Bien hecho.

Vocabulario

## 3 PRACTICE

## ¿Qué palabra necesito?

**¡OJO!** When students are doing the **¿Qué palabra necesito?** activities, accept any answer that makes sense. The purpose of these activities is to have students use the new vocabulary. They are not factual recall activities. Thus, it is not necessary for students to remember specific factual information from the vocabulary presentation when answering. If you wish, have students use the illustrations on this page as a stimulus, when possible.

**1 and 2** Do Activities 1 and 2 with books open.

**¡OJO!** Note that the activities are color-coded. All the activities in the text are communicative. However, the ones with blue titles are guided communication. The red titles indicate that the answers to the activity are more open-ended and can vary more. You may wish to correct students' mistakes more so in the guided activities than in the activities with a red title, which lend themselves to a freer response.

Vocabulario

## ¿Qué palabra necesito?

**1 ¿Qué es?** Identifiquen.

1. 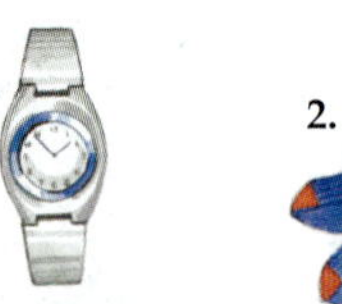
2. 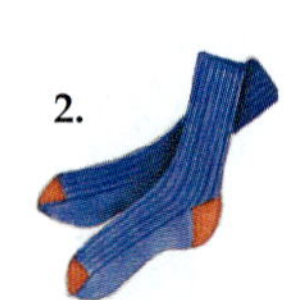
3. 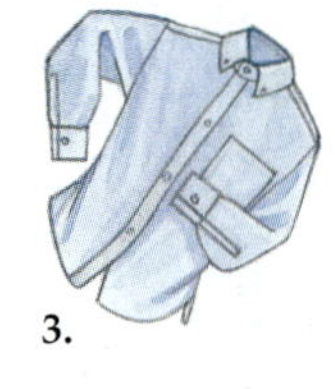
4. 
5. 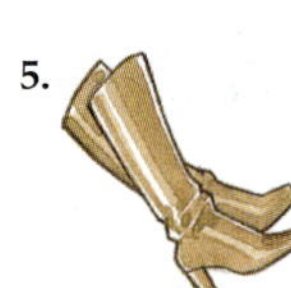
6. 
7. 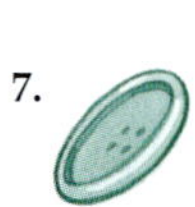
8. 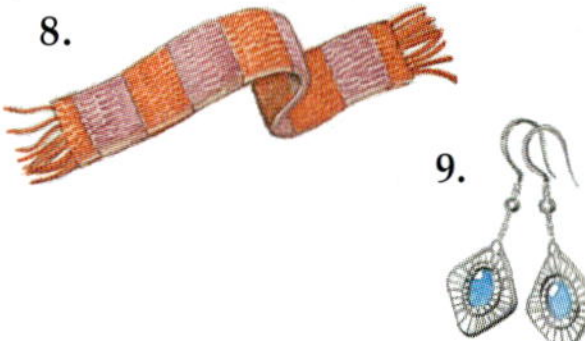
9. 
10.

**2 La ropa que llevamos** Escojan.

1. Es el verano y hace calor. Tadeo quiere comprar ____.
   **a.** un abrigo **b.** una camisa de mangas largas **c.** una camisa de mangas cortas
2. Llevamos ____ cuando llueve.
   **a.** una bufanda **b.** un impermeable **c.** sandalias
3. ____ tiene botones.
   **a.** Un calcetín **b.** Una blusa **c.** Un pañuelo
4. Llevo ____ cuando voy a la playa.
   **a.** zapatos **b.** sandalias **c.** botas
5. Es necesario llevar ____ con algunos pantalones.
   **a.** corbata **b.** calcetines **c.** cinturón
6. Los zapatos que está llevando Elena tienen un tacón muy ____.
   **a.** largo **b.** caro **c.** alto
7. Isabel no compró los zapatos porque ____.
   **a.** le quedaban bien **b.** eran un poco estrechos **c.** le gustaban
8. Uno puede llevar ____ en el dedo.
   **a.** una cadena **b.** un arete **c.** un anillo
9. Uno lleva una pulsera en ____.
   **a.** la oreja **b.** la muñeca **c.** el cuello



## Answers to ¿Qué palabra necesito?

**1**

1. un reloj
2. unos calcetines
3. una manga (larga)
4. un cinturón
5. unas botas
6. un saco (una chaqueta)
7. un botón
8. una bufanda
9. unos aretes (pendientes)
10. un suéter

**2**

1. c
2. b
3. b
4. b
5. c
6. c
7. b
8. c
9. b

**3 Historieta En la tienda de ropa**
Contesten según se indica.

1. ¿Adónde fue Juan? (a la tienda de ropa)
2. ¿Qué vio en el escaparate? (un traje)
3. ¿Le gustó? (sí, mucho)
4. ¿De qué color era? (azul oscuro)
5. ¿Cuántos botones tenía la chaqueta? (tres)
6. ¿Entró Juan en la tienda? (sí)
7. ¿Con quién habló? (el dependiente)
8. ¿Qué le enseñó el dependiente? (el traje que vio en el escaparate)
9. ¿Qué hizo Juan? (se probó el traje)
10. ¿Cómo le quedó? (muy bien)

Málaga, España

**4 Preguntas personales** Contesten.

1. La última ropa que compraste, ¿dónde la compraste?
2. ¿Te atendió un(a) dependiente(a)?
3. ¿Viste el artículo que querías en una vitrina?
4. ¿Qué artículos de ropa te enseñó el/la dependiente(a)?
5. ¿Tenían lo que querías en tu tamaño?
6. ¿Cuánto te costó?

**5 Todo nuevo** Un(a) amigo(a) te invitó al baile en tu escuela. Vas a la tienda de ropa a comprar algo especial para la ocasión. Habla con el/la dependiente(a) (tu compañero[a]). Describe todo lo que quieres. Él o ella te va a ayudar. Luego cambien de rol.

**6 Juego ¿Qué es?** Piensa en un artículo de ropa o en algo que ves en una joyería. Descríbelo a tu compañero(a). Él o ella va a adivinar lo que estás describiendo. Luego cambien de rol. Puedes usar el modelo como guía.

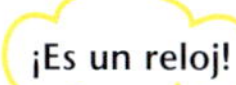

**3** You can do Activity 3 once giving the cues and a second time without the cues. When not giving cues, accept any answer that makes sense.

## Writing Development

After going over Activity 3, have students write the answers in an organized paragraph.

**4** You can do this activity as a paired activity. One student can ask the questions and another can respond.

**Expansion:** After going over Activity 4, have one student retell the story in his or her own words.

**6 Juego** You can alter this game and have students ask questions to guess the item the person is thinking of. Example: **¿Tiene mangas? No. ¿Es de oro? No. ¿Tiene un tacón? Sí. Es un zapato.**

**LEVELING**

**E:** Activities 1, 2, 5

**A:** Activities 2, 3, 4, 5, 6

## FUN FACTS

The **bufanda** is an important article of clothing in Hispanic countries. At the first sign of a chill, people will put on a scarf to protect against a cold or sore throat. It is very common to see men in a suit or sport coat with a scarf wrapped around their neck.

## ANSWERS TO ¿Qué palabra necesito?

**3**

1. Juan fue a la tienda de ropa.
2. Vio un traje en el escaparate.
3. Sí, le gustó mucho.
4. Era azul oscuro.
5. La chaqueta tenía tres botones.
6. Sí, Juan entró en la tienda.
7. Habló con el dependiente.
8. El dependiente le enseñó el traje que vio en el escaparate.
9. Juan se probó el traje.
10. Le quedó muy bien.

**4** *Answers will vary but may include:*

1. La última ropa que compré, la compré en ___.
2. Sí, (No, no) me atendió un dependiente.
3. Sí, (No, no) ví el artículo que quería en una vitrina.
4. El dependiente me enseñó ___.
5. Sí, (No, no) tenían lo que quería en mi tamaño.
6. Me costó ___.

**5** *Answers will vary. Students will use the vocabulary from* Palabras 1.

**6** *Answers will vary. Students will use the model as a guide.*

## 1 PREPARATION

### Resource Manager

Vocabulary Transparencies 4.4–4.5
Audio Activities TE, pages 41–43
Audio CD 3
Workbook, pages 35–36
Quizzes, page 17
ExamView® Pro

### Bellringer Review

*Use BRR Transparency 4.2 or write the following on the board.*
List as many food items as you can under each of the following categories: **carnes, pescados y mariscos, legumbres, frutas.**

## 2 PRESENTATION

**Step 1** After presenting the vocabulary using suggestions from previous chapters, you may wish to have a more able student come to the front of the room, play teacher, and ask questions about the illustrations and photos on Vocabulary Transparencies 4.4–4.5.

### Recycling

As they learn new vocabulary in this section, students are also reviewing many words from **¡Buen viaje! Level 1.**

# Vocabulario

PALABRAS 2

## La compra de comestibles

el mercado

el colmado, la tienda de abarrotes, la tienda de ultramarinos

el supermercado

el hipermercado

En la panadería se vende pan.

En la carnicería se vende carne.

En la pescadería se vende pescado. Se venden también mariscos.

En la pastelería se venden pasteles.

En la verdulería se venden legumbres (vegetales).

En la frutería se venden frutas.



### Vocabulary Expansion

Students have probably figured out that the ending **-ería** usually refers to a place, especially a kind of shop. Ask them what they think the following places are:
**una dulcería**
**una heladería**
**una camisería**
**una sombrerería**
**una perfumería**

### FUN FACTS

**Hipermercados** are giant markets that have parking for thousands of cars. They sell food and a wide variety of other merchandise, from furniture to textbooks. There are chains of **hipermercados** in Spain and other countries (see page 111).

La señora iba de compras todos los días. Compraba pan en la panadería.

A veces la señora hacía sus compras en el supermercado.
Empujaba el carrito por los pasillos.
Hoy compró:

- seis tajadas (rebanadas) de jamón
- un paquete de guisantes congelados
- seis latas de refrescos
- una botella de agua mineral
- un frasco de mayonesa
- una caja de detergente

Y compraba vegetales frescos en la verdulería.

En el supermercado la señora siempre pagaba en la caja.
La empleada ponía sus compras en bolsas de plástico.



## Vocabulario

**Step 2** Point out to students the following items in the **carrito:**

**seis tajadas de jamón**
**un paquete de guisantes congelados**
**seis latas de refrescos**
**una botella de agua mineral**
**un frasco de mayonesa**
**una caja de detergente**

### Fun Facts

Bread has enormous symbolic value in Hispanic culture. Someone who is very kind and good is called **un pedazo de pan.** Governments have often subsidized the cost of wheat to bakers so that reasonable prices could be maintained. Riots and civil unrest have often been the result of an increase in the price of bread.

### Chapter Projects

**Anuncios** Have students prepare some magazine advertisements for clothing.

## Reaching All Students

### Total Physical Response

*(Student 1),* levántate.
Ven acá, por favor.
Vas a ir de compras hoy. Vas al supermercado.
Toma un carrito.
Empuja el carrito por los pasillos.
Pon unas latas de refrescos en tu carrito.
Pon un frasco de mayonesa en tu carrito.
Mira los vegetales.
Toca los tomates.
Pon unos tomates en tu carrito.
Paga tus compras en la caja.
Toma la bolsa de plástico y sal del supermercado.
Gracias, *(Student 1).* Puedes volver a tu asiento.

# Vocabulario

## 3 PRACTICE

## ¿Qué palabra necesito?

7 Do Activity 7 orally with books closed. Then assign it for homework and go over it again quickly the following day.

8 Do Activity 8 orally with books closed. Then have students open their books, read the questions, and give their answers again.
**Expansion:** After going over this activity, have a student retell the entire story in his or her own words.

9 You can have pairs of students do Activity 9 together as if they were conducting an interview.

### Learning from Photos

*(page 98 top)* Today in **una panadería** you can buy sweet rolls and other pastries. The traditional **panadería**, however, would sell only bread. Indeed, many traditional **panaderías** would open only in the morning and would close by noon.

**LEVELING**

**E:** Activities 7, 8, 10
**A:** Activities 11, 12
**C:** Activity 13



## ¿Qué palabra necesito?

**7 De compras** Contesten.

1. Alicia necesitaba pan. ¿Adónde fue ella?
2. Ella quería comprar un biftec. ¿Adónde fue?
3. Quería ostras frescas y un filete de pescado. ¿Adónde fue?
4. Necesitaba una docena de naranjas. ¿Adónde fue?
5. Quería comprar un pastel delicioso. ¿Adónde fue?

Una panadería, México

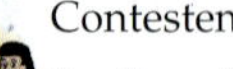

**8 Historieta Al supermercado**
Contesten.

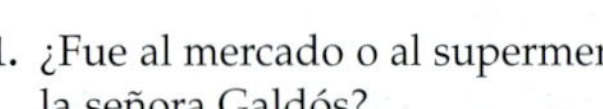

1. ¿Fue al mercado o al supermercado la señora Galdós?
2. ¿Empujó un carrito por los pasillos?
3. ¿Fue de un departamento a otro?
4. ¿Qué compró en la carnicería?
5. ¿Qué compró en el departamento de productos congelados?
6. Quería hacer un bocadillo de jamón y queso. ¿Cuántas rebanadas de jamón compró?
7. ¿Compró un frasco de mayonesa?
8. ¿Dónde pagó?
9. ¿En qué puso la señora sus compras?

Un supermercado, San José, Costa Rica

**9 Preguntas personales** Contesten.

1. ¿Quién en tu familia compra la comida?
2. ¿Hace las compras en un mercado o en un supermercado?
3. ¿Qué productos congelados compra con frecuencia?
4. ¿Compra la carne en una carnicería o en el supermercado?
5. En el supermercado donde ustedes compran, ¿usan bolsas de plástico o de papel?



## ANSWERS TO ¿Qué palabra necesito?

**7**

1. Ella fue a la panadería.
2. Ella fue a la carnicería.
3. Ella fue a la pescadería.
4. Ella fue a la frutería.
5. Ella fue a la pastelería.

**8**

1. La señora Galdós fue al supermercado (mercado).
2. Sí, (No, no) empujó un carrito por los pasillos.
3. Sí, (No, no) fue de un departamento a otro.
4. En la carnicería compró ___.
5. En el departamento de productos congelados compró un paquete de guisantes congelados.
6. Compró ___ rebanadas de jamón.
7. Sí, (No, no) compró un frasco de mayonesa.
8. Pagó en la caja.
9. La señora puso sus compras en bolsas de plástico.

**9** *Answers will vary but may include:*

1. En mi familia, mi ___ compra la comida.
2. Hace las compras en un mercado (un supermercado).
3. Compra ___ con frecuencia.
4. Compra la carne en una carnicería (un supermercado).
5. En el supermercado donde nosotros compramos, usan bolsas de plástico (de papel).

Vocabulario

**10** **¿A cuánto está?** Contesten según el anuncio.

1. la bolsa de patatas fritas
2. la lata de tomate
3. el jamón serrano
4. la caja de queso castellano
5. el frasco de mermelada

**10** Students have to refer to the realia as they do Activity 10. Tell them that this is an advertisement for a Spanish supermarket and that the prices are therefore in **pesetas.** Obviously newer advertisements will reflect the change to euros.

**FUN FACTS**

The best **jamón serrano** is **jamón ibérico.** This ham comes from a free-range pig native to the Iberian Peninsula. The favorite food of these pigs is the **bellota,** or *acorn,* plentiful in the cork oak forests of Andalucía and Extremadura. The ham was traditionally cured in the snows of the **sierra.**

**11** **¿Cuánto?** Tú eres el/la dependiente(a) en el mercado. El/La cliente (tu compañero[a]) pide uno de los siguientes productos y tú le preguntas la cantidad que quiere, en kilos, latas, paquetes, bolsas, botellas, etc. Luego cambien de rol.

zanahorias congeladas

mayonesa

**12** **Los favoritos** Prepara dos listas: una lista de los comestibles que te gustan y otra de los comestibles que no te gustan. Luego trabaja con un(a) compañero(a). Comparen sus listas y determinen los gustos que tienen en común.

**13** **¡Qué invitación!** Estás viviendo con los Menéndez, una familia mexicana. ¡Qué coincidencia! Los «Dallas Cowboys» están en México y los señores Menéndez invitan a los «Cowboys» a cenar. Con el señor o la señora Menéndez (tu compañero[a]), planeen el menú para la comida que van a servir. Discutan las cantidades que van a necesitar. A propósito, *a ton* en español es «una tonelada».

UN POCO MÁS *For more practice using words from **Palabras 2**, do Activity 4 on page H5 at the end of this book.*

Plaza San Jacinto, Ciudad de México

UN POCO MÁS This *InfoGap* Activity will allow students to practice in pairs. The activity should be very manageable for them, since all vocabulary and structures are familiar.



## Answers to ¿Qué palabra necesito?

**10**

1. La bolsa de patatas fritas está a 0, 53 euros.
2. La lata de tomate está a 1, 15 euros.
3. El jamón serrano está a 7, 58 euros por kilo.
4. La caja de queso castellano está a 4, 95 euros.
5. El frasco de mermelada está a 1, 85 euros.

**11** *Answers will vary but may include:*

—Por favor, necesito zanahorias congeladas.
—¿Cuántos paquetes quiere ustedes?
—Dos paquetes, por favor.

**12** *Answers will vary. Students should use the vocabulary from* Palabras 2 *as well as food vocabulary previously learned in* **¡Buen viaje! Level 1.**

**13** *Answers will vary. Students should use the vocabulary from* Palabras 2 *as well as food vocabulary previously learned in* **¡Buen viaje! Level 1.**

# Estructura

## 1 PREPARATION

### Resource Manager

Audio Activities TE, pages 44–45
Audio CD 3
Workbook, pages 37–41
Quizzes, pages 18–21
ExamView® Pro

### Bellringer Review

*Use BRR Transparency 4.3 or write the following on the board.*

Write the following.

1. **cuatro cosas que hiciste ayer en la escuela**
2. **cuatro cosas que hiciste ayer después de las clases**

## 2 PRESENTATION

### El pretérito y el imperfecto

**Step 1** Have students open their books to page 100. Lead them through Items 1–4.

**Step 2** For Item 2 draw a timeline on the board. Each time you give a verb in the preterite, draw an abrupt slash through the timeline to indicate completion or termination in the past.

**Step 3** As you go over the model sentences in Item 3, put another timeline on the board. Each time you give a verb in the imperfect, draw a long shaded box alongside it to indicate duration.

# Estructura

## El pretérito y el imperfecto
### Talking about past events

1. The choice of whether to use the preterite or imperfect depends upon whether the speaker is describing an action completed in the past or a continuous, recurring action in the past.

2. You use the preterite to express actions or events that began and ended at a specific time in the past.

   **Anoche Carmen fue al supermercado.**
   **Compró una caja de detergente y unos productos congelados.**
   **El dependiente puso todo en una bolsa.**

3. You use the imperfect to talk about a continuous, habitual, or repeated action in the past. The moment when the action began or ended is unimportant.

   **Carmen iba al supermercado con frecuencia.**
   **Cada día compraba las cosas que necesitaba.**
   **Casi siempre pagaba con tarjeta de crédito.**

4. Compare the following sentences.

| REPEATED, HABITUAL ACTION | COMPLETED ACTION |
|---|---|
| **Ellos iban al cine todos los sábados.** | **Ellos fueron al cine el sábado pasado.** |
| **Siempre se sentaban en la primera fila.** | **Ayer se sentaron en la última fila.** |
| **Todas las noches se acostaban tarde.** | **Anoche se acostaron temprano.** |

Un supermercado, Estepona, España

# ¿Cómo lo digo?

**14** **¿Una vez o frecuentemente?** Contesten.

1. ¿Fue la señora al mercado ayer por la mañana?
   ¿Cuándo fue la señora al mercado?
   ¿Iba la señora al mercado cada mañana?
   ¿Cuándo iba la señora al mercado?
2. ¿Jugaste al tenis ayer por la tarde?
   ¿Cuándo jugaste al tenis?
   ¿Jugabas al tenis cada tarde?
   ¿Cuándo jugabas al tenis?
3. Anoche, ¿se comunicaron por correo electrónico los amigos?
   ¿Cuándo se comunicaron por correo electrónico los amigos?
   ¿Se comunicaban por correo electrónico casi todas las noches?
   ¿Cuándo se comunicaban por correo electrónico los amigos?

**15** **¿Cuándo?** Sigan el modelo.

**todas las semanas / la semana pasada →**
**Bárbara, ¿ibas al cine todas las semanas?**
**Bárbara, ¿fuiste al cine la semana pasada?**

1. todas las noches / anoche

2. todos los días / ayer

3. todas las mañanas / esta mañana

4. todas las tardes / ayer por la tarde

5. todos los sábados / el sábado pasado



**Estructura**

## 3 PRACTICE

## ¿Cómo lo digo?

**14** Note that the sequencing of questions in Activity 14 forces students to concentrate on the time element.

**14 and 15** While doing Activities 14 and 15, gesture with a slash of the hand to indicate completion with the preterite. Wave your hand back and forth to indicate duration with the imperfect.

## Answers to ¿Cómo lo digo?

**14**

1. Sí, la señora fue al mercado ayer por la mañana.
   Fue al mercado ayer por la mañana.
   Sí, la señora iba al mercado cada mañana.
   Iba al mercado cada mañana.
2. Sí, jugué al tenis ayer por la tarde.
   Jugué al tenis ayer por la tarde.
   Sí, jugaba al tenis cada tarde.
   Jugaba al tenis cada tarde.
3. Sí, los amigos se comunicaron por correo electrónico anoche.
   Se comunicaron por correo electrónico anoche.
   Sí, se comunicaban por correo electrónico casi todas las noches.
   Se comunicaban por correo electrónico casi todas las noches.

**15**

1. Bárbara, ¿mirabas la televisión todas las noches?
   Bárbara, ¿miraste la televisión anoche?
2. ¿Te ponías (Llevabas) aretes todos los días?
   ¿Te pusiste (Llevaste) aretes ayer?
3. ¿Tomabas el desayuno todas las mañanas?
   ¿Tomaste el desayuno esta mañana?
4. ¿Ibas de compras todas las tardes?
   ¿Fuiste de compras ayer por la tarde?
5. ¿Te levantabas tarde todos los sábados?
   ¿Te levantaste tarde el sábado pasado?

# Estructura

## 3 PRACTICE *(continued)*

16 You may wish to give students a few minutes to prepare this activity before going over it in class.

17 You may wish to have different pairs of students present their conversations to the class.

18 Tell students to take a look at the realia before trying to do Activity 18.

**SPANISH Online**

The Glencoe Spanish Web site **(spanish.glencoe.com)** offers options that enable you and your students to experience the Spanish-speaking world via the Internet. For each **Capítulo,** there are activities, games, and quizzes. In addition, an *Enrichment* section offers students an opportunity to visit Web sites related to the theme of the chapter.

## 1 PREPARATION

### Bellringer Review

*Use BRR Transparency 4.4 or write the following on the board.*

Complete with the preterite.

1. **Ayer yo ___ de compras. (ir)**
2. **Yo ___ al mercado solo(a). Mi hermano no ___. (ir, ir)**
3. **Yo ___ algunas frutas muy ricas. (comprar)**
4. **Cuando yo ___ a casa, ___ una naranja. (volver, comer)**

# Estructura

16 **Historieta Los sábados de Juan Antonio** Cambien **Todos los sábados** a **El sábado pasado.** Hagan los cambios necesarios.

Todos los sábados Juan Antonio se levantaba muy temprano. Bajaba a la cocina y él mismo preparaba el desayuno. Después de comer, subía a su cuarto y prendía su computadora. Cuando hacía la conexión a Internet mandaba un correo electrónico a un buen amigo en España. En pocos segundos se comunicaba con su amigo. Los dos escribían de muchas cosas durante horas.

17 **Entrevista** Vas a entrevistar *(interview)* a un(a) compañero(a). Pregúntale lo que le gustaba hacer cuando era joven y dos cosas que le impresionaron como niño(a). Luego cambien de rol.

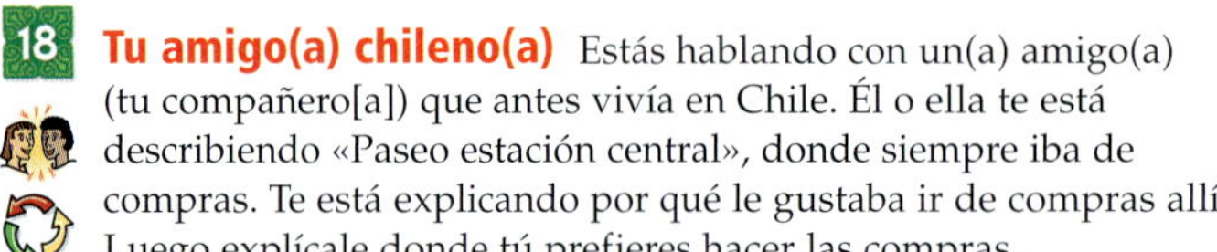

18 **Tu amigo(a) chileno(a)** Estás hablando con un(a) amigo(a) (tu compañero[a]) que antes vivía en Chile. Él o ella te está describiendo «Paseo estación central», donde siempre iba de compras. Te está explicando por qué le gustaba ir de compras allí. Luego explícale donde tú prefieres hacer las compras.

## Answers to ¿Cómo lo digo?

16

El sábado pasado Juan Antonio se levantó muy temprano. Bajó a la cocina y él mismo preparó el desayuno. Después de comer, subió a su cuarto y prendió su computadora. Cuando hizo la conexión, entonces entró la dirección de un buen amigo en España. En pocos minutos se comunicó con su amigo. Los dos hablaron de muchas cosas durante horas.

17 *Answers will vary, but students will use the imperfect tense and any vocabulary previously learned.*

18 *Answers will vary, but students will use the advertisement as a stimulus for discussing shopping in a typical mall.*

# Dos acciones en una oración

## Narrating a sequence of events

1. Often a sentence may have two or more verbs in the past. The verbs may be in the same tense or in different tenses. In the sentence below, both verbs are in the preterite. Both describe simple actions that began and ended at a specific time in the past.

   **Laura llegó ayer y Pepe la vio.**

2. In the sentence below, the two verbs are in the imperfect because they both describe habitual or continuous actions. The moment when the actions began or ended is unimportant.

   **Durante los inviernos, Adela iba a las montañas a esquiar, pero yo trabajaba.**

3. In the sentence below, the verb **estudiaba** is in the imperfect; it describes the background—what was going on. The verb in the preterite, **entró,** expresses the action or event that interrupted the ongoing action.

   **Yo estudiaba cuando Julia entró.**

## ¿Cómo lo digo?

**19 Historieta ¿Qué hacías cuando... ?**

Contesten.

1. ¿Estabas en casa cuando sonó el teléfono?
2. ¿Mirabas un video cuando sonó?
3. ¿Contestaste el teléfono cuando sonó?
4. ¿Hablabas por teléfono cuando tu padre volvió a casa?
5. ¿Preguntó tu padre con quién hablabas?
6. ¿Con quién hablabas cuando tu padre entró?

# Estructura

## 2 PRESENTATION

### Dos acciones en una oración

**Step 1** When explaining the difference between the preterite and the imperfect, you may wish to have students think of a play. Explain that the stage background, the description, and the scenery are in the imperfect. What the actors and actresses actually do on stage is in the preterite.

**Step 2** Give some examples to show the difference between background information and acting. Background: **Él era muy guapo. Había una fiesta. Todo el mundo se divertía. José y Elena bailaban.** Acting: **En ese momento Carlos entró. Dijo «Buenos días» a todo el mundo. Saludó a todos.**

**Step 3** Now use two verbs in one sentence to contrast the background information with the actions on stage. For example: **Ana y Paco bailaban cuando Carlos entró.**

## 3 PRACTICE

### ¿Cómo lo digo?

**19** When going over Activity 19, have students identify the background, descriptive activity, and the activity that intervened or interrupted.

**LEVELING**

**E:** Activity 19
**A:** Activities 16, 17, 18
**C:** Activity 17

## Answers to ¿Cómo lo digo?

**19**

1. Sí, (No, no) estaba en casa cuando sonó el teléfono.
2. Sí, (No, no) miraba un video cuando sonó.
3. Sí, (No, no) contesté el teléfono cuando sonó.
4. Sí, (No, no) hablaba por teléfono cuando mi padre volvió a casa.
5. Sí (No), mi padre (no) preguntó con quién hablaba.
6. Hablaba con ___ cuando mi padre entró.

# Estructura

## 3 PRACTICE *(continued)*

20 **Expansion:** After going over Activity 20, have students look at the illustrations and make up an original story about them.

21 Tell students to be as creative as possible and to make up as many statements as they can when doing Activity 21. It is recommended that you do this activity orally and then have students write the answers.

23 *Juego* This is a good end-of-class activity that students should enjoy doing.

### About the Spanish Language

Students know the greetings **Hola** and **Buenos días.** They may not realize that **Adiós** is a greeting as well as a way of saying good-bye. When two friends or acquaintances pass each other and do not intend to stop to talk, an appropriate greeting is **Adiós,** accompanied by a wave of the hand.

**LEVELING**

**E:** Activities 20, 21, 24, 25, 26, 27

**A:** Activities 20, 21

**C:** Activity 22



**20 Historieta En la tienda de ropa**
Contesten según los dibujos.

1. ¿Adónde fue Susana para hacer sus compras?
2. ¿Qué quería comprar?
3. ¿Qué tomó para subir al segundo piso?
4. Cuando ella llegó a la caja, ¿con quién hablaba la dependienta?
5. Cuando Susana pagaba, ¿quiénes la saludaron?

**21 Yo hacía esto cuando eso pasó.** Sigan el modelo.

jugar → **Yo jugaba cuando sonó el teléfono.**

**22 Lo que hacía cuando...** Habla con un(a) compañero(a). Dile algo que hacías ayer. Tu compañero(a) te va a decir algo que ocurrió e interrumpió lo que hacías. Luego en una sola oración, describe lo que hacías y lo que pasó (ocurrió). ¡Usen la imaginación!

**23 *Juego* Vicente el perezoso** Lazy Vicente needs excuses for not turning in his homework. Something always interferes with his studying, reading, writing, etc. Help him out. Give him half a dozen good excuses like: **¡Yo estudiaba cuando el presidente me llamó!** You get the idea. See who can come up with the most original excuse in the class!



### ANSWERS TO ¿Cómo lo digo?

**20**

1. Susana fue a una tienda de ropa para señoras para hacer sus compras.
2. Quería comprar un vestido.
3. Tomó el ascensor para subir al segundo piso.
4. Cuando ella llegó a la caja, la dependienta hablaba con una señora.
5. Cuando Susana pagaba, unas amigas la saludaron.

**21** *Answers will vary. Students should use the preterite and imperfect for the provided verbs in the colored boxes.*

**22 and 23** *Answers will vary. Students will use previously learned vocabulary as they practice the use of the preterite and the imperfect.*

## Verbos como **querer** y **creer** en el pasado
### Expressing feelings in the past

Since most mental processes involve duration or continuance, verbs that deal with mental activities or conditions are most often expressed in the imperfect tense in the past. The most common of these verbs are:

| | |
|---|---|
| **creer** | **pensar** *(to think)* |
| **desear** | **preferir** |
| **querer** | **poder** |
| **tener ganas de** *(to feel like)* | **saber** |

**Él sabía lo que preferíamos.**
**Yo tenía ganas de salir.**
**Él creía que yo estaba enfermo.**

## ¿Cómo lo digo?

24 **Yo quería...** Preparen una lista de las cosas que querían hacer.

25 **Yo sabía...** Preparen una lista de las cosas que sabían hacer cuando eran niños(as).

26 **Y yo no podía...** Preparen una lista de las cosas que no podían hacer cuando eran niños(as).

27 **Sabía y podía...** Preparen una lista de las cosas que sabían hacer y que podían hacer.

Caracas, Venezuela



## Estructura

### 1 PREPARATION

#### Bellringer Review

*Use BRR Transparency 4.5 or write the following on the board.*
Your best friend got into trouble. Use preterite forms to tell what happened: **levantarse tarde, no hacer la tarea, hablar mucho en clase, no estudiar para el examen, sacar una nota mala en el examen.**

### 2 PRESENTATION

#### Verbos como **querer** y **creer** en el pasado

**Step 1** Have students open their books to page 105 and lead them through the explanation. Provide and elicit additional examples.

### 3 PRACTICE

#### ¿Cómo lo digo?

**¡OJO!** You may wish to assign these activities for homework and go over them the following day in class.

#### Assessment

As an informal assessment, you may wish to have students make up as many original sentences as they can, using the preterite and the imperfect.

### ANSWERS TO ¿Cómo lo digo?

24, 25, 26, and 27 *Answers will vary. Students will practice the imperfect as they discuss things they wanted to, knew how to, and could or couldn't do when they were younger.*

### Learning from Photos

*(page 105)* Have students compare the Venezuelan students in the photo to American students of the same age. They will see little, if any, difference. Then discuss the idea of a "youth culture" that crosses borders.

Estructura

## 1 PREPARATION

### Bellringer Review

*Use BRR Transparency 4.6 or write the following on the board.*
Write four sentences telling what you wanted to do yesterday.

## 2 PRESENTATION

### La voz pasiva con se

**Step 1** Read the definition of the passive voice in Item 1.

**Step 2** Write the model sentences from Item 2 on the board. Indicate that **pescado** is singular, therefore **se vende** is used. **Papas** is plural, therefore **se venden** is used.

**Step 3** As you go over Item 3, ask additional questions such as: **¿Qué idioma se habla en la clase de español? ¿Y en la clase de matemáticas, ¿Se habla qué idioma?**

## 3 PRACTICE

### ¿Cómo lo digo?

28 Make sure that students understand why the verb is singular or plural; explain that it depends on the subject.



Estructura

## La voz pasiva con se
### Talking in general terms

1. When we talk about something being done without saying who does it, we use the passive voice in English.

   *Fish is sold at the fish market.*

2. In Spanish, the pronoun **se** is used to express this idea.

   **Se vende pescado en la pescadería.**
   **Se venden papas en la verdulería.**

   The verb is singular or plural depending on the subject.

3. You will often see the **se** construction used to express ideas such as:

   *They speak Spanish here.*
   *Spanish is spoken here.*
   *One speaks Spanish here.*
   *People speak Spanish here.*
   } **Aquí se habla español.**

Una pescadería, Puerto Montt, Chile

Una panadería, Málaga, España

### ¿Cómo lo digo?

**28 ¿Dónde se venden?** Contesten.

1. ¿Se vende pan en la panadería?
2. ¿Se venden suéteres en la tienda de ropa?
3. ¿Se vende carne en la carnicería?
4. ¿Se venden guisantes en la verdulería?
5. ¿Se vende fruta en la frutería?
6. ¿Se venden productos congelados en el supermercado?
7. ¿Se vende pescado en la pescadería?
8. ¿Se venden bolígrafos en la papelería?



### Answers to ¿Cómo lo digo?

28

1. Sí, se vende pan en la panadería.
2. Sí, se venden suéteres en la tienda de ropa.
3. Sí, se vende carne en la carnicería.
4. Sí, se venden guisantes en la verdulería.
5. Sí, se vende fruta en la frutería.
6. Sí, se venden productos congelados en el supermercado.
7. Sí, se vende pescado en la pescadería.
8. Sí, se venden bolígrafos en la papelería.

**29** **¿Qué idioma se habla dónde?** Escojan.

| | | |
|---|---|---|
| **francés** | **español** | **portugués** |
| **inglés** | **árabe** | **alemán** |

1. ¿Qué idioma se habla en México?
2. ¿Qué idioma se habla en el Brasil?
3. ¿Qué idioma se habla en Egipto?
4. ¿Qué idioma se habla en Irlanda?
5. ¿Qué idioma se habla en Alemania?
6. ¿Qué idiomas se hablan en Quebec?

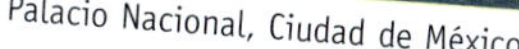

Palacio Nacional, Ciudad de México

El Zócalo, la Ciudad de México

**30** **El «Hipercor»** Tú estás en un hipermercado y no puedes encontrar las cosas que necesitas. Hablas con un(a) dependiente(a) (tu compañero[a]). Pídele a él o a ella los productos que necesitas. Tu compañero(a) te va a decir dónde se encuentran en la tienda. Luego cambien de rol.

**—Busco el atún.**
**—Ah, sí. El atún se encuentra en el pasillo dos.**

## Answers to ¿Cómo lo digo?

**29**

1. Se habla español en México.
2. Se habla portugués en el Brasil.
3. Se habla árabe en Egipto.
4. Se habla inglés en Irlanda.
5. Se habla alemán en Alemania.
6. Se hablan inglés y francés en Quebec.

**30** *Answers will vary. Students will use vocabulary relating to food and shopping.*

## Estructura

**29** You may wish to point to each location mentioned in Activity 29, using the world map on pages xxii–xxiii or Map Transparency M 1.

### Learning from Photos

*(page 106 top)* Puerto Montt is the major port of southern Chile and the country's most important fishing port. Chile is one of the world's major fishing nations. Chile exports fish and fish products around the world.
*(page 107 left)* **El Zócalo**, a square with the Mexican flag flying in the middle, is the heart of Mexico City.
*(page 107 right)* **Palacio Nacional** occupies the eastern side of **El Zócalo**. It houses the Presidential offices and many murals by Diego Rivera. Diego Rivera painted on the walls of public buildings in order to directly communicate with his countrymen, telling them about the turbulent history of their land—the pre-Colombian civilizations through the Mexican Revolution.

### ¡Adelante!

At this point in the chapter, students have learned all the vocabulary and structure necessary to complete the chapter. The conversation and cultural readings that follow recycle all the material learned up to this point.

Conversación

## 1 PREPARATION

### Resource Manager

Audio Activities TE, pages 45–46
Audio CD 3

### Bellringer Review

*Use BRR Transparency 4.7 or write the following on the board.*
Answer the following questions.

1. **¿Qué hiciste esta mañana?**
2. **¿A qué hora saliste de casa?**
3. **¿Adónde fuiste?**
4. **¿Con quién fuiste?**

## 2 PRESENTATION

**Step 1** Tell students they are going to hear a conversation between a young woman and her grandmother. Then have them listen to the recording on Audio CD 3 with books closed.

**Step 2** Have them listen to the recording again as they follow along in their books.

**LEVELING**

**E:** Conversation

# Conversación

## Naranjas para abuelita   

**Leonor** Abuelita, te compré unas naranjas preciosas en el supermercado.

**Abuelita** Ay, gracias, mi cielito. Pero, ¿por qué no fuiste a la frutería del mercado San Miguel? Es donde yo siempre iba.

**Leonor** Yo fui allí una vez y no me gustó. ¿Por qué tú siempre hacías tus compras allí, abuelita?

**Abuelita** Ay, niña. Allí todo el mundo me conocía. Y todo era tan fresco. Todo lo podías ver. No estaba en paquetes de plástico. A propósito, ¿a cuánto estaban las naranjas?

**Leonor** No sé, abuelita.

**Abuelita** Sí, sabes. Yo sé que son muy caras. Recuerdo cuando estaban a diez pesos la docena.

### ¿Comprendes?

Contesten.

1. ¿Dónde hizo sus compras Leonor?
2. ¿Para quién compró las naranjas?
3. ¿Adónde iba la abuelita para hacer sus compras?
4. ¿Fue Leonor alguna vez al mercado? ¿Le gustó?
5. ¿Por qué le gustaba a la abuela comprar en San Miguel?
6. ¿Cómo era todo allí?
7. ¿Sabe Leonor a cuánto estaban las naranjas?
8. ¿Qué recuerda la abuelita?



### ANSWERS TO ¿Comprendes?

1. Leonor hizo sus compras en el supermercado.
2. Compró las naranjas para su abuelita.
3. La abuelita iba a la frutería del mercado San Miguel.
4. Sí, Leonor fue una vez al mercado. No, no le gustó.
5. A la abuela le gustaba comprar en San Miguel porque todo el mundo la conocía.
6. Todo allí era fresco.
7. No, Leonor no sabe a cuánto estaban las naranjas.
8. La abuelita recuerda cuando estaban a diez pesos la docena.

## Vamos a hablar más

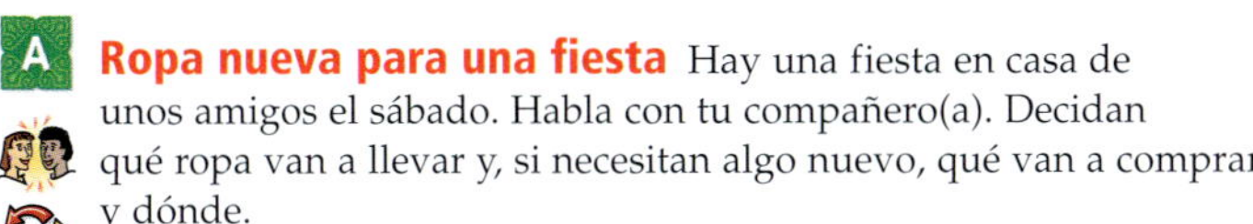

**A Ropa nueva para una fiesta** Hay una fiesta en casa de unos amigos el sábado. Habla con tu compañero(a). Decidan qué ropa van a llevar y, si necesitan algo nuevo, qué van a comprar y dónde.

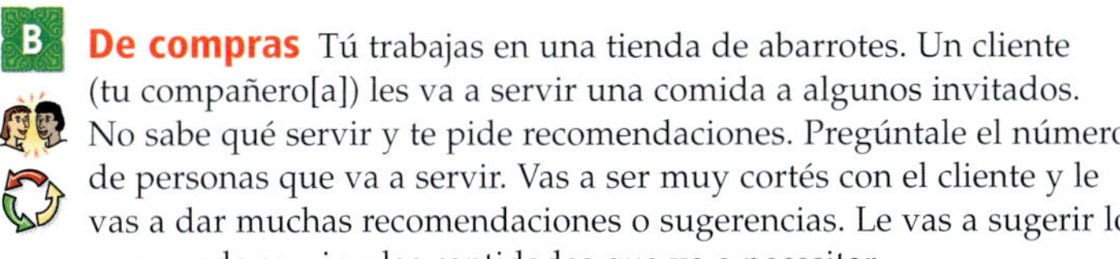

**B De compras** Tú trabajas en una tienda de abarrotes. Un cliente (tu compañero[a]) les va a servir una comida a algunos invitados. No sabe qué servir y te pide recomendaciones. Pregúntale el número de personas que va a servir. Vas a ser muy cortés con el cliente y le vas a dar muchas recomendaciones o sugerencias. Le vas a sugerir lo que puede servir y las cantidades que va a necesitar.

**C Un recuerdo de la niñez** Piensa en unas cosas que te gustaba hacer de niño(a). Luego cuenta a tu compañero(a) de una ocasión en la que hiciste una de estas cosas. Luego tu compañero(a) te va a decir lo mismo.

Barcelona, España



## Conversación

**Step 3** Call on two students to read the conversation aloud. Intersperse their reading with questions from the **¿Comprendes?** activity.

**Step 4** After going over the **¿Comprendes?** activity, have students retell the story of the conversation in their own words.

## 3 PRACTICE

### Vamos a hablar más

**A** If Spanish-language publications are available in your area, you might bring some fashion magazines or clothing catalogs to class to help stimulate the students' conversations.

**B** You may wish to have students working on Activity B present their conversations to the entire class.

### Learning from Photos

*(page 109)* The children are in a park overlooking the port of Barcelona. The port is the busiest and most important in Spain. Barcelona is Spain's second most populous city after Madrid. It is the chief city of Cataluña. The **catalanes** have their own language and literature and have always been fiercely independent.

### About the Spanish Language

The usual word for *orange* is **la naranja.** In Puerto Rico, however, the **naranja** is a bitter variety of orange used for preserves. The sweet orange is called **la china.** The name comes from **la naranja de la China** that originally referred to the sweet orange. Over time, the word **china** by itself came to refer to the sweet orange.

### Answers to Vamos a hablar más

**A** *Answers will vary. Students will use the vocabulary from* Palabras 1 *as well as the clothing vocabulary previously learned in* **¡Buen viaje! Level 1.**

**B** *Answers will vary. Students will use vocabulary relating to food shopping.*

**C** *Answers will vary. Students will use the preterite and imperfect tenses.*

### Glencoe Technology

On the CD-ROM, students can watch a dramatization of this conversation. They can then play the role of either one of the characters and record themselves in the converation.

# Lecturas culturales

## Resource Manager

Audio Activities TE, page 47
Audio CD 3

## National Standards

**Cultures**
The reading about markets and the related activities familiarize students with both traditional and modern types of markets in Spanish-speaking countries.

## Bellringer Review

*Use BRR Transparency 4.8 or write the following on the board.*
You are planning lunch for a friend. Make a shopping list and note where you are going to buy each item.

## PRESENTATION

### Pre-reading

**Step 1** Have students read the Reading Strategy and then have them look at the title and subheads.

**Step 2** Give students a brief synopsis of the **Lectura** in Spanish.

**Step 3** Ask them some questions about your synopsis.

### Reading

**Step 1** Have students open their books. Call on an individual to read three or four sentences.

**Step 2** After the student has read, ask other members of the class questions about the sentences just read.

# Lecturas culturales

**Reading Strategy**

**Skimming** Skimming is the quickest way to find out what a reading selection is about. When you skim, look at the titles, subtitles, and any words in bold print. Also look at the photographs. All of these will indicate to you the topic of the reading and will help you understand it better.

Sant Feliu de Guixols, España

## De compras  

### Mercados

En los países hispanos la gente tradicionalmente compraba la comida en el mercado. Los mercados municipales tenían puestos para los diferentes productos. Había pescaderías, carnicerías, fruterías, verdulerías, etc. La señora hacía sus compras todos los días—generalmente temprano por la mañana. En el mercado iba de un puesto a otro. Conocía a todos los vendedores y conversaba (charlaba) con ellos. Llevaba una bolsa o un capacho[1] para sus compras. Los vendedores no las ponían en bolsas de plástico.

### Supermercados

En todas las ciudades hispanas hay supermercados también. Son modernos, limpios[2] y sobre todo convenientes. En el supermercado uno toma un carrito. Lo empuja por los pasillos y en un solo establecimiento puede comprar todo lo que necesita.

[1]capacho *a cloth shopping bag*
[2]limpios *clean*

Caracas, Venezuela



## Learning from Photos

*(page 110 top)* This outdoor market is in the port town of **Sant Feliu de Guixols** in Cataluña. The name of the town is in **catalán.**
*(page 110 bottom)* This supermarket is in Caracas, the capital of Venezuela. Caracas is a magnificent, modern city with a population of over two million. It was founded by the Spaniards in 1567.

**LEVELING**

**E:** Reading

### Hipermercados

Recientemente llegó otra posibilidad para hacer las compras—el hipermercado. El hipermercado es un enorme establecimiento comercial, normalmente en las afueras[3] de la ciudad. El hipermercado tiene lugar para miles de automóviles.

En el hipermercado se puede comprar comida, obviamente. Pero también se puede comprar de todo: ropa, aparatos electrónicos, libros, casi cualquier[4] tipo de producto. El hipermercado tiene docenas de pasillos y cajas registradoras. Si uno quiere, puede pagar sus compras con tarjeta de crédito.

Estepona, España

Hoy en día nadie tiene bastante tiempo. Todos estamos muy ocupados. El hipermercado ayuda a conservar tiempo. Podemos comprar todo lo que necesitamos sin tener que ir a más de una tienda.

Pero todavía hay muchos que prefieren el mercado donde todo es muy fresco y todo el mundo se conoce. Los mercados municipales todavía existen y muchas personas siguen haciendo sus compras allí.

[3]afueras *outskirts* [4]cualquier *any*

## ¿Comprendes?

**A De compras** Contesten.

1. ¿Dónde compraba la gente la comida?
2. ¿Cuáles son tres puestos que se encuentran en el mercado?
3. ¿Cuándo hacía sus compras la señora?
4. ¿Con quiénes conversaba en el mercado?
5. ¿Para qué llevaba ella un capacho?
6. ¿Dónde hay supermercados?
7. ¿Por qué prefieren algunas personas el supermercado?
8. ¿Qué es un hipermercado?
9. ¿Dónde están los hipermercados normalmente?
10. ¿Por qué prefieren algunas personas el hipermercado?

**B El hipermercado y el mercado tradicional**

Comparen el mercado tradicional y el hipermercado.



## Lecturas culturales

### Post-reading

**Step 1** After going over the entire **Lectura,** ask about six salient questions whose answers provide a synopsis of the story. Call on several individuals to answer one question each.

**Step 2** Call on one student to answer all six questions. The answers will give an oral synopsis.

**Step 3** Have students do the **¿Comprendes?** activities for homework. Go over them in class the next day.

### Critical Thinking Activity

**Giving opinions** Have two groups of students debate the following issue: **¿Cuál es preferible, el mercado tradicional o el hipermercado moderno?** Allow time for the students to develop their arguments, and then have them present the debate to the class with a student moderator.

## Answers to ¿Comprendes?

**A**

1. La gente compraba la comida en el mercado.
2. Tres puestos que se encuentran en el mercado son: la pescadería, la carnicería y la frutería.
3. La señora hacía sus compras todos los días—generalmente temprano por la mañana.
4. Conversaba con todos los vendedores.
5. Llevaba un capacho para sus compras.
6. Hay supermercados en todas las ciudades hispanas.
7. Algunas personas prefieren el supermercado porque es moderno, limpio y sobre todo conveniente.
8. Un hipermercado es un enorme establecimiento comercial.
9. Los hipermercados están normalmente en las afueras de la ciudad.
10. Algunas personas prefieren el hipermercado porque se puede comprar todo allí y el hipermercado ayuda a conservar tiempo.

**B** *Answers will vary. Students should use the information presented in the reading to form the comparisons.*

Lectura opcional

## National Standards

**Cultures**
This reading about the open-air market and the dress of the indigenous women in Chichicastenango, Guatemala, and the related activities on page 113 familiarize students with a typical traditional market and the clothing of one group of indigenous people in Latin America.

**¡OJO!** This reading is optional. You may skip it completely, have the entire class read it, have only several students read it and report to the class, or assign it for extra credit.

## PRESENTATION

**Step 1** You may wish to have any student or students who read this optional selection present the material briefly to the class.

## Literature Connection

For any students interested in contemporary life of the Indians of Guatemala, you might recommend that they read ***me llamo Rigoberta Menchú y así me nació la conciencia*** by the Nobel Prize-winning author. The book is available in English.
Note: There is an excerpt from this book in **¡Buen viaje! Level 3.**

Lectura opcional

# El mercado de Chichicastenango

## El mercado

Los jueves y los domingos son días de mercado en la plaza del pequeño pueblo de Chichicastenango en Guatemala. Antes de levantarse el sol[1], individuos y grupos de indígenas llegan al pueblo. Muchos llevan en la cabeza o en los hombros[2] los productos que van a vender. Antes, la gente caminaba muchas horas por las montañas para llegar temprano al mercado. Todavía hay muchos que llegan a pie, pero hoy día hay muchos que toman el autobús para ir al mercado.

En el mercado hay puestos de verduras y carne. Además de comestibles también venden joyas, cajas decoradas y preciosas mantas[3] y huipiles. Los huipiles son las blusas que llevan las indígenas.

[1]levantarse el sol *the sun rises*
[2]hombros *shoulders*
[3]mantas *blankets*

Una señora de la aldea de Sololá, Guatemala

Iglesia de Santo Tomás, Chichicastenango

### La ropa indígena

Las mujeres de cada grupo indígena llevan ropa que las identifica como miembros del grupo. Las mujeres de Chichicastenango llevan un huipil que tiene muchos diseños[4] geométricos y figuras de flores y plantas. Su falda tiene rayas azules. Hoy la mayoría de los hombres no llevan el traje tradicional. Antes llevaban un pantalón de lana negra, una faja roja y una chaqueta negra con diseños rojos. En la cabeza llevaban un «tzut», un tipo de bufanda roja.

[4]diseños *designs*

## ¿Comprendes?

**A La palabra, por favor.** Completen.

1. Los dos días de mercado en Chichicastenango son ____ y ____.
2. El mercado está en la ____ del pueblo pequeño.
3. Los ____ llegan al pueblo muy temprano por la mañana.
4. Llevan en la cabeza o en los ____ los productos que van a vender.
5. Algunos llegan al mercado a pie pero hoy en día muchos toman el ____.
6. Además de comestibles, en el mercado venden ____.
7. Un huipil es una ____ que llevan las mujeres de Chichicastenango.
8. Las mujeres llevan ____ que las identifica como miembros del grupo.
9. En el pasado, los hombres de Chichicastenango llevaban un tipo de ____ roja en la cabeza.

**B El mercado de Chichicastenango**
Describan la foto del mercado de «Chichi».

Chichicastenango



## Lectura opcional

### Assessment

You may wish to give the following quiz to students who read the selection.

**Contesten.**

1. **¿Qué días hay mercado en Chichicastenango?**
2. **¿Cómo llegaban los indígenas al mercado?**
3. **¿Hay muchos que todavía llegan a pie?**
4. **¿Qué toman otros?**
5. **¿Qué hay en el mercado?**
6. **¿Qué es un huipil?**

### Learning from Photos

*(page 113 top right)* The man in the photo is playing a marimba. The marimba is similar to the xylophone. The player strikes graduated wooden slabs arranged like a keyboard. This instrument is native to both Central America and southern Africa.

**LEVELING**

**E:** Reading

**A:** Reading

## Answers to ¿Comprendes?

**A**

1. el jueves, el domingo
2. plaza
3. indígenas
4. hombros
5. autobús
6. joyas, cajas decoradas y preciosas mantas y huipiles
7. blusa
8. ropa
9. bufanda

**B** *Answers will vary but may include:*

Es el mercado de Chichicastenango en Guatemala. Hay muchas personas en el mercado. Hay puestos de verduras y frutas.

## National Standards

**Connections**
This reading about marketing and advertising in the Spanish-speaking world establishes a connection with another discipline, allowing students to reinforce and further their knowledge of business through the study of Spanish.

**¡OJO!** The readings in the **Conexiones** section are optional. They focus on some of the major disciplines taught in schools and universities. The vocabulary is useful for discussing such topics as history, literature, art, economics, business, science, etc. You may choose any of the following ways to do the readings in the **Conexiones** sections.

**Independent reading** Have students read the selections and do the post-reading activities as homework, which you collect. This option is least intrusive on class time and requires a minimum of teacher involvement.

**Homework with in-class follow-up** Assign the readings and post-reading activities as homework. Review and discuss the material in class the next day.

**Intensive in-class activity** This option includes a pre-reading vocabulary presentation, in-class reading and discussion, assignment of the activities for homework, and a discussion of the assignment in class the following day.

# Conexiones

## *El comercio*

### El mercadeo

One of the most important subjects for business students is marketing. **Mercadeo** is the Spanish word for *marketing,* but the English word is more often used all over the Spanish-speaking world—**el marketing.** A major focus of marketing is the promotion and advertising of a product or service.

### El mercado

Antes de definir el término «marketing», es necesario dar una definición de la palabra «mercado». El mercado es el conjunto de todos los posibles compradores (los consumidores) de un producto o de un servicio. Ejemplos de un producto son un coche o un pantalón. Ejemplos de un servicio son un banco o una agencia de viajes.

**El marketing**

En términos generales, el marketing es la creación de un mercado para un producto o servicio antes de comenzar a producir el producto o servicio. Es la responsabilidad del departamento de marketing de informar a los posibles compradores sobre la existencia del producto y las características del producto.

**LEVELING**
**C:** Reading

## La promoción

Para informar al público de la existencia y de las características de un producto, un aspecto muy importante del marketing es la promoción. Y la propaganda[1] juega un rol primordial, muy importante, en la promoción. Para lanzar[2] un buen programa de promoción, el personal de marketing tiene que emplear muchos medios de comunicación como la radio, la televisión, los anuncios en los periódicos y en las revistas.

**Diferentes productos y mercados**

Hay algunos productos y servicios que la gente necesita. Hay otros que la gente no necesita pero quiere. No es necesario convencer a la gente de comprar comida o gasolina. ¡Pero otra cosa es el perfume!

La industria de la ropa es un caso muy interesante. La gente necesita ropa porque todos tenemos que vestirnos. Pero hay también ropa que la gente no necesita pero que quiere. Uno puede comprar un pantalón que cuesta treinta dólares. O puede comprar un pantalón que cuesta trescientos dólares. Los dos satisfacen la necesidad de vestirse. Pero la persona que paga trescientos dólares no compra solamente algo que necesita—un artículo de ropa. Compra algo que quiere—prestigio. Y la propaganda tiene que convencer a los clientes que la belleza, la calidad y el prestigio valen el precio que les ponen.

[1]propaganda *advertising* [2]lanzar *to launch*

### ¿Comprendes?

**A El mercadeo**

Digan que sí o que no.

1. El coche es un producto.
2. El banco es otro producto.
3. Los consumidores compran sólo productos que necesitan.
4. Los consumidores no tienen que conocer las características de un producto.
5. El perfume se considera una necesidad.
6. El prestigio es una necesidad.

**B Definiciones** Den una definición de las siguientes palabras.

1. el consumidor
2. el comprador
3. el mercado
4. el producto
5. el servicio
6. la necesidad

**C Un anuncio** Preparen un anuncio para un artículo de ropa.



### Answers to ¿Comprendes?

**A**

1. Sí
2. No
3. No
4. No
5. No
6. No

**B**

1. un comprador
2. una persona que compra
3. el conjunto de todos los posibles compradores
4. algo que se puede comprar, por ejemplo un coche
5. algo que provee un servicio, por ejemplo, un banco
6. algo que se necesita, por ejemplo la comida

**C** *Answers will vary. Students can use vocabulary related to the article or any other words previously learned in the* **¡Buen viaje! Level 1** *and* **Level 2** *textbooks.*

# Conexiones

## PRESENTATION

### *El comercio*
### El mercadeo

**Step 1** You may wish to have only those students interested in a career in business or merchandising read this selection. However, since marketing and advertising affect everyone's life, this information could be of interest to all students.

**Step 2** Have students give a list of products that they know in Spanish that are really **necesidades.**

**Step 3** Have them give another list of products that are luxury items.

### Reaching All Students

**Additional Practice** You may wish to ask additional comprehension questions such as:
**¿Para qué sirve la promoción?**
**¿Cuáles son algunos medios de comunicación?**
**¿Cuáles son ejemplos de productos que son una necesidad?**
**¿Cuáles son algunos productos que no son una necesidad?**

### ¿Comprendes?

**C** When students create their advertisements, you may wish to have them prepare them for the different media mentioned in the reading—print, radio, or television.

## Use what you have learned

### Recycling

These activities allow students to use the vocabulary and structure from this chapter in completely open-ended, real-life situations.

### PRESENTATION

Encourage students to say as much as possible when they do these activities. Tell them not to be afraid to make mistakes, since the goal of the activities is real-life communication. If someone in the group makes an error, allow the others to politely correct him or her. Let students choose the activities they would like to do.

You may wish to divide students into pairs or groups. Encourage students to elaborate on the basic theme and to be creative. They may use props, pictures, or posters if they wish.

### Writing Development

Have students keep a notebook or portfolio containing their best written work from each chapter. These selected writings can be based on assignments from the Student Textbook and the Workbook. The activities on page 117 are examples of writing assignments that may be included in each student's portfolio. On page 44 in the Workbook, students will begin to develop an organized autobiography **(Mi autobiografía)**. These workbook pages may also become a part of their portfolio.

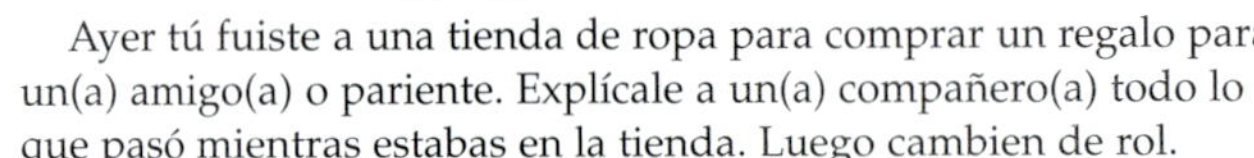

# Use what you have learned

HABLAR 1

### Una experiencia interesante

***✔ Talk about a market in a Spanish-speaking country***

Tú viajabas por un país hispanohablante y fuiste a un mercado interesante. Explícales a unos compañeros dónde estabas, con quién y cuándo. Diles todo lo que pasó en el mercado y descríbeles todo lo que viste allí.

HABLAR 2

### En la tienda de ropa

***✔ Talk about a shopping excursion***

Ayer tú fuiste a una tienda de ropa para comprar un regalo para un(a) amigo(a) o pariente. Explícale a un(a) compañero(a) todo lo que pasó mientras estabas en la tienda. Luego cambien de rol.

HABLAR 3

### Tantas interrupciones

***✔ Talk about two activities happening at once***

Trabaja con un(a) compañero(a) de clase. Ayer ustedes hacían muchas cosas. Pero siempre había interrupciones. Hablen de todo lo que hacían y todo lo que interrumpió lo que hacían.



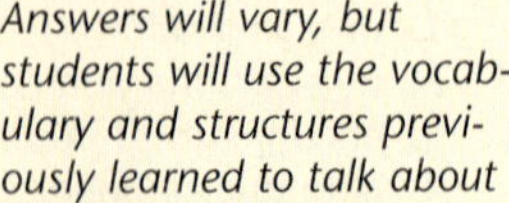

### Answers to ¡Te toca a ti!

 and 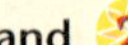 *Answers will vary, but students will use the vocabulary and structures previously learned to talk about shopping.*

 *Answers will vary, but students will practice speaking about past events.*

¡Te toca a ti!

## Una gran apertura

✔ *Describe a supermarket*

Un supermercado americano quiere abrir sucursales *(branches)* en España. Prepara un anuncio para el nuevo supermercado. Incluye en el anuncio lo que se puede comprar, los precios, las ventas *(sales)* especiales, etc.

## Un anuncio

✔ *Describe some articles of clothing*

Estás trabajando en el departamento de publicidad *(advertising)* de una gran revista. Tienes que escribir un anuncio sobre cada una de las prendas que ves aquí.

### Writing Strategy

**Writing with graphics**
Sometimes words alone do not convey adequate information about a topic. Including maps, diagrams, tables, or graphs can help illustrate your expository writing. Pictures and text work well together. Often the graphic will show quickly what might take many paragraphs to describe. When using graphics, be sure to label clearly and accurately to help readers recognize and understand information.

## Las compras en distintos países

You have read about shopping habits in Spanish-speaking countries. List the kinds of shops and the products people buy in each in one column. Now think about your family and the places where you do your shopping. List those stores and products in the second column.

In a Venn Diagram like this one, put those shopping practices that are exclusive to Spanish-speaking countries in the left, those of your family on the right, and those common to both in the middle, overlapping section of the diagram. Now write a paragraph, comparing your family's buying habits with those of families in Spanish-speaking countries.

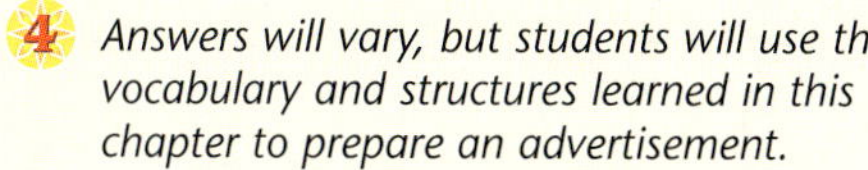
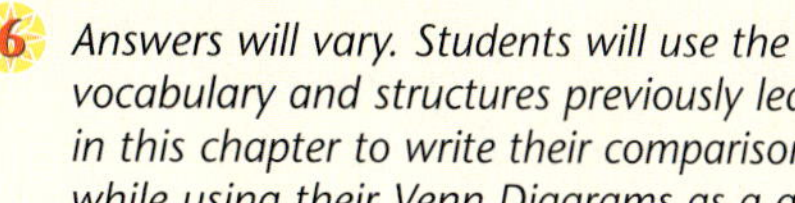

ANSWERS TO ¡Te toca a ti!

4 *Answers will vary, but students will use the vocabulary and structures learned in this chapter to prepare an advertisement.*

5 *Answers will vary. Students should use the vocabulary and structures from the chapter to write about the products in the advertisements.*

6 *Answers will vary. Students will use the vocabulary and structures previously learned in this chapter to write their comparisons while using their Venn Diagrams as a guide.*

### Writing Strategy

**Writing with graphics** Have students read the Writing Strategy and the directions to the activity on page 117. You may wish to work with the class in preparing their graphics. It can be done as a group effort. Have students read their paragraphs aloud, displaying their Venn Diagrams to the class as they do so. Students can compare their family's shopping habits with those of others in the class. When everyone has finished, students can make a more general comparison (including another Venn Diagram) of their shopping habits with those in Spanish-speaking countries.

### National Standards

**Communities and Comparisons**
Have students bring in Spanish-language newspapers available in the community and read the advertisements. They should discuss the content of the advertisements, the differences between the products advertised in the Spanish-language newspapers and those advertised in English-language newspapers, and any other similarities and differences they find.

### LEVELING

These activities encompass all three levels. All students will be able to do them at a sophistication level commensurate with their ability in Spanish. Some students will be able to speak for several minutes, and others may be able to give just a few sentences. This is to be expected when students are functioning completely on their own generating their own language to the best of their ability.

## Assessment

### Resource Manager

Communication Transparency C 4
Quizzes, pages 16–21
Performance Assessment, Task 4
Tests, pages 45–60
Situation Cards, Chapter 4
**Maratón mental** Videoquiz, Chapter 4
ExamView® Pro, Chapter 4

### Assessment

This is a pre-test for students to take before you administer the chapter test. Note that each section is cross-referenced so students can easily find the material they have to review in case they made errors. You may use Assessment Answers Transparency A 4 to do the assessment in class, or you may assign this assessment for homework. You can correct the assessment yourself, or you may prefer to project the answers on the overhead in class.

### Glencoe Technology

**MINDJOGGER VHS/DVD**

You may wish to help your students prepare for the chapter test by playing the MindJogger game show. Teams will compete against each other to review chapter vocabulary and structure and sharpen listening comprehension skills.

## Assessment

# Vocabulario

**1 Identifiquen.**

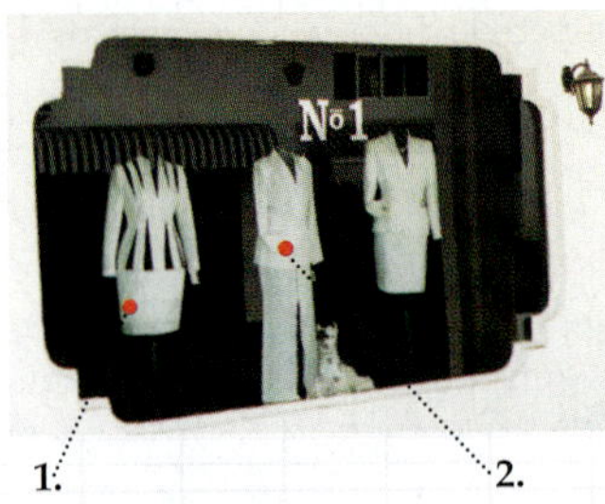


1. 2.

3.

4. 5.

To review **Palabras 1**, turn to pages 92–93.

**2 Completen.**

—No, estos zapatos no me __6__ bien.

—No, ¿por qué?

—Son demasiado grandes, demasiado __7__.

**3 ¿Sí o no?**

8. Un hipermercado es aún más grande que un supermercado.
9. La tienda de abarrotes es una panadería.
10. Un mercado tiene muchos puestos diferentes.
11. La señora quería comprar seis tajadas de detergente.
12. Ella quiere comprar los tomates porque tienen muy mala pinta.

To review **Palabras 2**, turn to pages 96–97.



## Answers to 

**1**

1. las sandalias
2. el pantalón
3. el escaparate
4. el bolsillo
5. la manga larga

**2**

6. quedan
7. anchos

**3**

8. Sí
9. No
10. Sí
11. No
12. No

# Estructura

**4** **Completen en el pasado.**

13. Él ____ al cine casi todos los viernes. (ir)
14. Pero ayer (él) no ____. (ir)
15. Ellos ____ todas sus vacaciones en las montañas. (pasar)
16. Pero el verano pasado (ellos) ____ un viaje a México. (hacer)

To review the preterite and the imperfect, turn to page 100.

**5** **Completen en el pasado.**

17–18. Nadie ____ en casa cuando ____ el teléfono. (estar, sonar)

19–20. Ellos ____ cuando yo ____. (trabajar, salir)

To review two actions in the same sentence, turn to page 103.

**6** **Completen.**

21. ____ frutas y vegetales en una verdulería. (vender)
22. ____ español en muchos países. (hablar)

To review the passive voice with se, turn to page 106.

# Cultura

**7** **¿Sí o no?**

23. En los países hispanos la gente hace sus compras sólo una vez a la semana. Van al mercado los lunes.
24. En un supermercado se puede comprar casi todo lo que se necesita en una sola tienda.
25. Un hipermercado es un mercado antiguo con muchos puestos diferentes.

To review this cultural information, turn to pages 110–111.

Un mercado, Málaga, España

## Assessment

**FOLDABLES™ Study Organizer** **Dinah Zike's Study Guides**

Your students may wish to use Foldable 6 to organize, display, and arrange data as they develop communication skills in Spanish. You may wish to encourage them to add information from each chapter as they continue to expand their ability to describe, explain, and discuss all the different topics they are studying.

A *miniature matchbook* foldable is ideal in helping students to give more complex descriptions about topics they have studied in Spanish.

## Answers to Assessment

**4**

13. iba
14. fue
15. pasaban
16. hicieron

**5**

17. estaba
18. sonó
19. trabajaban
20. salí

**6**

21. Se venden
22. Se habla

**7**

23. No
24. No
25. No

# ¡Hablo como un pro!

This unique page gives students the opportunity to speak freely and say whatever they can, using the vocabulary and structures they have learned in the chapter. The illustration serves to remind students of precisely what they know how to say in Spanish. There are no activities that students do not have the ability to describe or talk about in Spanish. The art not only depicts the vocabulary and content of this chapter, but also reinforces what they learned in previous chapters.

You may wish to use this page in many ways. Some possibilities are to have students do the following:

1. Look at the illustration and identify items by giving the correct Spanish words.
2. Make up sentences about what they see in the illustration.
3. Make up questions about the illustration. They can call on another class member to respond if you do this as a class activity, or you may prefer to allow students to work in small groups. This activity is extremely beneficial because it enables students to actively use interrogative words.
4. Answer questions you ask them about the illustration.
5. Work in pairs and make up a conversation based on the illustration.
6. Look at the illustration and give a complete oral review of what they see.
7. Look at the illustration and write a paragraph (or essay) about it.

You can also use this page as an assessment or testing tool, taking into account individual differences by having students go from simple to quite complicated tasks. The assessment can be either oral or written. You may wish to use the rubrics provided on pages T20–T21 as you give students the following directions.

1. Identify the topic or situation of the illustration.
2. Give the Spanish words for as many items as you can.
3. Think of as many sentences as you can to describe the illustration.
4. Go over your sentences and put them in the best sequencing to give a coherent story based on the illustration.

# ¡Hablo como un pro!

Tell all you can about this illustration.

# Vocabulario

**Identifying more stores**

la zapatería
la joyería

**Shopping for clothes and jewelry**

mirar en el escaparate (la vitrina)
probarse la ropa
¿En qué puedo servirle?
Quisiera…
No me (le) queda(n) bien.

**VIDEOTUR**

**Episodio 4**

In this video episode, you will join Francisco and Julián on a trip to the supermarket. See page 483 for more information.

**Identifying more clothing**

el bolsillo
el saco, la chaqueta
el abrigo
el impermeable, la gabardina
el suéter
la camisa de mangas cortas (largas)
el vestido
el cinturón
el pañuelo
la ropa interior
la bufanda
los botones
las sandalias
las botas
el tacón

**Identifying jewelry**

las joyas
una pulsera
una cadena
un anillo
un arete, un pendiente
un reloj

**Identifying more parts of the body**

la muñeca
el cuello
el dedo
la oreja, el oído

**How well do you know your vocabulary?**

- Choose any type of store you like to shop in.
- Tell what you like to buy there.

**Describing clothing and jewelry**

mediano(a)
ancho(a)
estrecho(a)
de oro

**Identifying more food stores**

el colmado, la tienda de abarrotes, la tienda de ultramarinos
el puesto
el supermercado
el hipermercado
la panadería
la carnicería
la pescadería
la pastelería
la verdulería
la frutería

**Foods**

el pan
la carne
el pescado
los mariscos
los pasteles
las legumbres, los vegetales

**Shopping for food**

hacer las compras, ir de compras
¿A cuánto están… ?
tener buena pinta
empujar el carrito
fresco(a)
la bolsa de plástico
una tajada, una rebanada
un frasco
una caja
una docena



# Reaching All Students

**For the Heritage Speakers**

If there are heritage speakers in the class, ask them to tell the words they use where there are choices in the vocabulary, for example: **colmado, tienda de abarrotes, tienda de ultramarinos;** or **saco, chaqueta; impermeable, gabardina,** and any others they may come up with.

# Vocabulario

## Vocabulary Review

The words and phrases in the **Vocabulario** have been taught for productive use in this chapter. They are summarized here as a resource for both student and teacher. This list also serves as a convenient resource for the **¡Te toca a ti!** activities on pages 116 and 117. There are approximately five cognates in this chapter. Have students find them.

¡OJO! You will notice that the vocabulary list here is not translated. This has been done intentionally, since we feel that by the time students have finished the material in the chapter they should be familiar with the meanings of all the words. If there are several words they still do not know, we recommend that they refer to the **Palabras 1** and **2** sections in the chapter or go to the dictionaries at the end of this book to find the meanings. However, if you prefer that your students have the English translations, please refer to Vocabulary Transparency 4.1, where you will find all these words with their translations.

**VIDEO VHS/DVD**

The Video Program allows students to see how the chapter vocabulary and structures are used by native speakers within an engaging story line. For maximum reinforcement, show the video episode as a final activity for Chapter 4.

Repaso

# Preview

This section reviews the salient points from Chapters 1–4. In the **Conversación** students will review train, restaurant, and shopping vocabulary and the preterite of some regular and irregular verbs. In the **Estructura** section, they will review the conjugations of irregular verbs in the preterite and the imperfect tense. They will practice these structures as they talk about train travel, eating in a restaurant, and a trip to Chichicastenango.

## Resource Manager

Workbook, pages 45–50
Tests, pages 61–67
Performance Assessment, Tasks 1–4

## PRESENTATION

### Conversación

**Step 1** Have students open their books to page 122. Call on two students to read the conversation aloud.

**Step 2** Go over the activities in the **¿Comprendes?** section.

### Learning from Photos

*(page 122)* For many years, **La Gran Vía** was Madrid's Fifth Avenue. Here were the city's most elegant shops, first-run movie theaters, and luxury hotels. Today, the **Gran Vía** has lost some of its glamour.

Repaso

La Gran Vía, Madrid

# Conversación

## ¿Cuándo volviste?

**Tadeo** ¿A qué hora llegaste?
**Anita** Pues, el tren llegó a tiempo, a las 18:10.
**Tadeo** ¿Viniste en tren?
**Anita** Sí, no quería tomar el avión. Tarda mucho tiempo el viaje del aeropuerto al centro.
**Tadeo** Con el tráfico, no hay duda. ¿Comiste en el tren?
**Anita** No. Fui a un restaurante cerca de la estación antes de salir. Pedí una tortilla y una ensalada. La tortilla estaba muy buena. Me gustó.
**Tadeo** ¿Qué hiciste desde que llegaste? Papá quería saber dónde estabas.
**Anita** ¿Te preguntó dónde estaba? Pues, fui a la Gran Vía. Le compré un regalo para su cumpleaños.
**Tadeo** Yo le compré un par de zapatos. Y tú, ¿qué le compraste?
**Anita** Una camisa blanca y azul. Tiene mangas cortas. Creo que le va a quedar muy bien y que le va a gustar.

### ¿Comprendes?

**Anita hizo mucho.** Contesten.

1. ¿A qué hora llegó Anita a Madrid?
2. ¿Cómo vino?
3. ¿Por qué no quería tomar el avión?
4. ¿Dónde comió?
5. ¿Qué pidió?
6. ¿Qué tal le gustó?
7. ¿Adónde fue cuando llegó a Madrid?
8. ¿Qué compró?

### Answers to ¿Comprendes?

1. Anita llegó a Madrid a las 18:10.
2. Vino en tren.
3. No quería tomar el avión porque tarda mucho tiempo el viaje del aeropuerto al centro.
4. Comió en un restaurante cerca de la estación.
5. Pidió una tortilla y una ensalada.
6. Le gustó mucho.
7. Cuando llegó a Madrid fue a la Gran Vía.
8. Compró un regalo (una camisa) para su papá.

CAPÍTULOS 1–4

# Estructura

## El pretérito

1. Review the following irregular verbs in the preterite.

| | | | | | |
|---|---|---|---|---|---|
| ESTAR | estuve | PONER | puse | HACER | hice |
| TENER | tuve | PODER | pude | VENIR | vine |
| ANDAR | anduve | SABER | supe | QUERER | quise |

2. The preceding irregular verbs all take the same endings in the preterite. Review the following.

| | | | | | | |
|---|---|---|---|---|---|---|
| TENER | tuve | tuviste | tuvo | tuvimos | *tuvisteis* | tuvieron |
| PONER | puse | pusiste | puso | pusimos | *pusisteis* | pusieron |
| VENIR | vine | viniste | vino | vinimos | *vinisteis* | vinieron |

3. Note that verbs with a **j** in the preterite have the ending **-eron**, not **-ieron**.

   **dijeron** **trajeron**

4. Review the verbs with the stem change **e → i** and **o → u** in the preterite.

| | | | | | | |
|---|---|---|---|---|---|---|
| SERVIR | serví | serviste | sirvió | servimos | *servisteis* | sirvieron |
| DORMIR | dormí | dormiste | durmió | dormimos | *dormisteis* | durmieron |

Other verbs conjugated like **servir** are **pedir, repetir, freír,** and **seguir. Morir** is conjugated like **dormir.**

 **Historieta Un viaje en tren** Contesten.

1. ¿Hiciste el viaje en tren?
2. ¿Viniste con tu hermano?
3. ¿Estuvieron ustedes mucho tiempo en la estación de ferrocarril?
4. ¿Tuvieron ustedes que hacer cola delante de la ventanilla para comprar sus billetes?
5. ¿Quién hizo las maletas? ¿Tú o tu hermano?
6. ¿Pudieron ustedes llevar las maletas o tuvieron que buscar ayuda?
7. ¿Le pidieron ayuda a un mozo?

El ferrocarril, Chile



## PRESENTATION

### El pretérito

**Step 1** Have students open their books to page 123. Lead them through Items 1–4.

**Step 2** You may wish to have students repeat the verb forms aloud.

## PRACTICE

**1** After students do Activity 1, you may have them retell the story in their own words.

## Answers to Repaso

1. Sí, (No, no) hice el viaje en tren.
2. Sí, (No, no) vine con mi hermano.
3. Sí, (No, no) estuvimos mucho tiempo en la estación de ferrocarril.
4. Sí, (No, no) tuvimos que hacer cola delante de la ventanilla para comprar nuestros billetes.
5. Yo hice (Mi hermano hizo) las maletas.
6. Nosotros pudimos llevar las maletas. (Tuvimos que buscar ayuda.)
7. Sí, (No, no) le pedimos ayuda a un mozo.

# Repaso

## PRACTICE *(continued)*

**2** If students have problems doing Activity 2, review the irregular preterite forms in the **Estructura** sections of Chapters 1 and 2.

## PRESENTATION

### El imperfecto

**Step 1** Lead students through Items 1–4 on page 124. Model the verb forms and have students repeat them after you.

**Step 2** For a more complete review of the imperfect, refer students to the **Estructura** sections in Chapter 3 (pages 68–75) and Chapter 4 (pages 100–105).



**2** **Historieta En el restaurante**

Completen.

El viernes pasado yo __1__ (ir) a un restaurante con mi amiga Julia. Ella __2__ (pedir) la especialidad de la casa. Yo __3__ (pedir) un plato con camarones y langosta. Nosotros dos __4__ (pedir) una ensalada de tomate y lechuga.

La comida estaba deliciosa. Julia __5__ (decir) que le gustaba mucho. Yo le __6__ (repetir) al mesero lo que ella __7__ (decir). El mesero nos __8__ (servir) muy bien.

Yo __9__ (pedir) la cuenta. El mesero la __10__ (traer) y nos __11__ (invitar) a tomar un postre. Yo __12__ (pedir) un helado y Julia __13__ (pedir) flan—un tipo de pudín español.

Lima, Perú

## El imperfecto

**1.** Review the forms of the imperfect tense of regular verbs.

| | | | | | | |
|---|---|---|---|---|---|---|
| **TOMAR** | tomaba | tomabas | tomaba | tomábamos | *tomabais* | tomaban |
| **COMER** | comía | comías | comía | comíamos | *comíais* | comían |
| **VIVIR** | vivía | vivías | vivía | vivíamos | *vivíais* | vivían |

**2.** Review the forms of the irregular verbs **ir** and **ser**.

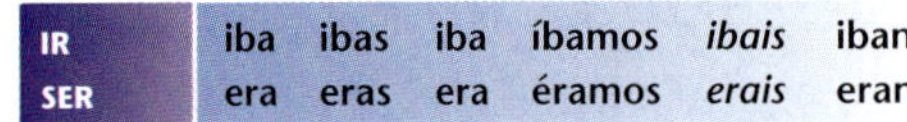

| | | | | | | |
|---|---|---|---|---|---|---|
| **IR** | iba | ibas | iba | íbamos | *ibais* | iban |
| **SER** | era | eras | era | éramos | *erais* | eran |

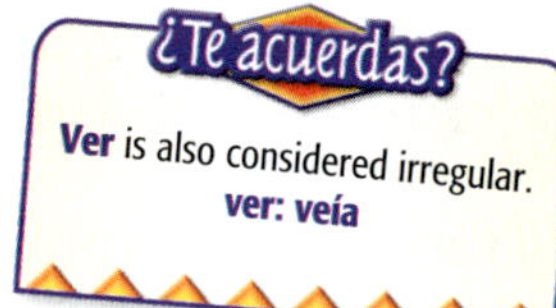

**¿Te acuerdas?**

**Ver** is also considered irregular.
**ver: veía**

**3.** The imperfect tense is used to express an action in the past that is continuous or repeated. The time the action began and ended is not important. The preterite tense is used to express an action that began and ended at a definite time in the past. A sentence will often have both types of past action. The action that was going on is expressed by the imperfect, and the action that intervened or interrupted is expressed by the preterite.

**Su hermano iba allí cada año pero Roberto fue solamente una vez.**
**Él miraba en el escaparate cuando vio a su amigo.**

**4.** The imperfect is used for description in the past.

**Él tenía ocho años y era muy inteligente.**



## Answers to Repaso

**2**

1. fui
2. pidió
3. pedí
4. pedimos
5. dijo
6. repetí
7. dijo
8. sirvió
9. pedí
10. trajo
11. invitó
12. pedí
13. pidió

**3 Cuando yo era niño(a)** Contesten personalmente.

1. Cuando tú eras niño(a), ¿dónde vivías?
2. ¿Cuántos cuartos tenía la casa donde vivía tu familia?
3. ¿A qué escuela ibas?
4. ¿A qué hora salías de casa para ir a la escuela?
5. ¿Quién hacía las compras en tu familia?
6. ¿Tenían ustedes una computadora?

**4 Historieta Un viaje estupendo** Completen.

1. El año pasado mis amigos y yo ___ (hacer) un viaje estupendo.
2. Nosotros ___ (ir) a Guatemala.
3. Yo ___ (tomar) un curso de español en Antigua.
4. Mis amigos ___ (estudiar) el español también.
5. Un día nosotros nos ___ (levantar) temprano y ___ (ir) a Chichicastenango.
6. Nosotros ___ (andar) por el mercado de Chichi.
7. Nosotros ___ (ver) a los indígenas.
8. Las mujeres de Chichicastenango ___ (llevar) una blusa y una falda de colores vivos.
9. En el mercado los indios ___ (vender) los productos que ___ (cultivar) o ___ (hacer) en casa.
10. Con el dinero que ___ (recibir) por las cosas que ___ (vender), ellos ___ (comprar) todas las provisiones que ___ (necesitar).

Antigua, Guatemala

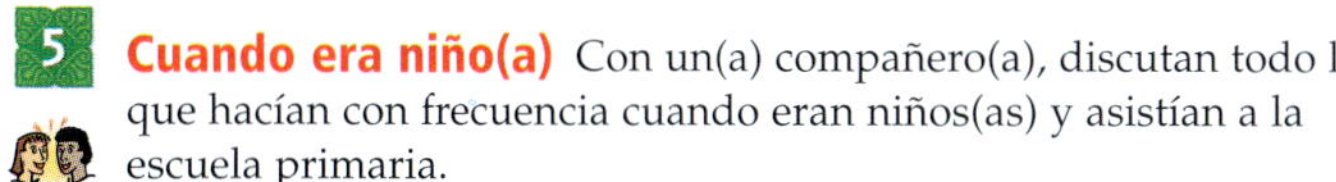

**5 Cuando era niño(a)** Con un(a) compañero(a), discutan todo lo que hacían con frecuencia cuando eran niños(as) y asistían a la escuela primaria.

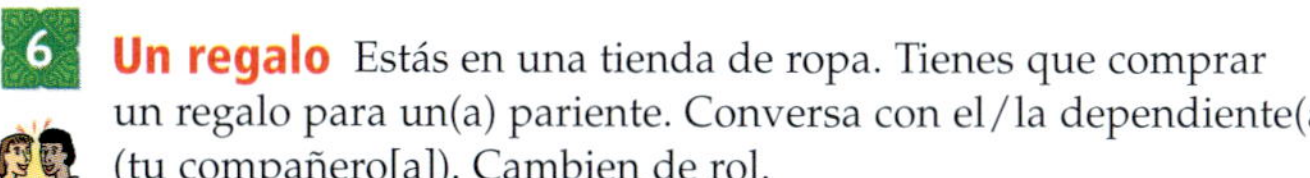

**6 Un regalo** Estás en una tienda de ropa. Tienes que comprar un regalo para un(a) pariente. Conversa con el/la dependiente(a) (tu compañero[a]). Cambien de rol.

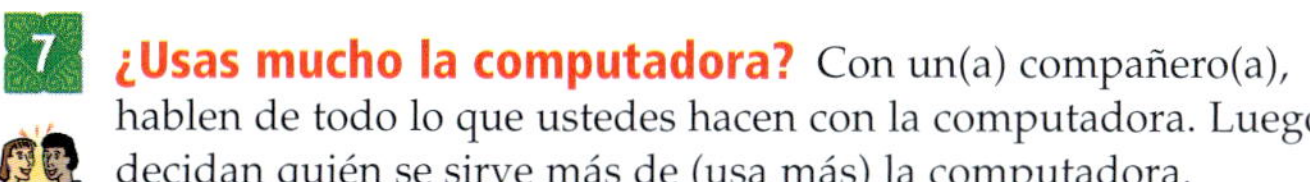

**7 ¿Usas mucho la computadora?** Con un(a) compañero(a), hablen de todo lo que ustedes hacen con la computadora. Luego decidan quién se sirve más de (usa más) la computadora.

**Literary Companion**

**You may wish to read the adaptation of *Platero y yo* by Juan Ramón Jiménez. You will find this literary selection on pages 460–463.**



## PRACTICE

**3** If students have problems doing Activity 3, review some of the activities in Chapter 3.

**4** After going over Activity 4, have students retell the story in their own words.

**5** Have students first make a list of things they did in elementary school.

**6** Students may want to review the vocabulary from Chapter 4 as they prepare to do this activity.

**7** Students may want to review the vocabulary from Chapter 3 as they prepare to do this activity.

### Literary Companion

When you finish this chapter, if you wish, have students read the adaptation of ***Platero y yo*** by Juan Ramón Jiménez on pages 460–463.

### Geography Connection

Antigua is a beautiful colonial city founded in 1524. It was the original capital of Guatemala, but after it suffered a number of earthquakes, the worst in 1773, the Spanish governors decided to move the capital to Guatemala City in 1776.

## Answers to Repaso

**3**

1. Cuando era niño(a) vivía en ___.
2. La casa donde vivía mi familia tenía ___ cuartos.
3. Iba a la Escuela ___.
4. Salía de casa a las ___ para ir a la escuela.
5. Mi ___ hacía las compras en mi familia.
6. Sí, (No, no) teníamos una computadora.

**4**

1. hicimos
2. fuimos
3. tomé
4. estudiaron
5. levantamos, fuimos
6. anduvimos
7. vimos
8. llevaban
9. vendían, cultivaban, hacían
10. recibían, vendían, compraban, necesitaban

**5** *Answers will vary. Students will use the vocabulary from the chapters as well as previously learned vocabulary from* **¡Buen viaje! Level 1.**

**6** *Answers will vary, but students will use the clothing vocabulary from Chapter 4.*

**7** *Answers will vary, but students will use the vocabulary from Chapter 3.*

People EN ESPAÑOL

## Entérate Estados Unidos

This section was prepared by Time Learning Ventures of Time Incorporated. Its purpose is to give students greater insight, through visual images and fun articles, into the Hispanic culture and people of the United States. You may want to begin by asking your students if they can identify regions in the United States that have large Hispanic populations.

Have students look at the photographs and read the articles. Encourage the students to talk about what they've seen and read. Let them say anything they can, using the vocabulary they have learned to this point.

Hispanics in the United States are among the fastest growing and politically, financially, and culturally influential communities. In addition to urban centers such as New York and Miami—which have a long history of Hispanic populations—many other U.S. regions are also experiencing an influx of Hispanic groups. The result is a fascinating hybrid U.S. culture that reflects many different customs, traditions, and voices.

**A Datos interesantes sobre los latinos en EE.UU.**

¿Verdadero o falso?

1. Los latinos son la minoría menos numerosa de EE.UU.
2. En 1970 el gobierno de EE.UU. inventó el término "hispanos".
3. Los valores culturales más importantes para los hispanos son la religión y el trabajo.
4. Estados Unidos es el segundo país de habla hispana en el mundo.
5. Los mexicanos son el mayor grupo de hispanos en Estados Unidos.
6. Todos los mexicanos del suroeste llegaron recientemente.

# People EN ESPAÑOL Entérate Estados Unidos

## Datos interesantes sobre los latinos en Estados Unidos

- En 1970 el gobierno de Estados Unidos inventó el término "hispanos" para dar un solo nombre a esta diversa población. Muchos "hispanos" prefieren el término "latinos" porque indica el origen de Latinoamérica.
- Estados Unidos es el 5° país de habla hispana en el mundo, y los latinos son la minoría más numerosa de este país.
- De mayor a menor, estos son los grupos que viven en Estados Unidos: mexicanos, puertorriqueños, cubanos, dominicanos, salvadoreños, colombianos; el resto son hispanos de orígenes diversos.
- Muchos mexicanos del suroeste tienen un origen diferente al resto de los hispanos, porque ellos ya vivían ahí cuando Estados Unidos conquistó[1] estos territorios.
- Los valores[2] culturales más importantes para los hispanos son preservar la lengua española y la unión de la familia.

[1]conquistó: *conquered*

[2]valores: *values*

## California, su pasado español

Santa Bárbara, fundada en 1786.

Los colonizadores[1] españoles dejaron su marca más obvia en los numerosos nombres españoles de los diferentes lugares. En la arquitectura también es notable su presencia. Las misiones californianas son un ejemplo del estilo español. Los indígenas construyeron estos bellos edificios de adobe. Hay 21 misiones en todo el estado y hoy día son una gran atracción turística.

[1]colonizadores: *settlers*

## Las tiendas latinas

Hay "bodegas" en todos los barrios latinos; son tiendas de comestibles donde la atención personal es muy importante. Como para los latinos es extremadamente importante "verse bien"[1], es una buena idea tener un salón de belleza en sus barrios. Las tiendas donde venden hierbas[2], medicamentos naturales, incienso y velas[3] especiales se llaman botánicas.

[1]"verse bien": *"looking good"* [2]hierbas: *herbs* [3]velas: *candles*



## SUCESOS

César Chávez

**César Chávez** es un líder muy respetado entre los chicanos y los trabajadores extranjeros. Latinos en su mayoría, los que recogen[1] las frutas en Estados Unidos hoy reciben un mejor salario gracias al trabajo de Chávez. Un momento importante en su carrera fue en 1970, cuando los rancheros aceptaron pagar más y mejorar las condiciones de trabajo para estas personas. César Chávez murió en 1993.

**Sábados Gigantes** es uno de los programas más famosos y populares de la televisión hispana. Desde hace 40 años, el chileno "Don Francisco" conduce el programa, un récord que pasó al Libro Guinness de los Récords.

[1]recogen: *pick*

**LEVELING**

**E:** Activity A

**A:** Activities B and C

**C:** Activity D

Chef Douglas Rodríguez

## El "Mango Gang"

Más y más estadounidenses conocen la diferencia entre una "tortilla" en un restaurante mexicano y en un restaurante español. Pero… ¿quién conoce al "Mango Gang"? Ellos hicieron popular la "Nuevo Latino Cuisine". En Miami, el chef cubanoamericano, Douglas Rodríguez, y sus colegas Norman Van Aken, Robin Haas, Allen Susser y Mark Militello re-inventaron la cocina tradicional latina. Ellos usan frijoles negros y arroz, mangos, aguacates[1], pescado caribeño y los preparan de una manera diferente.

[1]aguacates: *avocados*

La parada puertorriqueña

## Calendario de fiestas

**5 de mayo** En el suroeste, y poco a poco[1] en otras partes de Estados Unidos, se celebra el patrimonio cultural mexicano. En México, la fiesta conmemora la victoria de los mexicanos sobre los invasores franceses.

**12 de octubre** En 1492 llegaron los españoles a América y hoy se celebra el "Día de la Raza[2]" en esta fecha. Esta fiesta conmemora el patrimonio cultural de todos los latinos en Estados Unidos. Además, el mes de octubre es el "Mes de la Hispanidad".

**1° de noviembre** "El Día de los Muertos[3]" era una fiesta exclusivamente de los mexicanos al sur de la frontera. Hoy día, más y más mexicanamericanos celebran esta fiesta en Estados Unidos porque les gusta recordar[4] a sus familiares en forma festiva.

**6 de junio** El segundo domingo del mes de junio se celebra "El día nacional de los puertorriqueños" en la Ciudad de Nueva York. Las estrellas del cine, del deporte y también el alcalde[5] y otras autoridades van a la parada en la Quinta Avenida, donde hay carrozas[6] y mucha música y baile.

[1]poco a poco: *little by little*
[2]raza: *race*
[3]muertos: *dead*
[4]recordar: *to remember*
[5]alcalde: *mayor*
[6]carrozas: *floats*

## micocina

**Primero, las tortillas y ahora ¡las pupusas!**
Esta comida típica salvadoreña se come con la mano y es muy popular entre los latinos de todas partes. Es como una tortilla gorda rellena[1] con carne, queso, frijoles o una combinación de todos estos ingredientes. *(Atención: No es bueno llamar "tortillas" a las pupusas frente a un salvadoreño.)*

**Pupusas de frijol con queso**

**Ingredientes**

*(Para la masa[2])*
2 tazas de harina de maíz
1 taza de agua tibia[3]
1 poco de sal

*(Para el relleno)*
1 lata de frijoles molidos[4]
250g de queso rallado[5]

**Preparación**
Mezclar la harina, el agua y la sal para hacer la masa. Formar 12 bolitas medianas. Ahuecar[6] el centro y rellenar con los frijoles y el queso. Luego, aplastar[7] y formar una tortilla gruesa (1/2 pulgada). Freír en aceite caliente y servir con salsa de tomates frescos.

[1]rellena: *filled*
[2]masa: *dough*
[3]tibia: *lukewarm*
[4]molidos: *ground*
[5]rallado: *grated*
[6]ahuecar: *hollow*
[7]aplastar: *flatten*

Pupusas de frijol con queso

127

**People EN ESPAÑOL**

**A Datos interesantes sobre los latinos en EE.UU.**
¿Verdadero o falso?
1. Los latinos son la minoría menos numerosa de EE.UU.
2. En 1970 el gobierno de EE.UU. inventó el término "hispanos".
3. Los valores culturales más importantes para los hispanos son la religión y el trabajo.

**B Sucesos y California, su pasado español** Escojan.
1. Hay ___ misiones en el estado de California.
   a. 21
   b. 42
   c. 12
2. ___ hoy tienen mejores condiciones de trabajo gracias a César Chávez.
   a. Los rancheros
   b. Don Francisco
   c. Los latinos que recogen las frutas
3. Los colonizadores españoles dejaron su marca en ___.
   a. los nombres españoles de los diferentes lugares
   b. barrios latinos
   c. el programa Sábados Gigantes

**C Calendario de fiestas**
Contesten.
1. ¿Qué conmemora el 5 de mayo en México?
2. ¿Anteriormente, para quién era "El Día de los Muertos"?
3. ¿Cuál es la fecha del "Día de la Raza"?

**LEVELING**
**E:** Activity A
**A:** Activity B
**C:** Activity C

### Answers to ¿Comprendes?

**A**
1. falso
2. verdadero
3. falso

**B**
4. a
5. c
6. a

**C**
1. Conmemora la victoria de los mexicanos sobre los invasores franceses.
2. Era una fiesta exclusivamente de los mexicanos al sur de la frontera.
3. Se celebra el "Día de la Raza" el 12 de octubre.

People EN ESPAÑOL

Hispanics have a strong tradition of artistic expression, but in recent years names formerly popular only within Hispanic populations, have become internationally recognizable. From music to literature to film and television, the richness and diversity of Hispanic contribution to the arts, have helped to transform the arts and give voice to the global Latino community.

**A ¡Acción! y en el set** Corrijan.

1. Nilo Cruz recibió el Premio Pulitzer en el año 1999.
2. Anthony Quinn, Raquel Welch y José Ferrer son escritores.
3. Nilo Cruz fue el tercer latino ganador del Premio Pulitzer.
4. Nilo Cruz, hoy día, es profesor en la Universidad de Brown.
5. Existe un mercado—hispano y anglosajón—que demanda el sabor anglosajón.

**B Cómo viajar a Latinoamérica sin salir de EE.UU.** Completen.

1. La calle más famosa de La Pequeña Habana es la ___.
2. El ___ ofrece programas de arte y cultura.
3. La mayoría de los dominicanos que viven en EE.UU. residen en ___.
4. Pilsen y Villita es una comunidad hispana de la ciudad de ___.
5. La comunidad mexicana más grande de Estados Unidos es ___ en California.
6. Si quieres hacer tus compras en "El Barrio" en Nueva York, debes visitar La ___.
7. "Quisqueya Heights" es donde viven muchos ___ en Nueva York.

Un latino ganador

## Nilo Cruz, el primer Premio Pulitzer latino de teatro

El escritor Nilo Cruz recibió el Premio Pulitzer en el año 2003 por su obra de teatro[1] "Anna in the Tropics". Nilo Cruz nació en Cuba, pero vivió en Miami desde los 10 años. Él estudió en la Universidad de Brown y hoy día es profesor en la Universidad de Yale. "¡Esto es increíble!", dijo al recibir el premio. Sí, es increíble porque Nilo Cruz fue el primer latino ganador[2] de este premio prestigioso.

[1]obra de teatro: *play* [2]ganador: *winner*

## EN EL SET

No solamente el público latino reconoce los nombres de Selma Hayek, Antonio Banderas, Rosie Pérez, Raúl Julia, Rubén Blades, Penélope Cruz y muchos más; también los conoce el público en general en Estados Unidos y en todo el mundo. En el pasado[1], actores como Anthony Quinn, Raquel Welch y José Ferrer también fueron famosos, pero su patrimonio cultural no era el foco de atención. Ahora el éxito de los actores latinos depende de su talento y también de su identidad porque hoy día existe un mercado – hispano y anglosajón – que demanda el sabor latino, una de las expresiones legítimas y modernas del multiculturalismo en Estados Unidos.

[1]en el pasado: *in the past*

128

## Cómo viajar a Latinoamérica sin salir de Estados Unidos

¿Quieres conocer Latinoamérica pero no tienes dinero para viajar? Aquí hay otras alternativas:

- En Miami tienes **La Pequeña Habana,** el centro de la comunidad cubana en Estados Unidos. Es una zona de 25 calles con muchos restaurantes, botánicas, tiendas de autos y de música. Su calle más famosa es la Calle Ocho. Gracias a sus residentes, este barrio está lleno de vida.
- En Chicago tienes **Pilsen y La Villita.** Después del Este de Los Ángeles en California, ésta es la comunidad mexicana más grande de Estados Unidos. En la Calle 18 hay restaurantes, panaderías, tiendas de comestibles y agencias sociales. Desde 1987 el Museo de Arte Mexicano ofrece programas de arte y cultura.

De compras en el barrio

- En Nueva York tienes **El Barrio** donde antes vivían principalmente puertorriqueños, pero desde 1990 también viven allí muchos mexicanos. Es interesante visitar la famosa Marqueta (un mercado) y el Museo del Barrio.
- En Washington Heights, en la ciudad de Nueva York, residen 3/4 de los dominicanos que viven en Estados Unidos. Por eso, a este barrio lo llaman afectuosamente "**Quisqueya**[1] **Heights**". Caminar por sus calles es como caminar por Santo Domingo. La gente, la música, los restaurantes y las tiendas le dan un tono tropical a este barrio de Manhattan.

[1]Quisqueya: *indigenous name for the island where Haiti and Dominican Republic are located today*

### Answers to ¿Comprendes?

**A**

1. Nilo Cruz recibió el Premio Pulitzer en el año 2003.
2. Anthony Quinn, Raquel Welch y José Ferrer son actores.
3. Nilo Cruz fue el primer latino ganador del Premio Pulitzer.
4. Nilo Cruz, hoy día, es profesor en la Universidad de Yale.
5. Existe un mercado—hispano y anglosajón—que demanda el sabor latino.

**B**

1. Calle Ocho
2. Museo de Arte Mexicano
3. Washington Heights, NY
4. Chicago
5. Este de Los Ángeles
6. Marqueta
7. dominicanos

Marc Anthony

# música

Paulina Rubio

## La explosión latina

Esta no es una moda transitoria; tampoco es simplemente el aumento de la población latina. Es la creciente[1] influencia de distintos elementos latinos en la cultura de Estados Unidos. Esto es evidente en la comida, en la moda, en todas las artes y especialmente en la música popular. Los latinos adoptaron rápidamente el estilo pop y hoy día artistas como Shakira, Marc Anthony, Juanes, Cristina Aguilera y Paulina Rubio son conocidos por el público en general. Otra consecuencia de esta explosión es la presencia de los ritmos latinos en la música anglosajona.

[1]creciente: *growing*

## Julia Álvarez, una escritora dominicana-americana

"Yo soy una dominicana 'guión[1]' americana", dice esta conocida escritora. "Para mí las cosas más interesantes pasan dentro de ese 'guión'; ahí es donde está la colisión y la combinación de dos mundos." Julia Álvarez nació en Nueva York, pero vivió en la República Dominicana hasta los 10 años de edad. Ella estudió en Nueva York y actualmente es profesora de inglés en Middlebury College. Sus novelas más famosas son: *How the García Girls Lost Their Accent* y *In the Time of the Butterflies.*

[1]guión: *hyphen*

## En la tele

George López

**George López, un gran comediante**
Este nativo de Los Ángeles creció en el valle de San Fernando, en Mission Hills. Él es el co-autor, escritor, productor y actor del programa cómico "George López". A los latinos, a los críticos y también al público en general les gusta mucho este programa. George es un artista con muchas habilidades porque también trabaja en el teatro, en el cine y en la radio. Además, ayuda a muchas organizaciones y fundaciones de caridad[1]. Por ejemplo, participa en el programa "Alto a la violencia" del Departamento de Policía de Los Ángeles (LAPD).

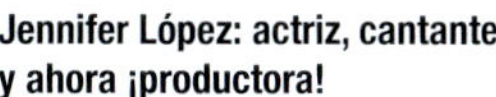
Jennifer López

**Jennifer López: actriz, cantante y ahora ¡productora!**
La latina más famosa y mejor pagada de Hollywood decidió trabajar como productora de programas televisivos. "En mi casa yo veía todas las novelas y los programas en español", dice la actriz y cantante. "Quiero narrar la historia de los latinos que viven aquí y tienen 'el sueño americano'[2]." Jennifer, como otros artistas, a veces basa su trabajo en sus experiencias personales.

[1]caridad: *charity*
[2]sueño americano: *American Dream*





**C Música, la tele y la literatura**
Contesten.

1. ¿En qué es evidente la influencia latina en la cultura de Estados Unidos?
2. ¿Qué es una consecuencia de la explosión latina en la música anglosajona?
3. ¿Cómo se describe Julia Álvarez?
4. ¿Cuáles son algunas obras de Julia Álvarez?
5. ¿Dónde y qué enseña Julia Álvarez?
6. ¿Qué tipo de trabajo benévolo hace George López?
7. Además de la televisión, ¿en qué trabaja George López?
8. ¿Qué trabajo decidió hacer Jennifer López?
9. ¿En qué basa su trabajo a veces Jennifer López?

**LEVELING**
**E:** Activity A
**A:** Activity B
**C:** Activity C

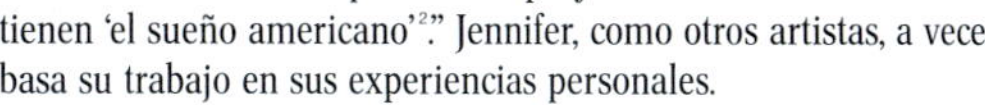

### Answers to ¿Comprendes?

**C**

1. Es evidente en la comida, en la moda, en las artes y en la música.
2. Hay una presencia de los ritmos latinos en la música anglosajona.
3. Dice que es "dominicana 'guión' americana".
4. *How the Garcia Girls Lost Their Accent y In the Time of the Butterflies*
5. Enseña inglés en Middlebury College.
6. George López participa en el programa "Alto a la violencia" del LAPD.
7. También trabaja en el teatro, en el cine y en la radio.
8. Decidió hacer el trabajo de productora.
9. A veces basa su trabajo en sus experiencias personales.

# Planning for Chapter 5

## SCOPE AND SEQUENCE, PAGES 130–159

### Topics

- ❖ Board games and hobbies
- ❖ Activities in the park

### Culture

- ❖ Sunday in the park in Spanish-speaking countries
- ❖ Chapultepec Park, Mexico, D.F.
- ❖ Palermo Park, Buenos Aires
- ❖ Game arcades in the Spanish-speaking world
- ❖ Domino
- ❖ Literary genres in Spanish
- ❖ Isabel Allende

### Functions

- ❖ How to talk about leisure time activities
- ❖ How to talk about going to the amusement park and the zoo
- ❖ How to talk about future events
- ❖ How to compare people and things

### Structure

- ❖ The future tense
- ❖ Comparatives and superlatives

### National Standards

- ❖ Communication Standard 1.1 pages 134, 135, 138, 139, 141, 142, 143, 145, 147, 154
- ❖ Communication Standard 1.2 pages 135, 139, 143, 146, 147, 148–149, 150, 151, 152–153, 154
- ❖ Communication Standard 1.3 pages 135, 147, 155
- ❖ Cultures Standard 2.1 pages 148–149, 150, 151
- ❖ Cultures Standard 2.2 pages 148–149
- ❖ Connections Standard 3.1 pages 152–153
- ❖ Comparisons Standard 4.2 pages 150, 151
- ❖ Communities Standard 5.1 page 159
- ❖ Communities Standard 5.2 page 147

## PACING AND PRIORITIES

**The chapter content is color coded below to assist you in planning.**

**■ required ■ recommended ■ optional**

**Vocabulario** *(required)* *Days 1–4*

- ■ Palabras 1
  - Los pasatiempos y hobbys
  - ¿Como pasarán el tiempo mañana?
- ■ Palabras 2
  - El parque

**Estructura** *(required)* *Days 5–7*

- ■ Futuro de los verbos regulares
- ■ Comparativo y superlativo

**Conversación** *(required)*

- ■ Una diferencia de opinión

**Lecturas culturales**

- ■ El domingo en el parque *(recommended)*
- ■ Las salas de juegos *(optional)*
- ■ El dominó *(optional)*

**Conexiones**

- ■ La literatura *(optional)*

■ **¡Te toca a ti!** *(recommended)*

■ **Assessment** *(recommended)*

■ **¡Hablo como un pro!** *(optional)*

## RESOURCE GUIDE

| Section | Pages | Section Resources |
|---|---|---|
| **Vocabulario PALABRAS 1** | | |
| Los pasatiempos y hobbys<br>¿Cómo pasarán el tiempo mañana? | 132, 134–135<br>133, 134–135 | Vocabulary Transparencies 5.2–5.3<br>Audio CD 4<br>Audio Activities TE, pages 51–53<br>Workbook, pages 51–52<br>Quiz 1, page 22<br>ExamView® Pro |
| **Vocabulario PALABRAS 2** | | |
| El parque | 136–139 | Vocabulary Transparencies 5.4–5.5<br>Audio CD 4<br>Audio Activities TE, pages 54–55<br>Workbook, pages 52–53<br>Quiz 2, page 23<br>ExamView® Pro |
| **Estructura** | | |
| Futuro de los verbos regulares<br>Comparativo y superlativo | 140–143<br>144–145 | Audio CD 4<br>Audio Activities TE, pages 55–58<br>Workbook, pages 54–57<br>Quizzes 3–4, pages 24–25<br>ExamView® Pro |
| **Conversación** | | |
| Una diferencia de opinión | 146–147 | Audio CD 4<br>Audio Activities TE, page 59<br>Interactive CD-ROM |
| **Lecturas culturales** | | |
| El domingo en el parque<br>Las salas de juegos<br>El dominó | 148–149<br>150<br>151 | Audio CD 4<br>Audio Activities TE, page 60<br>Tests, pages 72, 75 |
| **Conexiones** | | |
| La literatura | 152–153 | Tests, pages 73–74 |
| **¡Te toca a ti!** | | |
| | 154–155 | **¡Viva el mundo hispano!** Video, Episode 5<br>Video Activities, pages 81–83<br>Spanish Online Activities spanish.glencoe.com |
| **Assessment** | | |
| | 156–157 | Communication Transparency C 5<br>Quizzes 1–4, pages 22–25<br>Performance Assessment, Task 5<br>Tests, pages 69–82<br>Situation Cards, Chapter 5<br>ExamView® Pro<br>**Maratón mental** Videoquiz |

# Using Your Resources for Chapter 5

## Transparencies

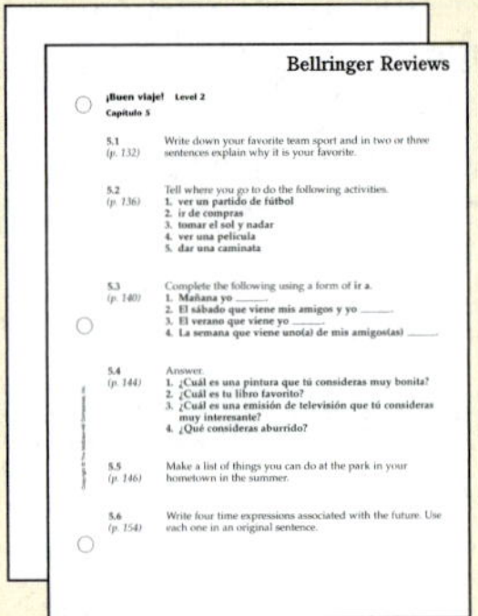
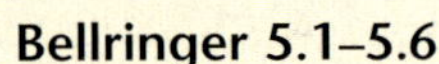
Bellringer 5.1–5.6

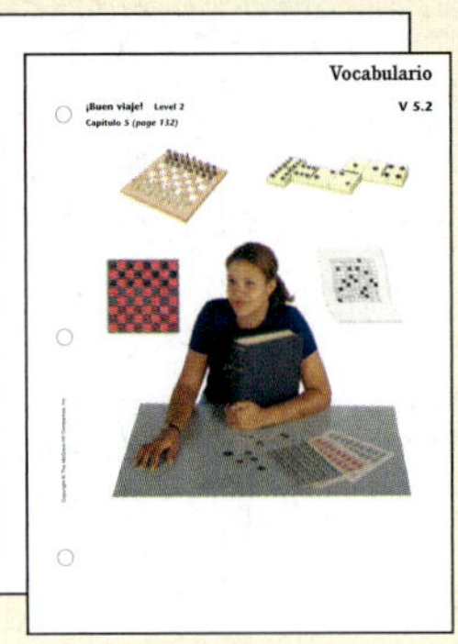
Vocabulary 5.1–5.5

Communication C 5

## Workbook

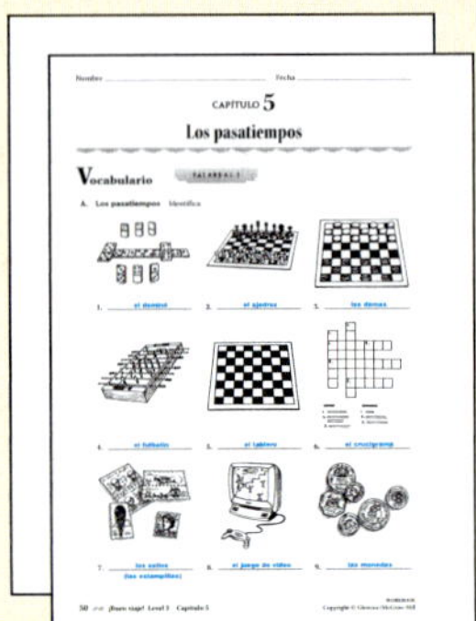
Vocabulary, pages 51–53

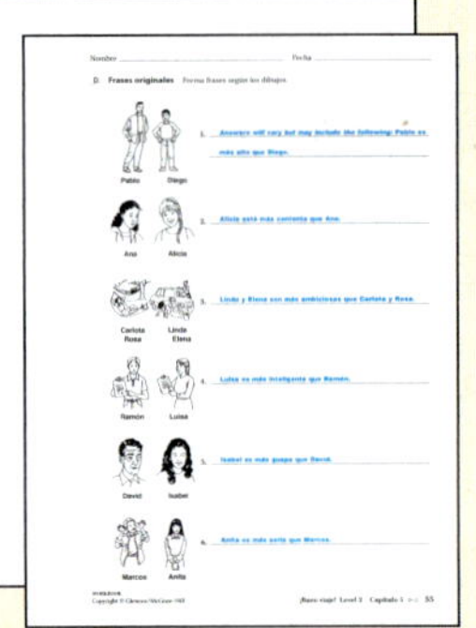
Structure, pages 54–57

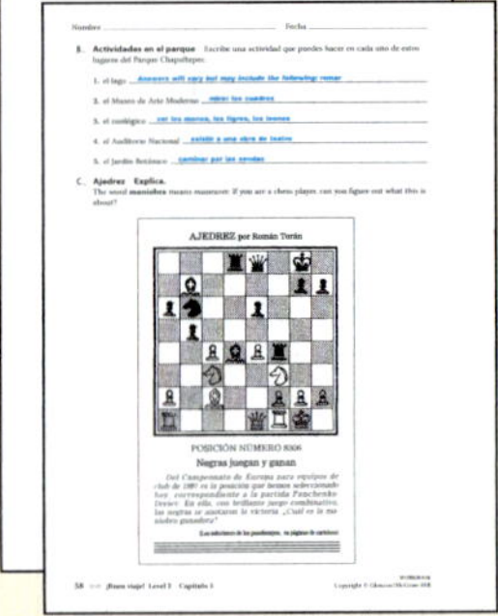
Enrichment, pages 58–60

## Audio Activities

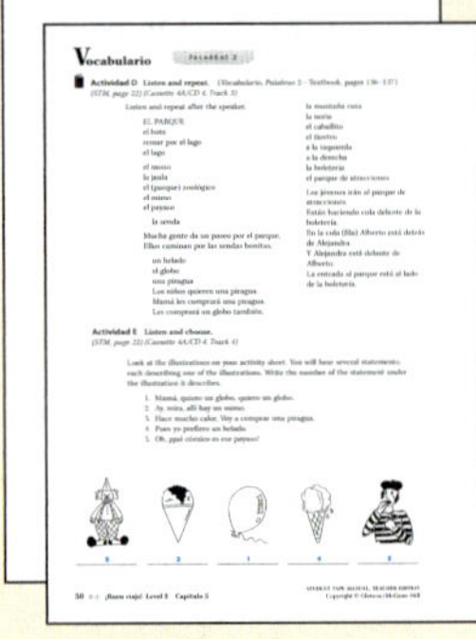
Vocabulary, pages 51–55

Structure, pages 55–58

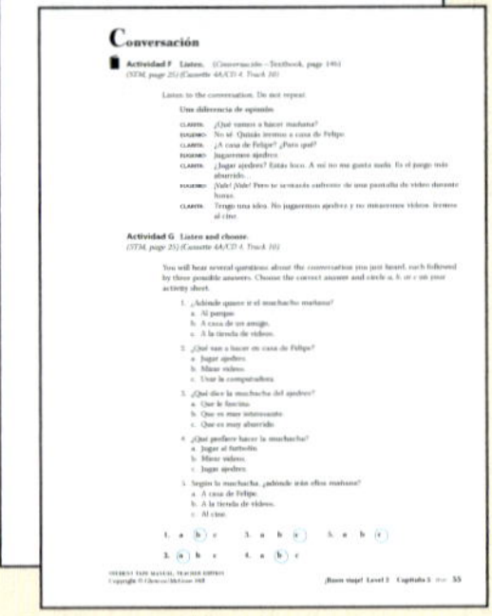
Conversation, page 59

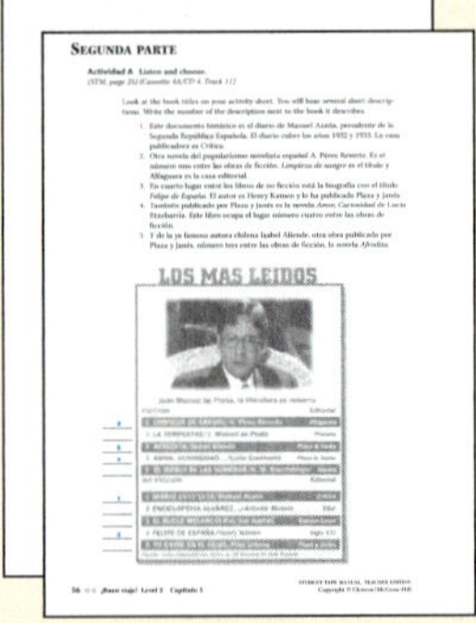
Additional Practice, pages 61–63

# Assessment

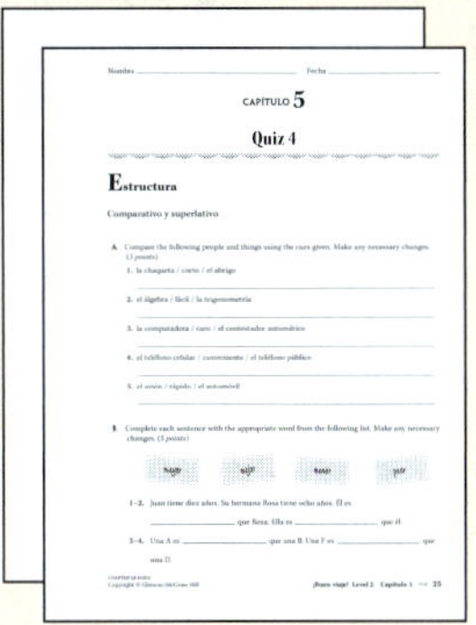

Vocabulary and Structure Quizzes, pages 22–25

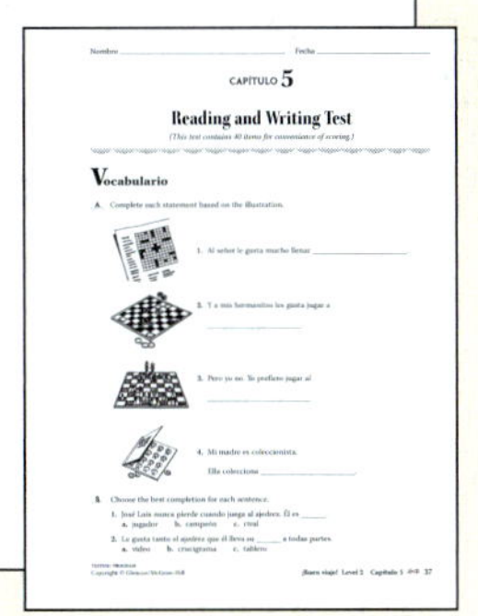

Chapter Tests, pages 69–82

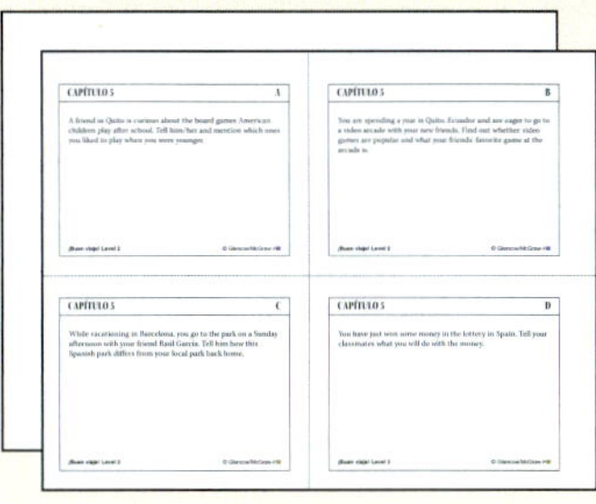

Situation Cards, Chapter 5

MindJogger Videoquiz, ExamView® Pro, Chapter 5

## Timesaving Teacher Tools

### TeacherWorks™

TeacherWorks™ is your all-in-one teacher resource center. Personalize lesson plans, access resources from the Teacher Wraparound Edition, connect to the Internet, or make a to-do list. These are only a few of the many features that can assist you in the planning and organizing of your lessons.

Includes:

- A calendar feature
- Access to all program blackline masters
- Standards correlations and more

### ExamView® Pro

Test Bank software for Macintosh and Windows makes creating, editing, customizing, and printing tests quick and easy.

## Technology Resources

In the Chapter 5 Internet Activity, you will have a chance to learn more about the Spanish-speaking world. Visit spanish.glencoe.com

On the interactive CD–ROM, students can listen to and take part in a recorded version of the conversation in Chapter 5.

**¡Viva el mundo hispano!** Video and Video Activities, Chapter 5. Available on VHS and DVD.

Help your students prepare for the chapter test by playing the **Maratón mental** Videoquiz game show. Teams will compete against each other to review chapter vocabulary and structure and sharpen listening comprehension skills. Available on VHS and DVD.

**¡Buen viaje!** is also available on CD or Online.

## Preview

In this chapter, students will learn to talk about their favorite indoor leisure activities as well as activities in a park. In addition to learning the formation of the future tense, students will learn how to compare people and things. The cultural focus of the chapter is on typical park activities and pastimes in the Spanish-speaking world.

### National Standards

**Communication**

In Chapter 5 students will learn to communicate in spoken and written Spanish on the following topics:

- playing games and pursuing hobbies
- participating in activities in a park

Students will obtain and provide information and engage in conversations dealing with indoor and outdoor leisure activities as they fulfill the chapter objectives listed on this page.

Capítulo 5

# Los pasatiempos

**Objetivos**

In this chapter you will learn to:

- talk about popular hobbies and games
- talk about activities in the park
- give details about location
- talk about what will happen in the future
- compare objects and people
- describe your favorite pastime
- talk about pastimes in Spanish-speaking countries

Gonzalo Cienfuegos *The Enchanted Crystal*

Capítulo 5

## Spotlight on Culture

**Arte** An important Latin American artist whose works are seldom seen in this country, Gonzalo Cienfuegos was born in Santiago de Chile in 1949. Cienfuegos paints characters that are shaped by his experience in metropolitan Chilean society.

**Fotografía** The **Parque María Luisa** is in Sevilla. The sunken gardens, with pools, fountains, and ceramic tiles, are magnificent. The elaborate buildings in the park were built for the **Exposición Ibero-americana** of 1929.

## LEVELING

The activities, conversations, and readings within each chapter are marked according to level of difficulty. **E** indicates easy. **A** indicates average. **C** indicates challenging. Some activities cover a range of difficulty. In some activities, for example, advanced students will be able to produce more extensive responses while students who learn at a different rate may give less detailed responses. The leveling indicators will help you individualize instruction to best meet your students' needs.

# Vocabulario

PALABRAS 1

## 1 PREPARATION

### Resource Manager

Vocabulary Transparencies 5.2–5.3
Audio Activities TE, pages 51–53
Audio CD 4
Workbook, pages 51–52
Quizzes, page 22
ExamView® Pro

### Bellringer Review

*Use BRR Transparency 5.1 or write the following on the board.*
Write down your favorite team sport and in two or three sentences explain why it is your favorite.

## 2 PRESENTATION

**Step 1** Have students close their books. Show Vocabulary Transparencies 5.2–5.3 for the initial presentation of vocabulary. Point to individual items and have students repeat each word or expression two or three times after you or the recording on Audio CD 4.

**Step 2** After presenting the vocabulary orally, have students open their books and read for additional reinforcement.

**Step 3** You may wish to ask the following questions as you present the new vocabulary: **¿Juegas (al) dominó? ¿Te gusta el dominó? Y el ajedrez, ¿te gusta? ¿Se usa un tablero para jugar (al) ajedrez? ¿Se usa un tablero para jugar (a las) damas?**

# Vocabulario

PALABRAS 1

## Los pasatiempos y hobbys

Luisa es coleccionista.
Colecciona sellos y monedas.

Mañana irá al centro.
Comprará unas monedas antiguas.



## Chapter Projects

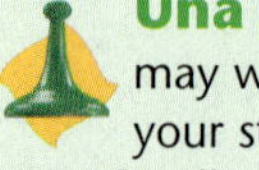

**Una partida de Scrabble** You may wish to reserve a class period for your students to play Scrabble in Spanish. Allow the students to use dictionaries as they play.

**Parques de atracciones** Have students write to their favorite amusement park and ask for information in Spanish about the park. Have them use this material to make posters advertising the amusement park.

## ¿Cómo pasarán el tiempo mañana?

Mañana Ramona jugará al ajedrez con un amigo.
Ella es más lista que su rival.
Ramona ganará. Será la campeona.

A Tomás le gustan los crucigramas.
Él llenará un crucigrama.

los juegos de video

la sala de juegos

el futbolín



# Vocabulario

**¡OJO!** The future tense is introduced in the **Vocabulario** section in the third person only. Students can immediately use this form to answer questions without having to change endings.

### Vocabulary Expansion

For the chess players in your class:

| | |
|---|---|
| **el rey** | *king* |
| **la reina/la dama** | *queen* |
| **el alfil** | *bishop* |
| **el caballo** | *knight* |
| **la torre** | *rook/castle* |
| **el peón** | *pawn* |

### About the Spanish Language

In Spain the word is **vídeo** with a written accent on the **í.** In Latin America the word is **video** with the stress on the **e.**

**LEVELING**

**E:** Vocabulary

Vocabulario

## 3 PRACTICE

## ¿Qué palabra necesito?

**¡OJO!** When students are doing the **¿Qué palabra necesito?** activities, accept any answer that makes sense. The purpose of these activities is to have students use the new vocabulary. They are not factual recall activities. Thus, it is not necessary for students to remember specific factual information from the vocabulary presentation when answering. If you wish, have students use the visuals on this page as a stimulus, when possible.

**Historieta** Each time **Historieta** appears, it means that the answers to the activity form a short story. Encourage students to look at the title of the **Historieta,** since it can help them do the activity.

**1** Have students refer to the illustrations as they do Activity 1.

**2** Do Activity 2 orally with books closed. Then have students retell the story in their own words.

Vocabulario

## ¿Qué palabra necesito?

**1** **Los pasatiempos** Contesten según los dibujos.

1. ¿A qué juegan las muchachas?
2. ¿Qué hay en el periódico?
3. ¿A qué juegan los señores?

4. ¿A qué juegan los niños?
5. ¿Dónde están los muchachos?

**2** **Historieta** **Un juego de ajedrez**
Contesten según se indica.

1. ¿Jugará Tomás a las damas o al ajedrez? (al ajedrez)
2. ¿Con quién jugará? (un amigo)
3. ¿Quién es el jugador más listo? (su amigo)
4. ¿Tomás ganará o perderá el juego? (perderá)
5. ¿Quién será el campeón? (su amigo)

Barcelona, España



### Answers to ¿Qué palabra necesito?

1. Las muchachas juegan a las damas.
2. Hay un crucigrama en el periódico.
3. Los señores juegan al ajedrez.
4. Los niños juegan al futbolín.
5. Los muchachos están en la sala de juegos.

**2**

1. Tomás jugará al ajedrez.
2. Jugará con un amigo.
3. Su amigo es el jugador más listo.
4. Tomás perderá el juego.
5. Su amigo será el campeón.

**3 ¿Qué será?** Adivinen.

1. Para completar uno de estos necesitas un lápiz o un bolígrafo.
2. Puedes participar en una carrera de automóviles, una aventura con monstruos, un viaje por las galaxias.
3. Hay juegos que duran horas. Los jugadores piensan mucho antes de mover una pieza.
4. Juegas con un tablero, como el ajedrez, y usas fichas, pero el juego es más fácil que el ajedrez.
5. Es un juego como el fútbol en miniatura. Puedes jugar con un amigo o con tres amigos más.

**4 Preguntas personales** Contesten.

1. ¿Te gustan los juegos de video? ¿Juegas en casa?
2. ¿Cuáles son los juegos más populares?
3. ¿Tú sabes jugar al ajedrez? ¿Es difícil?
4. ¿Quién es el / la mejor jugador(a) entre tus amigos?
5. ¿Alguien en tu familia llena los crucigramas?
6. ¿A ti te gustan los crucigramas o crees que son aburridos?
7. ¿Eres coleccionista?
8. ¿Qué coleccionas?

Una sala de juegos

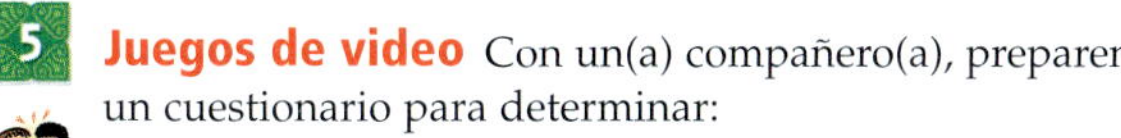

**5 Juegos de video** Con un(a) compañero(a), preparen un cuestionario para determinar:

- cuántos alumnos en tu clase usan juegos de video
- cuántos juegan con los juegos de video en casa y cuántos en salas de juegos
- cuáles son los tres juegos de video más populares

Luego preparen un informe sobre los resultados de su encuesta *(survey)* para la clase.

**6 Los gemelos con gustos distintos**
Eugenio y Eugenia son gemelos *(twins)*. Ellos tienen la misma apariencia pero no los mismos gustos. Con un(a) compañero(a), hagan el papel de los gemelos. Digan lo que cada uno hace después de las clases y en los fines de semana con su tiempo libre. Usen la imaginación.



## Vocabulario

**3** You can have students do Activity 3 together as a game.

**4** Students can come to the front of the room and go over Activity 4 in pairs, as if it were an interview.

**¡OJO!** Note that the activities are color-coded. All the activities in the text are communicative. However, the ones with blue titles are guided communication. The red titles indicate that the answers to the activity are more open-ended and can vary more. You may wish to correct students' mistakes more so in the guided activities than in the activities with a red title, which lend themselves to a freer response.

**Expansion:** After completing Activity 6, you may wish to ask students the following questions:
**¿Conoces a algunos gemelos? ¿Quiénes son?**
**¿Hay gemelos en tu familia?**
**Los gemelos que conoces, ¿tienen los mismos intereses o no?**
**¿Son muy diferentes o son idénticos?**

**LEVELING**
**E:** Activities 1, 2, 3, 4, 5
**A:** Activities 3, 4, 5, 6

### About the Spanish Language

Twins are **gemelos** in most places, but in Mexico they are **cuates.** Mexicans also use the word **cuate** to mean *pal* or *buddy.*

### Vocabulary Expansion

A few other games are:

| | |
|---|---|
| **el chaquete** | *backgammon* |
| **las damas chinas** | *Chinese checkers* |
| **el Bingo** | *Bingo* |

## Answers to ¿Qué palabra necesito?

**3**

1. un crucigrama
2. un juego de video
3. el ajedrez
4. las damas
5. el futbolín

**4**

1. Sí, (No, no) me gustan los juegos de video. Sí, (No, no) juego en casa.
2. Los juegos más populares son ___.
3. Sí, (No, no) sé jugar al ajedrez. Es fácil (difícil).
4. El / La mejor jugador(a) entre mis amigos es ___.
5. Sí, mi ___ llena los crucigramas. (No, nadie en mi familia llena los crucigramas.)
6. Sí, me gustan los crucigramas. (Creo que son aburridos.)
7. Sí, (No, no) soy coleccionista.
8. Colecciono ___.

**5** *Answers will vary, but students should use vocabulary presented in* Palabras 1.

**6** *Answers will vary. Students will use the vocabulary in* Palabras 1.

# Vocabulario

PALABRAS 2

## 1 PREPARATION

### Resource Manager

Vocabulary Transparencies 5.4–5.5
Audio Activities TE, pages 54–55
Audio CD 4
Workbook, pages 52–53
Quizzes, page 23
ExamView® Pro

### Bellringer Review

*Use BRR Transparency 5.2 or write the following on the board.*
Tell where you go to do the following activities.

1. **ver un partido de fútbol**
2. **ir de compras**
3. **tomar el sol y nadar**
4. **ver una película**
5. **dar una caminata**

## 2 PRESENTATION

**Step 1** Have students close their books. Then model the new vocabulary using Vocabulary Transparencies 5.4–5.5. Have students repeat each word or expression two or three times after you or the recording on Audio CD 4.

**Step 2** After presenting the vocabulary, have students open their books and read the new vocabulary aloud. You can have the class read in chorus or call on individuals to read.

# Vocabulario

PALABRAS 2

## El parque

## Reaching All Students

### Total Physical Response

*(Student 1),* **levántate.**
**Ven acá.**
**Vas a ir al parque hoy.**
**Da un paseo por el parque.**
**Compra una piragua.**
**Come la piragua.**
**Ahora rema por el lago en un bote.**
**Rema a la derecha.**
**Rema a la izquierda.**
**Baja del bote.**
**Gracias,** *(Student 1).* **Regresa a tu asiento.**

la senda

Mucha gente da un paseo por el parque.
Ellos caminan por las sendas bonitas.

el globo
una piragua
un helado

Los niños quieren una piragua.
Mamá les comprará una piragua.
Les comprará un globo también.

el parque de atracciones

Los jóvenes irán al parque de atracciones.
Están haciendo cola delante de la boletería.
En la cola (fila) Alberto está detrás de Alejandra.

Y Alejandra está delante de Alberto.
La entrada al parque está al lado de la boletería.



## Learning from Photos

*(page 136)* The park in the photo is the **Parque del Buen Retiro** in the heart of Madrid. Atop the pavilion overlooking the lake is an equestrian statue of Alfonso XII (1857–1885). The statue, by the famous sculptor Mariano Benlliure, was dedicated in 1922.

## Fun Facts

The **piragüero** is a summertime fixture, especially in the tropics. From his little cart he sells paper cupfuls of shaved ice over which he pours syrup flavorings.

## About the Spanish Language

There are a number of words for *ticket.* An airline, train, or bus ticket is usually called **un boleto** in Latin America. In Spain it's **un billete.** A theater, movie, or other admission ticket is **una entrada.** However, **tique, tiquet,** and **tiquete** are becoming very common as generic terms for *ticket.*

## Spanish Online

The Glencoe Spanish Web site **(spanish.glencoe.com)** offers options that enable you and your students to experience the Spanish-speaking world via the Internet. For each **Capítulo,** there are activities, games, and quizzes. In addition, an *Enrichment* section offers students an opportunity to visit Web sites related to the theme of the chapter.

# Vocabulario

## 3 PRACTICE

## ¿Qué palabra necesito?

**7** Go over Activity 7 orally with books closed.

**8** After going over Activity 8, call on more able students to make up original sentences using the words that did not fit.

**Writing Development**
After going over Activity 8, have students write the answers in an organized paragraph to illustrate how all the items tell a story.

Vocabulario

## ¿Qué palabra necesito?

**7** **Historieta Al parque**

Contesten.

1. ¿Irán los niños al parque mañana?
2. ¿Visitarán el zoológico?
3. ¿Verán los monos en el zoológico?
4. ¿Se divertirán los niños con los monos?
5. ¿Tomarán los niños una piragua?
6. ¿Les comprarán sus padres un globo?

El Retiro, Madrid

**8** **Historieta Un día en el parque**

Escojan la palabra apropiada.

1. La gente da un paseo por ____ del parque.
   **a.** las avenidas **b.** los lagos **c.** las sendas
2. Algunos ____ por el lago en un bote.
   **a.** compran **b.** hacen **c.** reman
3. Hay muchos animales en el ____.
   **a.** lago **b.** zoológico **c.** parque de atracciones
4. La gente hace cola ____ la boletería.
   **a.** detrás de **b.** a la derecha de **c.** delante de
5. Hay muchas ____ en un parque zoológico.
   **a.** jaulas **b.** atracciones **c.** norias
6. El ____ hace muchos gestos cómicos y extravagantes.
   **a.** tiovivo **b.** payaso **c.** caballito
7. A los niños les gusta tomar ____.
   **a.** lagos **b.** atracciones **c.** piraguas

El padre y su hijo se divierten.



## Answers to ¿Qué palabra necesito?

**7**

1. Sí, los niños irán al parque mañana.
2. Sí, (No, no) visitarán el zoológico.
3. Sí, (No, no) verán los monos en el zoológico.
4. Sí (No), los niños (no) se divertirán con los monos.
5. Sí (No), los niños (no) tomarán una piragua.
6. Sí (No), sus padres (no) les comprarán un globo.

**8**

1. c
2. c
3. b
4. c
5. a
6. b
7. c

**9** **¿Dónde está?** Contesten según el plano.

1. ¿Qué hay en el centro del parque?
2. ¿Dónde está la boletería? ¿Delante del lago o al lado del lago?
3. ¿Dónde está la entrada al parque?
4. Y el parque zoológico, ¿dónde está?
5. Estás delante de la boletería. El parque de atracciones, ¿está a tu derecha o a tu izquierda?

**10** **En el parque** Con un(a) compañero(a), miren el dibujo. Describan todo lo que ven en el dibujo. Tu compañero(a) te va a hacer preguntas. Contesta a sus preguntas. Entonces tú le puedes hacer preguntas y él o ella contestará.

**11** **Haciendo planes** Habla con un(a) compañero(a). Ustedes van a hacer algo el domingo. Tengan una conversación y decidan si van a ir al zoológico, al parque de atracciones o simplemente a un parque cerca de donde ustedes viven. Expliquen por qué prefieren ir adonde van.

UN POCO MÁS *For more practice using words from **Palabras 2**, do Activity 5 on page H6 at the end of this book.*



## Vocabulario

**9** **Expansion:** After going over Activity 9, have students make up sentences telling where things are located in relation to other things.

**10** Encourage students to write as many sentences as possible to describe the illustration. You may wish to have a contest to see which pair comes up with the longest list.

### Writing Development

Have students write a paragraph about what they see in the illustration that accompanies Activity 10.

UN POCO MÁS This *InfoGap* Activity will allow students to practice in pairs. The activity should be very manageable for them, since all vocabulary and structures are familiar to them.

### LEVELING

**E:** Activities 7, 8, 10
**A:** Activities 8, 9, 10, 11
**C:** Activity 11

## Answers to ¿Qué palabra necesito?

**9**

1. Hay un parque de atracciones.
2. La boletería está al lado del lago.
3. La entrada al parque está al lado de la boletería.
4. El parque zoológico está detrás del parque de atracciones.
5. El parque de atracciones está a mi izquierda.

**10** and **11** *Answers will vary. Students will use the vocabulary in* Palabras 1.

# Estructura

## 1 PREPARATION

### Resource Manager

Audio Activities TE, pages 55–58
Audio CD 4
Workbook, pages 54–57
Quizzes, pages 24–25
ExamView® Pro

### Bellringer Review

*Use BRR Transparency 5.3 or write the following on the board.*
Complete the following using a form of **ir a**.

1. **Mañana yo ___.**
2. **El sábado que viene mis amigos y yo ___.**
3. **El verano que viene yo ___.**
4. **La semana que viene uno(a) de mis amigos(as) ___.**

## 2 PRESENTATION

### Futuro de los verbos regulares

**Step 1** Ask students to open their books to page 140. Read Items 1 and 2 to them.

**Step 2** Have students repeat the verb forms after you.

**Step 3** Have students repeat the model sentences in Item 2 after you.

**¡OJO!** You may wish to de-emphasize this structure point with some groups because it is a low-frequency structure in comparison to the periphrastic future **ir a** + *infinitive.* You may want to present this tense more for receptive purposes.

# Estructura

## Futuro de los verbos regulares
### Talking about future events

**1.** The future tense is used to tell what will take place in the future. To form the future tense of regular verbs, you add the future endings to the infinitive. Study the following forms.

| INFINITIVE | estudiar | leer | escribir | ENDINGS |
|---|---|---|---|---|
| STEM | estudiar- | leer- | escribir- | |
| yo | estudiaré | leeré | escribiré | -é |
| tú | estudiarás | leerás | escribirás | -ás |
| él, ella, Ud. | estudiará | leerá | escribirá | -á |
| nosotros(as) | estudiaremos | leeremos | escribiremos | -emos |
| *vosotros(as)* | *estudiaréis* | *leeréis* | *escribiréis* | *-éis* |
| ellos, ellas, Uds. | estudiarán | leerán | escribirán | -án |

**Mañana jugaré al ajedrez.**
**Tú me verás jugar, ¿no?**
**Yo seré el campeón.**

**2.** You have already learned the construction **ir a** + *infinitive* to express events that will take place in the near future. In everyday conversation, this construction is actually used more frequently than the future tense.

**El año que viene voy a estudiar en Puerto Rico.**
**Me vas a escribir, ¿no?**
**Y yo voy a leer todas tus cartas.**

Universidad de Puerto Rico



### Learning from Photos

*(page 140)* This is the main campus of the **Universidad de Puerto Rico** in Río Piedras. The university was founded in 1903. A second campus was founded in 1911 in Mayagüez, followed later on by various others. The University of Puerto Rico is an accredited American university.

## ¿Cómo lo digo?

**12 Historieta Daniel viajará a España.**
Contesten.

1. ¿Adónde irá Daniel el año que viene?
2. ¿Estudiará en Alcalá de Henares?
3. ¿Asistirá a clases en la universidad?
4. ¿Leerá muchos libros?
5. ¿Su amiga le escribirá con frecuencia?
6. ¿Recibirá las cartas en algunos días?
7. ¿Responderá a las cartas de su amiga?

Universidad de Alcalá, España

**13 ¡A divertirse esta noche!**
Formen oraciones según el modelo.

**los muchachos →**
**Los muchachos verán la televisión.**

1. Raúl

2. El señor Fornos

3. Los niños

4. Nosotros

5. Leonor

6. Los monos

7. Tú

8. Yo



## Estructura

### 3 PRACTICE

### ¿Cómo lo digo?

**12** Go over this activity orally with books closed.
**Expansion:** Have a student or students retell the story in Activity 12 in their own words.

**13** Allow students to prepare Activity 13 before going over it in class.

### History Connection

The **Universidad de Alcalá, España,** was founded in 1598 by Cardinal Cisneros. However, the oldest university in Spain is **la Universidad de Salamanca**, founded in 1230. Salamanca served as the model for the first universities of the Americas: Santo Domingo (1538), Mexico (1553), and Lima (1553).

### LEVELING

**E:** Activities 12, 13
**A:** Activity 13

## Answers to ¿Cómo lo digo?

**12**

1. Daniel irá a España el año que viene.
2. Sí, estudiará en Alcalá de Henares.
3. Sí, asistirá a clases en la universidad.
4. Sí, leerá muchos libros.
5. Sí, su amiga le escribirá con frecuencia.
6. Sí, recibirá las cartas en algunos días.
7. Sí, responderá a las cartas de su amiga.

**13**

1. Raúl leerá un libro.
2. El señor Fornos llenará un crucigrama.
3. Los niños jugarán a las damas.
4. Nosotros jugaremos con un juego de video.
5. Leonor dará un paseo por el parque.
6. Los monos dormirán.
7. Tú hablarás por teléfono.
8. Yo escribiré una carta.

# Estructura

## 3 PRACTICE (continued)

14 You may wish to have students prepare Activity 14 before going over it in class.

15 Have students do Activity 15 with books open.

16 Activity 16 is somewhat difficult, going from preterite to future, but it is a very natural exchange since we so often tell someone what we didn't do but will do.

### Writing Development

You may wish to have students write Activity 15 as a unified paragraph.

# Estructura

### 14 Historieta El coleccionista

Sigan el modelo.

**Mañana voy a ir al centro. →**
**Mañana iré al centro.**

1. Mañana Carlos va a ir al centro.
2. Yo voy a ir con él.
3. Vamos a visitar los puestos de los coleccionistas.
4. Sé que Carlos va a comprar monedas.
5. Él cree que va a encontrar unas monedas raras.
6. Y yo voy a buscar sellos.
7. Yo sé quien me va a vender los sellos.
8. Y no voy a pagar mucho.

Una casa de campo, Mucuchíes, Venezuela

### 15 Historieta El sábado que viene

Completen con el futuro.

El sábado que viene yo __1__ (viajar) al campo. Allí __2__ (visitar) a mis abuelos. Ellos __3__ (estar) muy contentos. Ellos me __4__ (esperar) en la estación. Entonces me __5__ (llevar) a su casa. Mi tía María Luisa __6__ (preparar) una comida deliciosa. Después de comer todos nosotros __7__ (jugar) al dominó. Abuelita __8__ (ganar) como siempre. Yo __9__ (pasar) dos o tres días con ellos. Yo __10__ (volver) a casa un poco triste. Me gusta mucho visitar a los abuelos.

### 16 Ayer no, pero mañana, sí

Contesten según el modelo.

1. ¿Fuiste al parque ayer?
2. ¿Viste al payaso ayer?
3. ¿Visitaste el zoológico?
4. ¿Caminaste por las sendas del parque?
5. ¿Te divertiste?



## Answers to ¿Cómo lo digo?

**14**

1. Mañana Carlos irá al centro.
2. Yo iré con él.
3. Visitaremos los puestos de los coleccionistas.
4. Sé que Carlos comprará monedas.
5. Él cree que encontrará unas monedas raras.
6. Y yo buscaré sellos.
7. Yo sé quien me venderá los sellos.
8. Y no pagaré mucho.

**15**

1. viajaré
2. visitaré
3. estarán
4. esperarán
5. llevarán
6. preparará
7. jugaremos
8. ganará
9. pasaré
10. volveré

**16**

1. No, pero iré mañana.
2. No, pero veré al payaso mañana.
3. No, pero visitaré el zoológico mañana.
4. No, pero caminaré por las sendas del parque mañana.
5. No, pero me divertiré mañana.

17 **Tengo mucho que hacer.** Prepara una lista de todo lo que piensas hacer mañana. Por ejemplo, **Mañana escribiré una composición para la clase de español.** Puedes escoger algunas palabras de la lista. Entonces compara tu lista con la lista de un(a) compañero(a). ¿Cuáles son las actividades que ustedes dos van a hacer mañana?

18 **Mi rutina** Prepara tu rutina para mañana. Luego prepara un informe para la clase. Incluye las siguientes actividades en tu informe: **despertarse, levantarse, prepararse para la escuela, lavarse, vestirse, divertirse, acostarse, dormirse.**

Colegio Santa Teresita, Santurce, Puerto Rico



# Estructura

17 and 18 Allow students to choose the activities that they would like to do.

## Learning from Photos

*(page 143)* You may wish to ask questions about the photo of the students from the **Colegio Santa Teresita** in Santurce, Puerto Rico.
**¿Qué son los muchachos?**
**¿En qué escuela son alumnos?**
**¿Dónde está la escuela?**
**¿Qué hacen los alumnos?**

## LEVELING

**E:** Activity 17

**A:** Activities 14, 15, 16, 18

## Answers to ¿Cómo lo digo?

 and  *Answers will vary. Students will use the cues provided to do the activities.*

## 1 PREPARATION

### Bellringer Review

*Use BRR Transparency 5.4 or write the following on the board.*
Answer.

1. **¿Cuál es una pintura que tú consideras muy bonita?**
2. **¿Cuál es tu libro favorito?**
3. **¿Cuál es una emisión de televisión que tú consideras muy interesante?**
4. **¿Qué consideras aburrido?**

## 2 PRESENTATION

### Comparativo y superlativo

**Step 1** Have students open their books to page 144. Lead them through Items 1–6 and the model sentences.

**Step 2** Have students make lists of words they know which can be used to describe people.

**Step 3** Draw two stick figures on the board and name them. Have students use their list of adjectives and make up sentences comparing the two stick figures.

**Step 4** Provide additional examples by comparing objects or students in the room. For example: **Miren. ¿Es Fernando más alto que Alberto? (Sí, es más alto que Alberto.)**

**Step 5** Tell students that the superlative is followed by **de** in Spanish. Do not compare it to *in* in English. When the comparison is made, students tend to get more confused.

## Comparativo y superlativo
### Comparing people and things

1. To compare people or things in English, you add *-er* to short adjectives and you use *more* before long adjectives. The word *than* follows.

   *She is taller than her brother.*
   *She is also more intelligent than her brother.*

   This construction is called the comparative.

2. To form the comparative in Spanish, you put **más** before the adjective or adverb and **que** after it.

   **Ella es más alta que su hermano.**
   **Y también es más inteligente que su hermano.**

3. The superlative is used to describe "the most." To form the superlative in English, you add *-est* to short adjectives and place *most* before long adjectives.

   *She is the nicest person of all.*
   *She is the most intelligent person in the world.*

4. In Spanish, the superlative is formed by using the appropriate definite article **(el, la, los, las)** plus **más** with the adjective. The preposition **de** follows the superlative.

   **Ella es la persona más simpática de todas.**
   **Ella es la persona más inteligente del mundo.**

5. The adjectives **bueno** and **malo** have irregular comparative and superlative forms.

   | | | |
   |---|---|---|
   | **bueno(a)** | **mejor** | **el/la mejor** |
   | **malo(a)** | **peor** | **el/la peor** |

6. The adjectives **mayor** and **menor** most often refer to age.

   **Yo soy mayor que mi hermana.**
   **Mi hermana es la menor de la familia.**

**¿Lo sabes?**

The comparative is often followed by **nadie.**
**Él sabe más que nadie.**
**Tiene más paciencia que nadie.**

**¿Te acuerdas?**

Remember to add **-es** to an adjective that ends in a consonant.
**mi mejor amigo**
**mis mejores amigos**

### Learning from Realia

*(page 144)* This family portrait provides a good opportunity to practice **a la derecha** and **a la izquierda.**
**¿Quién está a la derecha de la madre?**
**¿Quién está a la derecha del padre?**
**¿Quién está a la izquierda del padre?**
**¿Quién está a la izquierda de la madre?**

# ¿Cómo lo digo?

**19** **Compararemos.** Sigan el modelo.

alto

**Luis / Pablo / Andrés →**
**Luis es alto.**
**Pablo es más alto que Luis.**
**Andrés es el más alto de todos.**

1. graciosa
   Susana / Lola / Anita
2. ricos
   los Gómez / los García / los Ramos
3. cómicos
   los mimos / los monos / los payasos
4. popular
   el ajedrez / el futbolín / los juegos de video

**20** **¿Cuál es más... ?** Sigan el modelo.

**grande** **la Ciudad de México / Nueva York →**
**La Ciudad de México es más grande que Nueva York.**

1. caro — el avión / el tren
2. rápido — el tren / el bus
3. difícil — el ajedrez / las damas
4. largo — un kilómetro / un metro
5. pequeña — una habichuela / una papa

Ciudad de México

**21** **¿Y tú?** Contesten.

1. ¿Quién es tu mejor amigo(a)?
2. ¿En qué clase recibes las mejores notas?
3. ¿Quién es el/la mayor de tu familia?
4. ¿Y el/la menor? ¿Quién es?
5. ¿Eres mayor o menor que tu padre?

Estructura

## 3 PRACTICE

### ¿Cómo lo digo?

**19** **and** **20** Have students prepare Activities 19 and 20 before going over them in class.

**21** **Expansion:** After going over Activity 21, have students give a description of their **mejor amigo(a), el / la mayor de su familia,** and **el / la menor de su familia.**

**¡Adelante!**
At this point in the chapter, students have learned all the vocabulary and structure necessary to complete the chapter. The conversation and cultural readings that follow recycle all the material learned up to this point.

**LEVELING**

**E:** Activities 19, 20, 21

## Answers to ¿Cómo lo digo?

**19**

1. Susana es graciosa.
   Lola es más graciosa que Susana.
   Anita es la más graciosa de todas.
2. Los Gómez son ricos.
   Los García son más ricos que los Gómez.
   Los Ramos son los más ricos de todos.
3. Los mimos son cómicos.
   Los monos son más cómicos que los mimos.
   Los payasos son los más cómicos de todos.
4. El ajedrez es popular.
   El futbolín es más popular que el ajedrez.
   Los juegos de video son los más populares de todos.

**20**

1. El avión es más caro que el tren.
2. El tren es más rápido que el bus.
3. El ajedrez es más difícil que las damas.
4. Un kilómetro es más largo que un metro.
5. Una habichuela es más pequeña que una papa.

**21** *Answers will vary but may include:*

1. Mi mejor amigo(a) es ___.
2. Recibo las mejores notas en la clase de ___.
3. El / La mayor de mi familia es ___.
4. El / La menor de mi familia es ___.
5. Soy menor que mi padre.

# Conversación

## 1 PREPARATION

### Resource Manager

Audio Activities TE, page 59
Audio CD 4

### Bellringer Review

*Use BRR Transparency 5.5 or write the following on the board.*
Make a list of things you can do at the park in your hometown in the summer.

## 2 PRESENTATION

**Step 1** With books closed, have students listen and repeat as you read the conversation aloud or play Audio CD 4.

**Step 2** Have students open their books. Call on volunteers to read the conversation in parts with as much expression as possible.

**Step 3** Call on individual students to retell the information in the conversation in their own words. This activity gives students important practice in going from dialogue to narrative form.

# Conversación

## Una diferencia de opinión   

**Clarita** ¿Qué vamos a hacer mañana?
**Eugenio** No sé. Quizás iremos a casa de Felipe.
**Clarita** ¿A casa de Felipe? ¿Para qué?
**Eugenio** Jugaremos ajedrez.
**Clarita** ¿Jugar ajedrez? Estás loco. A mí no me gusta nada. Es el juego más aburrido...
**Eugenio** ¡Vale! ¡Vale! Pero te sentarás enfrente de una pantalla de video durante horas.
**Clarita** Tengo una idea. No jugaremos ajedrez y no miraremos videos. Iremos al cine.

### ¿Comprendes?

Contesten.

1. ¿Adónde quiere ir mañana Eugenio?
2. Según Eugenio, ¿qué jugarán?
3. ¿Quiere ir Clarita?
4. ¿Le gusta a Clarita jugar ajedrez?
5. ¿Qué dice Clarita del ajedrez?
6. ¿Qué prefiere hacer Clarita?
7. Según Clarita, ¿adónde irán?



### About the Spanish Language

Eugenio says **¡Vale! ¡Vale!** It is the equivalent of *OK! OK!* in English. The expression **vale** is much more common in Spain than in Latin America, where people will often say **OK.**

### Answers to ¿Comprendes?

1. Mañana Eugenio quiere ir a casa de Felipe.
2. Según Eugenio, jugarán ajedrez.
3. No, Clarita no quiere ir.
4. No, a Clarita no le gusta jugar ajedrez.
5. Dice que el ajedrez es el juego más aburrido.
6. Clarita prefiere ver un video.
7. Según Clarita, irán al cine.

# Vamos a hablar más

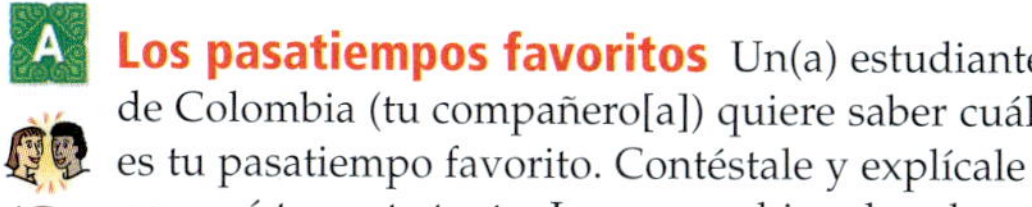
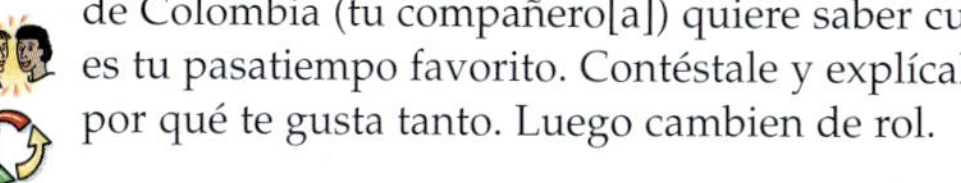

**A** **Los pasatiempos favoritos** Un(a) estudiante de Colombia (tu compañero[a]) quiere saber cuál es tu pasatiempo favorito. Contéstale y explícale por qué te gusta tanto. Luego cambien de rol.

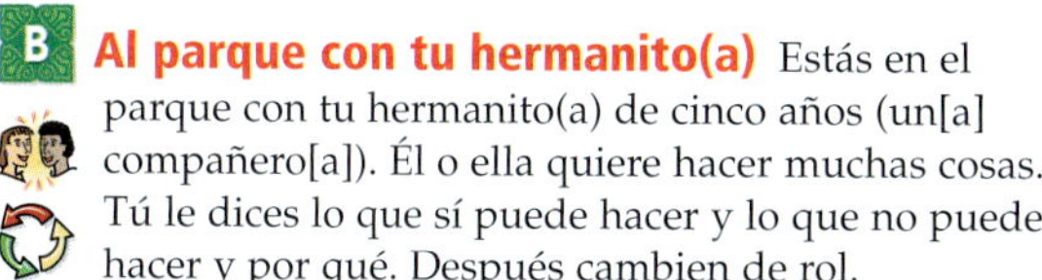

**B** **Al parque con tu hermanito(a)** Estás en el parque con tu hermanito(a) de cinco años (un[a] compañero[a]). Él o ella quiere hacer muchas cosas. Tú le dices lo que sí puede hacer y lo que no puede hacer y por qué. Después cambien de rol.

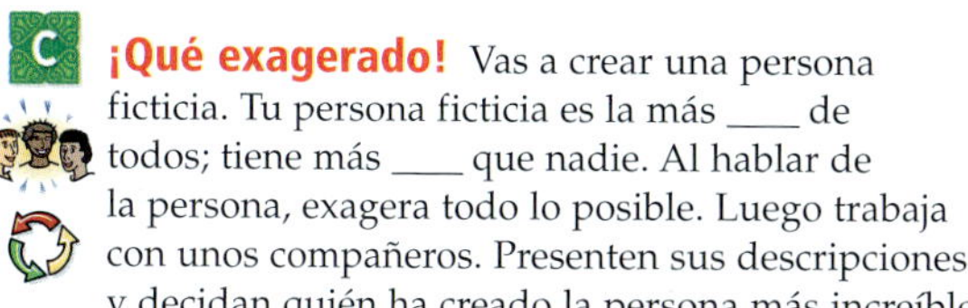

**C** **¡Qué exagerado!** Vas a crear una persona ficticia. Tu persona ficticia es la más ____ de todos; tiene más ____ que nadie. Al hablar de la persona, exagera todo lo posible. Luego trabaja con unos compañeros. Presenten sus descripciones y decidan quién ha creado la persona más increíble.

Cartagena, Colombia

**D** **No, de ninguna manera** Con un(a) compañero(a), miren esta foto. Los dos amigos están hablando de unos planes. Parece que a uno de ellos no le interesa nada el proyecto. Entablen la conversación entre los dos.

For more information about parks and other attractions in Spanish-speaking countries, go to the Glencoe Spanish Web site: spanish.glencoe.com



## 3 PRACTICE

### Vamos a hablar más

**A** You may wish to have students circulate in the classroom and ask various classmates what their favorite pastimes are until they find another person who has the same favorite pastime as they do.

### Geography Connection

Have students find Cartagena on the coast of Colombia. (See the map on page xxxi or use Map Transparency M 3.)

Cartagena is one of the oldest cities in the Americas. It was founded by the Spaniards in 1533 and was originally called **Cartagena de Indias,** in contrast to the city of Cartagena in Murcia, Spain.

### Writing Development

Have students write the description of the **persona más increíble** from Activity C.

### Glencoe Technology

On the CD-ROM, students can watch a dramatization of this conversation. They can then play the role of either one of the characters and record themselves in the conversation.

**LEVELING**

**E:** Conversation

## Answers to Vamos a hablar más

**A** *Answers will vary, but students will use vocabulary previously learned to talk about what they like to do in their free time.*

**B** *Answers will vary, but students will use vocabulary learned in this chapter to talk about what their younger siblings like to do at the park.*

**C** *Answers will vary, but students will use the superlative to describe an incredible person.*

**D** *Answers will vary, but students can use the conversation on page 146 as a model.*

# Lecturas culturales

## Resource Manager

Audio Activities TE, page 60
Audio CD 4

## National Standards

**Cultures**
The reading on page 148 and the related activities on page 149 familiarize students with a typical Sunday excursion to the park in a Spanish-speaking country.

## PRESENTATION

### Pre-reading
Have students open their books and do the Reading Strategy on page 148. Then ask them what genre they think this passage will most closely resemble—a novel, a short story, a poem, or an essay.

### Reading
**Step 1** To vary the presentation of the reading, you may wish to have students read this selection silently.

**Step 2** Have them tell something about what they read.

### Post-reading
Assign the **¿Comprendes?** activities on page 149 for homework and go over them the following day.

# Lecturas culturales

## Reading Strategy

**Being familiar with the genre** Be familiar with the kind of passage you are reading—the genre. Examples of genre are novel, short story, essay, and poem. A genre is somewhat predictable. For example, novels, short stories, and other types of prose will all tell a story. A poem will tend to evoke emotion. Knowing the genre will help you to know what to expect in the reading.

## El domingo en el parque

Casi todas las ciudades hispanas tienen uno o más parques bonitos. Los parques son un centro de recreo[1] para jóvenes y viejos, especialmente los domingos.

Si vas a un parque como el Retiro en Madrid o Chapultepec en México, verás a los viejos jugando al dominó hora tras hora. Y los niños estarán en fila delante del vendedor de helados o piraguas.

En algunos parques, como Palermo en Buenos Aires, hay un zoológico. El domingo que viene los Rodríguez llevarán a los niños al zoológico. Se divertirán mucho mirando a los cómicos monos. Pero se asustarán[2] un poco al ver los leones y tigres en sus jaulas grandes.

A veces hay también un parque de atracciones. A los niños les gusta subir al tiovivo. Los caballitos suben y bajan al acompañamiento del organillo.

El parque no es sólo para viejos y niños. En el parque verás a muchos jóvenes. Los jóvenes se encuentran y dan un paseo por el parque. Charlan (Hablan) con otros jóvenes que conocen en el parque y hacen nuevos amigos. A veces alquilan (rentan) un bote y reman por el lago del parque.

También veremos en el parque a las personas que demostrarán su arte: caricaturistas que te dibujarán[3] en un momento; fotógrafos que te tomarán una foto; mimos y payasos que te van a hacer reír[4] y vendedores ambulantes vendiendo de todo: globos, dulces, refrescos, camisetas.

[1]recreo *recreation*
[2]se asustarán *they will be frightened*
[3]dibujarán *will draw*
[4]reír *laugh*

Parque de Chapultepec, Ciudad de México

Palermo, Buenos Aires, Argentina



## Learning from Photos

*(page 148 top)* This is Mexico City's most popular park. On Sunday afternoons it is filled with strollers and picnickers. *(page 148 bottom)* Palermo is the main park of Buenos Aires, Argentina.

## History Connection

Within the **Bosque de Chapultepec** in Mexico City is the **Castillo de Chapultepec.** During the nineteenth century it was the residence of the Emperor Maximilian. In the early 1500s the grounds of the park were the favorite gardens of the Aztec emperor Montezuma.

## ¿Comprendes?

**A En el parque** Contesten.

1. ¿Quiénes van a los parques en las ciudades hispanas?
2. ¿Cuándo van?
3. ¿Qué juegan los viejos?
4. ¿Qué compran los niños?
5. ¿Qué hay en el zoológico?
6. ¿Qué hay en el parque de atracciones?
7. ¿Qué hacen los jóvenes en el parque?
8. ¿Qué venden los vendedores ambulantes?

**B Personajes interesantes** Contesten.

1. ¿Qué hacen los caricaturistas?
2. ¿Qué hacen los mimos y los payasos?
3. ¿Qué hacen los fotógrafos?

Buenos Aires, Argentina

**C ¿Qué es?** Adivinen.

1. un tipo de helado que es en realidad hielo con sirope
2. cualquier lugar adonde va la gente a divertirse
3. un animal bastante gracioso o cómico
4. personas que andan por las calles o parques vendiendo cosas
5. lugar donde exhiben muchos animales
6. dos animales salvajes de la misma familia que el gato

Sevilla, España



## Lecturas culturales

### Learning from Photos

*(page 149 top)* You may wish to ask questions like these about this photo:

**¿Qué hace el hombre en el centro?**
**¿Cómo se viste él?**
**¿Por qué están el señor y la señora a cada lado del hombre?**

*(page 149 bottom)* You may wish to ask:

**¿Qué hace el hombre?**
**¿Qué edificio ves en la foto?**

### Geography Connection

The twelve-sided tower seen in the bottom photo is the **Torre del Oro.** It was built in 1220 and was used to close off the harbor by means of a chain stretched across the Guadalquivir to another tower, which is no longer in existence.

### Writing Development

You may wish to have some students write a summary of the **Lectura.**

**LEVELING**

**E:** Reading

## Answers to ¿Comprendes?

**A**

1. Los jóvenes y los viejos van a los parques en las ciudades hispanas.
2. Van especialmente los domingos.
3. Los viejos juegan (al) dominó.
4. Los niños compran helados o piraguas.
5. En el zoológico hay monos, leones y tigres.
6. En el parque de atracciones hay un tiovivo.
7. Los jóvenes se encuentran y dan un paseo por el parque. Charlan con otros jóvenes que conocen y hacen nuevos amigos. A veces alquilan un bote y reman por el lago del parque.
8. Los vendedores ambulantes venden de todo: globos, dulces, refrescos, camisetas.

**B**

1. Los caricaturistas dibujan a la gente.
2. Los mimos y los payasos hacen reír a la gente.
3. Los fotógrafos toman fotos de la gente.

**C**

1. una piragua
2. un parque
3. un mono
4. vendedores ambulantes
5. un (parque) zoológico
6. un león y un tigre

# Lectura opcional 1

## National Standards

**Cultures**
This reading and the related activities on this page familiarize students with game arcades and games, both traditional and modern, in Spanish-speaking countries.

**Comparisons**
In this selection students learn that, despite the advent of video games of the kind that are so popular in the United States, the time-honored game of table soccer remains for many Spanish-speaking teens the game of choice.

**¡OJO!** This reading is optional. You may skip it completely, have the entire class read it, have only several students read it and report to the class, or assign it for extra credit.

## PRESENTATION

**Step 1** You may tell students that if they are interested in video games or games such as dominos, they can read one of these selections and do the **¿Comprendes?** activities for extra credit.

## About the Spanish Language

Video games are called either **juegos de video** or **videojuegos.** Remember, in Spain the word is **vídeo** with an accent on the **í,** while in Latin America it is **video** with the stress on the **e.**

# Lectura opcional 1

El futbolín

## Las salas de juegos

Las salas de juegos son muy populares en muchos países hispanos. No son nuevas. Hace muchos años que los jóvenes van a las salas de juegos para jugar al tenis de mesa y al futbolín.

Hoy las salas tienen los más modernos juegos de video. Los jóvenes meten una moneda en la ranura. Pulsan un botón y salen en la pantalla monstruos, guerras intergalácticas y carreras de automóviles. Color, sonido, moción. Para los juegos de video se necesita buena coordinación de ojo y mano y excelentes reflejos[1].

Pero de todos los juegos antiguos y modernos, el juego que les gusta mucho a los jóvenes hispanos es el futbolín. Pueden jugar dos o cuatro y hasta seis muchachos a la vez. El juego es sencillo (fácil). Hay que meter el baloncito en la portería opuesta[2]. Los jugadores humanos mueven los jugadores de madera[3] o plástico para lanzar o bloquear el balón. Un partido entre buenos jugadores puede durar mucho tiempo.

[1]reflejos *reflexes* [2]opuesta *opposite* [3]madera *wood*

Una sala de juegos, Caracas, Venezuela

## ¿Comprendes?

**A ¿Qué es?** Describan.
1. el juego de video
2. el tenis de mesa
3. el futbolín

**B Las salas de juegos** Contesten.
1. ¿Dónde son populares las salas de juegos?
2. ¿A qué jugaban los jóvenes en las salas en el pasado?
3. ¿Qué juegos hay en las salas modernas que no había en las salas antiguas?
4. ¿Dónde salen los monstruos y las guerras intergalácticas?
5. ¿Qué tienes que tener para ser buen jugador de juegos de video?
6. ¿Cuáles son algunas características de los juegos de video?

**C El futbolín** Explica el objetivo del futbolín y cómo se juega.



## Answers to ¿Comprendes?

**A** *Answers will vary.*
1. un juego electrónico con una pantalla
2. el ping-pong o pimpón
3. un juego de fútbol con jugadores de madera que se mueven para meter el balón en la portería

**B**
1. Las salas de juegos son populares en muchos países hispanos.
2. En el pasado los jóvenes jugaban al tenis de mesa y al futbolín.
3. En las salas modernas hay juegos de video.
4. Los monstruos y las guerras intergalácticas salen en la pantalla.
5. Tienes que tener buena coordinación de ojo y mano y excelentes reflejos.
6. Color, sonido y moción son algunas características de los juegos de video.

**C** *Answers will vary, but students will use the reading as a guide.*

# Lectura opcional 2

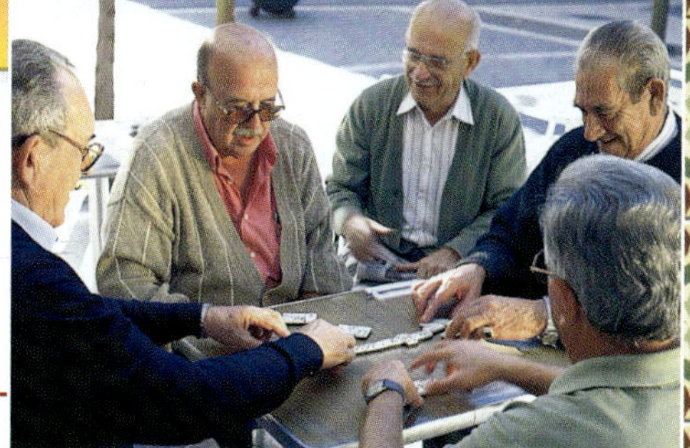
Estepona, España

## El dominó

El juego es antiguo. Jugaban al dominó en Venecia en el siglo XVIII. Las reglas[1] del juego son las mismas del siglo XVIII. Pero las veintiocho fichas modernas serán de plástico. Las antiguas eran de madera[2], o las más elegantes de marfil[3].

En las plazas de pueblos y ciudades en todo el mundo hispano podemos oír el «cli, cli» de las fichas que los jugadores golpean contra la mesa. Grupos de jugadores pasan horas jugando partida tras partida de dominó. Alrededor de la mesa siempre hay un grupo de «mirones».

Pero, ¿quiénes son los jugadores? Generalmente son señores mayores. Todos los días van a las mismas mesas, a la misma hora, con los mismos compañeros. Los señores son muy serios. Y juegan casi siempre sin expresión en la cara. Para ellos, el dominó es más que un pasatiempo, es un rito[4].

[1]reglas *rules*
[2]madera *wood*
[3]marfil *ivory*
[4]rito *ritual*

### ¿Comprendes?

**A El dominó** Completen.

1. El dominó es un juego muy ____.
2. En Venecia jugaban al dominó en el siglo ____.
3. Las ____ para jugar al dominó son las mismas del siglo XVIII.
4. Hay ____ fichas en el dominó.
5. Las fichas más elegantes eran de ____.
6. Las fichas modernas generalmente son de ____.
7. Los jugadores ____ las fichas contra la mesa.
8. Los jugadores se sientan a la mesa y los ____ están de pie alrededor de la mesa.
9. Los jugadores generalmente son señores ____.
10. Ellos son muy ____; no tienen ____ en la cara.

**B Los mirones** La lectura habla de «los mirones». ¿Sabes quiénes son?



# Lectura opcional 2

## National Standards

**Cultures**
This reading and the related activities on this page familiarize students with the popularity of the game of dominos in Spanish-speaking countries.

**Comparisons**
In this selection students learn that, unlike in the United States where dominos is regarded for the most part as a child's game, in Spanish-speaking countries it is played chiefly by adults in a very competitive fashion.

**¡OJO!** This reading is optional. You may skip it completely, have the entire class read it, have only several students read it and report to the class, or assign it for extra credit.

## About the Spanish Language

Both **partido** and **partida** mean a game or a match. However, **un partido** is a sports competition, **un partido de fútbol**, for example, while **una partida** is a match or game of chess, checkers, dominos, or a similar, nonathletic pastime.

**LEVELING**
**A:** Reading 1
**C:** Reading 2

### Answers to ¿Comprendes?

**A**
1. antiguo
2. XVIII
3. reglas
4. veintiocho
5. marfil
6. plástico
7. golpean
8. mirones
9. mayores
10. serios, expresión

**B** *Answers will vary. Students will use the reading and their personal opinions to answer the question.*

## National Standards

**Connections**

This reading about literary genres and their characteristics establishes a connection with another discipline, allowing students to reinforce and further their knowledge of literature and the arts through the study of Spanish.

**¡OJO!** The readings in the **Conexiones** section are optional. They focus on some of the major disciplines taught in schools and universities. The vocabulary is useful for discussing such topics as history, literature, art, economics, business, science, etc. You may choose any of the following ways to do the readings in the **Conexiones** sections.

**Independent reading** Have students read the selections and do the post-reading activities as homework, which you collect. This option is least intrusive on class time and requires a minimum of teacher involvement.

**Homework with in-class follow-up** Assign the readings and post-reading activities as homework. Review and discuss the material in class the next day.

**Intensive in-class activity** This option includes a pre-reading vocabulary presentation, in-class reading and discussion, assignment of the activities for homework, and a discussion of the assignment in class the following day.

# Conexiones

## *Las bellas artes*

### La literatura

The literary genres that we learn about in our English classes are the same ones that students in Spain and Latin America study: the novel, the short story, and poetry. People everywhere enjoy reading for pleasure. It is a very worthwhile pastime during one's leisure hours.

Casa de García Lorca, Granada, España

### Los géneros literarios

La literatura les interesa a los jóvenes y a los viejos. Hay personas que pasan horas leyendo novelas, cuentos y poesía.

**La novela**

La novela es una obra[1] literaria en prosa bastante larga que narra eventos ficticios. La primera novela importante en español es *El Quijote* (1605), obra de Miguel de Cervantes. Hay diferentes tipos de novela. Hay novelas de amor y novelas de aventura. Hoy las novelas policíacas y las novelas de ciencia-ficción son especialmente populares.

Isabel Allende, novelista chilena

**El cuento**

El cuento, como la novela, es una narración de eventos ficticios. Pero el cuento es mucho más corto que la novela. El cuento, igual que la novela, tiene uno o más protagonistas. El protagonista es el personaje más importante de la obra. El argumento es una narración de lo que pasa o lo que sucede en la novela o en el cuento.

[1]obra *work*



## Learning from Photos

*(page 152 top)* Federico García Lorca is considered one of Spain's greatest poets and playwrights. He was killed at the outbreak of the Spanish Civil War in 1936. *(page 152 bottom)* Isabel Allende is the author of a number of best-sellers, including ***La casa de los espíritus*** and ***Eva Luna.*** She is related to Salvador Allende, the former President of Chile, who was killed during a military coup.

**La poesía**

El cuento y la novela son obras en prosa. La prosa es el tipo de lenguaje que la gente usa en su habla diaria. La poesía, los poemas, son obras en verso, no en prosa. El poeta usa imágenes, métrica, ritmo y sonidos[2] para crear una reacción emocional en la persona que lee el poema.

A la gente de habla española le gusta mucho la poesía. Muchas veces, en una fiesta familiar, alguien se levanta y recita un poema. Y no es raro encontrar a un dentista o a una profesora que es también poeta.

[2]sonidos *sounds*

**A La literatura** Contesten.

1. ¿Cuáles son tres géneros literarios?
2. ¿Qué escribió Miguel de Cervantes?
3. ¿Cuáles son cuatro tipos de novela?
4. ¿Cuál es la mayor diferencia entre una novela y un cuento?
5. ¿Qué recitan algunas personas en fiestas familiares?

**B ¿Verso o prosa?** Digan si es verso o prosa.

1. una poesía
2. un poema lírico
3. una novela de ciencia-ficción
4. un cuento corto
5. un poema épico
6. un artículo de periódico

**C Un cuento** Vas a escribir un cuento. Para escribir el cuento, haz lo siguiente.

- **Protagonista** El o la protagonista es el personaje más importante del cuento. Le vas a dar un nombre y explicar quién es. Tienes que describir a tu protagonista. Explica cómo es físicamente y da algunos detalles sobre su personalidad.
- **Lugar o ambiente** Tienes que indicar de dónde es el o la protagonista. Indica también dónde tiene lugar la acción de tu cuento. Es necesario dar una descripción del lugar. Puedes describir la casa del protagonista, su pueblo o su ciudad. Incluye todo lo necesario o importante para el desarrollo *(development)* de la acción de tu cuento.
- **Argumento** Di lo que hace el o la protagonista. Escribe todo lo que sucede. Explica a los lectores (a los que leen tu cuento) cómo es la actuación del (de la) protagonista.
- **Desenlace** Explica lo que pasa al final y cómo termina la acción.



# Conexiones

## PRESENTATION

## *Las bellas artes*

### La literatura

**Step 1** Although this material is optional, you may wish to go over it with all students. This information will be beneficial to them in their future study of Spanish.

**Step 2** Ask students if they read the story about ***El Quijote*** in **¡Buen viaje! Level 1.** Call on students to tell as much as they remember about the story.

**¿Comprendes?**

**A and B** Quickly go over these activities with the class.

**C** You may wish to give students time in class to write their short story, or you may have them write it at home. If they write it at home, it is suggested that you tell them not to use a bilingual dictionary because, more often than not, they will choose the wrong word. Tell them to use only words they know, and if once in a while they must use an unknown word, tell them to leave a space and you will fill it in.

**LEVELING**

**E:** Reading

**A:** Reading

## Answers to ¿Comprendes?

**A**

1. Tres géneros literarios son la novela, el cuento y la poesía.
2. Escribió *El Quijote.*
3. Cuatro tipos de novela son la novela de amor, la novela de aventura, la novela policíaca y la novela de ciencia-ficción.
4. El cuento es mucho más corto que la novela.
5. Recitan un poema.

**B**

1. verso
2. verso
3. prosa
4. prosa
5. verso
6. prosa

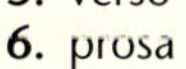

**C** *Answers will vary. Students should follow the guidelines provided.*

# ¡Te toca a ti!

## Use what you have learned

### 1 PREPARATION

**Bellringer Review**

*Use BRR Transparency 5.6 or write the following on the board.*
Write four time expressions associated with the future. Use each one in an original sentence.

### Recycling

These activities allow students to use the vocabulary and structure from this chapter in completely open-ended, real-life situations.

### 2 PRESENTATION

Encourage students to say as much as possible when they do these activities. Tell them not to be afraid to make mistakes, since the goal of the activities is real-life communication. If someone in the group makes an error, allow the others to politely correct him or her. Let students choose the activities they would like to do.

You may wish to divide students into pairs or groups. Encourage students to elaborate on the basic theme and to be creative. They may use props, pictures, or posters if they wish.

### 3 PRACTICE

1 You may wish to have one of the groups who did Activity 1 present their plans to the class.

2 One of the groups can present their conversation to the class.

4 Have students share with the class the events they have planned. The others can give their opinions about the plans.

5 Have students edit each other's e-mail messages.



# ¡Te toca a ti!

## Use what you have learned

### El parque de atracciones

*✔ Describe an amusement park*

Con un(a) compañero(a), miren este anuncio para un parque de atracciones. Discutan sus planes para visitar el parque. Decidan cuándo irán, cómo llegarán y lo que verán.

Buenos Aires, Argentina

### A un restaurante

*✔ Talk about a forthcoming visit to a restaurant*

Vas a estar libre el viernes por la noche. Quieres ir a un restaurante. Llama a un(a) amigo(a) por teléfono para ver si él o ella quiere ir también. Dile a tu amigo(a) a qué restaurante irás, lo que pedirás, si tomarás postre, cuánto costará, etc. Explica a tu amigo(a) como es que conoces el restaurante y por qué te gusta tanto que volverás a comer allí.

### Mis pasatiempos favoritos

*✔ Talk about your favorite pastimes*

Trabaja con un(a) compañero(a) de clase. Discutan sus pasatiempos favoritos. Decidan si tienen muchos intereses en común.

### Writing Development

Have students keep a notebook or portfolio containing their best written work from each chapter. These selected writings can be based on assignments from the Student Textbook and the Workbook. The activities on page 155 are examples of writing assignments that may be included in each student's portfolio. On page 59 in the Workbook, students will begin to develop an organized autobiography **(Mi autobiografía).** These workbook pages may also become a part of their portfolio.

### Answers to ¡Te toca a ti!

1 *Answers will vary. Students will use the vocabulary from* Palabras 2 *as well as the visuals as a guide.*

2 *Answers will vary. Students will use structures and vocabulary previously learned in the chapter.*

3 *Answers will vary but will include the vocabulary from this chapter.*

## El programa de actividades escolares

*✔ Describe extra curricular school activities*

Tú y dos compañeros de la clase de español son miembros de un comité que hace los planes para todas las actividades de su escuela. Escriban una lista de todos los eventos que están planeando para el próximo año escolar.

## Los pasatiempos de tu comunidad

*✔ Describe recreational activities in your community*

Prepara un e-mail para una alumna española que viene a tu escuela el semestre que viene. Pregúntale cuáles son los pasatiempos que le interesan; dile también lo que hay en tu comunidad para pasar el tiempo libre.

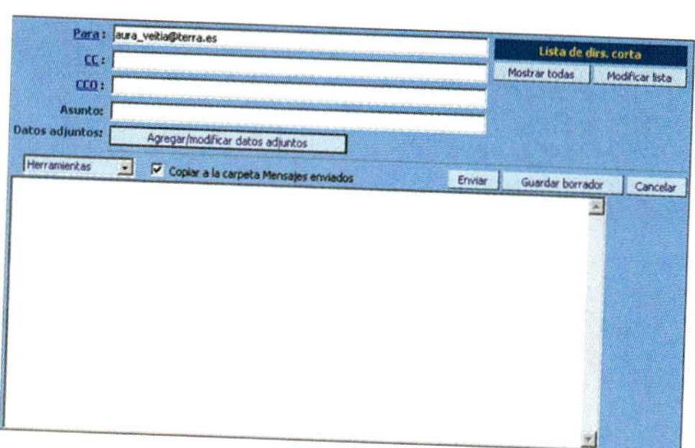


### Writing Strategy

**Writing about dreams and wishes—the future** To imagine the future, it is helpful to look at yourself as you are now. One way to do that is to use clusters to record your likes, interests, feelings, and reactions and how they relate to one another. These connections may help you learn more about yourself and help you see yourself years from now as you begin to think about the future. You can also use clusters to evaluate things as they are now and how you think they will be in the future. Evaluating these changes may help you understand how changes in the world may affect the way your own personal dreams are fulfilled.

## Algunas predicciones para el futuro

You're going to write a composition called **Algunas predicciones para el futuro.** First choose some topics to include in your predictions, such as transportation, family, hobbies and leisure-time activities, communication, education, medicine and hygiene, home, and vacation. If you want you can even predict your own future. Then prepare two lists: one titled **El presente** and the other titled **El futuro.** For each topic describe what it is like now and what you think it will be like in the future. When you finish the two lists, write your composition using the information from the lists.

### Writing Strategy

**Writing about dreams and wishes—the future** Have students read the Writing Strategy on page 155. Since their essays will cover a variety of areas, encourage students to use as much vocabulary as possible from what they have learned so far in their study of Spanish.

### About the Spanish Language

Several terms are used to describe the regions and peoples of the Americas south of the United States. The most common are **Latinoamérica** and **latinoamericanos.** Some Spanish speakers feel that this is too broad, since it includes Portuguese-speaking Brazil and French-speaking Haiti and Martinique. **Iberoamérica** and **iberoamericanos** exclude the French speakers but still include Brazil. **Hispanoamérica** and **hispanoamericanos** would be the appropriate terms for just the Spanish-speaking countries of the Americas and their people.

### Answers to ¡Te toca a ti!

4. *Answers will vary, but students will use the future tense.*
5. *Answers will vary, but students will use the vocabulary from the chapter.*
6. *Answers will vary. Students will use the vocabulary and structure previously learned in this chapter.*

### LEVELING

These activities encompass all three levels. All students will be able to do them at a sophistication level commensurate with their ability in Spanish. Some students will be able to speak for several minutes, and others may be able to give just a few sentences. This is to be expected when students are functioning completely on their own generating their own language to the best of their ability.

Assessment

## Resource Manager

Communication Transparency C 5
Quizzes, pages 22–25
Performance Assessment, Task 5
Tests, pages 69–82
Situation Cards, Chapter 5
**Maratón mental** Videoquiz, Chapter 5
ExamView® Pro, Chapter 5

## Assessment

This is a pre-test for students to take before you administer the chapter test. Note that each section is cross-referenced so students can easily find the material they have to review in case they made errors. You may use Assessment Answers Transparency A 5 to do the assessment in class, or you may assign this assessment for homework. You can correct the assessment yourself, or you may prefer to project the answers on the overhead in class.

## Glencoe Technology

### MINDJOGGER VHS/DVD

You may wish to help your students prepare for the chapter test by playing the MindJogger game show. Teams will compete against each other to review chapter vocabulary and structure and sharpen listening comprehension skills.

Assessment

# Vocabulario

To review **Palabras 1**, turn to pages 132–133.

### 1 Identifiquen.

1.  
2. 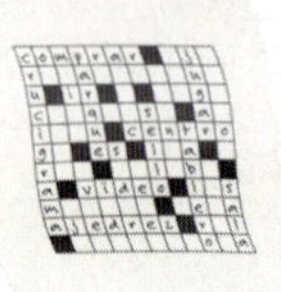
3. 
4. 

### 2 Completen.

5. Los jóvenes ____ el bote por el lago.
6. Hay muchos animales en un ____.
7. Los monos y los tigres están en ____.
8. El ____ es muy cómico.
9. La gente camina por las sendas del parque. Ellos dan un ____.

To review **Palabras 2**, turn to pages 136–137.

### 3 Identifiquen.

## Answers to Assessment

**1**
1. el ajedrez
2. un crucigrama
3. el tablero
4. una sala de juegos

**2**
5. reman
6. zoológico
7. jaulas
8. payaso
9. paseo

**3**
10. la noria
11. el globo
12. una piragua

# Estructura

**4** Escriban en el futuro.

13. Ellos estudian para sus exámenes.
14–15. Él lee la novela. No la escribe.
16. Yo contesto la carta.
17. ¿Ves la emisión deportiva en la televisión?
18. Hablamos con él.

To review the future tense, turn to page 140.

**5** Completen.

19. Elena es muy simpática. Yo creo que ella es ____ simpática ____ todas mis amigas.
20. Él no es muy alto. Pero es ____ alto ____ su hermano. La verdad es que su hermano es muy bajo.
21. Él es un alumno bastante bueno pero no es ____ de la clase.
22. Mi hermana tiene quince años y yo tengo diecisiete. Yo soy ____ mi hermana.

To review the comparative and the superlative, turn to page 144.

# Cultura

**6** Contesten.

23. ¿Qué tienen casi todas las ciudades hispanas?
24. ¿Qué hacen los jóvenes en el parque?
25. ¿Qué venden los vendedores ambulantes?

To review this cultural information, turn to page 148.

## Assessment

**FOLDABLES™ Study Organizer** Dinah Zike's Study Guides

Your students may wish to use Foldable 12 to organize, display, and arrange data as they learn to describe cultural events. You may wish to encourage them to add information from each chapter as they continue to watch movies in Spanish.

A *project board with tabs* foldable is also ideal for having students illustrate and describe scenes from other events that they will be learning about.

## Answers to Assessment

**4**

13. estudiarán
14. leerá
15. escribirá
16. contestaré
17. Verás
18. Hablaremos

**5**

19. la más, de
20. más, que
21. el mejor
22. mayor que

**6**

23. parques
24. Ellos se encuentran y dan un paseo por el parque. Charlan con otros jóvenes que conocen y hacen nuevos amigos. A veces alquilan un bote y reman por el lago del parque.
25. Venden de todo: globos, dulces, refrescos, camisetas.

# ¡Hablo como un pro!

This unique page gives students the opportunity to speak freely and say whatever they can, using the vocabulary and structures they have learned in the chapter. The illustration serves to remind students of precisely what they know how to say in Spanish. There are no activities that students do not have the ability to describe or talk about in Spanish. The art not only depicts the vocabulary and content of this chapter, but also reinforces what they learned in previous chapters.

You may wish to use this page in many ways. Some possibilities are to have students do the following:

1. Look at the illustration and identify items by giving the correct Spanish words.
2. Make up sentences about what they see in the illustration.
3. Make up questions about the illustration. They can call on another class member to respond if you do this as a class activity, or you may prefer to allow students to work in small groups. This activity is extremely beneficial because it enables students to actively use interrogative words.
4. Answer questions you ask them about the illustration.
5. Work in pairs and make up a conversation based on the illustration.
6. Look at the illustration and give a complete oral review of what they see.
7. Look at the illustration and write a paragraph (or essay) about it.

You can also use this page as an assessment or testing tool, taking into account individual differences by having students go from simple to quite complicated tasks. The assessment can be either oral or written. You may wish to use the rubrics provided on pages T20–T21 as you give students the following directions.

1. Identify the topic or situation of the illustration.
2. Give the Spanish words for as many items as you can.
3. Think of as many sentences as you can to describe the illustration.
4. Go over your sentences and put them in the best sequencing to give a coherent story based on the illustration.

¡Hablo como un pro!

Tell all you can about this illustration.

# Vocabulario

### Talking about pastimes and hobbies

| | |
|---|---|
| el pasatiempo | el campeón |
| el hobby | la campeona |
| el ajedrez | la sala de juegos |
| el tablero | el juego de video |
| las damas | el futbolín |
| el dominó | pasar el tiempo |
| la ficha | coleccionar sellos (monedas) |
| el/la coleccionista | llenar un crucigrama |

### Talking about activities in the park

| | |
|---|---|
| el parque | el caballito |
| el bote | la montaña rusa |
| el (parque) zoológico | la noria |
| el mono | el mimo |
| la jaula | el payaso |
| la boletería | el globo |
| el parque de atracciones | el helado |
| el tiovivo | la piragua |

### Discussing what one does in the park

dar un paseo
caminar por la senda
remar por el lago
hacer cola

### Giving location

delante de
detrás de
al lado de
a la derecha
a la izquierda

### Other useful expressions

listo(a)
la fila
la entrada

**How well do you know your vocabulary?**

- Choose words to describe a visit to a park.
- Write a brief description of a recent visit to a local park.

**VIDEOTUR**

## Episodio 5

In this video episode, you will join Francisco and Alejandra as they spend free time in the park. See page 484 for more information.

# Vocabulario

## Vocabulary Review

The words and phrases in the **Vocabulario** have been taught for productive use in this chapter. They are summarized here as a resource for both student and teacher. This list also serves as a convenient resource for the **¡Te toca a ti!** activities on pages 154 and 155. There are approximately six cognates in this vocabulary list. Have students find them.

**¡OJO!** You will notice that the vocabulary list here is not translated. This has been done intentionally, since we feel that by the time students have finished the material in the chapter they should be familiar with the meanings of all the words. If there are several words they still do not know, we recommend that they refer to the **Palabras 1** and **2** sections in the chapter or go to the dictionaries at the end of this book to find the meanings. However, if you prefer that your students have the English translations, please refer to Vocabulary Transparency 5.1, where you will find all these words with their translations.

**VIDEO VHS/DVD**

The Video Program allows students to see how the chapter vocabulary and structures are used by native speakers within an engaging story line. For maximum reinforcement, show the video episode as a final activity for Chapter 5.

# Planning for Chapter 6

## SCOPE AND SEQUENCE, PAGES 160–189

### Topics

- ❖ Hotel terminology

### Culture

- ❖ Inns (paradors) in Spain
- ❖ Youth hostels in the Spanish-speaking world
- ❖ Hotel de la Reconquista, Oviedo, Spain
- ❖ Physical fitness

### Functions

- ❖ How to check into and out of a hotel
- ❖ How to ask for things you need at a hotel
- ❖ How to express future actions
- ❖ How to refer to previously mentioned people or things

### Structure

- ❖ Irregular verbs in the future
- ❖ Indirect and direct object pronouns in the same sentence

### National Standards

- ❖ Communication Standard 1.1 pages 164, 165, 168, 169, 171, 172, 173, 174, 175, 177, 184
- ❖ Communication Standard 1.2 pages 165, 169, 173, 176, 177, 178–179, 180, 181, 182–183, 184
- ❖ Communication Standard 1.3 pages 177, 185
- ❖ Cultures Standard 2.2 pages 178–179, 180, 181
- ❖ Connections Standard 3.1 pages 182–183
- ❖ Connections Standard 3.2 page 181
- ❖ Comparisons Standard 4.2 pages 178–179
- ❖ Communities Standard 5.1 page 189
- ❖ Communities Standard 5.2 page 170

## PACING AND PRIORITIES

**The chapter content is color coded below to assist you in planning.**

**■ required ■ recommended ■ optional**

**Vocabulario** *(required)* *Days 1–4*

- ■ Palabras 1
  - La llegada al hotel
  - La salida del hotel
- ■ Palabras 2
  - En el cuarto
  - En el baño

**Estructura** *(required)* *Days 5–7*

- ■ Futuro de los verbos irregulares
- ■ **Me lo, te lo, nos lo**

**Conversación** *(required)*

- ■ La llegada al hotel

**Lecturas culturales**

- ■ Los paradores de España *(recommended)*
- ■ Los albergues *(optional)*

**Conexiones**

- ■ El ejercicio *(optional)*

■ **¡Te toca a ti!** *(recommended)*

■ **Assessment** *(recommended)*

■ **¡Hablo como un pro!** *(optional)*

## RESOURCE GUIDE

| SECTION | PAGES | SECTION RESOURCES |
|---|---|---|
| **Vocabulario PALABRAS 1** | | |
| La llegada al hotel<br>La salida del hotel | 162–165<br>163–165 | Vocabulary Transparencies 6.2–6.3<br>Audio CD 4<br>Audio Activities TE, pages 64–65<br>Workbook, pages 61–62<br>Quiz 1, page 26<br>ExamView® Pro |
| **Vocabulario PALABRAS 2** | | |
| En el cuarto<br>En el baño | 166, 168–169<br>167, 168–169 | Vocabulary Transparencies 6.4–6.5<br>Audio CD 4<br>Audio Activities TE, pages 66–67<br>Workbook, pages 63–64<br>Quiz 2, page 27<br>ExamView® Pro |
| **Estructura** | | |
| Futuro de los verbos irregulares<br>**Me lo, te lo, nos lo** | 170–173<br>173–175 | Audio CD 4<br>Audio Activities TE, pages 67–69<br>Workbook, pages 65–67<br>Quizzes 3–4, pages 28–29<br>ExamView® Pro |
| **Conversación** | | |
| La llegada al hotel | 176–177 | Audio CD 4<br>Audio Activities TE, pages 69–70<br>Interactive CD-ROM |
| **Lecturas culturales** | | |
| Los paradores de España<br>Los albergues<br>El Hotel de la Reconquista | 178–179<br>180<br>181 | Audio CD 4<br>Audio Activities TE, page 71<br>Tests, pages 86, 89 |
| **Conexiones** | | |
| El ejercicio | 182–183 | Tests, page 90 |
| **¡Te toca a ti!** | | |
| | 184–185 | **¡Viva el mundo hispano!** Video, Episode 6<br>Video Activities, pages 84–87<br>Spanish Online Activities spanish.glencoe.com |
| **Assessment** | | |
| | 186–187 | Communication Transparency C 6<br>Quizzes 1–4, pages 26–29<br>Performance Assessment, Task 6<br>Tests, pages 83–96<br>Situation Cards, Chapter 6<br>ExamView® Pro<br>**Maratón mental** Videoquiz |

# Using Your Resources for Chapter 6

## Transparencies

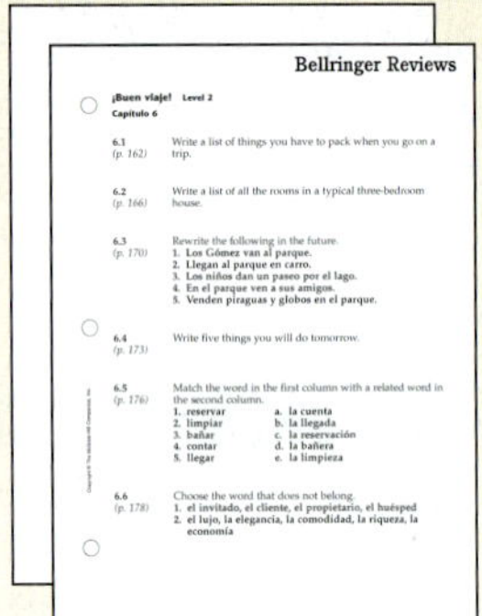
Bellringer 6.1–6.6

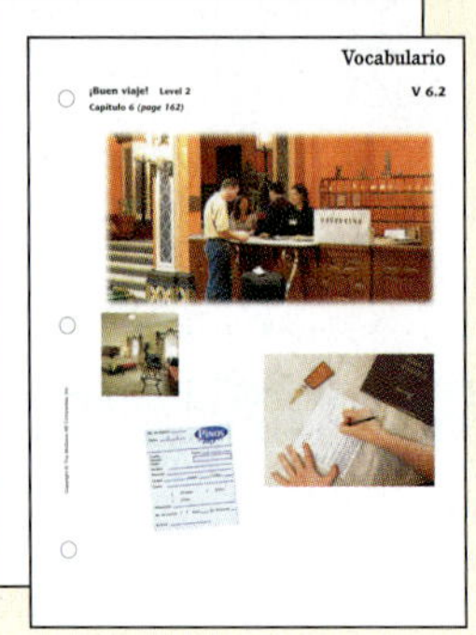
Vocabulary 6.1–6.5

Communication C 6

## Workbook

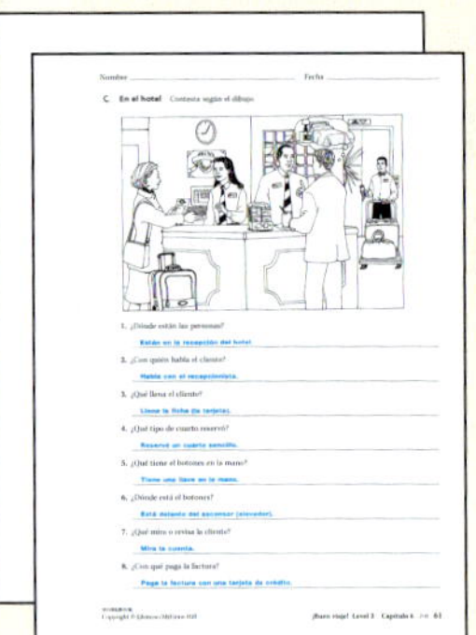
Vocabulary, pages 61–64

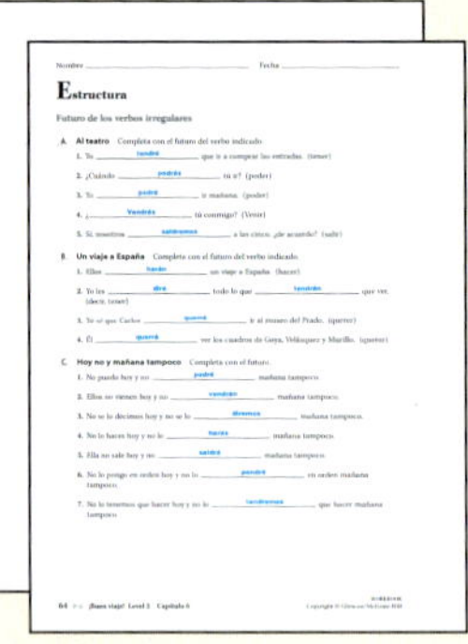
Structure, pages 65–67

Enrichment, pages 68–72

## Audio Activities

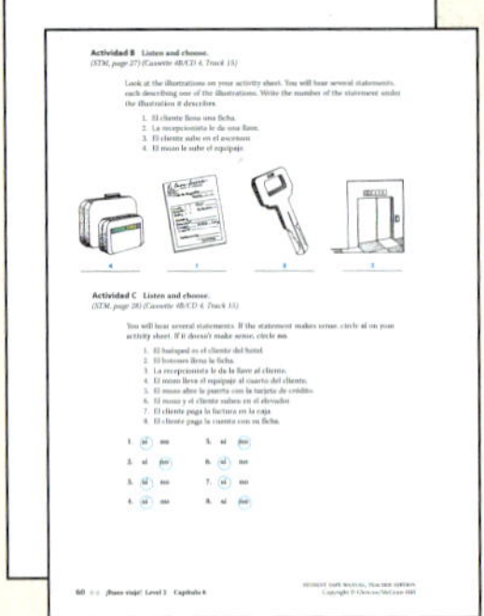
Vocabulary, pages 64–67

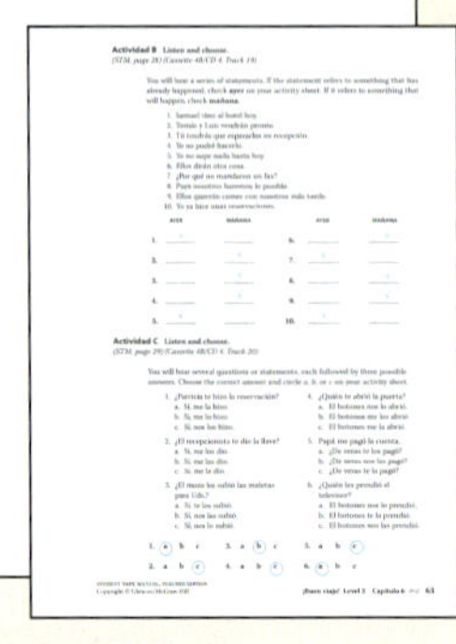
Structure, pages 67–69

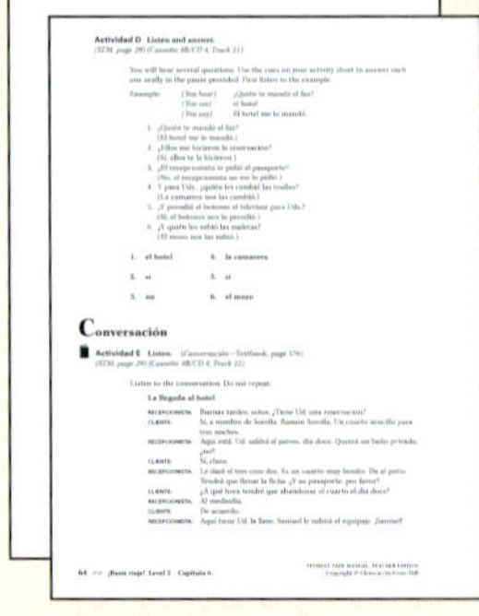
Conversation, pages 69–71

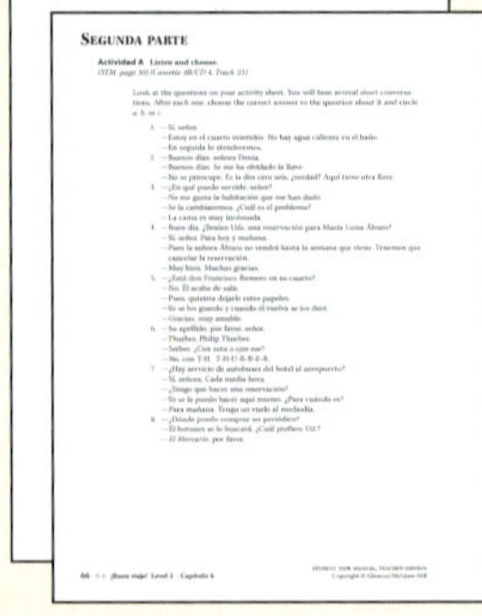
Additional Practice, pages 72–76

# Assessment

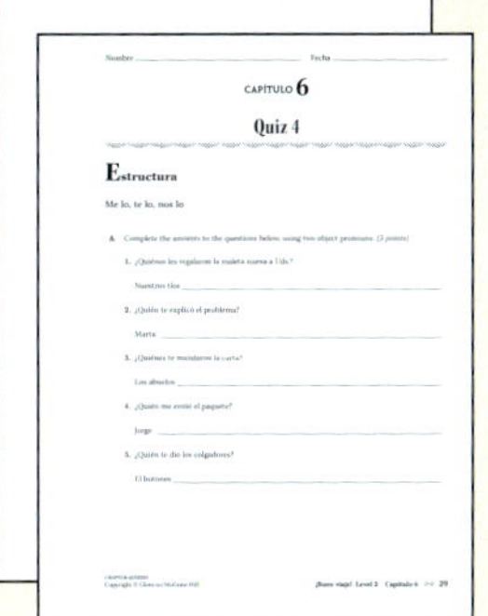
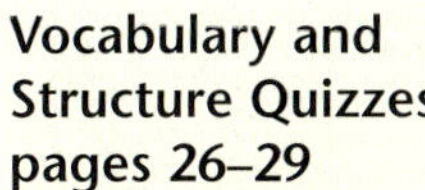

Vocabulary and Structure Quizzes, pages 26–29

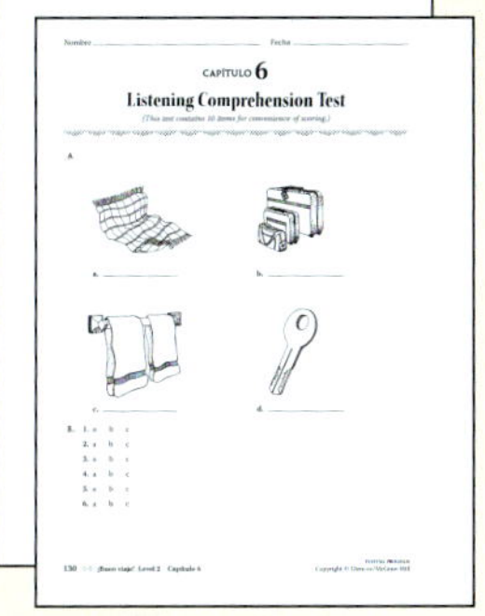

Chapter Tests, pages 83–96

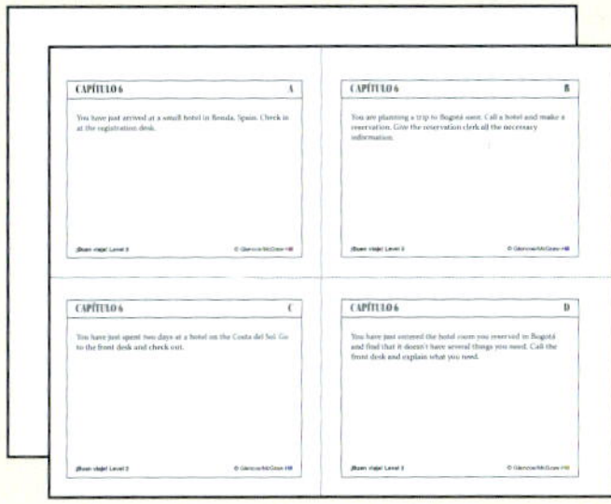

Situation Cards, Chapter 6

MindJogger Videoquiz, ExamView® Pro, Chapter 6

## Timesaving Teacher Tools

### TeacherWorks™

TeacherWorks™ is your all-in-one teacher resource center. Personalize lesson plans, access resources from the Teacher Wraparound Edition, connect to the Internet, or make a to-do list. These are only a few of the many features that can assist you in the planning and organizing of your lessons.

Includes:

- A calendar feature
- Access to all program blackline masters
- Standards correlations and more

### ExamView® Pro

Test Bank software for Macintosh and Windows makes creating, editing, customizing, and printing tests quick and easy.

## Technology Resources

In the Chapter 6 Internet Activity, you will have a chance to learn more about the Spanish-speaking world. Visit spanish.glencoe.com

On the interactive CD–ROM, students can listen to and take part in a recorded version of the conversation in Chapter 6.

**¡Viva el mundo hispano!** Video and Video Activities, Chapter 6. Available on VHS and DVD.

Help your students prepare for the chapter test by playing the **Maratón mental** Videoquiz game show. Teams will compete against each other to review chapter vocabulary and structure and sharpen listening comprehension skills. Available on VHS and DVD.

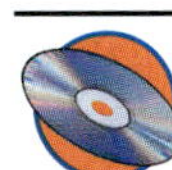

**¡Buen viaje!** is also available on CD or Online.

# Preview

In this chapter, students will learn vocabulary associated with making a hotel reservation, checking in and out, identifying features of a hotel room, and requesting various hotel services. They will continue to narrate in the future and to talk about people and things already mentioned. The cultural focus of the chapter is on the different types of hotel accommodations available in the Spanish-speaking world.

## National Standards

### Communication

In Chapter 6 students will learn to communicate in spoken and written Spanish on the following topics:

- making a reservation and checking into and out of a hotel
- requesting various hotel services
- discussing basic hotel features and facilities

Students will obtain and provide information about these topics and engage in conversations that would typically take place in a hotel as they fulfill the chapter objectives listed on this page.

### LEVELING

The activities, conversations, and readings within each chapter are marked according to level of difficulty. E indicates easy. A indicates average. C indicates challenging. Some activities cover a range of difficulty. In some activities, for example, advanced students will be able to produce more extensive responses while students who learn at a different rate may give less detailed responses. The leveling indicators will help you individualize instruction to best meet your students' needs.



Capítulo 6

# En el hotel

## Objetivos

**In this chapter you will learn to:**

- check into and out of a hotel
- ask for things you may need while at a hotel
- talk about future events
- refer to previously mentioned people or things
- talk about lodging in the Hispanic world

José Agustín Arrieta *View of the Patio*

## Spotlight on Culture

**Arte** José Agustín Arrieta (1803–1874) was a 19th Century Mexican painter. Arrieta is known for his still lifes and **costumbrista** works. The word **costumbrista** refers to art or literature that focuses on regional customs and traditions.

**Fotografía** You may wish to ask these questions about the photo of the **Hotel Residencia La Casa Grande** in Guatemala City:

**¿Está el hotel en una ci udad o en el campo?**
**¿Cuántos pisos tiene el hotel?**
**¿Es un hotel muy moderno o de estilo tradicional?**

# Vocabulario

PALABRAS 1

## 1 PREPARATION

### Resource Manager

Vocabulary Transparencies 6.2–6.3
Audio Activities TE, pages 64–65
Audio CD 4
Workbook, pages 61–62
Quizzes, page 26
ExamView® Pro

### Bellringer Review

*Use BRR Transparency 6.1 or write the following on the board.*
Write a list of things you have to pack when you go on a trip.

## 2 PRESENTATION

**Step 1** Have students close their books. Present **Palabras 1** by using Vocabulary Transparencies 6.2–6.3. Lead students through the new vocabulary by asking: **¿Qué es esto?** or **¿Quién es?** Model the response and have students repeat after you. For example: **¿Qué es? Es un hotel.**

**Step 2** Now have students open their books and repeat in unison as you model the entire **Palabras 1** vocabulary or play Audio CD 4.

### FUN FACTS

When checking into a hotel in Spain and other countries you are required to leave your passport at the desk. Passport information is then submitted to the police.

# Vocabulario

PALABRAS 1

## La llegada al hotel

Diego ya reservó un cuarto.
Reservó un cuarto sencillo, no un cuarto doble.

el cuarto, la habitación

Diego llena la ficha.

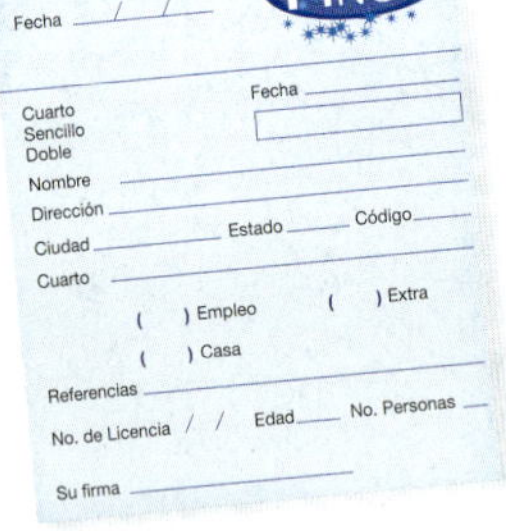

No. de Registro
Fecha / /
PINOS
Cuarto
Sencillo
Doble
Fecha
Nombre
Dirección
Ciudad Estado Código
Cuarto
( ) Empleo ( ) Extra
( ) Casa
Referencias
No. de Licencia / / Edad No. Personas
Su firma

la ficha,
la tarjeta



## Reaching All Students

**Total Physical Response** Set up places in the classroom in order to create a hotel. You might use a room key and a small suitcase as props

*(Student 1)* **y** *(Student 2)*, **vengan ustedes, por favor.**
*(Student 1)*, **llegas al hotel.**
*(Student 2)*, **eres el / la recepcionista.**
*(Student 1)*, **ve a la recepción. Pide una habitación.**
*(Student 2)*, **dale la ficha.**
*(Student 1)*, **llena la ficha.**
**Dale la ficha al / a la recepcionista.**
*(Student 2)*, **dale la llave al / a la cliente.**
*(Student 1)*, **toma tu equipaje. Sube la escalera.**
**Gracias,** *(Student 1)* **y** *(Student 2)*.

el ascensor, el elevador

el botones, el mozo

El mozo le subirá el equipaje.
Subirá el equipaje en el ascensor.

El mozo le abrirá la puerta al cliente.
Él le pondrá el equipaje en el cuarto.

## La salida del hotel

Diego saldrá del hotel hoy.
Tendrá que abandonar el cuarto antes del mediodía.

Él pedirá la cuenta y la pagará en la caja.
Pagará su factura con una tarjeta de crédito.



# Vocabulario

**Step 3** Project Vocabulary Transparencies 6.2–6.3 again. Ask for volunteers to read the new words or phrases from their books in random order while other volunteers go to the screen and point out the corresponding images.

**Step 4** Make *true / false* statements about the material and have students respond. For example: **La recepción está en el jardín del hotel. (falso) La recepción está en el pasillo. (falso) El cliente llena la ficha. (verdad)**

**Teaching Tip**

For additional practice in *true / false* activities, have students correct false statements.

## About the Spanish Language

- The traditional term for *elevator* is **ascensor,** and that is the term used in Spain. The word **elevador** is more common in Latin America.
- A *bellhop* is often called a **botones.** The term comes from the rows of brass buttons on the uniforms of old-time bellboys.

## Chapter Projects

**Planes de viaje**

Have students plan hotel stays in different Hispanic cities. If possible have them collect, or provide them with, pictures and travel brochures of these places.

## Reaching All Students

**Total Physical Response**

*(Student 1),* **ven acá, por favor.**
**Tú eres un(a) turista. Estás en un hotel, delante de la puerta de tu habitación.**
**Toma tu llave.**
**Abre la puerta con la llave.**
**Toma tu equipaje.**
**Entra en la habitación.**
**Pon tu equipaje sobre la cama.**
**Cierra la puerta.**
**Mira bien la habitación.**
**Indica que estás contento(a) con la habitación.**
**Gracias,** *(Student 1).* **Bien hecho.**

**LEVELING**

**E:** Vocabulary

**A:** Vocabulary

# Vocabulario

## 3 PRACTICE

## ¿Qué palabra necesito?

**¡OJO!** When students are doing the **¿Qué palabra necesito?** activities, accept any answer that makes sense. The purpose of these activities is to have students use the new vocabulary. They are not factual recall activities. Thus, it is not necessary for students to remember specific factual information from the vocabulary presentation when answering. If you wish, have students use the visuals on this page as a stimulus, when possible.

**Historieta** Each time **Historieta** appears, it means that the answers to the activity form a short story. Encourage students to look at the title of the **Historieta,** since it can help them do the activity.

**1** Have students refer to the illustrations as you go over Activity 1.

**2** Go over this activity orally with books closed. Then have students read all the answers to the activity for reinforcement. **Expansion:** After going over Activity 2, have one or more students retell the story in their own words.

**3** Have students prepare the activity before going over it in class.

### Writing Development

Have students write out Activity 3 as though these were definitions in a dictionary. For example: **El / La recepcionista: la persona que saluda a los clientes y busca la reservación.** Have students put the entries in alphabetical order. This is a good copying exercise in disguise. As we know, many students do not copy accurately.



# Vocabulario

## ¿Qué palabra necesito?

**1** **¿Qué o quién será?** Identifiquen.

1. ¿Es una llave o una tarjeta de crédito?

2. ¿Es el mozo o el recepcionista?
3. ¿Es la caja o la recepción?

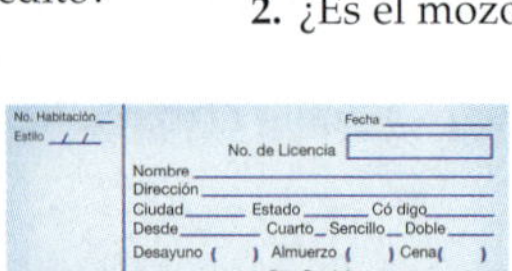

No. Habitación __
Estilo _/_/_
Fecha ____
No. de Licencia
Nombre ____
Dirección ____
Ciudad ___ Estado ___ Có digo ___
Desde ___ Cuarto _ Sencillo _ Doble ___
Desayuno ( ) Almuerzo ( ) Cena( )
( ) Otro Servicio
Desde ___ Hasta ___
Expiración _/_/_ Tarjeta de crédito ☐ Visa ☐ MC
PINOS

4. ¿Es la ficha o el equipaje?

Mantega una copia para su información
PINOS
392102130
Avenida sucursal de Los Pinos
Culiacán, México

| No. Habitación | Sencillo | Doble |
| --- | --- | --- |
| | | |

Nombre ____
Dirección ____

| No. de Licencia | Ciudad | Estado | Código |
| --- | --- | --- | --- |
| | | | |

Impuestos ___ Habitación ___
Extras ___ Comidas ___
Servicios ___
Tarjeta de Crédito ___ Total $ ___

5. ¿Es el equipaje o la cuenta?

**2** **Historieta Una visita al hotel**

Contesten.

1. ¿Reservó un cuarto el señor?
2. ¿Tiene él una reservación?
3. ¿Quién lo saludó en la recepción?
4. ¿Qué tendrá que llenar el señor?
5. ¿Quién le subirá el equipaje?
6. ¿Quién le abrirá la puerta?
7. ¿Cuándo tendrá que abandonar el cuarto el señor?
8. ¿Qué pedirá y dónde la pagará?
9. ¿Cómo pagará su cuenta el señor?

Fiesta Inn, Aguascalientes, México

**3** **¿Cómo se llama... ?** Identifiquen.

1. la persona que saluda a los clientes y busca la reservación
2. la persona que sube y baja las maletas
3. lo que se usa para abrir la puerta
4. un cuarto para una persona
5. un cuarto para dos personas
6. lo que se puede usar para pagar la cuenta
7. donde uno paga su cuenta

## ANSWERS TO ¿Qué palabra necesito?

1. Es una llave.
2. Es el mozo.
3. Es la recepción.
4. Es la ficha.
5. Es la cuenta.

**2**

1. Sí, el señor reservó un cuarto.
2. Sí, tiene una reservación.
3. El / La recepcionista lo saludó en la recepción.
4. El señor tendrá que llenar una ficha.
5. El mozo (botones) le subirá el equipaje.
6. El mozo (botones) le abrirá la puerta.
7. Tendrá que abandonar el cuarto antes del mediodía.
8. Pedirá la cuenta y pagará en la caja.
9. Pagará su cuenta con una tarjeta de crédito.

1. el / la recepcionista
2. el mozo (el botones)
3. la llave
4. un cuarto sencillo
5. un cuarto doble
6. una tarjeta de crédito
7. la caja

## 4 Historieta Al hotel

Contesten.

1. Cuando el cliente llega al hotel, ¿va primero a la caja?
2. ¿Lleva el mozo el equipaje al cuarto?
3. ¿Hay que llenar una ficha o tarjeta al llegar al hotel?
4. Un cuarto sencillo, ¿es para dos personas?
5. ¿Abandona el cuarto el cliente cuando llega al hotel?
6. Cuando uno paga la cuenta, ¿le da el dinero al botones?

Villa Real, Madrid, España

## 5 Una reservación

Tu clase de español está pensando en hacer un viaje a España. Todos están muy entusiasmados y todos tienen una tarea para ayudar a planear el viaje. Tú y un(a) compañero(a) tienen la responsabilidad de reservar las habitaciones (los cuartos). Van a llamar al Hotel Regente. Uno(a) de ustedes será el/la alumno(a) y el/la otro(a) será el/la empleado(a) del Hotel Regente. Discutan las fechas, el número de alumnos, el número de habitaciones, las comidas, los precios.

## 6 El huésped abandona su cuarto.

Eres el/la cajero(a) en el Hotel Regente. Un(a) compañero(a) es un(a) huésped. Está abandonando su cuarto. Preséntale al huésped su factura y explícale los cargos *(charges)*. Tu compañero(a) te hará algunas preguntas sobre los cargos. Después tú le preguntarás cómo quiere pagar la cuenta. Él o ella te dirá.

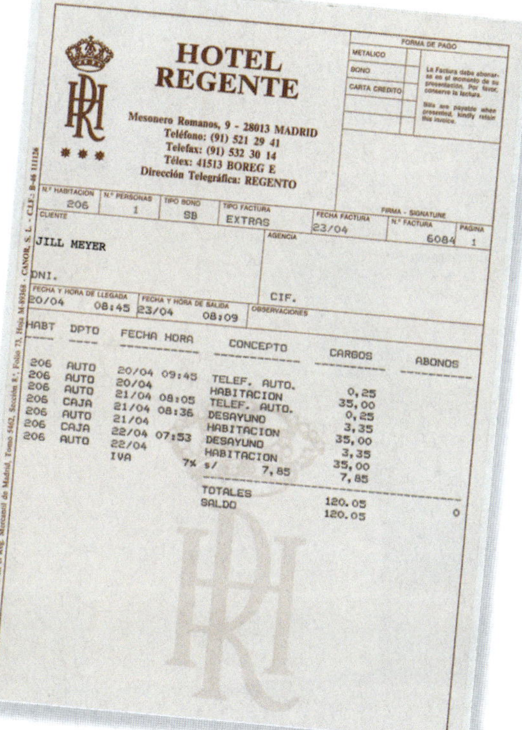

HOTEL REGENTE
★★★
Mesonero Romanos, 9 - 28013 MADRID
Teléfono: (91) 521 29 41
Telefax: (91) 532 30 14
Télex: 41513 BOREG E
Dirección Telegráfica: REGENTO

FORMA DE PAGO: METALICO / BONO / CARTA CREDITO

La Factura debe abonarse en el momento de su presentación. Por favor, conserve la factura.

Bills are payable when presented, kindly retain this invoice.

N.º HABITACION: 206 · N.º PERSONAS: 1 · TIPO BONO: SB · TIPO FACTURA: EXTRAS · FECHA FACTURA: 23/04 · FIRMA - SIGNATURE · N.º FACTURA: 6084 · PAGINA: 1

CLIENTE: JILL MEYER

AGENCIA

DNI.

CIF.

FECHA Y HORA DE LLEGADA: 20/04 08:45 · FECHA Y HORA DE SALIDA: 23/04 08:09 · OBSERVACIONES

| HABT | DPTO | FECHA HORA | CONCEPTO | CARGOS | ABONOS |
|---|---|---|---|---|---|
| 206 | AUTO | 20/04 09:45 | TELEF. AUTO. | | |
| 206 | AUTO | 20/04 | HABITACION | 0,25 | |
| 206 | AUTO | 21/04 08:05 | TELEF. AUTO. | 35,00 | |
| 206 | CAJA | 21/04 08:36 | DESAYUNO | 0,25 | |
| 206 | AUTO | 21/04 | HABITACION | 3,35 | |
| 206 | CAJA | 22/04 07:53 | DESAYUNO | 35,00 | |
| 206 | AUTO | 22/04 | HABITACION | 3,35 | |
| | | IVA 7% | s/ 7,85 | 35,00 | |
| | | | | 7,85 | |
| | | | TOTALES | 120.05 | |
| | | | SALDO | 120.05 | 0 |

Sociedad Inscrita en el Reg. Mercantil de Madrid, Tomo 5462, Sección 8.ª, Folio 73, Hoja M-89368 · CANOR, S.L. · C.I.F.: B-46 111126



## Vocabulario

**4** Do Activity 4 orally with books closed. Have students write the answers for homework. Review the activity the next day.

**¡OJO!** Note that the activities are color-coded. All the activities in the text are communicative. However, the ones with blue titles are guided communication. The red titles indicate that the answers to the activity are more open-ended and can vary more. You may wish to correct students' mistakes more so in the guided activities than in the activities with a red title, which lend themselves to a freer response.

**5** You may want to involve the entire class in this activity. **¿Quiénes quieren hacer el viaje? ¿Adónde quieren ir? ¿Cuánto pueden pagar?**, etc.

### LEVELING

**E:** Activities 1, 2, 3, 4
**A:** Activities 3, 4, 5, 6
**C:** Activity 6

### Learning from Realia

*(page 165)* Ask questions about the **Hotel Regente** bill:
**¿En qué ciudad está el hotel?**
**¿Cuál es la dirección?**
**¿Cuál era el precio de la habitación?**

## Answers to ¿Qué palabra necesito?

**4**

1. No, cuando el cliente llega al hotel, va primero a la recepción.
2. Sí, el mozo lleva el equipaje al cuarto.
3. Sí, hay que llenar una ficha o tarjeta al llegar al hotel.
4. No, un cuarto sencillo es para una persona.
5. No, el cliente abandona el cuarto cuando sale del hotel.
6. No, cuando uno paga la cuenta no le da el dinero al botones.

**5** *Answers will vary but should include vocabulary from* Palabras 1.

**6** *Answers will vary. Students will use vocabulary from* Palabras 1 *as well as the realia as a prompt.*

# 1 PREPARATION

## Resource Manager

Vocabulary Transparencies 6.4–6.5
Audio Activities TE, pages 66–67
Audio CD 4
Workbook, pages 63–64
Quizzes, page 27
ExamView® Pro

## Bellringer Review

*Use BRR Transparency 6.2 or write the following on the board.*
Write a list of all the rooms in a typical three-bedroom house.

# 2 PRESENTATION

**Step 1** Have students close their books. Model the **Palabras 2** vocabulary using Vocabulary Transparencies 6.4–6.5. Have students repeat the new material after you or Audio CD 4. Have them repeat each word or expression twice.

## About the Spanish Language

- Another word for *blanket* is **la frisa.**
- Another word for *closet* is **el ropero.** In a number of countries the *closet* is **el clóset.** The original **armario** was a piece of furniture, a *wardrobe.*

# Vocabulario PALABRAS 2

## En el cuarto

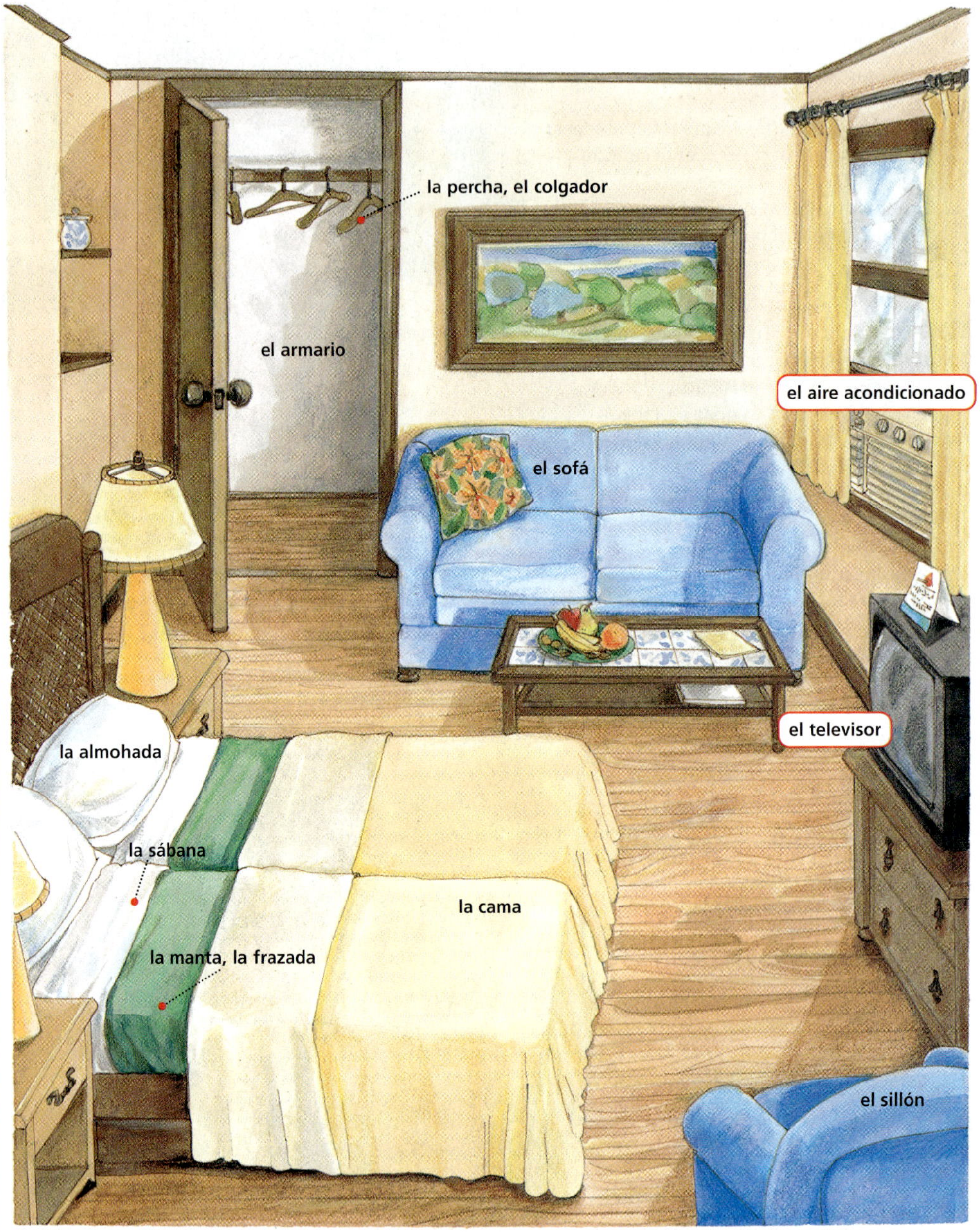

## Reaching All Students

### Total Physical Response

*(Student 1),* ven acá, por favor.
Estás en un hotel.
Estás en tu cuarto.
Abre la puerta del armario.
Toma una percha.
Cuelga tu abrigo.
Ponlo en el armario.
Cierra la puerta del armario.
Ve al baño.
Mírate en el espejo.
Toma el jabón. Lávate la cara.
Toma una toalla.
Sécate la cara con la toalla.
Gracias, *(Student 1).* Bien hecho.
Ahora, vuelve a tu asiento, por favor.

## En el baño

La camarera limpiará el cuarto.
Ella hará la cama.

Y cambiará las toallas.



## Vocabulario

**Step 2** Point to the appropriate illustration or photo on page 167 and ask questions, beginning with *yes / no* and *either / or* and then progressing to more open-ended ones such as: **¿Qué hará la camarera? ¿Quién hará las camas?**

**Step 3** Use props such as a pillow, soap, a hanger, etc., as cues. Ask students what one needs in order to do various things. For example: **Va a tomar una ducha. Va a bañarse. Se lava la cara. Va a dormir. Pone la ropa en el armario.**

### About the Spanish Language

The word **inodoro** comes from a brand name for an American-made toilet. The brand name became the generic name for *toilet* in much of Latin America. In Spain, the word **váter** is a corruption of *water closet* or *w.c.,* the British term for *toilet.*

### SPANISH Online

The Glencoe Spanish Web site **(spanish.glencoe.com)** offers options that enable you and your students to experience the Spanish-speaking world via the Internet. For each **Capítulo,** there are activities, games, and quizzes. In addition, an *Enrichment* section offers students an opportunity to visit Web sites related to the theme of the chapter.

### Reaching All Students

**Cooperative Learning** Allow students time to prepare this activity. Two team members are having a great time in an expensive hotel. The other two are having a terrible time in an inexpensive hotel. The four meet at a café and take turns describing their experiences. For example: **¡Nuestra habitación es enorme! ¡Nuestra habitación es como un armario! ¡Las camas son muy cómodas! ¡Nuestras camas son horribles!**, etc.

Vocabulario

## 3 PRACTICE

## ¿Qué palabra necesito?

**7** Have students refer to the illustrations as they do Activity 7. They can use the future tense in their responses.

**8** You can go over Activity 8 without having students prepare it beforehand.

**9** Have students prepare Activity 9 before going over it in class.

### FUN FACTS

Some of the world's finest soaps come from Spain. The term *castile soap* originally referred to soaps from Spain—fine, hard, bland soaps made from olive oil and sodium hydroxide.

### Chapter Projects

**Compartir experiencias** Invite a native Spanish-speaker or a North American who has traveled in Hispanic countries to share hotel experiences with the class.

Vocabulario

## ¿Qué palabra necesito?

**7 ¿Qué hará nuestra camarera?**
Expliquen las cosas que hará la camarera según los dibujos.

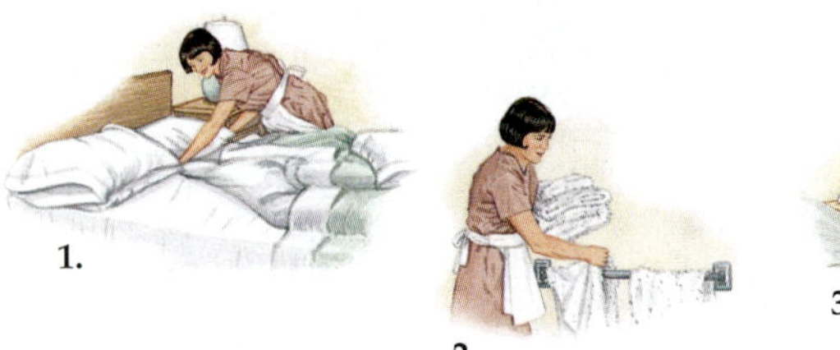

1. 2. 3. 4.

**8 ¿En el baño, en el armario o en el cuarto?**
Digan si las cosas se encuentran en el baño, el armario o el cuarto.

1. la ducha
2. el jabón
3. las sábanas
4. la percha
5. el lavabo
6. las toallas
7. la cama
8. el inodoro
9. el aire acondicionado
10. la manta

The word **el gancho** means *hook*, but in many areas of the Spanish-speaking world it can also mean *hanger*.

**9 ¿Qué necesitarás?** Pareen.

a. 
b. 
c. 
d. 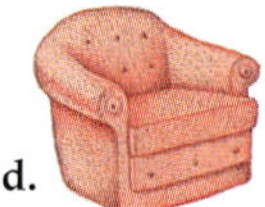
e. 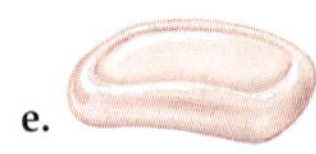
f. 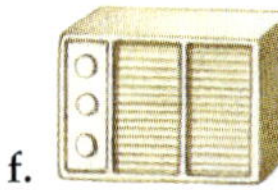
g. 

1. Tienes que lavarte las manos.
2. Después de lavarte las manos, tienes que secarlas.
3. Hace mucho frío esta noche.
4. Quieres ver tu programa favorito.
5. Hace calor en el cuarto.
6. Tienes que poner tu chaqueta en el armario.
7. Estás cansado(a) y quieres sentarte.



## ANSWERS TO ¿Qué palabra necesito?

**7**

1. La camarera hará la cama.
2. Cambiará las toallas.
3. Limpiará el cuarto.
4. Pondrá las perchas en el armario.

**8**

1. La ducha se encuentra en el baño.
2. El jabón se encuentra en el baño.
3. Las sábanas se encuentran en el cuarto.
4. La percha se encuentra en el armario.
5. El lavabo se encuentra en el baño.
6. Las toallas se encuentran en el baño.
7. La cama se encuentra en el cuarto.
8. El inodoro se encuentra en el baño.
9. El aire acondicionado se encuentra en el cuarto.
10. La manta se encuentra en el cuarto.

**9**

1. e
2. g
3. b
4. a
5. f
6. c
7. d

 **Un hotel bueno** Con un(a) compañero(a), discutan lo que les importa cuando se quedan en un hotel. Usen las siguientes expresiones en su discusión.

Hotel El Olivar de San Isidro, Lima, Perú

 **11** **Un desastre de hotel** Pasaste unas vacaciones en San Juan de Puerto Rico. Lo pasaste muy bien y te gustó todo menos el hotel. ¡Qué horror! Fue un desastre total. Un(a) compañero(a) quiere saber todo lo que pasó. Dile. Usa tu imaginación y exagera todo lo posible. Luego cambien de rol y decidan quién tuvo la experiencia más desastrosa.

 *For more practice using words from **Palabras 1** and **2**, do Activity 6 on page H7 at the end of this book.*



## Vocabulario

**11** You may wish to have students present their "experience" to the entire class.

### Geography Connection

The hotel in the photo is in the San Isidro section of Lima, one of the city's most important commercial districts. Lima is the capital and major city of Peru, with over seven million inhabitants. The city was founded in 1535 by Francisco Pizarro, the **conquistador,** who gave it the name **Ciudad de los Reyes.**

UN POCO MÁS This *InfoGap* Activity will allow students to practice in pairs. The activity should be very manageable for them, since all vocabulary and structures are familiar to them.

**LEVELING**

**E:** Activities 7, 8, 9, 10

**A:** Activity 10

**C:** Activity 11

### Chapter Projects

**Un hotel imaginario** Have groups create their own imaginary hotel and describe it to the class. The class can rate each different hotel as to quality, value-for-price, and cuisine.

## Answers to ¿Qué palabra necesito?

 *Answers will vary but may include:*

—No me importa si el hotel tiene una piscina.
—Me importa el servicio.
—A mí, me importa mucho el precio del cuarto.

 *Answers will vary. Students will use vocabulary learned in the chapter.*

# Estructura

## 1 PREPARATION

### Resource Manager

Audio Activities TE, pages 67–69
Audio CD 4
Workbook, pages 65–67
Quizzes, pages 28–29
ExamView® Pro

### Bellringer Review

*Use BRR Transparency 6.3 or write the following on the board.*
Rewrite the following in the future.

1. **Los Gómez van al parque.**
2. **Llegan al parque en carro.**
3. **Los niños dan un paseo por el lago.**
4. **En el parque ven a sus amigos.**
5. **Venden piraguas y globos en el parque.**

## 2 PRESENTATION

### Futuro de los verbos irregulares

**Step 1** Ask students to open their books to page 170. Lead them through the explanation and have them repeat the verb forms after you.

**Step 2** You may wish to write some of the verbs on the board and underline the endings.

**¡OJO!** Although you will want to familiarize students with the forms of these irregular verbs in the future, you may remind students that the **ir a** + *infinitive* construction is a simple and valid way to express future action and that it is more frequently used than the future tense in informal speech.



# Estructura

## Futuro de los verbos irregulares
### Expressing more future actions

**¿Te acuerdas?**
Regular verbs in the future use the infinitive as the stem.
**hablaré, comeré, escribiré**

**1.** Study the following forms of verbs that have an irregular stem in the future tense. Note that the endings for all irregular verbs are the same as those for the regular verbs.

| INFINITIVE | tener | salir | venir | ENDINGS |
|---|---|---|---|---|
| STEM | tendr- | saldr- | vendr- | |
| yo | tendré | saldré | vendré | -é |
| tú | tendrás | saldrás | vendrás | -ás |
| él, ella, Ud. | tendrá | saldrá | vendrá | -á |
| nosotros(as) | tendremos | saldremos | vendremos | -emos |
| *vosotros(as)* | *tendréis* | *saldréis* | *vendréis* | *-éis* |
| ellos, ellas, Uds. | tendrán | saldrán | vendrán | -án |

**2.** Other verbs that follow the same pattern are **poner, saber,** and **poder.**

**poner → pondré** **saber → sabré** **poder → podré**

**3.** The verbs **decir, hacer,** and **querer** also have an irregular future stem.

| INFINITIVE | decir | hacer | querer | ENDINGS |
|---|---|---|---|---|
| STEM | dir- | har- | querr- | |
| yo | diré | haré | querré | -é |
| tú | dirás | harás | querrás | -ás |
| él, ella, Ud. | dirá | hará | querrá | -á |
| nosotros(as) | diremos | haremos | querremos | -emos |
| *vosotros(as)* | *diréis* | *haréis* | *querréis* | *-éis* |
| ellos, ellas, Uds. | dirán | harán | querrán | -án |

For more information about popular vacation spots in the Spanish-speaking world, go to the Glencoe Spanish Web site: spanish.glencoe.com

## ¿Cómo lo digo?

**12** **Historieta La huésped llegará mañana.**
Contesten según se indica.

1. ¿Cuándo vendrá la huésped? (mañana)
2. ¿Quién sabrá si tiene una reservación? (el recepcionista)
3. ¿Qué tendrá que llenar la huésped? (una ficha)
4. ¿Quién podrá abrirle la puerta? (el mozo)
5. ¿Dónde le pondrá su equipaje? (en el cuarto)
6. ¿Cuándo saldrá la huésped? (en dos días)

**13** **Y mañana, ¿qué?** Contesten según el modelo.

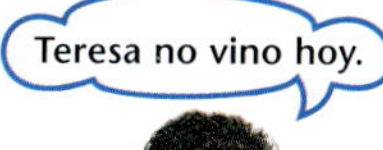

1. Ella no salió de casa a tiempo.
2. Yo no sabía la hora de su llegada.
3. Ella no nos mandó un fax.
4. Nosotros no pudimos ir a buscarla.

**14** **Historieta Las vacaciones de Ricardo**
Completen.

El invierno que viene Ricardo Valbuena __1__ (tener) dos semanas de vacaciones. Él y su familia __2__ (hacer) un viaje a México. Allí ellos __3__ (poder) pasar unos días con sus parientes. El padre de Ricardo __4__ (llamar) a México y les __5__ (decir) a sus parientes la hora de su llegada. Todos los parientes de Ricardo __6__ (querer) ir al aeropuerto a recibirlos. Ricardo y sus padres __7__ (salir) en el vuelo de las once. El vuelo __8__ (hacer) escala en Dallas antes de llegar a México.

Acapulco, México



# Estructura

## 3 PRACTICE

## ¿Cómo lo digo?

**12** Go over this activity orally first with books closed.
**Expansion:** After going over Activity 12, call on a student to retell the story in his or her own words.

**13** Activity 13 is a bit difficult, but the logical sequence of past to future is used often in free communication: "No, I didn't, but I will . . ."

**14** Have students prepare Activity 14 and then read it aloud.

### Writing Development

After going over Activity 14, give students a few minutes in class to rewrite the information from the story in their own words.

### Learning from Photos

*(page 171)* Acapulco is an ideal holiday resort 260 miles south of Mexico City, on the Pacific coast. The beautiful, picturesque Acapulco bay is one of the world's best natural harbors.

### LEVELING

**E:** Activity 12
**A:** Activities 13, 14
**C:** Activity 14

## Answers to ¿Cómo lo digo?

**12**

1. La huésped vendrá mañana.
2. El recepcionista sabrá si tiene una reservación.
3. La huésped tendrá que llenar una ficha.
4. El mozo podrá abrirle la puerta.
5. Le pondrá su equipaje en el cuarto.
6. La huésped saldrá en dos días.

**13**

1. No, pero saldrá de casa a tiempo mañana.
2. No, pero sabrás la hora de su llegada mañana.
3. No, pero ella nos pondrá un fax mañana.
4. No, pero nosotros podremos ir a buscarla mañana.

**14**

1. tendrá
2. harán
3. podrán
4. llamará
5. dirá
6. querrán
7. saldrán
8. hará

## 3 PRACTICE *(continued)*

**15** Have students prepare Activity 15 before going over it in class. Then have two students read the conversation to the class.
**Expansion:** Call on two very able students to present their own conversation to the class, based on the information from the activity.

**16** Have students prepare Activity 16 before going over it in class.

### Learning from Photos

*(page 172)* You may wish to ask students questions about the photos:

**¿Qué tipo de teléfono usa la señorita?**
**¿Qué es la señora a la derecha?**
**¿Dónde está ella?**

### Vocabulary Expansion

The stand of cubbyholes behind the desk clerk is called **un casillero** and each of the boxes is **una casilla.** In some places a **casilla** is also a post office box.



### 15 Historieta Una reservación

Completen la conversación con el futuro.

| | |
|---|---|
| CLIENTE | Buenos días. Soy Elena Sánchez. ¿Quién __1__ (poder) confirmar mi reservación? |
| RECEPCIONISTA | Pues, yo, señorita. ¿Cuándo __2__ (venir) usted al hotel? |
| CLIENTE | El jueves. Yo __3__ (saber) la hora exacta más tarde. |
| RECEPCIONISTA | Un momentito y le __4__ (decir) si tiene reservación. Sí, sí, aquí está. Usted __5__ (venir) el jueves y __6__ (salir) el domingo, ¿verdad? |
| CLIENTE | Así es. Yo __7__ (tener) que salir a primera hora el domingo. Yo __8__ (querer) transporte al aeropuerto. |
| RECEPCIONISTA | No hay problema. El conserje le __9__ (hacer) una reservación en la limusina. |
| CLIENTE | Muchas gracias. |

### 16 El pronóstico del tiempo para mañana

Completen.

1. Hoy hace calor pero mañana ____ frío.
2. Hoy no tienen que llevar abrigo, pero mañana sí que ____ que llevar abrigo.
3. Hoy no pueden esquiar, pero mañana ____ esquiar.
4. Hoy yo no quiero ir a clase, pero mañana ____ ir.
5. Hoy no me pongo el suéter, pero mañana me lo ____.
6. Hoy todo el mundo sale a la calle, pero mañana nadie ____ a la calle.



### ANSWERS TO ¿Cómo lo digo?

**15**

1. podrá
2. vendrá
3. sabré
4. diré
5. vendrá
6. saldrá
7. tendré
8. querré
9. hará

**16**

1. hará
2. tendrán
3. podrán
4. querré
5. pondré
6. saldrá

**17** **Un trabajo para el verano** Este verano trabajarás en un hotel o motel cerca de donde tú vives. El hotel tiene muchos clientes de Latinoamérica. Por eso, el director del hotel (un[a] compañero[a]) te da una entrevista (una interviú) en español. Pregúntale al director todo lo que tendrás que hacer. El modelo les servirá de guía.

**18** **El fin de semana que viene** No sabes por qué pero no hay duda que siempre tienes mucho que hacer. Con un(a) compañero(a), hagan planes para el próximo fin de semana. Discutan todo lo que harán. Dividan sus actividades en las siguientes categorías.

## Me lo, te lo, nos lo
### Talking about things already stated

1. Many sentences have both a direct and an indirect object pronoun. In these sentences the indirect object pronoun always precedes the direct object pronoun in Spanish. Both pronouns precede the conjugated form of the verb.

| | |
|---|---|
| **Ella nos sirvió el helado.** | **Ella nos lo sirvió.** |
| **El mozo me dio la llave.** | **El mozo me la dio.** |
| **Él me vendió los libros.** | **Él me los vendió.** |
| **Papá te hizo las reservaciones.** | **Papá te las hizo.** |

2. Note that the indirect object **me, te,** or **nos** comes before the direct object **lo, la, los, las.**



# Estructura

## 1 PREPARATION

### Bellringer Review

*Use BRR Transparency 6.4 or write the following on the board.*
Write five things you will do tomorrow.

## 2 PRESENTATION

### Me lo, te lo, nos lo

**Step 1** Have students open their books. Lead them through Items 1 and 2 on page 173.

**Step 2** Call on volunteers to read the model sentences aloud.

**Step 3** You may wish to write the model sentences on the board. Circle the objects as is done on page 173. Draw an arrow from the pronoun to the noun it replaces. Have students note that the second pronoun comes after the one that was already there.

### Answers to ¿Cómo lo digo?

**17** *Answers will vary. Students will use the model in the textbook as a guide.*

**18** *Answers will vary. Students will use the future tense with previously learned vocabulary to form sentences.*

### LEVELING

**E:** Activities 17, 18
**A:** Activities 15, 16, 17, 18
**C:** Activity 15

# Estructura

## 3 PRACTICE

## ¿Cómo lo digo?

**¡OJO!** All the activities on pages 174 and 175 can be gone over orally in class with books closed. They can then be read for additional reinforcement. **Note:** You can decide to what extent you wish to emphasize this particular point. Students should be able to recognize the double object pronouns, but when speaking on their own (producing language) they could say, for example, **Mi tío Lucas me regaló la computadora.**

### History Connection

The original **Alcázar de Toledo** was heavily damaged during the Spanish Civil War and subsequently reconstructed. In 1936, Nationalist forces withstood a Republican siege of over two months within the ruins of the fortress. The tour of the **Alcázar** focuses on the siege.

### Learning from Realia

*(page 174)* A *keycard* in Spanish is **una tarjeta llave.**



## ¿Cómo lo digo?

**19 El generoso tío Lucas** Contesten según el modelo.

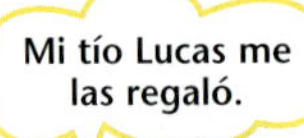

1. ¿Quién te regaló la computadora?
2. ¿Quién te regaló los videos?
3. ¿Quién te regaló el balón?
4. ¿Quién te regaló las damas?
5. ¿Quién te regaló los esquís?
6. ¿Quién te regaló el televisor?
7. ¿Quién te regaló las botas?

**20 El mozo del hotel** Contesten con pronombres.

1. ¿Te subió las maletas?
2. ¿Te abrió la puerta?
3. ¿Te dio la llave el mozo?
4. ¿Te prendió el aire acondicionado?

**21 ¿Quién te compró todo eso?**
Formen preguntas según el modelo.

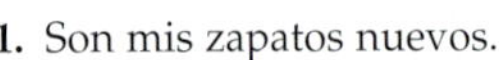

1. Son mis zapatos nuevos.
2. Es mi equipaje nuevo.
3. Es mi computadora nueva.
4. Son mis revistas nuevas.
5. Es mi bufanda nueva.

## Answers to ¿Cómo lo digo?

**19**

1. Mi tío Lucas me la regaló.
2. Mi tío Lucas me los regaló.
3. Mi tío Lucas me lo regaló.
4. Mi tío Lucas me las regaló.
5. Mi tío Lucas me los regaló.
6. Mi tío Lucas me lo regaló.
7. Mi tío Lucas me las regaló.

**20**

1. Sí, (No, no) me las subió.
2. Sí, (No, no) me la abrió.
3. Sí, (No, no) me la dio.
4. Sí, (No, no) me lo prendió.

**21**

1. ¿Quién te los compró?
2. ¿Quién te lo compró?
3. ¿Quién te la compró?
4. ¿Quién te las compró?
5. ¿Quién te la compró?

## 22 Doña Flor, la profesora

Contesten con pronombres según el modelo.

**Doña Flor nos explicó el sistema. →**
**Doña Flor nos lo explicó.**

1. Doña Flor nos enseñó los poemas.
2. Doña Flor nos explicó la teoría.
3. Doña Flor nos enseñó el vocabulario.
4. Doña Flor nos dio la interpretación.
5. Doña Flor nos explicó las diferencias.

## 23 No oigo bien.

Usen dos pronombres en cada oración.

1. —Carlos me hizo la reservación
   —Perdón, ¿quién ___?
2. —Carlos. Y él me confirmó la reservación ayer.
   —Perdón, ¿cuándo ___?
3. —Ayer. Y también me dio las direcciones.
   —Perdón, ¿Carlos ___?
4. —Sí, Carlos. Y me envió las direcciones por fax.
   —Perdón, ¿cómo ___?

Hotel Libertador, Trujillo, Perú

### Paired Activity

Activity 22 can be done in pairs. One student says the sentences with rising intonation, making them questions, and the other responds using double object pronouns.

### Learning from Photos

**Hotel Libertador** is located on the main square in the once walled-in historical city of Trujillo, Peru. Only ten minutes from the hotel, you will find Chan Chan, the clay city and capital of the ancient Chimu culture, as well as the **Huaca del Sol y la Luna** (*Temple of the Sun and Moon*).

### ¡Adelante!

At this point in the chapter, students have learned all the vocabulary and structure necessary to complete the chapter. The conversation and cultural readings that follow recycle all the material learned up to this point.

## Answers to ¿Cómo lo digo?

**22**

1. Doña Flor nos los enseñó.
2. Doña Flor nos la explicó.
3. Doña Flor nos lo enseñó.
4. Doña Flor nos la dio.
5. Doña Flor nos las explicó.

**23**

1. te la hizo
2. te la confirmó
3. te las dio
4. te las envió

### Leveling

**E:** Activities 19,21
**A:** Activities 20, 21, 22
**C:** Activity 23

# Conversación

## 1 PREPARATION

### Resource Manager

Audio Activities TE, pages 69–70
Audio CD 4

### Bellringer Review

*Use BRR Transparency 6.5 or write the following on the board.*
Match the word in the first column with a related word in the second column.

| | |
|---|---|
| 1. reservar | a. la cuenta |
| 2. limpiar | b. la llegada |
| 3. bañar | c. la reservación |
| 4. contar | d. la bañera |
| 5. llegar | e. la limpieza |

## 2 PRESENTATION

**Step 1** Tell students they are going to hear a conversation between a hotel clerk and a guest.

**Step 2** Have students open their books to page 176 and follow along as you play Audio CD 4.

**Step 3** Have pairs of students create hotel-centered skits based on the conversation. Then have them present their skits to the class. They can make any changes they wish.

**Step 4** Now go over the **¿Comprendes?** activity. If students can answer the questions with relative ease, move on. Students should not be expected to memorize the conversation.

**LEVELING**

**E:** Conversation

# Conversación

## La llegada al hotel   

**Recepcionista** Buenas tardes, señor. ¿Tiene usted una reservación?

**Cliente** Sí, a nombre de Sorolla, Ramón Sorolla. Un cuarto sencillo para tres noches.

**Recepcionista** Aquí está. Usted saldrá el jueves, día doce. Querrá un baño privado, ¿no?

**Cliente** Sí, claro.

**Recepcionista** Le daré el tres cero dos. Es un cuarto muy bonito. Da al patio. Tendrá que llenar la ficha. ¿Y su pasaporte, por favor?

**Cliente** ¿A qué hora tendré que abandonar el cuarto el día doce?

**Recepcionista** Al mediodía.

**Cliente** De acuerdo.

**Recepcionista** Aquí tiene usted la llave. Samuel le subirá el equipaje. ¡Samuel!

### ¿Comprendes?

Contesten.

1. ¿Cómo se llama el cliente?
2. ¿Cuántos días estará en el hotel?
3. ¿Qué día saldrá del hotel?
4. ¿Qué tipo de cuarto reservó?
5. ¿Qué tendrá que llenar el cliente y qué le dará a la recepcionista?
6. ¿A qué hora tendrá que abandonar el cuarto?
7. ¿Quién es Samuel y qué hará él?



### Answers to ¿Comprendes?

1. El cliente se llama Ramón Sorolla.
2. Estará tres noches en el hotel.
3. Saldrá del hotel el jueves
4. Reservó un cuarto sencillo.
5. Tendrá que llenar la ficha y le dará su pasaporte a la recepcionista.
6. Tendrá que abandonar el cuarto al mediodía.
7. Samuel es el mozo y le subirá el equipaje.

### Learning from Photos

*(page 176)* You may wish to ask students questions about the photo:
**¿Cómo se viste la señorita?**
**¿Dónde están ellos?**
**¿Qué hay en el mostrador?**
**¿Qué hace el señor?**

# Vamos a hablar más

**A** **Un hotel en Madrid** Tú y tu familia estarán en Madrid este verano. Aquí hay folletos de dos hoteles madrileños que ofrecen muchos servicios a sus clientes. Dile a un(a) compañero(a) en cuál de los dos hoteles quieres quedarte. Explica por qué. Luego tu compañero(a) te dirá su preferencia y te dirá por qué. Discutan por qué se quedarán o no se quedarán en el mismo hotel.

MADRID

HOTEL ORENSE

* * * *

DIRECCION

Pedro Teixeira, 5 (esq. Orense)
28020 Madrid
Tel. (91) 597 15 68
Fax. (91) 597 12 95

SITUACION

El Hotel está situado en el corazón de Azca (zona de negocios y centro financiero), junto al Palacio de Congresos, el Paseo de la Castellana y el Estadio Santiago Bernabeu. A 5 minutos de la estación de Chamartín. Acceso directo a la M-40, a 10 minutos del aeropuerto e Ifema.

CAPACIDAD

- 140 habitaciones todas dobles (incluye 10 suites estilo)

SERVICIOS GENERALES

- Restaurante
- Bar Cafetería
- Comedor privado
- Salón social
- Fax
- Amplio garaje propio
- Desayuno Buffet
- Circuito cerrado de T.V.

SERVICIOS HABITACIONES

- Todas exteriores e insonorizadas
- Teléfono directo
- T.V. color con mando a distancia
- Antena parabólica / Canal +
- Hilo musical
- Radio
- Aire acondicionado
- Climatizador individual
- Cuarto de baño en dos volúmenes
- Secador de pelo
- Caja de seguridad
- Mini-bar
- Room service
- Línea de fax opcional

MADRID

GRAN HOTEL COLON

* * * *

DIRECCION

Pez Volador, 11 (semiesquina con Dr. Ezquerdo)
28007 Madrid
Tel. (91) 573 59 00 / 573 86 00
Fax. (91) 573 08 09
Telex 22984 COLON E

SITUACION

Ubicado en una zona céntrica y residencial, junto al Parque del Retiro. A 5 minutos de la estación de Atocha, del Centro Comercial de Goya y, del Triángulo del Arte. Acceso directo a la M-30 y M-40, (por la nueva prolongación O'Donnell) a 10 minutos del aeropuerto y del Parque Ferial Juan Carlos I.

CAPACIDAD

- 380 habitaciones (incluidas suites)

SERVICIOS GENERALES

Restaurante, Bar, Cafetería / Hall, Terraza con jardín, Sauna / Masajes, Peluquería, Rayos uva, Gimnasio panorámico (próxima apertura), Solarium, Agencia de viajes, Alquiler de coches, Garaje privado.

SERVICIOS HABITACIONES

Todas exteriores, Habitaciones con Terraza, Teléfono directo, T.V. color con mando a distancia, Antena parabólica, Radio / Hilo musical, Mini-bar, Caja de seguridad, Aire acondicionado, Servicio de habitaciones.

INSTALACIONES PARA CONFERENCIAS Y REUNIONES

El hotel permite la posibilidad de múltiples transformaciones, debido a que dispone de grandes espacios dedicados a salones. Todo ello contando con retroproyectores de transparencias, traducción simultánea, pantallas, videos, T.V., Megafonía y azafatas.

**B** **¿Cómo podré hacerlo todo?** Vas a preparar un *skit* muy cómico y divertido con un(a) compañero(a). Uno de ustedes será el ama de llaves *(head housekeeper)* de un hotel y el otro será una camarera nueva. Dentro de poco estarán llegando unos clientes. La pobre camarera no sabe qué hacer. Te hará muchas preguntas. Contesta a sus preguntas. Explícale todo lo que tendrá que hacer y cómo.

Conversación

## 3 PRACTICE

### Vamos a hablar más

**¡OJO!** These activities enable students to use the language creatively on their own as if they were communicating in real-life situations. Let students choose the activities they wish to do.

**A** Tell students working on Activity A to take a look at the brochures before getting started.

**B** You may wish to have some groups present their skits to the entire class, especially if they are comical.

### Learning from Realia

*(page 177)* You may wish to ask students questions about the two hotels:

**¿Cuál de los hoteles es más grande?**

**¿En cuál te quedarás si quieres ver un partido de fútbol?**

**Si tienes un coche, ¿en cuál de los hoteles puedes aparcar?**

**¿Cuál de los hoteles ofrece más servicios?**

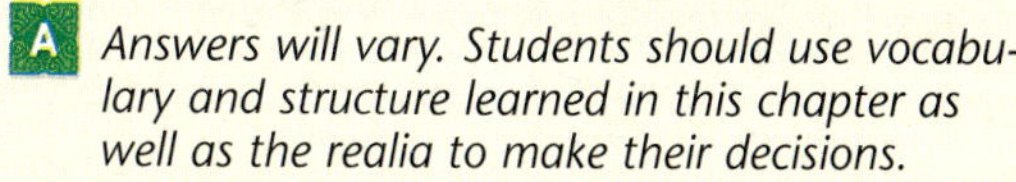

### Answers to Vamos a hablar más

**A** *Answers will vary. Students should use vocabulary and structure learned in this chapter as well as the realia to make their decisions.*

**B** *Answers will vary but will include vocabulary and structure from Chapter 6.*

### Glencoe Technology

On the CD-ROM, students can watch a dramatization of this conversation. They can then play the role of either one of the characters and record themselves in the conversation.

# Lecturas culturales

## Resource Manager

Audio Activities TE, page 71
Audio CD 4

## Bellringer Review

*Use BRR Transparency 6.6 or write the following on the board.*
Choose the word that does not belong.

1. **el invitado, el cliente, el propietario, el huésped**
2. **el lujo, la elegancia, la comodidad, la riqueza, la economía**

## National Standards

**Cultures**
The reading on pages 178–179 and the related activities on page 179 familiarize students with the attractive, culturally interesting chain of government-run hotels known as **paradores** in Spain.

## PRESENTATION

### Pre-reading

**Step 1** Before starting the reading, give students some information about **paradores. En España hay paradores. Los paradores son hoteles. Son muy buenos. Y son del gobierno. Hay paradores en todas partes de España. Algunos son muy grandes y otros son muy pequeños. Vamos a leer ahora sobre unos planes que tiene una familia americana. Ellos piensan pasar algunas noches en un parador.**

**Step 2** Ask some questions in Spanish about what you just told the students.

# Lecturas culturales

### Reading Strategy

**Using background knowledge to predict**
Before reading a selection, think about what you already know about the topic before you read in depth. Try to guess what new things it will tell you. You can base your guesses on background knowledge and intuition. Making predictions will help prepare you for the reading.

## Los paradores de España

El verano que viene Sandra, Roberto y sus padres harán un viaje a España. Saldrán el 28 de junio. Al llegar a España alquilarán un coche. Viajarán por todas partes del país. Pasarán una semana en el norte y otra en Madrid y sus alrededores. Pasarán la última semana en el sur, en Andalucía.

La señora White, la madre de Sandra y Roberto, está planeando el viaje. Dice que podrán pasar varias noches en algunos paradores.

Hay unos setenta paradores en España. Algunos son muy pequeños como el Parador de Villalba en Lugo, Galicia. Tiene sólo seis habitaciones. Otros son bastante grandes. El Parador de Cádiz tiene 147 habitaciones. Pero lo importante no es el tamaño. Lo más atractivo de los paradores es que son únicos. No son todos iguales. Cada uno tiene su carácter propio.

Algunos paradores son antiguos castillos[1] o monasterios. La madre de Sandra y Roberto dice que hará una reservación en el Parador San Francisco en Granada. Antes era un convento fundado por los Reyes Católicos, Fernando e Isabel. El parador está dentro de las murallas[2] y los jardines de la famosa Alhambra. Pero el Parador San Francisco es tan popular que los White tendrán que reservar una habitación con unos seis meses de anticipación.

[1]castillos *castles*
[2]murallas *walls*

Parador de Cádiz

Parador San Francisco, Granada



## Learning from Photos

*(page 178)* Ask students to study the photos of the two **paradores** on this page. Then ask them to contrast one with the other.

Los paradores nacionales son del gobierno[3] español. Los restaurantes de muchos paradores son muy buenos. Sirven platos típicos de las regiones donde se encuentran. Muchos turistas dicen que pasar una noche en un parador es como pasar una noche en un museo—pero un museo con todas las comodidades de un hotel de cuatro estrellas[4]. A ver lo que dirán Sandra, Roberto y sus padres al volver de su viaje a España.

[3]gobierno *government*
[4]estrellas *stars*

Parador de Cardona, España

## ¿Comprendes?

**A Un viaje a España** Contesten.

1. ¿Quiénes harán un viaje a España?
2. ¿Qué día saldrán?
3. ¿Qué alquilarán?
4. ¿Cuánto tiempo pasarán en Madrid y sus alrededores?
5. ¿Quién está planeando el viaje?
6. ¿Dónde podrán pasar algunas noches?
7. ¿Cómo son los paradores?
8. ¿De quién son los paradores?
9. ¿Qué sirven en los restaurantes de los paradores?

**B ¿Cómo es?** Describan.

1. Describe el Parador de Villalba en Lugo, Galicia.
2. Describe el Parador San Francisco en Granada, Andalucía.

**C Lo magnífico de los paradores** Expliquen.

1. Lo más atractivo de los paradores es que son únicos.
2. Pasar una noche en un parador es como pasar una noche en un museo—pero un museo con todas las comodidades de un hotel de cuatro estrellas.

Parador San Francisco, Granada



# Lecturas culturales

### Reading

Have students open their books. Call on individuals to read several sentences aloud.

### Post-reading

**Step 1** After having finished the reading, ask questions such as: **¿Cuándo harán un viaje a España Sandra, Roberto y sus padres? ¿Cuándo saldrán?**

**Step 2** After completing the **Lectura** as suggested above, have students prepare the **¿Comprendes?** activities at home. Go over them the following day in class.

### ¿Comprendes?

**A, B, and C** Allow students to refer to the reading to look up the answers, or you may use these activities as testing devices for factual recall.

**LEVELING**

**E:** Reading

**A:** Reading

## Answers to ¿Comprendes?

**A**

1. Sandra, Roberto y sus padres harán un viaje a España.
2. Saldrán el 28 de junio.
3. Alquilarán un coche.
4. Pasarán una semana en Madrid y sus alrededores.
5. La señora White está planeando el viaje.
6. Podrán pasar algunas noches en algunos paradores.
7. Los paradores son únicos. No son todos iguales.
8. Los paradores son del gobierno español.
9. Sirven platos típicos de las regiones donde se encuentran.

**B**

1. El Parador de Villalba en Lugo, Galicia, es muy pequeño. Tiene sólo seis habitaciones.
2. El Parador San Francisco en Granada, Andalucía, era un convento fundado por los Reyes Católicos, Fernando e Isabel. Está dentro de las murallas y los jardines de la famosa Alhambra.

**C** *Answers will vary but may include:*

1. Los paradores no son todos iguales. Cada uno tiene su carácter propio.
2. Algunos paradores son antiguos castillos o monasterios. Es porque se pueden comparar con un museo. Los cuartos son muy bonitos, y los restaurantes de muchos paradores son muy buenos, como los restaurantes de los hoteles de cuatro estrellas.

# Lectura opcional 1

## National Standards

**Cultures**

This reading about youth hostels and the related activities familiarize students with an appealing, low-budget type of accommodations for youth in many Spanish-speaking countries.

**¡OJO!** This reading is optional. You may skip it completely, have the entire class read it, have only several students read it and report to the class, or assign it for extra credit.

## PRESENTATION

You may wish to have a student or students who read this optional selection present the material briefly to the class.

### Learning from Realia

*(page 180)* Hotels in Spain are rated by the government, from five stars, for luxury hotels, to no stars. **Un hostal** is a simple hotel without amenities such as a restaurant. The card says: **Hostal R.** The **R** stands for **Residencia.** This **hostal** is named for the great Spanish playwright Lope de Vega (1562–1635).

# Lectura opcional 1

## Los albergues

En España y en algunos países de Latinoamérica hay albergues juveniles. Los albergues ofrecen cuartos limpios y económicos para jóvenes. La mayoría de los jóvenes que se hospedan (pasan la noche) en un albergue son estudiantes. Les gustan mucho los albergues porque no cuestan mucho y allí pueden conocer a otros estudiantes de todas partes del mundo. En los albergues hay casi siempre un salón central donde todos se reúnen para charlar y hacer amigos nuevos.

Cuartos en albergues juveniles, España

## ¿Comprendes?

**A Los albergues juveniles** Digan que sí o que no.

1. Todos los países latinoamericanos tienen albergues juveniles.
2. Un albergue juvenil es para viejos o ancianos.
3. Los albergues son bastante caros.
4. La mayoría de los jóvenes que se hospedan en un albergue juvenil son estudiantes.

**B Para pensar** Contesten.

¿Por qué a los estudiantes les gustan mucho los albergues juveniles?



### Answers to ¿Comprendes?

**A**

1. No
2. No
3. No
4. Sí

**B** *Answers will vary but may include:*

A los estudiantes les gustan mucho los albergues juveniles porque no cuestan mucho y pueden conocer a otros estudiantes de todas partes del mundo.

# Lectura opcional 2

HOTEL DE
LA RECONQUISTA

*El Hotel de la Reconquista, construido sobre la traza de un singular edificio del Siglo XVIII, antiguo Hospicio y Hospital del Principado de Asturias, Monumento Nacional, está situado en la zona más céntrica, residencial y comercial de la ciudad de Oviedo.*

*El Hotel dispone de un total de 142 habitaciones, incluyendo Junior suites y suites, algunas de ellas con preciosas vistas sobre el Patio de la Reina. Todas las habitaciones están perfectamente equipadas con hilo musical y TV vía satélite.*

*El Hotel le ofrece la oportunidad de disfrutar de la mejor cocina en su Restaurante.*

*El Hotel ofrece una amplia gama de instalaciones para Reuniones, congresos y Banquetes. Cuenta con una sala de proyecciones, con servicio de traducción simultánea disponible, ocho espléndidas salas de reuniones de 25 a 550 m² y encantadores patios para la celebración de todo tipo de conferencias y acontecimientos sociales como congresos, certámenes, exposiciones, banquetes y comidas de empresa con capacidad para albergar hasta 800 personas.*

## ¿Comprendes?

**¿Dónde nos dice...?**

Busquen la información en el folleto.

1. el nombre del hotel
2. de qué siglo data el edificio
3. dónde está ubicado (situado)
4. el número de habitaciones
5. algunos servicios que ofrece el hotel



# Lectura opcional 2

## National Standards

**Cultures**

This reading and the related activity familiarize students with the upscale accommodations offered by a hotel in Spain.

**¡OJO!** This reading is optional. You may skip it completely, have the entire class read it, have only several students read it and report to the class, or assign it for extra credit.

**Teaching Tips**

This reading is an actual brochure from the **Hotel de la Reconquista** in Oviedo, Spain. You may wish to have students take a look at it just to get an idea of what the hotel is like, exactly as if they were perusing a brochure in a travel agency.

## PRESENTATION

**Step 1** Have students read the brochure to themselves.

**Step 2** After they have read it, have them do the **¿Comprendes?** activity on this page.

**¿Comprendes?**

Students can quickly scan the brochure to get the information.

**LEVELING**

**E:** Reading 1
**A:** Reading 2
**C:** Reading 3

## Answers to ¿Comprendes?

1. Hotel de la Reconquista
2. del siglo XVIII
3. en la zona más céntrica, residencial y comercial de la ciudad de Oviedo
4. 142 habitaciones
5. salas para reuniones, congresos, banquetes y conferencias con capacidad para albergar hasta 800 personas

## History Connection

The **Hotel de la Reconquista** is in Asturias. The **Reconquista,** or reconquest of Spain from the Moors, began in the mountains of Asturias. Tradition has it that don Pelayo began the reconquest from Covadonga in Asturias in 722.

# Conexiones

## National Standards

**Connections**
This reading about physical fitness and various kinds of exercises establishes a connection with another discipline, allowing students to reinforce and further their knowledge of physical education through the study of Spanish.

**¡OJO!** The readings in the **Conexiones** section are optional. They focus on some of the major disciplines taught in schools and universities. The vocabulary is useful for discussing such topics as history, literature, art, economics, business, science, etc. You may choose any of the following ways to do the readings in the **Conexiones** sections.

**Independent reading** Have students read the selections and do the post-reading activities as homework, which you collect. This option is least intrusive on class time and requires a minimum of teacher involvement.

**Homework with in-class follow-up** Assign the readings and post-reading activities as homework. Review and discuss the material in class the next day.

**Intensive in-class activity** This option includes a pre-reading vocabulary presentation, in-class reading and discussion, assignment of the activities for homework, and a discussion of the assignment in class the following day.

# Conexiones

## *La educación física*

### El ejercicio

Physical fitness is a concern for everyone. Our health depends upon our fitness. Maintaining muscle tone and cardiovascular health and avoiding weight gain are important to our well-being and to our enjoyment of life. Sometimes it's difficult to stay in shape when traveling. For this reason, many hotels in major cities in Spain and Latin America provide exercise rooms or temporary membership in healthclubs for their guests.

### El ejercicio

Los hombres y las mujeres que viajan mucho quieren mantenerse en forma. Por eso, muchos hoteles tienen un gimnasio para el uso de sus clientes donde pueden hacer ejercicio. Hay dos tipos de ejercicio, el ejercicio aeróbico o cardiovascular y el ejercicio de fortaleza muscular.

**Ejercicios aeróbicos**

Los ejercicios aeróbicos como el jogging, el caminar, la natación, el «step» y el «spinning» aumentan temporalmente la respiración. Aumentan también el ritmo del corazón. Hacen más fuertes el corazón y todo el sistema cardiovascular. Algunos ejercicios aeróbicos son muy entretenidos[1] como, por ejemplo, el patinaje lineal[2] y el ciclismo.

[1]entretenidos *entertaining*
[2]patinaje lineal *roller blading*



### Learning from Realia

*(page 182)* Have students look at the yoga brochure pictured on this page. Ask them which words in the list of benefits of yoga are cognates. Ask if they can guess what **estiramientos,** the only word that is not a cognate, means. *(stretching)*

**Ejercicios de fortaleza muscular**

Los ejercicios de fortaleza muscular aumentan el tamaño y la fuerza de los músculos como los bíceps y tríceps y los músculos pectorales. Para hacer ejercicios de fortaleza muscular usamos una serie de aparatos—pesas y barras, tubos, ligas y bandas elásticas.

Un buen programa de ejercicios alterna el ejercicio aeróbico con el ejercicio de fortaleza muscular. Es decir, se practica un día aeróbicos y otro día fortaleza. Lo más importante es hacer ejercicio todos los días, aunque por sólo unos veinte minutos. También es importante no hacer demasiado ejercicio. Demasiado ejercicio te puede hacer daño. Tu cuerpo te dice cuando debes descansar[3]. Todo en moderación es siempre una buena idea.

[3]descansar *rest*

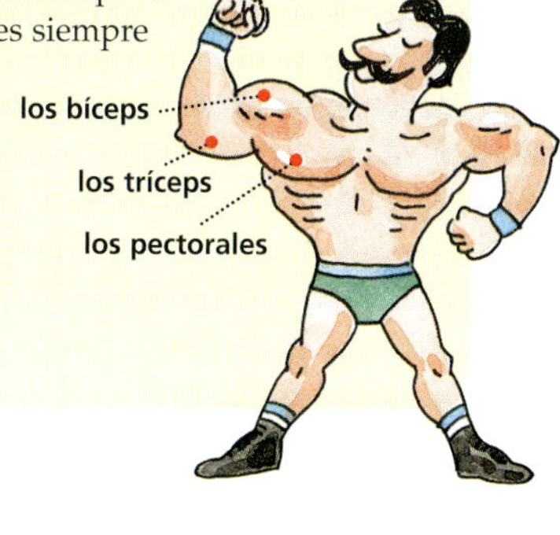

los bíceps

los tríceps

los pectorales

## ¿Comprendes?

**A Para mantenerse en forma** Completen.

1. Muchas personas que viajan quieren mantenerse en ____.
2. Los hoteles tienen un gimnasio donde los huéspedes pueden hacer ____.
3. Otro nombre para el «ejercicio aeróbico» es «ejercicio ____».
4. El tipo de ejercicio que no es aeróbico es el ejercicio de ____.
5. El ejercicio aeróbico aumenta el ritmo del ____.
6. El ejercicio de fortaleza muscular aumenta el tamaño de los ____.
7. Un programa que ____ el ejercicio aeróbico y el ejercicio de fortaleza muscular es recomendable.
8. Es importante hacer ejercicio ____ pero también es importante ____.
9. Si haces demasiado ejercicio, puedes hacer ____ a tu cuerpo.

**B ¿Aeróbico o fortaleza muscular?**

Identifiquen el tipo de ejercicio.

1. pesas y barras
2. patinaje lineal
3. «step»
4. bandas elásticas
5. jogging
6. ligas

# Conexiones

## PRESENTATION

### *La educación física*
### El ejercicio

Since students are probably familiar with most of the information in this reading from their health and physical education classes, you may wish to have all students scan the selection quickly. They should have little trouble understanding it.

**LEVELING**

**A:** Reading

## Answers to ¿Comprendes?

**A**

1. forma
2. ejercicio
3. cardiovascular
4. fortaleza muscular
5. corazón
6. músculos
7. alterna
8. todos los días, no hacer demasiado ejercicio
9. daño

**B**

1. fortaleza muscular
2. aeróbico
3. aeróbico
4. fortaleza muscular
5. aeróbico
6. fortaleza muscular

# ¡Te toca a ti!

## Use what you have learned

### Recycling

These activities allow students to use the vocabulary and structure from this chapter in completely open-ended, real-life situations.

### PRESENTATION

Encourage students to say as much as possible when they do these activities. Tell them not to be afraid to make mistakes, since the goal of the activities is real-life communication. If someone in the group makes an error, allow the others to politely correct him or her. Let students choose the activities they would like to do.

You may wish to divide students into pairs or groups. Encourage students to elaborate on the basic theme and to be creative. They may use props, pictures, or posters if they wish.

### PRACTICE

1 You may call on one group of students to present their conversation for Activity 1 to the class.

3 Activity 3 could be a fun activity to have pairs of students perform for the entire class.



# ¡Te toca a ti!

## Use what you have learned

HABLAR 1

### Una habitación, por favor.

✔ *Reserve a hotel room*

Tú has llegado a Burgos. Necesitas una habitación en un hotel. Llama al Hotel Mesón del Cid. Habla con el/la recepcionista (un[a] compañero[a]). Quieres saber si tienen una habitación disponible *(available)*. Necesitas saber el precio. Como no conoces a Burgos, no sabes dónde está el hotel. El/La recepcionista te ayudará y contestará cortésmente a todas tus preguntas.

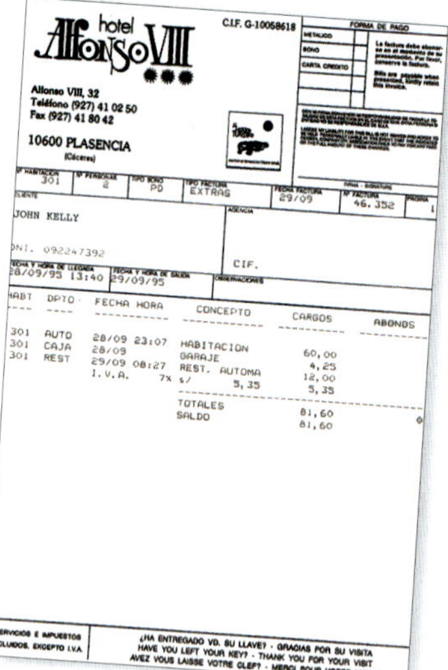

hotel Alfonso VIII
C.I.F. G-10058618
Alfonso VIII, 32
Teléfono (927) 41 02 50
Fax (927) 41 80 42
10600 PLASENCIA
(Cáceres)

FORMA DE PAGO: METALICO / BONO / CARTA CREDITO

Nº HABITACION 301 | Nº PERSONAS 2 | TIPO BONO PD | TIPO FACTURA EXTRAS | FECHA FACTURA 29/09 | Nº FACTURA 46.352 | PAGINA 1

CLIENTE: JOHN KELLY
DNI. 092247392
CIF.
FECHA Y HORA DE LLEGADA 28/09/95 13:40
FECHA Y HORA DE SALIDA 29/09/95

| HABT | DPTO | FECHA HORA | CONCEPTO | CARGOS | ABONOS |
|---|---|---|---|---|---|
| 301 | AUTO | 28/09 23:07 | HABITACION | 60,00 | |
| 301 | CAJA | 28/09 | GARAJE | 4,25 | |
| 301 | REST | 29/09 08:27 | REST. AUTOMA | 12,00 | |
| | | I.V.A. 7% | s/ 5,35 | 5,35 | |
| | | | TOTALES | 81,60 | |
| | | | SALDO | 81,60 | 0 |

SERVICIOS E IMPUESTOS INCLUIDOS, EXCEPTO I.V.A.

¿HA ENTREGADO VD. SU LLAVE? - GRACIAS POR SU VISITA
HAVE YOU LEFT YOUR KEY? - THANK YOU FOR YOUR VISIT
AVEZ VOUS LAISSE VOTRE CLEF? - MERCI POUR VOTRE VISITE

HABLAR 2

### La cuenta, por favor.

✔ *Check out of a hotel*

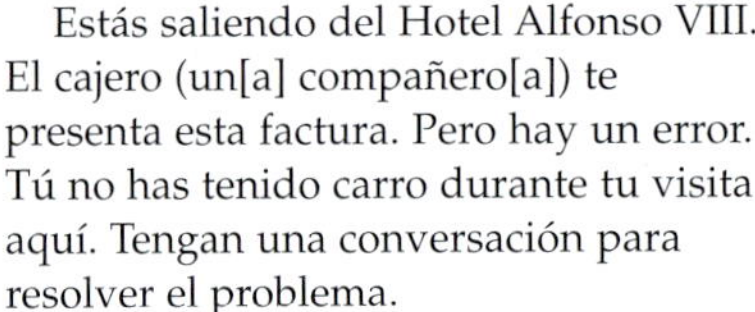

Estás saliendo del Hotel Alfonso VIII. El cajero (un[a] compañero[a]) te presenta esta factura. Pero hay un error. Tú no has tenido carro durante tu visita aquí. Tengan una conversación para resolver el problema.

HABLAR 3

### La buenaventura

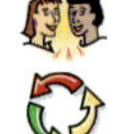

✔ *Tell what will happen in the future*

Trabaja con un(a) compañero(a). Él o ella te hará muchas preguntas porque quiere saber todo lo que le pasará. Tendrás que usar tu imaginación. Después de terminar con las preguntas de tu compañero(a), cambien de rol y tú harás preguntas sobre tu futuro.



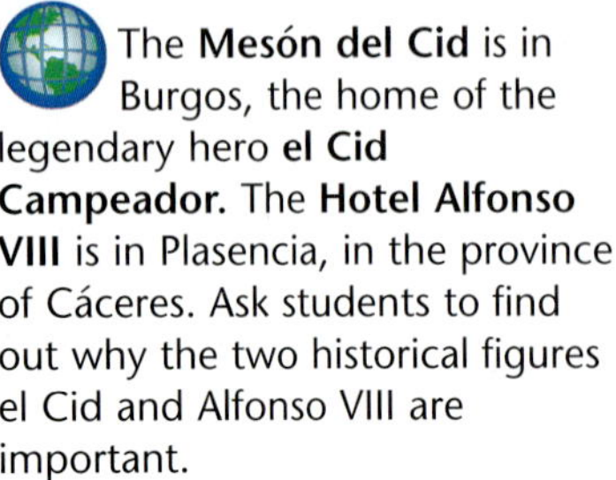

### Geography Connection

The **Mesón del Cid** is in Burgos, the home of the legendary hero **el Cid Campeador.** The **Hotel Alfonso VIII** is in Plasencia, in the province of Cáceres. Ask students to find out why the two historical figures el Cid and Alfonso VIII are important.

### Answers to ¡Te toca a ti!

1 *Answers will vary. Students will use vocabulary and structure from the chapter to request a hotel room.*

2 *Answers will vary. Students will use the realia as they question one of the charges on the bill.*

3 *Answers will vary but will include structure previously learned in this chapter to talk about what will happen in the future.*

## 4 Un fax para el hotel Excelsior

***✔ Obtain information about a hotel***

Los padres de uno de tus amigos van a México. Quieren quedarse (hospedarse, alojarse) en el Hotel Excelsior. Saben que tú estás estudiando el español y te piden ayuda. Tú les vas a preparar un fax para el Hotel Excelsior. Para preparar el fax, escribe una lista de toda la infomación que necesitan los padres de tu amigo. Luego prepara todas las preguntas que tienes que incluir en el fax. Al terminar tus dos listas, prepara la copia final para el fax que vas a enviar.

## 5 Un anuncio

A hotel in your community wants to encourage Spanish-speaking guests to stay there. They have asked you to prepare an advertisement describing the hotel and listing its best features. Use the advertisement for the Parador Reyes Católicos in Santiago de Compostela, Galicia, as a guide, but be as original as you can. Be sure your ad reflects services offered by the hotel as well as activities and events in your community.

### Writing Strategy

**Creating an advertisement**

The purpose of an advertisement is to persuade people to buy a product or service. An effective ad will attract attention, arouse interest, and create desire. You can use a striking design to draw readers in. You can use facts and opinions to explain the product's features and to show why readers should be interested in your product—why it is better than the competition. And you can appeal to your readers' reason and emotion to make them want your product.

## ¡Te toca a ti!

**4** Tell students that in preparing their list of the information they need, they can very often use just one word.

### Writing Strategy

**Creating an advertisement**

Have students read the Writing Strategy on page 185.

### History Connection

**Santiago de Compostela** was one of the major sites of Christian pilgrimage during the Middle Ages, along with Rome and Jerusalem.

### Writing Development

Have students keep a notebook or portfolio containing their best written work from each chapter. These selected writings can be based on assignments from the Student Textbook and the Workbook. The activities on page 185 are examples of writing assignments that may be included in each student's portfolio. On page 70 in the Workbook, students will begin to develop an organized autobiography **(Mi autobiografía).** These workbook pages may also become a part of their portfolio.

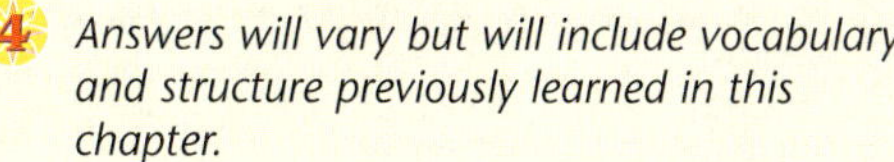

### Answers to ¡Te toca a ti!

**4** *Answers will vary but will include vocabulary and structure previously learned in this chapter.*

**5** *Answers will vary. Students will use vocabulary relating to hotels to create the advertisement.*

### LEVELING

These activities encompass all three levels. All students will be able to do them at a sophistication level commensurate with their ability in Spanish. Some students will be able to speak for several minutes, and others may be able to give just a few sentences. This is to be expected when students are functioning completely on their own generating their own language to the best of their ability.

Assessment

## Resource Manager

Communication Transparency C 6
Quizzes, pages 26–29
Performance Assessment, Task 6
Tests, pages 83–96
Situation Cards, Chapter 6
**Maratón mental** Videoquiz, Chapter 6
ExamView® Pro, Chapter 6

## Assessment

This is a pre-test for students to take before you administer the chapter test. Note that each section is cross-referenced so students can easily find the material they have to review in case they made errors. You may use Assessment Answers Transparency A 6 to do the assessment in class, or you may assign this assessment for homework. You can correct the assessment yourself, or you may prefer to project the answers on the overhead in class.

## Glencoe Technology

**MINDJOGGER VHS/DVD**

You may wish to help your students prepare for the chapter test by playing the MindJogger game show. Teams will compete against each other to review chapter vocabulary and structure and sharpen listening comprehension skills.

# Assessment

## Vocabulario

To review **Palabras 1**, turn to pages 162–163.

**1 Completen.**

1. Diego está viajando sólo. No lo acompaña nadie. Así reservó un cuarto ____.
2. Es necesario tener una ____ para abrir la puerta del cuarto.
3. El ____ subirá el equipaje al cuarto.
4. Diego sale hoy. Tiene que ____ el cuarto antes del mediodía.
5. Diego pedirá la ____ y pagará con su tarjeta de crédito.

To review **Palabras 2**, turn to pages 166–167.

**2 Identifiquen.**

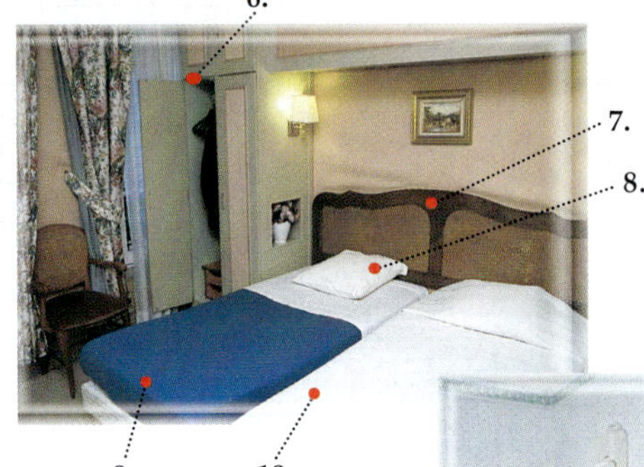


## Estructura

To review the future of irregular verbs, turn to page 170.

**3 Completen con el futuro.**

14. Él ____ que reservar un cuarto. (tener)
15–16. Ellos ____ saber qué día (tú) ____. (querer, salir)
17. Nosotros ____ el viaje en avión. (hacer)
18. Yo ____ ir también. (poder)
19. ¿Tú le ____ cuánto va a costar el hotel? (decir)



## Answers to Assessment

**1**

1. sencillo
2. llave
3. mozo (botones)
4. abandonar
5. cuenta

**2**

6. el armario
7. la cama
8. la almohada
9. la manta (la frazada)
10. la sábana
11. las toallas
12. el jabón
13. el lavabo

**3**

14. tendrá
15. querrán
16. saldrás
17. haremos
18. podré
19. dirás

 **Contesten con un pronombre.**

20. ¿El mozo te abrió la puerta?
21. ¿Abuelita me envió los regalos?
22. ¿Mamá te dio las entradas al zoológico?

To review direct and indirect object pronouns, turn to page 173.

## Cultura

 **Completen.**

23. Lo más atractivo de los paradores españoles es que ____.
24. Antes, el Parador San Francisco en Granada era ____.
25. Los restaurantes de muchos paradores sirven ____.

To review this cultural information, turn to pages 178–179.

Parador San Francisco, Granada



## Assessment

**FOLDABLES Study Organizer** **Dinah Zike's Study Guides**

Your students may wish to use Foldable 10 to organize, display, and arrange data as they learn to describe many situations in Spanish. You may wish to encourage them to draw a picture from each chapter as they continue to gather facts and make observations about all the different topics they will be studying.

An *envelope fold* is also ideal for collecting and reviewing information students have learned about particular subjects.

## Answers to Assessment

20. Sí, el mozo me la abrió.
21. Sí, abuelita te los envió.
22. Sí, mamá me las dio.

23. son todos únicos.
24. un convento
25. platos típicos

# ¡Hablo como un pro!

This unique page gives students the opportunity to speak freely and say whatever they can, using the vocabulary and structures they have learned in the chapter. The illustration serves to remind students of precisely what they know how to say in Spanish. There are no activities that students do not have the ability to describe or talk about in Spanish. The art not only depicts the vocabulary and content of this chapter, but also reinforces what they learned in previous chapters.

You may wish to use this page in many ways. Some possibilities are to have students do the following:

1. Look at the illustration and identify items by giving the correct Spanish words.
2. Make up sentences about what they see in the illustration.
3. Make up questions about the illustration. They can call on another class member to respond if you do this as a class activity, or you may prefer to allow students to work in small groups. This activity is extremely beneficial because it enables students to actively use interrogative words.
4. Answer questions you ask them about the illustration.
5. Work in pairs and make up a conversation based on the illustration.
6. Look at the illustration and give a complete oral review of what they see.
7. Look at the illustration and write a paragraph (or essay) about it.

You can also use this page as an assessment or testing tool, taking into account individual differences by having students go from simple to quite complicated tasks.

# ¡Hablo como un pro!

Tell all you can about this illustration.

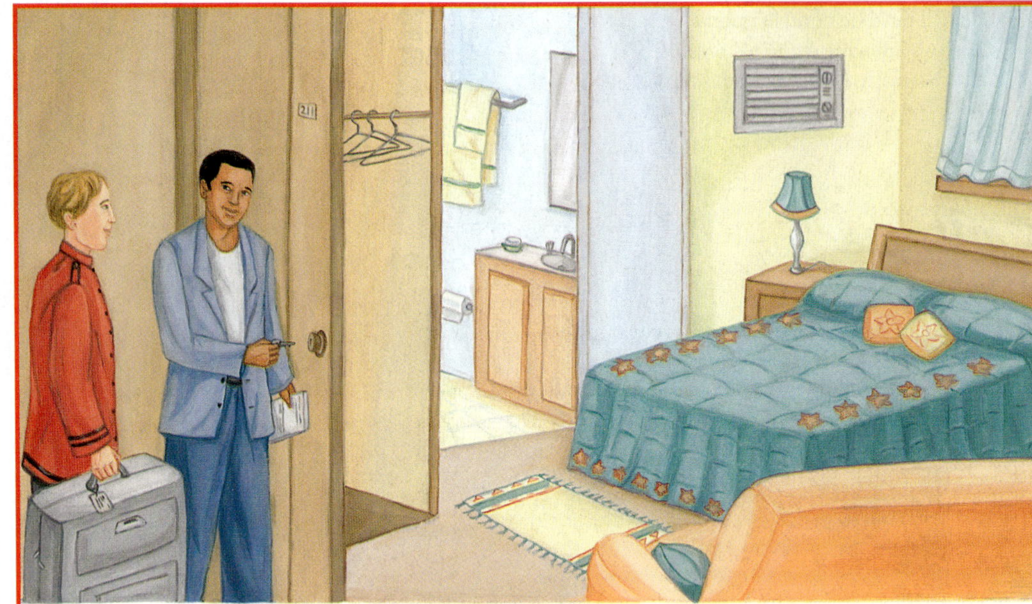

The assessment can be either oral or written. You may wish to use the rubrics provided on pages T20–T21 as you give students the following directions.

1. Identify the topic or situation of the illustration.
2. Give the Spanish words for as many items as you can.
3. Think of as many sentences as you can to describe the illustration.
4. Go over your sentences and put them in the best sequencing to give a coherent story based on the illustration.

# Vocabulario

### Making a hotel reservation

reservar
la reservación
el cuarto, la habitación
un cuarto sencillo
un cuarto doble

### Checking into a hotel

el hotel
la recepción
el/la recepcionista
el/la cliente, el/la huésped
la ficha, la tarjeta
la llave
la puerta
el botones, el mozo
el equipaje
el ascensor, el elevador

### Checking out of a hotel

abandonar el cuarto
bajar las maletas
pedir la cuenta
pagar la factura

**How well do you know your vocabulary?**

- Identify words you would use when reserving a hotel room.
- Describe the type of room you would like to have and how you will pay for it.

### Talking about a hotel room

la puerta
la cama
la sábana
la almohada
la manta, la frazada
el televisor
el aire acondicionado
el armario
la percha, el colgador
el sillón
el sofá

### Talking about a bathroom

la bañera
la ducha
el inodoro, el váter
el lavabo
el jabón
la toalla

### Talking about cleaning a hotel room

la camarera
limpiar el cuarto
hacer la cama
cambiar las toallas

**VIDEOTUR**

**Episodio 6**

In this video episode, you will join Francisco on an overnight excursion to a nearby city. See page 485 for more information.



# Vocabulario

## Vocabulary Review

The words and phrases in the **Vocabulario** have been taught for productive use in this chapter. They are summarized here as a resource for both student and teacher. This list also serves as a convenient resource for the **¡Te toca a ti!** activities on pages 184 and 185. There are at least ten cognates in this vocabulary list. Have students find them.

**¡OJO!** You will notice that the vocabulary list here is not translated. This has been done intentionally, since we feel that by the time students have finished the material in the chapter they should be familiar with the meanings of all the words. If there are several words they still do not know, we recommend that they refer to the **Palabras 1** and **2** sections in the chapter or go to the dictionaries at the end of this book to find the meanings. However, if you prefer that your students have the English translations, please refer to Vocabulary Transparency 6.1, where you will find all these words with their translations.

**VIDEO VHS/DVD**

The Video Program allows students to see how the chapter vocabulary and structures are used by native speakers within an engaging story line. For maximum reinforcement, show the video episode as a final activity for Chapter 6.

# Planning for Chapter 7

## SCOPE AND SEQUENCE, PAGES 190–221

### Topics

- ❖ Airplane terminology
- ❖ Airport terminology
- ❖ Geographical terms

### Culture

- ❖ El Alto Airport and La Paz, Bolivia
- ❖ La Paz, El Alto, and Lake Titicaca
- ❖ Capitán Emilio Carranza: A Mexican hero
- ❖ The geography of Spain
- ❖ **Vistas de Costa Rica**

### Functions

- ❖ How to talk about air travel
- ❖ How to talk about geographical features
- ❖ How to express conditions
- ❖ How to talk about things stated earlier

### Structure

- ❖ The conditional of regular verbs
- ❖ The conditional of irregular verbs
- ❖ Two object pronouns with **se**

### National Standards

- ❖ Communication Standard 1.1 pages 194, 195, 198, 199, 201, 202, 203, 204, 205, 206, 207, 209, 216
- ❖ Communication Standard 1.2 pages 195, 199, 205, 207, 208, 209, 210–211, 212, 213, 214–215, 216
- ❖ Communication Standard 1.3 page 217
- ❖ Cultures Standard 2.1 page 212
- ❖ Cultures Standard 2.2 pages 210–211
- ❖ Connections Standard 3.1 pages 213, 214–215
- ❖ Communities Standard 5.1 page 221
- ❖ Communities Standard 5.2 page 202

## PACING AND PRIORITIES

**The chapter content is color coded below to assist you in planning.**

■ **required** ■ **recommended** ■ **optional**

**Vocabulario** *(required)* *Days 1–4*

- ■ Palabras 1
  - En el avión
  - La cabina
- ■ Palabras 2
  - En el aeropuerto
  - Un poco de geografía

**Estructura** *(required)* *Days 5–7*

- ■ Modo potencial o condicional de verbos regulares
- ■ Modo potencial de verbos irregulares
- ■ Dos complementos con **se**

**Conversación** *(required)*

- ■ En el avión

**Lecturas culturales**

- ■ El aeropuerto que se llama «El Alto» *(recommended)*
- ■ Los alrededores de La Paz *(optional)*
- ■ Un héroe de la aviación latinoamericana *(optional)*

**Conexiones**

- ■ La geografía *(optional)*

■ **¡Te toca a ti!** *(recommended)*

■ **Assessment** *(recommended)*

■ **¡Hablo como un pro!** *(optional)*

## RESOURCE GUIDE

| Section | Pages | Section Resources |
|---|---|---|
| **Vocabulario PALABRAS 1** | | |
| En el avión<br>La cabina | 192, 194–195<br>192–195 | Vocabulary Transparencies 7.2–7.3<br>Audio CD 5<br>Audio Activities TE, pages 77–78<br>Workbook, pages 73–74<br>Quiz 1, page 30<br>ExamView® Pro |
| **Vocabulario PALABRAS 2** | | |
| En el aeropuerto<br>Un poco de geografía | 196–199<br>197–199 | Vocabulary Transparencies 7.4–7.5<br>Audio CD 5<br>Audio Activities TE, pages 79–80<br>Workbook, pages 75–76<br>Quiz 2, page 31<br>ExamView® Pro |
| **Estructura** | | |
| Modo potencial o condicional de verbos regulares<br>Modo potencial de verbos irregulares<br>Dos complementos con **se** | 200–202<br>203–205<br>205–207 | Audio CD 5<br>Audio Activities TE, pages 80–83<br>Workbook, pages 77–79<br>Quizzes 3–5, pages 32–34<br>ExamView® Pro |
| **Conversación** | | |
| En el avión | 208–209 | Audio CD 5<br>Audio Activities TE, pages 83–84<br>Interactive CD-ROM |
| **Lecturas culturales** | | |
| El aeropuerto que se llama «El Alto»<br>Los alrededores de La Paz<br>Un héroe de la aviación latinoamericana | 210–211<br>212<br>213 | Audio CD 5<br>Audio Activities TE, page 85<br>Tests, pages 99–100, 103 |
| **Conexiones** | | |
| La geografía | 214–215 | Tests, pages 104–105 |
| **¡Te toca a ti!** | | |
| | 216–217 | **¡Viva el mundo hispano!** Video, Episode 7<br>Video Activities, pages 88–91<br>Spanish Online Activities spanish.glencoe.com |
| **Assessment** | | |
| | 218–219 | Communication Transparency C 7<br>Quizzes 1–5, pages 30–34<br>Performance Assessment, Task 7<br>Tests, pages 97–110<br>Situation Cards, Chapter 7<br>ExamView® Pro<br>**Maratón mental** Videoquiz |

# Using Your Resources for Chapter 7

## Transparencies

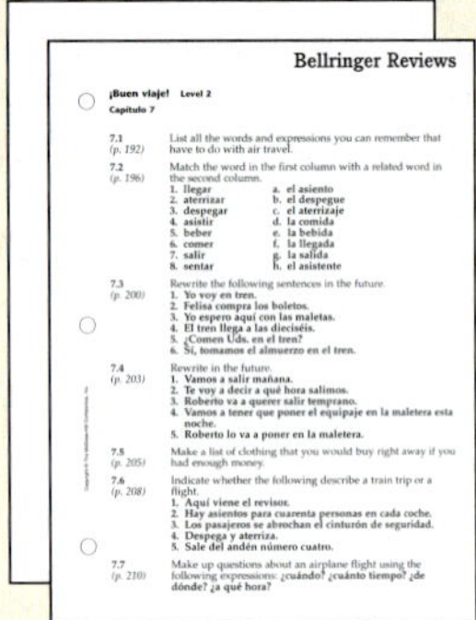
Bellringer 7.1–7.7

Vocabulary 7.1–7.5

Communication C 7

## Workbook

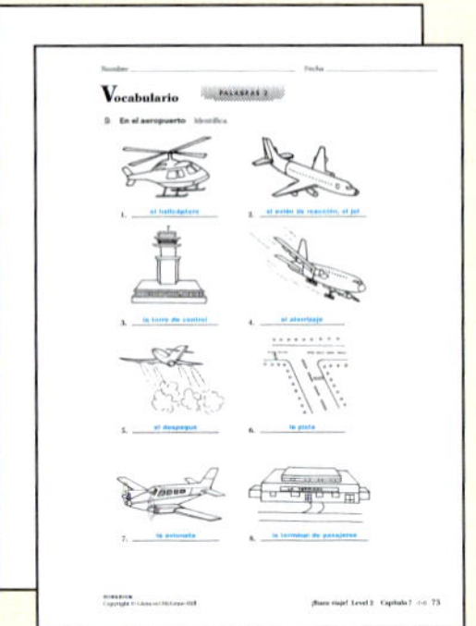
Vocabulary, pages 73–76

Structure, pages 77–79

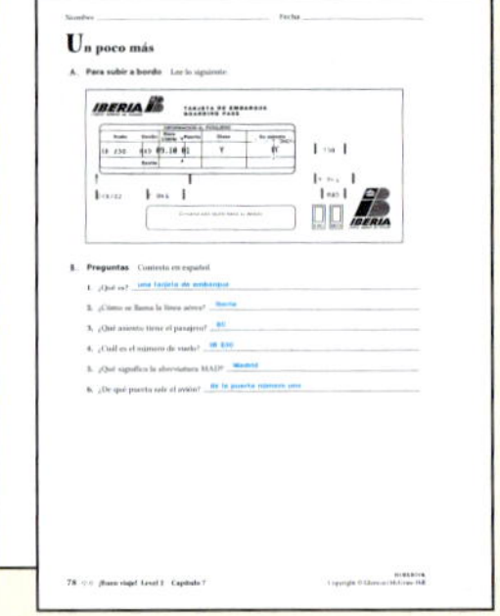
Enrichment, pages 80–83

## Audio Activities

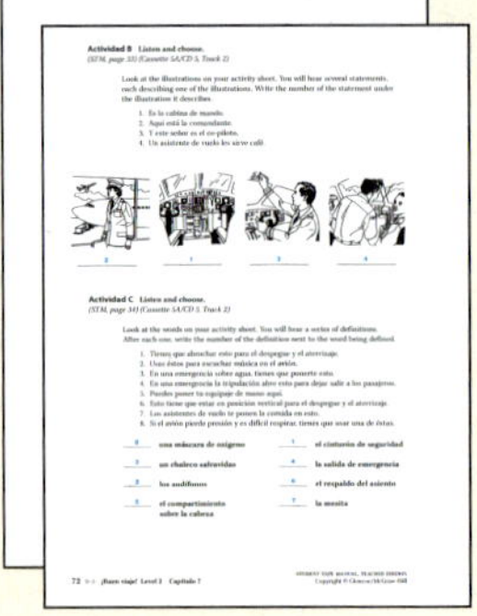
Vocabulary, pages 77–80

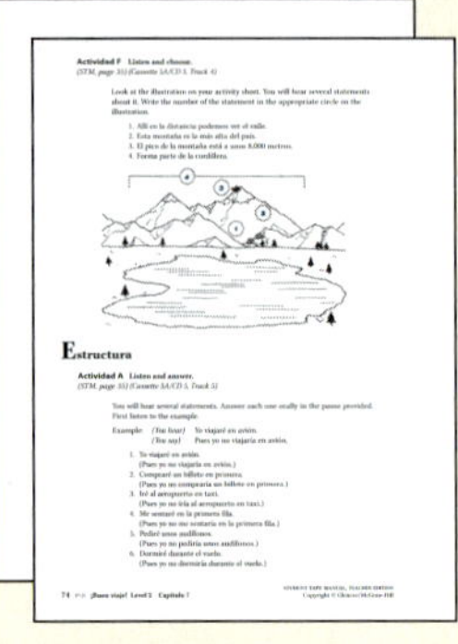
Structure, pages 80–83

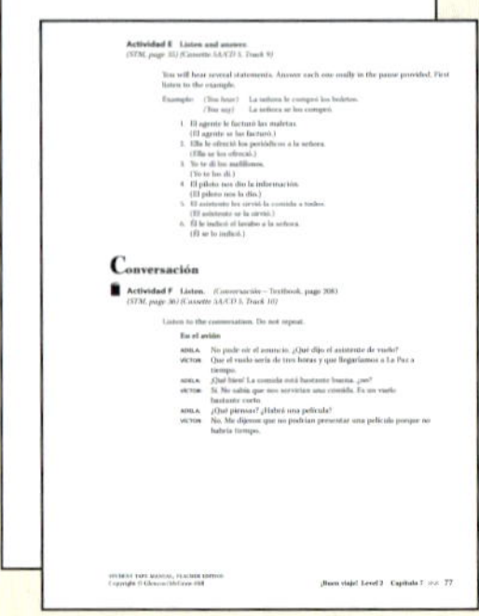
Conversation, pages 83–84

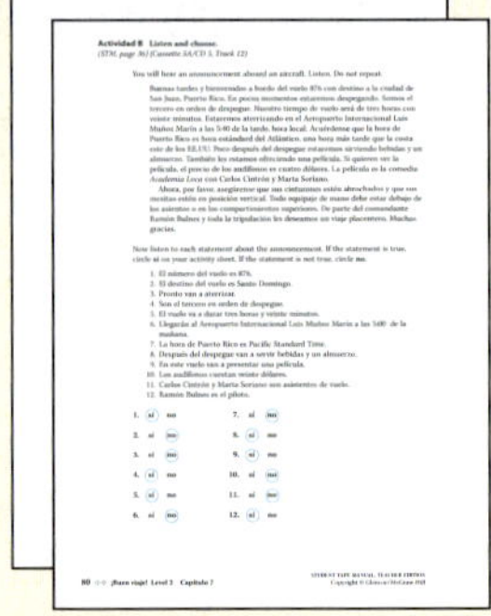
Additional Practice, pages 86–88

# Assessment

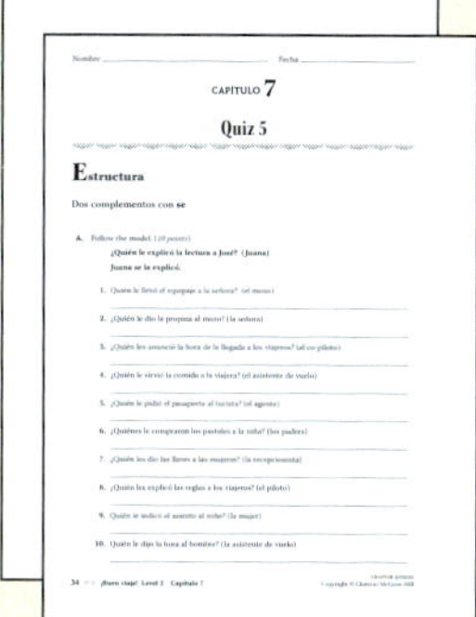

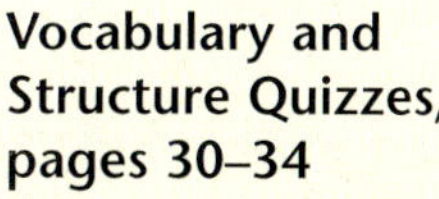

Vocabulary and Structure Quizzes, pages 30–34

Chapter Tests, pages 97–110

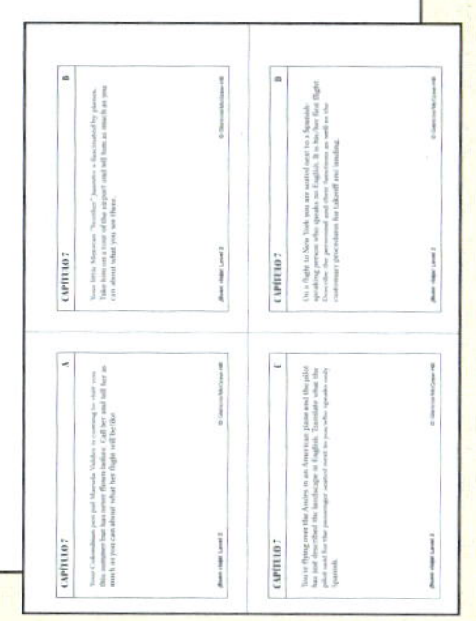

Situation Cards, Chapter 7

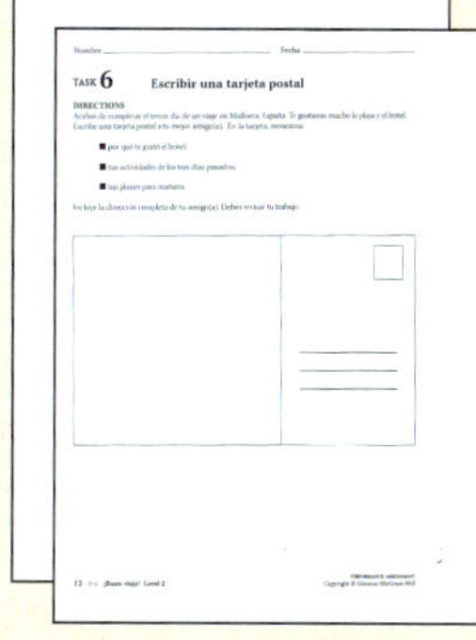

Performance Assessment, pages 9–14

MindJogger Videoquiz, ExamView® Pro, Chapter 7

## Timesaving Teacher Tools

### TeacherWorks™

TeacherWorks™ is your all-in-one teacher resource center. Personalize lesson plans, access resources from the Teacher Wraparound Edition, connect to the Internet, or make a to-do list. These are only a few of the many features that can assist you in the planning and organizing of your lessons.

Includes:

- A calendar feature
- Access to all program blackline masters
- Standards correlations and more

### ExamView® Pro

Test Bank software for Macintosh and Windows makes creating, editing, customizing, and printing tests quick and easy.

## Technology Resources

In the Chapter 7 Internet Activity, you will have a chance to learn more about the Spanish-speaking world. Visit spanish.glencoe.com

On the interactive CD–ROM, students can listen to and take part in a recorded version of the conversation in Chapter 7.

**¡Viva el mundo hispano!** Video and Video Activities, Chapter 7. Available on VHS and DVD.

Help your students prepare for the chapter test by playing the **Maratón mental** Videoquiz game show. Teams will compete against each other to review chapter vocabulary and structure and sharpen listening comprehension skills. Available on VHS and DVD.

**¡Buen viaje!** is also available on CD or Online.

# Preview

In this chapter, students will learn to talk about air travel, in-flight services, and geography. They will learn the formation of the conditional and the use of **se** when combining direct and indirect object pronouns. The cultural focus of the chapter is on air travel in Latin America and how it is influenced by geographical features of the land.

## National Standards

**Communication**

In Chapter 7 students will learn to communicate in spoken and written Spanish on the following topics:

- air travel
- services aboard a flight
- geography

Students will obtain and provide information about these topics and engage in conversations that would typically take place aboard a plane as they fulfill the chapter objectives listed on this page.

Capítulo 7

# El vuelo

## Objetivos

In this chapter you will learn to:

- talk about air travel
- discuss the influence of geography on travel in Latin America
- talk about things that would happen under certain conditions
- talk about air travel in Hispanic countries

Susana González-Pagliere *Village with Volcano*

# Capítulo 7

## Spotlight on Culture

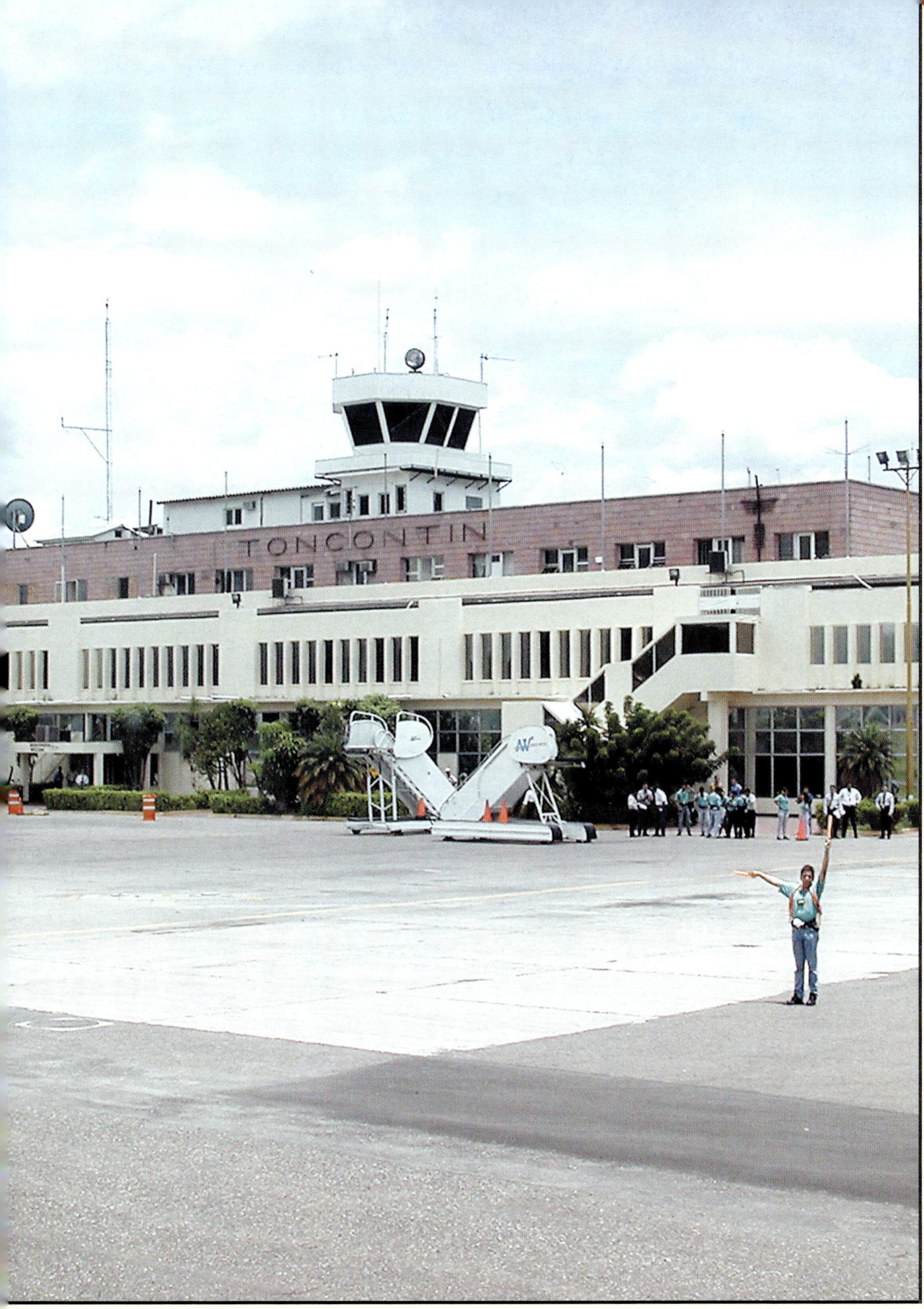

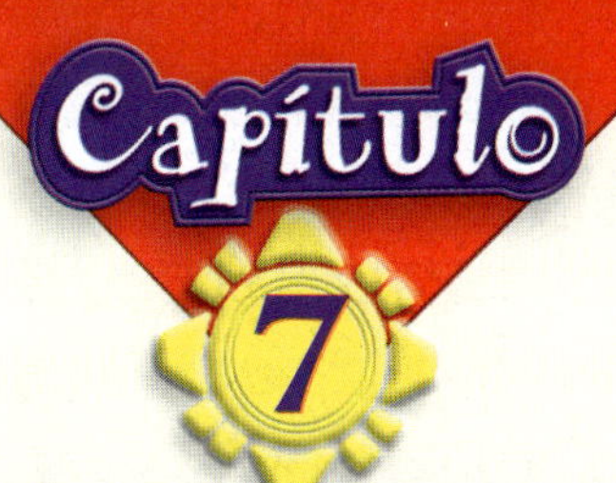

**Fotografía** Toncontin is the international airport that serves Tegucigalpa, the capital of Honduras. Tegucigalpa takes its name from two Indian words, **teguz** meaning *hill* and **galpa** meaning *silver.* For many years, Tegucigalpa was a small mining town. It became the capital in 1880. The entire **Distrito Central** has a population of over one million. Tegucigalpa has the flavor of a small colonial city. Clusters of colorful houses are built into the hills that surround the city.

## LEVELING

The activities, conversations, and readings within each chapter are marked according to level of difficulty. **E** indicates easy. **A** indicates average. **C** indicates challenging. Some activities cover a range of difficulty. In some activities, for example, advanced students will be able to produce more extensive responses while students who learn at a different rate may give less detailed responses. The leveling indicators will help you individualize instruction to best meet your students' needs.

PALABRAS 1

## 1 PREPARATION

### Resource Manager

Vocabulary Transparencies 7.2–7.3
Audio Activities TE, pages 77–78
Audio CD 5
Workbook, pages 73–74
Quizzes, page 30
ExamView® Pro

### Bellringer Review

*Use BRR Transparency 7.1 or write the following on the board.*
List all the words and expressions you can remember that have to do with air travel.

## 2 PRESENTATION

**Step 1** Project Vocabulary Transparencies 7.2–7.3 and have students repeat the new words, phrases, and sentences after you or Audio CD 5.

**Step 2** Model the new vocabulary again, calling out vocabulary words in random order. Have volunteers point to the appropriate image on the screen as you say the words.

**Step 3** Use the usual questioning techniques to present the material on page 192. Begin with simple *yes / no* and *either / or* questions.

**Step 4** When students have produced the new vocabulary on pages 192–193 several times, progress to open-ended questions such as: **¿Qué estaba haciendo el asistente de vuelo? ¿Qué les estaba dando a los pasajeros? ¿Qué estaba distribuyendo la asistente de vuelo? ¿Qué estaban sirviendo los asistentes de vuelo?**

# Vocabulario

PALABRAS 1

## En el avión

la tripulación

la cabina de mando, la cabina de vuelo

los asistentes de vuelo

## La cabina

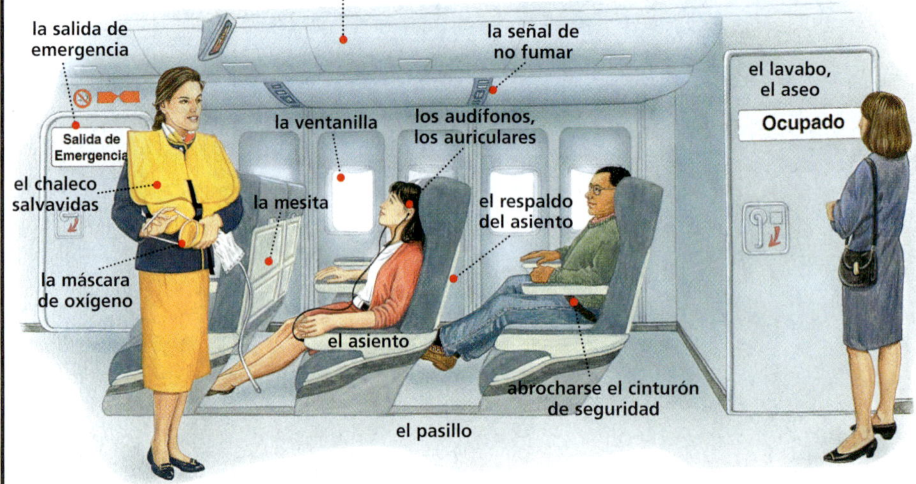


La señora iría al lavabo, pero no puede.
Está ocupado.



### Reaching All Students

**Total Physical Response**
*(Student 1),* ven acá. Estás en el avión.
Busca tu asiento.
Abre el compartimiento superior.
Pon tu equipaje en el compartimiento.
Cierra el compartimiento superior.
Siéntate.
Abróchate el cinturón de seguridad.
Pon el respaldo de tu asiento en posición vertical.
El asistente de vuelo llega. Va a darte los auriculares. Tómalos.
Pónte los auriculares.
Escoge un canal de música.
Gracias, *(Student 1)*. Bien hecho. Regresa a tu asiento.

El asistente de vuelo hizo algunos anuncios.
Dijo que los asistentes de vuelo:

pasarían por la cabina con los audífonos;
distribuirían los audífonos;
se los distribuirían a los pasajeros;

servirían bebidas y una comida durante el vuelo;

y que en el caso de una emergencia las máscaras de oxígeno caerían automáticamente.

También dijo que el equipaje de mano tendría que caber debajo del asiento o en el compartimiento superior.

Durante el vuelo los asistentes de vuelo sirvieron una comida a los pasajeros.

Se la sirvieron de un carrito.
Se la sirvieron en una bandeja.



## Reaching All Students

**Additional Practice** You may wish to ask the following questions about the photos and illustrations on pages 192–193:
**¿Iría al lavabo la señora?**
**¿Adónde iría?**
**¿Por qué no puede?**
**¿Qué dijo el asistente de vuelo?**
**¿Dijo que los asistentes pasarían por la cabina?**
**¿Qué distribuirían a los pasajeros?**
**¿Qué servirían?**
After presenting the vocabulary, have students say as many things as they can that the flight attendant said would take place during the flight.



## Vocabulary Expansion

Other words for *flight attendants* are:
- **la azafata** (female only, used in Spain)
- **los sobrecargos**
- **los auxiliares de vuelo**
- **los aeromozos**

Other terms for *lavatory* are **los servicios (sanitarios)** and **el retrete,** but this last term is considered old-fashioned and is less common.

## Reaching All Students

**Additional Practice** You may wish to have students write a short paragraph on this topic: **Hace cuarenta años los vuelos intercontinentales eran muy raros y sólo para la gente rica. Hoy hay vuelos relativamente baratos entre todos los continentes. ¿Qué influencia ha tenido esto en la manera en que la gente piensa? ¿Nos ha cambiado o no? ¿Qué opinas?**

## Chapter Projects

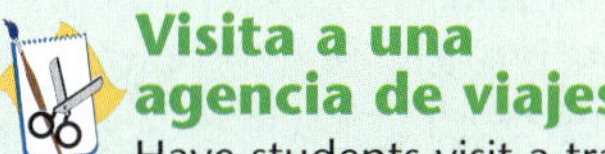

### Visita a una agencia de viajes

Have students visit a travel agency and obtain brochures on Bolivia and other countries in the Andes region of South America. Have them write captions for the brochures in Spanish and design a bulletin board display.

**LEVELING**
**E:** Vocabulary

Vocabulario

## 3 PRACTICE

## ¿Qué palabra necesito?

**¡OJO!** When students are doing the **¿Qué palabra necesito?** activities, accept any answer that makes sense. The purpose of these activities is to have students use the new vocabulary. They are not factual recall activities. Thus, it is not necessary for students to remember specific factual information from the vocabulary presentation when answering. If you wish, have students use the visuals on this page as a stimulus, when possible.

**Historieta** Each time **Historieta** appears, it means that the answers to the activity form a short story. Encourage students to look at the title of the **Historieta,** since it can help them do the activity.

**1** Have students refer to the illustrations as they do Activity 1.

**2** Activity 2 can be done first orally with books closed.

**3** and **4** Have students prepare Activities 3 and 4 before you go over them in class.

Vocabulario

# ¿Qué palabra necesito?

**1** **¿Qué es o quién es?** Identifiquen.

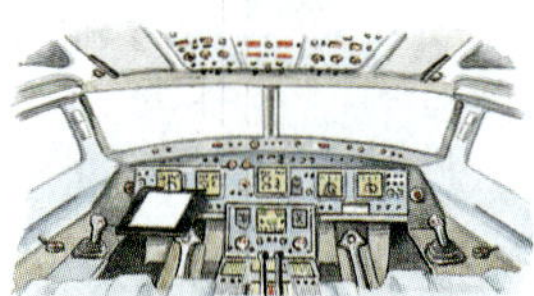

1. ¿Es el lavabo o la cabina de mando?
2. ¿Es la máscara de oxígeno o la señal de no fumar?
3. ¿Es el asistente de vuelo o el comandante?

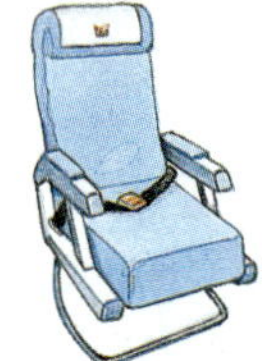

4. ¿Es el chaleco salvavidas o el cinturón de seguridad?
5. ¿Es el pasillo o el compartimiento superior?
6. ¿Es el asiento o la mesita?

**2** **Historieta La tripulación** Contesten según se indica.

1. ¿Dónde en el avión está el piloto? (en la cabina de vuelo o en la cabina de mando)
2. ¿Quiénes componen la tripulación? (el piloto o el comandante, el co-piloto y los asistentes de vuelo)
3. ¿Quiénes sirven a los pasajeros durante el vuelo? (los asistentes de vuelo)
4. ¿De qué se responsabilizan los asistentes de vuelo? (de la seguridad de los pasajeros)
5. En el caso de una emergencia, ¿por dónde salen los pasajeros? (por las salidas de emergencia)

**3** **A bordo del avión** Pareen.

1. donde uno va para lavarse las manos en el avión
2. donde se pone el equipaje de mano
3. lo que se usa para oír música o ver una película
4. la persona que sirve a los pasajeros en el avión
5. lo que usa el asistente de vuelo para servir la comida
6. donde pone el asistente de vuelo la comida que le sirve al pasajero

a. el lavabo
b. la bandeja
c. el asistente de vuelo
d. la mesita
e. el compartimiento superior
f. los audífonos



## ANSWERS TO ¿Qué palabra necesito?

**1**

1. Es la cabina de mando.
2. Es la máscara de oxígeno.
3. Es el comandante.
4. Es el chaleco salvavidas.
5. Es el compartimiento superior.
6. Es el asiento.

**2**

1. El piloto está en la cabina de vuelo o en la cabina de mando.
2. El piloto o el comandante, el co-piloto y los asistentes de vuelo componen la tripulación.
3. Los asistentes de vuelo sirven a los pasajeros durante el vuelo.
4. Los asistentes de vuelo se responsabilizan de la seguridad de los pasajeros.
5. En el caso de una emergencia, los pasajeros salen por las salidas de emergencia.

**3**

1. a
2. e
3. f
4. c
5. b
6. d

**4** **Algunas reglas a bordo del avión** Contesten.

1. ¿Qué abrocharías durante el despegue y el aterrizaje?
   a. el cinturón de seguridad
   b. el respaldo del asiento
   c. la máscara de oxígeno
2. Durante el despegue y el aterrizaje, ¿dónde pondrías tu equipaje de mano?
   a. debajo del asiento
   b. en el pasillo
   c. en el lavabo
3. En caso de un cambio en la presión del aire en el avión, ¿qué usarías?
   a. el cinturón de seguridad
   b. los audífonos
   c. la máscara de oxígeno
4. ¿Cómo pondrías el respaldo de tu asiento durante el despegue y el aterrizaje?
   a. en posición vertical
   b. debajo del asiento
   c. en el compartimiento sobre la cabeza
5. En caso de un aterrizaje de emergencia en el mar, ¿qué te pondrías?
   a. el lavabo
   b. la señal de no fumar
   c. el chaleco salvavidas

La aerolínea Avensa

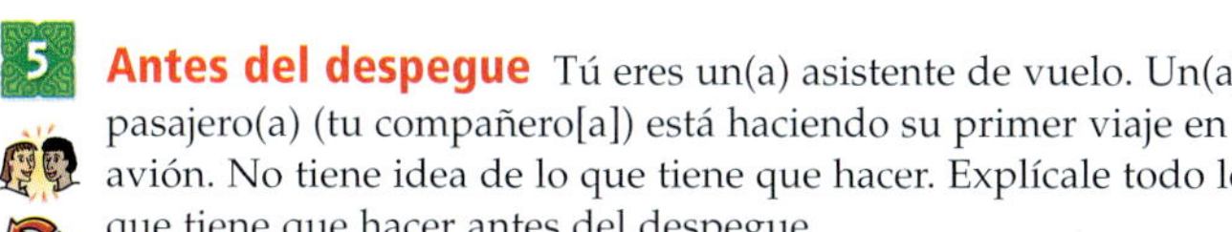

**5** **Antes del despegue** Tú eres un(a) asistente de vuelo. Un(a) pasajero(a) (tu compañero[a]) está haciendo su primer viaje en avión. No tiene idea de lo que tiene que hacer. Explícale todo lo que tiene que hacer antes del despegue.

**6** **A bordo del avión** Con un(a) compañero(a), mira el dibujo. Juntos describan todo lo que ven en el dibujo. Luego decidan si quieren hacer un viaje en avión. Expliquen por qué.



Vocabulario

**¡OJO!** Note that the activities are color-coded. All the activities in the text are communicative. However, the ones with blue titles are guided communication. The red titles indicate that the answers to the activity are more open-ended and can vary more. You may wish to correct students' mistakes more so in the guided activities than in the activities with a red title, which lend themselves to a freer response.

## Learning from Photos

*(page 195)* AVENSA is a Venezuelan airline serving a dozen destinations in Venezuela and offering flights to many other destinations in Europe and North and South America.

## Fun Facts

The **SA** in AVENSA and in the names of many companies in Spain and Latin America—LACSA, ATESA, etc.—stands for **Sociedad Anónima,** the Spanish equivalent of *incorporated.*

## Chapter Projects

**Algo sobre la historia** Have individuals or groups prepare reports on different aspects of the history of the Andean countries, such as Bolivia, Perú, Chile, or Ecuador.

**Informes turísticos** Have groups prepare reports on Lake Titicaca and the Aymara and Quechua peoples.

## Answers to ¿Qué palabra necesito?

**4**

1. a
2. a
3. c
4. a
5. c

**5** *Answers will vary but will include the vocabulary from* Palabras 1.

**6** *Answers will vary. Students will use vocabulary presented in* Palabras 1 *to describe the illustration.*

## Leveling

**E:** Activities 1, 2, 3, 4, 5, 6
**A:** Activities 3, 4, 5, 6

## 1 PREPARATION

### Resource Manager

Vocabulary Transparencies 7.4–7.5
Audio Activities TE, pages 79–80
Audio CD 5
Workbook, pages 75–76
Quizzes, page 31
ExamView® Pro

### Bellringer Review

*Use BRR Transparency 7.2 or write the following on the board.*
Match the word in the first column with a related word in the second column.

| | |
|---|---|
| **1. llegar** | **a. el asiento** |
| **2. aterrizar** | **b. el despegue** |
| **3. despegar** | **c. el aterrizaje** |
| **4. asistir** | **d. la comida** |
| **5. beber** | **e. la bebida** |
| **6. comer** | **f. la llegada** |
| **7. salir** | **g. la salida** |
| **8. sentar** | **h. el asistente** |

## 2 PRESENTATION

**Step 1** Have students close their books. Project Vocabulary Transparencies 7.4–7.5. Point to each item and have students repeat each word two or three times after you or the recording on Audio CD 5.

**Step 2** Now point to items at random on the transparencies as you ask **¿Qué es?** and call on individuals to respond.

# Vocabulario

PALABRAS 2

## En el aeropuerto

### Chapter Projects

**La actualidad** Have groups research modern-day Bolivia, compiling their findings for a class bulletin board display on that country.

El comandante les habló a los pasajeros.
Les anunció que:
despegarían a tiempo.
el avión volaría a una altura de 10.000 metros.
sería un vuelo directo; no harían escala.
sobrevolarían los Andes.
habría muy poca turbulencia durante el vuelo.

## Un poco de geografía

## Vocabulario

**Step 3** You may wish to ask the following questions about the sentences on this page:

**¿Dijo el piloto que despegarían a tiempo?**
**¿Dijo que despegarían a tiempo o con retraso?**
**¿A qué altura volaría?**
**¿Dijo que sería un vuelo directo?**
**¿Harían escala o no?**

### Learning from Photos

*(page 196 bottom left)* Iberia is the national airline of Spain. It was founded in 1927, with flights between Madrid and Barcelona. In 1946 Iberia began service between Madrid and Buenos Aires and in 1954 between Madrid and New York. The Iberia plane taking off in the photo is a DC10.
*(page 196 bottom right)* Avianca is the national airline of Colombia and one of the oldest airlines in Latin America. It began in collaboration with Pan American World Airways. Today it flies to multiple cities in North and South America and Europe. The Avianca plane landing is a Boeing 767.

### About the Spanish Language

Explain to students that the term **altiplano** is used to refer to the entire Andean region in general.

Vocabulario

## 3 PRACTICE

## ¿Qué palabra necesito?

¡OJO! It is recommended that you go over the activities orally in class before assigning them for homework.

**7** Go over Activity 7 orally with books closed. Then have students read the activity aloud for additional reinforcement.

**8** Activity 8 can be done without prior preparation but with books open.

### LEVELING

**E:** Activities 7, 8, 9, 10, 11

**A:** Activities 7, 8, 9, 10, 11, 12



Vocabulario

Caracas, Venezuela

## ¿Qué palabra necesito?

**7 Historieta A bordo del avión**
Contesten según se indica.

1. ¿De dónde hizo el comandante algunos anuncios? (de la cabina de vuelo)
2. ¿Dijo que despegarían con una demora? (no, a tiempo)
3. ¿Dijo que habría mucha turbulencia durante el vuelo? (no, poca)
4. ¿Dijo que el tiempo de vuelo sería de tres horas? (no, de tres horas y treinta minutos)
5. ¿Dijo que sobrevolarían los Andes? (sí)
6. ¿Qué dijo que podrían ver los pasajeros? (los picos de las montañas)

**8 En el aeropuerto** Escojan.

1. El avión va a llegar en pocos momentos. Esperamos ____.
   **a.** el despegue **b.** el aterrizaje **c.** la salida
2. Los controladores le dan instrucciones al piloto. Se las dan desde la ____.
   **a.** cabina de mando **b.** terminal **c.** torre de control
3. Los amigos y parientes de los pasajeros los esperan en la ____.
   **a.** terminal **b.** torre de control **c.** pista
4. Otro avión ya va a salir. En pocos minutos veremos ____.
   **a.** la llegada **b.** el despegue **c.** el aterrizaje
5. ____ despega y aterriza verticalmente.
   **a.** La avioneta **b.** El avión de reacción **c.** El helicóptero

Granada, España



## ANSWERS TO ¿Qué palabra necesito?

**7**

1. El comandante hizo algunos anuncios de la cabina de vuelo.
2. No, dijo que despegarían a tiempo.
3. No, dijo que habría poca turbulencia durante el vuelo.
4. No, dijo que el tiempo de vuelo sería de tres horas y treinta minutos.
5. Sí, dijo que sobrevolarían los Andes.
6. Dijo que los pasajeros podrían ver los picos de las montañas.

**8**

1. b
2. c
3. a
4. b
5. c

**9** **Definiciones** Pareen.

1. parte superior de una montaña
2. extensión de tierra que no tiene altos ni bajos
3. espacio de tierra entre montañas
4. agua que comienza en la tierra y va al mar
5. serie de montañas, una tras otra
6. elevación de tierra que termina en un pico

a. río
b. cordillera
c. pico
d. llanura
e. valle
f. montaña

Los Andes

**10** **¿Qué son... ?** Contesten.

1. los Andes, los Apalaches, las Rocosas
2. el Amazonas, el Misisipí, el Nilo
3. Aconcagua, Everest, McKinley
4. Huron, Ontario, Michigan, Erie, Superior

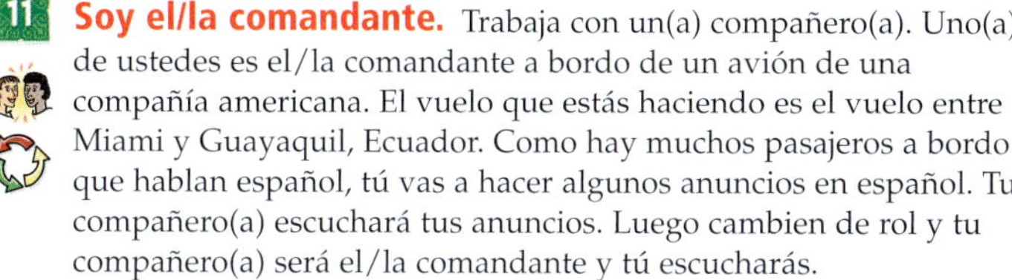

**11** **Soy el/la comandante.** Trabaja con un(a) compañero(a). Uno(a) de ustedes es el/la comandante a bordo de un avión de una compañía americana. El vuelo que estás haciendo es el vuelo entre Miami y Guayaquil, Ecuador. Como hay muchos pasajeros a bordo que hablan español, tú vas a hacer algunos anuncios en español. Tu compañero(a) escuchará tus anuncios. Luego cambien de rol y tu compañero(a) será el/la comandante y tú escucharás.

**12** **Donde vivimos** Trabaja con un(a) compañero(a). Den una descripción de la geografía de la región donde viven. Pueden usar las siguientes palabras.

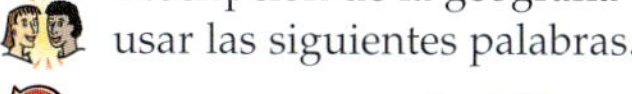

*For more practice using words from* ***Palabras 1*** *and* ***2****, do Activity 7 on page H8 at the end of this book.*



**9** You may wish to have students prepare Activity 9 before going over it in class.

## Critical Thinking Activity

**Identifying causes** Read the following to the class or write it on the board:

**¿Por qué razones se cancela o se anula un vuelo?**

## Learning from Photos

*(page 199)* The Andes are among the highest mountains in the world. They extend the entire length of South America, 8,500 kilometers (5,000 miles), from Cape Horn in the south to the Caribbean in the north. The average height of the mountains is 4,500 meters (14,763 feet). The highest peak is Aconcagua in Argentina at 6,960 meters (22,834 feet).

UN POCO MÁS This *InfoGap* Activity will allow students to practice in pairs. The activity should be very manageable for them, since all vocabulary and structures are familiar to them.

## Answers to ¿Qué palabra necesito?

**9**

1. c
2. d
3. e
4. a
5. b
6. f

**10**

1. Son cordilleras.
2. Son ríos.
3. Son montañas.
4. Son lagos.

**11** *Answers will vary, but students will use the vocabulary presented in* Palabras 2 *to make announcements a pilot would make during a flight.*

**12** *Answers will vary, but students will use the cues provided to describe the area where they live.*

# Estructura

## 1 PREPARATION

### Resource Manager

Audio Activities TE, pages 84–87
Audioc CD 5
Workbook, pages 75–77
Quizzes, pages 32–34
ExamView® Pro

### Bellringer Review

*Use BRR Transparency 7.3 or write the following on the board.*
Rewrite the following sentences in the future.

1. **Yo voy en tren.**
2. **Felisa compra los boletos.**
3. **Yo espero aquí con las maletas.**
4. **El tren llega a las dieciséis.**
5. **¿Comen ustedes en el tren?**
6. **Sí, tomamos el almuerzo en el tren.**

## 2 PRESENTATION

### Modo potencial o condicional de verbos regulares

**Step 1** Have students open their books to page 200. Lead them through Items 1–3.

**Step 2** Have them repeat the verb forms after you.

**Step 3** Call on individuals to read the model sentences or have the class read them in unison.

**¡OJO!** This structure point should not prove difficult for students. They are already familiar with the verb stems from the future tense and with the endings from the imperfect. The uses of the conditional are the same in Spanish and English.

# Estructura

## Modo potencial o condicional de verbos regulares
### Expressing conditions

1. As with the future, the infinitive is used as the stem for the conditional of regular verbs. Study the following forms.

| INFINITIVE | llegar | ver | servir | ENDINGS |
|---|---|---|---|---|
| STEM | llegar- | ver- | servir- | |
| yo | llegaría | vería | serviría | -ía |
| tú | llegarías | verías | servirías | -ías |
| él, ella, Ud. | llegaría | vería | serviría | -ía |
| nosotros(as) | llegaríamos | veríamos | serviríamos | -íamos |
| *vosotros(as)* | *llegaríais* | *veríais* | *serviríais* | *-íais* |
| ellos, ellas, Uds. | llegarían | verían | servirían | -ían |

Note that the endings for the conditional are the same as those for the imperfect of **-er** and **-ir** verbs.

**¿Te acuerdas?**

Remember that the stem for the future tense of regular verbs is the infinitive.
**volaré** **comeré** **serviré**

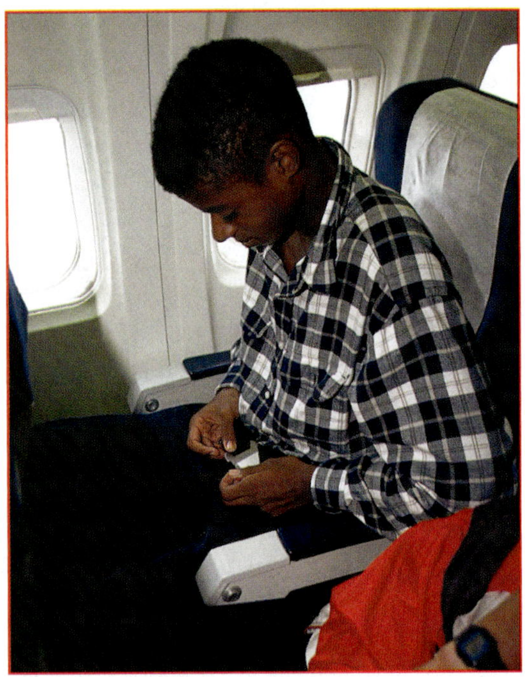
La aerolínea LACSA, Costa Rica

2. You use the conditional, as you do in English, to tell what would take place under certain circumstances.

**El avión despegaría ahora pero no puede porque hace mal tiempo.**
**Nosotros viajaríamos a Europa pero no tenemos suficiente dinero.**

3. The conditional is also used to soften requests.

**¿Me pasaría usted los audífonos, por favor?**
**¿Se abrocharía el cinturón de seguridad, por favor, señor?**



### Learning from Photos

*(page 200)* You may wish to ask students the following questions about the photo:
**¿Dónde está el asiento del muchacho, al lado de la ventanilla o del pasillo?**
**¿Qué está haciendo el muchacho?**
**¿Está el respaldo de su asiento en posición vertical?**
**¿Qué lleva el muchacho?**
Tell students that **LACSA** stands for **Líneas Aéreas Centroamericanas SA.** It is based in Costa Rica. Recently **LACSA** formed an alliance with **Aviateca, Nica,** and **Taca,** all Central American airlines, to create a Central American airline consortium.

## ¿Cómo lo digo?

**13** **Historieta** **Imaginándome millonario(a)**

Contesten.

1. ¿Vivirías en la ciudad o en el campo?
2. ¿Viajarías mucho?
3. ¿Adónde irías?
4. ¿Cómo irías?
5. ¿Con quién irías?
6. ¿Comprarías una casa grande?
7. ¿Cómo sería la casa?
8. ¿Trabajarías?

**14** **Historieta** **Las vacaciones del muchacho**

Contesten.

1. ¿Adónde iría el muchacho para las vacaciones?
2. ¿Cómo viajaría?
3. ¿Cuánto pagaría?
4. ¿Dónde nadaría él?
5. ¿A qué jugaría?
6. ¿Qué subiría él?
7. ¿Qué comería?
8. ¿Dónde dormiría?

En una agencia de viajes, España

Lima, Perú





## Estructura

### 3 PRACTICE

### ¿Cómo lo digo?

**13** Activity 13 can be done orally with books closed. Tell students to be as original as possible when they respond.

**14** Activity 14 can also be done orally with books closed. **Expansion:** Call on a student or students to tell in his or her own words all about the vacation described in this activity.

**Paired Activity** Have students ask one another questions about what they would do on vacation.

### Learning from Photos

*(page 201 middle)* You may wish to ask students these questions about the photo:
**¿Quiénes son las dos personas?**
**¿Qué usa el agente?**
**Describe lo que ves en la foto.**
*(page 201 bottom)* Ask these questions about the photo taken in Lima:
**¿De qué es la foto de abajo?**
**¿Qué serán las personas en la foto?**

**LEVELING**

**E:** Activities 13, 14

**A:** Activities 15, 16

### Answers to ¿Cómo lo digo?

**13**

1. Viviría en la ciudad (en el campo).
2. Sí, (No, no) viajaría mucho.
3. Iría a ___.
4. Iría en ___.
5. Iría con ___.
6. Sí, (No, no) compraría una casa grande.
7. La casa sería ___.
8. Sí, (No, no) trabajaría.

**14** *Answers will vary but may include:*

1. El muchacho iría a ___ para las vacaciones.
2. Viajaría en ___.
3. Pagaría ___.
4. Nadaría ___.
5. Jugaría a ___.
6. Subiría ___.
7. Comería ___.
8. Dormiría ___.

## 3 PRACTICE *(continued)*

**15** Have students present Activity 15 as a series of miniconversations.

**16** Activity 16 can be done orally with books closed.
**Note:** This activity incorporates all forms of the conditional.

### Learning from Realia

*(page 202)* Have students identify some of the destinations on the route map of Mexicana Airlines and tell which ones they would like to visit. Have them tell what they know about some of the cities Mexicana flies to.

### Learning from Photos

The Torres del Paine National Park is known for being one of the most beautiful, unspoiled and remote places in the world. Attractions include a spectacular mountain range, lakes, flora and fauna that make this a popular spot for Eco-tourism and adventure. Tourist activities include sightseeing, hiking, kayaking, glacier crossing, and climbing.

### SPANISH Online

The Glencoe Spanish Web site **(spanish.glencoe.com)** offers options that enable you and your students to experience the Spanish-speaking world via the Internet. For each **Capítulo,** there are activities, games, and quizzes. In addition, an *Enrichment* section offers students an opportunity to visit Web sites related to the theme of the chapter.





**15** **No, no.** Contesten según el modelo.

1. Ellos piensan llamar. ¿Y tú?
2. Yo pienso escribir. ¿Y ustedes?
3. Carolina piensa visitar a sus primos. ¿Y su hermano?
4. Nosotros pensamos ir. ¿Y ustedes?
5. Ellos piensan viajar por avión. ¿Y ustedes?
6. Teresa piensa manejar. ¿Y tú?

**16** **Historieta Un viaje con unos amigos**
Contesten según se indica.

1. ¿Irían tus amigos a la playa o a las montañas? (a las montañas)
2. ¿Los acompañarías? (sí)
3. ¿Cómo irían ustedes, en tren o en carro? (en carro)
4. ¿Quién manejaría? (Teresa)
5. ¿Cuánto tiempo pasarían ustedes en las montañas? (unos cinco días)
6. ¿Dónde se quedarían ustedes? (en un hotel económico)

Torres del Paine, Chile

For more information about Argentina and its different geographical regions, go to the Glencoe Spanish Web site: spanish.glencoe.com



### ANSWERS TO ¿Cómo lo digo?

**15**

1. No, yo no llamaría.
2. No, nosotros no escribiríamos.
3. No, su hermano no visitaría a sus primos.
4. No, nosotros no iríamos.
5. No, nosotros no viajaríamos por avión.
6. No, yo no manejaría.

**16**

1. Mis amigos irían a las montañas.
2. Sí, los acompañaría.
3. Iríamos en carro.
4. Teresa manejaría.
5. Pasaríamos unos cinco días en las montañas.
6. Nos quedaríamos en un hotel económico.

## Modo potencial de verbos irregulares
### Expressing more conditions

The same verbs that are irregular in the future tense are irregular in the conditional. Study the following.

| INFINITIVE | FUTURE | CONDITIONAL |
|---|---|---|
| TENER | tendré | tendría |
| PONER | pondré | pondría |
| SALIR | saldré | saldría |
| VENIR | vendré | vendría |
| PODER | podré | podría |
| SABER | sabré | sabría |
| HACER | haré | haría |
| DECIR | diré | diría |
| QUERER | querré | querría |

## ¿Cómo lo digo?

**17 Historieta ¿Vendrá tu hermana o no?**

Contesten según el modelo.

1. ¿Vendrá tu hermana?
2. ¿Hará el viaje?
3. ¿Podrá pagar el viaje?
4. ¿Saldrá el viernes?
5. ¿Tendrá bastante tiempo?

## 1 PREPARATION

### Bellringer Review

*Use BRR Transparency 7.4 or write the following on the board.*

Rewrite in the future.

1. **Vamos a salir mañana.**
2. **Te voy a decir a qué hora salimos.**
3. **Roberto va a querer salir temprano.**
4. **Vamos a tener que poner el equipaje en la maletera esta noche.**
5. **Roberto lo va a poner en la maletera.**

## 2 PRESENTATION

### Modo potencial de verbos irregulares

**Step 1** Have students open their books to page 203. Lead them through the explanation and have them repeat the verb forms after you.

## 3 PRACTICE

## ¿Cómo lo digo?

**17** Have students present Activity 17 as a miniconversation.

## Answers to ¿Cómo lo digo?

**17**

1. Dijo que vendría.
2. Dijo que haría el viaje.
3. Dijo que podría pagar el viaje.
4. Dijo que saldría el viernes.
5. Dijo que tendría bastante tiempo.

# Estructura

## 3 PRACTICE *(continued)*

**18** and **19** These activities must be done with books open. You can go over them without prior preparation or have students prepare them first.

**20** This activity can be done orally with books closed. **Expansion:** Call on a student or students to give a summary of the information the pilot and the flight attendant gave in Activity 20.

**LEVELING**

**E:** Activity 20

**A:** Activities 17, 18, 19, 20



**18 Uno sí y el otro no** Completen con el condicional.

1. Él sabría la dirección pero su hermano no la ____.
2. Yo te lo diría pero ellos nunca te lo ____.
3. Nosotros lo haríamos pero ellos no lo ____ nunca.
4. Yo podría ir pero mis amigos no ____.
5. Ustedes lo pondrían en orden pero él no lo ____.
6. Yo tendría que volver pero tú no ____.

**19 Ahora lo hará pero antes no lo haría.**
Completen con el condicional.

1. Carlos podrá pero antes no ____.
2. Los muchachos vendrán pero antes no ____.
3. Tú lo harás pero antes no lo ____.
4. Ustedes saldrán pero antes no ____.
5. Usted me lo dirá pero antes no me lo ____.

**20 Historieta A bordo del avión**
Contesten con **sí**.

1. ¿Dijo el comandante que el avión podría despegar a tiempo?
2. ¿Dijo que saldrían dentro de cinco minutos?
3. ¿Dijo el asistente de vuelo que los pasajeros tendrían que poner su equipaje de mano en el compartimiento superior?
4. ¿Dijo que no podríamos fumar cigarrillos durante el vuelo?
5. ¿Dijo que yo podría usar mi computadora durante el vuelo?
6. ¿Dijo el comandante que nos diría la hora exacta de nuestra llegada?
7. ¿Dijo que haríamos escala en Bogotá?

| PLAN DE VUELOS Y HORARIOS | | |
|---|---|---|
| DE LUNES A VIERNES | SALIDA | LLEGADA |
| Santiago - Bilbao | 07:45 | 09:05 |
| Bilbao - Santiago | 09:35 | 10:55 |
| Santiago - Bilbao | 17:15 | 18:35 |
| Bilbao - Santiago | 19:05 | 20:25 |
| Santiago - Asturias | 11:25 | 12:10 |
| Asturias - Santiago | 12:40 | 13:25 |
| Santiago - Asturias | 20:55 | 21:40 |
| Asturias - Santiago | 22:10 | 22:55 |
| Santiago - Santander | 13:55 | 15:05 |
| Santander - Santiago | 15:35 | 16:45 |

LA LINEA AEREA QUE PRIMA

primair

## Answers to ¿Cómo lo digo?

**18**

1. sabría
2. dirían
3. harían
4. podrían
5. pondría
6. tendrías

**19**

1. podría
2. vendrían
3. harías
4. saldrían
5. diría

**20**

1. Sí, el comandante dijo que el avión podría despegar a tiempo.
2. Sí, el comandante dijo que saldrían dentro de cinco minutos.
3. Sí, el asistente de vuelo dijo que los pasajeros tendrían que poner su equipaje de mano en el compartimiento superior.
4. Sí, dijo que no podríamos fumar cigarrillos durante el vuelo.
5. Sí, dijo que tú podrías usar tu computadora durante el vuelo.
6. Sí, el comandante dijo que nos diría la hora exacta de nuestra llegada.
7. Sí, dijo que haríamos escala en Bogotá.

**21** **Una encuesta** Trabaja con un(a) compañero(a). Van a hacer una encuesta *(survey)*. Ésta es la situación. Hay un billete de cien dólares en la calle. Cada uno(a) de ustedes preguntará a cinco compañeros qué harían al encontrar los cien dólares. Luego organicen las respuestas para informar a la clase sobre los resultados.

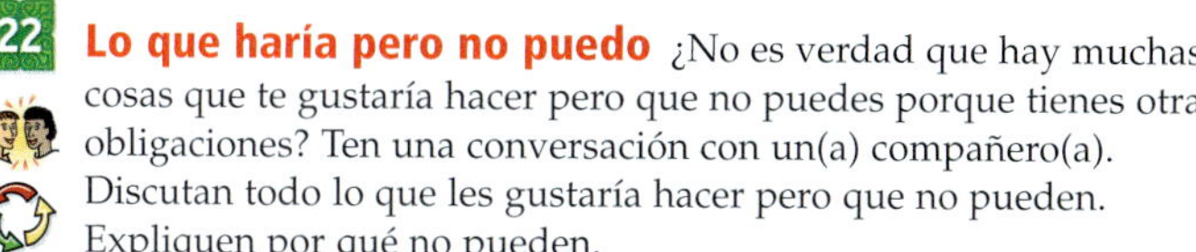

**22** **Lo que haría pero no puedo** ¿No es verdad que hay muchas cosas que te gustaría hacer pero que no puedes porque tienes otras obligaciones? Ten una conversación con un(a) compañero(a). Discutan todo lo que les gustaría hacer pero que no pueden. Expliquen por qué no pueden.

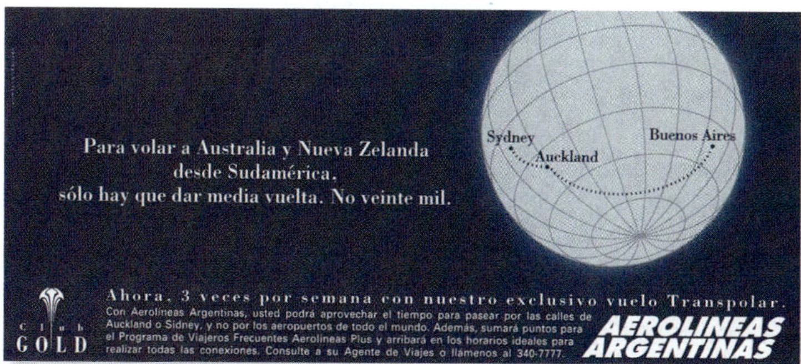


## Dos complementos con se
### Talking about things stated before

1. The indirect object pronouns **le** and **les** change to **se** when used in the same sentence with either **lo, la, los,** or **las.**

   **El asistente de vuelo les sirvió la comida a los pasajeros.**
   **El asistente de vuelo se la sirvió.**
   **El joven le dio los audífonos a su mamá.**
   **El joven se los dio.**

2. Because the pronoun **se** can refer to many different people, it is often clarified with a prepositional phrase.

   **El asistente se la pasó a él (a ella, a usted, a ellos, a ellas, a ustedes).**

**¿Te acuerdas?**

When there are two object pronouns in the same sentence, the indirect object always precedes the direct object.

**Él me lo dio.**
**Yo te lo explicaría.**



# Estructura

**21** and **22** Allow students to choose the activities they would like to do.

## 1 PREPARATION

### Bellringer Review

*Use BRR Transparency 7.5 or write the following on the board.*
Make a list of clothing that you would buy right away if you had enough money.

## 2 PRESENTATION

### Dos complementos con se

**Step 1** Have students open their books to page 205. Lead them through Items 1 and 2.

**Step 2** You may want to write the model sentences on the board to reinforce this concept. Draw an arrow from the pronoun to the noun it replaces.

### Geography Connection

Have students read the **Aerolíneas Argentinas** ad on page 205. They should look at the world map on pages xxii–xxiii or Map Transparency M 1 and determine the distance between Buenos Aires and Auckland, New Zealand. Buenos Aires is much closer to New Zealand and Australia than New York is, for example.

### Answers to ¿Cómo lo digo?

**21** and **22** *Answers will vary, but students should answer using the conditional.*

### LEVELING

**E:** Activities 21, 22
**A:** Activities 21, 22, 23, 24
**C:** Activities 24, 25, 26, 27

# Estructura

## 3 PRACTICE

## ¿Cómo lo digo?

¡OJO! You may decide to what extent you wish to emphasize the practice of this particular structure point. Although students should recognize the **se lo** construction, it is not always necessary for them to produce it, since they could respond with nouns: **El asistente le dio la manta a la señora.** It takes students quite a bit of time to use the **se lo** construction actively.

23 This activity can be done orally with books closed. Students can then write the answers for additional reinforcement.

24 Students can present this activity as a series of mini-conversations.

### Learning from Photos

The **Plaza de Armas** is located in the center of the city of Cuzco, Peru. The **Plaza** is on the former Incan ceremonial site of Huacaypata. The **Plaza de Armas** is close to many of the historic and cultural attractions of the age-old city; it is lined by the Cathedral and the Iglesia de la Compañia, as well as various restaurants, cafés, hotels, souvenir shops and travel agencies.

Estructura

## ¿Cómo lo digo?

Una aerolínea española, Madrid

### 23 Historieta Durante el vuelo

Contesten según el modelo.

**¿Quién le dio la revista al pasajero? → El asistente se la dio.**

1. ¿Quién le dio la manta a la señora?
2. ¿Quién le pasó la bandeja a la señorita?
3. ¿Quién le ofreció los audífonos al pasajero?
4. ¿Quién les explicó las reglas de seguridad a los pasajeros?
5. ¿Quién les sirvió la comida a los pasajeros?
6. ¿Quién les anunció la hora de llegada a los viajeros?

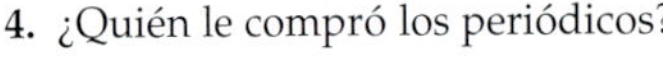

### 24 Su abuelita se lo compró. Contesten según el modelo.

**—¿Quién le compró el regalito?**
**—Su abuelita se lo compró.**

1. ¿Quién le compró la bicicleta?
2. ¿Quién le compró el billete?
3. ¿Quién le compró las entradas?
4. ¿Quién le compró los periódicos?

Plaza de Armas, Cuzco, Perú



### Answers to ¿Cómo lo digo?

23

1. El asistente se la dio.
2. El asistente se la pasó.
3. El asistente se los ofreció.
4. El asistente se las explicó.
5. El asistente se la sirvió.
6. El asistente se la anunció.

24

1. Su abuelita se la compró.
2. Su abuelita se lo compró.
3. Su abuelita se las compró.
4. Su abuelita se los compró.

25 **A mí, no. A Carlos.** Sigan el modelo.

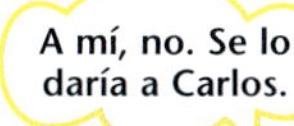

1. ¿Tu papá te regalaría las entradas?
2. ¿Te darían la computadora?
3. ¿Tus abuelos te enviarían el dinero?
4. ¿Los muchachos te darían los esquís?
5. ¿Maribel te compraría los periódicos?

26 **Historieta Tomás se los llevó.**
Sigan el modelo.

**Tomás le llevó los vegetales a su mamá. →**
**Tomás se los llevó a ella.**

1. Tomás le llevó los vegetales a su mamá.
2. Tomás le pidió dinero a su mamá.
3. Su madre le dio el dinero a Tomás.
4. Tomás le dio las legumbres congeladas a su mamá.
5. Tomás le devolvió el cambio a su mamá.

El Corte Inglés, Sevilla

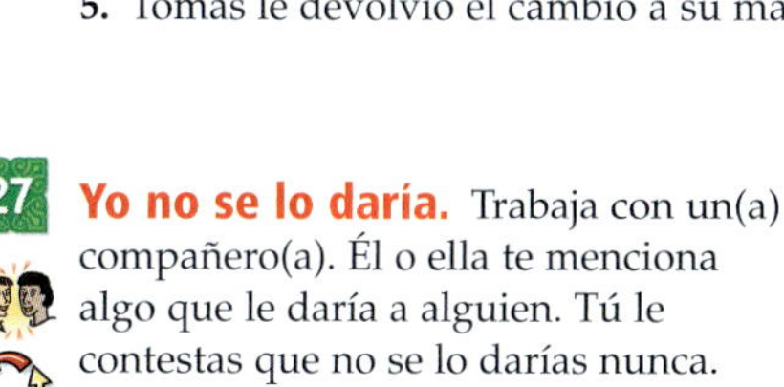

27 **Yo no se lo daría.** Trabaja con un(a) compañero(a). Él o ella te menciona algo que le daría a alguien. Tú le contestas que no se lo darías nunca. Usen el modelo como guía.

**—Yo le daría este disco a Elena.**
**—Yo nunca se lo daría a ella.**

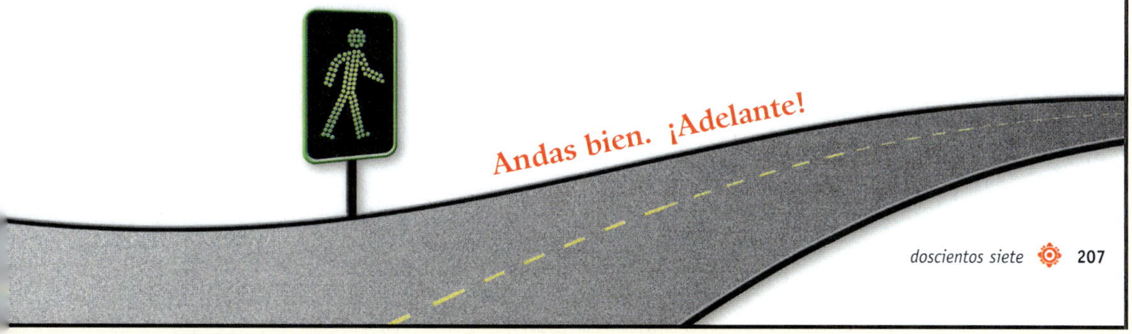

## Estructura

25 Have students work in pairs to do this activity.

26 You may wish to have students prepare Activity 26 before going over it in class.

### Learning from Photos

*(page 207)* **El Corte Inglés** is Spain's major department store chain with large stores in all major cities. Most include a food section, as does this one in Seville. You may wish to ask students to identify as many produce items as they can. **El Corte Inglés** literally means *the English cut* (or *style of clothing*).

### ¡Adelante!

At this point in the chapter, students have learned all the vocabulary and structure necessary to complete the chapter. The conversation and cultural readings that follow recycle all the material learned up to this point.

## Answers to ¿Cómo lo digo?

25

1. A mí, no. Se las regalaría a Carlos.
2. A mí, no. Se la darían a Carlos.
3. A mí, no. Se lo enviarían a Carlos.
4. A mí, no. Se los darían a Carlos.
5. A mí, no. Se los compraría a Carlos.

26

1. Tomás se los llevó a ella.
2. Tomás se lo pidió a ella.
3. Su madre se lo dio a él.
4. Tomás se las dio a ella.
5. Tomás se lo devolvió a ella.

27 *Answers will vary. Students will use the model as a guide.*

Conversación

## 1 PREPARATION

### Resource Manager

Audio Activities TE, pages 83–84
Audio CD 5

### Bellringer Review

*Use BRR Transparency 7.6 or write the following on the board.*
Indicate whether the following describe a train trip or a flight.

1. **Aquí viene el revisor.**
2. **Hay asientos para cuarenta personas en cada coche.**
3. **Los pasajeros se abrochan el cinturón de seguridad.**
4. **Despega y aterriza.**
5. **Sale del andén número cuatro.**

## 2 PRESENTATION

**Step 1** Tell students they will hear a conversation between Adela and Víctor, two passengers on a commercial airliner.

**Step 2** Have students close their books and listen as you read the conversation or play Audio CD 5.

**Step 3** Now have students open their books. Allow pairs a few minutes to practice reading the conversation.

**Step 4** Call on one or two pairs of volunteers to read the conversation to the class with as much expression as possible.

**Step 5** Then go over the **¿Comprendes?** activity.

**Step 6** After going over the conversation, have a student retell all the information in his or her own words in narrative form.

# Conversación

## En el avión   

**Adela** No pude oír el anuncio. ¿Qué dijo el asistente de vuelo?
**Víctor** Que el vuelo sería de tres horas y que llegaríamos a La Paz a tiempo.
**Adela** ¡Qué bien! La comida es bastante buena, ¿no?
**Víctor** Sí. No sabía que nos servirían una comida. Es un vuelo bastante corto.
**Adela** ¿Qué piensas? ¿Habrá una película?
**Víctor** No. Me dijeron que no podrían presentar una película porque no habría tiempo.

### ¿Comprendes?

Contesten.

1. ¿Dónde están Adela y Víctor?
2. ¿Adónde van ellos?
3. ¿Qué dijo el asistente de vuelo?
4. ¿Cuánto tiempo dura el vuelo?
5. Según Adela, ¿cómo es la comida?
6. ¿Qué no sabía Víctor?
7. ¿Habrá una película?
8. ¿Por qué le dijeron a Víctor que no podrían presentar una película?



### ANSWERS TO ¿Comprendes?

1. Adela y Víctor están en el avión.
2. Ellos van a La Paz.
3. El asistente de vuelo dijo que el vuelo sería de tres horas y que llegarían a La Paz a tiempo.
4. El vuelo dura tres horas.
5. Según Adela la comida es bastante buena.
6. Víctor no sabía que les servirían una comida.
7. No, no habrá una película.
8. Le dijeron a Víctor que no podrían presentar una película porque no habría tiempo.

### History Connection

The full name of La Paz is La Paz de Ayacucho, so named for a Bolivian victory over the Spaniards at Ayacucho, Peru, in the War for Independence (1809–1825).

# Vamos a hablar más

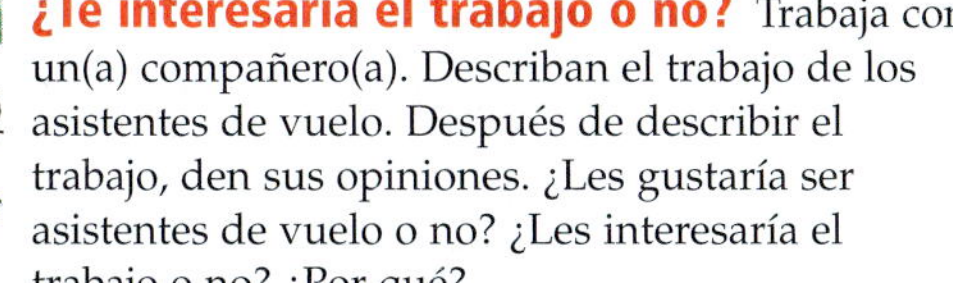

**A** **¿Te interesaría el trabajo o no?** Trabaja con un(a) compañero(a). Describan el trabajo de los asistentes de vuelo. Después de describir el trabajo, den sus opiniones. ¿Les gustaría ser asistentes de vuelo o no? ¿Les interesaría el trabajo o no? ¿Por qué?

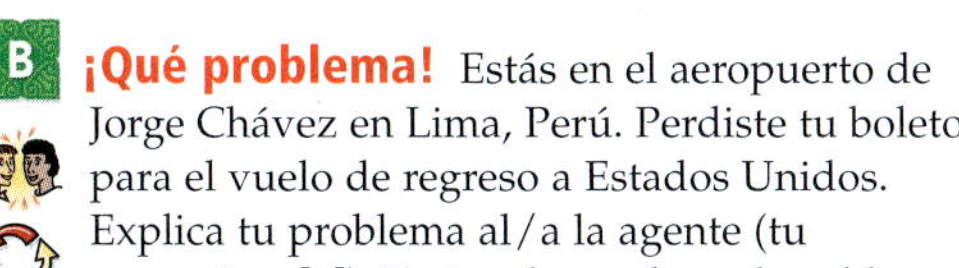

**B** **¡Qué problema!** Estás en el aeropuerto de Jorge Chávez en Lima, Perú. Perdiste tu boleto para el vuelo de regreso a Estados Unidos. Explica tu problema al/a la agente (tu compañero[a]). Traten de resolver el problema.

Lima, Perú

**C** **¡Por favor!** Trabaja con un(a) compañero(a). Uno(a) de ustedes será pasajero(a) y el/la otro(a) será asistente de vuelo. Preparen una conversación basada en lo que ven en cada dibujo.

1.

2.

3.

4.



## Conversación

### 3 PRACTICE

## Vamos a hablar más

**¡OJO!** Although the communicative activities are based on the chapter vocabulary and structures, encourage students to use any language they have learned up to this point.

### Learning from Photos

*(page 208)* Have students talk about the photo. Have them describe the two passengers, who they might be, and where they are seated.

*(page 209)* The Lima airport is named for a famous Peruvian, Jorge Chávez. Ask students:

**¿Qué otros aeropuertos conoces con el nombre de una persona famosa?**

**¿Por qué es famosa la persona?**

### Glencoe Technology

On the CD-ROM, students can watch a dramatization of this conversation. They can then play the role of either one of the characters and record themselves in the conversation.

### Answers to Vamos a hablar más

**A** *Answers will vary. Students will use vocabulary related to airplanes and flight attendants.*

**B** *Answers will vary. Students will use vocabulary and structure previously learned to solve the problem.*

**C** *Answers will vary, but students will use the vocabulary presented in the chapter to create conversations based on the illustrations.*

### LEVELING

**E:** Conversation

# Lecturas culturales

## Resource Manager

Audio Activities TE, page 85
Audio CD 5

## Bellringer Review

*Use BRR Transparency 7.7 or write the following on the board.*
Make up questions about an airplane flight using the following expressions: **¿cuándo? ¿cuánto tiempo? ¿de dónde? ¿a qué hora?**

## National Standards

### Cultures

The reading about the **El Alto** airport on pages 210–211 and the related activities on page 211 familiarize students with Bolivian geography and some interesting aspects of the world's highest commercial airport.

## PRESENTATION

### Pre-reading

Tell students that they are going to read about a very interesting airport. Tell them that as they read they should concentrate on why it is so interesting.

### Reading

**Step 1** Read the selection to the students. You may have them just listen as you read or have them follow along in their books.

**Step 2** Have students open their books. Call on an individual to read a few sentences. Then stop and ask questions about what the student read.

### Post-reading

Have students read the **Lectura** at home and prepare the **¿Comprendes?** activities. Go over them the next day in class.

# Lecturas culturales

## El aeropuerto que se llama «El Alto»

El aeropuerto El Alto en La Paz, Bolivia, está en una llanura del altiplano andino. Es el aeropuerto comercial más alto del mundo. Está a 13.450 pies o 4.100 metros sobre el nivel del mar[1]. A estas alturas del altiplano hay menos oxígeno en el aire que al nivel del mar. Por esta razón cuando un viajero baja del avión en El Alto, puede tener dificultad en respirar[2]. En el aeropuerto hay botellas de oxígeno para los pasajeros que lo necesitan.

¿Te gustaría hacer un viaje a La Paz algún día? Te aseguro[3] que sería una experiencia maravillosa. Al aterrizar tendrías una vista magnífica de la ciudad de La Paz. La Paz, la capital del país, está a una altura 1.000 pies más abajo del aeropuerto. La ciudad parece estar en un cráter. Y encima de la ciudad el cielo es claro, limpio y muy azul—sobre todo en el invierno.

[1]nivel del mar *sea level*
[2]respirar *breathing*
[3]Te aseguro *I assure you*

### Reading Strategy

**Distinguishing between fact and opinion** When writing, an author will sometimes include his or her opinions among facts. It is important to distinguish between facts and the author's opinions. You must watch for expressions that indicate when an author is expressing an opinion rather than a fact. Some of these expressions in Spanish are: **creo que, prefiero, pienso, en mi opinión.**

Aeropuerto El Alto

El altiplano, Bolivia



## Fun Facts

Planes taking off from airports at high altitudes such as **El Alto** airport need longer runways because of the lower air density at high altitudes.

## Geography Connection

The **altiplano** is the great high plateau of South America. It is 4,000 meters high and covers an area of 100,000 square kilometers. The **altiplano** falls between the two **cordilleras** of the Andes, the Oriental and the Occidental, and is located primarily in Bolivia, with parts extending into Peru, Chile, and Argentina.

Al terminar tu viaje y salir de La Paz, el avión despegará de una de las pistas más largas del mundo. A esta altura el aire tiene muy poca densidad y no puede sostener el peso[4] del avión. Por consiguiente el avión tiene que alcanzar una gran velocidad antes de poder despegar. Y para poder alcanzar esta velocidad la pista tiene que ser muy larga.

[4]sostener el peso *support the weight*

La Paz, Bolivia

## ¿Comprendes?

**A Un aeropuerto interesante** Contesten.

1. ¿Cómo se llama el aeropuerto que sirve a La Paz, Bolivia?
2. ¿Por qué puede tener un pasajero dificultad en respirar al bajar de un avión en La Paz?
3. ¿Qué tienen en el aeropuerto para su uso?
4. Al aterrizar en El Alto, ¿qué tendrías?
5. ¿Cómo es la pista del aeropuerto El Alto?
6. ¿Por qué es tan larga?

**B ¿Sí o no?** Digan que sí o que no.

1. El aeropuerto El Alto está en la Sierra Nevada.
2. El aeropuerto de La Paz es el aeropuerto comercial más alto del mundo.
3. A esta altura el aire contiene más oxígeno que al nivel del mar.
4. La ciudad de La Paz está a una altura aún más alta que el aeropuerto.
5. En el verano el cielo sobre La Paz es claro, limpio y muy azul.
6. A esta altura el aire no puede sostener el peso del avión si no alcanza una gran velocidad antes de despegar.



# Lecturas culturales

### Writing Development

Have students write a brief summary of the information from the **Lectura.**

### Learning from Photos

*(page 211)* The view in the photo is of La Paz, with the snowcapped Mount Illimani behind it. La Paz is the largest city in Bolivia, with a population of about two million. It is the highest capital in the world, at an altitude of 3,660 meters (12,000 feet). Although La Paz is the administrative capital of Bolivia, the legal capital is Sucre.

### Critical Thinking Activity

**Drawing conclusions**

Read the following to the class or write it on the board.

**¿Por qué es muy apropiado darle el nombre «El Alto» al aeropuerto de La Paz?**

**LEVELING**

**E:** Activity

## Answers to ¿Comprendes?

**A**

1. Se llama El Alto.
2. Un pasajero puede tener dificultad en respirar al bajar de un avión en La Paz porque a estas alturas del altiplano hay menos oxígeno en el aire que al nivel del mar.
3. Tienen botellas de oxígeno.
4. Tendrías una vista magnífica de la ciudad de La Paz.
5. La pista es muy larga.
6. A esta altura el aire no puede sostener el peso del avión. El avión tiene que alcanzar una gran velocidad antes de despegar. Por eso la pista tiene que ser muy larga.

**B**

1. No
2. Sí
3. No
4. No
5. No
6. Sí

# Lectura opcional 1

## National Standards

**Cultures**

This reading and the related activities on this page familiarize students with La Paz, Bolivia, and its surroundings.

## PRESENTATION

You may wish to have students who read this selection present some information about the area around Lake Titicaca to the class.

### Learning from Photos

*(page 212 top)* The Aymaras live in the Titicaca basin of Bolivia and Peru. Though subjugated by the Incas in the fifteenth century, they still dominate the region and continue to speak their own languages. Contemporary Aymara and Quechua cultures are related.

*(page 212 middle)* Titicaca is the world's highest large lake, at 3,810 meters (12,500 ft.) above sea level. It has been a center of Indian cultures from pre-Incan times. The islands of Titicaca and Coati, the birthplace of the Incas, are in the lake.

*(page 212 bottom)* Related to the camel, the llama thrives in the cold climate of the Andean foothills.

# Lectura opcional 1

Indios quechua

India aymara

## Los alrededores de La Paz

Antiguamente la ciudad de La Paz estaba situada donde hoy está el aeropuerto. En este lugar siempre había mucho viento. A los conquistadores españoles no les gustaba el viento fuerte y decidieron trasladar la ciudad a un valle más abajo donde haría menos viento. Es por esta razón que el aeropuerto está a una altura más elevada que la ciudad. Para ir del aeropuerto a la ciudad el viajero tiene que bajar unos 1.000 pies.

En la carretera que enlaza la ciudad con el aeropuerto se ven muchos anuncios para aerodeslizadores. Estos aerodeslizadores o hidrofoils cruzan el lago Titicaca. El lago Titicaca está entre Bolivia y Perú. Igual que el aeropuerto El Alto es el aeropuerto comercial más alto del mundo, el lago Titicaca es el lago navegable más alto del mundo. Cruzar el lago Titicaca es una experiencia extraordinaria. Al cruzar el lago verías los pueblos de los indios aymara y quechua. Verías también muchas alpacas, llamas, vicuñas y chinchillas. ¿Te interesan los animales y la naturaleza? ¿Sí? Pues, te encantaría un viaje por esta región interesante de la cordillera andina.

El lago Titicaca

Cuzco, Perú

## ¿Comprendes?

**A Los alrededores de La Paz** Contesten.

1. ¿Qué se ve en la carretera que enlaza la ciudad de La Paz con el aeropuerto?
2. ¿Por qué hay muchos aerodeslizadores?
3. ¿Dónde está el lago Titicaca?
4. ¿Cuál es una característica interesante del lago Titicaca?
5. ¿Quiénes viven a orillas del lago?
6. ¿Cuáles son algunos animales de esta región andina?

**B Análisis** Expliquen.

Expliquen cómo y por qué el aeropuerto está a una altura más elevada que la ciudad de La Paz.



## Answers to ¿Comprendes?

**A**

1. Se ven muchos anuncios para aerodeslizadores.
2. Hay muchos aerodeslizadores porque el lago Titicaca está cerca del aeropuerto.
3. El lago Titicaca está entre Bolivia y el Perú.
4. El lago Titicaca es el lago navegable más alto del mundo.
5. Los indios aymara y quechua viven a orillas del lago.
6. Algunos animales de esta región andina son alpacas, llamas, vicuñas y chinchillas.

**B** *Answers will vary but may include:*

El aeropuerto está a una altura más alta que la ciudad de La Paz porque a los conquistadores españoles no les gustaba el viento fuerte y decidieron trasladar la ciudad—
que estaba situada donde hoy está el aeropuerto—a un valle más abajo donde haría menos viento.

# Lectura opcional 2

## Un héroe de la aviación latinoamericana

Emilio Carranza enfrente de su avión Excelsior

En 1928 Charles Lindbergh, «El Águila[1] Solitaria», voló de Wáshington a México D.F. en el mismo avión con el que cruzó el Atlántico. Los mexicanos querían responder a tan fino gesto. El 11 de junio de 1928 Emilio Carranza, de 22 años de edad, capitán de las Fuerzas Aéreas Mexicanas y sobrino del ex-presidente Venustiano Carranza, salió de México en su avión Excelsior. Llegó a Wáshington como héroe.

El joven piloto pasó un mes en Estados Unidos. A las 7:05 de la noche del 12 de julio de 1928 despegó del aeropuerto Roosevelt de Nueva York para volver a México. Nunca llegó a México. Cerca de Chatsworth, Nueva Jersey, encontraron los restos del Excelsior y el cuerpo del valiente capitán.

Diez mil soldados y marinos norteamericanos marcharon con el cuerpo del héroe mexicano a la Pennsylvania Station donde un tren lo llevaría a México.

En las escuelas de México hicieron una colecta para levantar un monumento en el lugar de la tragedia. Allí está todavía. Y cada año, en el aniversario de su muerte, militares y representantes de las dos repúblicas dejan flores en honor de Emilio Carranza.

[1]Águila *Eagle*

Venustiano Carranza (a la izquierda)

## ¿Comprendes?

**Dos aviadores** Completen.

1. A Charles Lindbergh se le llamaba ____.
2. En 1928 Lindbergh voló de ____ a la Ciudad de México.
3. Emilio Carranza era ____ en las Fuerzas Aéreas Mexicanas.
4. Su tío fue ____.
5. Carranza voló en su avión de ____ a Wáshington.
6. El avión cayó del cielo cerca de ____ en el estado de Nueva Jersey.
7. Los soldados y marinos americanos llevaron su cuerpo a la ____.
8. Los alumnos mexicanos hicieron una colecta para levantar un ____ en Nueva Jersey.
9. Todos los años representantes norteamericanos y mexicanos ponen ____ en el monumento.



### Answers to ¿Comprendes?

1. «El Águila Solitaria»
2. Wáshington
3. capitán
4. el ex-presidente, Venustiano Carranza
5. la Ciudad de México
6. Chatsworth
7. Pennsylvania Station
8. monumento
9. flores

**LEVELING**

**E:** Reading 1
**A:** Reading 1
**C:** Reading 1

# Lectura opcional 2

### National Standards

**Cultures**
This reading and the related activities on this page familiarize students with a Mexican hero of aviation, Emilio Carranza.

**¡OJO!** The readings on pages 212 and 213 are optional. You may skip them completely, have the entire class read them, have only several students read them and report to the class, or assign either of them for extra credit.

**Teaching Tips**
Ask students if they know anything about Charles Lindbergh. Have them tell in Spanish what they know.

### History Connection

The period from 1911 through the 1920s was one of the most turbulent periods in Mexican history. Francisco Ignacio Madero, Emiliano Zapata, Francisco (Pancho) Villa, and Venustiano Carranza were major players in the Mexican Revolution that began with the overthrow of Porfirio Díaz in 1911.

### Reaching All Students

**Cooperative Learning**
The historical figure of Venustiano Carranza is very interesting, especially his relations with the United States during World War I. Have a pair of students prepare a brief biography of Venustiano Carranza and report to the class.

# Conexiones

## National Standards

**Connections**

This reading about the geography and climate of the Iberian Peninsula establishes a connection with another discipline, allowing students to reinforce and further their knowledge of the natural sciences through the study of Spanish.

¡OJO! The readings in the **Conexiones** section are optional. They focus on some of the major disciplines taught in schools and universities. The vocabulary is useful for discussing such topics as history, literature, art, economics, business, science, etc. You may choose any of the following ways to do the readings in the **Conexiones** sections.

**Independent reading** Have students read the selections and do the post-reading activities as homework, which you collect. This option is least intrusive on class time and requires a minimum of teacher involvement.

**Homework with in-class follow-up** Assign the readings and post-reading activities as homework. Review and discuss the material in class the next day.

**Intensive in-class activity** This option includes a pre-reading vocabulary presentation, in-class reading and discussion, assignment of the activities for homework, and a discussion of the assignment in class the following day.

# Conexiones

## *Las ciencias naturales*

### La geografía

Geography, the science, deals with the description, distribution, and interaction of the various physical, biological, and cultural features of the Earth's surface. However, for most people, geography is simply "physical geography" that studies the world's surface, the distribution and description of its land and water areas. The climate and the physical features of a country or region obviously have a great influence on the economy and even on the culture of a people.

La península ibérica

The geography of Spain has affected its people enormously. The Pyrenees, separating Spain from the rest of Europe—the French have said that "Africa begins at the Pyrenees"—have often insulated Spain from European influence. Spain was a maritime nation in part because of its unique situation as a peninsula with coasts on the Atlantic and the Mediterranean. As you read, you will find out some things you probably did not know about Spain's geography.

### La geografía de España

España, con Portugal, forman la península ibérica. La meseta central cubre más de la mitad del país con una altura media de 600 a 800 metros. Una serie de sierras cruza el país de este a oeste. En el extremo norte están los Pirineos, en el centro, no lejos de Madrid, la Sierra de Guadarrama, y continuando hacia el sur, la Sierra Morena y la Sierra Nevada.

Andalucía, España



## History Connection

The Iberians were the original inhabitants of the peninsula before the arrival of the Celts, Phoenicians, Carthaginians, and Romans. They fought ferociously against the Carthaginians and the Romans.

## Reaching All Students

**Additional Practice** You may wish to have students refresh their geography vocabulary by asking:

**¿Qué es una península?**
**¿Cuál es la diferencia entre una isla y una península?**
**¿Qué es un continente?**
**¿Cuáles son los cinco continentes?**
**¿Cuáles son dos océanos?**
**¿Qué es una cordillera o una sierra?**

De todos los países de Europa, sólo Suiza es más montañosa que España. Aunque mucha gente no lo cree, hay importantes estaciones de esquí en la Sierra Nevada y la Sierra de Guadarrama.

La península ibérica se divide en dos, la Iberia seca[1] y la Iberia húmeda. La Iberia húmeda es la región de los Pirineos, el noroeste de España y casi todo Portugal. La mayor parte de España está en la Iberia seca. Por eso, en el verano, si vuelas sobre España, verás un paisaje mayormente árido y pardo[2]. Los ríos, en el verano, llevan poca agua. Los ríos importantes que desembocan[3] en el Atlántico son el Duero, el Tajo, el Guadiana y el Guadalquivir. El río más importante que desemboca en el Mediterráneo es el Ebro. El agua tiene una importancia enorme. Sin agua, no se podría cultivar nada. Y España, hasta años recientes, era un país agrícola, y la agricultura sigue siendo un importante factor económico.

[1]seca *dry*
[2]pardo *brown*
[3]desembocan *empty into*

Sierra Nevada, España

Toledo, España

## ¿Comprendes?

**A Un poco de geografía** Completen según la lectura.

1. Los países que constituyen la península ibérica son ____ y ____.
2. Las montañas que están entre Francia y España son los ____.
3. Las sierras importantes van de este a ____.
4. La sierra más cerca de Madrid es la ____.
5. Portugal está en la Iberia húmeda, y la mayor parte de España está en la Iberia ____.
6. Muchos ríos en España desembocan en el ____.
7. Pero el Ebro desemboca en el ____.

**B ¿Lo saben?** Contesten.

1. Nombra tres ríos importantes de España.
2. Nombra dos sierras donde hay estaciones de esquí.
3. Di lo que uno vería desde un avión volando sobre la meseta central en verano.



# Conexiones

## PRESENTATION

### *Las ciencias naturales*
### La geografía

**Step 1** Since this geography selection is very specific to Spain, you may wish to have all students read it, at least quickly, as an additional cultural reading.

**Step 2** You may wish to have students locate all the places mentioned in the reading on the map of Spain on page xxx or on Map Transparency M 2.

### History Connection

Toledo, known in ancient times as **Toletum,** was conquered by the Romans in 193 B.C. Later, it became the capital of Visigothic Spain. During Moorish domination it was part of the Caliphat of Córdoba until reconquered in 1085. Pictured here is the Roman bridge over the **Río Tajo.** The Cathedral of Toledo and its ancient synagogues are world-famous. Toledo is also closely connected with El Greco and his art.

### LEVELING

**E:** Reading

## ANSWERS TO ¿Comprendes?

**A**

1. España, Portugal
2. Pirineos
3. oeste
4. Sierra de Guadarrama
5. seca
6. Atlántico
7. Mediterráneo

**B**

1. el Ebro, el Duero, el Tajo (el Guadiana, el Guadalquivir)
2. La Sierra Nevada y la Sierra de Guadarrama
3. un paisaje mayormente árido y pardo

## ¡Te toca a ti!

### Use what you have learned

**Recycling**

These activities allow students to use the vocabulary and structure from this chapter in completely open-ended, real-life situations.

**PRESENTATION**

Encourage students to say as much as possible when they do these activities. Tell them not to be afraid to make mistakes, since the goal of the activities is real-life communication. If someone in the group makes an error, allow the others to politely correct him or her. Let students choose the activities they would like to do.

You may wish to divide students into pairs or groups. Encourage students to elaborate on the basic theme and to be creative. They may use props, pictures, or posters if they wish.

**PRACTICE**

## ¡Te toca a ti!

# Use what you have learned

HABLAR 1

### Yo conozco la América Latina.

*✔ Describe a Latin American country you would like to visit*

Tú y tu compañero(a) ya saben mucho sobre varios países hispanos. Cada uno(a) de ustedes va a seleccionar el país que te gustaría visitar. Dile a tu compañero(a) por qué te gustaría viajar a ese país. Dile también todo lo que harías allí. Luego cambien de rol.

Patagonia, Argentina

HABLAR 2

### Un viaje estupendo

*✔ Talk about air travel*

Habla con algunos compañeros sobre un viaje que hiciste en avión. Diles adonde ibas y descríbales todo lo que pasó en el aeropuerto de salida, en el aeropuerto de llegada y a bordo del avión.

HABLAR 3

### ¡Un millón de dólares! ¡Increíble!

*✔ Tell what you would do with a million dollars*

Tú y tu compañero(a) acaban de recibir un millón de dólares. Cada uno(a) de ustedes va a hacer una lista de las cosas que harían con el dinero. Comparen sus listas. Luego decidan quién haría las cosas más interesantes.



**Learning from Photos**

*(page 216)* The southern part of Patagonia has dry, stony countryside with rugged, dark mountains. The area is inhabited by English and Welsh who live in isolated **estancias** that often cover thousands of acres of land used for grazing sheep.

ANSWERS TO 

1. *Answers will vary but will include vocabulary and structure learned in the chapter.*
2. *Answers will vary. Students will use vocabulary relating to airplanes and travel to describe a trip that they have taken.*
3. *Answers will vary, but students will use the conditional to describe what they would do with the money they just won.*

## Un vuelo excelente o terrible

✔ *Write about an airline trip*

Tú acabas de volver de un viaje a Costa Rica. Tu vuelo de regreso fue tan excelente (o terrible) que decides escribir una carta a la línea aérea. Describe el vuelo y diles lo que piensas de la tripulación y los servicios que ofrecen. Da ejemplos de lo que pasó (ocurrió) durante el vuelo.

•Visite San José con conexiones a Guatemala.
Salidas los jueves y lunes 8:20 a.m.
Tels. 724-3330/3444. Consulte a su agente de viajes
Desde $289.00 a San José y $299.00 a Panamá*
*ciertas restricciones aplican
Infórmese sobre nuestro exclusivo servicio de carga a través del
Tel. 723-3160
Con el estilo de... LACSA
Lineas Aereas de Costa Rica/The Airline of Costa Rica
¡NOS ENCANTA LA GENTE!

### Writing Strategy

**Identifying sources for a research paper** To write a research paper, you must plan, set goals, and gather information. When you find a source, skim it to see whether it has any useful information. If it does, record the publication information on an index card so you can find the source easily when you begin your research. Be sure to use all resources available to you—both print and nonprint. Your school library will be an excellent place to begin looking for sources for your research paper.

## La geografía del estado de...

You have been asked to write a brief description of the geography of your state for a Spanish-speaking audience. Your school librarian will help you select the most appropriate print resources—encyclopedias, almanacs, and, of course, geography books. The Internet will be an excellent nonprint resource. Log in and go to your state's Web sites. Once you have assembled your resources, scan them for the essential information you will need. Jot down the information you will need for your report. Remember to include references. Prepare a draft of your report in Spanish and ask your Spanish teacher to review it for you. After you have seen your teacher's recommendations, prepare your final version.

Agua Azul, México

## ¡Te toca a ti!

4 You may wish to call on a few students to read their letters to the class.

### LEVELING

These activities encompass all three levels. All students will be able to do them at a sophistication level commensurate with their ability in Spanish. Some students will be able to speak for several minutes, and others may be able to give just a few sentences. This is to be expected when students are functioning completely on their own generating their own language to the best of their ability.

### Writing Strategy

**Identifying sources for a research paper** You may wish to have students work in groups to research and write this report or assign it for extra credit to more able students. When students have prepared their drafts, you may wish to have them review each other's work before handing the reports in to you.

### Reaching All Students

**Additional Practice** Have pairs of students compose a letter to a Latin American airline inquiring about positions. The letters should request the following information:

- what positions are available
- the training needed
- the salary and benefits
- what positions require English and Spanish skills

## Answers to ¡Te toca a ti!

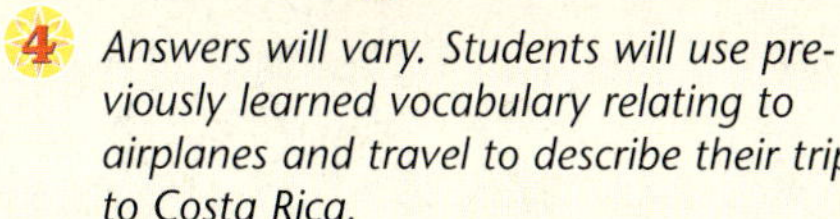

4 *Answers will vary. Students will use previously learned vocabulary relating to airplanes and travel to describe their trip to Costa Rica.*

5 *Answers will vary based on where students live.*

### Learning from Realia

*(page 217)* You may wish to ask questions such as:
**¿Qué es LACSA?**
**¿Qué días tiene vuelos?**
**¿A qué hora son los vuelos?**
**¿Cuál de los destinos cuesta más?**
**¿Quién llamaría al 723–3160?**

# Assessment

## Resource Manager

Communication Transparency C 7
Quizzes, pages 30–34
Performance Assessment, Task 7
Tests, pages 97–110
Situation Cards, Chapter 7
**Maratón mental** Videoquiz, Chapter 7
ExamView® Pro, Chapter 7

## Assessment

This is a pre-test for students to take before you administer the chapter test. Note that each section is cross-referenced so students can easily find the material they have to review in case they made errors. You may use Assessment Answers Transparency A 7 to do the assessment in class, or you may assign this assessment for homework. You can correct the assessment yourself, or you may prefer to project the answers on the overhead in class.

## Glencoe Technology

**MINDJOGGER VHS/DVD**

You may wish to help your students prepare for the chapter test by playing the MindJogger game show. Teams will compete against each other to review chapter vocabulary and structure and sharpen listening comprehension skills.

# Assessment

## Vocabulario

**1 Identifiquen.**

To review **Palabras 1**, turn to pages 192–193.

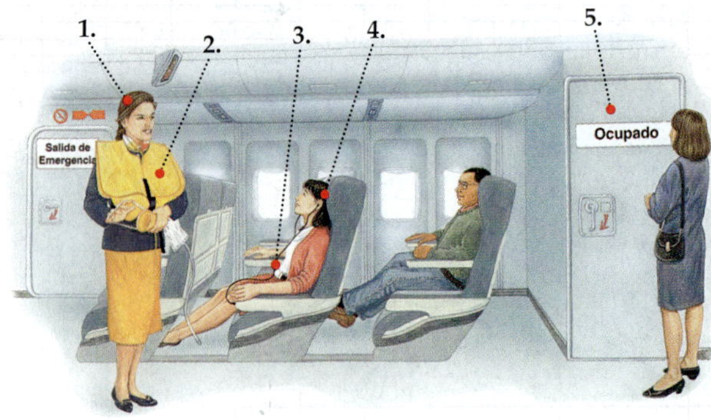


**2 Identifiquen.**

To review **Palabras 2**, turn to pages 196–197.

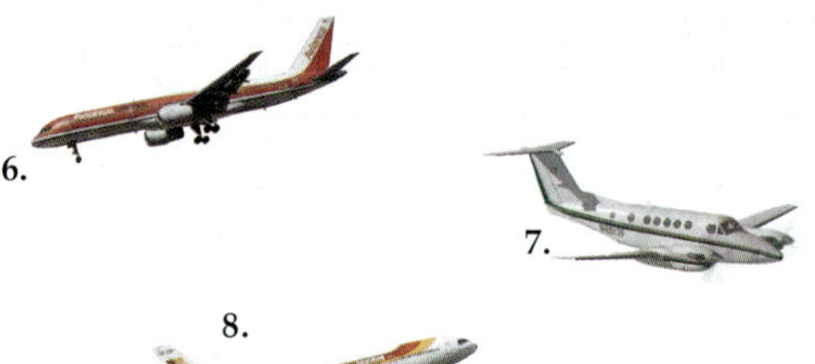


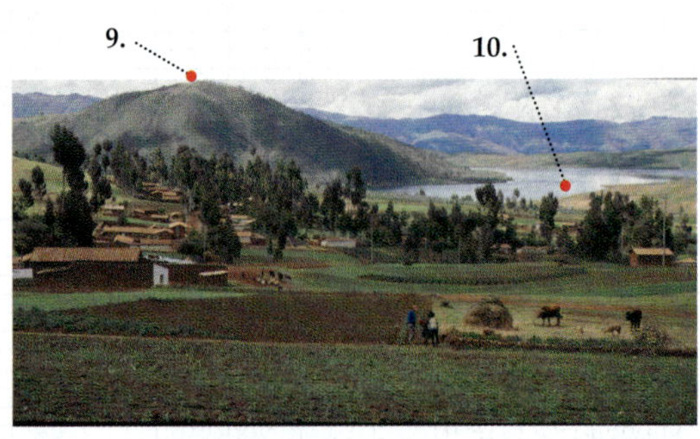




### Answers to Assessment

1. la asistente de vuelo
2. el chaleco salvavidas
3. el cinturón de seguridad
4. los audífonos (los auriculares)
5. el lavabo (el aseo)

6. el aterrizaje
7. la avioneta
8. el despegue
9. el pico
10. el lago

## Estructura

**3 Escriban en el condicional.**

11. Ellos llegan a tiempo.
12. Yo sirvo la comida.
13. Vemos una película.
14. Tú no lo sabes.
15. ¿Lo pone (él) debajo de su asiento?

To review the conditional, turn to pages 200 and 203.

**4 Contesten con pronombres.**

16. ¿Quién les serviría la comida a los pasajeros? (los asistentes de vuelo)
17. ¿Quién le daría el dinero al niño? (su padre)
18. ¿Quién le compró los boletos? (yo)

To review the use of two object pronouns, turn to page 205.

## Cultura

**5 Escriban dos frases sobre el aeropuerto en La Paz, Bolivia.**

19–20. El aeropuerto en La Paz, Bolivia...

To review this cultural information, turn to page 210.

El altiplano, Bolivia



## Assessment

**FOLDABLES Study Organizer** **Dinah Zike's Study Guides**

Your students may wish to use Foldable 3 to organize, display, and arrange data as they learn about the vast Spanish-speaking world. You may wish to encourage them to add information from each chapter as they continue to gather facts and make observations about all the different countries they will be studying.

A *pocket book* foldable is also ideal for having students differentiate between masculine and feminine forms.

## Answers to Assessment

11. Ellos llegarían a tiempo.
12. Yo serviría la comida.
13. Veríamos una película.
14. Tú no lo sabrías.
15. ¿Lo pondría (él) debajo de su asiento?

16. Los asistentes de vuelo se la servirían (a los pasajeros).
17. Su padre se lo daría (al niño).
18. Yo se los compré.

19–20. *Answers will vary, but they will be based on the information in the cultural reading on pages 210–211.*

# ¡Hablo como un pro!

This unique page gives students the opportunity to speak freely and say whatever they can, using the vocabulary and structures they have learned in the chapter. The illustration serves to remind students of precisely what they know how to say in Spanish. There are no activities that students do not have the ability to describe or talk about in Spanish. The art not only depicts the vocabulary and content of this chapter, but also reinforces what they learned in previous chapters.

You may wish to use this page in many ways. Some possibilities are to have students do the following:

1. Look at the illustration and identify items by giving the correct Spanish words.
2. Make up sentences about what they see in the illustration.
3. Make up questions about the illustration. They can call on another class member to respond if you do this as a class activity, or you may prefer to allow students to work in small groups. This activity is extremely beneficial because it enables students to actively use interrogative words.
4. Answer questions you ask them about the illustration.
5. Work in pairs and make up a conversation based on the illustration.
6. Look at the illustration and give a complete oral review of what they see.
7. Look at the illustration and write a paragraph (or essay) about it.

You can also use this page as an assessment or testing tool, taking into account individual differences by having students go from simple to quite complicated tasks. The assessment can be either oral or written. You may wish to use the rubrics provided on pages T20–T21 as you give students the following directions.

1. Identify the topic or situation of the illustration.
2. Give the Spanish words for as many items as you can.
3. Think of as many sentences as you can to describe the illustration.
4. Go over your sentences and put them in the best sequencing to give a coherent story based on the illustration.

¡Hablo como un pro!

Tell all you can about this illustration.

# Vocabulario

### Describing an airplane

el avión de reacción, el jet
la avioneta
el helicóptero
la cabina de mando, la cabina de vuelo
la ventanilla
el compartimiento sobre la cabeza, el compartimiento superior
la señal de no fumar
la salida de emergencia
el pasillo
el asiento
el respaldo del asiento
el cinturón de seguridad
el chaleco salvavidas
la máscara de oxígeno
el carrito
la mesita
la bandeja
el equipaje de mano
el lavabo, el aseo

### Identifying some crew members

la tripulación
el/la comandante, el/la piloto
el/la copiloto
el/la asistente de vuelo

### Describing a flight and on-board services

el vuelo
el anuncio
el/la pasajero(a)
el aterrizaje
el despegue
la escala
la altura
la turbulencia
volar
sobrevolar
despegar
aterrizar
anunciar
pasar por la cabina
distribuir audífonos (auriculares)
servir bebidas
servir una comida
abrochar
caber
a tiempo
con una demora

**How well do you know your vocabulary?**

- Choose your words to describe a trip by plane.
- Write a brief description of a trip by plane for someone who is traveling for the first time.

### Describing some things at an airport

la pista
la terminal de pasajeros
la torre de control

### Talking about geography

la geografía
la altura, la altitud
el pico
la montaña
la cordillera
el altiplano
la meseta
la llanura
el valle
el río
el lago

**VIDEOTUR**

## Episodio 7

In this video episode, you will watch Alberto's friends "help" him get over his fear of flying. See page 486 for more information.

# Vocabulario

## Vocabulary Review

The words and phrases in the **Vocabulario** have been taught for productive use in this chapter. They are summarized here as a resource for both student and teacher. This list also serves as a convenient resource for the **¡Te toca a ti!** activities on pages 216 and 217. There are approximately ten cognates in this vocabulary list. Have students find them.

**¡OJO!** You will notice that the vocabulary list here is not translated. This has been done intentionally, since we feel that by the time students have finished the material in the chapter they should be familiar with the meanings of all the words. If there are several words they still do not know, we recommend that they refer to the **Palabras 1** and **2** sections in the chapter or go to the dictionaries at the end of this book to find the meanings. However, if you prefer that your students have the English translations, please refer to Vocabulary Transparency 7.1, where you will find all these words with their translations.

**VIDEO VHS/DVD**

The Video Program allows students to see how the chapter vocabulary and structures are used by native speakers within an engaging story line. For maximum reinforcement, show the video episode as a final activity for Chapter 7.

Repaso

# Preview

This section reviews the salient points from Chapters 5–7. In the **Conversación** students will review forms of the future tense and direct and indirect object pronouns. In the **Estructura** section, they will review the regular and irregular forms of the future and the conditional. They will also review direct and indirect object pronouns used in the same sentence. They will practice these structures as they talk about air travel and hotel situations.

## Resource Manager

Workbook, Check-Up, pages 84–88
Tests, pages 111–119
Performance Assessment, Tasks 5–7

## PRESENTATION

### Conversación

**Step 1** Have students open their books to page 222. Ask two students to read the conversation aloud using as much expression as possible.

**Step 2** Go over the questions in the **¿Comprendes?** section.

### Learning from Photos

*(page 222 top)* You may wish to ask these questions about the photo:
**¿Dónde está la gente?**
**¿Por qué están en fila?**
**¿Qué harán ellos?**
**¿Quiénes están detrás de los mostradores?**
*(page 222 bottom)* Caracas is Venezuela's capital and major city. At 950 meters (3,100 feet) above sea level, the climate is springlike. Caracas is the economic and cultural hub of the nation. Caracas was founded in 1567 by Diego de Losada.

Repaso

# Conversación

## En el aeropuerto

**Diego** ¿De cuántas horas será el vuelo?
**Susana** Llegaremos a Caracas a las diez. Es un vuelo de cuatro horas.
**Diego** No sé lo que está pasando. Me parece que no saldremos a tiempo.
**Susana** Entonces podré hacer un crucigrama más.
**Diego** A ti te gusta mucho pasar el tiempo llenando tus crucigramas.
**Susana** ¿Me darías mi maletín?
**Diego** Te lo doy con mucho placer. ¿Qué quieres? ¿Tus crucigramas?
**Susana** No. Quiero ver si la confirmación para el hotel está en el maletín.
**Diego** Yo la tenía pero te la di en el taxi.
**Susana** Sí, sí. La tengo. Aquí está.
**Diego** A propósito, ¿cuántas noches vamos a estar en el Hotel Tamanaco?
**Susana** Cuatro. Es bastante caro el cuarto, ¿sabes?

## ¿Comprendes?

**Antes del vuelo** Contesten.

1. ¿Dónde están Diego y Susana?
2. ¿A qué hora llegarán a Caracas?
3. ¿De cuántas horas será el vuelo?
4. ¿Parece que saldrá a tiempo?
5. Si tiene más tiempo, ¿qué podrá hacer Susana?
6. ¿Por qué quería Susana su maletín?
7. ¿Dónde le dio la confirmación Diego?
8. ¿Cuántas noches estarán en el Hotel Tamanaco?

Caracas, Venezuela



## Answers to ¿Comprendes?

1. Diego y Susana están en el aeropuerto.
2. Llegarán a Caracas a las diez.
3. El vuelo será de cuatro horas.
4. Parece que no saldrá a tiempo.
5. Si tiene más tiempo Susana podrá hacer un crucigrama más.
6. Susana quería su maletín para buscar la confirmación para el hotel.
7. Diego le dio la confirmación en el taxi.
8. Estarán cuatro noches en el Hotel Tamanaco.

# Estructura

## El futuro y el condicional

1. Review the following forms of the future and conditional of regular verbs.

| | FUTURE | | | | | |
|---|---|---|---|---|---|---|
| MIRAR | **miraré** | **mirarás** | **mirará** | **miraremos** | *mirareis* | **mirarán** |
| COMER | **comeré** | **comerás** | **comerá** | **comeremos** | *comereis* | **comerán** |
| VIVIR | **viviré** | **vivirás** | **vivirá** | **viviremos** | *vivireis* | **vivirán** |

| | CONDITIONAL | | | | | |
|---|---|---|---|---|---|---|
| MIRAR | **miraría** | **mirarías** | **miraría** | **miraríamos** | *miraríais* | **mirarían** |
| COMER | **comería** | **comerías** | **comería** | **comeríamos** | *comeríais* | **comerían** |
| VIVIR | **viviría** | **vivirías** | **viviría** | **viviríamos** | *viviríais* | **vivirían** |

2. Review the stems for irregular verbs in the future and conditional. The endings for irregular verbs are the same as those for the regular verbs.

| INFINITIVE | STEM | FUTURE | CONDITIONAL |
|---|---|---|---|
| TENER | **tendr-** | **tendré** | **tendría** |
| SALIR | **saldr-** | **saldré** | **saldría** |
| VENIR | **vendr-** | **vendré** | **vendría** |
| PONER | **pondr-** | **pondré** | **pondría** |
| SABER | **sabr-** | **sabré** | **sabría** |
| PODER | **podr-** | **podré** | **podría** |
| DECIR | **dir-** | **diré** | **diría** |
| HACER | **har-** | **haré** | **haría** |
| QUERER | **querr-** | **querré** | **querría** |

**1 Historieta A México** Contesten.

1. ¿Irá Catalina a México?
2. ¿La acompañarás?
3. ¿Tomarán ustedes el avión?
4. ¿Leerás durante el vuelo o llenarás un crucigrama?
5. ¿Buscarán ustedes un taxi para ir al hotel?

Ciudad de México



CAPÍTULOS 5-7

## PRESENTATION

### El futuro y el condicional

**Step 1** Quickly review the verb paradigms on page 223. You may want to have students repeat the forms after you.

**Step 2** Write the regular future and conditional verb forms on the board. Underline the endings.

**Step 3** Remind students that all of the irregular verbs in Item 2 are verbs that are used frequently.

## PRACTICE

**1** This activity gives students practice with regular verbs in the future. Ask for volunteers to continue the **Historieta.**

### FUN FACTS

The *Beetle* is known as **un escarabajo.** It is the most popular taxi in Mexico City. The front passenger seat is removed to allow easier access for the customers. All the taxis are painted green and white. In some Latin American countries the *Beetle* is called **un volky.**

### Answers to Repaso

1. Sí (No), Catalina (no) irá a México.
2. Sí (No, no) la acompañaré.
3. Sí (No), nosotros (no) tomaremos el avión.
4. Leeré (Llenaré un crucigrama) durante el vuelo.
5. Sí, (No, no) buscaremos un taxi para ir al hotel.

## PRACTICE *(continued)*

**2** Activity 2 reviews regular forms of the conditional.

**3** Activity 3 reviews irregular forms of the future.

**4** Activity 4 reviews irregular forms of the conditional.

## PRESENTATION

### Los complementos

**Step 1** Lead students through Items 1 and 2 on page 224.

**Step 2** When reviewing Item 2, write the example on the board. Ask a volunteer to come to the board and explain to the class how **se** and **las** take the place of the direct and indirect objects.

### Learning from Photos

*(page 224)* Miraflores is one of Lima's more elegant neighborhoods and the site of many international hotels. There are also numerous art galleries as well as sidewalk art exhibits.

### Learning from Realia

*(page 224)* You may wish to ask students questions about the moist towelette:
**¿Qué es LanChile?**
**¿Qué será una toalla refrescante?**
You may wish to tell the students that the **Lan** in **LanChile** means **Línea Aérea Nacional.**

Repaso

**2 Pasatiempos** Sigan el modelo.

**leer una novela o una revista →**
**Nosotros leeríamos una novela pero él leería una revista.**

1. jugar ajedrez o dominó
2. ir al zoológico o al parque de atracciones
3. comer en casa o en un restaurante
4. coleccionar sellos o monedas antiguas
5. mirar al mimo o al payaso

Miraflores, Perú

**3 Unas vacaciones** Completen con el futuro.

PEPE Sandra, ¿por qué no me dices tú lo que __1__ (hacer) durante tus vacaciones?

SANDRA No te __2__ (poder) decir nada hasta la semana que viene.

PEPE ¿No __3__ (saber) hasta entonces?

SANDRA No, porque yo __4__ (tener) que hablar con Maripaz. Yo sé que ella __5__ (querer) hacer algo y yo lo __6__ (hacer) con ella.

PEPE ¿__7__ (Hacer) ustedes un viaje?

**4 Uno sí y el otro no** Completen con el condicional.

1. Él sabría el número del vuelo pero su hermano no lo ____.
2. Yo te lo diría pero ellos nunca te lo ____.
3. Nosotros lo haríamos pero ellos no lo ____.
4. Yo podría ir pero tú no ____.
5. Ustedes lo pondrían en orden pero él no lo ____.
6. Yo tendría que volver pero tú no ____.

### Los complementos

1. When both a direct and an indirect object pronoun are used in the same sentence, the indirect object pronoun always precedes the direct object pronoun.

   **El agente me devolvió el billete.**
   **El agente me lo devolvió.**

2. The indirect object pronouns **le** and **les** change to **se** when used with the direct object pronouns **lo, la, los,** or **las.** Because **se** can mean **a él, a ella, a usted, a ellos, a ellas,** or **a ustedes,** the prepositional phrase is often added for clarity.

   **¿A quién le diste las llaves del cuarto?**
   **Se las di a Teresa.**



## ANSWERS TO Repaso

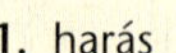

**2**
1. Nosotros jugaríamos al ajedrez pero él jugaría al dominó.
2. Nosotros iríamos al zoológico pero él iría al parque de atracciones.
3. Nosotros comeríamos en casa pero él comería en un restaurante.
4. Nosotros coleccionaríamos sellos pero él coleccionaría monedas antiguas.
5. Nosotros miraríamos al mimo pero él miraría al payaso.

**3**
1. harás
2. podré
3. sabrás
4. tendré
5. querrá
6. haré
7. Harán

**4**
1. sabría
2. dirían
3. harían
4. podrías
5. pondría
6. tendrías

**5** **A bordo del avión** Contesten según el modelo.

**¿Quién te sirvió la comida? →**
**El asistente de vuelo me la sirvió.**

1. ¿Quién te sirvió los refrescos?
2. ¿Quién te dio los audífonos?
3. ¿Quién te buscó la manta?
4. ¿Quién te explicó las reglas de seguridad?
5. ¿Quién te mostró el chaleco salvavidas?

**6** **En el hotel** Contesten según el modelo.

**¿Quién le dio la tarjeta al cliente? (la recepcionista) →**
**La recepcionista se la dio.**

1. ¿Quién le dio la llave al cliente? (el recepcionista)
2. ¿Quién le abrió la puerta? (el mozo)
3. ¿Quién le subió las maletas? (el mozo)
4. ¿Quién le limpió el cuarto? (la camarera)
5. ¿Quién le cambió las toallas? (la camarera)

Hotel Oro Verde, Manta, Ecuador

**7** **En el hotel** Trabaja con un(a) compañero(a). Están en la recepción de un hotel. Uno(a) de ustedes será el/la recepcionista y el/la otro(a) será el/la cliente. Discutan el precio, el número de noches, el cuarto, etc.

**8** **Un vuelo** Trabaja con un(a) compañero(a) de clase. Dentro de poco ustedes van a hacer un viaje juntos. Van a ir en avión. Discutan todo lo que tienen que hacer y todo lo que pasará o sucederá en el aeropuerto y durante el vuelo.

**Literary Companion**

**You may wish to read the adaptation of *La muralla* by Nicolás Guillén. This literary selection is found on pages 464–467.**



## PRACTICE

**5** Activity 5 practices using two object pronouns together.

**Expansion:** After doing this activity, ask students to imagine they were in a restaurant last week with a group of friends. Now ask them: **¿Quién les trajo el menú? ¿Quién les sirvió los refrescos? ¿Quién les sirvió la comida? ¿Quién les trajo la cuenta?**

**6** Activity 6 uses the **se la, se los,** etc. combination.

**7** This activity reviews the vocabulary presented in Chapter 6.

**8** This activity reviews the vocabulary presented in Chapter 7.

**Literary Companion**

When you finish this chapter, if you wish, have students read the adaptation of ***La muralla*** by Nicolás Guillén on pages 464–467.

## ANSWERS TO 

**5**

1. El asistente de vuelo me los sirvió.
2. El asistente de vuelo me los dio.
3. El asistente de vuelo me la buscó.
4. El asistente de vuelo me las explicó.
5. El asistente de vuelo me lo mostró.

**6**

1. El recepcionista se la dio.
2. El mozo se la abrió.
3. El mozo se las subió.
4. La camarera se lo limpió.
5. La camarera se las cambió.

**7** *Answers will vary. Students will use previously learned vocabulary relating to hotels and reservations.*

**8** *Answers will vary. Students will use previously learned vocabulary relating to airplanes, airports, and travel.*

## Entérate El Caribe

This section was prepared by Time Learning Ventures of Time Inc. Its purpose is to give students greater insight, through visual images and fun articles, into the culture and people of the **Caribe.** You may wish to explain to your students that Puerto Rico, Cuba, and the Dominican Republic are the three Spanish-speaking areas included when we talk about this region.

Have students look at the photographs and read the articles. Encourage them to discuss what they have read. Let them say anything they can, using the vocabulary they have learned to this point.

Besides its gentle beauty, the **Caribe** has a fascinating history. For centuries, people from South America who had arrived in canoes populated the islands. In 1492, when Christopher Columbus first set foot in today's Dominican Republic, the **Caribe** also became the place where the civilizations of Europe and the Americas first met. Since then, the extraordinary mixture of races and cultures in this part of the world is its greatest strength and a great attraction for international visitors.



# Entérate El Caribe

## El renacimiento de una identidad indígena

Monolitos y petroglifos taínos en Utuado, Puerto Rico.

En 1492, los taínos eran uno de los grupos indígenas más numerosos y tenían la cultura más avanzada de las Antillas Mayores. Cincuenta años después casi no quedaban personas de origen taíno; murieron por las enfermedades que trajeron los españoles a América y por el maltrato[1]. Pero la cultura taína fue, y todavía es, un tema importante para los profesores y académicos de las universidades. Los estudios recientes de ADN[2] confirman que hay un alto nivel de material genético taíno en los puertorriqueños. Hoy día existen descendientes directos de los taínos en el Caribe. Por ejemplo, los habitantes de la tribu taína Jatibonicu dicen: "Somos el pueblo original de la isla de Borikén (Puerto Rico), los verdaderos herederos[3] de la cultura taína". Los Jatibonicu tienen un sitio en la Internet. "Tau Ah Taiguey Guaitiao" (¡Hola y buenos días, amigos!).

[1] maltrato: *mistreatment*  [2] ADN: *DNA*  [3] herederos: *heirs*

## Un coleccionista de historia africana

**A. Schomburg, puertorriqueño**

En Nueva York está la "Colección Schomburg", una de las más completas del mundo. Tiene libros, objetos, artefactos y muchas piezas de arte de origen africano. Y… ¿quién coleccionó todo esto? Un puertorriqueño. Arturo Alfonso Schomburg nació en 1874. Cuando era un niño y después un joven, en su escuela no había libros ni clases sobre la historia de los descendientes de africanos. Así empezó su gran pasión por coleccionar información sobre sus antepasados[1] para combatir el racismo. Su colección mostró al mundo las extraordinarias contribuciones de estas personas a la historia.

[1] antepasados: *ancestors*

Fortaleza San Felipe en Puerto Plata, República Dominicana.

## Ciudades coloniales, fortalezas y piratas

La UNESCO declaró a las ciudades de Santo Domingo, La Habana y San Juan Patrimonio Cultural de la Humanidad. Los españoles construyeron estas bellas ciudades a principios del siglo XVI. Aunque cada una tiene su propia personalidad, estas tres joyas caribeñas también tienen muchas cosas en común. La zona histórica de estas ciudades tiene monumentales morros o fortalezas[1] militares, sus iglesias, los edificios de gobierno y las plazas públicas. Santo Domingo es la ciudad colonial más antigua del continente y es también la más "intelectual" de las tres porque ahí se estableció la primera universidad de las Américas.

Francis Drake

España construyó esas fortalezas alrededor de las ciudades para proteger los territorios coloniales de sus rivales imperiales y de los piratas. El legendario pirata Francis Drake atacó San Juan varias veces, pero nunca pudo entrar a la ciudad. Roberto Cofresí era menos conocido pero dio muchos dolores de cabeza a los españoles. Era un "Robin Hood" caribeño y como no estaba de acuerdo con el sistema de gobierno español, atacaba los barcos y distribuía el botín[2] entre sus amigos y los pobres de Puerto Rico. En 1825, el capitán norteamericano John Sloat lo capturó.

[1] morros o fortalezas: *fortresses*
[2] botín: *booty*

## ¿Restaurante o monumento histórico?

Muy cerca de la Plaza de la Catedral en La Habana Vieja está la "La Bodeguita del Medio". Este restaurante cubano clásico abrió sus puertas después de la Segunda Guerra Mundial[1]. Era una gran atracción para los bohemios, artistas, políticos y escritores. Ellos iban a comer y a conversar con sus amigos para "mejorar" el mundo. Muchas personas famosas tales como Gabriel García Márquez y Ernest Hemingway escribieron sus nombres en las paredes. Hoy día, La Bodeguita del Medio es igualmente popular; miles de turistas visitan el restaurante durante todo el año, porque ahí la comida es muy sabrosa y el ambiente[2]... ¡incomparable!

[1] Segunda Guerra Mundial: *Second World War*
[2] ambiente: *atmosphere*

## Calendario de fiestas

Carnaval dominicano

**1° de mayo: Día Internacional del Trabajo** *(Cuba)*

Esta celebración conmemora a los trabajadores del mundo. Mucha gente va con banderas[1] a la Plaza de la Revolución en La Habana. Allí escuchan los discursos[2] de sus líderes y de otros líderes internacionales.

**27 de febrero: Carnaval y Día de la Independencia** *(República Dominicana)*

Los dominicanos celebran la Independencia de la dominación del gobierno de Haití (1822–1824) y el fin del carnaval el mismo día. El carnaval es la fiesta más popular en ese país. La gente usa máscaras, se viste con disfraces[3], baila y canta en las calles de las ciudades.

**3ª semana de julio, Fiesta de Santiago Apóstol** *(Loíza, Puerto Rico)*

En Loíza, Puerto Rico, se celebra la fiesta patronal con una gran parada. La gente se viste con ropa tradicional, baila y canta y hace una parodia de las guerras entre moros y cristianos en España.

[1] banderas: *flags* [2] discursos: *speeches* [3] disfraces: *costumes*

## micocina

**Un platillo verdaderamente caribeño**

Los españoles trajeron a América el arroz y los frijoles. Los caribeños adoptaron rápidamente esta comida y hoy es el plato tradicional de estas tres islas. Este delicioso platillo se llama "arroz moro" en la República Dominicana, "congrí" en Cuba y "arroz con habichuelas" en Puerto Rico. *(El congrí y el arroz moro se preparan con frijoles negros.)*

**Arroz con habichuelas**[1] *(Puerto Rico)*

**Ingredientes**

*(Para el arroz)*
- 2 tazas de arroz blanco
- 3 tazas de agua
- 1 cucharada de aceite
- sal al gusto

*(Para las habichuelas)*
- 2 cucharaditas de aceite de oliva
- 2 cucharadas de jamón de cocinar, en cubos
- 1 lata de habichuelas coloradas
- 1 lata de salsa de tomate
- 1 paquete de sazón[2]
- 2 cucharadas de sofrito[3]
- 7 aceitunas rellenas con pimiento
- 1 cucharadita de alcaparrado[4]
- 2 papas medianas, en cubos
- 1 taza de agua

**Preparación**

Hervir las 3 tazas de agua en una olla. Agregar el arroz blanco, el aceite y la sal. Tapar la olla y reducir la temperatura. Cocinar durante 20 minutos. En una sartén con aceite, freír el jamón y el sofrito. Agregar la salsa de tomate, la sazón, las aceitunas y el alcaparrado. Revolver durante 2 minutos. Agregar las habichuelas, las papas, el agua y revolver. Calentar bien la mezcla, tapar la sartén, reducir la temperatura y cocinar durante 20 minutos.

[1] habichuelas: *beans in the Caribbean*
[2] sazón: *seasoning*
[3] sofrito: *mix of lightly fried onions, garlic, and herbs*
[4] alcaparrado: *capers with diced red peppers*

227

People EN ESPAÑOL

**A Una identidad indígena**
¿Verdadero o falso?

1. Los taínos tenían la cultura más avanzada de las Antillas Mayores.
2. El pirata Roberto Cofresí estaba de acuerdo con el sistema de gobierno español.
3. Arturo Schomburg era de Nueva York, pero le encantaba Puerto Rico.

**B ¿Restaurante o monumento histórico?**
Escojan.

1. "La Bodeguita del Medio" está abierta ___.
   a. en verano
   b. los fines de semana
   c. todo el año
2. Este restaurante era una gran atracción para ___.
   a. los niños del lugar
   b. los artistas
   c. los piratas
3. También hoy día es ___.
   a. muy popular
   b. una escuela
   c. un parque

**C Calendario de fiestas**
Contesten.

1. ¿Adónde conmemoran los cubanos a los trabajadores del mundo?
2. ¿Qué celebran los dominicanos el 27 de febrero?
3. ¿Cómo celebran en Loíza, Puerto Rico, la fiesta de Santiago Apóstol?

**LEVELING**

**E:** Activity A
**A:** Activity B
**C:** Activity C

**ANSWERS TO**

**A**

1. verdadero
2. falso
3. falso

**B**

1. c
2. b
3. a

**C**

1. Los conmemoran en la Plaza de la Revolución en La Habana.
2. Ellos celebran la independencia del gobierno de Haití.
3. Se visten con ropa tradicional, usan máscaras, disfraces, bailan y cantan en las calles.

People en español

As African descendants, Caribbeans have maintained close ties with African musical traditions and some of the finest musicians in the world come from that region. Their music has also been influenced by the United States. Caribbean musicians often adopt a musical style, such as jazz, and then masterfully enrich it with their own harvest of rhythms and instrumentation. Lately, the hottest export from Cuba has been *Orishas*, a group of Cuban rappers. Their music is a soulful combination of African-American rap and Afro-Cuban percussion. Their songs' lyrics have pushed social-criticism to a new level.

**A La Habana—capital caribeña del rap**

Corrijan.

1. En el festival de rap en La Habana sólo participan grupos cubanos.
2. El rap es un estilo musical típico de Cuba.
3. Instinto es un grupo de raperas que viven en Francia.
4. Ocho cubanos forman el grupo "Orishas".
5. "Orishas" ganó el Oscar en 2003.

**B En el set**

¿Quién es?

1. Cuando filmó su primera película todo cambió para ___.
2. Es famoso por su rol en El Padrino.
3. ___ no es cubano. Él no es feliz cuando no tiene libros ni comida.
4. Estudió actuación en California y en Nueva York. Recibió un Oscar en 2001.
5. Esta cubana emplea la "diáspora" africana y cubana como tema de sus películas.
6. Ella es puertorriqueña, pero ha tenido roles en inglés en telenovelas. Ahora es cantante.

People en español **¡Acción!**

El Grammy para *Orishas*

## La Habana, capital caribeña del Rap

¿Rap en Cuba? ¡Así es! Desde 1995 se celebra en el Anfiteatro Alamar de La Habana un festival de Rap. Ahí participan muchos grupos internacionales. El rap, un estilo musical típico de Nueva York, es popular en Cuba. "Instinto" es el primer grupo de mujeres cubanas "raperas". Pero los más famosos son cuatro cubanos del grupo "Orishas". Ellos viven en Francia y en 2003 recibieron el Grammy por sus composiciones, donde combinan el hip-hop y los ritmos cubanos "para escuchar el 'sonido' de la isla en su música".

## En la tele y la radio

**Charytín Goyco y el "escándalo[1] del mediodía"**

Goyco

**Charytín** es la presentadora[2] de un programa muy popular: "El escándalo del mediodía". Ella es una persona muy divertida y además tiene otros talentos: es bailarina y cantante. Nació en la República Dominicana y vivió mucho tiempo en Puerto Rico, donde también es famosa. Charytín y su familia viven en Miami desde 1989.

[1] escándalo: *scandal, shock*
[2] presentadora: *host of a TV show*

228

## En el set

del Toro

**Benicio del Toro** es puertorriqueño y a los 13 años llegó a Estados Unidos; estudió actuación[2] en California y después en *The Stella Adler Conservatory of Acting* en Nueva York. Le gustan los deportes, le gusta leer y también le encanta comer. Pero lo que más le gusta es actuar y en 2001 recibió un Óscar por su rol en *Traffic*. Él va a Puerto Rico cuando puede y si tiene tiempo, participa en campañas de ayuda social.

Rolando

**Gloria Rolando** es una cineasta[1] cubana de origen africano. Trabajar en el cine no es fácil en Cuba. "Muchas veces empiezo un proyecto sin dinero para completarlo. Pero siempre termino mis películas," dice Gloria. El tema de sus películas es la "diáspora" de los africanos y de los cubanos. Gloria escribió y trabajó como directora en el documental *Los ojos del arco iris*.

Sánchez

**Roselyn Sánchez** es bailarina, actriz, productora y ahora ¡cantante! "Para mí cantar era un sueño[3]", dice Sánchez. "Borinqueña", su primer CD, es una combinación de ritmos caribeños tradicionales, gospel y elementos del hip-hop y rap. Ella nació en Puerto Rico y sus primeros roles en inglés fueron en la telenovela[4] *As the World Turns* y en la serie de televisión *Fame L.A.* "*Rush Hour II*, mi primera película me cambió la vida", dice ella con una gran sonrisa.

García

**Andy García** nació en Cuba, pero vivió en Miami desde los 5 años. Estudió y trabajó como actor en Florida y después en Los Angeles, donde hizo varias series de televisión. Andy es famoso por su rol en Los Intocables, El Padrino, Parte III y muchas otras. Le encanta la música de su país y por eso hizo "Cachao… como su ritmo no hay dos", un film documental[5] sobre el músico cubano Israel "Cachao" López. Andy recibió excelentes críticas por la dirección de este film.

[1] cineasta: *filmmaker*
[2] actuación: *acting (theater)*
[3] sueño: *dream*
[4] telenovela: *soap opera*
[5] documental: *documentary*

### Answers to

**A**

1. En el festival de rap en La Habana participan grupos internacionales.
2. El rap es un estilo musical típico de Nueva York.
3. Instinto es un grupo de raperas que viven en Cuba.
4. Cuatro cubanos forman el grupo "Orishas".
5. "Orishas" ganó el Grammy en 2003.

**B**

1. Roselyn Sánchez
2. Andy García
3. Benicio del Toro
4. Benicio del Toro
5. Gloria Rolando
6. Roselyn Sánchez

República Dominicana

## Una isla, un regalo

En su 2º viaje, Cristóbal Colón regaló una isla a un marinero savonés[1] porque éste la vio por primera vez. El nombre original fue Isla Savona pero con el tiempo los dominicanos cambiaron su nombre por **Isla Saona**. Ahora es un Parque Nacional muy atractivo para los turistas por sus playas solitarias, sus aguas cristalinas y por las 13 horas de sol al día. Aquí vive poca gente, pero hay 112 especies de aves[2], muchos otros animales y una vegetación exuberante. Por su clima, su belleza y su paz[3], Isla Saona también hoy es un regalo para todos.

[1] marinero savonés: *seaman from Savona, an Italian city*
[2] paz: *peace*
[3] aves: *birds*

# SUCESOS

■ **El béisbol, un fenómeno caribeño** El lucrativo deporte del bate y la pelota obtiene del Caribe sus más brillantes estrellas[1]. El béisbol es una antigua tradición en las Antillas Mayores. Hoy muchos peloteros[2] caribeños juegan en las Grandes Ligas de béisbol. Ahora en el béisbol (deporte que antes era fundamentalmente anglosajón), los nombres de Roberto Clemente, Juan Marichal, Bernie Williams y Pedro Martínez forman parte de su historia.

[1] estrellas: *stars*
[2] peloteros: *baseball players*

Bernie Williams

■ **El museo de Ernest Hemingway en La Habana** "Finca La Vigía", al este de La Habana, fue la casa de este famoso escritor. Él vivió 20 años en Cuba (1940–1960). A su casa iba mucha gente famosa y ahí él escribió *El viejo y el mar*. Durante mucho tiempo no era posible visitarla, pero en el 2002 las autoridades cubanas la declararon un museo.

Finca La Vigía

# música

Tito Puente

## El jazz latino

Fernando Trueba, un director de cine español, realizó el film "Calle 54" en el 2000. La importante presencia de los músicos caribeños en el Jazz Latino es el tema de este documental "musical". El director muestra a músicos como el percusionista puertorriqueño Tito Puente y a los virtuosos del piano: el dominicano Michele Camilo y el cubano Chucho Valdés. Este film está en muchas tiendas donde alquilan[1] videocintas.

[1] alquilan: *they rent*

Chucho Valdés



People en español

**A La Habana—capital caribeña del rap**

Corrijan.

1. En el festival de rap en La Habana sólo participan grupos cubanos.
2. El rap es un estilo musical típico de Cuba.
3. Instinto es un grupo de raperas que viven en Francia.

**B En el set**

¿Quién es?

1. Cuando filmó su primera película todo cambió para ___.
2. Es famoso por su rol en El Padrino.
3. ___ no es cubano. Él no es feliz cuando no tiene libros ni comida.

**C El museo de Ernest Hemingway en La Habana**

Contesten.

1. Él vivió un tercio de su vida en Cuba. ¿Cuántos años tenía cuando murió?
2. ¿Quién visitaba al escritor en su casa en Cuba?
3. ¿En qué año abrieron "Finca La Vigía" al público?

**LEVELING**

**E:** Activity A
**A:** Activity B
**C:** Activity C

## Answers to

**A**

1. En el festival de rap en La Habana participan grupos internacionales.
2. El rap es un estilo musical típico de Nueva York.
3. Instinto es un grupo de raperas que viven en Cuba.

**B**

1. Roselyn Sánchez
2. Andy García
3. Benicio del Toro

**C**

1. Él tenía 60 años.
2. Mucha gente famosa visitaba al escritor.
3. En el año 2002 abrieron su casa al público.

# Planning for Chapter 8

## SCOPE AND SEQUENCE, PAGES 230–259

### Topics

- Minor accidents
- Parts of the body
- Emergency hospital care

### Culture

- Medical practitioners in remote areas of the Spanish-speaking world
- Buena Vista Hospital
- Contemporary medical problems
- Medical terms in Spanish

### Functions

- How to talk about minor accidents and medical procedures
- How to refer to parts of the body
- How to talk about emergency medical care
- How to talk about recent events
- How to compare people and things

### Structure

- The present perfect
- Irregular participles
- Making comparisons of equal value

### National Standards

- Communication Standard 1.1 pages 234, 235, 238, 239, 241, 242, 243, 244, 245, 247, 254
- Communication Standard 1.2 pages 235, 239, 242, 243, 245, 246, 247, 248–249, 250, 251, 252–253, 254
- Communication Standard 1.3 pages 235, 254, 255
- Cultures Standard 2.1 pages 248–249, 251
- Cultures Standard 2.2 page 250
- Connections Standard 3.1 pages 252–253
- Comparisons Standard 4.2 pages 248–249, 251
- Communities Standard 5.1 page 259
- Communities Standard 5.2 page 239

## PACING AND PRIORITIES

**The chapter content is color coded below to assist you in planning.**

**■ required ■ recommended ■ optional**

**Vocabulario** *(required)* *Days 1–4*

- ■ Palabras 1
  - Más partes del cuerpo
  - Un accidente
  - Una picadura
  - La cara
  - ¡A la sala de emergencia!
- ■ Palabras 2
  - En el hospital

**Estructura** *(required)* *Days 5–7*

- ■ El presente perfecto
- ■ Los participios irregulares
- ■ Comparación de igualdad

**Conversación** *(required)*

- ■ Una fractura

**Lecturas culturales**

- ■ Practicantes *(recommended)*
- ■ El Hospital Buena Vista *(optional)*
- ■ Problemas médicos de hoy *(optional)*

**Conexiones**

- ■ La medicina *(optional)*

■ **¡Te toca a ti!** *(recommended)*

■ **Assessment** *(recommended)*

■ **¡Hablo como un pro!** *(optional)*

## RESOURCE GUIDE

| Section | Pages | Section Resources |
|---|---|---|
| **Vocabulario PALABRAS 1** | | |
| Más partes del cuerpo<br>Un accidente<br>Una picadura<br>La cara<br>¡A la sala de emergencia! | 232, 234–235<br>232, 234–235<br>233, 234–235<br>233, 234–235<br>233, 234–235 | Vocabulary Transparencies 8.2–8.3<br>Audio CD 5<br>Audio Activities TE, pages 89–91<br>Workbook, pages 89–90<br>Quiz 1, page 35<br>ExamView® Pro |
| **Vocabulario PALABRAS 2** | | |
| En el hospital | 236–239 | Vocabulary Transparencies 8.4–8.5<br>Audio CD 5<br>Audio Activities TE, pages 92–93<br>Workbook, pages 90–91<br>Quiz 2, page 36<br>ExamView® Pro |
| **Estructura** | | |
| El presente perfecto<br>Los participios irregulares<br>Comparación de igualdad | 240–242<br>242–243<br>244–245 | Audio CD 5<br>Audio Activities TE, pages 94–96<br>Workbook, pages 91–93<br>Quizzes 3–5, pages 37–39<br>ExamView® Pro |
| **Conversación** | | |
| Una fractura | 246–247 | Audio CD 5<br>Audio Activities TE, pages 96–97<br>Interactive CD-ROM |
| **Lecturas culturales** | | |
| Practicantes<br>El Hospital Buena Vista<br>Problemas médicos de hoy | 248–249<br>250<br>251 | Audio CD 5<br>Audio Activities TE, page 97<br>Tests, pages 124, 127 |
| **Conexiones** | | |
| La medicina | 252–253 | Tests, page 129 |
| **¡Te toca a ti!** | | |
| | 254–255 | **¡Viva el mundo hispano!** Video, Episode 8<br>Video Activities, pages 92–96<br>Spanish Online Activities spanish.glencoe.com |
| **Assessment** | | |
| | 256–257 | Communication Transparency C 8<br>Quizzes 1–5, pages 35–39<br>Performance Assessment, Task 8<br>Tests, pages 121–134<br>Situation Cards, Chapter 8<br>ExamView® Pro<br>**Maratón mental** Videoquiz |

# Using Your Resources for Chapter 8

## Transparencies

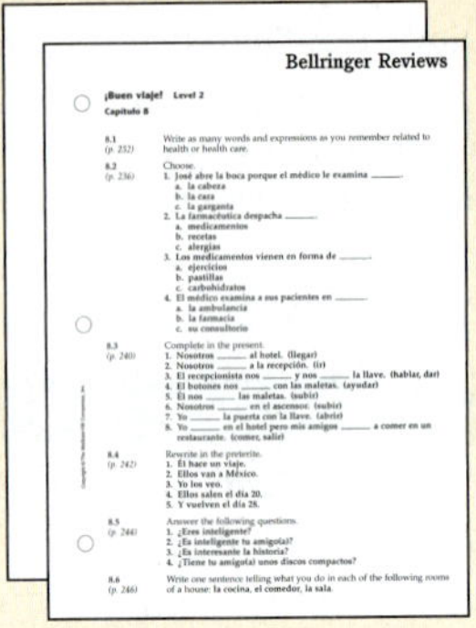

Bellringer 8.1–8.6

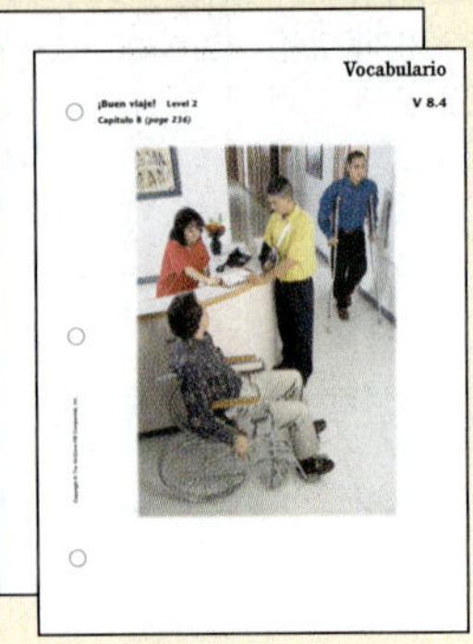

Vocabulary 8.1–8.5

Communication C 8

## Workbook

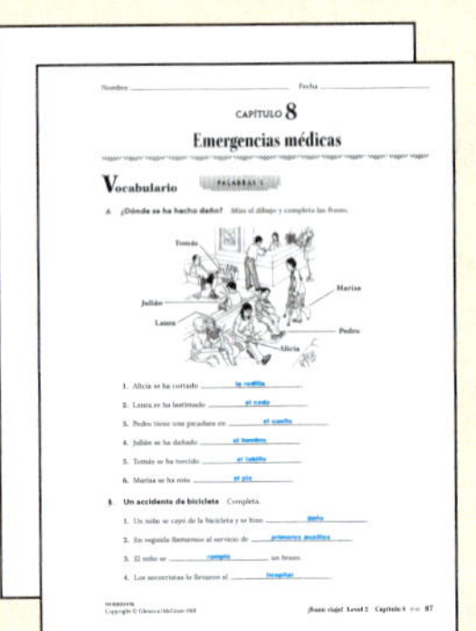

Vocabulary, pages 89–91

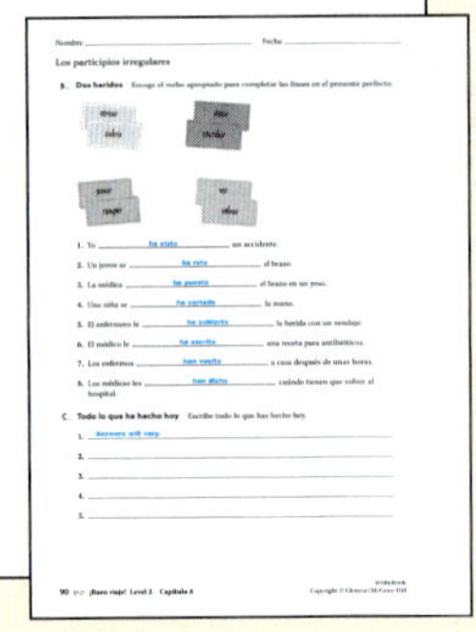

Structure, pages 91–93

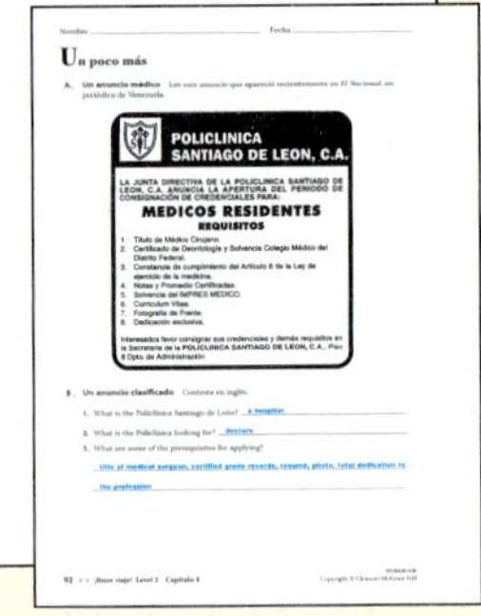

Enrichment, pages 94–96

## Audio Activities

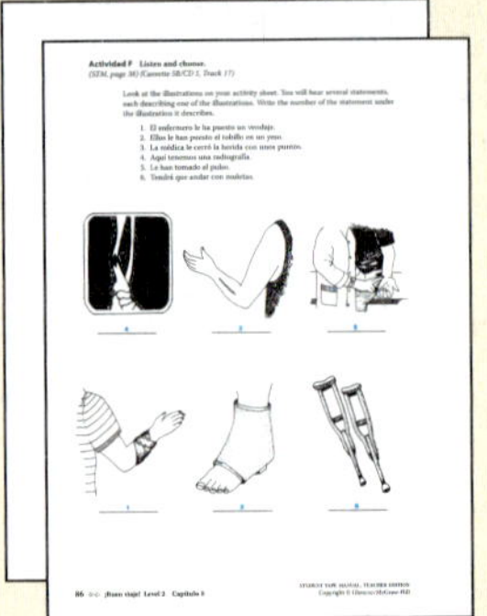

Vocabulary, pages 89–93

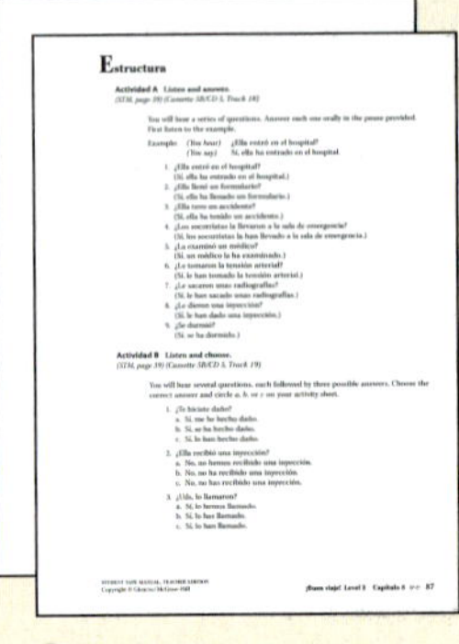

Structure, pages 94–96

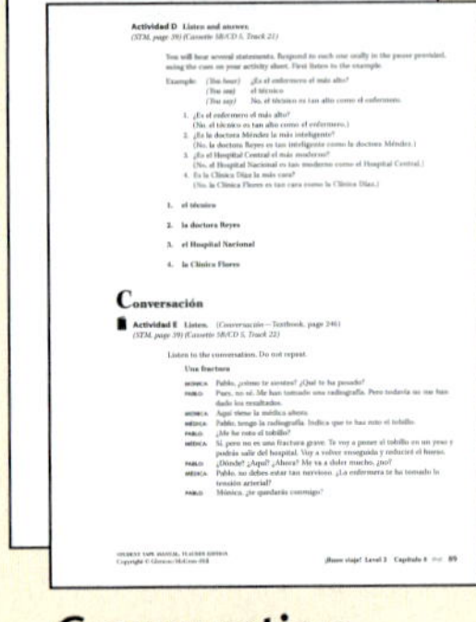

Conversation, pages 96–98

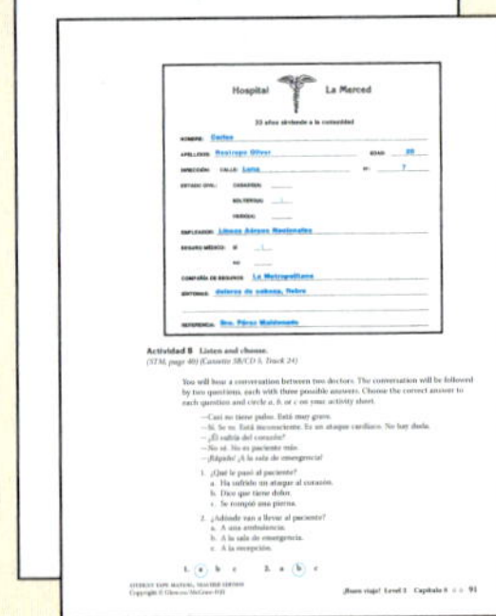

Additional Practice, pages 98–103

## Assessment

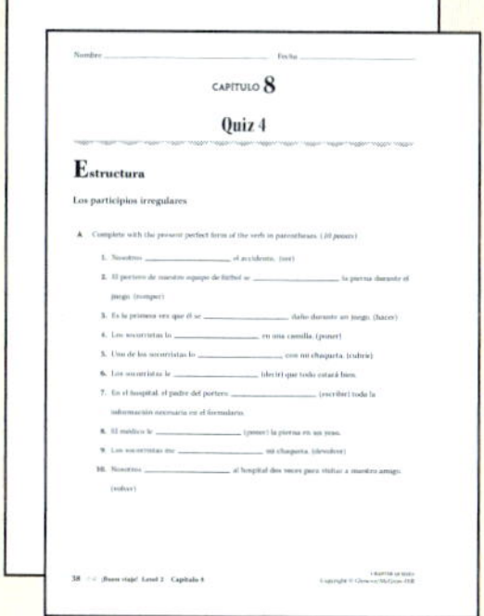
Vocabulary and Structure Quizzes, pages 35–39

Chapter Tests, pages 121–134

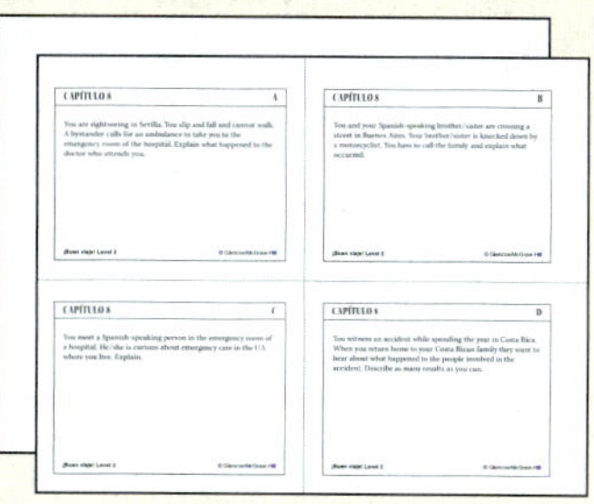
Situation Cards, Chapter 8

MindJogger Videoquiz, ExamView® Pro, Chapter 8

## Timesaving Teacher Tools

### TeacherWorks™

TeacherWorks™ is your all-in-one teacher resource center. Personalize lesson plans, access resources from the Teacher Wraparound Edition, connect to the Internet, or make a to-do list. These are only a few of the many features that can assist you in the planning and organizing of your lessons.

Includes:

- A calendar feature
- Access to all program blackline masters
- Standards correlations and more

### ExamView® Pro

Test Bank software for Macintosh and Windows makes creating, editing, customizing, and printing tests quick and easy.

## Technology Resources

In the Chapter 8 Internet Activity, you will have a chance to learn more about the Spanish-speaking world. Visit spanish.glencoe.com

On the interactive CD–ROM, students can listen to and take part in a recorded version of the conversation in Chapter 8.

**¡Viva el mundo hispano!** Video and Video Activities, Chapter 8. Available on VHS and DVD.

Help your students prepare for the chapter test by playing the **Maratón mental** Videoquiz game show. Teams will compete against each other to review chapter vocabulary and structure and sharpen listening comprehension skills. Available on VHS and DVD.

**¡Buen viaje!** is also available on CD or Online.

Capítulo 8

## Preview

In this chapter, students will learn to describe certain accidents and minor injuries and to talk about emergency hospital treatment. Students will learn how to speak about recent events in the past using the present perfect tense. They will also learn how to make comparisons of equality between people and things. The cultural focus of the chapter is on health practitioners and services in the Spanish-speaking world.

### National Standards

**Communication**

In Chapter 8 students will learn to communicate in spoken and written Spanish on the following topics:

- accidents and injuries
- emergency room treatment
- health issues in Spanish-speaking countries

Students will obtain and provide information about these topics and engage in conversations that would typically take place at the scene of an accident or in a hospital emergency room as they fulfill the chapter objectives listed on this page.

Capítulo 8

# Emergencias médicas

**Objetivos**

**In this chapter you will learn to:**

- talk about accidents and medical problems
- talk about hospital stays
- discuss things that you and others have done recently
- compare things with like characteristics
- talk about health care in various areas of the Spanish-speaking world

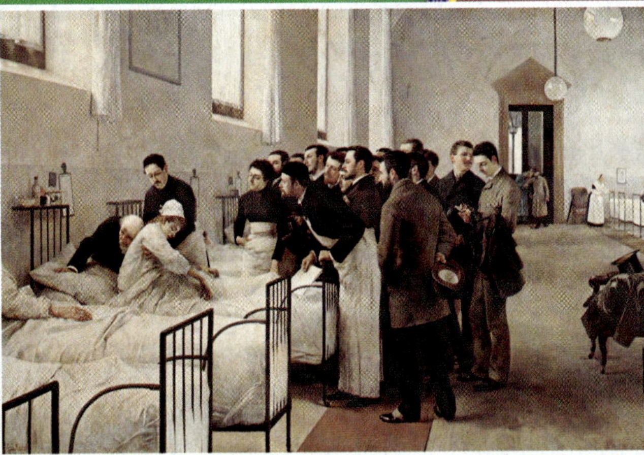

Manuel Jiménez Prieto *Hospital Visit*

230 doscientos treinta

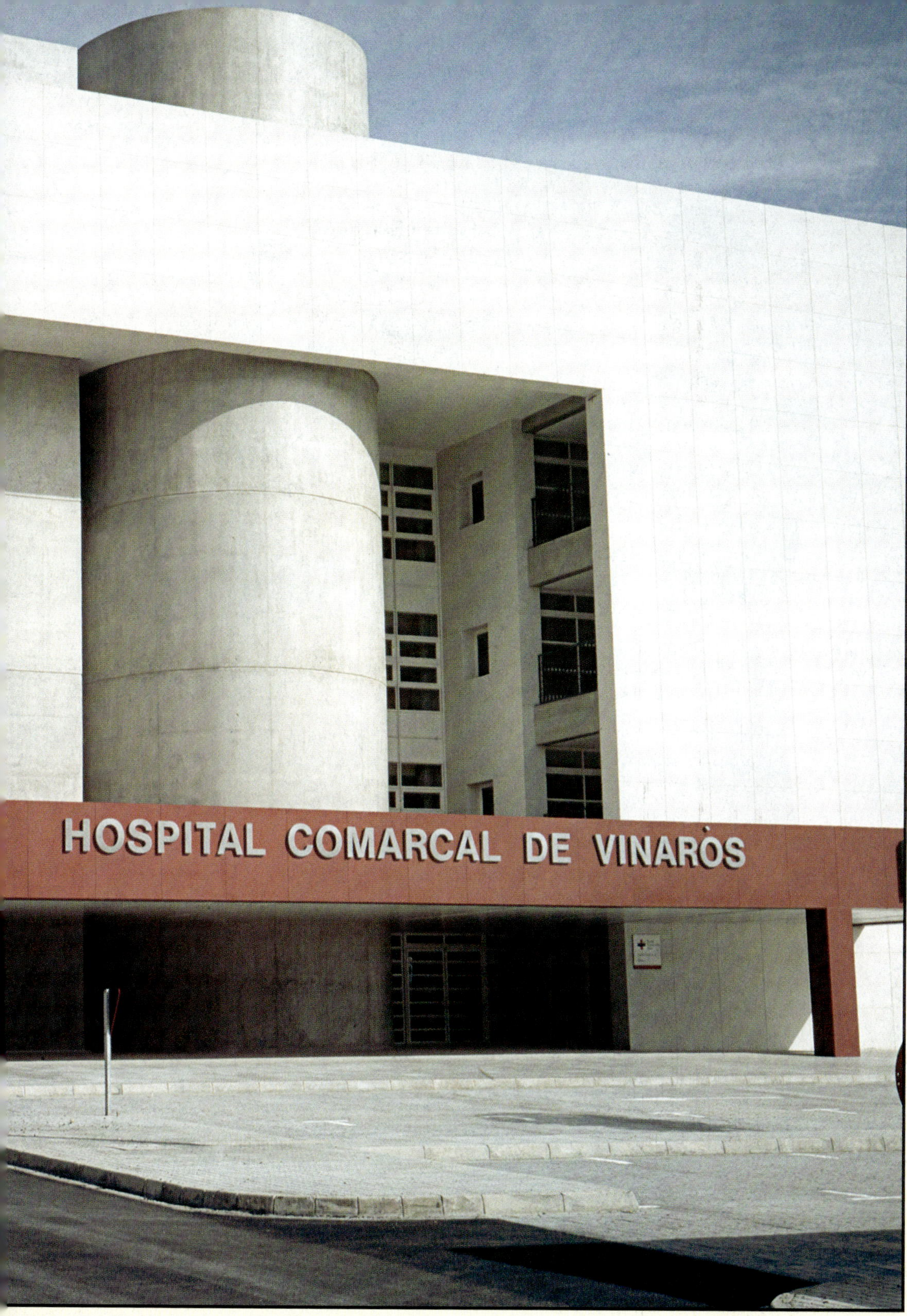

**Fotografía** Hospital Comarcal serves as the primary medical treatment facility for the small, coastal town of Vinaroz, located in the Valencia region of Spain.

## LEVELING

The activities, conversations, and readings within each chapter are marked according to level of difficulty. **E** indicates easy. **A** indicates average. **C** indicates challenging. Some activities cover a range of difficulty. In some activities, for example, advanced students will be able to produce more extensive responses while students who learn at a different rate may give less detailed responses. The leveling indicators will help you individualize instruction to best meet your students' needs.

# Vocabulario

PALABRAS 1

## 1 PREPARATION

### Resource Manager

Vocabulary Transparencies 8.2–8.3
Audio Activities TE, pages 89–91
Audio CD 5
Workbook, pages 89–90
Quizzes, page 35
ExamView® Pro

### Bellringer Review

*Use BRR Transparency 8.1 or write the following on the board.*
Write as many words and expressions as you remember related to health or health care.

## 2 PRESENTATION

**Step 1** In addition to using Vocabulary Transparencies 8.2–8.3 in your presentation, you may use gestures or dramatization to introduce many of these terms. Those which lend themselves to easy dramatizations are: **caerse, hacerse daño (lastimarse), torcerse el tobillo,** and **cortarse el dedo.**

**Step 2** Refer to yourself or a student model to demonstrate the parts of the body.

**Step 3** Have students repeat the vocabulary after you or the recording on Audio CD 5.

**Step 4** Call on volunteers to read the sentences from **Palabras 1** with as much expression as possible.

# Vocabulario

PALABRAS 1

## Más partes del cuerpo

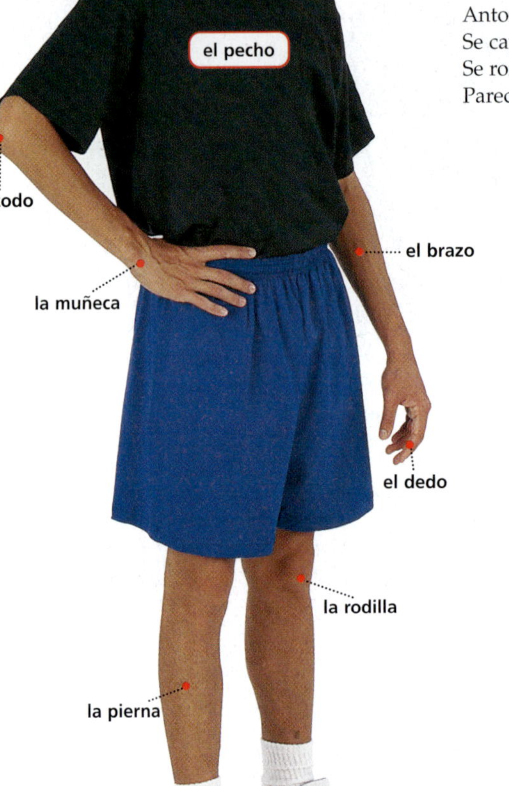


## Un accidente

Antonio ha tenido un accidente.
Se cayó de su bicicleta y se hizo daño (se lastimó).
Se rompió el dedo.
Parece que no se ha roto la pierna.

Anita se ha torcido el tobillo.
Tiene el tobillo muy hinchado.
Pero no tiene fractura.

Tomás tiene una herida.
Se ha cortado el dedo.



### Reaching All Students

**Total Physical Response**

*(Student 1),* **levántate.**
**Ven acá, por favor.**
**Muéstrame el brazo.**
**Muéstrame el dedo.**
**Muéstrame el hombro.**
**Muéstrame el tobillo.**
**Muéstrame la rodilla.**
**Muéstrame la muñeca.**
**Gracias,** *(Student 1).* **Siéntate.**
*(Student 2),* **levántate.**
**Ven acá, por favor.**
**Ve al teléfono.**
**Descuelga.**
**Marca el número.**
**Habla. Di lo que pasó.**
**Gracias,** *(Student 2).* **Siéntate.**

## Una picadura

Una abeja le ha picado a Tere.
Le ha picado en el hombro.
Ella no se siente bien. Le duele mucho.

## La cara

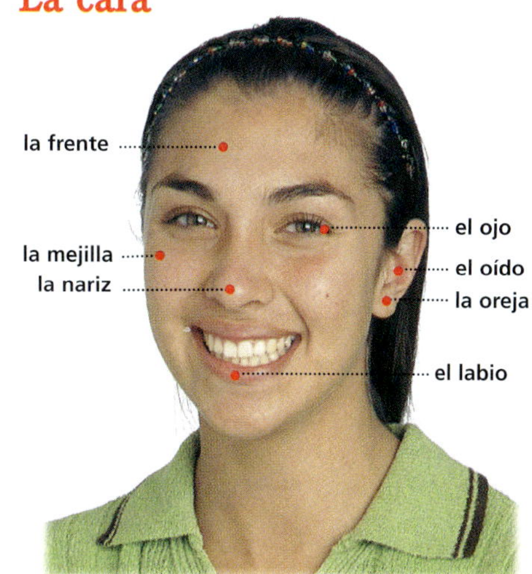


## ¡A la sala de emergencia!

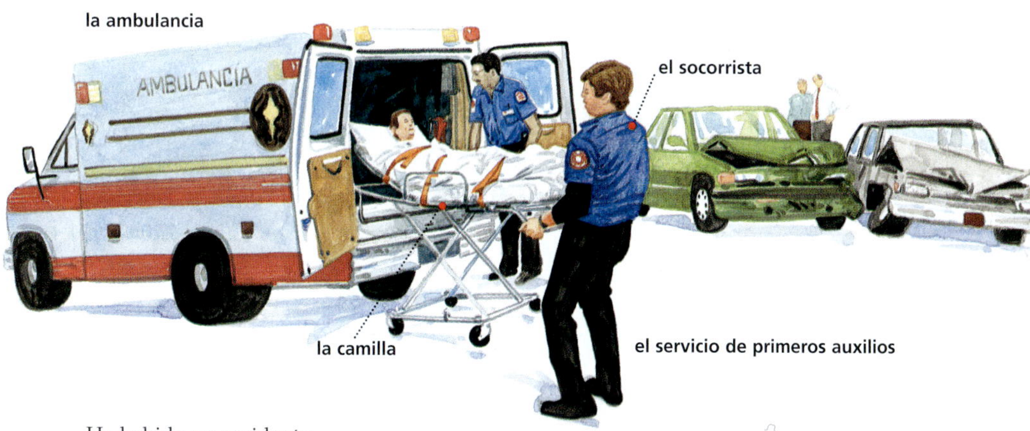


Ha habido un accidente.
El accidente acaba de tener lugar.
Ha llegado el servicio de primeros auxilios.
Los socorristas han ayudado a la víctima.
La van a llevar al hospital en una ambulancia.

## Vocabulario

**Step 5** Have students look at Vocabulary Transparencies 8.2–8.3 again and ask them questions to elicit the new vocabulary. For example:
**¿Es la pierna o el brazo?**
**¿Qué ha tenido Antonio?**
**¿Se cayó él?**
**¿De qué se cayó?**
**¿Se hizo daño o no?**
**¿Se ha roto la pierna?**
**¿Qué se rompió?**

### Teaching Tip

When introducing **El accidente acaba de tener lugar,** repeat **acaba de tener lugar—acaba de—no en el pasado—sólo hace dos minutos.**

### Assessment

As an informal assessment, you may wish to call on volunteers to draw human figures on the board. Ask other students to supply labels of as many parts of the body as they can.

### About the Spanish Language

- You may wish to remind students of the difference between **oreja** and **oído. La oreja** refers to the *external ear* only, and **el oído** refers to the *inner ear* and also means *hearing* in general. An *earache* is **un dolor de oídos.**
- The **camilla** *(gurney)* shown in the illustration is **una camilla de ruedas.** A **camilla** is a *stretcher.*

### Chapter Projects

**Un accidente** Have students select one of the accidents or injuries that they will learn about in this chapter and have them write a paragraph about it.

**LEVELING**
**E:** Vocabulary

Vocabulario

## 3 PRACTICE

## ¿Qué palabra necesito?

**¡OJO!** When students are doing the **¿Qué palabra necesito?** activities, accept any answer that makes sense. The purpose of these activities is to have students use the new vocabulary. They are not factual recall activities. Thus, it is not necessary for students to remember specific factual information from the vocabulary presentation when answering. If you wish, have students use the photos on this page as a stimulus, when possible.

**Historieta** Each time **Historieta** appears, it means that the answers to the activity form a short story. Encourage students to look at the title of the **Historieta,** since it can help them do the activity.

**Teaching Tip**
It is recommended that you go over the activities before assigning them for homework.

**2** This activity can be done orally with books open.
**Expansion:** Have a student retell the story from Activity 2 in his or her own words.



Vocabulario

## ¿Qué palabra necesito?

**1** **Unas heridas** Contesten según los dibujos.

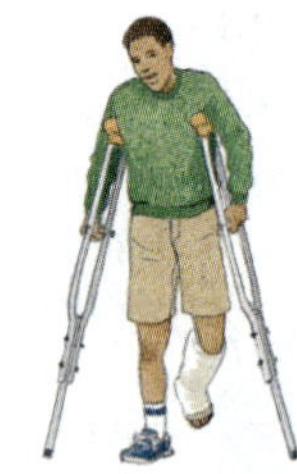

1. ¿Qué se ha roto Carlos?

2. ¿Qué se ha torcido Pablo?

3. ¿Qué se ha cortado Elena?

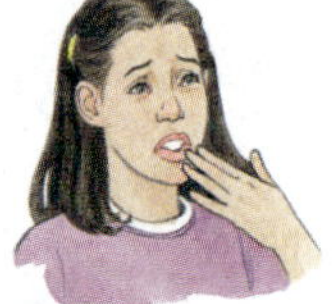

4. ¿Qué se ha cortado Diana?

**2** **Historieta Un accidente**
Contesten con **sí**.

1. ¿Ha habido un accidente?
2. ¿Acaba de tener lugar el accidente?
3. ¿Se ha caído de su bicicleta un niño?
4. ¿Se ha lastimado?
5. ¿Parece que se ha roto la pierna?
6. ¿Ha llegado el servicio de primeros auxilios?
7. ¿Han ayudado los socorristas al niño?
8. ¿Lo van a llevar al hospital en la ambulancia?
9. ¿Lo ponen en una camilla?

Madrid, España



### ANSWERS TO ¿Qué palabra necesito?

**1**

1. Carlos se ha roto la pierna.
2. Pablo se ha torcido el tobillo.
3. Elena se ha cortado el dedo.
4. Diana se ha cortado el labio.

**2**

1. Sí, ha habido un accidente.
2. Sí, el accidente acaba de tener lugar.
3. Sí, un niño se ha caído de su bicicleta.
4. Sí, se ha lastimado.
5. Sí, parece que se ha roto la pierna.
6. Sí, el servicio de primeros auxilios ha llegado.
7. Sí, los socorristas han ayudado al niño.
8. Sí, lo van a llevar al hospital en la ambulancia.
9. Sí, lo ponen en una camilla.

**3** **Historieta** **Una picadura** Contesten.

1. ¿Tiene Anita una picadura?
2. ¿Qué le ha picado?
3. ¿Dónde le ha picado?
4. ¿Le duele mucho la picadura?
5. ¿Tiene Anita alergia a las picaduras?

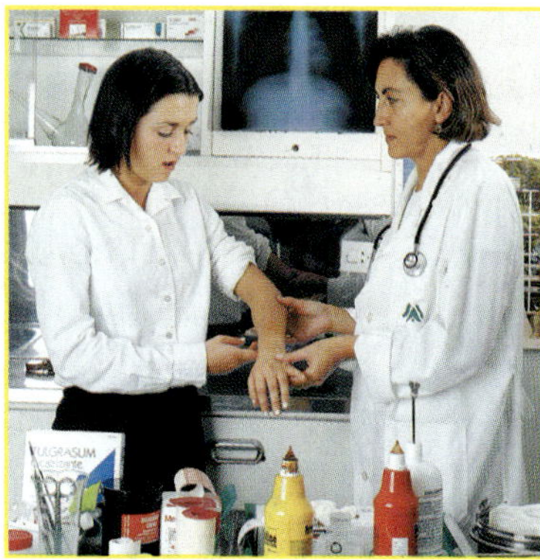

Granada, España

**4** **Partes del cuerpo** Completen.

1. La niña se ha torcido el ____; así no puede andar bien.
2. ____, ____ y ____ son partes del brazo.
3. ____, ____ y ____ son partes de la pierna.
4. Tenemos cinco ____ en cada mano.
5. Vemos con los ____.
6. Y oímos con los ____.

Asturias, España

**5** **Un accidente en el extranjero**

Tú y un(a) amigo(a) están viajando por España. Van en bicicleta. Tu amigo se ha caído de la bicicleta y tú crees que se ha roto el brazo. Llega un(a) socorrista (un compañero[a]). Explícale lo que ha pasado y contesta a todas sus preguntas.

**6** **Juego** Trabaja con un(a) compañero(a) de clase. Dibujen un monstruo. Luego describan su monstruo a otros miembros de la clase.

**LEVELING**

**E:** Activities 1, 2, 3, 4, 6

**A:** Activity 5

**2** and **3** These activities have students use the third person forms of the present perfect. They will learn the other forms to express themselves in the present perfect in the **Estructura** section of this chapter.

**4** Have students prepare this activity before going over it in class.

**¡OJO!** Note that the activities are color-coded. All the activities in the text are communicative. However, the ones with blue titles are guided communication. The red titles indicate that the answers to the activity are more open-ended and can vary more. You may wish to correct students' mistakes more so in the guided activities than in the activities with a red title, which lend themselves to a freer response.

## Learning from Photos

*(page 235 top)* Ask students to describe what is happening in the photo. You might ask them:

**¿Quiénes son las personas en la foto?**
**¿Dónde están ellas?**
**¿Cuál será el problema?**

*(page 235 middle)* Have students say as much as they can about the photo.

## Answers to ¿Qué palabra necesito?

**3**

1. Sí, Anita tiene una picadura.
2. Una abeja le ha picado.
3. Le ha picado en el brazo (el hombro, etc.).
4. Sí, (No, no) le duele mucho la picadura.
5. Sí (No), Anita (no) tiene alergia a las picaduras.

**4**

1. tobillo
2. La muñeca, el codo, el hombro
3. El tobillo, la rodilla, el pie
4. dedos
5. ojos
6. oídos

**5** *Answers will vary, but students will use the vocabulary from* Palabras 1.

**6** *Answers will vary depending on each student's drawing.*

## Writing Development

Have students write the information in Activity 2 as if it were a newspaper article.

# Vocabulario

PALABRAS 2

## 1 PREPARATION

### Resource Manager

Vocabulary Transparencies 8.4–8.5
Audio Activities TE, pages 92–93
Audio CD 5
Workbook, pages 90–91
Quizzes, page 36
ExamView® Pro

### Bellringer Review

*Use BRR Transparency 8.2 or write the following on the board.*
Choose.

1. **José abre la boca porque el médico le examina ___.**
   a. la cabeza
   b. la cara
   c. la garganta
2. **La farmacéutica despacha ___.**
   a. medicamentos
   b. recetas
   c. alergias
3. **Los medicamentos vienen en forma de ___**
   a. ejercicios
   b. pastillas
   c. carbohidratos
4. **El médico examina a sus pacientes en ___.**
   a. la ambulancia
   b. la farmacia
   c. su consultorio

## 2 PRESENTATION

**Step 1** To present the vocabulary, you may wish to follow some suggestions presented in previous chapters, using Vocabulary Transparencies 8.4–8.5 and Audio CD 5.

# Vocabulario

PALABRAS 2

## En el hospital

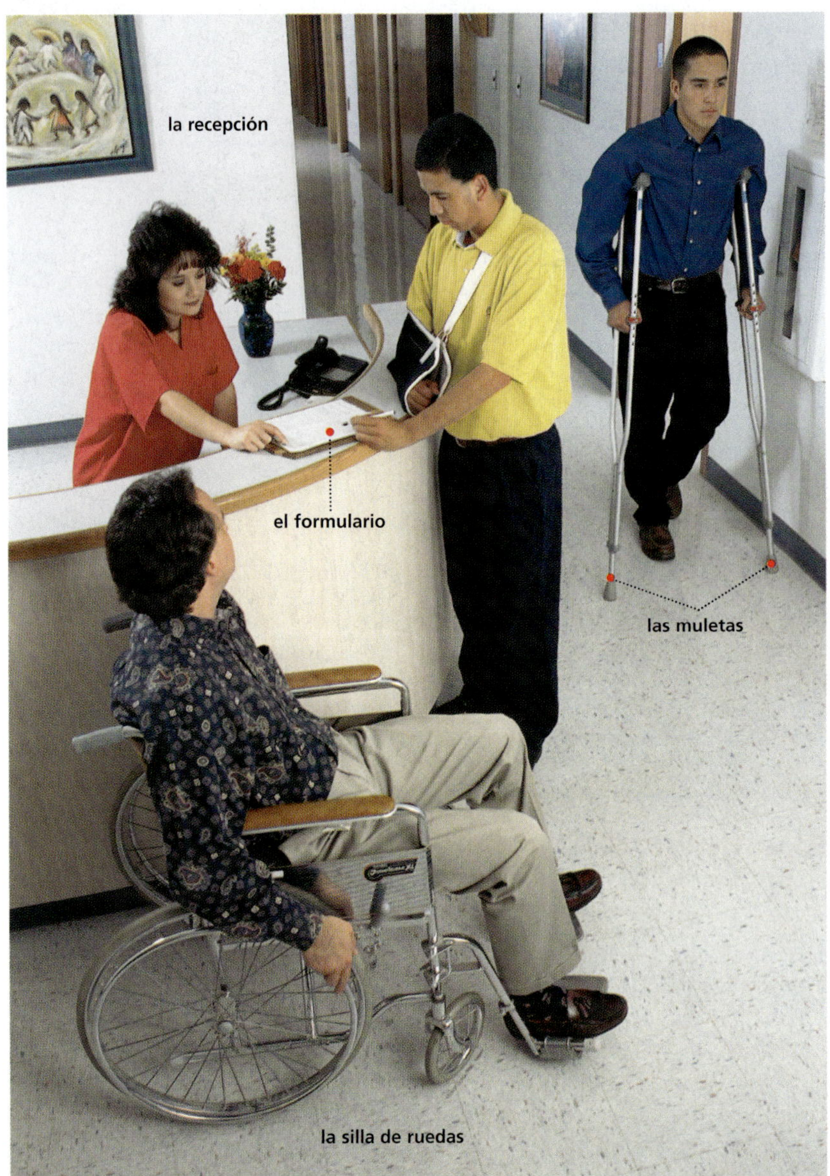


José ha llenado un formulario.
Lo ha llenado en la recepción.



### Chapter Projects

**La ciencia y la medicina** In **¡Buen viaje! Level 1**, students read about the contributions of Hispanics to the world of medicine. Have those students interested in science and medicine do a report on one of the following people: Miguel Servet, Carlos Juan Finlay y Barres, or Santiago Ramón y Cajal.

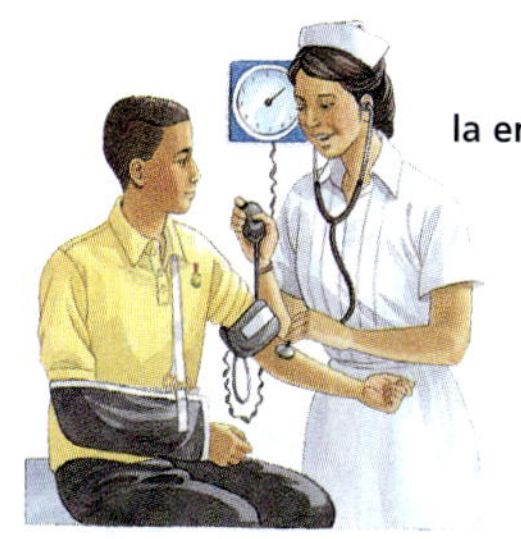


La enfermera le ha tomado la tensión (presión) arterial.

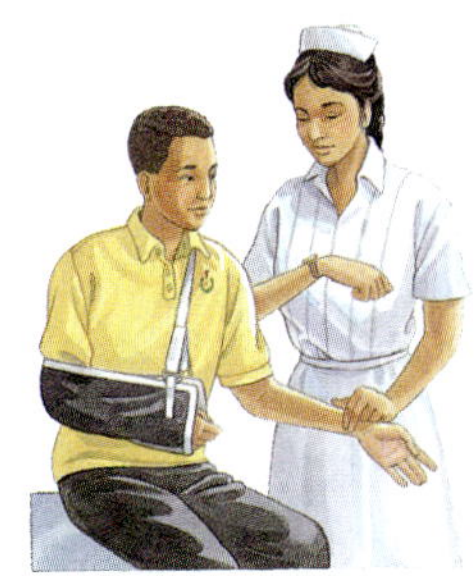

Le ha tomado el pulso también.

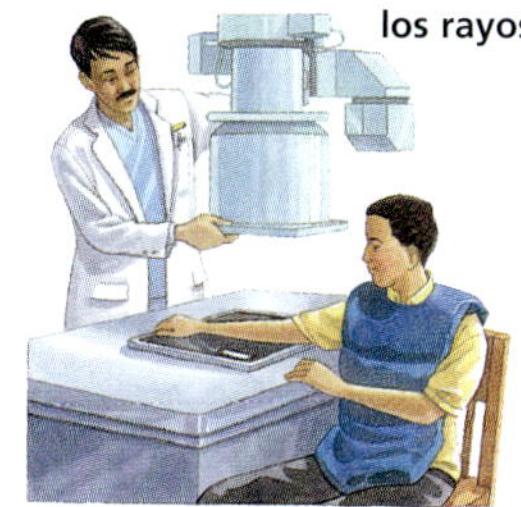


El técnico le ha tomado una radiografía.
El joven tiene una fractura.

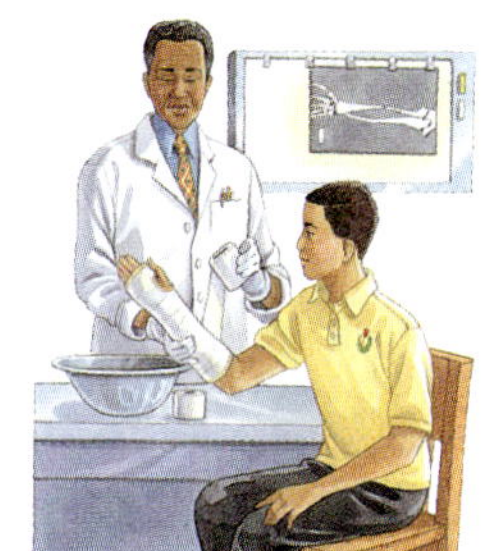

El cirujano ortopédico le ha reducido el hueso.
Ha puesto el brazo en un yeso.

un vendaje

Paco tiene una herida.
La médica le ha cerrado la herida.
La ha cerrado con unos puntos.
Y le ha puesto un vendaje.

Los dos jóvenes están enfermos.
El uno está tan enfermo como el otro.
José tiene tantos dolores como Paco.



## Vocabulario

### About the Spanish Language

The word **muleta** is also used to refer to the red cloth used by a **matador** during a bullfight.

**Step 2** You may wish to have students repeat some of the expressions in isolation before having them repeat the entire sentence. For example: **La enfermera / la tensión arterial / ha tomado. La enfermera ha tomado la tensión arterial.** Then ask questions such as the following: **¿Quién es? ¿Qué le ha tomado la enfermera?**

**Step 3** After presenting the vocabulary orally, have students open their books and read the sentences for additional reinforcement.

**Expansion:** Project the transparencies again. Have one student go to the screen and ask questions about the illustrations and photo. He or she calls on other members of the class to answer.

### SPANISH Online

The Glencoe Spanish Web site **(spanish.glencoe.com)** offers options that enable you and your students to experience the Spanish-speaking world via the Internet. For each **Capítulo,** there are activities, games, and quizzes. In addition, an *Enrichment* section offers students an opportunity to visit Web sites related to the theme of the chapter.

### Vocabulary Expansion

You may wish to give students additional medical vocabulary:

| | |
|---|---|
| **el seguro médico** | *medical insurance* |
| **la prueba de sangre** | *blood test* |
| **la muestra de sangre** | *blood sample* |
| **el análisis** | *analysis* |
| **la infección** | *infection* |
| **los mareos** | *dizziness* |

# Vocabulario

## 3 PRACTICE

## ¿Qué palabra necesito?

**7** and **8** These activities can be done orally with books closed. After the oral presentation, students can write the answers to these activities as a homework assignment.

**Expansion:** Call on a student or students to retell the information from either Activity 7 or Activity 8 in their own words.

### Learning from Realia

*(page 238)* You may wish to ask students to say as much as they can about the OMRON pamphlet.

### Learning from Photos

*(page 238)* You may wish to ask the following questions about the photo:

**¿Dónde están estas personas?**
**¿Quién será la señora?**
**¿Qué hace ella?**
**¿Quién será el señor?**

**LEVELING**

**E:** Activities 7, 8, 9, 10, 11

**A:** Activities 8, 9, 11, 12

Vocabulario

## ¿Qué palabra necesito?

**7** **Historieta El pobre Joselito**

Contesten con **sí.**

1. ¿Acaba de tener un accidente Joselito?
2. ¿Le duele mucho la pierna?
3. ¿Lo han puesto en una camilla los socorristas?
4. ¿Lo han llevado a la sala de emergencia del hospital municipal?
5. ¿Le ha tomado una radiografía un técnico?
6. ¿Se ha roto la pierna Joselito?
7. ¿Le ha reducido la fractura el cirujano ortopédico?
8. ¿Tendrá que andar con muletas Joselito?

**8** **Historieta Andrea va al hospital.**

Contesten según se indica.

1. ¿Qué tiene que llenar Andrea cuando llega al hospital? (un formulario)
2. ¿Dónde lo llena? (en la recepción)
3. ¿Qué le toma un enfermero? (la tensión arterial y el pulso)
4. ¿Ha tenido Andrea un accidente? (no)
5. ¿Qué le duele mucho a Andrea? (el estómago)
6. ¿Qué le ha tomado un técnico? (una radiografía)
7. ¿De qué sufre Andrea? (un ataque de apendicitis)

Hospital Santrix, Caracas

*For more practice using words from* ***Palabras 1*** *and* ***2****, do Activity 8 on page H9 at the end of this book.*



## ANSWERS TO ¿Qué palabra necesito?

**7**

1. Sí, Joselito acaba de tener un accidente.
2. Sí, le duele mucho la pierna.
3. Sí, los socorristas lo han puesto en una camilla.
4. Sí, lo han llevado a la sala de emergencia del hospital municipal.
5. Sí, un técnico le ha tomado una radiografía.
6. Sí, Joselito se ha roto la pierna.
7. Sí, el cirujano ortopédico le ha reducido la fractura.
8. Sí, Joselito tendrá que andar con muletas.

**8**

1. Andrea tiene que llenar un formulario cuando llega al hospital.
2. Lo llena en la recepción.
3. Un enfermero le toma la tensión arterial y el pulso.
4. No, Andrea no ha tenido un accidente.
5. A Andrea le duele mucho el estómago.
6. Un técnico le ha tomado una radiografía.
7. Andrea sufre de un ataque de apendicitis.

9 **El hospital** Digan que sí o que no.

1. Al llegar al hospital, el enfermo o paciente tiene que llenar o completar un formulario.
2. La enfermera le ha tomado la tensión arterial al paciente en la cara.
3. La enfermera le ha tomado el pulso en la muñeca.
4. Los rayos equis son fotografías.
5. El joven ha tenido que andar con muletas porque se ha cortado el dedo.
6. El médico le ha puesto unos puntos porque se cortó la mejilla.
7. Han puesto al herido en una camilla porque lo tienen que llevar al hospital en la ambulancia.
8. Lo han puesto en una silla de ruedas porque no puede caminar.

**SPANISH Online**

For more information about Ponce and other cities in Puerto Rico, go to the Glencoe Spanish Web site: spanish.glencoe.com

10 **Sinónimos** Pareen.

| | |
|---|---|
| 1. la sala de emergencia | a. la presión arterial |
| 2. los rayos equis | b. la sala de urgencias |
| 3. la tensión arterial | c. las suturas |
| 4. los puntos | d. se hizo daño |
| 5. se lastimó | e. la radiografía |

11 **¡Socorro!** Tú estás en la Calle Sol en Ponce, Puerto Rico. Acaba de ocurrir un accidente de tráfico. No es muy grave, pero las víctimas necesitan ayuda. Desde un teléfono público, llama al 911. Explícale al/a la operador(a) (tu compañero[a]) lo que pasó y contesta a cualquier pregunta.

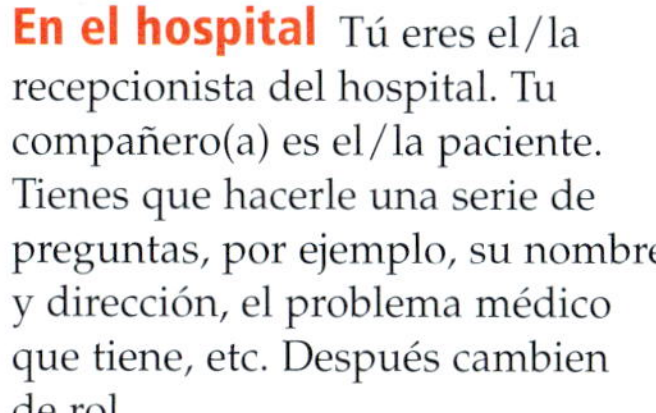

12 **En el hospital** Tú eres el/la recepcionista del hospital. Tu compañero(a) es el/la paciente. Tienes que hacerle una serie de preguntas, por ejemplo, su nombre y dirección, el problema médico que tiene, etc. Después cambien de rol.

Ponce, Puerto Rico

## Vocabulario

**UN POCO MÁS** This *InfoGap* Activity will allow students to practice in pairs. The activity should be very manageable for them, since all vocabulary and structures are familiar to them.

9 After going over Activity 9 you may wish to call on more able students to correct the false statements.

10 Activity 10 can be done in class with or without prior preparation.

### Learning from Photos

*(page 239)* Ponce is Puerto Rico's second largest city, located on the south coast of the island. It was named for the first governor of Puerto Rico, Ponce de León. Ponce is noted for its colonial architecture, its fine art museum, and its charming plaza.

## ANSWERS TO ¿Qué palabra necesito?

**9**

1. Sí
2. No
3. Sí
4. Sí
5. No
6. Sí
7. Sí
8. Sí

**10**

1. b
2. e
3. a
4. c
5. d

**11** *Answers will vary. Students will use vocabulary from* Palabras 1 *and* Palabras 2.

**12** *Answers will vary, but students will use vocabulary from* Palabras 2.

# Estructura

## 1 PREPARATION

### Resource Manager

Audio Activities TE, pages 94–96
Audio CD 5
Workbook, pages 91–93
Quizzes, pages 37–39
ExamView® Pro

### Bellringer Review

*Use BRR Transparency 8.3 or write the following on the board.*
Complete in the present.

1. **Nosotros ___ al hotel. (llegar)**
2. **Nosotros ___ a la recepción. (ir)**
3. **El recepcionista nos ___ y nos ___ la llave. (hablar, dar)**
4. **El botones nos ___ con las maletas. (ayudar)**
5. **Él nos ___ las maletas. (subir)**
6. **Nosotros ___ en el ascensor. (subir)**
7. **Yo ___ la puerta con la llave. (abrir)**
8. **Yo ___ en el hotel pero mis amigos ___ a comer en un restaurante. (comer, salir)**

## 2 PRESENTATION

### El presente perfecto

**Step 1** Go over the formation of the past participle as you write the examples on the board.

**Step 2** As you go over Item 2, you may wish to give students just the forms of the verb **haber.** Then go over the present perfect forms in the book. Have students read them aloud in unison.

# Estructura

## El presente perfecto
### Talking about recent events

1. The present perfect tense in Spanish is formed by using the present tense of the verb **haber** and the past participle. The past participle of regular verbs is formed by adding **-ado** to the infinitive stem of **-ar** verbs and **-ido** to the infinitive stem of **-er** and **-ir** verbs.

| | | | | | |
|---|---|---|---|---|---|
| LLAMAR | **llamado** | COMER | **comido** | SUFRIR | **sufrido** |
| CORTAR | **cortado** | TENER | **tenido** | SUBIR | **subido** |

2. The present perfect is called a compound tense because it is made up of two verb forms. They are the present tense of the verb **haber** and the past participle.

| INFINITIVE | llegar | comer | salir |
|---|---|---|---|
| yo | he llegado | he comido | he salido |
| tú | has llegado | has comido | has salido |
| él, ella, Ud. | ha llegado | ha comido | ha salido |
| nosotros(as) | hemos llegado | hemos comido | hemos salido |
| *vosotros(as)* | *habéis llegado* | *habéis comido* | *habéis salido* |
| ellos, ellas, Uds. | han llegado | han comido | han salido |

3. The present perfect tense is used to describe an action completed very recently in the past. Some time expressions frequently used with the present perfect are:

| | | | |
|---|---|---|---|
| **ya** | *already, yet* | **jamás** | *ever, never* |
| **todavía no** | *not yet* | **nunca** | *never* |

**—En tu vida, ¿has tenido un accidente?**
**—No, nunca he tenido un accidente.**
**—Todavía no has tenido un accidente. ¡Qué suerte!**
**—Y yo ya he tenido tres.**

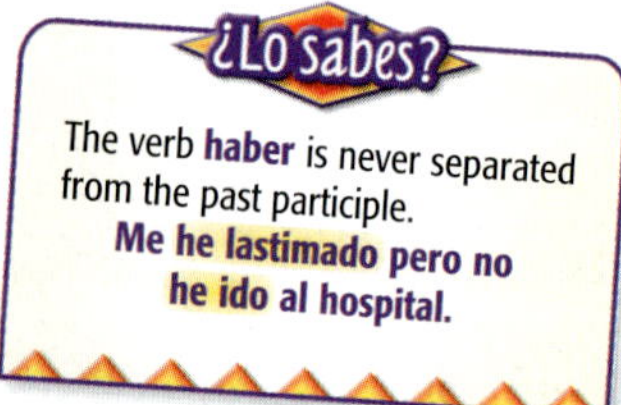




### Reaching All Students

**For the Heritage Speakers**
For those students who learned their grammar in a Spanish-speaking country, you may wish to remind them that the present perfect is also called **el pretérito perfecto compuesto.**

**LEVELING**
**E:** Activities 13, 14
**A:** Activities 14, 15

## ¿Cómo lo digo?

**13** **Historieta El accidente** Contesten.

1. ¿Ha tenido un accidente Diego?
2. ¿Se ha caído de la bicicleta?
3. ¿Se ha lastimado?
4. ¿Ha llegado la ambulancia?
5. ¿Lo han atendido los socorristas?
6. ¿Adónde lo han llevado?

**14** **Sí, ya la he llamado.** Contesten según el modelo.

1. ¿Has hablado con ella?
2. ¿Le has preguntado qué le pasó?
3. ¿Le has mandado unas flores?
4. ¿Has buscado sus libros?
5. ¿Los has llevado a su casa?

**15** **Historieta En el hospital**

Completen con el presente perfecto.

Adela __1__ (llegar) al hospital. Ella __2__ (presentarse) en la recepción y __3__ (llenar) unos formularios. Una abeja le __4__ (picar) en el brazo. Los socorristas la __5__ (llevar) al hospital porque ella __6__ (tener) una reacción a la picadura. La médica la __7__ (examinar) y le __8__ (permitir) volver a casa.

La alergia respiratoria se produce cuando una persona reacciona al contacto con determinadas sustancias (alergenos), como el polvo, polen, alimentos, algunos medicamentos o la pelusa de animales. Estas reacciones pueden variar, pues es posible que afecten órganos importantes como ojos, nariz, pulmones y piel.

## Estructura

**Step 3** As students read the model sentences in Item 3, you may want to draw a timeline on the board. Put a line through the past and bring the line right up to the present. Have a student read the information in the **¿Lo sabes?** box on page 240.

### 3 PRACTICE

### ¿Cómo lo digo?

**13** Activity 13 can be done orally with books closed.

**14** Have students present Activity 14 as a series of miniconversations.

**15** Call on students to read Activity 15 aloud.

### Writing Development

After going over Activity 15, have students rewrite the information in their own words.

### Learning from Realia

*(page 241)* You may wish to call on a heritage speaker or one of the more able students to explain the content of the **Alergias** article in simpler Spanish.

You may also wish to ask students:

1. ¿Quién sufre de alergias?
2. ¿A qué tienes alergia?
3. ¿Qué síntomas tienes?
4. ¿Tomas algún medicamento para la alergia?

### Answers to ¿Cómo lo digo?

**13**

1. Sí, Diego ha tenido un accidente.
2. Sí, se ha caído de la bicicleta.
3. Sí, se ha lastimado.
4. Sí, la ambulancia ha llegado.
5. Sí, los socorristas lo han atendido.
6. Lo han llevado al hospital.

**14**

1. Sí, ya he hablado con ella.
2. Sí, ya le he preguntado qué le pasó.
3. Sí, ya le he mandado unas flores.
4. Sí, ya he buscado sus libros.
5. Sí, ya los he llevado a su casa.

**15**

1. ha llegado
2. se ha presentado
3. ha llenado
4. ha picado
5. han llevado
6. ha tenido
7. ha examinado
8. ha permitido

## PRACTICE *(continued)*

**16** This activity can be done orally with books closed.
**Expansion:** After going over Activity 16, have any student who wishes tell a story in his or her own words about a hospital experience.

## 1 PREPARATION

### Bellringer Review

*Use BRR Transparency 8.4 or write the following on the board.*
Rewrite in the preterite.
1. **Él hace un viaje.**
2. **Ellos van a México.**
3. **Yo los veo.**
4. **Ellos salen el día 20.**
5. **Y vuelven el día 28.**

## 2 PRESENTATION

### Los participios irregulares

**Step 1** Have students read these participles aloud several times. The more they hear them and practice them, the easier it will be to produce them.

## 3 PRACTICE

### ¿Cómo lo digo?

**18** Activity 18 can be done as a series of miniconversations.



**16** **Preguntas personales** Contesten.

1. ¿Has tenido un accidente alguna vez?
2. ¿Te han examinado los socorristas?
3. ¿Te han metido en una ambulancia?
4. ¿Te han llevado al hospital?
5. ¿Has tenido que pasar unos días en el hospital?

**17** **Un accidente** Un amigo se ha lastimado y lo han llevado al hospital. Tú llamas por teléfono y hablas con el/la enfermero(a) (tu compañero[a]). Quieres saber lo que le ha pasado a tu amigo, si lo han examinado, etc. Después cambien de rol.

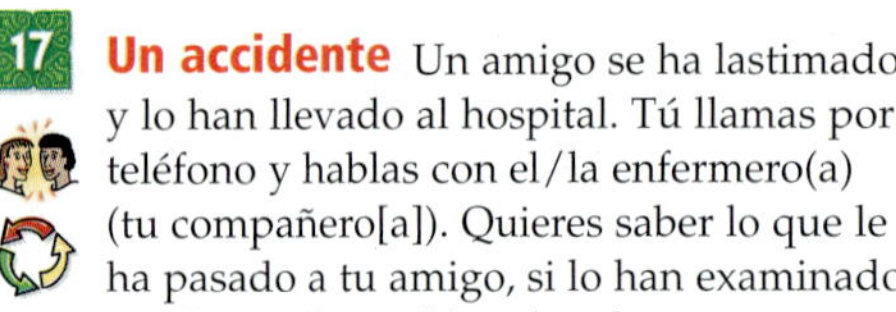

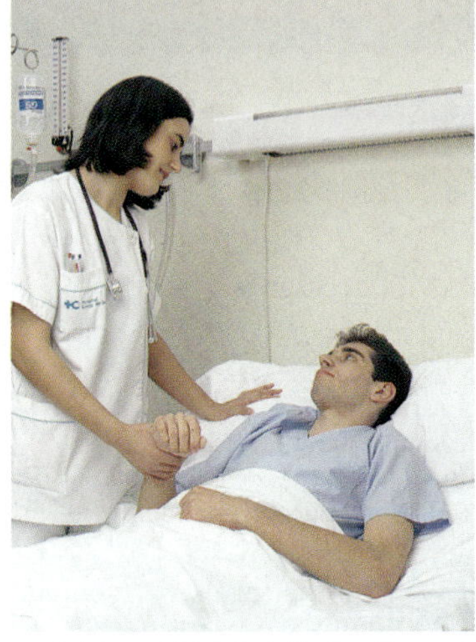

Hospital Costa del Sol, Marbella, España

## Los participios irregulares

### Talking about recent events

The following verbs have irregular past participles.

| | | | |
|---|---|---|---|
| DECIR | dicho | VOLVER | vuelto |
| HACER | hecho | DEVOLVER | devuelto |
| VER | visto | MORIR | muerto |
| ESCRIBIR | escrito | ABRIR | abierto |
| PONER | puesto | CUBRIR | cubierto |
| ROMPER | roto | | |

**¿Lo sabes?**

**Volver** *means to return to a place and* **devolver** *means to return something.*
**He vuelto a casa.**
**Le he devuelto sus libros.**

## ¿Cómo lo digo?

**18** **Ya lo han hecho.**
Contesten según el modelo.

¿Verlo? 
Pero ya lo han visto.

1. ¿Abrirlo?
2. ¿Ponerlo?
3. ¿Devolverlo?
4. ¿Escribirlo?
5. ¿Decirlo?
6. ¿Hacerlo?

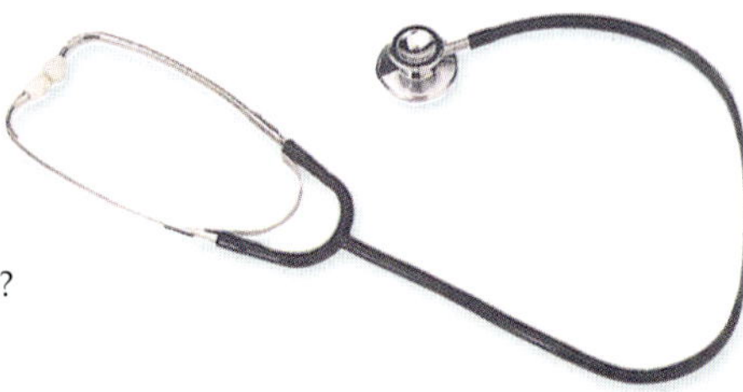



## ANSWERS TO ¿Cómo lo digo?

**16**

1. Sí, he tenido un accidente una vez. (No, no he tenido un accidente nunca.)
2. Sí, (No, no) me han examinado los socorristas.
3. Sí, (No, no) me han metido en una ambulancia.
4. Sí, (No, no) me han llevado al hospital.
5. Sí, (No, no) he tenido que pasar unos días en el hospital.

**17** *Answers will vary, but students will use the present perfect with vocabulary from the chapter.*

**18**

1. Pero ya lo han abierto.
2. Pero ya lo han puesto.
3. Pero ya lo han devuelto.
4. Pero ya lo han escrito.
5. Pero ya lo han dicho.
6. Pero ya lo han hecho.

19 **Historieta Pobre Antonio** Contesten.

1. ¿Antonio se ha hecho daño?
2. ¿Se ha roto el brazo?
3. ¿Ha ido Antonio a la sala de emergencia?
4. ¿Lo ha visto un médico?
5. ¿Le han puesto un vendaje en el hospital?
6. ¿Ha dicho algo Antonio?
7. ¿Ha vuelto a casa Antonio?

20 **He estado muy ocupado(a).** Siempre estás muy ocupado(a). Siempre tienes algo que hacer. Trabaja con un(a) compañero(a). Cada uno(a) de ustedes va a preparar una lista de las cosas que ya han hecho hoy. Luego comparen sus listas. Determinen cuáles son las actividades que ustedes dos han hecho. Y decidan quién en realidad ha estado más ocupado(a).

Barcelona, España

21 **Algún día** Hay tantas cosas que nos gustaría hacer algún día que hasta ahora no hemos hecho. Trabaja con un(a) compañero(a). Hablen de las cosas que quieren hacer algún día pero que hasta ahora no han hecho nunca. Si es posible, expliquen por qué no las han hecho.

## Estructura

### Learning from Photos

(*page 242*) You may wish to ask students the following questions about the photo:
**¿Quiénes son estas personas?**
**¿Por qué está el hombre en la cama?**
**¿Qué hace la médica?**

19 Activity 19 can be done orally with books closed.

20 **and** 21 Allow students to select the activity they wish to do.

### FUN-FACTS

The Barcelona subway was inaugurated in 1924 by combining two private companies, **El Gran Metro** and **El Metro Transversal.** Today there are 5 subway lines with 111 stations in the city and nearby suburbs.

### Reaching All Students

**For the Heritage Speakers** Students will often try to make irregular past participles into regular past participles. You may hear **"rompido,"** **"ponido,"** and **"cubrido."** Remind them that verbs derived from verbs with irregular past participles maintain that irregularity:

| | |
|---|---|
| **prever** | **previsto** |
| **describir** | **descrito** |
| **posponer** | **pospuesto** |
| **descubrir** | **descubierto** |
| **revolver** | **revuelto** |

## Answers to ¿Cómo lo digo?

19

1. Sí (No), Antonio (no) se ha hecho daño.
2. Sí, (No, no) se ha roto el brazo.
3. Sí (No), Antonio (no) ha ido a la sala de emergencia.
4. Sí, (No, no) lo ha visto un médico.
5. Sí, (No, no) le han puesto un vendaje en el hospital.
6. Sí (No), Antonio (no) ha dicho algo (nada).
7. Sí (No), Antonio (no) ha vuelto a casa.

20 *Answers will vary, but students will use the present perfect tense with previously learned vocabulary to form their lists.*

21 *Answers will vary, but students will use vocabulary and tenses previously learned to talk about things they would like to do in the future that they have not yet done.*

### LEVELING

**E:** Activities 17, 18, 19, 20
**A:** Activities 16, 17, 18, 20, 21
**C:** Activity 21

# Estructura

## 1 PREPARATION

### Bellringer Review

*Use BRR Transparency 8.5 or write the following on the board.*
Answer the following questions.

1. **¿Eres inteligente?**
2. **¿Es inteligente tu amigo(a)?**
3. **¿Es interesante la historia?**
4. **¿Tiene tu amigo(a) unos discos compactos?**

## 2 PRESENTATION

### Comparación de igualdad

**Step 1** Have students open their books to page 244. Lead them through the explanation.

**Step 2** Have them repeat all the model sentences after you.

## 3 PRACTICE

### ¿Cómo lo digo?

**¡OJO!** After going over the activities, have students make up their own sentences using the comparative structures they just learned.

### National Standards

**Comparisons**
Students develop an insight into their own language as they learn that the subject pronoun always follows a comparison in Spanish: **Ella es más alta que yo.** It is the same as the English construction: *She is taller than I.* English speakers often erroneously use the object pronoun: *She is taller than "me."*

# Estructura

## Comparación de igualdad
### Comparing people and things

1. To compare equal quantities in English you use *as much . . . as* or *as many . . . as.*

   *He has as much money as I.*
   *He has as many problems as I.*

   In Spanish you use **tanto… como.** Because **tanto** is an adjective it has to agree with the noun it modifies.

   **Elena tiene tanta energía como yo.**
   **Pero ella no tiene tantos accidentes como yo.**

2. To compare equal qualities in English you use *as . . . as.*

   *I am as smart as he is.*

   In Spanish you use **tan… como** with either the adjective or adverb.

   **Él está tan enfermo como su amigo.**
   **Él se va a curar tan rápido como ella.**

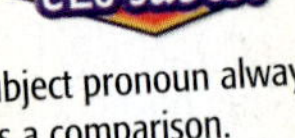

**¿Lo sabes?**
The subject pronoun always follows a comparison.
**Él tiene tanto dinero como yo.**
**Y yo estudio tanto como tú.**
**Soy tan inteligente como tú.**

## ¿Cómo lo digo?

**22 Dos hospitales** Contesten.

1. ¿Tiene el hospital en la ciudad tantas camas como el hospital en las afueras?
2. ¿Tiene el doctor López tanta experiencia como el doctor Salas?
3. ¿Tienen tantos pacientes aquí como en el hospital nuevo?
4. ¿Tiene el hospital nuevo tantas enfermeras como el otro?
5. ¿Tienen tantos técnicos aquí como en el otro?
6. ¿Pagan tanto dinero aquí como en el otro hospital?

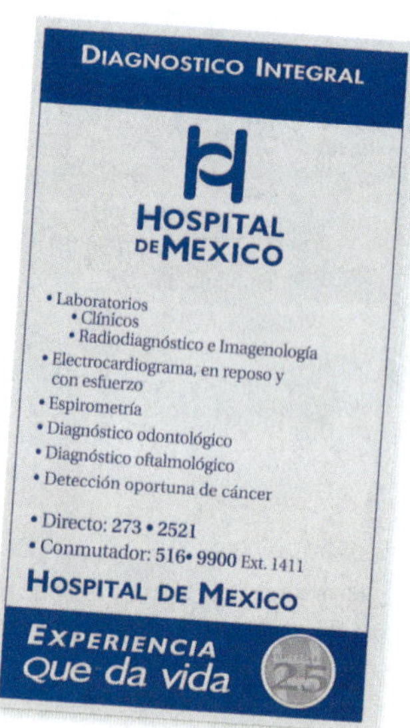




## Answers to ¿Cómo lo digo?

**22**

1. Sí (No), el hospital en la ciudad (no) tiene tantas camas como el hospital en las afueras.
2. Sí (No), el doctor López (no) tiene tanta experiencia como el doctor Salas.
3. Sí, (No, no) tienen tantos pacientes aquí como en el hospital nuevo.
4. Sí (No), el hospital nuevo (no) tiene tantas enfermeras como el otro.
5. Sí, (No, no) tienen tantos técnicos aquí como en el otro.
6. Sí, (No, no) pagan tanto dinero aquí como en el otro hospital.

## 23 Historieta Los dos son buenos.

Completen con **tanto... como** o **tan... como.**

1. El Hospital San José es ____ bueno ____ el Hospital Municipal.
2. Pero el Hospital San José no es ____ grande ____ el Hospital Municipal.
3. Y el Hospital Municipal no tiene ____ enfermeros ____ el Hospital San José.
4. Pero el Hospital San José tiene ____ pacientes ____ el Municipal.
5. La sala de emergencia del San José es ____ moderna ____ la sala de emergencia del Municipal.
6. El Hospital San José está ____ cerca de nuestra casa ____ el Hospital Municipal.

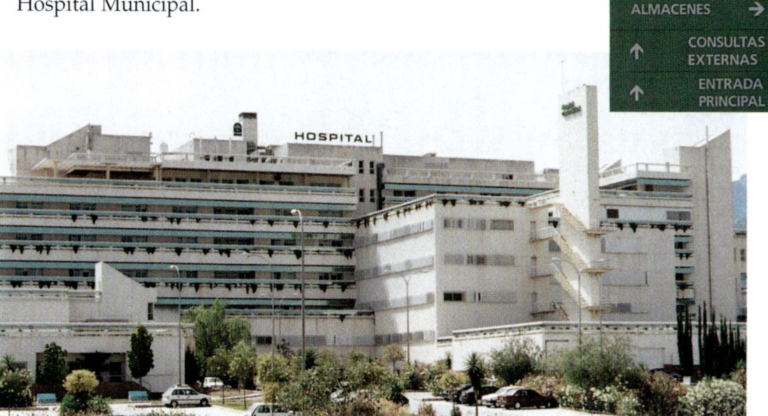


Hospital Costa del Sol, Marbella, España

## 24 Son muy parecidas.

Trabaja con un(a) compañero(a). Piensen en algunas personas que ustedes conocen que, en su opinión, tienen mucho en común o que tienen las mismas características físicas. Comparen a estas personas.

# Estructura

**Learning from Realia**

*(page 244)* You may wish to ask students questions about the **Hospital de México** pamphlet:

**¿Qué clases de laboratorios tiene?**
**¿Cuál es la diferencia entre los dos electrocardiogramas?**
**¿Cuáles son dos diagnósticos que hacen?**
**¿Qué quiere decir detección «oportuna»?**

**23** Do this activity with books open.

**¡Adelante!** At this point in the chapter, students have learned all the vocabulary and structure necessary to complete the chapter. The conversation and cultural readings that follow recycle all the material learned up to this point.

**LEVELING**

**E:** Activity 22
**A:** Activities 23, 24

## Answers to ¿Cómo lo digo?

**23**

1. tan, como
2. tan, como
3. tantos, como
4. tantos, como
5. tan, como
6. tan, como

**24** *Answers will vary, but students will use comparatives to talk about and compare people.*

## 1 PREPARATION

### Resource Manager

Audio Activities TE, pages 96–97
Audio CD 5

### Bellringer Review

*Use BRR Transparency 8.6 or write the following on the board.*
Write one sentence telling what you do in each of the following rooms of a house: **la cocina, el comedor, la sala.**

## 2 PRESENTATION

**Step 1** Have students close their books. Ask them to listen and repeat as you read the conversation aloud or play Audio CD 5.

**Step 2** Open books and call on volunteers to read the conversation in parts with as much expression as possible.

**Step 3** Call on individual students to answer the questions that follow the conversation.

**Step 4** Call on a student to retell the information from the conversation in his or her own words. This activity gives students important practice in going from dialogue to narrative form.

# Conversación

## Una fractura   

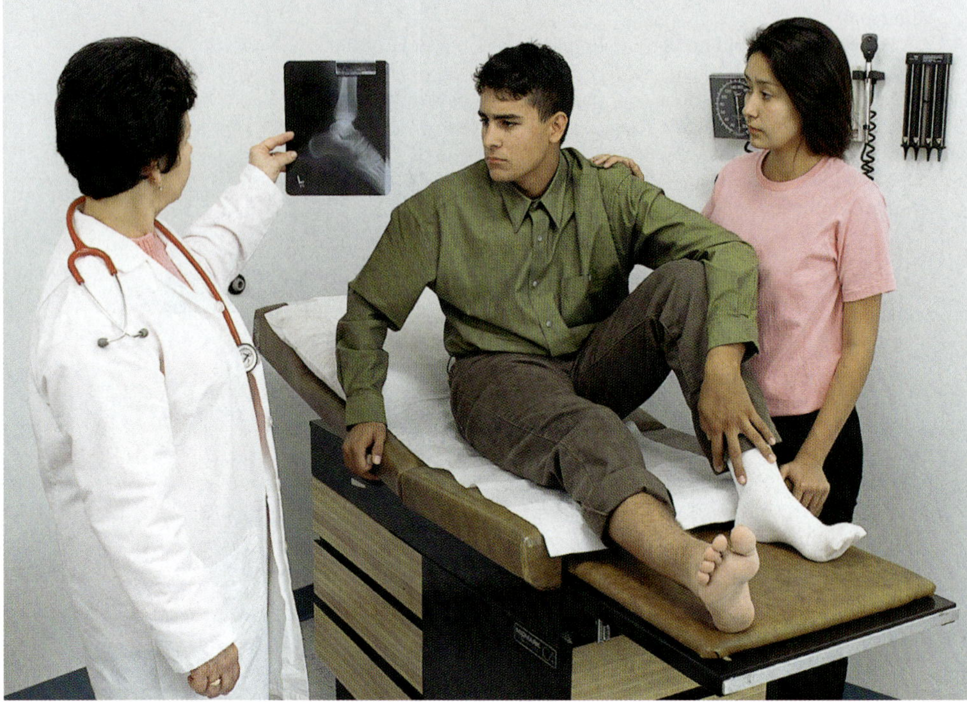

**Mónica** Pablo, ¿cómo te sientes? ¿Qué te ha pasado?
**Pablo** Pues, no sé. Me han tomado una radiografía. Pero todavía no me han dado los resultados.
**Mónica** Aquí viene la médica ahora.
**Médica** Pablo, tengo la radiografía. Indica que te has roto el tobillo.
**Pablo** ¿Me he roto el tobillo?
**Médica** Sí, pero no es una fractura grave. Te voy a poner el tobillo en un yeso y podrás salir del hospital. Voy a volver enseguida y reduciré el hueso.
**Pablo** ¿Dónde? ¿Aquí? ¿Ahora? Me va a doler mucho, ¿no?
**Médica** Pablo, no debes estar tan nervioso. ¿La enfermera te ha tomado la tensión arterial?
**Pablo** Mónica, ¿te quedarás conmigo?

### ¿Comprendes?

Contesten.

1. ¿Quién ha venido a visitar a Pablo?
2. ¿Qué le ha pasado a Pablo?
3. ¿Le han tomado una radiografía?
4. ¿Sabe Pablo los resultados?
5. ¿Qué le dice la médica a Pablo?
6. ¿Qué va a hacer la médica?
7. ¿Tiene que quedarse en el hospital Pablo?
8. ¿Está nervioso Pablo? ¿Por qué o por qué no?



### Answers to ¿Comprendes?

1. Mónica ha venido a visitar a Pablo.
2. Él no sabe qué le ha pasado.
3. Sí, le han tomado una radiografía.
4. No, él no sabe los resultados.
5. La médica le dice que se ha roto el tobillo.
6. La médica le va a poner el tobillo en un yeso y reducirá el hueso.
7. No, Pablo no tiene que quedarse en el hospital.
8. Sí, Pablo está nervioso porque piensa que le va a doler mucho.

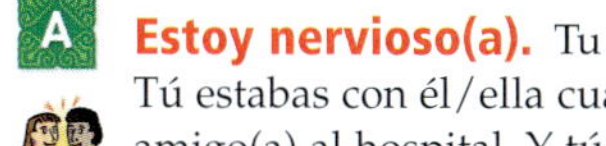

# Vamos a hablar más

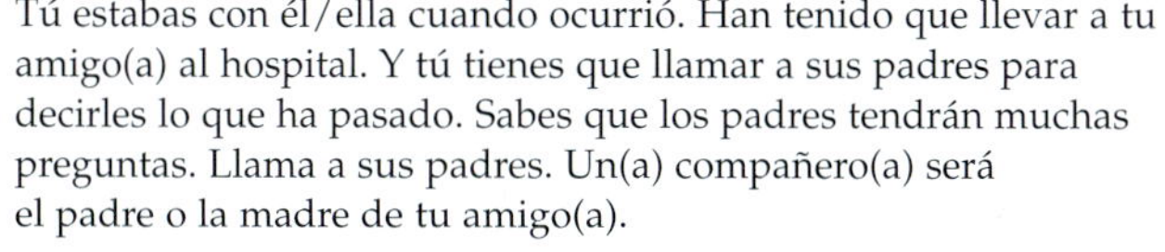

**A Estoy nervioso(a).** Tu amigo(a) ha tenido un pequeño accidente. Tú estabas con él/ella cuando ocurrió. Han tenido que llevar a tu amigo(a) al hospital. Y tú tienes que llamar a sus padres para decirles lo que ha pasado. Sabes que los padres tendrán muchas preguntas. Llama a sus padres. Un(a) compañero(a) será el padre o la madre de tu amigo(a).

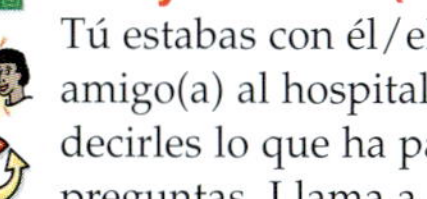

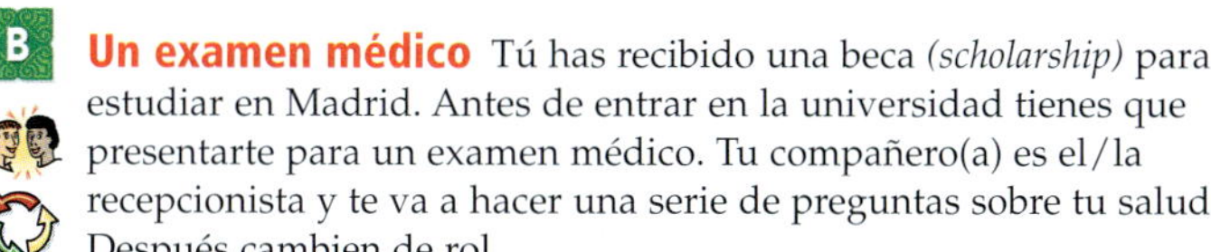

**B Un examen médico** Tú has recibido una beca *(scholarship)* para estudiar en Madrid. Antes de entrar en la universidad tienes que presentarte para un examen médico. Tu compañero(a) es el/la recepcionista y te va a hacer una serie de preguntas sobre tu salud. Después cambien de rol.

Universidad de Madrid

**C ¿Qué te ha pasado?** Tú vas a ser el/la médico(a). Un(a) compañero(a) es el/la paciente. Él/Ella ha tenido un accidente. Hazle preguntas sobre su accidente: dónde, cuándo, cómo ha ocurrido. Pregúntale dónde le duele. Luego dale una diagnosis y explícale el tratamiento—es decir, lo que vas a hacer.

## Conversación

### 3 PRACTICE

## Vamos a hablar más

**A**, **B**, and **C** These activities allow students to use the chapter vocabulary and structures in open-ended situations. You may select those you consider most appropriate. You may also allow students to select the activity or activities they wish to take part in.

**A** Students may have fun working on this activity in groups and presenting their conversations to the entire class.

**B** Have students make a list of questions before they begin the activity.

### Reaching All Students

**Cooperative Learning**
Have team members take turns being "injured." The other members will ask questions to determine the symptoms and to figure out what the "injured" student needs.

### Glencoe Technology

On the CD-ROM, students can watch a dramatization of this conversation. They can then play the role of either one of the characters and record themselves in the conversation.

## Answers to Vamos a hablar más

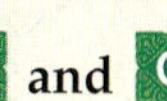

**A** and **C** *Answers will vary, but students will use material learned in the chapter to talk about an accident.*

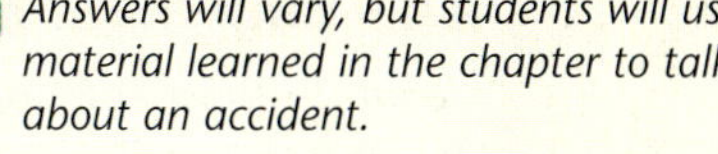

**B** *Answers will vary, but students will use material learned in the chapter to talk about their health.*

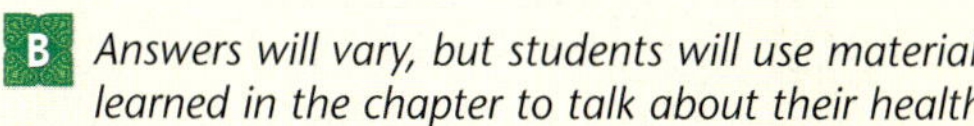

**LEVELING**

**E:** Conversation

# Lecturas culturales

## Resource Manager

Audio Activities TE, page 97
Audio CD 5

## National Standards

**Cultures**

The reading about **practicantes** on page 248 and the related activities on page 249 familiarize students with a type of traditional medical professional in Latin American countries.

**Comparisons**

Students learn that, unlike in the United States, where few areas today are inaccessible, many villages in Latin America are isolated owing to certain rugged features of the geography there. The need for **practicantes,** such as the one described in this reading, is therefore especially urgent. In North America, the *physician assistant* plays a role similar to that of the **practicante** in Spain and Latin America.

## PRESENTATION

### Pre-reading

**Step 1** Give students a brief synopsis of the reading selection in Spanish.

**Step 2** Ask questions about the brief synopsis.

### Reading

**Step 1** Have students open their books and repeat several sentences after you or call on individuals to read.

**Step 2** Ask questions about what was just read.

**Step 3** Have students read the selection at home and write the answers to the activities that accompany the **Lectura.**

**LEVELING**

**A:** Reading

# Lecturas culturales

## Reading Strategy

**Using context to determine meanings of words** Sometimes when reading you will come across words that you do not know. In this situation it is best to attempt to guess the most general meaning of the word or its category. To do this, it is helpful to rely on the words and sentences around the word. By doing this, you will probably be able to accurately guess those words you do not know.

## Practicantes 

Estefanía Reyes es practicante. Ella vive en un pueblo pequeño cerca de Puno en los Andes de Perú. Vamos a ver lo que ha hecho Estefanía esta mañana. Ha estado muy ocupada. Son las once de la mañana y ya ha visto a muchos pacientes.

Le ha tomado la tensión arterial a un señor mayor. Tiene la tensión bastante elevada y Estefanía le ha recomendado una dieta.

Una niña de tres años se ha cortado el pie. Su mamá estaba muy nerviosa. Pero Estefanía le ha puesto cinco puntos para cerrar la herida. Y le ha puesto una inyección contra el tétano.

Ha visto a un señor que tiene dolores abdominales muy fuertes. Le duele tanto el estómago que Estefanía cree que está sufriendo de un ataque de apendicitis. Puede ser algo muy serio. Estefanía lo ha mandado al hospital para ver a un médico.

Pero, ¿qué es Estefanía? Es una practicante. En los países hispanos siempre ha habido practicantes. Son profesionales en el campo de la medicina. El o la practicante es un(a) diplomado(a) en enfermería. Puede poner inyecciones y practicar curas médicas simples y rutinarias. En caso de heridas o enfermedades serias, el practicante manda al paciente a un médico.

En muchos pueblos pequeños de áreas remotas, el practicante es muy importante. A veces es el único profesional médico que tienen los habitantes.

Un pueblo andino, Perú



## Learning from Photos

*(page 248 top)* Ask students questions about the photo such as:
**¿Quién será la señora?**
**¿Quiénes son los niños?**
**¿Hay más niños o niñas en el grupo?**
*(page 248 bottom)* The houses in this village are made of stone. Trees are uncommon high in the Andes, and timber is not abundant for building. Stone houses are common.

## Learning from Realia

*(page 249)* Ask students to tell as much as they can about the **Servicio de A.T.S. / Practicante a domicilio.**

## ¿Comprendes?

**A Un trabajo interesante** Contesten.

1. ¿Qué es Estefanía Reyes?
2. ¿De dónde es?
3. ¿Qué es un(a) practicante?
4. ¿En qué es diplomado(a)?
5. ¿Cuándo manda al paciente a ver al médico el practicante?
6. ¿Por qué es muy importante el practicante en muchas áreas?

**B Pacientes** Expliquen.

Son las once de la mañana y Estefanía ya ha visto a muchos pacientes. Identifiquen a todos los pacientes que ella ha examinado y describan lo que ha hecho a cada uno.

**C Palabras**

Empleen las siguientes palabras en una oración.

1. el practicante
2. la tensión arterial
3. le ha puesto puntos
4. el tétano
5. un ataque de apendicitis

SERVICIO DE
A.T.S. / PRACTICANTE
A DOMICILIO
"TODO MADRID"
INYECCIONES
SONDAS
SUEROS
PRESIÓN ARTERIAL
CURAS QUIRÚRGICAS
(ÚLCERAS, HERIDAS, QUEMADURAS...)
SUTURAS
ETC.
Para comunicar su aviso llame al teléfono:
☎ 908 – 72 88 83
(Este teléfono móvil sustituye al anterior servicio de "busca" 450 28 12, abonado nº 3516)

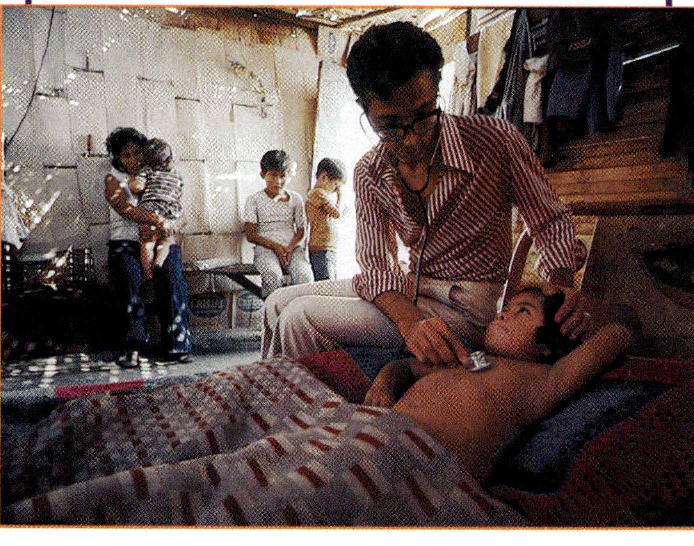

Una zona rural en Bolivia



# Lecturas culturales

### Post-reading

**Step 1** Go over the **¿Comprendes?** activities in class the next day.

**Step 2** Call on a student to give a summary of the reading in his or her own words. If necessary, ask five or six questions to review the salient points of the reading selection in order to enable him or her to do this more easily. After the oral summary, the more able students can write a synopsis of the **Lectura** in their own words.

## Reaching All Students

### For Heritage Speakers

In many Hispanic countries medical services are paid for by the government. Yet many people who can afford it prefer to get private medical care. Ask students to write a paragraph addressing the following: **¿Cuáles son algunas ventajas y desventajas del servicio médico pagado por el gobierno? ¿Para quiénes es un beneficio? ¿Para quiénes no lo es?**

## Answers to ¿Comprendes?

**A**

1. Es una practicante.
2. Es del Perú.
3. Es un(a) profesional en el campo de la medicina.
4. Es diplomado(a) en enfermería.
5. El practicante manda al paciente a ver al médico en caso de heridas o enfermedades serias.
6. Es muy importante en muchas áreas porque a veces es el único profesional médico que tienen los habitantes.

**B** *Answers will vary but may include:*

1. Un señor mayor: Estefanía le ha tomado la tensión arterial y le ha recomendado una dieta.
2. Una niña de tres años que se ha cortado el pie: Estefanía le ha puesto cinco puntos para cerrar la herida y le ha puesto una inyección contra el tétano.
3. Un señor que tiene dolores abdominales muy graves: lo ha mandado al hospital para ver a un médico.

**C** *Answers will vary. Students can use the reading as well as the vocabulary from* Palabras 2 *to help write their sentences.*

# Lectura opcional 1

## National Standards

**Cultures**
This reading about the opening of a new hospital and the related activities on this page familiarize students with some modern medical services in the Spanish-speaking world.

**¡OJO!** This reading is optional. You may skip it completely, have the entire class read it, have only several students read it and report to the class, or assign it for extra credit.

## PRESENTATION

This reading is an actual newspaper article about the opening of a new hospital.

## FUN FACTS

**Quirófano, cirugía,** and **cirujano** are all derived from the Greek word for *hand.* The English words *surgery* and *surgeon* have the same root. Ask students why they think this is so.

# Lectura opcional 1

## EL HOSPITAL BUENA VISTA

La mañana del jueves de esta semana se han abierto por primera vez las puertas del nuevo Hospital Buena Vista. La alcaldesa de la ciudad, doña Emilia Porras Narváez, ha cortado la cinta ceremonial en frente de la entrada principal.

Este modernísimo hospital cuenta con doscientas camas, un quirófano[1] con un equipo técnico muy avanzado, salas de recuperación, una unidad de cuidado intensivo, y departamentos especializados, entre ellos los de cardiología, ginecología, ortopedia, y pediatría. El director del hospital, el doctor Elías Maldonado, ha dicho que la primera responsabilidad del hospital es la salud de la comunidad. Después de la ceremonia de apertura, los invitados fueron a la cafetería del hospital para una recepción.

[1]quirófano *operating room*

Hospital Buena Vista

## ¿Comprendes?

**A ¿Cómo se dice en inglés... ?** Pareen.

| | |
|---|---|
| 1. la alcaldesa | a. ribbon |
| 2. la cinta | b. advanced |
| 3. avanzado | c. intensive care |
| 4. cuidado intensivo | d. recovery rooms |
| 5. salas de recuperación | e. the mayor (female) |

**B Especialidades médicas** Contesten.

1. ¿Cuáles son cuatro especialidades médicas que mencionan en el artículo?
2. ¿Cómo se llaman esas cuatro especialidades en inglés?

**C El hospital nuevo** Contesten según el artículo.

1. ¿Cuándo inauguraron el nuevo hospital?
2. ¿Cuántos pacientes pueden dormir en el hospital?
3. ¿Qué hay en el quirófano?
4. ¿Qué ha dicho el doctor Maldonado?
5. ¿Por qué fueron los invitados a la cafetería?



## ANSWERS TO ¿Comprendes?

**A**

1. e
2. a
3. b
4. c
5. d

**B**

1. la cardiología, la ginecología, la ortopedia y la pediatría
2. cardiology, gynecology, orthopedics, and pediatrics

**C**

1. Inauguraron el nuevo hospital la mañana del jueves de esta semana.
2. Doscientos pacientes pueden dormir en el hospital.
3. En el quirófano hay un equipo técnico muy avanzado.
4. Ha dicho que la primera responsabilidad del hospital es la salud de la comunidad.
5. Los invitados fueron a la cafetería para una recepción.

# Lectura opcional 2

## Problemas médicos de hoy

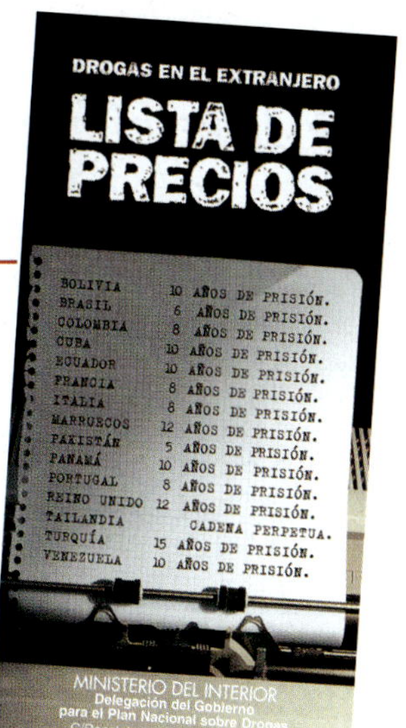


Al hablar de la salud y la medicina hay tres problemas graves que todos tenemos que confrontar. Son la adicción a las drogas, el abuso del alcohol y el sida.

En todos los países hispanos, igual que en Estados Unidos, verás anuncios que dicen «No a las drogas».

En España y en otros países hispanos hay campañas de castigos[1] rigurosos contra los conductores de automóviles que manejan (conducen) bajo la influencia del alcohol. El número de muertes[2] causadas por accidentes vehiculares excede la tasa[3] de mortalidad de muchas enfermedades.

Se considera el sida la plaga de nuestro siglo. Esta enfermedad contagiosa está matando[4] a miles de personas cada día en todos los continentes del mundo. En todas partes hay programas y campañas para educar a la gente sobre los peligros[5] del uso de las drogas y la promiscuidad sexual, las dos causas principales del sida.

La drogadicción, el alcoholismo y el sida son problemas que todos tenemos que confrontar, resolver y vencer.

[1]castigos *punishments*
[2]muertes *deaths*
[3]tasa *rate*
[4]matando *killing*
[5]peligros *dangers*

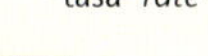

TU DERECHO A FUMAR ACABA DONDE EMPIEZA MI NECESIDAD DE RESPIRAR

### ¿Comprendes?

**Problemas de hoy**

Digan que sí o que no.

1. Actualmente hay tres problemas médicos que son muy graves.
2. El sida es una enfermedad venérea contagiosa.
3. El número de muertes causadas por conductores de automóviles bajo la influencia del alcohol es muy bajo.
4. El sida no existe en muchas partes del mundo.



# Lectura opcional 2

## National Standards

**Cultures**

This reading and the related activity on this page familiarize students with three serious medical and social problems—alcoholism, drug addiction, and AIDS—in the Spanish-speaking world.

**¡OJO!** This reading is optional. You may skip it completely, have the entire class read it, have only several students read it and report to the class, or assign it for extra credit.

## PRESENTATION

**Note:** Since this reading deals with some very contemporary problems, you may wish to have all students scan it. There are many cognates, so students should not have any difficulty understanding it.

## About the Spanish Language

**SIDA** is the acronym for **Síndrome de inmunodeficiencia adquirida.** It is the equivalent of the English *AIDS.* The Spanish equivalent of *HIV* is **VIH, Virus de inmunodeficiencia humana.**

**LEVELING**

**E:** Reading 1
**A:** Reading 2
**C:** Reading 3

### Answers to ¿Comprendes?

1. Sí
2. Sí
3. No
4. No

### Learning from Realia

*(page 251 bottom)* Ask students the following questions about the anti-smoking material:

**¿Qué quiere decir: Tu derecho de fumar acaba donde empieza mi necesidad de respirar? Explica.**

# Conexiones

## National Standards

**Connections**
This reading about medical specialties and diseases in the Spanish-speaking world establishes a connection with another discipline, allowing students to reinforce and further their knowledge of science, specifically medicine, through the study of Spanish.

**Comparisons**
This reading illustrates the prevalence of English / Spanish cognates, thereby giving students a better understanding of the nature of language.

**¡OJO!** The readings in the **Conexiones** section are optional. They focus on some of the major disciplines taught in schools and universities. The vocabulary is useful for discussing such topics as history, literature, art, economics, business, science, etc. You may choose any of the following ways to do the readings in the **Conexiones** sections.

**Independent reading** Have students read the selections and do the post-reading activities as homework, which you collect. This option is least intrusive on class time and requires a minimum of teacher involvement.

**Homework with in-class follow-up** Assign the reading and post-reading activities as homework. Review and discuss the material in class the next day.

**Intensive in-class activity** This option includes a pre-reading vocabulary presentation, in-class reading and discussion, assignment of the activities for homework, and a discussion of the assignment in class the following day.

# Conexiones
## *Las ciencias*

### La medicina

As you know, many English and Spanish words are cognates. They are similar in form and mean the same thing because both have the same source, usually Latin. Much medical terminology comes directly from Latin. Therefore the number of English/Spanish cognates is particularly great in this field. You will also note a pattern in the endings. The **ía** ending in Spanish is usually *y* in English. The **ólogo(a)** ending is usually *ologist* in English. Let's go over a few of these cognates.

| ESPECIALIDADES MÉDICAS | MÉDICOS ESPECIALISTAS |
|---|---|
| **la cardiología** | **el/la cardiólogo(a)** |
| **la ginecología** | **el/la ginecólogo(a)** |
| **la psiquiatría** | **el/la psiquiatra** |
| **la pediatría** | **el/la pediatra** |
| **la oncología** | **el/la oncólogo(a)** |
| **la oftalmología** | **el/la oftalmólogo(a)** |
| **la urología** | **el/la urólogo(a)** |
| **la dermatología** | **el/la dermatólogo(a)** |

It shouldn't be too hard to figure out what the names of these specialties and specialists are in English. If you don't know what they are in English, check with your science teacher or the school nurse. Here are a few hints.

| | |
|---|---|
| **la cardiología** | *cardiology* |
| **el cardiólogo** | *the cardiologist* |

Una pediatra, Estepona, España



### Learning from Photos

*(page 252)* Ask students the following questions about this photo: **¿Quién es el paciente, el niño o su madre? ¿Qué tratan los pediatras? ¿Qué opinas, al niño le duele el estómago?**

Now see whether you can guess the meaning of these diseases or illnesses:

| LAS ENFERMEDADES | |
|---|---|
| **la tuberculosis** | **la artritis** |
| **el cáncer** | **la meningitis** |
| **la apendicitis** | **la esquizofrenia** |
| **la hepatitis** | **las úlceras** |

See whether you can answer these questions.

1. ¿Cómo se llama el especialista que trata las enfermedades de los niños?
2. ¿Quién es el especialista que trata las enfermedades mentales?
3. ¿A qué médico deben ir las personas que sufren de cáncer?
4. Si tienes un problema con los ojos, ¿a qué especialista debes consultar?

Now let's see how much you understand about certain diseases.

1. La esquizofrenia es una enfermedad ____.
   **a.** de los ojos **b.** mental **c.** de niños
2. Los médicos les ponen a dieta a las víctimas de ____.
   **a.** úlceras **b.** artritis **c.** esquizofrenia
3. Esta enfermedad afecta más a las personas viejas. Se les hace difícil usar las manos. La enfermedad es ____.
   **a.** la artritis **b.** la tuberculosis **c.** la hepatitis
4. Si una persona come mariscos contaminados puede sufrir de ____.
   **a.** apendicitis **b.** tuberculosis **c.** hepatitis

# Conexiones

## PRESENTATION

### *Las ciencias*
### La medicina

**Step 1** You may wish to have students interested in medicine do this reading along with the accompanying activities.

**Step 2** Students who are not particularly interested in medicine can take a quick look at the terms to familiarize themselves with them. They are all cognates.

### Learning from Realia

*(page 253 top)* Have students look at the advertisement with the frog and ask them: **¿De qué trata el anuncio?** Then ask them to list all the benefits mentioned that come from stopping smoking. *(page 253 bottom)* Ask students: **¿Cuál es la especialización de los médicos en el Centro Barraquer? ¿Quiénes tienen que ir al Centro Barraquer?**

### ANSWERS

**Note:** These are the answers to the questions in the reading above.

1. el / la pediatra
2. el / la psiquiatra
3. el / la oncólogo(a)
4. el / la oftalmólogo(a)

1. b
2. a
3. a
4. c

### LEVELING

**A:** Reading

## ¡Te toca a ti!

### Use what you have learned

### Recycling

These activities allow students to use the vocabulary and structure from this chapter in completely open-ended, real-life situations.

### PRESENTATION

Encourage students to say as much as possible when they do these activities. Tell them not to be afraid to make mistakes, since the goal of the activities is real-life communication. If someone in the group makes an error, allow the others to politely correct him or her. Let students choose the activities they would like to do.

You may wish to divide students into pairs or groups. Encourage students to elaborate on the basic theme and to be creative. They may use props, pictures, or posters if they wish.

### PRACTICE

Let students choose the activities they would like to do.

#### Writing Development

Have students keep a notebook or portfolio containing their best written work from each chapter. These selected writings can be based on assignments from the Student Textbook and the Workbook. The activities on page 255 are examples of writing assignments that may be included in each student's portfolio. On page 94 in the Workbook, students will begin to develop an organized autobiography **(Mi autobiografía).** These workbook pages may also become a part of their portfolio.

## ¡Te toca a ti!

## Use what you have learned

HABLAR **1**

### Servicios médicos de tu comunidad

✔ *Describe medical services*

Hay un(a) estudiante de intercambio en tu escuela (tu compañero[a]). Es de Panamá. Tiene algunas preguntas sobre los servicios médicos que ofrece tu comunidad. Descríbele el hospital local. Si no sabes nada del hospital que sirve a tu comunidad, ve a buscar un folleto sobre el hospital para poder contestar a las preguntas del/de la estudiante de intercambio.

Canal de Panamá

HABLAR **2**

### Voy a ser intérprete.

✔ *Ask questions about medical problems*

El hospital local tiene un problema. Su intérprete de español ha estado enfermo. Tú vas a ayudar. Vas a trabajar a tiempo parcial en el hospital. Vas a ayudar a los pacientes hispanohablantes. Tu compañero(a) va a ser tu primer(a) paciente. Ayúdale a llenar el formulario en la recepción.

HABLAR **3**

### Una comedia

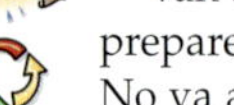

✔ *Talk about emergency room procedures and accidents*

Van a divertirse. Trabajando en grupos de cuatro o cinco personas, preparen un «skit». Su «skit» se llama «Un día en la sala de emergencia». No va a ser muy serio. Va a ser muy cómico. Presenten su comedia a la clase.



#### History Connection

The Panama Canal could not have been built without controlling yellow fever in the Canal Zone. The ravages of this disease contributed to the failure of a French effort to build the canal. Two important names in connection with the victory over yellow fever are Carlos J. Finlay (1833–1915), of Cuba, and the American William Gorgas (1854–1920). You may wish to assign biographies of these two medical heroes to some of your more able students.

## ¡Te toca a ti!

ESCRIBIR **4**

### Un formulario

✔ *Fill out a medical form*

En una hoja de papel, escribe la información que te pide el formulario.

HOSPITAL ABC

Apellidos __________ Nombre __________

Dirección __________ Edad ______

Problema médico que tiene __________

Nombres y dirección de padres u otros parientes __________

Nombre de la compañía de seguros __________

ESCRIBIR **5**

### Las noticias

Your local Spanish language newspaper has asked you to write a feature story on a person or place in your community. Your parents recently had an accident and had to go to the emergency room. They were transported there by the First Aid Squad in your community. You were extremely pleased with the quality of service, beginning with the paramedics who arrived promptly and administered treatment at the scene. The care your parents received in the emergency room from the staff was equally as good. Write an article about this experience to share with the Spanish-speaking members of your community and to perhaps offer a refreshing perspective to an otherwise unpleasant event.

#### Writing Strategy

**Writing a feature article**
When writing a feature article, writers have two challenges: first, they must identify current topics that will be of interest; they must gather the information that will bring the topic to life and give readers the background they need. An important aspect of feature writing is the use of an effective "lead" to describe the opening of the story. This will catch the readers' attention and draw them in.



## ¡Te toca a ti!

#### Career Connection

**Intérpretes** Activity 2 on page 254 shows the importance of Spanish in the medical profession. You may wish to invite an interpreter from a local hospital to speak to your class about his or her job and training.

#### Critical Thinking Activity

**Identifying causes** **El Canal de Panamá no tiene hoy la misma importancia que tenía en el pasado. ¿Cuáles serán algunas razones?**

**4** You may wish to photocopy this form for your students.

#### Writing Strategy

**Writing a feature article**
Have students read the Writing Strategy on page 255. In order to help them understand what a "lead" is, bring in Spanish-language newspapers and have them read the lead sentences of several articles.

### ANSWERS TO ¡Te toca a ti!

**1**, **2**, and **3** *Answers will vary, but students will use the vocabulary from* Palabras 1 *and* Palabras 2.

**4** and **5** *Answers will vary.*

### LEVELING

These activities encompass all three levels. All students will be able to do them at a sophistication level commensurate with their ability in Spanish. Some students will be able to speak for several minutes, and others may be able to give just a few sentences. This is to be expected when students are functioning completely on their own generating their own language to the best of their ability.

## Resource Manager

Communication Transparency C 8
Quizzes, pages 35–39
Performance Assessment, Task 8
Tests, pages 121–134
Situation Cards, Chapter 8
**Maratón mental** Videoquiz, Chapter 8
ExamView® Pro, Chapter 8

## Assessment

This is a pre-test for students to take before you administer the chapter test. Note that each section is cross-referenced so students can easily find the material they have to review in case they made errors. You may use Assessment Answers Transparency A 8 to do the assessment in class, or you may assign this assessment for homework. You can correct the assessment yourself, or you may prefer to project the answers on the overhead in class.

## Glencoe Technology

### MINDJOGGER VHS/DVD

You may wish to help your students prepare for the chapter test by playing the MindJogger game show. Teams will compete against each other to review chapter vocabulary and structure and sharpen listening comprehension skills.

# Assessment

## Vocabulario

**1 Identifiquen.**

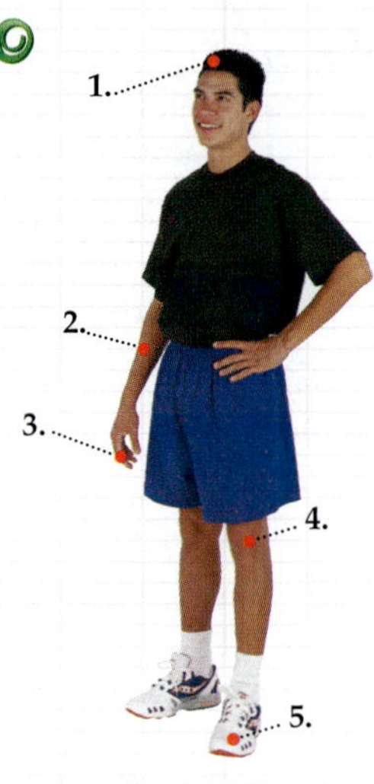


To review **Palabras 1**, turn to pages 232–233.

**2 ¿Sí o no?**

6. Cuando alguien se ha torcido el tobillo, tiene una fractura.
7. El servicio de primeros auxilios llega en una camilla al escenario de un accidente.

**3 Pareen.**

To review **Palabras 2**, turn to pages 236–237.

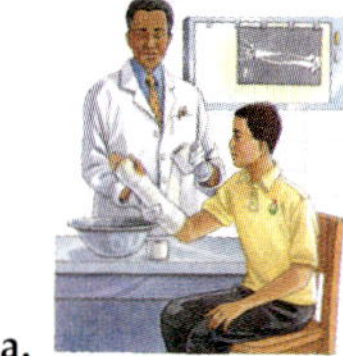
a.

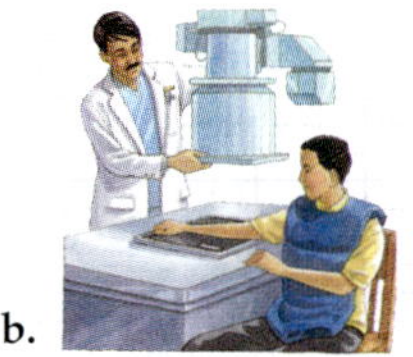
b.

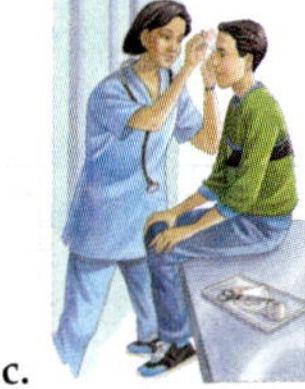
c.

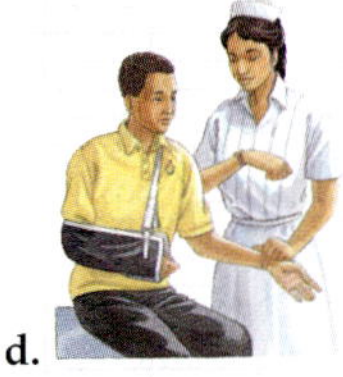
d.

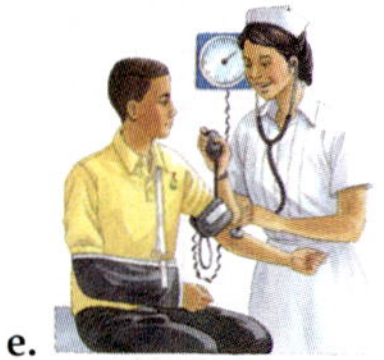
e.

8. ____ Le toma una radiografía.
9. ____ Le toma el pulso.
10. ____ Le pone el brazo en un yeso.
11. ____ Le toma la tensión arterial.
12. ____ Le pone un vendaje.



## Answers to Assessment

**1**
1. la cabeza
2. el brazo
3. el dedo
4. la rodilla
5. el pie

**2**
6. No
7. No

**3**
8. b
9. d
10. a
11. e
12. c

# Estructura

**4 Completen con el presente perfecto.**

13. Ellos ____. (salir)
14–15. Yo no ____ porque no ____ apetito. (comer, tener)
16. Nosotros ya ____ en Puerto Rico. (estar)
17. ¿Tú ____ a tu prima? (llamar)

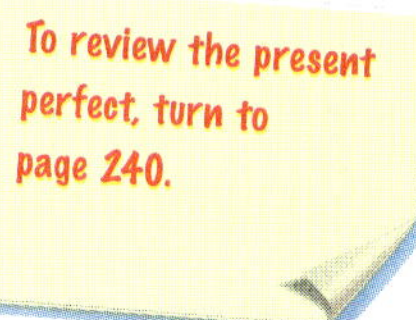

To review the present perfect, turn to page 240.

**5 Den el participio pasado.**

18. decir
19. ver
20. volver
21. abrir

To review irregular participles, turn to page 242.

**6 Completen.**

22–23. Él es ____ simpático ____ yo pero no tiene ____ paciencia ____ yo.
24. Ella tiene ____ trabajo ____ tú.

To review comparison of equality, turn to page 244.

# Cultura

**7 ¿Sí o no?**

25. Un(a) practicante es un(a) profesional en el campo de la medicina que hace mucho trabajo que hace el/la médico(a); sobre todo en las áreas rurales donde no hay muchos médicos.
26. Si un(a) paciente está muy enfermo(a), el/la practicante le puede operar.

To review this cultural information, turn to page 248.

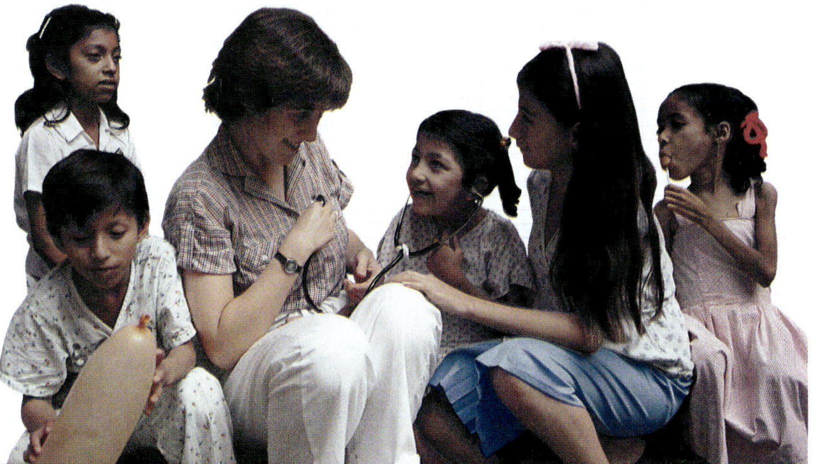



## Assessment

**FOLDABLES Study Organizer** **Dinah Zike's Study Guides**

Your students may wish to use Foldable 4 to organize, display, and arrange data as they expand their Spanish vocabulary. You may wish to encourage them to add information from each chapter as they continue to learn new words related to the different topics they will be studying.

A *vocabulary book* foldable is an ideal reference, especially as students begin to make word associations and write simple passages in Spanish.

Note: You may wish to have students store their foldables in a plastic bag in their notebooks.

## Answers to Assessment

**4**

13. han salido
14. he comido
15. he tenido
16. hemos estado
17. has llamado

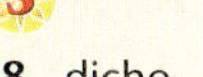
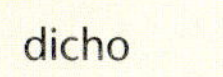

**5**

18. dicho
19. visto
20. vuelto
21. abierto

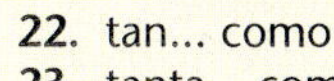

**6**

22. tan... como
23. tanta... como
24. tanto... como

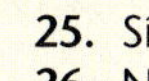
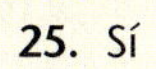

**7**

25. Sí
26. No

# ¡Hablo como un pro!

This unique page gives students the opportunity to speak freely and say whatever they can, using the vocabulary and structures they have learned in the chapter. The illustration serves to remind students of precisely what they know how to say in Spanish. There are no activities that students do not have the ability to describe or talk about in Spanish. The art not only depicts the vocabulary and content of this chapter, but also reinforces what they learned in previous chapters.

You may wish to use this page in many ways. Some possibilities are to have students do the following:

1. Look at the illustration and identify items by giving the correct Spanish words.
2. Make up sentences about what they see in the illustration.
3. Make up questions about the illustration. They can call on another class member to respond if you do this as a class activity, or you may prefer to allow students to work in small groups. This activity is extremely beneficial because it enables students to actively use interrogative words.
4. Answer questions you ask them about the illustration.
5. Work in pairs and make up a conversation based on the illustration.
6. Look at the illustration and give a complete oral review of what they see.
7. Look at the illustration and write a paragraph (or essay) about it.

You can also use this page as an assessment or testing tool, taking into account individual differences by having students go from simple to quite complicated tasks. The assessment can be either oral or written. You may wish to use the rubrics provided on pages T20–T21 as you give students the following directions.

1. Identify the topic or situation of the illustration.
2. Give the Spanish words for as many items as you can.
3. Think of as many sentences as you can to describe the illustration.
4. Go over your sentences and put them in the best sequencing to give a coherent story based on the illustration.

## ¡Hablo como un pro!

Tell all you can about this illustration.

# Vocabulario

### Talking about an accident

tener un accidente
hacerse daño, lastimarse
caerse
romperse
torcerse
cortarse
picar
ocurrir
tener lugar
acabar de

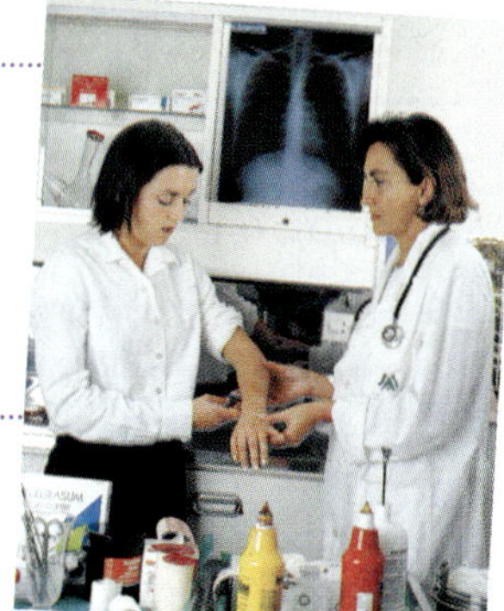

### Talking about medical emergencies and a hospital

el servicio de primeros auxilios
la ambulancia
la camilla
el hospital
la sala de emergencia, la sala de urgencias
la recepción
la silla de ruedas
las muletas
la víctima
llenar el formulario

### Talking about medical professionals

el/la médico(a)
el/la cirujano(a) ortopédico(a)
el/la enfermero(a)
el/la técnico(a)
el/la socorrista

**How well do you know your vocabulary?**

- Identify words that describe emergency room procedures.
- Write a few sentences about the steps a doctor takes to treat a medical emergency of your choice.

### Talking about medical problems

una fractura
una herida
una picadura
el dolor
hinchado(a)

### Talking about medical care

ayudar
doler
sentirse
tomar la tensión (presión) arterial
tomar el pulso
tomar una radiografía
tomar unos rayos equis
reducir el hueso
poner en un yeso
poner un vendaje
cerrar la herida
poner puntos (suturas)
parecer

### Identifying parts of the body

el cuerpo
el hombro
el brazo
el cuello
el pecho
el codo
la muñeca
el dedo
la pierna
la rodilla
el tobillo
el pie

### Identifying parts of the face

la cara
la frente
la mejilla
la nariz
el labio
el oído, la oreja
el ojo

**VIDEOTUR**

## Episodio 8

In this video episode, you will watch "daredevil" Vicky. See page 487 for more information.



# Vocabulario

## Vocabulary Review

The words and phrases in the **Vocabulario** have been taught for productive use in this chapter. They are summarized here as a resource for both student and teacher. This list also serves as a convenient resource for the **¡Te toca a ti!** activities on pages 254 and 255. There are approximately eight cognates in this vocabulary list. Have students find them.

**¡OJO!** You will notice that the vocabulary list here is not translated. This has been done intentionally, since we feel that by the time students have finished the material in the chapter they should be familiar with the meanings of all the words. If there are several words they still do not know, we recommend that they refer to the **Palabras 1** and **2** sections in the chapter or go to the dictionaries at the end of this book to find the meanings. However, if you prefer that your students have the English translations, please refer to Vocabulary Transparency 8.1, where you will find all these words with their translations.

**VIDEO VHS/DVD**

The Video Program allows students to see how the chapter vocabulary and structures are used by native speakers within an engaging story line. For maximum reinforcement, show the video episode as a final activity for Chapter 8.

## Reaching All Students

### For the Heritage Speakers

Have students write down any words they know from their own experience in the categories listed on the **Vocabulario** page. They could define their words and share them with the class.

# Planning for Chapter 9

## SCOPE AND SEQUENCE, PAGES 260–289

### Topics

- Life in the city
- Life in the country

### Culture

- Buenos Aires, Argentina
- Lima, Peru
- Santa Fe, New Mexico
- The demography of Latin America

### Functions

- How to get around in the city
- How to talk about common agricultural topics
- How to describe what was going on
- How to refer to things already mentioned
- How to point out people and things

### Structure

- The imperfect progressive
- Placement of object pronouns
- Demonstrative adjectives and pronouns

### National Standards

- Communication Standard 1.1 pages 264, 265, 268, 270, 271, 272, 273, 275, 277, 284
- Communication Standard 1.2 pages 265, 269, 271, 275, 276, 277, 278–279, 280, 281, 282–283, 284
- Communication Standard 1.3 page 285
- Cultures Standard 2.1 pages 278–279, 280
- Connections Standard 3.2 pages 282–283
- Comparisons Standard 4.2 pages 281, 282–283
- Communities Standard 5.1 page 289
- Communities Standard 5.2 page 269

## PACING AND PRIORITIES

**The chapter content is color coded below to assist you in planning.**

**■ required ■ recommended ■ optional**

**Vocabulario** *(required)* *Days 1–4*

- ■ Palabras 1
  - En la ciudad
  - La estación del metro
- ■ Palabras 2
  - En el campo

**Estructura** *(required)* *Days 5–7*

- ■ El imperfecto progresivo
- ■ Colocación de los pronombres de complemento
- ■ Adjetivos y pronombres demostrativos

**Conversación** *(required)*

- ■ El campo y la ciudad

**Lecturas culturales**

- ■ Buenos Aires, Argentina *(recommended)*
- ■ Lima, Perú *(optional)*
- ■ Una ciudad norteamericana con profundas raíces hispanas *(optional)*

**Conexiones**

- ■ La demografía *(optional)*

■ **¡Te toca a ti!** *(recommended)*

■ **Assessment** *(recommended)*

■ **¡Hablo como un pro!** *(optional)*

## RESOURCE GUIDE

| Section | Pages | Section Resources |
|---|---|---|
| **Vocabulario PALABRAS 1** | | |
| En la ciudad<br>La estación del metro | 262–265<br>263–265 | Vocabulary Transparencies 9.2–9.3<br>Audio CD 6<br>Audio Activities TE, pages 104–106<br>Workbook, pages 97–98<br>Quiz 1, page 40<br>ExamView® Pro |
| **Vocabulario PALABRAS 2** | | |
| En el campo | 266–269 | Vocabulary Transparencies 9.4–9.5<br>Audio CD 6<br>Audio Activities TE, pages 106–108<br>Workbook, pages 99–100<br>Quiz 2, page 41<br>ExamView® Pro |
| **Estructura** | | |
| El imperfecto progresivo<br>Colocación de los pronombres de complemento<br>Adjetivos y pronombres demostrativos | 270–271<br>272–273<br>274–275 | Audio CD 6<br>Audio Activities TE, pages 108–110<br>Workbook, pages 101–104<br>Quizzes 3–5, pages 42–44<br>ExamView® Pro |
| **Conversación** | | |
| El campo y la ciudad | 276–277 | Audio CD 6<br>Audio Activities TE, page 111<br>Interactive CD-ROM |
| **Lecturas culturales** | | |
| Buenos Aires, Argentina<br>Lima, Perú<br>Una ciudad norteamericana con profundas raíces hispanas | 278–279<br>280<br>281 | Audio CD 6<br>Audio Activities TE, page 112<br>Tests, pages 138, 141 |
| **Conexiones** | | |
| La demografía | 282–283 | Tests, page 142 |
| **¡Te toca a ti!** | | |
| | 284–285 | **¡Viva el mundo hispano!** Video, Episode 9<br>Video Activities, pages 97–100<br>Spanish Online Activities spanish.glencoe.com |
| **Assessment** | | |
| | 286–287 | Communication Transparency C 9<br>Quizzes 1–5, pages 40–44<br>Performance Assessment, Task 9<br>Tests, pages 135–148<br>Situation Cards, Chapter 9<br>ExamView® Pro<br>**Maratón mental** Videoquiz |

# Using Your Resources for Chapter 9

## Transparencies

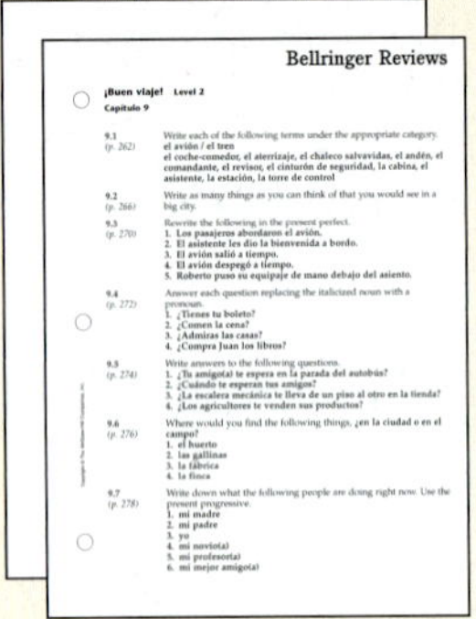
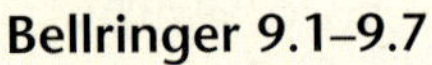
Bellringer 9.1–9.7

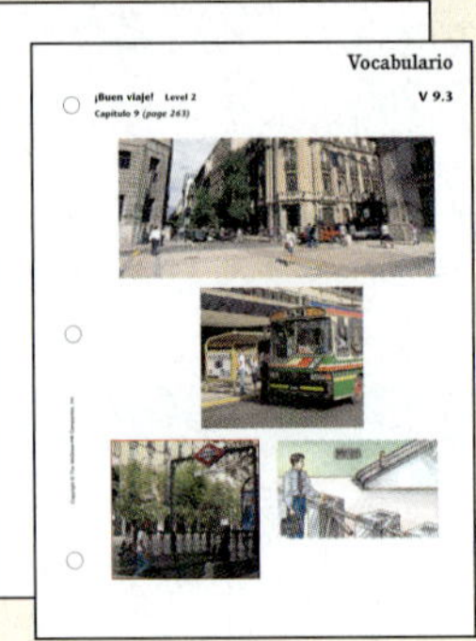
Vocabulary 9.1–9.5

Communication C 9

## Workbook

Vocabulary, pages 97–100

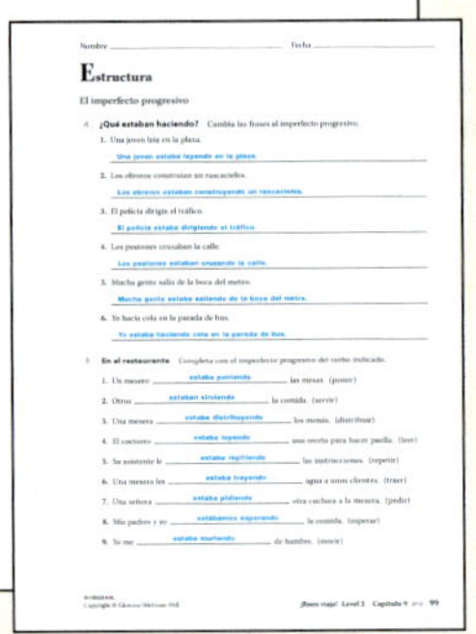
Structure, pages 101–104

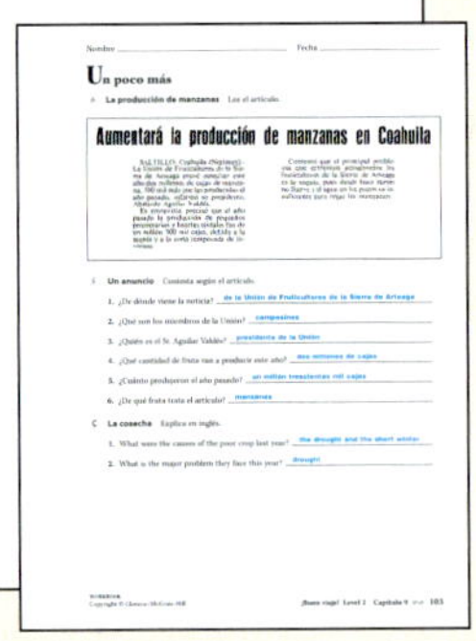
Enrichment, pages 105–108

## Audio Activities

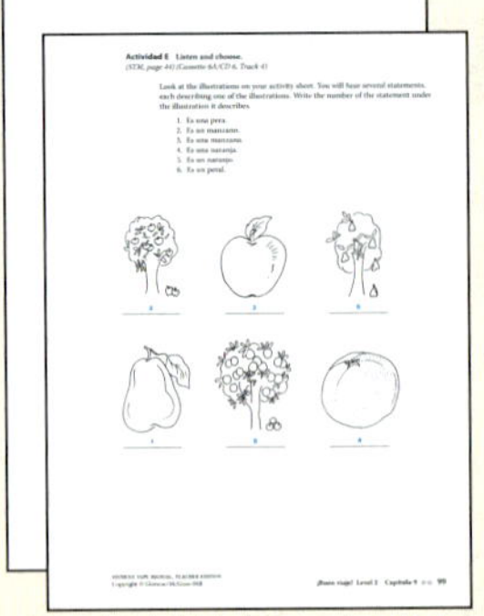
Vocabulary, pages 104–108

Structure, pages 108–110

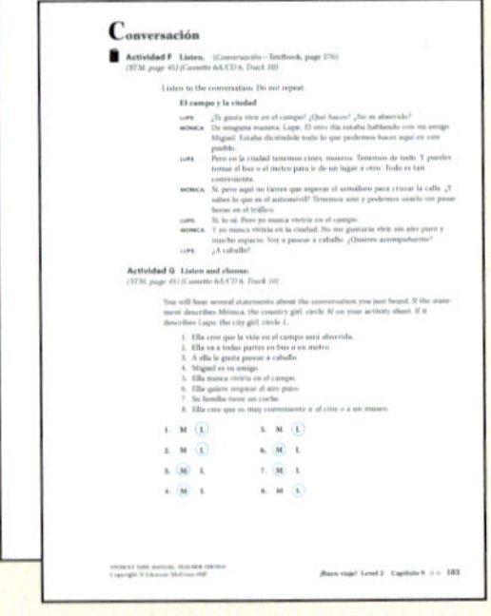
Conversation, page 111

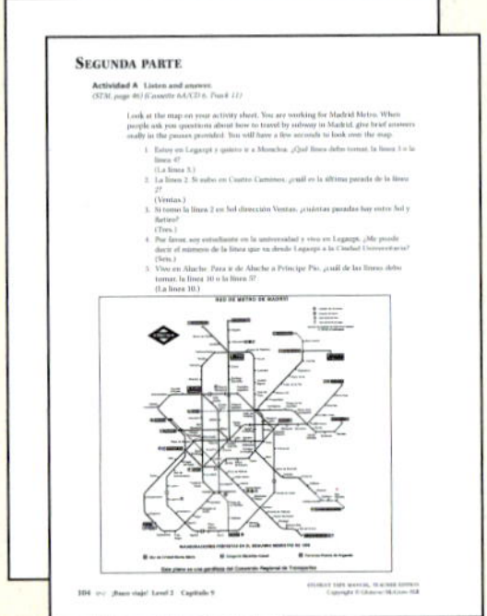
Additional Practice, pages 113–116

# Assessment

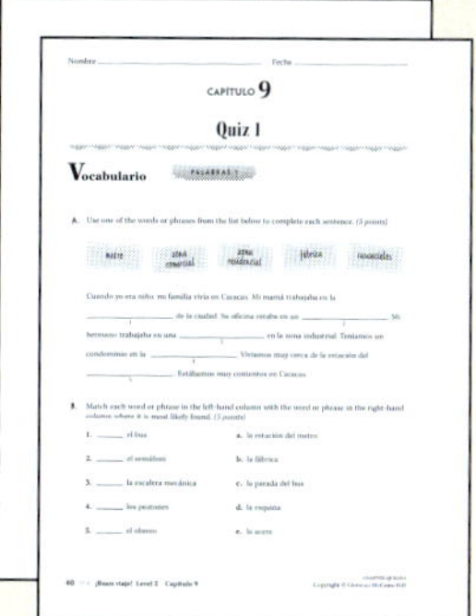
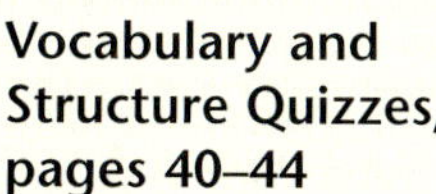

Vocabulary and Structure Quizzes, pages 40–44

Chapter Tests, pages 135–148

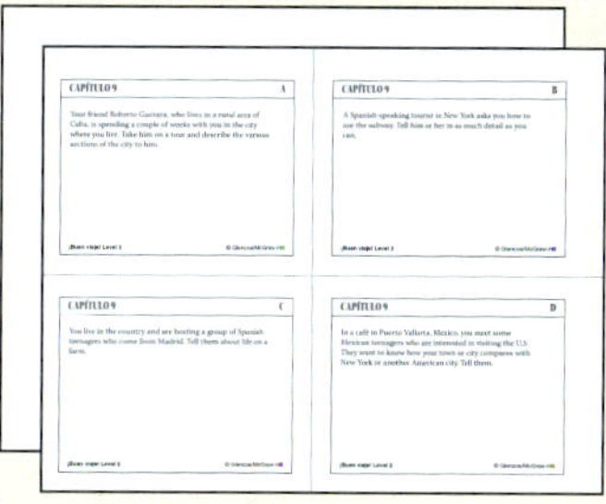

Situation Cards, Chapter 9

MindJogger Videoquiz, ExamView® Pro, Chapter 9

## Timesaving Teacher Tools

### TeacherWorks™

TeacherWorks™ is your all-in-one teacher resource center. Personalize lesson plans, access resources from the Teacher Wraparound Edition, connect to the Internet, or make a to-do list. These are only a few of the many features that can assist you in the planning and organizing of your lessons.

Includes:

- A calendar feature
- Access to all program blackline masters
- Standards correlations and more

### ExamView® Pro

Test Bank software for Macintosh and Windows makes creating, editing, customizing, and printing tests quick and easy.

## Technology Resources

In the Chapter 9 Internet Activity, you will have a chance to learn more about the Spanish-speaking world. Visit spanish.glencoe.com

On the interactive CD–ROM, students can listen to and take part in a recorded version of the conversation in Chapter 9.

**¡Viva el mundo hispano!** Video and Video Activities, Chapter 9. Available on VHS and DVD.

Help your students prepare for the chapter test by playing the **Maratón mental** Videoquiz game show. Teams will compete against each other to review chapter vocabulary and structure and sharpen listening comprehension skills. Available on VHS and DVD.

**¡Buen viaje!** is also available on CD or Online.

Capítulo 9

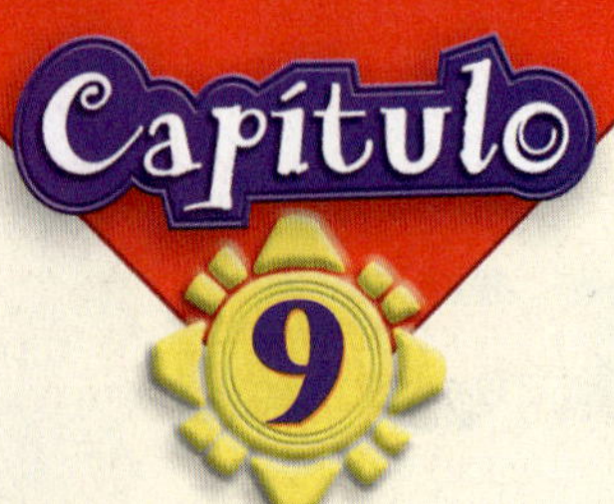

## Preview

In this chapter, students will learn to compare and contrast city and country life. Students will learn how to describe an action as it was taking place in the past, using the imperfect progressive tense. They will also expand their knowledge of how to refer to people and things already mentioned. In addition, they will learn to point out people or things by using demonstrative adjectives and pronouns.

The cultural focus of the chapter is on urban life in the Spanish-speaking world, in particular in Buenos Aires, Argentina, and Lima, Peru.

### National Standards

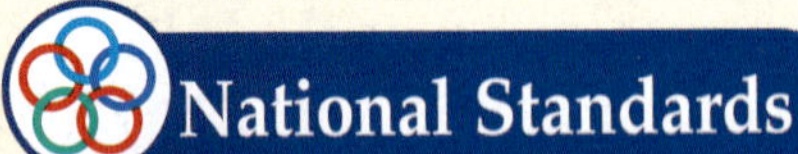

**Communication**

In Chapter 9 students will learn to communicate in spoken and written Spanish on the following topics:

- city life
- country life
- cities in the Spanish-speaking world

Students will obtain and provide information about these topics and engage in conversations that would typically take place in urban or rural settings as they fulfill the chapter objectives listed on this page.

Capítulo 9

# Ciudad y campo

### Objetivos

**In this chapter you will learn to:**

- **talk about life in the city**
- **talk about life in the country**
- **describe things that were happening**
- **refer to things already mentioned**
- **indicate where things are located**
- **talk about some cities in the Spanish-speaking world**

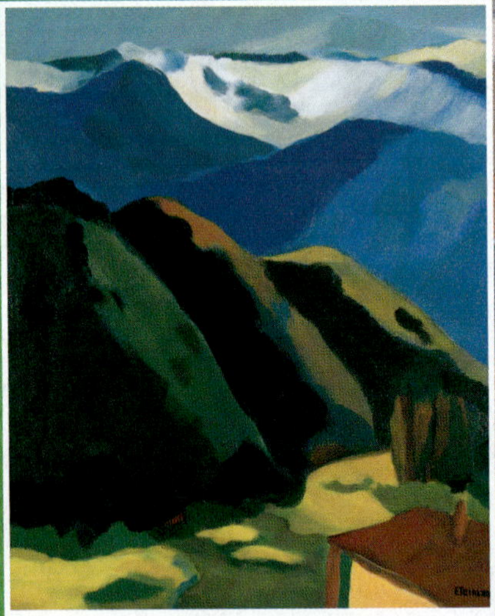

María Eugenia Terrazas *Inmensidad cordillerana*

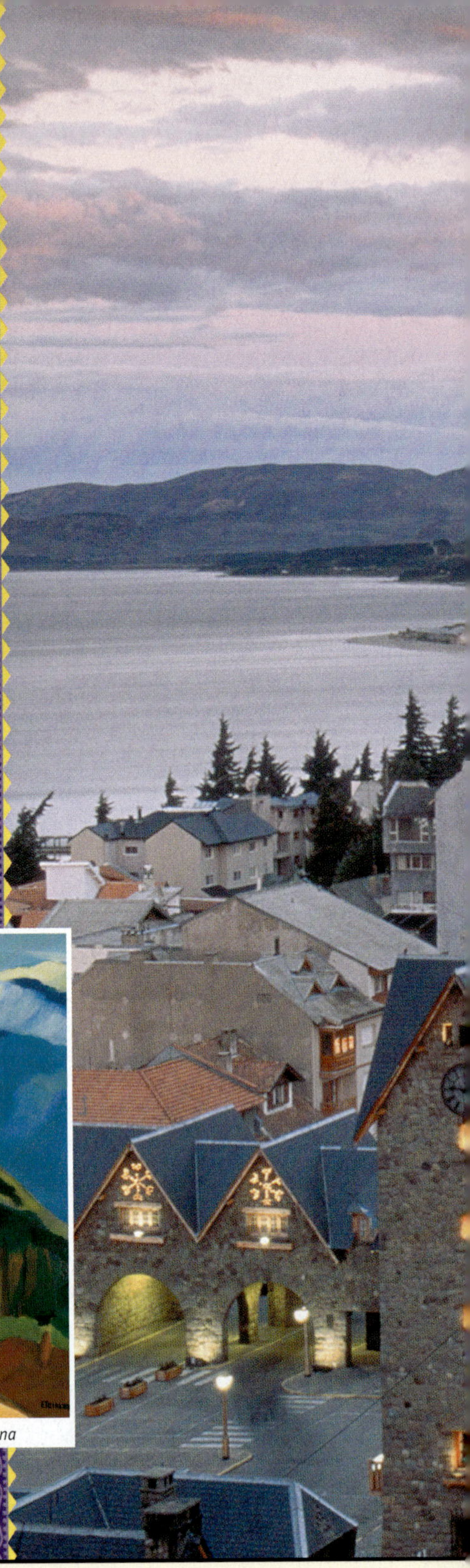

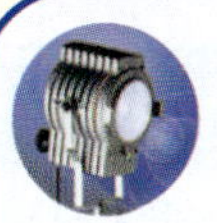

## Spotlight on Culture

**Fotografía** San Carlos de Bariloche is located in the very northern part of the Argentine Patagonia. Bariloche, in the beautiful lake region, is a year-round resort. Skiing is popular in the winter and the famous Snow Festival is held every August. Fishing is popular from mid-November to mid-March. The lakes are well stocked with several types of trout and salmon. Campers, swimmers, anglers, and other fans of the outdoors flock to Bariloche in the summer. Many people compare Bariloche to a Swiss village.

## LEVELING

The activities, conversations, and readings within each chapter are marked according to level of difficulty. **E** indicates easy. **A** indicates average. **C** indicates challenging. Some activities cover a range of difficulty. In some activities, for example, advanced students will be able to produce more extensive responses while students who learn at a different rate may give less detailed responses. The leveling indicators will help you individualize instruction to best meet your students' needs.

# Vocabulario

PALABRAS 1

## 1 PREPARATION

### Resource Manager

Vocabulary Transparencies 9.2–9.3
Audio Activities TE, pages 104–106
Audio CD 6
Workbook, pages 97–98
Quizzes, page 40
ExamView® Pro

### Bellringer Review

*Use BRR Transparency 9.1 or write the following on the board.*
Write each of the following terms under the appropriate category.
**el avión / el tren**
**el coche-comedor, el aterrizaje, el chaleco salvavidas, el andén, el comandante, el revisor, el cinturón de seguridad, la cabina, el asistente, la estación, la torre de control**

## 2 PRESENTATION

**Step 1** Have students close their books. Project Vocabulary Transparencies 9.2–9.3 to present the **Palabras 1** vocabulary. Model each new word or expression and have students repeat them two or three times after you or Audio CD 6.

**Step 2** When the new words are used in sentences, ask questions about each sentence: **¿Dónde hay muchas oficinas? ¿Qué más hay en una zona comercial? ¿Es alto un rascacielos?**

**LEVELING**
**E:** Vocabulary

# Vocabulario

PALABRAS 1

## En la ciudad

En la zona comercial hay muchas oficinas y tiendas.
Eran las siete y media de la tarde y mucha gente estaba saliendo de sus oficinas.

La zona industrial está en las afueras de la ciudad.
Los obreros estaban trabajando todo el día en la fábrica.

En la zona residencial hay muchos apartamentos (departamentos) y condominios.
Hay pocas casas privadas.

Muchas calles y avenidas desembocan en la plaza.
Las avenidas son anchas.

Esta calle o callecita angosta es muy pintoresca.
Está en el barrio viejo de la ciudad.



## Reaching All Students

**Total Physical Response**
*(Student 1)*, **ven acá, por favor.**
**Estás en la ciudad hoy.**
**Camina en la acera.**
**Ve a la esquina.**
**Espera en la esquina. El semáforo está rojo.**
**El semáforo está verde ahora. Cruza la calle en el cruce de peatones.**
**Ve a la boca del metro.**
**Baja la escalera mecánica.**
**Mete tu tique en la ranura del torniquete.**
**Sube al metro.**
**Gracias,** *(Student 1)*. **Puedes regresar a tu asiento.**

Hay un semáforo en la esquina
Los peatones caminan en la acera.
Cruzan la calle en el cruce de peatones.

La gente estaba esperando en la parada del bus.

## La estación del metro

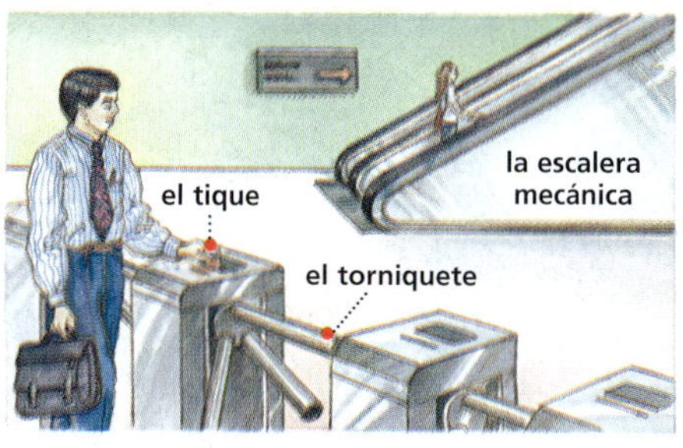


La señorita estaba subiendo la escalera mecánica.
El señor estaba metiendo el tique en la ranura del torniquete.



**Step 3** After presenting the vocabulary orally, have students open their books and read for additional reinforcement.

**Step 4** Call a student to the front of the room. Show the Vocabulary Transparencies again. Have the student play teacher and ask questions about what he or she sees in the illustrations and photos.

### Learning from Photos

*(page 262 bottom right)* The street scene pictured in the photo is from one of the picturesque **Pueblos Blancos** of Andalucía. What can be seen in the photo are:

| | |
|---|---|
| **macetas** | *flowerpots* |
| **balcones** | *balconies* |
| **un escudo** | *heraldic shield* |
| **rejas** | *iron grilles on the windows* |

### About the Spanish Language

- **Un plano** is a map or diagram of a city, town, fortress, park, or similar area. **Un mapa** is a *road map* or map of a relatively large geographic area, a province or state, for example.
- **El semáforo** is also called **la luz roja** in many places.
- **Un torniquete** is, of course, a *turnstile,* but it is also the word for *tourniquet,* the bandage used to stop bleeding.
- In Mexico a *bus* is **un camión,** in Puerto Rico it's **una guagua,** in Spain it's **un autobús.** In other places it may be called **un bus, un ómnibus** or **un colectivo.** In Chile **una guagua** is a *baby.* In Spain, a *long-distance bus* is **un autocar.**

### Reaching All Students

**Additional Practice** Give students the following definitions and have them supply the correct words.

1. **un edificio muy alto, que tiene muchos pisos**
2. **donde trabajan los obreros para hacer o manufacturar productos**
3. **una calle pequeña y angosta**
4. **una casa donde vive sólo una familia**
5. **donde se encuentran dos calles**
6. **donde cruzan los peatones la calle**
7. **donde se puede subir a un autobús o bajar de un autobús**
8. **la entrada del metro**

## 3 PRACTICE

## ¿Qué palabra necesito?

**¡OJO!** When students are doing the **¿Que palabra necesito?** activities, accept any answer that makes sense. The purpose of these activities is to have students use the new vocabulary. They are not factual recall activities. Thus, it is not necessary for students to remember specific factual information from the vocabulary presentation when answering. If you wish, have students use the visuals on this page as a stimulus, when possible.

**Teaching Tip**

It is recommended that you go over the activities before assigning them for homework.

**1** This activity can be done first orally with books closed.

**Expansion:** After going over Activity 1, call on a student to tell all about **el señor Salas** in his or her own words.

**2** Have students refer to the illustration to do Activity 2.

### Writing Development

Have students write the information in Activity 2 in an organized paragraph, as a description of a city scene.



## ¿Qué palabra necesito?

### 1 Historieta El señor Salas de Caracas

Contesten.

1. ¿Estaba viviendo el señor Salas en Caracas?
2. ¿Tenía un apartamento en una zona residencial de la ciudad?
3. ¿Estaba su apartamento en un edificio alto?
4. ¿Trabajaba él en una oficina cerca de la Plaza Simón Bolívar?
5. ¿Estaba su oficina en un rascacielos?
6. ¿Tomaba el señor Salas el metro a su trabajo?
7. ¿Había una boca de metro cerca de su apartamento?
8. ¿Compraba el señor Salas tiques para el metro?

Caracas, Venezuela

### 2 El plano de la ciudad

Contesten según el dibujo.

1. ¿Desembocan muchas calles en la Plaza San Martín?
2. ¿Es ancha o angosta la calle Mina?
3. ¿Hay un semáforo en la esquina de Mina y Luz?
4. ¿Hay una parada de bus en la plaza?
5. ¿Hay muchos coches en la plaza?
6. ¿Hay peatones en la acera?



## Answers to ¿Qué palabra necesito?

**1**

1. Sí, el señor Salas estaba viviendo en Caracas.
2. Sí, (No, no) tenía un apartamento en una zona residencial de la ciudad.
3. Sí (No), su apartamento (no) estaba en un edificio alto.
4. Sí (No), él (no) trabajaba en una oficina cerca de la Plaza Simón Bolívar.
5. Sí (No), su oficina (no) estaba en un rascacielos.
6. Sí (No), el señor Salas (no) tomaba el metro a su trabajo.
7. Sí, (No, no) había una boca de metro cerca de su apartamento.
8. Sí (No), el señor Salas (no) compraba tiques para el metro.

**2**

1. Sí, muchas calles desembocan en la Plaza San Martín.
2. La calle Mina es angosta.
3. No, no hay un semáforo en la esquina de Mina y Luz.
4. No, no hay una parada de bus en la plaza.
5. No, no hay muchos coches en la plaza.
6. No, no hay peatones en la acera.

## 3 En la ciudad Digan que sí o que no.

1. Frecuentemente el barrio viejo de una ciudad es también una zona histórica.
2. Una zona comercial de una ciudad tiene muchas fábricas.
3. La zona industrial siempre se encuentra en el centro mismo de la ciudad.
4. Un obrero trabaja en una oficina.
5. Hay muchas oficinas en la zona comercial de la ciudad.
6. Un rascacielos es un edificio muy alto que tiene muchos apartamentos u oficinas.
7. Los semáforos se encuentran por lo general en una esquina y ayudan a controlar el tráfico.
8. La gente espera el bus en la boca del metro.
9. Los peatones caminan en la calle.
10. Los peatones pueden cruzar la calle en el cruce de peatones.

La Habana, Cuba

## 4 El transporte en la ciudad Contesten.

1. ¿Qué toman los pasajeros para bajar y subir de una estación de metro?
2. ¿Dónde meten los pasajeros el tique antes de abordar el metro?
3. ¿Dónde esperan los pasajeros el bus?
4. ¿Dónde caminan los peatones?
5. ¿Dónde pueden cruzar la calle los peatones?

Santiago, Chile

## 5 Una ciudad cercana Trabaja con un(a) compañero(a). Si ustedes viven en una ciudad, conversen juntos y describan su ciudad. Si no viven en una ciudad, hablen de una ciudad que han visitado cerca de donde viven.

## 6 Opiniones Trabaja con un(a) compañero(a). Discutan lo que ustedes consideran las ventajas y las desventajas de la vida en una ciudad. ¿Están ustedes de acuerdo o no?

## Answers to ¿Qué palabra necesito?

**3**

| | |
|---|---|
| 1. Sí | 6. Sí |
| 2. No | 7. Sí |
| 3. No | 8. No |
| 4. No | 9. No |
| 5. Sí | 10. Sí |

**4**

1. Toman la escalera mecánica.
2. Meten el tique en la ranura del torniquete.
3. Los pasajeros esperan el bus en la parada del bus.
4. Los peatones caminan en la acera.
5. Pueden cruzar la calle en el cruce de peatones.

**5** *Answers will vary. Students will use the vocabulary from* Palabras 1 *to describe their city or one nearby.*

**6** *Answers will vary. Students will use the vocabulary from* Palabras 1 *to write their opinions.*

# Vocabulario

**3** Have students correct any false statements in Activity 3.

**4** Activity 4 can be done first orally with books closed.

### Writing Development

After going over Activity 4, have students write a short paragraph about urban transportation.

**¡OJO!** Note that the activities are color-coded. All the activities in the text are communicative. However, the ones with blue titles are guided communication. The red titles indicate that the answers to the activity are more open-ended and can vary more. You may wish to correct students' mistakes more so in the guided activities than in the activities with a red title, which lend themselves to a freer response.

**5 and 6** One student in each pair should take notes about the discussion and report to the class.

### Learning from Photos

*(page 265 top)* **La Habana** is the capital of Cuba and one of the oldest cities in the Americas. It was founded in 1514 and named **San Cristóbal de la Habana.**
*(page 265 bottom)* Today Santiago, the capital of Chile, is a mixture of grand colonial buildings and modern corporate high-rises. However, because Santiago is in an earthquake zone, skyscrapers are not as tall as those in other cities.

## 1 PREPARATION

### Resource Manager

Vocabulary Transparencies 9.4–9.5
Audio Activities TE, pages 106–108
Audio CD 6
Workbook, pages 99–100
Quizzes, page 41
ExamView® Pro

### Bellringer Review

*Use BRR Transparency 9.2 or write the following on the board.*
Write as many things as you can think of that you would see in a big city.

## 2 PRESENTATION

**Step 1** To present the vocabulary, you may wish to follow some suggestions presented in previous chapters, using Vocabulary Transparencies 9.4–9.5 and Audio CD 6.

**Step 2** Point to the appropriate visual on the Vocabulary Transparencies and begin by asking *yes / no* and *either / or* questions and then progress to more open-ended ones such as: **¿Qué está sembrando el campesino? ¿En qué estación va a cosechar los cereales? ¿Qué animales crían los agricultores?**

**Step 3** After presenting the vocabulary orally, have students open their books and read the sentences for additional reinforcement.

# Vocabulario

PALABRAS 2

## En el campo

el campesino
una casa de campo
un pueblo pequeño
el campo
una finca

Los campesinos viven en el campo.
Ellos tienen una finca.
Ellos cultivan los campos.

El cultivo de los cereales es muy importante.

El campesino va a sembrar cereales.
No está sembrándolos ahora.
Va a sembrarlos en la primavera.

Y va a cosecharlos en el otoño.



### Reaching All Students

**Total Physical Response**
*(Student 1)*, ven acá, por favor.
Vas a ser campesino(a).
Da de comer a las gallinas.
Ve al campo.
Siembra los cereales.
Ve a la huerta.
Cosecha los vegetales.
Vuelve a tu casa de campo.
Gracias, *(Student 1)*. Bien hecho. Regresa a tu asiento ahora.

Los agricultores crían animales domésticos.

el ganado

las vacas

los cerdos

las gallinas

## Vocabulary Expansion

**El ganado** is the generic word for *livestock,* but there are different kinds of **ganado:**

| | |
|---|---|
| **ganado vacuno** | *beef or dairy cattle* |
| **ganado porcino** | *hogs* |
| **ganado ovino** | *sheep* |

## Learning from Photos

*(pages 266–267)* You may wish to ask students the following questions about the photos:

**¿Qué llevan en la cabeza el campesino en la foto de abajo en la página 266 y el campesino en la foto en la página 267? (una boina)**

**¿Qué animal tiene el campesino en la foto?**

**¿Qué ropa lleva el campesino?**

## Chapter Projects

**¿Prefieres la ciudad o el campo?** Have students choose a Spanish-speaking city or town that they would like to live in, according to whether they prefer urban or rural life. Have them prepare a report on their city or town and ask them to explain why they selected it. Students should include photos and maps of the city or town in their report, if possible. The Internet is a good source for this information.

**LEVELING**

**E:** Activities 1, 2, 3, 4, 5

**A:** Activities 3, 4, 5, 6

## Vocabulary Expansion

- **El campo** is both the *country* or the *countryside* and a *field,* **un campo de trigo,** for example.
- The people who work on farms are also called **labradores.**
- **Un pueblo pequeño** can also be called **una aldea.**
- In some parts of South America **el maíz** is called **el choclo.**

## 3 PRACTICE

## ¿Qué palabra necesito?

**7** Activity 7 can be done first orally with books closed. Students can then write the answers for additional reinforcement.
**Expansion:** After going over this activity, have students tell the story about **los Ayala** in their own words.

**8** Activity 8 has students review and recall a great deal of previously learned vocabulary.

### Learning from Photos

*(page 268 top)* Echalar is a town in the region of Navarra, in the province of Pamplona. The provincial capital, Pamplona, is famous for the yearly running of the bulls the week of July 7. *(page 268 bottom)* Andalucía is one of Spain's most important agricultural regions. It is a major producer of olives and olive oil, wheat and other cereals, cotton, sugar cane, citrus fruits, and wine.

Have students locate each of the areas shown in the photographs on the map of Spain on page xxx or on Map Transparency M 2.

Vocabulario

## ¿Qué palabra necesito?

Echalar, España

**7 Historieta Los Ayala**
Contesten según se indica.

1. ¿Dónde viven los Ayala? (en un pueblo pequeño en el campo)
2. ¿Qué tienen ellos? (una finca)
3. ¿Qué hay en la finca? (campos de cereales)
4. ¿Qué siembran los Ayala? (trigo y maíz)
5. ¿Cuándo siembran? (en la primavera)
6. ¿Cuándo es la cosecha? (en el otoño)
7. ¿Qué crían los Ayala en su finca? (animales domésticos)
8. ¿Qué animales tienen? (vacas y cerdos)

**8 Ya sabemos mucho.** Contesten.

1. ¿Cuáles son todos los vegetales o todas las legumbres que ya conoces en español?
2. ¿Cuáles son las frutas que ya conoces en español?
3. ¿Cuáles son los animales que ya conoces en español?
4. ¿Cuáles son las cuatro estaciones del año?

Andalucía, España



## ANSWERS TO ¿Qué palabra necesito?

**7**

1. Los Ayala viven en un pueblo pequeño en el campo.
2. Ellos tienen una finca.
3. En la finca hay campos de cereales.
4. Los Ayala siembran trigo y maíz.
5. Siembran en la primavera.
6. La cosecha es en el otoño.
7. Los Ayala crían animales domésticos en su finca.
8. Tienen vacas y cerdos.

**8** *Answers will vary but may include:*

1. vegetales: los tomates, las zanahorias, las habichuelas, etc.
2. frutas: las manzanas, las peras, las naranjas, etc.
3. animales: la vaca, el cerdo, la gallina, etc.
4. estaciones: la primavera, el verano, el otoño, el invierno

## 9 Cosas del campo Digan que sí o que no.

1. Las vacas nos dan leche.
2. Las gallinas ponen huevos.
3. El tomate es un vegetal.
4. Hay muchas fincas en la ciudad.
5. Los obreros son campesinos.
6. Los campesinos cultivan los campos en una fábrica.
7. El manzano es un árbol y la manzana es la fruta que da el árbol.
8. Una carne que nos da el cerdo es el jamón.
9. Los campesinos viven en una casa de campo.
10. Una huerta produce muchos vegetales.

## 10 En el campo No importa si vives en el campo o no.

A casi todos nosotros nos gusta de vez en cuando pasar un día tranquilo en el campo. Trabaja con un(a) compañero(a). Describan un día fabuloso en el campo. Hablen de lo que ven y lo que hacen.

## 11 Opiniones Trabaja con un(a) compañero(a). Discutan lo que ustedes consideran las ventajas y las desventajas de la vida en el campo. ¿Están ustedes de acuerdo o no? ¿Quién preferiría vivir en el campo?

For more information about the countryside of Mexico and other countries in the Spanish-speaking world, go to the Glencoe Spanish Web site: spanish.glencoe.com

Oaxaca, México

Sinaloa, México

*For more practice using words from **Palabras 1** and **2**, do Activity 9 on page H10 at the end of this book.*



## Vocabulario

**9** Whenever possible, have students correct the false statements.

**11** You may wish to have students share their opinions in this activity with the entire class.

### LEVELING

**E:** Activities 7, 8, 9, 10

**A:** Activities 7, 9, 10, 11

**C:** Activity 11

### Learning from Photos

*(page 269 left)* Oaxaca is in southern Mexico. The villages surrounding Oaxaca are famous for their artisans. Near Oaxaca are two extraordinary pre-Columbian sites, Monte Albán and Mitla.

*(page 269 right)* The state of Sinaloa is on the northern Mexican Pacific coast. Mazatlán is the major city as well the major seaport. The climate of Sinaloa is varied. Near the coast it is warm and wet most of the year. Nearer the mountains the weather is cooler. Near Sonora it's a semidesert.

This *InfoGap* Activity will allow students to practice in pairs. The activity should be very manageable for them, since all vocabulary and structures are familiar to them.

## Answers to ¿Qué palabra necesito?

**9**

1. Sí
2. Sí
3. No
4. No
5. No
6. No
7. Sí
8. Sí
9. Sí
10. Sí

**10** *Answers will vary. Students will use vocabulary learned in* Palabras 2 *to describe a fantastic day in the country.*

**11** *Answers will vary. Students will use vocabulary relating to the country to make their lists.*

# Estructura

## 1 PREPARATION

### Resource Manager

Audio Activities TE, pages 108–110
Audio CD 6
Workbook, pages 101–104
Quizzes, pages 42–44
ExamView® Pro

### Bellringer Review

*Use BRR Transparency 9.3 or write the following on the board.*
Rewrite the following in the present perfect.

1. **Los pasajeros abordaron el avión.**
2. **El asistente les dio la bienvenida a bordo.**
3. **El avión salió a tiempo.**
4. **El avión despegó a tiempo.**
5. **Roberto puso su equipaje de mano debajo del asiento.**

## 2 PRESENTATION

### El imperfecto progresivo

**Step 1** Have students open their books to page 270. Lead them through Items 1–3. Model the examples and have students repeat.

**Step 2** Write the forms of the verb **estar** on the board in the present, imperfect, and future tenses.

**Step 3** Add the present participles to the forms of **estar** and have students repeat the forms of the progressive tenses.

# Estructura

## El imperfecto progresivo
### Describing what was going on

1. The imperfect progressive is used to describe an action as it was taking place. It is formed by using the imperfect tense of **estar** and the present participle.

   **El obrero estaba trabajando en la fábrica.**
   **Los muchachos estaban comiendo las frutas del huerto.**

2. Most verbs that have a stem change in the preterite have the same stem change in the present participle.

| E → I | | O → U | |
|---|---|---|---|
| pedir | pidiendo | dormir | durmiendo |
| servir | sirviendo | morir | muriendo |
| repetir | repitiendo | | |
| decir | diciendo | | |

3. The following verbs have a **y** in the present participle.

| | | | |
|---|---|---|---|
| caer | cayendo | distribuir | distribuyendo |
| leer | leyendo | construir | construyendo |
| traer | trayendo | contribuir | contribuyendo |
| oír | oyendo | | |

**¿Te acuerdas?**

The present progressive is used to describe events actually taking place.
**El obrero está saliendo de la fábrica.**
**El campesino está cultivando los campos.**

## ¿Qué palabra necesito?

**Historieta Un día típico en la ciudad**

Contesten con **sí**.

1. ¿Estaba circulando mucho tráfico por la ciudad?
2. ¿Estaba dirigiendo el tráfico un policía?
3. ¿Estaban caminando por las aceras muchos peatones?
4. ¿Estaban cruzando las calles?
5. ¿Estaban cruzando las calles en el cruce de peatones?
6. ¿Estaba haciendo cola mucha gente en la parada del bus?
7. ¿Estaba saliendo mucha gente de la boca del metro?
8. ¿Estaba subiendo mucha gente en la escalera mecánica?

Madrid, España



## Answers to ¿Cómo lo digo?

1. Sí, mucho tráfico estaba circulando por la ciudad.
2. Sí, un policía estaba dirigiendo el tráfico.
3. Sí, muchos peatones estaban caminando por las aceras.
4. Sí, estaban cruzando las calles.
5. Sí, estaban cruzando las calles en el cruce de peatones.
6. Sí, mucha gente estaba haciendo cola en la parada del bus.
7. Sí, mucha gente estaba saliendo de la boca del metro.
8. Sí, mucha gente estaba subiendo en la escalera mecánica.

## 13 Historieta Durante el vuelo

Contesten según el modelo.

1. ¿Servían refrescos los asistentes de vuelo?
2. ¿Servían una comida?
3. ¿Daban anuncios?
4. ¿Leían las reglas de seguridad?
5. ¿Oían música estereofónica los pasajeros?
6. ¿Leían revistas algunos pasajeros?
7. ¿Dormían otros?

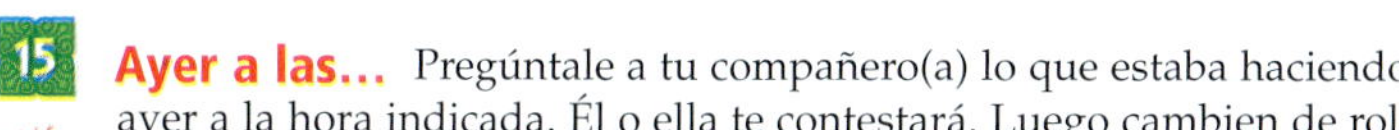

## 14 Historieta El túnel nuevo

Completen con el imperfecto progresivo.

Los ingenieros __1__ (construir) el túnel nuevo. El público __2__ (esperar) la apertura del túnel. Muchos hombres y mujeres __3__ (trabajar) en su construcción. Este proyecto les __4__ (pagar) un buen salario. Pero algunas personas __5__ (decir) que no era buena idea. Ellos __6__ (pensar) en el impacto ecológico del túnel. Pero nadie __7__ (escuchar) a los ecologistas. El público __8__ (ver) que con el túnel los viajes al centro serían más cortos.

## 15 Ayer a las...

Pregúntale a tu compañero(a) lo que estaba haciendo ayer a la hora indicada. Él o ella te contestará. Luego cambien de rol.

## 16 Tienes un problema.

Un(a) compañero(a) va a ser tu padre o tu madre. Está muy enfadado(a) *(angry)* porque tú volviste a casa muy tarde anoche. Él o ella tiene muchas preguntas para ti. Tienes que decirle todo lo que estabas haciendo para explicar por qué no podías volver a casa más temprano. Luego cambien de rol.



# Estructura

## 3 PRACTICE

## ¿Cómo lo digo?

**12** This activity can be done first orally while books are closed.

### Paired Activity

Activity 13 can be done as a paired activity. One student asks the question and the other student answers.

**14** You may wish to have students prepare this activity before going over it in class.

### Writing Development

After going over Activity 14, have students write it in paragraph form.

### Reaching All Students

**For the Heritage Speakers** Ask your students to do Activities 15 and 16, changing the verbs in the **imperfecto progresivo** to the **futuro progresivo** and the **condicional progresivo:** **¿Estará circulando... ? ¿Estaría circulando... ?**

**15** Encourage students to use all the cues in the colored boxes.

**16** **Expansion:** Students could prepare funny skits based on this activity and present them to the class.

### LEVELING

**E:** Activities 12, 15

**A:** Activities 13, 14, 15, 16

**C:** Activity 16

## Answers to ¿Cómo lo digo?

**13**

1. Sí, estaban sirviendo refrescos.
2. Sí, estaban sirviendo una comida.
3. Sí, estaban dando anuncios.
4. Sí, estaban leyendo las reglas de seguridad.
5. Sí, los pasajeros estaban oyendo música estereofónica.
6. Sí, algunos pasajeros estaban leyendo revistas.
7. Sí, otros estaban durmiendo.

**14**

1. estaban construyendo
2. estaba esperando
3. estaban trabajando
4. estaba pagando
5. estaban diciendo
6. estaban pensando
7. estaba escuchando
8. estaba viendo

**15** *Answers will vary. Students will answer in the imperfect progressive tense for the times provided.*

**16** *Answers will vary, but students will use the imperfect progressive tense to make up their excuses.*

# Estructura

## 1 PREPARATION

### Bellringer Review

*Use BRR Transparency 9.4 or write the following on the board.*
Answer each question replacing the italicized noun with a pronoun.
1. ¿Tienes tu *boleto*?
2. ¿Comen la *cena*?
3. ¿Admiras las *casas*?
4. ¿Compra Juan los *libros*?

## 2 PRESENTATION

### Colocación de los pronombres de complemento

**Step 1** Ask students to open their books to page 272. Lead them through Items 1–2.

**Step 2** Students should realize that the pronouns are often attached to the participle. For productive purposes, however, they need only place them before the auxiliary.

## 3 PRACTICE

### ¿Cómo lo digo?

**17** and **18** It is recommended that these activities be done with books open. You may wish to have students prepare these activities before going over them in class.

# Estructura

## Colocación de los pronombres de complemento
### Referring to things already mentioned

1. When the object pronouns are used with the present participle, they may precede the helping verb or they may be attached to the participle.

| | |
|---|---|
| **Estaban comiendo el maíz.** | **Me estaba mostrando la finca.** |
| **Lo estaban comiendo.** | **Me la estaba mostrando.** |
| **Estaban comiéndolo.** | **Estaba mostrándomela.** |

2. When the object pronouns are used with the infinitive, they may precede the helping verb that accompanies the infinitive or they may be attached to the infinitive.

| | |
|---|---|
| **Voy a cruzar la calle.** | **Voy a dar el plano a José.** |
| **La voy a cruzar.** | **Se lo voy a dar.** |
| **Voy a cruzarla.** | **Voy a dárselo.** |

**¿Lo sabes?**

To maintain the same stress, a participle carries a written accent when either one or two pronouns are attached to it.
**Está sirviéndolo.**
**Está sirviéndomelo.**

**¿Lo sabes?**

To maintain the same stress, an infinitive carries a written accent only when two pronouns are attached to it.
**Quiere darme el plano.**
**Quiere dármelo.**

## ¿Qué palabra necesito?

### 17 Historieta En la finca

Contesten según el modelo.

**¿Estaba mostrándote la finca el señor? →**
**Sí, estaba mostrándomela.**
**Sí, me la estaba mostrando.**

1. ¿Estaba mostrándote la casa de campo el señor?
2. ¿Te estaba describiendo la casa?
3. ¿Estabas admirando la casa?
4. ¿Estabas mirando a los campesinos en la finca?
5. ¿Estaban ellos sembrando los campos?
6. ¿Estaban criando los animales también?

### 18 Buena higiene

Sigan el modelo.

**Me voy a lavar *el pelo*. →**
**Voy a lavármelo.**

1. Me voy a lavar *el pelo*.
2. Quiero comprarme *el nuevo champú* en la farmacia.
3. No puedo recordar *el nombre del champú*.
4. El farmacéutico podrá darme *el nombre*.
5. Tengo que lavarme *el pelo* esta noche.



## Answers to ¿Cómo lo digo?

**17**

1. Sí, estaba mostrándomela. Sí, me la estaba mostrando.
2. Sí, estaba describiéndomela. Sí, me la estaba describiendo.
3. Sí, estaba admirándola. Sí, la estaba admirando.
4. Sí, estaba mirándolos en la finca. Sí, los estaba mirando en la finca.
5. Sí, estaban sembrándolos. Sí, los estaban sembrando.
6. Sí, estaban criándolos también. Sí, los estaban criando también.

**18**

1. Voy a lavármelo.
2. Quiero comprármelo en la farmacia.
3. No puedo recordarlo.
4. El farmacéutico podrá dármelo.
5. Tengo que lavármelo esta noche.

Estructura

**19** **Historieta** **En el cine** Contesten con pronombres.

1. ¿Quiere ver la película Marisol?
2. ¿Va a ver la película?
3. ¿Está comprando las entradas ahora?
4. ¿Está comprando las entradas en la taquilla del cine?
5. ¿Quiere Marisol ver la película desde la primera fila?
6. Desde la primera fila, ¿puede ver la película bien?

**20** **¿Acabas de hacerlo?** Contesten según el modelo.

¿Acabas de hacer el crucigrama o vas a hacer el crucigrama?

Acabo de hacerlo.

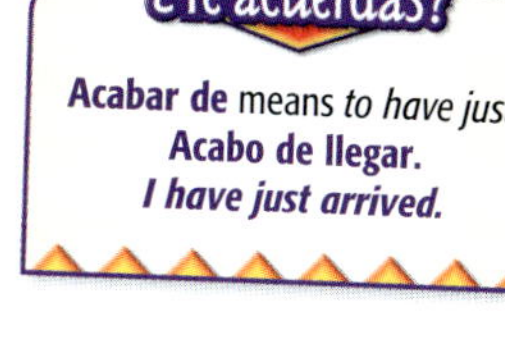


1. ¿Acabas de leer el periódico o vas a leer el periódico?
2. ¿Acabas de escribir la carta o vas a escribir la carta?
3. ¿Acabas de tomar el examen o vas a tomar el examen?
4. ¿Acabas de hacer tus tareas o vas a hacer tus tareas?
5. ¿Acabas de llamar a tu amigo o vas a llamar a tu amigo?

**21** **Historieta** **Una carta**

Contesten según se indica.

1. ¿Está escribiendo la carta Elena? (no)
2. ¿Cuándo va a escribírtela? (mañana)
3. ¿Está comprando los sellos ahora? (no)
4. ¿Ya los ha comprado? (sí)
5. ¿Cuándo va a enviarte la carta? (mañana)
6. ¿La vas a abrir enseguida? (sí)
7. ¿Cómo vas a leerla? (con mucho interés)
8. ¿La vas a contestar enseguida? (sí)
9. ¿Vas a enviarle la carta enseguida? (sí)

**19** This activity can be done orally with books closed.

**20** Have students present this activity as a series of miniconversations.

**21** This activity can be done first orally with books closed.

## LEVELING

**A:** Activities 17, 18, 19, 20, 21

## Answers to ¿Cómo lo digo?

**19**

1. Sí (No), Marisol (no) quiere verla. Sí (No), Marisol (no) la quiere ver.
2. Sí, (No, no) va a verla. Sí, (No, no) la va a ver.
3. Sí, (No, no) está comprándolas ahora. Sí, (No, no) las está comprando ahora.
4. Sí, (No, no) está comprándolas en la taquilla del cine. Sí, (No, no) las está comprando en la taquilla del cine.
5. Sí, (No, no) quiere verla desde la primera fila. Sí, (No, no) la quiere ver desde la primera fila.
6. Sí, (No, no) puede verla bien desde la primera fila. Sí, (No, no) la puede ver bien desde la primera fila.

**20**

1. Acabo de leerlo.
2. Acabo de escribirla.
3. Acabo de tomarlo.
4. Acabo de hacerlas.
5. Acabo de llamarlo.

**21**

1. No, Elena no está escribiendo la carta. (No, Elena no está escribiéndola.) (No, Elena no la está escribiendo.)
2. Va a escribírmela (Me la va a escribir) mañana.
3. No, no está comprando los sellos ahora. (No, no está comprándolos ahora.) (No, no los está comprando ahora.)
4. Sí, ya los ha comprado.
5. Va a enviarme la carta mañana. (Va a enviármela mañana.) (Me la va a enviar mañana.)
6. Sí, voy a abrirla (la voy a abrir) enseguida.
7. Voy a leerla (La voy a leer) con mucho interés.
8. Sí, la voy a contestar (voy a contestarla) enseguida.
9. Sí, se la voy a enviar (voy a enviársela) la carta enseguida. (Sí, voy a enviarle la carta enseguida.)

# Estructura

## 1 PREPARATION

### Bellringer Review

*Use BRR Transparency 9.5 or write the following on the board.*
Write answers to the following questions.

1. **¿Tu amigo(a) te espera en la parada del autobús?**
2. **¿Cuándo te esperan tus amigos?**
3. **¿La escalera mecánica te lleva de un piso al otro en la tienda?**
4. **¿Los agricultores te venden sus productos?**

## 2 PRESENTATION

### Adjetivos y pronombres demostrativos

**Step 1** Use a boy, a girl, a book, and a magazine to illustrate the meaning of **este, ese, aquel.** Have the boy stand near you as you say **este muchacho.** Have him stand near another student as you say **ese muchacho.** Have the boy stand in the back of the room away from everyone as you say **aquel muchacho.** Do the same with a girl, a book, and a magazine. Explain to students that the forms used for the demonstrative pronouns are the same as those used for the demonstrative adjectives.

**Step 2** Then have students open their books and read the explanation in Items 1–3 aloud.

**Step 3** Write the forms of the demonstrative adjectives and pronouns on the board.

**Step 4** Have students read all the model sentences aloud.

**LEVELING**

**E:** Activities 22, 24, 25

**A:** Activities 22, 23, 24, 25

Estructura

## Adjetivos y pronombres demostrativos

### Pointing out people or things

1. You use the demonstrative adjectives *this, that, these,* and *those* to point out people or things. In Spanish, the demonstrative adjective, like all adjectives, agrees with the noun it modifies.

2. All forms of **este** indicate someone or something close to the speaker. They mean *this* or *these* in English.

   **Este boleto que tengo aquí es para el metro.**

   All forms of **ese** indicate someone or something close to the person being spoken to.

   **Ese boleto que tú tienes allí es para el bus.**

   All forms of **aquel** indicate someone or something away from both the speaker and the listener. The forms of both **ese** and **aquel** mean *that* or *those* in English.

   **Aquellos boletos en aquella mesa allá no son usados.**

   Note that the adverbs **aquí, allí,** and **allá** indicate relative position—*here, there, over there.*

3. The forms used for the demonstrative pronouns—*this one, that one, these, those*—are the same as those used for demonstrative adjectives.

   **No me gusta este (aquí).**
   **Pero aquellos (allá), sí, me gustan.**

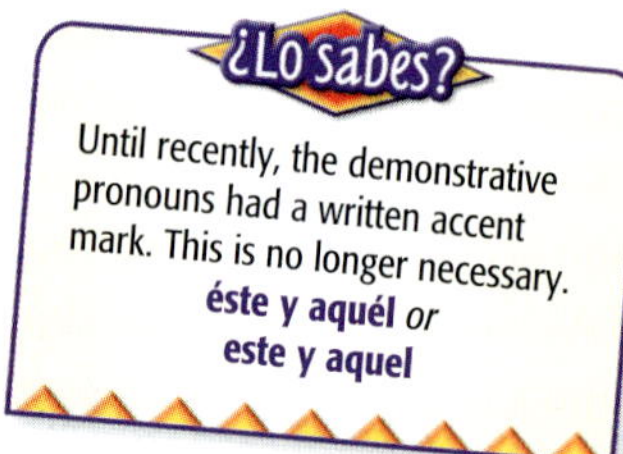




### About the Spanish Language

- The **Real Academia** has recently ruled that it is no longer necessary to put a written accent on the demonstrative pronouns. It is only required when there would be ambiguity.
- Another important decision was made in 1994, to no longer consider the **ch** and the **ll** as separate letters of the Spanish alphabet.

### Answers to ¿Cómo lo digo?

**22** *All answers begin with* ¿Qué precio tienen... ?

1. ¿Cuáles? ¿Estos guantes aquí?
   No, aquellos guantes en el escaparate.
2. ¿Cuál? ¿Esta falda aquí?
   No, aquella falda en el escaparate.
3. ¿Cuál? ¿Este suéter aquí?
   No, aquel suéter en el escaparate.
4. ¿Cuáles? ¿Estas corbatas aquí?
   No, aquellas corbatas en el escaparate.
5. ¿Cuál? ¿Este cinturón aquí?
   No, aquel cinturón en el escaparate.

# ¿Cómo lo digo?

**22** **¿Qué precio tienen?** Sigan el modelo.

**el abrigo →**
**¿Qué precio tiene el abrigo?**
**¿Cuál? ¿Este abrigo aquí?**
**No, aquel abrigo en el escaparate.**

1. los guantes
2. la falda
3. el suéter
4. las corbatas
5. el cinturón
6. los pantalones
7. la blusa
8. los calcetines

Buenos Aires, Argentina

**23** **El plano que tú tienes** Completen con **este, ese** o **aquel.**

1. ____ plano de la ciudad que tú estás mirando es bueno pero ____ que tiene Felipe es malo. No sirve para nada.
2. ____ calle aquí es una calle peatonal pero ____ allá no es sólo para peatones. Y tiene mucho tráfico.
3. ____ estación de metro aquí en el centro de la ciudad es mucho más grande que ____ estación en las afueras.
4. ____ edificios aquí en el centro mismo de la ciudad son muy altos. ____ que están más lejos en las afueras no son tan altos.
5. ____ novela que yo estoy leyendo tiene lugar aquí en ____ ciudad. Pero ____ novela que tiene Pedro, no la conozco. No sé dónde tiene lugar.

**24** **Preferencias** Trabaja con un(a) compañero(a). Miren esta foto de un escaparate de una tienda de ropa en Caracas. Discutan lo que a cada uno(a) de ustedes le gusta y no le gusta. Luego comparen sus preferencias.

Caracas, Venezuela

**25** **Juego** **¿Cuál?** Trabaja con un(a) compañero(a). Haz una frase usando **este, ese** o **aquel.** Tu compañero(a) te dirá si hablas de algo **aquí, allí** o **allá.** Luego cambien de rol.

## Estructura

### 3 PRACTICE

### ¿Cómo lo digo?

**22** Have students present this activity as a miniconversation.

**23** The information in each sentence of this activity allows students to determine which demonstrative must be used. Have students prepare Activity 23 before going over it in class.

**25** **Juego** This is a good end-of-class activity.

**¡Adelante!**
At this point in the chapter, students have learned all the vocabulary and structure necessary to complete the chapter. The conversation and cultural readings that follow recycle all the material learned up to this point.

## Answers to ¿Cómo lo digo?

6. ¿Cuáles? ¿Estos pantalones aquí?
No, aquellos pantalones en el escaparate.
7. ¿Cuál? ¿Esta blusa aquí?
No, aquella blusa en el escaparate.
8. ¿Cuáles? ¿Estos calcetines aquí?
No, aquellos calcetines en el escaparate.

**23**

1. Ese, aquel
2. Esta, aquella
3. Esta, aquella
4. Estos, Aquellos
5. Esta, esta, aquella

**24** *Answers will vary, but students will use demonstrative adjectives and pronouns to list their preferences. Refer to Chapter 4 to review the clothing vocabulary if needed.*

**25** *Answers will vary. Have students use objects in the classroom as models if they need a prompt.*

Conversación

# 1 PREPARATION

## Resource Manager

Audio Activities TE, page 111
Audio CD 6

## Bellringer Review

*Use BRR Transparency 9.6 or write the following on the board.*
Where would you find the following things, **¿en la ciudad o en el campo?**

1. **el huerto**
2. **las gallinas**
3. **la fábrica**
4. **la finca**

# 2 PRESENTATION

**Step 1** Have two students with good pronunciation read the conversation to the class.

**Step 2** Have students listen to the recording on Audio CD 6 once.

**Step 3** Call on individuals to read parts of the conversation aloud.

**Step 4** After a student reads, intersperse some questions. You can make up questions or use those in the **¿Comprendes?** section.

**Step 5** After presenting the conversation, have students write answers to the **¿Comprendes?** questions for homework.

# Conversación

## El campo y la ciudad   

**Lupe** ¿Te gusta vivir en el campo? ¿Qué haces? ¿No es aburrido?

**Mónica** De ninguna manera. El otro día estaba hablando con mi amigo Miguel. Estaba diciéndole todo lo que podemos hacer aquí en este pueblo.

**Lupe** Pero en la ciudad tenemos cines, museos. Tenemos de todo. Y puedes tomar el bus o el metro para ir de un lugar a otro. Todo es tan conveniente.

**Mónica** Sí, pero aquí no tienes que esperar el semáforo para cruzar la calle. ¿Y sabes lo que es el automóvil? Tenemos uno y podemos usarlo sin pasar horas en el tráfico.

**Lupe** Sí, lo sé. Pero yo nunca viviría en el campo.

**Mónica** Y yo nunca viviría en la ciudad. No me gustaría vivir sin aire puro y mucho espacio. Voy a pasear a caballo. ¿Quieres acompañarme?

**Lupe** ¿A caballo?

### ¿Comprendes?

Contesten.

1. ¿Qué le pregunta Lupe a Mónica?
2. ¿Con quién estaba hablando Mónica el otro día?
3. ¿Cree Mónica que el campo es aburrido?
4. ¿Por qué prefiere Lupe la ciudad?
5. ¿Por qué dice ella que todo es tan conveniente?
6. Según Mónica, ¿hay mucho tráfico en el campo?
7. ¿Quién no viviría nunca en el campo? ¿Por qué no?
8. ¿Qué va a hacer Mónica?
9. ¿Qué crees? ¿La va a acompañar Lupe?



### Answers to ¿Comprendes?

1. Lupe le pregunta a Mónica si le gusta vivir en el campo.
2. Mónica estaba hablando con su amigo Miguel el otro día.
3. Mónica cree que el campo no es aburrido.
4. Lupe prefiere la ciudad porque todo es tan conveniente.
5. Dice que todo es tan conveniente porque en la ciudad puedes tomar el bus o el metro para ir de un lugar a otro.
6. No, según Mónica, no hay mucho tráfico en el campo.
7. Lupe nunca viviría en el campo porque prefiere la ciudad y cree que el campo es aburrido.
8. Mónica va a pasear a caballo.
9. Sí (No), Lupe (no) la va a acompañar.

# Vamos a hablar más

**A** **Donde quiere vivir** Trabaja con un(a) compañero(a). Discutan si preferirían vivir en la ciudad o en el campo. Den sus razones.

El Alcázar, Segovia, España

Palacio de Bellas Artes, Ciudad de México

**B** **Explica por qué.** Trabaja con un(a) compañero(a). Él o ella te preguntará por qué no hiciste algo ayer. Explica que no lo hiciste ayer porque estabas haciendo otra cosa. Dile lo que estabas haciendo. Luego cambien de rol. Pueden usar el modelo como guía.

**—¿Por qué no me llamaste ayer?**
**—No te llamé porque estaba leyendo un libro interesante.**



Conversación

## 3 PRACTICE

## Vamos a hablar más

**A** With more able groups you can have students prepare a debate on the topic in this activity.

### Learning from Photos

*(page 277 top)* This storybook castle, **El Alcázar**, looks like a huge ship rising atop a rock 80 meters (262 feet) high. It was built during the time of **El Cid** by King Alfonso VI. You may wish to ask students these questions about the photo:
**¿Qué animales hay en la foto?**
**¿Qué es el hombre?**
**¿Qué hace el perro?**
*(page 277 bottom)* Construction on the **Palacio de Bellas Artes** began in 1904 during the dictatorship of Porfirio Díaz. Work was interrupted by the revolution and was not resumed until 1932. In the building there are works by most of the great Mexican muralists: Rivera, Orozco, Siqueiros, and Tamayo. It is considered one of the world's great theaters.

### Glencoe Technology

On the CD-ROM, students can watch a dramatization of this conversation. They can then play the role of either one of the characters and record themselves in the conversation.

### Answers to Vamos a hablar más

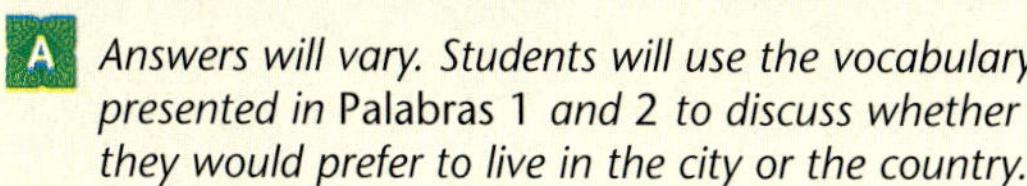

**A** *Answers will vary. Students will use the vocabulary presented in* Palabras 1 *and 2 to discuss whether they would prefer to live in the city or the country.*

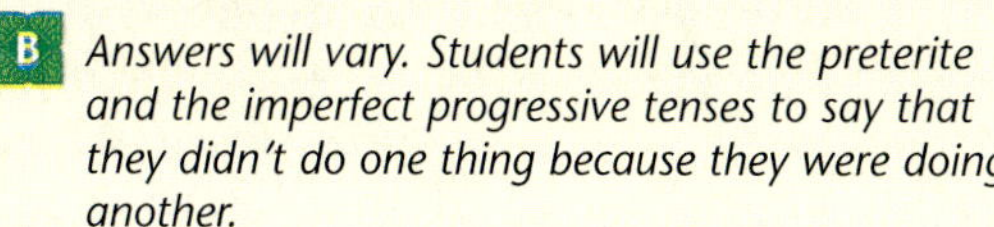

**B** *Answers will vary. Students will use the preterite and the imperfect progressive tenses to say that they didn't do one thing because they were doing another.*

### LEVELING

**E:** Conversation

# Lecturas culturales

## Resource Manager

Audio Activities TE, page 112
Audio CD 6

## Bellringer Review

*Use BRR Transparency 9.7 or write the following on the board.*
Write down what the following people are doing right now. Use the present progressive.

1. **mi madre**
2. **mi padre**
3. **yo**
4. **mi novio(a)**
5. **mi profesor(a)**
6. **mi mejor amigo(a)**

## National Standards

**Cultures**
The reading about Buenos Aires and the related activity familiarize students with life in a vibrant Latin American city.

**Comparisons**
Students learn that, as in many cities in the United States, urban poverty is a persistent problem in Latin America.

## PRESENTATION

### Pre-reading

Before reading the **Lectura,** have students look at the photographs on these pages. Have them scan the book quickly and look at all the photographs of Buenos Aires and Argentina. You might also wish to have them locate Buenos Aires on the map of South America on page xxxi or on Map Transparency M 3.

# Lecturas culturales

**Reading Strategy**

**Taking notes to remember what has been read** If you are reading material that you do not know much about, it is often a good idea to take notes to help you remember and organize what you read. One way to take notes is to summarize the content of a selection. Another way is to jot down key words and ideas about the topic. These notes will come in handy later when you need to study for a test.

## Buenos Aires, Argentina 

Buenos Aires, la capital de la Argentina, es una ciudad muy bonita. Se dice que esta ciudad es la más europea de todas las ciudades de Latinoamérica.

Recientemente Sandra Connors, una americana, estaba visitando a Buenos Aires. Un día, mientras estaba caminando por el centro de la ciudad, les dijo a algunos conocidos porteños[1] que no sabía si estaba en Buenos Aires, Londres o Madrid.

La calle Florida es una calle peatonal en la zona comercial de la ciudad. En esta calle no permiten carros. Si te gusta ir de compras tienes que caminar por esta calle con sus cientos de tiendas.

La avenida más ancha del mundo es la Avenida 9 de Julio. Aquí puedes sentarte en una confitería[2] y mirar a la gente que pasa. Si tienes hambre, puedes ir a uno de los carritos de la Costanera norte. Los verdaderos carritos del pasado se han transformado en una fila de restaurantes al borde del río de la Plata. Aquí sirven el delicioso bife argentino.

[1]porteños *inhabitants of Buenos Aires*
[2]confitería *café, tea room*

Calle Florida y Avenida Córdoba

Avenida 9 de Julio, Buenos Aires



## About the Spanish Language

In Argentina the slum communities of the poor mentioned in the **Lectura** are called **villas miseria.** In other countries they have different names: in Peru, **pueblos jóvenes;** in Chile, **callampas;** and in Brazil, **favelas.**

El bife argentino viene del ganado que cuidan los gauchos en las pampas argentinas. Muchos porteños ricos tienen estancias en las pampas. Una estancia es una finca grande donde crían ganado. Los ricos van a su estancia para divertirse en sus lujosas[3] casas de campo.

Es imposible hablar de las ciudades de Latinoamérica sin mencionar el problema de los pobres que vienen a las ciudades desde el campo en busca de trabajo. Estos pobres viven en chabolas que se encuentran principalmente en las afueras. En Buenos Aires se llaman «villas miseria».

[3]lujosas *luxurious*

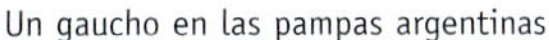

Un gaucho en las pampas argentinas

Una estancia, Argentina

## ¿Comprendes?

**Buenos Aires** Identifiquen y describan.

1. la calle Florida
2. la Avenida 9 de Julio
3. los carritos de la Costanera norte
4. las pampas
5. una estancia
6. una «villa miseria»

Una villa miseria, Buenos Aires

## Lecturas culturales

### Reading

**Step 1** Call on a student to read three or four sentences aloud. Then stop and ask other members of the class questions about the material that was just read.

**Step 2** If students have any trouble understanding the information about the **carritos,** explain the following to them. The **Costanera norte** is a street that runs along the **Río de la Plata.** Until recently there were many little carts where meats were grilled and people would come to feast. Slowly but surely, these little carts have given way to a whole series of barbecue restaurants that line the shore of the **Río de la Plata.** It is still a very popular family eating area.

**Step 3** Have students read the selection at home and write the answers to the **¿Comprendes?** activity that accompanies the **Lectura.**

### Post-reading

**Step 1** Go over the **¿Comprendes?** activity in class the next day.

**Step 2** Call on a student to give a summary of the reading in his or her own words. If necessary, ask five or six questions to review the salient points of the reading selection in order to enable him or her to do this more easily. After the oral summary, the more able students can write a synopsis of the **Lectura** in their own words.

### LEVELING

**E:** Reading

## Answers to ¿Comprendes?

1. La Calle Florida es una calle peatonal en la zona comercial de la ciudad. Tiene cientos de tiendas.
2. La Avenida 9 de Julio es la avenida más ancha del mundo.
3. Los carritos de la Costanera norte se han transformado en una fila de restaurantes al borde del Río de la Plata.
4. Los gauchos crían ganado en las pampas y muchos porteños ricos tienen estancias allí.
5. Una estancia es una finca grande donde crían ganado.
6. Una «villa miseria» es un lugar en las afueras de la ciudad donde viven en chabolas los pobres que vienen a las ciudades en busca de trabajo.

# Lectura opcional 1

**¡OJO!** This reading is optional. You may skip it completely, have the entire class read it, have only several students read it and report to the class, or assign it for extra credit.

## National Standards

**Cultures**
This reading about Lima and its surroundings and the related activity on page 280 familiarize students with another important city in Latin America.

## PRESENTATION

**Step 1** Have students who are going to read the **Lectura** on Lima peruse the book and look at all the photographs of Lima or Peru that appear in it. You may also wish to have them find Lima on the map of South America on page xxxi or on Map Transparency M 3.

### Recycling

Have students give any information they remember about Peru. Some may have read the selections on **Machu Picchu** or the **Nazca** lines in **¡Buen viaje! Level 1.**

### FUN FACTS

**La garúa** is a curious weather phenomenon affecting Lima. The cold Peru current offshore helps maintain the stability of the atmosphere, but it gives rise to frequent fogs. During the months of June, July, and August, Lima's winter, the mist is constant. This constant fog is called **la garúa.**

# Lectura opcional 1

## Lima, Perú

Lima, la capital de Perú, es una ciudad muy hermosa. En el centro mismo de la ciudad hay un gran barrio histórico. Muchos de los edificios de este barrio datan de la época colonial.

Hay dos plazas importantes en el centro de Lima—la Plaza de Armas y la Plaza San Martín. El famoso Jirón de la Unión enlaza[1] estas dos plazas. El Jirón de la Unión es una calle peatonal con muchas tiendas y centros o galerías comerciales. Hoy día hay también muchos vendedores ambulantes. Estos vendedores ambulantes han venido a la capital de los pueblos pequeños del altiplano.

En los alrededores de Lima cerca de las playas del Pacífico hay muchas zonas residenciales muy bonitas. En las calles bordeadas de palmas hay edificios altos con apartamentos y condominios. Hay también casas lujosas[2].

Una vez más, es imposible hablar de las ciudades de Latinoamérica sin mencionar el problema de los pobres que vienen a las ciudades desde el campo en busca de trabajo. Como hemos aprendido, los barrios pobres donde viven se llaman «villas miseria» en Buenos Aires. En Perú se llaman «pueblos jóvenes».

[1]enlaza *joins* [2]lujosas *luxurious*

Lima, Perú

## ¿Comprendes?

**Lima** Contesten.

1. ¿Cuál es la capital de Perú?
2. ¿Cómo es el centro de Lima?
3. ¿De qué época datan muchos de los edificios?
4. ¿Cuáles son dos plazas importantes en el centro de Lima?
5. ¿Qué calle enlaza estas dos plazas?
6. ¿Qué es el Jirón de la Unión?
7. ¿Quiénes son los vendedores ambulantes?
8. ¿Qué hay en los alrededores de Lima?
9. ¿Por qué van los campesinos a la ciudad?
10. ¿Qué es un «pueblo joven»?

Jirón de la Unión, Lima



## Answers to ¿Comprendes?

1. La capital del Perú es Lima.
2. Hay un gran barrio histórico en el centro de Lima.
3. Muchos de los edificios datan de la época colonial.
4. Dos plazas importantes en el centro de Lima son la Plaza de Armas y la Plaza San Martín.
5. El Jirón de la Unión enlaza estas dos plazas.
6. El Jirón de la Unión es una calle peatonal con muchas tiendas y centros o galerías comerciales.
7. Los vendedores ambulantes han venido a la capital de los pueblos pequeños del altiplano.
8. En los alrededores de Lima hay muchas zonas residenciales muy bonitas.
9. Los campesinos van a la ciudad en busca de trabajo.
10. Un «pueblo joven» es una «villa miseria»—un lugar en las afueras de la ciudad donde viven los pobres.

# Lectura opcional 2

Plaza Central, Santa Fe

## Una ciudad norteamericana con profundas raíces hispanas

Santa Fe, la capital de Nuevo México, está al pie de las montañas Sangre de Cristo. Esta ciudad fue fundada[1] por los españoles en 1609 sobre unas ruinas indígenas prehistóricas. Durante doscientos años Santa Fe fue un centro para el comercio entre los españoles y varios grupos indígenas. En 1680 los indios pueblo se levantaron contra los españoles. Querían echarlos[2] de Santa Fe y así hicieron. Pero doce años después, los españoles, bajo Diego de Vargas, volvieron a Santa Fe y restablecieron su dominio.

Si abres la guía telefónica o simplemente miras los nombres en las casas, verás que la influencia hispana todavía vive en Santa Fe. Sigue existiendo no solamente en los museos sino en carne y hueso. Las familias hispanas predominan en esta ciudad que es la capital más antigua de Estados Unidos.

[1]fundada *founded*
[2]echarlos *throw them out*

### ¿Comprendes?

**A La geografía** Busquen en un mapa dónde está la ciudad de Santa Fe y dónde están las montañas Sangre de Cristo.

**B Santa Fe** Contesten.

1. ¿Qué edad tiene Santa Fe?
2. Antes de la fundación de Santa Fe, ¿qué había en el mismo sitio?
3. ¿Para qué servía la ciudad durante dos siglos?
4. ¿Qué hicieron los indios pueblo en 1680?
5. ¿Qué hicieron los españoles en 1692?

**C El significado** En tus propias palabras, explica lo que dice el último párrafo de la lectura.

Calle comercial, Santa Fe



Lectura opcional 2

**¡OJO!** This reading is optional. You may skip it completely, have the entire class read it, have only several students read it and report to the class, or assign it for extra credit.

### National Standards

**Cultures**
This reading and the related activities on page 281 familiarize students with the Hispanic heritage of Santa Fe, New Mexico.

### Learning from Photos

*(page 281)* The city of Santa Fe is on the old **Camino Real,** the *Royal Road* that led from Mexico City to Spain's northern settlements in the American Southwest.

**LEVELING**
**E:** Reading 1
**A:** Reading 3

### Answers to ¿Comprendes?

**B**

1. Santa Fe tiene casi cuatrocientos años. (Fue fundada en 1609.)
2. Había unas ruinas indígenas prehistóricas en el mismo sitio.
3. Durante dos siglos la ciudad fue un centro para el comercio entre los españoles y varios grupos indígenas.
4. En 1680 los indios pueblo se levantaron contra los españoles. Los echaron de Santa Fe.
5. En 1692 los españoles volvieron a Santa Fe y restablecieron su dominio.

**C** *Answers will vary but may include:*

La influencia hispana todavía vive en Santa Fe, no solamente en los museos pero también con las familias hispanas que predominan en Santa Fe.

# Conexiones

## National Standards

**Connections**
This reading about demographics in Latin America establishes a connection with another discipline, allowing students to reinforce and further their knowledge of the social sciences through the study of Spanish.

**Comparisons**
This reading contrasts certain demographic statistics of the United States with those of Latin America, affording students a better understanding of the nature of both the size and age of the two populations.

**¡OJO!** The readings in the **Conexiones** section are optional. They focus on some of the major disciplines taught in schools and universities. The vocabulary is useful for discussing such topics as history, literature, art, economics, business, science, etc. You may choose any of the following ways to do the readings in the **Conexiones** sections.

**Independent reading** Have students read the selections and do the post-reading activities as homework, which you collect. This option is least intrusive on class time and requires a minimum of teacher involvement.

**Homework with in-class follow-up** Assign the readings and post-reading activities as homework. Review and discuss the material in class the next day.

**Intensive in-class activity** This option includes a pre-reading vocabulary presentation, in-class reading and discussion, assignment of the activities for homework, and a discussion of the assignment in class the following day.



# Conexiones

## *Las ciencias sociales*

Bogotá, Colombia

### La demografía

Demography is the study of human populations, of their distribution, density, and vital statistics. Demographics explain where people choose to live and why. They also explain population shifts—why people move around.

The demography of Latin America is particularly interesting. You will see some marked contrasts between the demographics of the two Americas.

Lima, Perú

### La demografía de Latinoamérica

La demografía es el estudio de las poblaciones humanas. El demógrafo nos explica dónde decide vivir la gente y por qué decide vivir allí. Nos explica también cuándo y por qué la gente decide mudarse para establecerse en otro lugar. Es decir que el demógrafo explica las razones por la migración.

**Algunas estadísticas**

Si contrastamos las poblaciones de Latinoamérica y Estados Unidos, lo primero que notamos es que Latinoamérica tiene una población mucho más numerosa. Durante muchos años Nueva York y Los Ángeles fueron las dos ciudades más grandes de las Américas. Ya no.

| | | | |
|---|---|---|---|
| **Nueva York** | 8.050.000 | **México D.F.** | 8.681.000 |
| **Los Ángeles** | 3.903.000 | **São Paulo, Brasil** | 17.900.000 |



### Learning from Photos

*(page 282 left)* Ask students the following questions about the photo: **¿Es una foto de qué zona de la ciudad? ¿Hay rascacielos en la foto? ¿Hay muchas fábricas en esta zona de la ciudad? Y detrás de la ciudad, ¿qué ves?**
*(page 282 right)* You may wish to ask students the following questions about the photo: **¿Es una foto de qué? ¿En qué zona está la plaza?**

**Patrones migratorios**

En las últimas décadas los centros urbanos de Latinoamérica han crecido dramáticamente. Los campesinos se han ido del campo a la ciudad en busca de trabajo y mejores condiciones de vida. En muchos casos ellos no han encontrado mejor vida, sino miseria. Las ciudades no pueden acomodar a todos los que allí buscan mejor vida. No hay bastante trabajo. Y no hay viviendas adecuadas. Los pobres tienen que vivir en barrios sin agua corriente ni electricidad.

**La edad**

Otra estadística significativa es la de la edad de las poblaciones de las Américas. Latinoamérica es una región de jóvenes, mientras que Estados Unidos es un país de envejecientes. Como ejemplo, vamos a comparar a México con Estados Unidos.

| | % menos de 5 años | % 5 a 14 años | % más de 65 años |
|---|---|---|---|
| EE.UU. | 7.5 | 14.1 | 12.4 |
| México | 13.8 | 25.1 | 4.1 |

## ¿Comprendes?

**A ¿Cuál es la palabra?** Busquen la palabra cuya definición sigue.

1. el acto de trasladarse para establecerse en otro lugar
2. personas que se están poniendo viejos
3. el estudio de las poblaciones humanas
4. casas, residencias donde la gente vive
5. una zona o parte de una ciudad

**B La demografía** Digan que sí o que no.

1. El demógrafo nos enseña dónde vive la gente y por qué decide vivir allí.
2. Las ciudades de Estados Unidos son más grandes que las ciudades de Latinoamérica.
3. Las ciudades latinoamericanas siempre han sido más grandes que las ciudades de Estados Unidos.
4. Los campesinos que se establecen en las ciudades de Latinoamérica siempre encuentran mejor vida.
5. No hay bastante trabajo para todos en el campo y no hay bastante trabajo en las ciudades.
6. Hay más viejos o ancianos en Latinoamérica que en Estados Unidos.
7. La población latinoamericana es más vieja (mayor) que la población estadounidense.



# Conexiones

## PRESENTATION

### *Las ciencias sociales*
### La demografía

**¡OJO!** Even if you don't have students read this section in depth, you may have them scan it quickly or tell them some of the most important information. Many of the problems facing some Latin American nations are due to demographic changes.

**Step 1** Have students read the introduction in English on page 282.

**Step 2** Now have them read the selection quickly.

**Step 3** Suggest to students that they look for cognates and attempt to guess the meaning from context.

**Step 4** Now do the **¿Comprendes?** activities on this page.

### ¿Comprendes?

**B** After going over this activity have students correct the false statements.

### Answers to ¿Comprendes?

**A**

1. la migración
2. envejecientes
3. la demografía
4. viviendas
5. barrio

**B**

1. Sí
2. No
3. No
4. No
5. Sí
6. No
7. No

**LEVELING**

**E:** Reading

**A:** Reading

# ¡Te toca a ti!

## Use what you have learned

### Recycling

These activities allow students to use the vocabulary and structure from this chapter in completely open-ended, real-life situations.

### PRESENTATION

Encourage students to say as much as possible when they do these activities. Tell them not to be afraid to make mistakes, since the goal of the activities is real-life communication. If someone in the group makes an error, allow the others to politely correct him or her. Let students choose the activities they would like to do.

You may wish to divide students into pairs or groups. Encourage students to elaborate on the basic theme and to be creative. They may use props, pictures, or posters if they wish.

# ¡Te toca a ti!

## Use what you have learned

### 1 La ciudad

✔ *Talk about life in the city*

Con un(a) compañero(a), miren esta foto de la ciudad de Barcelona. Hablen juntos y describan todo lo que ven en la foto. Luego decidan si es una ciudad que les gustaría visitar.

Barcelona, España

### 2 Transporte público

✔ *Talk about public transportation*

Tu compañero(a) es un(a) joven ecuatoriano(a) que está visitando tu pueblo o ciudad. Quiere saber algo sobre los medios de transporte público. Si no hay transporte público donde vives, describe los medios de transporte en una ciudad cercana.

### 3 Una ciudad hispana

✔ *Talk about life in an interesting Spanish-speaking city*

Tú ya conoces muchas ciudades hispanas. Selecciona una que a ti te gusta y descríbela a un(a) compañero(a). Luego tu compañero(a) describirá una ciudad que a él o a ella le gusta.

### 4 ¿Hablas de la ciudad o del campo?

✔ *Talk about city or country life*

Trabaja con un(a) compañero(a). Haz una frase que describe algún aspecto de la ciudad o del campo. Tu compañero(a) te dirá de qué hablas—la ciudad o el campo. Luego cambien de rol.



## Answers to ¡Te toca a ti!

1 *Answers will vary but may include:*

—Hay una plaza en la ciudad.
—Los peatones cruzan en los cruces de peatones.
—Los coches esperan un semáforo en verde.
—La gente camina en la senda.

2 *Answers will vary. Students will explain public transportation available in their city or one nearby using the vocabulary from* Palabras 1.

3 *Answers will vary. Suggest to students other photos of cities in the chapter to describe and use as a stimulus.*

4 *Answers will vary but may include:*

—Cosechan en el otoño aquí.
—Es el campo.
—Camino en la acera.
—Es la ciudad.

## 5 Yo nunca viviría en...

✔ *Give your opinion about city life versus country life*

Vas a escribir una composición titulada «Yo nunca viviría en... ». Tienes que completar el título con **la ciudad** o **el campo.**

### Writing Strategy

**Comparing and contrasting**
Comparing and contrasting involves writing about similarities and differences between two or more related things. A Venn diagram will help you do this. First draw two intersecting circles; title the circles with the subject to be compared. List unique features of each subject. Then list the similarities of the two subjects in the area where the circles intersect. This tool, or any other similar one you can think of, will help you organize your thoughts so you can clearly and effectively write your comparison.

## 6 Dos ciudades

Think of two cities you have visited. Write a paper, comparing the two places. If you are not familiar with two different cities, compare the town where you live with a nearby city or other town. Be sure to organize your thoughts with a list or a graphic, showing the similarities and differences.

Viña del Mar, Chile

Santiago, Chile





## ¡Te toca a ti!

### PRACTICE

**LEVELING**

These activities encompass all three levels. All students will be able to do them at a sophistication level commensurate with their ability in Spanish. Some students will be able to speak for several minutes, and others may be able to give just a few sentences. This is to be expected when students are functioning completely on their own generating their own language to the best of their ability.

5 Encourage students to have fun with this activity and give as many reasons as possible why they would never live in either the city or the country.

### Writing Strategy

**Comparing and contrasting**
Have students read the Writing Strategy on page 285. Have students read aloud their papers, displaying their Venn Diagrams to the class as they do so. They can compare and contrast the cities or towns they wrote about with those that other students wrote about.

6 You may wish to work with the class in preparing their graphic. It can be done as a group effort.

### Answers to ¡Te toca a ti!

5 *Answers will vary. Students will use vocabulary from* Palabras 1 *and* 2 *to support their opinions.*

6 *Answers will vary. Students will use vocabulary from this chapter and other previously learned words to compare and contrast two cities.*

### Writing Development

Have students keep a notebook or portfolio containing their best written work from each chapter. These selected writings can be based on assignments from the Student Textbook and the Workbook. The two activities on page 285 are examples of writing assignments that may be included in each student's portfolio. On page 106 in the Workbook, students will begin to develop an organized autobiography **(Mi autobiografía).** These workbook pages may also become a part of their portfolio.

Assessment

## Resource Manager

Communication Transparency C 9
Quizzes, pages 40–44
Performance Assessment, Task 9
Tests, pages 135–148
Situation Cards, Chapter 9
**Maratón mental** Videoquiz, Chapter 9
ExamView® Pro, Chapter 9

## Assessment

This is a pre-test for students to take before you administer the chapter test. Note that each section is cross-referenced so students can easily find the material they have to review in case they made errors. You may use Assessment Answers Transparency A 9 to do the assessment in class, or you may assign this assessment for homework. You can correct the assessment yourself, or you may prefer to project the answers on the overhead in class.

## Glencoe Technology

**MINDJOGGER VHS/DVD**

You may wish to help your students prepare for the chapter test by playing the MindJogger game show. Teams will compete against each other to review chapter vocabulary and structure and sharpen listening comprehension skills.

Assessment

# Vocabulario

To review **Palabras 1**, turn to pages **262–263**.

**1 Contesten.**

1. ¿Qué hay en una zona comercial de una ciudad?
2. ¿Qué hay en las esquinas de muchas ciudades que ayudan a controlar el tráfico?

**2 Completen.**

3. Los obreros trabajan en una ____ en una zona industrial en las afueras de la ciudad.
4. Muchas calles y avenidas ____ en la plaza.
5. Los ____ andan (a pie) por la acera.
6. La gente espera el bus en la ____.

**3 Identifiquen.**

7. 

8. 

To review **Palabras 2**, turn to pages **266–267**.

9. 

10. 

**4 Completen.**

11. El ____ es el árbol que da manzanas.
12. Los agricultores ____ animales domésticos.
13. Los campesinos ____ los campos.



Answers to Assessment

**1**

1. En una zona comercial hay muchas oficinas y tiendas.
2. Hay semáforos en las esquinas de muchas ciudades.

**2**

3. fábrica
4. desembocan
5. peatones
6. parada del bus

**3**

7. las gallinas
8. las vacas
9. el maíz
10. los cerdos

**4**

11. manzano
12. crían
13. cultivan

# Estructura

**5** **Escriban según el modelo.**

**Ellos cosechan el arroz. →**
**Estaban cosechando el arroz.**

14. Ellos construyen una fábrica.
15. Yo repito las direcciones.
16. La gallina duerme.
17. Yo no leo nada.
18. ¿Quién lo dice?

To review the imperfect progressive, turn to page 270.

**6** **Escriban de otra manera.**

19. ¿El plano de la ciudad? Yo quería dárselo.
20. ¿Los campos? Estaban cultivándolos.
21. ¿El tique? Él estaba metiéndolo en la ranura del torniquete.

To review the placement of object pronouns, turn to page 272.

**7** **Contesten con adjetivos o pronombres demostrativos.**

22. ¿Qué casa prefieres? (la casa que veo allá lejos)
23. ¿Qué periódicos te interesan más? (los periódicos que tengo aquí)

To review demonstrative adjectives and pronouns, turn to page 274.

# Cultura

**8** **Identifiquen.**

24. la capital de Argentina
25. la avenida que tiene fama de ser la más ancha del mundo.

To review this cultural information, turn to pages 278–279.

## Assessment

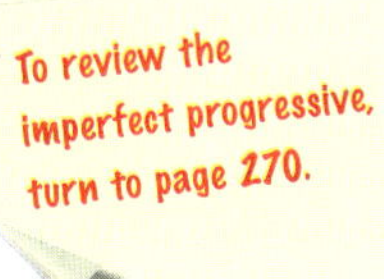

**Dinah Zike's Study Guides**

Your students may wish to use Foldable 2 to organize, display, and arrange data as they learn about the seasons in Spanish. You may wish to encourage them to add information from each chapter as they continue to learn vocabulary that can be used to describe seasons and weather.

A *forward-backward book* foldable is also an ideal reference for students to organize what they know about two related subjects.

**SPANISH Online**

The Glencoe Spanish Web site **(spanish.glencoe.com)** offers options that enable you and your students to experience the Spanish-speaking world via the Internet. For each Capítulo, there are activities, games, and quizzes. In addition an *Enrichment* section offers students an opportunity to visit Web sites related to the theme of the chapter.

## Answers to Assessment

14. Ellos estaban construyendo una fábrica.
15. Yo estaba repitiendo las direcciones.
16. La gallina estaba durmiendo.
17. Yo no estaba leyendo nada.
18. ¿Quién lo estaba diciendo?

19. Yo se lo quería dar.
20. Los estaban cultivando.
21. Él lo estaba metiendo en la ranura del torniquete.

22. Prefiero aquella casa.
23. Estos periódicos me interesan más.

24. Buenos Aires
25. la Avenida 9 de Julio

# ¡Hablo como un pro!

This unique page gives students the opportunity to speak freely and say whatever they can, using the vocabulary and structures they have learned in the chapter. The illustration serves to remind students of precisely what they know how to say in Spanish. There are no activities that students do not have the ability to describe or talk about in Spanish. The art not only depicts the vocabulary and content of this chapter, but also reinforces what they learned in previous chapters.

You may wish to use this page in many ways. Some possibilities are to have students do the following:

1. Look at the illustration and identify items by giving the correct Spanish words.
2. Make up sentences about what they see in the illustration.
3. Make up questions about the illustration. They can call on another class member to respond if you do this as a class activity, or you may prefer to allow students to work in small groups. This activity is extremely beneficial because it enables students to actively use interrogative words.
4. Answer questions you ask them about the illustration.
5. Work in pairs and make up a conversation based on the illustration.
6. Look at the illustration and give a complete oral review of what they see.
7. Look at the illustration and write a paragraph (or essay) about it.

You can also use this page as an assessment or testing tool, taking into account individual differences by having students go from simple to quite complicated tasks. The assessment can be either oral or written. You may wish to use the rubrics provided on pages T20–T21 as you give students the following directions.

1. Identify the topic or situation of the illustration.
2. Give the Spanish words for as many items as you can.
3. Think of as many sentences as you can to describe the illustration.
4. Go over your sentences and put them in the best sequencing to give a coherent story based on the illustration.

## ¡Hablo como un pro!

Tell as much as you can about this illustration.

# Vocabulario

### Talking about the city

la ciudad
la zona comercial
el rascacielos
el edificio
la oficina
la zona industrial
las afueras
la fábrica
el/la obrero(a)
la zona residencial
el apartamento (departamento)
el condominio
la casa privada

### Talking about the layout of a city

el plano
la plaza
la avenida, el bulevar
la calle
el barrio viejo
la esquina
la acera
los peatones
el semáforo
el cruce de peatones
caminar
cruzar
desembocar
pintoresco(a)
ancho(a)
angosto(a)

### Talking about public transportation

la estación del metro
la boca del metro
la escalera mecánica
el tique
el torniquete
la ranura
la parada del bus
el autobús, la guagua, el camión

### Talking about the country

el campo
el pueblo
la finca
la casa de campo
el campesino

**How well do you know your vocabulary?**

- Choose a word from the list.
- Have a classmate tell whether it relates more to the city, the country, or both.
- Take turns.

### Talking about farming

la siembra
la cosecha
el maíz
el trigo
los cereales
la huerta
los vegetales
el huerto
el manzano
el peral
cultivar
sembrar
cosechar
criar los animales

### Identifying some farm animals

el ganado
la vaca
el cerdo
la gallina

**VIDEOTUR**

## Episodio 9

In this video episode, you will join Claudia and Julian as they do a school assignment. See page 488 for more information.



# Vocabulario

## Vocabulary Review

The words and phrases in the **Vocabulario** have been taught for productive use in this chapter. They are summarized here as a resource for both student and teacher. This list also serves as a convenient resource for the **¡Te toca a ti!** activities on pages 284 and 285. There are approximately twelve cognates in this vocabulary list. Have students find them.

**¡OJO!** You will notice that the vocabulary list here is not translated. This has been done intentionally, since we feel that by the time students have finished the material in the chapter they should be familiar with the meanings of all the words. If there are several words they still do not know, we recommend that they refer to the **Palabras 1** and **2** sections in the chapter or go to the dictionaries at the end of this book to find the meanings. However, if you prefer that your students have the English translations, please refer to Vocabulary Transparency 9.1, where you will find all these words with their translations.

**VIDEO VHS/DVD**

The Video Program allows students to see how the chapter vocabulary and structures are used by native speakers within an engaging story line. For maximum reinforcement, show the video episode as a final activity for Chapter 9.

# Planning for Chapter 10

## SCOPE AND SEQUENCE, PAGES 290–319

### Topics

- ❖ Kitchen appliances
- ❖ Kitchen utensils
- ❖ Foods and food preparation

### Culture

- ❖ A recipe for paella
- ❖ The tomato: Food or poison?
- ❖ The origin of corn and potatoes
- ❖ A healthy diet

### Functions

- ❖ How to talk about kitchen appliances
- ❖ How to talk about foods and food preparation
- ❖ How to give formal commands
- ❖ How to refer to things already stated

### Structure

- ❖ Formal imperative: Regular forms
- ❖ Formal imperative: Irregular forms
- ❖ Placement of object pronouns

### National Standards

- ❖ Communication Standard 1.1 pages 294, 295, 299, 301, 302, 303, 304, 305, 307, 314
- ❖ Communication Standard 1.2 pages 295, 299, 302, 304, 306, 307, 308–309, 310, 311, 312–313, 314
- ❖ Communication Standard 1.3 pages 309, 315
- ❖ Cultures Standard 2.1 page 310
- ❖ Cultures Standard 2.2 pages 306, 308–309, 311
- ❖ Connections Standard 3.1 pages 310, 311, 312–313
- ❖ Comparisons Standard 4.2 pages 312–313, 315
- ❖ Communities Standard 5.1 page 319
- ❖ Communities Standard 5.2 page 304

## PACING AND PRIORITIES

**The chapter content is color coded below to assist you in planning.**

■ **required** ■ **recommended** ■ **optional**

**Vocabulario** *(required)* *Days 1–4*

- ■ Palabras 1
  - La cocina
  - ¡A cocinar!
  - Algunos comestibles
- ■ Palabras 2
  - ¡A preparar la comida!
  - Más comestibles

**Estructura** *(required)* *Days 5–7*

- ■ Imperativo formal: formas regulares
- ■ Imperativo formal: formas irregulares
- ■ Colocación de los pronombres de complemento

**Conversación** *(required)*

- ■ ¿Yo? ¿En la cocina?

**Lecturas culturales**

- ■ Una receta española *(recommended)*
- ■ El tomate, ¿comida o veneno? *(optional)*
- ■ El maíz y la papa, regalos de las Américas *(optional)*

**Conexiones**

- ■ La nutrición *(optional)*

■ **¡Te toca a ti!** *(recommended)*

■ **Assessment** *(recommended)*

■ **¡Hablo como un pro!** *(optional)*

## RESOURCE GUIDE

| Section | Pages | Section Resources |
|---|---|---|
| **Vocabulario PALABRAS 1** | | |
| La cocina<br>¡A cocinar!<br>Algunos comestibles | 292, 294–295<br>292, 294–295<br>293, 294–295 | Vocabulary Transparencies 10.2–10.3<br>Audio CD 6<br>Audio Activities TE, pages 117–119<br>Workbook, pages 109–110<br>Quiz 1, page 45<br>ExamView® Pro |
| **Vocabulario PALABRAS 2** | | |
| ¡A preparar la comida!<br>Más comestibles | 296, 298–299<br>297, 298–299 | Vocabulary Transparencies 10.4–10.5<br>Audio CD 6<br>Audio Activities TE, pages 120–121<br>Workbook, pages 111–113<br>Quiz 2, page 46<br>ExamView® Pro |
| **Estructura** | | |
| Imperativo formal: formas regulares<br>Imperativo formal: formas irregulares<br>Colocación de los pronombres de complemento | 300–302<br>303–304<br>305 | Audio CD 6<br>Audio Activities TE, pages 122–124<br>Workbook, pages 114–116<br>Quizzes 3–5, pages 47–49<br>ExamView® Pro |
| **Conversación** | | |
| ¿Yo? ¿En la cocina? | 306–307 | Audio CD 6<br>Audio Activities TE, page 125<br>Interacting CD-ROM |
| **Lecturas culturales** | | |
| Una receta española<br>El tomate, ¿comida o veneno?<br>El maíz y la papa, regalos de las Américas | 308–309<br>310<br>311 | Audio CD 6<br>Audio Activities TE, page 126<br>Tests, pages 152, 155 |
| **Conexiones** | | |
| La nutrición | 312–313 | Tests, page 157 |
| **¡Te toca a ti!** | | |
| | 314–315 | **¡Viva el mundo hispano!** Video, Episode 10<br>Video Activities, pages 101–103<br>Spanish Online Activities spanish.glencoe.com |
| **Assessment** | | |
| | 316–317 | Communication Transparency C 10<br>Quizzes 1–5, pages 45–49<br>Performance Assessment, Task 10<br>Tests, pages 149–162<br>Situation Cards, Chapter 10<br>ExamView® Pro<br>**Maratón mental** Videoquiz |

# Using Your Resources for Chapter 10

## Transparencies

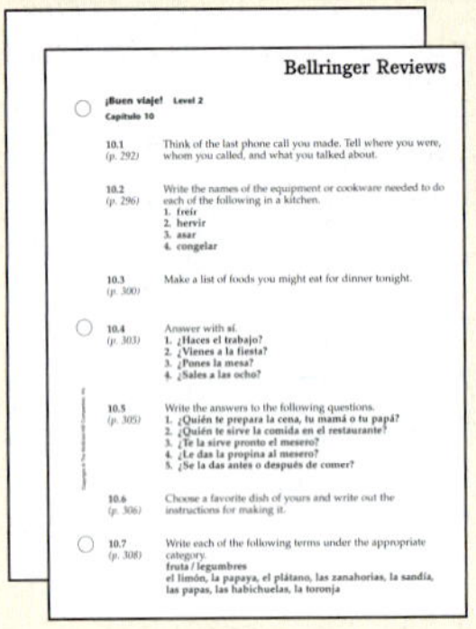
Bellringer 10.1–10.6

Vocabulary 10.1–10.5

Communication C 10

## Workbook

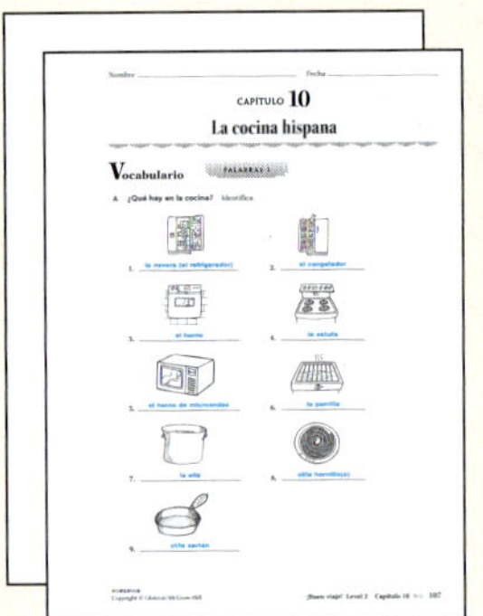
Vocabulary, pages 109–113

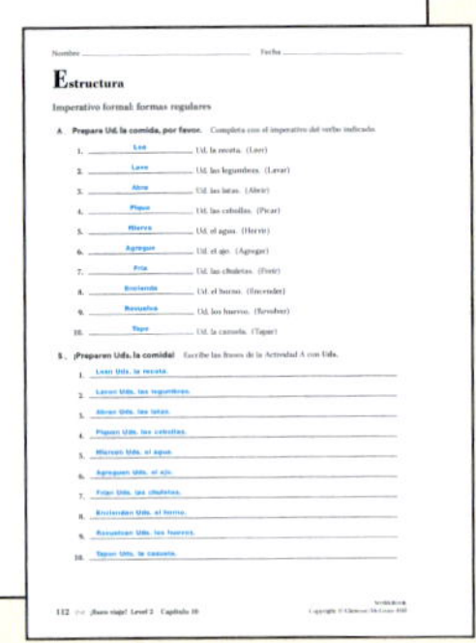
Structure, pages 114–116

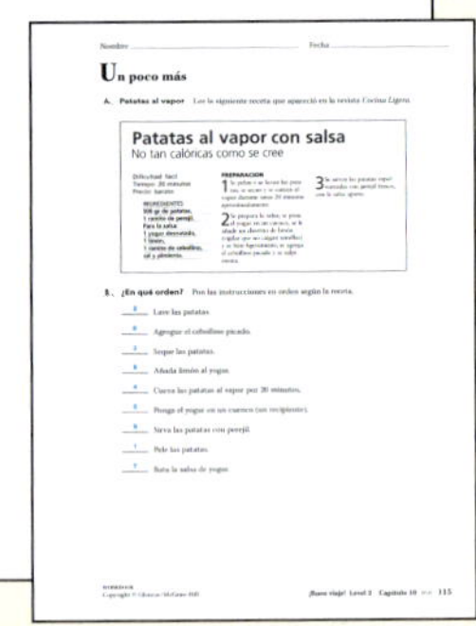
Enrichment, pages 117–120

## Audio Activities

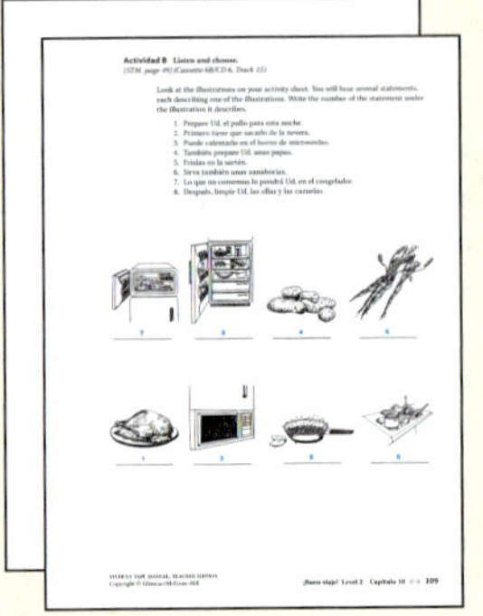
Vocabulary, pages 117–121

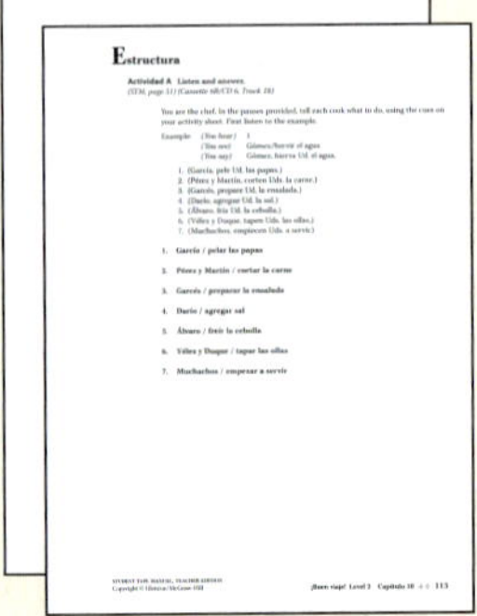
Structure, pages 122–124

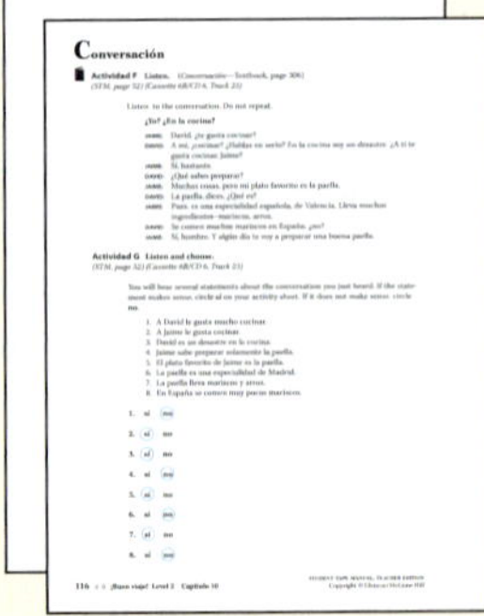
Conversation, page 125

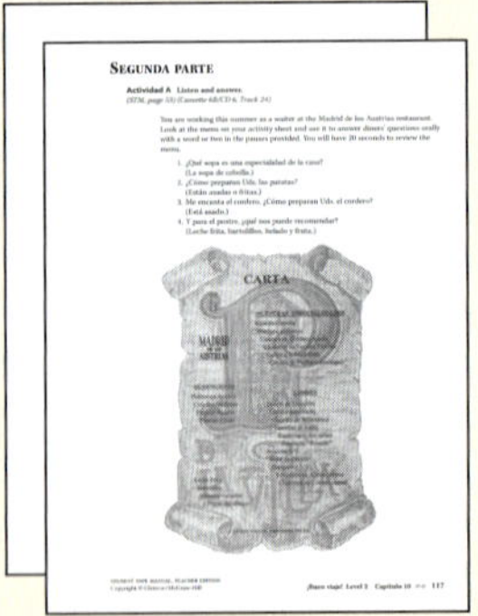
Additional Practice, pages 127–130

# Assessment

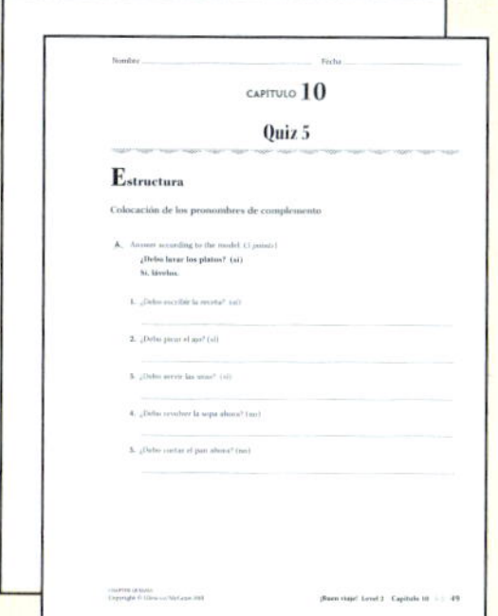
Vocabulary and Structure Quizzes, pages 45–49

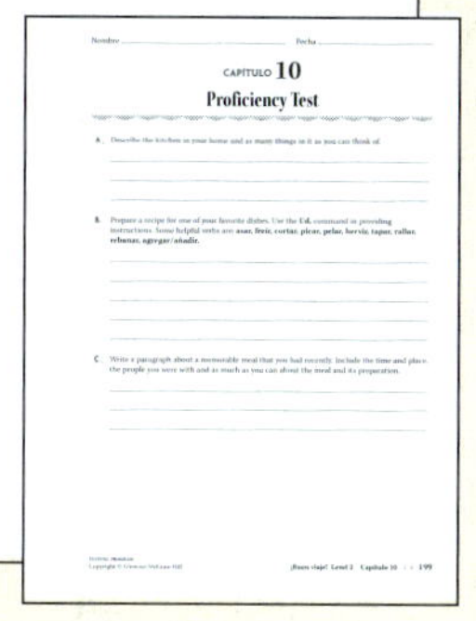
Chapter Tests, pages 149–162

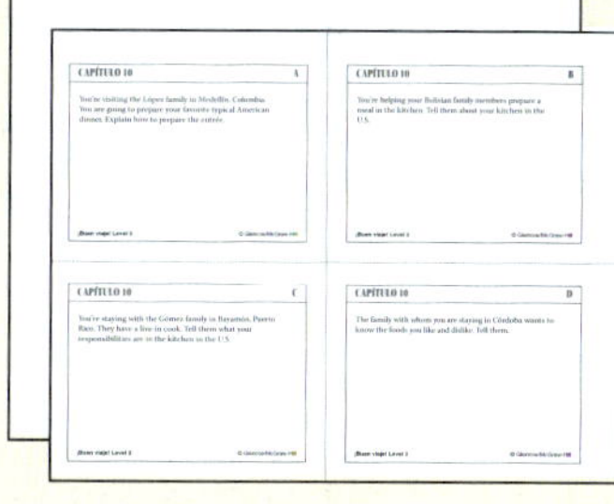
Situation Cards, Chapter 10

MindJogger Videoquiz, ExamView® Pro, Chapter 10

## Timesaving Teacher Tools

### TeacherWorks™

TeacherWorks™ is your all-in-one teacher resource center. Personalize lesson plans, access resources from the Teacher Wraparound Edition, connect to the Internet, or make a to-do list. These are only a few of the many features that can assist you in the planning and organizing of your lessons.

Includes:

- A calendar feature
- Access to all program blackline masters
- Standards correlations and more

### ExamView® Pro

Test Bank software for Macintosh and Windows makes creating, editing, customizing, and printing tests quick and easy.

## Technology Resources

In the Chapter 10 Internet Activity, you will have a chance to learn more about the Spanish-speaking world. Visit spanish.glencoe.com

On the interactive CD–ROM, students can listen to and take part in a recorded version of the conversation in Chapter 10.

**¡Viva el mundo hispano!** Video and Video Activities, Chapter 10. Available on VHS and DVD.

Help your students prepare for the chapter test by playing the **Maratón mental** Videoquiz game show. Teams will compete against each other to review chapter vocabulary and structure and sharpen listening comprehension skills. Available on VHS and DVD.

**¡Buen viaje!** is also available on CD or Online.

## Preview

In this chapter, students will learn to talk about food and its preparation. Students will also increase their communication skills by learning the formal imperative forms as well as the placement of object pronouns with them. The cultural focus of this chapter is on the variety of foods and recipes available in the Spanish-speaking world and the important role that cuisine plays in it.

### National Standards

**Communication**

In Chapter 10 students will learn to communicate in spoken and written Spanish on the following topics:

- foods
- food preparation
- the origins of specific foods

Students will obtain and provide information about these topics and engage in conversations that would typically take place in a kitchen as they fulfill the chapter objectives listed on this page.

Capítulo 10

# La cocina hispana

**Objetivos**

In this chapter you will learn to:

- talk about foods and food preparation
- give commands
- refer to people and things previously mentioned
- prepare some regional specialties
- talk about the origin of several foods

Manuel Serrano *A Mexican Kitchen in 1885*

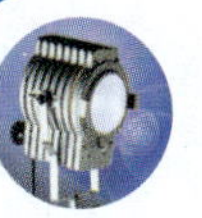

## Spotlight on Culture

**Fotografía** The photo shows traditional Spanish foods. Pictured are varieties of **embutidos** (the generic word for *sausages*): **chorizos, salchichones,** and others. There is also a whole **jamón serrano**. On the wall is a **ristra** (*string of hot peppers*) called **chiles picantes** in Mexico or **guindillas** in Spain.

The poster is of Trujillo in the province of Cáceres, in the region of Extremadura. Trujillo was the home of three of the most famous **conquistadores**, Francisco Pizarro and his brothers Gonzalo and Hernando.

## LEVELING

The activities, conversations, and readings within each chapter are marked according to level of difficulty. **E** indicates easy. **A** indicates average. **C** indicates challenging. Some activities cover a range of difficulty. In some activities, for example, advanced students will be able to produce more extensive responses while students who learn at a different rate may give less detailed responses. The leveling indicators will help you individualize instruction to best meet your students' needs.

# Vocabulario
PALABRAS 1

## 1 PREPARATION

### Resource Manager

Vocabulary Transparencies 10.2–10.3
Audio Activities TE, pages 117–119
Audio CD 6
Workbook, pages 109–110
Quizzes, page 45
ExamView® Pro

### Bellringer Review

*Use BRR Transparency 10.1 or write the following on the board.*
Think of the last phone call you made. Tell where you were, whom you called, and what you talked about.

## 2 PRESENTATION

**Step 1** Have students close their books. Project Vocabulary Transparencies 10.2–10.3 and have them repeat the new words, phrases, and sentences after you or Audio CD 6. You may wish to use your own props, such as photos of kitchens or items from your own kitchen.

**Step 2** Intersperse the presentation with questions which elicit the new vocabulary.

**Step 3** After students have produced the new vocabulary several times, have them open their books to pages 292–293. Call on volunteers to read the new words, phrases, and sentences.

# Vocabulario
PALABRAS 1

## La cocina

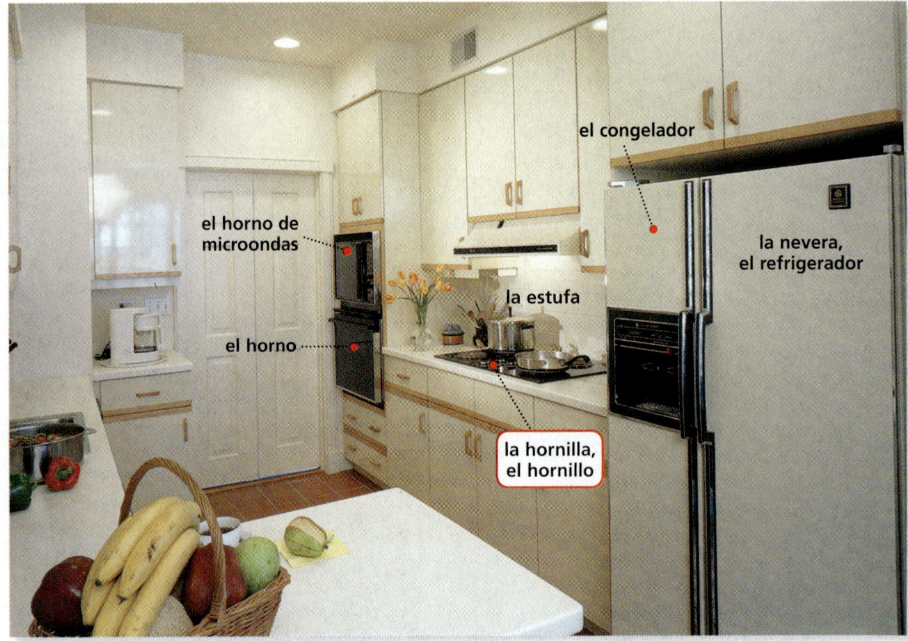


## ¡A cocinar!

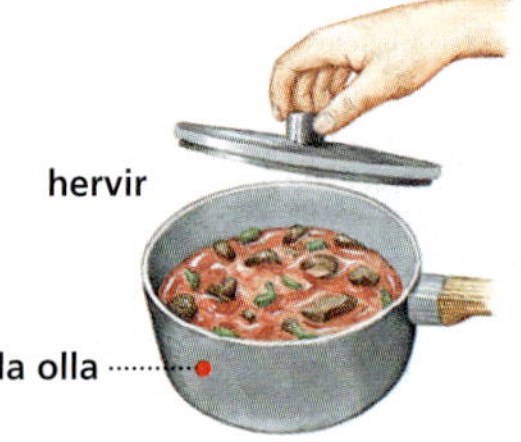


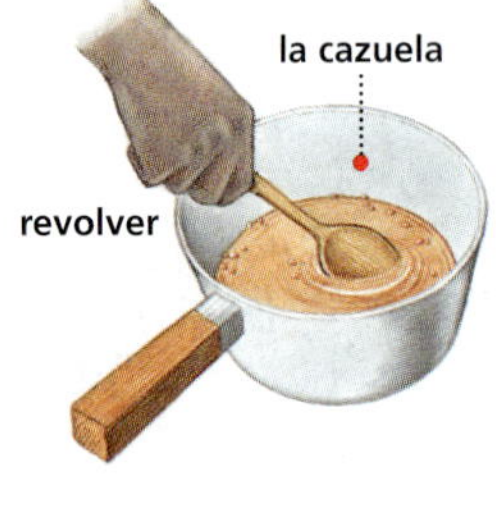


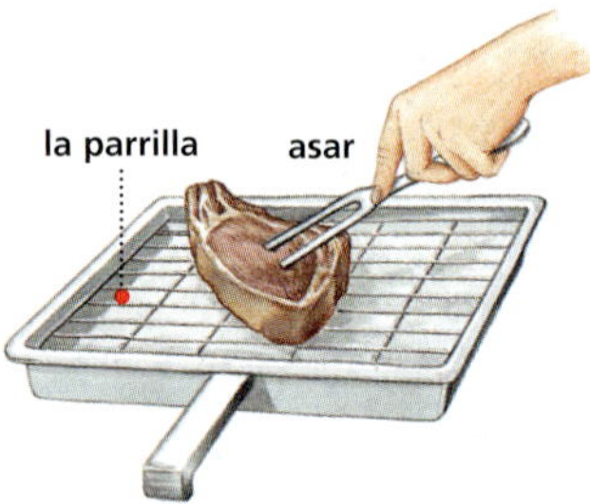




## Reaching All Students

**Total Physical Response**

*(Student 1),* levántate.
Ven acá, por favor.
Vas a cocinar.
Pon la sartén en la hornilla.
Pon las papas en la sartén y fríelas.
Pon las habichuelas en la olla.
Revuelve las habichuelas.
Abre el horno.
Asa el pollo en el horno.
Ahora come.
Gracias, *(Student 1).* Bien hecho. Regresa a tu asiento.

# Vocabulario

## Algunos comestibles

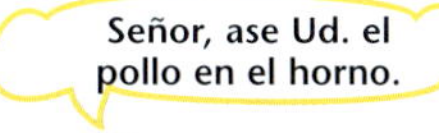

## Reaching All Students

**Cooperative Learning**
Have half the teams in the class make lists of food items. Have the other half make lists of kitchen items. Teams exchange papers and write sentences using the items on their new lists. When finished, they can check and correct their sentences with the team that drew up the original list.

## About the Spanish Language

The names for kitchen appliances and foods often vary from region to region. A *range* can be **una cocina (eléctrica / de gas),** a *refrigerator* can be **un frigorífico. La toronja** in Spain is **el pomelo.** Ask heritage speakers what name they give to each of the vocabulary items shown.

## Chapter Projects

**Cocina hispana**
Make a **paella** using the recipe on page 308 or prepare another dish from a Spanish-speaking country with your class.

**LEVELING**

**A:** Vocabulary

Vocabulario

## 3 PRACTICE

## ¿Qué palabra necesito?

**¡OJO!** When students are doing the **¿Que palabra necesito?** activities, accept any answer that makes sense. The purpose of these activities is to have students use the new vocabulary. They are not factual recall activities. Thus, it is not necessary for students to remember specific factual information from the vocabulary presentation when answering. If you wish, have students use the photos on this page as a stimulus, when possible.

**Historieta** Each time **Historieta** appears, it means that the answers to the activity form a short story. Encourage students to look at the title of the **Historieta,** since it can help them do the activity.

**1** **Expansion:** After going over this activity, have students write a short description of the kitchen in the photograph.

**2** You may wish to have students prepare the activity before going over it in class.

Vocabulario

## ¿Qué palabra necesito?

### 1 Historieta En la cocina Contesten.

1. ¿Está la señora en la cocina?
2. ¿Es una cocina moderna o anticuada?
3. ¿Cuántas hornillas tiene la estufa?
4. ¿Es una estufa eléctrica o de gas?
5. ¿Hay un refrigerador moderno en la cocina?
6. ¿Cuántas puertas tiene el refrigerador?
7. ¿Tiene congelador un refrigerador moderno?
8. ¿Qué haces tú en la cocina?

Restaurante El Sur, Estepona, España

### 2 ¿Qué necesita el cocinero? Completen.

1. El cocinero necesita una ___ porque va a freír algo.
2. El cocinero necesita una parrilla porque va a ___ algo.
3. El cocinero necesita una ___ porque va a hervir algo.
4. El cocinero va a ___ el agua.
5. El cocinero va a ___ las chuletas de cerdo.
6. El cocinero va a ___ los huevos.

### 3 Lo que me gusta y lo que no me gusta

Contesten.

1. ¿Te gustan las uvas?
2. ¿Te gusta la ensalada de lechuga y tomates?
3. ¿Te gustan las papas asadas?
4. ¿Te gustan más las toronjas o las naranjas?
5. ¿Te gustan más las legumbres o las frutas?
6. ¿Te gusta el limón?
7. ¿Te gusta más el pollo frito o el pollo asado?
8. ¿Te gusta más la carne o el pescado?

## ANSWERS TO ¿Qué palabra necesito?

1. No, la señora no está en la cocina.
2. Es una cocina moderna.
3. La estufa tiene cuatro hornillas.
4. Es una estufa de gas (eléctrica).
5. Sí, hay un refrigerador moderno en la cocina.
6. El refrigerador tiene dos puertas.
7. Sí, un refrigerador moderno tiene un congelador.
8. En la cocina yo ___.

1. sartén
2. asar
3. olla
4. hervir
5. freír (asar)
6. freír (revolver, hervir)

1. Sí, (No, no) me gustan las uvas.
2. Sí, (No, no) me gusta la ensalada de lechuga y tomates.
3. Sí, (No, no) me gustan las papas asadas.
4. Me gustan más las naranjas (toronjas).
5. Me gustan más las legumbres (las frutas).
6. Sí, (No, no) me gusta el limón.
7. Me gusta más el pollo frito (asado).
8. Me gusta más la carne (el pescado).

### 4 ¿A qué grupo pertenece?

Digan la categoría a la cual pertenece cada comestible.

1. la cebolla
2. la toronja
3. la zanahoria
4. el cerdo
5. la papa
6. el cordero
7. el limón
8. las uvas
9. la pimienta

Mercado de San Miguel, Madrid, España

### 5 Nuestras comidas favoritas

Con un(a) compañero(a) hagan una lista de sus comidas favoritas. Luego decidan a cuál de los dos le gustan más las comidas que son buenas para la salud.

### 6 Una cocina

Trabaja con un(a) compañero(a). Miren esta foto de una cocina. Juntos describan la cocina. Indiquen si es una cocina moderna o anticuada.

## Vocabulario

**3** This activity reincorporates food vocabulary from previous chapters and reviews the verb **gustar.** Activity 3 can be done first orally with books closed.

**4** This activity can also be done without prior preparation.

**¡OJO!** Note that the activities are color-coded. All the activities in the text are communicative. However, the ones with blue titles are guided communication. The red titles indicate that the answers to the activity are more open-ended and can vary more. You may wish to correct students' mistakes more so in the guided activities than in the activities with a red title, which lend themselves to a freer response.

### Learning from Photos

*(page 294 middle)* Ask students to tell what the man's profession is and what he is doing.
*(page 295 middle)* **El Mercado de San Miguel** is in Old Madrid, just off the **Calle Mayor.** It is a wonderfully preserved municipal market dating from the early 1900s.
*(page 294 top and page 295 bottom)* You may wish to ask students to describe each of the two modern kitchens.

### LEVELING

**E:** Activities 1, 2, 3, 4, 6
**A:** Activities 4, 5, 6

## Answers to ¿Qué palabra necesito?

**4**

1. legumbre
2. fruta
3. legumbre
4. carne
5. legumbre
6. carne
7. fruta
8. fruta
9. especia

**5** *Answers will vary. Students will use the food vocabulary from* Palabras 1 *to write their lists. For more food vocabulary tell students to skip ahead to* Palabras 2.

**6** *Answers will vary. Students will use the kitchen vocabulary from* Palabras 1 *to describe the kitchen in the photo.*

# Vocabulario
PALABRAS 2

## 1 PREPARATION

### Resource Manager

Vocabulary Transparencies 10.4–10.5
Audio Activities TE, pages 120–121
Audio CD 6
Workbook, pages 111–113
Quizzes, page 46
ExamView® Pro

### Bellringer Review

*Use BRR Transparency 10.2 or write the following on the board.*
Write the names of the equipment or cookware needed to do each of the following in a kitchen.

1. **freír**
2. **hervir**
3. **asar**
4. **congelar**

## 2 PRESENTATION

**Step 1** Have students close their books. Model the **Palabras 2** vocabulary using Vocabulary Transparencies 10.4–10.5. Have students repeat the new material after you or Audio CD 6.

**Step 2** Dramatize the meaning of these words: **limpiar, pelar, rallar, rebanar, cortar, agregar, picar, tapar, retirar.**

**Step 3** When students have produced the new vocabulary several times, have them open their books to pages 296–297 and call on volunteers to read the words, phrases, and sentences. Model pronunciation as necessary.

# Vocabulario
PALABRAS 2

## ¡A preparar la comida!

limpiar

pelar

rallar

rebanar

cortar

agregar, añadir

los pedacitos, los trocitos

tapar

Anita pone la cacerola al fuego.

Anita quita (retira) la cacerola del fuego. Apaga el fuego.



## Reaching All Students

**Total Physical Response**

*(Student 1),* **ven acá, por favor.**
**Ve a la cocina.**
**Saca la carne del refrigerador.**
**Asa la carne en el horno.**
**Pela las papas.**
**Pon el aceite en la sartén.**
**Pica el ajo.**
**Agrega las papas y el ajo al aceite.**
**Fríe las papas y el ajo.**
**Limpia la lechuga.**
**Prepara la ensalada.**
**Pon la olla al fuego.**
**Pela las zanahorias y córtalas en rebanadas.**
**Agrega las zanahorias.**
**Gracias,** *(Student 1).* **Vuelve a tu asiento.**

## Más comestibles

### About the Spanish Language

- In Mexico and some other countries all *peppers* are called **chiles,** not **pimientos.** *Bell peppers,* in most Spanish-speaking countries, are called **pimientos.** *Small hot peppers* are **ajíes.**
- In Puerto Rico *sweet bananas* for eating are **guineos. Plátanos** are *big cooking bananas.* In Venezuela a *banana* is called **un cambur.**
- While in most places any *lobster* is called **una langosta,** the word really refers to the clawless, spiny lobster. The *Atlantic lobster* is called **un bogavante.**

### Chapter Projects

**Mi comida favorita**
Have students make a list of their favorite foods. As they go through the chapter, have them observe and jot down differences between Hispanic and North American eating habits.

## Vocabulario

### 3 PRACTICE

## ¿Qué palabra necesito?

**7** This activity can be done without prior preparation.
**Note:** In Activity 7 students hear the formal command form but they do not have to use it.

**8** Have students refer to the photos as they do the activity. This activity also reviews the present progressive.

**LEVELING**

**E:** Activities 8, 9, 10, 12
**A:** Activities 7, 9, 10, 11, 12
**C:** Activity 11



## ¿Qué palabra necesito?

### 7 Una receta buena o mala

¿Es algo que se hace o no?

1. Corte el pan en rebanadas para tostarlo.
2. Hierva el agua para preparar el té.
3. Fría bien la sandía.
4. Limpie la lechuga antes de comerla.
5. Pele las cebollas antes de comerlas.
6. Apague el fuego antes de empezar a cocinar.
7. Fría las papas en aceite.
8. Ponga la sartén al fuego para hervir el agua.

Lima, Perú

### 8 Preparando la comida

Contesten según las fotos.

1. ¿Qué está picando la señora?

2. ¿Qué está rebanando el señor?

3. ¿Qué está cortando la señorita?

4. ¿Qué está pelando el joven?

5. ¿Qué está limpiando la muchacha?



### Answers to ¿Qué palabra necesito?

**7**

1. Sí
2. Sí
3. No
4. Sí
5. Sí
6. No
7. Sí
8. No

**8**

1. La señora está picando los tomates.
2. El señor está rebanando el pan.
3. La señorita está cortando los pimientos.
4. El joven está pelando las zanahorias.
5. La muchacha está limpiando la papa.

**9** **¿Qué opinas?** Digan si se puede o no.

1. ¿Se puede hervir o freír el arroz?
2. ¿Se puede rallar la lechuga?
3. ¿Se puede rallar el queso o el coco?
4. ¿Se puede rebanar la sandía?
5. ¿Se puede picar la carne de res?
6. ¿Se puede freír la chuleta?
7. ¿Se puede asar el arroz?
8. ¿Se puede tapar la olla?

**10** **Historieta Cocinando algo**
Contesten según se indica.

1. ¿Qué estás preparando? (un pollo)
2. ¿Lo vas a asar o freír? (asar)
3. ¿Qué tienes que hacer con el pollo antes de asarlo? (lavarlo)
4. ¿Lo vas a asar entero? (no)
5. ¿Qué vas a hacer? (cortarlo en pedazos)
6. ¿Vas a sazonar el pollo? (sí, con ajo, sal y pimienta)
7. ¿Dónde lo vas a asar? (en el horno)
8. ¿Lo vas a asar a fuego lento? (sí)
9. ¿Qué vas a servir con el pollo? (una ensalada)
10. Y de postre, ¿qué hay? (frutas)

**11** **Una comida norteamericana** Estás en Lima, Perú, con la familia Sandoval. Ellos quieren comer una comida típica norteamericana. La señora Sandoval (tu compañero[a]) te pide describir una comida típica norteamericana. Describe la comida y dile a la señora cómo prepararla. Después cambien de rol.

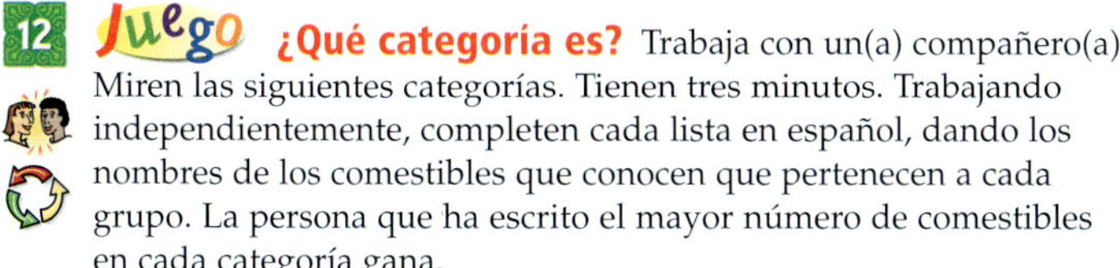

**12** **Juego ¿Qué categoría es?** Trabaja con un(a) compañero(a). Miren las siguientes categorías. Tienen tres minutos. Trabajando independientemente, completen cada lista en español, dando los nombres de los comestibles que conocen que pertenecen a cada grupo. La persona que ha escrito el mayor número de comestibles en cada categoría gana.

*For more practice using words from **Palabras 1** and **2**, do Activity 10 on page H11 at the end of this book.*



## Vocabulario

**9** Have students correct the false statements in this activity.

**10** This activity can be done first orally with books closed.
**Expansion:** After going over Activity 10, have students retell the story in their own words.

### Learning from Realia

*(page 299)* Rice is an important staple in Spanish cuisine. It is the basis of the **paella** and many other traditional dishes. There are restaurants in Madrid and Valencia that specialize almost exclusively in rice-based dishes. Spain is a major producer.

UN POCO MÁS This *InfoGap* Activity will allow students to practice in pairs. The activity should be very manageable for them, since all vocabulary and structures are familiar to them.

## ANSWERS TO ¿Qué palabra necesito?

**9**

1. Sí, se puede hervir o freír el arroz.
2. No, no se puede rallar la lechuga.
3. Sí, se puede rallar el queso o el coco.
4. Sí, se puede rebanar la sandía.
5. Sí, se puede picar la carne de res.
6. Sí, se puede freír la chuleta.
7. No, no se puede asar el arroz.
8. Sí, se puede tapar la olla.

**10**

1. Estoy preparando un pollo.
2. Lo voy a asar.
3. Tengo que lavarlo antes de asarlo.
4. No, no lo voy a asar entero.
5. Voy a cortarlo en pedazos.
6. Sí, voy a sazonar el pollo con ajo, sal y pimienta.
7. Lo voy a asar en el horno.
8. Sí, lo voy a asar a fuego lento.
9. Voy a servir una ensalada con el pollo.
10. De postre hay frutas.

**11** *Answers will vary. Students can use the sequence of events presented at the bottom of page 297 as a guide for giving directions to prepare their favorite meal.*

**12** *Answers will vary. Students can use food vocabulary from both* Palabras 1 *and* Palabras 2 *to make their lists.*

# Estructura

## 1 PREPARATION

### Resource Manager

Audio Activities TE, pages 122–124
Audio CD 6
Workbook, pages 114–116
Quizzes, pages 47–49
ExamView® Pro

### Bellringer Review

*Use BRR Transparency 10.3 or write the following on the board.*
Make a list of foods you might eat for dinner tonight.

## 2 PRESENTATION

### Imperativo formal: formas regulares

**Step 1** Have students open their books to pages 300–301 and lead them through Items 1 and 2.

**Step 2** Illustrate the difference between singular and plural imperatives by giving a command to an individual and then the same command to a group of students. For example: **María, tome usted su libro de español. María y José, tomen ustedes su libro de español.**

**Step 3** Practice negative forms by calling out affirmative commands and having students change them to the negative. Then reverse the procedure.

# Estructura

## Imperativo formal: formas regulares

### Telling people what to do

1. You use the command form of the verb—the imperative—to tell someone what to do. To form the **usted** and **ustedes** commands, you drop the **o** from the present tense **yo** form and add the following endings.

| INFINITIVE | YO—PRESENT | UD. COMMAND | UDS. COMMAND |
|---|---|---|---|
| preparar | preparø | prepare Ud. | preparen Uds. |
| leer | leø | lea Ud. | lean Uds. |
| abrir | abrø | abra Ud. | abran Uds. |

You form the imperative of stem-changing verbs in the same way. The **yo** form of the present tense serves as the stem.

| | | | |
|---|---|---|---|
| **pensar** | **piensø** | **piense Ud.** | **piensen Uds.** |
| **volver** | **vuelvø** | **vuelva Ud.** | **vuelvan Uds.** |
| **hervir** | **hiervø** | **hierva Ud.** | **hiervan Uds.** |
| **pedir** | **pidø** | **pida Ud.** | **pidan Uds.** |

**¿Te acuerdas?**

Remember the following spelling patterns.

| | |
|---|---|
| **busca** | **busque** |
| **agrega** | **agregue** |
| **empieza** | **empiece** |

Note that the endings used for the formal commands have the vowel opposite to the vowel usually associated with the conjugation. The **-ar** verbs have **e** and the **-er** and **-ir** verbs have **a.**

2. To make these commands negative, simply place **no** before the verb.

| | | | |
|---|---|---|---|
| **prepare Ud.** | **no prepare Ud.** | **preparen Uds.** | **no preparen Uds.** |
| **pida Ud.** | **no pida Ud.** | **pidan Uds.** | **no pidan Uds.** |
| **abra Ud.** | **no abra Ud.** | **abran Uds.** | **no abran Uds.** |

ENCHILADAS DE CHILE ANCHO

(6 porciones)

| | | | |
|---|---|---|---|
| 2 | cucharadas de aceite | 1 | cubo de Maggi Pollo |
| 1 | diente de ajo | 1 | lata de **Media Crema** |
| ¼ | de cebolla | 12 | tortillas pasadas por aceite caliente |
| 3 | pimientas grandes | 1 | pechuga de pollo cocida y deshebrada |
| 1 | rajita de canela | ¼ | de cebolla picada |
| 3 | chiles anchos lavados y sin semillas | 50 | g de queso blanco rallado |
| 3 | tazas de agua | | |

Calienta el aceite y sofríe el ajo y la cebolla, agrega las pimientas, la canela, los chiles y el agua, sazona con el Maggi Pollo y cocina durante 5 minutos, deja enfriar y licua lo anterior con la **Media Crema**. Regrésala al fuego para que se caliente. Rellena las tortillas con el pollo, dóblalas y sirve bañando con la salsa anterior. Espolvorea la cebolla y el queso. Sirve caliente.

TIP

Puedes asar los chiles en lugar de freírlos.



### Learning from Photos

*(page 300)* The recipe is for enchiladas made with **chile ancho**. The **chile ancho** is a relatively mild, delicious pepper grown in Mexico and New Mexico.

You may wish to prepare this dish with your class.

# ¿Cómo lo digo?

**13** **La ensalada** Contesten según el modelo.

1. ¿Preparo la comida?
2. ¿Limpio la lechuga?
3. ¿Pelo los tomates?
4. ¿Pico el ajo?
5. ¿Hiervo el agua?
6. ¿Frío el pollo?
7. ¿Tapo la sartén?
8. ¿Retiro la sartén del fuego?

Gazpacho

Caracas, Venezuela

**14** **¿Preparamos la comida?**

Contesten según el modelo.

**¿Preparamos la comida?**
**No, no preparen ustedes la comida. Yo la voy a preparar.**

1. ¿Preparamos la comida?
2. ¿Limpiamos la lechuga?
3. ¿Pelamos los tomates?
4. ¿Picamos el ajo?
5. ¿Hervimos el agua?
6. ¿Freímos el pollo?
7. ¿Tapamos la sartén?
8. ¿Retiramos la sartén del fuego?



Estructura

## 3 PRACTICE

## ¿Cómo lo digo?

**13** **and** **14** Have pairs of students present these activities as miniconversations.

### Learning from Photos

*(page 301 top)* **Gazpacho** is often described as a liquid salad. It is made from tomatoes, olive oil, vinegar, and each of the ingredients surrounding it on the table, which also serve as garnishes. **Gazpacho** is always served cold. *(page 301 bottom)* You may wish to ask students to describe the kitchen pictured, the people in it, and the activities going on.

### LEVELING

**E:** Activities 13, 16
**A:** Activities 13, 14, 15, 16, 17

## Answers to ¿Cómo lo digo?

**13**

1. Sí, prepare usted la comida.
2. Sí, limpie usted la lechuga.
3. Sí, pele usted los tomates.
4. Sí, pique usted el ajo.
5. Sí, hierva usted el agua.
6. Sí, fría usted el pollo.
7. Sí, tape usted la sartén.
8. Sí, retire usted la sartén del fuego.

**14**

1. No, no preparen ustedes la comida. Yo la voy a preparar.
2. No, no limpien ustedes la lechuga. Yo la voy a limpiar.
3. No, no pelen ustedes los tomates. Yo los voy a pelar.
4. No, no piquen ustedes el ajo. Yo lo voy a picar.
5. No, no hiervan ustedes el agua. Yo lo voy a hervir.
6. No, no frían ustedes el pollo. Yo lo voy a freír.
7. No, no tapen ustedes la sartén. Yo la voy a tapar.
8. No, no retiren ustedes la sartén del fuego. Yo la voy a retirar.

# Estructura

## 3 PRACTICE *(continued)*

**15** and **16** Have students work in pairs and present these activities as miniconversations.

### Art Connection

El Greco (Doménikos Theotokópoulos) was born on the island of Crete in 1541. He studied in Italy, where he came in contact with artists of the Venetian school: Titian, Tintoretto, and Bassano. He arrived in Spain around 1576 and established himself in Toledo. Among his most important works are: *El Entierro del Conde de Orgaz* (in the church of Santo Tomé), *El Martirio de San Mauricio* (El Escorial), *El Caballero de la mano en el pecho* (Museo del Prado), *Vista de Toledo* (Metropolitan Museum, NY).
**Expansion:** Show the Fine Art Transparency of this painting by El Greco from the Transparency Binder. You may wish to have students read the background information accompanying this transparency and have them do the related activities.
**Note:** For *Vista de Toledo* and related activities, see the Fine Art Transparency.

# Estructura

**15** **¿Qué debo hacer con la carta?** Contesten con el imperativo.

1. ¿Debo aceptar la carta?
2. ¿Debo abrir la carta?
3. ¿Debo leer la carta?
4. ¿Debo contestar la carta?
5. ¿Debo escribir la carta en inglés?

*San Martín y el pordiosero* de El Greco

**16** **Debe hacer lo que quiere hacer.** Sigan el modelo.

1. Quiero viajar a España.
2. Quiero pasar un mes en Madrid.
3. Quiero tomar el tren a Toledo.
4. Quiero visitar la capital.
5. Quiero ver los cuadros de El Greco.
6. Quiero aprender el español.
7. Quiero comer una paella.
8. Quiero beber horchata.
9. Quiero vivir con una familia española.

**17** **Soy yo el/la profesor(a).** Trabajen en grupos de tres. Uno(a) de ustedes va a ser el/la profesor(a). Los otros serán los alumnos. El/La profesor(a) les va a dar una orden. Los alumnos van a decir si quieren hacerlo o no. El/La profesor(a) puede usar las siguientes palabras.

## Answers to ¿Cómo lo digo?

**15**
1. Sí, acepte usted la carta.
2. Sí, abra usted la carta.
3. Sí, lea usted la carta.
4. Sí, conteste usted la carta.
5. Sí, escriba usted la carta en inglés.

**16**
1. Entonces, ¡viaje usted a España!
2. Entonces, ¡pase usted un mes en Madrid!
3. Entonces, ¡tome usted el tren a Toledo!
4. Entonces, ¡visite usted la capital!
5. Entonces, ¡vea usted los cuadros de El Greco!
6. Entonces, ¡aprenda usted el español!
7. Entonces, ¡coma usted una paella!
8. Entonces, ¡beba usted horchata!
9. Entonces, ¡viva usted con una familia española!

**17** *Answers will vary. Students will use the verbs in the colored boxes to do the activity.*

# Imperativo formal: formas irregulares

## Telling people what to do

1. A verb that has an irregularity in the **yo** form of the present tense will keep the same irregularity in the command form, since the **yo** form of the present tense serves as the root for the command. Study the following.

| INFINITIVE | YO—PRESENT | UD. COMMAND | UDS. COMMAND |
|---|---|---|---|
| hacer | hagø | haga Ud. | hagan Uds. |
| poner | pongø | ponga Ud. | pongan Uds. |
| salir | salgø | salga Ud. | salgan Uds. |
| venir | vengø | venga Ud. | vengan Uds. |
| decir | digø | diga Ud. | digan Uds. |
| introducir | introduzcø | introduzca Ud. | introduzcan Uds. |

2. The following verbs are the only ones in Spanish that have irregular command forms.

| INFINITIVE | UD. COMMAND | UDS. COMMAND |
|---|---|---|
| ir | vaya Ud. | vayan Uds. |
| ser | sea Ud. | sean Uds. |
| saber | sepa Ud. | sepan Uds. |
| estar | esté Ud. | estén Uds. |
| dar | dé Ud. | den Uds. |

Málaga, España

## ¿Cómo lo digo?

**18** **Voy de compras.** Sigan el modelo.

1. Quiero hacer las compras.
2. Quiero salir ahora.
3. Quiero ir al mercado de Santa Tecla.
4. Quiero poner mis compras en esta bolsa.
5. Quiero ir a pie.

# Estructura

## 1 PREPARATION

### Bellringer Review

*Use BRR Transparency 10.4 or write the following on the board.*
Answer with **sí**.

1. **¿Haces el trabajo?**
2. **¿Vienes a la fiesta?**
3. **¿Pones la mesa?**
4. **¿Sales a las ocho?**

## 2 PRESENTATION

### Imperativo formal: formas irregulares

**Step 1** Have students open their books to page 303. Lead them through Items 1 and 2.

**Step 2** Have them repeat the command forms after you.

## 3 PRACTICE

### ¿Cómo lo digo?

**18** Have students present the activity as a series of miniconversations.

## ANSWERS TO ¿Cómo lo digo?

**18**

1. Pues, haga usted las compras.
2. Pues, salga usted ahora.
3. Pues, vaya usted al mercado de Santa Tecla.
4. Pues, ponga usted sus compras en esta bolsa.
5. Pues, vaya usted a pie.

# Estructura

## 3 PRACTICE *(continued)*

### Recycling

Activity 20 reintroduces vocabulary from Chapter 3.

**Expansion:** After going over Activity 20, call on a student to explain how to use a public telephone.

**21** After students have done the activity in pairs, have them do it as a whole-class activity. One student describes a recipe and the class has to guess what the dish is.

**22** *Juego* This is a good end-of-class activity that students will enjoy.

**LEVELING**

**E:** Activity 22

**A:** Activities 18, 19, 20, 21, 22

**C:** Activities 23, 24



**19 ¿Podemos salir?** Sigan el modelo.

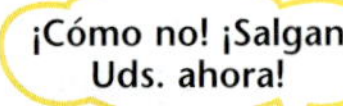

1. ¿Podemos salir mañana?
2. ¿Podemos usar el carro?
3. ¿Podemos llevar a Anita?
4. ¿Podemos volver?
5. ¿Podemos poner las maletas en la maletera?

**20 Una llamada telefónica**

Completen con el imperativo.

1. ____ (llamar) usted por teléfono.
2. ____ (hacer) usted la llamada esta noche.
3. ____ (ir) usted a una cabina telefónica.
4. ____ (descolgar) usted el auricular.
5. ____ (introducir) usted la tarjeta telefónica en la ranura.
6. ____ (esperar) usted el tono.
7. ____ (marcar) usted el número.
8. ____ (esperar) usted la contestación.
9. ____ (decir) usted quien es.
10. ____ (preguntar) usted por Antonio.
11. ____ (hablar) usted con él.

Estepona, España

**21 Dos recetas** Trabaja con un(a) compañero(a). Selecciona (Escoge) uno de tus platos favoritos—un plato no muy complicado. Luego dile a tu compañero(a) cómo se prepara el plato—es decir, le vas a dar la receta. Luego tu compañero(a) te dará la receta para su plato favorito.

**22** *Juego* **¡Hágalo!** Have some fun. Get together in small groups and make up commands telling your teacher what to do. Now it's your turn because a teacher always tells you what to do. **¿Verdad?**

**SPANISH *Online***

For more information about typical dishes and recipes from the Spanish-speaking world, go to the Glencoe Spanish Web site: spanish.glencoe.com

## ANSWERS TO ¿Cómo lo digo?

**19**

1. ¡Cómo no! ¡Salgan ustedes mañana!
2. ¡Cómo no! ¡Usen ustedes el carro!
3. ¡Cómo no! ¡Lleven ustedes a Anita!
4. ¡Cómo no! ¡Vuelvan ustedes!
5. ¡Cómo no! ¡Pongan ustedes las maletas en la maletera!

**20**

1. Llame
2. Haga
3. Vaya
4. Descuelgue
5. Introduzca
6. Espere
7. Marque
8. Espere
9. Diga
10. Pregunte
11. Hable

**21** *Answers will vary. Students will use the food preparation vocabulary from* Palabras 2 *to create a recipe for their favorite dishes.*

**22** *Answers will vary. Suggest that students give you commands that you can perform in class. Commands might include:* Abra usted el libro. Cierre usted la puerta.

## Colocación de los pronombres de complemento
### Referring to things already stated

The object pronouns are attached to the affirmative command. They come before, or precede, the negative command.

| | | |
|---|---|---|
| Lave los platos. | Lávelos. | No los lave Ud. |
| Coma la ensalada. | Cómala. | No la coma Ud. |
| Sirva el postre. | Sírvalo. | No lo sirva Ud. |
| Déme la receta. | Démela. | No me la dé Ud. |

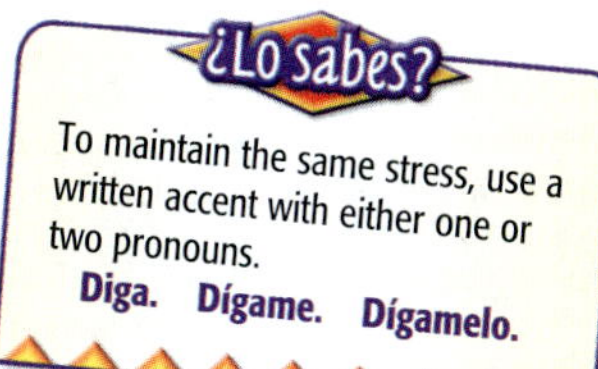


## ¿Cómo lo digo?

**23 ¿Qué debo hacer?** Contesten según el modelo.

**¿Debo limpiar la lechuga? ⟶**
**Sí, límpiela.**
**No, no la limpie usted.**

1. ¿Debo lavar los cuchillos?
2. ¿Debo pelar las naranjas?
3. ¿Debo abrir la lata?
4. ¿Debo leer la receta?
5. ¿Debo picar el ajo?
6. ¿Debo rallar el queso?
7. ¿Debo revolver los huevos?
8. ¿Debo poner el pollo en la nevera?

**24 Ellos no lo hicieron.**
Sigan el modelo.

**Ellos no cortaron la carne. ⟶**
**Pues, córtenla ustedes.**

1. Ellos no rebanaron el pan.
2. Ellos no hirvieron la sopa.
3. Ellos no frieron los huevos.
4. Ellos no taparon las ollas.
5. Ellos no añadieron azúcar.
6. Ellos no pusieron el pollo en el horno.

Una merienda, España

### Answers to ¿Cómo lo digo?

**23**

1. Sí, lávelos.
   No, no los lave usted.
2. Sí, pélelas.
   No, no las pele usted.
3. Sí, ábrala.
   No, no la abra usted.
4. Sí, léala.
   No, no la lea usted.
5. Sí, píquelo.
   No, no lo pique usted.
6. Sí, rállelo.
   No, no lo ralle usted.
7. Sí, revuélvalos.
   No, no los revuelva usted.
8. Sí, póngalo en la nevera.
   No, no lo ponga usted en la nevera.

**24**

1. Pues, rebánenlo ustedes.
2. Pues, hiérvanla ustedes.
3. Pues, fríanlos ustedes.
4. Pues, tápenlas ustedes.
5. Pues, añádanlo ustedes.
6. Pues, pónganlo ustedes en el horno.

## Estructura

### 1 PREPARATION

#### Bellringer Review

*Use BRR Transparency 10.5 or write the following on the board.*
Write the answers to the following questions.

1. **¿Quién te prepara la cena, tu mamá o tu papá?**
2. **¿Quién te sirve la comida en el restaurante?**
3. **¿Te la sirve pronto el mesero?**
4. **¿Le das la propina al mesero?**
5. **¿Se la das antes o después de comer?**

### 2 PRESENTATION

#### Colocación de los pronombres de complemento

**Step 1** Ask students to open their books to page 305. Lead them through the explanation.

**Step 2** Choose examples and write them on the board. Have students repeat the sentences.

### 3 PRACTICE

#### ¿Cómo lo digo?

**23** and **24** Have students work in pairs and present these activities to the class as miniconversations.

**¡Adelante!**
At this point in the chapter, students have learned all the vocabulary and structure necessary to complete the chapter. The conversation and cultural readings that follow recycle all the material learned up to this point.

## Conversación

## 1 PREPARATION

### Resource Manager

Audio Activities TE, page 125
Audio CD 6

### Bellringer Review

*Use BRR Transparency 10.6 or write the following on the board.*
Choose a favorite dish of yours and write out the instructions for making it.

## 2 PRESENTATION

**Step 1** To vary the procedure for presenting the conversation, don't tell students what it is about. Have them listen to Audio CD 6. Now ask them questions to see how much they understood.

**Step 2** Have students open their books. Call on two students to take the parts and read the conversation to the class.

**Step 3** After every six to eight sentences, ask some comprehension questions from the **¿Comprendes?** section.

**Step 4** Have students make up a conversation on the same theme—who does or doesn't like to cook.

### Glencoe Technology

On the CD-ROM, students can watch a dramatization of this conversation. They can then play the role of either one of the characters and record themselves in the conversation.

## Conversación

### ¿Yo? ¿En la cocina?   

**Jaime** David, ¿te gusta cocinar?
**David** A mí, ¿cocinar? ¿Hablas en serio? En la cocina soy un desastre. ¿A ti te gusta cocinar?
**Jaime** Sí, bastante.
**David** ¿Qué sabes preparar?
**Jaime** Muchas cosas, pero mi plato favorito es la paella.
**David** La paella, dices. ¿Qué es?
**Jaime** Pues, es una especialidad española, de Valencia. Lleva muchos ingredientes—mariscos, arroz.
**David** Se comen muchos mariscos en España, ¿no?
**Jaime** Sí, hombre. Y algún día te voy a preparar una buena paella.

### ¿Comprendes?

Contesten.

1. ¿A quién le gusta cocinar?
2. ¿Quién es un desastre en la cocina?
3. ¿Cuál es el plato que a Jaime le gusta mucho preparar?
4. ¿Dónde se come la paella?
5. ¿De qué región de España es la paella una especialidad?
6. ¿Qué opinas? ¿Te gustaría la paella o no?



### Answers to ¿Comprendes?

1. A Jaime le gusta cocinar.
2. David es un desastre en la cocina.
3. A Jaime le gusta mucho preparar la paella.
4. La paella se come en España.
5. La paella es una especialidad de Valencia.
6. Sí, (No, no) me gustaría la paella.

# Vamos a hablar más

**A** **La cafetería de la escuela**

Tu compañero(a) es la persona responsable de la cafetería de tu escuela. Dile cuáles son los platos que sirven en la cafetería que te gustan y cuáles son los platos que no te gustan. Dale algunas sugerencias *(suggestions)*. Dile lo que debe preparar y servir en la cafetería. Luego cambien de rol.

Colegio Santa Teresita, Santurce, Puerto Rico

Un restaurante, Ronda, España

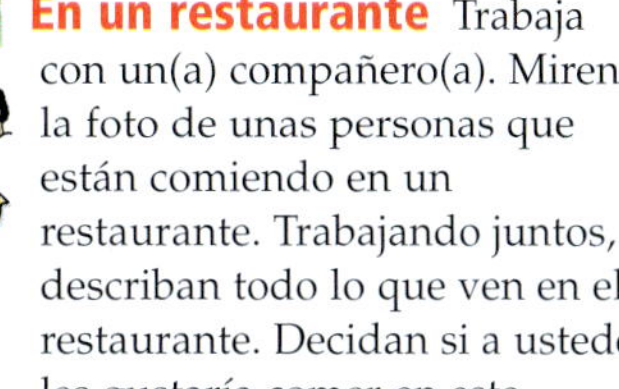

**B** **En un restaurante** Trabaja con un(a) compañero(a). Miren la foto de unas personas que están comiendo en un restaurante. Trabajando juntos, describan todo lo que ven en el restaurante. Decidan si a ustedes les gustaría comer en este restaurante.

**C** **Una comida española** Aquí ves una foto de un plato típico español. Trabaja con un(a) compañero(a). Identifiquen todos los ingredientes que ven. Luego expliquen cómo creen que se prepara este plato.

## Learning from Photos

*(page 307 top)* You may wish to ask these questions about the photo:

**¿Qué son las dos personas?**
**¿Dónde están ellos?**
**¿Viven en una zona muy fría?**
**¿Qué ropa llevan ellos?**
**¿Qué están haciendo?**

*(page 307 middle)* Ask students:

**¿Dónde está el restaurante?**
**¿Tiene una terraza el restaurante?**
**¿Hay algunas mesas libres?**
**¿Lee el menú el señor?**

*(page 307 bottom)* You may wish to ask students to look at the bottom photo on this page and do the following:

**Describe el plato que vemos.**

**LEVELING**

**E:** Conversation

## Answers to Vamos a hablar más

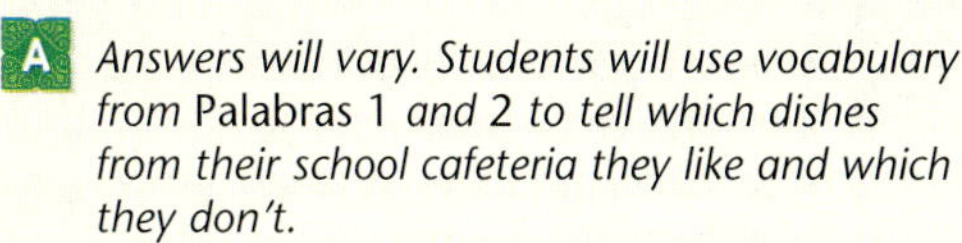

**A** *Answers will vary. Students will use vocabulary from* Palabras 1 *and 2 to tell which dishes from their school cafeteria they like and which they don't.*

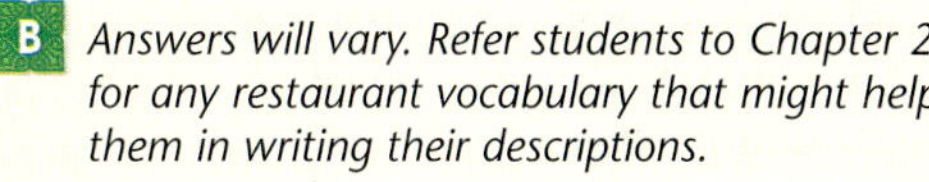

**B** *Answers will vary. Refer students to Chapter 2 for any restaurant vocabulary that might help them in writing their descriptions.*

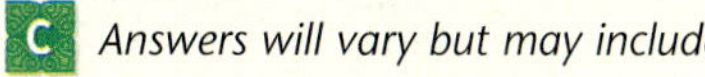

**C** *Answers will vary but may include:*

—Hay carne de res en el plato.
—También tiene maíz, tomates, zanahorias, habichuelas.
—Para preparar el plato, ase el carne. Pele las zanahorias.

# Lecturas culturales

## Resource Manager

Audio Activities TE, page 126
Audio CD 6

## Bellringer Review

*Use BRR Transparency 10.7 or write the following on the board.*
Write each of the following terms under the appropriate category.
**frutas / legumbres**
**el limón, la papaya, el plátano, las zanahorias, la sandía, las papas, las habichuelas, la toronja**

## National Standards

### Cultures

The reading about **paella** and the related activities familiarize students with a world-renowned specialty of Spanish cuisine.

### Comparisons

In this recipe, one of the measures is metric, in contrast with the English measures with which students are more familiar.

## PRESENTATION

### Pre-reading

Prior to reading the recipe you may wish to have students figure out the English equivalent of 1/2 kilo of shrimp. Tell them **un kilo** = 2.2 lbs.

### Reading

While going through the selection, have students repeat after you the new vocabulary in the recipe.

# Lecturas culturales

## Una receta española

Como le dijo Jaime a David, la paella es un plato delicioso que es una especialidad de la cocina española. Quien no ha comido una paella no sabe lo que se ha perdido. La paella valenciana lleva muchos ingredientes. Aquí tiene usted una receta bastante sencilla para preparar una paella. Decida si a usted le gustaría comer este plato delicioso.

### Reading Strategy

**Reading for detailed information** Some readings require a reader to focus in on details. When you need to do so, you will need to read a selection more than once and pay close attention. Sometimes when you need to be aware of details, it is helpful to take notes on what you read or make a list of the important details. Reading for detail is especially necessary with recipes. You must understand each step and follow the procedure carefully to ensure that the final product is as good as it can be.

### LA PAELLA

INGREDIENTES

3 tomates
2 cebollas grandes
2 pimientos (uno verde y uno rojo)
4 dientes[1] de ajo
1/2 kilo de camarones
4 calamares
12 almejas
12 mejillones
langosta (opcional)
1 pollo en partes
3 chorizos
1 paquete de guisantes congelados
1 bote de pimientos morrones
1 1/2 tazas de arroz
3 tazas de consomé de pollo
4 pizcas[2] de azafrán[3]
1/4 taza de aceite de oliva

PREPARACIÓN

1. Pique los tomates, los pimientos, las cebollas y el ajo.
2. Lave las almejas y los mejillones en agua fría.
3. Limpie y pele los camarones.
4. Limpie y corte en rebanadas los calamares.
5. Corte en rebanadas los chorizos.
6. Fría o ase el pollo aparte.

COCCIÓN

Se usa una paellera o una olla.

1. Fría ligeramente[4] en el aceite los pimientos y las cebollas picadas.
2. Agregue el ajo y los tomates y fría ligeramente a fuego lento unos dos o tres minutos.
3. Agregue el arroz.
4. Revuelva el arroz con los tomates, las cebollas, los pimientos y el ajo.
5. Agregue el consomé de pollo y llévelo a la ebullición[5].
6. Baje el fuego y agregue los camarones, los calamares, el chorizo, el pollo, las almejas y los mejillones.
7. Agregue el azafrán.
8. Ponga sal y pimienta a su gusto.

Si se prepara la paella en una olla, tape la olla y cocine a fuego lento encima de la estufa unos 40 minutos. En una paellera, ase la paella en el horno sin tapa o cocine a fuego lento encima de la estufa. Al final agregue los guisantes y los pimientos y sirva. Usted notará que el arroz tiene un bonito color amarillo. Es del azafrán.

[1]dientes *cloves*
[2]pizcas *pinches*
[3]azafrán *saffron*
[4]ligeramente *lightly*
[5]a la ebullición *to a boil*



## FUN-FACTS

The dish *paella* derives its name from the word **paella** in the Valencian language. In **valenciano, paella** means the special **sartén** or *large flat pan* in which it is prepared. In Spanish, the pan is called **una paellera.**

## ¿Comprendes?

**A ¿Cuál es la palabra?** Completen según la receta.

1. una ____ para hacer la paella
2. medio ____ de camarones
3. un ____ de guisantes congelados
4. tres ____ de ajo
5. una ____ de sal
6. una ____ de consomé de pollo

**B La paella** Preparen una lista de los ingredientes que lleva una paella.

**C La cocción** Digan que sí o que no.

1. Se puede asar la paella en el horno.
2. La paella lleva muchas papas.
3. Hay muchas especias en una paella.
4. El arroz de una paella se pone amarillo.
5. El chorizo es un tipo de salchicha española.

**D Para pensar** Miren el mapa de España en la página xxx y expliquen por qué se comen muchos mariscos en España.

Valencia, España



## Lecturas culturales

### Post-reading

**Step 1** Have students re-read the recipe at home and write the answers to the accompanying **¿Comprendes?** activities.

**Step 2** Go over the **¿Comprendes?** activities in class the next day.

### FUN FACTS

Saffron, a basic ingredient of paella, is probably the world's most expensive spice. Only the stigma or the pistils of the flower are used. It is estimated that it takes the pistils of four thousand plants to produce one ounce of saffron powder. (See photo, page 319.) Saffron gives the rice of paella its distinctive orange-yellow tint.

### Critical Thinking Activity

**Making inferences, drawing conclusions**

Read the following to the class or write it on the board or on an overhead transparency: **La paella viene de Valencia. La paella tradicional lleva muchos mariscos. Busca Valencia en el mapa en la página xxx. ¿Por qué crees que hay muchos mariscos en la paella?**

## Answers to ¿Comprendes?

**A**

1. paellera (una olla)
2. kilo
3. paquete
4. dientes
5. pizca
6. taza

**B**

tomates, cebollas, pimientos (verdes y rojos), ajo, camarones, calamares, almejas, mejillones, langosta, pollo, chorizos, guisantes, arroz, consomé de pollo, azafrán, aceite de oliva, sal y pimienta

**C**

1. No
2. No
3. No
4. Sí
5. Sí

**D** *Answers will vary but may include:*

Se comen muchos mariscos en España porque hay muchas costas en España. Hay tres océanos o mares: el Atlántico, el Mediterráneo y el Mar Cantábrico.

# Lectura opcional 1

## National Standards

### Cultures

This reading and the related activities on this page familiarize students with some interesting information about the tomato.

### Comparisons

In this reading students learn that, although the Spaniards and Italians eventually realized tomatoes were not poisonous and began to eat them, the English and North Americans avoided eating them until the nineteenth century.

**¡OJO!** This reading is optional. You may skip it completely, have the entire class read it, have only several students read it and report to the class, or assign it for extra credit.

### Teaching Tip

Even if students do not read this selection, you may wish to tell them this interesting bit of information about tomatoes.

### About the Spanish Language

- The word **tomate** comes from the Nahuatl word **tomatl.** The Nahuatl civilization at different times and places was known as Toltec, Chichimec, and Aztec.
- The *potato* is called **una papa** or **una patata.** *Corn* is called **el maíz** or **el choclo.**

# Lectura opcional 1

Ica, Perú

## El tomate, ¿comida o veneno?

¿Sabías que durante muchos años los ingleses y los norteamericanos no comían el tomate? Ellos creían que el tomate era venenoso[1]. Creían que al comer un tomate, uno se moriría[2]. Comer un tomate era fatal.

Cuando los españoles llevaron los primeros tomates de América a Europa, los usaban solamente como adorno, y no como comida. Pero en poco tiempo los españoles y los italianos descubrieron que el tomate era delicioso y no venenoso. Pero los ingleses, no. Hasta el siglo XIX, los ingleses y los norteamericanos seguían creyendo que el tomate era veneno.

[1]venenoso *poisonous* [2]se moriría *would die*

## ¿Comprendes?

**A El tomate** Contesten según la lectura.

1. El tomate, ¿es de origen europeo o americano?
2. ¿Qué creían los ingleses que pasaría a la persona al comer un tomate?
3. ¿Para qué se usaban los tomates en Europa originalmente?
4. ¿Quiénes, en Europa, fueron los primeros en comer el tomate?
5. ¿Hasta cuándo creían los norteamericanos que el tomate era venenoso?

**B La superstición** ¿Conoces tú alguna superstición acerca de alguna comida? ¿Cuál es? ¿Podrías decirnos?



## Answers to ¿Comprendes?

**A**

1. El tomate es de origen americano.
2. Creían que la persona que comía un tomate se moriría.
3. Se usaban como adorno.
4. Los españoles y los italianos fueron los primeros en comer el tomate.
5. Los norteamericanos creían que el tomate era venenoso hasta el siglo XIX.

**B** *Answers will vary.*

# Lectura opcional 2

Santiago Atitlán, Guatemala

## El maíz y la papa, regalos de las Américas

Los españoles llegaron a las Américas en el siglo XV. En Europa no había maíz ni papas. Los europeos no cultivaban estos vegetales. Los europeos no los conocían. La papa y el maíz tienen su origen en las Américas.

Los indios cultivaban el maíz en toda la América. El maíz era la base de la dieta de muchos indios. La tortilla de maíz sigue siendo muy importante en la cocina mexicana y centroamericana.

La papa tiene su origen en el altiplano sudamericano. Los incas cultivaban la papa en la región que hoy es Perú y Bolivia. Los españoles llevaron la papa a Europa donde, en poco tiempo, llegó a ser la base de la dieta de varios países, como Irlanda y Polonia.

### ¿Comprendes?

**A ¿Sí o no?** Contesten.

1. En el siglo XVIII los primeros españoles llegaron a las Américas.
2. Los europeos cultivaban la papa y el maíz antes del siglo XV.
3. La tortilla se hace de papa.
4. Los incas cultivaban la papa en el altiplano.
5. La tortilla es muy importante en la dieta de Perú y Bolivia.
6. La tortilla de maíz se come mucho en México.
7. La papa era muy importante en Irlanda y Polonia.

**B ¿Qué país es?** Identifiquen.

1. Irlanda está en Europa. Está cerca de Inglaterra. Su capital es Dublín. ¿Cómo se llama Irlanda en inglés?
2. Polonia está en el noreste de Europa. Está cerca de Rusia. Su capital es Varsovia. Los polacos son de Polonia. ¿Cómo se llama Polonia en inglés?

Urubamba, Perú



# Lectura opcional 2

### National Standards

**Cultures**
This reading and the related activities on this page familiarize students with information about the growing of corn and potatoes in the Americas.

**Comparisons**
Students learn that corn and potatoes were unknown in Europe prior to the Spanish exploration of the Americas.

**¡OJO!** This reading is optional. You may skip it completely, have the entire class read it, have only several students read it and report to the class, or assign it for extra credit.

### FUN FACTS

Other products unknown in Europe before the arrival of the Spaniards in the Americas are:

| | |
|---|---|
| **tabaco** | *tobacco* |
| **maní, cacahuates, cacahuetes** | *peanuts* |
| **cacao** | *cacao* (the bean from which cocoa and chocolate are made) |

### Answers to ¿Comprendes?

**A**

1. No
2. No
3. No
4. Sí
5. No
6. Sí
7. Sí

**B**

1. Ireland
2. Poland

### LEVELING

**E:** Readings 1, 2

**A:** Reading

# Conexiones

## National Standards

**Connections**
This reading about diet and nutrition establishes a connection with another discipline, allowing students to reinforce and further their knowledge of science through the study of Spanish.

**Comparisons**
In this reading students learn how the consumption of certain categories of foods in the United States differs from that in Spain.

**¡OJO!** The readings in the **Conexiones** section are optional. They focus on some of the major disciplines taught in schools and universities. The vocabulary is useful for discussing such topics as history, literature, art, economics, business, science, etc. You may choose any of the following ways to do the readings in the **Conexiones** sections.

**Independent reading** Have students read the selections and do the post-reading activities as homework, which you collect. This option is least intrusive on class time and requires a minimum of teacher involvement.

**Homework with in-class follow-up** Assign the readings and post-reading activities as homework. Review and discuss the material in class the next day.

**Intensive in-class activity** This option includes a pre-reading vocabulary presentation, in-class reading and discussion, assignment of the activities for homework, and a discussion of the assignment in class the following day.

# Conexiones

## Las ciencias

### La nutrición

Everyone is aware of the importance of a healthy diet. What constitutes a healthy diet? What effect does diet have on our lives? How does the diet of Hispanic countries differ from ours?

Madrid, España

### La dieta

Vamos a comparar la dieta típica de un español y un norteamericano.

**Carnes y legumbres:** El norteamericano come bastante carne, especialmente carne roja, como el biftec. También consume legumbres como los guisantes, las zanahorias y las papas, pero casi siempre en pequeñas cantidades con la carne. El español come poca carne, y muy poca carne roja. Las carnes que consume, en pequeñas cantidades, son el pollo, la ternera y el cordero. Las legumbres que come son, muchas veces, el plato principal, basado en frijoles, garbanzos[1], lentejas[2], y similares. Una de las mayores diferencias es en el consumo de pescado y mariscos. El español come pescado y mariscos tres o cuatro veces a la semana. Muchos españoles consumen más pescado que carne. El norteamericano come poco pescado.

**Frutas y verduras:** El norteamericano come frutas con el cereal por la mañana y cuando tiene hambre entre comidas. Para el español las frutas son postre, y las come todos los días. Los norteamericanos y los españoles comen mucha ensalada. La ensalada de lechuga y tomate es tradicional en España. En Latinoamérica se añade el aguacate o la palta a la ensalada. Muchos platos de los países sudamericanos llevan vegetales, tales como las papas y el maíz.

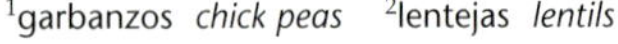

[1]garbanzos *chick peas* [2]lentejas *lentils*

Otavalo, Ecuador

**Productos lácteos (de la leche):** El norteamericano consume mucha mantequilla. El español come poquísima mantequilla y nunca cocina con mantequilla. El español consume menos mantequilla que cualquier otro europeo. El norteamericano toma leche. En España y en Latinoamérica solamente los bebés y los niños pequeños toman leche. Pero el español consume bastante queso. El queso con frutas es un postre popular. Los españoles también toman yogur como postre. Al norteamericano le gusta mucho el helado. También les gusta a los españoles, pero ellos consumen mucho menos.

**Pan y cereales:** Los norteamericanos y los españoles comen mucho pan, pero el español casi nunca come pan con mantequilla. El norteamericano come cereales para el desayuno. El español come pan con su café con leche. Los espaguetis y otras pastas son más y más populares en EE.UU. Pero el norteamericano, a diferencia del español, come poco arroz. El español consume grandes cantidades de arroz.

Es importante notar que muchos jóvenes, españoles y norteamericanos, tienen una dieta muy diferente a la dieta de la gente mayor. Muchos jóvenes son vegetarianos. Consumen poca grasa y muchas verduras, cereales y legumbres.

## ¿Comprendes?

**A ¿Es español o norteamericano?**
Escojan.
1. Pide un plato de garbanzos.
2. Está comiendo un biftec grande.
3. No quiere mantequilla con su pan.
4. Come pescado tres veces a la semana.
5. Pide un vaso de leche.
6. Quiere camarones con arroz.
7. Para el desayuno toma cereal con fruta, pan con mantequilla y un vaso de leche.
8. Para el postre pide queso y fruta.
9. Usa aceite de oliva para freír, no mantequilla.

**B ¿Qué opinas?** Contesten.
1. Para ti, ¿en qué consiste una dieta buena?
2. ¿Qué opinas? ¿Tienen los norteamericanos una dieta buena? ¿Por qué o por qué no?



# Conexiones

## PRESENTATION

### *Las ciencias*
### La nutrición

**Step 1** You may wish to tell those students who are going to read this selection to take notes on a sheet of paper with a double column. The titles of the columns could be: **Comida hispana / Comida norteamericana.**

**Step 2** Have students read the introduction in English on page 312.

**Step 3** Now have them read the selection quickly.

**Step 4** Suggest to students that they look for cognates and attempt to guess the meaning from context.

**Step 5** Now do the **¿Comprendes?** activities on this page.

**LEVELING**

**A:** Reading

## ANSWERS TO ¿Comprendes?

**A**
1. Es español.
2. Es norteamericano.
3. Es español.
4. Es español.
5. Es norteamericano.
6. Es español.
7. Es norteamericano.
8. Es español.
9. Es español.

**B** *Answers will vary but may include:*
1. Para mí, una dieta buena consiste en ___.
2. Yo creo que los norteamericanos tienen una dieta buena (mala) porque ___.

## ¡Te toca a ti!

### Use what you have learned

 **Recycling**

These activities allow students to use the vocabulary and structure from this chapter in completely open-ended, real-life situations.

### PRESENTATION

Encourage students to say as much as possible when they do these activities. Tell them not to be afraid to make mistakes, since the goal of the activities is real-life communication. If someone in the group makes an error, allow the others to politely correct him or her. Let students choose the activities they would like to do.

You may wish to divide students into pairs or groups. Encourage students to elaborate on the basic theme and to be creative. They may use props, pictures, or posters if they wish.

### Writing Development

Have students keep a notebook or portfolio containing their best written work from each chapter. These selected writings can be based on assignments from the Student Textbook and the Workbook. The two activities on page 315 are examples of writing assignments that may be included in each student's portfolio. On page 118 in the Workbook, students will begin to develop an organized autobiography **(Mi autobiografía).** These workbook pages may also become a part of their portfolio.

## ¡Te toca a ti!

# Use what you have learned

### 1 En el mercado

*✔ Talk about foods and food preparation*

Tú estás en un mercado en México. Quieres comprar los ingredientes que necesitas para un plato favorito. Tu compañero(a) es el/la empleado(a) en el mercado. Dile todo lo que quieres y en qué cantidades. Dile también lo que vas a preparar.

Guanajuato, México

### 2 Comidas étnicas

*✔ Describe an ethnic dish that you like*

¿Hay restaurantes étnicos, restaurantes que sirven comida de otras partes del mundo, en tu comunidad? Si los hay, con un(a) compañero(a) preparen una lista de estos restaurantes y el tipo de comida que sirven. Luego describan un plato típico de uno de los restaurantes.

### 3 Simón dice...

*✔ Use commands*

Trabajen en grupos de cinco. Van a jugar **Simón dice.** Cada líder dará cinco órdenes y luego escogerán a otro líder.



### Answers to ¡Te toca a ti!

1 *Answers will vary. Students will use vocabulary from* Palabras 1 *and* 2 *to talk about which foods they need and in what quantities.*

2 *Answers will vary. If there aren't any ethnic restaurants in your area, have students describe typical dishes from a Mexican, Italian, and Chinese restaurant.*

3 *Answers will vary.*

## PRACTICE

### Writing Strategy

**Writing about a process**
Have students read the Writing Strategy on page 315. Have students translate the measures for their recipes into the metric system if necessary.

### National Standards

**Communities**
You may wish to invite a Hispanic chef from a local restaurant or a member of the local Hispanic community to tell students about the favorite foods in his or her culture and how they are prepared. Encourage students to ask questions.

ESCRIBIR 4

## ¡Qué comida más deliciosa!

*✔ Describe a dish you really liked*

Estás viajando por México. Anoche fuiste a cenar en un restaurante y pediste algo que salió delicioso, muy rico. Te gustó mucho. Escribe una tarjeta postal a tus padres. Descríbeles el restaurante y el plato que te gustó tanto. Si puedes, explícales cómo crees que el cocinero preparó el plato.

San Miguel de Allende, México

### Writing Strategy

**Writing about a process**
When you write about a process or how to do something, you must remember to tell all the little details involved. Describe the process accurately and thoroughly. In this type of expository writing, be sure to define any terms you think your readers will not be familiar with and also to put the various steps of the process in logical order.

ESCRIBIR 5

## Un(a) americano(a) en Aranjuez

You are living with a Spanish family in Aranjuez, near Madrid. One day last week you prepared your favorite American dish for them. They loved it! They want you to write out the recipe for them before you leave to return to the United States. Since they don't speak much English, you will have to write the recipe in Spanish. Be sure to explain all the steps as clearly as possible so that they prepare something delicious rather than a disaster!



### Answers to ¡Te toca a ti!

 *Answers will vary. Students will use vocabulary from the chapter to describe their delicious Mexican meal and how it is prepared.*

 *Answers will vary. Students will use the vocabulary and structure from the chapter to write their American recipe.*

### LEVELING

These activities encompass all three levels. All students will be able to do them at a sophistication level commensurate with their ability in Spanish. Some students will be able to speak for several minutes, and others may be able to give just a few sentences. This is to be expected when students are functioning completely on their own generating their own language to the best of their ability.

Assessment

## Resource Manager

Communication Transparency C 10
Quizzes, pages 45–49
Performance Assessment, Task 10
Tests, pages 149–162
Situation Cards, Chapter 10
**Maratón mental** Videoquiz, Chapter 10
ExamView® Pro, Chapter 10

## Assessment

This is a pre-test for students to take before you administer the chapter test. Note that each section is cross-referenced so students can easily find the material they have to review in case they made errors. You may use Assessment Answers Transparency A 10 to do the assessment in class, or you may assign this assessment for homework. You can correct the assessment yourself, or you may prefer to project the answers on the overhead in class.

## Glencoe Technology

**MINDJOGGER VHS/DVD**

You may wish to help your students prepare for the chapter test by playing the MindJogger game show. Teams will compete against each other to review chapter vocabulary and structure and sharpen listening comprehension skills.

# Assessment

## Vocabulario

To review **Palabras 1**, turn to pages 292–293.

**1 Identifiquen.**

1. 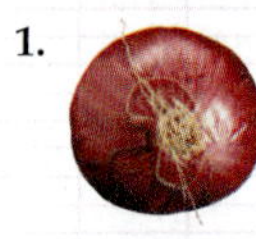
2. 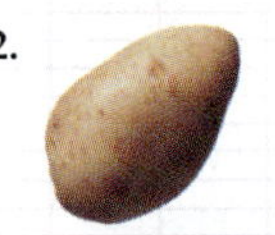
3. 
4. 

**2 Pareen.**

5. freír     a. la parrilla
6. hervir     b. la olla
7. asar     c. el/la sartén

To review **Palabras 2**, turn to pages 296–297.

**3 Identifiquen.**

8. 
9. 
10. 
11. 
12. 
13. 
14. 

### Answers to Assessment

1. la cebolla
2. la papa
3. el / la sartén
4. la parrilla

5. c
6. b
7. a

8. pelar
9. cortar
10. tapar
11. el aceite
12. el plátano (la banana)
13. los camarones (las gambas)
14. el arroz

# Estructura

**4 Completen con el imperativo.**

15. ____ usted la comida. (preparar)
16. ____ usted la receta. (leer)
17. ____ usted otra vez. (volver)
18. ____ ustedes el menú. (pedir)
19. ____ usted el aceite en la sartén. (poner)
20. ____ ustedes con nosotros. (salir)

To review the imperatives, turn to pages 300 and 303.

**5 Escriban con el pronombre.**

21. Sirva usted el postre.
22. No sirva usted las papas.
23. Déme la receta.

To review object pronouns with commands, turn to page 305.

# Cultura

**6 Contesten.** *(Answer.)*

24–25. ¿Cuáles son algunos ingredientes que lleva una paella?

To review this cultural information, turn to page 308.

## Assessment

**FOLDABLES Study Organizer** **Dinah Zike's Study Guides**

Your students may wish to use Foldable 8 to organize, display, and arrange data as they learn about new topics in Spanish. You may wish to encourage them to add information from each chapter as they continue to learn how to discuss many different aspects of their lives in Spanish.

Encourage students to keep this *minibook* foldable in a safe place so they can refer to it and add content as they acquire more knowledge.

**SPANISH Online**

The Glencoe Spanish Web site **(spanish.glencoe.com)** offers options that enable you and your students to experience the Spanish-speaking world via the Internet. For each **Capítulo,** there are activities, games, and quizzes. In addition, an *Enrichment* section offers students an opportunity to visit Web sites related to the theme of the chapter.

## Answers to Assessment

15. Prepare
16. Lea
17. Vuelva
18. Pidan
19. Ponga
20. Salgan

21. Sírvalo usted.
22. No las sirva usted.
23. Démela.

24–25. tomates, cebollas, pimientos, ajo, camarones, calamares, almejas, mejillones, langosta, pollo, chorizo, guisantes, pimientos morrones, consomé de pollo, azafrán, aceite de oliva.

# ¡Hablo como un pro!

This unique page gives students the opportunity to speak freely and say whatever they can, using the vocabulary and structures they have learned in the chapter. The illustration serves to remind students of precisely what they know how to say in Spanish. There are no activities that students do not have the ability to describe or talk about in Spanish. The art not only depicts the vocabulary and content of this chapter, but also reinforces what they learned in previous chapters.

You may wish to use this page in many ways. Some possibilities are to have students do the following:

1. Look at the illustration and identify items by giving the correct Spanish words.
2. Make up sentences about what they see in the illustration.
3. Make up questions about the illustration. They can call on another class member to respond if you do this as a class activity, or you may prefer to allow students to work in small groups. This activity is extremely beneficial because it enables students to actively use interrogative words.
4. Answer questions you ask them about the illustration.
5. Work in pairs and make up a conversation based on the illustration.
6. Look at the illustration and give a complete oral review of what they see.
7. Look at the illustration and write a paragraph (or essay) about it.

You can also use this page as an assessment or testing tool, taking into account individual differences by having students go from simple to quite complicated tasks.

# ¡Hablo como un pro!

Tell all you can about this illustration.

The assessment can be either oral or written. You may wish to use the rubrics provided on pages T20–T21 as you give students the following directions.

1. Identify the topic or situation of the illustration.
2. Give the Spanish words for as many items as you can.
3. Think of as many sentences as you can to describe the illustration.
4. Go over your sentences and put them in the best sequencing to give a coherent story based on the illustration.

# Vocabulario

### Talking about some kitchen appliances and utensils

la cocina
el congelador
la nevera, el refrigerador
la estufa
el horno
el horno de microondas
la hornilla, el hornillo
la cazuela, la cacerola
el/la sartén
la parrilla
la olla

### Talking about food preparation

limpiar
pelar
rallar
picar
cortar
rebanar
agregar, añadir
tapar
los pedacitos, los trocitos
las rebanadas

### Talking about some cooking procedures

cocinar
revolver
freír
asar
hervir
poner al fuego
quitar del fuego
apagar el fuego

**How well do you know your vocabulary?**

- Choose words from the list and describe a meal you would like to serve.
- Describe as many steps as you can in the preparation of the meal.

### Identifying more foods

la coliflor
las cebollas
el pepino
las zanahorias
la lechuga
las papas
los pimientos
el aguacate
el ajo
el arroz
las habichuelas negras, los frijoles negros
la lima
el limón
la toronja
las uvas
la papaya
el coco
la sandía
el plátano, la banana
la carne de res
el cerdo
el cordero
la salchicha, el chorizo
la ternera
el pollo
la costilla
la chuleta
el pescado
los mariscos
la langosta
los camarones, las gambas
las almejas
los calamares
los mejillones
las ostras
la sal
la pimienta
el azúcar
el aceite
la mantequilla

**VIDEOTUR**

**Episodio 10**

In this video episode, you will join Alejandra and Vicky as they show off their culinary talents. See page 489 for more information.

# Vocabulario

## Vocabulary Review

The words and phrases in the **Vocabulario** have been taught for productive use in this chapter. They are summarized here as a resource for both student and teacher. This list also serves as a convenient resource for the **¡Te toca a ti!** activities on pages 314 and 315. There are approximately four cognates in this vocabulary list. Have students find them.

**¡OJO!** You will notice that the vocabulary list here is not translated. This has been done intentionally, since we feel that by the time students have finished the material in the chapter they should be familiar with the meanings of all the words. If there are several words they still do not know, we recommend that they refer to the **Palabras 1** and **2** sections in the chapter or go to the dictionaries at the end of this book to find the meanings. However, if you prefer that your students have the English translations, please refer to Vocabulary Transparency 10.1, where you will find all these words with their translations.

**VIDEO VHS/DVD**

The Video Program allows students to see how the chapter vocabulary and structures are used by native speakers within an engaging story line. For maximum reinforcement, show the video episode as a final activity for Chapter 10.

**Learning from Photos**

*(page 319 top left)* The paella shown in the photo contains, in addition to the **camarones,** some shellfish that students may not know. They are **langostinos** (the pink ones) and **cangrejos de río** (the red ones).

# Planning for Chapter 11

## SCOPE AND SEQUENCE, PAGES 320–349

### Topics

- ❖ Automobile terminology and driving
- ❖ Service station terminology
- ❖ Giving directions on the road and in the city

### Culture

- ❖ The Panamerican Highway
- ❖ Parking your car in Spanish-speaking countries
- ❖ Spanish traffic signs
- ❖ Pollution and the environment
- ❖ **Vistas del Perú**

### Functions

- ❖ How to talk about car models and parts of an automobile
- ❖ How to talk about routine services at a gas station
- ❖ How to talk about driving on the highway and in the city
- ❖ How to tell friends what to do and what not to do

### Structure

- ❖ The familiar imperative: Regular forms
- ❖ The familiar imperative: Irregular forms
- ❖ Negative imperatives

### National Standards

- ❖ Communication Standard 1.1 pages 324, 325, 328, 329, 330, 331, 332, 333, 334, 335, 337, 344
- ❖ Communication Standard 1.2 pages 325, 329, 333, 336, 337, 338, 339, 340, 341, 342–343, 344
- ❖ Communication Standard 1.3 page 345
- ❖ Cultures Standard 2.1 pages 339, 340
- ❖ Cultures Standard 2.2 pages 338–339, 340, 341
- ❖ Connections Standard 3.1 pages 342–343
- ❖ Comparisons Standard 4.2 pages 340, 341, 343
- ❖ Communities Standard 5.1 page 349
- ❖ Communities Standard 5.2 page 329

## PACING AND PRIORITIES

**The chapter content is color coded below to assist you in planning.**

**■ required ■ recommended ■ optional**

**Vocabulario** *(required)* *Days 1–4*

- ■ Palabras 1
  - El coche
  - La estación de servicio, La gasolinera
- ■ Palabras 2
  - En la carretera
  - En la ciudad

**Estructura** *(required)* *Days 5–7*

- ■ Imperativo familiar: formas regulares
- ■ Imperativo familiar: formas irregulares
- ■ Imperativo negativo

**Conversación** *(required)*

- ■ Un sitio para estacionar

**Lecturas culturales**

- ■ La carretera panamericana *(recommended)*
- ■ El estacionamiento *(optional)*
- ■ Las señales de tránsito *(optional)*

**Conexiones**

- ■ La ecología *(optional)*

■ **¡Te toca a ti!** *(recommended)*

■ **Assessment** *(recommended)*

■ **¡Hablo como un pro!** *(optional)*

## RESOURCE GUIDE

| Section | Pages | Section Resources |
|---|---|---|
| **Vocabulario PALABRAS 1** | | |
| El coche<br>La estación de servicio, La gasolinera | 322, 324–325<br>323, 324–325 | Vocabulary Transparencies 11.2–11.3<br>Audio CD 7<br>Audio Activities TE, pages 131–133<br>Workbook, pages 121–122<br>Quiz 1, page 51<br>ExamView® Pro |
| **Vocabulario PALABRAS 2** | | |
| En la carretera<br>En la ciudad | 326, 328–329<br>327, 328–329 | Vocabulary Transparencies 11.4–11.5<br>Audio CD 7<br>Audio Activities TE, pages 133–135<br>Workbook, pages 123–124<br>Quiz 2, page 52<br>ExamView® Pro |
| **Estructura** | | |
| Imperativo familiar: formas regulares<br>Imperativo familiar: formas irregulares<br>Imperativo negativo | 330–331<br>332–333<br>334–335 | Audio CD 7<br>Audio Activities TE, pages 135–136<br>Workbook, pages 125–128<br>Quizzes 3–5, pages 53–55<br>ExamView® Pro |
| **Conversación** | | |
| Un sitio para estacionar | 336–337 | Audio CD 7<br>Audio Activities TE, page 137<br>Interactive CD-ROM |
| **Lecturas culturales** | | |
| La carretera panamericana<br>El estacionamiento<br>Las señales de tránsito | 338–339<br>340<br>341 | Audio CD 7<br>Audio Activities TE, page 138<br>Tests, pages 165, 169 |
| **Conexiones** | | |
| La ecología | 342–343 | Tests, page 170 |
| **¡Te toca a ti!** | | |
| | 344–345 | **¡Viva el mundo hispano!** Video, Episode 11<br>Video Activities, pages 104–108<br>Spanish Online Activities spanish.glencoe.com |
| **Assessment** | | |
| | 346–347 | Communication Transparency C 11<br>Quizzes 1–5, pages 51–55<br>Performance Assessment, Task 11<br>Tests, pages 163–178<br>Situation Cards, Chapter 11<br>ExamView® Pro<br>**Maratón mental** Videoquiz |

# Using Your Resources for Chapter 11

## Transparencies

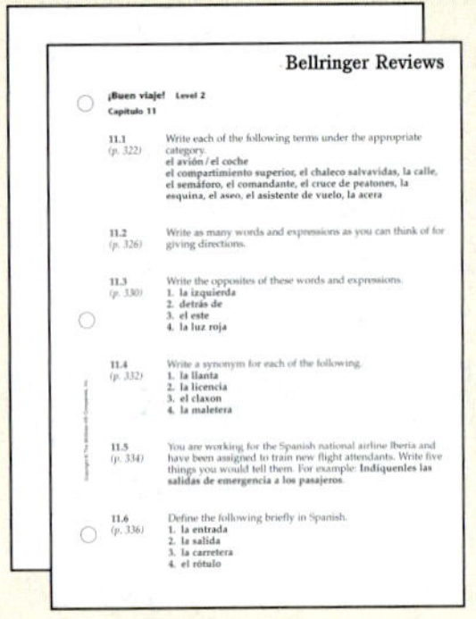


Bellringer 11.1–11.6

Vocabulary 11.1–11.5

Communication C 11

## Workbook

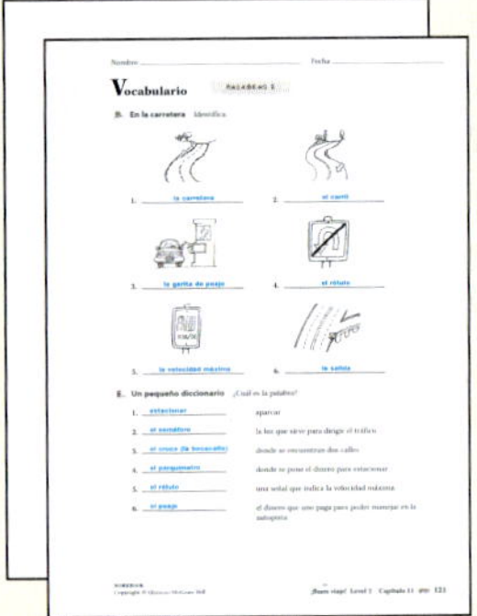

Vocabulary, pages 121–124

Structure, pages 125–128

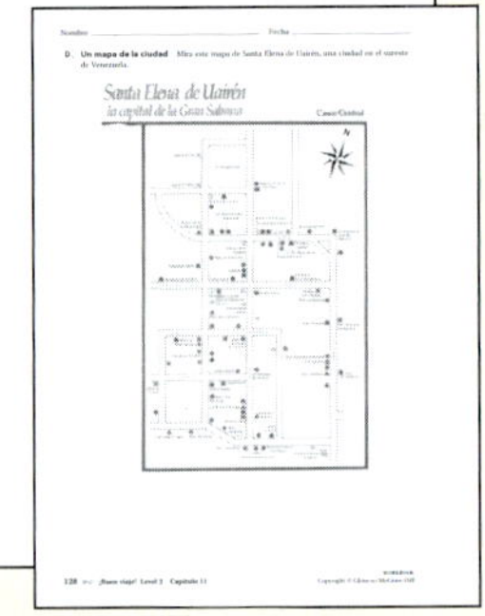

Enrichment, pages 129–132

## Audio Activities

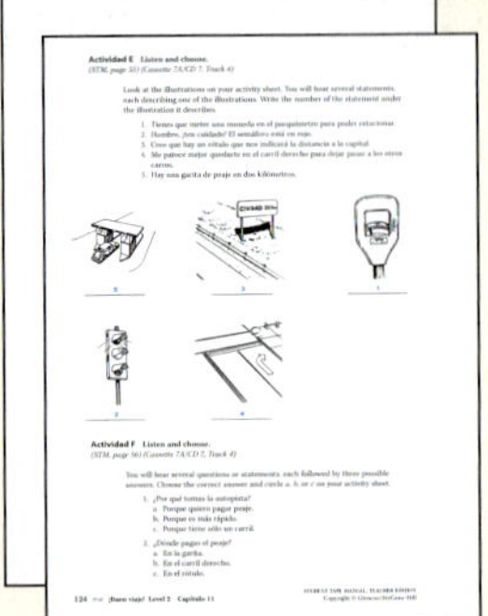

Vocabulary, pages 131–135

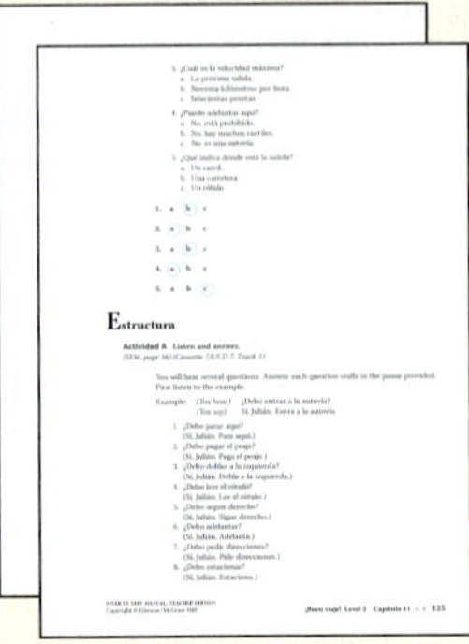

Structure, pages 135–136

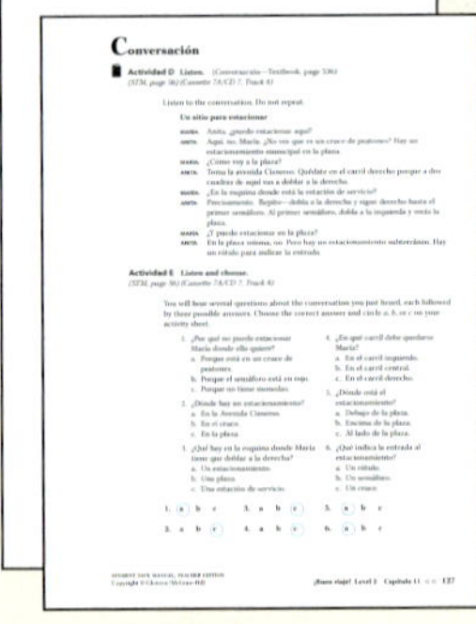

Conversation, page 137

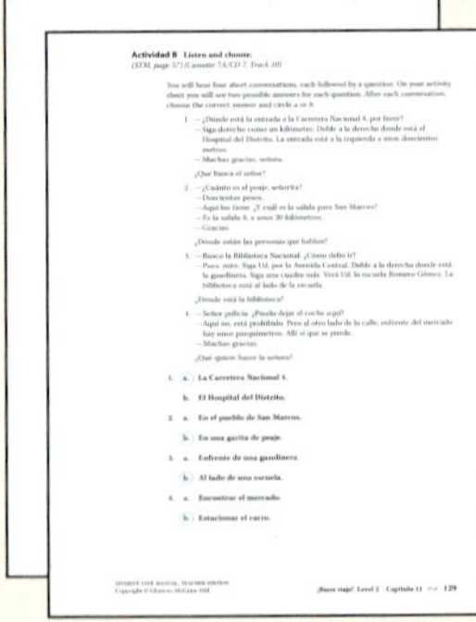

Additional Practice, pages 139–143

# Assessment

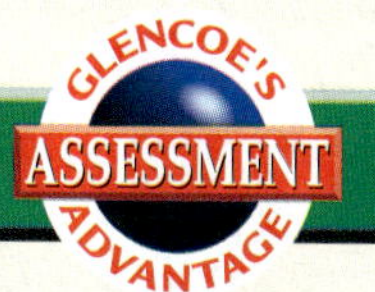


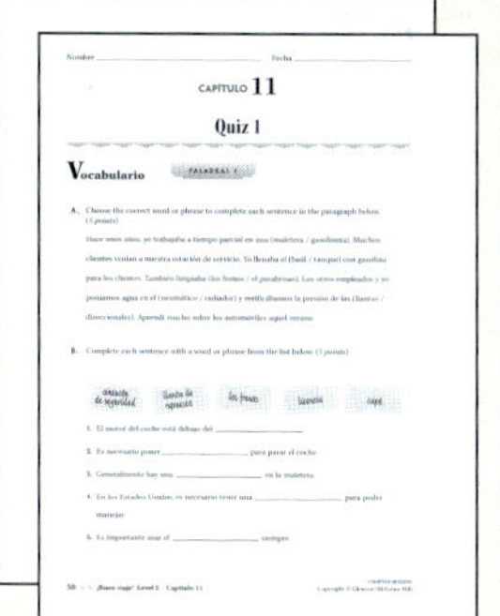

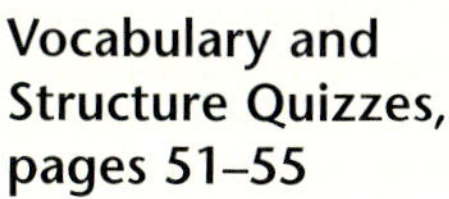

Vocabulary and Structure Quizzes, pages 51–55

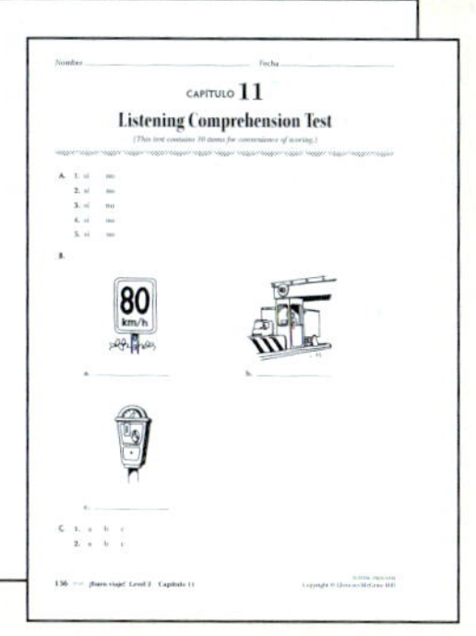

Chapter Tests, pages 163–178

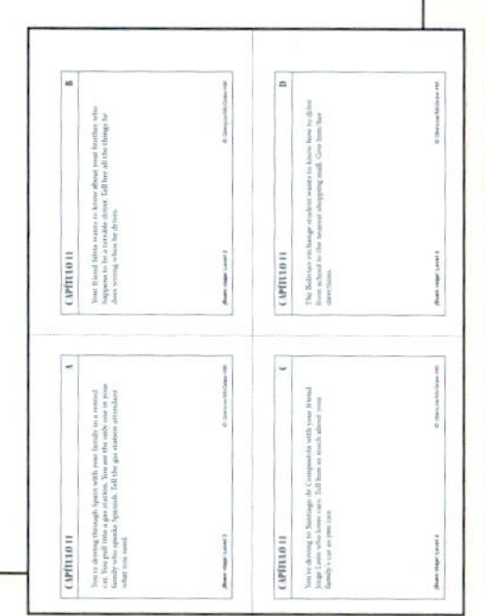

Situation Cards, Chapter 11

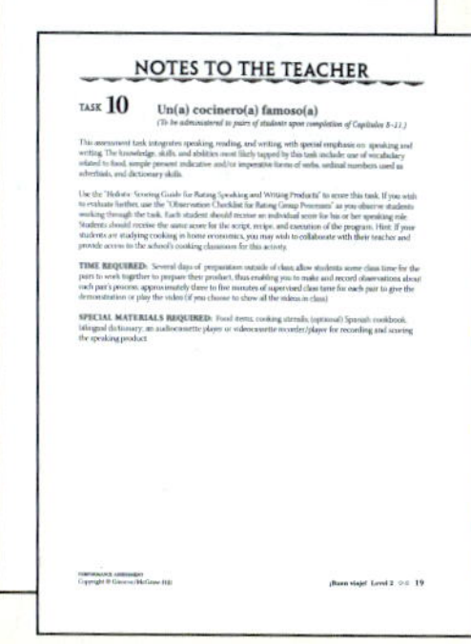

Performance Assessment, pages 15–22

MindJogger Videoquiz, ExamView® Pro, Chapter 11

## Timesaving Teacher Tools

### TeacherWorks™

TeacherWorks™ is your all-in-one teacher resource center. Personalize lesson plans, access resources from the Teacher Wraparound Edition, connect to the Internet, or make a to-do list. These are only a few of the many features that can assist you in the planning and organizing of your lessons.

Includes:

- A calendar feature
- Access to all program blackline masters
- Standards correlations and more

### ExamView® Pro

Test Bank software for Macintosh and Windows makes creating, editing, customizing, and printing tests quick and easy.

## Technology Resources

In the Chapter 11 Internet Activity, you will have a chance to learn more about the Spanish-speaking world. Visit spanish.glencoe.com

On the interactive CD–ROM, students can listen to and take part in a recorded version of the conversation in Chapter 11.

**¡Viva el mundo hispano!** Video and Video Activities, Chapter 11. Available on VHS and DVD.

Help your students prepare for the chapter test by playing the **Maratón mental** Videoquiz game show. Teams will compete against each other to review chapter vocabulary and structure and sharpen listening comprehension skills. Available on VHS and DVD.

**¡Buen viaje!** is also available on CD or Online.

## Preview

In this chapter, students will learn to talk about cars, roads, and driving. They will learn vocabulary associated with different types of cars, gas station services, and city and highway driving. They will also learn both the affirmative and negative forms of the familiar imperative. The cultural focus of this chapter is on driving customs and highways in the Spanish-speaking world.

### National Standards

**Communication**

In Chapter 11 students will learn to communicate in spoken and written Spanish on the following topics:

- cars and driving
- giving directions
- road travel in the Spanish-speaking world

Students will obtain and provide information about these topics and engage in conversations that would typically take place behind the wheel of a car as they fulfill the chapter objectives listed on this page.

Capítulo 11

# El coche y la carretera

**Objetivos**

In this chapter you will learn to:

- talk about cars and driving
- give directions on the road
- tell family and friends what to do and what not to do
- talk about highways in the Hispanic world

Norberto Russo *De mi Buenos Aires*

Capítulo 11

## Spotlight on Culture

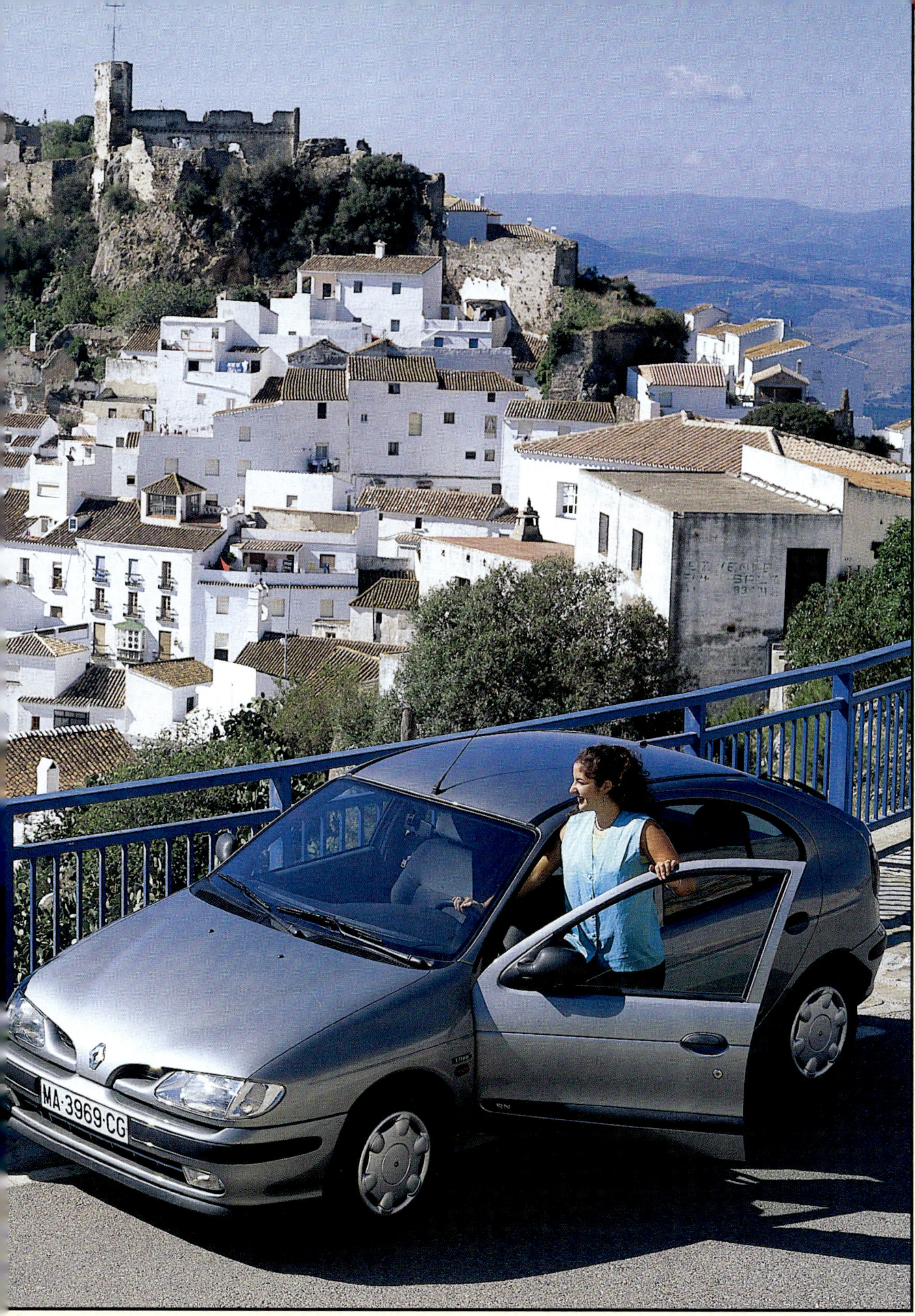

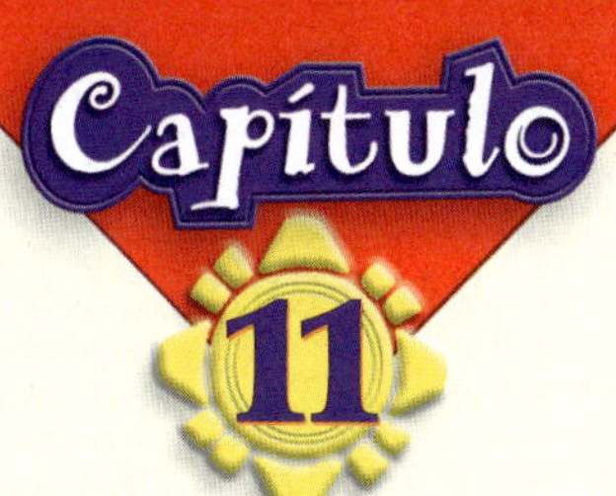

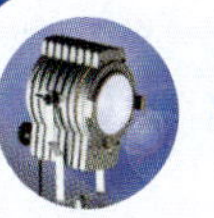

**Arte** Norberto Russo (1934) is an award-winning contemporary Argentine artist.

**Fotografía** The view is of Casares, one of the famous **Pueblos Blancos** of Andalucía. There is a **Ruta de los Pueblos Blancos** that connects these villages from south to north. Many of these towns have **de la Frontera** as part of their names. The **frontera** was the frontier between Christian and Moorish Spain and was moved as territory was taken or lost by one side or the other. As is typical of many of the **Pueblos Blancos,** this town is dominated by a medieval castle set on high ground.

## LEVELING

The activities, conversations, and readings within each chapter are marked according to level of difficulty. E indicates easy. A indicates average. C indicates challenging. Some activities cover a range of difficulty. In some activities, for example, advanced students will be able to produce more extensive responses while students who learn at a different rate may give less detailed responses. The leveling indicators will help you individualize instruction to best meet your students' needs.

# Vocabulario

PALABRAS 1

## 1 PREPARATION

### Resource Manager

Vocabulary Transparencies 11.2–11.3
Audio Activities TE, pages 131–133
Audio CD 7
Workbook, pages 121–122
Quizzes, page 51
ExamView® Pro

### Bellringer Review

*Use BRR Transparency 11.1 or write the following on the board.*
Write each of the following terms under the appropriate category.
**el avión / el coche**
**el compartimiento superior, el chaleco salvavidas, la calle, el semáforo, el comandante, el cruce de peatones, la esquina, el aseo, el asistente de vuelo, la acera**

## 2 PRESENTATION

**¡OJO!** More than the usual number of alternate words appear in this vocabulary presentation. All the variants taught here are commonly used.

**Step 1** Have students close their books. Using Vocabulary Transparencies 11.2–11.3, point to each illustration or photo and have students repeat the corresponding word or phrase two or three times.

**Step 2** Point to items at random and ask *yes / no* or *either / or* questions. After some practice, progress to more open-ended questions, such as **¿Qué es esto?**

# Vocabulario

PALABRAS 1

## El coche

El conductor maneja (conduce) con cuidado.

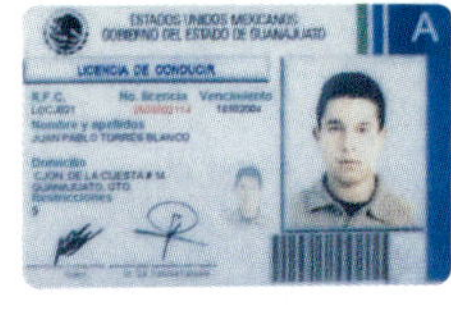

## Reaching All Students

**Total Physical Response** Set up a chair in the classroom as a driver's seat. Pieces of paper on the floor can serve as the accelerator and brake pedals.

*(Student 1),* **levántate, por favor. Ven acá. Es tu coche.**
**Abre la puerta de tu coche.**
**Sube.**
**Siéntate.**
**Cierra la puerta.**
**Pon el cinturón de seguridad.**
**Pon el pie en el acelerador.**
**Conduce con cuidado. Ve a la gasolinera.**
**Pon los frenos. Necesitas gasolina.**
*(Student 2),* **ven acá. Eres el empleado(a).**
**Llena el tanque de gasolina.**
**Limpia el parabrisas.**
**Pon aire en las llantas.**
**Gracias,** *(Students 1 and 2).* **Bien hecho. Pueden volver a su asiento.**

## La estación de servicio, La gasolinera

El muchacho llenó el tanque de gasolina.
La muchacha limpió el parabrisas.
El otro muchacho puso aire en las llantas.



## Vocabulario

**Step 3** Have students open their books to pages 322–323 and repeat the vocabulary after you or the recording on Audio CD 7.

**Step 4** Call on volunteers to read the new words and sentences.

**Step 5** Show students a photo of your own car or a magazine picture of one and describe it, using as much of the new vocabulary as possible. For example: **Tengo un coche deportivo de color rojo. Es un descapotable americano. Es una marca americana. Acelera rápidamente, pero siempre conduzco con cuidado.**

### Teaching Tips

When an individual cannot respond to a question, try getting the answer from a volunteer by gesturing silently to the class or asking **¿Quién sabe?** Always have the original student repeat the correct model and come back to him or her soon with the same question.

### Vocabulary Expansion

Additional vocabulary items related to cars include:

| | |
|---|---|
| **el retrovisor** | *rearview mirror* |
| **los parachoques** | *bumpers* |
| **el gato** | *(tire) jack* |

Remind students that the **para** in **parabrisas** and **parachoques** means *to stop.* Others words with this meaning of **para** are: **paracaídas** *(parachute)* and **paraguas** *(umbrella).*

### LEVELING

**A:** Vocabulary

### Reaching All Students

**Additional Practice** Have students use the **favor de** expression with other words learned in this section that they could use at a service station.

### Fun Facts

Diesel powered cars are very popular in Spain because of their excellent gas mileage. Fuel is extremely expensive by American standards. A gallon of gasoline can cost the equivalent of $4.00 to $5.00 or more. The difference in price is attributable to very high taxes on fuel. For that reason, large cars are far less common on the road in Spain than in the United States.

Vocabulario

## 3 PRACTICE

## ¿Qué palabra necesito?

¡OJO! When students are doing the **¿Qué palabra necesito?** activities, accept any answer that makes sense. The purpose of these activities is to have students use the new vocabulary. They are not factual recall activities. Thus, it is not necessary for students to remember specific factual information from the vocabulary presentation when answering. If you wish, have students use the visuals on this page as a stimulus, when possible.

**Historieta** Each time **Historieta** appears, it means that the answers to the activity form a short story. Encourage students to look at the title of the **Historieta,** since it can help them do the activity.

**1** This activity can be done first orally with books closed. **Expansion:** After going over Activity 1, have students prepare the activity silently. Now call on individuals to give the information about themselves in their own words.

**2** Have students correct the false statements in the activity.

**3** **Expansion:** Students can also make up questions about the illustrations in Activity 3. They can call on other members of the class to answer their questions.

**LEVELING**

**E:** Activities 1, 2, 3, 4, 5

**A:** Activities 1, 2, 4, 6, 7



Vocabulario

## ¿Qué palabra necesito?

Un coche clásico, La Habana, Cuba

**1** **Historieta Mi coche** Contesten.

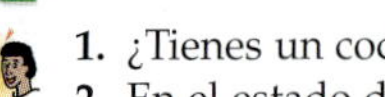

1. ¿Tienes un coche o quieres tener un coche algún día?
2. En el estado donde vives, ¿cuántos años tienes que cumplir para tener el permiso de conducir?
3. ¿Qué tipo de coche quieres?
4. ¿Tienes un modelo favorito? ¿Cuál es?
5. ¿Vas a manejar con cuidado?
6. ¿Vas a llevar tu coche a la estación de servicio con frecuencia?

**2** **Coches** Digan que sí o que no.

1. El motor de un coche está en la maletera.
2. El motor del coche está debajo del capó.
3. Es una buena idea tener una llanta de repuesto en la maletera del carro.
4. Es necesario tocar la bocina cada vez que pasas por un hospital.
5. Es necesario tener el cinturón abrochado cuando estás en un asiento delantero del carro.
6. Es necesario poner los frenos para parar el coche.
7. Los coches tienen tres neumáticos.
8. Se limpia el parabrisas con gasolina.

**3** **Historieta En la gasolinera**

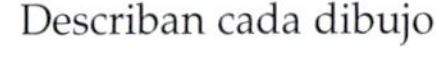

Describan cada dibujo.

1.

2.

3.



## ANSWERS TO ¿Qué palabra necesito?

**1**

1. Sí, (No, no) tengo un coche. Sí, (No, no) quiero tener un coche algún día.
2. Tengo que cumplir ___ años para tener el permiso de conducir.
3. Quiero un ___.
4. Sí, (No, no) tengo un modelo favorito. Mi modelo favorito es ___.
5. Sí, (No, no) voy a manejar con cuidado.
6. Sí, (No, no) voy a llevar mi coche a la estación de servicio con frecuencia.

**2**

1. No
2. Sí
3. Sí
4. No
5. Sí
6. Sí
7. No
8. No

**3** *Answers will vary but may include:*

1. Ella limpia el parabrisas.
2. El empleado va a llenar el tanque de gasolina.
3. Él revisa el aceite.

## 4 En la gasolinera Escojan.

1. En la gasolinera el señor llena el tanque de ____.
   a. agua  b. aceite  c. gasolina
2. El muchacho revisa ____.
   a. el agua en los neumáticos  b. el tanque  c. el nivel del aceite
3. El señor nunca pondría agua en ____.
   a. la batería  b. el radiador  c. el tanque
4. La señora podría verificar ____.
   a. la presión de los neumáticos  b. el aire del radiador
   c. el parabrisas
5. El parabrisas está muy sucio. No puedo ver nada. ¿Me lo ____ usted, por favor?
   a. llenaría  b. revisaría  c. limpiaría

## 5 Mi carro

¿Tienes un carro (coche) o no? Si no tienes carro, ¿te comprarás uno algún día? Trabaja con un(a) compañero(a). Cada uno de ustedes describirá el carro de sus sueños.

## 6 Un carro nuevo

Estás pasando un año estudiando en Puerto Rico. Decides comprarte un carro. Como tienes muy poco dinero, tienes que comprar un carro usado (de ocasión). Visitas una agencia. Estás hablando con el/la vendedor(a) (tu compañero[a]). Él o ella te quiere vender un carro—cualquier carro, no importa la calidad ni la condición. Discutan juntos.

## 7 Trabajo a tiempo parcial

Imagínate que trabajas en una gasolinera. Tu compañero(a) cree que a él o a ella le gustaría trabajar a tiempo parcial en una gasolinera para ganar unos dólares extra. Te va a hacer preguntas sobre el trabajo que haces. Contesta a sus preguntas.

Una gasolinera, Miraflores, Perú



## Vocabulario

**4** Have students prepare Activity 4 before going over it in class.

**¡OJO!** Note that the activities are color-coded. All the activities in the text are communicative. However, the ones with blue titles are guided communication. The red titles indicate that the answers to the activity are more open-ended and can vary more. You may wish to correct students' mistakes more so in the guided activities than in the activities with a red title, which lend themselves to a freer response.

### Learning from Photos

*(pages 324–325)* You may wish to ask students to say as much as they can about the two photos.

### Chapter Projects

**Mi coche favorito** Have students bring in a large magazine photo of their favorite kind of car. Have them label all the parts of the car and elements from the setting in Spanish, when appropriate.

## Answers to ¿Qué palabra necesito?

**4**

1. c
2. c
3. c
4. a
5. c

**5** *Answers will vary. Students will use vocabulary from* Palabras 1 *to describe the car of their dreams.*

**6** *Answers will vary. Students should try to use as much of the vocabulary from* Palabras 1 *as possible to ask questions about different cars and their quality and condition.*

**7** *Answers will vary. Students will use vocabulary relating to gas stations to discuss what work is done there.*

# Vocabulario

PALABRAS 2

## 1 PREPARATION

### Resource Manager

Vocabulary Transparencies 11.4–11.5
Audio Activities TE, pages 133–135
Audio CD 7
Workbook, pages 123–124
Quizzes, page 52
ExamView® Pro

### Bellringer Review

*Use BRR Transparency 11.2 or write the following on the board.*
Write as many words and expressions as you can think of for giving directions.

## 2 PRESENTATION

**Step 1** Have students act out the monologues in this vocabulary section.

**Step 2** As you present the vocabulary, you may wish to ask questions such as the following:

**¿Se queda en qué carril para salir de la autopista? ¿En el carril derecho o en el carril izquierdo?**

**¿Indica un rótulo dónde está la salida de la autopista?**

**¿Se puede adelantar en una carretera donde hay solamente un carril en cada sentido?**

**¿Es necesario parar cuando hay una luz roja o una luz verde?**

**En una calle de sentido único, ¿puede el tráfico ir en dos direcciones?**



# Vocabulario

PALABRAS 2

## En la carretera

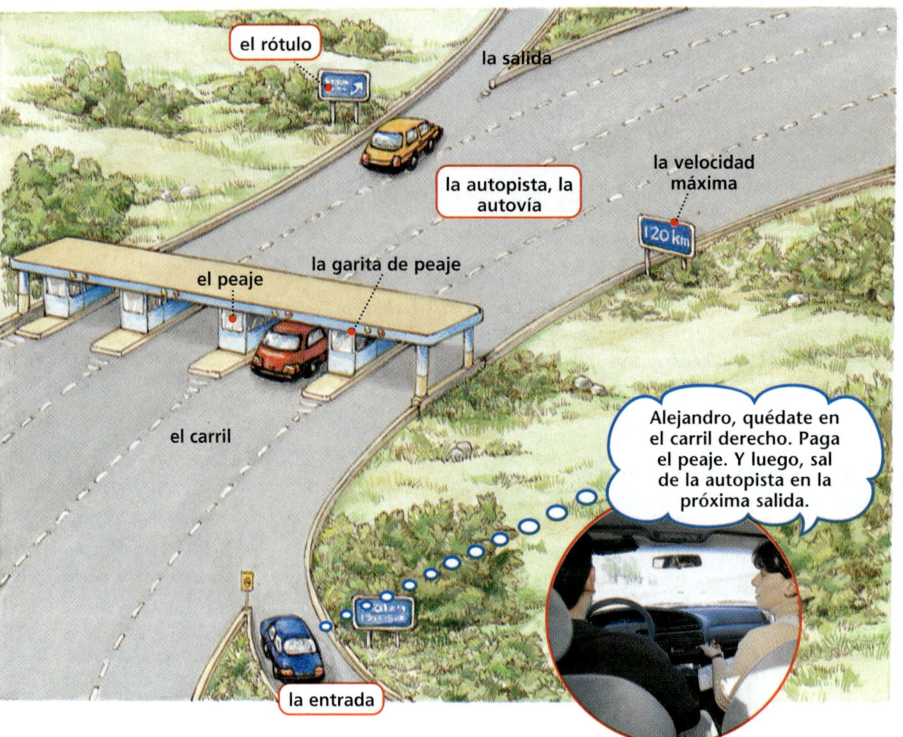

## En la ciudad

Es necesario parar cuando hay una luz roja.

### Vocabulary Expansion

You may wish to give students a few extra words that are useful on the road:

| | |
|---|---|
| **la flecha** | *arrow* |
| **virar** | *to turn (synonym of* **doblar***)* |
| **dar la vuelta** | *to turn around* |
| **ceder el paso** | *yield (right-of-way)* |
| **el arcén** | *shoulder (of the road)* |

### About the Spanish Language

Both **coche** and **carro** are common words for *car.* **Coche** is more commonly used in Spain and southern South America, **carro** in most other places. The original **coche** was a horse-drawn coach designed to carry passengers, a stagecoach, for example. The **carro** was also a horse-drawn vehicle, a *cart,* but it was used for carrying produce or other goods, not people.

# Vocabulario

## 3 PRACTICE

## ¿Qué palabra necesito?

**8** This activity can be done orally with books closed.
**Expansion:** After going over Activity 8, have students describe some rules of the road in their own words.

**9** This activity can be done in class without prior preparation.
**Note:** Activity 9 has many informal commands, but students do not have to use them actively.

### Learning from Photos

*(page 328)* You may wish to ask these questions about the photo:
**¿Dónde están estas personas?**
**¿Quién es el señor que está de pie?**
**¿Qué está haciendo él?**
**¿Quiénes son las otras personas?**
**¿Qué están haciendo ellos?**

**LEVELING**
**E:** Activities 8, 9
**A:** Activities 9, 10, 11, 12
**C:** Activity 12

# Vocabulario

## ¿Qué palabra necesito?

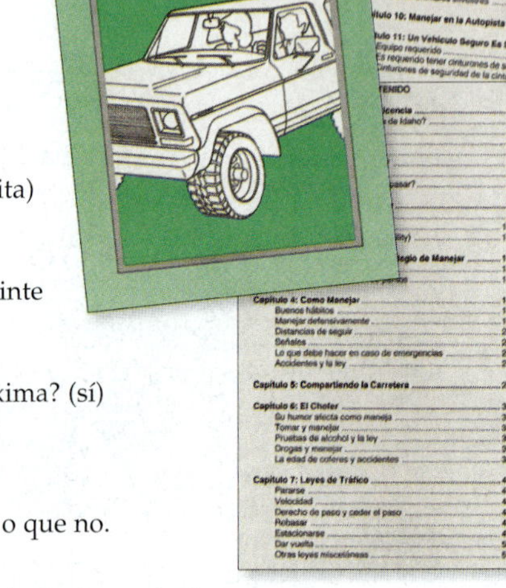


**8** **Historieta En la carretera**
Contesten según se indica.

1. ¿Qué vamos a tomar? (la autopista)
2. ¿Qué tendremos que pagar? (el peaje)
3. ¿Dónde lo tenemos que pagar? (en la garita)
4. ¿Cuántos carriles tiene la autopista en cada sentido? (tres)
5. ¿Cuál es la velocidad máxima? (ciento veinte kilómetros por hora)
6. ¿Está prohibido adelantar? (no)
7. ¿Está prohibido exceder la velocidad máxima? (sí)

**9** **Buenos o malos consejos** Digan que sí o que no.

1. Maneja con cuidado.
2. Estaciona el coche donde está prohibido el estacionamiento.
3. Excede la velocidad indicada en el rótulo.
4. Quédate en el carril derecho para adelantar un carro.
5. Mete una moneda en la ranura del parquímetro.
6. Paga el peaje en la garita.
7. Al llegar a un cruce, para y mira a la derecha y a la izquierda antes de seguir.
8. Cuando vas a parar, pon las direccionales.
9. Pon las direccionales porque vas a doblar a la izquierda.

Motril, España



## ANSWERS TO ¿Qué palabra necesito?

**8**

1. Vamos a tomar la autopista.
2. Tendremos que pagar el peaje.
3. Lo tenemos que pagar en la garita.
4. La autopista tiene tres carriles en cada sentido.
5. La velocidad máxima es ciento veinte kilómetros por hora.
6. No, no está prohibido adelantar.
7. Sí, está prohibido exceder la velocidad máxima.

**9**

1. Sí
2. No
3. No
4. No
5. Sí
6. Sí
7. Sí
8. No
9. Sí

**10** **Historieta Donde vivo yo** Contesten.

1. ¿Cuál es una autopista cerca de donde tú vives?
2. ¿Es una autopista de peaje?
3. ¿Cuánto es el peaje?
4. ¿Dónde tienes que pagar peaje? ¿En la salida de la autopista? Si no, ¿a cada cuántos kilómetros hay garitas de peaje?
5. ¿Cuál es el número de la salida más cerca de tu casa?
6. ¿Cuál es la velocidad máxima en la autopista?
7. ¿Cuántos carriles tiene?
8. A la salida, ¿hay un rótulo que indica los pueblos cercanos?

**11** **Las autopistas** Estás viajando por Ecuador. Un(a) amigo(a) ecuatoriano(a) (tu compañero[a]) te hace preguntas sobre las autopistas donde tú vives. Contesta a todas sus preguntas y descríbele las autopistas de tu estado.

**SPANISH Online**

For more information about Ecuador, go to the Glencoe Spanish Web site: spanish.glencoe.com

**12** **Ventajas** En las autopistas es casi siempre necesario pagar peaje. En las carreteras secundarias no hay peaje. Con un(a) compañero(a), discutan por qué es mejor tomar la autopista y pagar el peaje. ¿Cuáles son las ventajas *(advantages)*?

La carretera panamericana, Perú

Zafra, España

*For more practice using words from **Palabras 1** and **2**, do Activity 11 on page H12 at the end of this book.*



**Vocabulario**

**10** This activity can be done orally with books closed.

## Writing Development

You can have students write a short paragraph about a superhighway near where they live using the information in Activity 10 as a guide.

**SPANISH Online**

The Glencoe Spanish Web site **(spanish.glencoe.com)** offers options that enable you and your students to experience the Spanish-speaking world via the Internet. For each **Capítulo,** there are activities, games, and quizzes. In addition, an *Enrichment* section offers students an opportunity to visit Web sites related to the theme of the chapter.

**Un poco más** This *InfoGap* Activity will allow students to practice in pairs. The activity should be very manageable for them, since all vocabulary and structures are familiar to them.

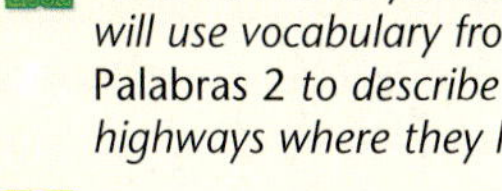

## Answers to ¿Qué palabra necesito?

**10**

1. Una autopista cerca de donde yo vivo es ___.
2. Sí, (No, no) es una autopista de peaje.
3. El peaje es ___.
4. Tengo que pagar el peaje en ___. Hay garitas de peaje cada ___ kilómetros.
5. El número de la salida más cerca de mi casa es ___.
6. La velocidad máxima en la autopista es ___.
7. Tiene ___ carriles.
8. Sí (No), a la salida (no) hay un rótulo que indica los pueblos cercanos.

**11** *Answers will vary. Students will use vocabulary from* Palabras 2 *to describe highways where they live.*

**12** *Answers will vary.*

## Estructura

## 1 PREPARATION

### Resource Manager

Audio Activities TE, pages 135–136
Audio CD 7
Workbook, pages 125–128
Quizzes, pages 53–55
ExamView ® Pro

### Bellringer Review

*Use BRR Transparency 11.3 or write the following on the board.*
Write the opposites of these words and expressions.

1. **la izquierda**
2. **detrás de**
3. **el este**

## 2 PRESENTATION

### Imperativo familiar: formas regulares

**Step 1** Have students open their books to page 330. Lead them through the explanation. Have students repeat the imperative forms.

**Step 2** Provide and elicit additional examples.

**¡OJO!** Students should not be expected to produce the command forms perfectly, since one who is not very fluent seldom tells someone what to do. You may wish to present this point more for receptive purposes.

## Estructura

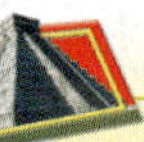

### Imperativo familiar: formas regulares
#### Telling friends what to do

You use the **tú** command when speaking with friends, family, people you know well, and children. The regular **tú** form of the command is the same form as the **usted** form in the present tense.

| PRESENT (UD.) | IMPERATIVE (TÚ) |
|---|---|
| Ud. maneja. | ¡Maneja! |
| Ud. aprende. | ¡Aprende! |
| Ud. escribe. | ¡Escribe! |
| Ud. comienza. | ¡Comienza! |
| Ud. vuelve. | ¡Vuelve! |
| Ud. sigue. | ¡Sigue! |

Estepona, España

## ¿Cómo lo digo?

**13 ¿Qué debo hacer?**

Sigan el modelo.

1. ¿Debo parar?
2. ¿Debo doblar?
3. ¿Debo dar la vuelta?
4. ¿Debo doblar a la derecha?
5. ¿Debo leer el rótulo?
6. ¿Debo seguir derecho?
7. ¿Debo volver?
8. ¿Debo pedir direcciones?



### Answers to ¿Cómo lo digo?

13

1. Sí, Pepe, para.
2. Sí, Pepe, dobla.
3. Sí, Pepe, da la vuelta.
4. Sí, Pepe, dobla a la derecha.
5. Sí, Pepe, lee el rótulo.
6. Sí, Pepe, sigue derecho.
7. Sí, Pepe, vuelve.
8. Sí, Pepe, pide direcciones.

### LEVELING

**A:** Activities 13, 14, 15

# Estructura

## 3 PRACTICE

## ¿Cómo lo digo?

**13** Have students present each item of the activity as a miniconversation.

**14** Have students prepare the activity before going over it in class.

**15** Have students present each item of the activity as a miniconversation.

**Learning from Photos**

*(page 331)* Have students look at the photo of the car. Tell them that the **L** on top of the car is the international symbol for *learner.*

**Learning from Realia**

*(page 331)* Prospective drivers in Venezuela must get a medical clearance. There are many questions you can ask students about this document. For example:
**¿Qué indica el certificado?**
**¿Para cuánto tiempo es válido el certificado?**
**¿Qué tiene que llevar el conductor?**

**14** **Historieta El instructor** Completen con el imperativo.

Estepona, España

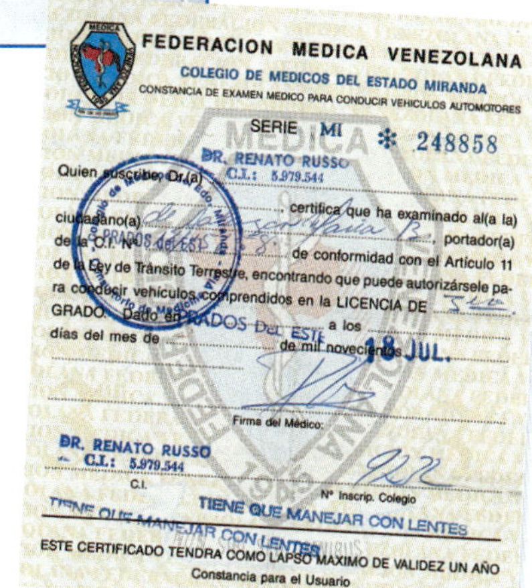
FEDERACION MEDICA VENEZOLANA
COLEGIO DE MEDICOS DEL ESTADO MIRANDA
CONSTANCIA DE EXAMEN MEDICO PARA CONDUCIR VEHICULOS AUTOMOTORES
SERIE MI ✻ 248858
Quien suscribe, Dr.(a) DR. RENATO RUSSO C.I.: 5.979.544
........ certifica que ha examinado al(a la) ciudadano(a) ........, portador(a) de la C.I. N° ........ de conformidad con el Articulo 11 de la Ley de Tránsito Terrestre, encontrando que puede autorizársele para conducir vehículos comprendidos en la LICENCIA DE ........ GRADO. Dado en PRADOS DEL ESTE a los ........ días del mes de ........ de mil novecientos 18 JUL.
Firma del Médico:
DR. RENATO RUSSO C.I.: 5.979.544
C.I.
N° Inscrip. Colegio
TIENE QUE MANEJAR CON LENTES
ESTE CERTIFICADO TENDRA COMO LAPSO MAXIMO DE VALIDEZ UN AÑO
Constancia para el Usuario

Luis, primero __1__ (prender) el motor. __2__ (Prestar) atención a la carretera. Ahora __3__ (entrar) en la carretera. Bien. __4__ (Adelantar) en el carril izquierdo. Ahora __5__ (volver) al carril derecho. __6__ (Seguir) derecho hasta la salida. __7__ (Manejar) siempre con calma. __8__ (Parar) aquí. __9__ (Apagar) el motor. __10__ (Tomar) este manual y __11__ (leer). Es todo para hoy.

**15** **Una visita a Argentina** Sigan el modelo.

1. Quiero viajar a Argentina.
2. Quiero tomar un avión.
3. Quiero pasar un mes allí.
4. Quiero visitar a Buenos Aires.
5. Quiero subir a la cordillera.
6. Quiero esquiar en Bariloche.
7. Quiero comer un biftec allí.
8. Quiero nadar en los lagos.



## ANSWERS TO ¿Cómo lo digo?

**14**

1. prende
2. Presta
3. entra
4. Adelanta
5. vuelve
6. Sigue
7. Maneja
8. Para
9. Apaga
10. Toma
11. lee

**15**

1. Pues, viaja a la Argentina.
2. Pues, toma un avión.
3. Pues, pasa un mes allí.
4. Pues, visita a Buenos Aires.
5. Pues, sube a la cordillera.
6. Pues, esquía en Bariloche.
7. Pues, come un biftec allí.
8. Pues, nada en los lagos.

# Estructura

## 1 PREPARATION

### Bellringer Review

*Use BRR Transparency 11.4 or write the following on the board.*
Write a synonym for each of the following.
1. **la llanta**
2. **la licencia**
3. **el claxon**
4. **la maletera**

## 2 PRESENTATION

### Imperativo familiar: formas irregulares

**Step 1** Have students open their books to page 332 and have them repeat the irregular forms of the **tú** command after you.

## 3 PRACTICE

### ¿Cómo lo digo?

**16** Have students present each item of the activity as a miniconversation.

**17** Have students prepare the activity before going over it in class.

### FUN-FACTS

The **autovías** in Spain are a series of modern highways inaugurated at the time of the Expo '92 international fair. The **autovías** do not charge tolls. The **autopistas** are a small number of superhighways on which there is no speed limit and which do require toll payments.



## Imperativo familiar: formas irregulares

### Telling friends what to do

The following verbs have irregular forms for the **tú** commands.

| INFINITIVE | IMPERATIVE (TÚ) |
|---|---|
| decir | di |
| ir | ve |
| ser | sé |
| salir | sal |
| hacer | haz |
| tener | ten |
| venir | ven |
| poner | pon |

## ¿Cómo lo digo?

### 16 A casa del abuelo

Contesten con **sí** y el imperativo.

1. ¿Debo venir mañana?
2. ¿Debo salir temprano?
3. ¿Debo hacer el viaje en carro?
4. ¿Debo poner aire en las llantas?
5. ¿Debo decir adiós a mi hermano?
6. ¿Debo ir por la carretera vieja?
7. ¿Debo tener cuidado?

La carretera panamericana, cerca de Riobamba, Ecuador

### 17 Historieta El mecánico experto y el mecánico nuevo

Completen con el imperativo.

__1__ (Oír), Paco. __2__ (Venir) aquí. Hay aceite en el piso, así es que __3__ (tener) cuidado. Bien, __4__ (mirar) lo que yo hago, y tú, __5__ (hacer) lo mismo. __6__ (Poner) la luz aquí y __7__ (ser) atento. Ahora, __8__ (decir) todo lo que aprendiste hoy.



### Answers to ¿Cómo lo digo?

**16**
1. Sí, ven mañana.
2. Sí, sal temprano.
3. Sí, haz el viaje en carro.
4. Sí, pon aire en las llantas.
5. Sí, di adiós a tu hermano.
6. Sí, ve por la carretera vieja.
7. Sí, ten cuidado.

**17**
1. Oye
2. Ven
3. ten
4. mira
5. haz
6. Pon
7. sé
8. di

**18** **Historieta Tito el tímido**
Sigan el modelo.

> **No sé si debo manejar. →**
> **¡Maneja, hombre!**

1. No sé si debo hacer el viaje.
2. No sé si debo salir de la ciudad.
3. No sé si debo manejar.
4. No sé si debo ir por la autopista.
5. No sé si debo pedir un día de vacación.
6. No sé si debo volver tarde.

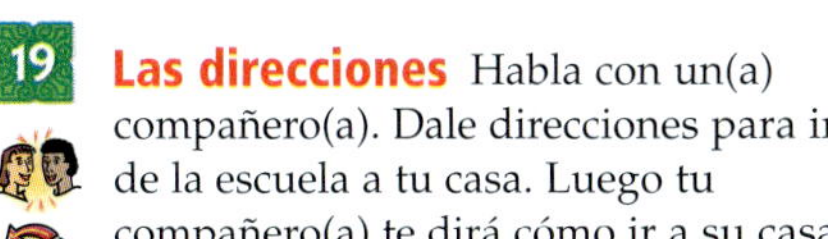

**19** **Las direcciones** Habla con un(a) compañero(a). Dale direcciones para ir de la escuela a tu casa. Luego tu compañero(a) te dirá cómo ir a su casa.

**20** **Una llamada telefónica** Estás hablando con un(a) estudiante de intercambio de Buenos Aires, Argentina. Él o ella quiere hacer una llamada desde un teléfono público. Dile lo que tiene que hacer.

Buenos Aires, Argentina

**21** **A la capital** Alicia acaba de recibir su permiso de conducir. Mañana sus padres le van a permitir usar el carro. Alicia tiene que ir a la capital y no conoce la ruta. Explícale cómo puede ir de tu pueblo a la capital de tu estado. Contesta a todas sus preguntas.

## Estructura

**18** Have students present this activity as a miniconversation.

**19**, **20**, and **21** Have students choose the activity or activities they wish to do.

### Learning from Photos

*(page 332)* Riobamba is situated in a broad valley on the southern slope of **El Chimborazo** volcano. The Pan American Highway descends from the eastern side of **El Chimborazo** to the city of Riobamba, the capital of Chimborazo Province—a mostly rural agricultural region in the center of Ecuador. It has the highest percentage (some 70 percent) of indigenous people in Ecuador.

### LEVELING

**A:** Activities 16, 17, 19, 20, 21
**C:** Activity 18

## Answers to ¿Cómo lo digo?

**18**

1. ¡Haz el viaje, hombre!
2. ¡Sal de la ciudad, hombre!
3. ¡Maneja, hombre!
4. ¡Ve por la autopista, hombre!
5. ¡Pide un día de vacación, hombre!
6. ¡Vuelve tarde, hombre!

**19** *Answers will vary. Students will use the tú form of the imperative to tell friends how to get from school to their houses.*

**20** *Answers will vary. Students will use the tú form of the imperative to give instructions on how to use a public telephone. Have students refer to Chapter 3 for any vocabulary that they might need.*

**21** *Answers will vary, but students will use vocabulary and structure from the chapter to give directions from their city to the capital.*

## Estructura

## 1 PREPARATION

### Bellringer Review

*Use BRR Transparency 11.5 or write the following on the board.*
You are working for the Spanish national airline Iberia and have been assigned to train new flight attendants. Write five things you would tell them. For example:
**Indíquenles las salidas de emergencia a los pasajeros.**

## 2 PRESENTATION

### Imperativo negativo

**Step 1** Have students open their books to page 334 and lead them through Items 1 and 2. Then have them repeat the forms after you.

**Step 2** Provide and elicit additional examples.

**¡OJO!** The use of the commands, and particularly the placement of pronouns with commands, is extremely difficult for students. Since they do not have to produce these forms until they are quite fluent, it is recommended that you present them primarily for recognition only.

## 3 PRACTICE

## ¿Cómo lo digo?

**22** Have students do this activity in pairs. Have different pairs present one item to the class.



## Estructura

# Imperativo negativo
## Telling friends what not to do

1. The negative **tú** commands are formed the same way as the formal **(usted, ustedes)** commands. You drop the **o** of the **yo** form of the present tense and add **es** to **-ar** verbs and **as** to **-er** and **-ir** verbs.

| INFINITIVE | PRESENT (YO) | NEGATIVE COMMAND (TÚ) |
|---|---|---|
| hablar | hablø | no hables |
| comer | comø | no comas |
| abrir | abrø | no abras |
| volver | vuelvø | no vuelvas |
| pedir | pidø | no pidas |
| hacer | hagø | no hagas |
| salir | salgø | no salgas |

2. The same verbs that are irregular in the formal command are irregular in the negative **tú** command.

| | |
|---|---|
| ir | no vayas |
| ser | no seas |
| saber | no sepas |
| estar | no estés |
| dar | no dés |

### ¿Te acuerdas?

Object pronouns are attached to affirmative formal commands and precede negative commands. The same is true of familiar commands.

**¡Levántate!**
**¡No te levantes!**
**¡Dámelo!**
**¡No me lo des!**
**¡Cómpramelo!**
**¡No me lo compres!**
**¡Mírame!**
**¡No me mires!**
**¡Díselo!**
**¡No se lo digas!**

## ¿Cómo lo digo?

**22** **Historieta ¿Hago el viaje o no?** Contesten según el modelo.

1. ¿Voy temprano o no?
2. ¿Salgo a las nueve o no?
3. ¿Tomo la carretera vieja o no?
4. ¿Manejo el convertible o no?
5. ¿Excedo la velocidad máxima o no?
6. ¿Le digo la verdad a Pepe o no?
7. ¿Vuelvo tarde o no?
8. ¿Hago el viaje o no?



## ANSWERS TO ¿Cómo lo digo?

1. No, no vayas temprano.
2. No, no salgas a las nueve.
3. No, no tomes la carretera vieja.
4. No, no manejes el convertible.
5. No, no excedas la velocidad máxima.
6. No, no le digas la verdad a Pepe.
7. No, no vuelvas tarde.
8. No, no hagas el viaje.

## LEVELING

**E:** Activity 2A
**A:** Activities 22, 23
**C:** Activities 25, 26

**23** **En la gasolinera** Contesten con **no** y el imperativo.

1. ¿Lleno el tanque?
2. ¿Abro el capó?
3. ¿Reviso el aceite?
4. ¿Pongo agua en el radiador?
5. ¿Limpio el parabrisas?
6. ¿Pongo aire en las llantas?

Ciudad de México

**24** **¡Qué dormilona es Marisa!**
Practiquen la conversación.

MAMÁ Marisa, levántate. Ya es hora.
MARISA ¡Ay, mamá! Que no. ¡Déjame, por favor!
MAMÁ Bien. No te levantes. Y no te laves ni te vistas. Quédate en cama.
MARISA Perdóname, mami, pero estoy muy cansada.

Un coche eléctrico, Puerto Banús, España

**25** **¿Lo compro o no?** Sigan el modelo.

**—¿Compro el carro o no?**
**—Sí, cómpralo. / No, no lo compres.**

1. ¿Compro las baterías o no?
2. ¿Compro el aceite o no?
3. ¿Compro la gasolina o no?
4. ¿Compro el convertible o no?
5. ¿Compro los neumáticos o no?

**26** **Sí, dámelas.** Contesten según el modelo.

**—¿Te doy las direcciones?**
**—Sí, dámelas.**

1. ¿Te doy el mapa?
2. ¿Te doy las instrucciones?
3. ¿Te doy el dinero para el parquímetro?
4. ¿Te doy los tiques?
5. ¿Te doy la licencia?

## Estructura

**23** You can go over the activity without prior preparation.
**Expansion:** Have two students present Activity 23 as a conversation in a service station.

**24** Call on two students to read this activity with as much expression as possible.

**25 and 26** Call on more able students to answer when going over these activities.

### Learning from Photos

*(page 335 top)* You may wish to ask these questions about the photo:
**¿Dónde están ellos?**
**¿Qué será uno de los hombres?**
**¿Qué están mirando ellos?**
**¿Cuál será el problema?**
*(page 335 middle)* Puerto Banús is a plush marina in Marbella with beautiful yachts and excellent hotels and restaurants.

**¡Adelante!**
At this point in the chapter, students have learned all the vocabulary and structure necessary to complete the chapter. The conversation and cultural readings that follow recycle all the material learned up to this point.

## ANSWERS TO ¿Cómo lo digo?

**23**

1. No, no llenes el tanque.
2. No, no abras el capó.
3. No, no revises el aceite.
4. No, no pongas agua en el radiador.
5. No, no limpies el parabrisas.
6. No, no pongas aire en las llantas.

**25**

1. Sí, cómpralas. No, no las compres.
2. Sí, cómpralo. No, no lo compres.
3. Sí, cómprala. No, no la compres.
4. Sí, cómpralo. No, no lo compres.
5. Sí, cómpralos. No, no los compres.

**26**

1. Sí, dámelo.
2. Sí, dámelas.
3. Sí, dámelo.
4. Sí, dámelos.
5. Sí, dámela.

# Conversación

## 1 PREPARATION

### Resource Manager

Audio Activities TE, page 137
Audio CD 7

## 2 PRESENTATION

**Step 1** Have students listen to the conversation on Audio CD 7.

**Step 2** Have the class repeat the conversation after you.

**Step 3** Call on two students to read the conversation aloud.

**Step 4** After students read a few lines, ask corresponding questions from the **¿Comprendes?** section.

### Glencoe Technology

On the CD-ROM, students can watch a dramatization of this conversation. They can then play the role of either one of the characters and record themselves in the conversation.

# Conversación

## Un sitio para estacionar   

**María** Anita, ¿puedo estacionar aquí?
**Anita** Aquí, no. ¿No ves que es un cruce de peatones? Hay un estacionamiento municipal en la plaza.
**María** ¿Cómo voy a la plaza?
**Anita** Toma la avenida Cisneros. Quédate en el carril derecho porque a dos cuadras de aquí vas a doblar a la derecha.
**María** ¿En la esquina donde está la estación de servicio?
**Anita** Precisamente. Repito—dobla a la derecha y sigue derecho hasta el primer semáforo. Al primer semáforo, dobla a la izquierda y verás la plaza.
**María** ¿Y puedo estacionar en la plaza?
**Anita** En la plaza misma, no. Pero hay un estacionamiento subterráneo. Hay un rótulo para indicar la entrada.

### ¿Comprendes?

Contesten.

1. ¿Qué quiere saber María?
2. Según Anita, ¿por qué no se puede estacionar allí?
3. ¿Dónde se puede estacionar?
4. ¿Sabe María ir allí?
5. ¿Por qué debe María quedarse en el carril derecho?
6. ¿Qué hay en la esquina donde debe doblar?
7. Después de doblar a la derecha, ¿qué debe hacer María?
8. ¿Cuándo debe doblar a la izquierda?
9. ¿Dónde se encuentra el estacionamiento?
10. ¿Qué hay para indicar la entrada?



### Answers to ¿Comprendes?

1. María quiere saber si puede estacionar allí.
2. Según Anita, no se puede estacionar allí porque es un cruce de peatones.
3. Se puede estacionar en un estacionamiento municipal en la plaza.
4. No, María no sabe cómo ir allí.
5. Debe quedarse en el carril derecho porque a dos cuadras de allí va a doblar a la derecha.
6. En la esquina donde debe doblar está la estación de servicio.
7. Después de doblar a la derecha María debe seguir derecho hasta el primer semáforo.
8. Debe doblar a la izquierda al primer semáforo.
9. El estacionamiento se encuentra en la plaza pero es un estacionamiento subterráneo.
10. Hay un rótulo para indicar la entrada.

# Vamos a hablar más

**A** **Las señales de tránsito** Trabaja con un(a) compañero(a). Tú escogerás una señal y explicarás a tu compañero(a) lo que significa. Tu compañero(a) tiene que adivinar cuál de las señales estás describiendo. Luego cambien de rol.

**B** **Juego** **¿No lo hago?** Have some fun. Your parents and teachers are always telling you what not to do. Get together in small groups and in a nice way imitate your parents and teachers. State all those things they do indeed tell each of you not to do.

Santo Domingo, República Dominicana



Conversación

## 3 PRACTICE

# Vamos a hablar más

¡OJO! These activities encourage students to use the chapter vocabulary and structures in open-ended situations. It is not necessary to have them do all the activities. Choose the ones you consider most appropriate.

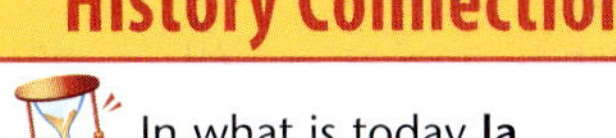

## About the Spanish Language

Two additional words that mean *to park* besides **estacionar** are **aparcar** and **parquear.**

## History Connection

In what is today **la República Dominicana,** Columbus established the first Spanish settlement in the Americas, **La Isabela,** on the island of **La Española** in 1493. The capital is Santo Domingo, but most Spanish speakers refer to the entire island as Santo Domingo despite the fact that a third of the island constitutes the Republic of Haiti. Dominican immigration to the United States is significant. New York City has a large Dominican population.

**LEVELING**

**E:** Conversation

## Answers to Vamos a hablar más

**A**

- Camiones
- Niños jugando
- Bicicletas
- Semáforo
- Cruce de peatones
- Fin del camino
- Cruce

**B** *Answers will vary. Students will use commands to imitate their parents and teachers. For more advanced students or to make the game more challenging, have students use the informal commands when impersonating their parents, the singular formal commands when being their teacher, and the plural for giving commands to more than one person.*

# Lecturas culturales

## Resource Manager

Audio Activities TE, page 138
Audio CD 7

## National Standards

**Cultures**
The reading about the Pan American Highway and the related activities familiarize students with the longest highway system in the world.

**Comparisons**
In this reading students learn that, unlike in the United States where roads are generally well-maintained, traveling on certain portions of the Pan American Highway may require caution and a sense of adventure.

## PRESENTATION

### Pre-reading

Tell students that they are going to read about the longest and possibly most interesting highway in the world. If possible, show students on a map or maps the route the Pan American Highway takes.

### Reading

**Step 1** Call on an individual to read several sentences aloud.

**Step 2** After two students have read aloud, ask questions such as: **¿Qué es la carretera panamericana? ¿Dónde empieza ¿Dónde termina?**



# Lecturas culturales

## La carretera panamericana

La carretera panamericana es la carretera más larga del mundo—47.516 kilómetros. La panamericana es un sistema de carreteras y caminos que se extiende desde la frontera de Estados Unidos y México hasta la ciudad de Puerto Montt en Chile. Además de extenderse del norte al sur de los continentes americanos, la carretera enlaza[1] la costa oriental con la costa occidental de la América del Sur. Enlaza también las capitales de diecisiete países latinoamericanos. Esta carretera es una ruta importante para el transporte de materias primas y productos agrícolas.

**Reading Strategy**

**Summarizing** When you read informative passages, you must develop ways to try to remember what you read. This is most important if you are reading about a topic you know nothing about. Summarizing is a good way to do this. The easiest way to summarize is to take notes as you begin to read. From your notes, you can write a sentence about each section or paragraph of the reading. From your paragraph sentences, it will be easy to write one sentence describing the main idea of the selection. Use all your summary sentences to help trigger your memory about the contents of each part of the reading.

La carretera panamericana cerca de Buenos Aires

En algunas partes la carretera panamericana es una carretera moderna con dos o más carriles en cada sentido. En su mayor parte la carretera está pavimentada—en algunos casos en buenas condiciones y en otros casos en malas condiciones. En muchos trayectos de la carretera la tierra es muy inhóspita. Se puede decir que la carretera también es inhóspita. Hay que manejar con mucho cuidado porque nunca sabes cuándo encontrarás un bache[2] muy profundo. A veces el pavimento desaparece repentinamente y te encuentras en un camino de rocas, piedras y lodo[3].

[1]enlaza *connects*
[2]bache *pothole*
[3]lodo *mud*

Una estación de servicio en la carretera panamericana, cerca de Icá, Perú

La carretera panamericana, Guatemala

¡Ten cuidado! Hay otro peligro. La mayor parte de la carretera no tiene borde. Por consiguiente cuando un carro o un camión tiene una avería[4], el conductor pone unas ramas[5] de árboles o plantas a unos metros detrás del carro. Estas ramas advierten[6] a los conductores que se están acercando que hay un carro averiado. Pero al reparar el carro o cambiar la llanta pinchada[7], el conductor sale y allí se quedan las ramas. Y de noche es difícil verlas.

Como ya hemos dicho, en muchas áreas la carretera panamericana es una carretera moderna y conveniente. Pero en las zonas remotas que recorre, tomar la panamericana es una verdadera aventura.

[4]avería *breakdown*
[5]ramas *branches*
[6]advierten *warn*
[7]pinchada *flat*

## ¿Comprendes?

**A La panamericana** Contesten.

1. ¿Cuál es la carretera más larga del mundo?
2. ¿Qué es la panamericana?
3. ¿Dónde empieza la panamericana y dónde termina?
4. ¿Enlaza a cuántas capitales?
5. ¿Cómo es la carretera en algunas partes?
6. ¿Cómo es en otras partes?

**B Palabras** Empleen las siguientes palabras en una oración.

1. carril
2. enlaza (hace enlace con)
3. bache
4. avería
5. llanta pinchada



## Lecturas culturales

### Post-reading

**Step 1** Go over the **¿Comprendes?** activities.

**Step 2** Have a few students give a description in their own words of the Pan American Highway.

### Geography Connection

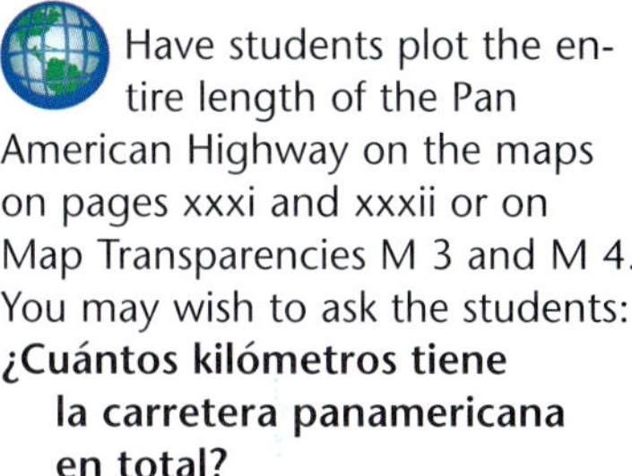

Have students plot the entire length of the Pan American Highway on the maps on pages xxxi and xxxii or on Map Transparencies M 3 and M 4. You may wish to ask the students:

**¿Cuántos kilómetros tiene la carretera panamericana en total?**

**¿Por qué países pasa la carretera?**

**¿Qué montañas tiene que cruzar?**

## Answers to ¿Comprendes?

**A**

1. La carretera más larga del mundo es la carretera panamericana.
2. Es un sistema de carreteras y caminos que se extiende desde la frontera de Estados Unidos y México hasta la ciudad de Puerto Montt en Chile.
3. Empieza en la frontera de Estados Unidos y México y termina en Puerto Montt, en Chile.
4. Enlaza a diecisiete capitales.
5. En algunas partes es una carretera moderna con dos o más carriles en cada sentido.
6. En otras partes la carretera está en malas condiciones. Hay que manejar con mucho cuidado.

**B**

*Answers will vary. Have students find the words in the reading and model their sentences after them using words from the chapter vocabulary.*

# Lectura opcional 1

## National Standards

**Cultures**

This reading and the related activities on this page familiarize students with parking in the Spanish-speaking world.

**¡OJO!** This reading is optional. You may skip it completely, have the entire class read it, have only several students read it and report to the class, or assign it for extra credit.

## PRESENTATION

**¡OJO!** Note that this selection reintroduces quite a few familiar command forms.

**Step 1** Have a student who read this selection explain in his or her own words how to use a parking meter where he or she lives.

### Learning from Realia

*(page 340)* Direct the students' attention to the blue ticket. You may wish to ask them:

**¿Para qué es el tique?**
**¿Cuánto cuesta?**
**¿Para cuánto tiempo es válido?**
**¿Es obligatorio tener un tique?**
**¿Qué anuncios o propaganda lleva el tique?**

# Lectura opcional 1

Buenos Aires, Argentina

## El estacionamiento

En todas las grandes ciudades de España y Latinoamérica es difícil estacionar. En algunas calles donde no está prohibido el estacionamiento hay parquímetros donde uno puede meter una moneda. Entonces el parquímetro indicará el tiempo que puedes estacionar.

Hay también aparcamientos públicos y garajes privados donde es necesario pagar. En muchas ciudades hay aparcamientos municipales donde no hay parquímetros pero tienes que pagar.

—Dime lo que tengo que hacer si voy a uno de estos estacionamientos.

—Busca la (máquina) distribuidora de tiques.
Introduce una o varias monedas en la distribuidora.
Pon suficiente dinero para el tiempo deseado.
Oprime el botón y saldrá un papelito o tique.
Indicará el tiempo que puedes estacionar.

Pon el papelito o el tique en el interior del parabrisas del coche donde lo pueden ver los guardias o policías. Si no lo ven, te darán una multa[1].

[1]multa *fine*

## ¿Comprendes?

**A ¿Qué hago para estacionar?**
Explica a un(a) amigo(a) todo lo que tiene que hacer para estacionar el coche (aparcar el carro) en un aparcamiento público con una distribuidora de tiques.

### Answers to ¿Comprendes?

**A** *Answers will vary but may include:*

Busco una distribuidora de tiques. Pongo varias monedas en la distribuidora. Pongo suficiente dinero para el tiempo deseado. Oprimo el botón y sale un papelito o tique que indica el tiempo que puedo estacionar. Pongo el tique en el interior del parabrisas del coche donde lo pueden ver los policías.

# Lectura opcional 2

## Las señales de tránsito

Desde hace muchos años, en España, Latinoamérica y en otras partes del mundo, se han usado las señales de tránsito internacionales. En Estados Unidos la introducción de estas señales fue más reciente, pero ahora se ven en todas partes. Lo bueno de las señales internacionales es que no es necesario saber el idioma del país, porque muchas de las señales no usan palabras.

Estas son las señales más comunes.

**¿Qué quiere decir... ?**
Identifiquen las señales de tránsito.



# Lectura opcional 2

## National Standards

**Cultures**
This reading and the related activity on this page familiarize students with international road signs and their use in the Spanish-speaking world.

**Comparisons**
Students learn that, unlike in Spain and the Latin American countries, international road signs were only recently introduced in the United States.

**¡OJO!** This reading is optional. You may skip it completely, have the entire class read it, have only several students read it and report to the class, or assign it for extra credit.

## PRESENTATION

**Step 1** Have students quickly read the selection. See how many of the signs they can identify.

**Step 2** Ask them if there are signs like these in their community.

### FUN FACTS

The stop signs in some Latin American countries say **Alto**, in others they say **Pare**, and in Spain they say **Stop**.

### ANSWERS TO ¿Comprendes?

*Answers will vary but may include:*
- Parar
- No doblar a la izquierda
- Curva. No exceder 40 km
- No doblar a la derecha
- Ceder el paso
- De sentido único
- Cruce de peatones

### LEVELING

**E:** Reading, Readings 1, 2

**A:** Reading, Reading 1

# Conexiones

## National Standards

**Connections**
This reading about air pollution, caused primarily by emissions of internal combustion engines in many parts of Latin America, establishes a connection with another discipline, allowing students to reinforce and further their knowledge of ecology through the study of Spanish.

**¡OJO!** The readings in the **Conexiones** section are optional. They focus on some of the major disciplines taught in schools and universities. The vocabulary is useful for discussing such topics as history, literature, art, economics, business, science, etc. You may choose any of the following ways to do the readings in the **Conexiones** sections.

**Independent reading** Have students read the selections and do the post-reading activities as homework, which you collect. This option is least intrusive on class time and requires a minimum of teacher involvement.

**Homework with in-class follow-up** Assign the readings and post-reading activities as homework. Review and discuss the material in class the next day.

**Intensive in-class activity** This option includes a pre-reading vocabulary presentation, in-class reading and discussion, assignment of the activities for homework, and a discussion of the assignment in class the following day.

**LEVELING**
**E:** Reading
**A:** Reading

# Conexiones

## *Las ciencias*

Ciudad de México

### La ecología

Ecology is a subject of great interest to people around the world. People are becoming more aware of the damage being done to our environment. Many of the ecological problems that exist in one area of the world are common in many other areas. People in Mexico City are as concerned about their polluted air as are the residents of Los Angeles.

Quito, Ecuador

### La ecología

El problema de la contaminación del medio ambiente[1] ha dado lugar al movimiento ecologista. El término «ecología» significa el equilibrio entre los seres vivientes y la naturaleza.

**La contaminación del aire**

La contaminación del aire es un problema serio en muchas partes del mundo. España y Latinoamérica no son ninguna excepción. El aire de muchas ciudades de España y Latinoamérica está contaminado. Los gases que salen de los tubos de escape de los automóviles, camiones y buses son una causa principal de la contaminación.

[1]medio ambiente *environment*



### Learning from Photos

*(page 342 bottom)* Ask students the following questions about the photo:

**¿Es una calle peatonal? ¿Cómo lo sabes? ¿Qué opinas? ¿Hay mucho tráfico en esta calle? En esta calle, ¿qué es más rápido, en tu opinión—andar a pie o en carro? ¿Es ancha o angosta la calle?**

**Campañas ecológicas**

Muchas ciudades están experimentando con programas para controlar o eliminar la contaminación. La Ciudad de México, que tiene uno de los problemas más serios en cuanto a la contaminación del aire, no permite a los autobuses de largo recorrido entrar en el centro de la ciudad.

En algunas ciudades los carros con placa de número par[2] circulan un día y los carros con placa de número impar circulan el otro. Es una manera de tratar de eliminar el número de vehículos y así reducir la emisión de gases que contaminan el aire.

[2]placa de número par *license plate with an even number*

Ciudad de México

037774
D F MEX

¿Comprendes?

## A ¿Cuál es la palabra?

Busquen la palabra equivalente en la lectura.

1. pollution
2. environment
3. human beings
4. campaign

## B Donde vivimos Contesten.

1. ¿Está muy contaminado el aire donde ustedes viven?
2. ¿Hay otros tipos de contaminación?
3. ¿Hay mucho o poco tráfico donde ustedes viven?
4. ¿Tiene su pueblo o ciudad un programa para controlar la contaminación?
5. En su ciudad o pueblo, ¿pueden circular todos los vehículos el mismo día?
6. ¿Sabes el número de la placa del carro de tu familia?
7. ¿Tiene un número par o impar?

SOLO PAPEL Y CARTON
Tu papel
Es importante
Delegación de R.S.U. y Medio Ambiente



# Conexiones

## PRESENTATION

### *Las ciencias*
### La ecología

You may wish to have all students scan this selection quickly. The topic is of great interest today, and the reading selection is quite easy. Tell students that the word **contaminación,** as it is used here, does not mean *contamination.* Ask them what it means. *(pollution)*

### Learning from Realia

*(page 343 top)* You may wish to ask students the following about the Mexican license plate: **La placa que vemos, ¿es un número par o un número impar?**

*(page 343 middle)* You may wish to ask students the following questions about the poster:

**¿Qué es la figura en la caricatura?**
**¿Qué pide él?**
**¿Quiénes son buenos ciudadanos?**
**¿Cuáles son algunos desperdicios sólidos?**
**¿Qué quiere decir «Reciclando hoy para un mejor mañana»?**

### National Standards

**Communities**

If there are exchange students from Spain or Latin America, ask them to report to the class on problems of pollution in their countries and what is being done or can be done about them. Encourage students to ask questions. If a student is unavailable, an adult member of the Hispanic community could be invited.

## ANSWERS TO ¿Comprendes?

**A**

1. la contaminación
2. el medio ambiente
3. los seres vivientes
4. la campaña

**B** *Answers will vary but may include:*

1. Sí (No), el aire (no) está muy contaminado donde vivimos.
2. Sí ,(No, no) hay otros tipos de contaminación.
3. Hay mucho (poco) tráfico donde vivimos.
4. Sí (No), nuestro pueblo (nuestra ciudad) (no) tiene un programa para controlar la contaminación.
5. Sí (No), en nuestro pueblo (nuestra ciudad), (no) pueden circular todos los vehículos el mismo día.
6. Sí, (No, no) sé el número de la placa del carro de mi familia.
7. Tiene un número par (impar).

## ¡Te toca a ti!

### Use what you have learned

### Recycling

These activities allow students to use the vocabulary and structure from this chapter in completely open-ended, real-life situations.

### PRESENTATION

Encourage students to say as much as possible when they do these activities. Tell them not to be afraid to make mistakes, since the goal of the activities is real-life communication. If someone in the group makes an error, allow the others to politely correct him or her. Let students choose the activities they would like to do.

You may wish to divide students into pairs or groups. Encourage students to elaborate on the basic theme and to be creative. They may use props, pictures, or posters if they wish.

### Writing Development

Have students keep a notebook or portfolio containing their best written work from each chapter. These selected writings can be based on assignments from the Student Textbook and the Workbook. The activities on page 345 are examples of writing assignments that may be included in each student's portfolio. On page 130 in the Workbook, students will begin to develop an organized autobiography **(Mi autobiografía).** These workbook pages may also become a part of their portfolio.

## ¡Te toca a ti!

# Use what you have learned

HABLAR 1

### Cerca de donde vives

✔ *Talk about cars and driving*

Con un(a) compañero(a) de clase, selecciona (escoge) una ciudad que está cerca de donde ustedes viven. Indiquen las carreteras que pueden tomar para ir a esa ciudad.

HABLAR 2

### Leyendo el mapa

✔ *Give directions*

Con un(a) compañero(a), miren el mapa de España. Han alquilado un coche y quieren ir de Madrid a otra ciudad que los dos escogen. Discutan cómo van a ir y las carreteras que van a tomar. ¡A ver si pueden adivinar cuánto tiempo durará *(will take)* el viaje!

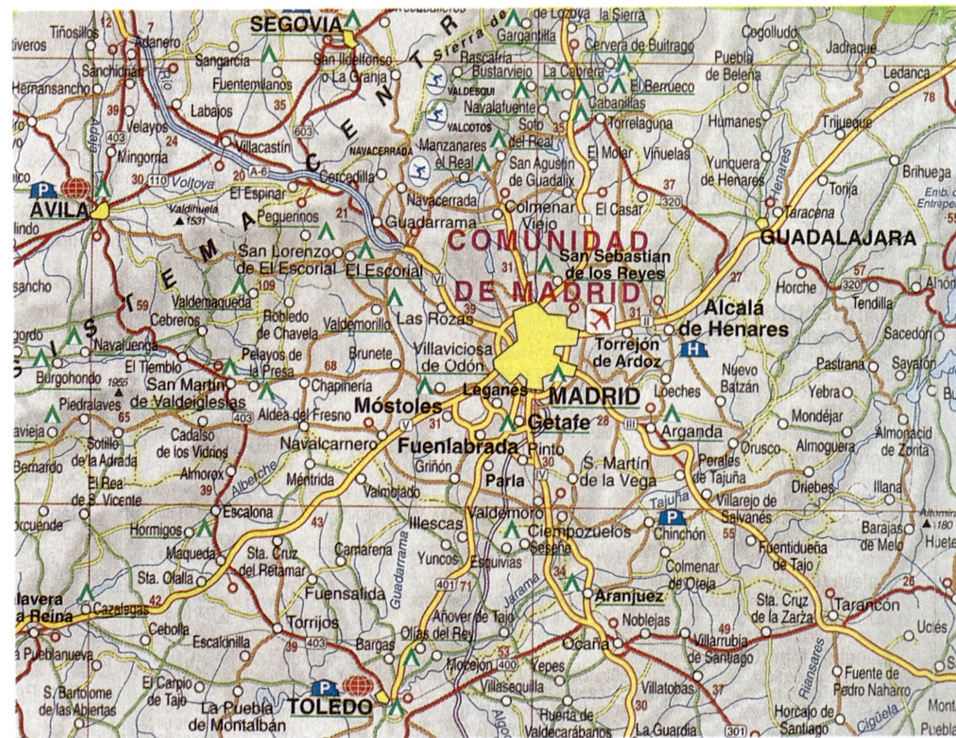




ANSWERS TO ¡Te toca a ti!

1 *Answers will vary. Students will use vocabulary from* Palabras 2 *and the imperative to give directions to a nearby city.*

2 *Answers will vary. Students will use the map provided to give directions to Madrid from a city of their choice.*

## Del aeropuerto a nuestra casa

✔ *Write directions*

Tú tienes un buen amigo que vive en Venezuela. Te va a visitar dentro de poco. Viene con su familia y al llegar al aeropuerto van a alquilar un carro. Escríbele a tu amigo(a) dándole direcciones para ir del aeropuerto a tu casa.

## Instrucciones

✔ *Write orders or commands*

Tus padres van a salir este fin de semana. Ellos te han escrito una lista de cosas que debes hacer y otra lista de cosas que no debes hacer. Escribe lo que dice la lista. Luego compara tu lista con la de un(a) compañero(a).

### Writing Strategy

**Developing a fictional narrative** Like any other narrative, a fictional narrative tells a story. A short story is one kind of fictional narrative, created in the writer's imagination. It tells about a made-up event built up around a complication. It has a plot, characters, and a setting, all of which are related from a certain point of view. For some writers, the hardest part is coming up with the idea, but once they do, they must be sure that their stories contain all these elements.

## Tú y Antonio llegaron muy tarde

You were driving to school with Antonio, the high school exchange student living with you. You missed your first period class, which happens to be your driver education class. And to make matters worse, you had a test that day. You tried to explain to your teacher what happened but he asked you to write it down for him because it seemed so complicated. Write an imaginative story to tell why you and Antonio were late. It might be fun to use the road signs below to help you make up excuses. Be as humorous and creative as you can. Remember, you have to be convincing enough so your teacher will let you make up the exam rather than take a zero.

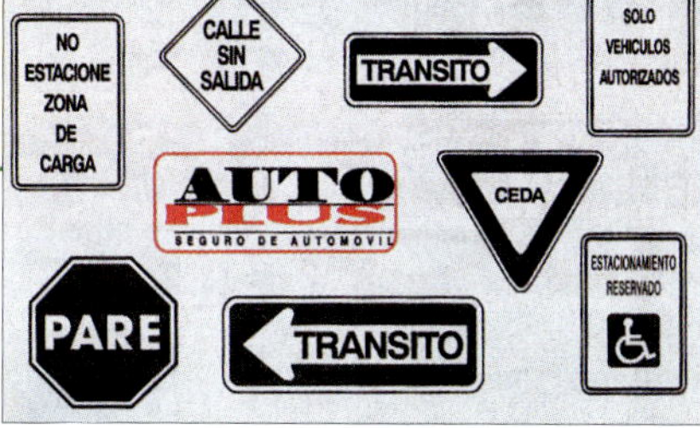




### Answers to ¡Te toca a ti!

 *Answers will vary. Students will use structure learned in the chapter to give directions from the airport to their house.*

 *Answers will vary. Students will practice using commands in the affirmative and the negative to write their lists of instructions from their parents.*

5 *Answers will vary.*

## ¡Te toca a ti!

5 Have individuals read their lists to the class. Have the other students raise their hands each time they have the same item on their lists. Then poll the class to see how many times each order was given.

### Writing Strategy

**Developing a fictional narrative** Have students read the Writing Strategy on page 345. Have students work in pairs to write this story.

### LEVELING

These activities encompass all three levels. All students will be able to do them at a sophistication level commensurate with their ability in Spanish. Some students will be able to speak for several minutes, and others may be able to give just a few sentences. This is to be expected when students are functioning completely on their own generating their own language to the best of their ability.

## Assessment

### Resource Manager

Communication Transparency C 11
Quizzes, pages 51–55
Performance Assessment, Task 11
Tests, pages 163–178
Situation Cards, Chapter 11
**Maratón mental** Videoquiz, Chapter 11
ExamView® Pro, Chapter 11

### Assessment

This is a pre-test for students to take before you administer the chapter test. Note that each section is cross-referenced so students can easily find the material they have to review in case they made errors. You may use Assessment Answers Transparency A 11 to do the assessment in class, or you may assign this assessment for homework. You can correct the assessment yourself, or you may prefer to project the answers on the overhead in class.

### Glencoe Technology

**MINDJOGGER VHS/DVD**

You may wish to help your students prepare for the chapter test by playing the MindJogger game show. Teams will compete against each other to review chapter vocabulary and structure and sharpen listening comprehension skills.

## Assessment

# Vocabulario

**Identifiquen.**

1. 

2. 

3. 

4. 

To review **Palabras 1**, turn to pages 322–323.

**2 Completen.**

5. El ___ tiene sólo dos puertas. Un sedán tiene cuatro.
6. El buen conductor ___ con cuidado.
7. El señor va a la gasolinera para ___ el tanque.

To review **Palabras 2**, turn to pages 326–327.

**3 Completen.**

8. Un ___ o una bocacalle es donde se encuentran dos calles.
9. En muchas autopistas, es necesario pagar el ___.
10. Una autopista tiene varios ___ en cada sentido.
11. Hay un ___ que indica la salida de la autopista.

ANSWERS TO Assessment

1. el permiso de conducir
2. la bocina (el claxon)
3. la llanta de repuesto (de recambio)
4. el descapotable (el convertible)

5. el cupé (el coche deportivo, el descapotable)
6. maneja (conduce)
7. llenar

8. cruce
9. peaje
10. carriles
11. rótulo

# Estructura

**4 Completen con el imperativo (tú).**

12. Francisco, ¡____ con cuidado! (manejar)
13. ____ la autopista. (tomar)
14. ____ derecho. (seguir)
15. ____ cuidado. (tener)
16. ____ de la autopista en la salida. (salir)

To review the familiar imperative, turn to pages 330 and 332.

**5 Escriban en la forma negativa.**

17. Entra en la carretera.
18. Escribe las direcciones.
19. Toma la carretera.
20. Vuelve por la misma carretera.

21–22. Sal de la carretera y toma las calles locales.

To review negative imperatives, turn to page 334.

# Cultura

**6 Completen.**

23. La ____ es la carretera más larga del mundo.
24. Esta carretera empieza en ____ y termina en ____.
25. Esta carretera enlaza ____.

To review this cultural information, turn to pages 338–339.

La carretera panamericana, Guatemala



## Assessment

**FOLDABLES™ Study Organizer** Dinah Zike's Study Guides

Your students may wish to use Foldable 7 to organize, display, and arrange data as they learn to write more extensively in Spanish. You may wish to encourage them to add information from each chapter as they continue to write about and illustrate all the different topics they will be studying.

A *single picture frame* foldable will help different types of learners organize. When it comes to writing, it may help students begin to gather their thoughts to depict what it is they want to write about.

## Answers to Assessment

 4

12. Maneja
13. Toma
14. Sigue
15. Ten
16. Sal

 5

17. No entres en la carretera.
18. No escribas las direcciones.
19. No tomes la carretera.
20. No vuelvas por la misma carretera.

21–22. No salgas de la carretera y no tomes las calles locales.

 6

23. carretera panamericana
24. México, Chile
25. diecisiete capitales

# ¡Hablo como un pro!

This unique page gives students the opportunity to speak freely and say whatever they can, using the vocabulary and structures they have learned in the chapter. The illustration serves to remind students of precisely what they know how to say in Spanish. There are no activities that students do not have the ability to describe or talk about in Spanish. The art not only depicts the vocabulary and content of this chapter, but also reinforces what they learned in previous chapters.

You may wish to use this page in many ways. Some possibilities are to have students do the following:

1. Look at the illustration and identify items by giving the correct Spanish words.
2. Make up sentences about what they see in the illustration.
3. Make up questions about the illustration. They can call on another class member to respond if you do this as a class activity, or you may prefer to allow students to work in small groups. This activity is extremely beneficial because it enables students to actively use interrogative words.
4. Answer questions you ask them about the illustration.
5. Work in pairs and make up a conversation based on the illustration.
6. Look at the illustration and give a complete oral review of what they see.
7. Look at the illustration and write a paragraph (or essay) about it.

You can also use this page as an assessment or testing tool, taking into account individual differences by having students go from simple to quite complicated tasks. The assessment can be either oral or written. You may wish to use the rubrics provided on pages T20–T21 as you give students the following directions:

# ¡Hablo como un pro!

Tell all you can about this illustration.

1. Identify the topic or situation of the illustration.
2. Give the Spanish words for as many items as you can.
3. Think of as many sentences as you can to describe the illustration.
4. Go over your sentences and put them in the best sequencing to give a coherent story based on the illustration.

## Reaching All Students

### For the Heritage Speakers

If there are heritage speakers in the class, ask them to tell which words they use when there are choices in the vocabulary. For example: **¿el descapotable o el convertible? ¿El permiso de conducir o la licencia? ¿La bocina o el claxon? ¿La estación de servicio o la gasolinera?**, etc.

# Vocabulario

### Talking about cars

el descapotable, el convertible
el coche (carro) deportivo
el permiso de conducir, la licencia
el sedán
el cupé
el conductor

### Identifying parts of a car

el cinturón de seguridad
el capó
la puerta
la maletera, el baúl
el parabrisas
las luces
los frenos
las direccionales
la bocina, el claxon
la goma, la llanta, el neumático
la llanta de repuesto (de recambio)

### Talking about services at a gas station

la estación de servicio, la gasolinera
el aceite
la gasolina
 súper
 diesel
 sin plomo
limpiar el parabrisas
llenar el tanque
poner agua en el radiador
revisar el aceite
verificar la presión

### Talking about driving on the highway

la carretera
la autopista, la autovía
el carril
el peaje
la garita de peaje
la entrada
la salida
el rótulo
la velocidad máxima

**How well do you know your vocabulary?**

- Choose words to describe getting around a city by car.
- Write three or four sentences about what a good driver should and should not do.

### Giving directions

seguir derecho
quedarse en el carril
doblar
estar prohibido
adelantar
entrar

### Talking about the city

la cuadra
el cruce, la bocacalle
el semáforo, la luz roja
estacionar el coche, aparcar
el parquímetro
una calle de sentido único

### Other useful expressions

favor de

**VIDEOTUR**

## Episodio 11

In this video episode, you will join Alejandra and Claudia on an evening out. See page 490 for more information.



# Vocabulario

## Vocabulary Review

The words and phrases in the **Vocabulario** have been taught for productive use in this chapter. They are summarized here as a resource for both student and teacher. This list also serves as a convenient resource for the **¡Te toca a ti!** activities on pages 344 and 345. There are approximately nine cognates in this vocabulary list. Have students find them.

**¡OJO!** You will notice that the vocabulary list here is not translated. This has been done intentionally, since we feel that by the time students have finished the material in the chapter they should be familiar with the meanings of all the words. If there are several words they still do not know, we recommend that they refer to the **Palabras 1** and **2** sections in the chapter or go to the dictionaries at the end of this book to find the meanings. However, if you prefer that your students have the English translations, please refer to Vocabulary Transparency 11.1, where you will find all these words with their translations.

**VIDEO VHS/DVD**

The Video Program allows students to see how the chapter vocabulary and structures are used by native speakers within an engaging story line. For maximum reinforcement, show the video episode as a final activity for Chapter 11.

Repaso

# Preview

This section reviews the salient points from Chapters 8–11. In the **Lectura** students will review the present perfect and the present progressive in context. In the **Estructura** section, they will review the present perfect, irregular past participles, object pronouns that are attached to infinitives or participles, and comparisons of equality. They will practice these structures as they talk about the topics that were presented in Chapters 8–11.

## Resource Manager

Workbook, Check-Up, pages 133–138
Tests, pages 179–187
Performance Assessment, Tasks 8–11

## PRESENTATION

**Step 1** Have students open their books to page 350. Ask a student to read aloud using as much expression as possible.

**Step 2** Go over the questions in the **¿Comprendes?** section.

## Learning from Photos

*(page 350 top)* You may wish to ask these questions about the photo.

**¿Qué es la señora?**
**¿Cómo es el uniforme que lleva?**
**¿Quién se ha lesionado?**
**¿En qué le han puesto a ella?**

*(page 350 bottom)* You may wish to ask these questions about the photo.

**¿Es una calle o una carretera?**
**¿Cuántos carriles vemos?**
**¿Qué tipos de vehículos puedes identificar?**

Repaso

## Lectura

### Accidente entre un camión y un coche

Ha habido un accidente entre un camión y un coche privado en el pueblo de Mirasierra en el kilómetro 55 de la carretera nacional 3A. La policía local ha cerrado dos carriles de la carretera en dirección norte. Los socorristas han llegado al escenario y en este momento están administrando los primeros auxilios a los lesionados (heridos). Parece que la conductora del coche ha sufrido heridas más graves. Ha sido transportado en ambulancia al Hospital del Sagrado Corazón en la ciudad de San Cristóbal.

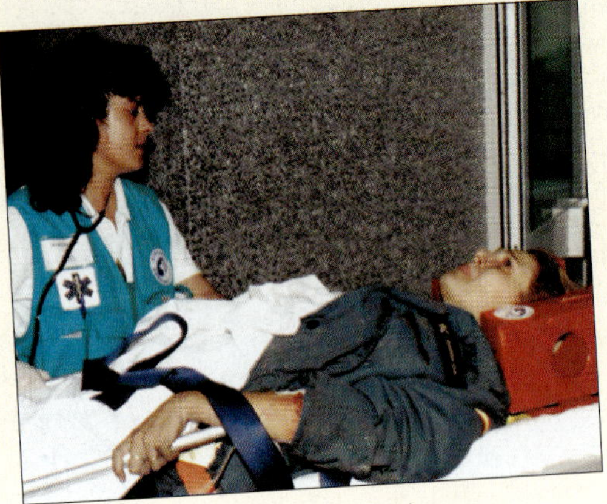

## ¿Comprendes?

**En la carretera** Contesten.

1. ¿Dónde ha habido un accidente?
2. ¿Qué ha cerrado la policía?
3. ¿Quiénes han llegado al escenario?
4. ¿Qué están haciendo los socorristas?
5. ¿Quién ha sufrido lesiones o heridas más graves?
6. ¿Adónde la han transportado?
7. ¿Cómo la han transportado?

Bogotá, Colombia



## Answers to ¿Comprendes?

1. Ha habido un accidente en el pueblo de Mirasierra.
2. La policía ha cerrado dos carriles de la carretera en dirección norte.
3. Los socorristas han llegado al escenario.
4. Los socorristas están administrando los primeros auxilios a los lesionados (heridos).
5. Parece que la conductora del coche ha sufrido heridas más graves.
6. La han transportado al Hospital del Sagrado Corazón.
7. La han transportado en ambulancia.

# Estructura

## El presente perfecto

1. The present perfect is used to express an action completed recently. The present perfect is formed by using the present tense of the verb **haber** and the past participle. Review the forms of regular verbs.

| HABLAR | COMER | VIVIR |
|---|---|---|
| he hablado | he comido | he vivido |
| has hablado | has comido | has vivido |
| ha hablado | ha comido | ha vivido |
| hemos hablado | hemos comido | hemos vivido |
| *habéis hablado* | *habéis comido* | *habéis vivido* |
| han hablado | han comido | han vivido |

2. The following verbs have irregular past participles.

| | | | |
|---|---|---|---|
| DECIR | **dicho** | VOLVER | **vuelto** |
| HACER | **hecho** | MORIR | **muerto** |
| VER | **visto** | CUBRIR | **cubierto** |
| ESCRIBIR | **escrito** | ABRIR | **abierto** |
| PONER | **puesto** | | |

### Historieta Una comida deliciosa

Contesten.

1. ¿Ha preparado una comida buena Lucinda?
2. ¿La has ayudado?
3. ¿Han hecho ustedes una paella?
4. ¿La han cocinado en el horno?
5. ¿Han llegado los invitados?
6. ¿Ya han comido?

Un restaurante, Ronda, España





## PRESENTATION

### El presente perfecto

**Step 1** Lead students through Items 1 and 2 on page 351. Have them repeat the forms after you. Remind students that the initial **h** is silent.

**Step 2** Tell students that most of the irregular past participles in Item 2 are high-frequency verbs.

## PRACTICE

**1** After doing this activity, have students retell the story in their own words.

## Answers to Repaso

1. Sí (No), Lucinda (no) ha preparado una comida buena.
2. Sí, (No, no) la he ayudado.
3. Sí, (No, no) hemos hecho una paella.
4. Sí, (No, no) la hemos cocinado en el horno.
5. Sí, (No, no) han llegado los invitados.
6. Sí, ya (No, todavía no) hemos comido.

Repaso

## PRESENTATION

### Pronombres con el participio y el infinitivo

**Step 1** Lead students through the explanation on page 352. Explain to students why the accent is sometimes added to the participle.

## PRACTICE

**2 and 3** After doing Activities 2 and 3 in class, assign them as homework. Go over the assignment the next day.

### Learning from Photos

*(page 352 top)* The reserved parking in front of the hospital in San Juan is for **impedidos.** In Spain the sign would say: **minusválidos.** Ask students what we call this in English.

### Literary Companion

When you finish this chapter, if you wish, have students read the adaptation of ***El cohítre: Una leyenda puertorriqueña*** by Ester M. Feliciano Mendoza on pages 468–471.

Repaso

## Pronombres con el participio y el infinitivo

When a sentence has an infinitive **(hablar)** or a present participle **(hablando),** the object pronouns can either be added to the infinitive or participle or they can precede the helping verb.

**El médico quiere examinarlo.**
**El médico lo quiere examinar.**

**El técnico está tomándole los rayos equis.**
**Está tomándoselos en el hospital.**
**Él se los está tomando.**

San Juan, Puerto Rico

### 2 En la sala de emergencia

Sigan el modelo.

**¿Quiere el médico examinarle la garganta? →**
**Sí, se la quiere examinar.**
**Sí, quiere examinársela.**

1. ¿Quiere el médico tomarle una radiografía?
2. ¿Está dándole una inyección contra el tétano la enfermera?
3. ¿Están ayudando al paciente los socorristas?
4. ¿Quiere el cirujano reducirle la fractura?
5. ¿Le está poniendo el vendaje el enfermero?
6. ¿Tiene que ponerle puntos el médico?

Plaza de España, Madrid, España

### 3 Historieta Una visita a la ciudad

Sigan el modelo.

**Él quiere ver el plano de la ciudad. →**
**Él lo quiere ver.**
**Él quiere verlo.**

1. Él está mirando el plano de la ciudad.
2. Quiere visitar la ciudad.
3. Tiene que cruzar la calle en el cruce para peatones.
4. Va a tomar el metro.
5. Está esperando el metro en la estación Plaza de España.
6. Muchos pasajeros están bajando la escalera mecánica.



## Answers to Repaso

**2**

1. Sí, se la quiere tomar. Sí, quiere tomársela.
2. Sí, se la está dando. Sí, está dándosela.
3. Sí, lo están ayudando. Sí, están ayudándolo.
4. Sí, se la quiere reducir. Sí, quiere reducírsela.
5. Sí, se lo está poniendo. Sí, está poniéndoselo.
6. Sí, se los tiene que poner. Sí, tiene que ponérselos.

**3**

1. Él lo está mirando. Él está mirándolo.
2. Él la quiere visitar. Él quiere visitarla.
3. Él la tiene que cruzar en el cruce para peatones. Él tiene que cruzarla en el cruce para peatones.
4. Él lo va a tomar. Él va a tomarlo.
5. Él lo está esperando en la estación Plaza de España. Él está esperándolo en la estación Plaza de España.
6. Muchos pasajeros la están bajando. Muchos pasajeros están bajándola.

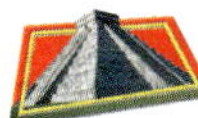

## Comparación de igualdad

The comparative of equality means that two items being compared have equal characteristics. Remember that **tan... como** is used with adjectives and adverbs and **tanto... como** is used with nouns. **Tanto** must agree with the noun it modifies.

**Él es tan rico como su hermano.**
**Él tiene tanto dinero y tanta fortuna como su hermano.**

**4 Comparaciones** Contesten según el modelo.

**¿Hay más tráfico en Lima que en Caracas? ⟶**
**No, hay tanto tráfico en Lima como en Caracas.**

1. ¿Es más alto el edificio Latar que el edificio Lamar?
2. ¿Tiene el edificio Latar más pisos que el edificio Lamar?
3. ¿Es la Plaza Simón Bolívar más bonita que la Plaza San Martín?
4. ¿Tiene la Plaza Simón Bolívar más estatuas que la Plaza San Martín?
5. ¿Es más larga la calle Luna que la calle Londres?
6. ¿Hay más tiendas en la calle Luna que en la calle Londres?
7. ¿Hay más gente en la boca del metro que en la parada del autobús?

Caracas, Venezuela

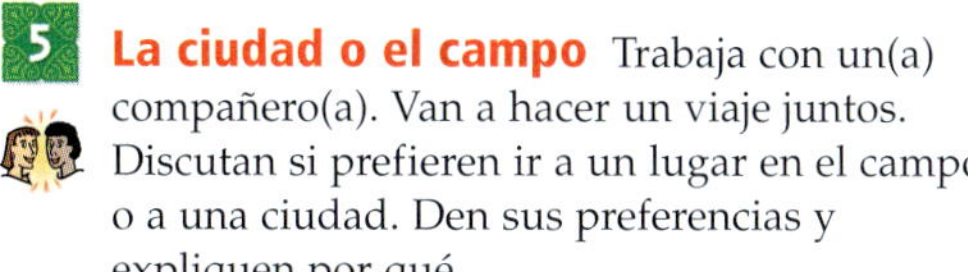

**5 La ciudad o el campo** Trabaja con un(a) compañero(a). Van a hacer un viaje juntos. Discutan si prefieren ir a un lugar en el campo o a una ciudad. Den sus preferencias y expliquen por qué.

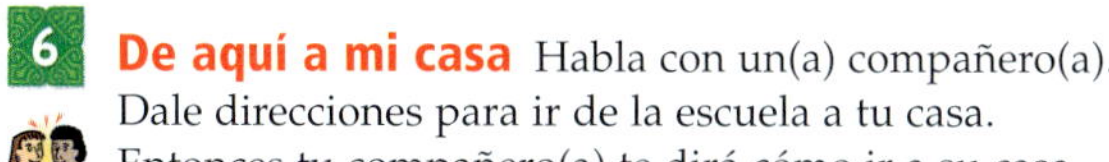

**6 De aquí a mi casa** Habla con un(a) compañero(a). Dale direcciones para ir de la escuela a tu casa. Entonces tu compañero(a) te dirá cómo ir a su casa.

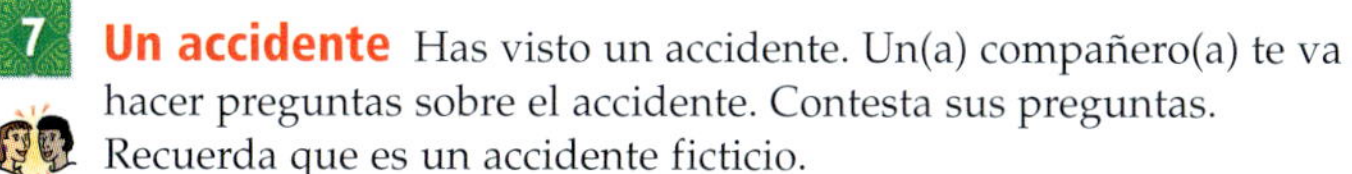

**7 Un accidente** Has visto un accidente. Un(a) compañero(a) te va a hacer preguntas sobre el accidente. Contesta sus preguntas. Recuerda que es un accidente ficticio.

**Literary Companion**

**You may wish to read the adaptation of *El cohítre: Una leyenda puertorriqueña* by Ester M. Feliciano Mendoza. This literary selection is found on pages 468–471.**



## PRESENTATION

### Comparación de igualdad

**Step 1** Have students open their books to page 353. Lead students through the explanation.

**Step 2** Write the two examples on the board. Underline **tan... como** and **tanto... como** in the examples.

## PRACTICE

**4** After doing this activity, ask volunteers to make up questions that compare anything they can think of. Have other students respond.

**5, 6, and 7** Allow students to select the activities that they want to do.

**5** Activity 5 reviews vocabulary presented in Chapter 9.

**6** Activity 6 reviews vocabulary presented in Chapter 11.

**7** Activity 7 reviews vocabulary presented in Chapter 8.

## ANSWERS TO 

**4**

1. No, el edificio Latar es tan alto como el edificio Lamar.
2. No, el edificio Latar tiene tantos pisos como el edificio Lamar.
3. No, la Plaza Simón Bolívar es tan bonita como la Plaza San Martín.
4. No, la Plaza Simón Bolívar tiene tantas estatuas como la Plaza San Martín.
5. No, la calle Luna es tan larga como la calle Londres.
6. No, hay tantas tiendas en la calle Luna como en la calle Londres.
7. No, hay tanta gente en la boca del metro como en la parada del autobús.

**5** *Answers will vary. Students will use vocabulary relating to the city and country to discuss where they would prefer to go.*

**6** *Answers will vary. Students will use the vocabulary and structure learned in Chapter 11 to give directions from the school to their houses.*

**7** *Answers will vary. Students will use vocabulary relating to accidents and hospitals to have a conversation about a fictitious accident.*

People EN ESPAÑOL

## Entérate Centroamérica

This section was prepared by Time Learning Ventures of Time Incorporated. Its purpose is to give students greater insight, through visual images and fun articles, into the culture and people of **Centroamérica.** You may wish to explain to your students that Guatemala, El Salvador, Honduras, Nicaragua, Costa Rica, and Panama are the Spanish-speaking countries included when we talk about this region.

Have students look at the photographs and read the articles. Encourage the students to talk about what they've seen and read. Let them say anything they can, using the vocabulary they have learned to this point.

Though it is a cluster of tightly-compacted, relatively small countries, **Centroamérica** is anything but homogenous. Travel just over the border from Honduras to Guatemala and virtually everything is different; take a day trip from Nicaragua to Costa Rica and you'll swear you've traveled a thousand miles. From ecology to archeaology to unique regional Spanish dialects, the countries of **Centroamérica** are a fascinating introduction to the Spanish-speaking world.

People EN ESPAÑOL

# Entérate Centroamérica

## Piedras que hablan

**Entérate de lo que cuentan dos grandes ciudades: Copán, de Honduras, y Tikal, de Guatemala. Por su "mensaje", son hoy Patrimonio de la Humanidad.**

Estela maya

### Copán

■ Ciudad fundada en el siglo V a.C.
■ Sus ruinas revelan que fue un importante centro cultural y observatorio astronómico. Por ello, se la conoce como "la Atenas[1] del Nuevo Mundo".
■ Aún hoy causan admiración sus plazas y templos: Su acrópolis —sitio alto y fortificado, como en las ciudades griegas—, cuenta con el Templo del Sol y la impresionante Escalera de los jaguares. La Escalera de los jeroglíficos contiene el texto más importante de la civilización maya. La cancha para el juego de pelota era el centro social de la ciudad.
■ Los pobladores de Copán comerciaban con lugares tan distantes como las regiones centrales de lo que hoy es México.
■ Copán fue el centro principal de la cultura maya durante tres siglos y medio.
■ De pronto[2] y en todo el esplendor de su grandeza cultural, artística y científica, sus habitantes se marcharon[3]. Existen varias conjeturas, pero hasta hoy se desconocen las razones por las que Copán fue abandonada. Todo ello forma parte del "misterio maya".

### Tikal

■ Ochenta y seis estelas[4] cuentan la historia de esta urbe[5] del imperio maya. Su mensaje aún no ha sido descifrado, pero es innegable[6] que estas piedras tienen mucho que contar. Calladamente nos hablan de una alta civilización cuyos logros[7] aún nos asombran.
■ Su símbolo es el Templo I, impresionante pirámide de 44 metros de altura. Otro de sus templos mide 70 metros de altura.
■ El Templo del gran jaguar, el Templo de la serpiente de dos cabezas, el Palacio de las siete ventanas y tres canchas de juegos de pelota son muestras del esplendor de Tikal.
■ Consta[8] además de numerosos palacios, residencias, calzadas[9], estelas y tumbas, que se extienden por 16 kilómetros.
■ Se sabe que Tikal fue un gran centro comercial.

Templo I, Tikal

[1] Atenas: *Athens*
[2] de pronto: *suddenly*
[3] se marcharon: *left*
[4] estelas: *stelae*
[5] urbe: *major city*
[6] innegable: *undeniable*
[7] logros: *accomplishments*
[8] consta: *It has*
[9] calzadas: *wide streets*

## Los asombrosos[1] mayas

Escultura, Copán

■ En Occidente[2], el concepto del número cero proviene de[3] la India. Los avances matemáticos de los mayas los llevaron al mismo concepto del cero, independientemente de la India.
■ Inventaron un calendario de 260 días con el que controlaban las tareas agrícolas y la vida diaria. Otro calendario se basaba en la rotación de la Tierra alrededor del Sol. Tenía 365 días y era tan exacto como el nuestro.
■ Los mayas eran excelentes "dentistas". Desarrollaron un empaste[4] muy duradero[5]. Los dentistas actuales[6] se alegrarían mucho al descubrir la composición química de esa mezcla.
■ El *Popol Vuh* es el libro sagrado[7] de los quiché. Estos descendientes de los mayas cuentan sus mitos[8] en ese libro.

[1] asombrosos: *amazing*
[2] Occidente: *Western world*
[3] proviene de: *comes from*
[4] empaste: *amalgam*
[5] duradero: *lasting*
[6] actuales: *present-day*
[7] sagrado: *sacred*
[8] mitos: *myths*

## el mundo salvaje

■ Si te gusta surfear, pensarás que las playas de Costa Rica son el paraíso de los surfeadores, o sea, "¡pura vida!", como dicen los costarricenses. Lugares como Playa Hermosa o Playa Guines tienen olas[1] ideales. Además, la temperatura del agua es tan agradable que no hay necesidad de llevar traje de surfear[2].

Playa de Costa Rica

■ El Cocibolca, también llamado lago de Nicaragua, es el segundo lago más grande de América latina. Tiene olas, una isla con dos volcanes ¡y hasta tiburones[3]! Sí, en este lago se encuentran los únicos tiburones de agua dulce[4] del planeta.

■ Una cadena[5] volcánica recorre la costa oeste de Centroamérica. El volcán Arenal de Costa Rica es uno de los más impresionantes. Noche a noche, es todo un espectáculo cuando la lava incandescente desciende por sus laderas[6]. Incluso, con un poco de suerte, ¡lo oirás rugir[7]!

Volcán Arenal

■ El territorio de Costa Rica mide 51,000 kilómetros cuadrados y el 25% de estos ¡está reservado para parques nacionales y áreas protegidas! El ecoturismo es tradición en este país centroamericano.

■ ¿Te gustaría ver delfines nadar libremente en las aguas transparentes del Caribe? En Roatán, Honduras, un instituto de ciencias marinas ofrece la oportunidad de nadar con estos bellos e inteligentes seres marinos.

[1] olas: *waves*
[2] traje de surfear: *wet suit*
[3] tiburones: *sharks*
[4] agua dulce: *freshwater*
[5] cadena: *chain*
[6] laderas: *slopes*
[7] rugir: *roar*

## SUCESOS

La paz se estudia en una universidad que queda en Costa Rica; se trata de la Universidad de la Paz. Costa Rica es una de las democracias más antiguas de América. ¡Es el único país del mundo que no tiene ejército[1]!

Centroamérica cuenta con dos ganadores del premio Nóbel de la Paz: la guatemalteca **Rigoberta Menchú** y el expresidente de Costa Rica, **Óscar Arias Sánchez.**

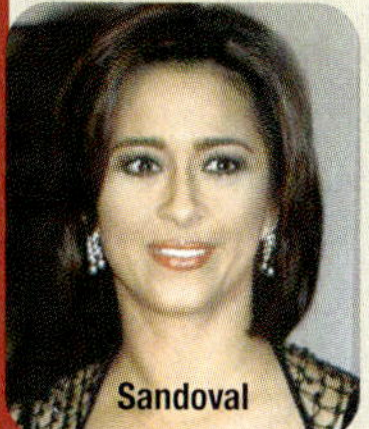
Sandoval

**Neida Sandoval** es presentadora de "Despierta América" (Univisión). Con la sonrisa y el profesionalismo de esta hondureña, los latinos de Estados Unidos reciben las noticias todas las mañanas. Neida obtuvo dos premios Emmy por su participación en este programa, el matutino[2] número uno de la televisión en español.

[1] ejército: *army*
[2] matutino: *morning [news]*

Atolillo de mamá Elsa

## micocina

Luis Enrique

**La dulzura de Luis Enrique**

El cantante nicaragüense **Luis Enrique** admite no ser buen cocinero. Sin embargo, es conocedor de la cocina de su país y no pierde ocasión de compartir recetas de su abuela, quien prepara — según él — el mejor atolillo. Hay muchas versiones de este reconfortante postre[1] en toda Latinoamérica. Anímate a preparar el atolillo de mamá Elsa y, ¡a ver qué opinas tú!

**Ingredientes**
- 1 litro de leche
- 2 yemas de huevo
- 1 taza de azúcar blanco
- 2 onzas de maizena (fécula de maíz)
- 1/8 cucharadita de sal
- 1/2 taza de pasas
- astillas de canela[2] al gusto

**Preparación**

En una taza y media de leche, mezclar bien la maizena y las yemas de huevo. Aparte, combinar el azúcar, la canela, las pasas y la sal con el resto de la leche. La segunda mezcla se pone a fuego lento, removiéndola[3] constantemente para evitar grumos. Cuando está hirviendo, incorporar la primera mezcla, pasándola por un colador[4], sin dejar de remover. Continuar la cocción[5] hasta lograr una consistencia espesa[6]. Servir caliente y, ¡buen provecho!

[1] postre: *dessert*
[2] astillas de canela: *cinnamon sticks*
[3] removiéndola: *stirring it*
[4] colador: *strainer*
[5] cocción: *cooking*
[6] espesa: *thick*

355

**People EN ESPAÑOL**

**A Piedras que hablan**
¿Verdadero o falso?
1. Copán está en Guatemala.
2. Tikal fue un gran centro comercial.
3. Los pobladores de Copán no comerciaban con lugares distantes.

**B Los asombrosos mayas**
Completen.
1. Los matemáticos mayas llegaron al concepto del número ___.
2. Los mayas tenían ___ calendarios.
3. Los mayas comprendían la ___ de la Tierra alrededor del Sol.

**C El mundo salvaje**
Escojan.
1. Las playas de Costa Rica son buenas para ___.
   a. nadar
   b. comer
   c. surfear
2. ___ es el segundo lago más grande de América latina.
   a. Roatán
   b. Cocibolca
   c. Playa Hermosa
3. En Costa Rica, ___ del territorio está reservado para parques nacionales y áreas protegidas.
   a. 25%
   b. 45%
   c. 10%

**D Sucesos**
Contesten.
1. ¿Cuál es el único país del mundo que no tiene ejército?
2. ¿Quiénes son dos centroamericanos ganadores del Premio Nóbel de la Paz?
3. ¿Quién recibió un par de Emmys por su trabajo en la televisión?
4. ¿Cuándo se presenta el programa "Despierta América"?

### ANSWERS

**A**
1. falso
2. verdadero
3. falso

**B**
1. cero
2. dos
3. rotación

**C**
1. c
2. b
3. a

**D**
1. Costa Rica
2. Rigoberta Menchú y Óscar Arias Sánchez
3. Neida Sandoval
4. todas las mañanas

### LEVELING

**E:** Activity A
**A:** Activities B, C
**C:** Activity D

What does it mean to **vosearse**? What's a **tico** and who are some famous Central Americans? The language and artistic expression of Guatemala, El Salvador, Honduras, Nicaragua, Costa Rica, and Panama are as diverse as the topography unique to each country. The complexity of their cultural identity makes these countries an important source of study for students and travelers alike.

**A El español antes y después**
Corrijan.
1. Rubén Darío es hondureño.
2. Los idiomas nacen solamente.
3. Rubén Darío es actor.
4. A finales del siglo XIX, el español era un idioma vigoroso y muy expresivo.
5. Rubén Darío es la gran figura literaria de Guatemala.

**B Centroamérica y su literatura**
¿Quién es?
1. Nació en Honduras pero es guatemalteco.
2. Es escritora y poeta nicaragüense.
3. Tradujo al lenguaje moderno todo el pasado cultural de su país.
4. Tenía pocos años cuando le enseñó sus escritos a don Juan Ramón Jiménez.
5. En 2001 este escritor guatemalteco recibió el Premio Príncipe de Asturias.

**C ¿Tú o vos?**
¿Se vosean aquí, o no?
1. Uruguay
2. Panamá
3. Costa Rica
4. España

Rubén Darío

## El español antes y después...

Ya conoces a Cervantes, el creador de *El Quijote.* Ahora tienes que conocer a **Rubén Darío.** Como todas las cosas vivas, los idiomas nacen, envejecen[1] y mueren. A finales del siglo XIX, el español era un idioma gastado[2], poco expresivo, débil[3]. Era necesario darle nueva vida.

Quien hace esa revolución y convierte al español en una lengua apta para expresar las cosas del siglo XX es Rubén Darío. El escritor nicaragüense logró que el español sonara como una orquesta capaz[4] de interpretar todos los tonos y melodías. Para ello empleó la mayor variedad de metros[5] que hasta ahora ha utilizado un solo poeta. ¡Sus estudiosos[6] han contado nada menos que 134 tipos distintos de versos!

[1] envejecen: *grow old*
[2] gastado: *worn-out*
[3] débil: *weak*
[4] capaz: *able*
[5] metros: *meters*
[6] estudiosos: *scholars*

## ¿Tú o vos?

¿Querés que te cuente algo? ¿Sabías vos que en todos los países centroamericanos, excepto Panamá, se dice casi siempre *vos* en vez de *tú?* Lo mismo ocurre en Argentina, Uruguay y en partes de Venezuela y Colombia. Los centroamericanos creen que es más "sabroso"[1] hablar de *vos,* o vosearse. ¿Qué creés vos?

## Gentilicios[2] chistosísimos[3]

Si conoces a alguien de Nicaragua, no lo llames nicaragüense, llámalo *nica.* Alguien de Costa Rica no es costarricense; mejor dile *tico.* A un hondureño, lo llamarás *catracho.* Si es de El Salvador, dile *guanaco.* Y nada de decir guatemalteco, se dice *chapín.* Sorprendentemente, los panameños se quedaron sin gentilicio chistoso. ¿Cómo los llamarías tú?

[1] sabroso: *fun*
[2] gentilicios: *name given to the people from a particular region or country*
[3] chistosísimos: *very funny*

356

## Centroamérica y su literatura

Belli

**Gioconda Belli** es escritora y poeta nicaragüense. Ha ganado varios premios internacionales. Sus obras se han traducido a varios idiomas.

Monterroso

**Augusto Monterroso,** escritor guatemalteco nacido en Honduras, ganó el Premio Príncipe de Asturias en 2001. Suyo es el cuento más corto que se conoce. ¿Quieres que te lo cuente?: "Cuando se despertó, el dinosaurio todavía estaba ahí".

Alegría

Cuando era jovencita, **Claribel Alegría** mostró sus escritos[1] al famoso escritor español Juan Ramón Jiménez. Actualmente, la obra de esta salvadoreña es conocida en todo el mundo.

**Miguel Ángel Asturias** tradujo al lenguaje moderno todo el rico pasado cultural de su país, Guatemala. Esta hazaña[2] lo llevó a ganar el Premio Nóbel de Literatura.

[1] escritos: *writings*
[2] hazaña: *achievement*

### Answers

**A**
1. Rubén Darío es nicaragüense.
2. Los idiomas nacen, envejecen y mueren.
3. Rubén Darío es escritor.
4. A finales del siglo XIX, el español era un idioma gastado y poco expresivo.
5. Rubén Darío es la gran figura literaria de Nicaragua.

**B**
1. Augusto Monterroso
2. Gioconda Belli
3. Miguel Ángel Asturias
4. Claribel Alegría
5. Augusto Monterroso

**C**
1. Sí
2. No
3. Sí
4. No

Cardenal

**Katia Cardenal** nació en Nicaragua, pero ahora vive muy lejos de allí. Ha llevado la dulzura de su canto a Noruega[1], donde la adoran.

**Ricardo Arjona,** de Guatemala, escribe poesía y la canta con toda el alma.

Al cantante, músico y compositor **Luis Enrique,** de Nicaragua, se lo conoce como el príncipe de la salsa. También ha sido percusionista de Ricky Martin y Gloria Estefan.

**Rubén Blades** es el salsero consentido[2]. Este cantante, actor de cine y compositor panameño es embajador de la salsa en todo el mundo.

**Álvaro Torres** es compositor y cantante salvadoreño. Cantó su canción "Buenos amigos" a dúo con Selena, hecho que lanzó a la fama a la cantante tejana.

Los roqueros[3] no podían faltar[4] en Centroamérica. La prueba[5] es **¡Rabanes!,** el grupo de rock panameño.

[1] Noruega: *Norway*
[2] consentido: *that makes sense*
[3] roqueros: *rock musicians*
[4] faltar: *be absent*
[5] prueba: *proof*

Álvaro Torres

Mujer kuna

## Escuela primitivista de Solentiname

Numerosos pintores nicaragüenses pintan en el estilo[1] primitivista. El pintor primitivista a veces carece de[2] conocimiento técnico, pero representa libremente el paisaje y la vida diaria de su país.

## El pueblo kuna

Los indios kunas viven en el archipiélago de San Blas, en Panamá. Han logrado mantener su identidad cultural desde tiempos ancestrales. Su manera de vestirse y adornar el cuerpo es toda una obra de arte. Las molas, vistosas blusas que llevan las mujeres, son artesanías[3] que cuentan tradiciones de la cultura kuna.

## Arte moderno

El arte moderno latinoamericano tiene un importante representante en la obra internacionalmente reconocida del pintor nicaragüense **Armando Morales.**

[1] estilo: *style*
[2] carece de: *lacks*
[3] artesanías: *crafts*

Chang Díaz

## Fanático de alto vuelo

El costarricense Franklin R. Chang Díaz es físico[1] y astronauta de la NASA. Uno de sus viajes a bordo del transbordador espacial[2], para la misión *Endeavour,* ocurrió durante el Campeonato Mundial de Fútbol que se llevó a cabo en Japón y Corea. Desde el espacio, el astronauta siguió atentamente los juegos donde participó el equipo de su país. ¡Hasta llevó una camiseta[3] del conjunto costarricense para honrarlo[4] desde las alturas!

[1] físico: *physicist*
[2] transbordador espacial: *space shuttle*
[3] camiseta: *t-shirt*
[4] honrarlo: *honor it*

357

People en Español

**D Gentilicios chistosísimos**
Y, ¿de dónde son estos?
1. los ticos
2. los guanacos
3. los nicas
4. los catrachos

**E Arte y cultura en Centroamérica** Contesten.
1. ¿Qué cuentan las molas?
2. ¿Qué tipo de arte pinta Armando Morales?
3. ¿Cómo es el arte de un pintor primitivista?
4. ¿Quiénes llevan la mola?

**F Fanático de alto vuelo**
¿Verdadero o falso?
1. Franklin R. Chang es astronauta y físico.
2. Uno de sus viajes abordo el Endeavor ocurrió durante las Olimpiadas.
3. El Campeonato Mundial de Fútbol se llevó a cabo en Costa Rica y Nicaragua.
4. Aunque estaba en el espacio, Chang siguió los juegos.
5. Él llevaba una camiseta del equipo costarricense.

**G Música**
Escojan.
1. En Noruega la gente adora a ___.
   a. Álvaro Torres
   b. Rabanes
   c. Katia Cardenal
2. Álvaro Torres cantó un dúo con ___ que le hizo a ella famosa.
   a. Katia Cardenal
   b. Selena
   c. Gloria Estefan
3. Cantante, actor y compositor es este gran hijo de Panamá, ___.
   a. Luis Enrique
   b. Ricardo Arjona
   c. Rubén Blades

## Answers

1. Costa Rica
2. El Salvador
3. Nicaragua
4. Honduras

**E**

1. La molas cuentan tradiciones de la cultura kuna.
2. Armando Morales pinta arte moderno.
3. Un pintor primitivista a veces carece de conocimiento técnico.
4. Las mujeres kunas llevan molas.

**F**

1. verdadero
2. falso
3. falso
4. verdadero
5. verdadero

1. c
2. b
3. c

**LEVELING**

**E:** Activities A, C, F
**A:** Activities B, D, G
**C:** Activity E

# Planning for Chapter 12

## SCOPE AND SEQUENCE, PAGES 358–389

### Topics

- ❖ Beauty salons and barber shops
- ❖ The dry cleaner
- ❖ The post office
- ❖ The bank

### Culture

- ❖ José Luis and his friends prepare for a trip to southern Spain
- ❖ La Alhambra, Granada
- ❖ La Mezquita, Córdoba
- ❖ El Alcázar, Sevilla
- ❖ La Moneda, Santiago, Chile
- ❖ Finances and Banking

### Functions

- ❖ How to talk about hairstyles and hair care
- ❖ How to have clothing dry-cleaned
- ❖ How to talk about common postal services
- ❖ How to conduct banking transactions
- ❖ How to tell what may or may not happen
- ❖ How to express wishes and orders
- ❖ How to express opinions

### Structure

- ❖ The subjunctive
- ❖ The subjunctive in nominal clauses
- ❖ The subjunctive with impersonal expressions

### National Standards

- ❖ Communication Standard 1.1 pages 362, 363, 366, 367, 370, 371, 372, 374, 377, 384
- ❖ Communication Standard 1.2 pages 363, 367, 373, 375, 376, 377, 378–379, 380, 381, 382–383, 384, 385
- ❖ Communication Standard 1.3 page 385
- ❖ Cultures Standard 2.1 pages 380, 381
- ❖ Cultures Standard 2.2 pages 376, 378–379, 380
- ❖ Connections Standard 3.1 pages 382–383
- ❖ Connections Standard 3.2 pages 378–379
- ❖ Comparisons Standard 4.1 page 381
- ❖ Communities Standard 5.1 page 389
- ❖ Communities Standard 5.2 page 368

## PACING AND PRIORITIES

**The chapter content is color coded below to assist you in planning.**

**■ required ■ recommended ■ optional**

**Vocabulario** *(required)* *Days 1–4*

- ■ Palabras 1
  - En la peluquería
  - En la tintorería
- ■ Palabras 2
  - El correo
  - El banco
  - La casa de cambio

**Estructura** *(required)* *Days 5–7*

- ■ El subjuntivo
- ■ El subjuntivo en cláusulas nominales
- ■ El subjuntivo con expresiones impersonales

**Conversación** *(required)*

- ■ En la casa de cambio

**Lecturas culturales**

- ■ Muchos quehaceres *(recommended)*
- ■ La Moneda: Un edificio con mucha historia *(optional)*
- ■ El pelo y el peinado *(optional)*

**Conexiones**

- ■ La banca *(optional)*

■ **¡Te toca a ti!** *(recommended)*

■ **Assessment** *(recommended)*

■ **¡Hablo como un pro!** *(optional)*

## RESOURCE GUIDE

| SECTION | PAGES | SECTION RESOURCES |
|---|---|---|
| **Vocabulario PALABRAS 1** | | |
| En la peluquería<br>En la tintorería | 360, 362–363<br>361, 362-363 | Vocabulary Transparencies 12.2–12.3<br>Audio CD 7<br>Audio Activities TE, pages 144–146<br>Workbook, pages 139–141<br>Quiz 1, page 57<br>ExamView® Pro |
| **Vocabulario PALABRAS 2** | | |
| El correo<br>El banco<br>La casa de cambio | 364, 366–367<br>365, 366–367<br>365, 366–367 | Vocabulary Transparencies 12.4–12.5<br>Audio CD 7<br>Audio Activities TE, pages 146–148<br>Workbook, pages 142–143<br>Quiz 2, page 58<br>ExamView® Pro |
| **Estructura** | | |
| El subjuntivo<br>El subjuntivo en cláusulas nominales<br>El subjuntivo con expresiones impersonales | 368–370<br>371–373<br>373–375 | Audio CD 7<br>Audio Activities TE, pages 148–150<br>Workbook, pages 144–148<br>Quizzes 3–5, pages 59–61<br>ExamView® Pro |
| **Conversación** | | |
| En la casa de cambio | 376–377 | Audio CD 7<br>Audio Activities TE, page 151<br>Interactive CD-ROM |
| **Lecturas culturales** | | |
| Muchos quehaceres<br>La Moneda: un edificio con mucha historia<br>El pelo y el peinado | 378–379<br>380<br>381 | Audio CD 7<br>Audio Activities TE, page 152<br>Tests, pages 192, 195 |
| **Conexiones** | | |
| La banca | 382–383 | Tests, page 196 |
| **¡Te toca a ti!** | | |
| | 384–385 | **¡Viva el mundo hispano!** Video, Episode 12<br>Video Activities, pages 109–112<br>Spanish Online Activities spanish.glencoe.com |
| **Assessment** | | |
| | 386–387 | Communication Transparency C 12<br>Quizzes 1–5, pages 57–61<br>Performance Assessment, Task 12<br>Tests, pages 189–202<br>Situation Cards, Chapter 12<br>ExamView® Pro<br>**Maratón mental** Videoquiz |

# Using Your Resources for Chapter 12

## Transparencies

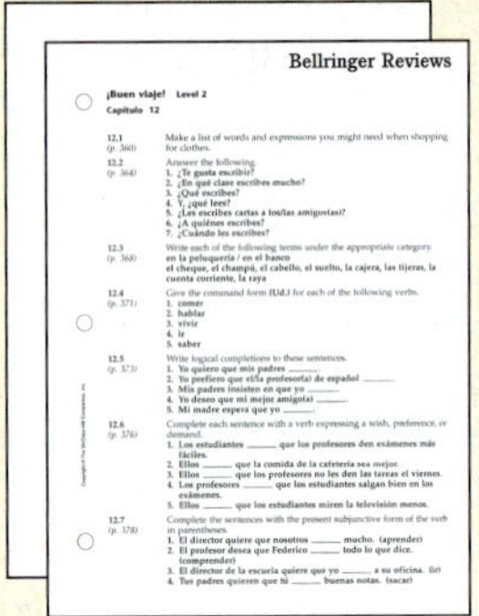
Bellringer 12.1–12.7

Vocabulary 12.1–12.5

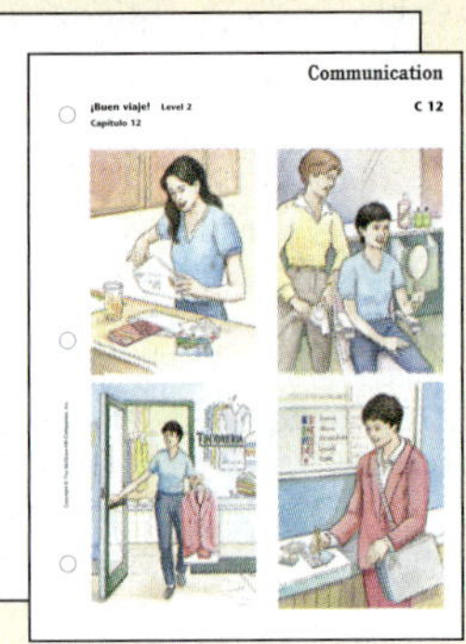
Communication C 12

## Workbook

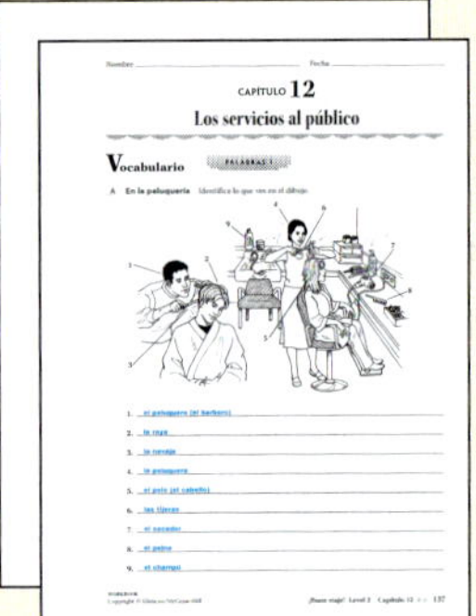
Vocabulary, pages 139–143

Structure, pages 144–148

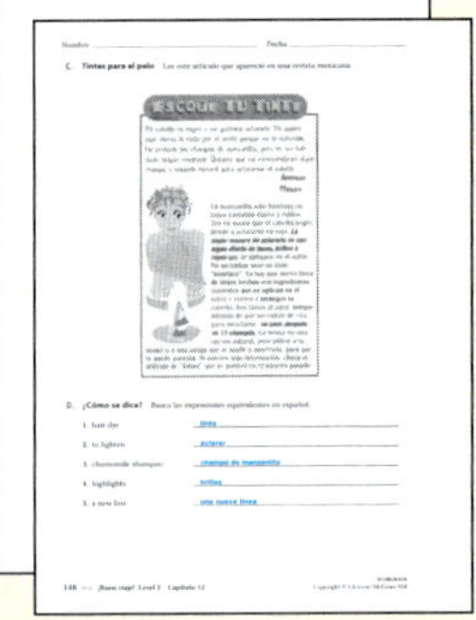
Enrichment, pages 149–152

## Audio Activities

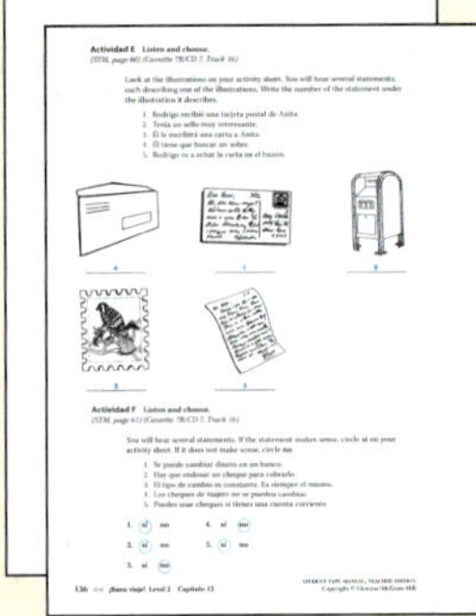
Vocabulary, pages 144–148

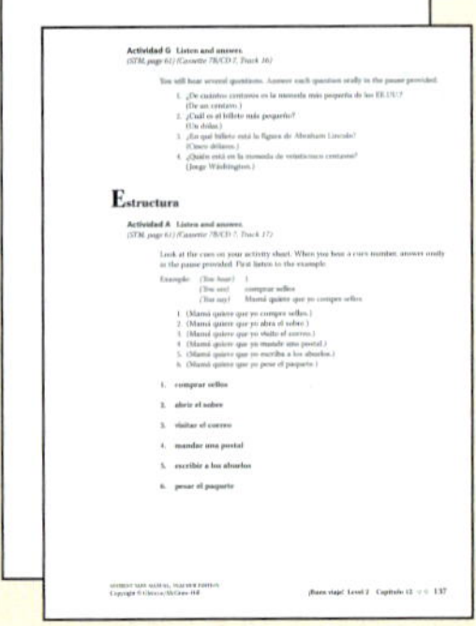
Structure, pages 148–150

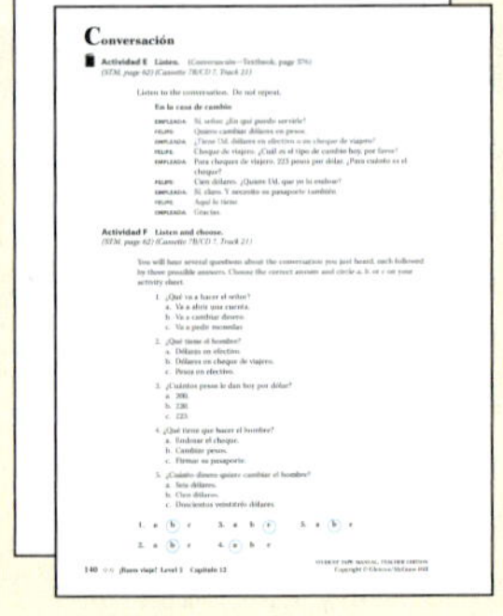
Conversation, page 151

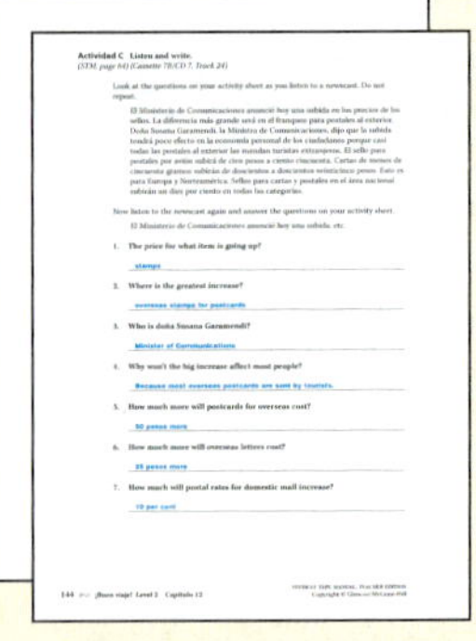
Additional Practice, pages 153–156

# Assessment

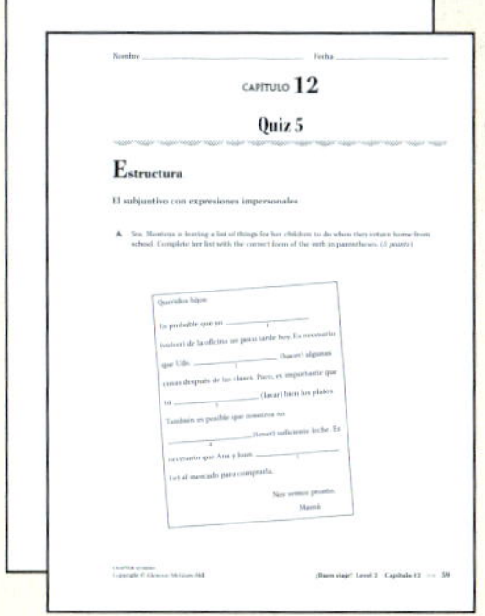

Vocabulary and Structure Quizzes, pages 57–61

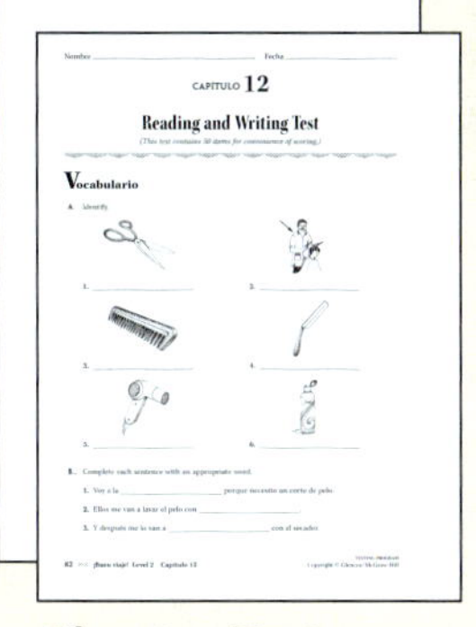

Chapter Tests, pages 189–202

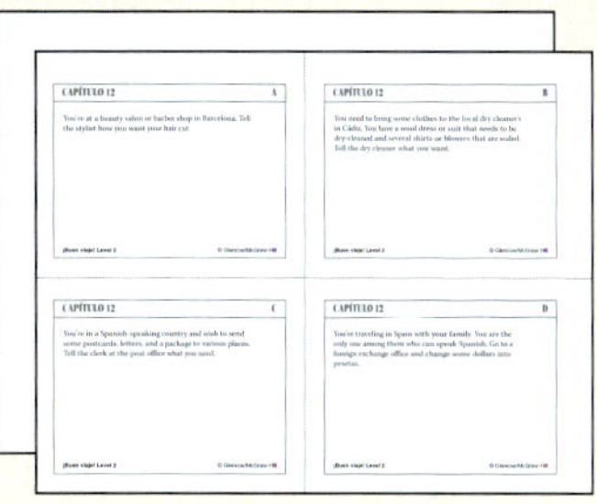

Situation Cards, Chapter 12

MindJogger Videoquiz, ExamView® Pro, Chapter 12

## Timesaving Teacher Tools

### TeacherWorks™

TeacherWorks™ is your all-in-one teacher resource center. Personalize lesson plans, access resources from the Teacher Wraparound Edition, connect to the Internet, or make a to-do list. These are only a few of the many features that can assist you in the planning and organizing of your lessons.

Includes:

- A calendar feature
- Access to all program blackline masters
- Standards correlations and more

### ExamView® Pro

Test Bank software for Macintosh and Windows makes creating, editing, customizing, and printing tests quick and easy.

## Technology Resources

In the Chapter 12 Internet Activity, you will have a chance to learn more about the Spanish-speaking world. Visit spanish.glencoe.com

On the interactive CD–ROM, students can listen to and take part in a recorded version of the conversation in Chapter 12.

**¡Viva el mundo hispano!** Video and Video Activities, Chapter 12. Available on VHS and DVD.

Help your students prepare for the chapter test by playing the **Maratón mental** Videoquiz game show. Teams will compete against each other to review chapter vocabulary and structure and sharpen listening comprehension skills. Available on VHS and DVD.

**¡Buen viaje!** is also available on CD or Online.

## Preview

In this chapter, students will learn how to talk about going to the hairstylist, the post office, the bank, and the dry cleaner's. They will learn to use the subjunctive mood to express actions that may or may not happen, wishes and orders, and opinions introduced by impersonal expressions. The cultural focus of the chapter is on personal services in the Spanish-speaking world.

### National Standards

**Communication**

In Chapter 12 students will learn to communicate in spoken and written Spanish on the following topics:

- hairstyling
- laundry and dry cleaning
- using the postal service
- personal banking

Students will obtain and provide information about these topics and engage in conversations that would typically take place in business establishments as they fulfill the chapter objectives listed on this page.

Capítulo 12

# Los servicios al público

**In this chapter you will learn to:**

- talk about going to the hairdresser/barbershop
- talk about having your clothes cleaned
- talk about using the services of the post office and bank
- talk about things that may or may not happen
- express what you would like, wish, or hope others would do

Hernán Miranda *Metro*

BANCO RIO

## Spotlight on Culture

**Fotografía** The photo is of the **Plaza de Mayo** in Buenos Aires. It is a beautiful open space with the monument to the 25th of May, 1810, the day on which armed citizens of the **cabildo,** or *town council,* demanded the resignation of the Spanish viceroy **(virrey)** and established a provisional representative government. This action marked the beginning of the Latin American revolt against Spanish rule. **El 25 de mayo** is a national holiday.

## LEVELING

The activities, conversations, and readings within each chapter are marked according to level of difficulty. **E** indicates easy. **A** indicates average. **C** indicates challenging. Some activities cover a range of difficulty. In some activities, for example, advanced students will be able to produce more extensive responses while students who learn at a different rate may give less detailed responses. The leveling indicators will help you individualize instruction to best meet your students' needs.

# Vocabulario
PALABRAS 1

## 1 PREPARATION

### Resource Manager

Vocabulary Transparencies 12.2–12.3
Audio Activities TE, pages 144–146
Audio CD 7
Workbook, pages 139–141
Quizzes, page 57
ExamView® Pro

### Bellringer Review

*Use BRR Transparency 12.1 or write the following on the board.*
Make a list of words and expressions you might need when shopping for clothes.

## 2 PRESENTATION

¡OJO! Note that many of the sentences introduce students to the use of the subjunctive. The subjunctive will be taught in this chapter. The subjunctive forms in the **Vocabulario** section are in the third person only.

**Step 1** Present the vocabulary by projecting Vocabulary Transparencies 12.2–12.3.

**Step 2** Have students repeat the new words and phrases two or three times after you or Audio CD 7.

**Step 3** Ask the following questions:

**¿Quiere Paco que el barbero le corte el pelo?**
**¿Quiere Teresa que la peluquera le lave el pelo?**
**¿Quiere Paco que el barbero le corte el pelo con navaja?**
**¿Y quiere Teresa que la peluquera le corte el pelo con tijeras?**



# Vocabulario
PALABRAS 1

## En la peluquería

Paco quiere un corte de pelo.

Quiere que el barbero le corte el pelo con navaja.

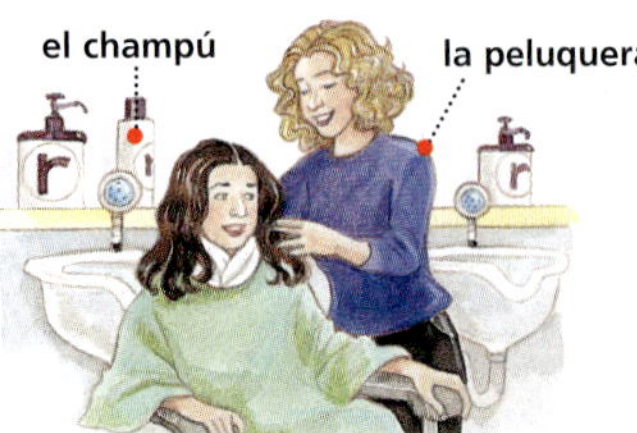


Teresa quiere que la peluquera le lave el pelo.
Quiere un champú.

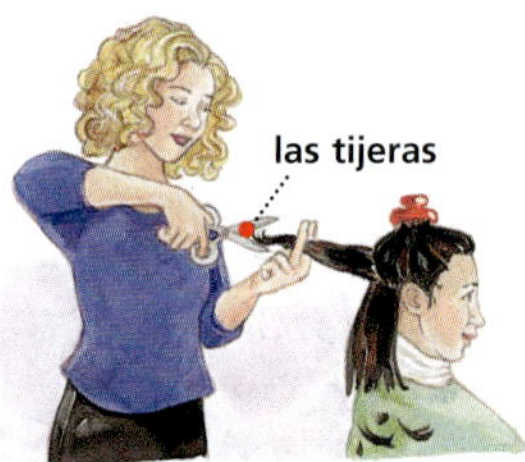


Quiere que le corte el pelo con tijeras.

Quiere que le seque el pelo con el secador.



## Reaching All Students

### Total Physical Response

*(Student 1)*, ven acá, por favor.
Eres peluquero(a).
Lávale el pelo a tu cliente.
Córtale el pelo con tijeras.
Ahora córtale los lados con tijeras.
El / La cliente lo quiere más corto por los lados.
Córtale más los lados con tijeras.
Toma el peine y ponle la raya a la derecha.
Sécale el pelo con el secador.
Gracias, *(Student 1)*. Regresa a tu asiento.

## En la tintorería

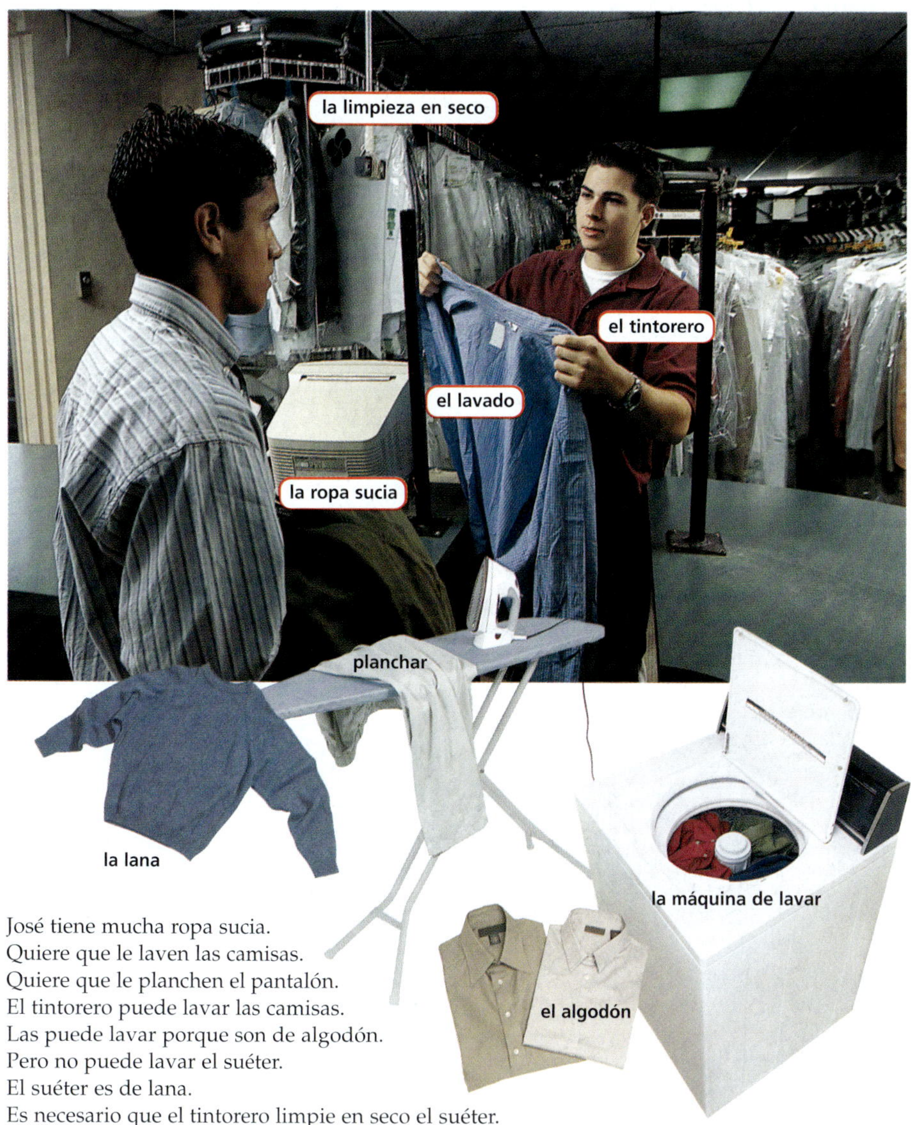


José tiene mucha ropa sucia.
Quiere que le laven las camisas.
Quiere que le planchen el pantalón.
El tintorero puede lavar las camisas.
Las puede lavar porque son de algodón.
Pero no puede lavar el suéter.
El suéter es de lana.
Es necesario que el tintorero limpie en seco el suéter.



# Vocabulario

**Step 4** After presenting the vocabulary orally, have students open their books and read the words, expressions, and sentences for additional reinforcement.

**Step 5** Call a student to the front of the room. Show the Vocabulary Transparencies again. Have the student play teacher and ask questions about what he or she sees in the illustrations and photos.

### Teaching Tip

Students may have trouble getting the meaning of **algodón.** Tell them: **La camisa no es de nilón. No es de poliéster. La camisa es de algodón. El algodón es una tela natural. ¿Qué es el algodón?** You can also point to some cotton shirts or blouses in the classroom.

### Fun Facts

- The **peluquería** was originally the place where you got your **peluca,** *wig,* cleaned and repaired. The **tintorería** was the dyer's shop, and the **tintorero** only dyed clothes.
- Una **navaja** can be either a *straight razor* or a *safety razor.* In many countries a *safety razor* is called **una gilette.** You may wish to ask students why this is so.

### Chapter Projects

**Presupuesto** Have students keep a diary of their expenditures as you do this chapter. At the chapter's end, have them tell or write what they learned about themselves by doing this.

**Note:** You may also have them check the Internet for the exchange rates for the euro or the Mexican peso and ask them to convert their expenses into one of these currencies.

### LEVELING

**A:** Vocabulary

### Vocabulary Expansion

A few more hairdressing terms are:

| | |
|---|---|
| **el espejo** | *mirror* |
| **el salón de belleza** | *beauty salon* |
| **la barbería** | *barbershop* |
| **el cepillo para el cabello** | *hairbrush* |
| **la maquinilla** | *hair clippers* |
| **la peluca** | *wig* |

Vocabulario

## 3 PRACTICE

## ¿Qué palabra necesito?

¡OJO! When students are doing the **¿Qué palabra necesito?** activities, accept any answer that makes sense. The purpose of these activities is to have students use the new vocabulary. They are not factual recall activities. Thus, it is not necessary for students to remember specific factual information from the vocabulary presentation when answering. If you wish, have students use the photos on this page as a stimulus, when possible.

1 Have students refer to the photos as they do this activity.

2 This activity can be gone over orally with books closed.

### Writing Development

After going over Activity 2, have students write their answers in a unified paragraph.

Vocabulario

# ¿Qué palabra necesito?

**1 ¿Qué prefieren los clientes?** Pareen.

a. 

b. 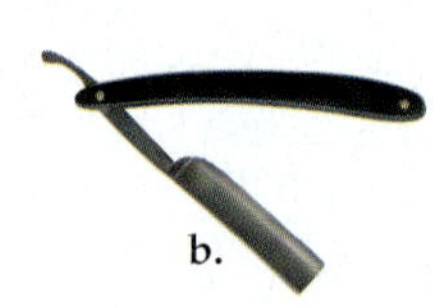

c. 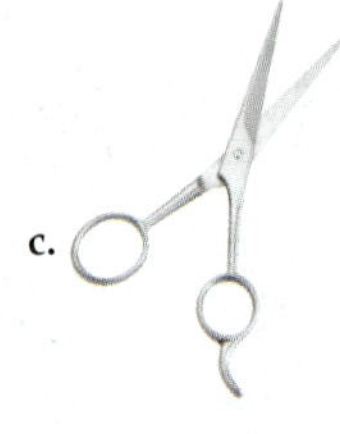

d. 

1. La señora quiere que le corten el pelo con tijeras.
2. Ella quiere que le laven el pelo.
3. Y después quiere que lo sequen.
4. El señor quiere que el barbero use la navaja.

**2 Historieta A la peluquería**

Contesten personalmente.

1. ¿Prefieres llevar el pelo largo o corto?
2. ¿A qué peluquería vas?
3. ¿Con qué frecuencia te cortas el pelo?
4. ¿Prefieres lavarte el pelo o que te lo laven en la peluquería?
5. ¿Prefieres que te corten el pelo con tijeras o con navaja?
6. Cuando te lavas el pelo, ¿prefieres secarlo con una toalla o con un secador?
7. ¿Cuántas veces al día te peinas?

San Miguel de Allende, México

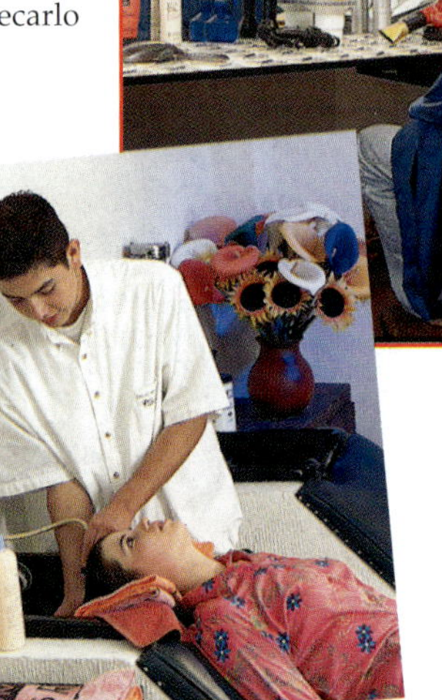

Ciudad de México



## ANSWERS TO ¿Qué palabra necesito?

**1**

1. c
2. a
3. d
4. b

**2**

1. Prefiero llevar el pelo largo (corto).
2. Voy a ___.
3. Me corto el pelo cada ___.
4. Prefiero lavarme el pelo (que me lo laven en la peluquería).
5. Prefiero que me corten el pelo con tijeras (con navaja).
6. Cuando me lavo el pelo, prefiero secarlo con una toalla (con un secador).
7. Me peino ___ veces al día.

## 3 Historieta En la tintorería Contesten.

1. ¿Tiene el joven mucha ropa sucia?
2. ¿La lleva a la tintorería?
3. ¿Quiere que la tintorera le lave las camisas?
4. ¿De qué material son las camisas?
5. ¿Puede lavarlas la tintorera?
6. ¿De qué material es el saco?
7. ¿Puede lavar el saco la tintorera?
8. ¿Es necesario que lo limpie en seco?
9. ¿Quiere el joven que la tintorera le planche el pantalón?
10. ¿Quiere que le planche las camisas también?

Lima, Perú

## 4 Preguntas personales Contesten.

1. ¿Qué ropa llevas a la tintorería?
2. ¿Qué ropa lavas en casa?
3. ¿Prefieres que te planchen o que no te planchen las camisas?
4. ¿Planchas los blue jeans o no?
5. ¿Tienes mucho lavado cada semana?

## 5 La peluquería

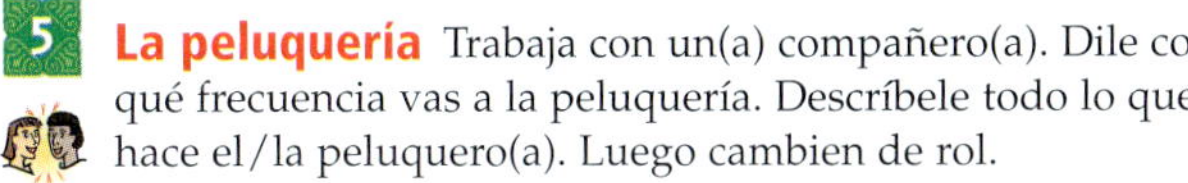

Trabaja con un(a) compañero(a). Dile con qué frecuencia vas a la peluquería. Descríbele todo lo que hace el/la peluquero(a). Luego cambien de rol.

## 6 En la tintorería

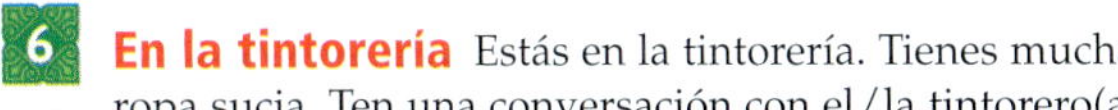

Estás en la tintorería. Tienes mucha ropa sucia. Ten una conversación con el/la tintorero(a) (tu compañero[a]). Dile todo lo que necesitas. Luego cambien de rol.

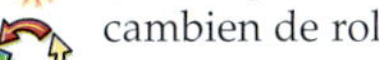

## 7 En una lavandería

Estás trabajando a tiempo parcial *(part time)* en una lavandería *(laundromat)* en tu comunidad donde hay muchos clientes hispanohablantes. Explícale a un(a) cliente (tu compañero[a]) cómo usar la máquina de lavar. Puedes usar las siguientes expresiones.

Lima, Perú

## Vocabulario

**3 and 4** You may wish to go over these activities orally in class with books closed before assigning them as written homework. Go over them once again the following day for additional reinforcement.

### Paired Activity

You can do Activity 4 as a paired activity. One student asks the questions and the other answers.

### Learning from Photos

*(page 362 middle)* You may ask students:
**¿Dónde están ellos?**
**¿Qué es la señorita en la foto?**
**¿Qué le da ella a su cliente?**
*(page 362 bottom)* You may ask the following questions about the photo:
**¿Qué hace el peluquero con su cliente?**
**¿Qué hay en las botellas de plástico?**
*(page 363 top)* You may wish to ask students the following questions about the photo:
**¿Dónde están los dos?**
**¿Qué trae el joven?**

## Answers to ¿Qué palabra necesito?

**3**

1. Sí, el joven tiene mucha ropa sucia.
2. Sí, la lleva a la tintorería.
3. Sí, quiere que la tintorera le lave las camisas.
4. Las camisas son de algodón.
5. Sí, la tintorera puede lavarlas.
6. El saco es de lana (algodón).
7. No, la tintorera no puede lavar el saco.
8. Sí, es necesario que lo limpie en seco.
9. Sí, el joven quiere que la tintorera le planche el pantalón.
10. Sí, quiere que le planche las camisas también.

**4** *Answers will vary but may include:*

1. Llevo ___ a la tintorería.
2. Lavo en casa mis ___.
3. Prefiero que (no) me planchen las camisas.
4. Sí, (No, no) plancho los blue jeans.
5. Sí, (No, no) tengo mucho lavado cada semana.

**5** *Answers will vary. Students will use vocabulary from page 360 to tell how often they get their hair cut and how they get it cut.*

**6** *Answers will vary. Students will use vocabulary from page 361 to have a conversation about what they need done at the dry cleaner's.*

**7** *Answers will vary. Students will use the vocabulary provided in the colored boxes to explain how to use a washing machine.*

# Vocabulario

PALABRAS 2

## 1 PREPARATION

### Resource Manager

Vocabulary Transparencies 12.4–12.5
Audio Activities TE, pages 146–148
Audio CD 7
Workbook, pages 142–143
Quizzes, page 58
ExamView® Pro

### Bellringer Review

*Use BRR Transparency 12.2 or write the following on the board.*
Answer the following.

1. **¿Te gusta escribir?**
2. **¿En qué clase escribes mucho?**
3. **¿Qué escribes?**
4. **Y, ¿qué lees?**
5. **¿Les escribes cartas a los / las amigos(as)?**
6. **¿A quiénes escribes?**
7. **¿Cuándo les escribes?**

## 2 PRESENTATION

**Step 1** After presenting the vocabulary using any of the suggestions given in previous chapters, show Vocabulary Transparencies 12.4–12.5 again.

**Step 2** Have students look at the Vocabulary Transparencies. Call on individuals to say as much as they can about what they see on them.

# Vocabulario

PALABRAS 2

## El correo

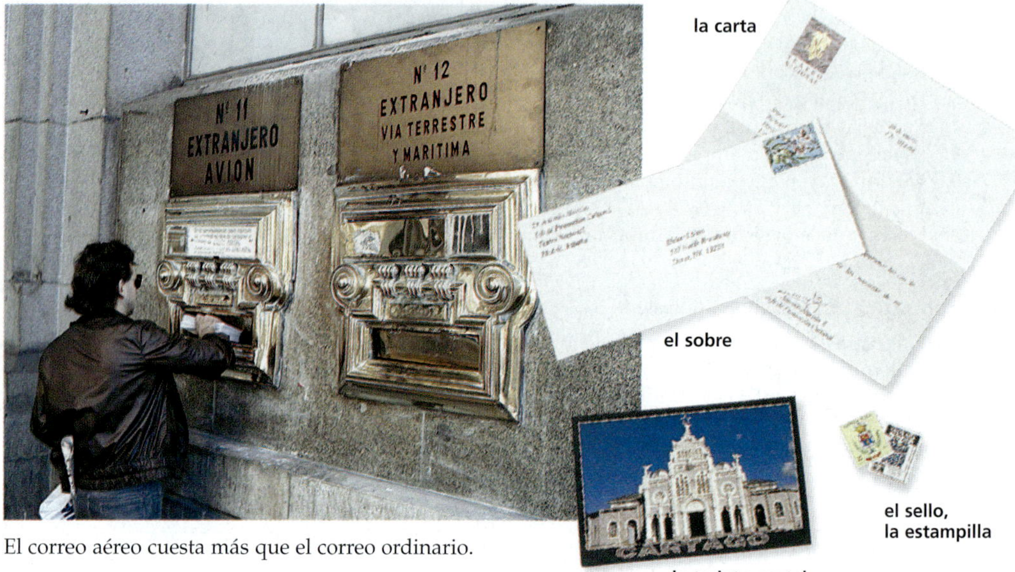


El correo aéreo cuesta más que el correo ordinario.

La señora echa la carta en el buzón.

La empleada pesa el paquete.



## Reaching All Students

### Total Physical Response

*(Student 1)* **y** *(Student 2)*, **vengan acá, por favor.**
*(Student 1)*, **eres un(a) empleado(a) de correo.**
*(Student 2)*, **tienes algo que mandar. Ve al correo. Dile «buenos días» al / a la empleado(a).**
*(Student 1)*, **contesta. Preguntale al / a la cliente qué quiere mandar.**
*(Student 2)*, **dile lo que quieres mandar. Dile adónde quieres mandarlo.**
*(Student 1)*, **dile cuánto va a costar.**
*(Student 2)*, **págale al / a la empleado(a). Dale el dinero.**
*(Student 1)*, **dale unos sellos.**
*(Student 2)*, **mira bien los sellos. Hay un problema. El / La empleado(a) no te dio bastantes sellos. Explícale el problema al / a la empleado(a).**

## El banco

La señorita quiere cobrar un cheque de viajero.
Ella endosa el cheque.
Ella firma el cheque.

## La casa de cambio

El joven quiere que le cambien dólares en pesos.

El cajero le da muchos billetes grandes.
El joven quiere cambio de un billete de cinco mil. Quiere suelto también.



### Vocabulary Expansion

You may give students the following additional vocabulary, which is useful in talking about the post office and the bank:

| | |
|---|---|
| **el cartero** | *letter carrier* |
| **el correo certificado** | *certified mail* |
| **el código postal** | *zip code* |
| **el apartado postal** | *postbox* |
| **la tasa de interés** | *interest rate* |
| **los préstamos** | *loans* |
| **la transacción** | *transaction* |

**LEVELING**

**E:** Activities 1, 2, 3, 4, 5, 6

**A:** Activities 3, 4, 5, 6

**C:** Activity 7

Vocabulario

## 3 PRACTICE

## ¿Qué palabra necesito?

**8** Students can work in pairs to do the activity as an interview.

**9** This activity can be prepared before going over it in class. You may wish to call on more able students to make up original sentences using the alternative words.

**10** This activity can be done orally with books closed. Then have students write the answers as a homework assignment.

### Learning from Realia

*(page 366)* You may wish to ask students to identify the historical figure depicted on the banknote and to find out something about him.

Vocabulario

## ¿Qué palabra necesito?

**8 Tu experiencia personal** Contesten.

1. ¿Tú escribes muchas cartas o prefieres hablar por teléfono?
2. Cuando viajas, ¿mandas tarjetas postales? ¿A quién?
3. ¿Quién te escribe a ti con frecuencia?
4. ¿Dónde está el buzón más cerca de tu casa?
5. ¿Cuánto cuesta un sello para una carta por correo ordinario?
6. ¿Cuándo fue la última vez que recibiste un paquete por correo?
7. ¿Qué había en el paquete?

Ciudad de México

**9 La correspondencia** Escojan.

1. Acabo de escribir esta carta, pero no tengo un ____ en que meterla.
   **a.** sello **b.** sobre **c.** buzón
2. Y ahora tengo que ponerle un ____ para correo aéreo.
   **a.** sello **b.** sobre **c.** buzón
3. Quiero echar la carta al correo. ¿Hay un ____ en esta calle?
   **a.** sello **b.** sobre **c.** buzón
4. El correo aéreo es caro. Es posible que sea mejor que yo la mande por correo ____.
   **a.** postal **b.** ordinario **c.** pesado

**10 Historieta Cosas bancarias** Contesten.

1. ¿Tiene tu familia una cuenta en el banco?
2. ¿Quién en tu familia escribe cheques?
3. ¿Tú has recibido un cheque alguna vez?
4. ¿De quién o para qué?
5. ¿Dónde cobraste el cheque?
6. ¿Tuviste que endosar el cheque?
7. ¿Te dio billetes grandes el cajero?
8. ¿Le pediste cambio?

## Answers to ¿Qué palabra necesito?

**8**

1. Yo escribo muchas cartas. (Yo prefiero hablar por teléfono.)
2. Sí (No), cuando viajo (no) mando tarjetas postales. Mando tarjetas postales a ___.
3. ___ me escribe con frecuencia.
4. El buzón más cerca de mi casa está ___.
5. Un sello para una carta por correo ordinario cuesta ___.
6. La última vez que recibí un paquete por correo fue ___.
7. En el paquete había ___.

**9**

1. b
2. a
3. c
4. b

**10**

1. Sí (No), mi familia (no) tiene una cuenta en el banco.
2. Mi ___ escribe cheques.
3. Sí, (No, no) he recibido un cheque (nunca).
4. De ___. Para ___.
5. Cobré el cheque en ___.
6. Sí, tuve que endosar el cheque.
7. Sí (No), el cajero (no) me dio billetes grandes.
8. Sí, (No, no) le pedí cambio.

**11** **La palabra, por favor.** Identifiquen.

1. Es necesario ponerlo en un sobre antes de enviar una carta.
2. Debes saberlo antes de cambiar una moneda por otra.
3. Lo necesitas cuando tienes solamente billetes grandes.
4. Lo necesitas cuando tienes solamente billetes.
5. Tienes que tener uno para escribir cheques.

**12** **En el correo** Estás en el correo en Chosica, no muy lejos de Lima. Tienes unas tarjetas postales que quieres mandar a casa. No sabes cuántos sellos necesitas ni cuánto te costará mandarlas. Y quieres tener una idea de cuándo van a llegar tus tarjetas. Ten una conversación con el/la empleado(a) en el correo (tu compañero[a]). Luego cambien de rol.

**13** **Cambio** Estás viajando por Guatemala y te quedan muy pocos quetzales. Ve al banco para cambiar dinero. Tu compañero(a) será el/la cajero(a) en el banco.

Una lavandería pública, Antigua, Guatemala

*For more practice using words from **Palabras 1** and **2**, do Activity 12 on page H13 at the end of this book.*



## Vocabulario

### Learning from Photos

*(page 367)* The **lavandería pública** shown here is in the Guatemalan town of Antigua not far from Guatemala City. Such **lavanderías,** usually located not far from the center of town, served as a social gathering place for the local women. Today there are fewer **lavanderías,** but they have not completely disappeared.

UN POCO MÁS This *InfoGap* Activity will allow students to practice in pairs. The activity should be very manageable for them, since all vocabulary and structures are familiar to them.

**LEVELING**

**E:** Activities 8, 9, 10, 11, 12, 13
**A:** Activities 8, 9, 10, 12, 13

## Answers to ¿Qué palabra necesito?

**11**

1. un sello
2. el tipo de cambio
3. el cambio
4. el suelto
5. la cuenta corriente

**12** *Answers will vary. Students will use vocabulary from* Palabras 2 *to ask the employee at the post office everything they want to know about sending their postcards.*

**13** *Answers will vary, but students will use the vocabulary from* Palabras 2 *to exchange dollars for* quetzales *in Guatemala.*

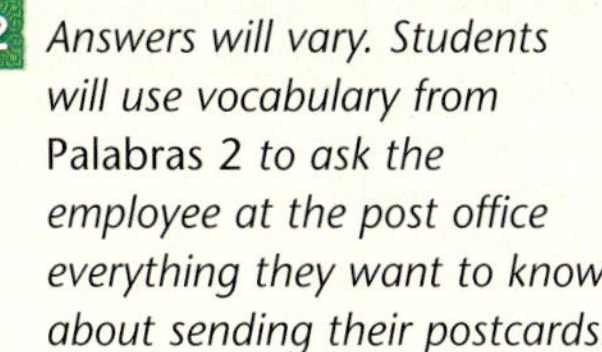

## Estructura

### 1 PREPARATION

**Resource Manager**

Audio Activities TE, pages 148–150
Audio CD 7
Workbook, pages 144–148
Quizzes, pages 59–61
ExamView® Pro

**Bellringer Review**

*Use BRR Transparency 12.3 or write the following on the board.*
Write each of the following terms under the appropriate category.
**en la peluquería / en el banco**
**el cheque, el champú, el cabello, el suelto, la cajera, las tijeras, la cuenta corriente, la raya**

### 2 PRESENTATION

**El subjuntivo**

**¡OJO!** The basic concept for students to understand is that the subjunctive is used when we do not know if the action will take place. If we know that it is or will be a reality, the indicative is used. If students understand this, it will not be necessary for them to memorize lists of phrases followed by the subjunctive. You may give students the following simple outline:

- **Indicative:** indicates or points something out; is factual; is objective, stands alone; is independent.
- **Subjunctive:** is subjective, is not objective; is not factual; cannot stand alone; is dependent on something else.



## Estructura

# El subjuntivo
## Telling what may or may not happen

**1.** All verb forms you have learned so far are in the indicative. All tenses of the indicative mood are used to express actions that actually do, did, or will take place. They are used to express real events.

**José tiene el pelo muy largo.**
**No fue a la peluquería ayer.**
**Irá mañana.**

All these statements express factual, real information.

*José has long hair. He didn't go to the barber's yesterday, but he will go tomorrow.*

**2.** Now you will learn the subjunctive mood. The subjunctive is used to express that which is not necessarily true or real. It expresses things that might happen, that you hope or want to happen. Let's compare the following two sentences.

**José tiene el pelo muy largo y va a la peluquería.**
**Los padres de José no quieren que él tenga el pelo tan largo y esperan que él vaya a la peluquería.**

The first sentence tells you that José has long hair and that he goes to the barber's. The information is factual. For this reason you use the indicative. The second sentence tells you that José's parents don't want him to have long hair, but that doesn't mean that his hair will necessarily be short. The sentence also tells us that they hope he goes to the barber, but this doesn't mean that he will. The second sentence tells you things that may happen. It does not present facts and, for this reason, you use the subjunctive.

For more information about paintings and art museums in the Spanish-speaking world, go to the Glencoe Spanish Web site: spanish.glencoe.com

*El peinado* de Pablo Picasso



**Art Connection**

Pablo Picasso Ruiz (1881–1973) is one of the most important artists of the twentieth century. Picasso was born in Málaga and studied in Barcelona and later in Paris. He spent most of his adult life in France. His art passed through various phases such as his blue period, his rose period, and cubism. *El peinado* is one of the artist's earlier works.
**Expansion:** Show the Fine Art Transparency of this painting by Picasso from the Transparency Binder.

3. To form the present tense of the subjunctive of regular verbs, you drop the **o** of the **yo** form of the present indicative. This is true of verbs that also have an irregular form in the present tense of the indicative. Add **e** endings to all **-ar** verbs and **a** endings to all **-er** and **-ir** verbs.

| INFINITIVE | PRESENT (YO) | STEM | PRESENT SUBJUNCTIVE (YO) |
|---|---|---|---|
| mirar | mirø | mir- | mire |
| comer | comø | com- | coma |
| vivir | vivø | viv- | viva |
| salir | salgø | salg- | salga |
| hacer | hagø | hag- | haga |
| decir | digø | dig- | diga |
| conducir | conduzcø | conduzc- | conduzca |

4. Study the forms for the present tense of the subjunctive.

| MIRAR | COMER | VIVIR | SALIR |
|---|---|---|---|
| mire | coma | viva | salga |
| mires | comas | vivas | salgas |
| mire | coma | viva | salga |
| miremos | comamos | vivamos | salgamos |
| *miréis* | *comáis* | *viváis* | *salgáis* |
| miren | coman | vivan | salgan |

**¿Te acuerdas?**

You are already familiar with these forms from your study of the commands.

**hable Ud., hablen Uds., no hables, venga Ud., vengan Uds., no vengas**

5. The following are the only verbs that do not follow the normal pattern for the formation of the present subjunctive.

| DAR | ESTAR | IR | SABER | SER |
|---|---|---|---|---|
| dé | esté | vaya | sepa | sea |
| des | estés | vayas | sepas | seas |
| dé | esté | vaya | sepa | sea |
| demos | estemos | vayamos | sepamos | seamos |
| *deis* | *estéis* | *vayáis* | *sepáis* | *seáis* |
| den | estén | vayan | sepan | sean |

## Estructura

**Step 1** Have students open their books to page 368. Go over Item 1 thoroughly and carefully. It is important for students to understand this concept.

**Step 2** Have students repeat the sentences after you.

**Step 3** Go over the explanation in Item 2 with your students.

**Step 4** Have students repeat each verb in the charts in Items 3–5.

**Step 5** Have students read the **¿Te acuerdas?** note to let them know that they are already familiar with the subjunctive verb forms from their study of the commands.

### Learning from Realia

*(page 369)* You may wish to ask students:
**¿Para qué se usa cada uno de los productos y el aparato en la página 369?**

### Reaching All Students

**For the Heritage Speakers** **Discusión: La gente mayor muchas veces se queja de los estilos de pelo de los jóvenes, especialmente de los varones. ¿Qué es lo que les molesta de los estilos de pelo de los jóvenes? ¿Qué preferirían los mayores? ¿Hay algo más en esto que el mero estilo?**

The Glencoe Spanish Web site **(spanish.glencoe.com)** offers options that enable you and your students to experience the Spanish-speaking world via the Internet. For each **Capítulo**, there are activities, games, and quizzes. In addition, an *Enrichment* section offers students an opportunity to visit Web sites related to the theme of the chapter.

# Estructura

## 3 PRACTICE

## ¿Cómo lo digo?

**14** The purpose of this activity is to give students initial practice with one form of the subjunctive.

### Learning from Realia

*(page 371 left)* The Chilean 300-peso stamp celebrates the 150th anniversary of German immigration. The Chilean government encouraged immigration from Germany in the nineteenth century to populate the virtually empty regions of the south. Today there are large populations of German descent in southern Chile who maintain their language and many of their traditional customs.
*(page 371 right)* You might ask students the following questions about the certified mail:
**¿Qué es el papel?**
**¿Quién manda la carta o paquete?**
**¿Dónde vive el remitente?**
**¿A quién o a quiénes manda la carta o paquete?**
**¿Dónde viven ellos?**

# Estructura

## ¿Cómo lo digo?

**14** **¿Qué quieren los padres de Adela? Quieren que ella haga muchas cosas.**
Sigan el modelo.

**estudiar →**
**Los padres de Adela quieren que ella estudie.**

1. estudiar mucho
2. trabajar duro
3. tomar cursos avanzados
4. leer mucho
5. comer bien
6. escribir a sus abuelos
7. recibir buenas notas
8. asistir a la universidad
9. salir bien en sus exámenes
10. decir la verdad
11. ser generosa
12. ir a una universidad buena
13. conducir con cuidado

Ciudad de Guatemala

**15** **Los profesores insisten.**
Sigan el modelo.

**estudiar →**
**Los profesores insisten en que estudiemos.**

1. trabajar
2. prestar atención
3. tomar apuntes
4. aprender
5. recibir buenas notas
6. hacer nuestras tareas
7. estar presentes
8. ser puntuales

Colegio Santa Teresita, Santurce, Puerto Rico



### Answers to ¿Cómo lo digo?

**14** *All answers begin with* Los padres de Adela quieren que ella…
1. … estudie mucho.
2. … trabaje duro.
3. … tome cursos avanzados.
4. … lea mucho.
5. … coma bien.
6. … escriba a sus abuelos.
7. … reciba buenas notas.
8. … asista a la universidad.
9. … salga bien en sus exámenes.
10. … diga la verdad.
11. … sea generosa.
12. … vaya a una universidad buena.
13. … conduzca con cuidado.

**15** *All answers begin with* Los profesores insisten en que…
1. … trabajemos.
2. … prestemos atención.
3. … tomemos apuntes.
4. … aprendamos.
5. … recibamos buenas notas.
6. … hagamos nuestras tareas.
7. … estemos presentes.
8. … seamos puntuales.

# El subjuntivo en cláusulas nominales

## Expressing wishes and orders

As you have seen, the subjunctive is used with the verbs **querer** and **insistir.** Even though someone wants or insists that something be done, it will not necessarily happen. The information in the clause introduced by either **querer** or **insistir** is not factual. It may or may not happen. Other verbs like **querer** and **insistir** that take the subjunctive are:

| | |
|---|---|
| **desear** *to wish* | **mandar** *to order* |
| **esperar** *to hope* | **temer** *to fear* |
| **preferir** *to prefer* | **tener miedo de** *to be afraid* |

**Quiero que mis amigos vayan a la fiesta.**
**Y espero que no lleguen tarde.**
**Tengo miedo de que no sepan las direcciones.**

## ¿Cómo lo digo?

**16 Historieta En la peluquería** Contesten.

1. ¿Quiere Antonio que el peluquero le corte el pelo?
2. ¿Quiere que le dé un champú?
3. ¿Quiere que use las tijeras?
4. ¿Quiere que le ponga la raya a la derecha o a la izquierda?
5. ¿Quiere que le seque el pelo con el secador?

**17 Historieta Una carta** Sigan el modelo.

**Tú le escribes. ⟶**
**Yo prefiero que tú le escribas.**

1. Le escribes en español.
2. Le mandas una tarjeta.
3. Pones un sello para correo aéreo.
4. Vas al correo.
5. Pones la tarjeta en el buzón delante del correo.

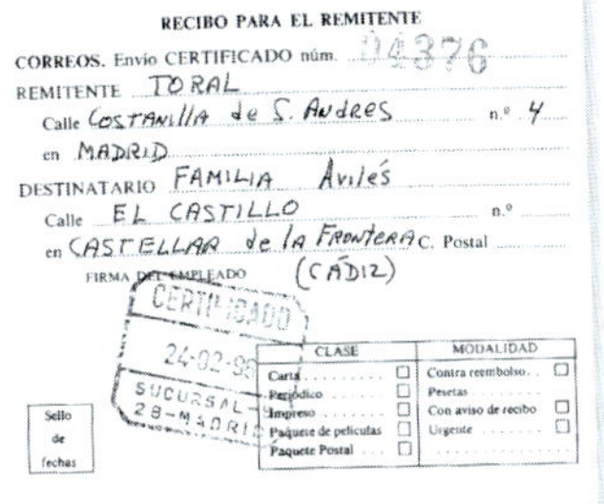

RECIBO PARA EL REMITENTE
CORREOS. Envío CERTIFICADO núm. 04376
REMITENTE TORAL
Calle COSTANILLA de S. ANDRES n.º 4
en MADRID
DESTINATARIO FAMILIA Avilés
Calle EL CASTILLO n.º
en CASTELLAR de la FRONTERA C. Postal
(CÁDIZ)
CERTIFICADO

| CLASE | | MODALIDAD | |
|---|---|---|---|
| Carta | ☐ | Contra reembolso | ☐ |
| Periódico | ☐ | Peritas | ☐ |
| Impreso | ☐ | Con aviso de recibo | ☐ |
| Paquete de películas | ☐ | Urgente | ☐ |
| Paquete Postal | ☐ | | |

## Answers to ¿Cómo lo digo?

**16**

1. Sí (No), Antonio (no) quiere que el peluquero le corte el pelo.
2. Sí, (No, no) quiere que le dé un champú.
3. Sí, (No, no) quiere que use las tijeras.
4. Quiere que le ponga la raya a la derecha (izquierda).
5. Sí, (No, no) quiere que le seque el pelo con el secador.

**17**

1. Yo prefiero que tú le escribas en español.
2. Yo prefiero que tú le mandes una tarjeta.
3. Yo prefiero que tú pongas un sello para correo aéreo.
4. Yo prefiero que tú vayas al correo.
5. Yo prefiero que tú pongas la tarjeta en el buzón delante del correo.

## Estructura

### 1 PREPARATION

**Bellringer Review**

*Use BRR Transparency 12.4 or write the following on the board.*
Give the command form **(Ud.)** for each of the following verbs.
1. **comer**
2. **hablar**
3. **vivir**
4. **ir**
5. **saber**

### 2 PRESENTATION

**El subjuntivo en cláusulas nominales**

**Step 1** Have students open their books to page 371 and lead them through the explanation. Have them read the verbs and model sentences aloud.

¡OJO! Stress the concept that even though someone wants or insists that something be done, it is not certain that it will take place. It may be helpful for students to relate *subjunctive* to *subjective,* relating to one's own perception of the world, not necessarily the world as it is. It is in cases of subjectivity that the subjunctive is used.

### 3 PRACTICE

**¿Cómo lo digo?**

**16** After going over Activity 16, have students retell the story in their own words. **Antonio quiere que...** They do not have to keep using the introductory clause. **Note:** This activity gives students practice using the third-person form of the subjunctive.

# Estructura

## 3 PRACTICE *(continued)*

**18** This activity gives students practice using the **yo** form of the subjunctive.

**19** This activity elicits the **tú** and **ustedes** forms of the subjunctive.

**20** This activity has students use many forms of the subjunctive. You may have students prepare this activity before going over it in class.

### LEVELING

**E:** Activities 14, 15, 16

**A:** Activities 14, 15, 17



### 18 Historieta ¿Qué temen ellos?

Sigan el modelo.

**Yo no tengo bastante dinero. ⟶**
**Temen que yo no tenga bastante dinero.**

1. Yo no voy al banco.
2. Yo no tengo bastante dinero en efectivo.
3. No compro cheques de viajero.
4. Cambio demasiados dólares en pesos.
5. No sé dónde firmar el cheque.

Valladolid, España

### 19 Historieta ¡Vamos todos! Contesten.

1. ¿Quieres que vayamos a Sevilla?
2. ¿Prefieres que yo conduzca?
3. ¿Insistes en que yo no exceda el límite de velocidad?
4. ¿Prefieres que yo tome la autopista?
5. ¿Temes que yo no pague el peaje?
6. ¿Esperas que lleguemos a Sevilla antes de la hora de cenar?

### 20 Historieta Cada uno quiere otra cosa.

Completen.

Yo no sé lo que vamos a hacer esta noche. Pablo quiere que nosotros __1__ (ir) al cine. Él insiste en que nosotros __2__ (ver) la película en el cine Apolo. Carlota teme que mañana __3__ (ser) el último día. Tiene miedo de que ellos __4__ (cambiar) las películas los sábados. Y tú, ¿quieres que nosotros __5__ (ir) al cine o que __6__ (hacer) otra cosa? ¿Qué me dices? Que Felipe quiere que ustedes __7__ (quedarse) en casa. ¿Por qué? Ah, él quiere que todo el grupo __8__ (ir) a su casa. Él prefiere que nosotros __9__ (escuchar) música y que __10__ (bailar). ¡Buena idea!



## ANSWERS TO ¿Cómo lo digo?

**18**

1. Temen que yo no vaya al banco.
2. Temen que yo no tenga bastante dinero en efectivo.
3. Temen que yo no compre cheques de viajero.
4. Temen que yo cambie demasiados dólares en pesos.
5. Temen que yo no sepa dónde firmar el cheque.

**19**

1. Sí, (No, no) quiero que vayan a Sevilla.
2. Sí, (No, no) prefiero que tú conduzcas.
3. Sí, (No, no) insisto en que tú no excedas el límite de velocidad.
4. Sí, (No, no) prefiero que tú tomes la autopista.
5. Sí, (No, no) temo que tú no pagues el peaje.
6. Sí, (No, no) espero que lleguen a Sevilla antes de la hora de cenar.

**20**

1. vayamos
2. veamos
3. sea
4. cambien
5. vayamos
6. hagamos
7. se queden
8. vaya
9. escuchemos
10. bailemos

**21** **Lo que quieren mis padres** Dile a un(a) compañero(a) de clase lo que tus padres siempre quieren que hagas. Tu compañero(a) te dirá lo que sus padres quieren que él o ella haga. Luego pongan sus dos listas juntas y decidan cuáles son los mismos consejos *(advice)* que ustedes reciben de sus padres. ¿Están ustedes de acuerdo con los deseos de sus padres? Den sus opiniones sobre sus consejos o deseos.

**22** **Mi mejor amigo(a)** Trabaja con un(a) compañero(a). Cada uno(a) de ustedes va a preparar una lista de características que ustedes quieren que tenga su mejor amigo(a). Luego comparen sus listas y determinen las características que ustedes dos buscan en su mejor amigo(a).

## El subjuntivo con expresiones impersonales
### Expressing opinions

1. The subjunctive is also used after the following impersonal expressions.

| | |
|---|---|
| es imposible | es probable |
| es posible | es necesario |
| es bueno | es fácil |
| es mejor | es difícil |
| es importante | |

2. These expressions are followed by the subjunctive because it is uncertain whether the action of the verb will take place or not.

   **Es necesario que cambiemos el dinero mañana.**
   **Es importante que sepas el tipo de cambio.**
   **Es posible que el banco esté cerrado.**

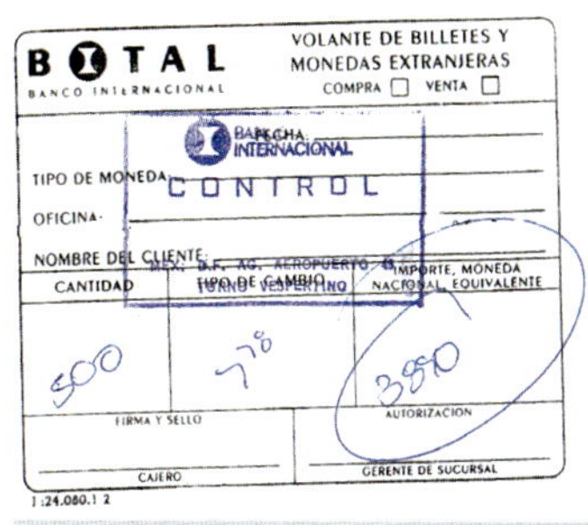

## Answers to ¿Cómo lo digo?

**21** *Answers will vary. Students will use the subjunctive to tell what their parents always want them to do.*

**22** *Answers will vary. Students will use the subjunctive to tell what qualities they want a best friend to have.*

**LEVELING**

**E:** Activity 19
**A:** Activities 18, 19, 20, 21, 22
**C:** Activity 20

## Estructura

### 1 PREPARATION

**Bellringer Review**

*Use BRR Transparency 12.5 or write the following on the board.*
Write logical completions to these sentences.

1. Yo quiero que mis padres ___.
2. Yo prefiero que el / la profesor(a) de español ___.
3. Mis padres insisten en que yo ___.
4. Yo deseo que mi mejor amigo(a) ___.
5. Mi madre espera que yo ___.

### 2 PRESENTATION

**El subjuntivo con expresiones impersonales**

**Step 1** Have students open their books to page 373 and lead them through the explanation. Then have them read the expressions and model sentences aloud.

¡OJO! You may emphasize here that even though an action is necessary (or important or good), it is not certain that it will occur. Therefore the subjunctive is used.

**Learning from Realia**

*(page 373 left)* You may wish to ask students these questions about the **volante de billetes y monedas extranjeras:**
¿Cuánto dinero cambiaron?
¿Cuál fue el tipo de cambio?
¿Cuánto recibió el cliente en moneda nacional?
¿Cómo se llama el banco?

# Estructura

## 3 PRACTICE

## ¿Cómo lo digo?

**23** and **24** You can go over these activities first orally with books closed. Then have students write them for homework and go over them again the following day.

### Learning from Realia

*(page 374)* Each of the three Mexican banknotes features an important figure in Mexican history.

For each banknote (the 20, 50, and 100 pesos), you may wish to ask students:

**¿Quién es la persona en el billete?**

**¿Por qué es importante esta persona?**

If students do not know who they are, you may have them look this information up for homework. (Benito Juárez is on the 20–peso note, José María Morelos is on the 50, and Nezahualcoyotl is on the 100.)

# Estructura

## ¿Cómo lo digo?

**23** **¿Sí o no? ¿Cuál es tu opinión?** Contesten.

1. ¿Es importante que los jóvenes estudien lenguas?
2. ¿Es fácil que reciban buenas notas?
3. ¿Es bueno que hablen mucho?
4. ¿Es posible que visiten otros países?
5. ¿Es mejor que aprendan el español?

Benidorm, España

**24** **Voy a la ciudad. Pues, es importante que…**
Sigan el modelo.

**tener cuidado** ⟶
**Pues, es importante que tengas cuidado.**

1. desayunar antes
2. tener cuidado
3. tomar el tren
4. llevar bastante dinero
5. llamar a los abuelos

**25** **Historieta Finanzas** Contesten.

1. ¿Es importante que tú tengas dinero en el banco?
2. ¿Es posible que tengas una cuenta corriente?
3. ¿Es importante que todos pongamos dinero en el banco?
4. ¿Es necesario que endosemos un cheque antes de cobrarlo?
5. ¿Es mejor que paguemos con una tarjeta de crédito?

## ANSWERS TO ¿Cómo lo digo?

**23**

1. Sí, (No, no) es importante que los jóvenes estudien lenguas.
2. Sí, (No, no) es fácil que reciban buenas notas.
3. Sí, (No, no) es bueno que hablen mucho.
4. Sí, es posible que visiten otros países.
5. Sí, (No, no) es mejor que aprendan el español.

**24**

1. Pues, es importante que desayunes antes.
2. Pues, es importante que tengas cuidado.
3. Pues, es importante que tomes el tren.
4. Pues, es importante que lleves bastante dinero.
5. Pues, es importante que llames a los abuelos.

**25**

1. Sí, (No, no) es importante que yo tenga dinero en el banco.
2. Sí, (No, no) es posible que tenga una cuenta corriente.
3. Sí, (No, no) es importante que todos pongamos dinero en el banco.
4. Sí, es necesario que endosemos un cheque antes de cobrarlo.
5. Sí, (No, no) es mejor que paguemos con una tarjeta de crédito.

**26** **Historieta ¿Dónde están los nietos?** Completen.

Abuelito está un poco nervioso. Es posible que sus nietos __1__ (llegar) mañana por la mañana. Es importante que abuelito __2__ (saber) cuándo van a llegar. Pero es difícil que abuelita le __3__ (decir) la hora precisa de la llegada de los nietos. Es posible que mañana __4__ (hacer) mal tiempo. Como los nietos vienen en carro será necesario que __5__ (manejar) despacio y con mucho cuidado si hay mucha nieve. Es mejor que ellos __6__ (llegar) un poco tarde. Abuelito no quiere que ellos __7__ (tener) un accidente. Es mejor que __8__ (llegar) tarde pero sanos y salvos.

Tolima, Colombia

**27** **Cosas fáciles y difíciles** Prepara una lista de cosas que es probable que tú hagas con frecuencia porque es fácil hacerlas. Prepara otra lista que indica lo que es difícil que tú hagas. Luego compara tus listas con las listas que ha preparado tu compañero(a).

**28** **Juego** **No, no. Es imposible.** Work in a small group. Talk together and tell one another what you think is important, necessary, or a good idea that some other member of the group do. Whoever is told to do it will answer with a good excuse as to why it's impossible.

Estructura

**26** Have students prepare this activity before going over it in class.

## LEVELING

**E:** Activities 23, 24, 25, 27

**A:** Activities 25, 27, 28

**C:** Activity 26

### ¡Adelante!

At this point in the chapter, students have learned all the vocabulary and structure necessary to complete the chapter. The conversation and cultural readings that follow recycle all the material learned up to this point.

## Answers to ¿Cómo lo digo?

**26**

1. lleguen
2. sepa
3. diga
4. haga
5. manejen
6. lleguen
7. tengan
8. lleguen

**27** *Answers will vary. Students will use the subjunctive to write two lists, one of things that are easy to do and another of things that are difficult to do.*

**28** *Answers will vary. Students will work in groups to discuss what's important, what's necessary or a good idea, and why it's impossible to do it.*

# Conversación

## 1 PREPARATION

### Resource Manager

Audio Activities TE, page 151
Audio CD 7

### Bellringer Review

*Use BRR Transparency 12.6 or write the following on the board.*
Complete each sentence with a verb expressing a wish, preference, or demand.

1. **Los estudiantes ___ que los profesores den exámenes más fáciles.**
2. **Ellos ___ que la comida de la cafetería sea mejor.**
3. **Ellos ___ que los profesores no les den las tareas el viernes.**
4. **Los profesores ___ que los estudiantes salgan bien en los exámenes.**
5. **Ellos ___ que los estudiantes miren la televisión menos.**

## 2 PRESENTATION

**Step 1** Tell students they will hear a conversation between a customer in an exchange bureau and a teller.

**Step 2** Have students close their books and listen as you read the conversation on page 376 or play Audio CD 7.

**Step 3** Divide the class into two groups, each of which assumes the role of one of the people in the conversation. Have each group repeat its part of the conversation in unison after you or the recording.

**Step 4** Choose a volunteer from each group to present the conversation to the class.

**Step 5** Supply substitutions for the amount of money exchanged and the rate of exchange. Call on pairs to present the conversation making these substitutions.

# Conversación

## En la casa de cambio   

**Empleada** Sí, señor. ¿En qué puedo servirle?
**Felipe** Quiero cambiar dólares en pesos.
**Empleada** ¿Tiene usted dólares en efectivo o en cheque de viajero?
**Felipe** Cheque de viajero. ¿Cuál es el tipo de cambio hoy, por favor?
**Empleada** Para cheques de viajero 223 pesos por dólar. ¿Para cuánto es el cheque?
**Felipe** Cien dólares. ¿Quiere usted que yo lo endose?
**Empleada** Sí, claro. Y necesito su pasaporte también.
**Felipe** Aquí lo tiene.
**Empleada** Gracias.

### ¿Comprendes?

Contesten.

1. ¿Qué va a hacer Felipe?
2. ¿Quiere cambiar dinero en efectivo o un cheque de viajero?
3. ¿Cuántos pesos recibirá Felipe por un dólar?
4. ¿Cuántos dólares quiere cambiar?
5. ¿Qué tiene que hacer Felipe con el cheque?
6. ¿Qué más tiene que darle a la empleada?



### Answers to ¿Comprendes?

1. Felipe va a cambiar dólares en pesos.
2. Quiere cambiar un cheque de viajero.
3. Felipe recibirá 223 pesos por un dólar.
4. Quiere cambiar 100 dólares.
5. Tiene que endosar el cheque.
6. Tiene que darle su pasaporte.

# Vamos a hablar más

**A** **En la peluquería** Estás en una peluquería en un país hispano. Habla con el/la peluquero(a) (tu compañero[a]). Dile cómo quieres el pelo. Dile todo lo que quieres que él o ella haga. Luego cambien de rol.

**B** **Sí, sí, pero...** Habla con un(a) compañero(a). Dile algunas cosas que quieres que él o ella haga. Tu compañero(a) te contestará que sabe que es bueno que él o ella haga lo que quieres pero en este momento es imposible que lo haga porque es importante que haga otra cosa. Luego cambien de rol.

Sevilla, España

Baños, Ecuador

Ávila, España



## Answers to Vamos a hablar más

**A** *Answers will vary. Students will use vocabulary from* Palabras 1 *to explain how they would like their hair cut.*

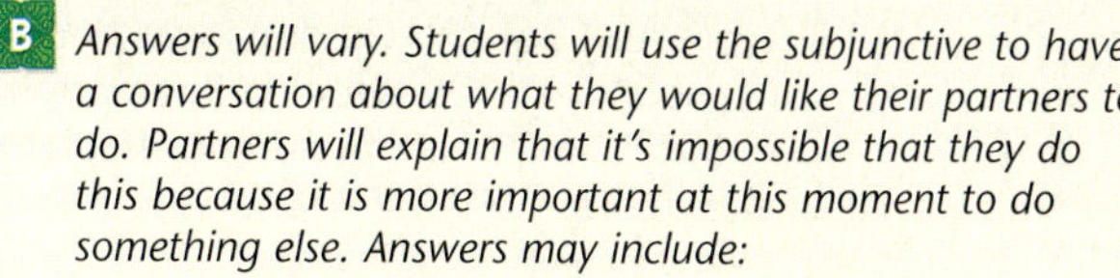

**B** *Answers will vary. Students will use the subjunctive to have a conversation about what they would like their partners to do. Partners will explain that it's impossible that they do this because it is more important at this moment to do something else. Answers may include:*

—Quiero que tú estudies.
—Sí, sé que es bueno que yo estudie pero en este momento, no puedo. Es imposible que yo estudie porque es importante que yo vaya al correo.

Conversación

**3 PRACTICE**

## Vamos a hablar más

### Learning from Photos

*(page 377)* You may wish to ask students to describe and tell as much as they can about each of the three photos.
*(page 377 left)* There are several towns in Ecuador named Baños. The Baños shown in this photo is a resort town known for its perpetually mild climate. It is in the central highlands at an elevation of 5,940 feet and serves as a gateway to both the high peaks of the Andes and to the **Oriente** or jungle region in the east. The **Volcán Tungurahua** towers over Baños. Baños is also known for its two popular hot springs or thermal baths that many Ecuadoreans believe can cure a variety of ailments.

### Geography Connection

Ask students to locate each of the three cities, Sevilla and Ávila, Spain, and Baños, Ecuador, on a map.

### Glencoe Technology

On the CD-ROM, students can watch a dramatization of this conversation. They can then play the role of either one of the characters and record themselves in the conversation.

**LEVELING**

**E:** Conversation

# Lecturas culturales

## Resource Manager

Audio Activities TE, page 152
Audio CD 7

## Bellringer Review

*Use BRR Transparency 12.7 or write the following on the board.*
Complete the sentences with the present subjunctive form of the verb in parentheses.

1. **El director quiere que nosotros ___ mucho. (aprender)**
2. **El profesor desea que Federico ___ todo lo que dice. (comprender)**
3. **El director de la escuela quiere que yo ___ a su oficina. (ir)**
4. **Tus padres quieren que tú ___ buenas notas. (sacar)**

## National Standards

**Cultures**
The reading on pages 378–379 and the related activities familiarize students with daily life in the Spanish-speaking world.

## PRESENTATION

### Pre-reading

Tell students: **Vamos a leer algo de un grupo de amigos de Madrid. Ellos van a hacer un viaje por el sur de España. Pero antes de salir de Madrid tienen muchas cosas que hacer.**

### Reading

You may wish to follow some of the suggestions outlined in previous chapters for the presentation of the **Lectura.** Assign the **¿Comprendes?** activities on page 379 for homework.

# Lecturas culturales

## Muchos quehaceres  

José Luis y un grupo de amigos de su colegio en Madrid han decidido que van a hacer una gira por el sur de España—por Andalucía. Van a ir a Córdoba, Granada y Sevilla donde quieren visitar los famosos monumentos de los árabes. Los árabes o los moros estuvieron en España por casi ocho siglos—desde 711 hasta 1492.

En Córdoba van a visitar la Mezquita.
En Granada, la Alhambra.
Y en Sevilla, el Alcázar.

Saben que en agosto va a hacer mucho calor en estas ciudades. Por consiguiente van a pasar unos días en una playa de la Costa del Sol antes de volver a casa.

### Reading Strategy

**Recognizing text organization** Before you begin to read a passage, take a look at it quickly to figure out how it is organized. Doing so will help you guess the meanings of words you do not know, because it will help you figure out the overall meaning of the material. In addition, knowing how a selection is organized will help you identify where in the reading you can find a certain piece of information.

La Mezquita, Córdoba

La Alhambra, Granada



### Learning from Photos

*(page 378 middle)* The Great Mosque of Córdoba was built during the reign of Abd er-Rahman in the eighth century upon the site of a Roman temple. The building is massive; 2,250 feet of wall surround it. Within are hundreds of columns and red- and white-striped arches that we see in the photo. Córdoba was, during the time of Abd er-Rahman, a city without equal in the West as a center of learning.
*(page 378 bottom)* **La Alhambra** overlooks the city of Granada. In it lived the Nazarí monarchs. Its construction dates from the thirteenth and fourteenth centuries. The towers and patios are marvelous: **la torre de las Infantas, la torre de las Damas, el patio de los Leones, el patio de los Arrayanes.** The gardens and grounds are of exceptional beauty.

El Alcázar, Sevilla

Como les quedan sólo dos días antes de salir para Andalucía, todos tienen muchos quehaceres[1]. José Luis tiene que ir a la peluquería. Quiere que el peluquero le corte el pelo. Tiene el pelo bastante largo y es mejor que tenga el pelo corto para la playa. Piensa nadar mucho en el Mediterráneo.

Teresa tiene mucho lavado. Tiene que llevar su ropa sucia a la lavandería. No es necesario que ella vaya a la tintorería. No es necesario limpiar en seco la ropa que va a llevar durante el viaje. Sólo tiene algunas camisetas, blusas y pantalones. Y Teresa no va a planchar la ropa tampoco[2]. Va a poner todo en su mochila y sabe que se va a arrugar[3].

Elena quiere ir al correo para comprar sellos. Querrá enviar unas postales a sus amigos y parientes y no quiere perder tiempo haciendo cola en el correo de Córdoba o Sevilla.

Y, ¿adónde tienen que ir todos? ¡Al banco! Sí, todos tienen que ir al banco porque necesitan dinero. En el banco no tienen que cambiar dinero porque estarán viajando dentro de España. Pero tienen que cobrar un cheque porque es necesario que tengan algún dinero en efectivo. Es probable que no compren cheques de viajero porque si no pagan sus cuentas en efectivo, pueden usar una tarjeta de crédito.

Pues, ¡buen viaje a todos! Y esperamos que lo pasen bien en Andalucía—¡que se diviertan!

[1]quehaceres *chores*
[2]tampoco *either*
[3]arrugar *to wrinkle*

## ¿Comprendes?

**A Preparativos para un viaje** Contesten.

1. ¿Quiénes han decidido hacer una gira por el sur de España?
2. ¿Por qué van a pasar unos días en la Costa del Sol?
3. ¿Qué tienen que hacer todos?
4. ¿Adónde tiene que ir José Luis?
5. ¿Qué quiere él?
6. ¿Cómo quiere el pelo para la playa?
7. ¿Adónde tiene que ir Teresa?
8. ¿Por qué no es necesario que ella vaya a la tintorería?
9. ¿Qué quiere hacer Elena en el correo?
10. ¿Qué van a hacer todos en el banco?

**B Una gira** Identifiquen.

1. una región del sur de España
2. tres ciudades de esta región
3. un monumento de Córdoba
4. un monumento de Granada
5. un monumento de Sevilla
6. el año 711



## Lecturas culturales

### Post-reading

**Step 1** Go over the **¿Comprendes?** activities in class the next day.

**Step 2** Call on a student to give a summary of the reading in his or her own words. If necessary, ask five or six questions to review the salient points of the reading selection in order to enable him or her to do this more easily. After the oral summary, the more able students can write a synopsis of the **Lectura** in their own words.

### Learning from Photos

*(page 379)* A great part of the Alcázar was built for King Pedro el Cruel of Castilla in the 1360s, using Moorish artisans. The original Alcázar was the palace of the Moorish governors who began its construction in the ninth century. It is an outstanding example of **mudéjar** art (art done by Muslims who lived in Christian areas of Spain in the twelfth to sixteenth centuries).

## Answers to ¿Comprendes?

**A**

1. José Luis y un grupo de amigos de su colegio en Madrid han decidido hacer una gira por el sur de España.
2. Van a pasar unos días en la Costa del Sol porque saben que va a hacer mucho calor y quieren ir a la playa.
3. Todos tienen que hacer muchos quehaceres.
4. José Luis tiene que ir a la peluquería.
5. Quiere que el peluquero le corte el pelo.
6. Quiere el pelo corto para la playa.
7. Teresa tiene que ir a la lavandería.
8. No es necesario que ella vaya a la tintorería porque no es necesario limpiar en seco la ropa que va a llevar durante el viaje.
9. Elena quiere comprar sellos en el correo.
10. En el banco todos tienen que cobrar un cheque porque es necesario que tengan algún dinero en efectivo.

**B**

1. Andalucía
2. Córdoba, Granada, y Sevilla
3. la Mezquita
4. la Alhambra
5. el Alcázar
6. el año que los árabes llegaron a España

# Lectura opcional 1

## National Standards

**Cultures**
This reading and the related activities on this page familiarize students with some interesting information about the Moneda Palace in Santiago de Chile.

**¡OJO!** This reading is optional. You may skip it completely, have the entire class read it, have only several students read it and report to the class, or assign it for extra credit.

**FUN FACTS**

Other Latin American countries have different names for their currencies.

- Venezuela: **el bolívar,** named for Simón Bolívar
- Guatemala: **el quetzal,** named for the national bird
- Panamá: **el balboa,** named for Vasco Nuñez de Balboa
- Costa Rica and El Salvador: **el colón,** named for Cristóbal Colón
- Nicaragua: **el córdoba,** named for Francisco Hernández de Córdoba
- Honduras: **el lempira,** named for the Indian chief who fought the Spaniards

# Lectura opcional 1

Palacio de la Moneda, Santiago de Chile

## La Moneda: un edificio con mucha historia

En pleno centro de Santiago, la capital de Chile, está el edificio de la Moneda. El edificio se construyó entre 1788 y 1805. Es un bello ejemplo de arquitectura colonial.

Desde 1846 hasta 1958 la Moneda sirvió de residencia a los presidentes de la República de Chile. Pero el edificio no se construyó para residencia presidencial. Era donde se acuñaba[1] la moneda en tiempos coloniales. Hasta 1929, los presidentes vivían en el edificio mientras se continuaba acuñando las monedas allí.

En 1973 el edificio de la Moneda apareció en los periódicos de todo el mundo. El 11 de septiembre durante un golpe[2] militar, unos aviones atacaron la Moneda y en las ruinas murió el presidente Salvador Allende.

La Moneda fue restaurada y hoy sirve de sede[3] al gobierno chileno.

[1]se acuñaba *they minted*
[2]golpe *a coup (the overthrow of a government)*
[3]sede *seat (of government)*

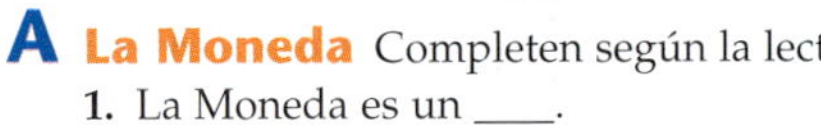

### ¿Comprendes?

**A La Moneda** Completen según la lectura.

1. La Moneda es un ____.
2. Está en el ____ de la ciudad.
3. Los presidentes del país vivían en el edificio desde ____ hasta ____.
4. El año 1929 fue el último año en que ____ dinero en el edificio.
5. La construcción del edificio tomó ____ años.

**B Las noticias de 1973** Expliquen lo que ocurrió de importancia en 1973.



### Answers to ¿Comprendes?

**A**

1. edificio con mucha historia
2. centro
3. 1846, 1958
4. se acuñó
5. diecisiete

**B** *Answers will vary but may include:*

El 11 de septiembre de 1973, durante un golpe militar, unos aviones atacaron (el palacio de) la Moneda y en las ruinas murió el presidente Salvador Allende.

Guatemala

# Lectura opcional 2

## El pelo y el peinado

En muchas culturas del mundo el pelo y el peinado siempre han tenido un gran significado. Aún hoy los jueces[1] en Gran Bretaña siguen llevando peluca[2] en la corte.

En las Américas, entre los indígenas, el peinado, igual que el vestido, frecuentemente identifica al grupo o a la tribu. Y el pelo largo no tiene nada que ver con el sexo de la persona. En algunos grupos las mujeres tienen el pelo largo y llevan trenzas[3] que adornan con cintas[4] de colores vivos. En otros grupos, como los indios otavaleños de Ecuador, son los hombres quienes llevan trenzas.

Y, ¿quién se encarga[5] del cuidado del pelo y de la barba[6]? Los barberos o peluqueros, por supuesto. En la literatura hispana, el barbero es un personaje especial. Ha tenido fama de ser muy independiente—casi anarquista. Trabaja por si mismo. No tiene jefe y conoce todos los secretos del pueblo. Y el hombre que pone el cuello bajo la navaja del barbero pone allí su vida. Este ha sido el tema o argumento de varios cuentos españoles y latinoamericanos.

[1]jueces *judges*
[2]peluca *wig*
[3]trenzas *braids*
[4]cintas *ribbons*
[5]se encarga *takes charge*
[6]barba *beard*

Ecuador

Barbados

### ¿Comprendes?

**Costumbres interesantes** Digan que sí o que no.

1. Los jueces en Gran Bretaña no tienen pelo.
2. Entre los indígenas de las Américas, el peinado identifica el grupo al que pertenecen.
3. Sólo las mujeres llevan el pelo largo.
4. En algunos grupos indígenas los señores llevan trenzas.
5. El barbero es un personaje especial en la literatura hispana.



Lectura opcional 2

### National Standards

**Cultures**

This reading and the related activities on this page familiarize students with information about hairstyles among some indigenous peoples of Latin America and the importance of barbers in Hispanic culture.

**¡OJO!** This reading is optional. You may skip it completely, have the entire class read it, have only several students read it and report to the class, or assign it for extra credit.

### Learning from Photos

*(page 381)* Have students say as much as they can about the photos on this page.

**LEVELING**

**E:** Reading
**A:** Reading 1
**C:** Reading 2

### Answers to ¿Comprendes?

1. No
2. Sí
3. No
4. Sí
5. Sí

# Conexiones

## National Standards

**Connections**
This reading about banking and finance establishes a connection with another discipline, allowing students to reinforce and further their knowledge of business through the study of Spanish.

**¡OJO!** The readings in the **Conexiones** section are optional. They focus on some of the major disciplines taught in schools and universities. The vocabulary is useful for discussing such topics as history, literature, art, economics, business, science, etc. You may choose any of the following ways to do the readings in the **Conexiones** sections.

**Independent reading** Have students read the selections and do the post-reading activities as homework, which you collect. This option is least intrusive on class time and requires a minimum of teacher involvement.

**Homework with in-class follow-up** Assign the readings and post-reading activities as homework. Review and discuss the material in class the next day.

**Intensive in-class activity** This option includes a pre-reading vocabulary presentation, in-class reading and discussion, assignment of the activities for homework, and a discussion of the assignment in class the following day.

# Conexiones

## *Las finanzas*

### La banca

At one time or another we must all get involved in matters of money and finances. A bank is a good provider of financial services. We may want to pay some bills by check or put some money aside and open a savings account. These are two of the many services offered by a bank. Today many of our banking needs can be taken care of without even entering the bank. We can do our transactions at the ATM, or Automated Teller Machine.

Let's learn a few very commonly used banking terms in Spanish.

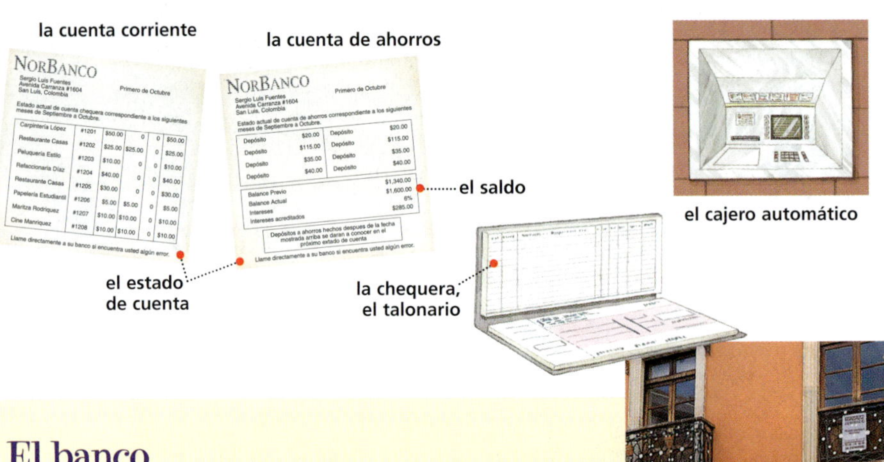


### El banco

**Una cuenta corriente**

El servicio que te da el banco es muy importante. Es muy conveniente pagar tus facturas de gas, electricidad, etc., con un cheque. Para escribir cheques es necesario tener una cuenta corriente en el banco. Pero hay que tener mucho cuidado. Es necesario que tengas suficientes fondos o dinero en tu cuenta para cubrir los cheques.

Cada mes el banco te envía un estado de cuenta. Es necesario conciliar el saldo—es decir, verificar que el saldo que tiene el banco es el mismo saldo que tú tienes.

Guanajuato, México



## About the Spanish Language

**El banco** is a specific banking institution or building. **La banca** refers to the entire banking industry.

**Una cuenta de ahorros**

¿Te gusta ahorrar[1] dinero? Entonces puedes abrir una cuenta de ahorros. Ingresas dinero (haces un depósito) en la cuenta de ahorros y el banco te paga interés. Así va subiendo el saldo de tu cuenta y vas haciéndote más rico.

**Préstamos**

A veces es necesario pedir prestado[2] dinero. Es posible que quieras comprar un carro o una casa. Es posible que no tengas bastante dinero. El banco te hará un préstamo[3].

Una hipoteca es un préstamo para comprar una casa. Es un ejemplo de un préstamo a largo plazo[4]. Durante unos veinte o veinticinco años tendrás que hacer pagos. Cada pago incluye el interés que el banco te cobra[5]. La tasa de interés varía. Por ejemplo, la tasa de interés para un préstamo a corto plazo es generalmente más alta que la tasa de interés para un préstamo a largo plazo.

Hoy día puedes efectuar casi todas las funciones bancarias sin entrar en el banco. El banco te dará una tarjeta para el cajero automático. Introduces la tarjeta en el cajero automático y aparecen en la pantalla las instrucciones para cualquier función bancaria.

[1]ahorrar *to save*
[2]pedir prestado *to borrow*
[3]préstamo *loan*
[4]a largo plazo *long-term*
[5]cobra *charges*

Un cajero automático, España

## ¿Comprendes?

**Ahorros para el futuro** Escojan.

1. Roberto quiere tener dinero para el futuro. Debe abrir ____.
   **a.** una cuenta corriente **b.** una cuenta de ahorros **c.** un banco
2. Si Roberto quiere ahorrar mucho dinero, tendrá que ____.
   **a.** retirar mucho dinero **b.** ingresar muchos fondos **c.** cobrar muchos cheques
3. Roberto no paga siempre con dinero en efectivo o con tarjeta de crédito. Él paga con ____.
   **a.** billetes **b.** libretas **c.** cheques
4. Roberto no tiene más cheques. Necesita ____.
   **a.** otra cuenta **b.** otro talonario **c.** otro estado
5. No se puede escribir otro cheque si no hay ____ en la cuenta corriente.
   **a.** fondos **b.** cheques **c.** depósitos
6. Una hipoteca es un préstamo ____.
   **a.** para un carro **b.** a largo plazo **c.** a corto plazo



# Conexiones

## PRESENTATION

### *Las finanzas*
### La banca

**Step 1** You may have students who are interested in finance, accounting, or banking read this selection.

**Step 2** You may wish to have all students look at the vocabulary words presented here since they are quite useful.

### Career Connection

Banking is an industry where knowledge of Spanish can be essential. Have students write to one of the large banks in the area, asking about careers in international banking. Be sure to have them ask what courses are necessary to be qualified for the positions.

**LEVELING**

**E:** Reading
**A:** Reading

### Answers to ¿Comprendes?

1. b
2. b
3. c
4. b
5. a
6. b

# ¡Te toca a ti!

## Use what you have learned

### Recycling

These activities allow students to use the vocabulary and structure from this chapter in completely open-ended, real-life situations.

### PRESENTATION

Encourage students to say as much as possible when they do these activities. Tell them not to be afraid to make mistakes, since the goal of the activities is real-life communication. Let students choose the activities they would like to do.

You may wish to divide students into pairs or groups. Encourage students to elaborate on the basic theme and to be creative. They may use props, pictures, or posters if they wish.

### Writing Development

Have students keep a notebook or portfolio containing their best written work from each chapter. These selected writings can be based on assignments from the Student Textbook and the Workbook. Activities 5 and 6 on page 385 are examples of writing assignments that may be included in each student's portfolio. On page 150 in the Workbook, students will begin to develop an organized autobiography **(Mi autobiografía).** These workbook pages may also become a part of their portfolio.

### Learning from Photos

*(page 385)* **La Universidad de Chile** was founded in 1843. The statue in front of the building depicts the founder of the university, the Venezuelan intellectual giant of the nineteenth century, Andrés Bello.

# ¡Te toca a ti!

## Use what you have learned

HABLAR 1

### Planes para un viaje

✔ *Talk about all you have to do to get ready for a trip*

Trabaja con un(a) compañero(a). Dentro de poco los dos van a hacer un viaje. Hablen de todo lo que tienen que hacer antes de salir para el viaje.

HABLAR 2

### Quehaceres

✔ *Discuss those chores you like or don't like to do*

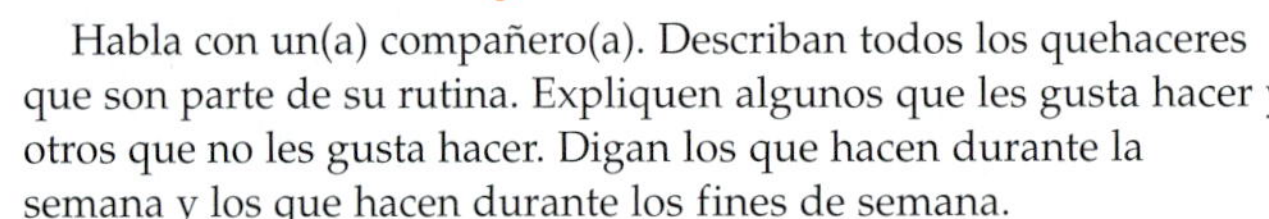

Habla con un(a) compañero(a). Describan todos los quehaceres que son parte de su rutina. Expliquen algunos que les gusta hacer y otros que no les gusta hacer. Digan los que hacen durante la semana y los que hacen durante los fines de semana.

HABLAR 3

### En la peluquería

✔ *Go to the hairdresser in a Spanish-speaking country*

Estás en una peluquería en México. Habla con el/la peluquero(a). Dile lo que necesitas y lo que quieres que él o ella haga.

Málaga, España



### ANSWERS TO ¡Te toca a ti!

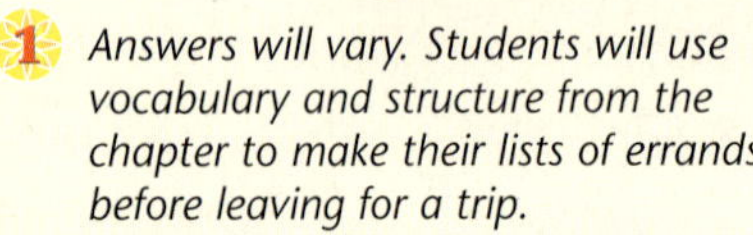

1 *Answers will vary. Students will use vocabulary and structure from the chapter to make their lists of errands before leaving for a trip.*

2 *Answers will vary. Students will use vocabulary from the chapter to discuss which chores they like to do and which ones they don't like.*

¡Te toca a ti!

## En la casa de correos

✔ *Use words and expressions related to postal services*

Estás viajando por España y quieres enviar unas tarjetas postales a tus amigos y parientes. Vas a la casa de correos donde hablas con el/la empleado(a) en la ventanilla (tu compañero[a]).

## Todo es fabuloso

✔ *Write to a friend telling what country you would like him or her to visit*

Estás viajando por un país hispano. Te encanta. Te gusta mucho. Quieres que un(a) amigo(a) venga a visitar el mismo país. Escríbele una carta diciéndole por qué te gusta tanto y por qué quieres que él o ella lo visite también. Luego dile todas las cosas que es posible o importante que él o ella haga durante su estadía *(stay)* en el país.

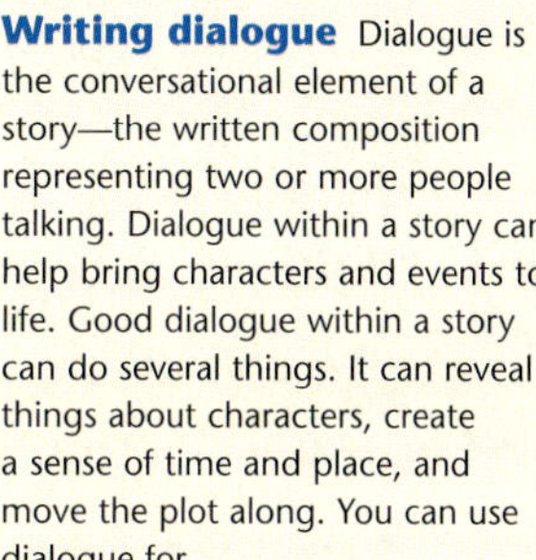

### Writing Strategy

**Writing dialogue** Dialogue is the conversational element of a story—the written composition representing two or more people talking. Dialogue within a story can help bring characters and events to life. Good dialogue within a story can do several things. It can reveal things about characters, create a sense of time and place, and move the plot along. You can use dialogue for these purposes and for many more.

## Un viaje con un(a) amigo(a)

You and a friend are going to Chile for a semester to study. Part of your credit for this coursework is writing about your entire trip, from beginning to end. This includes, of course, the planning stage as well. You are going to leave soon and your Spanish teacher would like you to submit a story about what it was like to prepare for this exciting upcoming adventure. Write about the meeting you and your friend had when you discussed everything you had to do to get ready. Use dialogue in your story to make it more lively. Be imaginative and creative.

Universidad de Chile



## PRACTICE

### Writing Strategy

**Writing dialogue**

Have students read the Writing Strategy on page 385. You may wish to have them work in pairs to do this activity.

## LEVELING

These activities encompass all three levels. All students will be able to do them at a sophistication level commensurate with their ability in Spanish. Some students will be able to speak for several minutes, and others may be able to give just a few sentences. This is to be expected when students are functioning completely on their own generating their own language to the best of their ability.

## ANSWERS TO ¡Te toca a ti!

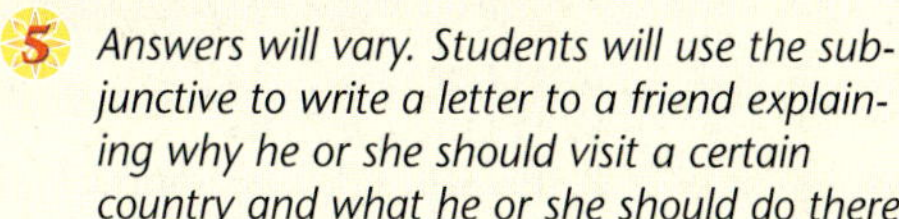

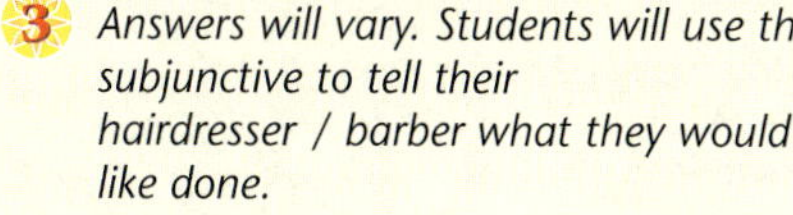

3 *Answers will vary. Students will use the subjunctive to tell their hairdresser / barber what they would like done.*

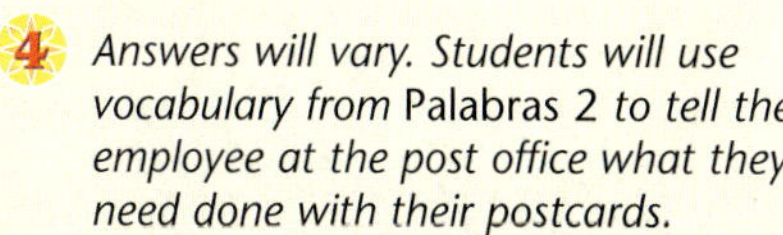

4 *Answers will vary. Students will use vocabulary from* Palabras 2 *to tell the employee at the post office what they need done with their postcards.*

5 *Answers will vary. Students will use the subjunctive to write a letter to a friend explaining why he or she should visit a certain country and what he or she should do there.*

6 *Answers will vary. Students will combine the vocabulary and structure from the chapter to write about their preparation for a trip to Chile. It is suggested that they include some dialogue in their paper.*

# Assessment

## Resource Manager

Communication Transparency C 12
Quizzes, pages 57–61
Performance Assessment, Task 12
Tests, pages 189–202
Situation Cards, Chapter 12
**Maratón mental** Videoquiz, Chapter 12
ExamView® Pro, Chapter 12

## Assessment

This is a pre-test for students to take before you administer the chapter test. Note that each section is cross-referenced so students can easily find the material they have to review in case they made errors. You may use Assessment Answers Transparency A 12 to do the assessment in class, or you may assign this assessment for homework. You can correct the assessment yourself, or you may prefer to project the answers on the overhead in class.

## Glencoe Technology

**MINDJOGGER VHS/DVD**

You may wish to help your students prepare for the chapter test by playing the MindJogger game show. Teams will compete against each other to review chapter vocabulary and structure and sharpen listening comprehension skills.

# Assessment

## Vocabulario

To review **Palabras 1**, turn to pages **360-361**.

### 1 Completen.

1. Cuando Juan necesita un corte de pelo, va a la ____.
2. El barbero le corta el pelo con una navaja o con ____.
3. Teresa quiere que la peluquera le lave el pelo. Quiere un ____.
4. Paco lava su ____ en la máquina de lavar.
5. Es necesario ____ el suéter porque es de lana.

### 2 Identifiquen.

To review **Palabras 2**, turn to pages **364-365**.

6. 

7. 

8. 

9. 

### 3 ¿Sí o no?

10. El dinero en efectivo es un cheque de viajero.
11. Es necesario tener una cuenta corriente en el banco para poder escribir un cheque.
12. El joven quiere cambio porque el cajero le da muchos billetes pequeños.



## Answers to Assessment

1. peluquería
2. tijeras
3. champú
4. ropa sucia
5. limpiar en seco

6. el buzón
7. la tarjeta postal
8. los sellos (las estampillas)
9. las monedas

10. No
11. Sí
12. No

# Estructura

**4 Completen.**

**13–14.** Los padres de Lucio quieren que él ____ mucho y que ____ mucha suerte. (escribir, tener)
**15–16.** El profesor insiste en que sus alumnos ____ puntuales y que ____ todas sus tareas. (ser, hacer)
**17.** Quiero que tú me lo ____. (decir)
**18.** Él prefiere que nosotros lo ____. (escribir)
**19.** Él tiene miedo de que yo no le ____. (hablar)

To review the subjunctive, turn to pages 368–369 and 371.

**5 Completen.**

**20.** Ustedes van. Es bueno que ____.
**21.** Cambiamos dinero. Es necesario que ____.
**22.** No tienes bastante dinero. Es posible que ____.

To review the subjunctive with impersonal expressions, turn to page 373.

# Cultura

**6 Identifiquen.**

**23.** dos ciudades famosas de Andalucía
**24.** un monumento famoso de los moros
**25.** las fechas de la ocupación mora en España

To review this cultural information, turn to pages 378–379.

JUNTA DE ANDALUCIA
CONSEJERIA DE CULTURA
PATRONATO DE LA ALHAMBRA Y GENERALIFE
Entrada al Conjunto Monumental de la Alhambra y Generalife
TARDE
VISITA GENERAL DIURNA. BILLETE DE TARDE.
HORARIO DE VISITA: 14:00 a 20:00
PERSONAS 3
FECHA: 05/08
TIPO DE ENTRADA: GENERAL — Entradas 3 — Precio 3€
TOTAL 3 3€
VISITA A LOS PALACIOS NAZARIES
HORA DE ENTRADA: 18:00 a 18:30
El acceso a los Palacios Nazaries sólo podrá realizarlo en la media hora indicada, de no hacerlo así perderá el derecho a la visita de los mismos.
116607



## Assessment

**FOLDABLES™ Study Organizer** Dinah Zike's Study Guides

Your students may wish to use Foldable 13 to organize, display, and arrange data as they review the vocabulary, verbs, and verb forms they know in Spanish. You may wish to encourage them to add information from each chapter as they continue to expand their vocabulary.

A *sentence strip holder* foldable is also ideal as students continue their study of Spanish and learn more and more words.

## Answers to Assessment

 **4**

**13.** escriba
**14.** tenga
**15.** sean
**16.** hagan
**17.** digas
**18.** escribamos
**19.** hable

**5**

**20.** vayan
**21.** cambiemos dinero
**22.** tengas bastante dinero

**6**

**23.** Córdoba, Granada, and Sevilla
**24.** la Mezquita, la Alhambra, and el Alcázar
**25.** 711–1492

# ¡Hablo como un pro!

This unique page gives students the opportunity to speak freely and say whatever they can, using the vocabulary and structures they have learned in the chapter. The illustration serves to remind students of precisely what they know how to say in Spanish. There are no activities that students do not have the ability to describe or talk about in Spanish. The art not only depicts the vocabulary and content of this chapter, but also reinforces what they learned in previous chapters.

You may wish to use this page in many ways. Some possibilities are to have students do the following:

1. Look at the illustration and identify items by giving the correct Spanish words.
2. Make up sentences about what they see in the illustration.
3. Make up questions about the illustration. They can call on another class member to respond if you do this as a class activity, or you may prefer to allow students to work in small groups. This activity is extremely beneficial because it enables students to actively use interrogative words.
4. Answer questions you ask them about the illustration.
5. Work in pairs and make up a conversation based on the illustration.
6. Look at the illustration and give a complete oral review of what they see.
7. Look at the illustration and write a paragraph (or essay) about it.

You can also use this page as an assessment or testing tool, taking into account individual differences by having students go from simple to quite complicated tasks. The assessment can be either oral or written. You may wish to use the rubrics provided on pages T20–T21 as you give students the following directions.

1. Identify the topic or situation of the illustration.
2. Give the Spanish words for as many items as you can.
3. Think of as many sentences as you can to describe the illustration.
4. Go over your sentences and put them in the best sequencing to give a coherent story based on the illustration.

# ¡Hablo como un pro!

Tell all you can about this illustration.

# Vocabulario

### Talking about the hairdresser

la peluquería
el/la peluquero(a), el barbero
el pelo, el cabello
un corte de pelo
el lado
la raya
la navaja
las tijeras
el secador
el champú
cortar
lavar
secar

### Talking about the dry cleaners

la tintorería
el/la tintorero(a)
la ropa sucia
el lavado
la máquina de lavar
de algodón
de lana
planchar
limpiar en seco

### Talking about the post office

el correo
el buzón
la ventanilla
la carta
el sobre
el sello, la estampilla
la tarjeta postal, la postal
el correo aéreo
el correo ordinario
pesar el paquete
echar la carta

### Talking about the bank

el/la cajero(a)
el dinero en efectivo
las monedas
los billetes
la cuenta corriente
el cheque de viajero
el suelto
endosar
firmar
cobrar

### Talking about changing currency

la casa de cambio
el/la cambista
el tipo (la tasa) de cambio
cambiar
estar a

**How well do you know your vocabulary?**

- Pick words from the list that relate to a chore you need to do.
- Write several sentences describing what chore you did.

**VIDEOTUR**

## Episodio 12

In this video episode, Claudia talks Francisco into getting his hair cut at a salon. See page 491 for more information.



# Vocabulario

## Vocabulary Review

The words and phrases in the **Vocabulario** have been taught for productive use in this chapter. They are summarized here as a resource for both student and teacher. This list also serves as a convenient resource for the **¡Te toca a ti!** activities on pages 384 and 385. There are two cognates in this vocabulary list. Have students find them.

**¡OJO!** You will notice that the vocabulary list here is not translated. This has been done intentionally, since we feel that by the time students have finished the material in the chapter they should be familiar with the meanings of all the words. If there are several words they still do not know, we recommend that they refer to the **Palabras 1** and **2** sections in the chapter or go to the dictionaries at the end of this book to find the meanings. However, if you prefer that your students have the English translations, please refer to Vocabulary Transparency 12.1, where you will find all these words with their translations.

**VIDEO VHS/DVD**

The Video Program allows students to see how the chapter vocabulary and structures are used by native speakers within an engaging story line. For maximum reinforcement, show the video episode as a final activity for Chapter 12.

# Planning for Chapter 13

## SCOPE AND SEQUENCE, PAGES 390–421

### Topics

- ❖ Birthdays
- ❖ Weddings
- ❖ Holidays

### Culture

- ❖ New Year's Eve at Puerta del Sol, Madrid
- ❖ How Angel and Monica came to be married
- ❖ The Freyssiner-Parada wedding: A newspaper account
- ❖ Spanish artists: Bartolomé Murillo and Diego Velázquez

### Functions

- ❖ How to talk about family celebrations
- ❖ How to discuss some important holidays
- ❖ How to tell what may or may not take place
- ❖ How to give advice and make suggestions
- ❖ How to express doubt or uncertainty
- ❖ How to express emotional reactions

### Structure

- ❖ Stem-changing verbs in the subjunctive
- ❖ The subjunctive with verbs such as **pedir** and **aconsejar**
- ❖ The subjunctive with expressions of doubt
- ❖ The subjunctive with expressions of emotion

### National Standards

- ❖ Communication Standard 1.1 pages 394, 395, 398, 399, 401, 402, 403, 404, 407, 409, 416
- ❖ Communication Standard 1.2 pages 395, 399, 403, 405, 407, 408, 409, 410–411, 412, 413, 414–415, 416
- ❖ Communication Standard 1.3 pages 399, 415, 417
- ❖ Cultures Standard 2.1 pages 410–411, 412, 413
- ❖ Connections Standard 3.1 pages 414–415
- ❖ Comparisons Standard 4.2 pages 412, 417
- ❖ Communities Standard 5.1 page 421
- ❖ Communities Standard 5.2 page 399

## PACING AND PRIORITIES

**The chapter content is color coded below to assist you in planning.**

**■ required ■ recommended ■ optional**

**Vocabulario** *(required)* *Days 1–4*

- ■ Palabras 1
  - El cumpleaños
  - La boda
- ■ Palabras 2
  - Navidad
  - Año Nuevo
  - Los Reyes Magos
  - Hanuka

**Estructura** *(required)* *Days 5–7*

- ■ El subjuntivo de los verbos de cambio radical
- ■ El subjuntivo con verbos como **pedir** y **aconsejar**
- ■ El subjuntivo con expresiones de duda
- ■ El subjuntivo con expresiones de emoción

**Conversación** *(required)*

- ■ Año Nuevo

**Lecturas culturales**

- ■ Las doce uvas de la felicidad *(recommended)*
- ■ La boda *(optional)*
- ■ Freyssiner-Parada *(optional)*

**Conexiones**

- ■ Las artes plásticas *(optional)*

■ **¡Te toca a ti!** *(recommended)*

■ **Assessment** *(recommended)*

■ **¡Hablo como un pro!** *(optional)*

## RESOURCE GUIDE

| SECTION | PAGES | SECTION RESOURCES |
|---|---|---|
| **Vocabulario PALABRAS 1** | | |
| El cumpleaños<br>La boda | 392, 394–395<br>393, 394–395 | Vocabulary Transparencies 13.2–13.3<br>Audio CD 8<br>Audio Activities TE, pages 157–158<br>Workbook, pages 153–154<br>Quiz 1, page 63<br>ExamView® Pro |
| **Vocabulario PALABRAS 2** | | |
| Navidad<br>Año Nuevo<br>Los Reyes Magos<br>Hanuka | 396, 398–399<br>396, 398–399<br>397, 398–399<br>397, 398–399 | Vocabulary Transparencies 13.4–13.5<br>Audio CD 8<br>Audio Activities TE, pages 159–161<br>Workbook, pages 155–156<br>Quiz 2, page 64<br>ExamView® Pro |
| **Estructura** | | |
| El subjuntivo de los verbos de cambio radical<br>El subjuntivo con verbos como **pedir** y **aconsejar**<br>El subjuntivo con expresiones de duda<br>El subjuntivo con expresiones de emoción | 400–401<br>402–403<br>404–405<br>406–407 | Audio CD 8<br>Audio Activities TE, pages 162–164<br>Workbook, pages 157–161<br>Quizzes 3–6, pages 65–68<br>ExamView® Pro |
| **Conversación** | | |
| Año Nuevo | 408–409 | Audio CD 8<br>Audio Activities TE, page 165<br>Interactive CD-ROM |
| **Lecturas culturales** | | |
| Las doce uvas de la felicidad<br>La boda<br>Freyssiner-Parada | 410–411<br>412<br>413 | Audio CD 8<br>Audio Activities TE, page 166<br>Tests, pages 205, 209 |
| **Conexiones** | | |
| Las artes plásticas | 414–415 | Tests, page 210 |
| **¡Te toca a ti!** | | |
| | 416–417 | **¡Viva el mundo hispano!** Video, Episode 13<br>Video Activities, pages 113–117<br>Spanish Online Activities spanish.glencoe.com |
| **Assessment** | | |
| | 418–419 | Communication Transparency C 13<br>Quizzes 1–6, pages 63–68<br>Performance Assessment, Task 13<br>Tests, pages 203–218<br>Situation Cards, Chapter 13<br>ExamView® Pro<br>**Maratón mental** Videoquiz |

# Using Your Resources for Chapter 13

## Transparencies

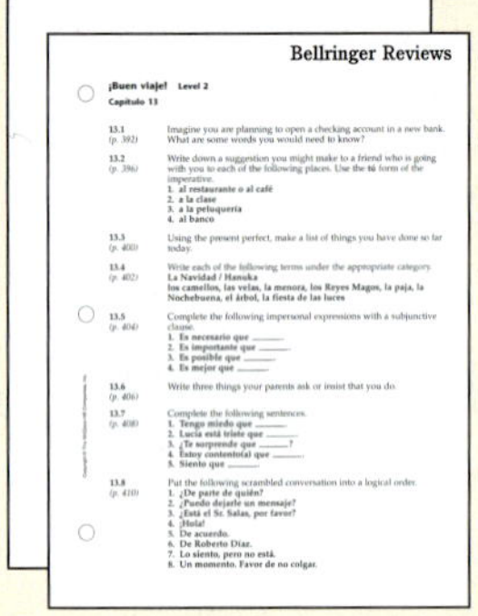
Bellringer 13.1–13.8

Vocabulary 13.1–13.5

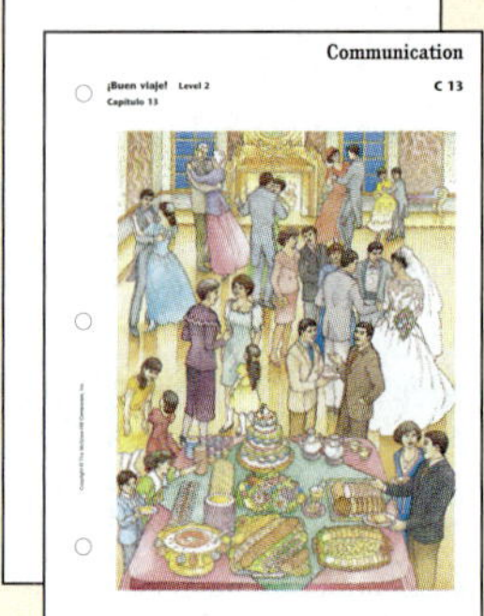
Communication C 13

## Workbook

Vocabulary, pages 153–156

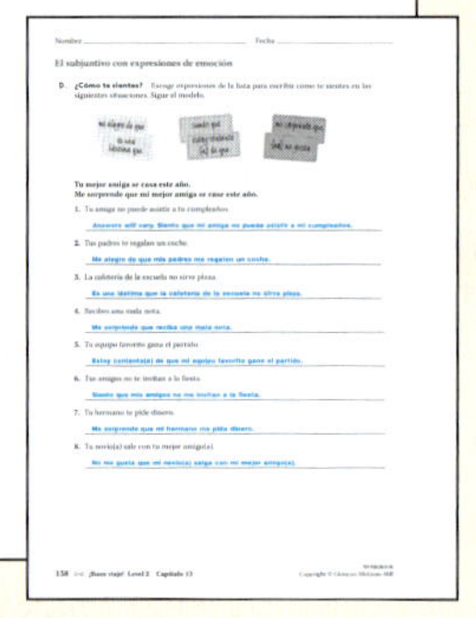
Structure, pages 157–161

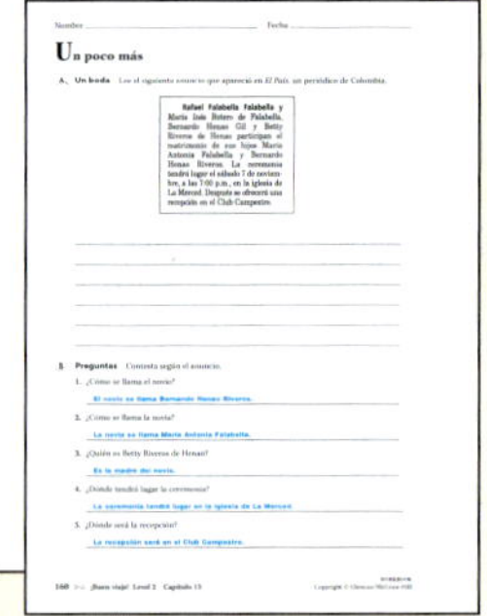
Enrichment, pages 162–164

## Audio Activities

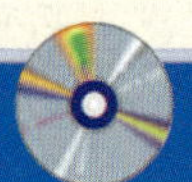

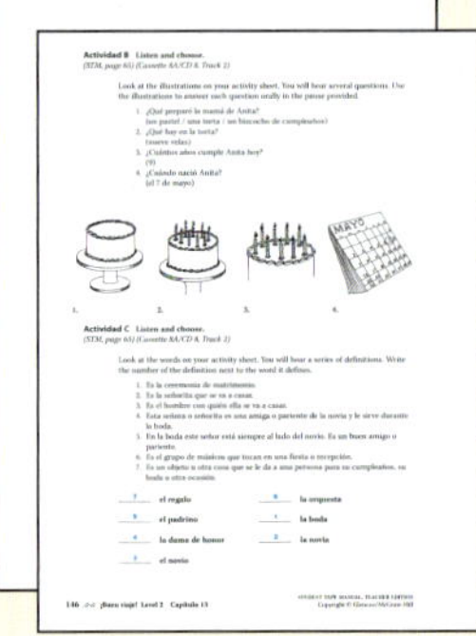
Vocabulary, pages 157–161

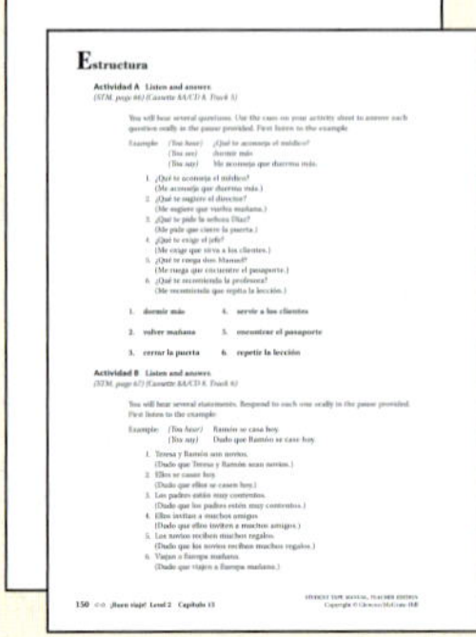
Structure, pages 162–164

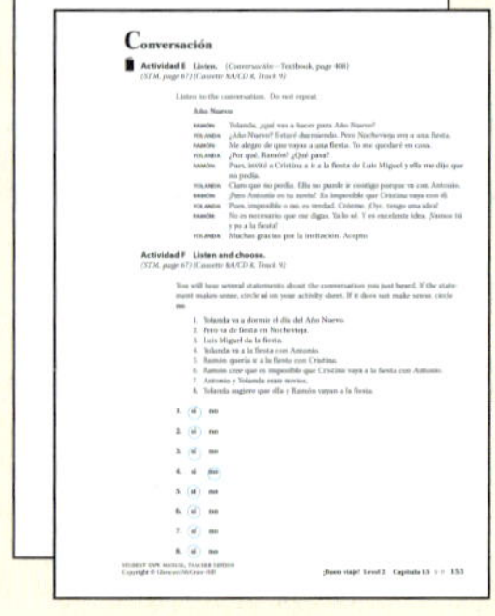
Conversation, page 165

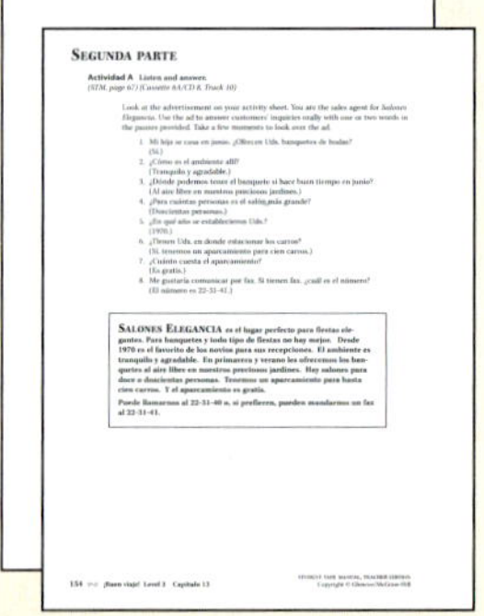
Additional Practice, pages 167–169

# Assessment

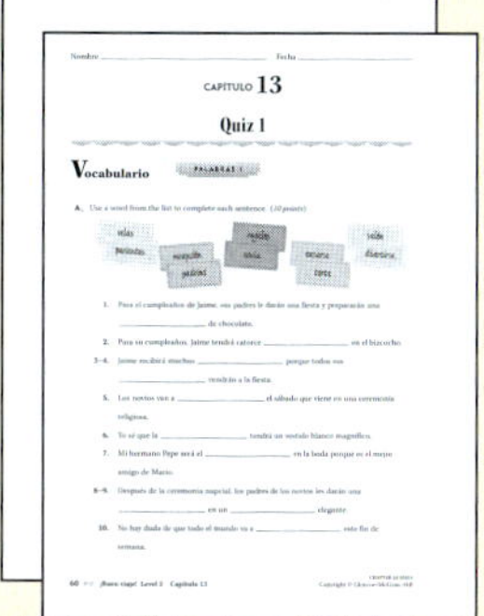

Vocabulary and Structure Quizzes, pages 63–68

Chapter Tests, pages 203–218

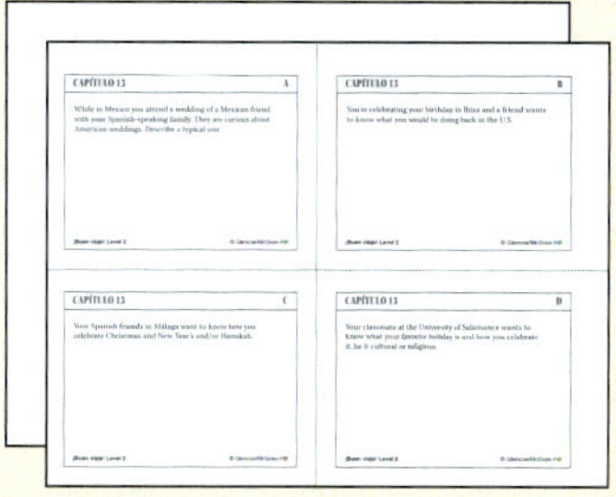

Situation Cards, Chapter 13

MindJogger Videoquiz, ExamView® Pro, Chapter 13

## Timesaving Teacher Tools

### TeacherWorks™

TeacherWorks™ is your all-in-one teacher resource center. Personalize lesson plans, access resources from the Teacher Wraparound Edition, connect to the Internet, or make a to-do list. These are only a few of the many features that can assist you in the planning and organizing of your lessons.

Includes:

- A calendar feature
- Access to all program blackline masters
- Standards correlations and more

### ExamView® Pro

Test Bank software for Macintosh and Windows makes creating, editing, customizing, and printing tests quick and easy.

## Technology Resources

In the Chapter 13 Internet Activity, you will have a chance to learn more about the Spanish-speaking world. Visit spanish.glencoe.com

On the interactive CD–ROM, students can listen to and take part in a recorded version of the conversation in Chapter 13.

**¡Viva el mundo hispano!** Video and Video Activities, Chapter 13. Available on VHS and DVD.

Help your students prepare for the chapter test by playing the **Maratón mental** Videoquiz game show. Teams will compete against each other to review chapter vocabulary and structure and sharpen listening comprehension skills. Available on VHS and DVD.

**¡Buen viaje!** is also available on CD or Online.

## Preview

In this chapter, students will learn how to talk about parties, weddings, and holidays. They will also expand their knowledge of the use of the subjunctive to express actions that may or may not happen, to give advice and offer suggestions, and to express doubt or uncertainty as well as emotional reactions to what others do. The cultural focus of the chapter is on family, social events, and significant holidays in the Hispanic world.

### National Standards

**Communication**

In Chapter 13 students will learn to communicate in spoken and written Spanish on the following topics:

- family social events
- weddings
- holiday customs

Students will obtain and provide information about these topics, express feelings, and engage in conversations that would typically take place at celebrations or on important holidays as they fulfill the chapter objectives listed on this page.

# Capítulo 13

# ¡Fiestas!

### Objetivos

**In this chapter you will learn to:**

- describe and talk about parties and weddings
- talk about some holidays
- give advice and make recommendations
- express doubt, uncertainty, or disbelief
- express emotional reactions to what others do
- talk about New Year's Eve in the Hispanic world

Alfredo Ramos Martínez *Casamiento indio*

## Spotlight on Culture

**Fotografía** The wedding is being performed at a lovely old church in Buenos Aires, Argentina. **Los novios** and **la comitiva** are arrayed before the altar. **La comitiva** consists of the **padrinos, el padrino y la madrina,** and any number of **damas** and ushers. **El sacerdote** or **cura** faces the members of the wedding party and officiates at the ceremony.

## LEVELING

The activities, conversations, and readings within each chapter are marked according to level of difficulty. **E** indicates easy. **A** indicates average. **C** indicates challenging. Some activities cover a range of difficulty. In some activities, for example, advanced students will be able to produce more extensive responses while students who learn at a different rate may give less detailed responses. The leveling indicators will help you individualize instruction to best meet your students' needs.

PALABRAS 1

# 1 PREPARATION

## Resource Manager

Vocabulary Transparencies 13.2–13.3
Audio Activities TE, pages 157–158
Audio CD 8
Workbook, pages 153–154
Quizzes, page 63
ExamView® Pro

## Bellringer Review

*Use BRR Transparency 13.1 or write the following on the board.*
Imagine you are planning to open a checking account in a new bank. What are some words you would need to know?

## National Standards

**Comparisons**
Students will compare traditional celebrations in their culture with those in Hispanic cultures.

While most families celebrate a person's **cumpleaños** or *birthday,* many traditional families still celebrate the **santo,** the person's *name day* or *saint's day.* There is a saint for every day of the year. For example, every José and Josefina celebrates his or her **santo** on March 19.

# Vocabulario

PALABRAS 1

## El cumpleaños

Anita nació el ocho de abril.
Su familia y sus amigos celebran su cumpleaños con una fiesta.
No hay duda que todos se divierten.
Anita se alegra de que todos sus parientes vengan a la fiesta.



## Reaching All Students

**Total Physical Response** Dramatize the meaning of **encender** and **apagar** before beginning.

*(Student 1),* **ven acá, por favor.**
**Es tu fiesta de cumpleaños hoy.**
**Pon las velas en la torta.**
**Enciende las velas.**
**Apaga las velas.**
**Ahora, come la torta.**
**Baila con tus amigos. ¡Diviértete!**
**Gracias,** *(Student 1).* **Bien hecho. Puedes volver a tu asiento.**

## La boda

Los novios acaban de casarse.
La recepción es en un salón elegante.
Los novios reciben muchos regalos.

Vocabulario

## 2 PRESENTATION

**Step 1** Have students close their books. Project Vocabulary Transparencies 13.2–13.3 and have students repeat the new words, phrases, and sentences after you or Audio CD 8.

**Step 2** Have students open their books and read the new vocabulary for additional reinforcement.

### Recycling

Remind students that they have already learned the word **padrino,** but its meaning was quite different. Ask them: **¿Quién es el padrino? «El padrino asiste al bebé durante el bautizo.»** Ask them the meaning of **padrino** in the context in which it is used in this chapter.

### FUN FACTS

Calendars in the Hispanic world usually have *Monday,* **lunes,** as the first day of the week.

### Chapter Projects

**Una boda** Have students prepare a wedding invitation or a wedding announcement in Spanish.

**¡Saludos!** Students can send electronic greeting cards in Spanish for various holidays from the Glencoe Spanish Web site (spanish.glencoe.com).

**LEVELING**

**A:** Vocabulary

## 3 PRACTICE

## ¿Qué palabra necesito?

**¡OJO!** When students are doing the **¿Que palabra necesito?** activities, accept any answer that makes sense. The purpose of these activities is to have students use the new vocabulary. They are not factual recall activities. Thus, it is not necessary for students to remember specific factual information from the vocabulary presentation when answering. If you wish, have students use the photo on this page as a stimulus, when possible.

**Historieta** Each time **Historieta** appears, it means that the answers to the activity form a short story. Encourage students to look at the title of the **Historieta,** since it can help them do the activity.

**¡OJO!** It is recommended that you go over all the activities in class before assigning them for homework.

**1** Activity 1 can be done as an interview. One student asks the questions and the other responds.

**1 and 2** After going over these activities orally, have students write the answers for homework.

**Expansion:** Call on students to give a summary in their own words about the stories in Activities 1 and 2.

### Writing Development

Have students write the answers to Activity 2 in a unified paragraph.



## ¿Qué palabra necesito?

### 1 Historieta Una fiesta

Contesten personalmente.

1. ¿Cuándo es tu cumpleaños?
2. ¿Cuándo naciste?
3. ¿Te preparan una torta para tu cumpleaños?
4. ¿Qué clase de torta te gusta?
5. ¿Cuántas velas tendrás en tu próxima torta?
6. ¿Te dan una fiesta para tu cumpleaños?
7. ¿Quiénes asisten a la fiesta?
8. ¿Recibes muchos regalos?
9. ¿Qué hacen ustedes en la fiesta?
10. ¿Qué regalo te gustaría recibir para tu próximo cumpleaños?

*Que el día de tu cumpleaños*
*Celebres con alegría*
*Y que tu vida esté siempre*
*Llena de dicha, Hija mía.*

*Que Seas Muy*
*Feliz Siempre*

Madrid, España

### 2 Historieta La boda

Contesten. Inventen una historia.

1. ¿Acaba de casarse la pareja?
2. ¿La mujer vestida de blanco es la dama de honor o la novia?
3. ¿Los novios dan o reciben regalos?
4. ¿Van a dar una recepción?
5. ¿La música será de CDs o de una orquesta?
6. ¿Dónde van a pasar los novios su luna de miel?



## Answers to ¿Qué palabra necesito?

**1**

1. Mi cumpleaños es el ___.
2. Nací el ___.
3. Sí, (No, no) me preparan una torta para mi cumpleaños.
4. Me gusta la torta de ___.
5. En mi próxima torta tendré ___ velas.
6. Sí, (No, no) me dan una fiesta para mi cumpleaños.
7. Mis amigos y mis parientes asisten a la fiesta.
8. Sí, (No, no) recibo muchos regalos.
9. En la fiesta nosotros comemos, bebemos y bailamos (nos divertimos).
10. Para mi próximo cumpleaños me gustaría recibir ___.

**2**

1. Sí, la pareja acaba de casarse.
2. La mujer vestida de blanco es la novia.
3. Los novios reciben regalos.
4. Sí, (No, no) van a dar una recepción.
5. La música será de una orquesta (de CDs).
6. Los novios van a pasar su luna de miel en ___.

**3** **Preguntas personales** Contesten.

1. ¿Has asistido a una boda alguna vez? ¿Quiénes se casaron?
2. ¿Cómo era la ropa de la novia?
3. ¿La ceremonia fue religiosa o civil?
4. ¿Quiénes fueron el padrino y la dama de honor?
5. ¿Fuiste a la recepción?
6. ¿Dónde tuvieron la recepción?
7. ¿Qué hiciste en la recepción?

Una boda, España

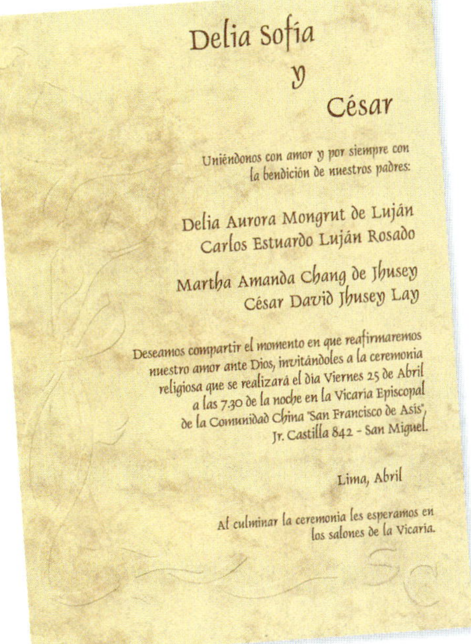

Delia Sofía
y
César

Uniéndonos con amor y por siempre con la bendición de nuestros padres:

Delia Aurora Mongrut de Luján
Carlos Estuardo Luján Rosado

Martha Amanda Chang de Jhusey
César David Jhusey Lay

Deseamos compartir el momento en que reafirmaremos nuestro amor ante Dios, invitándoles a la ceremonia religiosa que se realizará el día Viernes 25 de Abril a las 7.30 de la noche en la Vicaria Episcopal de la Comunidad China "San Francisco de Asís", Jr. Castilla 842 - San Miguel.

Lima, Abril

Al culminar la ceremonia les esperamos en los salones de la Vicaria.

**4** **Una boda** Trabaja con un(a) compañero(a). Cada uno(a) de ustedes va a describir una boda a la que ha asistido. Luego comparen las dos bodas. ¿Había algunas diferencias entre las dos? ¿Cuáles eran las diferencias?

**5** **Fiestas de cumpleaños** A muchas personas les gusta mucho tener fiestas en su honor. A otras no les gusta. Trabaja con un(a) compañero(a). Dile si a ti te gustan las fiestas en tu honor o no. Explica por qué. Luego tu compañero(a) te dará sus opiniones. ¿Están de acuerdo o no?

**3** Students can do Activity 3 on their own and then read their answers aloud to the class.

**¡OJO!** Note that the activities are color-coded. All the activities in the text are communicative. However, the ones with blue titles are guided communication. The red titles indicate that the answers to the activity are more open-ended and can vary more. You may wish to correct students' mistakes more so in the guided activities than in the activities with a red title, which lend themselves to a freer response.

### Learning from Realia

*(page 395)* Ask questions about the wedding invitation such as:

**¿Para qué ocasión es la tarjeta?**

**¿Quiénes son Delia Sofía y César?**

### LEVELING

**E:** Activities 1, 2, 4

**A:** Activities 1, 3, 4, 5

## Answers to ¿Qué palabra necesito?

**3** *Answers will vary but may include:*

1. Sí, (No, no) he asistido a una boda. ___ se casaron.
2. La ropa de la novia era ___.
3. La ceremonia fue religiosa (civil).
4. El padrino fue ___ y la dama de honor fue ___.
5. Sí, (No, no) fui a la recepción.
6. Tuvieron la recepción en ___.
7. En la recepción yo ___.

**4** *Answers will vary. Students should use vocabulary related to weddings to describe their experiences.*

**5** *Answers will vary. Students should use vocabulary relating to parties to describe why they do or do not like parties given in their honor.*

# Vocabulario

PALABRAS 2

## 1 PREPARATION

### Resource Manager

Vocabulary Transparencies 13.4–13.5
Audio Activities TE, pages 159–161
Audio CD 8
Workbook, pages 155–156
Quizzes, page 64
ExamView® Pro

### Bellringer Review

*Use BRR Transparency 13.2 or write the following on the board.*
Write down a suggestion you might make to a friend who is going with you to each of the following places. Use the **tú** form of the imperative.

1. **al restaurante o al café**
2. **a la clase**
3. **a la peluquería**
4. **al banco**

## 2 PRESENTATION

**Step 1** Have students close their books. Model the **Palabras 2** vocabulary using Vocabulary Transparencies 13.4–13.5. Have students repeat the new material two or three times after you or Audio CD 8.

**Step 2** As you present the new vocabulary ask questions such as:
**¿Cuándo es la Navidad?**
**¿Qué tiene la familia en la sala para Navidad?**
**¿Hay regalos debajo del árbol?**
**¿Qué es Hanuka?**
**¿Quién enciende las velas de la menora?**



# Vocabulario

PALABRAS 2

## Navidad

La Navidad es el veinticinco de diciembre.

**Diciembre**

| L | M | M | J | V | S | D |
|---|---|---|---|---|---|---|
| | 1 | 2 | 3 | 4 | 5 | 6 |
| 7 | 8 | 9 | 10 | 11 | 12 | 13 |
| 14 | 15 | 16 | 17 | 18 | 19 | 20 |
| 21 | 22 | 23 | 24 | 25 | 26 | 27 |
| 28 | 29 | 30 | 31 | | | |

Nochebuena es el veinticuatro de diciembre.

## Año Nuevo

La víspera de Año Nuevo (Nochevieja) es el treinta y uno de diciembre.
La gente celebra cuando el reloj da las doce.

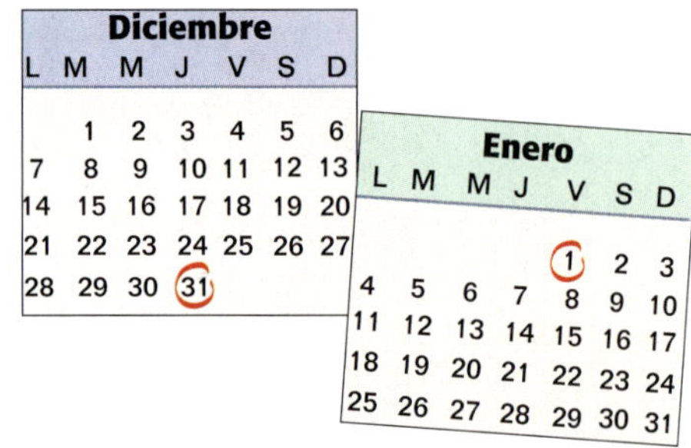


Año Nuevo es el primero de enero, el primer día del año.

## Los Reyes Magos

El seis de enero es el Día de los Reyes.
Los padres les dicen a los niños que pongan paja para los camellos en sus zapatos.
Los niños esperan que los Reyes les traigan regalos.

## Hanuka

Hanuka es la fiesta de las luces.
Es una fiesta hebrea. La fiesta dura ocho días.
Durante la fiesta le piden al hijo mayor que encienda las velas de la menora.
La menora tiene nueve brazos.





### FUN FACTS

Hispanic children know the names of each of the Three Wise Men: Gaspar, Melchor, and Baltasar. Tradition has it that the Wise Men brought the baby Jesus gifts of gold **(oro),** frankincense **(olíbano),** and myrrh **(mirra).** Parents will often be very imaginative in creating the impression that the Wise Men and their animals have visited. They remove the straw from the shoes and leave signs leading to where gifts may be. Many families in Mexico give children toys and playthings on Christmas **(la Navidad)** and practical gifts, such as clothing, on January 6 **(el Día de los Reyes).**

Even though most Spanish-speaking countries are predominately Catholic, there are sizable Jewish populations in several countries in Latin America, particularly in Mexico, Panama, and Argentina.

### Vocabulary Expansion

You may wish to give students the names of a few Christmas carols in Spanish:

| | |
|---|---|
| **Noche de Paz** | *Silent Night* |
| **Navidad** | *Deck the Halls* |
| **Paz en la Tierra** | *Joy to the World* |

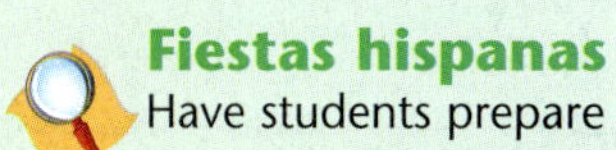

### Chapter Projects

**Fiestas hispanas** Have students prepare a report on either **el dos de noviembre** or **el seis de enero.**

**Feliz Navidad** Have students select a holiday that is celebrated in the Spanish-speaking world and the United States. Ask them to prepare a report comparing and contrasting the ways in which the holiday is celebrated in the two different cultures.

# Vocabulario

## 3 PRACTICE

## ¿Qué palabra necesito?

**6** Have students refer to the illustrations while doing Activity 6.

**7** Activity 7 can be done first orally with books closed. **Expansion:** Have a student retell all the information from Activity 7 in his or her own words.

### Writing Development

Have students write the answers to Activity 7 in a unified paragraph.

### National Standards

**Comparisons**

Students will compare traditional holiday customs in their culture with those in Hispanic cultures. Service workers of all kinds expect an **aguinaldo** *(a money gift)* at Christmastime. People receive Christmas greetings from the plumber, the mail carrier, the trash collector, etc. An envelope with **un aguinaldo** is expected in return. Ask students if they have ever heard of Boxing Day in Great Britain, Canada, and other Commonwealth countries. It's the day after Christmas and the day service workers there get their gifts.

UN POCO MÁS This *InfoGap* Activity will allow students to practice in pairs. The activity should be very manageable for them, since all vocabulary and structures are familiar to them.

Vocabulario

## ¿Qué palabra necesito?

**6** **¿Qué celebran?** Identifiquen según se indica.

1.

2.

3.

4.

5.

**7** **Historieta Los regalos** Contesten.

1. En Estados Unidos, ¿quién les trae regalos a los niños, San Nicolás o los Reyes?
2. ¿Quiénes traen regalos a los niños hispanos?
3. ¿Qué decoran para Navidad las familias norteamericanas?
4. ¿Cuándo reciben sus regalos los niños norteamericanos?
5. ¿Cuándo reciben sus regalos los niños hispanos?
6. ¿Para quiénes es la paja en los zapatos?
7. ¿Quiénes les dicen a los niños que pongan la paja en sus zapatos?
8. ¿Están contentos los niños que los Reyes les traigan regalos?

Paja para los camellos

*For more practice using words from **Palabras 1** and **2**, do Activity 13 on page H14 at the end of this book.*



### ANSWERS TO ¿Qué palabra necesito?

**6**

1. Es Hanuka.
2. Es un cumpleaños.
3. Es una boda.
4. Es la Navidad.
5. Es el Día de los Reyes.

**7**

1. En Estados Unidos San Nicolás les trae regalos a los niños.
2. Los Reyes (Magos) les traen regalos a los niños hispanos.
3. Las familias norteamericanas decoran el árbol de Navidad para Navidad.
4. Los niños norteamericanos reciben sus regalos el veinticinco de diciembre.
5. Los niños hispanos reciben sus regalos el seis de enero, el Día de los Reyes.
6. La paja en los zapatos es para los camellos.
7. Los padres les dicen a los niños que pongan la paja en sus zapatos.
8. Sí, los niños están contentos que los Reyes les traigan regalos.

**8** **Algunas tradiciones** Completen.

1. La «fiesta de las luces» se llama ____.
2. La menora lleva ____ brazos.
3. En cada brazo hay una ____.
4. La persona que enciende las velas es el ____.
5. Esta fiesta dura ____ días.

Girona, España

**9** **Una fiesta de invierno** El/La alumno(a) de intercambio (tu compañero[a]) quiere saber qué fiesta celebra tu familia en el invierno y cómo la celebran. Descríbele las costumbres y tradiciones de tu familia para Navidad, Hanuka, Kwanza o cualquier otra fiesta de invierno. Después cambien de rol.

**10** **Entrevista** Si es posible, busca en tu comunidad a una persona mayor hispana. Prepara una entrevista con esta persona sobre las costumbres de Navidad o Reyes en su país. Luego prepara un reportaje y preséntalo a la clase.

**SPANISH Online**

For more information about winter holidays celebrated throughout the Spanish-speaking world, go to the Glencoe Spanish Web site: spanish.glencoe.com



Vocabulario

## Writing Development

After going over Activity 8 in class, have students write a paragraph about **Hanuka** in their own words.

## SPANISH Online

The Glencoe Spanish Web site **(spanish.glencoe.com)** offers options that enable you and your students to experience the Spanish-speaking world via the Internet. For each **Capítulo,** there are activities, games, and quizzes. In addition, an *Enrichment* section offers students an opportunity to visit Web sites related to the theme of the chapter.

## LEVELING

**E:** Activities 6, 7, 8, 9

**A:** Activities 7, 8, 10

## Answers to ¿Qué palabra necesito?

**8**

1. Hanuka
2. nueve
3. vela
4. hijo mayor
5. ocho

**9** *Answers will vary. Students should use the vocabulary presented inthis chapter to describe their family traditions.*

**10** *Answers will vary. Students should use vocabulary presented in* Palabras 2 *to prepare interview questions.*

## Learning from Photos

*(page 399)* Have students tell what holiday these people are celebrating and tell as much about the holiday **(Hanuka)** as they can.

# Estructura

## 1 PREPARATION

### Resource Manager

Audio Activities TE, pages 162–164
Audio CD 8
Workbook, pages 157–161
Quizzes, pages 65–68
ExamView® Pro

### Bellringer Review

*Use BRR Transparency 13.3 or write the following on the board.*
Using the present perfect, make a list of things you have done so far today.

## 2 PRESENTATION

### El subjuntivo de los verbos de cambio radical

**Step 1** Have students open their books to page 400 and lead them through Items 1–2.

**Step 2** Write the forms of one or two of the verbs on the board.

**Step 3** Have students repeat the verb forms.

**Step 4** With books closed, call on volunteers to write conjugations of other verbs, following the model(s) which you have provided. Have the class repeat these forms.

# Estructura

## El subjuntivo de los verbos de cambio radical
### Telling what may or may not take place

**1.** Verbs that have a stem change in the present indicative also have a stem change in the present subjunctive.

| | E → IE | | O → UE | |
|---|---|---|---|---|
| INFINITIVE | cerrar | perder | encontrar | poder |
| yo | cierre | pierda | encuentre | pueda |
| tú | cierres | pierdas | encuentres | puedas |
| él, ella, Ud. | cierre | pierda | encuentre | pueda |
| nosotros(as) | cerremos | perdamos | encontremos | podamos |
| *vosotros(as)* | *cerréis* | *perdáis* | *encontréis* | *podáis* |
| ellos, ellas, Uds. | cierren | pierdan | encuentren | puedan |

Other verbs with the **e → ie** stem change like **cerrar** are:

**sentarse, comenzar, empezar, pensar**

Other **o → ue** verbs like **encontrar** are:

**acostarse, recordar, volver**

**2.** The verbs **sentir (e → ie), dormir (o → ue),** and **pedir (e → i)** have a stem change in every person of the present subjunctive.

| | E → IE | O → UE | E → I |
|---|---|---|---|
| INFINITIVE | sentir | dormir | pedir |
| yo | sienta | duerma | pida |
| tú | sientas | duermas | pidas |
| él, ella, Ud. | sienta | duerma | pida |
| nosotros(as) | sintamos | durmamos | pidamos |
| *vosotros(as)* | *sintáis* | *durmáis* | *pidáis* |
| ellos, ellas, Uds. | sientan | duerman | pidan |

Other verbs with the **e → i** stem change like **pedir** are:

**repetir, freír, seguir, servir**

# ¿Cómo lo digo?

**11 Historieta Yo quiero.** Sigan el modelo.

**Él vuelve pronto. ⟶**
**Yo quiero que él vuelva pronto.**

1. Él vuelve mañana.
2. Él nos encuentra en el restaurante.
3. Él se sienta a nuestra mesa.
4. Él pide algo bueno.
5. Él me recomienda un plato.
6. El mesero nos sirve atentamente.

RESTAURANT
de: José Antonio Lema Molina
Plaza Avaroa · Telf. 328892
FACTURA
Válido para Crédito Fiscal
Nº 147080
Orden No. 6361005
Original Cliente

Ronda, España

**12 Historieta Necesitamos a Luis.** Completen.

Espero que Luis __1__ (volver) mañana. Quiero que él __2__ (encontrar) un vuelo temprano. Esperamos que él __3__ (poder) llegar por la mañana. Es posible que el partido __4__ (comenzar) a las dos de la tarde. Para nosotros, es mejor que el partido __5__ (empezar) más tarde. Temo que Luis no __6__ (poder) jugar si llega tarde. Y sin Luis, es probable que nosotros __7__ (perder) el partido.



## Estructura

### 3 PRACTICE

## ¿Cómo lo digo?

**11** Go over this activity first orally with books closed.
**Expansion:** Call on a student to retell in his or her own words what he or she wants a friend to do at a restaurant, based on the information in Activity 11.

**12** Have students prepare this activity before going over it in class.

### Writing Development

After going over Activity 12 orally, have students rewrite the story in their own words.

### Learning from Realia

*(page 401)* You may wish to ask students:
**¿Para qué es la factura?**
**¿Quién recibe el original de la factura?**
**¿Cuánto fue el total de la cuenta?**

## Answers to ¿Cómo lo digo?

**11**

1. Yo quiero que él vuelva mañana.
2. Yo quiero que él nos encuentre en el restaurante.
3. Yo quiero que él se siente a nuestra mesa.
4. Yo quiero que él pida algo bueno.
5. Yo quiero que él me recomiende un plato.
6. Yo quiero que el mesero nos sirva atentamente.

**12**

1. vuelva
2. encuentre
3. pueda
4. comience
5. empiece
6. pueda
7. perdamos

Estructura

# 1 PREPARATION

## Bellringer Review

*Use BRR Transparency 13.4 or write the following on the board.*
Write each of the following terms under the appropriate category.
**La Navidad / Hanuka**
**los camellos, las velas, la menora, los Reyes Magos, la paja, la Nochebuena, el árbol, la fiesta de las luces**

# 2 PRESENTATION

## El subjuntivo con verbos como **pedir** y **aconsejar**

**Step 1** Have students open their books to page 402 and lead them through Items 1–3.

**Step 2** Have students repeat the model sentences after you.

**Step 3** Emphasize that we use the subjunctive because we do not know if the action of the verb will take place or not.

# 3 PRACTICE

## ¿Cómo lo digo?

13 You may wish to have students prepare Activity 13 before going over it in class.
**Expansion:** Have students do the activity again with **Mi mamá me pide que...**

Estructura

# El subjuntivo con verbos como **pedir** y **aconsejar**
## Giving advice and making suggestions

1. The subjunctive is used with the following verbs because even though you may advise, recommend, suggest, ask, or order someone to do something, he or she may not do it.

| | |
|---|---|
| **pedir** *to ask* | **rogar** *to beg, to plead* |
| **aconsejar** *to advise* | **exigir** *to demand* |
| **sugerir** *to suggest* | |

**Él pide que yo vaya.**
**Y yo le aconsejo que se quede aquí.**
**Mamá nos sugiere que salgamos ahora.**

2. An indirect object pronoun often goes with these verbs. The pronoun serves as the subject of the dependent clause.

**Él me pide que (yo) sirva de padrino.**
**Les ruego que (ustedes) no se casen en junio porque no voy a estar.**

3. The verbs **decir** and **escribir** call for the subjunctive only when they imply a command or request, such as: "He writes me to come right away."

**Ellos me dicen que no me case.**
**Yo le escribo que venga pronto.**

## ¿Cómo lo digo?

### 13 Mamá te pide que...

Completen según el modelo.

**limpiar tu cuarto →**
**Mamá te pide que limpies tu cuarto.**

1. levantarte temprano
2. limpiar tu cuarto
3. bañarte
4. tomar el desayuno
5. no jugar hoy
6. dormir bastante
7. volver a casa en el bus

Coyoacán, México



## Learning from Realia

*(page 402)* Have students say whatever they can about the magazine cover. Ask questions such as: **¿Para quiénes es la revista? ¿De qué trata el artículo principal de la revista?**

## Answers to ¿Cómo lo digo?

13

1. Mamá te pide que te levantes temprano.
2. Mamá te pide que limpies tu cuarto.
3. Mamá te pide que te bañes.
4. Mamá te pide que tomes el desayuno.
5. Mamá te pide que no juegues hoy.
6. Mamá te pide que duermas bastante.
7. Mamá te pide que vuelvas a casa en el bus.

Estructura

**14** **¿Qué te escribe tu primo?** Sigan el modelo.

**ir a la fiesta →**
**Mi primo me escribe que vaya a la fiesta.**

1. ir al cine
2. tomar el tren
3. llegar un día antes de la fiesta
4. no ir a un hotel
5. quedarse en casa de mis tíos

**15** **El profesor exige que…** Sigan el modelo.

**Estudiamos mucho. →**
**El profesor nos exige que estudiemos mucho.**

1. Llegamos temprano a clase.
2. Hacemos preguntas.
3. Estudiamos.
4. No perdemos el tiempo.
5. Pensamos antes de hablar.

Parking gratuito
Hasta 24 horas GRATIS
Hasta 48 horas GRATIS
• Clase Club
• Clase Preferente
• TARJETA Club AVE ORO
• Coche Cama y Preferente de Trenes de Grandes Líneas
P
Nuevo Servicio
Sin Esperas
Ahora puede formalizar su plaza de aparcamiento al dejar su coche. Le evitará la espera al regreso.
AVE

**16** **Consejos de mis padres** Contesten.

1. ¿Tus padres te aconsejan que seas bueno?
2. ¿Tus padres te piden que ayudes un poco con las tareas domésticas?
3. ¿Te piden que les digas adónde vas y con quiénes?
4. ¿Tus padres te sugieren que hagas tus tareas antes de poner la televisión?
5. ¿Te dicen que te acuestes antes de las once?

Santurce, Puerto Rico

**17** **Los consejos de don o doña Sabelotodo**

Tú vas a ser don o doña Sabelotodo—y no hay duda que tú lo sabes todo. Además sabes lo que todo el mundo debe hacer. Trabaja con un(a) compañero(a). Dale muchos consejos, sugerencias y recomendaciones. Tu compañero(a) te dirá si va a seguir tus consejos o no. Luego cambien de rol.



**14** and **15** Before going over these activities in class, have students prepare them. Or if you prefer, do them orally with books open.

**15** **Expansion:** Have students redo Activity 15 with **Yo sé que el profesor siempre te exige que…**

**16** You may wish to have students prepare Activity 16 before going over it in class.

## Learning from Realia

*(page 403)* Ask students to tell you as much as they can about the ad. You may wish to remind them that the AVE is the high-speed train that operates in Spain.

### LEVELING

**E:** Activity 11
**A:** Activities 12, 13, 14, 15, 16, 17

## Answers to ¿Cómo lo digo?

1. Mi primo me escribe que vaya al cine.
2. Mi primo me escribe que tome el tren.
3. Mi primo me escribe que llegue un día antes de la fiesta.
4. Mi primo me escribe que no vaya a un hotel.
5. Mi primo me escribe que me quede en casa de mis tíos.

1. El profesor nos exige que lleguemos temprano a clase.
2. El profesor nos exige que hagamos preguntas.
3. El profesor nos exige que estudiemos.
4. El profesor nos exige que no perdamos el tiempo.
5. El profesor nos exige que pensemos antes de hablar.

1. Sí, mis padres me aconsejan que sea bueno(a).
2. Sí (No), mis padres (no) me piden que ayude un poco con las tareas domésticas.
3. Sí, (No, no) me piden que les diga adónde voy y con quiénes.
4. Sí (No), mis padres (no) me sugieren que haga mis tareas antes de poner la televisión.
5. Sí, (No, no) me dicen que me acueste antes de las once.

*Answers will vary but may include:*

Te aconsejo que estudies mucho. Te sugiero que te acuestes temprano. Te aconsejo que duermas ocho horas cada noche.

Estructura

## 1 PREPARATION

### Bellringer Review

*Use BRR Transparency 13.5 or write the following on the board.*
Complete the following impersonal expressions with a subjunctive clause.

1. **Es necesario que ___.**
2. **Es importante que ___.**
3. **Es posible que ___.**
4. **Es mejor que ___.**

## 2 PRESENTATION

### El subjuntivo con expresiones de duda

**Step 1** Have students open their books to page 404 and lead them through Items 1–3.

**Step 2** Have students repeat the model sentences in Items 1 and 2 after you.

## 3 PRACTICE

### ¿Cómo lo digo?

**18** Activity 18 can be done in class without prior preparation.

### Learning from Realia

*(page 404)* Ask students to give their interpretation of **Este motor... no contamina** on the book cover shown on this page.

Estructura

## El subjuntivo con expresiones de duda

### Expressing doubt or uncertainty

1. The subjunctive is always used after expressions that imply doubt or uncertainty.

   **Dudo que ellos se casen.**
   **No creo que ellos tengan una recepción.**

2. If the statement implies certainty, however, the indicative rather than the subjunctive is used. The verb is frequently in the future tense.

   **No dudo que ellos se casarán.**
   **Creo que tendrán una gran recepción.**

3. Study the following expressions of doubt and certainty.

| SUBJUNCTIVE | INDICATIVE |
|---|---|
| dudar | no dudar |
| es dudoso | no es dudoso |
| no estar seguro(a) | estar seguro(a) |
| no creer | creer |
| no es cierto | es cierto |

Parque del Amor, Lima, Perú

### ¿Cómo lo digo?

**18 ¿Lo crees o no lo crees?**

Introduzcan la oración con **creo** o **no creo.**

1. Los aviones vuelan a un millón de millas por hora.
2. Las bicicletas contaminan el aire.
3. Hace mucho calor en Siberia.
4. Todos los españoles hablan inglés.
5. Todos los compañeros de clase bailan muy bien.
6. Sirven comida excelente en la cafetería.
7. Las muchachas son más inteligentes que los muchachos.

### ANSWERS TO ¿Cómo lo digo?

**18**

1. No creo que los aviones vuelen a un millón de millas por hora.
2. No creo que las bicicletas contaminen el aire.
3. No creo que haga mucho calor en la Siberia.
4. No creo que todos los españoles hablen inglés.
5. No creo que todos los compañeros de clase bailen muy bien.
6. No creo que sirvan comida excelente en la cafetería.
7. No creo que las muchachas sean más inteligentes que los muchachos.

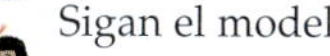

## 19 Martín nunca dice la verdad.

Sigan el modelo.

**Yo soy el más inteligente de la clase.** ⟶
**No, Martín. Dudo que seas el más inteligente de la clase.**

1. Yo tengo mucho talento.
2. También soy muy guapo.
3. Recibo las mejores notas de la clase.
4. Yo bailo como un profesional.
5. Mis padres son millonarios.
6. Las muchachas me adoran.
7. Voy a Madrid mañana.
8. Me quieren en Hollywood.

## 20 Historieta La boda de mi mejor amigo(a)

Contesten con **creo** o **dudo**.

1. Tu mejor amigo(a) se casa pronto.
2. Te invita a la recepción.
3. La recepción es en un gran hotel.
4. La orquesta toca música clásica.
5. Tú le regalas un coche.
6. Los novios viajan a Buenos Aires.

## 21 ¿Pasará o no pasará?

Con un(a) compañero(a), determinen las cosas o los eventos que ustedes creen que van a pasar u ocurrir en su vida y cosas que no creen que pasen ni ocurran. Luego comparen sus dos listas para determinar lo que ustedes creen que tienen en común.



# Estructura

**19** Have students present each item of Activity 19 as a miniconversation. Insist that they use as much expression as possible.

**20** You may go over Activity 20 with or without prior preparation.

## Critical Thinking Activity

**Giving opinions** Read the following to the class or write it on the board.

**Las bodas lujosas y elegantes, y muy caras, están otra vez de moda. Algunos dicen que esto representa un deseo de volver al formalismo y tradición del pasado. Otros dicen que es cuestión de «status» social. ¿Qué opinas tú? ¿Quiénes deben determinar el tipo de boda que tienen los novios, los novios o los padres de los novios? ¿Por qué?**

### LEVELING

**E:** Activity 19

**A:** Activities 18, 19, 20, 21

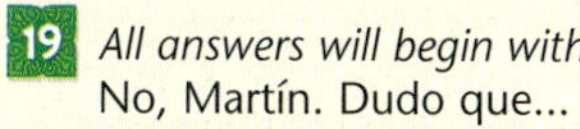

## Answers to ¿Cómo lo digo?

**19** *All answers will begin with* No, Martín. Dudo que...

1. tengas mucho talento.
2. seas muy guapo.
3. recibas las mejores notas de la clase.
4. bailes como un profesional.
5. tus padres sean millonarios.
6. las muchachas te adoren.
7. vayas a Madrid mañana.
8. te quieran en Hollywood.

**20**

1. Creo que tu mejor amigo(a) se casará pronto. Dudo que tu mejor amigo(a) se case pronto.
2. Creo que te invitará a la recepción. Dudo que te invite a la recepción.
3. Creo que la recepción será en un gran hotel. Dudo que la recepción sea en un gran hotel.
4. Creo que la orquesta tocará música clásica. Dudo que la orquesta toque música clásica.
5. Creo que tú le regalarás un coche. Dudo que tú le regales un coche.
6. Creo que los novios viajarán a Buenos Aires. Dudo que los novios viajen a Buenos Aires.

**21** *Answers will vary. Students should use the indicative (future tense) to describe what they believe will happen and the subjunctive to describe what they do not believe will happen.*

# Estructura

## 1 PREPARATION

### Bellringer Review

*Use BRR Transparency 13.6 or write the following on the board.*
Write three things your parents ask or insist that you do.

## 2 PRESENTATION

### El subjuntivo con expresiones de emoción

**Step 1** Have students open their books to page 406 and lead them through Items 1 and 2.

**Step 2** Call on volunteers to read the model sentences aloud.

¡OJO! The use of the subjunctive after these expressions does not fit the general rule that it be used when it is uncertain whether or not an event will take place. Emphasize here that the subjunctive is used due to the subjective nature of the statements, as explained in Item 1.

## 3 PRACTICE

### ¿Cómo lo digo?

**22** Have students prepare Activity 22 before going over it in class. Call on three students and have them present each item.

# Estructura

## El subjuntivo con expresiones de emoción
### Expressing emotional reactions

**1.** The subjunctive is used in a dependent clause that is introduced by a verb or expression of emotion.

**Me alegro de que tú celebres tu cumpleaños.**
**Siento que tu hermano no pueda asistir.**
**Es una lástima que él tenga que trabajar.**

**2.** The following are verbs and expressions that convey emotion.

**alegrarse de**
**estar contento**
**sorprender**
**gustar**
**sentir**
**ser una lástima**

Santiago de Chile

## ¿Cómo lo digo?

**22** **Sara, sí, y Nora, no.** Sigan el modelo.

**Tenemos un examen mañana. ⟶**
**Sara se alegra de que tengamos un examen mañana.**
**Nora siente que tengamos un examen mañana.**

1. Tenemos clase mañana.
2. El profesor nos da un examen.
3. El examen es difícil.
4. No podemos usar los libros.
5. Escribimos una composición.
6. Hacemos una presentación oral.
7. El profesor lee las composiciones.



## Answers to ¿Cómo lo digo?

**22**

1. Sara se alegra de que tengamos clase mañana. Nora siente que tengamos clase mañana.
2. Sara se alegra de que el profesor nos dé un examen. Nora siente que el profesor nos dé un examen.
3. Sara se alegra de que el examen sea difícil. Nora siente que el examen sea difícil.
4. Sara se alegra de que no podamos usar los libros. Nora siente que no podamos usar los libros.
5. Sara se alegra de que escribamos una composición. Nora siente que escribamos una composición.
6. Sara se alegra de que hagamos una presentación oral. Nora siente que hagamos una presentación oral.
7. Sara se alegra de que el profesor lea las composiciones. Nora siente que el profesor lea las composiciones.

**23** **¿Se alegra o no se alegra Andrés?** Contesten. Empiecen las frases con **Andrés se alegra** o **Andrés no se alegra.**

1. La escuela cierra temprano.
2. Los chicos pueden jugar.
3. Va a llover.
4. Acaba de llover.
5. Su equipo pierde.
6. Los padres les compran pizza.
7. Juegan otra vez mañana.

**24** **Historieta El Día de los Reyes y Hanuka** Contesten.

1. ¿Están contentos los niños que llegue el seis de enero?
2. ¿Se alegran de que vengan los Reyes?
3. ¿Están alegres que los Reyes les traigan regalos?
4. ¿Les sorprende que los camellos coman la paja en los zapatos?
5. ¿Te sorprende que la fiesta de Hanuka dure ocho días?
6. ¿Los niños se alegran de que los padres les den un regalo cada uno de los ocho días?
7. ¿Se alegran los padres de que su hijo mayor encienda las velas de la menora?

**25** **Emociones** Trabaja con un(a) compañero(a). Van a hablar de su escuela y de su vida escolar. Es cierto que en la escuela hay cosas que les ponen contentos y hay otras cosas que les ponen tristes. Al hablar de su vida escolar usen las expresiones **Me alegro de que, Siento que, Estoy contento(a) que, Estoy triste que** y den sus opiniones.

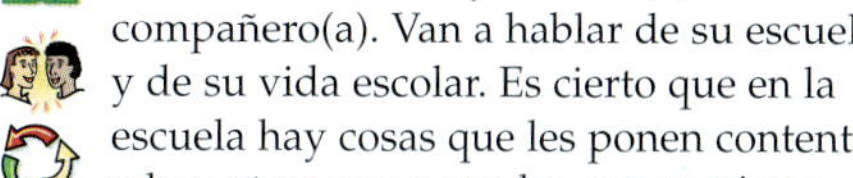

Santurce, Puerto Rico

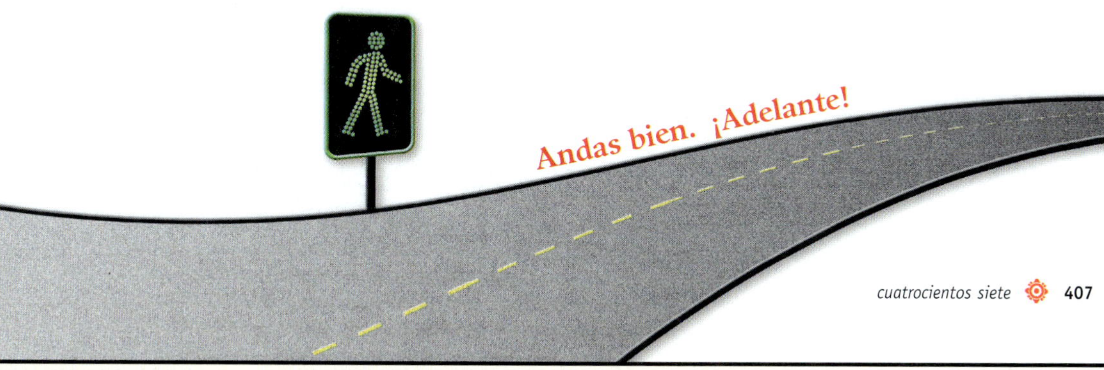




## Learning from Photos

*(pages 406–407)* Ask students to describe and say as much as they can about the photos. You may wish to prompt responses by asking questions such as: **¿Qué están haciendo las dos muchachas? ¿Para quién serán los regalos? ¿Dónde están los muchachos? ¿Qué hacen ellos? ¿Llevan uniforme? ¿Cómo es el uniforme?**

**23** Activity 23 can be done orally in class with books closed.

**24** Because of the length of the sentences, it is recommended that you go over Activity 24 with books open.

**¡Adelante!** At this point in the chapter, students have learned all the vocabulary and structure necessary to complete the chapter. The conversation and cultural readings that follow recycle all the material learned up to this point.

## Answers to ¿Cómo lo digo?

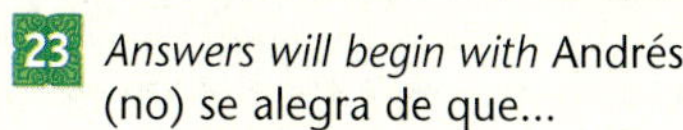

**23** *Answers will begin with* Andrés (no) se alegra de que...

1. la escuela cierre temprano.
2. los chicos puedan jugar.
3. vaya a llover.
4. acabe de llover.
5. su equipo pierda.
6. los padres les compren pizza.
7. jueguen otra vez mañana.

**24**

1. Sí, los niños están contentos que llegue el seis de enero.
2. Sí, se alegran de que vengan los Reyes.
3. Sí, están alegres que los Reyes les traigan regalos.
4. No, no les sorprende que los camellos coman la paja en los zapatos.
5. Sí, (No, no) me sorprende que la fiesta de Hanuka dure ocho días.
6. Sí, los niños se alegran de que sus padres les den un regalo cada uno de los ocho días.
7. Sí, los padres se alegran de que su hijo mayor encienda las velas de la menora.

**25** *Answers will vary. Students should use the phrases given followed by the subjunctive.*

# Conversación

## 1 PREPARATION

**Resource Manager**

Audio Activities TE, page 165
Audio CD 8

**Bellringer Review**

*Use BRR Transparency 13.7 or write the following on the board.*
Complete the following sentences.

1. **Tengo miedo que ___.**
2. **Lucía está triste que ___.**
3. **¿Te sorprende que ___?**
4. **Estoy contento(a) que ___.**
5. **Siento que ___.**

## 2 PRESENTATION

**Step 1** Tell students they are going to hear a conversation about plans for New Year's Eve. Something interesting comes out in the conversation. Tell them to listen for what it is.

**Step 2** Have students listen to Audio CD 8 or read the conversation aloud to the class.

**Step 3** Call on pairs of individuals to read the conversation aloud using as much expression as possible.

**Step 4** Go over the **¿Comprendes?** questions.

**Step 5** Have students write the answers to the **¿Comprendes?** questions for homework.

**Step 6** Call on a student to tell all about the conversation in his or her own words.

# Conversación

## Año Nuevo   

**Ramón** ¿Qué vas a hacer para Año Nuevo?
**Yolanda** ¿Año Nuevo? Estaré durmiendo. Pero Nochevieja voy a una fiesta.
**Ramón** Me alegro de que vayas a una fiesta. Yo me quedaré en casa.
**Yolanda** ¿Por qué? ¿Qué pasa?
**Ramón** Pues, invité a Cristina a ir a la fiesta de Luis Miguel y ella me dijo que no podía.
**Yolanda** Claro que no podía. Ella no puede ir contigo porque va con Antonio.
**Ramón** ¡Pero Antonio es tu novio! Es imposible que Cristina vaya con él.
**Yolanda** Pues, imposible o no, es verdad. Créeme. ¡Oye, tengo una idea!
**Ramón** No es necesario que me digas. Ya lo sé. Y es excelente idea. ¡Vamos tú y yo a la fiesta!
**Yolanda** Muchas gracias por la invitación. Acepto.

### ¿Comprendes?

Contesten.

1. ¿Qué va a hacer Yolanda durante Año Nuevo?
2. ¿Cuándo va ella a una fiesta?
3. ¿Quién da la fiesta?
4. ¿Qué piensa hacer Ramón?
5. ¿A quién pensaba Ramón invitar a la fiesta?
6. ¿Qué le dijo ella?
7. ¿Por qué no puede Cristina ir a la fiesta con Ramón?
8. ¿Quién es Antonio?
9. ¿Cuál es la idea que tiene Yolanda?
10. ¿Qué van a hacer Yolanda y Ramón?



### Answers to ¿Comprendes?

1. Yolanda va a dormir durante Año Nuevo.
2. Ella va a una fiesta Nochevieja.
3. Luis Miguel da la fiesta.
4. Ramón piensa quedarse en casa.
5. Ramón invitó a Cristina.
6. Le dijo que no podía.
7. Cristina no puede ir a la fiesta con Ramón porque va con Antonio.
8. Antonio es el novio de Yolanda.
9. La idea que tiene Yolanda es de ir a la fiesta con Ramón.
10. Yolanda y Ramón van a ir a la fiesta juntos.

# Vamos a hablar más

**A** **¡Qué horror!** Trabaja con un(a) compañero(a). Uno(a) de ustedes va a ser (tomar el papel de) Yolanda en la conversación en la página 408. El/La otro(a) tomará el papel de Antonio que va a salir con otra. Yolanda va a decirle a Antonio todo lo que ella piensa de él. Antonio va a tratar de defenderse.

Ciudad de México

**B** **La víspera de Año Nuevo** Trabaja con un(a) compañero(a). Discutan todo lo que ustedes hacen o no hacen para celebrar el Año Nuevo.

Conversación

## 3 PRACTICE

# Vamos a hablar más

**A and B** Allow students to choose the activities that they would like to participate in.

### FUN FACTS

Mexicans usually refer to their capital city simply as **México** if the context is clear. In print the capital city is usually just **México, D.F.**

In Spain, Mexico is often spelled with a **j, Méjico.** In most other countries, as in Mexico itself, it is spelled **México.**

### Glencoe Technology

On the CD-ROM, students can watch a dramatization of this conversation. They can then play the role of either one of the characters and record themselves in the conversation.

**LEVELING**

**E:** Conversation

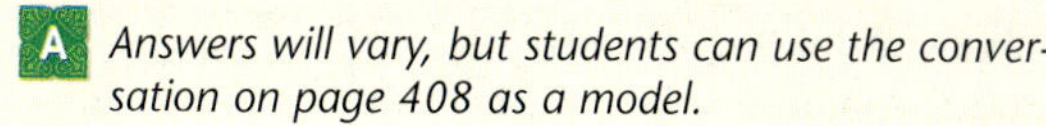

**A** *Answers will vary, but students can use the conversation on page 408 as a model.*

**B** *Answers will vary. Students should use party vocabulary to describe their typical New Year's celebrations.*

# Lecturas culturales

## Resource Manager

Audio Activities TE, page 166
Audio CD 8

## Bellringer Review

*Use BRR Transparency 13.8 or write the following on the board.*
Put the following scrambled conversation into a logical order.

1. **¿De parte de quién?**
2. **¿Puedo dejarle un mensaje?**
3. **¿Está el Sr. Salas, por favor?**
4. **¡Hola!**
5. **De acuerdo.**
6. **De Roberto Díaz.**
7. **Lo siento, pero no está.**
8. **Un momento. Favor de no colgar.**

## National Standards

**Cultures**
The reading on page 410 and the related activities on page 411 familiarize students with an interesting Spanish New Year's Eve custom.

**Comparisons**
Students learn that the citizens of Madrid gather in the city center every New Year's Eve and eat the twelve "grapes of happiness" as a golden ball descends in the clock tower at the stroke of midnight. This is similar to the tradition in New York, where crowds watch the ball descend in Times Square on New Year's Eve.

# Lecturas culturales

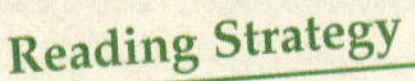

### Reading Strategy

**Visualizing while reading** When you are reading a passage, making a mental picture of what you are reading about will help you remember. This is called "visualizing," that is, allowing yourself to imagine the setting and events and picture them in your mind. This is especially helpful when reading about a topic that is new to you or one about which you have no background information.

## Las doce uvas de la felicidad

Madrid, la capital de España, está en el centro del país. Y en el mismo centro de Madrid está la Puerta del Sol. La Puerta del Sol es una plaza donde desembocan muchas calles. La Puerta del Sol tiene gran importancia histórica. Es allí donde los madrileños se reúnen cuando algo importante ha ocurrido o va a ocurrir.

Cada Nochevieja miles y miles de madrileños llenan la Puerta del Sol para esperar la llegada del Año Nuevo. Todos miran el reloj que está en la torre de la antigua Casa de Correos. Están contentos que llegue otro año. En los momentos antes de las doce de la noche, una bola dorada[1] comienza a bajar, segundo por segundo. Cuando baja completamente, el año ha terminado, y un año nuevo comienza. Mientras el reloj da las doce los madrileños tienen la costumbre de comerse doce uvas, una por una. Estas uvas se llaman las uvas de la felicidad. Comerlas es garantía de un año nuevo próspero y feliz.

[1]dorada *golden*

Puerta del Sol, Madrid



## PRESENTATION

### Pre-reading

**Step 1** Tell students that they are going to learn how some **madrileños** spend New Year's Eve.

**Step 2** Have students read the Reading Strategy on this page. Have them look at the photos as well. Visualizing this New Year's Eve custom can help in understanding the **Lectura.**

### Learning from Photos

*(page 410 bottom)* The building shown is the **Dirección General de Seguridad** or *police headquarters.* The building was originally the **Casa de Correos** built during the reign of Carlos III in the eighteenth century. The clock tower, from which the golden ball descends on New Year's Eve, was added in 1866.

### Fun Facts

The **Puerta del Sol** is the 0-kilometer marker for all national highways in Spain. All distances are measured from this point. If you are on **Nacional V** and the marker says 220, you are 220 kilometers from the **Puerta del Sol.**

**LEVELING**
**E:** Reading

## ¿Comprendes?

**A Nochevieja en Madrid** Contesten según la lectura.

1. ¿Qué tienen en común Madrid y la Puerta del Sol?
2. ¿Por qué es importante históricamente la Puerta del Sol?
3. ¿Qué día del año llenan los madrileños la Puerta del Sol?
4. ¿Qué hacen ellos allí?
5. ¿Qué hay en la antigua Casa de Correos?

**B ¿Cómo es Nochevieja?** Expliquen en sus propias palabras las tradiciones de Nochevieja en España.

Puerta del Sol, Madrid



## Lecturas culturales

### Reading

**Step 1** Call on a student to read three or four sentences aloud. Then stop and ask other members of the class questions about the material that was just read.

**Step 2** Have students read the selection at home and write the answers to the **¿Comprendes?** activities that accompany the **Lectura.**

### Post-reading

**Step 1** Go over the **¿Comprendes?** activities in class the next day.

**Step 2** Call on a student to give a summary of the reading in his or her own words. If necessary, ask five or six questions to review the salient points of the reading selection in order to enable him or her to do this more easily. After the oral summary, the more able students can write a synopsis of the **Lectura** in their own words.

### History Connection

**La Puerta del Sol** is regarded as the geographical center of Spain. It has also been the scene of great events in Spanish history. One of the most significant was the uprising by the people of Madrid against Napoleon's Mamelukes and Imperial Guard on May 2, 1808. This event was immortalized by Goya in his painting ***El Dos de Mayo.*** For further enrichment, you may wish to refer to the Fine Art Transparency from **¡Buen viaje! Level 1.**

## Answers to ¿Comprendes?

**A**

1. Madrid está en el centro del país y la Puerta del Sol está en el centro de Madrid.
2. La Puerta del Sol es importante históricamente porque es allí donde los madrileños se reúnen cuando algo importante ha ocurrido o va a ocurrir.
3. Los madrileños llenan la Puerta del Sol la Nochevieja.
4. Esperan la llegada del Año Nuevo.
5. Hay un reloj en la torre de la antigua Casa de Correos.

**B** *Answers will vary but may include:*

Los madrileños esperan el Año Nuevo en La Puerta del Sol. Miran el reloj y una bola dorada que baja en los momentos antes de las doce. Mientras el reloj da las doce, ellos comen doce uvas, las uvas de la felicidad. Comerlas es garantía de un año nuevo próspero y feliz.

# Lectura opcional 1

## National Standards

**Cultures**
This reading about wedding customs and the related activity familiarize students with an important family and social event in the Spanish-speaking world.

**Comparisons**
Students learn that, in the Spanish-speaking world, it is very important for the young couple's families to get to know each other better during the engagement period. Also, the couple usually has both a religious and a civil wedding ceremony.

**¡OJO!** This reading is optional. You may skip it completely, have the entire class read it, have only several students read it and report to the class, or assign it for extra credit.

**Learning from Photos**
*(page 412)* You may wish to ask students to describe what they see in the photo of the wedding.

**LEVELING**
**E:** Reading 1
**A:** Reading 2

# Lectura opcional 1

## La boda

Ángel y Mónica seguían saliendo juntos y cada mes se querían más. Sabían que querían casarse. Ángel fue a la casa de Mónica y le pidió al padre la mano de su hija. Poco después los padres anunciaron el compromiso[1] de sus hijos. Hubo un cóctel elegante en el que fijaron la fecha para su boda y todos los parientes de las dos familias y los amigos íntimos festejaron a los nuevos comprometidos. Estas fiestas y reuniones familiares son muy importantes porque el matrimonio es el enlace de las dos familias y durante las fiestas antenupciales las dos familias van conociéndose.

Se casaron un año después. El día de la boda hay generalmente dos ceremonias—la civil y la religiosa. Los novios van a la iglesia acompañados del padrino y de la madrina, de sus pajes de honor y de sus damas de honor. La madre de Mónica le sirvió de madrina y el padre de Ángel le sirvió de padrino. Después de la ceremonia Ángel y Mónica salieron de la iglesia como esposo y esposa y fueron a una recepción en donde sus familiares y sus amigos íntimos les dieron la enhorabuena.

Al terminar la recepción, Ángel y Mónica salieron para su viaje de novios. Fueron a Europa a pasar su luna de miel[2].

[1]compromiso *engagement*
[2]luna de miel *honeymoon*

### ¿Comprendes?

**Los novios** Contesten.

1. ¿Quiénes son Ángel y Mónica?
2. ¿Qué hizo Ángel cuando supo que él y Mónica iban a comprometerse?
3. ¿Qué hubo para anunciar su compromiso?
4. ¿Para qué sirven las fiestas antenupciales?
5. ¿Cuántas ceremonias hay para la boda?
6. ¿A quiénes escogieron Ángel y Mónica para su padrino y madrina?
7. ¿Adónde fueron los recién casados para su luna de miel?



### Answers to ¿Comprendes?

1. Ángel y Mónica son novios.
2. Fue a la casa de Mónica y le pidió al padre la mano de su hija.
3. Hubo un cóctel elegante para anunciar su compromiso.
4. Sirven para que las familias de los novios se conozcan.
5. Hay dos ceremonias—la civil y la religiosa.
6. Escogieron a la madre de Mónica para su madrina y al padre de Ángel para su padrino.
7. Los recién casados fueron a Europa para su luna de miel.

# Lectura opcional 2

## Freyssiner–Parada

El reverendo Manuel Belman Robles, S.J., impartió la bendición nupcial a Sandra Freyssiner y César Parada, durante una ceremonia que tuvo lugar el pasado sábado por la tarde en la iglesia de Nuestra Señora del Socorro.

A la hora señalada llegaron los novios con su comitiva y en la puerta fueron recibidos por el sacerdote[1], quien les acompañó hasta el altar mayor, donde participaron del calvario de Cristo.

La iglesia fue profusamente iluminada y decorada con arreglos de flores naturales mientras el coro interpretó trozos de música sacra, lo que dio mayor lucimiento a la ceremonia.

El sacerdote oficiante pronunció un emotivo fervorín en donde dio consejos a los novios para su vida espiritual.

Estuvieron los padres de los contrayentes Jaime Freyssiner de la Barrera, Gloria Márquez Marrón, Francisco Javier Parra Jiménez y Amelia López de Parada.

Asimismo fueron madrinas Gloria Freyssiner Márquez, Karu Noval de Freyssiner, Amelia Parada de Hernández, Leticia Parada de Alba y Beatriz Alvarez.

Como pajes actuaron los niños Elvira Parada Dommarco y Cristina Hernández Parada.

Al finalizar el acto religioso, los nuevos esposos desfilaron[2] por el pasillo central y en el atrio[3] recibieron felicitaciones de amigos y parientes.

Más tarde se ofreció una recepción en su honor en donde se brindó[4] por la felicidad de la pareja, la que más tarde salió de viaje de bodas.

[1]sacerdote *priest*
[2]desfilaron *paraded*
[3]atrio *vestibule, entrance*
[4]se brindó *everyone toasted*

### ¿Comprendes?

**La boda** Contesten.

1. ¿Cómo se llama el sacerdote que le dio la bendición nupcial a la pareja?
2. ¿Dónde tuvo lugar la ceremonia?
3. ¿Cuándo tuvo lugar?
4. ¿Dónde recibió a la pareja el sacerdote?
5. ¿Adónde los acompañó?
6. ¿Con qué fue decorada la iglesia?
7. Después de la ceremonia, ¿dónde recibieron felicitaciones los nuevos esposos?
8. ¿Qué se ofreció después de la ceremonia en la iglesia?
9. ¿Para dónde salió la pareja después de la recepción?



### Answers to ¿Comprendes?

1. El sacerdote se llama Manuel Belman Robles, S.J.
2. La ceremonia tuvo lugar en la iglesia de Nuestra Señora del Socorro.
3. La boda tuvo lugar el (pasado) sábado por la tarde.
4. El sacerdote recibió a la pareja en la puerta.
5. Los acompañó hasta el altar mayor.
6. La iglesia fue decorada con (arreglos de) flores naturales.
7. Después de la ceremonia los nuevos esposos recibieron felicitaciones en el atrio.
8. Después de la ceremonia en la iglesia se ofreció una recepción en honor de la pareja.
9. Después de la recepción la pareja salió de viaje de bodas.

# Lectura opcional 2

## National Standards

**Cultures**
This reading and the related activity on this page familiarize students with a typical wedding ceremony in the Hispanic world.

**¡OJO!** This reading is optional. You may skip it completely, have the entire class read it, have only several students read it and report to the class, or assign it for extra credit.

## PRESENTATION

**Step 1** Have any students who are interested in the topic of weddings do the reading and then discuss any differences they may have noted between the wedding described in this article and weddings they themselves may have attended.

**Step 2** This is an actual wedding announcement that appeared in a newspaper. Have students bring in a wedding announcement from a local newspaper and compare it with the Spanish one.

## Fun Facts

In Madrid there was a refrain: **Él que no pasa por la calle de la Pasa no se casa.** The church offices for registering marriages were on **la calle de la Pasa** in Old Madrid. The saying meant that if one didn't marry in the Church, one wasn't married.

# Conexiones

## National Standards

**Connections**

This reading about the lives and works of two of Spain's most important artists, Diego Velázquez and Bartolomé Murillo, establishes a connection with another discipline, allowing students to reinforce and further their knowledge of the fine arts through the study of Spanish.

**¡OJO!** The readings in the **Conexiones** section are optional. They focus on some of the major disciplines taught in schools and universities. The vocabulary is useful for discussing such topics as history, literature, art, economics, business, science, etc. You may choose any of the following ways to do the readings in the **Conexiones** sections.

**Independent reading** Have students read the selections and do the post-reading activities as homework, which you collect. This option is least intrusive on class time and requires a minimum of teacher involvement.

**Homework with in-class follow-up** Assign the readings and post-reading activities as homework. Review and discuss the material in class the next day.

**Intensive in-class activity** This option includes a pre-reading vocabulary presentation, in-class reading and discussion, assignment of the activities for homework, and a discussion of the assignment in class the following day.

# Conexiones

## *Las bellas artes*

### Las artes plásticas

From earliest times, religion has had a profound influence on art. The temples of the Far East, the Gothic cathedrals of Europe, the pyramids of the Mayas, and the great mosques of Cordoba and Cairo are artistic expressions of profound religious feeling. Throughout the centuries, the painters of Europe, especially the Spaniards, often employed religious themes in their work. *The Adoration of the Magi* by Velázquez and *The Return of the Prodigal Son* by Murillo are two notable examples.

Diego Velázquez

Bartolomé Murillo

### La escuela española

Como ya saben ustedes, hay diferentes épocas y «escuelas» de arte y, en particular, de pintura. Velázquez y Murillo son representantes de la «escuela española». Pero también se puede decir que eran clásicos. Cuando hablamos de los clásicos en el arte, nos referimos a los artistas que se notan por su claridad, elegancia y atención a las formas de los griegos y los romanos.

Los dos artistas nacieron[1] en Sevilla. Velázquez (1599–1660) era de una familia noble. Murillo (1617–1682) era de una familia pobre. Perdió a sus padres cuando tenía sólo diez años. Velázquez fue a Madrid a pintar para la corte donde su talento artístico fue reconocido enseguida. Murillo se quedó en Sevilla donde se ganó la vida pintando y vendiendo sus cuadros en el mercado. En poco tiempo ganó fama y fue reconocido como el pintor principal de la ciudad.

[1]nacieron *were born*



## FUN-FACTS

The statue of Velázquez is at the entrance to the Museo del Prado, one of the world's most important art museums. The collection began as the royal collections of both Hapsburg and Bourbon monarchs. The building was designed during the reign of Carlos III and opened in 1819 during the reign of Fernando VII. The museum possesses more than 5,000 pictures, of which about 2,300 are on display to the public in 120 rooms on three floors. The Museo del Prado houses the finest collection of Spanish masters: El Greco, Velázquez, Murillo, Zurbarán, Ribera, and Goya.

*La adoración de los Magos* de Diego Velázquez

Los temas favoritos de la escuela española eran la mitología y la religión. Este cuadro de Velázquez, *La adoración de los Magos,* representa a los tres Reyes Magos—Melchor, Gaspar y Baltasar—ofreciendo sus regalos al Niño Jesús. Notarán ustedes los anacronismos en esta obra. Por ejemplo, la época del evento es del primer siglo. Las ropas son contemporáneas con la época del pintor del siglo XVII. Noten los colores que emplea el artista. Velázquez es maestro de colorido.

Este cuadro de Murillo, *El regreso del hijo pródigo,* describe la historia bíblica del mismo nombre. Todos los personajes y objetos que aparecen[2] en la historia bíblica están incluidos en el cuadro. Vemos al padre que recibe a su hijo que regresa y los sirvientes que le traen zapatos y ropa nueva. El cuadro no tiene líneas definidas ni un fuerte contraste de colores. El pintor quería una composición sencilla y armoniosa. No hay nada en el cuadro que nos distraiga[3] de la contemplación de la alegría del padre.

[2]aparecen *appear* [3]distraiga *distracts*

*El regreso del hijo pródigo* de Bartolomé Murillo

## ¿Comprendes?

**A La escuela española** Contesten.

1. ¿Quiénes son representantes de la «escuela española»?
2. ¿Dónde nacieron?
3. ¿Quién era de una familia noble y rica?
4. ¿Quién era de una familia pobre?
5. ¿Dónde pintó Velázquez?
6. ¿Dónde pintó Murillo?
7. ¿Cuáles eran los temas favoritos de la «escuela española»?
8. ¿Cómo se llama el cuadro de Velázquez?
9. ¿Qué representa?
10. ¿Cómo se llama el cuadro de Murillo?

**B Tu preferencia** ¿Cuál de los dos cuadros te gusta más? ¿Por qué?



# Conexiones

## PRESENTATION

### *Las bellas artes*
### Las artes plásticas

**Step 1** Even though this material is optional, you may wish to go over this selection at least quickly with the entire class.

**Step 2** Have students who read the selection on ***Las Meninas*** in **¡Buen viaje! Level 1,** Chapter 6, retell any information they remember.

**Step 3** When discussing these paintings you may wish to show Fine Art Transparency F 6 of the painting by Murillo. You may wish to have students read the background information and do the related activities that accompany the Fine Art Transparency.

**LEVELING**

**A:** Reading

## Answers to ¿Comprendes?

**A**

1. Velázquez y Murillo son representantes de la «escuela española».
2. Nacieron en Sevilla.
3. Velázquez era de una familia noble.
4. Murillo era de una familia pobre.
5. Velázquez pintó en Madrid.
6. Murillo pintó en Sevilla.
7. Los temas favoritos de la «escuela española» eran la mitología y la religión.
8. El cuadro de Velázquez se llama «La adoración de los Magos».
9. Representa a los tres Reyes Magos—Melchor, Gaspar y Baltasar—ofreciendo sus regalos al Niño Jesús.
10. El cuadro de Murillo se llama «El regreso del hijo pródigo».

**B** *Answers will vary. Students should give reasons for their preference.*

# ¡Te toca a ti!

## Use what you have learned

### Recycling

These activities allow students to use the vocabulary and structure from this chapter in completely open-ended, real-life situations.

### PRESENTATION

Encourage students to say as much as possible when they do these activities. Tell them not to be afraid to make mistakes, since the goal of the activities is real-life communication. If someone in the group makes an error, allow the others to politely correct him or her. Let students choose the activities they would like to do.

You may wish to divide students into pairs or groups. Encourage students to elaborate on the basic theme and to be creative. They may use props, pictures, or posters if they wish.

### PRACTICE

#### Writing Development

Have students keep a notebook or portfolio containing their best written work from each chapter. These selected writings can be based on assignments from the Student Textbook and the Workbook. The activities on page 417 are examples of writing assignments that may be included in each student's portfolio. On page 164 in the Workbook, students will begin to develop an organized autobiography **(Mi autobiografía).** These workbook pages may also become a part of their portfolio.



# ¡Te toca a ti!

## Use what you have learned

HABLAR 1

### Una situación delicada

✔ *Give someone advice*

Tu mejor amigo(a) (tu compañero[a]), iba a casarse. Pero ahora ha cambiado de idea. Él o ella no sabe qué hacer. Te pide consejos. Conversen juntos.

HABLAR 2

### Mi fiesta favorita

✔ *Talk about your favorite holiday*

Trabaja con un(a) compañero(a). Descríbele tu fiesta favorita. Explícale por qué te gusta tanto. Luego cambien de rol.

HABLAR 3

### Resoluciones para el Año Nuevo

✔ *Tell what you believe or doubt what one another will do.*

Trabaja con un(a) compañero(a) de clase. Cada uno(a) de ustedes le dirá al/a la otro(a) lo que crees que él o ella hará en el Año Nuevo y lo que dudas que él o ella haga.



### Answers to ¡Te toca a ti!

1. *Answers will vary. Students should give advice using verbs such as* aconsejar, sugerir, *or* pedir, *followed by the subjunctive.*

2. *Answers will vary. Students should use vocabulary presented in* Palabras 1 *and* Palabras 2.

3. *Answers will vary. Students should use the subjunctive to express doubts and the indicative to express certainty.*

¡Te toca a ti!

## 4 Una invitación

*✔ Write an invitation*

Escribe una invitación para un cumpleaños, una boda o cualquier otra fiesta. Da todos los informes necesarios.

### Writing Strategy

**Classifying a subject** When writing, one way to effectively organize your material is to classify your subject. For example, if you are writing about clothing, there are several categories your subject could fit into: clothing for school, clothing for weekends, clothing for doing chores, and many more. By choosing a category and classifying your subject, you will be able to organize your information more appropriately and use this classification to construct a good paragraph or paper.

## 5 Las fiestas

Obviously you celebrate many holidays throughout the year. This does not mean, however, that you and your classmates celebrate the same ones. Write a paper about some of the holidays you celebrate and describe what these celebrations entail. It would be impossible to write about all the holidays you celebrate; therefore, narrow your list by selecting a category for your holidays: holidays I like best, religious holidays, winter holidays, summer holidays, or any other you can think of. Include an introduction and a conclusion.



### Writing Strategy

**Classifying a subject** Have students read the Writing Strategy on page 417. You may wish to have students do the Chapter 13 Internet Activity on Hispanic holidays before you assign this composition. Students can do this writing activity as a follow-up to the Internet Activity.

### LEVELING

These activities encompass all three levels. All students will be able to do them as a sophistication level commensurate with their ability in Spanish. Some students will be able to speak for several minutes, and others may be able to give just a few sentences. This is to be expected when students are functioning completely on their own generating their own language to the best of their ability.

### ANSWERS TO ¡Te toca a ti!

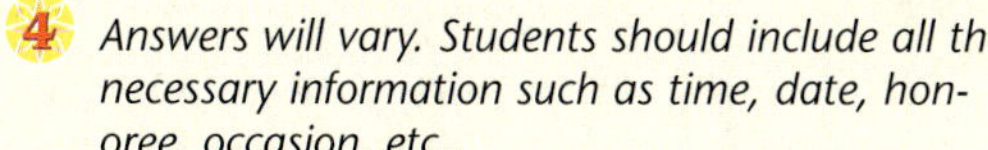

4 *Answers will vary. Students should include all the necessary information such as time, date, honoree, occasion, etc.*

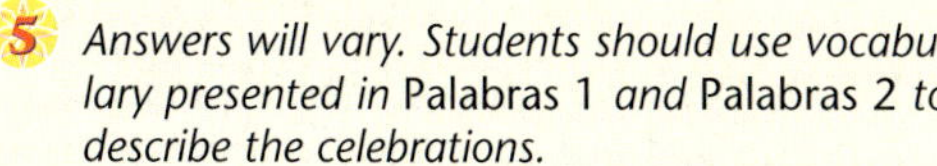

5 *Answers will vary. Students should use vocabulary presented in* Palabras 1 *and* Palabras 2 *to describe the celebrations.*

# Assessment

## Resource Manager

Communication Transparency C 13
Quizzes, pages 63–68
Performance Assessment, Task 13
Tests, pages 203–218
Situation Cards, Chapter 13
**Maratón mental** Videoquiz, Chapter 13
ExamView® Pro, Chapter 13

## Assessment

This is a pre-test for students to take before you administer the chapter test. Note that each section is cross-referenced so students can easily find the material they have to review in case they made errors. You may use Assessment Answers Transparency A 13 to do the assessment in class, or you may assign this assessment for homework. You can correct the assessment yourself, or you may prefer to project the answers on the overhead in class.

## Glencoe Technology

**MINDJOGGER VHS/DVD**

You may wish to help your students prepare for the chapter test by playing the MindJogger game show. Teams will compete against each other to review chapter vocabulary and structure and sharpen listening comprehension skills.

# Assessment

## Vocabulario

To review **Palabras 1**, turn to pages 392–393.

**1 Contesten.**

1. ¿En qué pones velas?
2. ¿Qué dices a una persona que celebra su cumpleaños?
3. ¿Quiénes van a casarse?
4. ¿Qué reciben los novios?

To review **Palabras 2**, turn to pages 396–397.

**2 ¿Sí o no?**

5. La víspera de Año Nuevo es la Nochevieja.
6. Año Nuevo es el mismo día que la Navidad.
7. Hanuka se llama también la fiesta de las luces y es una fiesta hebrea.
8. Los niños hispanos ponen paja en sus zapatos el 31 de diciembre cuando el reloj da las doce.

## Estructura

To review the subjunctive of stem-changing verbs, turn to page 400.

**3 Escriban cada oración de nuevo.**

9. Mis padres quieren que nos acostemos temprano.
   Mis padres quieren que yo ________.
10. Es necesario que tú duermas aquí.
   Es necesario que nosotros ________.
11. Ellos prefieren que tú lo pidas.
   Ellos prefieren que ustedes ________.
12. Es posible que volvamos temprano.
   Es posible que yo ________.



## Answers to Assessment

1. Pongo velas en el pastel (la torta, el bizcocho).
2. Digo «Feliz cumpleaños» a una persona que celebra su cumpleaños.
3. Los novios van a casarse.
4. Los novios reciben regalos.

5. Sí
6. No
7. Sí
8. No

9. Mis padres quieren que yo me acueste temprano.
10. Es necesario que nosotros durmamos aquí.
11. Ellos prefieren que ustedes lo pidan.
12. Es posible que yo vuelva temprano.

## 4 Completen.

13. Él se va a casar y pide que (yo) le ___ de padrino. (servir)
14. Yo les ruego a ustedes que ___ a la celebración. (asistir)
15. El profesor te ruega que ___ tus tareas con cuidado. (hacer)

To review the subjunctive for giving advice and making suggestions, turn to page 402.

## 5 Escriban cada oración de nuevo.

16. Dudo que ellos vengan.
    No dudo ___.
17. Es cierto que él saldrá.
    No es cierto ___.
18. Creo que él lo sabrá.
    No creo ___.

To review the subjunctive with expressions of doubt, turn to page 404.

## 6 Completen.

19. Estoy contento que ustedes ___ asistir. (poder)
20. Me sorprende que él no ___ nada. (saber)
21. Me alegro de que tú ___ de acuerdo. (estar)
22. Sandra siente que yo no ___ el viaje. (hacer)

To review the subjunctive with expressions of emotion, turn to page 406.

# Cultura

## 7 Contesten.

23. ¿Dónde tiene lugar la celebración de las doce uvas de la felicidad?
24. ¿Cuándo tiene lugar?
25. ¿Dónde está la Puerta del Sol?

To review this cultural information, turn to page 410.

## Assessment

**FOLDABLES™ Study Organizer** **Dinah Zike's Study Guides**

Your students may wish to use Foldable 9 to organize, display, and arrange data as they learn how to talk about how they feel in Spanish. You may wish to encourage them to add information from each chapter as they continue to expand upon their ability to describe situations and emotions.

A *paper file folder organizer* foldable is also ideal for having students add information to different categories over a period of time.

## Answers to Assessment

13. sirva
14. asistan
15. hagas

16. No dudo que ellos vendrán.
17. No es cierto que él salga.
18. No creo que él lo sepa.

19. puedan
20. sepa
21. estés
22. haga

23. La celebración de las doce uvas de la felicidad tiene lugar en la Puerta del Sol.
24. Tiene lugar en Nochevieja.
25. La Puerta del Sol está en el centro de Madrid.

# ¡Hablo como un pro!

This unique page gives students the opportunity to speak freely and say whatever they can, using the vocabulary and structures they have learned in the chapter. The illustration serves to remind students of precisely what they know how to say in Spanish. There are no activities that students do not have the ability to describe or talk about in Spanish. The art not only depicts the vocabulary and content of this chapter, but also reinforces what they learned in previous chapters.

You may wish to use this page in many ways. Some possibilities are to have students do the following:

1. Look at the illustration and identify items by giving the correct Spanish words.
2. Make up sentences about what they see in the illustration.
3. Make up questions about the illustration. They can call on another class member to respond if you do this as a class activity, or you may prefer to allow students to work in small groups. This activity is extremely beneficial because it enables students to actively use interrogative words.
4. Answer questions you ask them about the illustration.
5. Work in pairs and make up a conversation based on the illustration.
6. Look at the illustration and give a complete oral review of what they see.
7. Look at the illustration and write a paragraph (or essay) about it.

You can also use this page as an assessment or testing tool, taking into account individual differences by having students go from simple to quite complicated tasks.

# ¡Hablo como un pro!

Tell as much as you can about this illustration.

The assessment can be either oral or written. You may wish to use the rubrics provided on pages T20–T21 as you give students the following directions.

1. Identify the topic or situation of the illustration.
2. Give the Spanish words for as many items as you can.
3. Think of as many sentences as you can to describe the illustration.
4. Go over your sentences and put them in the best sequencing to give a coherent story based on the illustration.

# Vocabulario

### Talking about a birthday party

el cumpleaños
el pastel, la torta, el bizcocho
las velas
el regalo
los parientes
nacer
venir a la fiesta
divertirse
¡Feliz cumpleaños!

### Talking about a wedding

la boda
la novia
el novio
la dama de honor
el padrino
la madrina
la recepción
el salón
la orquesta
casarse
¡Felicitaciones!
¡Enhorabuena!

### Talking about Christmas

la Navidad
el árbol de Navidad
la Nochebuena
los Reyes Magos
los camellos
la paja
¡Feliz Navidad!

### Talking about Chanukah

la fiesta de las luces
la menora
hebreo
encender las velas
durar
¡Feliz Hanuka!

**How well do you know your vocabulary?**

- Choose words that describe a holiday you enjoy.
- Write a few sentences about how you and your family or friends celebrate this holiday.

### Talking about New Year's

el Año Nuevo
La víspera de Año Nuevo (Nochevieja)
el reloj
dar las doce
celebrar
¡Feliz Año Nuevo!

### Other useful expressions

alegrarse

**VIDEOTUR**

**Episodio 13**

In this video episode you will join Vicky in her new business adventure. See page 492 for more information.



# Vocabulario

## Vocabulary Review

The words and phrases in the **Vocabulario** have been taught for productive use in this chapter. They are summarized here as a resource for both student and teacher. This list also serves as a convenient resource for the **¡Te toca a ti!** activities on pages 416 and 417. There are approximately five cognates in this vocabulary list. Have students find them.

**¡OJO!** You will notice that the vocabulary list here is not translated. This has been done intentionally, since we feel that by the time students have finished the material in the chapter they should be familiar with the meanings of all the words. If there are several words they still do not know, we recommend that they refer to the **Palabras 1** and **2** sections in the chapter or go to the dictionaries at the end of this book to find the meanings. However, if you prefer that your students have the English translations, please refer to Vocabulary Transparency 13.1, where you will find all these words with their translations.

**VIDEO VHS/DVD**

The Video Program allows students to see how the chapter vocabulary and structures are used by native speakers within an engaging story line. For maximum reinforcement, show the video episode as a final activity for Chapter 13.

# Planning for Chapter 14

## SCOPE AND SEQUENCE, PAGES 422–449

### Topics

- ❖ Professions and occupations
- ❖ Job interviews

### Culture

- ❖ A young man named Bobby
- ❖ The importance of knowing a second language
- ❖ The science of economics
- ❖ **Vistas de Guatemala**

### Functions

- ❖ How to talk about professions and occupations
- ❖ How to prepare for job interviews
- ❖ How to say what you would like to do and what you would like others to do
- ❖ How to say "perhaps" or "maybe"
- ❖ How to describe indefinite persons or things

### Structure

- ❖ Infinitive or subjunctive
- ❖ The subjunctive with **ojalá** and **quizá(s)**

### National Standards

- ❖ Communication Standard 1.1 pages 426, 427, 430, 431, 432, 433, 434, 435, 444
- ❖ Communication Standard 1.2 pages 427, 431, 433, 434, 436, 437, 438–439, 440, 441, 442–443, 444
- ❖ Communication Standard 1.3 pages 440, 443, 445
- ❖ Cultures Standard 2.1 pages 438–439
- ❖ Cultures Standard 2.2 pages 441, 444
- ❖ Connections Standard 3.1 pages 442–443
- ❖ Comparisons Standard 4.1 page 440
- ❖ Comparisons Standard 4.2 pages 438–439, 441
- ❖ Communities Standard 5.1 page 449
- ❖ Communities Standard 5.2 page 437

## PACING AND PRIORITIES

**The chapter content is color coded below to assist you in planning.**

**■ required ■ recommended ■ optional**

**Vocabulario** *(required)* *Days 1–4*

- ■ Palabras 1
  - La oficina
  - La tienda
  - La corte
  - El gobierno municipal
  - Otras profesiones
  - Algunos oficios
- ■ Palabras 2
  - En busca de un puesto

**Estructura** *(required)* *Days 5–7*

- ■ Infinitivo o subjuntivo
- ■ El subjuntivo con **ojalá** y **quizá(s)**
- ■ El subjuntivo en cláusulas relativas

**Conversación** *(required)*

- ■ Planes para el futuro

**Lecturas culturales**

- ■ Un muchacho que se llama Bobby *(recommended)*
- ■ La importancia de las lenguas extranjeras *(optional)*
- ■ Gerentes de restaurante, gerente de tienda, gerente de ventas y un chef *(optional)*

**Conexiones**

- ■ La economía *(optional)*

■ **¡Te toca a ti!** *(recommended)*

■ **Assessment** *(recommended)*

■ **¡Hablo como un pro!** *(optional)*

## RESOURCE GUIDE

| SECTION | PAGES | SECTION RESOURCES |
|---|---|---|
| **Vocabulario PALABRAS 1** | | |
| La oficina<br>La tienda<br>La corte<br>El gobierno municipal<br>Otras profesiones<br>Algunos oficios | 424, 426–427<br>424, 426–427<br>424, 426–427<br>424, 426–427<br>424, 426–427<br>425, 426–427 | Vocabulary Transparencies 14.2–14.3<br>Audio CD 8<br>Audio Activities TE, pages 170–172<br>Workbook, pages 165–166<br>Quiz 1, page 69<br>ExamView® Pro |
| **Vocabulario PALABRAS 2** | | |
| En busca de un puesto | 428–431 | Vocabulary Transparencies 14.4–14.5<br>Audio CD 8<br>Audio Activities TE, pages 172–173<br>Workbook, pages 166–167<br>Quiz 2, page 70<br>ExamView® Pro |
| **Estructura** | | |
| Infinitivo o subjuntivo<br>El subjuntivo con **ojalá** y **quizá(s)**<br>El subjuntivo en cláusulas relativas | 432–433<br>434<br>435 | Audio CD 8<br>Audio Activities TE, pages 174–176<br>Workbook, pages 168–170<br>Quizzes 3–5, pages 69–73<br>ExamView® Pro |
| **Conversación** | | |
| Planes para el futuro | 436–437 | Audio CD 8<br>Audio Activities TE, pages 176–177<br>Interactive CD-ROM |
| **Lecturas culturales** | | |
| Un muchacho que se llama Bobby<br>La importancia de las lenguas extranjeras<br>Gerentes de restaurante, gerente de tienda, gerente de ventas y un chef | 438–439<br>440<br>441 | Audio CD 8<br>Audio Activities TE, page 177<br>Tests, pages 223, 227 |
| **Conexiones** | | |
| La economía | 442–443 | Tests, page 228 |
| **¡Te toca a ti!** | | |
| | 444–445 | **¡Viva el mundo hispano!** Video, Episode 14<br>Video Activities, pages 118–121<br>Spanish Online Activities spanish.glencoe.com |
| **Assessment** | | |
| | 446–447 | Communication Transparency C 14<br>Quizzes 1–5, pages 69–73<br>Performance Assessment, Task 14<br>Tests, pages 221–234<br>Situation Cards, Chapter 14<br>ExamView® Pro<br>**Maratón mental** Videoquiz |

# Using Your Resources for Chapter 14

## Transparencies

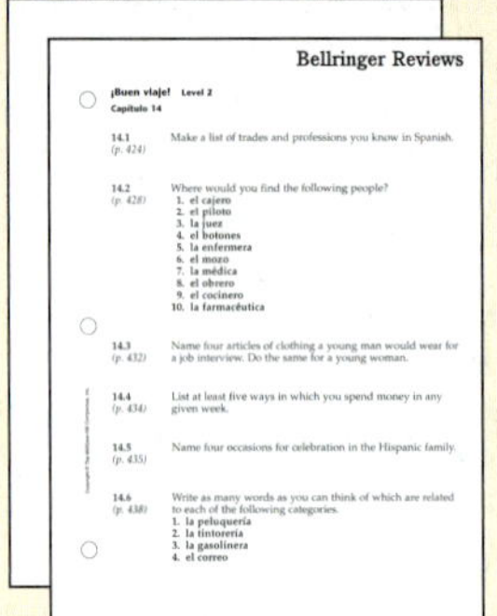

Bellringer 14.1–14.6

Vocabulary 14.1–14.5

Communication C 14

## Workbook

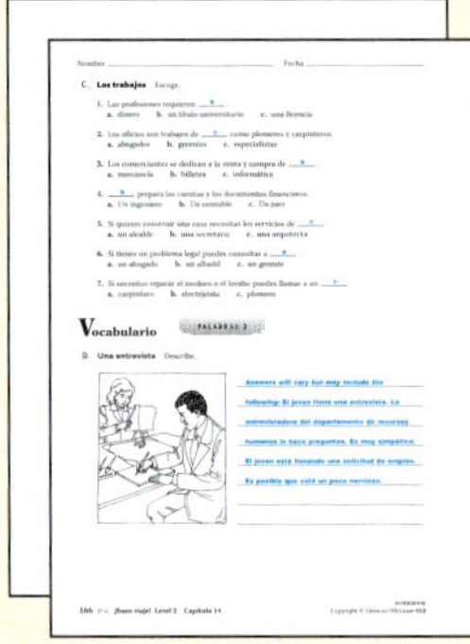

Vocabulary, pages 165–167

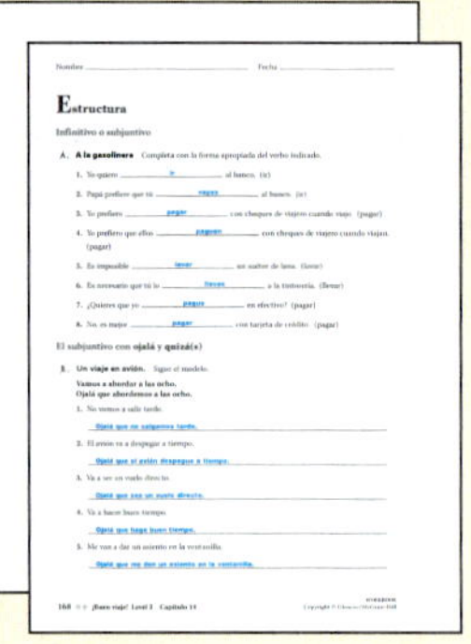

Structure, pages 168–170

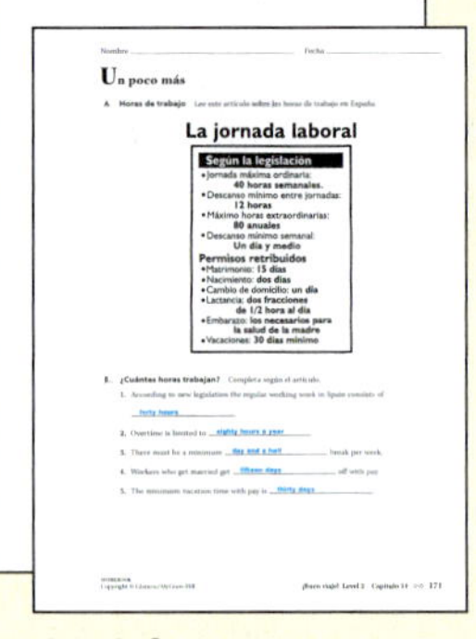

Enrichment, pages 171–174

## Audio Activities

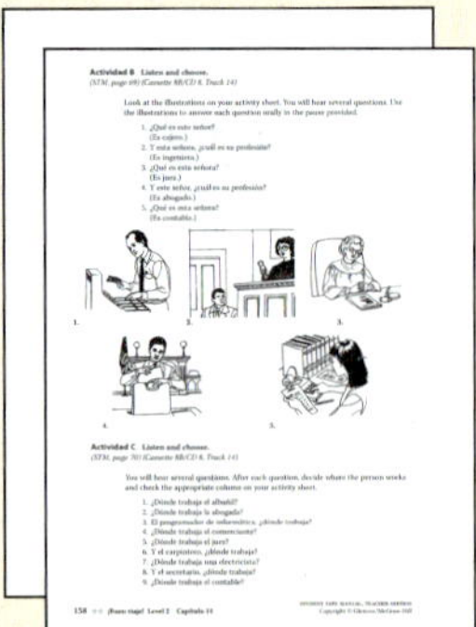
Vocabulary, pages 170–173

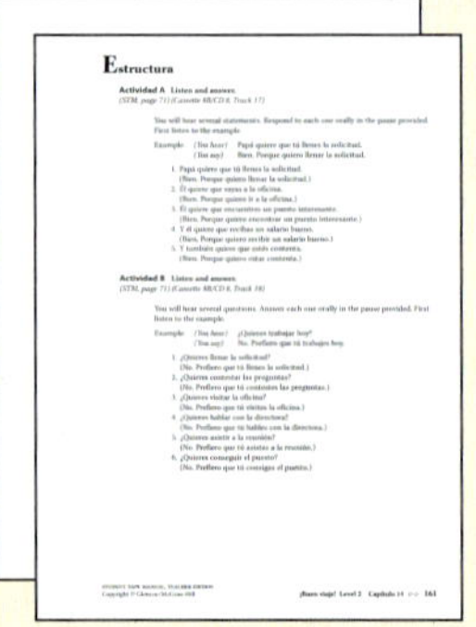

Structure, pages 174–176

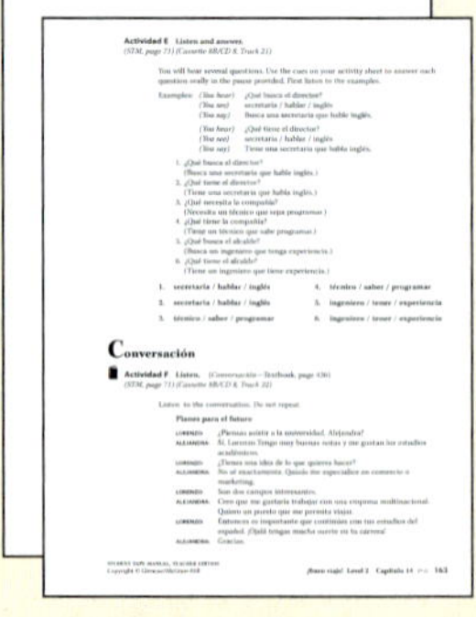

Conversation, pages 176–177

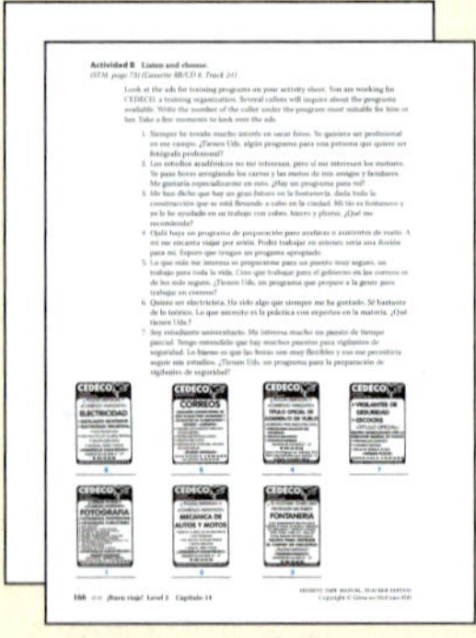
Additional Practice, pages 178–181

# Assessment

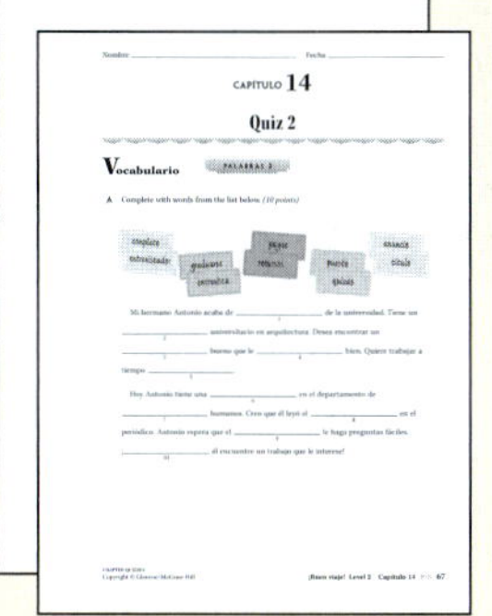
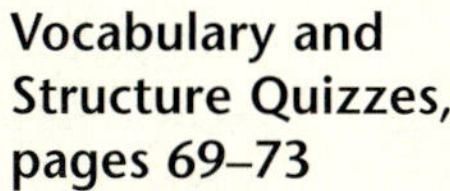

Vocabulary and Structure Quizzes, pages 69–73

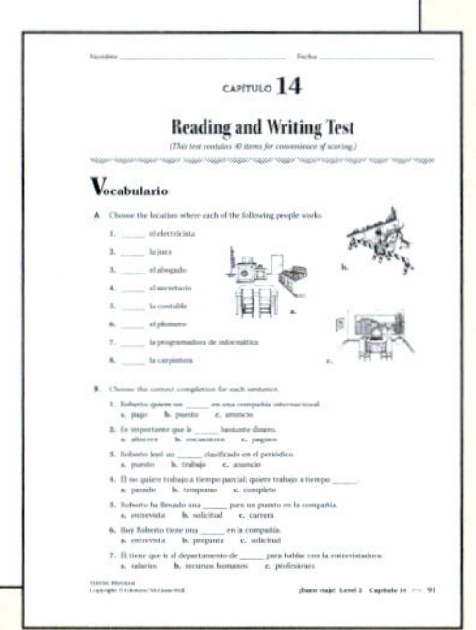

Chapter Tests, pages 221–234

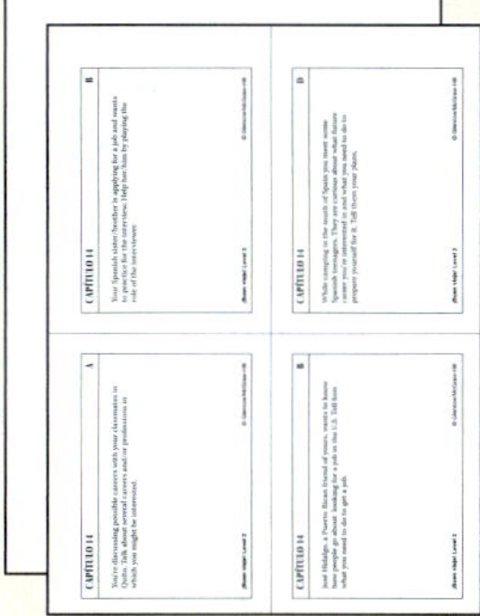

Situation Cards, Chapter 14

MindJogger Videoquiz, ExamView® Pro, Chapter 14

## Timesaving Teacher Tools

### TeacherWorks™

TeacherWorks™ is your all-in-one teacher resource center. Personalize lesson plans, access resources from the Teacher Wraparound Edition, connect to the Internet, or make a to-do list. These are only a few of the many features that can assist you in the planning and organizing of your lessons.

Includes:

- A calendar feature
- Access to all program blackline masters
- Standards correlations and more

### ExamView® Pro

Test Bank software for Macintosh and Windows makes creating, editing, customizing, and printing tests quick and easy.

## Technology Resources

In the Chapter 14 Internet Activity, you will have a chance to learn more about the Spanish-speaking world. Visit spanish.glencoe.com

On the interactive CD–ROM, students can listen to and take part in a recorded version of the conversation in Chapter 14.

**¡Viva el mundo hispano!** Video and Video Activities, Chapter 14. Available on VHS and DVD.

Help your students prepare for the chapter test by playing the **Maratón mental** Videoquiz game show. Teams will compete against each other to review chapter vocabulary and structure and sharpen listening comprehension skills. Available on VHS and DVD.

**¡Buen viaje!** is also available on CD or Online.

## Preview

In this chapter, students will learn to talk about professions, occupations, and looking for work, including interviewing for a position. They will also expand their knowledge of the use of the subjunctive to say what they would like others to do, in contrast to the use of the infinitive to say what they would like to do. Additionally, they will learn to use the subjunctive to state *perhaps* or *maybe.* The cultural focus of this chapter is on future careers, in particular those that may require knowledge of Spanish.

### National Standards

**Communication**

In Chapter 14 students will learn to communicate in spoken and written Spanish on the following topics:

- professions and occupations
- looking for work
- interviewing for a job

Students will obtain and provide information about these topics and engage in conversations that would typically take place when discussing their future plans.

Capítulo 14

# Profesiones y oficios

**Objetivos**

In this chapter you will learn to:

- talk about professions and occupations
- interview for a job
- state work qualifications
- talk about future events
- talk about probable events

Antonio Gattorno *Agricultores*

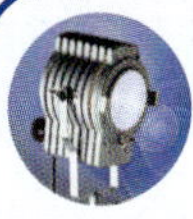

## Spotlight on Culture

**Arte** Cuban painter Antonio Gattorno (1904–1980) was one of the founding members of **El Grupo Minorista**—an early 20th century Cuban artistic, literary, and political movement.

**Fotografía** In this photo we see José Alicea, a graphic artist, at work in his studio in Puerto Rico.

The Museum of History, Anthropology, and Art in the Río Piedras campus of the University of Puerto Rico has a good collection of paintings by Puerto Rican artists.

# Vocabulario

PALABRAS 1 

## 1 PREPARATION

### Resource Manager

Vocabulary Transparencies 14.2–14.3
Audio Activities TE, pages 170–172
Audio CD 8
Workbook, pages 165–166
Quizzes, page 69
ExamView® Pro

### Bellringer Review

*Use BRR Transparency 14.1 or write the following on the board.*
Make a list of trades and professions you know in Spanish.

## 2 PRESENTATION

**Step 1** Have students close their books. Project Vocabulary Transparencies 14.2–14.3 and have students repeat the new words, phrases, and sentences after you or the recording on Audio CD 8.

**Step 2** Have students open their books to pages 424–425 and ask them to read the new words, phrases, and sentences.

**Step 3** Using the Vocabulary Transparencies, call on volunteers to point to various illustrations and photos at random and name the professions.

# Vocabulario

PALABRAS 1

## La oficina

el secretario

la contable

la programadora de informática

el gerente

## Otras profesiones

la ingeniera

el arquitecto

## La tienda

la cajera

el comerciante

## El gobierno municipal

el funcionario

el alcalde

la alcaldía

## La corte

el juez

la abogada

el tribunal

el bufete del abogado



## Reaching All Students

**Total Physical Response** Write the following sentences on cards, one to a card, and distribute them for students to mime the actions. Have the rest of the class guess what profession each individual is miming.

**Tú eres artista.**
**Tú eres juez.**
**Tú eres escultor(a).**
**Tú eres secretario(a).**
**Tú eres profesor(a).**
**Tú eres programador(a) de informática.**
**Tú eres carpintero(a).**
**Tú eres albañil.**
**Tú eres plomero(a).**
**Tú eres contable.**

## Algunos oficios

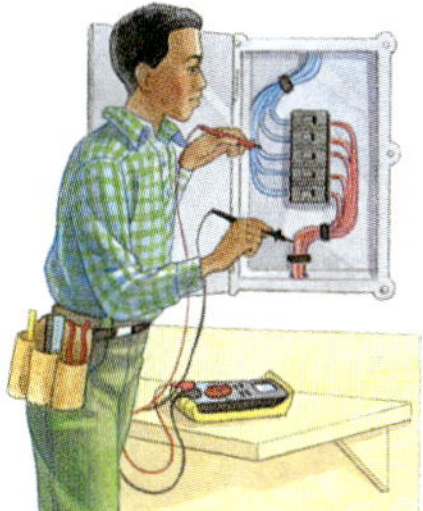

el electricista

el plomero, el fontanero

la carpintera

el albañil

Los oficios son los trabajos de especialistas como plomeros y carpinteros.
Estos especialistas tienen que tener (poseer) un talento.

Las profesiones son los trabajos que requieren un título universitario.
Es necesario que los profesionales tengan un título universitario.

Los comerciantes se dedican a la compra y venta de mercancía.
Quieren que sus clientes compren mucho.
¡Ojalá estén satisfechos!

### National Standards

**Comparisons**
Students learn to understand the nature of language through comparisons of Spanish and English. Both **fontanero** and **plomero** mean *plumber.* **Plomero** is not an anglicism. The word comes from the same Latin root as the English word *plumber:* **plumbum,** meaning *lead,* the metal used by the ancient Romans in their plumbing.

### Learning from Photos

*(page 425)* You may wish to ask students to describe the scenes in the two photos on this page.

### About the Spanish Language

You may wish to tell students that the names of most professions have both masculine and feminine forms: **el / la ingeniero(a), el / la abogado(a), el / la doctor(a), el / la farmacéutico(a),** etc. Some change only in the article: **el / la contable, el / la juez,** etc. All those that end in **a** will change in the article only: **el / la artista, el / la electricista, el / la anestesista,** etc.

**LEVELING**
**E:** Vocabulary
**A:** Vocabulary

Vocabulario

## 3 PRACTICE

## ¿Qué palabra necesito?

¡OJO! When students are doing the **¿Que palabra necesito?** accept any answer that makes sense. The purpose of these activities is to have students use the new vocabulary. They are not factual recall activities. Thus, it is not necessary for students to remember specific factual information from the vocabulary presentation when answering. If you wish, have students use the illustrations on this page as a stimulus, when possible.

**1** Have students refer to the illustrations as they do the activity.

**2** This activity also reviews other professions learned in previous chapters.

**Expansion:** You can do Activity 2 a second time and not allow students to look at the illustrations.

Vocabulario

## ¿Qué palabra necesito?

**1** **¿Qué es y quiénes trabajan aquí?** Contesten.

1. 

2. 

3. 

4. 

5. 

**2** **¿Quién trabaja dónde?** Escojan.

**a.** el mecánico

**b.** la funcionaria

**c.** el cocinero

**d.** la profesora

**e.** el mesero

**f.** el contable

**g.** la juez

**h.** el pintor

**i.** el campesino

**j.** la obrera

**k.** el médico

**l.** la veterinaria

1. ¿Quién trabaja en una fábrica?
2. ¿Quién trabaja en la sala de consulta?
3. ¿Quién cuida de los animales?
4. ¿Quién siembra los campos?
5. ¿Quién pinta cuadros?
6. ¿Quién enseña?
7. ¿Quién repara el carro?
8. ¿Quién prepara los platos en el restaurante?
9. ¿Quién les sirve a los clientes en el restaurante?
10. ¿Quién prepara cuentas y documentos financieros?
11. ¿Quién trabaja en la corte y decide quién es inocente o no?
12. ¿Quién trabaja para el gobierno municipal, estatal o federal?



## Answers to ¿Qué palabra necesito?

**1** *Answers will vary but may include:*

1. Es una oficina. Los secretarios, los contables, los programadores de informática y los gerentes trabajan aquí.
2. Es una tienda. Los comerciantes y los empleados (dependientes) trabajan aquí.
3. Es un cuarto de baño. Los plomeros (fontaneros) trabajan aquí.
4. Es una corte (un tribunal). Los jueces y los abogados trabajan aquí.
5. Es un cuarto. Los electricistas trabajan aquí.

**2**

1. j
2. k
3. l
4. i
5. h
6. d
7. a
8. c
9. e
10. f
11. g
12. b

**3**

1. Necesito un carpintero.
2. Necesito un abogado.
3. Necesito un farmacéutico.
4. Necesito un mozo.
5. Necesito un asistente de vuelo.
6. Necesito un dependiente.

## 3 ¿A quién necesitas si... ? Contesten.

1. quieres construir un garaje para tu casa
2. tienes un problema legal
3. necesitas medicina y tienes una receta del médico
4. quieres ayuda con tus maletas en el aeropuerto
5. quieres unos audífonos en el avión
6. estás buscando ayuda en una tienda

## 4 Una carrera que me interesaría Sigan el modelo.

**agente de policía ⟶**
**Sí, me gustaría ser agente de policía. Me interesaría./ No, no me gustaría ser agente de policía. No me interesaría nada.**

1. médico
2. arquitecto
3. gerente de una gran empresa o compañía
4. abogado
5. dentista
6. contable
7. electricista
8. programador
9. funcionario en una agencia del gobierno
10. veterinario

Un cocinero, Marbella

Una abogada, Ciudad de México

AMALIA ANAYA
Coordinadora General
Equipo Técnico de Apoyo a la Reforma Educativa - ETARE
MINISTERIO DE PLANEAMIENTO Y COORDINACION
Av. Sánchez Lima No. 2647 - Tel. 376051 - Fax 392399 - Casilla 8406 - La Paz - Bolivia

## 5 Una profesión Trabaja con un(a) compañero(a). Hablen de las profesiones u oficios que les interesarían. Expliquen por qué les interesaría cierta profesión.

## 6 Juego ¿Qué soy? Piensa en un oficio o profesión. Tu compañero(a) te puede hacer un máximo de cinco preguntas para adivinar o acertar el oficio o la profesión en que estás pensando. Luego cambien de rol.

*For more practice using words from **Palabras 1**, do Activity 14 on page H15 at the end of this book.*



## Vocabulario

**3** You may wish to have students prepare this activity before going over it in class.

**4** This activity reviews the verbs **interesar** and **gustar.**

### Learning from Realia

*(page 427)* The card is called **una tarjeta de visita.** You may wish to ask students to tell you as much as they can about it.

## Answers to ¿Qué palabra necesito?

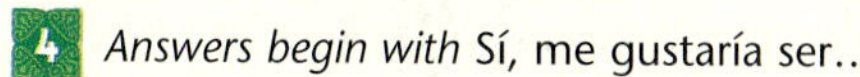

**4** *Answers begin with* Sí, me gustaría ser...

1. ... médico. Me interesaría. No, no me gustaría ser médico. No me interesaría nada.
2. ... arquitecto. Me interesaría. No, no me gustaría ser arquitecto. No me interesaría nada.
3. ... gerente de una gran empresa o compañía. Me interesaría. No, no me gustaría ser gerente de una gran empresa o compañía. No me interesaría nada.
4. ... abogado. Me interesaría. No, no me gustaría ser abogado. No me interesaría nada.
5. ... dentista. Me interesaría. No, no me gustaría ser dentista. No me interesaría nada.
6. ... contable. Me interesaría. No, no me gustaría ser contable. No me interesaría nada.
7. ... electricista. Me interesaría. No, no me gustaría ser electricista. No me interesaría nada.
8. ... programador. Me interesaría. No, no me gustaría ser programador. No me interesaría nada.
9. ... funcionario en una agencia del gobierno. Me interesaría. No, no me gustaría ser funcionario en una agencia del gobierno. No me interesaría nada.
10. ... veterinario. Me interesaría. No, no me gustaría ser veterinario. No me interesaría nada.

**5** *Answers will vary. Students will use vocabulary from* Palabras 1 *to talk about the professions and trades that interest them and why.*

**6** *Answers will vary. Students will use vocabulary from* Palabras 1 *to play the game.*

# Vocabulario
PALABRAS 2

## 1 PREPARATION

### Resource Manager

Vocabulary Transparencies 14.4–14.5
Audio Activities TE, pages 172–173
Audio CD 8
Workbook, pages 166–167
Quizzes, page 70
ExamView® Pro

### Bellringer Review

*Use BRR Transparency 14.2 or write the following on the board.*
Where would you find the following people?

1. **el cajero**
2. **el piloto**
3. **la juez**
4. **el botones**
5. **la enfermera**
6. **el mozo**
7. **la médica**
8. **el obrero**
9. **el cocinero**
10. **la farmacéutica**

## 2 PRESENTATION

**Step 1** You may follow some of the suggestions given in previous chapters to introduce the vocabulary.

# Vocabulario
PALABRAS 2

## En busca de un puesto

Jorge está buscando un puesto que sea interesante.
Quiere que le paguen bien.
Es posible que vea un anuncio en el periódico.
¡Quizás encuentre algo que le interese!

Jorge no quiere trabajar a tiempo completo (cuarenta horas por semana).
Quizás le ofrezcan un trabajo a tiempo parcial.

### Learning from Photos

*(page 428)* Jorge is looking in the **Anuncios clasificados.** He is probably looking under the heading of **Ofrezco.** Under this heading are listed the job offerings. The other heading is **Busco empleo.** The advertisements under **Busco empleo** are placed by people looking for jobs.

### LEVELING

**E:** Activities 1, 2, 3, 4, 5, 6
**A:** Activities 3, 4, 5

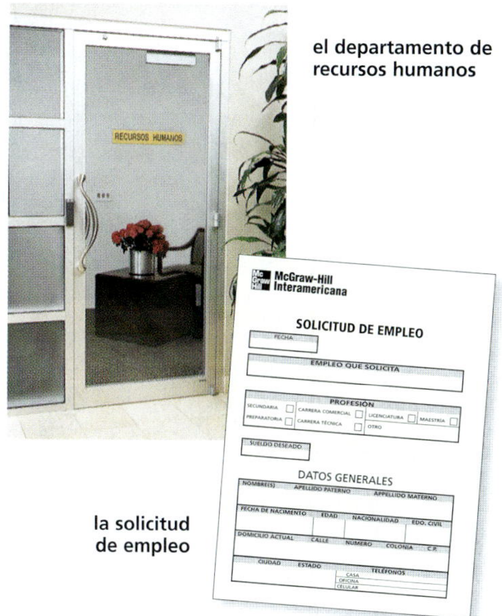


McGraw-Hill Interamericana

SOLICITUD DE EMPLEO

FECHA

EMPLEO QUE SOLICITA

PROFESIÓN

SECUNDARIA / CARRERA COMERCIAL / LICENCIATURA / MAESTRÍA

PREPARATORIA / CARRERA TÉCNICA / OTRO

SUELDO DESEADO

DATOS GENERALES

NOMBRE(S) / APELLIDO PATERNO / APELLIDO MATERNO

FECHA DE NACIMIENTO / EDAD / NACIONALIDAD / EDO. CIVIL

DOMICILIO ACTUAL / CALLE / NÚMERO / COLONIA / C.P.

CIUDAD / ESTADO / TELÉFONOS

CASA / OFICINA / CELULAR

el departamento de recursos humanos

la solicitud de empleo

Catalina busca un puesto también.
Ella llena una solicitud de empleo.

El candidato tiene una entrevista.
La entrevistadora le hace preguntas.
¡Ojalá (que) conteste bien a las preguntas!
Es posible que esté un poco nervioso.
Quizás esté nervioso durante la entrevista.



## Vocabulario

**Step 2** The following are questions you can ask when presenting the sentences:

**¿Qué está buscando Jorge?**
**¿Qué tipo de puesto está buscando?**
**¿Quiere un puesto que le pague bien?**
**¿Dónde es posible que haya un anuncio?**
**¿Quiere Jorge trabajar a tiempo completo o a tiempo parcial?**
**¿Y qué busca Catalina?**
**¿Qué llena ella?**
**¿Con quién tiene el candidato una entrevista?**
**¿Es posible que el candidato esté un poco nervioso durante la entrevista?**

### Paired Activities

Have students create a conversation between the **entrevistador(a)** and the **aspirante** based on the photo on page 429. Allow pairs time to practice their conversation and then have them present it to the class.

## Chapter Projects

### Currículum vitae

Have students prepare their curriculum vitae in Spanish.

## Reaching All Students

### Total Physical Response

*(Student 1)* y *(Student 2)*, vengan acá.
*(Student 1)*, buscas trabajo.
*(Student 2)*, trabajas en el departamento de recursos humanos. Vas a ser entrevistador(a).
*(Student 1)*, toma el periódico. Lee los anuncios clasificados.
Ve al departamento de personal. Llena una solicitud de empleo.
*(Student 2)*, invita al / a la aspirante a sentarse en el sillón en tu oficina. Hazle preguntas.
*(Student 1)*, estás nervioso(a). Contesta a sus preguntas.
Gracias, *(Student 1)* y *(Student 2)*, pueden regresar a su asiento.

Vocabulario

## 3 PRACTICE

## ¿Qué palabra necesito?

**Historieta** Each time **Historieta** appears, it means that the answers to the activity form a short story. Encourage students to look at the title of the **Historieta,** since it can help them do the activity.

**7**, **8**, and **9** These activities can be done first orally with books closed. Students can then write answers to each activity for homework.

**Expansion:** After going over the activities, call on a student or several students to retell all the information from each activity in their own words.

### Learning from Realia

*(page 430)* You may wish to ask questions about the want ads:

**¿Qué tipo de compañía es? ¿Qué tipo de profesional busca? ¿Cuáles son tres cosas que son importantes para el puesto? ¿Cuánto es el salario?**

Vocabulario

## ¿Qué palabra necesito?

### 7 Historieta Una entrevista

Contesten según la foto.

1. ¿Están entrevistando a la señorita?
2. ¿Estará buscando ella un puesto que sea interesante y que le pague bien?
3. ¿Tiene la candidata una carta de recomendación?
4. ¿Tiene que llenar una solicitud de empleo?
5. ¿Quiere la señorita que la entrevistadora lea su carta de recomendación?
6. ¿Es posible que la candidata esté un poco nerviosa?

Caracas, Venezuela

### 8 Historieta Mi trabajo

Contesten.

1. ¿Trabajas?
2. ¿Dónde trabajas?
3. ¿Trabajas a tiempo completo o a tiempo parcial?
4. ¿Prefieres trabajar a tiempo completo o a tiempo parcial?
5. ¿Recibes un salario?
6. ¿Cuánto te pagan?

Empresa de primer orden de INGENIERIA Y SISTEMAS DE CONTROL DE TRAFICO Y TRANSPORTE, con presencia consolidada en ámbitos internacionales, ofrece puesto de

**ingeniero de compras y logística**

- Buscamos un profesional, con formación de **Ingeniero Superior o Técnico**, dominio del **inglés** y disponibilidad para viajar por España y el extranjero.
- **Se valorará:**
  - La experiencia adquirida en el área de compras y logística en Empresa Industrial.
  - La formación específica sobre la materia.
  - La capacidad de negociación con proveedores nacionales y extranjeros.
- La remuneración es a convenir, en función de la formación y experiencia aportada por los candidatos.

***Rogamos envíen Historial Profesional detallado, con pretensiones económicas, fotografía, señas y teléfono de contacto, indicando la Ref.: 22.229 a:***

**GM&A Selección** C/ Don Ramón de la Cruz, 33 28001 Madrid

**SE SOLICITA RECEPCIONISTA**

Para importante empresa. Presentarse de lunes a viernes, en Av. 20 de Octubre # 1743 (esq. Conchitas) de 9 a 10:30 con currículum y referencias.



## ANSWERS TO ¿Qué palabra necesito?

**7**

1. Sí, están entrevistando a la señorita.
2. Sí, estará buscando un puesto que sea interesante y que le pague bien.
3. Sí, la candidata tiene una carta de recomendación.
4. Sí, tiene que llenar una solicitud de empleo.
5. Sí, la señorita quiere que la entrevistadora lea su carta de recomendación.
6. Sí, es posible que la candidata esté un poco nerviosa.

**8** *Answers will vary but may include:*

1. Sí, (No, no) trabajo.
2. Trabajo en ___.
3. Trabajo a tiempo completo (parcial).
4. Prefiero trabajar a tiempo completo (parcial).
5. Sí, (No, no) recibo un salario.
6. Me pagan ___.

**9** **Historieta Él solicita trabajo.** Contesten según se indica.

1. ¿Juan busca trabajo? (sí)
2. ¿Qué ha leído? (un anuncio en el periódico)
3. ¿Qué compañía está buscando (reclutando) empleados? (Austral)
4. ¿Adónde va Juan? (al departamento de recursos humanos de Austral)
5. ¿Qué tiene que llenar? (una solicitud de empleo)
6. ¿A quién le da la solicitud? (a la recepcionista)
7. ¿Qué va a tener? (una entrevista)

**10** **Una entrevista** Eres un(a) empleado(a) en una agencia de empleos. Un(a) compañero(a) es un(a) candidato(a) para un empleo. Tú vas a darle una entrevista. Pregúntale sobre sus estudios, experiencia, aptitudes personales, talentos artísticos, etc. Luego cambien de rol.

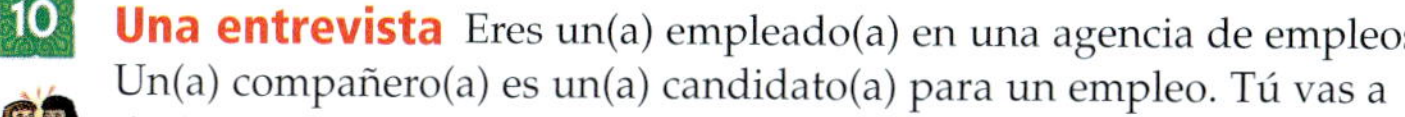

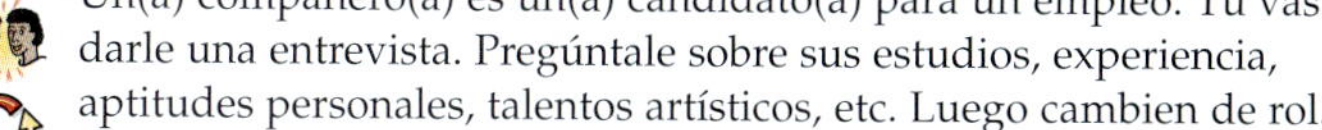

**11** **En la oficina del/de la consejero(a) de orientación**
El/La consejero(a) de orientación *(guidance counselor)* de tu escuela te ha pedido ayudar a un(a) estudiante hispanohablante que acaba de llegar de un país latinoamericano. Quiere que le hagas preguntas para determinar una carrera que le interesaría. Luego quiere que le expliques todo lo que tiene que hacer para prepararse para esa carrera.

Guadalajara, México



## Vocabulario

### Writing Development

After going over Activity 9, have students write the story about Juan in a unified paragraph using the activity as a guide.

**10 and 11** These activities encourage students to use the chapter vocabulary and structures in open-ended situations. It is not necessary to have them do both activities. Choose the one you consider most appropriate.

### Chapter Projects

**Tu futuro** Have students prepare a report on what they think they would like to do when they complete their education and how Spanish might help them in their careers.

**Note:** You might like to do this project in conjunction with the **Lecturas**, pages 438–440.

### LEVELING

**E:** Activities 7, 8, 9, 10

**A:** Activities 10, 11

## Answers to ¿Qué palabra necesito?

**9**

1. Sí, Juan busca trabajo.
2. Ha leído un anuncio en el periódico.
3. Austral está buscando (reclutando) empleados.
4. Juan va al departamento de recursos humanos de Austral.
5. Tiene que llenar una solicitud de empleo.
6. Le da la solicitud a la recepcionista.
7. Va a tener una entrevista.

**10** *Answers will vary. Students will use vocabulary from* Palabras 2 *to conduct a job interview.*

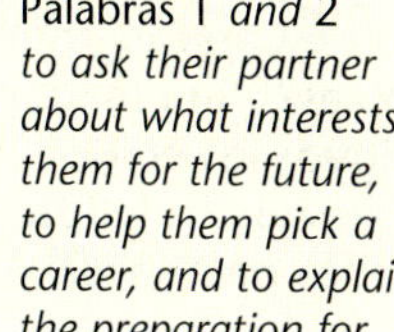

**11** *Answers will vary. Students will use vocabulary from* Palabras 1 *and* 2 *to ask their partner about what interests them for the future, to help them pick a career, and to explain the preparation for the career.*

# Estructura

## 1 PREPARATION

### Resource Manager

Audio Activities TE, pages 174–176
Audio CD 8
Workbook, pages 168–170
Quizzes, pages 71–73
ExamView® Pro

### Bellringer Review

*Use BRR Transparency 14.3 or write the following on the board.*
Name four articles of clothing a young man would wear for a job interview. Do the same for a young woman.

## 2 PRESENTATION

### Infinitivo o subjuntivo

**Step 1** Lead students through Items 1 and 2 on page 432.

**Step 2** Call on volunteers to read the model sentences aloud.

## 3 PRACTICE

### ¿Cómo lo digo?

**12** and **13** Have students present each item in these activities as a miniconversation. Students must do these activities with books open so they can read the first line of each miniconversation.

# Estructura

## Infinitivo o subjuntivo
### Saying what you would like to do and what you would like others to do

1. With any verbs or expressions that require the subjunctive, the subjunctive is used only when there is a change of subject. In other words, the subjunctive is used when the subject of the main clause is different from the subject of the dependent clause that follows **que.**

| MAIN CLAUSE | | DEPENDENT CLAUSE |
|---|---|---|
| **Tú quieres** | **que** | **yo vaya al banco.** |
| **Nosotros preferimos** | **que** | **ustedes cambien dinero.** |
| **Es necesario** | **que** | **alguien decida.** |

2. If there is no change of subject, the infinitive is used.

**Tú quieres ir al banco.**
**Nosotros preferimos cambiar dinero.**
**Es necesario decidir.**

Caracas, Venezuela

## ¿Cómo lo digo?

**12** **Historieta No. Yo quiero hacerlo.**

Contesten según el modelo.

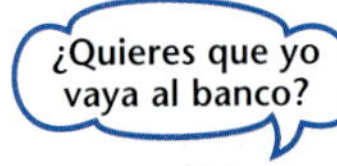

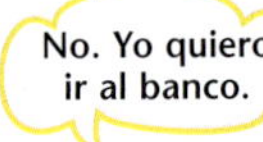

1. ¿Quieres que yo vaya al banco?
2. ¿Quieres que yo endose el cheque?
3. ¿Quieres que yo cobre el cheque?
4. ¿Quieres que yo pida la tasa de cambio?
5. ¿Quieres que yo cambie dólares?
6. ¿Quieres que yo abra una cuenta?



### Learning from Photos

*(page 432)* Ask students to say all they can about the photo. Some questions you might ask are: **En la foto de Caracas, ¿qué tipo de zona es? ¿Son modernos o antiguos los edificios? ¿Hay rascacielos en la foto? ¿Hay muchos peatones?**

### Answers to ¿Cómo lo digo?

**12**

1. No, yo quiero ir al banco.
2. No, yo quiero endosar el cheque.
3. No, yo quiero cobrar el cheque.
4. No, yo quiero pedir la tasa de cambio.
5. No, yo quiero cambiar dólares.
6. No, yo quiero abrir una cuenta.

# Estructura

**13** **Historieta** **Nosotros también** Sigan el modelo.

Yo espero que Uds. hagan el viaje.

Nosotros también esperamos hacer el viaje.

1. Yo espero que ustedes hagan el viaje.
2. Espero que ustedes viajen en avión.
3. Espero que tomen un vuelo directo.
4. Espero que lleguen a tiempo.
5. Espero que visiten los museos.
6. Espero que vean los monumentos.
7. Espero que coman bien.
8. Espero que tengan bastante dinero.
9. Espero que vuelvan en una semana.

Ciudad de México

Museo de Arte Contemporáneo, Ciudad de México

**14** **Historieta** **La ropa sucia** Contesten.

1. ¿Quieres lavar la ropa sucia?
2. ¿O prefieres que yo la lave?
3. ¿Quieres ir a la lavandería?
4. ¿O prefieres que yo vaya?
5. ¿Quieres que yo te lave el suéter?
6. ¿O es necesario limpiarlo en seco?
7. ¿Quieres que yo lo lleve a la tintorería?

**15** **Este fin de semana** Pregúntale a tu compañero(a) lo que él o ella quiere hacer este fin de semana. Después, pregúntale lo que quiere que sus padres hagan. Luego cambien de rol.

**14** This activity can be done first orally with books closed.

## Learning from Photos

*(page 433 top)* Ask students to say all they can about the photo. Some questions you might ask are: **¿Dónde están las personas en la foto de arriba en la página 433? ¿Qué están haciendo ellos?**
*(page 433 bottom)* Ask students to do the following. **Describe lo que ves en la foto del Museo de Arte Contemporáneo.**

## LEVELING

**E:** Activities 12, 13, 14, 15

**A:** Activities 12, 13, 14, 15

## Answers to ¿Cómo lo digo?

**13**

1. Nosotros también esperamos hacer el viaje.
2. Nosotros también esperamos viajar en avión.
3. Nosotros también esperamos tomar un vuelo directo.
4. Nosotros también esperamos llegar a tiempo.
5. Nosotros también esperamos visitar los museos.
6. Nosotros también esperamos ver los monumentos.
7. Nosotros también esperamos comer bien.
8. Nosotros también esperamos tener bastante dinero.
9. Nosotros también esperamos volver en una semana.

**14**

1. Sí, (No, no) quiero lavar la ropa sucia.
2. Sí, (No, no) prefiero que tú la laves.
3. Sí, (No, no) quiero ir a la lavandería.
4. Sí, (No, no) prefiero que tú vayas.
5. Sí, (No, no) quiero que tú me laves el suéter.
6. Sí, (No, no) es necesario limpiarlo en seco.
7. Sí, (No, no) quiero que tú lo lleves a la tintorería.

**15** *Answers will vary. Students will practice using the subjunctive and the infinitive by explaining what they want to do this weekend versus what their parents would like them to do.*

## 1 PREPARATION

### Bellringer Review

*Use BRR Transparency 14.4 or write the following on the board.*
List at least five ways in which you spend money in any given week.

## 2 PRESENTATION

### El subjuntivo con ojalá y quizá(s)

**Step 1** Have students open their books to page 434. Lead them through the explanation.

**Step 2** Have volunteers read the model sentences aloud.

## 3 PRACTICE

### ¿Cómo lo digo?

**16** and **17** These activities can be done orally with books closed. Students can then write the answers at home. Have students use as much expression as possible when using **ojalá** and **quizás.**

### Learning from Realia

*(page 434)* You may wish to ask these questions about the realia.

**¿Para qué irías a Carlos Durán? ¿Qué será Luisa Fernanda?**

### LEVELING

**E:** Activity 20

**A:** Activities 16, 17, 18, 19



## El subjuntivo con ojalá y quizá(s)

### Stating *perhaps* or *maybe*

The expressions **ojalá** *(I wish* or *I hope)* and **quizá(s)** *(perhaps* or *maybe)* are always followed by the subjunctive.

**¡Ojalá que tengas una entrevista!**
**¡Ojalá que te salga bien!**
**¡Quizá te ofrezcan el puesto!**

Ciudad de México

### ¿Cómo lo digo?

**16 Historieta ¡Ojalá que sí!** Contesten con **ojalá.**

1. ¿Él va a buscar un puesto?
2. ¿Va a ir al departamento de recursos humanos?
3. ¿Va a pedir una solicitud de empleo?
4. ¿Va a llenar la solicitud?
5. ¿Le van a dar una entrevista?
6. ¿No va a estar muy nervioso?
7. ¿Le van a ofrecer el puesto?
8. ¿Le va a pagar bien el trabajo?

**17 El corte de pelo** Contesten según el modelo.

**¿Dónde estará Marta? (la peluquería) →**
**Quizás esté en la peluquería.**

1. ¿Dónde estará Marta? (la peluquería)
2. ¿Qué pedirá ella? (un corte de pelo)
3. ¿Qué usarán para cortarle el pelo? (tijeras)
4. ¿Qué más le darán? (un champú)
5. ¿Quién le cortará el pelo? (Nilda)
6. ¿Cuánto tiempo tomará? (media hora)
7. ¿Cuánto le cobrarán? (20 pesos)

**18 Quizá y ojalá** Habla con un(a) compañero(a). Usando **quizá,** dile algunas cosas que es posible que ocurran en el futuro. Si es algo que quieres que ocurra, sigue hablando usando **ojalá.** Por ejemplo, **¡Quizá seas rico(a)! ¡Ojalá sea rico(a)!** Luego cambien de rol.



### Answers to ¿Cómo lo digo?

**16**

1. ¡Ojalá que él busque un puesto!
2. ¡Ojalá que vaya al departamento de recursos humanos!
3. ¡Ojalá que pida una solicitud de empleo!
4. ¡Ojalá que llene la solicitud!
5. ¡Ojalá que le den una entrevista!
6. ¡Ojalá que no esté muy nervioso!
7. ¡Ojalá que le ofrezcan el puesto!
8. ¡Ojalá que le pague bien el trabajo!

**17**

1. Quizá(s) esté en la peluquería.
2. Quizá(s) pida un corte de pelo.
3. Quizá(s) usen tijeras para cortarle el pelo.
4. Quizá(s) le den un champú.
5. Quizá(s) Nilda le corte el pelo.
6. Quizá(s) tome media hora.
7. Quizá(s) le cobren 20 pesos.

*Answers will vary. Students will use* quizá *to speculate on things that are possible in the future. If the event is something that they also would like to happen, students should repeat the idea substituting* ojalá *for* quizá.

## El subjuntivo en cláusulas relativas
### Describing indefinite persons or things

A grouping of words that modifies a noun is called a relative clause. A relative clause can modify or describe a noun that refers to a specific, definite person or thing or an indefinite person or thing. When the clause describes a definite person or thing, the verb in the clause is in the indicative. If, however, it modifies an indefinite person or thing, the verb is in the subjunctive. Note too that the **a personal** is omitted when the object is indefinite.

**Conocemos a una secretaria que habla bien el español.**
**Buscamos una secretaria que hable bien el español.**

## ¿Cómo lo digo?

**19 Un conocido** Contesten según el modelo.

**una persona que habla español →**
**No necesito una persona que hable español.**
**Conozco a una persona que habla español.**

1. una persona que es bilingüe
2. una persona que tiene experiencia
3. una persona que conoce el mercado
4. una persona que puede viajar

**20 Historieta Están buscando empleados.** Contesten.

1. ¿Está ofreciendo la compañía Vensa un puesto que paga bien?
2. ¿Buscan alguien que tenga experiencia en ventas?
3. ¿Quieren alguien que pueda viajar?
4. ¿Necesitan una persona que conozca más de un idioma?

### Answers to ¿Cómo lo digo?

1. No necesito una persona que sea bilingüe. Conozco a una persona que es bilingüe.
2. No necesito una persona que tenga experiencia. Conozco a una persona que tiene experiencia.
3. No necesito una persona que conozca el mercado. Conozco a una persona que conoce el mercado.
4. No necesito una persona que pueda viajar. Conozco a una persona que puede viajar.

1. Sí (No), la compañía Vensa (no) está ofreciendo un puesto que paga bien.
2. Sí, (No, no) buscan alguien que tenga experiencia en ventas.
3. Sí, (No, no) quieren alguien que pueda viajar.
4. Sí, (No, no) necesitan una persona que conozca más de un idioma.

## Estructura

### 1 PREPARATION

**Bellringer Review**

*Use BRR Transparency 14.5 or write the following on the board.*
Name four occasions for celebration in the Hispanic family.

### 2 PRESENTATION

**El subjuntivo en cláusulas relativas**

**Step 1** Have students open their books to page 435. Lead them through the explanation.

**Step 2** Call on volunteers to read the model sentences aloud.

### 3 PRACTICE

**¿Cómo lo digo?**

**19** Have students prepare this activity before going over it in class.

**20** This activity can be done orally with books closed.

**Learning from Realia**

*(page 435)* You may wish to ask students the following questions about the advertisement. **¿Para qué es el anuncio? ¿Qué aprenderías allí? ¿Con qué máquinas podrías practicar?**

**¡Adelante!**
At this point in the chapter, students have learned all the vocabulary and structure necessary to complete the chapter. The conversation and cultural readings that follow recycle all the material learned up to this point.

# Conversación

## 1 PREPARATION

**Resource Manager**

Audio Activities TE, pages 176–177
Audio CD 8

## 2 PRESENTATION

**Step 1** Have students listen once to Audio CD 8.

**Step 2** Call on two students to read. One can take the part of Lorenzo, the other the part of Alejandra.

**Step 3** After going over the entire conversation, do the **¿Comprendes?** activity.

**Step 4** Have students retell Alejandra's plans in their own words.

**LEVELING**

**E:** Conversation

# Conversación

## Planes para el futuro   

**Lorenzo** ¿Piensas asistir a la universidad, Alejandra?

**Alejandra** Sí. Tengo muy buenas notas y me gustan los estudios académicos.

**Lorenzo** ¿Tienes una idea de lo que quieres hacer?

**Alejandra** No sé exactamente. Quizás me especialice en comercio o marketing.

**Lorenzo** Son dos campos interesantes.

**Alejandra** Creo que me gustaría trabajar con una empresa multinacional. Quiero un puesto que me permita viajar.

**Lorenzo** Entonces es importante que continúes con tus estudios del español. ¡Ojalá tengas mucha suerte en tu carrera!

**Alejandra** Gracias.

### ¿Comprendes?

Contesten.

1. ¿Qué piensa hacer en el futuro Alejandra?
2. ¿Por qué quiere asistir a la universidad?
3. ¿Sabe Alejandra lo que quiere hacer después?
4. ¿En qué campos piensa especializarse?
5. ¿Por qué dice que le gustaría trabajar con una empresa multinacional?
6. ¿Qué le aconseja Lorenzo?



### Answers to ¿Comprendes?

1. Alejandra piensa asistir a la universidad.
2. Tiene buenas notas y le gustan los estudios académicos.
3. No, Alejandra no sabe exactamente qué quiere hacer después.
4. Piensa especializarse en comercio o marketing.
5. Quiere un puesto que le permita viajar.
6. Lorenzo le aconseja que continúe con sus estudios del español.

### Glencoe Technology

On the CD-ROM, students can watch a dramatization of his conversation. They can then play the role of either one of the characters and record themselves in the conversation.

# Vamos a hablar más

**A** **Un trabajo ideal** Piensa en lo que tú considerarías un trabajo ideal, algo que a ti te gustaría mucho hacer. Describe tu trabajo ideal a un(a) compañero(a). Luego cambien de rol.

**B** **Posibles carreras** Trabaja con un(a) compañero(a). Cada uno(a) de ustedes va a preparar una lista de las cosas que le interesan y de las materias o asignaturas que le gustan. Luego miren sus listas. Determinen los intereses que tienen en común. Luego discutan las profesiones o los oficios que les interesarían a los dos.

**C** **Buscando un puesto** Trabaja con un(a) compañero(a). Miren las fotos y describan lo que pasa en cada una.

**SPANISH Online**

For more information about professions available in the Spanish-speaking world, go to the Glencoe Spanish Web site: spanish.glencoe.com

a.

b.

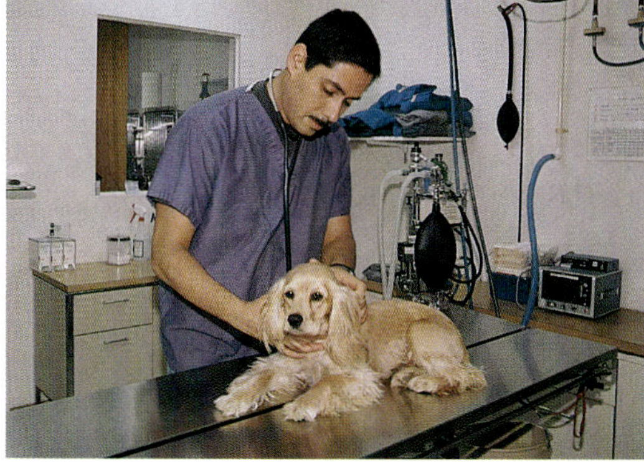

c.



## Answers to Vamos a hablar más

 *Answers will vary. Students will use vocabulary from* Palabras 1 *to describe what would be their favorite job to do.*

 *Answers will vary. Students will use* Palabras 1 *and* 2 *to make lists of their interests and favorite classes. Then with their partner, they'll try to match their interests with possible careers.*

 *Answers will vary. Students will use the vocabulary from the chapter to describe the photos.*



## 3 PRACTICE

### Vamos a hablar más

**A**, **B**, and **C** Have students choose the activity or activities they would like to do.

### Learning from Photos

*(page 437)* You may wish to ask pairs of students to create a conversation based on Photo B.

### About the Spanish Language

Dog lovers may want to know the names of some popular dog breeds in Spanish. Ask them to try to figure out what the following are.

| | |
|---|---|
| **un cócker** | *Cocker Spaniel* |
| **el gran danés** | *Great Dane* |
| **el galgo** | *Greyhound* |
| **el pastor alemán** | *German shepherd* |
| **el perro de Terranova** | *Newfoundland* |
| **el perrito pequinés** | *Pekinese* |
| **el chihuahua** | *Chihuahua* |

The Glencoe Spanish Web site **(spanish.glencoe.com)** offers options that enable you and your students to experience the Spanish-speaking world via the Internet. For each **Capítulo,** there are activities, games, and quizzes. In addition an *Enrichment* section offers students an opportunity to visit Web sites related to the theme of the chapter.

# Lecturas culturales

## Resource Manager

Audio Activities TE, page 177
Audio CD 8

## Bellringer Review

*Use BRR Transparency 14.6 or write the following on the board.*
Write as many words as you can think of which are related to each of the following categories.

1. **la peluquería**
2. **la tintorería**
3. **la gasolinera**
4. **el correo**

## National Standards

**Cultures**
The reading on pages 438–439 and the related activity on page 439 allow students to see how, by combining Spanish with his college major, one young man was able to pursue a successful career in diplomacy.

## PRESENTATION

### Pre-reading

**Step 1** Have students read the Reading Strategy on page 438.

**Step 2** Then have them scan the selection and ask them to tell you in Spanish what they think it is about.

### Reading

**Step 1** Have students open their books and call on individuals to read.

**Step 2** Ask questions about what was just read.

# Lecturas culturales

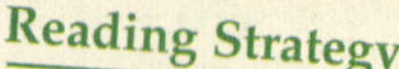

## Reading Strategy

**Scanning for specific information** An important strategy is using titles and pictures to preview a reading selection and to help you know what it is about. Previewing a passage will help give an idea as to its purpose, organization, and content.

## Un muchacho que se llama Bobby

Esta historia no es ficción. Bobby, a quien hoy le llaman don Roberto, es norteamericano. Asistió a una escuela pública donde estudió el español por cuatro años. Siguió con sus estudios del español en la universidad, aunque el español no era su campo de especialización. Se especializó en ciencias políticas.

Después de graduarse de la universidad Bobby entró al Cuerpo de Paz[1] como voluntario. Pasó unos meses de entrenamiento[2] en Puerto Rico. Después fue a Centroamérica donde trabajaba con campesinos en proyectos de irrigación y reforestación. Cuando terminó su período de voluntario, Bobby tomó el examen para el Departamento de Estado.

Bobby fue a trabajar con el Departamento de Estado y ascendió rápidamente. Fue cónsul en Costa Rica y agregado cultural en España. Él ha representado a Estados Unidos en Centroamérica, Sudamérica y España. Y hoy Bobby es embajador.

[1]Cuerpo de Paz *Peace Corps*
[2]entrenamiento *training*

Bolivia

Ecuador



## Learning from Photos

*(pages 438–439)* Ask students to describe what they see and to say all they can about the photos.

## FUN FACTS

The Peace Corps was founded in 1961 by executive order of President Kennedy. Volunteers serve for twenty-seven months. Volunteers serve in a number of countries in Latin America. They work in project sectors such as agriculture, language teaching, math and science education, business development, public administration, vocational training, healthcare, and natural-resource management.

¿Dónde y cómo comenzó esta ilustre carrera diplomática? Según don Roberto, «en el noveno grado, en mi clase de español uno».

¡Ojalá que tú también tengas una carrera tan interesante como la de Bobby! ¡Quizás seas nuestro embajador o embajadora en España o en México! ¿Qué opinas? ¿Te interesa la posibilidad de un puesto que te pague bien y que te permita ver el mundo al mismo tiempo?

Perú

Embajada norteamericana, Santiago, Chile

## ¿Comprendes?

**Una carrera interesante** Contesten.

1. ¿Cómo le llaman a Bobby hoy?
2. ¿De qué nacionalidad es?
3. ¿Cuántos años estudió el español en la escuela secundaria?
4. ¿Dónde siguió con sus estudios del español?
5. ¿En qué se especializó?
6. ¿Qué hizo en el Cuerpo de Paz?
7. Al terminar su período con el Cuerpo de Paz, ¿adónde fue a trabajar Bobby?
8. ¿Qué ha sido él?



## Lecturas culturales

### Post-reading

**Step 1** Ask students to answer the question posed in the last paragraph of the reading.

**Step 2** Have students read the selection at home and write the answers to the **¿Comprendes?** activity. Go over it in class the next day.

### Career Connection

In this reading students learned about some careers in foreign service and the Peace Corps that require knowledge of Spanish. For more information about these careers, you may wish to have students write to the State Department and Peace Corps or have the school guidance counselor talk to your class. If there is a Peace Corps office in your community, you might also like to invite a former Peace Corps Volunteer to class to talk about his or her experiences.

**LEVELING**

**E:** Reading

### Answers to ¿Comprendes?

1. Hoy le llaman don Roberto.
2. Es norteamericano.
3. Estudió el español cuatro años en la escuela secundaria.
4. Siguió con sus estudios del español en la universidad.
5. Se especializó en ciencias políticas.
6. Trabajó con campesinos en proyectos de irrigación y reforestación.
7. Fue a trabajar con el Departamento de Estado.
8. Fue cónsul en Costa Rica y agregado cultural en España. Ha representado a Estados Unidos en Centroamérica, Sudamérica y España. Y hoy es embajador.

# Lectura opcional 1

## National Standards

**Cultures**

This reading and the related activity on this page familiarize students with the importance of knowing foreign languages in international business.

**¡OJO!** This reading is optional. You may skip it completely, have the entire class read it, have only several students read it and report to the class, or assign it for extra credit.

## About the Spanish Language

The expression **¡Ojalá!** is used to indicate the fervent desire that something happen. The origin of the expression is **wa-sa'Allah** meaning *would that God will it.* This is another vivid example of the influence of the Arabic language and culture in Spain.

## Career Connection

Have students research which American companies have offices in Spanish-speaking countries and what types of positions are available. Have them pool the information and decide which company they would like to work for and what type of job they would be interested in.

# Lectura opcional 1

Caracas, Venezuela

## La importancia de las lenguas extranjeras

No hay duda que el conocimiento de un idioma extranjero como el español puede ser un beneficio en muchas carreras. Hoy en día el comercio internacional tiene más y más importancia. No es suficiente sólo exportar nuestros productos al extranjero. Hay que tener una presencia real en muchos países. Por consiguiente muchas grandes empresas norteamericanas han llegado a ser multinacionales. Quiere decir que tienen instalaciones o sucursales[1] y filiales[2] en el extranjero. ¡Imagínate! Es posible que algún día tú trabajes con una compañía americana y que tu oficina esté en Caracas, Lima o Madrid.

Quizás el español en sí[3] no sea una carrera. Pero el español con otra especialización le da a uno una ventaja incalculable. Si tú conoces la contabilidad, el marketing o la informática, por ejemplo, y además dominas bien el español, podrás trabajar con una empresa multinacional. El español y tu otra especialización te permitirán encontrar un trabajo que te pague bien, que te sea interesante y que te dé la oportunidad de viajar y ver el mundo. ¡Ojalá! ¿No?

[1]sucursales *branches* [2]filiales *subsidiaries* [3]en sí *in itself*

Caracas, Venezuela

Ceuta

## ¿Comprendes?

**La importancia de una lengua extranjera**

Discutan.

¿Por qué es importante estudiar una lengua extranjera? ¿Cómo te puede ayudar en tu vida?



## Learning from Photos

*(page 440)* You may wish to call students' attention to the calling card, then ask: **¿Cuáles son tres formas de comunicarse con la oficina de la UNESCO en Santiago de Chile?**

## Answers to ¿Comprendes?

*Answers will vary.*

# Lectura opcional 2

Málaga, España

AHORA EN MADRID LA LUNA
ABRE SUS PUERTAS

**y para integrar su equipo profesional te necesitamos en los puestos de**

**GERENTES DE RESTAURANTE, GERENTE DE TIENDA, GERENTE DE VENTAS Y UN CHEF**

**Requisitos para chef:**

- Inglés (nivel medio).
- Edad no mayor de 40 años.
- Escolaridad mínima de BUP o Secundaria, con estudios de especialización en alimentos y bebidas.
- Experiencia mínima comprobable de 4 años como chef en restaurantes de medio o alto volumen, con conocimientos de control de costos, gastos y manejo de personal.
- Buena presencia.

**Requisitos para gerentes de tienda, gerente de ventas y gerente de restauración:**

- Inglés (dominio).
- Edad entre 28 y 35 años.
- Estudios en administración, turismo, mercadotecnia o comercio (requisito sustituible únicamente con experiencia comprobable).
- Experiencia mínima comprobable de dos años como responsable del área.
- Con excelente actitud de servicio y ventas.
- Excelente presentación.

**Ofrecemos para todos los puestos:**

- Sueldo a convenir.
- Bonificación semestral y otras ventajas sociales.

**Los interesados** deberán enviar *currículum vitae*, con fotografía, por correo, a: C/ Antonio Maura, 12, 4.° derecha, 28014 MADRID, a la atención de La Luna Madrid. Fax 91 522 08 53.

**La confirmación** de los expedientes seleccionados se realizará telefónicamente para un proceso de entrevistas que se efectuará en Madrid.

**LA FECHA LÍMITE PARA RECEPCIÓN DE DATOS ES EL 14 DE OCTUBRE**

## ¿Comprendes?

**El restaurante «La Luna»** Contesten.

1. ¿Qué abre sus puertas en Madrid?
2. ¿Quién necesita saber más inglés, el chef o el gerente de ventas?
3. ¿Cuál es la edad máxima para el chef? ¿Y para los otros puestos?
4. ¿Cuántos años de experiencia tiene que tener el chef? ¿Y los otros?
5. ¿Dónde tendrán lugar las entrevistas?
6. ¿Qué deben enviar los interesados con su currículum vitae?
7. ¿Cómo van a informar a las personas que seleccionan para presentarse para una entrevista?



# Lectura opcional 2

## National Standards

**Cultures**

This reading and the related activity on this page familiarize students with a want ad that might be found in a typical newspaper in the Spanish-speaking world.

**¡OJO!** This reading is optional. You may skip it completely, have the entire class read it, have only several students read it and report to the class, or assign it for extra credit.

**LEVELING**

**E:** Reading 1

**A:** Reading 2

## Answers to ¿Comprendes?

1. La Luna abre sus puertas en Madrid.
2. El gerente de ventas necesita saber más inglés.
3. La edad máxima para el chef es 40 años. Y para los otros puestos, entre 28 y 35 años.
4. El chef tiene que tener cuatro años de experiencia. Los otros tienen que tener dos años de experiencia.
5. Las entrevistas tendrán lugar en Madrid.
6. Deben enviar una fotografía.
7. Van a informar a las personas que seleccionan por teléfono.

# Conexiones

## National Standards

**Connections**

This reading about basic concepts in economics such as opportunity cost establishes a connection with another discipline, allowing students to reinforce and further their knowledge of the social sciences through the study of Spanish.

**¡OJO!** The readings in the **Conexiones** section are optional. They focus on some of the major disciplines taught in schools and universities. The vocabulary is useful for discussing such topics as history, literature, art, economics, business, science, etc. You may choose any of the following ways to do the readings in the **Conexiones** sections.

**Independent reading** Have students read the selections and do the post-reading activities as homework, which you collect. This option is least intrusive on class time and requires a minimum of teacher involvement.

**Homework with in-class follow-up** Assign the readings and post-reading activities as homework. Review and discuss the material in class the next day.

**Intensive in-class activity** This option includes a pre-reading vocabulary presentation, in-class reading and discussion, assignment of the activities for homework, and a discussion of the assignment in class the following day.

# Conexiones

## *Las ciencias sociales*

### La economía

Economics is the science that deals with the production, distribution, and consumption of goods and services for the welfare of humankind. It is an interesting and complex science. People need or desire all kinds of goods and services. However, we do not have at our disposal all the resources we would need to produce all that society would like to have. For this reason, economists provide the information necessary to those who must make crucial decisions as to what will and will not be produced.

### La economía

**¿Qué es la economía?**

Hay varias definiciones de economía. La economía es el estudio de las decisiones que tomamos en la producción, distribución y consumo de bienes y servicios[1]. Es el estudio de las maneras en que las sociedades deciden lo que van a producir y para quién. También es el estudio del uso y control de recursos[2] para satisfacer las necesidades y los deseos humanos. Este es un aspecto muy importante de la economía porque los deseos humanos no tienen límite. Las necesidades humanas pueden ser de primera necesidad como la comida y la ropa. Hay también bienes y servicios que no son de primera necesidad pero que son importantes para algunas personas—los diamantes y un chófer, por ejemplo. Si las necesidades y los deseos humanos no tienen límite, no es el caso con los recursos. Los recursos son limitados. La verdad es que hay una escasez[3] de recursos.

[1]bienes y servicios *goods and services*
[2]recursos *resources*
[3]escasez *shortage*

Barcelona, España



## Critical Thinking Activity

**Supporting statements with reasons** Have pairs of students work together to consider other examples of **costo de oportunidad** either from their own lives or on a wider scale. They should present their examples to the class.

**Recursos económicos**

Los recursos económicos son el total de los recursos naturales, fabricados[4] y humanos que se emplean en la producción de bienes y la provisión de servicios. Los recursos naturales son la materia prima[5], lo que viene de la Tierra. Los recursos fabricados incluyen las fábricas, los edificios comerciales y todo tipo de equipo mecánico y técnico. Los recursos humanos incluyen la mano de obra[6] de toda clase—profesional, técnica, gerencial y obrera.

Una fábrica, Barcelona, España

**Costo de oportunidad**

Como todos los recursos son limitados, es imposible dar a la sociedad todos los bienes y servicios que desea. La escasez de materiales y recursos nos obliga a escoger lo que vamos a producir porque no podemos producir todo. Si usamos los recursos disponibles[7] para producir una cosa, perdemos la oportunidad de usar estos mismos recursos para producir otra cosa. Este sacrificio se llama «el costo de oportunidad». Si todos los trabajadores en una fábrica van a producir televisores, la fábrica no puede producir otro producto. Es el costo de oportunidad. Todo lo que hacemos tiene su costo de oportunidad. Si decides ir al cine en vez de estudiar para un examen, estás sacrificando la oportunidad de estudiar. Es el costo de oportunidad de ir al cine.

[4]fabricados *manufactured*
[5]materia prima *raw material*
[6]mano de obra *workforce*
[7]disponibles *available*

## ¿Comprendes?

**A Términos económicos** Contesten.

1. ¿Cuál es un ejemplo de una necesidad esencial?
2. ¿Cuál es un ejemplo de una necesidad que no es esencial?
3. ¿Cuáles son algunos recursos económicos?
4. ¿Cuál es un ejemplo de una materia prima?

**B Costo de oportunidad** Expliquen.

Explica lo que significa «el costo de oportunidad».



## Answers to ¿Comprendes?

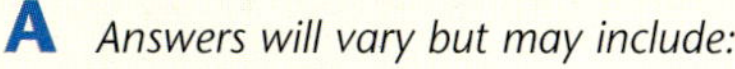

**A** *Answers will vary but may include:*

1. la comida (la ropa)
2. diamantes (un chófer)
3. La materia prima, las fábricas, los edificios comerciales, todo tipo de equipo mecánico y técnico y la mano de obra de toda clase son algunos recursos económicos.
4. la madera, el algodón

**B** *Answers will vary but may include:*

El «costo de oportunidad» es el uso de los recursos disponibles para producir una cosa, perdiendo la oportunidad de producir otra.

# Conexiones

## PRESENTATION

### *Las ciencias sociales*
### La economía

You may wish to have only students interested in economics do this reading, along with the accompanying activities.

### Fun Facts

Many American manufacturing companies have plants in Mexico near the border, where final assembly is performed on a number of products ranging from VCRs to automobiles. These assembly plants are known as **maquiladoras.** After assembly, the products return to the United States for distribution and sale.

### LEVELING

**C:** Reading

# ¡Te toca a ti!

## Use what you have learned

### Recycling

These activities allow students to use the vocabulary and structure from this chapter in completely open-ended, real-life situations.

### PRESENTATION

Encourage students to say as much as possible when they do these activities. Tell them not to be afraid to make mistakes, since the goal of the activities is real-life communication. If someone in the group makes an error, allow the others to politely correct him or her. Let students choose the activities they would like to do.

You may wish to divide students into pairs or groups. Encourage students to elaborate on the basic theme and to be creative. They may use props, pictures, or posters if they wish.

### PRACTICE

Let students choose the activities they would like to do.

### Writing Development

Have students keep a notebook or portfolio containing their best written work from each chapter. These selected writings can be based on assignments from the Student Textbook and the Workbook. The two activities on page 445 are examples of writing assignments that may be included in each student's portfolio. On page 174 in the Workbook, students will begin to develop an organized autobiography **(Mi autobiografía).** These workbook pages may also become a part of their portfolio.

# ¡Te toca a ti!

## Use what you have learned

### La importancia del español

✔ *Talk about the advantages of learning Spanish for your future employment*

Tú y un(a) compañero(a) van a hablarles a los alumnos en una clase del primer año de español. Les van a decir por qué deben continuar con sus estudios del español. Les van a explicar por qué es muy importante el estudio del español. Traten de ser creativos y usen su sentido del humor.

### Ventajas y desventajas

✔ *Talk about professions*

Trabaja con un(a) compañero(a) de clase. Piensen en varias carreras. Hablen de lo que consideran las ventajas y desventajas de cada una. Decidan cuáles son algunas carreras que les interesarían.

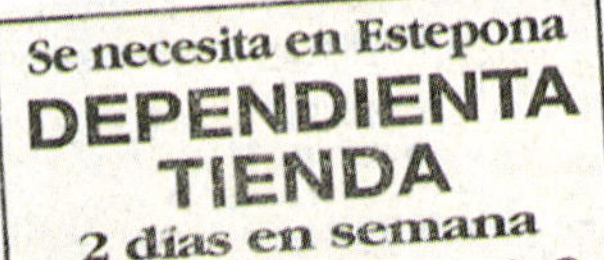

*Empresa Constructora en pleno proceso de expansión precisa incorporar para su delegación en CATALUÑA*

**Ingeniero de Caminos**

Con el objetivo de dirigir un grupo de Obras Edificación y Obra Civil

SI TIENES:

• Entre 25 y 35 años.

• Experiencia en obras.

• Ganas de crecer con nosotros.

*Envía tu Currículum Vitae al Apdo. de Correos 48061, 28080 Madrid.*



### Learning from Realia

*(page 444)* Have students describe in as much detail as possible what they see in the ads on this page.

# ¡Te toca a ti!

## 3 Mi currículum vitae

*✔ Write your personal resumé*

Vas a preparar tu currículum vitae o resumen personal en español. En tu resumen incluye los siguientes detalles: nombre, dirección, preparación académica, título, talentos, intereses y hobbys.

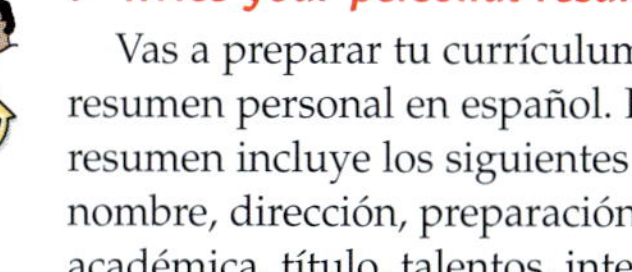

CURRICULUM VITAE

1. DATOS PERSONALES

Nombre: Yolanda
Apellidos: Amer Dengra
Dirección: C/Fco. Martin Mora, nº1-7º-2ª ESC.B
C.P.:07011
Fecha de nacimiento: 21-04-73
N.I.F.: 43.090.440-D
Estado Civil: Soltera
Tlf. de Contacto: (971) 73.60.54

2. DATOS ACADEMICOS

2.A. Enseñanza oficial
Graduado Escolar: C.P. Jaime 1, en la localidad de Palma de Mca, provincia de Baleares.

2.B. Formación complementaria
Curso de Informática de gestión. Centro de estudios "Didact 1", C/Naranjas 3, en la localidad de Jerez de la Fra., Provincia de Cádiz.

3. EXPERIENCIA LABORAL

Aux. Administrativo en la empresa "Rucoplasti Andalucía", Plz. Madre de Dios S/N. (Duración: 1 año)
Localidad: Jerez de la Fra. (CADIZ)

Aux. De Clínica en la residencia geriátrica "Los Angeles", C/Granados, 7 Urb. El Almendral. (Duración 6 meses).
Localidad: Mairena de Aljarafe (SEVILLA).

Depependienta en cafetería-pub "Sin comentarios", Urb. San Joaquín. (Duración 7 meses)
Localidad: Jerez de la Fra. (CÁDIZ)

Dependienta en tienda de moda "Detalles". Vía Sindicato, 4. (Duración 1 mes)
Localidad: Palma de Mca. (BALEARES)

4. OTROS DATOS

Incorporación inmediata
Don de gentes

### Writing Strategy

**Using visuals** Well-organized writing that is clearly expressed is the key to good communication. However, visuals can help organize, clarify, and expand many different kinds of data. A visual can help you illustrate an important concept. Good visuals can portray at a glance an idea that might take several paragraphs to express in words.

## 4 ¿Cuáles son los intereses de la clase?

It is likely that many of your classmates have varied plans for the future. Prepare a survey to administer to your classmates, asking what they would like to do. After you have gathered the data, prepare a visual that gives an overview of the possible careers and job interests your class has. You may wish to use a computer to help you create your visual to convey your information to your readers.

### Writing Strategy

**Using visuals** Have students read the Writing Strategy on page 445. Once students have completed the survey, you might have them enlist the help of the computer science or graphic arts teacher at your school to help them prepare their visuals.

### LEVELING

These activities encompass all three levels. All students will be able to do them at a sophistication level commensurate with their ability in Spanish. Some students will be able to speak for several minutes, and others may be able to give just a few sentences. This is to be expected when students are functioning completely on their own generating their own language to the best of their ability.

## Answers to ¡Te toca a ti!

1 *Answers will vary. Students will use vocabulary from the chapter to explain to first-year Spanish students why they should continue to study Spanish.*

2 *Answers will vary. Students will use the advertisements provided to discuss the advantages and disadvantages of each job.*

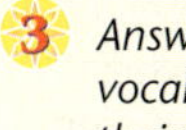

3 *Answers will vary. Students will use vocabulary from the chapter to write their resumé.*

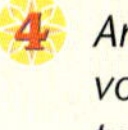

4 *Answers will vary. Students will use vocabulary and structure from the chapter to write a survey and interpret the results.*

## Assessment

### Resource Manager

Communication Transparency C 14
Quizzes, pages 69–73
Performance Assessment, Task 14
Tests, pages 221–234
Situation Cards, Chapter 14
**Maratón mental** Videoquiz, Chapter 14
ExamView® Pro, Chapter 14

### Assessment

This is a pre-test for students to take before you administer the chapter test. Note that each section is cross-referenced so students can easily find the material they have to review in case they made errors. You may use Assessment Answers Transparency A 14 to do the assessment in class, or you may assign this assessment for homework. You can correct the assessment yourself, or you may prefer to project the answers on the overhead in class.

### Glencoe Technology

**MINDJOGGER VHS/DVD**

You may wish to help your students prepare for the chapter test by playing the MindJogger game show. Teams will compete against each other to review chapter vocabulary and structure and sharpen listening comprehension skills.

## Assessment

# Vocabulario

### 1 Identifiquen.

1.

2.

3.

4.

5.

To review **Palabras 1**, turn to pages 424–425.

### 2 Completeen.

6. Los ____ son los trabajos de especialistas como albañiles y electricistas.
7. Las ____ son los trabajos que requieren un título universitario.
8. Los comerciantes se dedican a la ____ de mercancía.

To review **Palabras 2**, turn to pages 428–429.

### 3 ¿Sí o no?

9. Hay anuncios para puestos vacantes en los periódicos.
10. Trabajar a tiempo parcial es trabajar cuarenta horas por semana.
11. Cuando uno busca un puesto es casi siempre necesario llenar una solicitud de empleo.
12. El candidato o aspirante es el que busca trabajo.



### Answers to Assessment

**1**

1. la contable
2. el tribunal (el juez, la abogada)
3. la carpintera
4. el plomero (el fontanero)
5. la ingeniera

**2**

6. oficios
7. profesiones
8. compra y venta

**3**

9. Sí
10. No
11. Sí
12. Sí

# Estructura

**4** **Completen.**

**13–14.** Él quiere ____ dinero. (cambiar)
Él quiere que nosotros ____ dinero.

**15–16.** Nosotros preferimos que tú lo ____. (hacer)
Nosotros lo preferimos ____.

To review the infinitive versus the subjunctive, turn to page 432.

**5** **Escojan.**

**17.** Están buscando una persona ____.
- **a.** que hable tres idiomas
- **b.** que habla tres idiomas

**18.** ¿Sí? Yo tengo un amigo ____.
- **a.** que hable tres idiomas
- **b.** que habla tres idiomas

**19.** Todos queremos un trabajo ____.
- **a.** que nos pague bien
- **b.** que nos paga bien

**20.** Yo sé que hay un puesto con nuestra compañía ____.
- **a.** que pague muy bien
- **b.** que paga muy bien

To review the subjunctive in relative clauses, turn to page 435.

## Assessment

**FOLDABLES™ Study Organizer** **Dinah Zike's Study Guides**

Your students may wish to use Foldable 5 to organize, display, and arrange data as they practice interrogative words. You may wish to encourage them to add information from each chapter as they continue to ask and answer questions in Spanish.

Encourage students to keep this *tab book* foldable in a safe place so they can refer to it and add content as they acquire more knowledge.

## Answers to Assessment

 4

13. cambiar
14. cambiemos
15. hagas
16. hacer

 5

17. a
18. b
19. a
20. b

# ¡Hablo como un pro!

This unique page gives students the opportunity to speak freely and say whatever they can, using the vocabulary and structures they have learned in the chapter. The illustration serves to remind students of precisely what they know how to say in Spanish. There are no activities that students do not have the ability to describe or talk about in Spanish. The art not only depicts the vocabulary and content of this chapter, but also reinforces what they learned in previous chapters.

You may wish to use this page in many ways. Some possibilities are to have students do the following:

1. Look at the illustration and identify items by giving the correct Spanish words.
2. Make up sentences about what they see in the illustration.
3. Make up questions about the illustration. They can call on another class member to respond if you do this as a class activity, or you may prefer to allow students to work in small groups. This activity is extremely beneficial because it enables students to actively use interrogative words.
4. Answer questions you ask them about the illustration.
5. Work in pairs and make up a conversation based on the illustration.
6. Look at the illustration and give a complete oral review of what they see.
7. Look at the illustration and write a paragraph (or essay) about it.

You can also use this page as an assessment or testing tool, taking into account individual differences by having students go from simple to quite complicated tasks. The assessment can be either oral or written. You may wish to use the rubrics provided on pages T20–T21 as you give students the following directions.

1. Identify the topic or situation of the illustration.
2. Give the Spanish words for as many items as you can.
3. Think of as many sentences as you can to describe the illustration.
4. Go over your sentences and put them in the best sequencing to give a coherent story based on the illustration.

## ¡Hablo como un pro!

Tell all you can about this illustration.

# Vocabulario

### Identifying some office personnel

el/la programador(a) de informática
el/la secretario(a)
la oficina
el/la gerente
el/la contable

### Talking about merchandising

el/la comerciante
el/la cliente
el/la cajero(a)
la venta
la compra
la mercancía
satisfecho(a)

### Discussing some legal professions

el tribunal
el/la juez
el/la abogado(a)
el bufete del abogado

### Identifying some municipal government workers

la alcaldía
el alcalde
el/la funcionario(a)

### Talking about some professions

la profesión
el título universitario
el/la ingeniero(a)
el/la arquitecto(a)

### Identifying some trades

el oficio
el/la especialista
el/la electricista
el/la albañil
el/la plomero(a), el/la fontanero(a)
el/la carpintero(a)

### Talking about job opportunities

un puesto
el anuncio
el departamento de recursos humanos
el/la candidato(a), el/la aspirante
el/la entrevistador(a)
la entrevista
la solicitud de empleo
ofrecer un trabajo
a tiempo completo
a tiempo parcial

### Other useful expressions

ojalá
quizá(s)

**How well do you know your vocabulary?**

- Choose an occupation from the list.
- Write a few sentences about the job and how you would apply for the position.

**VIDEOTUR**

**Episodio 14**

In this video episode, you will join our friends as they peek into the future. See page 493 for more information.



# Vocabulario

## Vocabulary Review

The words and phrases in the **Vocabulario** have been taught for productive use in this chapter. They are summarized here as a resource for both student and teacher. This list also serves as a convenient resource for the **¡Te toca a ti!** activities on pages 444 and 445. There are approximately thirteen cognates in this vocabulary list. Have students find them.

**¡OJO!** You will notice that the vocabulary list here is not translated. This has been done intentionally, since we feel that by the time students have finished the material in the chapter they should be familiar with the meanings of all the words. If there are several words they still do not know, we recommend that they refer to the **Palabras 1** and **2** sections in the chapter or go to the dictionaries at the end of this book to find the meanings. However, if you prefer that your students have the English translations, please refer to Vocabulary Transparency 14.1, where you will find all these words with their translations.

**VIDEO VHS/DVD**

The Video Program allows students to see how the chapter vocabulary and structures are used by native speakers within an engaging story line. For maximum reinforcement, show the video episode as a final activity for Chapter 14.

Repaso

## Preview

This section reviews the salient points from Chapters 12–14. In the **Conversación** students will review subjunctive forms as well as vocabulary having to do with public services. In the **Estructura** section, they will review the uses of the subjunctive.

### Resource Manager

Workbook, pages 175–178
Tests, pages 235–243
Performance Assessment, Tasks 12–14

### National Standards

**Comparisons**
Students will develop insight into the nature of language through comparisons of Spanish and English. You may wish to remind students that there is a subjunctive in English although it is rarely used since we usually use the infinitive instead.

*I insist that he go* is an example of the subjunctive in English. *I want him to go* is the more typical infinitive construction. The subjunctive is often encountered in more formal language: *It is imperative that they attend. We demand that he surrender.*

## PRESENTATION

**Step 1** Have students open their books to page 450. Call on two students to read the conversation aloud.

**Step 2** Ask the questions from the **¿Comprendes?** section.

Repaso

# Conversación

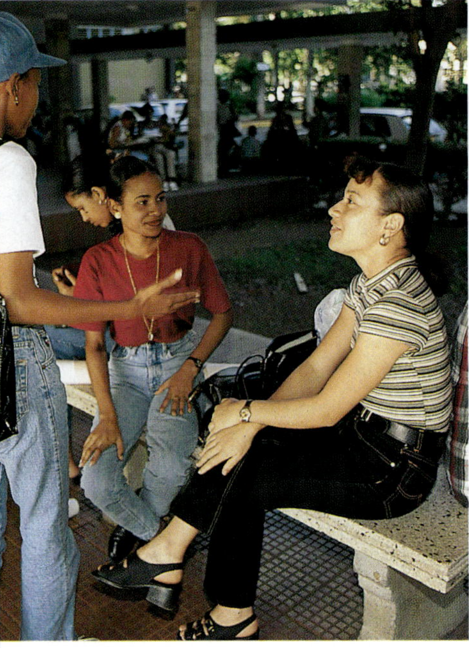

## La futura jefa de banquetes

**Antonia** ¿Adónde vas, Isabel?
**Isabel** Voy a la peluquería. Tengo el pelo un poco largo. Necesito un corte. Y después voy al correo.
**Antonia** ¿Por qué es necesario que vayas al correo?
**Isabel** Tengo que enviar las invitaciones. Quiero que lleguen a tiempo.
**Antonia** ¿Qué invitaciones?
**Isabel** Pues, el día 13 voy a dar una gran fiesta.
**Antonia** ¿Qué estás celebrando?
**Isabel** No te voy a decir. ¡Ya verás!
**Antonia** Ay, pero siempre estás dando fiestas.
**Isabel** Pues, me gustan las fiestas y me gusta darlas.
**Antonia** Algún día, ¡quizás seas una jefa de banquetes que planee fiestas y recepciones para bodas y bautizos.
**Isabel** ¡Tal vez! ¿Quién sabe?

### ¿Comprendes?

**Un trabajo para Isabel** Contesten.

1. ¿Adónde va Isabel?
2. ¿Por qué va allí?
3. Y después, ¿adónde va?
4. ¿Por qué es necesario que ella vaya allí?
5. ¿Cuándo será la fiesta?
6. ¿Para qué es?
7. ¿Por qué da muchas fiestas Isabel?
8. Un día, ¿es posible que ella haga qué tipo de trabajo?

### Answers to ¿Comprendes?

1. Isabel va a la peluquería.
2. Tiene el pelo un poco largo.
3. Después va al correo.
4. Es necesario que ella vaya porque tiene que enviar invitaciones para una fiesta.
5. La fiesta será el día 13.
6. Isabel no quiere decir para qué es la fiesta.
7. Le gustan las fiestas.
8. Algún día quizás sea jefa de banquetes.

# Estructura

## Usos del subjuntivo

The indicative mood of the verb is used to express events and actions that actually have taken, are taking, or will take place. The subjunctive, on the other hand, is used to express events that may or may not take place. Some introductory statement makes the actual event uncertain. The following are some expressions that are followed by the subjunctive.

| | | |
|---|---|---|
| **querer** | **es posible** | **alegrarse de** |
| **esperar** | **es imposible** | **sentir** |
| **temer** | **es probable** | **estar contento** |
| **preferir** | **es necesario** | **estar triste** |
| **pedir** | **es importante** | |
| **sugerir** | **es bueno, es mejor** | |
| **aconsejar** | **es fácil** | |
| **exigir** | **es difícil** | |
| **mandar** | | |
| **insistir** | | |

**Quiero que él vaya. Espero que él vaya. Le pido que vaya. La verdad es que insisto en que él vaya porque es importante que él vaya. Más que importante, es necesario que él vaya. Pero la verdad es que yo no sé si va a ir o no.**

### 1 Historieta En la peluquería

Contesten.

1. ¿Quiere José que el peluquero le corte el pelo?
2. ¿Prefiere que el peluquero use la navaja o las tijeras para cortarle el pelo?
3. ¿Le pide que le dé un champú también?
4. ¿Quiere el peluquero que José le diga cómo quiere el pelo?
5. ¿Insiste José en que el peluquero le ponga una raya?

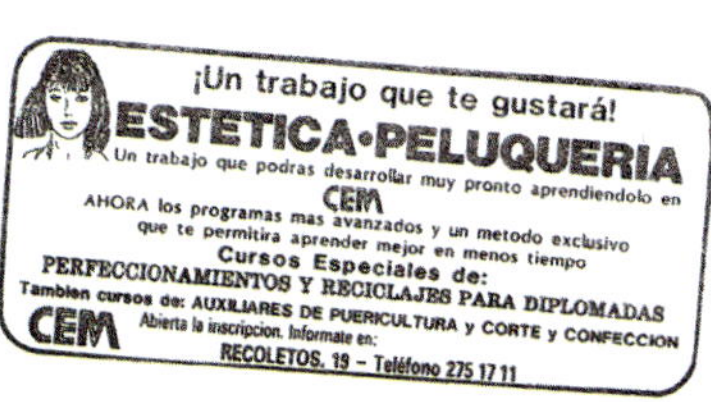


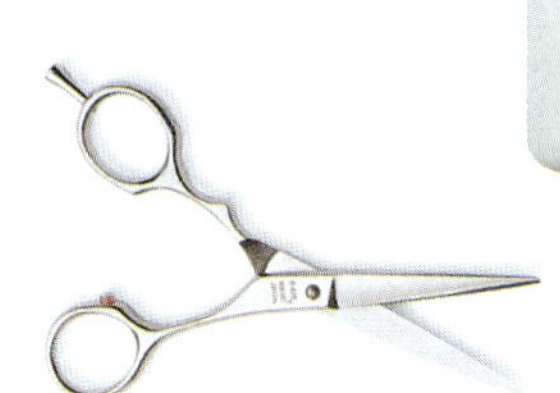





## PRESENTATION

### Usos del subjuntivo

**Step 1** Have students open their books to page 451. Lead students through the explanation of the subjunctive.

**Step 2** Have students repeat the sentences on page 451. Ask volunteers to make up additional sentences, choosing from the list of words and expressions. Write their sentences on the board.

## PRACTICE

**1** After doing this activity, ask for volunteers to retell the story in their own words.

## Answers to Repaso

1. Sí (No), José (no) quiere que el peluquero le corte el pelo.
2. Prefiere que el peluquero use la navaja (las tijeras).
3. Sí, (No, no) le pide que le dé un champú también.
4. Sí (No), el peluquero (no) quiere que José le diga cómo quiere el pelo.
5. Sí (No), José (no) insiste en que el peluquero le ponga una raya.

# Repaso

## PRACTICE (continued)

**2** After doing this activity, divide the class into pairs and do this activity again for additional practice with the subjunctive.

**3** After going over Activity 3, have students retell the story in their own words.

## PRESENTATION

### Más usos del subjuntivo

**Step 1** Go over Items 1–2 on page 452 with students. You may want to write the examples on the board or on an overhead transparency in order to explain the concepts.

**Step 2** You may want to use additional examples from Chapter 13, pages 404–405, and Chapter 14, page 435.

Repaso

**2 Consejos** Contesten.

1. ¿Quieren tus padres que escojas una buena carrera?
2. ¿Te aconseja tu profesor que sigas con tus estudios del español?
3. ¿Te sugiere que tomes un curso de informática?
4. ¿Están contentos tus padres que estudies mucho y que saques buenas notas?
5. ¿Es probable que tú vayas a la universidad?
6. ¿Es importante que tú sepas la carrera que vas a escoger antes de ir a la universidad?

**3 Historieta En la estación de servicio**

Sigan el modelo.

**Yo quiero / él / llenar el tanque ⟶**
**Yo quiero que él llene el tanque.**

1. Yo quiero / él / poner gasolina sin plomo
2. Le pido / revisar el aceite
3. Me alegro de que / él / limpiar el parabrisas
4. Es necesario / él / poner aire en las llantas
5. Es importante / nosotros / manejar con cuidado
6. El empleado prefiere / yo / pagar con cheque

Universidad Nacional Autónoma de México, Ciudad de México

## Más usos del subjuntivo

1. The subjunctive is also used when introduced by a statement that conveys doubt. When the statement implies certainty, however, the indicative is used.

   **Dudo que él asista a la boda.**
   **Pero creo que los novios van a recibir muchos regalos.**

2. The subjunctive is also used in a clause that modifies an indefinite antecedent. If the antecedent refers to a specific person or thing, the indicative is used.

   **La compañía está buscando un candidato que hable inglés.**
   **La compañía tiene un candidato que habla inglés.**

## ANSWERS TO Repaso

1. Sí, mis padres quieren que escoja una buena carrera.
2. Sí, mi profesor me aconseja que siga con mis estudios de español.
3. Sí, (No, no) me sugiere que tome un curso de informática.
4. Sí, mis padres están contentos que estudie mucho y que saque buenas notas.
5. Sí, (No, no) es probable que vaya a la universidad.
6. Sí, (No, no) es importante que sepa la carrera que voy a escoger antes de ir a la universidad.

1. Yo quiero que él ponga gasolina sin plomo.
2. Le pido que revise el aceite.
3. Me alegro de que él limpie el parabrisas.
4. Es necesario que él ponga aire en las llantas.
5. Es importante que nosotros manejemos con cuidado.
6. El empleado prefiere que yo pague con cheque.

**4 Historieta Una carta** Contesten.

1. ¿Crees que José te ha escrito?
2. ¿Piensas que él ha puesto la carta en un buzón?
3. ¿Dudas que él vaya al correo para mandar la carta?
4. ¿Es dudoso que la carta llegue hoy?
5. ¿Es cierto que la carta tiene bastantes sellos?

**5 Hay que tener ciertas calificaciones.** Completen.

1. La compañía Vensa está buscando alguien que ____ (tener) experiencia, que ____ (conocer) bien el español y el inglés y que ____ (poder) viajar.
2. El director de recursos humanos me dijo que necesitan alguien que ____ (estar) libre inmediatamente.
3. Han entrevistado a dos candidatos. Hay un candidato que ____ (tener) experiencia, que ____ (querer) y ____ (poder) trabajar enseguida.
4. Desgraciadamente él no habla inglés y la compañía sigue buscando alguien que ____ (hablar) inglés y que ____ (conocer) el mercado norteamericano.

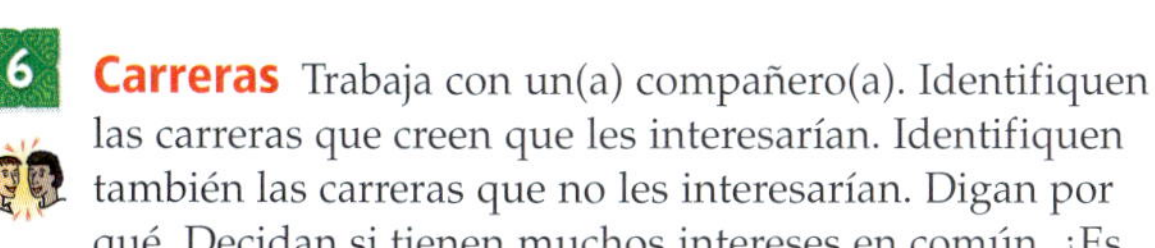

**6 Carreras** Trabaja con un(a) compañero(a). Identifiquen las carreras que creen que les interesarían. Identifiquen también las carreras que no les interesarían. Digan por qué. Decidan si tienen muchos intereses en común. ¿Es posible que sigan o escojan la misma carrera?

**7 Fiestas** Trabaja con un(a) compañero(a). Planeen una gran fiesta. Discutan por qué van a dar la fiesta y todo lo que van a hacer durante la fiesta. Entonces decidan todo lo que tienen que hacer antes de la fiesta.

**8 En la peluquería** Con un(a) compañero(a), entablen una conversación que tiene lugar en una peluquería. Uno(a) de ustedes será el/la peluquero(a) y el/la otro(a) será el/la cliente.

**Literary Companion**

You may wish to read the adaptation of ***Tierra*** by Gregorio López y Fuentes. This literary selection is found on pages 472–477.



## PRACTICE

**4** Have students answer the items in the activity in the affirmative.
**Expansion:** After doing this activity, have students retell the story in their own words.

**5** After doing this activity, have volunteers read all of the items together, in paragraph form.

**6** This activity reviews the vocabulary from Chapter 14.

**7** This activity reviews the vocabulary from Chapter 13. Have students share their ideas for a **fiesta** with the class. Everyone will be interested in hearing the details!

**8** This activity reviews vocabulary from Chapter 12. Students can view the Chapter 12 video episode as a model for their conversation.

**Literary Companion**

When you finish this chapter, if you wish, have students read the adaptation of ***Tierra*** by Gregorio López y Fuentes on pages 472–477.

## Answers to Repaso

**4**

1. Sí, creo que José me ha escrito.
2. Sí, pienso que él ha puesto la carta en un buzón.
3. Sí, dudo que el vaya al correo para mandar la carta.
4. Sí, es dudoso que la carta llegue hoy.
5. Sí, es cierto que la carta tiene bastantes sellos.

**5**

1. tenga, conozca, pueda
2. esté
3. tiene, quiere, puede
4. hable, conozca

**6** *Answers will vary. Students will use vocabulary from Chapter 14* Palabras 1 *to discuss careers that are and aren't interesting with their partner.*

**7** *Answers will vary. Students will use the subjunctive to make a list of what needs to be done to plan a party.*

**8** *Answers will vary. Students will use vocabulary from Chapter 12* Palabras 1 *and the subjunctive to have a conversation with their hairdresser/barber.*

People EN ESPAÑOL

## Entérate
## Venezuela y Colombia

This section was prepared by Time Learning Ventures of Time Incorporated. Its purpose is to give students greater insight, through visual images and fun articles, into the culture and people of Venezuela and Colombia. You may want to ask your students if they know anything about these countries before they begin reading.

Have students look at the photographs and read the articles. Encourage the students to talk about what they've seen and read. Let them say anything they can, using the vocabulary they have learned to this point.

Venezuela and Colombia have some of the most spectacular natural wonders in the world: massive savannahs, breathtaking waterfalls, unspoiled tropical rainforests, and much more. In addition to the natural beauty of these countries, they are also notable for the distinct presence of traditional cultures. Today, there are still over twenty-five indigenous languages spoken in Venezuela and three hundred dialects present in Colombia.

# People EN ESPAÑOL Entérate Colombia y Venezuela

Salto Ángel

## De la mano de la naturaleza

La UNESCO declaró estos sitios Patrimonio de la Humanidad.

**Parque Nacional Los Katíos** Existe un paso natural entre Centro y Suramérica. Es la puerta de entrada a América del Sur. Para pasar, los viajeros tienen que tomar un barco de Panamá a Colombia. ¿Sabes por qué es imposible cruzar en automóvil por la región? Este "puente" es uno de los terrenos más inhóspitos[1] y lluviosos del planeta. Llueve tanto que las aguas alimentan uno de los ríos más caudalosos[2] del mundo: el Atrato. El Atrato vierte[3] al Caribe casi 5,000 metros cúbicos de agua por segundo. El parque tiene una gran riqueza de flora y fauna que debe protegerse.

**Parque Nacional Canaima** El piloto norteamericano Jimmy Ángel va en su avión. De pronto, las nubes lo envuelven y pierde el rumbo. Al despejarse[4] el día, Ángel descubre la séptima maravilla[5] natural del planeta, que hoy lleva su nombre. Imagínate un río que cae, con una caída libre[6] de casi 1,000 metros. ¿Te lo imaginas? ¡Es el salto más alto del mundo: el Salto Ángel! Es el tesoro que guarda celosamente[7] este parque, donde además viven especies animales y vegetales únicas en el planeta. También viven allí en armonía con la naturaleza, los pueblos nativos de la región.

## De la mano del ser humano

**Cartagena de Indias** Visitar esta bellísima ciudad colonial, sus plazas, fuertes y castillos, es pasear por 500 años de historia.

Cartagena de Indias

**Coro** Esta ciudad, la más antigua de Venezuela, fue fundada en 1527. Su arquitectura demuestra muchas de las posibilidades de la construcción en barro[8].

Coro

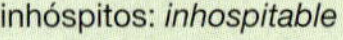

[1] inhóspitos: *inhospitable*
[2] caudalosos: *with large volume of water*
[3] vierte: *pours*
[4] despejarse: *clear up*
[5] maravilla: *marvel*
[6] caída libre: *free fall*
[7] guarda celosamente: *keeps zealously*
[8] barro: *mud, adobe*

## Los "hermanos mayores" hablan de ecología

Representantes del pueblo kogi

En las altas montañas de la Sierra Nevada de Colombia vive un pueblo precolombino muy pacífico: los kogis. Su aislamiento[1] es total y voluntario. ¿Por qué? Quieren vivir en total armonía con la naturaleza. Desde hace tiempo, los kogis observan los cambios climáticos que ocurren en nuestro planeta. Hace unos años, los sabios[2] del pueblo, que se consideran nuestros hermanos mayores, decidieron enviar un mensaje al resto de los habitantes del planeta, sus hermanos menores. Es necesario que oigamos su mensaje, dicen ellos. De eso depende nuestro futuro. En el documental de Alan Ereira *Desde el corazón de la Tierra: Nuestros hermanos mayores*, los kogis piden que cuidemos de nuestro planeta. Dicen que la solución está en nuestras manos.

[1] aislamiento: *isolation* [2] sabios: *wise ones*

## Calendario de fiestas

Carnaval de Barranquilla

**Carnaval de Barranquilla**
¡Cumbia…! Al grito de la desbordante[1] música caribeña se celebra el famoso Carnaval de Barranquilla, uno de los más importantes del mundo. La fiesta dura cuatro días, en los que la gente de esta ciudad festeja su herencia[2] africana y europea. Como dicen los colombianos, el Carnaval de Barranquilla se celebra sana y alegremente "hasta que el cuerpo aguante[3]".

**Feria del Orinoco**
Esta fiesta gira alrededor de un pez. La sapoara es un pez que sólo se encuentra en el río Orinoco. Las aguas del gran río bajan de caudal[4] en el mes de agosto. Entonces los habitantes de Ciudad Bolívar, en Venezuela, pescan sapoaras. La persona que pesque la sapoara más grande gana un premio. Alegres bailes, competencias de otros deportes acuáticos y exposiciones industriales y ganaderas[5] son también parte de la diversión. ¡A pescar se ha dicho!

**Tambores de San Juan**
Así se llama una fiesta popular de la zona central de Venezuela, donde se mezclan bailes afroantillanos y costumbres españolas. Los tambores resuenan[6] y los pobladores y miles de visitantes no dejan de bailar por las calles.

[1] desbordante: *bursting*
[2] herencia: *heritage*
[3] hasta que el cuerpo aguante: *as long as the body can take it*
[4] caudal: *volume of water*
[5] ganaderas: *cattle*
[6] resuenan: *resound*

## Museos

**El Museo del Oro** Al entrar al museo, las luces están apagadas. Se encienden las luces y se escucha: "¡Ah!". El brillo de una barca en miniatura hecha de oro puro y otras extraordinarias reliquias[1] indígenas asombran[2] al mundo entero en Bogotá.

Fernando Botero

**Museo de Arte Contemporáneo de Caracas**
Los maestros de las artes plásticas modernas, tanto extranjeros como venezolanos, han encontrado su casa en este museo de importancia internacional.

**Fernando Botero y sus gorditos** Botero cuida muy bien su figura pero envía a sus "gorditos" a recorrer el mundo. Hace unos años, sus gatos, figuras humanas y otras esculturas gigantescas impresionaron a los neoyorquinos desde la avenida Park. En 2003, el mismo asombro se apoderó[3] de italianos y turistas que paseaban por Venecia[4].

[1] reliquias: *relics*
[2] asombran: *amaze*
[3] apoderó: *took hold*
[4] Venecia: *Venice*

Arepas

## micocina

### Una reina pepeada, por favor

La arepa es la "hamburguesa" venezolana. Realmente, la arepa es un pan. Los venezolanos acompañan sus comidas con este pan de maíz. También es un plato principal. Todo depende del relleno. Se acompaña con mantequilla, frijoles, queso, pescado, huevo y todo tipo de carnes. Una de las más famosas es la reina pepeada. Disfruta de una y tú también dirás: "¡Déme una reina pepeada, por favor!"

**Ingredientes**

2 tazas de harina de maíz blanco precocida
1 cucharadita de sal
1 taza y 1/2 de agua
1 cucharada de aceite

**Preparación**
En un recipiente hondo, poner el agua, la sal y el aceite. Agregar poco a poco la harina, evitando[1] que se formen grumos[2]. Amasar con las manos hasta obtener una masa suave que no se pegue[3] a las manos. Hacer bolas medianas y aplanarlas[4] formando las arepas. Ponerlas en una plancha[5] caliente y engrasada y cocinarlas por ambos lados. Luego ponerlas al horno precalentado a 350°. Dejarlas hasta que, al golpearlas suavemente, suenen a huecas[6] y estén doradas.

**Relleno**
Hacer una mezcla de pollo hervido y desmenuzado[7], aguacate en trozos y mayonesa.

Servir las arepas en el momento, acompañadas del relleno, ¡y a disfrutar del banquete!

[1] evitando: *avoiding*
[2] grumos: *lumps*
[3] pegue: *stick*
[4] aplanarlas: *flatten*
[5] plancha: *skillet*
[6] huecas: *hollow*
[7] desmenuzado: *shredded*



People EN ESPAÑOL

**A De la mano de la naturaleza**
¿Verdadero o falso?

1. El Atrato vierte al Caribe casi 5,000 metros cúbicos de agua por segundo.
2. JimmyÁngel es piloto colombiano.
3. El Parque Nacional Los Katíos es un sitio Patrimonio de la Humanidad.

**B Los "hermanos mayores" hablan de ecología** Completen.

1. Los ___ viven en las altas montañas de la Sierra Nevada de Colombia.
2. Los kogis desean vivir en ___ con la naturaleza.
3. Los "hermanos mayores" piden que ___ de nuestro planeta.

**C Calendario de fiestas**
Contesten.

1. ¿Dónde se encuentra la sapoara?
2. ¿Cómo se llama la fiesta popular de la zona central de Venezuela?
3. ¿Cuántos días dura el Carnaval de Barranquilla?

**D Museos**
Corrijan.

1. Cuando uno entra en el Museo del Oro, todas las luces están encendidas.
2. En el Museo del Oro hay muchas reliquias españolas.
3. El Museo del Oro está en Barranquilla.
4. En el Museo de Arte Contemporáneo de Caracas podemos ver las obras de los maestros de las artes plásticas antiguas.
5. Las figuras en las obras de Fernando Botero tienden a ser muy delgadas.

**LEVELING**

**E:** Activities A, D
**A:** Activity B
**C:** Activity C

### ANSWERS TO ¿Comprendes?

**A**

1. verdadero
2. falso
3. verdadero

**B**

1. kogis
2. armonía
3. cuidemos

**C**

1. La sapoara se encuentra en el río Orinoco.
2. La fiesta popular se llama Tambores de San Juan.
3. El Carnaval de Barranquilla dura cuatro días.

**D**

1. Cuando uno entra en el Museo del Oro, todas las luces están apagadas.
2. En el Museo del Oro hay muchas reliquias indígenas.
3. El Museo del Oro está en Bogotá.
4. En el Museo de Arte Contemporáneo de Caracas podemos ver las obras de los maestros de las artes plásticas modernas.
5. Las figuras en las obras de Fernando Botero tienden a ser gorditas.

People en español

Venezuelan and Colombian culture have embraced a fascinating fusion of indigenous, European, and African roots. Through music, artisanal crafts, theatre, literature, and studio art, both countries have become hotbeds of unique cultural expression. Though they continue to weather severe political and economic crises, Venezuela and Colombia remain prolific contributors to the international artistic community.

**A Nóbel para una "canción"**
Corrijan.

1. Gabriel García Márquez es autor de una novela poca conocida.
2. Gabriel García Márquez siempre escribe con una flor azul en su escritorio.
3. Gabriel García Márquez recibe el Premio Nóbel en su traje de baño.
4. Los amigos de García Márquez le llaman "Marco".
5. El autor ha dicho que *Cien años de soledad* es un tipo de música llamado bolero.
6. Algo curioso es que él nunca lee sus obras en voz alta.
7. Salma Hayek aparece en la versión cinematográfica de *El amor en los tiempos del cólera*.

**B En el set** ¿Quién es?

1. A esta persona, le fascinan las momias.
2. Es el Toulouse Lautrec de *Moulin Rouge*.
3. Este actor que nació en Colombia tomó el rol de un animal en la película *Ice Age*.
4. Esta excelente actriz ha actuado con Robin Williams y Arnold Schwarzenegger.
5. Esta colombiana dedica su talento a una campaña nacional contra el SIDA.

People en español

Gabriel García Márquez

## Nóbel para una "canción"

Gabriel García Márquez es autor de una novela considerada entre las mejores del siglo XX. Gabo, como le dicen sus amigos, es una persona muy particular. Por ejemplo:

- Recibe el Premio Nóbel vestido de liqui-liqui, traje típico de los llanos[1] venezolanos.
- Siempre escribe con una flor amarilla en su escritorio.
- Es fanático de Shakira. ¡Hasta ha escrito sobre ella!
- Tanto le gusta la música, que dice que *Cien años de soledad* es un vallenato—música de acordeón típica de la región de Valledupar—de 400 páginas, y *El amor en los tiempos del cólera* —otra novela famosa—es un bolero de 380 páginas. Confiesa leer en voz alta todos sus escritos, aún el más pequeño párrafo que escribe: "...un relato literario es un instrumento hipnótico, como lo es la música..." dice, y agrega: "...cualquier tropiezo[2] del ritmo puede malograr[3] el hechizo[4]. De esto me cuido hasta el punto de que no mando un texto a la imprenta mientras no lo lea en voz alta para estar seguro de su fluidez[5]".
- El cine es otra de sus pasiones. Gabo ha escrito guiones[6] de cine. Su novela *El coronel no tiene quien le escriba* es también película; Salma Hayek aparece en esa versión cinematográfica.

[1] llanos: *plains*
[2] tropiezo: *slip, mistake*
[3] malograr: *spoil*
[4] hechizo: *spell*
[5] fluidez: *smooth flow*
[6] guiones: *scripts*

Gabriel García Márquez

Velázquez

**Patricia Velázquez** Actúa en las películas *La momia* y *El regreso de la momia*. Sí, el personaje que interpreta esta artista venezolana ¡es quien hace despertar[1] la venganza de la momia!

Alonso

**María Conchita Alonso** Tiene gran trayectoria en Hollywood y en la televisión estadounidense. Figura al lado de grandes estrellas como Arnold Schwarzenegger y Robin Williams.

Vergara

**Sofía Vergara** Si buscas a una artista de cine y televisión que sea talentosa y altruista[2], te presentamos a Sofía Vergara. La famosa colombiana es la portavoz[3] de una campaña nacional contra el SIDA. ¡Bravo, Sofía!

Leguizamo

**John Leguizamo** Su nombre brilla tanto en Hollywood como en Broadway. Es el Toulouse Lautrec de *Moulin Rouge*, al lado de Nicole Kidman; actuó como Tibaldo, acompañando a Leonardo di Caprio en la más reciente versión llevada al cine de Romeo y Julieta. Además, Leguizamo anima con su voz a *Sid the Sloth*, en la película de dibujos animados *Ice Age*. Recientemente, debutó como director de cine en una película en la que también actúa. ¿Hay algo más que se pueda decir de este triunfador? Sí, ¡nació en Colombia!

[1] hace despertar: *awakens*
[2] altruista: *altruistic*
[3] portavoz: *spokeswoman*

## Answers to ¿Comprendes?

**A**

1. Gabriel García Márquez es autor de una novela considerada entre las mejores del siglo XX.
2. Gabriel García Márquez siempre escribe con una flor amarilla en su escritorio.
3. Gabriel García Márquez recibe su Premio Nóbel en un traje liqui-liqui.
4. Los amigos de García Márquez le llaman "Gabo".
5. El autor ha dicho que *Cien años de soledad* es un tipo de música llamado vallenato.
6. Algo curioso es que él siempre lee sus obras en voz alta.
7. Salma Hayek aparece en la versión cinematográfica de *El coronel no tiene quien le escriba*.

**B**

1. Patricia Velázquez
2. John Leguizamo
3. John Leguizamo
4. María Conchita Alonso
5. Sofía Vergara

# música

## Súbele el volumen

Juanes

**Juanes** Aunque su nombre indique que se trata de más de una persona, Juanes es sólo uno, pero vale por[1] cinco… Fíjate bien en este cantante colombiano. En la más reciente entrega de los Grammys latinos, ¡cinco premios fueron para Juanes! Entre estos, ganó el del Mejor álbum y el de la Mejor canción.

**Shakira** ¿Dudas que alguien no sepa que esta joven colombiana es la diva indiscutible[2] de la actualidad?

**Aterciopelados** La música de este grupo de rock colombiano no es nada aterciopelada[3], pero los jóvenes la escuchan a todo volumen.

**Oscar de León** La mejor música de salsa y el venezolano Oscar de León son una sola cosa.

[1] vale por: *he's worth* [2] indiscutible: *undeniably* [3] aterciopelada: *velvety*

Shakira

## Atletas que destacan

Baena

**Cecilia Baena** "La Chechi Baena", como la llaman cariñosamente los colombianos, es campeona mundial de patinaje sobre ruedas[1] del maratón juvenil.

**Juan Carlos Montoya** El corredor colombiano de autos de Fórmula Uno, en 2003, ocupó el tercer puesto en el campeonato mundial de automovilismo.

Cabrera

**Miguel Cabrera** Tenía tan sólo 17 años, cuando sus padres negociaron el contrato para que este venezolano jugara en las Grandes ligas. Recientemente, a los 20 años, se puso en el camino de los poderosos Yankees, y su actuación fue decisiva para que los Marlins de la Florida ganaran la Serie Mundial de 2003.

Larreal

**Daniela Larreal** La ciclista venezolana sabe que el cielo es el límite. Después de ganar dos medallas de plata en los pasados Juegos Panamericanos, se prepara para conquistar medallas en las Olimpíadas de Atenas.

[1] patinaje sobre ruedas: *roller blading*

## SUCESOS

Herrera

**Carolina Herrera** El traje de novia, sobrio[1] y elegante, que Carolina Kennedy vistió el día de su boda fue creación de la diseñadora venezolana.

**Gimnasio de altura** Jóvenes y adultos hacen montañismo[2] en un "gimnasio" que mide 2,500 metros de altura: el Monte Ávila. A los pies de esta imponente montaña, se encuentra la ciudad de Caracas.

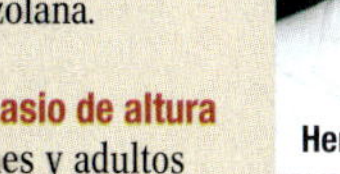

**Rodrigo García** El hijo de García Márquez es talentoso como su padre. Es camarógrafo, escritor y director de cine. Trabajó en películas tan exitosas como *Danzón* y *Frida*.

[1] sobrio: *unassuming*
[2] montañismo: *mountain climbing*

457

People EN ESPAÑOL

**C Atletas que destacan**

Contesten.

1. ¿Quién jugó en la Serie Mundial de 2003?
2. ¿Cuál es el deporte de Cecilia Baena?
3. ¿Cuántos medallas de plata ha ganado Daniela Larreal?
4. ¿En qué deporte participa Daniela Larreal?
5. ¿Quién es un famoso automovilista colombiano?

**D Sucesos**

¿Verdadero o falso?

1. Carolina Herrera diseñó el traje de novia para Carolina Kennedy.
2. El Monte Ávila es un famoso gimnasio de Caracas.
3. Rodrigo García es novelista y cuentista igual que su padre Gabriel García Márquez.
4. *Danzón* y *Frida* son dos novelas de García Márquez.

**E Música**

Completen.

1. Cuando entregaron los Grammys latinos, Juanes ganó ___ premios.
2. La "diva" de la actualidad, hasta García Márquez es un fanático de ella, es la colombiana ___.
3. El grupo colombiano, "Aterciopelados" se dedica a la música ___.
4. En Venezuela Oscar de León es la estrella de la música ___.

**LEVELING**

**E:** Activities A, D
**A:** Activities B, E
**C:** Activity C

### Answers to ¿Comprendes?

**C**

1. Miguel Cabrera jugó en la Serie Mundial de 2003.
2. Cecilia Baena hace patinaje sobre ruedas.
3. Daniela Larreal ha ganado dos medallas de plata.
4. Participa en ciclismo.
5. Juan Carlos Montoya es un famoso automovilista.

**D**

1. verdadero
2. verdadero
3. falso
4. falso

**E**

1. cinco
2. Shakira
3. rock
4. salsa

## Preview

All literary selections are optional. You may wish to skip them or present them very thoroughly. In some cases you may have students read the selection quickly just to get the general idea.

# Literary Companion

These literary selections develop reading and cultural skills and introduce students to Hispanic literature.



Barranco, Lima, Perú

## Literary Companion

¡OJO! The exposure to literature early in one's study of another language should be a pleasant experience. As students read these selections, it is not necessary for them to understand every word. Explain to them that they should try to enjoy the experience of reading literature in a new language. As they read they should look for the following:

- who the main characters are
- what they are like
- what they are doing—the plot
- what happens to them—the outcome of the story

### Learning from Photos

*(pages 458–459)* This colorful library is in the Barranco section of Lima. Barranco is a lovely section some two miles south of Miraflores. It has many old mansions with beautiful balconies and gables. Some one hundred years ago, Barranco was a summer resort, but today it is part of metropolitan Lima.

# Literatura 1

## *Platero y yo (fragmento)*

### National Standards

**Cultures**
Students experience, discuss, and analyze an expressive product of the culture: a selection from the poetic narrative ***Platero y yo*** by Juan Ramón Jiménez.

**¡OJO!** This literary selection is optional. You may wish to present it after students have completed Chapters 1–4, as they will have acquired the vocabulary and structures necessary to read the selection by this point.

You may present the piece thoroughly as a class activity or you may have some or all students read it on their own. If you present it as a class activity, you may wish to vary presentation procedures from section to section. Some options are:

- Students read silently.
- Students read after you in unison.
- Call on individuals to read aloud.
- When dialogue appears in the story, call on students to take parts.

With any of the above procedures, intersperse some comprehension questions. Call on a student or students to give a brief synopsis of a section in Spanish.

**Note:** The following teaching suggestions are for a thorough presentation of *Platero y yo.*

## Teaching Vocabulary

**¡OJO!** Students merely need to be familiar with the vocabulary to help them understand the story. This vocabulary does not have to be a part of their active, productive vocabulary. All high-frequency words will be reintroduced in **¡Buen viaje! Level 3** as new vocabulary.



# Literatura 1

## *Platero y yo (fragmento)* de Juan Ramón Jiménez

## Vocabulario

El burro anda por el prado.
Acaricia las florecitas con su hocico.

**el cascabeleo** el sonido de los cascabeles
**la pena** algo triste
**los gemelos** dos cosas iguales o dos hermanos nacidos al mismo tiempo
**el acero** un metal muy duro
**la plata** un metal blanco, valioso; se usa para monedas

**blando(a)** lo contrario de «duro(a)»
**suelto(a)** libre
**peludo(a)** con mucho pelo
**tibiamente** suavemente
**acariciar** tocar suavemente
**la abeja** un insecto que produce la miel del néctar de las flores

# Actividades

**A** **¿Sí o no?** Digan que sí o que no.

1. Los higos son una flor.
2. A veces un gato lleva un collar de cascabeles.
3. Las abejas son insectos.
4. Los escarabajos producen la miel del néctar de las flores.
5. Otro nombre para «celeste» es blanco.
6. Otro nombre para «gualda» es amarillo.
7. Se hacen monedas de la plata.

**B** **La palabra, por favor.** Completen.

1. Yo tengo un dólar, pero no es de papel; es de ____.
2. Los dos hermanos nacieron el mismo día; ellos son ____.
3. No es blando; es muy ____.
4. Pero el otro es duro, muy duro, duro como el ____.
5. El animal puede ir adonde quiera; siempre anda ____.
6. Está muy triste; tiene muchas ____.
7. El hombre pasa la mano sobre el burrito; lo ____.



## Literatura 1

**Step 1** Present the new vocabulary on pages 460 and 461 using the teaching suggestions given in the regular chapters in this textbook.

**Step 2** Quickly go over Activities A and B with the class.

## About the Spanish Language

Some colors have more than one name in Spanish. For example, for *yellow* there is **gualda** (the yellow in the flag of Spain) in addition to **amarillo.** Other colors include:

| | |
|---|---|
| **azul marino** | *navy blue* |
| **celeste** | *light blue* |
| **rosa, color de rosa, rosado** | *pink* |
| **marrón, castaño, moreno, pardo** | *brown* |

## Answers to Actividad

 A

1. No
2. Sí
3. Sí
4. No
5. No
6. Sí
7. Sí

 B

1. plata
2. gemelos
3. duro
4. acero
5. suelto
6. penas
7. acaricia

Literatura 1

## Discussing Literature

### Introducción

**Step 1** You may go over the **Introducción** with the students or you may decide to omit it and just have them read the narrative.

**Step 2** You can ask the following questions about the **Introducción.**

**¿Es *Platero y yo* una obra para niños?**

**¿Qué recibió Juan Ramón Jiménez en 1956?**

**¿En qué pueblo español vive Platero?**

**¿En qué región de España está Moguer? ¿Está en el norte o en el sur de España?**

### *Platero y yo*

**Step 1** Read the selection to the class. Use as much expression as you can.

**Step 2** Have students open their books to page 462. Have them read the selection silently. Then call on individuals to read a paragraph each.

**Step 3** Now go over the **¿Comprendes?** activities.

Andalucía, España

**INTRODUCCIÓN** Esta obra no es prosa, ni es poesía. Se puede decir que es prosa poética. Muchos creen que don Juan Ramón escribió la obra para niños, pero en su prólogo el autor dice: «Ese breve libro, en donde la alegría y la pena son gemelos, cual las orejas de Platero, estaba escrito para... qué sé yo para quien... para quien escribimos los poetas líricos». Juan Ramón Jiménez recibió el Premio Nóbel de Literatura en 1956.

El fragmento que sigue se titula «Platero», y es uno de 139 capítulos. Es una descripción del burrito, amigo y compañero constante de don Juan Ramón en el pequeño pueblo de Moguer en Andalucía, España.

## *Platero y yo*

Platero es pequeño, peludo, suave; tan blando por fuera que se diría todo de algodón, que no lleva huesos. Sólo los espejos de azabache° de sus ojos son duros cual dos escarabajos de cristal negro.

Lo dejo suelto, y se va al prado, y acaricia tibiamente con su hocico, rozándolas° apenas, las florecillas rosas, celestes y gualdas. Lo llamo dulcemente: —¿Platero?— y viene a mí con un trotecillo alegre que parece que se ríe, en no sé qué cascabeleo ideal... Come cuanto le doy. Le gustan las naranjas mandarinas, las uvas moscateles°, todas de ámbar, los higos morados, con su cristalina gotita de miel...

Es tierno° y mimoso° igual que un niño, que una niña... ; pero fuerte y seco por dentro, como de piedra. Cuando paso sobre él, los domingos, por las últimas callejas del pueblo, los hombres del campo, vestidos de limpio y despaciosos°, se quedan mirándolo: —Tien´ asero—... Tiene acero. Acero y plata de luna, al mismo tiempo.

espejos de azabache *black mirrors*

rozándolas *brushing against them*

uvas moscateles *tipo de uva muy dulce*

tierno *tender*

mimoso *pampered*

despaciosos *con calma*

Moguer, Andalucía

## ¿Comprendes?

**A La palabra, por favor.** Completen.

1. Platero no es grande; es ____.
2. Y no es duro; es ____.
3. Las uvas moscateles son del color de ____.
4. Platero acaricia las florecillas con su ____.
5. El día de la semana que el autor pasa sobre su burro es el ____.

**B Platero** Contesten.

1. Cuando el autor suelta al burro, ¿adónde va el animalito?
2. ¿Con quiénes compara el autor a Platero?
3. ¿Qué le gusta comer a Platero?
4. ¿Quiénes miran a Platero cuando pasa por el pueblo?

**C Para pensar** Discutan.

1. El autor describe a Platero en formas contradictorias, especialmente cuando habla de lo exterior y de lo interior del animalito. Explica.
2. Describe a Platero.
3. Los campesinos dicen que el burrito «Tien´ asero… » ¿Qué quiere decir esa frase, y por qué lo escribe de esa forma el autor?
4. Al final del capítulo don Juan Ramón dice: «Acero y plata de luna, al mismo tiempo». Interpreta esa frase.

**D Recursos literarios** Contesten.

A metaphor is a figure of speech in which a word that means one thing is substituted for another to indicate a similarity or likeness, for example, "In the springtime of life." A simile is a figure of speech in which two very different things are compared to each other, usually using the word *like* **(como),** for example, "eyes like stars, hands like hams," etc. What metaphors and similes can you identify in this selection?

Un campesino con su burro, Andalucía, España

### FUN-FACTS

The legendary Spanish **burro** is now an endangered species. Today, machines are much more common in farming than animal labor is. A preserve has been established to protect the **burros** that have been abandoned by their former owners.



## Answers to ¿Comprendes?

**A**

1. pequeño
2. blando
3. ámbar
4. hocico
5. domingo

**B**

1. El animalito se va al prado.
2. El autor compara a Platero con un niño, con una niña.
3. A Platero le gusta comer las naranjas mandarinas, las uvas moscateles, los higos morados.
4. Los hombres del campo miran a Platero cuando pasa por el pueblo.

**C**

1. *Answers will vary. Students should explain and interpret the meaning of the burro's soft exterior and hard interior.*
2. *Answers will vary but may include:* Platero es pequeño, suave, parece de algodón. Tiene ojos negros. Es tierno y mimoso, pero fuerte como la piedra.
3. Quiere decir que es fuerte como el acero. El autor lo dice de esa forma porque repite la forma de hablar de los campesinos.
4. *Answers will vary. Students may comment on the symbolism of comparing the burro to* plata, *showing that it is highly valuable.*

**D** *Answers will vary but may include:*

Espejos de azabache de sus ojos
Es fuerte y seco por dentro, como de piedra

## La muralla

**National Standards**

**Cultures**
Students experience, discuss, and analyze an expressive product of the culture: the poem *La muralla* by the Cuban poet Nicolás Guillén.

**¡OJO!** This literary selection is optional. You may wish to present it after students have completed Chapters 5–7, as they will have acquired the vocabulary and structures necessary to read the selection by this point.

You may present the piece thoroughly as a class activity or you may have some or all students read it on their own. If you present it as a class activity, you may wish to vary presentation procedures from section to section. Some options are:

- Students read silently.
- Students read after you in unison.
- Call on individuals to read aloud.
- When dialogue appears in the story, call on students to take parts.

With any of the above procedures, intersperse some comprehension questions. Call on a student or students to give a brief synopsis of a section in Spanish.
**Note:** The following teaching suggestions are for a thorough presentation of *La muralla.*

### Teaching Vocabulary

**Step 1** Have students open their books to page 464. Have them repeat the new vocabulary words and sentences after you.

**Step 2** It is not necessary for students to become as thoroughly familiar with this vocabulary as with the vocabulary in a typical chapter. It is presented to help students understand the reading, but it is not necessary for them to learn the vocabulary for productive purposes.



Literatura 2

# *La muralla* de Nicolás Guillén

## Vocabulario

Las dos niñas están cerca de la muralla.
Ellas juntaban las manos.

**el veneno** una sustancia que puede matar, como el arsénico
**el puñal** un tipo de cuchillo
**alzar** levantar

# Actividades

**A** **Estudio de palabras** Pareen.

1. el horizonte — a. poison, venom
2. la serpiente — b. horizon
3. la rosa — c. mountain
4. el veneno — d. rose
5. el monte — e. serpent

**B** **¿Sabes?** Identifiquen.

1. dos flores
2. dos pájaros
3. un reptil
4. dos insectos

**C** **¿Cuál es?** Escojan.

1. Entre las flores había unos preciosos ____.
   a. claveles b. puñales c. venenos
2. La serpiente podría matar con su ____.
   a. flor b. veneno c. cuchillo
3. Sí, sí, el criminal tenía un cuchillo; era un ____.
   a. alacrán b. clavel c. puñal
4. No, no lo va a bajar; al contrario, lo va a ____.
   a. alzar b. matar c. abrir

Cañaverales, Cuba

## Literatura 2

### Actividades

**A**, **B**, **and C** Quickly go over these activities orally to be sure that students will understand the words in the reading.

### About the Spanish Language

There are different words for various kinds of walls.

- **Una pared** is an interior wall in a house or other building.
- **Un muro** is a fortified outer wall such as that found on fortresses or around walled towns.
- **Una muralla** is a synonym of **un muro.**
- **Una verja** is an outer wall or fence.
- **Una tapia** is an outer wall, usually an earthen wall.

### Fun Facts

In Spanish times, Cape Canaveral, the Florida launch site for astronauts, was the location of large sugar cane fields.

## Answers to Actividades

**A**

1. b
2. e
3. d
4. a
5. c

**B** *Answers will vary but may include:*

1. la rosa, el clavel
2. la paloma, el ruiseñor
3. la serpiente
4. el alacrán, el ciempiés

**C**

1. a
2. b
3. c
4. a

Literatura 2

## Discussing Literature

### Introducción

**Step 1** You may go over the **Introducción** with students or you may decide to omit it and just have them read the poem.

### *La muralla*

**Step 1** Before reading this selection you may wish to discuss with students the symbols in the photos on page 466. For example: **¿Cómo son las manos en la foto? ¿Son manos blancas o negras? ¿Cómo se llaman las flores en la foto?**

**Step 2** If you are presenting the story as a class activity, you can use many gestures or expressions to help students with comprehension.

**Step 3** Have students close their books. Read the poem aloud to the class with as much expression as possible.

**Step 4** Now have students open their books. Have them read the poem silently to themselves.

**Step 5** Have students locate the line in the poem that corresponds to each photo on page 466.

**INTRODUCCIÓN** El poeta cubano Nicolás Guillén presenta, en sus versos, elementos de folklore negro. Él es uno de los cultivadores de la poesía «afrocubana». En el poema que sigue, el poeta nos presenta un lindo mensaje de comprensión y tolerancia.

## *La muralla*

Para hacer esta muralla,
tráiganme todas las manos:
los negros sus manos negras,
los blancos sus blancas manos.
Ay,
una muralla que vaya
desde la playa hasta el monte,
desde el monte hasta la playa, bien,
allá sobre el horizonte.
—¡Tun, tun!
—¿Quién es?
—Una rosa y un clavel...

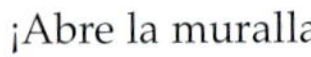

¡Abre la muralla!
—¡Tun, tun!
—¿Quién es?
—El sable° del coronel°...
—¡Cierra la muralla!
—¡Tun, tun!
—¿Quién es?
—La paloma y el laurel...
—¡Abre la muralla!
—¡Tun, tun!
—¿Quién es?
—El alacrán y el ciempiés...
—¡Cierra la muralla!

sable *sword, saber*
coronel *colonel*

Al corazón del amigo,
abre la muralla;
al veneno y al puñal,
cierra la muralla;
al mirto° y la yerbabuena°,
abre la muralla;
al diente de la serpiente,
cierra la muralla;
al ruiseñor en la flor,
abre la muralla…
Alcemos una muralla
juntando todas las manos;
los negros, sus manos negras,
los blancos sus blancas manos.
Una muralla que vaya
desde la playa hasta el monte,
desde el monte hasta la playa, bien,
allá sobre el horizonte…

mirto *myrtle*
yerbabuena *mint*

## ¿Comprendes?

**A La muralla** Escojan.

1. Para hacer la muralla se necesitan muchas ____.
   **a.** flores **b.** manos **c.** palomas
2. La muralla estará entre el monte y ____.
   **a.** la playa **b.** el coronel **c.** el horizonte
3. Los primeros que llegan son ____.
   **a.** el coronel y el alacrán **b.** la rosa y el clavel
   **c.** el ciempiés y el ruiseñor
4. El coronel lleva ____.
   **a.** un sable **b.** una flor **c.** un diente

**B Cosas en común** Contesten.

1. ¿Qué tienen en común la rosa, el clavel, el mirto y el laurel?
2. ¿Qué tienen en común el ruiseñor y la paloma?
3. ¿Qué tienen en común el alacrán y el ciempiés?
4. ¿Qué tienen en común el sable y el puñal?

**C Rima** ¿Qué rima con… ?

1. muralla
2. monte
3. clavel
4. quién es



**Answers to ¿Comprendes?**

**A**
1. b
2. a
3. b
4. a

**B**
1. Son plantas.
2. Cantan.
3. Pican.
4. Cortan.

**C**
1. playa
2. horizonte
3. coronel
4. ciempiés

## National Standards

**Comparisons**
Students will develop an understanding of the nature of language through comparisons of Spanish and English. Onomatopoeia is the use of words whose sound suggests the meaning. In this poem, **tun, tun** is an example of onomatopoeia. Ask students what the equivalent of **tun, tun** is in English. Ask them for other examples of onomatopoeia in English.

## ¿Comprendes?

**Note:** Students should read the entire poem on pages 466 and 467 before doing the **¿Comprendes?** activities.

Literatura 3

## El cohítre

**National Standards**

**Cultures**
Students experience, discuss, and analyze an expressive product of the culture: the Puerto Rican legend *El cohítre,* as re-told by the Puerto Rican scholar Ester M. Feliciano Mendoza.

**¡OJO!** This literary selection is optional. You may wish to present it after students have completed Chapters 8–11, as they will have acquired the vocabulary and structures necessary to read the selection by this point.

You may present the piece thoroughly as a class activity or you may have some or all students read it on their own. If you present it as a class activity, you may wish to vary presentation procedures from section to section. Some options are:

- Students read silently.
- Students read after you in unison.
- Call on individuals to read aloud.
- When dialogue appears in the story, call on students to take parts.

With any of the above procedures, intersperse some comprehension questions. Call on a student or students to give a brief synopsis of a section in Spanish.

**Note:** The following teaching suggestions are for a thorough presentation of *El cohítre.*



# El cohítre
# Una leyenda puertorriqueña

**de Ester M. Feliciano Mendoza**

## Vocabulario

La niña hacía un castillo.
Era muy feliz.

A lo lejos había un cerro.
No lo podía ver bien porque era muy neblinoso.

La niña veía su reflejo en el agua.

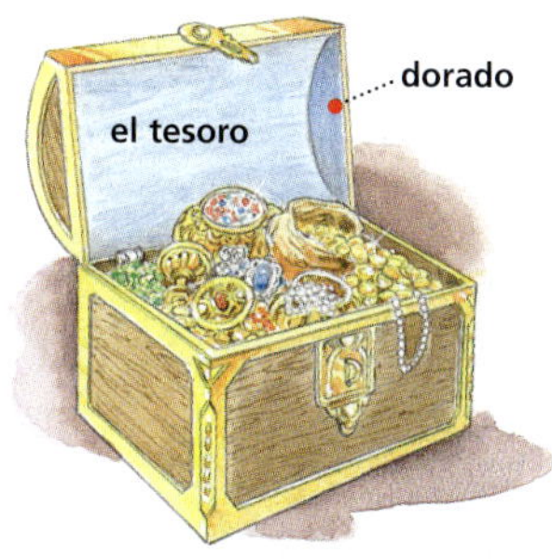

El padre lloraba. Lloraba porque su hija murió.

**liláceo(a)** del color de las lilas
**el alma** el espíritu, no el cuerpo
**el barro** la combinación de tierra y agua
**reidor(a)** que se ríe
**enjugar** secar, lavar
**la súplica** la petición, el ruego
**rogar, rezar** decir u ofrecer una oración a Dios
**ofrendar** ofrecer
**brotar** salir

# Actividades

**A** **Otra manera de decirlo** Expresen la parte indicada de otra manera.

1. Los ojos de la niña eran *del color de las lilas.*
2. El padre y la hija subieron *el pequeño monte.*
3. Allí encontraron *muchas riquezas.*
4. En ese monte los indios *ofrecían* regalos a sus dioses.
5. Con los regalos también hacían *peticiones* a los dioses.

**B** **La palabra, por favor.** Escojan.

1. El niño lloraba y su madre le ____ las lágrimas.
   **a.** enjugó **b.** ofrendó **c.** modeló
2. Donde cayeron las lágrimas pronto ____ unas flores de la tierra.
   **a.** ofrecieron **b.** ofrendaron **c.** brotaron
3. Era difícil ver el cerro claramente porque era muy ____.
   **a.** neblinoso **b.** reidor **c.** liláceo
4. Los religiosos creen que ____ es más importante que el cuerpo.
   **a.** el alma **b.** la ofrenda **c.** el reflejo
5. La niña vio ____ de su cara en el agua.
   **a.** el barro **b.** el reflejo **c.** la figurita
6. La familia puso flores en ____ del abuelo.
   **a.** la tumba **b.** el alma **c.** el caracol



# Literatura 3

## Teaching Vocabulary

**Step 1** Have students open their books to page 468. Have them repeat the new vocabulary words and sentences after you.

**Step 2** Students merely need to be familiar with the vocabulary to help them understand the story. This vocabulary does not have to be a part of their active, productive vocabulary. All high-frequency words will be reintroduced in **¡Buen viaje! Level 3.**

## Actividades

**A and B** Quickly go over these activities orally to be sure that students will understand the words in the reading.

## Answers to Actividades

1. liláceos
2. el cerro
3. muchos tesoros
4. ofrendaban
5. súplicas

1. a
2. c
3. a
4. a
5. b
6. a

Literatura 3

## Discussing Literature

### Introducción

**Step 1** The **Introducción** on page 470 gives students a concise summary of the legend. Before doing the reading, go over the introduction with the students.

### *El cohítre*

**Step 1** Tell students they are going to read a legend about a young girl who, during Spanish colonial times, lived on the island now known as Puerto Rico. The legend explains how the **cohítre** flower, native to Puerto Rico, came into being.

**Step 2** You may wish to have students take a few minutes to read the selection silently before going over it orally in class.

**Step 3** Call on a more able student to give a synopsis of each paragraph. This helps less able students understand the selection.

Los indios taínos

**INTRODUCCIÓN** Ester Feliciano Mendoza (1918–1988) escribió en varios géneros, pero se destacó más como poeta. Esta selección viene de una de sus colecciones de leyendas. Esta leyenda nos habla de una flor típica de Puerto Rico y cómo llegó a ser. Los indios de Puerto Rico eran los taínos. La niña de la leyenda es hija de un español y una india. El padre de la niña quiere marcharse a Perú en busca de tesoro. La niña quiere quedarse en su isla amada.

Un cerro neblinoso

## *El cohítre*°

Tenía los ojos azules y la piel dorada. Cuando nació, su padre creyó ver en sus pupilas los mismos reflejos liláceos de las tardes de Castilla. La amó por él y por la india que se murió rogando por su niña que no era ni india ni española.

La niña criolla fue tímida y amorosa. Amiga de los cerros neblinosos y las playas reidoras, conoció los secretos de las flores y de los caracoles. Aprendió a modelar cemíes° con la carne dócil del barro y a hacer castillos con las arenas escurridizas°. Amó al indio tanto como al español y a unos y otros enjugó las heridas del cuerpo y del alma. La niña criolla era feliz.

Un día el padre oyó hablar de las riquezas de Perú. Por primera vez la niña sintió el temor de la ausencia. Lloró los días que vendrían lejos de la isla querida. Se arrodilló ante la Virgen blanca y ofrendó flores y frutas a Yocahu, en una misma súplica: «No me dejen marchar». A los pies del altar cristiano rogaba también el padre español: «Dios nos lleve a Perú». Mirando a lo lejos el neblinoso monte Yukiyú, pensaba sin embargo: ¿Valdrá la pena marcharme?

Enfermó de angustia la niña criolla. Veía los cielos de Castilla en las pupilas azules, pero el padre no vio cómo la muerte lentamente las cubría de nubes… Y la niña, un día claro, se murió de pena.

Desde los brazos del padre voló a las regiones de Yocahu y de la virgencita blanca. Y pasaron los días… Sobre la tumba amada vio el padre español brotar, apretadita a la tierra, con sus florecitas azules reflejando el cielo de la isla, la yerba del cohítre… Y así fue para siempre en la tierra de Puerto Rico.

cohítre *wild herb*

cemíes *clay figures made by Taíno Indians of Puerto Rico*

escurridizas *slippery*

Un cementerio, Viejo San Juan, Puerto Rico



### ANSWERS TO ¿Comprendes?

**A**

1. b
2. d
3. f
4. a
5. c
6. e

**B**

1. Sí
2. Sí
3. No, el padre de la niña era español.
4. Sí
5. No, la madre rogaba por su niña.

**C**

1. c
2. a
3. c
4. a
5. b

## ¿Comprendes?

**A Estudio de palabras** Pareen.

1. las pupilas
2. modelar
3. dócil
4. la ausencia
5. la tumba
6. los reflejos

a. absence
b. pupils (eyes)
c. tomb
d. to model
e. reflections
f. docile, obedient

**B ¿Sí o no?** Corrijan las oraciones incorrectas.

1. La niña tenía los ojos azules.
2. La piel de la niña era del color del oro.
3. El padre de la niña era indio.
4. La madre de la niña murió.
5. La madre rogaba por su marido.

**C ¿Qué comprendieron?** Escojan.

1. La niña hacía figuritas de ____.
   a. arena b. agua c. barro
2. Para construir castillos usaba ____.
   a. arena b. agua c. barro
3. El padre de la niña se interesó en Perú por sus ____.
   a. castillos b. cerros c. riquezas
4. La niña le ofreció a Yocahu ____.
   a. flores y frutas b. riquezas c. caracoles
5. La niña murió de ____.
   a. una herida b. pena c. temor

**D Según la leyenda...** Contesten.

1. ¿Por qué dice la leyenda «que la niña no era ni india ni española»?
2. ¿Por qué sintió la niña el temor de la ausencia?
3. ¿Por qué lloraba ella?
4. ¿A quiénes rogaba la niña?
5. ¿Qué quería la niña?
6. ¿Dónde rogaba el padre?
7. ¿Cuál era el conflicto entre padre e hija?
8. ¿Qué serán «las regiones de la Virgen blanca y Yocahu»?
9. ¿Qué será Yocahu?

**E Interpretación** Contesten.

1. ¿Qué significa que la niña «modelaba cemíes y hacía castillos»?
2. ¿Qué significa que la niña «rogaba a la Virgen blanca y a Yocahu»?
3. ¿Qué es lo que veía el padre cada vez que miraba los ojos de su hija?

### About the Spanish Language

The literal meaning of **criollo** is a child born in the Americas of European, especially Spanish, parents. In Puerto Rico, however, **criollo** means native Puerto Rican, regardless of ethnic background.

### ¿Comprendes?

**Note:** Students should read the entire selection on page 470 before doing the **¿Comprendes?** activities.

## Answers to ¿Comprendes?

**D**

1. La leyenda dice «que la niña no era ni india ni española» porque era criolla.
2. La niña sintió el temor de la ausencia porque el padre pensaba en irse al Perú.
3. Lloraba porque no quería irse lejos de su isla querida.
4. La niña rogaba a la Virgen blanca y a Yocahu.
5. La niña quería que no la dejaran marchar. (Quería quedarse en la isla.)
6. El padre rogaba a los pies del altar cristiano.
7. El padre quería irse, la niña no.
8. El cielo.
9. Un dios de los indios taínos.

**E** *Answers will vary but may include:*

1. La niña hacía cosas de los indios y de los españoles.
2. Rogaba a los dioses españoles y a los dioses indios.
3. El padre veía los mismos reflejos liláceos de las tardes de Castilla.

# Literatura 4

## Tierra

**National Standards**

**Cultures**
Students experience, discuss, and analyze an expressive product of the culture: an excerpt from the novel of the Mexican Revolution, *Tierra*, by Gregorio López y Fuentes.

**¡OJO!** This literary selection is optional. You may wish to present it after students have completed Chapters 11–14, as they will have acquired the vocabulary and structures necessary to read the selection by this point.

You may present the piece thoroughly as a class activity or you may have some or all students read it on their own. If you present it as a class activity, you may wish to vary presentation procedures from section to section. Some options are:

- Students read silently.
- Students read after you in unison.
- Call on individuals to read aloud.
- When dialogue appears in the story, call on students to take parts.

With any of the above procedures, intersperse some comprehension questions. Call on a student or students to give a brief synopsis of a section in Spanish.

**Note:** The following teaching suggestions are for a thorough presentation of *Tierra.*

### Teaching Vocabulary

**Step 1** Have students open their books to page 472. Have them repeat the new vocabulary words after you.

**Step 2** Quickly go over Activities A and B on page 473 orally to make sure that the students can recognize the vocabulary for receptive purposes.



Literatura 4

# *Tierra* de Gregorio López y Fuentes

## Vocabulario

**el portal** puerta principal
**el tianguis** un mercado indio
**el corneta** soldado que toca la corneta
**el cabo** rango inferior al de sargento
**voltear** dar la vuelta
**alargarse** hacer más largo
**la esperanza** hope

# Actividades

**A** **La hacienda** Completen.

1. En ese espacio grande los indios hacían el ____; compraban y vendían sus productos.
2. Cuando abrieron el ____ todos entraron al patio.
3. Cerca del patio estaba la ____ donde estaban los caballos y los coches.
4. Había seis soldados, un ____ y un sargento.
5. El sargento no tenía barba, pero sí tenía un gran ____.

**B** **¿Cuál es?** Expliquen.

1. ¿Cuáles son dos suboficiales militares?
2. ¿Cuál será la diferencia entre «el corneta» y «la corneta»?

Una hacienda, México

Literatura 4

## Actividades

**A** Have students point to the objects in the illustration on page 472 as they answer each item in Activity A.

**B** In Activity B, Item 2, have students identify the two terms using the illustration on page 472.

## About the Spanish Language

The word **tianguis** comes from the Aztec **tianquiztli.** It is not a physical market, in the sense of a building or structure. In the story, the author says **un espacio... en él se hace el tianguis.** It is a place where the indigenous people gather on fixed days to buy and sell.

## Answers to Actividades

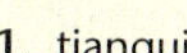

**A**

1. tianguis
2. portal
3. cuadra
4. cabo
5. bigote

**B**

1. el cabo, el sargento
2. «El corneta» es la persona que toca «la corneta». La corneta es un instrumento musical.

Literatura 4

## Discussing Literature

### Introducción

**Step 1** You may go over the **Introducción** with the class or you may decide to omit it and just have them read the story.

### *Tierra*

**Step 1** You may wish to have students take a few minutes to read each paragraph silently before going over it orally in class.

**Step 2** Since this reading is rather long, you may wish to go over only certain sections orally and just have students read the other parts silently.

**Step 3** Call on a more able student to give a synopsis of each paragraph. This helps less able students understand the selection.

Estatua de Emiliano Zapata, Chinameca, México

**INTRODUCCIÓN** Gregorio López y Fuentes (1895–1966) escribió la novela *Tierra* inspirada en la lucha de Emiliano Zapata por los indígenas del sur de México. Zapata fue traicionado y asesinado por tropas bajo el mando del Coronel Jesús María Guajardo. Guajardo le invitó a Zapata a cenar con él en la hacienda de Chinameca. Le dijo que quería unirse a su movimiento. El fragmento que sigue nos dice lo que pasó.

Emiliano Zapata

## *Tierra*

La casa de la hacienda, en Chinameca, es enorme, con un portal inmenso. Tiene habitaciones para las visitas y una gran cuadra para coches y caballos. Frente a la casa, un espacio cuadrangular, tan grande, que en él se hace el tianguis. El rectángulo está encerrado por una muralla. A derecha e izquierda, la muralla tiene anchas puertas. En Chinameca esperaba Guajardo al general Zapata. Dentro de la casa estaban los soldados, situados en los mejores y más ocultos lugares. La persona que llegara no vería más que seis hombres armados en cada una de las puertas de la muralla. Allí también había un corneta.

El general Zapata tardaba en llegar. Pronto llegó un emisario. No se le permitió entrar. Pocos momentos después comenzó a llegar la escolta del general. También a estos hombres se les negó entrar al patio. Los soldados tenían órdenes de no dejarlos pasar porque tenían que hacer los honores al jefe. El general entraría por la puerta derecha. Los seis soldados estaban formados impecablemente, en actitud de firmes.

Apareció el jefe. Se le conocía por la bravura de su caballo, por sus grandes bigotes y por algo que siempre se nota en los acompañantes de un jefe. Cuando estaban a veinte metros de la puerta el corneta comenzó a tocar «marcha de honor». En cuanto sonó la corneta el cabo ordenó con voz enérgica:

—Presenten… ¡armas!

El caballo se adelantó, todo nervioso, todo electrizado con el toque de la corneta. Los soldados seguían presentando armas. El general había avanzado cinco metros y estaba dentro del patio. Entonces, los seis hombres que presentaban armas hicieron un pequeño movimiento,… y se escuchó una descarga.

El general Zapata, violentamente, intentó voltear el caballo, quizás con la idea de salir de allí. Pero él se quedó a la mitad del movimiento. Se cayó al suelo. Pero el animal salió y se escapó. El cabo se acercó al general. Con la carabina le dio el tiro de gracia. Pusieron el cadáver en una mula. Los pies por un lado y los brazos por el otro lado. Tomaron el camino a Cuautla. Al trotar de la mula, las piernas hacían un movimiento como el de andar, como si Zapata seguía corriendo por el Estado de Morelos. Los brazos parecían alargarse, quizás queriendo tocar la tierra para sus muchachos, por la que tanto luchó, tan cerca y al mismo tiempo tan distante.

En Cuautla fue exhibido el cadáver y en voz baja comenzó la leyenda:

No es el general.

¡No va a ser! Está así, deformado, por haber venido como vino. La sangre se le fue a la cabeza.

No, compadre, el general tenía una seña muy particular, allí en la cara, y éste no la tiene.

¡Claro! Allí mismo le entró el tiro de gracia.

¡Quién sabe!

Y el «quién sabe» lleno de esperanzas, era como un lamento. Pero otros decían, muy contentos: —¡Vaya, por fin cayó este bandido!

Hacienda de San Juan Bautista, Taxco, México

## History Connection

Emiliano Zapata was one of the giants of the Mexican Revolution of the first two decades of the twentieth century. He was born in 1883 in San Miguel Anenecuilco and died in Chinameca in 1919. He was a fighter for agrarian reform. He wanted to wrest the land from wealthy landowners and distribute it to the peasants.

## Art Connection

You may wish to show the Fine Art Transparencies entitled ***Campamento Zapatista*** and ***Emiliano Zapata*** from the Transparency Binder for **¡Buen viaje! Level 3.** You may also want students to do the activities accompanying these transparencies.

# Literatura 4

## ¿Comprendes?

**Note:** Students should read the entire selection before doing the **¿Comprendes?** activities.

## ¿Comprendes?

**A Estudio de palabras** Pareen.

| | |
|---|---|
| **1.** el espacio | **a.** lament |
| **2.** encerrado | **b.** discharge, gunshot |
| **3.** oculto | **c.** companion |
| **4.** armado | **d.** space |
| **5.** el emisario | **e.** enclosed |
| **6.** impecablemente | **f.** occult, hidden |
| **7.** en actitud de firmes | **g.** deformed |
| **8.** el acompañante | **h.** armed |
| **9.** avanzar | **i.** to trot |
| **10.** la descarga | **j.** to advance |
| **11.** trotar | **k.** emissary, representative |
| **12.** deformado | **l.** impeccably, perfectly |
| **13.** el lamento | **m.** escort |
| **14.** la escolta | **n.** at attention |

**B ¿Sí o no?** Si no es verdad, hagan la corrección.

1. La casa de la hacienda en Chinameca es pequeña.
2. El portal de la casa es grande.
3. El tianguis se hace en un espacio enfrente de la casa.
4. El espacio donde se hace el tianguis es triangular.
5. Guajardo era general.
6. La casa donde Guajardo esperaba estaba en Chinameca.

**C La palabra, por favor.** Escojan.

1. Alrededor del espacio donde hacían el tianguis había ____.
   **a.** una cuadra **b.** una muralla **c.** un portal
2. La muralla tiene dos ____, una a la derecha y la otra a la izquierda.
   **a.** puertas **b.** habitaciones **c.** cornetas
3. Los soldados dentro de la casa estaban en lugares muy ____.
   **a.** anchos **b.** firmes **c.** ocultos
4. Antes de llegar el general, llegó un ____.
   **a.** cabo **b.** emisario **c.** soldado
5. En la cara del general se le veía unos grandes ____.
   **a.** ojos **b.** bigotes **c.** tiros



## Answers to ¿Comprendes?

**A**

1. d
2. e
3. f
4. h
5. k
6. l
7. n
8. c
9. j
10. b
11. i
12. g
13. a
14. m

**B**

1. No, la casa de la hacienda en Chinameca es enorme.
2. Sí
3. Sí
4. No, el espacio donde se hace el tianguis es cuadrangular.
5. No, Guajardo era coronel.
6. Sí

**C**

1. b
2. a
3. c
4. b
5. b

**D Comprensión** Completen.

1. Al llegar a la casa, una persona podría ver solamente a ____ soldados.
2. Junto con los soldados había otro que tocaba la ____.
3. Primero llegó el emisario del general y después llegaron los hombres de su ____.
4. Pero ni al emisario ni a la escolta les permitieron ____.
5. El general iba a entrar por la puerta de la ____.

**E Discusión** Reaccionen.

1. En tus propias palabras explica las dos oraciones que comienzan con: «Al trotar de la mula... » y terminan con «... tan cerca y al mismo tiempo tan distante».
2. ¿Cómo reaccionó la gente en Cuautla al ver el cadáver?

**F Interpretación** ¿Qué crees que representan los comentarios de la gente de Cuautla?

Las tropas de Emiliano Zapata

## Learning from Photos

*(page 477)* Ask students to identify Zapata in the photo and then to describe him, in Spanish, in as much detail as possible. (Zapata is the man seated in the middle of the front row.)

## Class Motivator

**¡Vamos a cantar!** After reading this selection you may want to play some Mexican ballads that became popular during the Mexican Revolution. Many of these ballads are well known even today in Mexico and parts of the United States.



## Answers to ¿Comprendes?

**D**

1. seis
2. corneta
3. escolta
4. entrar
5. derecha

**E**

1. *Answers will vary. Students should describe the image of Zapata's legs moving as if he were still alive and his arms reaching toward the ground in honor of his soldiers.*
2. *Answers will vary. Students should describe the mixed reactions of the people—disbelief and celebration.*

**F** *Answers will vary. Students will interpret the mixed reactions of the people—disbelief and celebration.*

# Video Companion

## Using video in the classroom

The use of video in the classroom can be a wonderful asset to the World Languages teacher and a most beneficial learning tool for the language student. Video enables students to experience whatever it is they are learning in their textbook in a real-life setting. With each lesson, they are able to take a vicarious field trip. They see people interacting at home, at school, at the market, etc., in an authentic milieu. Students sitting in a classroom can see real people going about their real life in real places. They may experience the target culture in many countries. The cultural benefits are limitless.

### Developing listening and viewing skills

In addition to its tremendous cultural value, video, when properly used, gives students much needed practice in developing good listening and viewing skills. Video allows students to look for numerous clues that are evident in a tone of voice, facial expressions, and gestures. Through video students can see and hear the diversity of the target culture and, as discerning viewers and listeners, compare and contrast the Spanish-speaking cultures to each other and to their own culture. Video introduces a dimension into classroom instruction that no other medium—teachers, overhead, text, audio CDs—can provide.

### Reinforcing learned language

Video that is properly developed for classroom use has speakers reincorporate the language students have learned in a given lesson. In keeping with reality, however, speakers introduce some new words, expressions, and structures because students functioning in a real-life situation would not know every word native speakers use with them in a live conversation. The lively and interactive nature of video allows students to use their listening and viewing skills to comprehend new language in addition to seeing and hearing the language they have learned come to life.

### Getting the most out of video

The intrinsic benefit of video is often lost when students are allowed to read the scripted material before viewing. In many cases, students will have come to understand language used by the speakers in the video by means of reading comprehension, thus negating the inherent benefits of video as a tool to develop listening and viewing skills. Because today's students are so accustomed to the medium of video as a tool for entertainment and learning, a well-written and well-produced video program will help them develop real-life language skills and confidence in those skills in an enjoyable way.

On Location
Soy Alberto.
Soy colombiano.
Soy de Bogota, Colombia.
Soy Alejandra.
Soy mexicana.
Soy de la Ciudad de México.
Soy Francisco.
Soy español.
Soy de Madrid, España.
Soy Vicky.
Soy argentina.
Soy de Buenos Aires.
Soy Claudia.
Soy argentina.
Soy de Buenos Aires, Argentina.
Soy Julián.
Soy venezolano.
Soy de Caracas, Venezuela.

## Video Synopsis

This episode begins with Francisco reading a book while waiting at a train station quai. Meanwhile, Claudia is at a kiosk buying chocolates made to look like gold coins. When Claudia approaches Francisco on the bench, he barely notices her and she takes his book to see why he is so engrossed. As she begins reading where Francisco left off, we see the enactment of the story about a mysterious, very elegant, international female spy. When the enactment of the spy story ends, Francisco wonders aloud about what the female spy had in her briefcase and as a joke, Claudia gives him her chocolate coins.

# VIDEOTUR

## ¡Viva el mundo hispano!

## Episodio 1

Francisco y Claudia leen un libro.

«Una mujer misteriosa» en la estación de ferrocarril

### Antes de mirar

¿Qué piensan ustedes? Inventen algo.

1. ¿Dónde están Francisco y Claudia?
2. ¿Qué tipo de libro leen?
3. ¿Hacen un viaje?
4. ¿Adónde van?
5. ¿Quién es el otro señor con «la mujer misteriosa»?

### Después de mirar

**Expansión** As you can see from the video, train travel is very popular in some Spanish-speaking countries. Do you think it is as popular where you live? What is your favorite means of transportation for long trips? Why? Survey your friends to find out their preferred means of travel. Share your results with the class.

### VIDEO VHS/DVD

The two photos above show highlights from the Chapter 1 video episode. Discuss the photos with your students before viewing the episode.

# VIDEOTUR

## ¡Viva el mundo hispano!

## Episodio 2

Alberto en el restaurante de su tío

Vicky y Alberto con cara de sorpresa

### Antes de mirar

¿Qué ven ustedes?

1. un camarero
2. un cliente
3. las papas
4. una propina
5. un vaso de agua

### Después de mirar

**Expansión** Are there many Hispanic restaurants in your community? Are they representative of a variety of different Spanish-speaking countries? Which ones are they? Do you have a favorite? Look at the menus of the different restaurants in your community or do research on the Internet to find some menus of Hispanic restaurants in this country. Are the foods very different? If any of the Hispanic restaurants in your community are run by a family, speak with one of the family members about the history of their business. Try to do this in Spanish if possible.



VIDEOTUR

### Video Synopsis

As this episode begins, we see Alberto working in a restaurant kitchen. Vicky arrives and reminds him that they are supposed to study together. Alberto explains that his uncle has had to leave the restaurant and left him in charge. Just at that moment, an important food critic calls to arrange a visit to the restaurant. Alberto panics but Vicky assures him that they can handle the situation. When two people simultaneously arrive at the restaurant, Alberto and Vicky make an incorrect assumption about which person is the critic. As a result, they offend the critic and only discover their mistake once the critic has left the restaurant.

The two photos above show highlights from the Chapter 2 video episode. Discuss the photos with your students before viewing the episode.

## Video Synopsis

Julián is working in an Internet café. Alejandra comes in and needs some help from him. A local television studio has an opening for a new soap opera actress and Alejandra wants to send them her photograph. Julián first tries to send the photo by fax but it doesn't go through. Next he tries to send a digital copy of the photo by email, but he cannot get the computer connected. Then Julián suggests calling the studio but Alejandra does not have her phone card with her. Finally, both Julián and Alejandra realize that the studio is only a few blocks away so they rush out to drop off the photo in person.

# VIDEOTUR

## ¡Viva el mundo hispano!

## Episodio 3

Alejandra y Julián están en el café Internet.

Julián trata de ayudar a Alejandra.

## Antes de mirar

¡Adivinen!

1. ¿Qué hacen Alejandra y Julián en el café Internet?
2. ¿De qué hablan Alejandra y Julián?
3. ¿Qué hace la otra gente en el café Internet

## Después de mirar

**Expansión** You are going to participate in a contest to appear in *People en español* with your favorite latino actor or musician. You have to send a photograph of yourself and a letter explaining why you admire the artist of your choice. Write the letter. Then explain how you are going to send the letter and the photograph. Think about ways you can do this with modern tecnology.

The two photos above show highlights from the Chapter 3 video episode. Discuss the photos with your students before viewing the episode.

## ¡Viva el mundo hispano!

# Episodio 4

Julián y Francisco van de compras.

Francisco y Julián están muy guapos.

## Antes de mirar

¿Qué ven ustedes?

1. flores
2. unos carritos
3. una caja
4. el pasillo
5. dos amigos muy bien vestidos

## Después de mirar

**Expansión** You see in the video that a fifteenth birthday is an important occasion for a young Hispanic girl. What is considered one of the most important birthdays for a young female in the United States? Do some research on the Internet to find out more information about a **quinceañera** and tell how it compares to a Sweet Sixteen celebration. Give similarities and differences.



VIDEOTUR

### Video Synopsis

This episode begins with Julián and Francisco standing at the entrance to a supermarket. They are shopping and talking about their plans for the evening. As Julián unravels his mother's long grocery list, Francisco tells him to hurry because he has been invited by to a **quinceañera** by a girl he likes. Julián says that he too has been invited to a **quinceañera** by a girl he likes but he seems to regard the formality of the occasion with less concern than Francisco. In the next scene, we see Julián and Francisco arrive at the same house and when a young woman opens the door, it is clear that both Julián and Francisco know her. At that moment, another identical young woman appears and the boys realize that they have been invited to the same birthday party by twin sisters.

### VIDEO VHS/DVD

The two photos above show highlights from the Chapter 4 video episode. Discuss the photos with your students before viewing the episode.

## Video Synopsis

As this episode begins, we see Francisco and Alejandra playing chess. Francisco is winning and enjoying the game, but Alejandra is bored. She decides to play a game with Francisco. While Francisco leaves momentarily to buy ice cream, Alejandra hides his queen and leaves behind a written clue. When Francisco returns, he reads the clue and follows the instructions that tell him to buy a balloon from a clown in a nearby park. Once Francisco buys the balloon, he finds another clue that instructs him to climb an artificial rock climbing wall. At the top of the wall, Francisco finds the final clue, which directs him back to the chessboard where he and Alejandra were playing earlier. In the end, Francisco finds his queen and Alejandra beats him in their game of chess.

# Videotur

## ¡Viva el mundo hispano!

## Episodio 5

Francisco y Alejandra andan en bicicleta.

Una aventura nueva para Francisco

## Antes de mirar

¿Sí o no?

1. Alejandra y Francisco están en el parque.
2. Hay un payaso en el parque.
3. Francisco está contento porque va a subir la pared de escala.
4. Alejandra va a subir también.

## Después de mirar

**Expansión** What are some leisure activities that you saw in the video? Are any of them leisure activities that you might enjoy? Do you and your friends go often to the beach or to the park? How do you spend your free time? Do you think Alejandra y Francisco would enjoy doing some of the things you enjoy doing in your free time?

### VIDEO VHS/DVD

The two photos above show highlights from the Chapter 5 video episode. Discuss the photos with your students before viewing the episode.

# VIDEOTUR

## ¡Viva el mundo hispano!

## Episodio 6

Francisco habla con el recepcionista en el hotel.

Francisco está en el cuarto del hotel.

## Antes de mirar

¡Usen su imaginación!

The name of the hotel that Francisco is going to stay in is **El Sportsman.** Try to think of what kind of a night he is going to have. In groups, act out what you think might happen if you were to stay in a hotel with that name. Then watch the video to find out what really happens.

## Después de mirar

**Expansión** In the video you visited **La Recoleta,** a cemetery in Buenos Aires. Do some research to find out more about this famous cemetery and some of the people who are buried there. Write a report about one of these people.



# VIDEOTUR

### Video Synopsis

Francisco has decided on go out of town and is unable to find a hotel with available rooms. At the very moment he begins to worry that he will have to sleep outside for the night, a flyer advertising a hotel lands at his feet. In the next scene, we see Francisco entering what appears to be a very old, strange hotel. Once inside the hotel, Francisco is greeted by a creepy concierge who explains to Francisco that if he spends the entire night in the hotel, he will not have to pay anything. As the concierge directs Francisco to his room, a series of bizarre events occur and Francisco realizes he is in a haunted hotel.

The two photos above show highlights from the Chapter 6 video episode. Discuss the photos with your students before viewing the episode.

# Videotur

## Video Synopsis

This episode begins with Alberto and Julián seated oustide. Vicky and Claudia arrive and Julián begins to tell his friends about a great deal he's gotten for a trip to Venezuela. Alberto teases Julián about being afraid to fly and Julián informs him that he's been cured of his phobia by listening to a series of CD recordings. Alberto, Vicky, and Claudia doubt the effectiveness of this, so they decide to test Julián by simulating an airplane experience. In the next scene, we see Julián's dream sequence as everything that could possibly go wrong during a flight, does. Julián tries to remain calm, but he eventually panics and when he wakes up, Alberto tries to calm him by reminding him that it was only a simulation.

# Videotur

## ¡Viva el mundo hispano!

## Episodio 7

Los amigos discuten algo importante.

¿Qué hacen los amigos?

## Antes de mirar

¡Usen su imaginación!

1. ¿Qué hacen los amigos?
2. ¿De qué hablan?
3. ¿Qué hace Julián?
4. ¿Qué ropa lleva Alberto? ¿Qué es?

## Después de mirar

**Expansión** In the Major Leagues in the United States, there are many Hispanic baseball players that have come from a number of Spanish-speaking countries, especially those in the Caribbean. Do some research on the Internet to find out some information about them. Have you ever seen any of them play either at a stadium or on television? Choose one whom you admire and give some information about his life.

**VIDEO VHS/DVD**

The two photos above show highlights from the Chapter 7 video episode. Discuss the photos with your students before viewing the episode.

# VIDEOTUR

## ¡Viva el mundo hispano!

## Episodio 8

Alberto y Vicky hablan con un chico.

El doctor Ernesto ayuda a Vicky.

## Antes de mirar

¡Usen su imaginación!

Completen el diálogo.

**Vicky:** Hola, chico.

**Chico:** ¿Qué tal?

## Después de mirar

**Expansión** Good health is associated with physical activity. Describe an exercise routine or participation in a sport that could keep you fit. Describe how the sport you play or the exercise you do helps different parts of your body. Describe a weekly schedule that you follow to keep physically fit. If you do not exercise regularly, discuss what type of schedule you would maintain if you were to begin.



# VIDEOTUR

### Video Synopsis

This episode begins with Alberto and Vicky passing by a skateboard park. Alberto and Vicky admire the skill of the skateboarders and Vicky brags that she can do what they do. Vicky then pays a skateboarder to loan her his equipment and almost immediately after starting to skateboard, she has an accident. Alberto runs over to to see if Vicky is okay and just at that moment, an older gentleman steps in and explains that he is a doctor. After briefly examining Vicky, the doctor determines that she has fractured her wrist and her ankle. Alberto warns Vicky that she needs to be more careful, but she doesn't listen and tries to make plans to go dancing.

### VIDEO VHS/DVD

The two photos above show highlights from the Chapter 8 video episode. Discuss the photos with your students before viewing the episode.

## Video Synopsis

In this episode, we switch back and forth between two different scenes: Julián in the city and Claudia in the country. Julián explains in detail and with several examples, why he loves city life. Claudia then lists the reasons why she loves the country. As Julián and Claudia each tell the many reasons why they love their respective environments, it becomes clear that they both enjoy switching places from time to time: Julián likes to escape to the country on the weekends and Claudia travels to the city on the weekends.

# VIDEOTUR

## ¡Viva el mundo hispano!

## Episodio 9

Julián está en la ciudad.

Claudia está en el campo.

## Antes de mirar

Contesten.

1. ¿Dónde están Julián y Claudia?
2. Describe el lugar donde está Julián.
3. Describe el lugar donde está Claudia.
4. ¿Son muy distintos los dos lugares?

## Después de mirar

**Expansión** ¿Prefieres la ciudad o el campo? ¿Por qué? ¿Qué te gusta hacer allí?

### VIDEO VHS/DVD

The two photos above show highlights from the Chapter 9 video episode. Discuss the photos with your students before viewing the episode.

## ¡Viva el mundo hispano!

# Episodio 10

Vicky y Alejandra preparan una comida.

Julián y Alberto llegan con una sorpresa.

## Antes de mirar

Contesten.

1. ¿Dónde están Vicky y Alejandra?
2. Escribe una lista de los ingredientes que hay en la mesa.
3. ¿Qué preparan ellas?
4. ¿Quiénes llegan a la puerta?
5. ¿Qué lleva Julián?

## Después de mirar

**Expansión** Encuentra en el Internet una receta para una comida hispana que te gusta. Prepara una lista de compras y si es posible prepara la comida para tu familia.



VIDEOTUR

### Video Synopsis

This episode begins with Vicky entering Alejandra's kitchen carrying grocery bags. Alejandra tells her to hurry because the dinner plans begin at eight o'clock. In the next scene, Vicky and Alejandra are hurriedly cooking and Vicky explains that she'll do the sausages because she has a special family recipe. The next scene shows Vicky and Alejandra getting ready for dinner. Alejandra notices a bottle in Vicky's bag and teases her that her family secret is in fact store bought. Suddenly, the two girls smell that something is burning. When Vicky and Alejandra enter the kitchen, they realize that the dinner is ruined and they worry about what to serve. Just at that moment the doorbell rings, and Julián arrives with Alberto. Julián surprises the girls with take-out dinner and teases Vicky about being a bad cook.

### VIDEO VHS/DVD

The two photos above show highlights from the Chapter 10 video episode. Discuss the photos with your students before viewing the episode.

VIDEOTUR

## Video Synopsis

When this episode begins, we see Claudia and Alejandra, dressed for a party and standing next to a convertible. Alejandra questions whether or not Claudia's brother will mind if they borrow the car to go to a party in the country. Claudia tells Alejandra not to worry about it. The girls try to start the car but discover that it doesn't have any gas, so they walk to the gas station. As they get ready to fill the gas tank, they realize that they need a key, which Claudia doesn't have. Claudia uses a bobby pin and the girls start the car, but it is clear that they are headed in a direction opposite of where they need to go. Once lost, they are stuck slowly driving behind a tractor, when a police cruiser pulls them over for going faster than the tractor speed limit. When the policeman asks them where they are going, Alejandra says that they have to attend to a family "tragedy" at which point the officer tells them that they will be late because they have a flat tire. Just as both girls lose all hope of getting to the party, the policeman smiles, explains that his daughter is going to the same party, and that he will help them get their tire repaired.

# VIDEOTUR

## ¡Viva el mundo hispano!

## Episodio 11

Alejandra y Claudia viajan por el campo.

Las dos amigas hablan con un policía.

## Antes de mirar

¡Usen su imaginación!

1. ¿Adónde van Claudia y Alejandra?
2. ¿Por qué hablan con un policía?

## Después de mirar

**Expansión** In the video you see some interesting things about transportation in Peru. Have you ever seen a llama? Is there a farm near you with llamas? Do some research on the Internet to find out more about how useful these animals were and still are in many parts of the Spanish-speaking world. Compare their use there with the way they might be used where you live. Are there many similarities?

The two photos above show highlights from the Chapter 11 video episode. Discuss the photos with your students before viewing the episode.

# ¡Viva el mundo hispano!

## Episodio 12

Francisco y Claudia están en una peluquería.

Chiquitín hace su «magia».

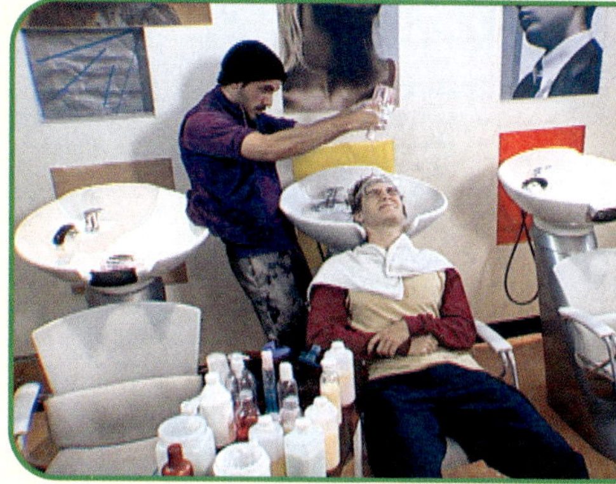

## Antes de mirar

Contesten.

1. ¿Qué miran Francisco y Claudia?
2. Describe la peluquería que ves en la foto.
3. ¿Está muy contento Francisco?

## Después de mirar

**Expansión** Find in a magazine a hairstyle that you like. Describe to the hairdresser the new haircut or hairstyle that you would like.





### Video Synopsis

The episode begins with Claudia and Francisco entering a hair salon. Francisco needs a haircut and would rather wait to have his mom cut it when he returns to Madrid, but Claudia assures him that she knows the owner of the salon. Francisco meets the owner of the salon, who looks somewhat like Marilyn Manson and is extremely flamboyant. Claudia leaves and the owner of the salon puts many different products in Francisco's hair. When Claudia returns, she explains that she has to run out again, despite Francisco's plees for her to stay. Once she is gone, the stylist cuts Francisco's hair. When Claudia returns, she realizes she's forgotten to pick up her mother's dry cleaning and quickly leaves again. After finishing all her errands, Claudia returns and the owner of the salon reveals Francisco's new look. Francisco's hair is now grey with blue stripes and he and Claudia are both horrified by the style.

### VIDEO VHS/DVD

The two photos above show highlights from the Chapter 12 video episode. Discuss the photos with your students before viewing the episode.

## Video Synopsis

This episode begins with Vicky sitting in an office and looking very bored. The phone rings—the call is from Alejandra—and Vicky begins to tell her why she regrets having started her own business. Just then, a mother and daughter duo walk in. The mother starts by explaining that her daughter is marrying a very rich, very handsome man and that she would like a video of the wedding. The mother continues to brag about the event and give instructions to Vicky about how to avoid filming the daughter's various "flaws". Meanwhile, the daughter becomes increasingly frustrated. The mother and daughter have a dispute, the daughter cancels the wedding, the mother blames Vicky for everything, and both women leave Vicky's office in a hurry. In the end, Vicky decides to change the nature of her business.

# Videotur

## ¡Viva el mundo hispano!

## Episodio 13

Vicky trabaja con dos clientes.

Vicky escucha atentamenta a sus clientes.

## Antes de mirar

Contesten.

1. Mira bien la foto. ¿Dónde trabaja Vicky?
2. ¿Qué hace Vicky en su trabajo?
3. Describe a los clientes.
4. Describe la oficina.

## Después de mirar

**Expansión** Look for a photograph of a fiesta—a wedding, a birthday, or any other celebration. The photograph can be of your family or from a magazine. Make up a story about the fiesta.

### VIDEO VHS/DVD

The two photos above show highlights from the Chapter 13 video episode. Discuss the photos with your students before viewing the episode.

## ¡Viva el mundo hispano!

## Episodio 14

Los amigos están en el parque.

Alejandra acepta un premio.

### Antes de mirar

¡Usen su imaginación!

1. ¿Qué hacen los amigos en el parque?
2. ¿De qué hablan?
3. ¿Qué premio acepta Alejandra?

### Después de mirar

**Expansión** Do you ever think about what you would like to do when you have finished with your education? How are you preparing yourself for this work? Where is it that you would like to work? Will you be famous? Do you know anyone who does the kind of work you are interested in? If so, interview him or her about the work.





### Video Synopsis

This episode opens with the entire main cast from the video series enjoying a picnic lunch together. Alejandra mentions what she'll be doing over their summer vacation and that leads to a discussion about where they will all be later in life. The camera cuts to a dream scene showing all six characters, still together, but elderly. In the subsequent scenes, we see that Vicky imagines being a veterinarian, Alberto thinks about being a famous doctor, Claudia envisions a successful career in banking and politics, Alejandra sees herself winning an Oscar, Julián dreams about being a professional soccer player, and Francisco will still be practicing his first love—sleeping.

### VIDEO VHS/DVD

The two photos above show highlights from the Chapter 14 video episode. Discuss the photos with your students before viewing the episode.

# Handbook

# InfoGap

## Activity 1

**CAPÍTULO 1, Palabras 2, pages 6–7**

**Alumno A** Ask your partner the following questions. Correct answers are in parentheses.

1. ¿Quién es el revisor? *(El señor Martínez es el revisor.)*
2. ¿El revisor está en el coche-cama o en el pasillo? *(El revisor está en el pasillo.)*
3. ¿Están Pablo y Ramona en el coche-comedor o en sus asientos? *(Están en sus asientos.)*
4. ¿Luis y Antonia van a bajar o van a subir? *(Luis y Antonia van a bajar.)*

**Alumno A** Answer your partner's questions based on the pictures below.

**Alberto**

**Señor Rivas**

**Susana y Pedro**

---

**Alumno B** Answer your partner's questions based on the pictures below.

**Ramona   Pablo   Señor Martínez**

**Luis y Antonia**

**Alumno B** Ask your partner the following questions. Correct answers are in parentheses.

1. ¿Dónde comen Susana y Pedro? *(Susana y Pedro comen en el coche-comedor/ coche-cafetería.)*
2. ¿Alberto sube al tren o baja del tren? *(Alberto baja del tren.)*
3. ¿El señor Rivas compra un billete o transborda? *(El señor Rivas transborda.)*
4. ¿El señor Rivas va a subir al tren o va a la sala de espera? *(El señor Rivas va a subir al tren.)*

## Activity 2

**CAPÍTULO 2, Palabras 2, Estructura, pages 36–37, 40**

**Alumno A** Ask your partner the following questions. Correct answers are in parentheses.

1. ¿Quién pide el pescado?
   *(Juanita pide el pescado.)*
2. ¿Qué piden Marta y Teresa?
   *(Marta y Teresa piden la langosta.)*
3. ¿Quién pide una ensalada?
   *(José pide una ensalada.)*
4. ¿Qué piden los muchachos?
   *(Los muchachos piden pollo.)*

**Alumno A** Answer your partner's questions based on the pictures below.

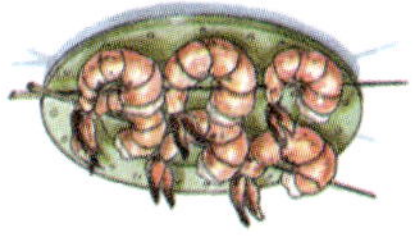

**Norma**

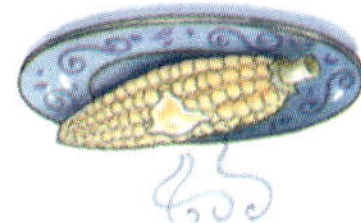

**Los turistas**

**Antonio**

**Paco y Mercedes**

---

**Alumno B** Answer your partner's questions based on the pictures below.

**Marta y Teresa**

**José**

**Juanita**

**Los muchachos**

**Alumno B** Ask your partner the following questions. Correct answers are in parentheses.

1. ¿Quién pide las almejas?
   *(Antonio pide las almejas.)*
2. ¿Qué piden Paco y Mercedes?
   *(Paco y Mercedes piden la carne.)*
3. ¿Qué piden los turistas?
   *(Los turistas piden el maíz.)*
4. ¿Quién pide los camarones?
   *(Norma pide los camarones.)*

## Activity 3

CAPÍTULO 3, Palabras 1, 2, pages 60–61, 64–65

**Alumno A** Ask your partner the following questions. Correct answers are in parentheses.

1. ¿El joven hace una llamada telefónica o manda un documento por fax?
   *(El joven hace una llamada telefónica.)*
2. ¿Introduce una moneda o una tarjeta telefónica?
   *(Introduce una tarjeta telefónica.)*
3. ¿Cuál es el prefijo de país del número de teléfono?
   *(El prefijo de país es cincuenta y seis.)*
4. ¿Cuál es la clave de área?
   *(La clave de área es treinta y dos.)*

**Alumno A** Answer your partner's questions based on the pictures below.

1–2.

3.

4.

**Alumno B** Answer your partner's questions based on the pictures below.

1.

2.

(056) 32 678-1945

3–4.

**Alumno B** Ask your partner the following questions. Correct answers are in parentheses.

1. ¿La joven hace una llamada telefónica o usa la computadora?
   *(La joven usa la computadora.)*
2. ¿Entra los datos con el teclado o el ratón? *(Entra los datos con el teclado.)*
3. ¿Qué mete en la ranura?
   *(Mete un CD en la ranura.)*
4. ¿Qué transmite por fax?
   *(Transmite un documento por fax.)*

## Activity 4

**CAPÍTULO 4, Palabras 2, pages 96–97**

**Alumno A** Ask your partner the following questions. Correct answers are in parentheses.

1. ¿Qué es, una carnicería o una verdulería? *(Es una carnicería.)*
2. ¿Qué se vende allí? *(Se vende carne.)*
3. ¿Qué es, una pastelería o una frutería? *(Es una frutería.)*
4. ¿Qué se vende allí? *(Se venden frutas.)*
5. ¿Qué es, una panadería o una pescadería? *(Es una pescadería.)*
6. ¿Qué se vende allí? *(Se vende pescado./Se venden mariscos.)*

**Alumno A** Answer your partner's questions based on the pictures below.

1–2.

3–4.

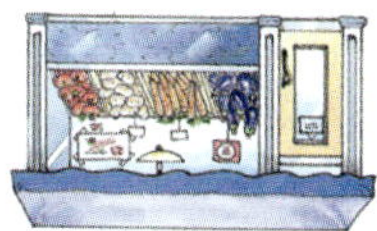

5–6.

**Alumno B** Answer your partner's questions based on the pictures below.

1–2.

3–4.

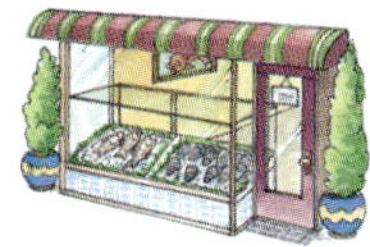

5–6.

**Alumno B** Ask your partner the following questions. Correct answers are in parentheses.

1. ¿Qué es, una pescadería o una panadería? *(Es una panadería.)*
2. ¿Qué se vende allí? *(Se vende pan.)*
3. ¿Qué es, una frutería o una pastelería? *(Es una pastelería.)*
4. ¿Qué se vende allí? *(Se venden pasteles.)*
5. ¿Qué es, una verdulería o una carnicería? *(Es una verdulería.)*
6. ¿Qué se vende allí? *(Se venden legumbres/vegetales.)*

InfoGap

## Activity 5

**CAPÍTULO 5, Palabras 2, pages 136–137**

**Alumno A** Ask your partner the following questions. Correct answers are in parentheses.

1. ¿Camina la gente por el parque o por el zoológico? *(La gente camina por el parque.)*
2. ¿Camina la gente por la senda? *(Sí, la gente camina por la senda.)*
3. ¿Qué hacen los jóvenes en el lago? *(Los jóvenes reman por el lago.)*
4. ¿En qué reman los jóvenes? *(Los jóvenes reman en el bote.)*

**Alumno A** Answer your partner's questions based on the pictures below.

**1–2.**

**3–4.**

---

**Alumno B** Answer your partner's questions based on the pictures below.

**1–2.**

**3–4.**

**Alumno B** Ask your partner the following questions. Correct answers are in parentheses.

1. ¿Quién toma una piragua, un muchacho o una muchacha? *(Un muchacho toma una piragua.)*
2. ¿Quién come un helado, un muchacho o una muchacha? *(Una muchacha come un helado.)*
3. ¿Dónde hacen cola en el parque de atracciones? *(Hacen cola en la boletería.)*
4. ¿Qué está detrás del tiovivo, la noria o la montaña rusa? *(La montaña rusa está detrás del tiovivo.)*

## Activity 6

**CAPÍTULO 6, Palabras 1, 2, pages 162–163, 166–167**

**Alumno A** Ask your partner the following questions. Correct answers are in parentheses.

1. ¿Es el recepcionista o el mozo? *(Es el mozo.)*
2. ¿Va a subir el equipaje o limpiar el cuarto? *(Va a subir el equipaje.)*
3. ¿El huésped paga la cuenta o llena la ficha? *(El huésped paga la cuenta.)*
4. ¿Cómo paga su factura? *(Paga con tarjeta de crédito.)*

**Alumno A** Answer your partner's questions based on the picture below.

**Alumno B** Answer your partner's questions based on the pictures below.

**1–2.**

**3–4.**

**Alumno B** Ask your partner the following questions. Correct answers are in parentheses.

1. ¿Es la camarera o la recepcionista? *(Es la camarera.)*
2. ¿Cambia las toallas o hace la cama? *(Hace la cama.)*
3. ¿Es un cuarto sencillo o doble? *(Es un cuarto sencillo.)*
4. ¿Tiene el cuarto un sofá o un sillón? *(El cuarto tiene un sillón.)*

# InfoGap

## Activity 7

**CAPÍTULO 7, Palabras 1, 2, pages 192–193, 196–197**

**Alumno A** Read your partner the following *true/false* statements. Correct responses are in parentheses.

1. La asistente de vuelo está en su asiento. *(No, la asistente de vuelo está en el pasillo.)*
2. Una señora usa audífonos. *(Sí, una señora usa audífonos.)*
3. El señor está en el pasillo. *(No, el señor está en su asiento.)*
4. La asistente de vuelo lleva un chaleco salvavidas. *(Sí, la asistente de vuelo lleva un chaleco salvavidas.)*

**Alumno A** Give your partner the correct information based on the pictures below.

**1–2.**

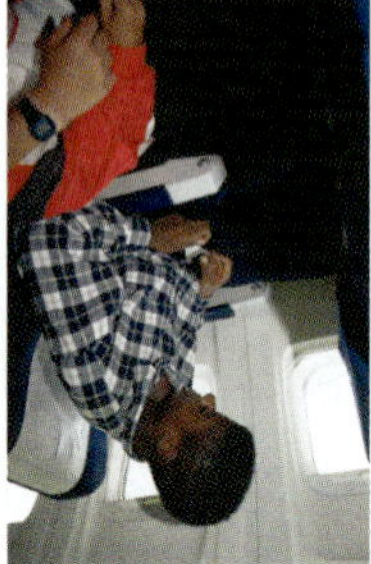

**3–4.**

---

**Alumno B** Give your partner the correct information based on the picture below.

**Alumno B** Read your partner the following *true/false* statements. Correct responses are in parentheses.

1. Es el despegue. *(No, es el aterrizaje.)*
2. Es un helicóptero. *(No, es un avión.)*
3. El muchacho está en la terminal de pasajeros. *(No, el muchacho está en el avión/en su asiento.)*
4. El muchacho se abrocha el cinturón de seguridad. *(Sí, el muchacho se abrocha el cinturón de seguridad.)*

InfoGap

## Activity 8

**CAPÍTULO 8, Palabras 1, 2, pages 232–233, 236–237**

**Alumno A** Ask your partner the following questions. Correct answers are in parentheses.

1. ¿Marta tiene una herida en la pierna o en el dedo? *(Marta tiene una herida en el dedo.)*
2. ¿La médica ha puesto un vendaje o un yeso? *(La médica ha puesto un vendaje.)*
3. ¿Alberto se lastimó la pierna o la cabeza? *(Alberto se lastimó la pierna.)*
4. ¿Cómo anda Alberto, en muletas o en una silla de ruedas? *(Alberto anda en una silla de ruedas.)*
5. ¿Quién llenó el formulario, Alberto o su amigo? *(Su amigo llenó el formulario.)*

**Alumno A** Answer your partner's questions based on the pictures below.

**Carlos**
**1–2.**

**Juanita**
**3–5.**

**Alumno B** Answer your partner's questions based on the pictures below.

**Marta**
**1–2.**

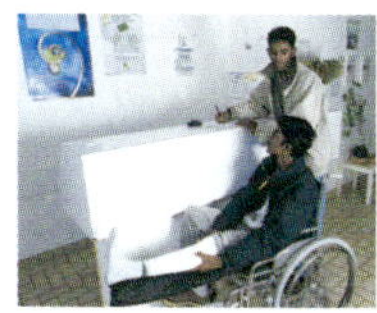

**Alberto**
**3–5.**

**Alumno B** Ask your partner the following questions. Correct answers are in parentheses.

1. ¿Carlos se rompió el brazo o la pierna? *(Carlos se rompió el brazo.)*
2. ¿La médica toma una radiografía o el pulso? *(La médica toma el pulso.)*
3. ¿Juanita se rompió el hombro o la pierna? *(Juanita se rompió la pierna.)*
4. ¿Tiene Juanita un yeso o un vendaje? *(Juanita tiene un yeso.)*
5. ¿Cómo anda Juanita, en muletas o en una silla de ruedas? *(Juanita anda en muletas.)*

# InfoGap

## Activity 9

CAPÍTULO 9, Palabras 1, 2, pages 262–263, 266–267

**Alumno A** Ask your partner the following questions. Correct answers are in parentheses.

1. ¿Qué animal es? *(Es un cerdo.)*
2. ¿Los obreros trabajan en una oficina o en una fábrica? *(Los obreros trabajan en una fábrica.)*
3. ¿La joven está en el campo o en la ciudad? *(La joven está en el campo.)*
4. ¿Es una zona industrial o residencial? *(Es una zona residencial.)*
5. ¿Hay muchos apartamentos? *(Sí, hay muchos apartamentos.)*

**Alumno A** Answer your partner's questions based on the pictures below.

1. 2. 3. 4–5.

**Alumno B** Answer your partner's questions based on the pictures below.

1.

2.

3.

4–5.

**Alumno B** Ask your partner the following questions. Correct answers are in parentheses.

1. ¿Qué animal es? *(Es una gallina.)*
2. ¿Qué animal es? *(Es una vaca.)*
3. ¿La gente trabaja en una oficina o en una fábrica? *(La gente trabaja en una oficina.)*
4. ¿Es una zona residencial o comercial? *(Es una zona comercial.)*
5. ¿Hay rascacielos en la zona? *(Sí, hay rascacielos en la zona.)*

## Activity 10

**CAPÍTULO 10, Palabras 1, 2, pages 292–293, 296–297**

**Alumno A** Ask your partner the following questions. Correct answers are in parentheses.

1. ¿La muchacha limpia o pela las papas? *(La muchacha pela las papas.)*
2. ¿Qué agrega a la olla el muchacho? *(El muchacho agrega sal.)*
3. ¿Qué lee el joven? *(El joven lee la receta.)*
4. ¿Qué es? *(Es langosta.)*

**Alumno A** Answer your partner's questions based on the picture below.

**Alumno B** Answer your partner's questions based on the pictures below.

**Alumno B** Ask your partner the following questions. Correct answers are in parentheses.

1. ¿Cuántas puertas tiene la nevera? *(La nevera tiene dos puertas.)*
2. ¿El refrigerador tiene un congelador? *(Sí, el refrigerador tiene un congelador.)*
3. ¿Hay plátanos en la cocina? *(Sí, hay plátanos en la cocina.)*
4. ¿Hay ollas en la estufa? *(Sí, hay ollas en la estufa.)*

# InfoGap

## Activity 11

**CAPÍTULO 11, Palabras 1, 2, pages 322–323, 326–327**

**Alumno A** Ask your partner the following questions. Correct answers are in parentheses.

1. ¿Dónde están las personas? *(Las personas están en la estación de servicio/la gasolinera.)*
2. ¿Qué llena Carlos? *(Carlos llena el tanque de gasolina.)*
3. ¿Luis limpia el parabrisas? *(No, Luis no limpia el parabrisas.)*
4. ¿Qué revisa Ricardo? *(Ricardo revisa el aceite.)*
5. ¿Antonio verifica la presión de las llantas? *(Sí, Antonio verifica la presión de las llantas.)*

**Alumno A** Answer your partner's questions based on the pictures below.

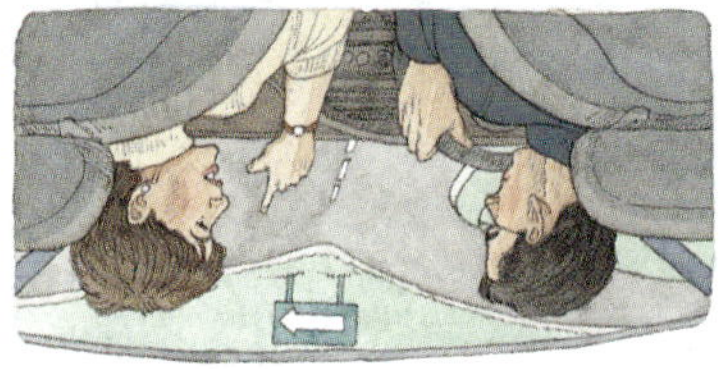

1–2.

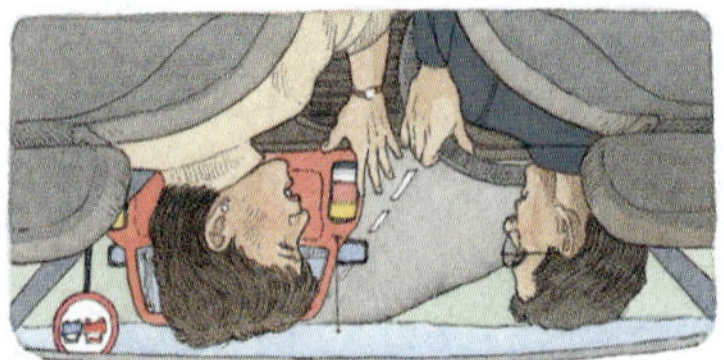

3–5.

**Alumno B** Answer your partner's questions based on the picture below.

**Alumno B** Ask your partner the following questions. Correct answers are in parentheses.

1. ¿El conductor tiene que doblar a la izquierda o a la derecha? *(El conductor tiene que doblar a la derecha.)*
2. ¿El rótulo indica una calle de sentido único o la velocidad máxima? *(El rótulo indica una calle de sentido único.)*
3. ¿Está el coche en la autopista o en una bocacalle? *(El coche está en la autopista.)*
4. ¿El rótulo indica una entrada a la autopista o un carril en cada sentido? *(El rótulo indica un carril en cada sentido.)*
5. ¿El conductor puede adelantar? *(No, el conductor no puede adelantar.)*

## Activity 12

**CAPÍTULO 12, Palabras 1, 2, pages 360–361, 364–365**

**Alumno A** Ask your partner the following questions. Correct answers are in parentheses.

1. ¿La peluquera lava o corta el pelo de la joven? (*La peluquera corta el pelo de la joven.*)
2. ¿La peluquera usa tijeras o una navaja? (*La peluquera usa tijeras.*)
3. ¿La peluquera seca o lava el pelo? (*La peluquera seca el pelo.*)
4. ¿Qué usa la peluquera para secar el pelo? (*La peluquera usa un secador.*)

**Alumno A** Answer your partner's questions based on the picture below.

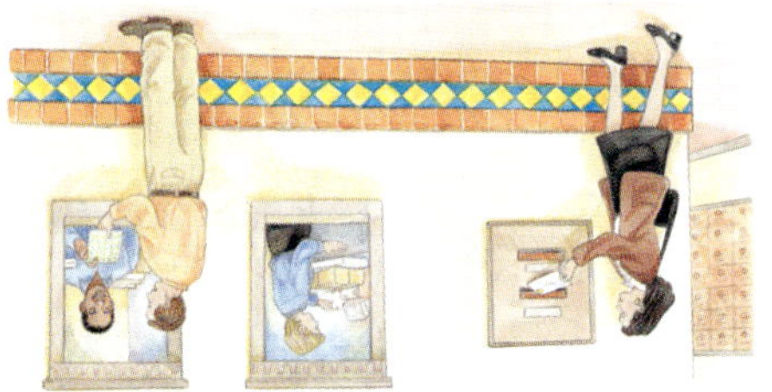

**Alumno B** Answer your partner's questions based on the pictures below.

**1–2.**

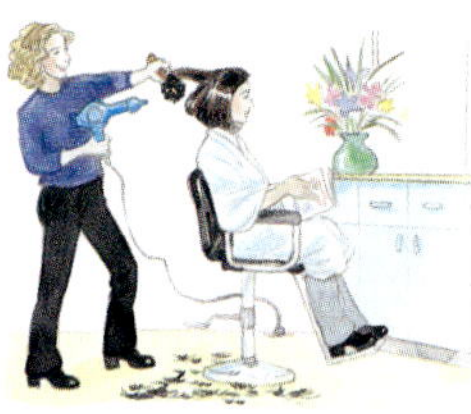

**3–4.**

**Alumno B** Ask your partner the following questions. Correct answers are in parentheses.

1. ¿Qué compra el señor, sellos o una tarjeta postal? (*El señor compra sellos.*)
2. ¿Qué echa la señora en el buzón? (*La señora echa una carta en el buzón.*)
3. ¿Cuántas ventanillas hay? (*Hay dos ventanillas.*)
4. ¿Qué hace la empleada? (*La empleada pesa el paquete.*)

## Activity 13

CAPÍTULO 13, Palabras 1, 2, pages 392–393, 396–397

**Alumno A** Ask your partner the following questions. Correct answers are in parentheses.

1. ¿Es una recepción de boda o una fiesta de cumpleaños? *(Es una recepción de boda.)*
2. ¿Los novios cantan o bailan? *(Los novios bailan.)*
3. ¿La familia celebra Hanuka o la Navidad? *(La familia celebra Hanuka.)*
4. ¿Qué tiene nueve brazos? *(La menora tiene nueve brazos.)*

**Alumno A** Answer your partner's questions based on the pictures below.

1–2.

3–4.

**Alumno B** Answer your partner's questions based on the pictures below.

1–2.

3–4.

**Alumno B** Ask your partner the following questions. Correct answers are in parentheses.

1. ¿La familia celebra Hanuka o la Navidad? *(La familia celebra la Navidad.)*
2. ¿Es Nochebuena o Nochevieja? *(Es Nochebuena.)*
3. ¿Celebran un cumpleaños o una boda? *(Celebran un cumpleaños.)*
4. ¿Qué llevan los amigos a la fiesta? *(Los amigos llevan regalos a la fiesta.)*

## Activity 14

**CAPÍTULO 14, Palabras 1, pages 424–425**

**Alumno A** Ask your partner the following questions. Correct answers are in parentheses.

1. ¿Qué hace la mecánica? *(La mecánica repara el coche.)*
2. ¿Qué hace el arquitecto? *(El arquitecto hace planes de construcción.)*
3. ¿Qué hace el plomero? *(El plomero repara el lavabo y el inodoro.)*
4. ¿Qué hace la contable? *(La contable calcula un plan financiero.)*

**Alumno A** Choose the correct information from the chart below to answer your partner's questions.

| ...repara las lámparas. |
|---|
| ...escribe programas en la computadora. |
| ...compra y vende mercancía. |
| ...defiende a los criminales en el tribunal. |

**Alumno B** Choose the correct information from the chart below to answer your partner's questions.

| ...repara el lavabo y el inodoro. |
|---|
| ...hace planes de construcción. |
| ...repara el coche. |
| ...calcula un plan financiero. |

**Alumno B** Ask your partner the following questions. Correct answers are in parentheses.

1. ¿Qué hace el comerciante? *(El comerciante compra y vende mercancía.)*
2. ¿Qué hace la abogada? *(La abogada defiende a los criminales en el tribunal.)*
3. ¿Qué hace el electricista? *(El electricista repara las lámparas.)*
4. ¿Qué hace la programadora? *(La programadora escribe programas en la computadora.)*

# Study Tips

## For students and parents/guardians

*This guide is designed to help you as students achieve success as you embark on the adventure of learning another language and to enable your parents or guardians to help you on this exciting journey. There are many ways to learn new information. You may find some of these suggestions more useful than others, depending upon which style of learning works best for you. Before you begin, it is important to understand how we acquire language.*

### Receptive Skills

Each day of your life you receive a great deal of information through the use of language. In order to get this information it is necessary to understand the language being used. It is necessary to understand the language in two different ways. First you must be able to understand what people are saying when they speak to you. This is referred to as oral or listening comprehension. Oral comprehension or listening comprehension is the ability to understand the spoken language.

You must also be able to understand what you read. This is referred to as reading comprehension. Reading comprehension is the ability to understand the written language.

Listening comprehension and reading comprehension are called *receptive skills*. They are receptive skills because as you listen to what someone else says or read what someone else has written you receive information without having to produce any language yourself.

It is usually very easy to understand your native language. It is a bit more problematic to understand a second language that is new to you. As a beginner you are still learning the sounds of the new language, and you recognize only a few words. Throughout **¡Buen viaje!** we will give you hints or suggestions to help you understand when people are speaking to you in Spanish or when you are reading in Spanish.

**Hints for Listening Comprehension** When you are listening to a person speaking Spanish, don't try to understand every word. It is not necessary to understand everything to get the idea of what someone is saying. Listen for the general message. If some details escape you, it doesn't matter. Also, never try to translate what people are saying in Spanish into English. It takes a great deal of experience and expertise to be a translator. Trying to translate will hinder your ability to understand.

**Hints for Reading Comprehension** Just as you will not always understand every word you hear in a conversation, you will not necessarily understand every word you encounter in a reading selection, either. In **¡Buen viaje!,** we have used only words you know or can easily figure out in the reading selections. This will make reading comprehension much easier for you. However, if at some time you wish to read a newspaper or magazine article in Spanish, you will most certainly come across some unfamiliar words. Do not stop reading. Continue to read to get the "gist" of the selection. Try to guess the meanings of words you do not know.

## Productive Skills

There are two productive skills in language. These two skills are speaking and writing. They are called *productive skills* because it is you who has to produce the language when you say or write something. When you speak or write, you have control over the language and which words you use. If you don't know how to say something, you don't have to say it. With the receptive skills, on the other hand, someone else produces the language that you listen to or read, and you have no control over the words they use.

There's no doubt that you can easily speak your native language. You can write, too, even though you may sometimes make errors in spelling and punctuation. In Spanish, there's not a lot you can say or write as a beginner. You can only talk or write about those topics you have learned in Spanish class.

**Hints for Speaking** Try to be as accurate as possible when speaking. Try not to make mistakes. However, if you do, it's not the end of the world. Spanish speakers will understand you. You're not expected to speak a language perfectly after a limited time. You have probably spoken with people from other countries who do not speak English perfectly, but you can understand them. Remember:

- Keep talking! Don't become inhibited for fear of making a mistake.
- Say what you know how to say. Don't try to branch out in the early stages and attempt to talk about topics or situations you have not yet learned in Spanish.

**Hints for Writing** There are many activities throughout each chapter of **¡Buen viaje!** that will help you to speak and write in Spanish. When you have to write something on your own, however, without the guidance or assistance of an activity in your book, be sure to choose a topic for which you know the vocabulary in Spanish. Never attempt to write about a topic you have not yet studied in Spanish. Write down the topic you are going to write about. Then think of the words you know that are related to the topic. Be sure to include some action words (verbs) that you will need.

From your list of words, write as many sentences as you can. Read them and organize them into a logical order. Fill in any gaps. Then proof your paragraph(s) to see if you made any errors. Correct any that you find.

When writing on your own, be careful not to rely heavily, if at all, on a bilingual dictionary. It's not that bilingual dictionaries are bad, but when you look up a word you will very often find that there are several translations for the same word. As a beginning language student, you do not know which translation to choose; the chances are great that you will pick the wrong one.

As a final hint, never prepare your paragraph(s) in English and attempt to translate word for word. Always write from scratch in Spanish.

# Study Tips

## Capítulo 1

### Vocabulario
PALABRAS 1 y 2 *(pages 2–9)*

1. Listen to the new words in **Palabras 1** and repeat them orally before reading them.
2. After learning the new words, match the following opposites.

| | |
|---|---|
| **la llegada** | **bajar de** |
| **de ida y vuelta** | **ocupado** |
| **subir a** | **la salida** |
| **libre** | **tarde** |
| **a tiempo** | **sencillo** |

3. Read the answers aloud to all the **Historieta** activities.

### Estructura
**El pretérito de los verbos irregulares**
*(pages 12–13)*

Note that these irregular verbs have the same endings in the preterite as regular verbs except in the **yo** and **él, ella, usted** forms.

| | Regular | Irregular |
|---|---|---|
| **yo** | **-í** | **-e** |
| **él, ella, Ud.** | **-ió** | **-o** |

### Lectura cultural
**En el AVE** *(pages 18-19)*

1. Before reading this selection, look at the photo of the bird—**el ave, el pájaro.** What's the association of the bird with the train?
2. Scan the reading selection to get just the general idea.
3. Read the selection again and look for some more precise details about a trip on the **AVE.**

## Capítulo 2

### Vocabulario
PALABRAS 1 y 2 *(pages 32–39)*

1. Do some review as you learn this new vocabulary. Think of all the foods you have learned in Spanish. You may wish to refer back to Chapter 5 in **¡Buen viaje!, Level 1.**

**Hint** If you´re the type of learner who has to write something before you can remember it, write the new words several times.

2. Activity 8 on page 39 reviews the use of **gustar.** You may review **interesar** and **gustar** on page 215 of **¡Buen viaje!, Level 1.**

### Estructura
**Verbos con el cambio e → i** *(pages 40–41)*

1. You have already come across this type of stem change in the irregular verb **decir.**
   **digo, dices, dice, decimos, *decís*, dicen**
2. As with other stem-changing verbs you have learned so far **(e → ie, o → ue),** these verbs take the same endings as any other verb that belongs to that conjugation.

**Hint** If you pronounce these verbs correctly, you will never have trouble spelling them. Remember **i** is pronounced like *ee* in English *see* and **e** is pronounced like the *a* in *ate.*

### Lectura cultural
**La comida mexicana** *(pages 46–47)*

If you have ever been to a Mexican restaurant, think about what you ate there. It will help you visualize what you are reading about.

## Capítulo 3

### Vocabulario

PALABRAS 1 *(pages 60–63)*

1. When studying the vocabulary on your own, be sure to pronounce the words orally. Then read them silently always concentrating on the illustration to ascertain meaning.

2. When you think you are quite familiar with the new words, cover up the Spanish and see what you can say about each illustration on your own.

3. If you are the type of learner who has to write something before you can retain it, copy each word two or three times on a piece of paper.

### Práctica

1. The first time you do these activities you may want to go back to pages 60–61 to look for the answers.

2. If you are a diligent student, however, you should get to know the material well enough that you can do these activities without having to look up the answers or at least the vast majority of them.

3. If you are studying at home with a classmate or person who knows Spanish, you can do Activities 4–6 on page 63 together.

PALABRAS 2 *(pages 64–67)*

1. Once again remember to go over the vocabulary orally as well as reading it.

**Hint** Think about the order of things you have to do to make a phone call from a public phone. After studying the vocabulary, determine if you can describe each step in Spanish without reading it.

# Study Tips

## Estructura

**Imperfecto de los verbos en –ar** *(pages 68–70)*

1. Repeat the verb forms *aloud.*
2. Take the verb **tomar** and write out the complete conjugation at least once.
3. Read the "model" sentences aloud.

**Hint** As you do, concentrate on the fact that it is not important when each action began nor when it ended, if it ever did.

4. To test your ability to use these new endings, try to do Activity 14 without having to look up any of the endings, that is to say without having to refer to the verb charts on page 68.

**Imperfecto de los verbos en –er e –ir** *(pages 70–71)*

1. Pronounce the endings aloud in isolation.
2. Write the endings at least once.
3. Read aloud all the forms in the verb chart.

**Hint** Read the verb forms down the first different endings. Then read them across to help you associate the ending with the subject.

Ex:

**tú leías comías escribías vivías**

**Imperfecto de los verbos *ser* y *ir*** *(pages 72–73)*

1. Follow the same suggestions given for the previous verb sections in the chapter.

**Usos del imperfecto** *(pages 74–75)*

**Hint** Concentrate on the fact that this tense, the imperfect, is used to describe or reminisce about the past. It is not used to describe what happened in the past.

**Conversación** *(page 76)*

1. Listen carefully to the conversation. You can listen to your teacher or use the CD-ROM. Listen more than once. Each time you'll pick up some more information
2. Read the conversation aloud several times.
3. Try to answer the questions that follow without looking up the answers in the conversation.

## Lectura cultural *(pages 78–79)*

**Futura ingeniera**

1. You should have no problem reading this selection since it only includes Spanish you have already learned.
2. Read the selection quickly to get the general idea.
3. Read it a second time to get more details.
4. Read all the questions on page 79.
5. Read the selection again. As you find the answer to each question, write it down.
6. As a final check read each question again. See how many questions you can answer without looking up the information. You should be able to answer at least eight of them.

## Capítulo 4

### Vocabulario

PALABRAS 1 y 2 *(pages 92–99)*

1. Look at each photo or illustration carefully.
2. Read the labels. What does each word refer to?
3. The words are then used in a meaningful context in a complete sentence. Repeat the sentence aloud as you look at the illustration.
4. To help you learn vocabulary, work with a friend or classmate. Have a contest. See who can say the most about each illustration or photo.
5. To review the vocabulary and see how much of it you know, cover the words and sentences and say as much as you can about each photo or illustration.
6. Do the activities that follow both orally and in writing.

**Hint** When you have finished studying the vocabulary, write a list of all the articles of clothing and a list of all the foods you can remember.

### Estructura

**El pretérito y el imperfecto** *(pages 100–102)*

**Hint** Always remember—if you know exactly when something happened, you use the preterite. If the precise time at which it happened is not important, you use the imperfect.

1. Read the model sentences on page 100, keeping in mind the above **Hint.** Relate the **Hint** to each of the sentences.
2. Exercises 14 and 15 on page 101 help you zero in on the time concept.

**Dos acciones en una oración** *(pages 103–104)*

**Hint** When trying to determine whether to use the imperfect or the preterite, pretend you are at the theater watching a play or that you are watching a movie. All the scenery or activity that is going on in the background is expressed by the imperfect. What the actors or actresses did is in the preterite. Just remember, background— imperfect; action—preterite.

1. As you do Activity 19 on page 103, keep in mind the above **Hint.** This will help you understand what you are doing.

**La voz pasiva con se.** *(pages 106–107)*

**Hint** Remember the **se** construction is used with only two verb forms— one singular, the other plural.

| | | | |
|---|---|---|---|
| **Aquí:** | **se habla español** | **se vende pescado** | **se escribe poesía** |
| **Aquí:** | **se hablan idiomas** | **se venden legumbres** | **se escriben novelas** |

**Conversación** *(page 108)*

1. Intonation is the melody of a language. Intonation is produced by the rise and fall of the voice. Each language has its own intonation patterns. English intonation is very different from Spanish intonation. Pay special attention to the rise and fall of the speaker's voice as you listen to the conversations on the CDs or CD-ROM.
2. Try to imitate the speakers' intonation as accurately as possible. If you do, you'll sound much more like a heritage Spanish speaker. Don't be inhibited. Pretend you are acting while you imitate the intonation.

# Study Tips

## Lectura cultural

**De compras** *(pages 110–111)*

1. Go over the Reading Strategy. Once you follow the suggestions in the Reading Strategy you will certainly know what this reading is about.

**Hint** Then think about what you already know about the topic. What's it like to shop in a supermarket? What's it like to shop in a small market, either a small vegetable stand or farmer's market? What's it like to shop in a gigantic outlet store?

2. Visualizing the answers to the above will help you understand rather easily the content of this reading selection.
3. When you think you know the information in the reading selection quite well, go over the questions on page 111 and see how many you can answer without having to look up information.

**Lectura opcional** *(page 112–113)*
Even if your teacher does not assign this optional reading you may wish to read it quickly. It gives you some interesting cultural information and once again reinforces language you have already learned. Remember, the more you are reintroduced to language you have already learned the easier Spanish will be.

**Vocabulario** *(page 120)*
Look at each word. Determine how many you know. If there are some you don't remember, go back to pages 92–93 and 96–97 to look for them.

# Capítulo 5

## Vocabulario

PALABRAS 1 y 2 *(pages 132–139)*

1. In **Palabras 1,** remember to listen to the words and repeat them orally before reading them.
2. After you have learned the new words in **Palabras 2,** look at each illustration, cover up the sentences, and say as much as you can about the illustration. If you can describe the illustration, you know your vocabulary. If you cannot describe it, you have to study some more.
3. Look at each sentence again. Find each verb. Verbs you will encounter are:

| | | |
|---|---|---|
| **irá** | **jugará** | **será** |
| **comprará** | **ganará** | **llenará** |

Since several sentences are introduced by **mañana,** what tense of the verb do you think this is?

a) present b) future c) past

If you chose future, you are correct.

## Estructura

**Futuro de los verbos regulares** *(pages 140–143)*

1. Remember that the entire infinitive serves as the root for the formation of the future tense. This is the first tense you have learned in which you add the ending to the infinitive.
2. In the verb charts, read the verb across to help you associate the ending with its corresponding subject:

**yo** **estudiaré** **leeré** **escribiré**

**Hint** Read or say aloud all the answers to the **Historieta** activities to give you some practice telling coherent stories in Spanish.

**Comparativo y superlativo** *(pages 144–145)*
In this section you are going to learn how to compare persons or things. Think of as many adjectives as you can. You have already learned quite a few. See how many you can come up with on your own before referring to the following list.

| | | | |
|---|---|---|---|
| **alto** | **serio** | **grande** | **fácil** |
| **bajo** | **ambicioso** | **inteligente** | **difícil** |
| **guapo** | **perezoso** | **interesante** | **popular** |
| **bonita** | **fantástico** | **joven** | **moderno** |
| **lindo** | **tímido** | **feo** | **sincero** |
| **moreno** | **honesto** | **rubio** | **generoso** |
| **flaco** | **simpático** | **gordo** | **aburrido** |
| **gracioso** | **pequeño** | **cómico** | **viejo** |

1. If you want to be a diligent student, after doing Activities 19 and 20 on page 145, you can make up many additional sentences in the comparative and superlative using the above adjectives.

# Study Tips

## Lectura cultural

**El domingo en el parque** *(pages 148–149)*

1. To reinforce the grammar point you learned in this chapter, skim the reading selection and find all the verbs in the future tense.
2. Be sure to write the answers to the Activities on page 149.
3. If you feel you are sufficiently familiar with the context of the reading selection, go over the questions on page 149 and see how many you can answer without having to look up information.

2. When doing the activities that follow each **Palabras** section, read aloud all the answers to each **Historieta** activity. By doing this you will be telling a story in Spanish. Always remember, the more you practice speaking Spanish, the better you'll be able to communicate.

3. In class, pay attention to the responses of the other students in class. Don't turn them off. The more you hear the new words used, the easier it will be for you to remember them.

# Capítulo 6

## Vocabulario

PALABRAS 1 y 2 *(pages 162-169)*

1. It can be fun to study with a classmate. You can do the following.
   - Ask one another questions in Spanish about the illustrations.
   - Have a contest. See who can give more Spanish words describing the illustrations in a three-minute period.
   - Tell your friend which of the items you would order if you were at a café.

## Estructura

**Futuro de los verbos irregulares** *(pages 170–173)*

1. This point should be easy for you since the endings are the same as those you already learned for the future of regular verbs in Chapter 5.
2. When going over the activities at home, be sure to do them aloud. Then write down the answers.
3. Retell the information in the **Historieta** activities in your own words.
4. See if you can give all of the future endings without having to look them up.

# Study Tips

**Me lo, te lo, nos lo** *(pages 173–175)*

**Hint** When learning another language it is often necessary to repeat the same thing many times before you can use it quickly and easily. The object pronouns you are learning in this lesson are a point in case. When you are carrying on a normal conversation it is impossible to ask yourself the gender of the object, the pronoun that replaces it and its place in the sentence—before or after the other pronoun. So, what's the solution? It's simple, practice makes perfect. Go over the activities as often as you can. Read the question aloud and then answer it. The more you hear **me lo, te lo,** etc. the easier it will be to use it.

**Hint** Be diligent in doing your Spanish homework. Work for at least a brief period of time each day. This enables you to learn everything in small doses. Do not let things pile up.

## Lectura cultural

**Los paradores de España** *(pages 178–179)*

1. As you read this selection find examples of the future tense to review the structure point of the lesson.
2. When you have finished studying the **Lectura,** just sit back and think about all the sentences you can make up to summarize the content of the reading selection.

## Capítulo 7

## Vocabulario

PALABRAS 1 y 2 *(pages 192–199)*

1. You already know some vocabulary related to airports and air travel from **¡Buen viaje!**, Level 1. Before going over the vocabulary, think of the words that you already know about this topic.

**Hint** If you're the type of learner who has to write something before you can remember it, copy the words in the **Palabras** section once or twice. Use the following learning sequence: listen, repeat, read, write.

2. Go over exercises 7, 8, 9, and 10 on pages 198–199 orally before writing them.
3. As you are about to finish studying the vocabulary at home, consult the vocabulary list on page 220. See how many words you understand without having to use the illustrations on pages 192, 193, 196, and 197.

## Estructura

**Modo potencial o condicional de verbos regulares** *(pages 200–202)*

1. See if you remember the endings for the imperfect of **–er** and **–ir** verbs. You will use these endings again with the conditional.
2. This grammatical point should be quite easy for you:
   - The conditional is used in Spanish in exactly the same way as it is in English.
   - You are already familiar with the root for the conditional – the entire infinitive. You have already used the root for the future tense.
   - You are also already familiar with the endings from your study of the imperfect.
3. Write the answers to the activities after doing them aloud.

**Modo potencial de verbos irregulares** *(pages 203–205)*

1. Remember, the root of irregular verbs is the same for the future and the conditional tenses.

**Dos complementos con se** *(pages 205–207)*

1. Re-read the **Hint** for **me lo, te lo, nos lo** on page H24. If you want to give yourself more practice, you can do the following substitution exercises: Follow the model:

   **Yo le di el boleto.**
   **Yo se lo di a él.**
   **(los boletos, la tarjeta de embarque, el maletín, las maletas, el periódico, las revistas, las fotografías, el carro, las llaves, la carta, el sello, el bolígrafo, el cuaderno, los lápices, la carpeta, la goma de borrar)**

# Capítulo 8

## Vocabulario

PALABRAS 1 y 2 *(pages 232–239)*

1. Think of all the parts of the body you have already learned.
2. Look at each photo or illustration carefully.
3. Read the labels. What does each word refer to?
4. The words are then used in a meaningful context in a complete sentence. Repeat the sentence aloud as you look at the illustration.
5. To help you learn vocabulary, work with a friend or classmate. Have a contest. See who can say the most about each illustration or photo.
6. To review the vocabulary and see how much of it you know, cover the words and sentences and say as much as you can about each photo or illustration.
7. Do the activities that follow both orally and in writing.

## Estructura

**El presente perfecto** *(pages 240–242)*

1. Give the past participle of the following verbs:

| | | |
|---|---|---|
| **hablar** | **aprender** | **vivir** |
| **estudiar** | **leer** | **salir** |
| **buscar** | **vender** | **servir** |
| **comprar** | **poder** | **reducir** |

2. After reading the explanation on page 240, go over Activities 13–16 on pages 241–242 first aloud and then write them out. It is suggested that you do one activity at a time.

**Los participios irregulares** *(pages 242–243)*

1. Repeat the irregular past participles aloud several times.
2. After you have gone over the activities, see if you can write all the verbs that have an irregular past participle without referring to the list on page 242.

**Comparación de igualdad** *(pages 244–245)*

1. Just remember:

   **tan... como** with an adjective.
   **tanto... como** with a noun
   **(tanto... como, tanta... como, tantos... como, tantas... como)**

2. Be sure to go over activities 22 and 23 orally.

# Study Tips

**Hint** If you're the type of learner who has to write something in order to remember it, copy the words in the **Estructura** section once or twice. Use the following learning sequence: listen, repeat, read, write.

**Conversación** *(page 246)*
When listening to people speak Spanish, the tone of voice can very often help you understand what the person is saying. When listening to this conversation, pay particular attention to the speaker's tone.

Intonation is the rising and dropping of the voice. As you know the intonation for a question is quite different than for a declarative sentence. This conversation includes quite a few questions and question words. Pay particular attention to the rising intonation.

## Capítulo 9

### Vocabulario

PALABRAS 1 y 2 *(pages 262–269)*

1. The **Palabras 1** section on pages 262 and 263 has many sentences. Only a small part of each sentence contains new words. An excellent study technique is to ask yourself questions about each sentence as you study.

   Example:
   **¿Qué hay en la zona comercial?**
   **¿Dónde hay muchas oficinas y tiendas?**
   **¿Qué hora es?**
   **¿Quién estaba saliendo?**
   **¿De dónde estaba saliendo la gente?**

   You can answer these questions with a complete sentence or with just the necessary words.

   Example:
   **La gente estaba saliendo de sus oficinas.**
   **De sus oficinas.**

This gives you the opportunity to use the words several times. The more you use them the easier it will be to remember them.

**Hint** Remember to go over the vocabulary activities at least once orally before writing them.

## Estructura

**El imperfecto progresivo** *(pages 270–271)*

**Hint** Remember that if you pronounce correctly, you will not misspell words. The vowel **i** is pronounced *ee* as in *see*. If you pronounce the following words correctly, you will never try to spell them with an **e**.

**pidiendo**
**sirviendo**
**repitiendo**
**diciendo**

1. This grammar point is quite easy. Pronounce the irregular past participles several times aloud. You may also want to copy them once in written form before doing the activities.

**Colocación de los pronombres de complemento** *(pages 272–273)*

1. As you have already read in previous Study Tips sections, the more you hear and use the object pronouns, the more comfortable you will be with them. For this reason it is suggested that you go over each activity twice.

**Adjetivos y pronombres demonstrativos** *(pages 274–275)*

1. Remember
   - something near you— a form of **este**
   - something near the person you're speaking to— a form of **ese**
   - something distant from the two of you— a form of **aquel**
2. You will often see the pronoun written with an accent to differentiate it from the adjective but current usage no longer requires this distinction.

## Lectura cultural

**Buenos Aires, Argentina** *(pages 278–279)*
After you read each paragraph, stop reading and think about the most important information you learned in the paragraph.

**Lecturas opcionales** *(pages 280–281)*
Even if your teacher does not assign either of these reading selections, you may want to read them very quickly not only to familiarize yourself with two other interesting cities but to give yourself the opportunity to be exposed once again to Spanish you have already learned. It cannot be emphasized enough that the more you are reintroduced to Spanish you have already learned, the easier the language will be.

## Vocabulario

PALABRAS 1 y 2 *(pages 292–299)*

1. Make a mental list of all the foods you have already learned in Spanish.
2. After studying the new words, cover each printed word and see if you can give the correct word by looking only at the illustration.

# Study Tips

## Estructura

**Imperativo formal: formas regulares**
*(pages 301–302)*

**Review** Since you will use the **yo** form of the present indicative to form the command for most verbs, review the following:

| | |
|---|---|
| **hablo** | **hago** |
| **como** | **pongo** |
| **escribo** | **traigo** |
| **vuelvo** | **salgo** |
| **empiezo** | **tengo** |
| **pido** | **vengo** |
| **sirvo** | |

1. Be sure to pronounce the command forms correctly. If you pronounce the **–e** and **–a** sounds clearly, you will never have a problem spelling the commands.

**Imperativo formal: formas irregulares**
*(pages 303–304)*

**Hint** Once again, say these forms aloud quite a few times. The more you hear them, the more automatic they will become and you will have no trouble using them. When speaking you do not have time to resort to the rule "take the **yo** form of the present, drop the **–o** ending, and add the vowel opposite to the typical vowel of that conjugation." The rule enables you to understand how the command is formed, but it is the practice that will enable you to use it.

**Colocación de los pronombres de complemento**
*(page 305)*

1. Go over the activities at least twice orally. Then write them out. Check your answers. Then read them at least once aloud.

## Lectura cultural

**Una receta española** *(pages 308–309)*
Pay particular attention to the command forms as you read this selection.

## Vocabulario

PALABRAS 1 y 2 *(pages 322–329)*

1. After studying the vocabulary, make three lists to determine how well you know the new vocabulary.
   - list 1 – car parts and models
   - list 2 – at a gas station
   - list 3 – on the road
2. Go over each activity at least once orally before writing it.

## Estructura

**Imperativo familiar: formas regulares**
*(pages 330–331)*

1. There is no doubt that the command forms of the verbs in Spanish are tricky even though they involve only two sounds: **–e** and **–a.** For starters, be sure to pronounce these sounds as carefully and clearly as you can. There is no substitute for good, old practice but the following may help you a bit:

   Verbs that take **–a** in the formal command (**usted**) take **–e** in the informal command.
2. Go over each activity several times.

**Imperativo familiar: formas irregulares**
*(pages 332–333)*
These verbs follow no set pattern and the only way to learn them is to use them.

1. Say them orally several times
2. Go over each activity at least twice.

**Classroom Suggestion** Listen to your classmates as they respond to the structure activities. The more you hear the form, the more readily you will be able to use it.

**Conversación** *(page 336)*
When listening to the conversation, pay particular attention to the intonation for the command.

## Lectura cultural

**La carretera panamericana** *(pages 338–339)*
When you have finished studying this selection, make a list of some of the interesting facts about the Panamerican Highway.

## Vocabulario

PALABRAS 1 y 2 *(pages 360–367)*

1. These vocabulary sections contain words that will be of great help to you when trying to get around in a Spanish-speaking area. After going over the vocabulary, make yourself a few "survival" lists.
   - Words I need to get my hair cut.
   - Words I need to get my clothes cleaned.
   - Words I need to mail something.
   - Words I need to get money.
2. Go over the activities both orally and in writing as you do your homework.

## Estructura

**El subjuntivo** *(pages 368–375)*

1. Many students learning Spanish consider the subjunctive to be very difficult. The subjunctive is traditionally presented as the verb form that is used following many different types of expressions such as: desire, volition, necessity, possibility, doubt, etc. It is difficult to keep all these categories in mind when speaking or using the subjunctive and it is not necessary.

   The subjunctive is almost always introduced by **que.** If what follows **que** may or may not take place, if it is not a reality, you will then use the subjunctive. Always ask yourself, "really or maybe?" If the answer is maybe, you will almost always have to use the subjunctive.
2. To contrast the indicative, which you have already learned, and the subjunctive, which you are about to learn, take into account the following regarding the meaning of these words:

   **Indicative** Indicates something – points something out – is objective – can stand alone – is independent.

   **Subjunctive** Subjective – does not indicate anything concrete – is not objective; it is the opposite of objective – cannot stand alone – is dependent upon something else.

   | Indicative | Subjunctive |
   |---|---|
   | He gets good grades. | I hope he *gets good marks.*<br>I want him to *get good marks.*<br>His parents insist that he *get good marks.*<br>It's necessary for him to *get good marks.*<br>He'll get a present when he *gets good marks.* |

3. You are already familiar with the subjunctive forms of the verb from your study of the command. The **usted, ustedes** and negative **tú** commands are actually subjunctive forms.
4. Once again, practice makes "perfect" in acquiring the subjunctive. Do each activity orally, then write it and after writing it, read your answers aloud.

# Study Tips

## Lectura cultural

**Muchos quehaceres** *(pages 378–379)*

1. Before reading the **Lectura** at home, read the questions in Activity A on page 379. As you read, focus on looking for the answers to these questions. When you finish reading, write down the answers to the questions.

## Vocabulario

PALABRAS 1 y 2 *(pages 392–399)*

1. Many of the activities in this vocabulary section are **Hisorieta** activities. As you complete each one, take a few minutes to retell the story in your own words.

## Estructura

**El subjuntivo de los verbos de cambio radical** *(pages 400–401)*

**Hint** Remember once again that if you pronounce your vowels carefully, you will have no problems with either the oral or written forms of these verbs.

**El subjuntivo con verbos como pedir y aconsejar** *(pages 402–407)*

1. If you refer to the explanation of the subjunctive given in the previous chapter you will note that the same explanation holds. You may, however, question why after a verb such as **creer** (to believe) the indicative, rather than the subjunctive, is used since there is still a bit of the "may or may not" involved. The only explanation is placed on the belief that what follows **creer** will indeed take place.

2. The expressions of emotion on pages 406–407 are somewhat different. They take the subjunctive because they are introduced by and thus dependent upon a subjective emotion.

   For example:

   **Estoy contento(a) que Juan asista.**

   You could be happy that John is attending but someone else could say:

   **Yo no estoy contento que Juan asista.**
   **Francamente, yo prefiero que no asista.**

## Vocabulario

PALABRAS 1 y 2 *(pages 424–431)*

**Hint** If you are the type of learner who has to write something before you remember it, write each new word two or three times.

1. Go over the vocabulary activities orally before you write them.
2. Retell the **Historieta** activities on pages 430–431 in your own words.

## Estructura

**Infinitivo o subjuntivo** *(pages 432–433)*

1. Make up additional sentences with:
   **Yo quiero....**
   **Yo quiero que tú...**
   **Ellos prefieren que yo...**
   **Nosotros preferemos...**

# Verb Charts

| REGULAR VERBS | | | |
|---|---|---|---|
| **INFINITIVO** | **hablar** *to speak* | **comer** *to eat* | **vivir** *to live* |
| **PRESENTE** | hablo<br>hablas<br>habla<br>hablamos<br>*habláis*<br>hablan | como<br>comes<br>come<br>comemos<br>*coméis*<br>comen | vivo<br>vives<br>vive<br>vivimos<br>*vivís*<br>viven |
| **PRETÉRITO** | hablé<br>hablaste<br>habló<br>hablamos<br>*hablasteis*<br>hablaron | comí<br>comiste<br>comió<br>comimos<br>*comisteis*<br>comieron | viví<br>viviste<br>vivió<br>vivimos<br>*vivisteis*<br>vivieron |
| **IMPERFECTO** | hablaba<br>hablabas<br>hablaba<br>hablábamos<br>*hablabais*<br>hablaban | comía<br>comías<br>comía<br>comíamos<br>*comíais*<br>comían | vivía<br>vivías<br>vivía<br>vivíamos<br>*vivíais*<br>vivían |
| **FUTURO** | hablaré<br>hablarás<br>hablará<br>hablaremos<br>*hablaréis*<br>hablarán | comeré<br>comerás<br>comerá<br>comeremos<br>*comeréis*<br>comerán | viviré<br>vivirás<br>vivirá<br>viviremos<br>*viviréis*<br>vivirán |
| **CONDICIONAL** | hablaría<br>hablarías<br>hablaría<br>hablaríamos<br>*hablaríais*<br>hablarían | comería<br>comerías<br>comería<br>comeríamos<br>*comeríais*<br>comerían | viviría<br>vivirías<br>viviría<br>viviríamos<br>*viviríais*<br>vivirían |
| **SUBJUNTIVO [PRESENTE]** | hable<br>hables<br>hable<br>hablemos<br>*habléis*<br>hablen | coma<br>comas<br>coma<br>comamos<br>*comáis*<br>coman | viva<br>vivas<br>viva<br>vivamos<br>*viváis*<br>vivan |

| REGULAR VERBS | | | |
|---|---|---|---|
| **INFINITIVO** | **hablar** *to speak* | **comer** *to eat* | **vivir** *to live* |
| PARTICIPIO PRESENTE | hablando | comiendo | viviendo |
| PARTICIPIO PASADO | hablado | comido | vivido |
| PRESENTE PERFECTO | he hablado<br>has hablado<br>ha hablado<br>hemos hablado<br>*habéis hablado*<br>han hablado | he comido<br>has comido<br>ha comido<br>hemos comido<br>*habéis comido*<br>han comido | he vivido<br>has vivido<br>ha vivido<br>hemos vivido<br>*habéis vivido*<br>han vivido |
| IMPERATIVO FORMAL | hable (Ud.)<br>no hable (Ud.)<br><br>hablen (Uds.)<br>no hablen (Uds.) | coma (Ud.)<br>no coma (Ud.)<br><br>coman (Uds.)<br>no coman (Uds.) | viva (Ud.)<br>no viva (Ud.)<br><br>vivan (Uds.)<br>no vivan (Uds.) |
| IMPERATIVO FAMILIAR | habla (tú)<br>no hables (tú) | come (tú)<br>no comas (tú) | vive (tú)<br>no vivas (tú) |

# Verb Charts

| STEM-CHANGING VERBS (-ar and -er verbs) | | | | |
|---|---|---|---|---|
| **INFINITIVO** | **empezar (e → ie)[1]** *to begin* | **almorzar (o → ue)[2]** *to eat lunch* | **perder (e → ie)[3]** *to lose* | **volver (o → ue)** *to return* |
| PRESENTE | empiezo<br>empiezas<br>empieza<br>empezamos<br>*empezáis*<br>empiezan | almuerzo<br>almuerzas<br>almuerza<br>almorzamos<br>*almorzáis*<br>almuerzan | pierdo<br>pierdes<br>pierde<br>perdemos<br>*perdéis*<br>pierden | vuelvo<br>vuelves<br>vuelve<br>volvemos<br>*volvéis*<br>vuelven |

[1] ***Comenzar, sentar,*** *and* ***pensar*** *are similar.*
[2] ***Acostar, costar,*** *and* ***jugar (ue → ue)*** *are similar.*
[3] ***Defender*** *and* ***entender*** *are similar.*

| STEM-CHANGING VERBS (-ir verbs) | | | |
|---|---|---|---|
| **INFINITIVO** | **preferir (e → ie, i)** *to prefer* | **dormir (o → ue, u)[4]** *to sleep* | **pedir (e → i, i)[5]** *to ask for* |
| PRESENTE | prefiero<br>prefieres<br>prefiere<br>preferimos<br>*preferís*<br>prefieren | duermo<br>duermes<br>duerme<br>dormimos<br>*dormís*<br>duermen | pido<br>pides<br>pide<br>pedimos<br>*pedís*<br>piden |
| PRETÉRITO | preferí<br>preferiste<br>prefirió<br>preferimos<br>*preferisteis*<br>prefirieron | dormí<br>dormiste<br>durmió<br>dormimos<br>*dormisteis*<br>durmieron | pedí<br>pediste<br>pidió<br>pedimos<br>*pedisteis*<br>pidieron |

[4] ***Morir*** *is similar.*
[5] ***Repetir, freír,*** *and* ***servir*** *are similar.*

| IRREGULAR VERBS[1] | |
|---|---|
| | **abrir** *to open* |
| PARTICIPIO PASADO | abierto |
| | **andar** *to walk* |
| PRETÉRITO | anduve anduviste anduvo anduvimos *anduvisteis* anduvieron |
| | **caer** *to fall, to drop* |
| PARTICIPIO PRESENTE | cayendo |
| | **conocer** *to know, to be familiar with* |
| PRESENTE | conozco conoces conoce conocemos *conocéis* conocen |
| | **cubrir** *to cover* |
| PARTICIPIO PASADO | cubierto |
| | **dar** *to give* |
| PRESENTE | doy das da damos *dais* dan |
| PRETÉRITO | di diste dio dimos *disteis* dieron |
| SUBJUNTIVO [PRESENTE] | dé des dé demos *deis* den |
| IMPERATIVO FORMAL | dé (Ud.) den (Uds.)<br>no dé (Ud.) no den (Uds.) |
| | **decir** *to say* |
| PRESENTE | digo dices dice decimos *decís* dicen |
| PRETÉRITO | dije dijiste dijo dijimos *dijisteis* dijeron |
| FUTURO | diré dirás dirá diremos *diréis* dirán |
| CONDICIONAL | diría dirías diría diríamos *diríais* dirían |

***(continued on H36)***

[1] *Note that only irregular forms are shown.*

## IRREGULAR VERBS

| | **decir** *to say* *(continued from H35)* | | | | | |
|---|---|---|---|---|---|---|
| PARTICIPIO PRESENTE | diciendo | | | | | |
| PARTICIPIO PASADO | dicho | | | | | |
| IMPERATIVO FAMILIAR | di (tú) | | | | | |
| | **escribir** *to write* | | | | | |
| PARTICIPIO PASADO | escrito | | | | | |
| | **estar** *to be* | | | | | |
| PRESENTE | estoy | estás | está | estamos | *estáis* | están |
| PRETÉRITO | estuve | estuviste | estuvo | estuvimos | *estuvisteis* | estuvieron |
| SUBJUNTIVO [PRESENTE] | esté | estés | esté | estemos | *estéis* | estén |
| IMPERATIVO FORMAL | esté (Ud.)<br>no esté (Ud.) | estén (Uds.)<br>no estén (Uds.) | | | | |
| | **hacer** *to do, to make* | | | | | |
| PRESENTE | hago | haces | hace | hacemos | *hacéis* | hacen |
| PRETÉRITO | hice | hiciste | hizo | hicimos | *hicisteis* | hicieron |
| FUTURO | haré | harás | hará | haremos | *haréis* | harán |
| CONDICIONAL | haría | harías | haría | haríamos | *haríais* | harían |
| PARTICIPIO PASADO | hecho | | | | | |
| IMPERATIVO FAMILIAR | haz (tú) | | | | | |

| IRREGULAR VERBS | |
|---|---|
| | **incluir** *to include* |
| PARTICIPIO PRESENTE | incluyendo |
| | **ir** *to go* |
| PRESENTE | voy vas va vamos *vais* van |
| PRETÉRITO | fui fuiste fue fuimos *fuisteis* fueron |
| IMPERFECTO | iba ibas iba íbamos *ibais* iban |
| SUBJUNTIVO [PRESENTE] | vaya vayas vaya vayamos *vayáis* vayan |
| PARTICIPIO PRESENTE | yendo |
| PARTICIPIO PASADO | ido |
| IMPERATIVO FORMAL | vaya (Ud.) vayan (Uds.)<br>no vaya (Ud.) no vayan (Uds.) |
| IMPERATIVO FAMILIAR | ve (tú)<br>no vayas (tú) |
| | **leer** *to read* |
| PARTICIPIO PRESENTE | leyendo |
| | **morir** *to die* |
| PARTICIPIO PRESENTE | muriendo |

| IRREGULAR VERBS | |
|---|---|
| | **oír** *to hear* |
| PRESENTE | oigo oyes oye oímos *oís* oyen |
| PRETÉRITO | oí oíste oyó oímos *oísteis* oyeron |
| PARTICIPIO PRESENTE | oyendo |
| | **poder** *to be able* |
| PRESENTE | puedo puedes puede podemos *podéis* pueden |
| PRETÉRITO | pude pudiste pudo pudimos *pudisteis* pudieron |
| FUTURO | podré podrás podrá podremos *podréis* podrán |
| CONDICIONAL | podría podrías podría podríamos *podríais* podrían |
| PARTICIPIO PRESENTE | pudiendo |
| | **poner** *to put* |
| PRESENTE | pongo pones pone ponemos *ponéis* ponen |
| PRETÉRITO | puse pusiste puso pusimos *pusisteis* pusieron |
| FUTURO | pondré pondrás pondrá pondremos *pondréis* pondrán |
| CONDICIONAL | pondría pondrías pondría pondríamos *pondríais* pondrían |
| PARTICIPIO PASADO | puesto |
| IMPERATIVO FAMILIAR | pon (tú) |

| IRREGULAR VERBS | |
|---|---|
| | **querer** *to want, to wish* |
| PRESENTE | quiero quieres quiere queremos *queréis* quieren |
| PRETÉRITO | quise quisiste quiso quisimos *quisisteis* quisieron |
| FUTURO | querré querrás querrá querremos *querréis* querrán |
| CONDICIONAL | querría querrías querría querríamos *querríais* querrían |
| | **romper** *to break* |
| PARTICIPIO PASADO | roto |
| | **saber** *to know* |
| PRESENTE | sé sabes sabe sabemos *sabéis* saben |
| PRETÉRITO | supe supiste supo supimos *supisteis* supieron |
| FUTURO | sabré sabrás sabrá sabremos *sabréis* sabrán |
| CONDICIONAL | sabría sabrías sabría sabríamos *sabríais* sabrían |
| SUBJUNTIVO [PRESENTE] | sepa sepas sepa sepamos *sepáis* sepan |
| IMPERATIVO FORMAL | sepa (Ud.) sepan (Uds.)<br>no sepa (Ud.) no sepan (Uds.) |
| | **salir** *to leave* |
| PRESENTE | salgo sales sale salimos *salís* salen |
| FUTURO | saldré saldrás saldrá saldremos *saldréis* saldrán |
| CONDICIONAL | saldría saldrías saldría saldríamos *saldríais* saldrían |
| IMPERATIVO FAMILIAR | sal (tú) |

| IRREGULAR VERBS | |
|---|---|
| | **ser** *to be* |
| PRESENTE | soy eres es somos *sois* son |
| PRETÉRITO | fui fuiste fue fuimos *fuisteis* fueron |
| IMPERFECTO | era eras era éramos *erais* eran |
| SUBJUNTIVO [PRESENTE] | sea seas sea seamos *seáis* sean |
| IMPERATIVO FORMAL | sea (Ud.) sean (Uds.)<br>no sea (Ud.) no sean (Uds.) |
| IMPERATIVO FAMILIAR | sé (tú)<br>no seas (tú) |
| | **tener** *to have* |
| PRESENTE | tengo tienes tiene tenemos *tenéis* tienen |
| PRETÉRITO | tuve tuviste tuvo tuvimos *tuvisteis* tuvieron |
| FUTURO | tendré tendrás tendrá tendremos *tendréis* tendrán |
| CONDICIONAL | tendría tendrías tendría tendríamos *tendríais* tendrían |
| IMPERATIVO FAMILIAR | ten (tú) |
| | **traer** *to bring* |
| PRESENTE | traigo traes trae traemos *traéis* traen |
| PRETÉRITO | traje trajiste trajo trajimos *trajisteis* trajeron |
| PARTICIPIO PRESENTE | trayendo |

## IRREGULAR VERBS

| | **venir** *to come* | | | | | |
|---|---|---|---|---|---|---|
| PRESENTE | vengo | vienes | viene | venimos | *venís* | vienen |
| PRETÉRITO | vine | viniste | vino | vinimos | *vinisteis* | vinieron |
| FUTURO | vendré | vendrás | vendrá | vendremos | *vendréis* | vendrán |
| CONDICIONAL | vendría | vendrías | vendría | vendríamos | *vendríais* | vendrían |
| PARTICIPIO PRESENTE | viniendo | | | | | |
| IMPERATIVO FAMILIAR | ven (tú) | | | | | |
| | **ver** *to see* | | | | | |
| PRESENTE | veo | ves | ve | vemos | *veis* | ven |
| PRETÉRITO | vi | viste | vio | vimos | *visteis* | vieron |
| IMPERFECTO | veía | veías | veía | veíamos | *veíais* | veían |
| PARTICIPIO PASADO | visto | | | | | |
| | **volver** *to return* | | | | | |
| PARTICIPIO PASADO | vuelto | | | | | |

## VERBS WITH A SPELLING CHANGE IN THE PRETERITE (-car, -gar, -zar)

| INFINITIVO | **practicar**[1] *to practice* | **llegar**[2] *to arrive* | **comenzar**[3] *to begin* |
|---|---|---|---|
| PRETÉRITO | practiqué<br>practicaste<br>practicó<br>practicamos<br>*practicasteis*<br>practicaron | llegué<br>llegaste<br>llegó<br>llegamos<br>*llegasteis*<br>llegaron | comencé<br>comenzaste<br>comenzó<br>comenzamos<br>*comenzasteis*<br>comenzaron |

[1]***Buscar*** *and* ***sacar*** *are similar.*
[2]***Jugar*** *and* ***pagar*** *are similar.*
[3]***Empezar*** *and* ***almorzar*** *are similar.*

# Spanish-English Dictionary

*The Spanish-English Dictionary contains all productive and receptive vocabulary from Levels 1 and 2. The numbers following each productive entry indicate the chapter and vocabulary section in which the word is introduced. For example, **3.2** in dark print means that the word was taught in this textbook **Capítulo 3, Palabras 2.** A light print number means that the word was introduced in **¡Buen viaje!**, Level 1. BV refers to the introductory **Bienvenidos** lessons in Level 1. If there is no number following an entry, this means that the word or expression is there for receptive purposes only.*

**a** at; to
**a bordo de** aboard, on board, **7.1**
**a eso de** at about (time), 4.1
**a fines de** at the end of
**a la española** Spanish style
**a lo menos**
**a menudo** often, **3.2**
**a pie** on foot, 4.1
**a plazos** in installments
**a propósito** by the way
**a solas** alone
**a tiempo** on time, 11.1
**a veces** sometimes, 7.1
**a ver** let's see
**abandonar el cuarto** to check out, **6.1**
**abarrotes: la tienda de abarrotes** grocery store, **4.2**
la **abeja** bee, **8.1**
el/la **abogado(a)** lawyer, **14.1**
**abordar** to get on, board
el **abrigo** overcoat, **4.1**
**abril** April, BV
**abrir** to open, 8.2
**abrocharse** to fasten, **7.1**
**abrocharse el cinturón de seguridad** to fasten one's seatbelt, **7.1**
la **abuela** grandmother, 6.1
el **abuelo** grandfather, 6.1
los **abuelos** grandparents, 6.1
**abundante** plentiful
**aburrido(a)** boring, 2.1
**aburrir** to bore
el **abuso** abuse
**acabar de** to have just (done something), **8.1**
la **academia** academy, school
**acariciar** to caress
el **acceso** access
el **accidente** accident, **8.1**
la **acción** action
el **aceite** oil, 14.2; **2.2**
**aceptar** to accept
la **acera** sidewalk, **9.1**
**acerca de** about, concerning
**acercarse(a)** to approach
**acertar (ie)** to guess right
**acomodar** to accommodate
el **acompañamiento** accompaniment
**acompañar** to accompany
**aconsejar** to advise
**acostarse (ue)** to go to bed, 12.1
el **acrílico** acrylic
la **actividad** activity
**activo(a)** active
el **actor** actor, 10.2
la **actriz** actress, 10.2
la **actuación** behavior
**actualmente** at the present time
la **acuarela** watercolor
**acuático(a): el esquí acuático** water-skiing, 9.1
**acuerdo: de acuerdo** OK, all right; in agreement
**acuñar** to coin, mint
**adaptar** to adapt
**adecuado(a)** adequate
**adelantar** to overtake, pass (car), **11.2**
**adelante** ahead
**además** moreover; besides
**además de** in addition to
la **adicción** addiction
**adiós** good-bye, BV
**adivinar** to guess
**admirar** to admire
**admitir** to admit, **8.2**
la **adolescencia** adolescence
el/la **adolescente** adolescent, teenager
**¿adónde?** where?, 1.1
la **adoración** adoration
**adorar** to adore
**adornar** to adorn
el **adorno** ornament
la **aduana** customs, 11.2
**advertir** to warn
**aérea: la línea aérea** airline
**aérobico(a)** aerobic
el **aerodeslizador** hydrofoil
el **aeropuerto** airport, 11.1
**afeitarse** to shave, 12.1
**la crema de afeitar** shaving cream, 12.1
**aficionado(a)** fond of, 10.1
el/la **aficionado(a)** fan (sports)
**afortunado(a)** fortunate
**africano(a)** African
**afroamericano(a)** African American
las **afueras** outskirts, **9.1**
la **agencia** agency
**la agencia de empleos** employment agency

el/la **agente** agent, 11.1
**el/la agente de aduana** customs agent, 11.2
**el/la agente de policía** police officer
**agosto** August, BV
**agradable** pleasant
**agregar** to add, **10.2**
**agrícola** agricultural
el/la **agricultor(a)** farmer, **9.2**
el **agua** *(f.)* water, 9.1
**el agua corriente** running water
**el agua mineral** mineral water, 12.2
**esquiar en el agua** to water-ski, 9.1
el **aguacate** avocado, **10.2**
el **águila** *(f.)* eagle
el **agujero** hole
**ahora** now, 4.2
**ahorrar** to save
el **aire** air, **11.1**
**al aire libre** outdoor *(adj.)*
el **aire acondicionado** air conditioning, **6.2**
el **ajedrez** chess, **5.1**
el **ají** chili pepper
el **ajo** garlic, 14.2; **2.2**
el **ajuar de novia** trousseau
**ajustar** to adjust
**al** to the
**al aire libre** outdoor *(adj.)*
**al bordo de** alongside, on the banks of (river)
**al contrario** on the contrary
**al lado de** beside, **5.2**
**al máximo** at the most
**al principio** at the beginning
**alarmarse** to be alarmed
el/la **albañil** bricklayer, **14.1**
la **alberca** swimming pool, 9.1
el **albergue para jóvenes (juvenil)** youth hostel, 12.2
el **álbum** album
la **alcachofa** artichoke, 14.2; **2.2**
el **alcalde** mayor, **14.1**
la **alcaldesa** female mayor
la **alcaldía** city hall, **14.1**
**alcanzar** to reach, attain
el **alcohol** alcohol
el **alcoholismo** alcoholism
**alegrarse de** to be glad about, **13.1**
**alegre** happy
la **alegría** happiness
el **alemán** German (language), 2.2
la **alergia** allergy, 8.2
el **álgebra** algebra, 2.2
**algo** something, 5.2
**¿Algo más?** Anything else?, 5.2
el **algodón** cotton, **12.1**
**alguien** someone
**algunos(as)** some, 4.1
el **alimento** food, 14.2; **2.2**
**allá** there
**allí** there
**almacenar** to store
la **almeja** clam, 14.2; **2.2**
la **almohada** pillow, **6.2**
**almorzar (ue)** to eat lunch
el **almuerzo** lunch, 5.2
**tomar el almuerzo** to have, eat lunch
**alojarse** to stay, lodge
la **alpargata** sandal
**alquilar** to rent, **5.2**
**alrededor** de around, 6.2
los **alrededores** outskirts
**alternar** to alternate
el **altiplano** high plateau, **7.2**
la **altitud** altitude, **7.2**
**altivo** arrogant, haughty
**alto(a)** tall, 1.1; high, 4.2
**en voz alta** aloud
**la nota alta** high grade, 4.2
la **altura** height; altitude, **7.2**
el/la **alumno(a)** student, 1.1
**amar** to love
**amarillo(a)** yellow, 3.2
**amazónico(a)** Amazonian
**ambicioso(a)** hardworking, 1.1
el **ambiente** environment; atmosphere
la **ambulancia** ambulance, **8.1**
**ambulante** itinerant
la **América Central** Central America
la **América del Norte** North America
la **América del Sur** South America
**americano(a)** American, 1.1
el/la **amigo(a)** friend, 1.1
el **amor** love
el **análisis** analysis
**analítico(a)** analytical
**analizar** to analyze
**anaranjado(a)** orange, 3.2
el/la **anarquista** anarchist
**ancho(a)** wide, **4.1**
**anciano(a)** old, 6.1
el/la **anciano(a)** old person
**andaluz(a)** Andalusian
**andante: el caballero andante** knight errant
el **andén** railway platform, 13.1; **1.1**
**andino(a)** Andean
la **anécdota** anecdote
**angosto(a)** narrow, **9.1**
el **anillo** ring, **4.1**
el **animal** animal
**el animal doméstico** farm animal, **9.2**
el **aniversario** anniversary
**anoche** last night, 9.2
el **anorak** parka, 9.2
la **Antártida** Antarctic
**anteayer** the day before yesterday
**antenupcial** prenuptial
los **anteojos de sol** sunglasses, 9.1
**antes de** before, 5.1
el **antibiótico** antibiotic, 8.2
**anticipación: de anticipación** ahead of time
**anticuado(a)** antiquated
la **antigüedad** antiquity

**antiguo(a)** old, ancient, **5.1**
**anunciar** to announce
el **anuncio** announcement; 7.1; advertisement, **14.2**
**dar anuncios** to make announcements, **7.1**
**añadir** to add, **10.2**
el **año** year, BV
**cumplir... años** to be . . . years old
**el año pasado** last year, 9.2
**este año** this year, 9.2
**tener... años** to be . . . years old, 6.1
el **Año Nuevo** New Year, **13.2**
**¡Próspero Año Nuevo!** Happy New Year!, **13.2**
**apagar** to turn off, **3.1**
el **aparato** appliance, device, **3.2**
el **aparcamiento** parking lot
**aparcar** to park, **11.2**
**aparecer** to appear
la **apariencia** appearance
el **apartamento** apartment, 6.2
**la casa de apartamentos** apartment house, 6.2
**apasionado(a)** passionate
el **apellido** last name
la **apendicitis** appendicitis
la **apertura** opening
**la apertura de clases** beginning of the school year
**aplaudir** to applaud, 10.2
el **aplauso** applause, 10.2
**dar aplausos** to applaud, **10.2**
**recibir aplausos** to receive applause, 10.2
**aplicar** to apply
el **apóstol** apostle
**aprender** to learn, 5.1
**apropiado(a)** appropriate
la **aptitud** aptitude
el **apunte: tomar apuntes** to take notes, 4.2
**aquel, aquella** that
**en aquel entonces** at that time
**aquí** here
**Aquí tiene (tienes, tienen)...** Here is (are) . . .
**por aquí** right this way
el/la **árabe** Arab
**aragonés(esa)** from Aragon (Spain)
el **árbol** tree
**el árbol de Navidad** Christmas tree, **13.2**
el **arco** arc
el **área** *(f.)* area
la **arena** sand, 9.1
el **arete** earring, **4.1**
**argentino(a)** Argentinian, 2.1
el **argumento** plot
**árido(a)** arid
la **aritmética** arithmetic, 2.2
el **arma** *(f.)* weapon
el **armario** closet, **6.2**
la **arqueología** archeology
**arqueológico(a)** archaeological
el/la **arqueólogo(a)** archaeologist
el/la **arquitecto(a)** architect, **14.1**
**arrancar** to pull out
**arrogante** arrogant
el **arroyo** stream, brook
el **arroz** rice, 5.2
**arrugar** to wrinkle
el **arsenal** arsenal
el **arte** *(f.)* art, 2.2
**las bellas artes** fine arts
el **artefacto** artifact
el/la **artista** artist, 10.2
**artístico(a)** artistic
**asado(a)** roasted
**asar** to roast, **10.1**
la **ascendencia** background
**de ascendencia mexicana (peruana, etc.)** of Mexican (Peruvian, etc.) ancestry
**ascender** to rise
el **ascensor** elevator, 6.2
**asegurar** to assure
el **aseo** restroom, **7.1**
**así** so; thus
el **asiento** seat, 11.1
**el número del asiento** seat number, 11.1
la **asignatura** subject, discipline, 2.2
el/la **asistente de vuelo** flight attendant, 11.2
**asistir** to attend
el **asno** donkey
el **aspa** sail (of a windmill)
el **aspecto** aspect
el/la **aspirante** candidate, **14.2**
la **aspirina** aspirin, 8.2
**astuto(a)** astute
**asustarse** to be frightened
**atacar** to attack
el **ataque** attack
la **atención: prestar atención** to pay attention, 4.2
**atender (ie)** to assist, wait on (customer), **4.1**
**atento(a)** polite, courteous
el **aterrizaje** landing, **7.2**
**aterrizar** to land, 11.2
el/la **atleta** athlete
**atlético(a)** athletic
la **atmósfera** atmosphere
las **atracciones** amusement park rides, **5.2**
**el parque de atracciones** amusement park, **5.2**
**atractivo(a)** attractive
**atrapar** to catch, 7.2
**atrás** behind, in the rear
**atravesar (ie)** to cross
el **atún** tuna, 5.2
los **audífonos** earphones, **7.1**
**aumentar** to increase
el **aumento** increase
**aun** even
**aún** yet
**aunque** although
el **auricular** telephone receiver, **3.2**; headphone, **7.1**
**austral** former Argentine unit of currency
**auténtico(a)** authentic

el **autobús** bus, 10.1
**perder el autobús (la guagua, el camión)** to miss the bus, 10.1
**automáticamente** automatically, **7.1**
el **automóvil** automobile
la **autopista** highway, **11.2**
el/la **autor(a)** author, 10.2
**autorizado(a)** authorized
el **autorretrato** self-portrait
la **autovía** highway, **11.2**
los **auxilios: los primeros auxilios** first aid
el **avance** advance
el **ave** *(f.)* bird
la **avenida** avenue, **9.1**
la **aventura** adventure
la **avería** breakdown
**averiado(a)** broken down
la **aviación** aviation
el **avión** airplane, 11.1
el **avión de reacción** jet, **7.2**
la **avioneta** small airplane, **7.2**
**ayer** yesterday, 9.2
**ayer por la mañana** yesterday morning, 9.2
**ayer por la tarde** yesterday afternoon, 9.2
la **ayuda** assistance, help
**ayudar** to help, 13.1; **1.1**
el **azafrán** saffron
el **azúcar** sugar, **10.1**
**azul** blue, 3.2
**azul oscuro** dark blue

el **bache** pothole
el **bachillerato** bachelor's degree
la **bacteria** bacteria
la **bahía** bay
**bailar** to dance, 4.2
el **baile** dance
**bajar** to lower; to go down, 9.2; to get off, 13.2; **1.2**
**bajar(se) del tren** to get off the train, 13.2; **1.2**
**bajar las maletas** to take the luggage down, **6.1**
**bajo: bajo cero** below zero, 9.2
**bajo(a)** short, 1.1; low, 4.2
**la planta baja** ground floor, 6.2
**la nota baja** low grade, 4.2
el **balneario** beach resort, 9.1
el **balón** ball, 7.1
**tirar el balón** to throw (kick) the ball, 7.2
el **baloncesto** basketball, 7.2
la **banana** banana, **10.2**
la **banca** banking
**bancario(a)** banking
el **banco** bank, **12.2**
la **banda** music band
la **banda elástica** elastic band
la **bandeja** tray, **7.1**
el **bando** team
el **bañador** bathing suit 9.1
**bañarse** to take a bath, 12.1
la **bañera** bathtub, **6.2**
el **baño** bathroom, 6.2; bath
**el cuarto de baño** bathroom, 6.2
**el traje de baño** bathing suit, 9.1
**barato(a)** cheap, inexpensive, 3.2
la **barba** beard
el/la **barbero(a)** barber, **12.1**
la **barra** bar
**la barra de jabón** bar of soap, 12.2
el **barrio** neighborhood, **9.1**
**basado(a)** based (on)
**basar** to base
**basarse** to be based
la **báscula** scale, 11.1
la **base** base, 7.2; basis
**básico(a)** basic
el **básquetbol** basketball, 7.2
**la cancha de básquetbol** basketball court, 7.2
**bastante** enough, rather, quite, 1.1
el **bastón** ski pole, 9.2
la **batalla** battle
el **bate** bat, 7.2
el/la **bateador(a)** batter, 7.2
**batear** to hit (baseball), 7.2
la **batería** battery
el **batú** Taíno Indian game
el **baúl** trunk, **11.1**
el **bautizo** baptism
el/la **bebé** baby
**beber** to drink, 5.1
la **bebida** beverage, drink, **7.1**
la **beca** scholarship
el **béisbol** baseball, 7.2
**el campo de béisbol** baseball field, 7.2
**el juego de béisbol** baseball game, 7.2
**el/la jugador(a) de béisbol** baseball player, 7.2
el/la **beisbolista** baseball player
la **belleza** beauty
**bello(a)** beautiful, pretty, 1.1
**las bellas artes** fine arts
la **bendición** blessing
el **beneficio** benefit
la **berenjena** eggplant, 14.2; **2.2**
**bíblico(a)** biblical
la **bicicleta** bicycle
**ir en bicicleta** to go by bike, 12.2
**bien** fine, well, BV
**muy bien** very well, BV
los **bienes y servicios** goods and services
la **bienvenida: dar la bienvenida** to welcome, 11.2
el **bife** beef
el **biftec** steak, 14.2; **2.2**
**bilingüe** bilingual
el **billete** ticket, 11.1; bill (currency), **12.2**
**el billete de ida y vuelta** round-trip ticket, 13.1; **1.1**
**el billete sencillo** one way ticket, 13.1; **1.1**

la **biografía** biography
la **biología** biology, 2.2
**biológico(a)** biological
el/la **biólogo(a)** biologist
el **bizcocho** cake, **13.1**
**blanco(a)** white, 3.2
el **blanqueador** bleach
el **bloc** notebook, writing pad, 3.1
**bloquear** to stop, block, 7.1
el **blue jean** jeans, 3.2
la **blusa** blouse, 3.2
la **boca** mouth, 8.2
**boca abajo** face down, **3.1**
**boca arriba** face up, **3.1**
la **boca del metro** subway entrance, **9.1**
la **bocacalle** intersection, **11.2**
el **bocadillo** sandwich, 5.1
la **bocina** horn, **11.1**
**tocar la bocina** to honk the horn
la **boda** wedding, **13.1**
la **bola** ball
la **boletería** ticket window, 9.2
el **boleto** ticket, 9.2
el **bolígrafo** ballpoint pen, 3.1
la **bolsa** bag, 5.2
**la bolsa de plástico** plastic bag, **4.2**
el **bolsillo** pocket, **4.1**
**bonito(a)** pretty, 1.1
el **borde** border, side, shoulder (road)
**bordear** to border
la **bota** boot, 9.2
el **bote** can, 5.2; boat, **5.2**
la **botella: la botella de agua mineral** bottle of mineral water, 12.2
el **botón** button (on a machine), **3.1**; (on clothing), **4.1**
el **botones** bellhop, **6.1**
el **brazo** arm, 7.1; branch (of candelabra, menorah, etc.), **13.2**
**breve** brief
**brillante** bright
**brillar** to shine, 9.1
el **bronce** bronze, 10.2
**bronceado(a)** tan
**bronceador(a): la loción bronceadora** suntan lotion, 9.1
**bucear** to dive; to swim underwater, 9.1
el **buceo** diving, underwater swimming, 9.1
**buen** good
**estar de buen humor** to be in a good mood, 8.1
**Hace buen tiempo.** The weather is nice., 9.1
la **buenaventura** fortune
**bueno(a)** good, 1.2
**Buenas noches.** Good evening., BV
**Buenas tardes.** Good afternoon., BV
**Buenos días.** Hello, Good morning., BV
**sacar una nota buena** to get a good grade, 4.2
**tener buena pinta** to look good (food), **4.2**
la **bufanda** scarf, **4.1**
el **bufete del abogado** lawyer's office, **14.1**
el **bulevar** boulevard, **9.1**
el **bus** bus, 4.1
**el bus escolar** school bus, 4.1
**busca: en busca de** in search of
**buscar** to look for, 3.1
la **butaca** seat (theater), 10.1
el **buzón** mailbox, **12.2**

el **caballero** knight; gentleman, man, **4.1**
**el caballero andante** knight errant
**la tienda de ropa para caballeros** men's clothing shop, **4.1**
el **caballete** easel
el **caballito** carousel horse, **5.2**
el **caballo** horse
**pasear a caballo** to go horsebook riding
el **cabello** hair, **12.1**
**caber** to fit, **7.1**
la **cabeza** head, 7.1
la **cabina** cabin, **7.1**
**la cabina de mando (vuelo)** cockpit, **7.1**
el **cacahuete (cacahuate)** peanut
la **cacerola** saucepan, **10.2**
**cada** each, every, 1.2
la **cadena** chain (necklace), **4.1**
**la cadena de oro** gold chain, **4.1**
**caerse** to fall, drop, **7.1**
el **café** coffee, BV; café, 5.1
**el café al aire libre** outdoor café
**el café con leche** coffee with milk, 5.1
**el café solo** black coffee, 5.1
la **cafetería** cafeteria
la **caja** cash register, 3.1; box, **4.2**
el/la **cajero(a)** teller, **12.2**; cashier, **14.1**
el **cajero automático** automatic teller
los **calamares** squid, **10.2**
los **calcetines** socks, 3.2
la **calculadora** calculator, 3.1
**calcular** to calculate
el **cálculo** calculus, 2.2
**calentarse (ie)** to heat
la **calidad** quality
la **calificación** qualification
la **calle** street, 6.2
**la calle de sentido único** one-way street, **11.2**
**la calle peatonal** pedestrian street
la **callecita** narrow street, alley, **9.1**
el **calor: Hace calor.** It's hot., 9.1

la **caloría** calorie
**calzar** to take, wear (shoe size), 3.2
la **cama** bed, 8.1
**guardar cama** to stay in bed, 8.1
**hacer la cama** to make the bed, **6.2**
la **camarera** maid, **6.2**
el/la **camarero(a)** waiter, waitress, 5.1
los **camarones** shrimp, 14.2; **2.2**
**cambiar** to change; exchange, **12.2**
**cambiar de tren** to change trains (transfer), 13.2; **1.2**
**cambiar las toallas** to change the towels, **6.2**
el **cambio** change, exchange, **12.2**
**la casa de cambio** foreign exchange office, **12.2**
**el tipo (la tasa) de cambio** exchange rate, **12.2**
el/la **cambista** money changer, **12.2**
el **camello** camel, **13.2**
la **camilla** stretcher, **8.1**
**caminar** to walk, **5.1**
**caminar por la senda** to walk along the path, **5.2**
la **caminata: dar una caminata** to take a hike, 12.2
el **camino** trail, path
el **camión** bus (Mexico), 10.1, truck
la **camisa** shirt, 3.2
**la camisa de mangas cortas** short-sleeved shirt, **4.1**
**la camisa de mangas largas** long-sleeved shirt, **4.1**
la **camiseta** T-shirt, undershirt, 3.2
la **campaña** campaign
el/la **campeón(ona)** champion, **5.1**
el **campeonato** championship
el/la **campesino(a)** farmer, peasant, **9.2**
el **campo** country; field, **9.2**
**el campo de béisbol** baseball field, 7.2
**el campo de fútbol** soccer field, 7.1
**la casa de campo** country home
**canadiense** Canadian
el **canal** channel (TV)
la **canasta** basket, 7.2
la **cancha** court, 7.2
**la cancha cubierta** enclosed court, 9.1
**la cancha de básquetbol** basketball court, 7.2
**la cancha de tenis** tennis court, 9.1
la **canción** song
el/la **candidato(a)** candidate, **14.2**
**cansado(a)** tired, 8.1
**cantar** to sing, 4.2
el **cante jondo** traditional flamenco singing
la **cantidad** amount
el **canto** singing
el **cañón** canyon
el **capacho** cloth shopping bag
la **capital** capital
el/la **capitán** captain
el **capítulo** chapter
el **capó** hood (automobile), **11.1**
la **cara** face, 12.1
el **carácter** character
la **característica** characteristic
el **carbohidrato** carbohydrate
**cardinal: los puntos cardinales** cardinal points
la **cardiología** cardiology
el/la **cardiólogo(a)** cardiologist
el **cardo** thistle
los **cargos** charges
el **Caribe** Caribbean
**el mar Caribe** Caribbean Sea
el/la **caricaturista** caricaturist
la **carne** meat, 5.2
**la carne de res** beef, 14.2; **2.2**
la **carnicería** butcher shop, meat market, **4.2**
**caro(a)** expensive, 3.2
la **carpeta** folder, 3.1
el/la **carpintero(a)** carpenter, **14.1**
la **carrera** race, career
la **carretera** highway, **11.2**
el **carril** lane (of highway), **11.2**
el **carrito** cart (shopping), **4.2**; (airplane), **7.1**
**empujar el carrito** to push the cart, **4.2**
el **carro** car, 4.1
**el carro deportivo** sports car, **11.1**
**en carro** by car, 4.1
la **carta** letter, **12.2**
**la carta de recomendación** letter of recommendation
la **casa** home, house, 6.2
**en casa** at home
**la casa de apartamentos (departamentos)** apartment house, 6.2
**la casa de campo** country home, **9.2**
**la casa privada (particular)** private house, 6.2
la **casa de cambio** foreign exchange office, **12.2**
**casado(a): estar casado(a)** to be married
**casarse** to get married, **13.1**
**casi** almost, practically
el **caso** case, **7.1**
**castellano(a)** Castillian
el **castigo** punishment
el **castillo** castle
el **catarro** cold (illness), 8.1
**tener catarro** to have a cold, 8.1
el/la **cátcher** catcher, 7.2
la **catedral** cathedral
la **categoría** category
**católico(a)** Catholic
**catorce** fourteen, BV
la **causa** cause
**causar** to cause
la **cazuela** pot, **10.1**
el **CD** compact disc

el **CD-ROM** CD-ROM, **3.1**
la **cebolla** onion, **10.1**
la **celebración** celebration
**celebrar** to celebrate, **13.1**
**célebre** famous
la **célula** cell
**celular: el teléfono celular** cell phone, **3.2**
la **cena** dinner, 5.2
**cenar** to have dinner
el **centavo** penny
**central** central
el **centro** downtown, **5.1**; center
**cepillarse** to brush one's hair, 12.1
**cepillarse los dientes** to brush one's teeth, 12.1
el **cepillo** brush, 12.2
**el cepillo de dientes** toothbrush, 12.2
**cerca de** near, 6.2
**cercano(a)** nearby
el **cerdo** pig (pork), 14.2; **2.2**
el **cereal** cereal, 5.2; grain, **9.2**
la **ceremonia** ceremony, **13**
**cero** zero, BV
**cerrar (ie)** to close, **8.2**
**cerrar la herida** to close the wound, **8.2**
la **cesta** basket (jai alai)
el **cesto** basket, 7.2
la **chabola** shack
el **chaleco** vest
el **chaleco salvavidas** life jacket, **7.1**
el **chalet** chalet
el **champú** shampoo, 12.2
**¡Chao!** Good-bye!, BV
la **chaqueta** jacket, 3.2
**charlar** to chat
la **chaucha** string beans
el **cheque de viajero** traveler's check, **12.2**
la **chequera** checkbook
el/la **chico(a)** boy (girl)
**chileno(a)** Chilean
la **chimenea** chimney
la **china** orange (fruit)
el **chisme** piece of gossip
**¡chist!** shh!
el **choclo** corn
el **chocolate: de chocolate** chocolate *(adj.)*, 5.1
el **chófer** chauffeur
el **chorizo** pork and garlic sausage, **10.1**
la **chuleta** chop, **10.1**
**la chuleta de cerdo** pork chop, **10.1**
el **churro** (type of) doughnut
el **ciclismo** cycling
el **cielo** sky, 9.1
la **ciencia-ficción** science fiction
las **ciencias** science, 2.2
**las ciencias naturales** natural sciences
**las ciencias políticas** political science
**las ciencias sociales** social sciences, 2.2
el/la **científico(a)** scientist
**científico(a)** scientific
**cien(to)** one hundred, 3.2
**cierto: Es cierto que...** It is certain that . . .
**cierto(a)** certain
**cinco** five, BV
**cincuenta** fifty, 2.2
el **cine** movie theater, 10.1
la **cinta** ribbon
el **cinturón** belt, **4.1**
**el cinturón de seguridad** seat belt, **7.1**
**circular** to circulate, travel, drive
el **círculo** circle
el/la **cirujano(a)** surgeon, **8.2**
**el/la cirujano(a) ortopédico(a)** orthopedic surgeon, **8.2**
**cítrico(a)** citric
la **ciudad** city, **9.1**
la **claridad** clarity
el **clarinete** clarinet
**claro(a)** clear
**¡Claro!** Certainly!, Of course!
**¡Claro que no!** Of course not!
la **clase** class (school), 2.1; class (ticket), 13.1; **1.1**; kind, type
**la apertura de clases** beginning of the school year
**la sala de clase** classroom, 4.1
**el salón de clase** classroom, 4.1
**primera clase** first class, 13.1; **1.1**
**segunda clase** second class, 13.1; **1.1**
**clásico(a)** classic
**clasificar** to classify
la **clave de área** area code, **3.2**
el **claxon** horn, **11.1**
el **clic** click
el/la **cliente** customer, 5.1; hotel guest, **6.1**
el **clima** climate
**climático(a)** climatic
la **clínica** clinic
el **club** club, 4.2
**el Club de español** Spanish Club, 4.2
**cobrar** to charge
**cobrar el cheque** to cash the check, **12.2**
la **cocción** cooking
el **coche** car, 4.1; train car, 13.2; **1.2**
**el coche deportivo** sports car, **11.1**
**en coche** by car, 4.1
el **coche-cafetería** cafeteria (dining) car, 13.2; **1.2**
el **coche-cama** sleeping car, 13.2; **1.2**
el **coche-comedor** dining car, 13.2; **1.2**
el **coche deportivo** sports car, **11.1**
el **cocido** stew
la **cocina** kitchen, 6.2
**cocinar** to cook, **10.1**
el/la **cocinero(a)** cook, 14.1; **2.1**
el **coco** coconut, **10.2**
el **cóctel** cocktail party
el **codo** elbow, **8.1**
la **coincidencia** coincidence

**cojo(a)** lame
el **cola** soda, soft drink, 5.1
la **cola** line (queue), 10.1
**hacer cola** to line up, to stand in line, 10.1
la **colección** collection
**coleccionar** to collect, **5.1**
el/la **coleccionista** collector, **5.1**
la **colecta: hacer una colecta** to take up a collection
el **colector** collector
el **colegio** school, 1.1
el **colesterol** cholesterol
el **colgador** clothes hanger, **6.2**
**colgar (ue)** to hang, hang up
la **coliflor** cauliflower, **10.1**
el **colmado** grocery store, **4.2**
la **colocación** placement
**colocar** to put, place
**colombiano(a)** Colombian, 1.1
la **colonia** suburb, colony
el **color** color, 3.2
**de color** colored
**de color marrón** brown, 3.2
**¿De qué color es?** What color is it?, 3.2
el/la **comandante** pilot, captain, 11.2
la **comedia** comedy
el **comedor** dining room, 6.2
**comenzar (ie)** to begin
**comer** to eat, 5.1
**comercial: la zona comercial** business district, **9.1**
el/la **comerciante** businessman (woman), **14.1**
el **comercio** business
el **comestible** food, 14.2; **2.2**
**cómico(a)** funny, 1.1
la **comida** food, meal, 5.2
la **comisión** commission
el **comité** committee
**como** like; as; since, 1.2
**¿cómo?** how?, what?, 1.1
**¿Cómo está... ?** How is . . . ?, 8.1
**¡Cómo no!** Of course!
la **comodidad** comfort

**compacto(a): el disco compacto** compact disk, CD, 4.2
el/la **compañero(a)** friend, 1.2
la **compañía** company
la **comparación** comparison
**comparar** to compare
el **compartimiento** compartment, 13.2; **1.2**
**el compartimiento sobre la cabeza** overhead compartment, **7.1**
**el compartimiento superior** overhead compartment, **7.1**
la **competencia** competition
la **competición** competition, contest
**competir (i, i)** to compete
**completar** to complete
**completo(a)** full (train), 13.2; **1.2**
**a tiempo completo** full time *(adj.)*, **14.2**
**componer** to compose
**comportarse** to behave
la **composición** composition
la **compra** buying, **4.1**
**comprar** to buy, 3.1
las **compras** shopping; purchases, **4.2**
**hacer las compras** to go shopping, **4.2**
**ir de compras** to go shopping, to shop, 5.2
**comprender** to understand, 5.1
**comprometerse** to get engaged
el **compromiso** engagement
la **computadora** computer, **3.1**
**común** common
la **comunicación** communication
**comunicarse** to communicate with each other, **3.1**
la **comunidad** community
**con** with
**con cuidado** carefully, cautiously, **11.1**

**con frecuencia** often, **3.2**
**con mucha plata** rich
**¿con quién?** with whom?
**con retraso** with a delay, 13.2; **1.2**
**con una demora** with a delay, late, 11.1
el **concierto** concert
**conciliar** to reconcile
el/la **conde(sa)** count(ess)
la **condición** condition
el **condimento** seasoning
el **condominio** condominium, **9.1**
**conducir** to drive, **11.1**
el/la **conductor(a)** driver, **11.1**
**conectar** to connect
la **conexión** connection
la **conferencia** lecture
**confirmar** to confirm
la **confitería** café, tearoom
**Conforme.** Agreed., Fine., 14.2; **2.2**
**confrontar** to confront
**congelado(a): los productos congelados** frozen food, 5.2
el **congelador** freezer, **10.1**
el **conjunto** set, collection
**conocer** to know, to be familiar with, 11.1
el/la **conocido(a)** acquaintance
el **conocimiento** knowledge
la **conquista** conquest
el **conquistador** conquerer
**conquistar** to conquer
el/la **consejero(a) de orientación** guidance counselor
el **consejo** advice
**consentir (ie, i)** to allow, tolerate
**conservar** to save
**considerar** to consider
**consiguiente: por consiguiente** consequently
**consistir (en)** to consist of
**construir** to construct
la **consulta del médico** doctor's office, 8.2
**consultar** to consult, 13.1; **1.1**

el **consultorio** medical office, 8.2
el/la **consumidor(a)** consumer
**consumir** to consume
el **consumo** consumption
la **contabilidad** accounting
el/la **contable** accountant, **14.1**
el **contacto** touch
**contagioso(a)** contagious
la **contaminación** pollution
**contaminado(a)** polluted
**contaminar** to pollute
**contemporáneo(a)** contemporary
**contener (ie)** to contain
**contento(a)** happy, 8.1
la **contestación** answer, response
el **contestador automático** answering machine, **3.2**
**contestar** to answer, **3.2**
el **continente** continent
**continuar** to continue, 7.2
**contra** against, 7.1
**contrario(a)** opposite
**lo contrario** the opposite
**contrastar** to contrast
**contribuir** to contribute
el **control** inspection, 11.1
**el control de pasaportes** passport inspection, 11.1
**el control de seguridad** security check, 11.1
el/la **controlador(a)** air traffic controller
**controlar** to control
**convencer** to convince
**conveniente** convenient
el **convento** convent
la **conversación** conversation
**conversar** to talk, speak
el **convertible** convertible, **11.1**
**convertir (ie, i)** to convert, transform
la **coordinación** coordination
la **copa: la Copa mundial** World Cup
la **copia** copy
**copiar** to copy
el/la **copiloto** copilot, 11.2
el **corazón** heart
la **corbata** tie, 3.2
el **cordero** lamb, 14.2; **2.2**
la **cordillera** mountain range, **7.2**
el **cordoncillo** piping (embroidery)
la **coreografía** choreography
**coreográfico(a)** choreographic
la **córnea** cornea
el **coro** choir, chorus
el **correo** mail; post office, **12.2**
**el correo aéreo** airmail, **12.2**
**el correo electrónico** e-mail, electronic mail, **3.1**
**el correo ordinario** regular mail, **12.2**
**correr** to run, 7.2
la **correspondencia** correspondence
**corriente: el agua corriente** running water
**cortar** to cut, **8.1**
**cortarse el pelo** to get one's hair cut
la **corte** court, **14.1**
el **corte de pelo** haircut, **12.1**
**cortés** courteous
la **cortesía** courtesy, BV
**corto(a)** short, 3.2
**el pantalón corto** shorts, 3.2
**las mangas cortas (largas)** short (long) sleeves, **4.1**
la **cosa** thing
la **cosecha** crop, harvest, **9.2**
**cosechar** to harvest, **9.2**
**coser** to sew
la **costa** coast
**costar (ue)** to cost, 3.1
**costarricense** Costa Rican
la **costilla** rib, **10.1**
la **costumbre** custom
la **costura** sewing
el **cráter** crater
la **creación** creation
**crear** to create
**crecer** to grow, increase
el **crecimiento** growth
**crédito: la tarjeta de crédito** credit card, 14.1; **2.1**
**creer** to believe, 8.2; to think so
la **crema: la crema de afeitar** shaving cream, 12.1
**la crema dentífrica** toothpaste, 12.2
**la crema protectora** sunblock, 9.1
**criar** to raise, **9.2**
**criollo(a)** Creole
**cristiano(a)** Christian
el **cruce** crossing, intersection, **11.2**
**el cruce de peatones** crosswalk, **9.1**
el **crucigrama** crossword puzzle, **5.1**
**llenar un crucigrama** to do a crossword puzzle, **5.1**
**cruel** cruel
**cruzar** to cross, **9.1**
el **cuaderno** notebook, 3.1
la **cuadra** (city) block, **11.2**
el **cuadro** painting, 10.2
**cuadros: a cuadros** check, plaid
**¿cuál?** which?, what?, BV
**¿Cuál es la fecha de hoy?** What is today's date?, BV
**¿cuáles?** which ones?, what?
**cualquier** any
**cuando** when, 4.2
**¿cuándo?** when?, 4.1
**cuanto: en cuanto a** in regard to
**¿cuánto?** how much?, 3.1
**¿A cuánto está(n)... ?** How much is (are) . . . ?, 5.2
**¿Cuánto cuesta(n)... ?** How much do(es) . . . cost?, 3.1
**¿Cuánto es?** How much does it cost?, 3.1

**¿cuántos(as)?** how many?, 2.1
**¿Cuántos años tienes?** How old are you?
**cuarenta** forty, 2.2
el **cuarto** room, bedroom 6.2; quarter, 2.2
**el cuarto de baño** bathroom, 6.2
**el cuarto de dormir** bedroom
**el cuarto doble** double room, **6.1**
**el cuarto sencillo** single room, **6.1**
**menos cuarto** a quarter to (the hour), 2.2
**y cuarto** a quarter past (the hour), 2.2
**cuarto(a)** fourth, 6.2
**cuatro** four, BV
**cuatrocientos(as)** four hundred, 3.2
**cubano(a)** Cuban
**cubanoamericano(a)** Cuban American
**cubrir** to cover
la **cuchara** tablespoon, 14.1; **2.1**
la **cucharita** teaspoon, 14.1; **2.1**
el **cuchillo** knife, 14.1; **2.1**
el **cuello** neck, **4.1**
la **cuenca** basin
la **cuenta** bill, check, 5.1
la **cuenta corriente** checking account, **12.2**
la **cuenta de ahorros** savings account
el/la **cuentista** short-story writer
el **cuento** story
la **cuerda** string (instrument)
el **cuerpo** body, **8.1**
el **Cuerpo de Paz** Peace Corps
el **cuestionario** questionnaire
**¡cuidado!** careful!
**con cuidado** carefully
**el cuidado intensivo** intensive care
**tener cuidado** to be careful
**cuidar** to raise, look after, care for
**cultivar** to cultivate, to grow, **9.2**
el **cultivo** cultivation, growing, **9.2**
**culto(a)** cultured
**cultural** cultural
el **cumpleaños** birthday, 6.1
**¡Feliz cumpleaños!** Happy birthday!, **13.1**
**cumplir: cumplir... años** to be . . . years old, 6.1
el **cupé** coupe, **11.1**
la **cura** cure, treatment
el/la **curandero(a)** folk healer
**curar** to heal, get well
el **curso** course, class, 2.1
**el curso obligatorio** required course
**el curso opcional** elective course

la **dama** lady-in-waiting, woman
**la dama de honor** maid of honor, **13.1**
las **damas** checkers, **5.1**
la **danza** dance
**dañar** to hurt
**daño: hacerse daño** to hurt oneself, **8.1**
**dar** to give, 4.2
**dar a** to open onto, look out on
**dar a entender** to imply that
**dar auxilio** to help
**dar énfasis** to emphasize
**dar la mano** to shake hands
**dar la vuelta** to turn around
**dar las doce** to strike twelve, **13.2**
**dar un examen** to give a test, 4.2
**dar un paseo** to take a walk, **5.2**
**dar una fiesta** to give (throw) a party, 4.2
**dar una representación** to put on a performance, 10.2
**datar** to date
los **datos** data, information, **3.1**
**entrar los datos** to enter, keyboard information, **3.1**
**de** of, from, for, BV
**de... a...** from (time) to (time), 2.2
**de joven** as a young person
**De nada.** You're welcome., BV
**de ninguna manera** by no means, 1.1
**¿De parte de quién?** Who's calling?, **3.2**
**de vez en cuando** sometimes
**debajo (de)** under, below, **7.1**
**deber** must; should; to owe
la **década** decade
**decidir** to decide
**décimo(a)** tenth, 6.2
**decir** to say, 13
**¡Diga!** Hello! (answering the telephone–Spain), 14.2; **2.2**
**declarar** to declare
la **decoración** decoration
**decorado(a)** decorated
**decorar** to decorate
**dedicarse** to devote oneself, **14.1**
el **dedo** finger, **4.1**
el **defecto** fault, flaw
**defender (ie)** to defend
la **definición** definition
**definir** to define
**definitivamente** once and for all
**dejar** to leave (something), 14.1; **2.1**; to let, allow
**dejar un mensaje** to leave a message, **3.2**

**del** of the, from the
**delante de** in front of, 10.1
**delantero(a)** front *(adj.)*
**delgado(a)** thin
**delicado(a)** delicate
**delicioso(a)** delicious
**demás** other, rest
**demasiado** too (much)
la **demografía** demography
el/la **demógrafo(a)** demographer
la **demora: con una demora** with a delay, 11.1
**demostrar (ue)** to demonstrate
la **densidad** density
**dentífrico(a): la pasta (crema) dentífrica** toothpaste, 12.2
el/la **dentista** dentist
**dentro de** within
**dentro de poco** soon
el **departamento** apartment, 6.2; department, **14.2**
**la casa de departamentos** apartment house, 6.2
**el departamento de recursos humanos** human resources department, **14.2**
**depender (ie) (de)** to depend (on)
el/la **dependiente(a)** salesperson, 3.1
el **deporte** sport, 7.1
**el deporte de equipo** team sport
**el deporte individual** individual sport
**deportivo(a)** (related to) sports, 6.2
**la emisión deportiva** sports program (TV), 6.2
el **depósito** deposit
**derecho(a)** right, 7.1
**a la derecha** to the right, 5.2
**derecho** straight (ahead), **11.2**
**seguir derecho** to go straight, **11.2**
la **dermatología** dermatology
el/la **dermatólogo(a)** dermatologist
**derrotar** to defeat
**desagradable** unpleasant
**desamparado(a): los niños desamparados** homeless children
**desaparecer** to disappear
el **desarrollo** development
el **desastre** disaster
**desastroso(a)** disastrous
**desayunarse** to eat breakfast, 12.1
el **desayuno** breakfast, 5.2
**tomar el desayuno** to eat breakfast, 12.1
**descansar** to rest
el **descapotable** convertible, **11.1**
el/la **descendiente** descendant
**descolgar (ue)** to pick up (the telephone), **3.2**
**describir** to describe
**descubrir** to discover
el **descuento** discount
**desde** since, from
**desear** to want, wish, 3.2
**¿Qué desea usted?** May I help you? (in a store), 3.2
los **desechos** waste
**desembarcar** to disembark, 11.2
**desembocar** to lead, go (one street into another), **9.1**; to empty
el **desenlace** conclusion
el **deseo** desire
el **desierto** desert
**despachar** to sell, 8.2
**despacio** slowly
**despegar** to take off (airplane), 11.2
el **despegue** take-off (airplane), **7.2**
**despertarse (ie)** to wake up, 12.1
**después (de)** after, 5.1; later
el **destino** destination, 11.1
**con destino a** to
la **desventaja** disadvantage
el **detalle** detail
el **detergente** detergent, **4.2**
**determinar** to determine
**detrás de** behind, **5.2**
**devolver (ue)** to return (something), 7.2
el **día** day, BV
**Buenos días.** Good morning., BV
**el Día de los Reyes** Epiphany (January 6), **13.2**
**hoy (en) día** nowadays, these days
**¿Qué día es (hoy)?** What day is it (today)?, BV
la **diagnosis** diagnosis, 8.2
el **diálogo** dialogue
el **diamante** diamond
**diario(a)** daily
**dibujar** to draw
el **dibujo** drawing
**diciembre** December, BV
**diecinueve** nineteen, BV
**dieciocho** eighteen, BV
**dieciséis** sixteen, BV
**diecisiete** seventeen, BV
el **diente** tooth
**cepillarse los dientes** to brush one's teeth, 12.1
**el cepillo de dientes** toothbrush, 12.2
**diesel** diesel (gas), **11.1**
la **dieta** diet
**diez** ten
la **diferencia** difference
**diferente** different
**difícil** difficult, 2.1
la **dificultad** difficulty
**¡Diga!** Hello! (telephone), 14.2; **2.2**
**diminuto(a)** tiny, minute
la **dinamita** dynamite
el **dinero** money, 14.1; **2.1**
**el dinero en efectivo** cash, **12.2**

¡**Dios mío!** Gosh!
el/la **diplomado(a)** graduate
**diplomático(a)** diplomatic
la **dirección** direction; address
**en dirección a** toward
las **direccionales** turn signals, **11.1**
**directo(a)** direct
el/la **director(a)** director, principal
**dirigir** to direct
la **disciplina** subject area (school), 2.2
el **disco** dial (of telephone), **3.2**
el **disco compacto** compact disk, CD, 14.2; **3.1**
**discutir** to discuss
el/la **diseñador(a)** designer
el **diseño** design
**disfrutar** to enjoy
**disponible** available
la **disputa** quarrel, argument
el **disquete** disk, diskette, 3.1
la **distancia** distance
**distinto(a)** different, distinct
**distraer** to distract
la **distribución** distribution
la **distribuidora** parking meter that dispenses tickets
**distribuir** to pass out, distribute, **7.1**
la **diversión** amusement
**divertido(a)** fun, amusing
**divertirse (ie, i)** to enjoy oneself, 12.2
**dividir** to divide
la **división** division
**divorciarse** to get divorced
**doblado(a)** dubbed, 10.1
**doblar** to turn, **11.2**
**doble: el cuarto doble** double room, **6.1**
**dobles** doubles, 9.1
**doce** twelve, BV
la **docena** dozen, **4.2**
el/la **doctor(a)** doctor
la **documentación** documentation
el **documento** document, **3.1**
el **dólar** dollar
**doler (ue)** to hurt, 8.2
**Me duele(n)...** My . . . hurt(s) me, 8.2
el **dolor** pain, ache, 8.1
**el dolor de cabeza** headache, 8.1
**el dolor de estómago** stomachache, 8.1
**el dolor de garganta** sore throat, 8.1
**Tengo dolor de...** I have a pain in my . . . , 8.2
**doméstico(a): los animales domésticos** farm animals, **9.2**
**la economía doméstica** home economics, 2.2
el **domingo** Sunday, BV
**dominicano(a)** Dominican, 2.1
**la República Dominicana** Dominican Republic
el **dominio** control, authority
el **dominó** dominos, **5.1**
**don** courteous way of addressing a man
**donde** where, 1.2
¿**dónde?** where?, 1.2
**doña** courteous way of addressing a woman
**dorado(a)** golden
**dormido(a)** asleep
el/la **dormilón(ona)** sleepy head
**dormir (ue, u)** to sleep
**el saco de dormir** sleeping bag, 12.2
**dormirse (ue, u)** to fall asleep, 12.1
el **dormitorio** bedroom, 6.2
**dos** two, BV
**doscientos(as)** two hundred, 3.2
la **dosis** dose, 8.2
el/la **dramaturgo(a)** playwright
**driblar** to dribble, 7.2
la **droga** drug
la **drogadicción** drug addiction
la **ducha** shower, 12.1
**tomar una ducha** to take a shower, 12.1
la **duda** doubt
**dudar** to doubt
**dudoso(a)** doubtful
**duele(n): Me duele(n) mucho.** It (They) hurt(s) me a lot., **8.2**
**dulce** sweet
**el pan dulce** sweet roll, 5.1
la **duración** duration
**durante** during
**durar** to last, **13.2**
**duro(a)** hard, difficult, 2.1
el **DVD** digital video disc (DVD)

## E

la **ebullición** boiling
**echar** to throw
**echar la carta (en el buzón)** to mail the letter, **12.2**
**echar (tomar) una siesta** to take a nap
**echarle flores** to pay someone a compliment
la **ecología** ecology
**ecológico(a)** ecological
la **economía** economics; economy
**la economía doméstica** home economics, 2.2
**económico(a)** economical, 12.2
la **ecuación** equation
**ecuatoriano(a)** Ecuadorean, 2.1
la **edad** age
el **edificio** building, **9.1**
la **educación** education
**la educación física** physical education, 2.2
**educar** to educate
**efectivo: el dinero en efectivo** cash
**efectuar** to carry out
**ejemplo: por ejemplo** for example

**ejercicio: hacer los ejercicios** to exercise
el **ejote** string beans
**el** the *(m. sing.)*, 1.1
**él** he, 1.1
la **electricidad** electricity
el/la **electricista** electrician, **14.1**
**eléctrico(a)** electric
**electrónico(a): el correo electrónico** e-mail, electronic mail
la **elegancia** elegance
**elegante** elegant, **13.1**
el **elemento** element
la **elevación** elevation
**elevado(a)** elevated, high
el **elevador** elevator, **6.1**
**elevar** to elevate
**eliminar** to eliminate
**ella** she, 1.1
**ellos(as)** they, 2.1
el **elote** corn (Mex.)
el/la **embajador(a)** ambassador
**embarcar** to board, 11.2
**embarque: la tarjeta de embarque** boarding pass, 11.1
**la puerta de embarque** departure gate
la **emergencia** emergency, **7.1**
**la sala de emergencia** emergency room, **8.1**
la **emisión** program (TV), 6.2; emission
**la emisión deportiva** sports program, 6.2
**emitir** to emit
la **emoción** emotion
**emocional** emotional
**empalmar** to connect
**empatado(a)** tied (score), 7.1
**El tanto queda empatado.** The score is tied., 7.1
**empezar (ie)** to begin, 7.1
el/la **empleado(a)** employee, clerk, 3.1
**emplear** to employ
el **empleo** employment, job
**una solicitud de empleo** a job application, **14.2**
la **empresa** business
el/la **empresario(a)** entrepreneur, businessperson
**empujar** to push, **4.2**
**empujar el carrito** to push the cart, **4.2**
**en** in; on
**en aquel entonces** at that time
**en caso de** in case of
**en punto** on the dot, sharp, 4.1
**en sí** in itself
el/la **enamorado(a)** sweetheart, lover
**encantador(a)** charming
**encantar** to delight
**encargarse** to take charge
**encender (ie)** to light, **13.2**
**encestar** to put in (make) a basket, 7.2
la **enchilada** enchilada, BV
**encima (de)** above
**por encima de** above, 9.1
**encontrar (ue)** to find
**encontrarse (ue)** to meet
la **encuesta** survey
**endosar** to endorse, **12.2**
el/la **enemigo(a)** enemy
la **energía** energy
**enero** January, BV
**enfadado(a)** angry
el **énfasis: dar énfasis** to emphasize
**enfatizar** to emphasize
la **enfermedad** illness
la **enfermería** nursing
el/la **enfermero(a)** nurse, **8.2**
**enfermo(a)** sick, 8.1
el/la **enfermo(a)** sick person, 8.1
**enfrente de** in front of
el **enganche** down payment
**¡Enhorabuena!** Congratulations!, **13.1**
el **enlace** union
**enlatado(a)** canned
**enlazar** to join, connect
**enorme** enormous
la **ensalada** salad, 5.1
**enseguida** right away, immediately, 5.1
**enseñar** to teach, 4.1; to show, **4.1**
**entablar** to start, begin
**entero(a)** entire, whole
**enterrar (ie)** to bury
el **entierro** burial
**entonces** then
**en aquel entonces** at that time
la **entrada** inning, 7.2; admission ticket, 10.1; entrance, **5.2**
**entrar** to enter, 4.1
**entrar en escena** to come (go) on stage, 10.2
**entre** between, 7.1
**entregar** to deliver
el **entrenamiento** training
**entretenido(a)** entertaining
la **entrevista** interview, **14.2**
el/la **entrevistador(a)** interviewer, **14.2**
**entrevistar** to interview
**entusiasmado(a)** enthusiastic
el/la **envejeciente** aging person
**enviar** to send
**envuelto(a)** wrapped
el **episodio** episode
la **época** period of time, epoch
el **equilibrio** equilibrium
el **equipaje** baggage, luggage, 11.1
**el equipaje de mano** carry-on luggage, 11.1
el **equipo** team, 7.1; equipment
**el deporte de equipo** team sport, 7.2
el **equivalente** equivalent
**erróneo(a)** wrong, erroneous
la **escala** stopover, **7.2**
**hacer escala** to stop over, make a stop, **7.2**
la **escalera** stairway, 6.2

la **escalera mecánica** escalator, **9.1**
los **escalofríos** chills, 8.1
**escamotear** to secretly take
**escapar** to escape
el **escaparate** shop window, **4.1**
la **escasez** shortage
la **escena** stage
**entrar en escena** to come (go) on stage, 10.2
el **escenario** scenery, set (theater), 10.2
**escoger** to choose
**escolar** (related to) school, 2.1
**el bus escolar** school bus, 4.1
**el horario escolar** school schedule
**la vida escolar** school life
**los materiales escolares** school supplies, 3.1
**esconder** to hide
**escribir** to write, 5.1
**escuchar** to listen (to), 4.2
el **escudero** squire, knight's attendant
la **escuela** school, 1.1
**la escuela intermedia** middle school
**la escuela primaria** elementary school
**la escuela secundaria** high school, 1.1
**la escuela superior** high school
el/la **escultor(a)** sculptor, 10.2
la **escultura** sculpture
**ese(a)** that
**esencial** essential
**eso** that (one)
**a eso de** at about (time), 4.1
**esos(as)** those
el **espacio** space
el **espagueti** spaghetti
**espantoso(a)** frightful
**España** Spain
el **español** Spanish (language), 2.2
**español(a)** Spanish *(adj.)*
la **espátula** palette knife, spatula
la **especia** spice
**especial** special
la **especialidad** specialty, specialization
el/la **especialista** specialist, **14.1**
**especializar** to specialize
**especialmente** especially
el **espectáculo** show, 10.2
**ver un espectáculo** to see a show, 10.2
el/la **espectador(a)** spectator, 7.1
el **espejo** mirror, 12.1
**espera: la sala de espera** waiting room, 13.1; **1.1**
**esperar** to wait (for), 11.1; to hope
**espontáneo(a)** spontaneous
la **esposa** wife, spouse, 6.1
el **esposo** husband, spouse, 6.1
el **esquí** skiing, 9.2; ski
**el esquí acuático** water skiing, 9.1
el/la **esquiador(a)** skier, 9.2
**esquiar** to ski, 9.2
**esquiar en el agua** to water-ski, 9.1
la **esquina** corner, **9.1**
**establecerse** to settle
el **establecimiento** establishment
la **estación** season, BV; station, 10.1
**la estación de esquí** ski resort, 9.2
**la estación de ferrocarril** train station, 13.1; **1.1**
**la estación del metro** subway station, 10.1
**la estación de servicio** service station, **11.1**
el **estacionamiento** parking
**estacionar** to park
la **estadía** stay
el **estadio** stadium, 7.1
la **estadística** statistic
el **estado** state
el **estado del banco** bank statement
**Estados Unidos** United States
**estadounidense** from the United States
la **estancia** ranch (Argentina)
**estar** to be, 4.1
**¿Está... ?** Is . . . there?, **3.2**
**estar cansado(a)** to be tired, **8.1**
**estar contento(a) (triste, etc.)** to be happy (sad, etc.), **8.1**
**estar de buen (mal) humor** to be in a good (bad) mood, **8.1**
**estar enfermo(a)** to be sick
**estar nervioso(a) (tranquilo[a])** to be nervous (calm), **8.1**
**estar resfriado(a)** to have a cold, 8.1
**estatal** pertaining to state *(adj.)*
la **estatua** statue, 10.2
**este(a)** this
el **este** east
**estereofónico(a)** stereo
el **estilo** style
**estimado(a)** esteemed
**esto** this (one)
el **estómago** stomach, 8.1
**estornudar** to sneeze, 8.1
**estos(as)** these
la **estrategia** strategy
**estrecho(a)** narrow, **4.1**
la **estrella** star
la **estructura** structure
el/la **estudiante** student
**el/la estudiante de intercambio** exchange student
**la residencia para estudiantes** student housing, dormitory, **3.2**
**estudiantil** (relating to) student
**estudiar** to study, 4.1

el **estudio** study, **14**
la **estufa** stove, **10.1**
**estupendo(a)** stupendous
**eterno(a)** eternal
**étnico(a)** ethnic
el **euro** euro (currency)
**Europa** Europe
**europeo(a)** European
**exactamente** exactly
**exacto(a)** exact
**exagerado(a)** exaggerated
**exagerar** to exaggerate
el **examen** test, exam, 4.2
**examinar** to examine, 8.2
la **excavación** excavation
**excavar** to dig, excavate
**exceder** to exceed
**excelente** excellent
la **excepción** exception
**exclamar** to exclaim
**exclusivamente** exclusively
la **exhibición** exhibition
**exigir** to demand
la **existencia** existence
**existir** to exist
el **éxito** success
la **expedición** expedition
la **experiencia** experience
**experimentar** to experiment
el/la **experto(a)** expert, 9.2
**explicar** to explain, 4.2
el/la **explorador(a)** explorer
la **explosión** explosion
**exportar** to export
la **exposición (de arte)** (art) exhibition, 10.2
la **expresión** expression
**el modo de expresión** means of expression
la **extensión** extension
**extranjero(a)** foreign
**el país extranjero** foreign country, 11.2
el/la **extranjero(a)** foreigner
**en el extranjero** abroad
**extraordinario(a)** extraordinary
**extravagante** strange
**extremo(a)** extreme

## F

la **fábrica** factory, **9.1**
**fabricado(a)** manufactured
**fabuloso(a)** fabulous
**fácil** easy, 2.1
**facilitar** to facilitate
el **facsímil** fax, **3.1**
la **factura** bill, **6.1**; invoice
**facturar el equipaje** to check luggage, 11.1
la **Facultad** school (of a university)
la **faja** sash
la **falda** skirt, 3.2
**falso(a)** false
la **fama: tener fama de** to have the reputation of
la **familia** family, 6.1
**familiar** (related to the) family
**famoso(a)** famous, 1.2
**fantástico(a)** fantastic, 1.2
el/la **farmacéutico(a)** druggist, pharmacist, 8.2
la **farmacia** drugstore, 8.2
**fascinar** to fascinate
**Favor de (+ infinitive)** Please (+ verb), **11.1**
**favorito(a)** favorite, **11**
el **fax** fax, **3.1**
**mandar (transmitir) un fax** to send a fax, to fax, **3.1**
**febrero** February, BV
la **fecha** date, BV
**¿Cuál es la fecha de hoy?** What is today's date?, BV
la **felicidad** happiness
**¡Felicitaciones!** Congratulations!, **13.1**
**feliz** happy
**¡Feliz cumpleaños!** Happy birthday!, **13.1**
**¡Feliz Hanuka!** Happy Chanukah!, **13.2**
**¡Feliz Navidad!** Merry Christmas!, **13.2**
**feo(a)** ugly, 1.1

el **ferrocarril** railroad, 13.1, **1.1**
**la estación de ferrocarril** train station, 13.1, **1.1**
**festejar** to celebrate
la **ficción** fiction
la **ficha** piece (game), **5.1**; registration card, **6.1**
**ficticio(a)** fictitious
la **fiebre** fever, 8.1
**tener fiebre** to have a fever, 8.1
**fiel** faithful
la **fiesta** party, **13.1**
**dar una fiesta** to give (throw) a party, 4.2
la **fiesta de las luces** The Festival of Lights, **13.2**
la **figura** figure
**figurativo(a)** figurative
**fijar** to fix
**fijo(a)** fixed
la **fila** row (of seats); line (queue), 10.1
el **filete** fillet
el **film** film, 10.1
el **fin** end
**a fines de** at the end of
**el fin de semana** weekend, BV
el **final: al final (de)** at the end (of)
**financiero(a)** financial
las **finanzas** finances
la **finca** farm, **9.2**
**fino(a)** fine
**firmar** to sign, **12.2**
la **física** physics, 2.1
**físico(a): la educación física** physical education, 2.2
**flaco(a)** thin, 1.2
**flamenco(a)** flamenco
la **flauta** flute
**flechar** to become enamored of (to fall for)
la **flor** flower
el **folleto** pamphlet
el **fondo** fund
el/la **fontanero(a)** plumber, **14.1**

la **forma** shape
**formar** to make up, to form
el **formulario** form, **8.2**
**llenar un formulario** to fill out a form, **8.2**
la **fortaleza** strength
la **fortificación** fortification
la **foto** photo
la **fotografía** photograph
el/la **fotógrafo(a)** photographer
la **fractura** fracture, **8.1**
el **fragmento** fragment
el **francés** French, 2.2
**franco(a)** frank, candid, sincere
el **frasco** jar, **4.2**
la **frase** phrase, sentence
la **frazada** blanket, **6.2**
**frecuentemente** frequently
**freír (i, i)** to fry, 14.1; **2.1**
los **frenos** brakes, **11.1**
la **frente** forehead, **8.1**
**fresco(a)** fresh, **4.2**
el **frijol** bean, 5.2
**los frijoles negros** black beans, **10.2**
el **frío: Hace frío.** It's cold., 9.2
**frito(a)** fried, 5.1
**las papas fritas** French fries, 5.1
el **frontón** wall (of a jai alai court)
la **fruta** fruit, 5.2
la **frutería** fruit store, **4.2**
el **fuego** fire, **10.2**
**a fuego lento** on a low flame, heat
**quitar (retirar) del fuego** to take (something) off the heat, **10.2**
la **fuente** source
**fuerte** strong
la **fuerza** strength; force
**fumar: la sección de (no) fumar** (no) smoking area, 11.1
**la señal de no fumar** no smoking sign, **7.1**
la **función** performance, 10.2; function
el **funcionamiento** functioning
el/la **funcionario(a)** city hall employee, **14.1**
la **fundación** foundation
**fundado(a)** founded, established
**fundar** to found, establish
la **furia** fury
**furioso(a)** furious
el **fútbol** soccer, 7.1
**el campo de fútbol** soccer field, 7.1
el **futbolín** table soccer, **5.1**
el **futuro** future

la **gabardina** raincoat, **4.1**
las **gafas de sol** sunglasses, 9.1
el **galán** beau, heartthrob
la **galaxia** galaxy
la **galería comercial** shopping mall
el **galón** gallon
**gallardo(a)** gallant, fine-looking
la **gallina** hen, **9.2**
las **gambas** shrimp, **10.2**
el **ganado** cattle, **9.2**
**ganar** to win, 7.1; to earn
**ganar la vida** to earn one's living
la **ganga** bargain
el **garaje** garage, 6.2
la **garantía** guarantee
la **garganta** throat, 8.1
la **garita de peaje** toll booth, **11.2**
la **gasolina** gasoline, **11.1**
la **gasolinera** service station, **11.1**
**gastar** to spend
el/la **gato(a)** cat, 6.1
el/la **gemelo(a)** twin
**general: en general** generally
**por lo general** in general, usually
**generalmente** usually, generally
el **género** genre
**generoso(a)** generous, 1.2
la **gente** people
la **geografía** geography, 2.2
la **geometría** geometry, 2.2
**geométrico(a)** geometric
**gerencial** managerial
el/la **gerente** manager, **14.1**
el **gesto** gesture
el **gigante** giant
el **gimnasio** gymnasium
la **ginecología** gynecology
el/la **ginecólogo(a)** gynecologist
la **gira** tour, 12.2
el **globo** balloon, **5.2**
el **gobierno** government, **14.1**
**el gobierno estatal** state government
**el gobierno federal** federal government
**el gobierno municipal** municipal government
el **gol: meter un gol** to score a goal, 7.1
el **golfo** gulf
el **golpe** coup (overthrow of a government)
**golpear** to hit, 9.2
la **goma** tire, **11.1**
la **goma de borrar** eraser, 3.1
**gordo(a)** fat, 1.2
la **gorra** cap, hat, 3.2
**gozar** to enjoy
**Gracias.** Thank you., BV
**gracioso(a)** funny, 1.1
el **grado** degree (temperature), 9.2; grade
**graduarse** to graduate
la **gramática** grammar
el **gramo** gram
**gran, grande** big, large, great
**las Grandes Ligas** Major Leagues
el **grano** grain

la **grasa** fat
**grave** serious, grave
el/la **griego(a)** Greek
la **gripe** flu, 8.1
**gris** gray, 3.2
el **grupo** group
la **guagua** bus (Puerto Rico, Cuba), 10.1
el **guante** glove, 7.2
**guapo(a)** handsome, 1.1
**guardar** to guard, 7.1; to keep, save, **3.1**
**guardar cama** to stay in bed, 8.1
el/la **guardia** police officer
**guatemalteco(a)** Guatemalan
la **guerra** war
la **guerrilla** band of guerrillas
el/la **guía** tour guide; guide
la **guía telefónica** telephone book, **3.2**
el **guisante** pea, 5.2
la **guitarra** guitar
**gustar** to like, to be pleasing
el **gusto** pleasure; taste
**Mucho gusto.** Nice to meet you.

**haber** to have (in compound tenses)
la **habichuela** bean, 5.2
**la habichuela tierna** string bean
**las habichuelas negras** black beans, **10.2**
la **habitación** bedroom, room, **6.1**
el/la **habitante** inhabitant
**habla: los países de habla española** Spanish-speaking countries
**hablar** to speak, talk, 3.1
**hace: Hace... años** . . . years ago
**Hace buen tiempo.** The weather is nice., 9.1
**Hace calor.** It's hot., 9.1
**Hace frío.** It's cold., 9.2
**Hace mal tiempo.** The weather is bad., 9.1
**Hace sol.** It's sunny., 9.1
**hacer** to do, to make
**hacer caso** to pay attention
**hacer cola** to line up, 10.1
**hacer la cama** to make the bed, **6.2**
**hacer la maleta** to pack one's suitcase
**hacer las compras** to shop, **4.2**
**hacer las tareas** to do homework, **3.1**
**hacer preguntas** to ask questions, **14.2**
**hacer un viaje** to take a trip, 11.1
**hacer una llamada telefónica** to make a telephone call, **3.2**
**hacerse daño** to hurt oneself, **8.1**
**hacia** toward
la **hacienda** ranch
**hallar** to find
**hambre: tener hambre** to be hungry, 14.1; **2.1**
la **hamburguesa** hamburger, 5.1
**Hanuka** Chanukah, **13.2**
**¡Feliz Hanuka!** Happy Chanukah!, **13.2**
**harmonioso(a)** harmonious
**hasta** until, BV
**¡Hasta luego!** See you later!, BV
**¡Hasta mañana!** See you tomorrow!, BV
**¡Hasta pronto!** See you soon!, BV
**hay** there is, there are, BV
**hay que** one must
**Hay sol.** It's sunny., 9.1
**No hay de qué.** You're welcome., BV
**hebreo(a)** Hebrew, **13.2**
**hecho(a)** made
**helado(a): el té helado** iced tea, 5.1
el **helado** ice cream, 5.1
**el helado de chocolate** chocolate ice cream, 5.1
**el helado de vainilla** vanilla ice cream, 5.1
el **helicóptero** helicopter, **7.2**
el **hemisferio norte** northern hemisphere
el **hemisferio sur** southern hemisphere
la **herencia** inheritance
la **herida** wound, **8.1**
el/la **herido(a)** injured person
la **hermana** sister, 6.1
el **hermano** brother, 6.1
**hermoso(a)** beautiful, pretty, 1.1
el/la **héroe** hero
**hervir (ie)** to boil, **10.1**
el **hidrofoil** hydrofoil
la **higiene** hygiene
**higiénico(a): el papel higiénico** toilet paper, 12.2
la **hija** daughter, 6.1
el **hijo** son, 6.1
**los hijos** children, 6.1
**hinchado(a)** swollen, **8.1**
el **hipermercado** hypermarket, **4.2**
la **hipoteca** mortgage
**hispano(a)** Hispanic
**hispanoamericano(a)** Spanish-American
**hispanohablante** Spanish-speaking
el/la **hispanohablante** Spanish speaker
la **historia** history, 2.2; story
el/la **historiador(a)** historian
**histórico(a)** historical
la **historieta** short story
el **hobby** hobby, **5.1**
la **hoja: la hoja de papel** sheet of paper, 3.1
**¡Hola!** Hello!, BV

el **hombre** man
**¡hombre!** good heavens!, you bet!
el **hombro** shoulder, **8.1**
**honesto(a)** honest, 1.2
el **honor** honor
la **hora** hour; time
**¿A qué hora?** At what time?, 2.2
**la hora de salida** departure hour
**la hora de la cena** dinner hour
el **horario** schedule, 13.1; **1.1**
**el horario escolar** school schedule
la **horchata** cold drink made from almonds, milk, and sugar
la **hornilla** stove burner, **10.1**
el **hornillo** portable stove, **10.1**
el **horno** oven, **10.1**
el **horno de microondas** microwave oven, **10.1**
**horrible** horrible
**hospedarse** to lodge, stay
el **hospital** hospital, **8.1**
el **hostal** inexpensive hotel, 12.2
la **Hostia** Host (religious)
el **hotel** hotel, **6.1**
**hoy** today, BV
**hoy (en) día** nowadays, these days
el **huarache** sandal
el/la **huerto(a)** vegetable garden, orchard, **9.2**
el **hueso** bone, **8.2**
el/la **huésped** guest, **6.1**
el **huevo** egg, 5.2
**humano(a): el ser humano** human being
**húmedo(a)** humid
**humilde** humble
el **humor** mood, 8.1
**estar de buen humor** to be in a good mood, 8.1
**estar de mal humor** to be in a bad mood, 8.1
el **huso horario** time zone

el **icono** icon
**ida: de ida y vuelta** round-trip (ticket), 13.1; **1.1**
la **idea** idea
**ideal** ideal, 1.2
el/la **idealista** idealist
**identificar** to identify
**idílico(a)** idyllic
el **idioma** language
la **iglesia** church
**igual** equal, alike
**igual que** like, as
la **ilusión** illusion
**ilustre** distinguished
la **imagen** image
la **imaginación** imagination
**imaginado(a)** imagined, dreamed of
**imaginar** to imagine
**imaginario(a)** imaginary
**impar: el número impar** odd number
el **imperativo** imperative
el **impermeable** raincoat, **4.1**
**importante** important
**importar** to be important
**imposible** impossible
**impresionar** to affect, influence
la **impresora** printer, **3.1**
**inaugurar** to inaugurate
el/la **inca** Inca
**incluido(a): ¿Está incluido el servicio?** Is the tip included?, 5.1
**incluir** to include, 5.1
**increíble** incredible
la **independencia** independence
el **indicador: el tablero indicador** scoreboard, 7.1
**indicar** to indicate, 11.1
**indígena** native, indigenous
el/la **indígena** native person
**indio(a)** Indian
**indispensable** indispensable
**individual** individual
**el deporte individual** individual sport
el **individuo** individual
**industrial: la zona industrial** industrial area, **9.1**
la **inferencia** inference
la **influencia** influence
la **información** information
**informar** to inform, 13.2; **1.2**
la **informática** computer science, 2.2
el **informe** report
la **ingeniería** engineering
el/la **ingeniero(a)** engineer, **14.1**
el **inglés** English, 2.2
el **ingrediente** ingredient
**ingresar** to make a deposit (bank)
**inhospital** inhospitable
**inhóspito(a)** desolate, inhospitable
**inmediatamente** immediately
**inmediato(a)** immediate
**inmenso(a)** immense
la **innovación** innovation
**inocente** innocent
el **inodoro** toilet, **6.2**
**insistir** to insist
**inspeccionar** to inspect, 11.1
la **instalación** installation
**instantáneo(a)** instantaneous
el **instante** instant
la **instrucción** instruction
el **instrumento** instrument
**el instrumento musical** musical instrument
**íntegro(a)** integral
**inteligente** intelligent, 2.1
el **intercambio** exchange
**el/la estudiante (alumno[a]) de intercambio** exchange student
el **interés** interest
**interesante** interesting, 2.1
**interesar** to interest

**intergaláctico(a)** intergalactic
**intermedio(a): la escuela intermedia** middle school
**internacional** international
**Internet** Internet, **3.1**
la **interpretación** interpretation
el/la **intérprete** interpreter
**interrumpir** to interrupt
la **interrupción** interruption
**intervenir** to intervene
**íntimo(a)** intimate, close
la **introducción** introduction
**introducir** to insert, **3.2**
**introducir la tarjeta telefónica** to insert the phone card, **3.2**
el **invento** invention
**inverso(a)** reverse
la **investigación** investigation
el/la **investigador(a)** researcher
el **invierno** winter, BV
la **invitación** invitation
el/la **invitado(a)** guest
**invitar** to invite, 6.1
la **inyección** injection, shot, 8.2
**poner una inyección** to give a shot
**ir** to go, 4.1
**ir a (+ infinitive)** to be going to (do something)
**ir a pie** to go on foot, to walk, 4.1
**ir de compras** to go shopping, 5.2
**ir en bicicleta** to go by bicycle, 12.2
**ir en carro (coche)** to go by car, 4.1
**ir en tren** to go by train
la **irrigación** irrigation
la **isla** island
**italiano(a)** Italian
**izquierdo(a)** left, 7.1
**a la izquierda** to the left, **5.2**

## J

el **jabón** soap, 12.2
**la barra (pastilla) de jabón** bar of soap, 12.2
**jamás** never
el **jamón** ham, 5.1
el **jardín** garden, 6.2
el/la **jardinero(a)** outfielder, 7.2
la **jaula** cage, **5.2**
el/la **jefe(a)** boss
el **jet** jet
el **jonrón** home run, 7.2
**joven** young, 6.1
**de joven** as a young person
el/la **joven** youth, young person, 10.1
la **joya** jewel, **4.1**
la **joyería** jewelry store, **4.1**
la **judía verde** green bean, 5.2
el **juego** game
**el juego de béisbol** baseball game, 7.2
**el juego de tenis** tennis game, 9.1
**el juego de video** video game, **5.1**
**los Juegos Olímpicos** Olympic Games
**la sala de juegos** game arcade, **5.1**
el **jueves** Thursday, BV
el/la **juez** judge, **14.1**
el/la **jugador(a)** player, 7.1
**el/la jugador(a) de béisbol** baseball player, 7.2
**jugar (ue)** to play, 7.1
**jugar (al) béisbol (fútbol, baloncesto, etc.)** to play baseball (soccer, basketball, etc.), 7.1
el **jugo** juice
**el jugo de naranja** orange juice, 12.1
el **juguete** toy
**julio** July, BV
la **jungla** jungle
**junio** June, BV
**juntos(as)** together
**juvenil: el albergue juvenil** youth hostel, 12.2
la **juventud** youth

## K

el **kilo** kilogram, 5.2
el **kilómetro** kilometer

## L

**la** the *(f. sing.)*, 1.1; it, her *(pron.)*
el **labio** lip, **8.1**
el **laboratorio** laboratory
el **lado** side
**al lado de** beside, next to, **5.2**
el **lago** lake, **5.2**
el **lamento** lament
la **lana** wool, **12.1**
la **langosta** lobster, 14.2; **2.2**
la **lanza** lance
el/la **lanzador(a)** pitcher, 7.2
**lanzar** to throw, 7.1; to launch
el **lápiz** pencil, 3.1
**largo(a)** long, 3.2
**de largo recorrido** long distance (trip)
**las** them *(f. pl. pron.)*
la **lástima: ser una lástima** to be a pity (a shame)
**lastimarse** to get hurt, **8.1**
la **lata** can, 5.2
**lateral** side *(adj.)*, 13.2; **1.2**
el **latín** Latin, 2.2
**latino(a)** Latin *(adj.)*
**Latinoamérica** Latin America, 1.1
**latinoamericano(a)** Latin American

el **lavabo** washbasin, **6.2**; restroom, **7.1**
el **lavado** laundry, **12.1**
la **lavandería** laundromat
**lavar: la máquina de lavar** washing machine, **12.1**
**lavarse** to wash oneself, 12.1
**lavarse los dientes** to brush one's teeth, 12.1
**le** to him, to her; to you *(formal) (pron.)*
la **lección** lesson, 4.2
la **leche** milk
**el café con leche** coffee with milk, 5.1
el **lechón** suckling pig
la **lechuga** lettuce, 5.2
la **lectura** reading
**leer** to read, 5.1
la **legumbre** vegetable
**lejos** far, **12.2**
la **lengua** language, 2.2
el **lenguaje** language
la **lenteja** lentil
**lento(a)** slow, **10.2**
el **león** lion
**les** to them; to you *(formal pl.) (pron.)*
el/la **lesionado(a)** injured person
la **letra** letter (of alphabet)
**levantar** to lift, to raise
**levantarse** to get up, 12.1; to rise up (against)
**levantarse el sol** the sun rises
el/la **libertador(a)** liberator
la **libra** pound
**libre** free, 5.1
**al aire libre** outdoor *(adj.)*
el **libro** book, 3.1
la **licencia** driver's license, **11.1**
el **liceo** high school
el **lienzo** canvas (painting)
la **liga** league
**las Grandes Ligas** Major Leagues
**ligero(a)** light (cheerful)
la **lima** lime, **10.1**
**limeño(a)** from Lima (Peru)
el **límite de velocidad** speed limit
el **limón** lemon, **10.1**
la **limonada** lemonade, BV
**limpiar** to clean, **6.2**
**limpiar el cuarto** to clean the room, **6.2**
**limpiar en seco** to dry clean, **12.1**
**limpio(a)** clean
la **limusina** limousine
**lindo(a)** pretty, 1.1
la **línea** line
**la línea aérea** airline
**la línea ecuatorial** equator
**la línea paralela** parallel line
**la línea telefónica** telephone line
el **lípido** lipid, fat
**líquido(a)** liquid
**lírico(a)** lyric
la **lista** list
**listo(a)** ready; clever, **5.1**
la **litera** berth, 13.2; **1.2**
**literal** literal
**literario(a)** literary
la **literatura** literature, 2.1
el **litro** liter
la **llamada larga** long distance call, **3.2**
la **llamada telefónica** telephone call, **3.2**
**hacer una llamada telefónica** to make a (telephone) call, 3.2
**poner la llamada** to put the call through
**llamado(a)** called
**llamar** to call; to telephone, **3.2**
**llamarse** to be named, to call oneself, 12.1
la **llanta** tire, **11.1**
**la llanta de recambio (repuesto)** spare tire, **11.1**
la **llanura** plain, **7.2**
la **llave** key, **6.1**
la **llegada** arrival, arriving, 11.1
**llegar** to arrive, 4.1
**llenar** to fill, fill out
**llenar un crucigrama** to do a crossword puzzle, **5.1**
**llenar el formulario** to fill out the form, **8.2**
**lleno(a)** full
**llevar** to carry, 3.1; to wear, 3.2; to bring, 6.1; to bear; to have (subtitles, ingredients, etc.); to take, 8.1
**llover (ue)** to rain
**Llueve.** It's raining., 9.1
la **lluvia** rain
**lo** it; him *(m. sing.) (pron.)*
**lo que** what, that which
**local** local, 13.2; **1.2**
la **loción: la loción bronceadora** suntan lotion, 9.1
**loco(a)** insane
el **lodo** mud
**lógico(a)** logical
**los** them *(m. pl.) (pron.)*
el **loto** lotto
las **luces** headlights, **11.1**
**luchar** to fight
**luego** later; then, BV
**¡Hasta luego!** See you later!, BV
el **lugar** place
**tener lugar** to take place, **8.1**
**lujo: de lujo** deluxe
**lujoso(a)** luxurious
la **luna** moon
la **luna de miel** honeymoon
**lunares: con lunares** with polka dots
el **lunes** Monday, BV
la **luz** light
**la luz roja** red light, **11.2**

la **madera** wood
la **madre** mother, 6.1
**madrileño(a)** native of Madrid
la **madrina** godmother
el/la **maestro(a)** teacher
**magnífico(a)** magnificent
el **maíz** corn, 14.2; **2.2**
**mal** bad, 14.2; **2.2**
**estar de mal humor** to be in a bad mood, 8.1
**Hace mal tiempo.** The weather's bad., 9.1
la **maleta** suitcase, 11.1
el/la **maletero(a)** trunk (of a car), 11.1; porter, 13.1; **1.1**
**malhumorado(a)** bad-tempered
**malo(a)** bad, 2.1
**sacar una nota mala** to get a bad grade, 4.2
la **mamá** mom
el **mambo** mambo
**mandar** to send, **3.1**; to order
**manejar** to drive, **11.1**
la **manera** way, manner, 1.1
**de ninguna manera** by no means, 1.1
la **manga** sleeve, **4.1**
**de manga corta (larga)** short- (long-) sleeved, **4.1**
el **maní** peanut
la **mano** hand, 7.1
**dar la mano** to shake hands
la **mano de obra** workforce
la **manta** blanket, **6.2**
el **mantel** tablecloth, 14.1; **2.1**
**mantener** to maintain
**mantenerse en forma** to keep in shape
la **mantequilla** butter, **10.2**
la **manzana** apple, 5.2
el **manzano** apple tree, **9.2**
**mañana** tomorrow, BV
**¡Hasta mañana!** See you tomorrow!, BV
la **mañana** morning
**de la mañana** A.M. (time), 2.2
**por la mañana** in the morning
el **mapa** map
el **maquillaje** makeup, 12.1
**ponerse el maquillaje** to put one's makeup on, 12.1
**maquillarse** to put one's makeup on, 12.1
la **máquina** machine, device
**la máquina de lavar** washing machine, **12.1**
**prender la máquina** to turn (a device) on, **3.1**
el **mar** sea, 9.1
**el mar Caribe** Caribbean Sea
**maravilloso(a)** marvelous
el **marcador** marker, 3.1
**marcar** to dial, **3.2**
**marcar el número** to dial the number, **3.2**
**marcar un tanto** to score a point, 7.1
**marchar** to march
el **marfil** ivory
el **marido** husband, 6.1
el/la **marino(a)** sailor
los **mariscos** shellfish, 5.2; **10.2**
**marrón: de color marrón** brown, 3.2
el **martes** Tuesday, BV
**marzo** March, BV
**más** more, 2.2
**más tarde** later
**más o menos** more or less
la **masa** mass
la **máscara de oxígeno** oxygen mask, **7.1**
**matar** to kill
las **matemáticas** mathematics, 2.1
la **materia** matter, subject; material
**la materia prima** raw material
el **material** supply, 3.1; material
**los materiales escolares** school supplies, 3.1
el **matrimonio** marriage
**máximo(a)** maximum, **11.2**
**la velocidad máxima** speed limit, **11.2**
el/la **maya** Maya
**mayo** May, BV
la **mayonesa** mayonnaise, **4.2**
**mayor** greater, greatest; elderly, older
**la mayor parte** the greater part, the most
la **mayoría** majority
**me** me *(pron.)*
el/la **mecánico(a)** mechanic
la **medalla** medal
**media** average
**y media** half-past (time)
**mediano(a)** medium, **4.1**
la **medianoche** midnight
las **medias** stockings, pantyhose
el **medicamento** medicine (drugs), 8.2
la **medicina** medicine (discipline), 8.2; medicine
el/la **médico(a)** doctor, 8.2
la **medida** measurement
el **medio** medium, means
**el medio de transporte** means of transportation
**medio(a)** half, 5.2; average
**media hora** half an hour
el **medio ambiente** environment
el **mediodía** noon
**medir (i, i)** to measure
la **mejilla** cheek, **8.1**
los **mejillones** mussels, **10.2**
**mejor** better
**el/la mejor** the best
**melancólico(a)** melancholic
el **melocotón** peach
la **memoria** memory
**mencionar** to mention
**menor** lesser, least

la **menora** menorah, **13.2**
**menos** less, fewer
**a menos que** unless
**menos cuarto** a quarter to (the hour)
el **mensaje** message, **3.2**
**dejar un mensaje** to leave a message, **3.2**
la **mensualidad** monthly installment
**mentiroso(a)** lying
el **menú** menu, 5.1
el **mercadeo** marketing
el **mercado** market, 5.2
la **mercancía** merchandise, **14.1**
el **merengue** merengue
la **merienda** snack, 4.2
**tomar una merienda** to have a snack, 4.2
la **mermelada** jam, marmalade
el **mes** month, BV
la **mesa** table, 5.1; plateau
la **mesera** waitress, 5.1
el **mesero** waiter, 5.1
la **meseta** plateau, **7.2**
la **mesita** tray table, **7.1**
el/la **mestizo(a)** mestizo
el **metabolismo** metabolism
el **metal: instrumentos de metal** brass (instruments in orchestra)
**meter** to put, place, 7.1; to put in, insert, **3.1**
**meter un gol** to score a goal, 7.1
el **método** method
la **métrica** metrics
el **metro** subway, 10.1; meter, **7.2**
**mexicano(a)** Mexican, 1.1
**mexicanoamericano(a)** Mexican American
la **mezcla** mixture
**mi** my
**mí** me
el **microbio** microbe
**microscópico(a)** microscopic
el **microscopio** microscope
el **miedo** fear
**tener miedo** to be afraid
el **miembro** member, 4.2
**mientras** while
el **miércoles** Wednesday, BV
la **migración** migration
**mil** (one) thousand, 3.2
el **militar** soldier
la **milla** mile
el **millón** million
el/la **millonario(a)** millionaire
el/la **mimo** mime, **5.2**
la **miniatura** miniature
la **miniaturización** miniaturization
el **ministerio** ministry
el **minuto** minute
**mirar** to look at, watch, 3.1
**mirarse** to look at oneself, 12.1
**¡Mira!** Look!
el/la **mirón(ona)** spectator
la **miseria** poverty
**mismo(a)** same, 2.1; myself, yourself, him/her/itself, ourselves, yourselves, themselves
el **misterio** mystery
**misterioso(a)** mysterious
la **mitad** half
la **mitología** mythology
**mixto(a)** co-ed (school)
la **mochila** backpack, 3.1; knapsack, 12.2
la **moción** motion
la **moda** style
**de moda** in style
la **modalidad** mode, type
el/la **modelo** model
el **módem** modem
la **moderación** moderation
**moderno(a)** modern
el **modo** manner, way
**el modo de expresión** means of expression
el **molino de viento** windmill
el **momento** moment
el **monasterio** monastery
la **moneda** coin, currency, **3.2**
el **monitor** monitor, computer screen, **3.1**
el **mono** monkey, **5.2**
**monocelular** single-celled
el **monstruo** monster
la **montaña** mountain, 9.2
la **montaña rusa** roller coaster, **5.2**
**montañoso(a)** mountainous
**montar (caballo)** horseback ride
el **monumento** monument
**moreno(a)** dark, brunette, 1.1
**morir (ue, u)** to die
el/la **moro(a)** Moor
**morrón: el pimiento morrón** sweet pepper
la **mortalidad** mortality
el **mostrador** counter, 11.1
**mostrar (ue)** to show
el **motivo** reason, motive; theme
el **motor** motor
**mover (ue)** to move
el **movimiento** movement
el/la **mozo(a)** porter (train station) 13.1; **1.1**; bellman (hotel), **6.1**
la **muchacha** girl, 1.1
el **muchacho** boy, 1.1
**mucho(a)** a lot; many, 2.1
**Mucho gusto.** Nice to meet you.
**mudarse** to move
los **muebles** furniture
la **muerte** death
la **mujer** wife, 6.1
la **muleta** crutch, **8.2**
la **multa** fine
**multinacional** multinational
la **multiplicación** multiplication
**multiplicar** to multiply
**mundial** worldwide, (related to the) world

**la Copa mundial** World Cup
**la Serie mundial** World Series
el **mundo** world
**todo el mundo** everyone
la **muñeca** wrist, **4.1**
el **mural** mural, 10.2
el/la **muralista** muralist
la **muralla** wall
**muscular** muscular
el **museo** museum, 10.2
la **música** music, 2.2
el/la **músico(a)** musician
**muy** very, BV
**muy bien** very well, BV

**nacer** to be born, **13.1**
**nacido(a)** born
**nacional** national
la **nacionalidad** nationality, 1.2
**¿de qué nacionalidad?** what nationality?
**nada** nothing, 5.2
**De nada.** You're welcome., BV
**Nada más.** Nothing else., 5.2
**Por nada.** You're welcome., BV
**nadar** to swim, 9.1
**nadie** no one
la **naranja** orange, 5.2
el **narcótico** narcotic
la **nariz** nose, **8.1**
la **narración** narration
**narrar** to narrate
la **natación** swimming, 9.1
**natural: los recursos naturales** natural resources, 2.1
**las ciencias naturales** natural sciences
la **naturaleza** nature
la **navaja** razor, 12.1
**navegar** to navigate
**navegar por la red** to surf the Net
la **Navidad** Christmas, **13.2**
**el árbol de Navidad** Christmas tree, **13.2**
**¡Feliz Navidad!** Merry Christmas!, **13.2**
**necesario(a)** necessary
la **necesidad** necessity
**necesitar** to need, 3.1
**negativo(a)** negative
**negro(a)** black, 3.2
**nervioso(a)** nervous, 8.1
el **neumático** tire, **11.1**
**nevar (ie)** to snow, 9.2
la **nevera** refrigerator, **10.1**
la **nieta** granddaughter, 6.1
el **nieto** grandson, 6.1
la **nieve** snow, 9.2
**ninguno(a)** not any, none
**de ninguna manera** by no means, 1.1
el/la **niño(a)** child
**los niños desamparados** homeless children
el **nivel** level
**el nivel del mar** sea level
**no** no, BV
**No hay de qué.** You're welcome., BV
**no hay más remedio** there's no other alternative
**noble** noble
la **noche** night, evening
**Buenas noches.** Good night., BV
**de la noche** P.M. (time), 2.2
**esta noche** tonight, 9.2
**por la noche** in the evening, at night
la **Nochebuena** Christmas Eve, **13.2**
la **Nochevieja** New Year's Eve, **13.2**
**nombrar** to mention
el **nombre** name
**¿a nombre de quién?** in whose name?, 14.2; **2.2**
la **noria** Ferris wheel, **5.2**
el **noroeste** northwest
el **norte** north
**norteamericano(a)** North American
**nos** (to) us *(pl. pron.)*
**nosotros(as)** we, 2.2
la **nota** grade, 4.2
**la nota buena (alta)** good (high) grade, 4.2
**la nota mala (baja)** bad (low) grade, 4.2
**sacar una nota buena (mala)** to get a good (bad) grade, 4.2
**notable** notable
**notar** to note
las **noticias** news, 6.2
**novecientos(as)** nine hundred, 3.2
la **novela** novel
el/la **novelista** novelist
**noveno(a)** ninth, 6.2
**noventa** ninety, 2.2
la **novia** bride, **13.1**; fiancée, girlfriend
**noviembre** November, BV
el **novio** groom, **13.1**; fiancé, boyfriend
los **novios** bride and groom, newlyweds, **13.1**
la **nube** cloud, 9.1
**Hay nubes.** It's cloudy., 9.1
**nublado(a)** cloudy, 9.1
**nuestro(a)** our
**nueve** nine, BV
**nuevo(a)** new
**de nuevo** again
el **número** number, 1.2; size (shoes), 3.2
**el número de teléfono** telephone number, **3.2**
**el número del asiento** seat number, 11.1

**el número del vuelo** flight number, 11.1
**el número equivocado** wrong number
**numeroso(a)** numerous
**nunca** never
**nupcial** nuptial, wedding
la **nutrición** nutrition

**o** or
**o sea** in other words
el **objetivo** objective
el **objeto** object
la **obligación** obligation
**obligatorio(a): el curso obligatorio** required course
la **obra** work
**la obra de arte** work of art
**la obra dramática** play
**la obra teatral** play, 10.2
el/la **obrero(a)** worker, **9.1**
la **observación** observation
el/la **observador(a)** observer
**observar** to observe
el **obstáculo** obstacle
**obtener** to obtain
**obvio(a)** obvious
la **ocasión** occasion
**occidental** western
el **océano** ocean
**ochenta** eighty, 2.2
**ocho** eight, BV
**ochocientos(as)** eight hundred, 3.2
**octavo(a)** eighth, 6.2
**octubre** October, BV
**ocupado(a)** taken, 5.1; busy (phone); occupied, **7.1**
**ocurrir** to happen
el **oeste** west
**oficial** official
la **oficina** office, **9.1**
el **oficio** trade, **14.1**
**ofrecer** to offer, **14.2**
la **oftalmología** ophthalmology
el/la **oftalmólogo(a)** ophthalmologist
el **oído** ear, **4.1**
**oír** to hear
**oír el tono** to hear the dial tone, **3.2**
**ojalá** I hope, **14.1**
el **ojo** eye, 8.2
la **ola** wave, 9.1
el **óleo** oil (religious)
la **oliva: el aceite de oliva** olive oil
la **olla** pot, **10.1**
**once** eleven, BV
la **oncología** oncology
el/la **oncólogo(a)** oncologist
la **onza** ounce
**opcional: el curso opcional** elective course
la **ópera** opera
el/la **operador(a)** operator
**operar** to operate
la **opereta** operetta
**opinar** to think, to express an opinion, **10.2**
la **opinión** opinion
la **oportunidad** opportunity
**oprimir** to push
**opuesto(a)** opposite
**oralmente** orally
la **orden** order (restaurant), 5.1
el **ordenador** computer, **3.1**
la **oreja** ear, **4.1**
el **orfanato** orphanage
el **organillo** organ
el **organismo** organism
**organizar** to organize
el **órgano** organ
**oriental** eastern
el **origen** origin
**original: en versión original** in its original (language) version, 10.1
la **orilla** bank (of a river, lake, etc.)
**a orillas de** on the shores of
el **oro** gold
**de oro** (made of) gold, **4.1**
la **orquesta** orchestra, **13.1**
**la orquesta sinfónica** symphony orchestra
la **ortiga** nettle
la **ortopedia** orthopedics
**oscuro(a)** dark
la **ostra** oyster, **10.2**
**otavaleño(a)** of or from Otavalo (Ecuador)
el **otoño** autumn, BV
**otro(a)** other, another
el **oxígeno** oxygen
**¡oye!** listen!

**P**

la **paciencia** patience
el/la **paciente** patient
el **padre** father, 6.1
**el padre (religioso)** father (religious)
**los padres** parents, 6.1
el **padrino** godfather; best man, **13.1**
**los padrinos** godparents
**pagar** to pay, 3.1
**pagar en la caja** to pay at the cashier, 3.1
**pagar la factura** to pay the bill, **6.1**
la **página** page
**la página Web** Web page
el **pago** payment
**el pago mensual** monthly payment
el **país** country, 11.2
**el país extranjero** foreign country
el **paisaje** landscape
la **paja** straw, **13.2**
el **pájaro** bird
el **paje** page (wedding)
la **palabra** word
el **palacio** palace
la **palma** palm tree

# Spanish-English Dictionary

el **pan** bread, **4.2**
**el pan dulce** sweet roll, 5.1
**el pan tostado** toast, 5.2
la **panadería** bakery, **4.2**
**panameño(a)** Panamanian, 2.1
**panamericano(a)** Panamerican
el **panqueque** pancake
la **pantalla** screen (movies), 10.1; computer monitor, **3.1**
**la pantalla de salidas y llegadas** arrival and departure screen, 11.1
el **pantalón** pants, trousers, 3.2
**el pantalón corto** shorts, 3.2
el **pañuelo** handkerchief, **4.1**
la **papa** potato, 5.1
**las papas fritas** French fries, 5.1
el **papá** dad
la **papaya** papaya, **10.2**
el **papel** paper, 3.1; role, part, **5.1**
**el papel higiénico** toilet paper, 12.2
**la hoja de papel** sheet of paper, 3.1
la **papelería** stationery store, 3.1
el **paquete** package, 5.2
**par: número par** even number
el **par** pair, **4.1**
**el par de tenis** pair of tennis shoes, 3.2
**para** for
**¿para cuándo?** for when?, 14.2; **2.2**
el **parabrisas** windshield, **11.1**
la **parada** stop, 13.2; **1.2**
**la parada de bus** bus stop, **9.1**
el **parador** inn
el **paraíso** paradise
**parar** to stop, to block, 7.1
**parcial: a tiempo parcial** part-time *(adj.)*, **14.2**
**pardo(a)** brown
**parear** to pair, match
**parecer** to look like; to seem, **8.1**
**parecido(a)** similar
la **pared** wall
la **pareja** couple
el/la **pariente** relative, 6.1
el **parque** park, **5.2**
**el parque de atracciones** amusement park, **5.2**
el **parquímetro** parking meter, **11.2**
el **párrafo** paragraph
la **parrilla** grill, **10.1**
la **parte** part, **8.1**
**¿De parte de quién?** Who's calling?, **3.2**
**la mayor parte** the greatest part, the most
**la parte superior** upper part
**por todas partes** everywhere
**particular** private, 6.2
**la casa particular** private house, 6.2
**particularmente** especially
la **partida** departure
el **partido** game, match, 7.1
el **pasado** the past
**pasado(a)** past; last
**el (año) pasado** last (year)
el/la **pasajero(a)** passenger, 11.1
el **pasaporte** passport, 11.1
**pasar** to pass, 7.2; to spend; to happen
**Lo están pasando muy bien.** They're having a good time., 12.2
**pasar por** to go through, 11.1
**pasar el tiempo** to spend time, 5.1
**¿Qué te pasa?** What's the matter (with you)?, 8.1
el **pasatiempo** hobby, **5.1**
el **pase** pass (permission)
**pasear a caballo** to go horseback riding
el **pasillo** aisle, 13.2; **1.2**
el **paso** step
la **pasta (crema) dentífrica** toothpaste, 12.2
el **pastel** pastry, **4.2**; cake, **13.1**
la **pastelería** bakery, **4.2**
la **pastilla** pill, 8.2
**la pastilla de jabón** bar of soap, 12.2
la **patata** potato, **10.1**
el **patinaje lineal** roller blading
el **patrón** pattern
**pavimentado(a)** paved
el **pavimento** pavement
el **payaso** clown, **5.2**
el **peaje** toll, **11.2**
**la garita de peaje** tollbooth, **11.2**
el **peatón** pedestrian, **9.1**
el **pecho** chest, **8.1**
el **pedacito** little piece, **10.2**
el **pedazo** piece
el/la **pediatra** pediatrician
la **pediatría** pediatrics
**pedir (i, i)** to ask for, 14.1; **2.1**
**pedir la cuenta** to ask for the bill, **6.1**
**pedir prestado** to borrow
el **peinado** hairdo
**peinarse** to comb one's hair, 12.1
el **peine** comb, 12.1
**pelar** to peel, **10.2**
la **película** film, movie, 6.2
**ver una película** to see a film, 10.1
el **peligro** danger
**peligroso(a)** dangerous
**pelirrojo(a)** redheaded
el **pelo** hair, 12.1
la **pelota** ball (tennis, baseball, etc.), 7.2
**la pelota vasca** jai alai
el/la **pelotari** jai alai player
la **peluca** wig
la **peluquería** hair salon, **12.1**
el/la **peluquero(a)** hair stylist, **12.1**

el **pendiente** earring, **4.1**
la **península** peninsula
el **pensamiento** thought
**pensar (ie)** to think
la **pensión** boarding house, 12.2
**peor** worse, worst
**el/la peor** the worst
el **pepino** cucumber, **10.1**
**pequeño(a)** small, 2.1
la **pera** pear, **9.2**
el **peral** pear tree, **9.2**
la **percha** clothes hanger, **6.2**
la **percusión** percussion
**perder (ie)** to lose, 7.1; to miss, 10.2
**perder el autobús** (la guagua, el camión) to miss the bus, 10.2
**perdón** excuse me
el/la **peregrino(a)** pilgrim
**perezoso(a)** lazy, 1.1
**perfeccionar** to perfect
el **periódico** newspaper, 6.2
el **período** period
el **permiso de conducir** driver's license, **11.1**
**permitir** to permit, 11.1
**pero** but
el **perrito** puppy
el **perro** dog, 6.1
la **persona** person, 1.2
el **personaje** character
el **personal** personnel, **14.2**
la **personalidad** personality
**personalmente** personally
**pertenecer** to belong
**peruano(a)** Peruvian
la **pesa** weight
**pesado(a)** heavy
**pesar** to weigh, **12.2**
la **pescadería** fish market, **4.2**
el **pescado** fish, 5.2
la **peseta** former monetary unit of Spain
el **peso** peso (monetary unit of several Latin American countries), BV; weight
la **petición** petition
el **petróleo** petroleum, oil
**petrolero(a)** oil (relating to)
el **piano** piano
la **picadura** sting, **8.1**
**picar** to sting, **8.1**; to dice, **10.2**
el/la **pícher** pitcher, 7.2
el **pico** peak, **7.2**
**y pico** just after (time)
el **pie** foot, 7.1; down payment
**a pie** on foot, 4.1
**al pie de** at the foot of
**de pie** standing
la **piedra** stone
la **pierna** leg, 7.1
la **pieza** room; piece
la **píldora** pill, 8.2
el/la **piloto** pilot, 11.2
la **pimienta** pepper, 14.1; **2.1**
el **pimiento** bell pepper, **10.2**
el **pimiento morrón** sweet pepper
**pinchado(a)** flat
el **pincel** brush, paintbrush
la **pinta** pint
**pinta: tener buena pinta** to look good (food), **4.2**
**pintar** to paint, **14.1**
el/la **pintor(a)** painter
**pintoresco(a)** picturesque, **9.1**
la **pintura** painting
la **piragua** crushed ice with syrup over it, **5.2**
los **pirineos** Pyrenees
la **pirueta** pirouette
la **piscina** swimming pool, 9.1
el **piso** floor, 6.2, apartment
la **pista** (ski) slope, 9.2; runway, **7.2**
la **pizarra** chalkboard, 4.2
el **pizarrón** chalkboard, 4.2
la **pizca** pinch
la **pizza** pizza, BV
la **placa** license plate
la **plaga** plague, menace
la **plancha de vela** sailboard, 9.1
**practicar la plancha de vela** to go windsurfing, 9.1
**planchar** to iron, **12.1**
**planear** to plan
el **plano** plan, map, **9.1**
la **planta** floor, 6.2; plant
**la planta baja** ground floor, 6.2
**plástico(a)** plastic, **4.2**
**la bolsa de plástico** plastic bag, **4.2**
la **plata** money (income)
el **plátano** banana, plantain, 5.2
el **platillo** home plate, 7.2; saucer, 14.1; **2.1**
el **plato** plate, dish, 14.1; **2.1**
la **playa** beach, 9.1
**playera: la toalla playera** beach towel, 9.1
la **plaza** seat, 13.2; **1.2**; town square, **9.1**
**plazo: a corto (largo) plazo** short- (long-)term
**pleno: en pleno +** (noun) in the middle of (noun)
el/la **plomero(a)** plumber, **14.1**
**plomo: sin plomo** unleaded, **11.1**
la **pluma** pen, 3.1
la **población** population, people
**pobre** poor
el/la **pobre** the poor boy (girl)
el/la **pobretón(ona)** poor man (woman)
**poco(a)** little, few, 2.1
**un poco (de)** a little
**poder (ue)** to be able, 7.1
el **poema** poem
la **poesía** poetry
el/la **poeta** poet
el/la **policía** police officer
**policíaco(a): novela policíaca** detective fiction, mystery
**político(a)** political

el **pollo** chicken, 5.2
el **poncho** poncho, shawl, wrap
**poner** to put, 11.1
**poner en un yeso** to put a cast on, **8.2**
**poner la mesa** to set the table, 14.1; **2.1**
**ponerse** to put on, 12.1
**ponerse el maquillaje** to put one's makeup on, 12.1
**ponerse la ropa** to dress oneself, to put on clothes, 12.1
**popular** popular, 2.1
la **popularidad** popularity
**por** for
**por aquí** over here
**por ciento** percent
**por ejemplo** for example
**por eso** therefore, for this reason, that's why
**por favor** please, BV
**por fin** finally
**por hora** per hour
**por la noche** in the evening
**por lo general** in general
**Por nada.** You're welcome., BV
**por tierra** overland
**¿por qué?** why?
el **porche** porch
el **pordiosero** beggar
el **poroto** string bean
**porque** because
**portátil** portable
el/la **porteño(a)** inhabitant of Buenos Aires
la **portería** goal line, 7.1
el/la **portero(a)** goalkeeper, goalie, 7.1
**poseer** to possess
la **posibilidad** possibility
**posible** possible
la **posición** position
la **postal** postcard, **12.2**
el **postre** dessert, 5.1
el/la **practicante** nurse practitioner
**practicar** to practice
**practicar el surfing (la plancha de vela, etc.)** to go surfing (windsurfing, etc.), 9.1
el **precio** price
**precioso(a)** precious, beautiful
**preciso(a)** precise
**precolombino(a)** pre-Columbian
la **predicción** prediction
**predominar** to predominate
el **predominio** predominance
**preferir (ie, i)** to prefer
el **prefijo de país** country code, **3.2**
la **pregunta** question
**preguntar** to ask (a question)
el **premio: el Premio Nóbel** Nobel Prize
**prender** to turn on, **3.1**
**prender la máquina** to turn (a device) on, **3.1**
la **preparación** preparation
**preparar** to prepare
la **presencia** presence
la **presentación** presentation
**presentar** to show (movie); to present
**presente** present *(adj.)*
el/la **presidente** president
la **presión** pressure, **11.1**
**la presión arterial** blood pressure, **8.2**
**prestado: pedir prestado** to borrow
el **préstamo** loan
**prestar: prestar atención** to pay attention, 4.2
el **prestigio** prestige
**prevalecer** to prevail
**primario(a): la escuela primaria** elementary school
la **primavera** spring, BV
**primero(a)** first, BV
**en primera (clase)** first-class, 13.1; **1.1**
**los primeros auxilios** first aid
el/la **primo(a)** cousin, 6.1
**primordial** fundamental
la **princesa** princess
**principal** main, principal
**principalmente** mainly
el/la **principiante** beginner, 9.2
**prisa: a toda prisa** as fast as possible
**privado(a)** private
**la casa privada** private house, 6.2
**probable** probable
**probarse (ue)** to try on, **4.1**
el **problema** problem
**procesar** to process
la **procesión** procession
el **proceso** process
**proclamar** to proclaim
**pródigo** prodigal
la **producción** production
**producido(a)** produced
**producir** to produce
el **producto** product, 5.2
**los productos congelados** frozen food, 5.2
la **profesión** profession, **14.1**
el/la **profesor(a)** teacher, professor, 2.1
**profundo(a)** deep
el **programa** program
el/la **programador(a) de informática** computer programmer, **14.1**
el **progreso** progress
**prohibido(a)** forbidden, **11.2**
la **promesa** promise
la **promoción** promotion
**promover (ue)** to promote
el **pronombre** pronoun
el **pronóstico** forecast
**pronto: ¡Hasta pronto!** See you soon!, BV
la **propaganda** publicity, advertising

la **propina** tip, 14.1; **2.1**
**propio(a)** (one's) own
la **prosa** prose
**próspero(a): ¡Próspero Año Nuevo!** Happy New Year, **13.2**
el/la **protagonista** protagonist
la **protección** protection
**protector(a): la crema protectora** sunblock, 9.1
la **proteína** protein
**protestar** to protest
el **protoplasma** protoplasm
el/la **proveedor(a)** provider
**proveer** to provide
la **provisión** provision
**próximo(a)** next, 13.2; **1.2**
**en la próxima parada** at the next stop, 13.2; **1.2**
**proyectar** to project, 10.1
el **proyecto** project
el/la **psiquiatra** psychiatrist
la **psiquiatría** psychiatry
**publicar** to publish
el **público** audience, 10.2
el **pueblo** town, **9.2**
**los pueblos jóvenes** shantytowns (Peru)
el **puerco** pork
la **puerta** gate, 11.1; door, **6.1**
**la puerta de salida** departure gate, 11.1
**puertorriqueño(a)** Puerto Rican
**pues** well
el **puesto** market stall, **4.2**; position, **14.2**
la **pulgada** inch
**pulsar: pulsar el botón** to push the button, **3.1**
la **pulsera** bracelet, **4.1**
el **pulso: tomar el pulso** to take one's pulse, **8.2**
el **punto** stitch, **8.1**; dot, point
**en punto** on the dot, sharp, 4.1
**los puntos cardinales** cardinal points
**poner puntos** to give (someone) stitches
**puntual** punctual
el **puré de papas** mashed potatoes
**puro(a)** pure

**que** who, that
**¿qué?** what? how?
**qué** what; how, BV
**¡Qué absurdo!** How absurd!
**¡Qué enfermo(a) estoy!** I'm so sick!
**¿Qué tal?** How are you?, BV
**¿Qué te pasa?** What's the matter (with you)?, 8.2
**quechua** Quechuan
**quedar** to remain, 7.1
**quedar: No me queda(n) bien.** It (They) doesn't (don't) look good on (fit) me., **4.1**
los **quehaceres** chores
**querer (ie)** to want, wish; to love
el **queso** cheese, 5.1
el **quetzal** quetzal (currency of Guatemala)
**¿quién?** who?, 1.1
**¿De parte de quién?** Who is calling?, **3.2**
**¿quiénes?** who? *(pl.)*, 2.1
la **química** chemistry, 2.2
**químico(a)** chemical
**quince** fifteen, BV
la **quinceañera** fifteen-year-old (girl)
**quinientos(as)** five hundred, 3.2
**quinto(a)** fifth, 6.2
el **quiosco** newsstand, 13.1; **1.1**
el **quirófano** operating room
**Quisiera...** I would like . . . , 14.2; **2.2**
**quitar** to take off, remove, **10.2**
**quizás** perhaps, **14.2**

el **radiador** radiator, **11.1**
la **radiografía** X-ray, **8.2**
la **raíz** root
**rallar** to grate, **10.2**
la **rama** branch
la **ranura** disk drive, **3.1**; slot, **3.2**
**rápidamente** quickly
**rápido** quickly
la **raqueta** racket (sports), 9.1
**raro(a)** rare
el **rascacielos** skyscraper, **9.1**
el **rato** while
el **ratón** mouse (computer), **3.1**
la **raya** part (in hair), **12.1**
**rayas: a rayas** striped
los **rayos equis** X-rays
la **razón** reason
**razonable** reasonable
la **reacción** reaction
**real** royal
**realista** realistic
el/la **realista** realist
**realmente** really
la **rebanada** slice, **4.2**
**rebanar** to slice, **10.2**
**rebotar** to rebound
la **recámara** bedroom, 6.2
la **recepción** front desk (hotel), 6.1; admissions (hospital), 8.2; reception (party)
el/la **recepcionista** hotel clerk, **6.1**
el/la **receptor(a)** catcher, 7.2
la **receta** prescription, 8.2; recipe, **10.2**
**recetar** to prescribe, 8.2
**recibir** to receive, 5.1
el **reciclaje** recycling
**recién** recently
**reciente** recent

**recitar** to recite
**reclamar** to claim (luggage), 11.2
el **reclamo de equipaje** baggage claim, 11.2
**reclutar** to recruit
**recoger** to pick up
**recoger el equipaje** to claim one's luggage, 11.2
la **recomendación** recommendation
**recomendar (ie)** to recommend
**reconocer** to recognize
**recordar (ue)** to remember
**recorrer** to travel through
el **recorrido** trip, distance traveled
**de largo recorrido** long distance
el **recreo** recreation
el **rectángulo** rectangle
el **recuerdo** memory, recollection
la **recuperación: la sala de recuperación** recovery room
el **recurso: los recursos naturales** natural resources
**el departamento de recursos humanos** human resources department, **14.2**
la **red** net, 9.1
**navegar por la red** to surf the Net
**reducido(a)** reduced (price)
**reducir** to set (bone), **8.2**
**reemplazar** to replace
**referir (ie, i)** to refer
**reflejar** to reflect
el **reflejo** reflection
**reflexionar** to reflect
la **reforestación** reforestation
el **refresco** drink, beverage, 5.1
el **refrigerador** refrigerator, **10.1**
el **refugio** refuge
**regalar** to give
el **regalo** gift, 6.1
la **región** region
**regional** regional
el **regionalismo** regionalism
**registrar** to register
la **regla** rule
**regresar** to return
el **regreso** return
**el viaje de regreso** return trip, trip back
**regular** regular, average, 2.2
la **reina** queen
**reír** to laugh
la **relación** relation
**relacionado(a)** related
**relativamente** relatively
**religioso(a)** religious
**rellenar** to fill
el **reloj** watch, **4.1**; clock, **13.2**
**remar** to row, **5.2**
el **remedio** solution
**renombrado(a)** well-known
**rentar** to rent
**renunciar** to renounce, give up
**reparar** to repair
**repentinamente** suddenly
**repetir (i, i)** to repeat; to take seconds (meal)
el **reportaje** report
la **representación** performance (theater), 10.2
**dar una representación** to put on a performance, 10.2
el/la **representante** representative
**representar** to represent
**representativo(a)** representative
la **república** republic
la **República Dominicana** Dominican Republic
**requerir (ie, i)** to require, **14.1**
el **requisito** requirement
la **reservación** reservation, **6.1**
**reservado(a)** reserved, 13.2; **1.2**
**reservar** to reserve, 14.2; **2.2**
**resfriado(a): estar resfriado(a)** to have a cold, 8.1
la **residencia: la residencia para estudiantes** student housing, dormitory, **3.2**
el/la **residente** resident
**resolver (ue)** to solve
el **respaldo** back (of seat), **7.1**
la **respiración** breathing
**respirar** to breathe
**responder** to respond
la **responsabilidad** responsibility
**responsabilizarse** to make oneself responsible
la **respuesta** answer
**restar** to subtract
el **restaurante** restaurant, 14.1; **2.1**
**restaurar** to restore
el **resto** rest, remainder
los **restos** remains
el **resultado** result
la **retina** retina
el **retintín** jingle
**retirar del fuego** to remove from the heat (stove), **10.1**
el **retraso: con retraso** with a delay, late, 13.2; **1.2**
el **retrato** portrait
la **reunión** gathering
**reunirse** to get together
**revisar** to inspect, 11.1; to check
**revisar el boleto** to check the ticket, 11.1
**revisar el aceite** to check the oil (car), **11.1**
el/la **revisor(a)** (train) conductor, 13.2; **1.2**
la **revista** magazine, 6.2
la **revolución** revolution

**revolver (ue)** to turn around; to stir, **10.1**
el **rey** king
los **Reyes Magos** Three Wise Men, **13.2**
**el Día de los Reyes** Epiphany (January 6), **13.2**
**rico(a)** rich; delicious, 14.2; **2.2**
el/la **rico(a)** rich person
**riguroso(a)** rigorous
el **río** river, **7.2**
el **ritmo** rhythm
el **rito** ritual
el **rival** rival
la **roca** rock
**rodar (ue)** to roll
la **rodilla** knee, 7.1
**rogar (ue)** to beg, to plead
**rojo(a)** red, 3.2
el **rol** role
el **rollo de papel higiénico** roll of toilet paper, 12.2
el/la **romano(a)** Roman
**romántico(a)** romantic
**romperse** to break, **8.1**
la **ropa** clothing, 3.2
**la ropa interior** underwear, **4.1**
**la ropa para caballeros (señoras)** men's (women's) clothing, **4.1**
**la ropa sucia** dirty laundry, **12.1**
**la tienda de ropa** clothing store, 3.2
la **rosa** rose
**rosado(a)** pink, 3.2
el **rótulo** sign, **11.2**
**rubio(a)** blond(e), 1.1
las **ruedas: la silla de ruedas** wheelchair, **8.2**
la **ruina** ruin
el **rumor** rumor
la **ruta** route
la **rutina** routine, 12.1
**rutinario(a)** routine *(adj.)*

## S

el **sábado** Saturday, BV
la **sábana** sheet, **6.2**
el/la **sabelotodo** know-it-all
**saber** to know (how), 11.2
**sabio(a)** wise
**sabroso(a)** delicious
**sacar** to get, 4.2; to take out, **3.1**
**sacar un billete** to buy a ticket
**sacar una nota buena (mala)** to get a good (bad) grade, 4.2
el **sacerdote** priest
el **saco** jacket, **4.1**
**el saco de dormir** sleeping bag, 12.2
**sacrificar** to sacrifice
el **sacrificio** sacrifice
la **sal** salt, 14.1; **2.1**
la **sala** room; living room, 6.2
**la sala de clase** classroom, 4.1
**la sala de consulta** doctor's office
**la sala de emergencia** emergency room, **8.1**
**la sala de espera** waiting room, 13.1; **1.1**
**la sala de juegos** game arcade, **5.1**
**la sala de recuperación** recovery room
**la sala de salida** departure area, 11.1
**la sala de urgencias** emergency room
el **salario** salary
la **salchicha** sausage, **10.1**
el **saldo** balance (bank)
la **salida** departure, leaving, 11.1; exit, **11.2**
**la hora de salida** departure hour, 13.1; **1.1**
**la pantalla de llegadas y salidas** arrival and departure screen, 11.1
**la sala de salida** departure area, 11.1
**la salida de emergencia** emergency exit, **7.1**
**salir** to leave, 10.1; to go out; to turn out
**salir a tiempo** to leave on time, 11.1
**salir bien (en un examen)** to do well (on an exam), 10.1
**salir tarde** to leave late, 11.1
el **salón** hall, **13.1**; room
**el salón de clase** classroom, 4.1
**saltar** to jump
la **salud** health
**saludar** to greet
el **saludo** greeting, BV
**salvaje** wild
**salvar** to save
**salvo(a)** safe
la **sandalia** sandal, **4.1**
la **sandía** watermelon, **10.2**
el **sándwich** sandwich, BV
la **sangre** blood
**sano(a)** healthy
el **santo** saint
el/la **sartén** frying pan, **10.1**
**satisfacer** to satisfy
**satisfecho(a)** satisfied, **14.1**
el **saxofono** saxophone
**sazonar** to season
el **secador** hair dryer, **12.1**
**secar** to dry, **12.2**
la **sección de (no) fumar** (no) smoking section, 11.1
**seco(a)** dry
el/la **secretario(a)** secretary, **14.1**
el **secreto** secret
**secundario(a)** secondary
**la escuela secundaria** high school, 1.1

**sed: tener sed** to be thirsty, 14.1; **2.1**
el **sedán** sedan, **11.1**
la **sede** seat (of government)
**seguir (i, i)** to follow, to continue, **11.2**
**Sigue derecho.** Go straight.
**según** according to
**segundo(a)** second, 6.2
**el segundo tiempo** second half (soccer), 7.1
**en segunda (clase)** second-class, 13.1; **1.1**
la **seguridad** security, **7.1**
**el control de seguridad** security (airport), 11.1
el **seguro** insurance
**seguro(a): estar seguro(a)** to be sure
**seis** six, BV
**seiscientos(as)** six hundred, 3.2
la **selección** selection
**seleccionar** to select
el **sello** stamp, **5.1**
la **selva** jungle
el **semáforo** traffic light, **9.1**
la **semana** week, BV
**el fin de semana** weekend, BV
**el fin de semana pasado** last weekend
**la semana pasada** last week, 9.2
**sembrar** to sow, plant, **9.2**
el **semestre** semester
el/la **senador(a)** senator
**sencillo(a)** easy, simple
**el billete sencillo** one-way ticket, 13.1; **1.1**
**el cuarto sencillo** single room, **6.1**
la **senda** path, **5.2**
**caminar por la senda** to walk along the path, **5.2**
**sentarse (ie)** to sit down, 12.1
el **sentido** meaning, significance; direction, **11.2**
**el sentido contrario** opposite way, **11.2**
**en cada sentido** in either direction, **11.2**
**una calle de sentido único** one-way street, **11.2**
**sentir (ie, i)** to be sorry
**sentirse (ie, i) bien (mal)** to feel well (ill), **8.1**
la **señal de no fumar** no smoking sign, **7.1**
la **señal de tránsito** traffic sign
el **señor** sir, Mr., gentleman, BV
la **señora** Ms., Mrs., madam, BV
la **señorita** Miss, Ms., BV
**separado(a)** separated
**septiembre** September, BV
**séptimo(a)** seventh, 6.2
**ser** to be
**ser una lástima** to be a pity
el **ser: el ser humano** human being
**el ser viviente** living creature, being
la **serie** series
**la Serie mundial** World Series
**serio(a)** serious, 1.1
**en serio** seriously
el **servicio** service, tip, 5.1
**¿Está incluido el servicio?** Is the tip included?, 5.1
el **servicio de primeros auxilios** first aid service, paramedics, **8.1**
la **servilleta** napkin, 14.1; **2.1**
**servir (i, i)** to serve, 14.1; **2.1**
**¿En qué puedo servirle?** How may I help you?, **4.1**
**sesenta** sixty, 2.2
la **sesión** show (movies), 10.1
**setecientos(as)** seven hundred, 3.2
**setenta** seventy, 2.2
el **sexo** sex
**sexto(a)** sixth, 6.2
el **show** show
**si** if
**sí** yes
el **sida** AIDS
la **siembra** sowing
**siempre** always, 7.1
**de siempre y para siempre** eternally, forever
la **sierra** sierra, mountain range
**siete** seven, BV
el **siglo** century
el **significado** meaning
**significante** meaningful
**significar** to mean
**significativo(a)** significant
**siguiente** following
la **silla** chair
la **silla de ruedas** wheelchair, **8.2**
el **sillón** armchair, **6.2**
**similar** similar
**simpático(a)** nice, 1.2
**simple** simple
**sin** without
**sin escala** nonstop
**sincero(a)** sincere, 1.2
**singles** singles, 9.1
el **síntoma** symptom, 8.2
el **sirope** syrup
el/la **sirviente(a)** servant
el **sistema** system
**el sistema métrico** metric system
el **sitio** place
la **situación** situation
**situar** to situate
**sobre** on top of; over; on, about
**sobre todo** especially
el **sobre** envelope, **12.2**
**sobresaltar** to jump up
**sobrevolar** to fly over, **7.2**
la **sobrina** niece, 6.1
el **sobrino** nephew, 6.1
**social: las ciencias sociales** social sciences
la **sociedad** society

la **sociología** sociology
**socorrer** to help
el/la **socorrista** paramedic, **8.1**
el **socorro** help
el **sofá** sofa, **6.2**
el **sol** Peruvian coin; sun, 9.1
**Hace (Hay) sol.** It's sunny., 9.1
**tomar el sol** to sunbathe, 9.1
**solamente** only
el/la **soldado** soldier
**soler (ue)** to be accustomed to, tend to
la **solicitud de empleo** job application, **14.2**
**solitario(a)** solitary, lone
**sólo** only
**solo(a)** alone
**a solas** alone
**el café solo** black coffee, 5.1
**soltero(a)** single, bachelor
la **solución** solution
el **sombrero** hat
**sonar (ue)** to ring, **3.2**
el **sonido** sound
la **sonrisita** little smile
la **sopa** soup, 5.1
el **sorbete** sherbet, sorbet
el/la **sordo(a)** deaf person
**sorprender** to surprise
**sostener** to support
**su** his, her, their, your
**subir** to go up, 6.2; to board, to get on; to take up
**subir al tren** to get on, to board the train, 13.1; **1.1**
**subterráneo(a)** underground
el **subtítulo** subtitle, 10.1
**con subtítulos** with subtitles, 10.1
el **suburbio** suburb
**suceder** to happen
**suceso: el buen suceso** great event
**sucio(a)** dirty
**la ropa sucia** dirty laundry, **12.1**
la **sucursal** branch (office)
**sudamericano(a)** South American
el **sudoeste** southwest
el **suegro** father-in-law
el **suelo** ground
el **suelto** change, **12.2**
el **sueño** dream
la **suerte** luck
**¡Buena suerte!** Good luck!
el **suéter** sweater, **4.1**
**suficiente** enough
**sufrir** to suffer
la **sugerencia** suggestion
**sugerir (ie, i)** to suggest
la **Suiza** Switzerland
**sumar** to add
**súper** super (gas), **11.1**
la **superficie** surface
**superior: la escuela superior** high school
el **supermercado** supermarket, 5.2
la **superstición** superstition
**supuesto: por supuesto** of course
el **sur** south
**sureste** southeast
el **surf de nieve** snowboarding
el **surfing** surfing, 9.1
**practicar el surfing** to surf, 9.1
el **suroeste** southwest
el **surtido** assortment
**sus** their, your *(pl.)*, 6.1
**suspirar** to sigh
la **sustancia: la sustancia controlada** controlled substance
la **sutura** stitch

el **T-shirt** T-shirt, 3.2
la **tabla: la tabla hawaiana** surfboard, 9.1
el **tablero** board, 7.1; gameboard, **5.1**
**el tablero de llegadas** arrival board, 13.1; **1.1**
**el tablero de salidas** departure board, 13.1; **1.1**
**el tablero indicador** scoreboard, 7.1
la **tableta** pill, 8.2
el **taco** taco, BV
el **tacón** heel, **4.1**
**taíno(a)** Taino
la **tajada** slice, **4.2**
**tal: ¿Qué tal?** How are you?, BV
el **talento** talent, **14.1**
la **talla** size (clothing), 3.2
el **talón** luggage claim ticket, 11.1
el **talonario** checkbook
el **tamal** tamale, BV
el **tamaño** size, 3.2
**también** also
**tampoco** either
**tan** so
**tan... como** as . . . as, **8.2**
el **tango** tango
el **tanque** gas tank, **11.1**
**llenar el tanque de gasolina** to fill the tank with gas, **11.1**
el **tanto** point, 7.1
**marcar un tanto** to score a point
**tanto(a)** so much
**tanto(a)... como** as much . . . as
**tantos(as)... como** as many . . . as, **8.2**
**tapar** to cover, **10.2**
la **taquilla** box office, 10.1
**tardar** to take time
**tarda el viaje** the trip takes (+ time)
**tarde** late
la **tarde** afternoon
**Buenas tardes.** Good afternoon., BV
**esta tarde** this afternoon, 9.2

**por la tarde** in the afternoon
la **tarea** task
**hacer las tareas** to do one's homework, **3.1**
la **tarifa** fare, rate
la **tarjeta** card, 11.1; registration card (hotel), **6.1**
**la tarjeta de crédito** credit card, 14.1; **2.1**
**la tarjeta de embarque** boarding pass, 11.1
**la tarjeta de identidad estudiantil** student I.D. card
**la tarjeta postal** postcard, **12.2**
**la tarjeta telefónica** telephone card, **3.2**
la **tasa** rate
**la tasa de cambio** exchange rate, **12.2**
**la tasa de desempleo** unemployment rate
el **taxi** taxi, 11.1
la **taza** cup, 14.1; **2.1**
**te** you *(fam. pron.)*
el **té** tea, 5.1
**el té helado** iced tea, 5.1
**teatral** theatrical, 10.2
el **teatro** theater, 10.2
**salir del teatro** to leave the theater, 10.2
la **tecla** key (on keyboard), **3.2**
el **teclado** keyboard, **3.1**; telephone keypad, **3.2**
el/la **técnico(a)** technician, **8.2**
la **tecnología** technology
la **telecomunicación** telecommunication, **3.1**
**telefonear** to telephone
**telefónico(a)** (related to the) telephone
**la línea telefónica** telephone line
**la llamada telefónica** telephone call, **3.2**
el **teléfono** telephone
**el teléfono celular** cellular telephone, **3.2**
**el teléfono de botones** push-button telephone, **3.2**
**el teléfono público** public (pay) telephone, **3.2**
**hablar por teléfono** to talk on the phone
el **telesilla** chairlift, 9.2
el **telesquí** ski lift, 9.2
la **televisión** television, 6.2
el **televisor** television set, **6.2**
el **telón** curtain (stage), 10.2
el **tema** theme, subject
**temer** to fear
la **temperatura** temperature, 9.2
**templado(a)** temperate
**temprano** early, 12.1
el **tenedor** fork, 14.1; **2.1**
**tener (ie)** to have, 6.1
**tener un accidente** to have an accident, **8.1**
**tener... años** to be . . . years old, 6.1
**tener buena pinta** to look good, **4.2**
**tener cuidado** to be careful
**tener hambre** to be hungry, 14.1; **2.1**
**tener lugar** to take place, occur, **8.1**
**tener miedo** to be afraid
**tener que** to have to
**tener sed** to be thirsty, 14.1; **2.1**
el **tenis** tennis, 9.1
los **tenis** tennis shoes, 3.2
**el par de tenis** pair of tennis shoes, 3.2
el/la **tenista** tennis player
la **tensión arterial** blood pressure, **8.2**
**tercer(o)(a)** third, 6.2
la **terminal: la terminal de pasajeros** passenger terminal, **7.2**
**terminar** to end, finish, **3.1**
el **término** term
la **ternera** veal, 14.2; **2.2**
la **terraza** terrace (sidewalk café)
**terrible** terrible
el **terror** terror, fear
el **tétano** tetanus
la **tía** aunt, 6.1
el **ticket** ticket, 9.2
el **tiempo** time; weather, 9.1; half (game)
**a tiempo** on time, 11.1
**a tiempo completo (parcial)** full- (part-) time *(adj.)*, **14.2**
**el segundo tiempo** second half (game), 7.1
**pasar el tiempo** to spend (pass) time, **5.1**
la **tienda** store, 3.2
**la tienda de abarrotes** grocery store, **4.2**
**la tienda de departamentos** department store
**la tienda de ropa** clothing store, 3.2
**la tienda de ropa para caballeros** men's clothing store, **4.1**
**la tienda de ropa para señoras** women's clothing store, **4.1**
**la tienda de ultramarinos** grocery store, **4.2**
**la tienda de videos** video store
**tierno(a)** tender
la **tierra** land
**por tierra** by land, overland
el **tigre** tiger
las **tijeras** scissors, **12.1**
el **tilde** accent
**tímido(a)** timid, shy, 1.2
la **tintorería** dry cleaner, **12.1**
el/la **tintorero(a)** dry cleaner, **12.1**
el **tío** uncle, 6.1
**los tíos** aunt and uncle, 6.1
el **tiovivo** merry-go-round, **5.2**
**típicamente** typically
**típico(a)** typical

el **tipo** type
el **tipo de cambio** exchange rate, **12.2**
el **tique** ticket, **9.1**
**tirar** to kick, 7.1; to throw
**tirar el balón** to kick (throw) the ball, 7.2
el **título universitario** university degree, **14.1**
la **toalla** towel, **6.2**
**la toalla playera** beach towel, 9.1
el **tobillo** ankle, **8.1**
**tocar** to touch; to play (music)
**tocar la bocina** to honk the horn
**todavía** yet, still
**todo: todo el mundo** everyone
**todos(as)** everybody, 2.2; everything, all
**por todas partes** everywhere
**tomar** to take, 4.1
**tomar agua (leche, café)** to drink water (milk, coffee)
**tomar apuntes** to take notes, 4.2
**tomar el bus (escolar)** to take the (school) bus, 4.1
**tomar el desayuno** to eat breakfast, 12.1
**tomar el pulso** to take one's pulse, **8.2**
**tomar el sol** to sunbathe, 9.1
**tomar fotos** to take photos
**tomar la tensión (presión) arterial** to take one's blood pressure, **8.2**
**tomar un refresco** to have (drink) a beverage
**tomar un vuelo** to take a flight, 11.1
**tomar una ducha** to take a shower, 12.1
**tomar una merienda** to have a snack, 4.2
**tomar una radiografía** to take an X-ray
el **tomate** tomato
el **tomo** volume
la **tonelada** ton
el **tono** dial tone, **3.2**; hue
**tonto(a)** foolish
**torcerse (ue)** to twist, **8.1**
el **torniquete** turnstile, **9.1**
la **toronja** grapefruit, **10.1**
**torpe** stupid
la **torre: la torre de control** control tower, **7.2**
la **torta** cake, **13.1**
la **tortilla** tortilla, 5.1
la **tos: tener tos** to have a cough, 8.1
**toser** to cough, 8.1
la **tostada** toast
**tostadito(a)** sunburned, tanned
**tostado(a): el pan tostado** toast, 5.2
**tostar** to toast
el **tostón** fried plantain slice
**totalmente** totally, completely
**tóxico(a)** toxic
el/la **trabajador(a)** worker
**trabajar** to work, 3.2
**trabajar a tiempo completo** to work full-time, **14.2**
**trabajar a tiempo parcial** to work part-time, **14.2**
el **trabajo** work; job, **14.2**
**el trabajo a tiempo completo (parcial)** full-time (part-time) job, **14.2**
la **tradición** tradition
**tradicional** traditional
**traer** to bring, 14.1; **2.1**
el **tráfico** traffic
la **tragedia** tragedy
el **traje** suit, 3.2
**el traje de baño** bathing suit, 9.1
**el traje de gala** evening gown, dress
el **tramo** stretch
**tranquilo(a)** peaceful; calm; quiet
**transbordar** to transfer, 13.2; **1.2**
**transformar** to transform
**transmitir** to send, to transmit, **3.1**
el **transporte** transportation
**tras** after
**trasladar** to transfer, move
el **tratamiento** treatment
**tratar** to treat; to try
el **trayecto** stretch (of road)
**trece** thirteen, BV
**treinta** thirty, BV
**treinta y uno** thirty-one, 2.2
el **tren** train, 13.2; **1.2**
**el tren directo** non-stop train, 13.2; **1.2**
**el tren local** local train, 13.2; **1.2**
la **trenza** braid
**tres** three, BV
**trescientos(as)** three hundred, 3.2
la **tribu** tribe
el **tribunal** court, **14.1**
el **trigo** wheat, **9.2**
la **tripulación** crew, 11.2
**triste** sad, 8.1
**triunfante** triumphant
el **trocito** piece, **10.2**
el **trombón** trombone
la **trompeta** trumpet
**tropical** tropical
**tu** your *(sing. fam.)*
**tú** you *(sing. fam.)*
el **tubo de escape** exhaust pipe
el **tubo de pasta (crema) dentífrica** tube of toothpaste, 12.2
la **turbulencia** turbulence, **7.2**
el/la **turista** tourist, 10.2

**u** or (used instead of **o** before words beginning with **o** or **ho**)
**Ud., usted** you *(sing. form.)* 3.2
**Uds., ustedes** you *(pl. form.)*, 2.2
**último(a)** last
**ultramarinos: la tienda de ultramarinos** grocery store, **4.2**
**un(a)** a, an, 1.1
la **una** one o'clock, 2.2
**único(a)** only; unique
la **unidad: la unidad de cuidado intensivo** intensive care unit
el **uniforme** uniform
la **universidad** university
**universitario(a)** (related to) university
**uno** one, BV
**unos(as)** some
**urbano(a)** urban
**urgencias: la sala de urgencias** emergency room
la **urología** urology
el/la **urólogo(a)** urologist
**usado(a)** used
**usar** to wear (size), 3.2; to use
**utilizar** to use
las **uvas** grapes, **10.1**

la **vaca** cow, **9.2**
la **vacación** vacation, **6.2**
el/la **vago(a)** loafer, idler
el **vagón** train car, 13.1; **1.1**
la **vainilla: de vainilla** vanilla *(adj.)*, 5.1
la **vainita** string bean
**¡vale!** OK!
**valer** to be worth
**valeroso(a)** brave
**valiente** brave
el **valle** valley, **7.2**
el **valor** value, worth
**el valor real** true value
**vamos** let's go
la **variación** variation
**variado(a)** varied
**variar** to vary, change
la **variedad** variety
**vario(a)** various
el **varón** male
**vasco(a)** Basque
**la pelota vasca** jai alai
el **vaso** (drinking) glass, 12.1
el **váter** toilet, **6.2**
el/la **vecino(a)** neighbor
el **vegetal** vegetable, 5.2
el/la **vegetariano(a)** vegetarian
**veinte** twenty, BV
**veinticinco** twenty-five, BV
**veinticuatro** twenty-four, BV
**veintidós** twenty-two, BV
**veintinueve** twenty-nine, BV
**veintiocho** twenty-eight, BV
**veintiséis** twenty-six, BV
**veintisiete** twenty-seven, BV
**veintitrés** twenty-three, BV
**veintiuno** twenty-one, BV
la **vela** candle, **13.1**
la **velocidad** speed, **11.2**
**la velocidad máxima** speed limit, **11.2**
**vencer** to conquer
el **vendaje** bandage, **8.2**
**poner un vendaje** to put a bandage on, **8.2**
el/la **vendedor(a)** salesperson, **11.1**
**vender** to sell, 5.2
el **veneno** poison
**venenoso(a)** poisonous
**venezolano(a)** Venezuelan
**venir** to come, 11.1
**el viernes (sábado, etc.) que viene** next Friday (Saturday, etc.)
la **venta** sale, **14.1**
la **ventaja** advantage
la **ventanilla** ticket window, 9.2; window (airplane), **7.1**; teller's window, **12.2**
**ver** to see; to watch, 5.1
el **verano** summer, BV
el **verbo** verb
la **verdad** truth
**¡verdad!** that's right (true)!
**verdadero(a)** true, real
**verde** green, 3.2
**la judía verde** green bean, 5.2
la **verdulería** greengrocer store, **4.2**
la **verdura** vegetable
**verificar** to check, 13.1; **1.1**
la **versión: en versión original** in (its) original version, 10.1
el **verso** verse
**vertical** vertical
**vestido(a)** dressed
el **vestido** dress, **4.1**
**los vestidos** clothes *(pl.)*
**vestirse (i, i)** to get dressed
el/la **veterinario(a)** veterinarian
la **vez** time
**a veces** at times, sometimes, 7.1
**de vez en cuando** now and then
**en vez de** instead of
**una vez más** one more time, again
la **vía** track, 13.1; **1.1**
**viajar** to travel
**viajar en avión** to travel by plane, 11.1
el **viaje** trip
**el viaje de novios** honeymoon
**el viaje de regreso** return trip

**hacer un viaje** to take a trip, 11.1
el/la **viajero(a)** traveler
**viceversa** vice versa
**víctima** victim, **8.1**
**victorioso(a)** victorious
la **vida** life
**la vida escolar** school life
el **video** video
**viejo(a)** old, 6.1
el/la **viejo(a)** old person
el **viento** wind
el **viernes** Friday, BV
**villa: villa miseria** shantytown (Arg.)
el **vinagre** vinegar
la **viola** viola
el **violín** violin
**visible** visible
**visitar** to visit
la **víspera de Año Nuevo** New Year's Eve, **13.2**
la **vista** view
**vital** vital
la **vitamina** vitamin
la **vitrina** shop window, **4.1**
la **vivienda** housing
**viviente: el ser viviente** living creature, being
**vivir** to live, 5.2
**vivo(a)** living, alive
la **vocal** vowel
**volar (ue)** to fly, **7.2**
el **voleibol** volleyball
el/la **voluntario(a)** volunteer
**volver (ue)** to return, 7.1
**volver a casa** to return home, 10.2
la **voz** voice
**en voz alta** aloud
el **vuelo** flight, 11.1
**el número del vuelo** flight number, 11.1
**el vuelo directo** direct flight, **7.2**
**el vuelo nacional** domestic flight
**tomar un vuelo** to take a flight, 11.1
la **vuelta: dar la vuelta** to turn around

**y** and, BV
**y cuarto** a quarter past (the hour)
**y media** half past (the hour)
**y pico** just after (the hour)
**ya** now; already
la **yarda** yard
el **yeso** cast, **8.2**
**yo** I, 1.1
el **yogur** yogurt

la **zanahoria** carrot, 5.2
la **zapatería** shoe store, **4.1**
el **zapato** shoe, 3.2
la **zona** zone, area, neighborhood
**la zona comercial** business zone, **9.1**
**la zona industrial** industrial area, **9.1**
**la zona residencial** residential area, **9.1**
el **zumo de naranja** orange juice (Spain)

# English-Spanish Dictionary

*This Spanish-English Dictionary contains all productive and receptive vocabulary from Levels 1 and 2. The numbers following each productive entry indicate the chapter and vocabulary section in which the word is introduced. For example, **3.2** in dark print means that the word was first taught in **Capítulo 3, Palabras 2.** A light print number means that the word was introduced in **¡Buen viaje!,** Level 1. BV refers to the introductory **Bienvenidos** lessons in Level 1. If there is no number following an entry, this means that the word or expression is there for receptive purposes only.*

**a, an** un(a), 1.1
**aboard, on board** a bordo de
**about** sobre; acerca de; **(time)** a eso de, **4.1**
**above** encima; por encima de, 9.1
**abroad** en el extranjero
**abstract** abstracto(a)
**abuse** el abuso
**academic** académico(a)
**academy** la academia
**accent** el tilde
to **accept** aceptar
**access** el acceso
**accident** el accidente, **8.1**
to **accommodate** acomodar
**accompaniment** el acompañamiento
to **accompany** acompañar
**according to** según
**account (bank)** la cuenta
**checking account** la cuenta corriente, **12.2**
**savings account** la cuenta de ahorros
**accountant** el/la contable, **14.1**
**ache** el dolor, 8.1
to **ache: My . . . ache(s).** Me duele(n)... , **8.2**
**acrylic** el acrílico
**action** la acción
**active** activo(a)
**activity** la actividad
**actor** el actor, 10.2
**actress** la actriz, 10.2
to **adapt** adaptar
to **add** sumar; agregar, añadir, **10.2**
**addiction** la adicción
**addition: in addition to** además de
**address** la dirección
**adequate** adecuado(a)
to **adjust** ajustar
to **admire** admirar
**admission ticket** la entrada, 10.1
to **admit** admitir, **8.2**
**adolescence** la adolescencia
**adolescent** el/la adolescente
**adorable** adorable
**adoration** la adoración
to **adore** adorar
to **adorn** adornar
**advance** el avance
**advantage** la ventaja
**adventure** la aventura
**advertisement** el anuncio, **14.2**
**advertising** la propaganda
**advice** el consejo
to **advise** aconsejar
**aerobic** aeróbico(a)
to **affect** impresionar
**African** africano(a)
**African American** afroamericano(a)
**after** después (de), 5.1; tras
**afternoon** la tarde
**Good afternoon.** Buenas tardes., BV
**in the afternoon** por la tarde
**this afternoon** esta tarde, 9.2
**again** de nuevo
**against** contra, 7.1
**age** la edad
**how old are you?** ¿Cuántos años tienes?
**agency** la agencia
**employment agency** la agencia de empleos
**agent** el/la agente, 11.1
**customs agent** el/la agente de aduana, 11.2
**aging person** el/la envejeciente
**agreed, Fine.** Conforme. 14.2
**agricultural** agrícola
**ahead** adelante
**AIDS** el sida
**air** el aire, **11.1**
**air conditioning** el aire acondicionado, **6.2**
**air traffic controller** el/la controlador(a), **7.2**
**airline** la línea aérea
**airmail** el correo aéreo, **12.2**
**airplane** el avión, 11.1
**small airplane** la avioneta, **7.2**
**airport** el aeropuerto, 11.1
**aisle** el pasillo, 13.2; **1.2**
**album** el álbum
**alcohol** el alcohol
**alcoholism** el alcoholismo
**algebra** el álgebra, 2.2

**alive** vivo(a)
**all** todos(as)
**allergy** la alergia, 8.2
to **allow** consentir (ie, i); dejar
**almost** casi
**alone** solo(a); a solas
**aloud** en voz alta
**already** ya
**also** también
to **alternate** alternar
**although** aunque
**altitude** la altitud, la altura, **7.2**
**always** siempre, 7.1
**ambassador** el/la embajador(a)
**ambulance** la ambulancia, **8.1**
**American** americano(a), 1.1
**amount** la cantidad
**amusement** la diversión
**amusement park** el parque de atracciones, **5.2**
**amusement park ride** la atracción, **5.2**
**amusing** divertido(a)
**analysis** el análisis
**analytical** analítico(a)
to **analyze** analizar
**ancient** antiguo(a), **5.1**
**and** y, BV
**Andalusian** andaluz(a)
**Andean** andino(a)
**anecdote** la anécdota
**angry** enfadado(a)
**animal** el animal
**farm animal** el animal doméstico, **9.2**
**ankle** el tobillo, **8.1**
**anniversary** el aniversario
to **announce** anunciar
**announcement** el anuncio, **7.1**
**another** otro(a)
to **answer** contestar, **3.2**
**answer** la respuesta
**answering machine** el contestador automático, **3.2**
**Antarctic** la Antártida
**antibiotic** el antibiótico, 8.2
**antiquated** anticuado(a)
**antiquity** la antigüedad
**any** cualquier
**apartment** el apartamento, el departamento, 6.2; el piso
**apartment house** la casa de apartamentos (departamentos), 6.2
**apostle** el apóstol
to **appear** aparecer
**appearance** la apariencia
**appendicitis** la apendicitis
to **applaud** aplaudir, 10.2
**applause** el aplauso, 10.2
**to receive applause** recibir aplausos, 10.2
**apple** la manzana, 5.2
**apple tree** el manzano, **9.2**
**application (job)** la solicitud (de empleo)
to **apply (for a job)** solicitar trabajo
to **approach** acercarse (de)
**appropriate** apropiado(a)
**April** abril, BV
**aptitude** la aptitud
**Arab** el/la árabe
**archaeological** arqueológico(a)
**archaeologist** el/la arqueólogo(a)
**archeology** la arqueología
**architect** el/la arquitecto(a), **14.1**
**area** el área *(f.)*; la zona
**area code** la clave de área, **3.2**
**Argentinian** argentino(a), 2.1
**argument** la disputa
**arid** árido(a)
**arithmetic** la aritmética, 2.2
**arm** el brazo, 7.1
**armchair** el sillón, **6.2**
**around** alrededor de, 6.2
**arrival** la llegada, 11.1
**arrival and departure screen** la pantalla de llegadas y salidas, 11.1
to **arrive** llegar, 4.1
**arrogant** altivo(a), arrogante
**art** el arte *(f.)*, 2.2
**fine arts** las bellas artes
**artichoke** la alcachofa, 14.2; **2.2**
**artifact** el artefacto
**artist** el/la artista, 10.2
**artistic** artístico(a)
**as** como, 1.2
**as . . . as** tan... como, **8.2**
**as many . . . as** tantos(as)... como, **8.2**
**as much . . . as** tanto(a)... como
to **ask (a question)** preguntar; (questions) hacer preguntas, **14.2**
to **ask for** pedir (i, i), 14.1
**to ask for the bill** pedir la cuenta, **6.1**
to **ask questions** hacer preguntas, **14.2**
**asleep** dormido(a)
**aspect** el aspecto
**aspirin** la aspirina, 8.2
to **assist** atender (ie), **4.1**
**assortment** el surtido
to **assure** asegurar
**astute** astuto(a)
**at** a
**at that time** en aquel entonces
**athlete** el/la atleta
**athletic** atlético(a)
**atmosphere** el ambiente; la atmósfera
to **attack** atacar
**attack** el ataque
to **attend** asistir
**attention: to pay attention** prestar atención, 4.2
**attractive** atractivo(a)
**audience** el público, 10.2
**August** agosto, BV
**aunt** la tía, 6.1
**aunt and uncle** los tíos, 6.1
**authentic** auténtico(a)
**author** el/la autor(a), 10.2
**automatic teller** el cajero automático

**automatically** automáticamente
**automobile** el automóvil
**autumn** el otoño, BV
**available** disponible
**avenue** la avenida, **9.1**
**average** medio(a); regular, 2.2
**aviation** la aviación
**avocado** el aguacate, **10.2**

**baby** el/la bebé
**bachelor's degree** el bachillerato
**back (of seat)** el respaldo, **7.1**
**background (ancestry)** la ascendencia
**backpack** la mochila, 3.1
**bacteria** la bacteria
**bad** malo(a), 2.1; mal, 14.2; **2.2**
**to be in a good (bad) mood** estar de buen (mal) humor, **8.1**
**bad-tempered** malhumorado(a)
**bag** la bolsa, 5.2
**cloth** shopping bag el capacho
**plastic bag** la bolsa de plástico, **4.2**
**baggage** el equipaje, 11.1
**baggage claim** el reclamo de equipaje, 11.2
**carry-on baggage** el equipaje de mano
**bakery** la panadería, la pastelería, **4.2**
**balance (bank)** el saldo
**ball (soccer, basketball)** el balón 7.1; **(baseball, tennis)** la pelota , 7.2
**balloon** el globo, **5.2**
**ballpoint pen** el bolígrafo, 3.1
**banana** el plátano, 5.2; la banana, **10.2**
**band (music)** la banda
**bandage** el vendaje, **8.2**
**to put a bandage on** poner un vendaje, **8.2**
**bank (of a river)** la orilla
**bank** el banco, **12.2**
**bank statement** el estado del banco
**banking** bancario(a)
**baptism** el bautizo
**bar: bar of soap** la barra de jabón, la pastilla de jabón, 12.2
**barber** el barbero, **12.1**
**bargain** la ganga
to **base** basar
**base** la base, 7.2
**baseball** el béisbol, 7.2
**baseball field** el campo de béisbol, 7.2
**baseball game** el juego de béisbol, 7.2
**baseball player** el/la beisbolista; el/la jugador(a) de béisbol, 7.2
**based (on)** basado(a)
**basic** básico(a)
**basket (basketball)** el canasto, la canasta, el cesto, 7.2; **(jai alai)** la cesta
**basketball** el baloncesto, el básquetbol, 7.2
**basketball court** la cancha de básquetbol, 7.2
**to put in (make) a basket** encestar, 7.2
**Basque** vasco(a)
**bat** el bate, 7.2
**bath** el baño
**to take a bath** bañarse, 12.1
**bathing suit** el bañador, el traje de baño, 9.1
**bathroom** el baño, el cuarto de baño, 6.2
**bathtub** la bañera, **6.2**
**batter** el/la bateador(a), 7.2
**battery** la batería
**battle** la batalla
**bay** la bahía
to **be** ser, 1.1; estar, 4.1
**to be afraid** tener miedo
**to be in a good (bad) mood** estar de buen (mal) humor
**to be happy (sad)** estar contento(a) (triste)
**to be hungry** tener hambre, 14.1; **2.1**
**to be married** estar casado(a)
**to be sick** estar enfermo(a)
**to be thirsty** tener sed, 14.1; 2.1
**to be tired** esta cansado(a)
**to be . . . years old** tener... años, 6.1
**to be able** poder (ue), 7.1
to **be accustomed to, tend to** soler (ue)
to **be alarmed** alarmarse
to **be based** basarse
to **be born** nacer, **13.1**
to **be called** llamarse, 12.1
to **be familiar with** conocer, 11.1
to **be frightened** asustarse
to **be glad about** alegrarse de, **13.1**
to **be going to (do something)** ir a + *infinitive*
to **be important** importar
to **be named** llamarse, 12.1
to **be sorry** sentir (i, i)
to **be worth** valer
**beach** la playa, 9.1
**beach resort** el balneario, 9.1
**beach towel** la toalla playera, 9.1
**bean** el frijol, la habichuela, 5.2
**black bean** la habichuela negra, el frijol negro, **10.2**
**string (green) bean** la habichuela tierna
to **bear** llevar
**beard** la barba
**beau, heartthrob** el galán
**beautiful** bello(a), hermoso(a), 1.1; precioso(a)
**beauty** la belleza
**because** porque
to **become enamored of (to fall for)** flechar

**bed** la cama, 8.1
**to go to bed** acostarse (ue), 12.1
**to make the bed** hacer la cama, **6.2**
**to stay in bed** guardar cama, 8.1
**bedroom** el cuarto de dormir; el cuarto, el dormitorio, la recámara, 6.2; la habitación, **6.1**
**bee** la abeja, **8.1**
**beef** la carne de res, 14.2; **2.2**
**before** antes de, 5.1
to **beg** rogar (ue)
to **begin** comenzar (ie); empezar (ie), 7.1
**beginner** el/la principiante, 9.2
**beginning: at the beginning** al principio
**beginning of the school year** la apertura de clases
to **behave** comportarse
**behavior** la actuación
**behind** atrás; detrás de, **5.2**
to **believe** creer, 8.2
**bell pepper** el pimiento, **10.2**
**bellhop** el botones, **6.1**
to **belong** pertenecer
**below** debajo (de), **7.1**
**below zero** bajo cero, 9.2
**belt** el cinturón, **4.1**
**seat belt** el cinturón de seguridad, **7.1**
**benefit** el beneficio
**berth** la litera, 13.2; **1.2**
**beside** al lado de, **5.2**
**besides** además
**best man** el padrino, **13.1**
**better, best** mejor
**between** entre, 7.1
**beverage** el refresco, 5.1; la bebida, **7.1**
**biblical** bíblico(a)
to **bicycle** ir en bicicleta, 12.2
**bicycle** la bicicleta
**big** gran, grande
**bilingual** bilingüe
**bill** la factura, **6.1**; **(money)** el billete, **12.2**; **(check)** la cuenta, 5.1
**biography** la biografía
**biological** biológico(a)
**biologist** el/la biólogo(a)
**biology** la biología, 2.2
**bird** el ave *(f.)*; el pájaro
**birthday** el cumpleaños, 6.1
**black** negro(a), 3.2
**blanket** la frazada, la manta, **6.2**
**bleach** el blanqueador
**blessing** la bendición
**block (city)** la cuadra, **11.2**
to **block** bloquear, parar, 7.1
**blond(e)** rubio(a), 1.1
**blood** la sangre
**blood pressure** la presión arterial, la tensión arterial, **8.2**
**blouse** la blusa, 3.2
**blue** azul , 3.2
**dark blue** azul oscuro
**blue jeans** el blue jean, 3.2
to **board** embarcar, 11.2; subir, 13.1; **1.1**; abordar
to **board the train** subir al tren, 13.1; **1.1**
**board** el tablero, 7.1
**arrival board** el tablero de llegadas, 13.1; **1.1**
**departure board** el tablero de salidas, 13.1; **1.1**
**scoreboard** el tablero indicador, 7.1
**boarding house** la pensión, 12.2
**boarding pass** la tarjeta de embarque, 11.1
**boat** el bote, **5.2**
**body** el cuerpo, **8.1**
to **boil** hervir (ie, i), **10.1**
**boiling** la ebullición
**bone** el hueso, **8.2**
**to set the bone** reducir el hueso, **8.2**
**book** el libro, 3.1
**boot** la bota, 9.2
to **border** bordear
**border** el borde
to **bore** aburrir
**boring** aburrido(a), 2.1
**born** nacido(a)
to **borrow** pedir prestado
**boss** el/la jefe(a)
**bottle** la botella, **4.2**
**bottle of mineral water** la botella de agua mineral, 12.2
**boulevard** el bulevar, **9.1**
**box office** la taquilla, 10.1
**boy** el muchacho, 1.1; el chico
**boyfriend** el novio
**bracelet** la pulsera, **4.1**
**braid** la trenza
to **brake** poner los frenos
**brakes** los frenos, **11.1**
**branch (office)** la sucursal; la filial
**branch (of menora)** el brazo, **13.2**
**branch (tree)** la rama
**brass (instruments in orchestra)** instrumentos de metal
**brave** valeroso(a); valiente
**bread** el pan, **4.2**
to **break** romperse, **8.1**
**breakdown** la avería
**breakfast** el desayuno, 5.2
to **breathe** respirar
**breathing** la respiración
**bricklayer** el/la albañil, **14.1**
**bride** la novia, **13.1**
**brief** breve
**bright** brillante
to **bring** llevar, 6.1; traer, 14.1; **2.1**
**broken down** averiado(a)
**bronze** el bronce, 10.2
**brook** el arroyo
**brother** el hermano, 6.1
**brown** de color marrón, 3.2; pardo(a)
**brunette** moreno(a), 1.1
**brush** el cepillo, 12.2; **(paint)** el pincel

# English-Spanish Dictionary

to **brush one's hair** cepillarse, 12.1
to **brush one's teeth** cepillarse los dientes, lavarse los dientes, 12.1
**building** el edificio, **9.1**
**burial** el entierro
**burner (stove)** la hornilla, **10.1**
to **bury** enterrar (ie)
**bus** el bus, 4.1; el autobús, 10.1; **(Mexico)** el camión, 10.1; **(Puerto Rico, Cuba)** la guagua, 10.1
**school bus** el bus escolar, 4.1
**bus stop** la parada de bus, **9.1**
**business** el comercio; la empresa, **14.1**
**business district** la zona comercial, **9.1**
**businessman (woman)** el/la comerciante, **14.1**; el/la empresario(a)
**busy (phone)** ocupado
**but** pero
**butcher shop** la carnicería, **4.2**
**butter** la mantequilla, **10.2**
**button** el botón, **3.1**
to **buy** comprar, 3.1
**buying** la compra, **14.1**
**by no means** de ninguna manera, 1.1
**by the way** a propósito

**cabin** la cabina, **7.1**
**café** el café, 5.1; la confitería
**outdoor café** el café al aire libre
**cafeteria** la cafetería
**cage** la jaula, **5.2**
**cake** el bizcocho, la torta, el pastel, **13.1**
to **calculate** calcular
**calculator** la calculadora, 3.1
**calculus** el cálculo, 2.2
to **call oneself, be named** llamarse, 12.1
to **call; to telephone** llamar, **3.2**
**Who is calling?** ¿De parte de quién?, **3.2**
**call** la llamada (telefónica), **3.2**
**long distance call** la llamada larga, **3.2**
**called** llamado(a)
**calm** tranquilo(a)
**calorie** la caloría
**camel** el camello, **13.2**
**campaign** la campaña
**can** el bote, la lata, 5.2
**Canadian** canadiense
**candid** franco(a)
**candidate** el/la aspirante, el/la candidato(a), **14.2**
**candle** la vela, **13.1**
**canned** enlatado(a)
**canvas (painting)** el lienzo
**canyon** el cañón
**cap** la gorra, 3.2
**capital** la capital
**captain (airplane)** el/la comandante, 11.2
**car** el carro, el coche, 4.1
**by car** en carro, 4.1
**dining car** el coche-comedor, el coche-cafetería, 13.2
**sleeping car** el coche cama, 13.2
**sports car** el carro deportivo, **11.1**
**train car** el coche, 13.2
**carbohydrate** el carbohidrato
**card** la tarjeta, 11.1
**credit card** la tarjeta de crédito, 14.1; **2.1**
**registration card (hotel)** la tarjeta, la ficha, **6.1**
**student I.D. card** la tarjeta de identidad estudiantil
**telephone card** la tarjeta telefónica, **3.2**
**cardinal points** los punto cardinales
**cardiologist** el/la cardiólogo(a)
**cardiology** la cardiología
**care: intensive care** el cuidado intensivo
**career** la carrera
**careful!** ¡cuidado!
**to be careful** tener cuidado
**carefully** con cuidado
to **caress** acariciar
**Caribbean** el Caribe
**Caribbean Sea** el mar Caribe
**caricaturist** el/la caricaturista
**carousel horse** el caballito, 5.2
**carpenter** el/la carpintero(a), **14.1**
**carrot** la zanahoria, 5.2
to **carry** llevar, 3.1
to **carry out** efectuar
**cart** el carrito, **4.2**
**case** el caso, **7.1**
**cash** el dinero en efectivo, **12.2**
**cash register** la caja, 3.1
to **cash the check** cobrar el cheque, **12.2**
**cashier** el/la cajero(a), **14.1**
**cast** el yeso, **8.2**
**castillian** castellano(a)
**castle** el castillo
**cat** el/la gato(a), 6.1
to **catch** atrapar, 7.2
**catcher** el/la cátcher, el/la receptor(a), 7.2
**category** la categoría
**cathedral** la catedral
**catholic** católico(a)
**cattle** el ganado, **9.2**
**cauliflower** la coliflor, **10.1**
to **cause** causar
**cause** la causa
**CD-ROM** el CD-ROM, **3.1**
to **celebrate** celebrar, **13.1**
**celebration** la celebración

**cell phone** el teléfono celular, **3.2**
**cellular** celular
**center** el centro
**central** central
**Central America** la América Central
**century** el siglo
**cereal** el cereal, 5.2
**ceremony** la ceremonia
**certain** cierto(a)
**Certainly!,** Of course! ¡Claro!
**chain (necklace)** la cadena, **4.1**
**gold chain** la cadena de oro, **4.1**
**chair** la silla
**armchair** el sillón, **6.2**
**chairlift** el telesilla, 9.2
**chalkboard** la pizarra, el pizarrón, 4.2
**champion** el/la campeón(ona), **5.1**
**championship** el campeonato
**change** el cambio, **12.2**
to **change** variar; cambiar, **12.2**
**to change the towels** cambiar las toallas, **6.2**
**to change trains (transfer)** transbordar, 13.2; **1.2**
**channel (TV)** el canal
**Chanukah** Hanuka, **13.2**
**Happy Chanukah!** ¡Feliz Hanuka!, **13.2**
**chapter** el capítulo
**character** el carácter; el personaje
**characteristic** la característica
to **charge** cobrar
**charges** los cargos
**charming** encantador(a)
to **chat** charlar
**chauffeur** el chófer
**cheap** barato(a), 3.2
**check (plaid)** a cuadros
to **check luggage** facturar el equipaje, 11.1
to **check out** abandonar el cuarto, **6.1**
to **check the oil** revisar el aceite, **11.2**
to **check the ticket** revisar el boleto, 11.1
**checkbook** la chequera; el talonario
**checkers** las damas, **5.1**
**checking account** la cuenta corriente, **12.2**
**cheek** la mejilla, **8.1**
**cheese** el queso, 5.1
**chemical** químico(a)
**chemistry** la química, 2.2
**chess** el ajedrez, **5.1**
**chest** el pecho, **8.1**
**chicken** el pollo, 5.2
**child** el/la niño(a)
**children** los hijos, 6.1
**chilean** chileno(a)
**chili pepper** el ají
**chills** los escalofríos, 8.1
**chimney** la chimenea
**chocolate** *(adj.)* de chocolate, 5.1
**choir** el coro
**cholesterol** el colesterol
to **choose** escoger
**chop** la chuleta, **10.1**
**chores** los quehaceres
**chorus** el coro
**Christian** cristiano(a)
**Christmas** la Navidad, **13.2**
**Merry Christmas!** ¡Feliz Navidad!, **13.2**
**Christmas Eve** la Nochebuena, **13.2**
**Christmas tree** el árbol de Navidad, **13.2**
**church** la iglesia
**circle** el círculo
to **circulate** circular
**citric** cítrico(a)
**city** la ciudad, **9.1**
**city hall** la alcaldía, **14.1**
**city hall employee** el/la funcionario(a), **14.1**
to **claim (luggage)** reclamar, 11.2
**to claim one's luggage** recoger el equipaje, 11.2
**clam** la almeja, 14.2; **2.2**
**clarinet** el clarinete
**clarity** la claridad
**class** la clase, el curso, 2.1
**first class** primera clase, 13.1; **1.1**
**second class** segunda clase, 13.1
**classic** clásico(a)
to **classify** clasificar
**classroom** la sala de clase, el salón de clase, 4.1
**clean** limpio(a)
to **clean** limpiar, **6.2**
**to clean the room** limpiar el cuarto, **6.2**
**clear** claro(a)
**clerk** el/la dependiente(a); el/la empleado(a), 3.1
**clever** listo(a), **5.1**
**click** el clic
**climate** el clima
**clinic** la clínica
**close** cercano(a)
to **close** cerrar (ie)
**to close the wound** cerrar la herida, **8.2**
**closet** el armario, **6.2**
**clothes** *(pl.)* la ropa, los vestidos
**to put on (one's) clothes** ponerse la ropa, **12.1**; vestirse (i, i)
**clothes hanger** el colgador, la percha, **6.2**
**clothing** la ropa, 3.2
**clothing store** la tienda de ropa, 3.2
**men's clothing store** la tienda de ropa para caballeros, **4.1**
**women's clothing store** la tienda de ropa para señoras, **4.1**
**cloud** la nube, 9.1
**cloudy** nublado(a), 9.1
**It's cloudy.** Hay nubes., 9.1
**clove (of garlic)** el diente (de ajo)
**clown** el payaso, **5.2**
**club** el club, 4.2
**Spanish Club** el Club de español, 4.2

**co-ed (school)** mixto(a)
**coast** la costa
**coat** el abrigo, **4.1**
**cockpit** la cabina de mando (vuelo), **7.1**
**coconut** el coco, **10.2**
**code: country code** el prefijo de país, **3.2**
**area code** la clave de área, **3.2**
**coffee** el café, BV
**black coffee** el café solo, 5.1
**coffee with milk** el café con leche, 5.1
**coin, currency** la moneda, **3.2**
**coincidence** la coincidencia
**cold (illness)** el catarro, 8.1
**It's cold.** Hace frío., 9.2
**to have a cold** tener catarro, estar resfriado(a), 8.1
to **collect** coleccionar, **5.1**
**collection** el conjunto; la colección; la colecta
**collector** el/la coleccionista, **5.1**
**Colombian** colombiano(a), 1.1
**colonial** colonial
**colony** la colonia
**color** el color, 3.2
**What color is it?** ¿De qué color es?, 3.2
**colored** de color
**comb** el peine, 12.1
to **comb one's hair** peinarse, 12.1
to **come** venir, 11.1
**to come (go) on stage** entrar en escena, 10.2
**comedy** la comedia
**comfort** la comodidad
**commission** la comisión
**committee** el comité
**common** común
to **communicate with each other** comunicarse, **3.1**
**communication** la comunicación
**community** la comunidad
**compact disk** CD, el disco compacto, 4.2
**company** la compañía
to **compare** comparar
**comparison** la comparación
**compartment** el compartimento, 13.2; **1.2**
**overhead compartment** el compartimiento superior, el compartimiento sobre la cabeza, 7.1
to **compete** competir (i, i)
**competition** la competencia; la competición
to **complete** completar
**completely** totalmente
**compliment: to pay someone a compliment** echarle flores
to **compose** componer
**composition** la composición
**computer** el ordenador, la computadora, **3.1**
**computer programmer** el/la programador(a) de informática, **14.1**
**computer science** la informática, 2.2
**concert** el concierto, 2.1
**conclusion** el desenlace
**condition** la condición
**condominium** el condominio, **9.1**
**conductor (train)** el/la revisor(a), 13.2; **1.2**
to **confirm** confirmar
to **confront** confrontar
**Congratulations!** ¡Enhorabuena!, ¡Felicitaciones!, **13.1**
to **connect** conectar; enlazar
**connection** la conexión
to **conquer** conquistar; vencer
**conqueror** el conquistador
**conquest** la conquista
**consequently** por consiguiente
to **consider** considerar
to **consist of** consistir (en)
to **construct** construir
to **consult** consultar, 13.1; **1.1**
to **consume** consumir
**consumer** el/la consumidor(a)
**consumption** el consumo
**contagious** contagioso(a)
to **contain** contener (ie)
**contemporary** contemporáneo(a)
**contest** la competición
**continent** el continente
to **continue** continuar, 7.2; seguir (i, i), **11.2**
**contrary: on the contrary** al contrario
to **contrast** contrastar
to **control** controlar
**control tower** la torre de control, **7.2**
**convenient** conveniente
**convent** el convento
**conversation** la conversación
to **convert** convertir (ie, i)
**convertible** el convertible, el descapotable, **11.1**
to **convince** convencer
to **cook** cocinar, **10.1**
**cook** el/la cocinero(a), 14.1; **2.1**
**cooking** la cocción
**coordination** la coordinación
**copilot** el/la copiloto, 11.2
to **copy** copiar
**copy** la copia
**corn (Mex.)** el elote; el choclo; el maíz, 14.2; **2.2**
**cornea** la córnea
**corner** la esquina, **9.1**
**correspondence** la correspondencia
**corridor** el pasillo, 13.2; **1.2**
to **cost** costar (ue), 3.1
**how much do(es) it (they) cost?** ¿Cuánto cuesta(n)?
**Costa Rican** costarricense
**cotton** el algodón, **12.1**
**cough** la tos, 8.1
**to have a cough** tener tos, 8.1

to **cough** toser, 8.1
**counter** el mostrador, 11.1
**country** el país, 11.2; el campo, **9.2**
**foreign country** el país extranjero
**coup (overthrow of a government)** el golpe
**coupe** el cupé, **11.1**
**couple** la pareja
**course** el curso, 2.1
**elective course** el curso opcional
**required course** el curso obligatorio
**court** la corte, el tribunal, **14.1**
**court** la cancha, 7.2
**basketball court** la cancha de básquetbol, 7.2
**enclosed court** la cancha cubierta, 9.1
**outdoor court** la cancha al aire libre, 9.1
**tennis court** la cancha de tenis, 9.1
**courteous** atento(a); cortés
**courtesy** la cortesía, BV
**cousin** el/la primo(a), 6.1
to **cover** cubrir; tapar, **10.2**
**cow** la vaca, **9.2**
to **create** crear
**credit card** la tarjeta de crédito, 14.1; **2.1**
**creole** criollo(a)
**crew** la tripulación, 11.2
**crop** la cosecha, **9.2**
to **cross** atravesar (ie); cruzar, **9.1**
**crossing** el cruce, **11.2**
**crosswalk** el cruce de peatones, **9.1**
**crossword puzzle** el crucigrama, **5.1**
**to do a crossword puzzle** llenar un crucigrama, **5.1**
**crutch** la muleta, **8.2**
**Cuban** cubano(a)
**Cuban American** cubanoamericano(a)
**cucumber** el pepino, **10.1**
to **cultivate** cultivar, **9.2**
**cultivation** el cultivo
**cultural** cultural
**cultured** culto(a)
**cup** la taza, 14.1; **2.1**
**cure** la cura
**curtain (stage)** el telón, 10.2
**custom** la costumbre
**customer** el/la cliente, 5.1
**customs** la aduana, 11.2
**customs agent** el/la agente de aduana, **11.2**
to **cut** cortar, **8.1**
**cycling** el ciclismo

**dad** el papá
**daily** diario(a)
to **dance** bailar, 4.2
**dance** el baile
**dance** la danza
**danger** el peligro
**dangerous** peligroso(a)
**dark** oscuro(a)
**dark-haired** moreno(a), 1.1
**data** los datos, **3.1**
to **date** datar
**date** la fecha, BV
**What is today's date?** ¿Cuál es la fecha de hoy?, BV
**daughter** la hija, 6.1
**day** el día, BV
**What day is it (today)?** ¿Qué día es (hoy)?, BV
**death** la muerte
**decade** la década
**December** diciembre, BV
to **decide** decidir
to **declare** declarar
to **decorate** decorar
**decorated** decorado(a)
**decoration** la decoración
to **dedicate** dedicar, **14.1**
**deep** profundo(a)
to **defeat** derrotar
to **defend** defender (ie)
to **define** definir
**definition** la definición
**degree (temperature)** el grado, 9.2
**delay: with a delay** con una demora, 11.1; con retraso, 13.2; **1.2**
**delicate** delicado(a)
**delicious** rico(a), 14.2; **2.2**; delicioso(a), sabroso(a)
to **delight** encantar
to **deliver** entregar
**deluxe** de lujo
to **demand** exigir
**demography** la demografía
to **demonstrate** demostrar (ue)
**density** la densidad
**dentist** el/la dentista
**department** el departamento, **14.2**
**department of human resources** el departamento de recursos humanos, **14.2**
**department store** la tienda de departamentos
**departure** la salida, 11.1; la partida
**departure area** la sala de salida, 11.1
**departure gate** la puerta de salida, 11.1; la puerta de embarque
**departure hour** la hora de salida, 13.1; **1.1**
to **depend (on)** depender (ie) (de)
**deposit** el depósito
**to make a deposit** ingresar
**dermatologist** el/la dermatólogo(a)
**dermatology** la dermatología
**descendant** el/la descendiente
to **describe** describir
**desert** el desierto
**design** el diseño

**designer** el/la diseñador(a)
**dessert** el postre, 5.1
**destination** el destino, 11.1
**detail** el detalle
**detective** policíaco(a)
**detergent** el detergente, **4.2**
to **determine** determinar
**development** el desarrollo
**device** el aparato, **3.1**
to **devote oneself to** dedicarse, **14.1**
**diagnosis** la diagnosis, 8.2
**dial (of telephone)** el disco, **3.2**
to **dial** marcar (el número), **3.2**
**dial tone** el tono, **3.2**
**dialogue** el diálogo
**diamond** el diamante
to **dice** picar, **10.2**
to **die** morir (ue, u)
**diesel gasoline** diesel, 11.1
**diet** la dieta
**difference** la diferencia
**different** diferente
**difficult** difícil, duro(a), 2.1
**difficulty** la dificultad
to **dig** excavar
to **dine, have dinner** cenar
**dining car** el coche comedor, el coche cafetería, 13.2
**dining room** el comedor, 6.2
**dinner** la cena, 5.2
**diplomatic** diplomático(a)
**direct** directo(a)
to **direct** dirigir
**direction** la dirección; el sentido, **11.2**
**in each direction** en cada sentido, **11.2**
**in the opposite direction** en el sentido contrario, **11.2**
**director** el/la director(a)
**dirty** sucio(a), **11.1**
**dirty laundry** la ropa sucia, **12.1**
**disadvantage** la desventaja
to **disappear** desaparecer
**disaster** el desastre
**disastrous** desastroso(a)
**discount** el descuento
to **discover** descubrir
to **discuss** discutir
to **disembark** desembarcar, 11.2
**dish** el plato, 14.1; **2.1**
**disk, diskette** el disquete, 3.1
**disk drive** la ranura, **3.1**
**distance** la distancia
**distinct** distinto(a)
**distinguished** ilustre
to **distract** distraer
to **distribute** distribuir, **7.1**
**distribution** la distribución
to **dive** bucear, 9.1
to **divide** dividir
**diving** el buceo, 9.1
**division** la división
**divorce: to get divorced** divorciarse
to **do** hacer
**to do homework** hacer las tareas, **3.1**
**to do well (on an exam)** salir bien (en un examen)
**doctor** el/la doctor(a); el/la médico(a), 8.2
**doctor's office** la consulta (el consultorio) del médico, 8.2; la sala de consulta
**document** el documento, **3.1**
**documentation** la documentación
**dog** el perro, 6.1
**dollar** el dólar, **11**
**Dominican** dominicano(a), 2.1
**Dominican Republic** la República Dominicana
**dominos** el dominó, **5.1**
**donkey** el asno
**door** la puerta, **6.1**
**dose** la dosis, 8.2
**dot** el punto
**on the dot, sharp** en punto, 4.1
**doubles** dobles, 9.1
to **doubt** dudar
**doubt** la duda
**doubtful** dudoso(a)
**down payment** el enganche
**downtown** el centro; en el centro (de la ciudad)
**dozen** la docena, **4.2**
to **draw** dibujar
**drawing** el dibujo
**dream** el sueño
**dress** el vestido, **4.1**
to **dress oneself, to put on clothes** ponerse la ropa, 12.1
**to get dressed** vestirse (i, i )
**dressed (in)** vestido(a) (de)
to **dribble** driblar, 7.2
to **drink** beber, 5.1
**to drink a beverage** tomar un refresco
**to drink water (milk, coffee)** tomar agua (leche, café)
**drink** el refresco, 5.1; la bebida, **7.1**
to **drive** conducir, manejar
**driver** el/la conductor(a), **11.1**
**driver's license** la licencia, el permiso de conducir, **11.1**
**drug** la droga
**drug addiction** la drogadicción
**druggist** el/la farmacéutico(a), 8.2
**drugstore** la farmacia, 8.2
to **dry** secar, **12.2**
**dry** seco(a)
to **dry clean** limpiar en seco, **12.1**
**dry cleaner** el/la tintorero(a), **12.1**
**dry cleaners** la tintorería, **12.1**
**dubbed** doblado(a), 10.1
**during** durante

**e-mail, electronic mail** el correo electrónico, **3.1**

**each** cada, 1.2
**in each direction** en cada sentido, **11.2**
**eagle** el águila *(f.)*
**ear** la oreja, **4.1**; el oído, **8.1**
**early** temprano, 12.1
to **earn** ganar
to earn one's living ganar la vida
**earphones** los audífonos, los auriculares, **7.1**
**earring** el arete, el pendiente, **4.1**
**easel** el caballete
**east** el este
**eastern** oriental
**easy** fácil, 2.1; sencillo(a)
to **eat** comer, 5.1
**to eat breakfast** desayunarse, tomar el desayuno, 12.1
**to eat dinner** cenar
**ecological** ecológico(a)
**ecology** la ecología
**economical** económico(a), 12.2
**economics** la economía
**home economics** la economía doméstica, 2.2
**economy** la economía
**Ecuadorean** ecuatoriano(a), 2.1
to **educate** educar
**education** la educación
physical education la educación física, 2.2
**egg** el huevo, 5.2
**eggplant** la berenjena, 14.2; **2.2**
**eight** ocho, BV
**eight hundred** ochocientos(as), 3.2
**eighteen** dieciocho, BV
**eighth** octavo(a), 6.2
**eighty** ochenta, 2.2
**either** tampoco
**elbow** el codo, **8.1**
**elective course** el curso opcional
**electric** eléctrico(a)
**electrician** el/la electricista, **14.1**
**electricity** la electricidad
**electronic** electrónico(a)
**electronic mail** el correo electrónico, **3.1**
**elegance** la elegancia
**elegant** elegante, **13.1**
**element** el elemento
**elementary school** la escuela primaria
to **elevate** elevar
**elevated** elevado(a)
**elevation** la elevación
**elevator** el ascensor, 6.2; el elevador, **6.1**
**eleven** once, BV
to **eliminate** eliminar
**emergency** la emergencia, **7.1**
**emergency exit** la salida de emergencia, **7.1**
**emergency room** la sala de emergencia, la sala de urgencias, **8.1**
**emission** la emisión
to **emit** emitir
**emotion** la emoción
**emotional** emocional
to **emphasize** dar énfasis; enfatizar
to **employ** emplear
**employee** el/la dependiente(a), el/la empleado(a), 3.1
**enchilada** la enchilada, BV
**end** el fin
**at the end (of)** al final (de); a fines de
to **end** terminar, **3.1**
to **endorse** endosar, **12.2**
**enemy** el/la enemigo(a)
**energy** la energía
**engagement** el compromiso
**engine** el motor
**engineer** el/la ingeniero(a), **14.1**
**engineering** la ingeniería
**English** el inglés, 2.2
to **enjoy** disfrutar; gozar
to **enjoy oneself** divertirse (ie, i), 12.2
**enormous** enorme
**enough** bastante, 1.1; suficiente
to **enter** entrar, 4.1
**entertaining** entretenido(a)
**enthusiastic** entusiasmado(a)
**entire** entero(a)
**entrance** la entrada, **5.2**
**entrepreneur** el/la empresario(a)
**envelope** el sobre, **12.2**
**environment** el ambiente; el medio ambiente
**episode** el episodio
**epoch** la época
**equal** igual; par
**equation** la ecuación
**equator** la línea ecuatorial
**equilibrium** el equilibrio
**equipment** el equipo
**equivalent** el equivalente
**eraser** la goma de borrar, 3.1
**erroneous** erróneo(a)
**escalator** la escalera mecánica, **9.1**
to **escape** escapar
**especially** especialmente; particularmente; sobre todo
**essential** esencial
to **establish** establecer, fundar
**establishment** el establecimiento
**eternal** eterno(a)
**eternally** de siempre y para siempre
**ethnic** étnico(a)
**euro** euro (currency)
**Europe** la Europa
**European** europeo(a)
**even** aun
**evening** la noche
**in the evening** por la noche
**evening gown** el traje de gala
**event: great event** el buen suceso

**every** cada, 1.2
**everybody** todos(as), 2.2
**everyone** todo el mundo
**everything** todos(as)
**everywhere** por todas partes
**exact** exacto(a)
**exactly** exactamente
to **exaggerate** exagerar
**exaggerated** exagerado(a)
**exam** el examen, 4.2
to **examine** examinar, 8.2
**example: for example** por ejemplo
to **excavate** excavar
**excavation** la excavación
to **exceed** exceder
**excellent** excelente
**exception** la excepción
to **exchange** cambiar, **12.2**
**exchange: exchange rate** el tipo (la tasa) de cambio, **12.2**
**exchange student** el/la estudiante de intercambio
to **exclaim** exclamar
**exclusively** exclusivamente
**excuse me** perdón
to **exercise** hacer los ejercicios
**exhaust pipe** el tubo de escape
**exhibition (art)** la exposición (de arte), 10.2; la exhibición
to **exist** existir
**existence** la existencia
**exit** la salida, **11.2**
**expedition** la expedición
**expensive** caro(a), 3.2
**experience** la experiencia
to **experiment** experimentar
**expert** el/la experto(a), 9.2
to **explain** explicar, 4.2
**explorer** el/la explorador(a)
**explosion** la explosión
to **export** exportar
to **express an opinion** opinar, **10.2**
**expression** la expresión
**means of expression** el modo de expresión
**expressway** la autopista, **11.2**
**extension** la extensión
**extraordinary** extraordinario(a)
**extreme** extremo(a)
**eye** el ojo, 8.2

**fabulous** fabuloso(a)
**face** la cara, 12.1
**face down** boca abajo, **3.1**
**face up** boca arriba, **3.1**
to **facilitate** facilitar
**factory** la fábrica, **9.1**
**factory worker** el/la obrero(a), **9.1**
**faithful** fiel
to **fall** caerse
to **fall asleep** dormirse, 12.1
**false** falso(a)
**fame** la fama
**family** la familia, 6.1
**family (related to the)** familiar
**famous** famoso(a), 1.2; célebre
**fan (sports)** el/la aficionado(a)
**fantastic** fantástico(a), 1.2
**far** lejos, **12.2**
**fare** la tarifa
**farm** la finca, **9.2**
**farm animals** los animales domésticos, **9.2**
**farmer** el/la agricultor(a)
to **fascinate** fascinar
**fast: as fast as possible** a toda prisa
to **fasten** abrocharse, **7.1**
**fat** gordo(a), 1.2
**fat** la grasa
**father** el padre, 6.1
**father-in-law** el suegro
**fault** el defecto
**favorite** favorito(a)
**fax** el facsímil, el fax, **3.1**
**fear** el miedo; el terror
to **fear** temer
**February** febrero, BV
to **feel** sentirse (ie, i), **8.1**
**Ferris wheel** la noria, **5.2**
to **fete** festejar
**fever** la fiebre, 8.1
**to have a fever** tener fiebre, 8.1
**few** poco(a), 2.1
**fewer** menos
**fiancé(e)** el/la novio(a)
**fiction** la ficción
**fictitious** ficticio(a)
**field** el campo, **9.2**
**baseball field** el campo de béisbol, 7.2
**soccer field** el campo de fútbol, 7.1
**fifteen** quince, BV
**fifteen-year-old (girl)** la quinceañera
**fifth** quinto(a), 6.2
**fifty** cincuenta, 2.2
to **fight** luchar
**figurative** figurativo(a)
**figure** la figura
to **fill** rellenar
to **fill out** llenar, **5.1**
to **fill out the form** llenar el formulario, **8.2**
**fillet** el filete
**film** la película, 6.2; el film, 10.1
**to see a film** ver una película, 10.1
**finally** por fin
**finances** las finanzas
**financial** financiero(a)
to **find** encontrar (ue); hallar
**fine** bien, BV
**fine** la multa
**finger** el dedo, **4.1**
to **finish** terminar, **3.1**
**fire** el fuego, **10.2**
**first** primero(a), BV
**first aid service** el servicio de primeros auxilios, **8.1**
**first class** en primera (clase), 13.1

**fish (food)** el pescado, 5.2
**fish market** la pescadería, **4.2**
to **fit** caber
**It (They) do(es)n't fit me.** No me queda(n) bien., **4.1**
**five** cinco, BV
**five hundred** quinientos(as), 3.2
to **fix** fijar
**fixed** fijo(a)
**flamenco** flamenco(a)
**traditional flamenco singing** el cante jondo
**flat (tire)** pinchado(a)
**flaw** el defecto
**flight** el vuelo, 11.1
**direct flight** el vuelo directo domestic flight el vuelo nacional
**flight number** el número del vuelo, 11.1
**to take a flight** tomar un vuelo, 11.1
**flight attendant** el/la asistente de vuelo, 11.2
**floor** el piso, la planta, 6.2
**ground floor** la planta baja, 6.2
**flower** la flor
**flu** la gripe, 8.1
**flute** la flauta
to **fly** volar (ue), **7.2**
to **fly over** sobrevolar, **7.2**
**folder** la carpeta, 3.1
**folk healer** el/la curandero(a)
to **follow** seguir (i, i)
**following** siguiente
**fond of** aficionado(a) a, 10.1
**food** la comida, 5.2; el alimento, el comestible, 14.2; **2.2**
**foolish** tonto(a)
**foot** el pie, 7.1
**on foot** a pie, 4.1
**for** de, BV; para; por
**for example** por ejemplo
**for when?** ¿para cuándo?, 14.2; **2.2**
**forbidden** prohibido(a), **11.2**
**forecast** el pronóstico
**forehead** la frente, **8.1**
**foreign** extranjero(a)
**foreign country** el país extranjero, 11.2
**foreign exchange office** la casa de cambio, **12.2**
**foreigner** el/la extranjero(a)
**forever** de siempre y para siempre
**fork** el tenedor, 14.1; **2.1**
**form** el formulario, **8.2**
to **form** formar
**fortification** la fortificación
**fortunate** afortunado(a)
**fortune** la buenaventura
**forty** cuarenta, 2.2
to **found** fundar
**foundation** la fundación
**four** cuatro, BV
**four hundred** cuatrocientos(as), 3.2
**fourteen** catorce, BV
**fourth** cuarto(a), 6.2
**fracture** la fractura, **8.1**
**fragment** el fragmento
**frank** franco(a)
**free** libre, 5.1
**freezer** el congelador, **10.1**
**French** el francés, 2.2
**French fries** las papas fritas, 5.1
**frequently** frecuentemente, con frecuencia, **3.2**
**fresh** fresco(a), **4.2**
**Friday** el viernes, BV
**fried** frito(a), 5.1
**friend** el/la amigo(a), 1.1; el/la compañero(a), 1.2
**frightful** espantoso(a)
**from** de, BV; desde
**from (time) to (time)** de... a..., 2.2
**front** delantero(a)
**in front of** delante de, 10.1
**frozen** congelado(a), **4.2**
**frozen food** los productos congelados, 5.2
**fruit** la fruta, 5.2
**fruit store** la frutería, **4.2**
to **fry** freír (i, i), 14.1; **2.1**
**frying pan** el/la sartén, **10.1**
**full** lleno(a)
**full (train)** completo(a), 13.2
**full-time job** un trabajo a tiempo completo, **14.2**
**fun** divertido(a)
**function** la función, 10.2
**functioning** el funcionamiento
**fund** el fondo
**fundamental** primordial
**funny** cómico(a), gracioso(a), 1.1
**furious** furioso(a)
**furniture** los muebles
**fury** la furia
**future** el futuro

**galaxy** la galaxia
**gallant** gallardo(a)
**gallon** el galón
**game** el juego; **(match)** el partido, 7.1; **(of dominos, etc.)** la partida
**baseball game** el juego de béisbol, 7.2
**Olympic Games** los Juegos Olímpicos
**tennis game** el juego de tenis, 9.1
**video game** el juego de video, **5.1**
**game arcade** la sala de juegos, **5.1**
**game board** el tablero, **5.1**
**game piece** la ficha, **5.1**
**garage** el garaje, 6.2
**garantee** la garantía
**garden** el jardín, 6.2
**garlic** el ajo, 14.2; **2.2**
**gas station** la gasolinera, **11.1**
**gas tank** el tanque, **11.1**
**gasoline** la gasolina, **11.1**
**regular (super) gasoline** súper, **11.2**
**unleaded** sin plomo, **11.1**

**gate** la puerta, 11.1
**gathering** la reunión
**generally** en general; generalmente
**in general,** usually por lo general
**generous** generoso(a), 1.2
**genre** el género
**gentleman** el caballero, **4.1**
**geography** la geografía, 2.2
**geometric** geométrico(a)
**geometry** la geometría, 2.2
**German (language)** el alemán, 2.2
**gesture** el gesto
to **get** sacar, 4.2
to **get a good (bad) grade** sacar una nota buena (mala), 4.2
to **get, buy a ticket** sacar un billete
to **get engaged** comprometerse
to **get off** bajar, 13.2; **1.2**
to **get off the train** bajar(se) del tren, 13.2; **1.2**
to **get on** subir, 13.2; abordar
to **get on the train** subir al tren, 13.1; **1.1**
to **get together** reunirse
to **get up** levantarse, 12.1
**giant** el gigante
**gift** el regalo, 6.1
**girl** la muchacha, 1.1; la chica
**girlfriend** la novia
to **give** dar, 4.2
**to give back** devolver (ue)
**to give (throw) a party** dar una fiesta, 4.2
**to give (someone) a present** regalar
**to give (someone) a shot (an injection)** poner una inyección
**to give a test** dar un examen, 4.2
to **give up** renunciar
**glass (drinking)** el vaso, 12.1
**glove** el guante, 7.2
to **go** ir, 4.1
**let's go** vamos
**to go back** volver (ue), 7.1
**to go back home** volver (ue) a casa, 10.2
**to go by bicycle** ir en bicicleta, 12.2
**to go by car** ir en carro (coche), 4.1
**to go by train** ir en tren
**to go on a trip** viajar, 11.1
**to go on foot** ir a pie, 4.1
**to go shopping** ir de compras, 5.2
**to go through** pasar por, 11.1
to **go down** bajar, 9.2
to **go surfing (windsurfing, etc.)** practicar el surfing (la plancha de vela, etc.), 9.1
to **go swimming** nadar, 9.1
to **go to bed** acostarse (ue), 12.1
to **go up** subir, 6.2
**goal line** la portería, 7.1
**goalkeeper, goalie** el/la portero(a), 7.1
**godfather** el padrino, **13.1**
**godmother** la madrina
**godparents** los padrinos
**gold** el oro
**gold chain** una cadena de oro, **4.1**
**golden** dorado(a)
**good** buen; bueno(a), 1.2
**Good afternoon.** Buenas tardes., BV
**Good evening.** Buenas noches., BV
**Good heavens!, You bet!** ¡hombre!
**Good morning. Hello.** Buenos días., BV
**to be in a good mood** estar de buen humor, 8.1
**good-bye** adiós, ¡Chao!, BV
**goods and services** los bienes y servicios
**Gosh!** ¡Dios mío!
**gossip item** el chisme
**government** el gobierno, **14.1**
**federal government** el gobierno federal
**municipal government** el gobierno municipal, **14.1**
**state government** el gobierno estatal
**grade** el grado; la nota, 4.2
**high grade** la nota alta, 4.2
**low grade** la nota baja, 4.2
**to get a good (bad) grade** sacar una nota buena (mala), 4.2
**graduate** el/la diplomado(a)
to **graduate** graduarse
**grain** el cereal, **9.2**
**grain** el grano
**gram** el gramo
**grammar** la gramática
**granddaughter** la nieta, 6.1
**grandfather** el abuelo, 6.1
**grandmother** la abuela, 6.1
**grandparents** los abuelos, 6.1
**grandson** el nieto, 6.1
**grapefruit** la toronja, **10.1**
**grapes** las uvas, **10.1**
to **grate** rallar, **10.2**
**grave (serious)** grave
**gray** gris, 3.2
**great** gran, grande
**greater, greatest** mayor
**greater part, the most** la mayor parte
**Greek** el/la griego(a)
**green** verde, 3.2
**green bean** la judía verde, 5.2
**greengrocer store** la verdulería, **4.2**
to **greet** saludar
**greeting** el saludo, BV
**grill** la parrilla, **10.1**
**grocery store** el colmado, la tienda de abarrotes, la tienda de ultramarinos, **4.2**
**groom** el novio, **13.1**
**ground** el suelo
**group** el grupo
to **grow** cultivar, **9.2**
**growth** el crecimiento

to **guard** guardar, 7.1
**Guatemalan** guatemalteco(a)
**guerrilla band** la guerrilla
to **guess** adivinar
to **guess right** acertar (ie)
**guest** el/la invitado(a); el/la huésped, **6.1**
**guidance counselor** el/la consejero(a) de orientación
**guide** el/la guía
**guitar** la guitarra
**gulf** el golfo
**gymnasium** el gimnasio
**gynecologist** el/la ginecólogo(a)
**gynecology** la ginecología

**hair** el pelo, **12.1**; el cabello, **12.1**
**hair dryer** el secador, **12.1**
**hair salon** la peluquería, **12.1**
**hair stylist** el/la peluquero(a), **12.1**
**haircut** el corte de pelo, **12.1**
**hairdo** el peinado
**half** la mitad
**half** medio(a), 5.2
**half an hour** media hora
**half-past (time)** y media
**half (game)** el tiempo
**second half (game)** el segundo tiempo, 7.1
**hall** el salón, **13.1**
**ham** el jamón, 5.1
**hamburger** la hamburguesa, 5.1
**hand** la mano, 7.1
**to hand out** distribuir, **7.1**
**to shake hands** dar la mano
**handkerchief** el pañuelo, **4.1**
**handsome** guapo(a), 1.1
to **hang, hang up** colgar (ue)
to **happen** ocurrir, suceder; pasar
**happiness** la alegría; la felicidad
**happy** contento(a), 8.1; alegre
**Happy birthday!** ¡Feliz cumpleaños!, **13.1**
**hard** duro(a), 2.1
**hardworking** ambicioso(a), 1.1
**harmonious** harmonioso(a)
to **harvest** cosechar, **9.2**
**harvest** la cosecha, **9.2**
**hat** el sombrero; la gorra, 3.2
to **have** tener (ie), 6.1
**to have (subtitles, ingredients, etc.)** llevar
**to have a cold** tener catarro, estar resfriado(a), 8.1
**to have a cough** tener tos, 8.1
**to have a headache** tener dolor de cabeza, 8.1
**to have a snack** tomar una merienda, 4.2
**to have a sore throat** tener dolor de garganta, 8.1
**to have to** tener que
to **have just (done something)** acabar de, **8.1**
**he** él, 1.1
**head** la cabeza, 7.1
**headache** el dolor de cabeza, 8.1
**health** la salud
**healthy** sano(a)
to **hear** oír
**to hear the dial tone** oír el tono, **3.2**
**heart** el corazón
**heat: on low heat** a fuego lento
**heavy** pesado(a)
**heel** el tacón, **4.1**
**height** la altura, **7.2**
**helicopter** el helicóptero, **7.2**
**Hello!** ¡Hola!, BV
**Hello! (answering the telephone–Spain)** ¡Diga!, 14.2; **2.2**
to **help** ayudar, 13.1; dar auxilio; socorrer
**help** el socorro, la ayuda
**hemisphere: northern hemisphere** el hemisferio norte
**southern hemisphere** el hemisferio sur
**hen** la gallina, **9.2**
**her** *(f. sing.) (pron.)* la
**her** su
**here** aquí
**Here is (are) . . .** Aquí tiene (tienes, tienen)...
**hero** el/la héroe
to **hide** esconder
**high** alto(a), 4.2; elevado
**high school** el liceo; la escuela secundaria, 1.1; la escuela superior
**highway** la carretera, la autovía, la autopista, **11.2**
**hike: to take a hike** dar una caminata, 12.2
**him** *(m. sing.) (pron.)* lo
**to him, to her; to you** *(pron.)* le
**his** su
**Hispanic** hispano(a), hispánico(a)
**historian** el/la historiador(a)
**historical** histórico(a)
**history** la historia, 2.2
to **hit** golpear, 9.2
to **hit (baseball)** batear, 7.2
**hobby** el pasatiempo, el hobby, 5.1
**hole** el agujero
**home** la casa, 6.2
**at home** en casa
**country home** la casa de campo, **9.2**
**home** economics la economía doméstica, 2.2
**home plate** el platillo, 7.2
**home run** el jonrón, 7.2
**honest** honesto(a), 1.2

**honeymoon** la luna de miel
to **honk the horn** tocar la bocina
**honor** el honor
**maid of honor** la dama de honor, **13.1**
**hood (automobile)** el capó, **11.1**
to **hope** esperar
**I hope** ojalá, **14.1**
**horn** el claxon, la bocina, **11.1**
**horrible** horrible
**horse** el caballo
**horseback: to go horseback riding** pasear a caballo; montar a caballo
**hospital** el hospital, **8.1**
**hot: It's hot.** Hace calor., 9.1
**hotel** el hotel, **6.1**
**inexpensive hotel** el hostal, 12.2
**hour** la hora
**departure hour** la hora de salida
**house** la casa, 6.2
**apartment house** la casa de apartamentos (departamentos), 6.2
**private house** la casa privada (particular), 6.2
**housing** la vivienda
**how?** ¿qué?, BV; ¿cómo?, 1.1
**How absurd!** ¡Qué absurdo!
**How are you?** ¿Qué tal?, BV
**How is ...?** ¿Cómo está...?, 8.1
**How may I help you?** ¿En qué puedo servirle?, **4.1**
**How much do(es) . . . cost?** ¿Cuánto cuesta(n)... ?, 3.1
**How much is (are) . . . ?** ¿A cuánto está(n)... ?, 5.2
**how many?** ¿cuántos(as)?, 2.1
**how much?** ¿cuánto?, 3.1
**human being** el ser humano
**humble** humilde
**humid** húmedo(a)
**hungry: to be hungry** tener hambre, 14.1; **2.1**
to **hurt** doler (ue), 8.2
**My . . . hurt(s) me** Me duele(n)..., 8.2
to **hurt oneself** hacerse daño, lastimarse, **8.1**
**husband** el marido, el esposo, 6.1
**hydrofoil** el aerodeslizador; el hidrofoil
**hygiene** la higiene
**hypermarket** el hipermercado, **4.2**

**I** yo, 1.1
**ice cream** el helado, 5.1
**chocolate ice cream** el helado de chocolate, 5.1
**vanilla ice cream** el helado de vainilla, 5.1
**icon** el icono
**idea** la idea
**ideal** ideal, 1.2
**idealist** el/la idealista
to **identify** identificar
**if** si
**illness** la enfermedad
**illusion** la ilusión
**image** la imagen
**imaginary** imaginario(a)
**imagination** la imaginación
to **imagine** imaginar
**imagined, dreamed of** imaginado(a)
**immediate** inmediato(a)
**immediately** enseguida, 5.1; inmediatamente
**immense** inmenso(a)
**imperative** el imperativo
to **imply that** dar a entender
**important** importante
**impossible** imposible
**in** en
**in case of** en caso de, **7.1**
**in general** por lo general
**in itself** en sí
**in regard to** en cuanto a
to **inaugurate** inaugurar
**Inca** el/la inca
**inch** la pulgada
to **include** incluir, 5.1
to **increase** aumentar
**incredible** increíble
**independence** la independencia
**Indian** indio(a)
to **indicate** indicar, 11.1
**indigenous** indígena
**indispensable** indispensable
**individual** el individuo
**individual: individual sport** el deporte individual
**industrial** industrial
**inexpensive** barato(a), 3.2
to **influence** impresionar
**influence** la influencia
to **inform** informar, 13.2; **1.2**
**information** la información; los datos, **3.1**
**ingredient** el ingrediente
**inhabitant** el/la habitante
**inheritance** la herencia
**inhospitable** inhospitable
**injection** la inyección, 8.2
**to give (someone) an injection** poner una inyección
**inn** el parador; el albergue
**inning** la entrada, 7.2
**innocent** inocente
**innovation** la innovación
**insane** loco(a)
to **insert** meter, **3.1**; introducir, **3.2**
to **inspect** inspeccionar, 11.1
**inspection** el control, 11.1
**installation** la instalación
**installments: in installments** a plazos
**instant** el instante
**instantaneous** instantáneo(a)
**instead of** en vez de
**instruction** la instrucción
**instrument** el instrumento
**insurance** el seguro
**integral** íntegro(a)

# English-Spanish Dictionary

**intelligent** inteligente, 2.1
**interest** el interés
to **interest** interesar
**interesting** interesante, 2.1
**international** internacional
**Internet** Internet, **3.1**
**interpretation** la interpretación
**interpreter** el/la intérprete
to **interrupt** interrumpir
**interruption** la interrupción
**intersection** el cruce, la bocacalle, **11.2**
to **intervene** intervenir
to **interview** entrevistar
**interview** la entrevista, **14.2**
**interviewer** el/la entrevistador(a), **14.2**
**introduction** la introducción
**invention** el invento
**investigation** la investigación
**invitation** la invitación
to **invite** invitar, 6.1
**invoice** la factura, **6.1**
to **iron** planchar, **12.1**
**irrigation** la irrigación
**island** la isla
**it** la, lo
**Italian** italiano(a)
**itinerant** ambulante
**ivory** el marfil

**jacket** la chaqueta, 3.2; el saco, **4.1**
**jai alai** la pelota vasca
**jai alai player** el/la pelotari
**jam** la mermelada
**January** enero, BV
**jar** el frasco, **4.2**
**jeans** el blue jean, **3.2**
**jet** el avión de reacción, el jet, **7.2**
**jewel** la joya, **4.1**
**jewelry store** la joyería, **4.1**
**Jewish** hebreo(a), **13.2**
**job** el trabajo
**job application** la solicitud de empleo, **14.2**
  **full- (part-) time job** el trabajo a tiemp completo (parcial), **14.2**
to **join** enlazar
**judge** el/la juez, **14.1**
**juice** el jugo
  **orange juice** el jugo de naranja, 12.1
**July** julio, BV
to **jump** saltar
**June** junio, BV
**jungle** la jungla; la selva
**just: just after (time)** y pico
  **to have just (done something)** acabar de *(+ infinitive)*, **8.1**

to **keep** guardar, **3.1**
to **keep in shape** mantenerse en forma
**key** la tecla, **3.2**; la llave, **6.1**
**keyboard** el teclado, **3.1**
to **keyboard** entrar los datos, **3.1**
to **kick** tirar, 7.1
  **to kick (throw) the ball** tirar el balón, 7.2
to **kill** matar
**kilogram** el kilo, 5.2
**kilometer** el kilómetro
**kind** la clase
**king** el rey
  **The Three Kings (Wise Men)** Los Reyes Magos, **13.2**
**kitchen** la cocina, 6.2
**knapsack** la mochila, 12.2
**knee** la rodilla, 7.1
**knife** el cuchillo, 14.1; **2.1**
**knight** el caballero
**knight errant** el caballero andante
to **know** conocer, 11.1
to **know (how)** saber, 11.2
**knowledge** el conocimiento

**laboratory** el laboratorio
**lady-in-waiting** la dama
**lake** el lago, **5.2**
**lamb** el cordero, 14.2; **2.2**
**lame** cojo(a)
**lament** el lamento
**lance** la lanza
to **land** aterrizar, 11.2
**land** la tierra
  **by land** por tierra
**landing** el aterrizaje, **7.2**
**landscape** el paisaje
**lane (of highway)** el carril, **11.2**
**language** la lengua, 2.2; el lenguaje; el idioma
**large** gran, grande
to **last** durar, **13.2**
**last** pasado(a); último(a)
**last (year)** el (año) pasado
**late** tarde; con una demora, 11.1; con retraso, 13.2; **1.2**
**later** luego, BV; después; más tarde
  **See you later!** ¡Hasta luego! , BV
**Latin** el latín, 2.2
**Latin** *(adj.)* latino(a)
**Latin America** Latinoamérica, 1.1
**Latin American** Latinoamericano(a)
to **laugh** reír
to **launch** lanzar
**laundromat** la lavandería
**laundry** el lavado, **12.1**
  **dirty laundry** la ropa sucia, **12.1**
**lavatory** el aseo, el lavabo, **7.1**
**lawyer** el/la abogado(a), **14.1**
**lawyer's office** el bufete del abogado, **14.1**
**lazy** perezoso(a), 1.1
to **lead, go (one street into another)** desembocar, **9.1**

# English-Spanish Dictionary

**league** la liga
**Major Leagues** las Grandes Ligas
to **learn** aprender, 5.1
to **leave (something)** dejar, 14.1; **2.1**
**to leave a tip** dejar una propina, 14.1; **2.1**
to **leave** salir, 10.1
**to leave late** salir tarde, 11.1
**to leave on time** salir a tiempo, 11.1
**to leave the theater** salir del teatro, 10.2
**lecture** la conferencia
**left** izquierdo(a), 7.1
**to the left** a la izquierda, **5.2**
**leg** la pierna, 7.1
**lemon** el limón, **10.1**
**lemonade** la limonada, BV
**lentil** la lenteja
**less** menos
**lesser, least** menor
**lesson** la lección, 4.2
to **let** dejar
**letter (of alphabet)** la letra
**letter** la carta, **12.2**
**letter of recommendation** la carta de recomendación
**lettuce** la lechuga, 5.2
**level** el nivel
**liberator** el/la libertador(a)
**license plate** la placa
**life** la vida
**school life** la vida escolar
**life jacket** el chaleco salvavidas, **7.1**
to **lift** levantar
**light (cheerful)** ligero(a)
to **light** encender (ie), **13.2**
**light** la luz, **11.1**
**red light** la luz roja, **11.2**
**like** como, 1.2
to **like, to be pleasing** gustar
**lime** la lima, **10.1**
**limousine** la limusina
**line (queue)** la cola, 10.1; la fila, **5.2**
**to stand (wait) in line** hacer cola, **10.1**
**line** la línea
**parallel line** la línea paralela
**telephone line** la línea telefónica
to **line up** hacer cola, 10.1
**lion** el león
**lip** el labio, **8.1**
**liquid** líquido(a)
**list** la lista
to **listen (to)** escuchar, 4.2
**Listen!** ¡Oye!
**liter** el litro
**literal** literal
**literary** literario(a)
**literature** la literatura, 2.1
**little** poco(a), 2.1
**a little** un poco (de)
to **live** vivir, 5.2
**living: to earn one's living** ganar la vida
**living room** la sala, 6.2
**loan** el préstamo
**lobster** la langosta, 14.2; **2.2**
**local** local, 13.2; **1.2**
to **lodge** alojarse; hospedarse
**logical** lógico(a)
**long** largo(a), 3.2
to **look at** mirar, 3.1
**Look!** ¡Mira!
to **look at oneself** mirarse, 12.1
to **look for** buscar, 3.1
to **look good (food)** tener buena pinta, **4.2**
to **look like** parecer, **8.1**
to **lose** perder (ie), 7.1
**lotto** el loto
**love** el amor
to **love** querer; amar; encantar
**low** bajo(a), 4.2
to **lower** bajar, 9.2
**luck** la suerte
**Good luck!** ¡Buena suerte!
**luggage** el equipaje, 11.1
**carry-on luggage** el equipaje de mano, 11.1
**to check luggage** facturar el equipaje, 11.1
**to claim luggage** reclamar
**lunch** el almuerzo, 5.2
**to have, eat lunch** tomar el almuerzo, almorzar (ue)
**luxurious** lujoso(a)
**lying** mentiroso(a)
**lyric** lírico(a)

**made** hecho(a)
**magazine** la revista, 6.2
**magnificent** magnífico(a)
**maid** la camarera, **6.2**
**maid of honor** la dama de honor, **13.1**
**mail** el correo, **12.2**
**air mail** el correo aéreo, **12.2**
**e-mail** el correo electrónico, **3.1**
**regular mail** el correo ordinario, **12.2**
to **mail the letter** echar la carta (en el buzón), **12.2**
**mailbox** el buzón, **12.2**
**main** principal
**mainly** principalmente
to **maintain** mantener
**majority** la mayoría
to **make** hacer
**to make a telephone call** hacer una llamada telefónica, **3.2**
**to make the bed** hacer la cama, **6.2**
to **make up** formar
**makeup** el maquillaje, 12.1
**to put one's makeup on** maquillarse, poner el maquillaje, 12.1
**male** el varón
**man** el hombre; el caballero, **4.1**
**manager** el/la gerente, **14.1**
**manner** el modo; la manera, 1.1
**manufactured** fabricado(a)

**many; a lot** muchos(as), 2.1
**map** el mapa; el plano, **9.1**
**March** marzo, BV
to **march** marchar
**marker** el marcador, 3.1
**market** el mercado, 5.2
**meat market** la carnicería, **4.2**
**marketing** el mercadeo
**marmalade** la mermelada
**marriage** el matrimonio
**to get married** casarse, **13.1**
**marvelous** maravilloso(a)
**mass** la masa
to **match** parear
**material** el material
**raw material** la material prima
**mathematics** las matemáticas, 2.1
**matter** la materia
**maximum** máximo(a), **11.2**
**May** mayo, BV
**Maya** el/la maya
**mayonnaise** la mayonesa
**mayor** el alcalde, **14.1**; la alcaldesa
**me** *(pron.)* me
**to me** a mí
**meal** la comida, 5.2
**to prepare the meal** preparar la comida
to **mean** significar
**meaning** el significado; el sentido
**meaningful** significante
**means** el medio
**means of expression** el modo de expresión
**means of transportation** el medio de transporte
to **measure** medir (i, i)
**measurement** la medida
**meat** la carne, 5.2
**mechanic** el/la mecánico(a)
**medal** la medalla
**medical office** el consultorio, 8.2
**medicine (discipline)** la medicina, 8.2
**medicine (drugs)** el medicamento, 8.2
**medium** mediano(a), **4.1**
**medium** el medio
to **meet** encontrarse (ue)
**melancholic** melancólico(a)
**member** el miembro, 4.2
**memory** la memoria; el recuerdo
**men: men's clothing store** la tienda de ropa para caballeros, **4.1**
**menace** la plaga
**menorah** la menora, **13.2**
to **mention** mencionar
**menu** el menú, 5.1
**merchandise** la mercancía, **14.1**
**merengue** el merengue
**merry-go-round** el tiovivo, **5.2**
**message** el mensaje, **3.2**
**mestizo** el/la mestizo(a)
**metabolism** el metabolismo
**meter** el metro
**method** el método
**metrics** la métrica
**metro entrance** la boca del metro, **9.1**
**Mexican** mexicano(a), 1.1
**Mexican American** mexicanoamericano(a)
**microbe** el microbio
**microscope** el microscopio
**microscopic** microscópico(a)
**microwave oven** el horno de microondas, **10.1**
**middle: in the middle of (noun)** en pleno + *noun*
**middle school** la escuela intermedia
**midnight** la medianoche
**migration** la migración
**mile** la milla
**milk** la leche
**million** el millón
**millionaire** el/la millonario(a)
**mime** el/la mimo, **5.2**
**miniature** la miniatura
**miniaturization** la miniaturización
**ministry** el ministerio
to **mint** acuñar
**minute** el minuto
**mirror** el espejo, 12.1
to **miss** perder (ie), 10.2
**to miss the bus** perder el autobús (la guagua, el camión), 10.1
**Miss, Ms.** la señorita, BV
**mixture** la mezcla
**mode** la modalidad
**model** el/la modelo
**modem** el módem
**moderation** la moderación
**modern** moderno(a)
**mom** la mamá
**moment** el momento
**monastery** el monasterio
**Monday** el lunes, BV
**money** el dinero, 14.1; **2.1**
**money (income)** la plata
**money changer** el/la cambista, **12.2**
**monitor** el monitor, **3.1**
**monkey** el mono, **5.2**
**monster** el monstruo
**month** el mes, BV
**monthly installment** la mensualidad
**monument** el monumento
**mood** el humor, 8.1
**to be in a bad (good) mood** estar de mal (buen) humor, 8.1
**moon** la luna
**Moor** el/la moro(a)
**more** más, 2.2
**more or less** más o menos
**moreover** además
**morning** la mañana
**A.M. (time)** de la mañana
**in the morning** por la mañana
**mortality** la mortalidad
**mortgage** la hipoteca
**mother** la madre, 6.1
**motion** la moción
**motive** el motivo

**motor** el motor
**mountain** la montaña, 9.2
**mountain range** la sierra; la cordillera, **7.2**
**mountainous** montañoso(a)
**mouse** el ratón, **3.1**
**mouth** la boca, 8.2
to **move** mover (ue), mudarse
**movement** el movimiento
**movie** la película, 6.2
**movie theater** el cine, 10.1
**Ms., Mrs., madam** la señora, BV
**much; a lot** mucho(a), 2.1
**mud** el lodo
**multinational** multinacional
**multiplication** la multiplicación
to **multiply** multiplicar
**mural** el mural, 10.2
**muralist** el/la muralista
**muscular** muscular
**museum** el museo, 10.2
**music** la música, 2.2
**musical instrument** el instrumento musical
**musician** el/la músico(a)
**mussels** los mejillones, **10.2**
**must** deber
**mute** mudo(a)
**my** mi
**mysterious** misterioso(a)
**mystery** el misterio
**mythology** la mitología

**name** el nombre
**in whose name?** ¿a nombre de quién?, 14.2; **2.2**
**last name** el apellido
**nap: to take a nap** echar (tomar) una siesta
**napkin** la servilleta, 14.1; **2.1**
**narcotic** el narcótico
to **narrate** narrar
**narration** la narración
**narrow** estrecho(a), **4.1**; angosto(a), **9.1**
**narrow street** la callecita, **9.1**
**national** nacional
**nationality** la nacionalidad, 1.2
**what nationality?** ¿de qué nacionalidad?
**native** indígena
**native person** el/la indígena
**natural resources** los recursos naturales, 2.1
**natural sciences** las ciencias naturales
**nature** la naturaleza
**navegable** navegable
to **navigate** navegar
**near** cerca de, 6.2
**nearby** cercano(a)
**necessary** necesario(a)
**necessity** la necesidad
**neck** el cuello, **4.1**
to **need** necesitar, 3.1
**negative** negativo(a)
**neighbor** el/la vecino(a)
**neighborhood** el barrio, **9.1**; la zona
**nephew** el sobrino, 6.1
**nervous** nervioso(a), 8.1
**net** la red, 9.1
**Net (Internet)** net
**nettle** la ortiga
**never** jamás; nunca
**new** nuevo(a)
**newlyweds** los novios, **13.1**
**New Year** el Año Nuevo, **13.2**
**Happy New Year!** ¡Próspero Año Nuevo!, **13.2**
**New Year's Eve** la Nochevieja, la víspera de Año Nuevo, **13.2**
**news** las noticias, 6.2
**newspaper** el periódico, 6.2
**newsstand** el quiosco, 13.1; **1.1**
**next** próximo(a),13.2; 1.2
**at the next stop** en la próxima parada, 13.2; 1.2
**nice** simpático(a), 1.2
**niece** la sobrina, 6.1
**night** la noche
**Good night.** Buenas noches., BV
**in the evening, at night** por la noche
**last night** anoche, 9.2
**P.M. (time)** de la noche
**nine** nueve, BV
**nine hundred** novecientos(as), 3.2
**nineteen** diecinueve, BV
**ninety** noventa, 2.2
**ninth** noveno(a), 6.2
**no** no, BV
**no one** nadie
**no smoking sign** la señal de no fumar, **7.1**
**Nobel Prize** el Premio Nóbel
**noble** noble
**none, not any** ninguno(a)
**by no means** de ninguna manera, 1.1
**nonstop** sin escala
**noon** el mediodía
**north** el norte
**North America** la América del Norte
**North American** norteamericano(a)
**northwest** el noroeste
**nose** la nariz, **8.1**
**notable** notable
to **note** notar
**notebook** el cuaderno, 3.1
**notes: to take notes** tomar apuntes, 4.2
**nothing** nada, 5.2
**Nothing else.** Nada más., 5.2
**novel** la novela
**novelist** el/la novelista
**November** noviembre, BV
**now** ahora, 4.2; ya
**now and then** de vez en cuando
**nowadays, these days** hoy (en) día
**number** el número, 1.2
**flight number** el número del vuelo, 11.1
**local number** el número local
**seat number** el número del asiento, 11.1

**telephone number** el número de teléfono
**wrong number** el número equivocado
**numerous** numeroso(a)
**nuptial, wedding** nupcial
**nurse** el/la enfermero(a), **8.2**; el/la practicante
**nutrition** la nutrición

**object** el objeto
**objective** el objetivo
**obligation** la obligación
**observation** la observación
to **observe** observar
**observer** el/la observador(a)
**obstacle** el obstáculo
to **obtain** obtener
**obvious** obvio(a)
**occasion** la ocasión
**occupied, taken** ocupado(a), 5.1
**ocean** el océano
**October** octubre, BV
**odd: odd number** el número impar
**of** de, BV
**Of course!** ¡Cómo no!; por supuesto
**of the, from the** del
to **offer** ofrecer, **14.2**
**office** la oficina, **9.1**
**official** oficial
**often** con frecuencia, a menudo, **3.2**
**oil** el aceite, 14.2; el óleo
**oil (relating to)** petrolero(a)
**OK, all right; in agreement** de acuerdo; ¡vale!
**old** viejo(a), anciano(a), 6.1; antiguo(a), **5.1**
**old person** el/la anciano(a); el/la viejo(a)
**olive oil** el aceite de oliva
**on** en; sobre
**on foot** a pie, 4.1
**on the dot, sharp** en punto, 4.1
**once and for all** definitivamente
**oncologist** el/la oncólogo(a)
**oncology** la oncología
**one** uno, BV
**one o'clock** la una
**one-way street** la calle de sentido único, **11.2**
**one-way ticket** el billete sencillo, 13.1; **1.1**
**one hundred** cien(to), 3.2
**onion** la cebolla, **10.1**
**only** único(a); sólo; solamente
to **open** abrir, 8.2
**opening** la apertura
**opera** la ópera
to **operate** operar
**operating room** el quirófano
**operator** el/la operador(a)
**operetta** la opereta
**ophthalmologist** el/la oftalmólogo(a)
**ophthalmology** la oftalmología
**opinion** la opinión
**opportunity** la oportunidad
**opposite** opuesto(a); contrario(a)
**the opposite** lo contrario
**the opposite direction** el sentido contrario, **11.2**
**or** o; u (used instead of **o** before words beginning with **o** or **ho**)
**orally** oralmente
**orange (fruit)** la china; la naranja, 5.2
**orange** anaranjado(a), 3.2
**orange juice** el jugo de naranja, 12.1; el zumo de naranja
**orchard** el/la huerto(a), **9.2**
**orchestra** la orquesta
**symphony orchestra** la orquesta sinfónica
**order (restaurant)** la orden, 5.1
to **order** mandar; **(restaurant)** pedir (i, i)
**organ** el órgano
**organism** el organismo
to **organize** organizar
**origin** el origen
**ornament** el adorno
**orthopedic surgeon** el/la cirujano(a) ortopédico(a), **8.2**
**orthopedics** la ortopedia
**other** otro(a)
**ounce** la onza
**our** nuestro(a)
**outdoor** *(adj.)* al aire libre
**outdoor café (market, etc.)** el café (mercado, etc.) al aire libre
**outfielder** el/la jardinero(a), 7.2
**outskirts** los alrededores; las afueras, **9.1**
**oven** el horno, **10.1**
**over** sobre
**overcoat** el abrigo, **4.1**
**overland** por tierra
to **overtake** adelantar, **11.2**
to **owe** deber
**own: one's own** propio(a)
**oxygen** el oxígeno
**oxygen mask** la máscara de oxígeno, **7.1**
**oyster** la ostra, **10.2**

to **pack one's suitcase** hacer la maleta
**package** el paquete, 5.2
**page** la página
**pain** el dolor, 8.1
**I have a pain in my . . .** Tengo dolor de..., 8.2
to **paint** pintar, **14.1**
**paintbrush** el pincel
**painter** el/la pintor(a)
**painting** el cuadro, 10.2; la pintura
**pair** el par, **4.1**
**pair of tennis shoes** el par de tenis, 3.2
**palace** el palacio
**palette knife** la espátula
**palm tree** la palma

**pamphlet** el folleto
**Panamanian** panameño(a), 2.1
**Panamerican** panamericano(a)
**pancake** el panqueque
**pants** el pantalón, 3.2
**papaya** la papaya, **10.2**
**paper** el papel, 3.1
**sheet of paper** la hoja de papel, 3.1
**toilet paper** el papel higiénico, 12.2
**paradise** el paraíso
**paragraph** el párrafo
**paramedics** el servicio de primeros auxilios, los socorristas, **8.1**
**parents** los padres, 6.1
to **park** aparcar, estacionar
**park** el parque, **5.2**
**parka** el anorak, 9.2
**parking** el estacionamiento
**parking lot** el aparcamiento
**parking meter** el parquímetro
**part (in hair)** la raya, 12.1
**part** la parte
**the greatest part, the most** la mayor parte
**upper part** la parte superior
**party** la fiesta, **13.1**
**to give (throw) a party** dar una fiesta, 4.2
**pass (permission)** el pase
to **pass** pasar, 7.2; **(car)** adelantar, **11.2**
**passenger** el/la pasajero(a), 11.1
**passionate** apasionado(a)
**passport** el pasaporte, 11.1
**passport inspection** el control de pasaportes, 11.1
**past** pasado(a)
**pastry** el pastel, **4.2**
**path** el camino; la senda, **5.2**
**to walk along the path** caminar por la senda, **5.2**
**patience** la paciencia
**patient** el/la paciente
**pattern** el patrón
**paved** pavimentado(a)
**pavement** el pavimento
to **pay** pagar, 3.1
**to pay at the cashier** pagar en la caja, 3.1
**to pay attention** hacer caso; prestar atención, 4.2
**to pay the bill** pagar la factura, **6.1**
**payment** el pago
**monthly payment** el pago mensual
**pea** el guisante, 5.2
**Peace Corps** el Cuerpo de Paz
**peaceful** tranquilo(a)
**peak** el pico, **7.2**
**peanut** el cacahuete (cacahuate); el maní
**pear** la pera, **9.2**
**pear tree** el peral, **9.2**
**pedestrian** el peatón, **9.1**
**pedestrian street** la calle peatonal, **9.1**
**pediatrician** el/la pediatra
**pediatrics** la pediatría
to **peel** pelar, **10.2**
**pen** la pluma, 3.1
**pencil** el lápiz, 3.1
**peninsula** la península
**penny** el centavo
**people** la gente
**pepper** la pimienta, 14.1; **2.1**
**bell pepper** el pimiento, **10.2**
**percent** por ciento
**percussion** la percusión
to **perfect** perfeccionar
**performance** la función, **(theater)** la representación, 10.2
**perhaps** quizás, **14.2**
**period** el período
**period of time** la época
to **permit** permitir, 11.1
**person** la persona, 1.2
**personality** la personalidad
**personally** personalmente
**Peruvian** peruano(a)
**petition** la petición
**petroleum** el petróleo
**pharmacist** el/la farmacéutico(a), 8.2
**phone** el teléfono
**cell phone** el teléfono celular, **3.2**
**pay phone** el teléfono público, **3.2**
**phone book** la guía telefónica, **3.2**
**phone call** la llamada telefónica, **3.2**
**push-button phone** el teléfono de botones, **3.2**
**photo** la foto
**photograph** la fotografía
**photographer** el/la fotógrafo(a)
**phrase** la frase
**physics** la física, 2.2
**piano** el piano
to **pick up** recoger
to **pick up (the telephone)** descolgar (ue), **3.2**
**picturesque** pintoresco(a), 9.1
**piece** el pedazo, 12.1; el trocito, **10.2**
**little piece** el pedacito, **10.2**
**pig (pork)** el cerdo, 14.2; **2.2**
**pilgrim** el/la peregrino(a)
**pill** la pastilla, la píldora, la tableta, 8.2
**pillow** la almohada, **6.2**
**pilot** el/la piloto, 11.2
**pinch** la pizca
**pink** rosado(a), 3.2
**pint** la pinta
**piping (embroidery)** el cordoncillo
**pirouette** la pirueta
**pitcher** el/la lanzador(a), el/la pícher, 7.2
**pity** la lástima
**pizza** la pizza, BV
to **place** colocar; meter, 7.1
**place** el lugar; el sitio
**placement** la colocación
**plague** la plaga

**plaid** a cuadros
**plain** la llanura, **7.2**
**plan** el plano, **9.1**
to **plan** planear
**plant** la planta
to **plant** sembrar, **9.2**
**plantain** el plátano, 5.2
**fried plantain slice** el tostón
**plastic** plástico(a), **4.2**
**plate** el plato, 14.1; **2.1**
**plateau** la mesa; la meseta, **7.2**
**high plateau** el altiplano, **7.2**
to **play (music)** tocar
**play** la obra teatral, 10.2; la obra dramática
to **play** jugar (ue), 7.1
**to play baseball (soccer, basketball, etc.)** jugar (al) béisbol (fútbol, baloncesto, etc.), 7.1
**player** el/la jugador(a), 7.1
**playwright** el/la dramaturgo(a)
to **plead** rogar (ue)
**pleasant** agradable
**please** por favor, BV; favor de, **11.2**
**pleasure** el gusto
**plentiful** abundante
**plot** el argumento
**plumber** el/la fontanero(a), el/la plomero(a), **14.1**
**pocket** el bolsillo, **4.1**
**poem** el poema
**poet** el poeta
**poetry** la poesía
**point** el tanto, 7.1; el punto
**poisonous** venenoso(a)
**police officer** el/la guardia; el/la agente de policía; el/la policía
**polite** atento(a)
**political** político(a)
**political science** las ciencias políticas
**polka dots: with polka dots** con lunares
to **pollute** contaminar
**polluted** contaminado(a)
**pollution** la contaminación
**poncho** el poncho
**poor** pobre
**poor boy (girl)** el/la pobre
**poor man (woman)** el/la pobretón(ona)
**popular** popular, 2.1
**popularity** la popularidad
**population, people** la población
**porch** el porche
**pork** el puerco
**portable** portátil
**porter** el/la maletero(a), el/la mozo(a), 13.1; **1.1**
**portrait** el retrato
**position** la posición; el puesto, **14.2**
to **possess** poseer
**possibility** la posibilidad
**possible** posible
**post office** el correo, **12.2**
**postcard** la postal, la tarjeta postal, **12.2**
**pot** la cazuela, la olla, **10.1**
**potato** la papa, 5.1; la patata
**mashed potatoes** el puré de papas
**pothole** el bache
**pound** la libra
**practically** casi
to **practice** practicar
**pre-Columbian** precolombino(a)
**precious** precioso(a)
**precise** preciso(a)
**prediction** la predicción
**predominance** el predominio
to **predominate** predominar
to **prefer** preferir (ie, i)
**prenuptial** antenupcial
**preparation** la preparación
to **prepare** preparar
to **prescribe** recetar, 8.2
**prescription** la receta, 8.2
**presence** la presencia
to **present** presentar
**present** *(adj.)* presente
**at the present time** actualmente
**presentation** la presentación
**president** el/la presidente
**pressure** la presión, **11.1**
**prestige** el prestigio
**pretty** bello(a), bonito(a), hermoso(a), lindo(a), 1.1
to **prevail** prevalecer
**price** el precio
to **prick** picar, **8.1**
**priest** el sacerdote
**princess** la princesa
**principal** el/la director(a)
**principal** principal
**printer** la impresora, **3.1**
**private** particular, 6.2; privado(a)
**private house** la casa particular, la casa privada, 6.2
**probable** probable
**problem** el problema
**process** el proceso
to **process** procesar
**procession** la procesión
to **proclaim** proclamar
**produced** producido(a)
**product** el producto, 5.2
**production** la producción
**profession** la profesión, **14.1**
**professor** el/la profesor(a), 2.1
**program (TV)** la emisión, 6.2; el programa
**sports program** la emisión deportiva, 6.2
**progress** el progreso
**project** el proyecto
to **project** proyectar, 10.1
**promiscuity** la promiscuidad
**promise** la promesa
to **promote** promover (ue)
**promotion** la promoción
**pronoun** el pronombre
**prose** la prosa
**prosperous** próspero(a)
**protagonist** el/la protagonista

**protection** la protección
**protein** la proteína
to **protest** protestar
**protoplasm** el protoplasma
to **provide** proveer
**provider** el/la proveedor(a)
**provision** la provisión
**psychiatrist** el/la psiquiatra
**psychiatry** la psiquiatría
**public** público(a)
**publicity** la propaganda
to **publish** publicar
**Puerto Rican** puertorriqueño(a)
to **pull out** arrancar
**pulse** el pulso, **8.2**
**punctual** puntual
**punishment** el castigo
**puppy** el perrito
**pure** puro(a)
to **push** oprimir; pulsar, **3.1**; empujar, **4.2**
to **put** poner, 11.1; colocar
to **put a cast on** poner en un yeso, **8.2**
to **put in** meter, **3.1**
to **put on** ponerse, 12.1
  **to put on a performance** dar una representación, 10.2
  **to put on makeup** ponerse el maquillaje, 12.1
**Pyrenees** los pirineos

## Q

**qualification** la calificación
**quality** la calidad
**quarrel** la disputa
**quarter** el cuarto, 2.2
  **quarter after (the hour)** y cuarto
  **quarter to (the hour)** menos cuarto
**queen** la reina
**question** la pregunta
**questionnaire** el cuestionario
**quickly** rápidamente; rápido
**quiet** tranquilo(a)
**quite** bastante, 1.1

## R

**race** la carrera
**racket (sports)** la raqueta, 9.1
**radiator** el radiador, **11.1**
**railroad** el ferrocarril, 13.1, **1.1**
**railway platform** el andén, 13.1; **1.1**
**rain** la lluvia
to **rain** llover (ue)
  **It's raining.** Llueve., 9.1
**raincoat** el impermeable, la gabardina, **4.1**
to **raise** criar, **9.2**
**ranch** la hacienda; **(Argentina)** la estancia
**rare** raro(a)
**rate** la tarifa; la tasa
  **exchange rate** el tipo de cambio, la tasa de cambio, **12.2**
  **unemployment rate** la tasa de desempleo
**rather** bastante, 1.1
**razor** la navaja, 12.1
**reaction** la reacción
to **read** leer, 5.1
**reading** la lectura
**ready** listo(a)
**realist** el/la realista
**realistic** realista
**really** realmente
**reason** el motivo; la razón
**reasonable** razonable
to **rebound** rebotar
to **receive** recibir, 5.1
**recent** reciente
**recently** recién
**reception** la recepción, **6.1**
**receptionist** el/la recepcionista, **6.1**
**recipe** la receta
to **recite** recitar
to **recognize** reconocer
**recollection** el recuerdo
to **recommend** recomendar (ie)
**recommendation** la recomendación
to **reconcile** conciliar
**recreation** el recreo
to **recruit** reclutar
**rectangle** el rectángulo
**recycling** el reciclaje
**red** rojo(a), 3.2
**redheaded** pelirrojo(a)
to **reduce (dislocated bone)** reducir, **8.2**
**reduced (price)** reducido(a)
to **refer** referir (ie, i)
to **reflect** reflejar; reflexionar
**reflection; reflex** el reflejo
**reforestation** la reforestación
**refrigerator** el refrigerador, la nevera, **10.1**
**refuge** el refugio
**region** la región
**regional** regional
**regionalism** el regionalismo
to **register** registrar
**registration card** la ficha, **6.1**
**regular (gasoline)** normal, **11.1**
**related** relacionado(a)
**relation** la relación
**relative** el/la pariente, 6.1
**relatively** relativamente
**religious** religioso(a)
to **remain** quedar, 7.1
**remainder** el resto
**remains** los restos
to **remember** recordar (ue)
to **renounce** renunciar
to **rent** alquilar, **5.2**; rentar
to **repair** reparar
to **repeat; to take seconds (meal)** repetir (i, i)
to **replace** reemplazar
**report** el informe; el reportaje
to **represent** representar
**representative** el/la representante
**representative** representativo(a)
**republic** la república

to **require** requerir (ie, i)
**requirement** el requisito
**researcher** el/la investigador(a)
**reservation** la reservación, **6.1**
to **reserve** reservar, 14.2; **2.2**
**reserved** reservado(a), 13.2; **1.2**
**residence** la residencia
**resident** el/la residente
**resort** la estación, 10.1
to **respond** responder
**responsibility** la responsabilidad
**to make oneself responsible** responsabilizarse
**rest** demás; el resto
to **rest** descansar
**restaurant** el restaurante, 14.1; **2.1**
to **restore** restaurar
**result** el resultado
**retina** la retina
**return** el regreso
**return trip, trip back** el viaje de regreso
to **return** regresar; volver (ue), 7.1
**to return home** volver a casa, 10.2
to **return (something)** devolver (ue), 7.2
**reverse** inverso(a)
**revolution** la revolución
**rhythm** el ritmo
**rib** la costilla, **10.1**
**ribbon** la cinta
**rice** el arroz, 5.2
**rich** rico(a), 14.2; **2.2**; con mucha plata
**rich person** el/la rico(a)
**ride** la atracción, **5.2**
**right** derecho(a), 7.1
**to the right** a la derecha, **5.2**
**right: that's right (true)!** ¡verdad!
**right away** enseguida, 5.1
**rigorous** riguroso(a)
**ring** el anillo, **4.1**
to **ring** sonar (ue), **3.2**
to **rise** ascender
**ritual** el rito
**rival** el rival
**river** el río, **7.2**
to **roast** asar, **10.1**
**roasted** asado(a)
**rock** la roca
**role** el rol; el papel
**roll of toilet paper** el rollo de papel higiénico, 12.2
to **roll** rodar (ue)
**roller blading** el patinaje lineal
**roller coaster** la montaña rusa, **5.2**
**Roman** el/la romano(a)
**romantic** romántico(a)
**room** el cuarto, la sala, 6.2; la pieza
**double room** el cuarto doble, **6.1**
**recovery room** la sala de recuperación
**single room** el cuarto sencillo, **6.1**
**waiting room** la sala de espera, 13.1; **1.1**
**root** la raíz
**rose** la rosa
**round-trip (ticket)** de ida y vuelta, 13.1; **1.1**
**route** la ruta
**routine** *(adj.)* la rutina, 12.1
**routine** rutinario(a)
**row (of seats)** la fila, 10.1
to **row** remar, **5.2**
**royal** real
**ruin** la ruina
**rule** la regla
**rumor** el rumor
to **run** correr, 7.2
**runway** la pista
**rural** rural

**sacrifice** el sacrificio
to **sacrifice** sacrificar
**sad** triste, 8.1
**safe** salvo(a)
**saffron** el azafrán
**sail (of a windmill)** el aspa
**sailboard** la plancha de vela, 9.1
**sailor** el/la marino(a)
**saint** el santo
**salad** la ensalada, 5.1
**salary** el salario
**sale** la venta, **14.1**
**salesperson** el/la dependiente(a), **4.1**; el/la vendedor(a), **11.1**
**salt** la sal, 14.1; **2.1**
**same** mismo(a), 2.1
**sand** la arena, 9.1
**sandal** el huarache; la alpargata; la sandalia, **4.1**
**sandwich** el sándwich, BV; el bocadillo, 5.1
**sash** la faja
**satisfied** satisfecho(a), **14.1**
to **satisfy** satisfacer
**Saturday** el sábado, BV
**saucepan** la cacerola, **10.2**
**saucer** el platillo, 14.1; **2.1**
**sausage (pork and garlic)** el chorizo, la salchicha, **10.1**
to **save** ahorrar; conservar; salvar; guardar, **3.1**
**savings account** la cuenta de ahorros
**saxophone** el saxofono
to **say** decir
**scales** la báscula, 11.1
**scarf** la bufanda, **4.1**
**scene** la escena
**scenery, set (theater)** el escenario, 10.2
**schedule** el horario, 13.1; **1.1**
**school schedule** el horario escolar
**scholarship** la beca
**school** el colegio, la escuela, 1.1; la academia
**elementary school** la escuela primaria
**high school** la escuela secundaria, 1.1; la escuela superior

**middle school** la escuela intermedia
**school (of a university)** la Facultad
**school (related to)** escolar, 2.1
**school bus** el bus escolar, 4.1
**school life** la vida escolar
**school schedule** el horario escolar
**school supplies** los materiales escolares, 3.1
**science** las ciencias, 2.2
**science fiction** la ciencia ficción
**scientific** científico(a)
**scientist** el/la científico(a)
**scissors** las tijeras, **12.1**
to **score a goal** meter un gol, 7.1
to **score a point** marcar un tanto, 7.1
**scoreboard** el tablero indicador, 7.1
**screen** la pantalla, 10.1
**arrival and departure screen** la pantalla de salidas y llegadas, 11.1
**sculptor** el/la escultor(a), 10.2
**sculpture** la escultura
**sea** el mar, 9.1
**sea level** el nivel del mar
**search: in search of** en busca de
**season** la estación, BV
to **season** sazonar
**seasoning** el condimento
**seat** el asiento, 11.1; la plaza, 13.2; **1.2**
**seat (of government)** la sede
**seat (theater)** la butaca, 10.1
**seat belt** el cinturón de seguridad, **7.1**
**seat number** el número del asiento, 11.1
**second** segundo(a), 6.2
**second class** en segunda (clase), 13.1; **1.1**
**second half (soccer)** el segundo tiempo, 7.1
**secondary** secundario(a)
**secret** el secreto
**secretary** el/la secretario(a), **14.1**
to **secretly take** escamotear
**security** la seguridad, **7.1**
**security check** el control de seguridad, 11.1
**sedan** el sedán, **11.1**
**see: See you later!** ¡Hasta luego!, BV
**See you soon!** ¡Hasta pronto!, BV
**See you tomorrow!** ¡Hasta mañana!, BV
to **see** ver, 5.1
**to see a show** ver un espectáculo, 10.2
to **seem** parecer, **8.1**
to **select** seleccionar
**selection** la selección
**self-portrait** el autorretrato
to **sell** vender, 5.2; despachar, 8.2
**semester** el semestre
**senator** el/la senador(a)
to **send** enviar; mandar, transmitir, **3.1**
**sentence** la frase
**separated** separado(a)
**September** septiembre, BV
**series** la serie
**World Series** la Serie mundial
**serious** serio(a), 1.1; grave
**servant** el/la sirviente
to **serve** servir (i, i), 14.1; **2.1**
**How may I help you?** ¿En qué puedo servirle?, **4.1**
**service** el servicio, 5.1
**service station** la estación de servicio, la gasolinera, **11.1**
**set** el conjunto
to **set the bone** reducir el hueso, **8.2**
to **set the table** poner la mesa, 14.1; **2.1**
**seven** siete, BV
**seven hundred** setecientos(as), 3.2
**seventeen** diecisiete, BV
**seventh** séptimo(a), 6.2
**seventy** setenta, 2.2
to **sew** coser
**sewing** la costura
**sex** el sexo
**shack** la chabola
to **shake hands** dar la mano
**shampoo** el champú, 12.2
**shantytown** la villa miseria **(Arg.);** el pueblo jóven **(Peru)**
**shape** la forma
to **shave** afeitarse, 12.1
**shaving cream** la crema de afeitar, 12.1
**shawl** el poncho
**she** ella, 1.1
**sheet** la sábana, **6.2**
**sheet of paper** la hoja de papel, 3.1
**shellfish** los mariscos, 5.2
**sherbet, sorbet** el sorbete
**shh!** ¡chist!
to **shine** brillar, 9.1
**shirt** la camisa, 3.2
**long-sleeved shirt** la camisa de mangas largas, **4.1**
**short-sleeved shirt** la camisa de mangas cortas, **4.1**
**shoe** el zapato, 3.2
**shoe store** la zapatería, **4.1**
to **shop** ir de compras, **5.2**; hacer las compras, **4.2**
**shop window** el escaparate, la vitrina, **4.1**
**shopping: to go shopping** hacer las compras, **4.2**; ir de compras, **5.2**
**shopping mall** la galería comercial
**short** bajo(a), 1.1; corto(a), 3.2
**short- (long-) term** a corto (largo) plazo
**shortage** la escasez
**shorts** el pantalón corto, 3.2
**shot: to give (someone) a shot** poner una inyección
**should** deber

**shoulder** el hombro, **8.1**
to **show (movie)** presentar; mostrar
**show (movies)** la sesión, 10.1
**show** el espectáculo, 10.2; el show
**shower** la ducha, 12.1
**to take a shower** tomar una ducha, 12.1
**shrimp** los camarones, 14.2; **2.2**; las gambas, **10.2**
**shy** tímido(a), 1.2
**sick** enfermo(a), 8.1
**sick person** el/la enfermo(a), 8.1
**side** *(adj.)* lateral, 13.2; **1.2**
**side** el borde; el lado
**sidewalk** la acera, **9.1**
to **sigh** suspirar
**sign** el rótulo, **11.2**
**traffic sign** la señal de tránsito
to **sign** firmar, **12.2**
**significance** el sentido, **11.2**
**significant** significativo(a)
**similar** parecido(a); similar
**simple** sencillo(a); simple
**since** como; desde
**sincere** franco(a); sincero(a), 1.2
to **sing** cantar, 4.2
**singing** el canto
**single** soltero(a)
**singles** singles, 9.1
**sir, Mr., gentleman** el señor, BV
**sister** la hermana, 6.1
to **sit down** sentarse (ie), 12.1
to **situate** situar
**situation** la situación
**six** seis, BV
**six hundred** seiscientos(as), 3.2
**sixteen** dieciséis, BV
**sixth** sexto(a), 6.2
**sixty** sesenta, 2.2
**size (shoes)** número, 3.2
**size** el tamaño, la talla, 3.2
**What size (shoe) do you wear (take)?** ¿Qué número calza usted?, **3.2**
**What size (clothing) do you wear (take)?** ¿Qué tamaño (talla) usa usted?, **3.2**
**ski** el esquí
to **ski** esquiar, 9.2
**ski lift** el telesquí, 9.2
**ski pole** el bastón, 9.2
**ski resort** la estación de esquí, 9.2
**ski slope** la pista, 9.2
**skier** el/la esquiador(a), 9.2
**skiing** el esquí, 9.2
**skirt** la falda, 3.2
**sky** el cielo, 9.1
**skyscraper** el rascacielos, **9.1**
to **sleep** dormir (ue, u)
**to fall asleep** dormirse (ue, u), 12.1
**sleeping bag** el saco de dormir, 12.2
**sleeve** la manga, **4.1**
**long- (short-) sleeved** de mangas largas (cortas), **4.1**
**slice** la rebanada, la tajada, **4.2**
to **slice** rebanar, **10.2**
**slot** la ranura, **3.1**
**slow** lento(a), **10.2**
**slowly** despacio
**small** pequeño(a), 2.1
**smile: little smile** la sonrisita
**smoking: (no) smoking area** la sección de (no) fumar, 11.1
**snack** la merienda, 4.2
**to have a snack** tomar una merienda, 4.2
to **sneeze** estornudar, 8.1
**snow** la nieve, 9.2
to **snow** nevar (ie), 9.2
**snowboarding** el surf de nieve
**so** así
**so, so much** tan, tanto(a)
**soap** el jabón, 12.2
**bar of soap** la barra (pastilla) de jabón, 12.2
**soccer** el fútbol, 7.1
**soccer field** el campo de fútbol, 7.1
**social sciences** las ciencias sociales, 2.2
**society** la sociedad
**sociology** la sociología
**socks** los calcetines, 3.2
**soda** el cola, 5.1
**sofa** el sofá, **6.2**
**soldier** el militar; el/la soldado
**solitary, lone** solitario(a)
**solution** el remedio; la solución
to **solve** resolver (ue)
**some** algunos(as), 4.1; unos(as)
**someone** alguien
**something** algo, 5.2
**sometimes** de vez en cuando; a veces, 7.1
**son** el hijo, 6.1
**song** la canción
**soon** dentro de poco
**sore throat** el dolor de garganta, 8.1
**sorry: to be sorry** sentir (ie, i)
**sound** el sonido
**soup** la sopa, 5.1
**source** la fuente
**south** el sur
**South America** la América del Sur
**South American** sudamericano(a)
**southeast** el sureste
**southwest** el sudoeste; el suroeste
to **sow** sembrar, **9.2**
**sowing** la siembra
**space** el espacio
**spaghetti** el espagueti
**Spain** la España, 1.2
**Spanish** *(adj.)* español(a)
**Spanish (language)** el español, 2.2
**Spanish American** hispanoamericano(a)
**Spanish speaker** el/la hispanohablante
**Spanish-speaking** hispanohablante

# English-Spanish Dictionary

**Spanish-speaking countries** los países de habla española
**Spanish-style** a la española
**spare tire** la llanta de recambia (repuesto), **11.1**
to **speak** hablar, 3.1; conversar
**special** especial
**specialist** el/la especialista, **14.1**
to **specialize** especializar
**specialty** la especialidad
**spectator** el/la espectador(a), 7.1; el/la mirón(ona)
**speed** la velocidad, **11.2**
**speed limit** el límite de velocidad
to **spend** pasar; gastar
to **spend time** pasar el tiempo, **5.1**
**spice** la especia
**spontaneous** espontáneo(a)
**sport** el deporte, 7.1
**individual sport** el deporte individual
**(related to) sports** deportivo(a), 6.2
**sports program (TV)** la emisión deportiva, 6.2
**team sport** el deporte de equipo
**spring** la primavera, BV
**squid** los calamares, **10.2**
**squire, knight's attendant** el escudero
**stadium** el estadio, 7.1
**stage: to come (go) on stage** entrar en escena, 10.2
**stairway** la escalera, 6.2
**stall** el puesto, **4.2**
**stamp** el sello, la estampilla **5.1**
to **stand on line** hacer cola
**standing** de pie
**star** la estrella
to **start** entablar
**state** el estado
**station** la estación, 10.1
**subway station** la estación del metro, **10.1**
**train station** la estación de ferrocarril, 13.1; **1.1**
**stationery store** la papelería, 3.1
**statistic** la estadística
**statue** la estatua, 10.2
**stay** la estadía
to **stay** alojarse
to **stay in bed** guardar cama, 8.1
**steak** el biftec, 14.2; **2.2**
**step** el paso
**stereo** estereofónico(a)
**still** todavía
**sting** la picadura, **8.1**
to **stir** revolver (ue), **10.1**
**stitch** el punto, la sutura, **8.1**
**stomach** el estómago, 8.1
**stomachache** el dolor de estómago, 8.1
**stone** la piedra
**stop** la parada, 13.2; **1.2**
to **stop** bloquear, parar, 7.1
**stopover** la escala, **7.2**
**store** la tienda, 3.2
to **store** almacenar
**story** el cuento; la historia
**short story** la historieta
**stove** la estufa, **10.1**
**stove burner** la hornilla, **10.1**
**straight** derecho, **11.2**
**to go straight** seguir derecho, **11.2**
**strange** extravagante
**strategy** la estrategia
**straw** la paja, **13.2**
**stream** el arroyo
**street** la calle, 6.2
**one-way street** la calle de sentido único, **11.2**
**pedestrian street** la calle peatonal
**strength** la fortaleza
**stretch (of road)** el trayecto; el tramo
**stretcher** la camilla, **8.1**
to **strike twelve** dar las doce, **13.2**
**string (instrument)** la cuerda
**string bean** la judía verde; el poroto; la vainita; el ejote; la chaucha
**striped** a rayas
**strong** fuerte
**structure** la estructura
**student (relating to)** estudiantil
**student** el/la alumno(a), 1.1; el/la estudiante
**student housing** la residencia para estudiantes, **3.2**
**study** el estudio
to **study** estudiar, 4.1
**stupendous** estupendo(a)
**stupid** torpe
**style** el estilo; la moda
**in style** de moda
**subject** la asignatura, 2.1; la materia; el tema
**subject area (school)** la disciplina, 2.2
**substance: controlled substance** la sustancia controlada
**subterranean** subterráneo(a)
**subtitle** el subtítulo, 10.1
**with subtitles** con subtítulos, 10.1
to **subtract** restar
**suburb** el suburbio; la colonia
**subway** el metro, 10.1
**subway station** la estación de metro, 10.1
**success** el éxito
**suckling pig** el lechón; el cochinillo
**suddenly** repentinamente
to **suffer** sufrir
**sugar** el azúcar, **10.1**
to **suggest** sugerir (ie, i)
**suggestion** la sugerencia
**suit** el traje, 3.2
**suitcase** la maleta, 11.1
**summer** el verano, BV
to **sunbathe** tomar el sol, 9.1
**sunblock** la crema protectora, 9.1

**sunburned, tanned** tostadito(a)
**Sunday** el domingo, BV
**sunglasses** las gafas de sol, los anteojos de sol, 9.1
**sunny: It's sunny.** Hace (Hay) sol., 9.1
**suntan lotion** la loción bronceadora, 9.1
**supermarket** el supermercado, 5.2
**supermarket cart** el carrito, **4.2**
**superstition** la superstición
to **support** sostener
**sure** seguro(a)
to **surf** practicar el surfing (la tabla hawaiana), 9.1
**to surf the Net** navegar por la red
**surface** la superficie
**surfboard** la tabla hawaiana, 9.1
**surfing** el surfing, 9.1
**surgeon** el/la cirujano(a), **8.2**
to **surprise** sorprender
**survey** la encuesta
**sweater** el suéter, **4.1**
**sweet** dulce
**sweet roll** el pan dulce, 5.1
**sweetheart, lover** el/la enamorado(a)
to **swim** nadar, 9.1
to **swim underwater** bucear, 9.1
**swimming** la natación, 9.1
**swimming pool** la alberca, la piscina, 9.1
**swollen** hinchado(a), **8.1**
**symptom** el síntoma, 8.2
**syrup** el sirope
**system** el sistema
**metric system** el sistema métrico

**T-shirt** la camiseta, el T-shirt, 3.2
**table** la mesa, 5.1
**table soccer** el futbolín, **5.1**
**tablecloth** el mantel, 14.1; **2.1**
**tablespoon** la cuchara, 14.1; **2.1**
**taco** el taco, BV
to **take** tomar, 4.1
**to take notes** tomar apuntes, 4.2
**to take one's blood pressure** tomar la tensión (presión) arterial, **8.2**
**to take one's pulse** tomar el pulso, **8.2**
**to take out** sacar, **3.1**
**to take photos** tomar fotos
**to take place** tener lugar, **8.1**
**to take the luggage down** bajar las maletas, **6.1**
**to take the (school) bus** tomar el bus (escolar), 4.1
to **take charge** encargarse
to **take off** quitar, **10.2**
**to take off (airplane)** despegar, **11.2**
**to take off the fire** retirar del fuego, **10.1**
to **take time** tardar
**takeoff (of an airplane)** el despegue, 7.2
**talent** el talento
to **talk** hablar, 3.1; conversar
**tall** alto(a), 1.1
**tamale** el tamal, BV
**tan** bronceado(a)
**tank** el tanque, **11.1**
**task** la tarea
**taxi** el taxi, 11.1
**tea** el té, 5.1
**iced tea** el té helado, 5.1
to **teach** enseñar, 4.1
**teacher** el/la maestro(a); el/la profesor(a), 2.1
**team** el bando; el equipo, 7.1
**team sport** el deporte de equipo, 7.2
**tearoom** la confitería
**teaspoon** la cucharita, 14.1; **2.1**
**technician** el/la técnico(a), **8.2**
**technology** la tecnología
**teenager** el/la adolescente
**telecommunication** la telecomunicación
to **telephone** telefonear
**to talk on the phone** hablar por teléfono
**telephone** el teléfono
**cell phone** el teléfono celular, **3.2**
**public (pay) telephone** el teléfono público, **3.2**
**push-button telephone** el teléfono de botones, **3.2**
**(related to the) telephone** telefónico(a)
**telephone book** la guía telefónica, **3.2**
**telephone call** la llamada telefónica, **3.2**
**telephone keypad** el teclado, **3.2**
**telephone line** la línea telefónica
**telephone receiver** el auricular, **3.2**
**television** la televisión, 6.2
**television set** el televisor, **6.2**
**teller** el/la cajero(a), **12.2**
**teller's window** la ventanilla, **12.2**
**temperate** templado(a)
**temperature** la temperatura, 9.2
**ten** diez
**tender** tierno(a)
**tennis** el tenis, 9.1
**pair of tennis shoes** el par de tenis, 3.2
**tennis player** el/la tenista
**tennis shoes** los tenis, 3.2
**tenth** décimo(a), 6.2
**term** el término
**terminal** el terminal
**passenger terminal** el terminal de pasajeros, **7.2**
**terrace (sidewalk café)** la terraza
**terrible** terrible

**terror** el terror
**test** el examen, 4.2
**tetanus** el tétano
**Thank you.** Gracias., BV
**that (one)** eso
**that** aquel, aquella; ese(a)
**the** la, el, 1.1
**theater** el teatro, 10.2
**theatrical** teatral, 10.2
**their** su, sus, 6.1
**them** las, los
**to them; to you** *(formal pl.) (pron.)* les
**theme** el motivo; el tema
**then** luego, BV; entonces
**there** allí, allá
**there is, there are** hay, BV
**therefore, for this reason, that's why** por eso
**these** estos(as)
**they** ellos(as), 2.1
**thin** delgado(a); flaco(a), 1.2
**thing** la cosa
to **think** pensar (ie); opinar, **10.2**
**third** tercer(o)(a), 6.2
**thirsty: to be thirsty** tener sed, 14.1; **2.1**
**thirteen** trece, BV
**thirty** treinta, BV
**thirty-one** treinta y uno, 2.2
**this (one)** esto
**this** este(a)
**thistle** el cardo
**those** aquellos(as), esos(as)
**thought** el pensamiento
**thousand** mil, 3.2
**three** tres, BV
**three hundred** trescientos(as), 3.2
**Three Wise Men** los Reyes Magos, **13.2**
**throat** la garganta, 8.1
to **throw** echar; lanzar, 7.1; tirar
**to throw (kick) the ball** tirar el balón, 7.2
**Thursday** el jueves, BV
**thus** así
**ticket** el boleto, el ticket, 9.2; el billete, 11.1; el tique, **9.1**
**luggage claim ticket** el talón, 11.1
**one-way ticket** el billete sencillo, 13.1; **1.1**
**round-trip ticket** el billete de ida y vuelta, 13.1; **1.1**
**ticket window** la boletería, la ventanilla, 9.2
**tie** la corbata, 3.2
**tied (score)** empatado(a), 7.1
**The score is tied.** El tanto queda empatado., 7.1
**tiger** el tigre
**time** la hora; el tiempo, **9.1**
**At what time?** ¿A qué hora?
**on time** a tiempo, 11.1
**What time is it?** ¿Qué hora es?
**time** la vez
**at times, sometimes** a veces, 7.1
**at that time** en aquel entonces
**one more time, again** una vez más
**time zone** el huso horario
**timid** tímido(a), 1.2
**tiny** diminuto(a)
**tip** el servicio, 5.1; la propina, 14.1; **2.1**
**Is the tip included?** ¿Está incluido el servicio?, 5.1
**tire** el neumático, la goma, la llanta, **11.1**
**flat tire** la llanta pinchada
**spare tire** la llanta de recambio (repuesto), **11.1**
**tired** cansado(a), 8.1
**to** a
**toast** la tostada; el pan tostado, 5.2
to **toast** tostar
**today** hoy, BV
**together** juntos(as)
**toilet** el inodoro, el váter, **6.2**
**toilet paper** el papel higiénico, 12.2
to **tolerate** consentir (ie, i)
**toll** el peaje, **11.2**
**toll booth** la garita de peaje, **11.2**
**tomato** el tomate
**tomorrow** mañana, BV
**ton** la tonelada
**tonight** esta noche, 9.2
**too much** demasiado
**tooth** el diente
**toothbrush** el cepillo de dientes, 12.2
**toothpaste** la pasta (crema) dentífrica, 12.2
**tortilla** la tortilla, 5.1
**totally** totalmente
**touch** el contacto
to **touch** tocar
**tour** la gira, 12.2
**tour guide** el/la guía
**tourist** el/la turista, 10.2
**toward** en dirección a; hacia
**towel** la toalla, 9.1; **6.2**
**beach towel** la toalla playera, 9.1
**tower** la torre
**control tower** la torre de control, **7.2**
**town** el pueblo, **9.2**
**town square** la plaza, **9.1**
**toxic** tóxico(a)
**toy** el juguete
**track** la vía, 13.1; **1.1**
**trade** el oficio, **14.1**
**tradition** la tradición
**traditional** tradicional
**traffic** el tráfico
**traffic light** el semáforo, **9.1**
**traffic sign** la señal de tránsito
**tragedy** la tragedia
**trail** el camino
**train** el tren, 13.2; **1.2**
**local train** el tren local, 13.2
**nonstop train** el tren directo, 13.2; **1.2**
**train car** el coche, el vagón, 13.1; **1.1**
**cafeteria (dining) car** el coche-cafetería, el coche-comedor, 13.2; **1.2**
**sleeping car** el coche-cama, 13.2
**train conductor** el/la revisor(a), 13.2; **1.2**

**train station** la estación de ferrocarril, 13.1; **1.1**
**training** el entrenamiento
to **transfer** transbordar, 13.2; **1.2**; trasladar
to **transform** convertir (ie, i); transformar
to **transmit** transmitir, **3.1**
**transportation** el transporte
to **travel** circular; recorrer; viajar
to **travel by air** viajar en avión, 11.1
**traveler** el/la viajero(a)
**traveler's check** el cheque de viajero, **12.2**
**tray** la bandeja, **7.1**
**tray table** la mesita, **7.1**
**treat** tratar
**treatment** el tratamiento; la cura
**tree** el árbol
**triangle** el triángulo
**tribe** la tribu
**trip** el viaje
**return trip** el viaje de regreso
**to take a trip** hacer un viaje, 11.1
**trip (distance traveled)** el recorrido
**triumphant** triunfante
**trombone** el trombón
**trousers** el pantalón, 3.2
**trousseau** el ajuar de novia
**true** verdadero(a)
**trumpet** la trompeta
**trunk (of a car)** el/la maletero(a), 11.1; la maletera, 13.1; **1.1**; el baúl, **11.1**
to **try** tratar
to **try on** probarse (ue), **4.1**
**tube of toothpaste** el tubo de pasta (crema) dentífrica, 12.2
**Tuesday** el martes, BV
**tuna** el atún, 5.2
**turbulance** la turbulencia, **7.2**
to **turn** doblar, **11.2**
to **turn around** revolver (ue), **10.1**
to **turn off** apagar (gu), **3.1**
to **turn on** prender, **3.1**
**turning signal** la direccional, **11.1**
**turnstile** el torniquete, **9.1**
**twelve** doce, BV
**twenty** veinte, BV
**twenty-eight** veintiocho, BV
**twenty-five** veinticinco, BV
**twenty-four** veinticuatro, BV
**twenty-nine** veintinueve, BV
**twenty-one** veintiuno, BV
**twenty-seven** veintisiete, BV
**twenty-six** veintiséis, BV
**twenty-three** veintitrés, BV
**twenty-two** veintidós, BV
**twin** el/la gemelo(a)
**twist** torcer (ue), **8.1**
**two** dos, BV
**two hundred** doscientos(as), 3.2
**type** el tipo; la modalidad típico(a)

**ugly** feo(a), 1.1
**uncle** el tío, 6.1
**under** debajo (de)
**undershirt** la camiseta, 3.2
to **understand** comprender, 5.1
**underwater swimming** el buceo, 9.1
**underwear** la ropa interior, **4.1**
**uniform** el uniforme
**union** el enlace
**unique** único(a)
**unit** la unidad
**United States** Estados Unidos
**from the United States** estadounidense
**university** la universidad
**related to university** universitario(a)
**university degree** el título universitario, **14.1**
**unleaded** sin plomo, **11.1**
**unless** a menos que
**unpleasant** desagradable
**until** hasta, BV
**urban** urbano(a)
**urologist** el/la urólogo(a)
**urology** la urología
**us** *(to) (pl. pron.)* nos
to **use** utilizar
**used** usado(a)
**usually** generalmente

**vacation** la vacación, **6.2**
**valley** el valle, **7.2**
**value** el valor
**vanilla** *(adj.)* de vainilla, 5.1
**variation** la variación
**varied** variado(a)
**variety** la variedad
**various** varios(as)
to **vary** variar
**veal** la ternera, 14.2; **2.2**
**vegetable** el vegetal, 5.2; la legumbre
**vegetable garden** el/la huerto(a), **9.2**
**vegetarian** el/la vegetariano(a)
**Venezuelan** venezolano(a)
**verse** el verso
**version: in its original (language) version** en versión original, 10.1
**very** muy, BV
**vest** el chaleco
**veterinarian** el/la veterinario(a)
**vice versa** viceversa
**victim** la víctima, **8.1**
**victorious** victorioso(a)
**video** el video
**video store** la tienda de videos
**view** la vista
**vinegar** el vinagre
**violin** el violín, 2.1
to **visit** visitar
**vitamin** la vitamina
**voice** la voz
**volleyball** el voleibol

**volume** el tomo
**volunteer** el/la voluntario(a)
**vowel** la vocal

to **wait (for)** esperar, 11.1
**waiter, waitress** el/la camarero(a), el/la mesero(a), 5.1
**waiting room** la sala de espera, 13.1; **1.1**
to **wake up** despertarse (ie), 12.1
to **walk** ir a pie, 4.1; andar; caminar, **9.1**
**to take a walk** dar un paseo, **5.2**
**wall** la muralla; la pared
to **want** desear, 3.2; querer (ie)
**I would like . . .** Quisiera... , 14.2; **2.2**
**war** la guerra
to **warn** advertir (ie,i)
to **wash oneself** lavarse, 12.1
**washbasin** el lavabo, **6.2**
**washing machine** la máquina de lavar
**waste** los desechos
**watch** el reloj, **4.1**
to **watch** mirar, 3.1
**water** el agua *(f.)*, 9.1
**mineral water** el agua mineral, 12.2
**running water** el agua corriente
to **water-ski** esquiar en el agua, 9.1
**water-skiing** el esquí acuático, 9.1
**watercolor** la acuarela
**watermelon** la sandía, **10.2**
**wave** la ola, 9.1
**way** el modo; la manera, 1.1
**we** nosotros(as), 2.2
**weapon** el arma (f.)
to **wear** llevar, 3.2
to **wear (size)** usar, 3.2; **(shoe size)** calzar, 3.2
**weather** el tiempo, 9.1
**It's cold.** Hace frío., 9.2
**It's hot.** Hace calor., 9.1
**It's sunny.** Hace sol., 9.1
**The weather is bad.** Hace mal tiempo., 9.1
**The weather is nice.** Hace buen tiempo., 9.1
**Web page** la página Web
**wedding** la boda, **13.1**
**Wednesday** el miércoles, BV
**week** la semana, BV
**last week** la semana pasada, 9.2
**weekend** el fin de semana, BV
**last weekend** el fin de semana pasado
to **weigh** pesar
**weight** la pesa; el peso
**welcome** dar la bienvenida, 11.2
**You're welcome.** De nada., Por nada., No hay de qué., BV
**well** bien, BV; pues
**very well** muy bien, BV
**well-known** renombrado(a)
**west** el oeste
**western** occidental
**what, that which** lo que
**what?** ¿qué?, BV
**What's the matter (with you)?** ¿Qué te pasa?, 8.2
**wheat** el trigo, **9.2**
**wheelchair** la silla de ruedas, **8.2**
**when** cuando, 4.2
**when?** ¿cuándo?, 4.1
**where** donde, 1.2
**where?** ¿adónde?, 1.1; ¿dónde?, 1.2
**which?, what?** ¿cuál?, BV
**while** el rato; mientras
**white** blanco(a), 3.2
**who?** ¿quién?, 1.1; *(pl.)* ¿quiénes?, 2.1
**Who is calling?** ¿De parte de quién?, **3.2**
**whole** entero(a)
**why?** ¿por qué?
**wide** ancho(a)
**wife** la mujer, la esposa, 6.1
**wig** la peluca
**wild** salvaje
to **win** ganar, 7.1
**wind** el viento
**windmill** el molino de viento
**window (post office, etc.)** la ventanilla; (shop) el escaparate, la vitrina, **4.1**
**windshield** el parabrisas, **11.1**
**winter** el invierno, BV
**wise** sabio(a)
**The Three Wise Men** Los Reyes Magos, **13.2**
to **wish** desear, 3.2
**with** con
**within** dentro de
**without** sin
**woman** la dama
**wood** la madera
**wool** la lana, **12.1**
**word** la palabra
**work** el trabajo
to **work** trabajar, 3.2
**to work full time** trabajar a tiempo completo, **14.2**
**to work part time** trabajar a tiempo parcial, **14.2**
**work** la obra
**work of art** la obra de arte
**worker** el/la trabajador(a); el/la obrero(a), **9.1**
**workforce** la mano de obra
**world** el mundo
**World Cup** la Copa mundial
**World Series** la Serie mundial
**worldwide, (related to the) world** mundial
**worse, worst** peor, el/la peor
**wound** la herida, **8.1**
**wounded person** el/la herido(a)
**wrapped** envuelto(a)
to **wrinkle** arrugar
**wrist** la muñeca, **4.1**

to **write** escribir, 5.1
**writing pad** el bloc, 3.1
**wrong** erróneo(a)

**X-ray** la radiografía, los rayos equis, **8.2**

**yard** la yarda
**year** el año, BV
**to be . . . years old** tener... años, 6.1; cumplir... años
**last year** el año pasado, 9.2
**this year** este año, 9.2
**yellow** amarillo(a), 3.2
**yes** sí
**yesterday** ayer, 9.2
**day before yesterday** anteayer
**yesterday afternoon** ayer por la tarde, 9.2
**yesterday morning** ayer por la mañana , 9.2
**yet** aún; todavía
**yogurt** el yogur
**you** *(sing. fam.)* tú; *(sing. form.)* Ud., usted, 3.2; *(pl. form.)* Uds., ustedes, 2.2
**You're welcome.** De nada., No hay de qué., BV
**young** joven, 6.1
**as a young person** de joven
**your** *(sing. fam.)* tu; *(form.)* su, sus, 6.1
**youth** la juventud
**youth, young person** el/la joven, 10.1
**youth hostel** el albergue para jóvenes (juvenil), 12.2

**zero** cero, BV
**zone** la zona
**commerical zone** la zona comercial, **9.1**
**industrial zone** la zona industrial, **9.1**
**residential zone** la zona residencial, **9.1**
**zoo** el parque zoológico, **5.2**

# Index

# Index

# Credits

**COVER** (l)Ed McDonald , (t)Galen Rowell/ CORBIS, (tc)Sergio Pitamitz/CORBIS, (bc)Michael Busselle/CORBIS, (b)Robert Holmes/CORBIS; **i** (l r)Ed McDonald , (t)Galen Rowell/CORBIS, (tc)Sergio Pitamitz/CORBIS, (bc)Michael Busselle/ CORBIS, (b)Robert Holmes/CORBIS; **iv** (t)Ken Karp, (b)Andrew Payti; **v** (l)Tim Fuller, (r)Patrick Ward/CORBIS; **vi** (t)Ken Karp, (bl)Luis Delgado, (br)Curt Fischer; **vii** Robert Frerck/Odyssey; **viii** (l)Robert Frerck/Odyssey, (r)Michelle Chaplow; **ix** (tl)Chad Ehlers/International Stock, (tr)Steve Vidler/Estock, (bl)Jeff Baker/FPG, (br)Robert Frerck/Odyssey; **x** (t)Tim Fuller, (bl)Doug Bryant/ DDB Stock Photo, (br)Michelle Chaplow; **xi** (l)Tim Fuller, (r)Michelle Chaplow; **xii** (t)Andrew Payti, (bl)C.J. Collins /Photo Researchers, (br)Robert Frerck/Odyssey; **xiii** (r)Chad Ehlers/International Stock, (tl)Michelle Chaplow, (bl)Robert Frerck/ Odyssey; **xiv** (l)Tim Fuller, (r)Robert Frerck/ Odyssey; **xv** (l)Michelle Chaplow, (r)Andrew Payti; **xvi** (t)Antoinette Jongen/FPG International, (b)Doug Bryant/DDB Stock Photo; **xvii** (l)Antonio Azcona West, (r)Michelle Chaplow; **xviii** (l)Tim Fuller, (r)Robert Frerck/Odyssey; **xix** Ed McDonald **xxi** (t)Randy Faris/CORBIS, (bl br)Andrew Payti, (bc)Photodisc; **xxxiv** (t)Timothy Fuller, (c)Mark Smestad, (b)Curt Fischer; **xxxv** (t)Timothy Fuller, (b)Ed McDonald; **xxxvi-xxxvii** Curt Fischer; **xxxvi** Schalkwijk/Art Resource, NY; **R3** Luis Delgado; **R4** Ken Karp; **R5** Andrew Payti; **R6** Morgan Cain & Associates; **R7** Michelle Chaplow; **R8** Kactus Foto, Santiago, Chile/SuperStock; **R8-R9** Doug Bryant/ DDB Stock Photo; **R10** (l)Ed McDonald, (r)Laura Sifferlin; **R11** (t)Ken Karp, (b)Suzanne Murphy-Larronde/FPG International; **R12** Robert Frerck/ Odyssey; **R13** Andrew Payti; **R14** (t)Ken Karp, (c b)Robert Frerck/Odyssey; **R15** (t)Ken Fisher/Tony Stone Images, (b)Luis Delgado; **R16** Christie's Images/SuperStock; **R16-R17** Robert Frerck/ Woodfin Camp & Assoc.; **R18** Doug Bryant/DDB Stock Photo; **R19** Tim Fuller; **R20** (t)Tim Fuller, (b)Michelle Chaplow; **R21 R22** Andrew Payti; **R23** Robert Frerck/Odyssey; **R25** Andrew Payti; **R26** Réunion des Musées Nationaux/Art Resource, NY; **R26-R27** David Leah/Allsport; **R28** (t)Doug Pensinger/Allsport, (bl)Aaron Haupt, (br)Jose Goitia/AP/Wide World Photos; **R29** Curt Fischer; **R30** Ken Karp; **R31** Stuart Cohen/Comstock; **R34** Christie's Images/CORBIS; **R34-R35** Robert Fried; **R37** (t)Cliff Hollenbeck, (b)Andrew Payti; **R38** Tim Fuller; **R39 R40** Andrew Payti; **R41** (t)Andrew Payti, (b)Getty Images; **R42** Christie's Images/ CORBIS; **R42-R43** Jeremy Horner/CORBIS; **R44** (t)Bob Daemmrich, (b)Aaron Haupt; **R46** Bob Daemmrich; **R47** Andrew Payti; **R48** Photodisc; **R49** (l)Bob Daemmrich, (r)file photo; **R50** Kactus Foto/SuperStock; **R50-R51** Demetrio Carrasco/ Tony Stone Images; **R52** Michelle Chaplow; **R53** (t)Getty Images, (b)CORBIS; **R54** (t)Tim Fuller, (c)Andrew Payti, (b)file photo; **R56** Curt Fischer; **0** The Stapleton Collection/ The Bridgeman Art Library; **0-1** Luis Delgado; **2** (tl b)Michelle Chaplow, (tr)Luis Delgado; **3** Andrew Payti; **4** Luis Delgado; **6** (t)Michelle Chaplow, (b)Doug Bryant/DDB Stock Photo; **7** (t)Andrew Payti, (bl)Doug Bryant/DDB Stock Photo, (br)Photodisc; **8** (t)Luis Delgado, (b)Michelle Chaplow; **9** (t)Ken Karp, (c)CORBIS, (b)Robert Fried/Robert Fried Photography; **10** Andrew Payti; **11** Ken Karp; **12** House of El Greco, Toledo Spain; **13** Yoichiro Miyazaki/FPG; **14** Robert Fried/Robert Fried Photography; **15** Ken Karp; **16 18** Luis Delgado; **19** (t b)Robert Fried/Robert Fried Photography, (c)Telegraph Color Library/FPG; **20** (t br)Robert Fried/Robert Fried Photography, (c)Robert Fried/Stock Boston, (bl)Robert Frerck/ Odyssey/Chicago; **21** Andrew Payti; **23** (tl)Curt Fischer, (bcr)Michelle Chaplow; (others)Luis Delgado; **24** Morgan Cain & Associates; **25** file photo; **26** Andrew Payti; **27** Robert Fried/Robert Fried Photography; **29** Luis Delgado; **30** Kactus Foto/Superstock **30-31** Luis Delgado; **32** Curt Fischer; **33** (t)Andrew Payti, (br)Aaron Haupt, (others)Doug Bryant/DDB Stock Photo; **34** (t)Ed McDonald, (b)Luis Delgado; **35** Luis Delgado; **36** Curt Fischer; **37** (t bl)Timothy Fuller, (br)Curt Fischer; **38** Michelle Chaplow; **41** (t)Ken Karp, (b)Morgan Cain & Associates; **43 44** Ken Karp; **46** (l)Curt Fischer, (r)Timothy Fuller; **47** National Palace, Mexico City; **48** (t)Michelle Chaplow, (c)Andrew Payti, (b)Curt Fischer; **49** (t)Robert Fried/Robert Fried Photography, (b) Laura Sifferlin **50** (bl)Andrew Payti, (others)Curt Fischer; **51** Michelle Chaplow; **52** file photo **54** Curt Fischer; **57** (t)Timothy Fuller, (b)Curt Fischer; **58** SuperStock; **58-59** Jose Fuste Raga/CORBIS; **60** (t)Esbin-Anderson/The Image Works, (mouse)file photo; **61** Tim Fuller; **62** (t)Robert Frerck/Odyssey, (b)Aaron Haupt; **64** (l)David Doyle, (r)Michelle Chaplow; **65** Michelle Chaplow; **66** Tim Fuller; **67** Michelle Chaplow; **68** Mark Smestad; **69** Getty Images; **71 72** Andrew Payti; **73** (t)Michelle Chaplow, (b)Melanie Carr/The Viesti Collection; **74** Ron Dahlquist/ SuperStock; **76** Andrew Payti; **77** (5)Michelle Chaplow, (others)file photo **78** Steve Torregrossa; **79** (t)Michelle Chaplow, (b)CORBIS; **81** Andrew Payti; **82** (l)Esbin-Anderson/The Image Works, (mouse)file photo, (r)UPI/CORBIS Bettman; **83** Michelle Chaplow; **84** (l)Steve Torregrossa, (c)Tim Fuller, (r)Jeff Smith/FOTOSMITH; **85** Michelle Chaplow; **86** David Doyle; **89** Robert Frerck/Odyssey; **90** Christie's Images/SuperStock; **90-91** Macduff Everton/CORBIS; **92** Dominic

## Credits

Oldershaw; **93** (l)Jeff Smith/FOTOSMITH, (r)Steve Torregrossa; **95** (t)Michelle Chaplow, (b)Ken Karp; **97** Tim Fuller; **98** (t)Don Smetzer/Tony Stone Images, (b)Tim Fuller; **99** Kelly-Mooney Photography/ CORBIS; **100** Andrew Payti; **105** Steve Torregrossa; **106** (t)Robert Fried, (b)Andrew Payti; **107** Getty Images; **108** Michelle Chaplow; **109** The Stock Market; **110** (t)Francis Morgan, (b)Tim Fuller; **111** Andrew Payti; **112** Robert Frerck/Odyssey; **113** (tl)M. Philip Kahl/Bruce Coleman, Inc., (tr)Robert Frerck/Odyssey, (b)Paul Edmondson/Tony Stone Images; **114** Aaron Haupt; **118** (tl r)Andrew Payti, (bl)Anthony Azcona; **119** Andrew Payti; **122** Dallas & John Heaton/Westlight; **123 124** Andrew Payti; **125** Antoinette Jogen/FPG International; **126** (t)Jack Hollingsworth/Getty Images, (bl)William S Heisel/Getty Images, (br)CORBIS Bettmann; **127** (t)KRT/Newscom, (c)AP Photo/ Damian Dovarganes, (b)FoodPix; **128** (t)AP Photo/Kathy Willens, (c)Jason Homa/Getty Images, (bl)AP Photo/Jim Cooper, (bcl)Zuma Press/Newscom, (bcr)Star Max Photos/Newscom, (br)Amanda Edwards/Getty Images; **129** (tl)Reuters Media Inc/CORBIS, (tr)Tim Mosen Felder/CORBIS, (cl)AP Photo/Alden Pellett, (cr)AP Photo/Krista Niles, (b)Evan Agostini/Getty Images; **130** Private Collection/Kactus Foto/SuperStock; **130-131** Robert Frerck/Odyssey; **132** Jeff Smith/FOTOSMITH; **133** (l)Tim Fuller, (r)Jeff Smith/FOTOSMITH; **134** Jeff Baker/FPG; **135 136** file photo **137** Chad Ehlers/ International Stock; **138** (t)Beryl Goldberg, (b)Jonathan Nourok/PhotoEdit; **140** David R. Frazier; **141** Michelle Chaplow; **142** (t)Steve Torregrossa, (c)Rob Crandall/The Image Works, (b)Ken Karp; **143** Mark Smestad; **144** Steve Torregrossa; **145** Margot Granitsas/The Image Works; **146** Doug Bryant/DDB Stock Photo; **147** (t)Greg Johnston/International Stock, (b)Doug Bryant/DDB Stock Photo; **148** (t)Steve Vidler/ Estock, (b)Bill Bachmann/Tony Stone Images; **149** (t)Robert Frerck/Odyssey, (b)Erica Lansner/Tony Stone Images; **150** Tim Fuller; **151** (t)Michelle Chaplow, (b) file photo **152** (t)Carma Casula/ Cover/The Image Works, (b)Blake Little/SYGMA; **153** Aaron Haupt; **154** Robert Frerck/Odyssey; **155** Gregory Edwards/International Stock; **157** Chad Ehlers/International Stock; **159** (t)Jeff Baker/FPG, (b)Jeff Smith/FOTOSMITH; **160** Christie's Images/ CORBIS; **160-161** Gail Shumway/FPG; **162** (t)Tim Fuller, (bl)Bob Daemmrich, (br)Tim Fuller; **163** Doug Bryant/DDB Stock Photo; **164** (t)Robert Fried, (b)Michelle Chaplow; **165** Michelle Chaplow; **167** Geoff Butler; **169** Tim Fuller; **171** (t)Ken Karp, (b)CORBIS; **172** Tim Fuller; **173** Ken Karp; **174** (t bl)Ken Karp, (br)Tim Fuller; **175** Andrew Payti; **176** Tim Fuller; **178** (l)Tourist Office of Spain, (r)Anthony Azcona; **179** (t)Tourist Office of Spain, (b)Michelle Chaplow; **180** (l)Nick Inman, (r)Michelle Chaplow; **183** file photo **186** (t)Catherine et Bernard Desjeux, (b)Steven Ferry; **187** Michelle Chaplow; **189** Robert Fried **190** (b)Kactus Foto, Santiago, Chile/SuperStock; **190-191** (bkgd)Thomas D. Mayes, Jr.; **192** (l)Larry Mangino/The Image Works, (r)Tim Fuller; **193** Doug Bryant/DDB Stock; **195** Tim Fuller; **196** (tl)David R. Frazier, (tr c)CORBIS, (b)Andrew Abshier; **197** (tl)Tim Fuller, (tr)Doug Bryant/DDB Stock, (b)Robert Frerck/Tony Stone Images; **198** (t)file photo, (b)Antonio Azcona West; **199** CORBIS; **200** Tim Fuller; **201** (l)Tim Fuller, (r)Michelle Chaplow; **202** (t)Ken Karp, (b)CORBIS; **203** Ken Karp; **204** Michelle Chaplow; **206** (t)Susan Van Etten/PhotoEdit, (b)Robert Frerck/Odyssey Productions; **207** (t)Ken Karp, (b)Robert Frerck/ Odyssey; **208** Michelle Chaplow; **209** Tim Fuller; **210** (l)Robert Frerck/Odyssey, (r)Norman Tomalin/ Bruce Coleman, Inc.; **211** Robert Frerck/Odyssey; **212** (tl b)Robert Frerck/Odyssey, (tr)Glen Allison/ Tony Stone Images, (c)Kevin Schafer/Tony Stone Images; **213** (t)Underwood & Underwood/ Bettman CORBIS, (b)UPI/ Bettman CORBIS; **214** (t)Telegraph Colour Library/FPG, (b)Anthony Azcona; **215** (t)Don & Pat Valenti/Tony Stone Images, (b)Robert Frerck/Odyssey; **216** Phillip & Karen Smith/Tony Stone Images; **217** (b)Sven Martson/The Image Works; **218** (tl c)Andrew Abshier, (tr)David R. Frazier, (b)Robert Frerck/Tony Stone Images; **219** Robert Frerck/Odyssey; **220** Tim Fuller; **222** (t)Tim Fuller, (b)CORBIS; **223** Getty Images; **224** Robert Fried; **225** Andrew Payti; **226** (tl)Stephanie Maze/CORBIS, (tr)Carl & Ann Parcel/CORBIS, (bl)Library of congress, (br)Hulton Archive/Getty Images; **227** (t)AP Photo/Cristobal Herrera, (c)AP Photo/Andres Leighton, (b)Studio Bonisolli/ Stockfood; **228** (tl)Newscom, (tr)William Claxton, (tcr)KRT/Newscom, (bcr)PGI/CORBIS Sygma, (bl)Manny Hernandez, (br)Newscom; **229**(tl)Richard Bickel/CORBIS, (tr)Reuters Photo Archive/ Newscom, (c)Jorge Alvarez, (bl)Giraud Philippe/ CORBIS Sygma, (br)Reuters Photo Archive/ Newscom; **230** Archivo Iconografico, S.A./CORBIS; **230-231** Manuel Bellver/CORBIS; **232 233** Jeff Smith/FOTOSMITH; **234** Anthony Azcona; **235** (l)Robert Frerck/Odyssey, (r)Michelle Chaplow; **236** Jeff Smith/FOTOSMITH; **238** Tim Fuller; **239** Mark Smestad; **241** Ken Karp; **242** (t)Michelle Chaplow, (b)Tim Fuller; **243** Michelle Chaplow; **245** Andrew Payti; **246** Jeff Smith/FOTOSMITH; **247** Michelle Chaplow; **248** (t)C.J. Collins/Photo Researchers, (b)Michele Burgess/The Stock Market; **249** Victor Englebert/Photo Researchers; **252** Michelle Chaplow; **253** file photo; **254** Andrew Payti; **256** Jeff Smith/FOTOSMITH; **257** C.J. Collins/Photo

Researchers; **259** Michelle Chaplow; **260** Kactus Foto/SuperStock; **260-261** Andrea Booher/Getty Images; **262** (l)Roberto Arakaki/International Stock, (r)Gordon R. Gainer/The Stock Market; **263** (t)Daniel Rivadamar/Odyssey, (c)Robert Fried, (b)Michelle Chaplow; **264** M. Antman/The Image Works; **265** (t)Bob Krist/eStock Photography, (b)Chad Ehlers/International Stock; **266** (l)Robert Fried, (c)Zbigniew Bzdak/The Image Works, (r)Steve Torregrossa; **267** (l)Robert Fried, (others)Grant Heilman Photography; **268** (t)Robert Fried, (b)Andrew Payti; **269** Robert Frerck/Odyssey; **270** Stuart Cohen/Comstock; **271** Ken Karp; **272** David Doyle; **273** Ken Karp; **275** (t)Stuart Cohen/Comstock, (b)Tim Fuller; **276** Michelle Chaplow; **277** (t)Robert Frerck/Odyssey, (b)R. Faris/Westlight; **278** (t)Robert Fried, (b)Robert Frerck/Odyssey; **279** (t)Chris Sharp/Photo Researchers, (c)Andrea Booher/Tony Stone Images, (b)Stuart Franklin/Magnum Photos; **280** (t)Andrew Payti, (b)Robert Frerck/Odyssey; **281** (t)Robert Reiff/FPG, (b)Haroldo Castro/FPG; **282** (l)Robert Frerck/Odyssey, (r)Andrew Payti; **283** Haroldo Castro/FPG; **284** Chuck Szymanski/International Stock; **285** file photo; **286** (9)Steve Torregrossa, (others)Grant Heilman Photography; **287** Robert Frerck/Odyssey; **289** Robert Fried; **290** Archivo Iconografico, S.A./CORBIS; **290-291** Daniel Aubry/Odyssey; **292** Stan Ries/International Stock; **293** (b)Laura Sifferlin, (others)Jeff Smith/FOTOSMITH; **294** (t)Maria Pape/FPG, (c)Michelle Chaplow, (b)Spencer Grant/FPG; **295** (t)Robert Frerck/Odyssey, (b)E.Alan McGee/FPG; **296** (b)Steve Torregrossa, (others)Laura Sifferlin; **297** Jeff Smith/FOTOSMITH; **298** (t)Tim Fuller, (others)Laura Sifferlin; **301** (t)Ken Karp, (c)Michelle Chaplow; (b)Tim Fuller; **302** (l)Ken Karp, (r)National Gallery of Art, Washington; **303** (t)Michelle Chaplow, (b)Ken Karp; **304** (l)Ken Karp, (r)Andrew Payti; **305** Anthony Azcona; **306** Raga/Corbis Stock Market, (inset)Geoff Butler; **307** (t)Mark Smestad, (c)Andrew Payti, (b)FoodPix; **308** Curt Fischer; **309** Miguel Raurich/Tony Stone Images; **310** (t)Alejandro Balaguer/Tony Stone Images, (b)Getty Images; **311** (t)Inga/DDB Stock, (c)Robert Fried, (b)Victor Englebert; **312** (t)Michelle Chaplow, (b)Andrew Payti; **313** David Doyle; **314** Robert Frerck/Odyssey; **315** Vladimir Pcholkin/FPG; **316** (1 2 4 12 14)PhotoDisc, (3)CORBIS, (8 9 10)Laura Sifferlin, (11 13)Curt Fischer; **317** Miguel Raurich/Tony Stone Images; **319** Michelle Chaplow; **320** Zurbaran Galleria/SuperStock; **320-321** Michelle Chaplow; **322** (cl)Doug Bryant/DDB Stock Photo, (others)Steve Torregrossa; **323** Andrew Payti; **324** Lorne Resnick/Tony Stone Images; **325** Andrew Payti; **326** (b)Michelle Chaplow, (inset)Tim Fuller; **327** (t)Andrew Payti, (b)Michelle Chaplow; **328** Michelle Chaplow; **329** Andrew Payti; **330** (t)Michelle Chaplow, (b)Ken Karp; **331** (t)Michelle Chaplow, (b)Ken Karp; **332** (t)Nick Inman, (b)Andrew Payti; **333** Andrew Payti; **334** Ken Karp; **335** (t)Tim Fuller, (b)Andrew Payti; **336** Michelle Chaplow; **337** Robert Frerck/Odyssey; **338** Andrew Payti; **339** (t)Andrew Payti, (b)Robert Frerck/Odyssey; **340** Andrew Payti; **341** (t l br)Francis Morgan, (cl)Michelle Chaplow, (cr bl bc)Andrew Payti; **342** (l)Marco/ASK Images/The Viesti Collection, (r)Jeff Greenberg/PhotoEdit; **343** (t)Robert Frerck/Odyssey, (c)Tim Fuller, (b)Andrew Payti; **346** (t)Doug Bryant/DDB Stock Photo, (others)Steve Torregrossa; **347** Byron Augustin/DDB Stock; **349** David Garcia/Cover/The Image Works; **350** (t)Sipa Press, (b)Maruka/International Stock; **351** Andrew Payti; **352** (t)Mark Smestad, (b)Andrew Payti; **353** Pablo Corral V/CORBIS; **354** (tl)Richard A. Cooke/CORBIS, (tr)Jan Butchofsky Houser/CORBIS, (b)Richard A. Cooke/CORBIS; **355** (tl)Dave G. Houser/CORBIS, (tr)Anita Calero, (cl)Kevin Schafer/CORBIS, (cr)Reuters/Shannon Stapleton, (b)Evaristo SA/AFP/Newscom; **356** (tl)Newscom, (tr)Notimex/Newscom, (c)AP Photo/Moises Castillo, (b)AFP/Newscom; **357** (tl)Courtesy Katia Cardena, (tr)Aurelia Ventura/Newscom, (cl)Peter Guttmannn/CORBIS, (cr)Tiziou Jacques/CORBIS Sygma, (b)Armando Morales; **358** Kactus Foto, Santiago, Chile/SuperStock; **358-359** Robert Fried; **360** (t)Michelle Chaplow, (inset)Clement Mok/PictureQuest; **361** (t b)Geoff Butler; (cl)KS studios, (c)Doug Martin; (cr)Jeff Smith/FOTOSMITH; **362** (tl)Andrew Payti, (tcl)Clement Mok/PictureQuest, (tcr)PhotoDisc, (tr)Geoff Butler, (b)Tim Fuller; **363** Tim Fuller; **364** (tl)Robert Frerck/Odyssey, (tr)Dominic Oldershaw, (b)Doug Bryant/DDB Stock Photo; **365** Dominic Oldershaw; **366** Tim Fuller; **367** (t)Andrew Payti, (b)Antoinette Jongen/FPG International; **368** Artists Rights Society (ARS), New York/SPADEM, Paris; **369** Nick Inman; **370** (t)Tim Fuller, (b)Mark Smestad; **372** Michelle Chaplow; **374** (t)Michelle Chaplow, (b)file photo; **375** Victor Englebert; **376** Michelle Chaplow; **377** (t)Robert Frerck/Odyssey, (b)Joe Viesti/The Viesti Collection; **378** Michelle Chaplow; **379** Robert Frerck/Odyssey; **380** Daniel Rivadamar/Odyssey; **381** (t)Robert Frerck/Odyssey, (c)Stuart Cohen/Comstock, (b)Kit Kittle/The Viesti Collection; **382** Doug Bryant/DDB Stock Photo; **383** Anthony Azcona; **384** Andrew Payti; **385** Daniel Rivadamar/Odyssey; **386** (6)Nick Inman, (others)Dominic Oldershaw; **389** Tim Fuller; **390** Christie's Images/SuperStock; **390-391** Robert Frerck/Odyssey **392** file photo; **393** (t)Antonio Azcona West, (b)Tim Fuller; **394** Anthony Azcona;